Frommer's

American Southwest
3rd Edition

by Lesley King & Karl Samson

Colorado & Utah coverage by Don & Barbara Laine

Las Vegas coverage by Mary Herczog

Here's what the critics say about Frommer's:

"Amazingly easy to use. Very portable, very complete."

—*Booklist*

"Detailed, accurate, and easy-to-read information for all price ranges."
—*Glamour Magazine*

"Hotel information is close to encyclopedic."

—*Des Moines Sunday Register*

"Frommer's Guides have a way of giving you a real feel for a place."
—*Knight Ridder Newspapers*

Wiley Publishing, Inc.

Published by:

Wiley Publishing, Inc.

111 River St.

Hoboken, NJ 07030-5774

ISBN: 978-0-470-13606-5

Editor: Matthew Brown
Production Editor: Lindsay Conner
Cartographer: Roberta Stockwell
Photo Editor: Richard Fox
Anniversary Logo Design: Richard Pacifico
Production by Wiley Indianapolis Composition Services

Front cover photo: Utah, Bryce Canyon National Park: sunlight and rock formations
Back cover photo: Arizona, Grand Canyon National Park, North Rim: North Kaibab Trail, mule ride into Bright Angel Canyon

For information on our other products and services or to obtain technical support, please contact our Customer Care Department within the U.S. at 800/762-2974, outside the U.S. at 317/572-3993 or fax 317/572-4002.

Wiley also publishes its books in a variety of electronic formats. Some content that appears in print may not be available in electronic formats.

Manufactured in the United States of America

5   4   3   2   1

Contents

10 UFOs & Carlsbad Caverns: Southern New Mexico from Top to Bottom

289

11 Tucson

338

12 Phoenix, Scottsdale & the Valley of the Sun

392

List of Maps

About the Authors

Lesley S. King (New Mexico coverage, plus chapters 2, 3, 4, and appendix) grew up on a ranch in northern New Mexico, where she still returns on weekends to help work cattle. A freelance writer and photographer, she's a contributor to *New Mexico Magazine* and an avid kayaker and skier. She has written for the *New York Times*, United Airlines' *Hemispheres* magazine, *American Cowboy*, and *Audubon*. She is writer and host of *Written on the Wind*, a television documentary series. She is also the author of *Frommer's Santa Fe, Taos & Albuquerque* and *Frommer's New Mexico*.

Karl Samson (Arizona coverage) finds that the sunny winter skies of the Arizona desert are the perfect antidote to the dreary winters of his Pacific Northwest home. Each winter, he flees the rain to explore Arizona's deserts, mountains, cities, and small towns. It is the state's unique regional style, Native American cultures, abundance of contemporary art, and, of course, boundless landscapes that keep him fascinated by Arizona. Summer finds him researching his other books, including *Frommer's Washington*, *Frommer's Oregon*, and *Frommer's Seattle & Portland*.

Residents of northern New Mexico for more than 30 years, **Don** and **Barbara Laine** (Colorado and Utah coverage) have traveled extensively throughout the Rocky Mountains and the Southwest. They are the authors of *Frommer's Colorado*, *Frommer's Utah*, *Frommer's Rocky Mountain National Park*, and *Frommer's Zion & Bryce Canyon National Parks;* are the lead authors of *Frommer's National Parks of the American West;* and have contributed to *Frommer's Texas* and *Frommer's USA*. The Laines have also written *Little-Known Southwest* and *New Mexico & Arizona State Parks* (both for The Mountaineers Books).

Mary Herczog (Las Vegas coverage) lives in Los Angeles and works in the film industry. She is the author of *Frommer's New Orleans* and *Las Vegas For Dummies*, and has contributed to *Frommer's Los Angeles*. She still isn't sure when to hit and when to hold when playing blackjack.

An Invitation to the Reader

In researching this book, we discovered many wonderful places—hotels, restaurants, shops, and more. We're sure you'll find others. Please tell us about them, so we can share the information with your fellow travelers in upcoming editions. If you were disappointed with a recommendation, we'd love to know that, too. Please write to:

Frommer's American Southwest, 3rd Edition
Wiley Publishing, Inc. • 111 River St. • Hoboken, NJ 07030-5774

An Additional Note

Please be advised that travel information is subject to change at any time—and this is especially true of prices. We therefore suggest that you write or call ahead for confirmation when making your travel plans. The authors, editors, and publisher cannot be held responsible for the experiences of readers while traveling. Your safety is important to us, however, so we encourage you to stay alert and be aware of your surroundings. Keep a close eye on cameras, purses, and wallets, all favorite targets of thieves and pickpockets.

Other Great Guides for Your Trip:

Frommer's Utah

Frommer's Arizona

Frommer's Colorado

Frommer's Las Vegas

Frommer's New Mexico

Frommer's Exploring America by RV

Frommer's National Parks of the American West

Frommer's Star Ratings, Icons & Abbreviations

Every hotel, restaurant, and attraction listing in this guide has been ranked for quality, value, service, amenities, and special features using a **star-rating system.** In country, state, and regional guides, we also rate towns and regions to help you narrow down your choices and budget your time accordingly. Hotels and restaurants are rated on a scale of zero (recommended) to three stars (exceptional). Attractions, shopping, nightlife, towns, and regions are rated according to the following scale: zero stars (recommended), one star (highly recommended), two stars (very highly recommended), and three stars (must-see).

In addition to the star-rating system, we also use **seven feature icons** that point you to the great deals, in-the-know advice, and unique experiences that separate travelers from tourists. Throughout the book, look for:

Finds	Special finds—those places only insiders know about
Fun Fact	Fun facts—details that make travelers more informed and their trips more fun
Kids	Best bets for kids and advice for the whole family
Moments	Special moments—those experiences that memories are made of
Overrated	Places or experiences not worth your time or money
Tips	Insider tips—great ways to save time and money
Value	Great values—where to get the best deals

The following **abbreviations** are used for credit cards:

AE	American Express	DISC	Discover	V	Visa
DC	Diners Club	MC	MasterCard		

Frommers.com

Now that you have this guidebook to help you plan a great trip, visit our website at **www.frommers.com** for additional travel information on more than 3,600 destinations. We update features regularly to give you instant access to the most current trip-planning information available. At Frommers.com, you'll find scoops on the best airfares, lodging rates, and car rental bargains. You can even book your travel online through our reliable travel booking partners. Other popular features include:

- Online updates of our most popular guidebooks
- Vacation sweepstakes and contest giveaways
- Newsletters highlighting the hottest travel trends
- Online travel message boards with featured travel discussions

What's New in the Southwest

THE FOUR CORNERS AREA Not far from Farmington, the **Soaring Eagle Lodge,** 48 C.R. 4370, off NM 511, Navajo Dam (© **800/866-2719** or 505/632-5621; www.soaringeaglelodge.net), offers cabins along the San Juan River and angling on private waters.

In Farmington, **Artifacts Gallery,** 302 E. Main St. (© **505/327-2907**), convenes a handful of artist's studios in a Victorian style lumber building— a great place to browse and schmooze with the creative set. See chapter 5.

SANTA FE The **Railyard Restaurant & Saloon,** 530 S. Guadalupe St. (© **505/989-3300;** www.railyardrestaurantand saloon.com), offers tasty steaks and fish in a refined warehouse ambience. The sesame-and-panko-crusted tuna is dynamite.

The City Different's newest way to relax is with an Indo-Asian spa treatment at **Absolute Nirvana Spa, Tea Room & Gardens,** 106 Faithway St. (© **505/983-7942;** www.absolutenirvana.com). The spa has master-level therapists who use plants, herbs, and spices in their treatments.

The **High Road Marketplace,** a co-op gallery off the Santuario de Chimayo plaza in Chimayo (© **866/343-5381** or 505/351-1078; www.highroadnewmexico. com), offers art and crafts from all over northern New Mexico, with an excellent collection of devotional crosses. See chapter 6.

TAOS For better or worse, condos seem to be taking over in the Taos Ski Valley. Last year, the Edelweiss made the move. This year, the Snakedance has become **Snakedance Condominiums,** 110 Sutton Place (© **800/332-9815** or 505/776-2277; www.snakedancecondos. com). These upscale condos at the very base of the mountain offer all the luxuries of home.

The Taos dining scene, always imaginative, has a few new notches on its hostess stand. Taoseños are bowled over by **Gutiz,** 812-B Paseo del Pueblo Norte (© **505/758-1226**), a French/Latin fusion spot in a modest space north of town. Some come for the fresh baked bread with brie at breakfast, or for the pork tenderloin with onion confit at lunch. Ice-cream lovers congregate at **Taos Cow,** 485 NM 150, Arroyo Seco (© **505/776-5640**). Breakfast tacos and sandwiches are a prelude to ice cream made with natural ingredients—flavors range from cherry ristra to simply good old chocolate.

The **Kit Carson Home and Museum,** 113 Kit Carson Rd (© **505/758-4613;** www.kitcarsonhome.com), has become a whole different museum than its predecessor, which closed in 2004. It now offers a glimpse of the sparseness of 19th-century frontier-town life. See chapter 7.

ALBUQUERQUE The city's new **Balloon Museum,** 9201 Balloon Museum Dr. NE (© **505/768-6020;** www.balloon museum.com), tells the history of ballooning from its first flight, in 1783, to the present, with authentic air-crafts displayed. Albuquerque's brightest new district—**Gold Avenue**—provides fun shopping and dining. See chapter 8.

NORTHERN NEW MEXICO At **Acoma Pueblo** (© 800/747-0181 or 505/552-6604; www.skycity.com), visitors now have more than the Sky City to see. A 40,000-square-foot museum presents the pueblo's history and present-day life with lovely artifacts.

In Chama, **Cookin' Books,** 2449 US 84/64 (© 505/756-1717), is the community's new hangout, offering tasty sandwiches such as roast turkey with goat cheese and pesto. The daily specials here are always a culinary adventure. See chapter 9.

SOUTHERN NEW MEXICO The biggest news in this part of the state is the **El Camino Real International Heritage Center,** C.R. 1598, 30 miles south of Socorro (© 505/854-3600; www. caminorealheritage.org). With artifacts and state-of-the-art exhibits, the museum presents the story of the 1,500-mile trade route from Mexico to near Santa Fe.

Certainly not new, but suddenly famous, **Manny's Buckhorn Tavern,** Building 68, NM 380, San Antonio (© 505/835-4423), serves what *GQ* magazine rated as one of the top 20 burgers in the United States. It's an atmospheric small-town tavern worth a stop.

The city of Las Cruces is talking about **Lemongrass,** 2540 El Paseo Rd. (© 505/ 523-8778). This Thai restaurant serves tasty pad Thai and other dishes made with fresh ingredients.

In Roswell, **Tia Juana's Mexican Grille & Cantina,** 3601 N. Main St. (© 505/627-6113), offers some of the liveliest food and ambience in the region. Try the enchiladas.

Finally, and of great note, is the resurrection of **Tinnie Silver Dollar Steakhouse and Saloon,** on US 70, 43 miles west of Roswell and 28 miles east of Ruidoso (© 505/653-4177). The restaurant offers excellent food in an elegant 1870s Victorian building. Try the coconut shrimp followed by filet mignon. See chapter 10.

TUCSON We've added a few new hotels in Tucson. These include the **Hyatt Place Tucson Airport,** 6885 S. Tucson Blvd. (© 800/492-8847 or 520/295-0405; www.hyattplace.com), which is a very pretty new business hotel near the airport. If you're looking for basic, inexpensive accommodations, try the **Extended StayAmerica Tucson,** 5050 E. Grant Rd. (© 800/804-3724 or 520/795-9510; www.extendedstayamerica.com).

We know the desert may not seem the place for sushi, but **Sky Blue Wasabi,** 250 S. Craycroft Rd., #100 (© 520/ 747-0228), is such a fun place and serves such great sushi that it's worth checking out. If you prefer your rolls with hot dogs rather than raw fish, be sure to eat at **El Guero Canelo,** 2480 N. Oracle Rd. (© 520/882-8977; www.elguerocanelo. com), which is known for its Mexican-style hot dogs. For much more upscale south-of-the-border fare, dine at **Miguel's,** 5900 N. Oracle Rd. (© 520/ 887-3777; www.miguelstucson.com), which is in La Posada hotel. If Mexican is too spicy for you, try **Le Delice,** 7245 E. Tanque Verde Rd. © 520/290-9714; www.le-delice.com), a casual little French place not far from Sabino Canyon. See chapter 11.

PHOENIX, SCOTTSDALE & THE VALLEY OF THE SUN Downtown Scottsdale has a couple of new hip business hotels this year, so if you're in town for the city's nightlife, the **Hyatt Place Scottsdale Old Town,** 7300 E. Third Ave., Scottsdale (© 888/492-8847 or 480/423-9944; www.hyattplace.com), and the **Hotel Indigo,** 4415 N. Civic Center Plaza, Scottsdale (© 866/2-INDIGO or 480/ 941-9400; scottsdalehiphotel.com), are both good bets. On the other hand, if you're looking for a deal on a hotel with a big pool, green lawns, and tall palms, check out the **Best Western Dobson Ranch Inn & Resort,** 1666 S. Dobson

Rd., Mesa (© **800/528-1356** or 480/ 831-7000; www.dobsonranchinn.com).

If you're going to be in Phoenix for a special occasion and want to splurge on dinner, we can think of no better place than **Kai**, 5594 W. Wild Horse Pass Blvd., Chandler (© **602/225-0100**; www.wild horsepassresort.com), which is at the Sheraton Wild Horse Pass Resort & Spa. The sophisticated southwestern-inspired menu relies on ingredients from Native American tribes around the country.

For the best flour tortillas in Phoenix, join the crowds standing in line at **Carolina's**, 1202 E. Mohave St., Phoenix (© **602/252-1503**; www.carolinasmex. com), which is located south of Chase Field.

It's a long way from north Scottsdale to the celebrated Heard Museum in downtown Phoenix, but you can get a taste for the museum at the new **Heard Museum North**, 32633 N. Scottsdale Rd., Scottsdale (© **480/488-9817**; www.heard.org), which is located just south of Carefree's el Pedregal Shops & Dining at The Boulders. If you do go to the main Heard Museum, be sure to also visit the recently expanded **Phoenix Art Museum**, 1625 N. Central Ave., Phoenix (© **602/257-1222**; www.phxart.org).

With suburban sprawl stretching for miles in every direction, it has become harder and harder to find any real desert in the Phoenix metropolitan area. For easy desert hikes, head to north Scottsdale's **McDowell Sonoran Preserve** (© **480/ 998-7971**; www.mcdowellsonoran.org), a large natural area that still has only limited public access. See chapter 12.

SOUTHERN ARIZONA In Tubac, there's now an upscale dining option in the form of the **Nob Hill Gourmet Market and Fine Dining**, 10 Avenida Goya, Suite B (© **520/398-1010**; www.nobhill tubac.com), which is located in the Plaza de Anza shopping center and has both a restaurant and a gourmet grocery store.

In Sonoita, be sure to stop in at **Dos Cabezas Wine Works** (© **602/622-0399**; www.doscabezaswinery.com), one of the area's newest wineries.

In Sierra Vista, **Adobe Southwestern Cuisine**, 5043 S. Hwy. 92., Sierra Vista (© **520/378-2762**), has become a hit with locals and should be on any bird-watcher's itinerary.

If you're looking for a pretty place to stay in Bisbee, check out the **Letson Loft Hotel**, 26 Main St., Bisbee (© **877/ 432-3210** or 520/432-3210; www.letson lofthotel.com), which is filled with interesting Asian antiques. For big breakfasts with the locals, head to the **Bisbee Breakfast Club**, 75A Erie St. (© **520/432-5885**; www.bisbeebreakfastclub.com). See chapter 13.

CENTRAL ARIZONA If you're looking for something to do after dark in Prescott, be sure to check the schedule at the **Raven Café**, 142 N. Cortez St. (© **928/717-0009**). This arty spot has an astonishing beer list. At night, the Raven has live-music performances and even shows vintage movies one night a week.

If you're heading to Sedona from Phoenix, you might want to avoid taking **Arizona 179**, which is the direct route from I-17 to Sedona. This narrow, winding, two-lane highway is being widened and improved, and construction is expected to last into 2009. To avoid the construction zone, take Arizona 260 from Camp Verde to Cottonwood and then Arizona 89A from Cottonwood to Sedona. Once you're in Sedona, you can avoid the traffic congestion and parking problems by hopping on the **Sedona Roadrunner**, a free shuttle bus that runs between uptown Sedona, Tlaquepaque, and the Hillside Shops.

You'd think that having some of the most awesome scenery in the world would be enough for Sedona, but no: This town is suffering from a case of pinot envy. It wants red rocks *and* red wine. Over the past few years, wineries have been sprouting along the banks of Oak Creek in the nearby community of Page Springs. Here you'll find **Page Springs Vineyards & Cellars,** 1500 N. Page Springs Rd. (© **928/639-3004;** www.pagespringscellars.com), and **Oak Creek Vineyards and Winery,** Page Springs Road (© **928/649-0290;** www.oakcreekvineyards.net), both of which produce some decent wines and have tasting rooms that are open to the public on a regular basis. If you'd like to visit **Echo Canyon Vineyard & Winery,** which isn't usually open to the public, book a wine tour with **Sun Country Adventures** (© **877/783-6000;** www.scadventures.net), which is affiliated with El Portal, our favorite Sedona lodge. If you're more interested in the Big Dipper than big reds, sign up for a stargazing tour with **Evening Sky Tours** (© **866/701-0398** or 928/203-0006; www.eveningskytours.com). See chapter 14.

THE GRAND CANYON & NORTH-ERN ARIZONA At Grand Canyon National Park, (© **928/638-7888;** www.nps.gov/grca) there are additional lanes at the south entrance to the park, so, hopefully, the summertime wait to get into the park won't be as long as it has sometimes been in the past. Also, **Bright Angel Lodge & Cabins** (© **888/297-2757** or 303/297-2757; www.xanterra.com or www.grandcanyonlodges.com), one of the park's two historic lodges, underwent an extensive renovation in 2007. The Bright Angel's rooms are now both a great value and quite comfortable.

For up-to-the-minute creative cuisine in Flagstaff, search out **Brix,** 413 N. San Francisco St. (© **928/213-1021;** www.brixflagstaff.com), which is inside an old carriage house.

The biggest news in the region is the Hualapai Indian Reservation's opening of the much-publicized **SkyWalk** at Grand Canyon West. However, with a sky-high admission price and a long drive for a short walk on a horseshoe-shaped pier, the SkyWalk is a less than grand attraction. If you're interested, the SkyWalk is operated by **Destination Grand Canyon** (© **877/716-9378** or 702/878-9378; www.destinationgrandcanyon.com). See chapter 15.

1

The Best of the Southwest

Planning a trip to a region as large and diverse as the American Southwest involves a lot of decision making, so in this chapter we've tried to give you some direction. We've chosen what we feel is the very best the region has to offer—the places and experiences you won't want to miss. Although the sights and activities listed here are written up in more detail elsewhere in this book, this chapter gives you an overview of the highlights and gets you started.

1 The Best of the Natural Southwest

- **Monument Valley Buttes at Sunset** (UT and AZ): These stark sentinels of the desert are impressive at any time, but they take on a particularly dignified aura when the setting sun casts its deep colors over them, etching their profiles against a darkening sky. Although the park generally closes before sunset, you can arrange a sunset tour—it's well worth the cost. See p. 112.
- **Rio Grande Gorge** (NM): A hike into this dramatic gorge is unforgettable. You'll first see it as you come over a rise heading toward Taos. It's a colossal slice in the earth formed during the late Cretaceous period (130 million years ago) and the early Tertiary period (about 70 million years ago). Drive about 35 miles north of Taos, near the village of Cerro, to the **Wild Rivers Recreation Area.** From the lip of the canyon, you descend through land inhabited by Indians since 16,000 B.C. If you're visiting during spring and early summer and like an adrenaline rush, be sure to find a professional guide and raft the

Taos Box, a 17-mile stretch of class IV white water. See "Getting Outside," in chapter 7.
- **Carlsbad Caverns National Park** (NM): One of the world's largest and most complex cave systems is in southeastern New Mexico. The 80 known caves have spectacular stalagmite and stalactite formations. Explore the Big Room on a 1-mile self-guided tour, then catch the massive bat flight from the cave entrance at sunset. See p. 311.
- **White Sands National Monument** (NM): Located 15 miles southwest of Alamogordo, White Sands National Monument preserves the best part of the world's largest gypsum dune field. For a truly unforgettable experience, camp overnight so that you can watch the sun rise on the smooth, endless dunes. See p. 296.
- **Arizona–Sonora Desert Museum** (AZ): The name is misleading—this is more zoo and botanical garden than museum. Naturalistic settings house dozens of species of desert animals, including a number of critters you

The American Southwest

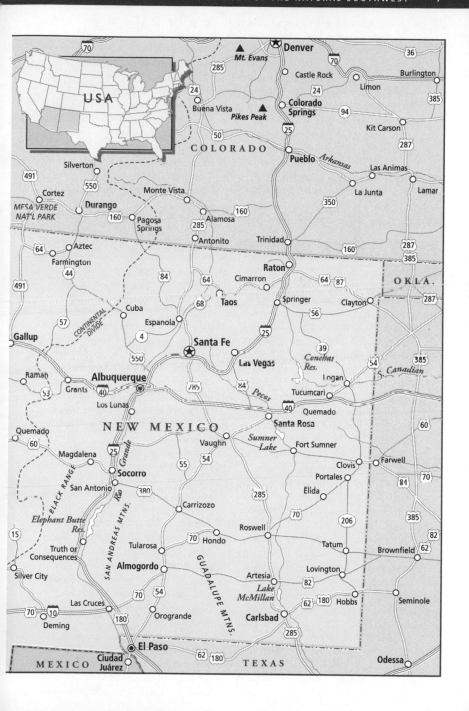

wouldn't want to meet in the wild (rattlesnakes, tarantulas, scorpions, black widows, and Gila monsters). See p. 366.

- **Saguaro National Park** (AZ): Lying both east and west of Tucson, this park preserves "forests" of saguaro cactuses and is the very essence of the desert as so many people imagine it. You can hike it, bike it, or drive it. See p. 367.

- **Desert Botanical Garden** (AZ): There's no better place to learn about the plants of Arizona's Sonoran Desert and the many other deserts of

the world. Displays at this Phoenix botanical garden explain plant adaptations and how indigenous tribes once used many of this region's wild plants. See p. 427.

- **Zion National Park** (UT): At the Narrows in Zion, sheer 1,000-foot-high walls enclose you in a 20-foot-wide world of hanging gardens, waterfalls, and sculpted sandstone arches, with the Virgin River beneath your feet. This is one of the park's many awe-inspiring experiences. See p. 562.

2 The Best Outdoor Activities

- **Hiking** (throughout the region): What's unique about hiking in the Southwest is the variety of terrain, from desert to alpine forest to badlands to canyons. In Utah, you can hike right past all three stone formations at Natural Bridges National Monument (p. 93) or explore the hoodoo formations in Bryce Canyon National Park (p. 568). Some of our favorite places for a hike in New Mexico are the El Malpais badlands (p. 268), the hauntingly sculpted rock formations at Abiquiu that artist Georgia O'Keeffe made famous in her paintings (p. 279), and White Sands National Monument (p. 296).

  In Arizona, a hike down into the Grand Canyon or Havasu Canyon is not for the unfit or the faint of heart, but it will take you on a journey through millions of years set in stone. This trip takes plenty of planning and requires some strenuous hiking. See "The Grand Canyon South Rim" and "Havasu Canyon & Grand Canyon West," in chapter 15.

- **Ballooning** (NM and AZ): With the International Balloon Fiesta in Albuquerque bringing more than 750 balloons to the area, Albuquerque has

become the sport's world capital. Fortunately, visitors can let loose the tethers and float free, too. Most of the operators are in Albuquerque; see p. 245 for recommendations. Ballooning is also popular in Arizona; see "Organized Tours," in chapter 11, "Organized Tours & Excursions," in chapter 12, and "Organized Tours," under "Sedona & Oak Creek Canyon," in chapter 14, for information on companies in Tucson, Phoenix, and Sedona.

- **Horseback riding** (NM and AZ): New Mexico's history is stamped with the hoof, dating from the Spanish conquistadors' introduction of horses to the New World. Riding in New Mexico still has that Old West feel, with trails that wind through wilderness, traversing passes and broad meadows. Some of the best rides are near Santa Fe, on Taos Pueblo land, and in Southern New Mexico. See "Getting Outside," in chapters 6, 7, and 10.

  Cowboys still ride ranges all over Arizona, and so can you if you book a stay at one of the state's many guest ranches (formerly known as dude ranches). You might even get to drive some cattle down the trail. After a long or short day in the saddle, you can soak in a hot tub, go for a swim, or play tennis before chowing down. See chapters 11, 13, and 14.

- **Mountain Biking** (NM and AZ): Almost anywhere you go in New Mexico, you'll find trails. We've hooked onto some fun old mining roads in the Black Range down south and explored sage forest on the rim of the Taos Gorge in the north. See the "Biking" sections under "Getting Outside," in each New Mexico chapter, especially chapter 7.

In Arizona, among the red rocks of Sedona, you can pedal through awesome scenery on some of the most memorable single-track trails in the Southwest. There's even plenty of slickrock. See "Getting Outside," under "Sedona & Oak Creek Canyon," in chapter 14.

- **River Rafting** (NM and AZ): Whether you go for 3 days or 2 weeks, no other active vacation in the region comes close to matching the excitement of a raft trip. In Arizona, nothing beats a Colorado River rafting trip through the Grand Canyon. Sure, the river is crowded with groups in the summer, but the grandeur of the canyon more than makes up for it. See "Other Ways of Seeing the Canyon," under "The Grand Canyon South Rim," in chapter 15. In New Mexico, the wild **Taos Box**, a steep-sided canyon south of the Wild Rivers Recreation Area, offers a series of class IV rapids that rarely lets up for some 17 miles, providing one of the most exciting 1-day white-water tours in the West. See "Getting Outside," in chapter 7.

3 The Best Scenic Drives

- **Monument Valley Navajo Tribal Park** (UT and AZ): This valley of sandstone buttes and mesas is one of the most photographed spots in America. It's familiar to people all over the world from countless movies, TV shows, and commercials. A 17-mile dirt road winds through the park, giving visitors close-up views of such landmarks as Elephant Butte, the Mittens, and Totem Pole. See "Monument Valley Navajo Tribal Park," in chapter 5.
- **High Road to Taos** (Santa Fe, NM): One of New Mexico's primo experiences, this road traverses the mountains from Santa Fe to Taos, passing by chile and apple farms in old Hispanic villages. Stop in Chimayo to see unique wool weaving, in Cordova to find lovely woodcarvings, and in renegade Truchas, where life remains

much as it did a century ago. Most important, the route crosses the base of New Mexico's grandest peaks. See "Taking the High Road to Taos," in chapter 6.
- **Turquoise Trail** (Albuquerque, NM): Meandering through the broad Galisteo basin, this is the scenic route from Albuquerque to Santa Fe. The two-lane road runs through piñon-studded hills and old mining towns such as Madrid and Cerrillos, where 2,000 years ago Native Americans hammered turquoise and silver from the hills. Today artists and craftspeople have revived the towns. See "En Route to Santa Fe: Along the Turquoise Trail," in chapter 8.
- **Lincoln Loop** (Ruidoso, NM): Elegant art, ancient petroglyphs, and Billy the Kid memorabilia draw road warriors to this 162-mile loop in

southeastern New Mexico. It begins in the mountain resort town of Ruidoso and cruises to Lincoln, where travelers can "walk in the footsteps" of the notorious punk Billy the Kid. Next it passes imaginative petroglyphs, through the Mescalero Apache Reservation, and back to Ruidoso. See "A Scenic Drive Around the Lincoln Loop," in chapter 10.

- **The Apache Trail** (east of Phoenix, AZ): Much of this winding road, which passes just north of the Superstition Mountains, is unpaved and follows a rugged route once ridden by Apaches. This is some of the most remote country in the Phoenix area, with far-reaching desert vistas and lots to see and do along the way. See "A Side Trip from Phoenix: The Apache Trail," in chapter 12.

- **Oak Creek Canyon** (Sedona, AZ): Slicing down from the pine country outside Flagstaff to the red rocks of Sedona, Oak Creek Canyon is a cool oasis. From the scenic overlook at the top of the canyon to the swimming holes and hiking trails at the bottom, this canyon road provides a rapid change in climate and landscape. See "Sedona & Oak Creek Canyon," in chapter 14.

- **Mount Lemmon** (Tucson, AZ): The views of Tucson from the city's northern foothills are great, but the vistas from Mount Lemmon are even better. With a ski area at its summit, Mount Lemmon rises from the desert like an island emerging from the sea. Along the way, the road climbs from cactus country to cool pine forests. See "Getting Outside," in chapter 11.

4 The Best Native American Sights

- **Ute Mountain Tribal Park** (CO): These ruins differ from others in Colorado because they're on the Ute Mountain Indian Reservation, and the only way to see the reservation is on a guided tour conducted by members of the tribe. You'll see ruins and petroglyphs similar to those in Mesa Verde, but with an informed personal guide and without crowds. See p. 85.

- **Mesa Verde National Park** (CO): Home to the most impressive prehistoric cliff dwellings in the Southwest, Mesa Verde (Spanish for "green table") overwhelms you with its size and complexity. The first national park set aside to preserve works created by humans, it covers some 52,000 acres just outside Cortez. Among the most compelling sites are Spruce Tree House, Square Tower House, and Cliff Palace, a four-story, apartment-style dwelling. See p. 87.

- **Hovenweep National Monument** (UT): This deserted valley contains some of the most striking and most isolated archaeological sites in the Four Corners area—the remains of curious sandstone towers built more than 700 years ago by the Anasazi (ancestral Puebloans). These mysterious structures still keep archaeologists guessing. See p. 85.

- **Monument Valley Navajo Tribal Park** (UT and AZ): For most of us, Monument Valley is the Old West. We've seen it dozens of times in movie theaters, on TV, in magazine advertisements, and on billboards. The Old West may be gone, but many Navajos still call this home. A Navajo guide will give you the Navajo perspective on this majestic land and take you into areas not otherwise open to visitors. See p. 112.

- **Chaco Culture National Historical Park** (NM): A combination of a stunning setting and well-preserved ruins makes the long drive to Chaco Canyon an incredible adventure into ancestral Puebloan culture. Many good hikes and bike rides are found in the area, and there's also a campground. See p. 131.

- **Indian Pueblo Cultural Center** (NM): Owned and operated as a nonprofit organization by the 19 pueblos of New Mexico, this is a fine place to begin an exploration of Native American culture. The Albuquerque museum is modeled after Pueblo Bonito, a spectacular 9th-century ruin in Chaco Culture National Historic Park, and contains art and artifacts old and new. See p. 240.
- **Petroglyph National Monument** (NM): This site has 25,000 petroglyphs (prehistoric rock carvings) and a variety of hiking trails geared to differing levels of difficulty. It's right on the outskirts of Albuquerque. See p. 243.
- **Bandelier National Monument** (NM): These ruins provide a spectacular peek into the lives of the Anasazi culture, which flourished in the area between A.D. 1100 and 1550. The most dramatic site is a dwelling and kiva (a room used for religious activities) in a cave 140 feet above the canyon floor—reached by a climb up long pueblo-style ladders. See p. 187.
- **Pecos National Historical Park** (NM): It's hard to rank New Mexico's many ruins, but this one, sprawled on a plain about 25 miles east of Santa Fe, is one of the most impressive. It resonates with the history of the Pueblo Revolt of 1680. You'll see evidence of where the Pecos people

burned the mission church before joining the attack on Santa Fe. You'll also see where the Spanish conquistadors later compromised, allowing sacred kivas to be built next to the reconstructed mission. See p. 186.
- **Heard Museum** (AZ): This Phoenix institution is one of the nation's premier museums devoted to Native American cultures. In addition to historical exhibits, a huge kachina collection, and an excellent store, it has annual exhibits of contemporary Native American art as well as dance performances and demonstrations of traditional skills. See p. 427.
- **Tonto National Monument** (AZ): East of Phoenix on the Apache Trail, this is one of the only easily accessible cliff dwellings in Arizona that you can still enter; you don't have to just observe from a distance. See p. 455.
- **Montezuma Castle National Monument** (AZ): Located just off I-17, this is the easiest cliff dwelling to get to in Arizona, but visitors cannot go inside the ruins. Nearby Montezuma Well also has some small ruins. See p. 495.
- **Canyon de Chelly National Monument** (AZ): Small cliff dwellings up and down the length of Canyon de Chelly are visible from overlooks, while a trip into the canyon itself offers a chance to see some of these ruins up close. See p. 106.
- **Navajo National Monument** (AZ): Keet Seel and Betatakin are some of the finest examples of Anasazi cliff dwellings in the state. Although the ruins are at the end of long hikes, their size and state of preservation make the sites well worth the effort you'll expend to see them. See p. 111.

5 The Best Family Experiences

- **Albuquerque Aquarium** (NM): For those of us born and raised in the desert, this attraction quenches years

of soul thirst. Exhibits focus on sea areas fed by the Rio Grande River. You'll pass by many large tanks and within an eels' den. The culminating show is a 285,000-gallon shark tank, where many species of fish and 15 to 20 sand tiger, brown, and nurse sharks swim around looking ominous. See p. 244.

- **Rio Grande Zoo** (NM): More than 1,200 animals of 300 species live on 60 acres of riverside bosque among ancient cottonwoods. Open-moat exhibits with animals in naturalized habitats are a treat for zoo-goers. During summer, a children's petting zoo is open, and the New Mexico Symphony Orchestra performs. See p. 245.

- **Santa Fe Children's Museum** (NM): Designed for the whole family, this museum offers interactive exhibits and hands-on activities focusing on the arts, humanities, science, and technology. Recently, *Family Life* magazine named this one of the 10 hottest children's museums in the nation. See p. 167.

- **Carlsbad Caverns National Park** (NM): Truly one of the world's natural wonders, these caverns swallow visitors as they embark on what feels like a journey to the center of the earth. Nocturnal creatures thrive, and water drips onto your body. Kids won't like the fact that they can't go climbing on the formations, but

they'll be too fascinated to complain much. See p. 311.

- **Arizona–Sonora Desert Museum** (AZ): This Tucson attraction is actually a zoo featuring the animals of the Sonoran Desert. It has rooms full of snakes, a prairie-dog town, bighorn sheep, mountain lions, and an aviary full of hummingbirds. Kids and adults love this place. See p. 366.

- **Shootouts at the O.K. Corral** (AZ): Tombstone may be "the town too tough to die," but poor Ike Clanton and his buddies the McLaury boys have to die over and over at frequent reenactments of the famous gunfight. See p. 472.

- **The Grand Canyon Railway** (AZ): Not only is this train excursion a fun way to get to the Grand Canyon, but it also lets you avoid wearisome parking problems and congestion. Shootouts and train robberies are to be expected in this corner of the Wild West. See p. 535.

- **Zion National Park** (UT): The Junior Ranger/Explorers program, available at most national parks, is particularly extensive here. Morning and afternoon activities all summer are geared toward teaching kids what makes this natural wonder so special. They'll have so much fun, they won't even notice they're learning. See p. 562.

6 The Best Luxury Hotels & Resorts

- **Inn of the Anasazi** (113 Washington Ave., Santa Fe; ℂ **800/688-8100** or 505/988-3030): Just steps from the plaza, this elegant hotel offers a taste of Anasazi architecture. The interior utilizes stacked sandstone with touches of Navajo artwork to create a warm ambience. Add to that excellent amenities and stellar service. See p. 138.

- **La Posada de Santa Fe Resort and Spa** (Santa Fe, NM; ℂ **800/727-5276** or 505/986-0000): With the feel of a meandering adobe village but the service of a fine hotel, this has become one of New Mexico's premier resorts. It has a Zen-Southwestern–style spa and pool and spacious spa rooms. See p. 141.

- **El Monte Sagrado** (Taos, NM; ℂ 800/828-TAOS or 505/758-3502): With guest rooms and casitas set around a grassy "Sacred Circle," this ecoresort is the quintessence of refinement. Every detail—from the waterfalls and chemical-free pool and hot tubs to the authentic theme decor in the rooms—has been created with conscious care. See p. 198.

- **Hyatt Regency Tamaya Resort and Spa** (Santa Ana Pueblo, NM; ℂ 800/55-HYATT or 505/867-1234): Situated on Santa Ana Pueblo land, this grand resort has all a person might need to get away from the world. Three swimming pools, a full-service spa and fitness center, an 18-hole golf course, and views of the Sandia Mountains make for plenty to do. Meanwhile, spacious rooms offer quiet for those who'd rather do nothing. It's only 25 minutes from Albuquerque and 45 minutes from Santa Fe. See p. 236.

- **Hyatt Regency Scottsdale Resort & Spa at Gainey Ranch** (Scottsdale, AZ; ℂ 800/55-HYATT or 480/444-1234): Contemporary desert architecture, dramatic landscaping, a water playground with its own beach, a staff that's always ready to assist you, several good restaurants, and even gondola rides—it all adds up to a lot of fun at one of the most smoothly run resorts in Arizona. See p. 400.

- **The Phoenician** (Scottsdale, AZ; ℂ 800/888-8234 or 480/941-8200): This Xanadu of the resort world brims with marble, crystal, and art. With staff members seemingly around every corner, the hotel offers its guests impeccable service. Mary Elaine's, the resort's premier dining room, is among the finest restaurants in the state, and the views are hard to beat. See p. 400.

- **The Boulders Resort and Golden Door Spa** (Carefree, AZ; ℂ 866/397-6520 or 480/488-9009): Taking its name from the massive blocks of eroded granite scattered about the grounds, the Boulders is among the most exclusive and expensive resorts in the state. Pueblo architecture fits seamlessly with the landscape, and the golf course is the most breathtaking in Arizona. See p. 403.

- **Arizona Biltmore Resort & Spa** (Phoenix, AZ; ℂ 800/950-0086 or 602/955-6600): Combining discreet service and the architectural styling of Frank Lloyd Wright, the Biltmore has long been one of Arizona's most prestigious resorts. This is a thoroughly old-money place, but it continues to keep pace with the times. See p. 405.

- **Loews Ventana Canyon Resort** (Tucson, AZ; ℂ 800/234-5117): With the Santa Catalina Mountains rising in the backyard and an almost-natural waterfall only steps away from the lobby, this is Tucson's most dramatic resort. Contemporary styling throughout makes constant reference to the desert setting. See p. 347.

- **Enchantment Resort** (Sedona, AZ; ℂ 800/826-4180 or 928/282-2900): A dramatic setting in a red-rock canyon makes this the most unforgettably situated resort in the state. If you want to feel as though you're vacationing in the desert, this place fills the bill. Guest rooms are constructed in pueblo architectural style; the spa is one of Arizona's finest. See p. 506.

7 The Best Bed & Breakfasts

- **Kokopelli's Cave** (Farmington, NM; ℂ 505/326-2461): This is an actual cave, but it's like no other cave you've ever seen. Carved deep into the side of a cliff, it's a three-room luxury apartment complete with carpet, VCR, kitchen, and space enough for a family. See p. 129.

- **Casa de las Chimeneas** (Taos, NM; © 877/758-4777 or 505/758-4777): This 1925 adobe home has been a model of Southwestern elegance since it opened as a B&B in 1988. The inn has lovely gardens, comfortable rooms, and a spa, as well as complete massage and facial treatments. The newest rooms have heated Saltillo tile floors, gas kiva fireplaces, and jetted tubs. See p. 202.

- **The Royal Elizabeth** (Tucson, AZ; © 877/670-9022 or 520/670-9022): In downtown Tucson just a block from the Temple of Music and Art, this Territorial-style historic home is filled with beautiful Victorian antiques and architectural details. Guest rooms have lots of touches not often seen in historic B&Bs, including "vintage" phones, TVs, fridges, and safes. See p. 346.

- **La Zarzuela** (Tucson, AZ; © 888/848-8225): Perched high on a hill on the west side of Tucson, this luxurious B&B boasts great views, colorful decor, and loads of outdoor spaces where guests can relax in the warmth of the desert. See p. 350.

- **Rocamadour Bed & Breakfast for (Rock) Lovers** (Prescott, AZ; © 888/771-1933 or 928/771-1933): Set amid the rounded boulders of the Granite Dells just north of Prescott, this inn combines a spectacular setting with French antiques and luxurious accommodations. You won't find a more memorable setting in the state. See p. 490.

- **Briar Patch Inn** (Sedona, AZ; © 888/809-3030 or 928/282-2342): Oak Creek Canyon, near Sedona, where you'll find this collection of luxurious cottages, is an oasis in the desert. Few experiences are more restorative than breakfast on the shady banks of the creek. See p. 507.

- **The Inn at 410** (Flagstaff, AZ; © 800/774-2008 or 928/774-0088): This restored 1907 bungalow offers a convenient location in downtown Flagstaff, pleasant surroundings, comfortable rooms, and delicious breakfasts. Rooms feature different, distinctive themes, and eight of them have their own fireplaces. See p. 555.

- **Cochise Stronghold B&B** (Cochise County, AZ; © 877/426-4141 or 520/826-4141): Surrounded by the national forest and mountainsides strewn with giant boulders, this B&B is one of the state's most remote inns. The passive solar building was built from straw bales and is not only energy-efficient but also quite beautiful. See p. 480.

8 The Best Places to Savor Southwest Flavors

- **The Compound** (Santa Fe, NM; © 505/982-4353): This reincarnation of one of Santa Fe's classic restaurants serves daring contemporary American food in a soulful setting. Such delicacies as monkfish chorizo with watercress or grilled beef tenderloin with Italian potatoes will please sophisticated palates—and probably simpler ones, too. See p. 152.

- **Geronimo** (Santa Fe, NM; © 505/982-1500): Set in the 1756 Borrego House on Canyon Road, this restaurant offers brilliant flavors in a serene adobe atmosphere. The elk tenderloin here is Santa Fe's most prized entree. Come for lunch and sit on the patio to watch the action on Canyon Road. See p. 153.

- **Santacafé** (Santa Fe, NM; © 505/984-1788): This restaurant, our all-time favorite, borrows from an international menu of preparations and offerings. The minimalist decor accentuates the beautiful architecture of the 18th-century Padre Gallegos House. One of their best dishes is the Alaskan halibut with English peas and saffron couscous. See p. 154.

- **The Shed** (Santa Fe, NM; ℂ 505/ 982-9030): A Santa Fe luncheon institution since 1953, this cafe occupies several rooms in part of a rambling hacienda that was built in 1692. The sauces here have been refined over the years, creating amazing flavors in basic dishes such as enchiladas, burritos, and stuffed *sopaipillas*. See p. 157. Its sister restaurant, **La Choza**, which has a similar menu, is just as good. See p. 156.

- **Joseph's Table** (Taos, NM; ℂ 505/ 751-4512): Now in new digs on Taos Plaza, this font of creativity serves delightful dishes with plenty of flair. Try the steak au poivre over mashed potatoes with a Madeira mushroom sauce. Delectable. See p. 206.

- **Diane's Bakery & Cafe** (Silver City, NM; ℂ 505/538-8722): Diane Barrett, who was once a pastry chef at La Traviata and Eldorado in Santa Fe, has brought refined flavors to the little mining town of Silver City. Come here to feast on sumptuous baked goods and sophisticated meals such as rack of lamb. See p. 334.

- **Roaring Fork** (Scottsdale, AZ; ℂ 480/947-0795): Roaring Fork has long been one of the most creative southwestern restaurants in the Phoenix area. The atmosphere is lively, and everything from the bread basket and bar snacks to the entrees and desserts shows an attention to detail. See p. 413.

- **Janos/J Bar** (Tucson, AZ; ℂ 520/ 615-6100): Serving a combination of regional and Southwestern dishes, Janos has for many years been one of Tucson's premier restaurants. It's just outside the front door of the Westin La Paloma resort, and is as formal a place as you'll find in this city. J Bar is Janos's less formal bar and grill. See p. 360, 363.

- **Terra Cotta** (Tucson, AZ; ℂ 520/ 577-8100): Terra Cotta was one of Arizona's pioneers in the realm of Southwestern cuisine. The beautiful, art-filled restaurant in the Tucson foothills continues to serve creative and reasonably priced meals. See p. 364.

- **Cowboy Club Grille & Spirits** (Sedona, AZ; ℂ 928/282-4200): In the building where the Cowboy Artists of America organization was founded, this thoroughly Western restaurant is a great place to try such Arizona specialties as buffalo filet mignon, rattlesnake, and cactus fries. See p. 512.

- **The Turquoise Room** (Winslow, AZ; ℂ 928/289-2888): Located in the little-visited town of Winslow in the restored La Posada historic hotel, this restaurant conjures up the days when the wealthy still traveled by railroad. Rarely will you find such excellent meals in such an off-the-beaten-path locale. See p. 98.

2

Planning Your Trip to the Southwest

As with any trip, a little preparation is essential before you start. This chapter provides you with a variety of planning tools, including information on when to go, how to get there, and how to get around once you're there.

1 The Regions in Brief

Four Corners   This region is the bull's-eye for this book. Containing some of the world's most cherished archaeological sites, the Four Corners area is the home to not only ancient cultures such as the Anasazi (or ancestral Puebloans), but also their modern-day descendants and other Native American people such as the Navajo and Apache. This region's other claim to fame is that it's the only place in the U.S. where four states—Colorado, Utah, New Mexico, and Arizona—meet. Each state has its own treasures. To name only a few, Colorado has Mesa Verde National Park, Utah has Monument Valley, New Mexico has Chaco Culture National Historic Park, and Arizona has Canyon de Chelly National Monument and the Hopi and Navajo reservations. These spectacular landmarks are set among painted canyons and poetic buttes, the perfect ambience to fulfill Southwestern fantasies.

Santa Fe, Taos & Albuquerque   Besides the Four Corners region, the main actor in New Mexico is its major art and cultural center, Santa Fe, with Taos and Albuquerque playing supporting roles. Santa Fe is a hip, artsy city that wears its 400-year-old mores on its sleeve. Nestled on the side of the **Sangre de Cristo**

Mountains, it's an adobe showcase of centuries-old buildings that hug the earth. Many of these are artist studios and galleries set on narrow streets, ideal for desultory browsing. And then there's upstart Taos, the little arts town and ski center of just 5,000 people that lies wedged between the 13,000-foot Sangre de Cristo Mountains and the 700-foot-deep **Rio Grande Gorge.** Albuquerque is the big city, New Mexico style, a place with good restaurants and fun attractions such as a tramway to the top of the Sandia Mountains and lava flows covered with petroglyphs.

Northern New Mexico   In this region, the lush **Rocky Mountains** rise directly out of parched plateaus, with the Rio Grande nourishing rich cultures. Woven throughout this terrain are 19 settlements and numerous ruins of the Native American Pueblo culture, an incredible testament to the resilience of a proud people. The Hispanic culture also has a legacy here; its cathedrals and missions, small mountain villages, and iconographic artwork date back over 400 years. Relics of the Old West are also prevalent, in mountain towns such as Chama and on the open plains of the northeast.

Southern New Mexico A land of wide-open spaces, this region is rich with natural wonders and Wild West and Native American history. To the east, the United States' first designated wilderness, the Gila, was once home to the Mogollon Indians; the Gila Cliff Dwellings National Monument preserves their past. The once-booming mining town of Silver City is at the heart of the region. Las Cruces, New Mexico's second-largest city, sits at the foot of the Organ Mountains, and not far east of there stand the blazing dunes of White Sands National Monument. At Carlsbad Caverns National Park, one of the nation's most elaborate cave systems offers the opportunity for underground exploration.

Tucson, Phoenix, Scottsdale & the Valley of the Sun These cities, which form a backbone across Arizona, offer desert beauty and sophisticated lifestyles. Tucson is in the lushest part of the Sonoran Desert and has all the highlights of a major city—excellent arts and culture, and plenty more. Encircled by mountain ranges, this desert oasis offers world-class golf resorts; historical treasures with Native American, Hispanic, and Anglo roots; and some of the Southwest's best hiking in Saguaro National Park. North of Tucson, Phoenix, Scottsdale, and the Valley of the Sun sprawl across the Sonoran desert. Twenty cities and communities nestle among several mountain rages. Resorts and golf courses abound here, as do retirement communities. But the sprawl has a positive note: The area boasts world-class shopping, museums, culture such as opera, dance, and theater, and professional sports.

Southern & Eastern Arizona Southern Arizona is a region of great contrasts, from desert lowlands to "sky islands," volcanic mountain ranges that seem to rise up from nowhere. The desert climate here attracts many retirees, and also many rare birds, which travel up from the tropics.

To the southwest, along the Mexican border, lies Organ Pipe Cactus National Monument, home to outlandish desert plant, bird, and animal life and one of the nation's best-kept secrets. To the north, what's known as eastern Arizona is a world apart from these desert lands. Made up of the Mogollon Rim, an escarpment that rises some 2,000 feet off the desert floor, as well as the White Mountains, this region offers tall forests and clear streams. It's home to the Sunrise Park Resort ski area on the White Mountain Apache Indian Reservation.

Central & Western Arizona At the center of Arizona, desert predominates. Parts of it are the desolate desert of Wile E. Coyote, but it has stunning variety. This region is home to the red-rock country of Sedona, which hosts a thriving arts scene and recreational opportunities, from hiking to hot-air ballooning. In the higher regions lie the quaint city of Prescott and the old mining town of Jerome, now an arts community. Arizona's West Coast region has miles of waterfront, and Lakes Mead and Mohave provide the state with plenty of watersports.

The Grand Canyon & Northern Arizona Few sights inspire as many superlatives as Grand Canyon National Park, which dominates this region. One of the world's natural wonders, the Grand Canyon is not only beautiful but also expansive, with numerous canyons stretching across hundreds of miles. The neighboring cities of Flagstaff, Williams, and Tusayan accommodate and feed millions of visitors each year. North of the Grand Canyon lies the state's most remote and untracked region, the Arizona Strip.

Las Vegas In high contrast to the nature-oriented slant of the Southwest is this glittery city in the desert, noted for its art, cuisine, and shows. Yeah, right. Most people, of course, come to gamble.

In recent years this city has become a master of illusion, with hotels posing as pyramids or Italian palaces, their structures providing whole worlds of fantasy. Some find Las Vegas a fun and convenient entryway to their Southwest vacation.

Southern Utah All five of Utah's national parks are in this region, and for good reason—it's undeniably beautiful. Ancient geologic forces, erosion, oxidation, and other natural processes have carved spectacular rock sculptures—delicate and intricate, bold and stately—and painted them in a riot of color. This is where you'll find Zion National Park, with its undulating landscapes; Bryce Canyon National Park, with its marvelous stone sculptures, called hoodoos; and the stunning red-rock country of Arches and Canyonlands National Parks. It's also the home of the bulk of Lake Powell and Glen Canyon National Recreation Area, a scenic play land for nearly every type of boater.

2 Visitor Information & Maps

Numerous agencies can assist you with planning your trip. For information on Arizona, contact the **Arizona Office of Tourism,** 1110 West Washington St., Suite 155, Phoenix, AZ 85007 (© **866/ 275-5816** or 602/364-3700; www.arizona guide.com). The Visitors Information Center for the **New Mexico Department of Tourism** is at 491 Old Santa Fe Trail, Santa Fe, NM 87501 (© **800/545-2070** or 505/827-7400; www.newmexico.org).

For Colorado, start by contacting the **Colorado Tourism Office,** 1625 Broadway, Suite 2700, Denver, CO 80202 (© **800/COLORADO** or 303/892-3885; www.colorado.com), for a free copy of the official state vacation guide, which includes a state map and describes attractions, activities, and lodgings throughout Colorado. Another good source for Colorado information is the website of the *Denver Post,* the state's major daily newspaper (www.denver post.com). For information on Utah as well as an official state map, contact the **Utah Office of Tourism,** Council Hall/ 300 North State St., Salt Lake City, UT 84114 (© **800/200-1160** or 801/538-1030; www.utah.com).

For information about Las Vegas, contact the **Las Vegas Convention and Visitors Authority,** 3150 Paradise Rd., Las Vegas, NV 89109 (© **877/VISITLV** or 702/892-7575; www.visitlv.com). Another excellent information source is the **Las Vegas Chamber of Commerce,** 3720 Howard Hughes Pkwy., No. 100, Las Vegas, NV 89109 (© **702/735-1616;** www.lvchamber.com). Request the *Visitor's Guide,* which contains extensive information about accommodations, attractions, excursions, children's activities, and more. The staff can answer all your Las Vegas questions, including those about weddings and divorces.

Convention and visitors' bureaus or chambers of commerce represent cities and regions throughout the Southwest. Their addresses, telephone numbers, and Internet addresses appear in the appropriate chapters in this book.

If you're a member of **AAA,** remember that you can get a map and guidebook covering Arizona and New Mexico. You can also request the club's free *Southwestern CampBook,* which includes campgrounds in Arizona, Utah, Colorado, and New Mexico.

Some regional **websites** that might be of help include the following:

- www.desertusa.com
- http://phoenix.about.com
- http://gosw.about.com/od/southwest miscelaneous/a/blogs.htm
- www.sfaol.com
- www.taosplaza.com

- www.ABQblogs.com
- www.southernnewmexico.com

Some new general **blogs** that might help in planning your trip include the following:

- www.gridskipper.com
- www.salon.com/wanderlust
- www.travelblog.com
- www.travelblog.org
- www.worldhum.com
- www.writtenroad.com

3 Entry Requirements

PASSPORTS

For information on how to get a passport, go to "**Passports**" in the "**Fast Facts**" section later in this chapter—the websites listed provide downloadable passport applications as well as the current fees for processing passport applications. For an up-to-date, country-by-country listing of passport requirements around the world, go to the "Foreign Entry Requirement" Web page of the U.S. State Department at **http://travel.state.gov**. International visitors can obtain a visa application at the same website. *Note:* Children are required to present a passport when entering the United States at airports. More information on obtaining a passport for a minor can be found at http://travel.state.gov.

VISAS

For specifics on how to get a visa, go to "**Visas**" in the "**Fast Facts**" section of this chapter.

The U.S. State Department has a **Visa Waiver Program (VWP)** allowing citizens of the following countries (at press time) to enter the United States without a visa for stays of up to 90 days: Andorra,

Australia, Austria, Belgium, Brunei, Denmark, Finland, France, Germany, Iceland, Ireland, Italy, Japan, Liechtenstein, Luxembourg, Monaco, the Netherlands, New Zealand, Norway, Portugal, San Marino, Singapore, Slovenia, Spain, Sweden, Switzerland, and the United Kingdom. Canadian citizens may enter the United States without visas; they will need to show passports and proof of residence, however. *Note:* Any passport issued on or after October 26, 2006, by a VWP country must be an **e-Passport** for VWP travelers to be eligible to enter the U.S. without a visa. Citizens of these nations also need to present a round-trip air or cruise ticket upon arrival. E-Passports contain computer chips capable of storing biometric information, such as the required digital photograph of the holder. (You can identify an e-Passport by the symbol on the bottom center cover of your passport.) If your passport doesn't have this feature, you can still travel without a visa if it is a valid passport issued before October 26, 2005, and includes a machine-readable zone, or between October 26, 2005, and October 25, 2006, and includes a digital photograph. For more

---

U.S. Entry: Passport Required

New regulations issued by the Homeland Security Department now require virtually every air traveler entering the U.S. to show a passport—and future regulations will cover land and sea entry as well. As of January 23, 2007, all persons, including U.S. citizens, traveling by air between the United States and Canada, Mexico, Central and South America, the Caribbean, and Bermuda are required to present a valid passport. Similar regulations for those traveling by land or sea (including ferries) are expected as early as January 1, 2008.

information, go to **www.travel.state. gov/visa.**

Citizens of all other countries must have (1) a valid passport that expires at least 6 months later than the scheduled end of their visit to the United States, and (2) a tourist visa, which may be obtained without charge from any U.S. consulate.

As of January 2004, many international visitors traveling on visas to the United States will be photographed and fingerprinted on arrival at Customs in airports and on cruise ships in a program created by the Department of Homeland Security called **US-VISIT.** Exempt from the extra scrutiny are visitors entering by land or those (mostly in Europe; p. 55) that don't require a visa for short-term visits. For more information, go to the Homeland Security website at **www.dhs. gov/dhspublic.**

MEDICAL REQUIREMENTS

Unless you're arriving from an area known to be suffering from an epidemic (particularly cholera or yellow fever), inoculations or vaccinations are not required for entry into the United States. If you have a medical condition that requires **syringe-administered medications,** carry a valid signed prescription from your physician; syringes in carry-on baggage will be inspected. Insulin in any form should have the proper pharmaceutical documentation. If you have a disease that requires treatment with **narcotics,** you should also carry documented proof with you—smuggling narcotics aboard a plane carries severe penalties in the U.S.

For **HIV-positive visitors,** requirements for entering the United States are somewhat vague and change frequently. For up-to-the-minute information, contact **AIDSinfo** (© 800/448-0440 or 301/519-6616 outside the U.S.; www.aids info.nih.gov) or the **Gay Men's Health Crisis** (© 212/367-1000; www.gmhc. org).

CUSTOMS

For information on what you can bring into and take out of the United States, go to "**Customs**" in the "**Fast Facts**" section of this chapter.

4 When to Go

THE CLIMATE The climate in the Southwest is, overall, a great pleasure. Though the parched air can dry your skin, the same aridness makes the heat and cold easier to handle and promises lots of sunny days. Summers are hot throughout most of the region, though distinctly cooler at higher elevations. Winters are relatively mild in the south, harsher in the north and in the mountains. Spring and fall have pleasant temperatures, though in spring the wind blows throughout the region. Rainfall is sparse except in the higher mountains; summer afternoon thunderstorms and winter snows account for most precipitation.

WHEN TO GO The Southwest is a year-round destination, although people head to different parts at different times of year. In Phoenix, Tucson, and other parts of the desert, the high season runs from October to mid-May, with the highest hotel rates during the holidays. Wintertime is also high season in the mountain areas of northern New Mexico and southern Colorado, where skiing is popular.

Summer is high season at most national parks, particularly Grand Canyon and Carlsbad Caverns, though the latter receives much less traffic than the former. In late summer, monsoon rains cool the region in afternoons. But beware: These storms can cause flash floods that make roads briefly impassable. Avoid entering low areas if it's raining anywhere nearby.

Spring and autumn are the best times to visit the region. Temperatures are cool in the mountains and warm in the desert, without extreme temperatures on either end. Still, snow can fall in the high regions well into spring, and in fall, thunderstorms can pound the desert.

New Mexico Average High/Low Temperatures in °F (°C) & Precipitation

	Jan	Apr	July	Oct	Annual Rainfall (inches)
Santa Fe	42 (6)/	62 (17)/	85 (29)/	65 (18)/	14.0
	18 (–7)	33 (1)	56 (13)	38 (3)	
Las Cruces	56 (13)/	77 (25)/	94 (34)/	78 (26)/	8.6
	25 (–4)	41 (5)	65 (18)	44 (7)	

Arizona Average High/Low Temperatures In °F (°C) & Precipitation

	Jan	Apr	July	Oct	Annual Rainfall (inches)
Flagstaff	41 (5)/	57 (14)/	81 (27)/	63 (17)/	22.91
	14 (–10)	27 (–3)	50 (10)	31 (–1)	
Phoenix	65 (18)/	84 (29)/	105 (41)/	88 (31)/	8.29
	38 (3)	52 (11)	78 (26)	57 (14)	

CALENDAR OF EVENTS

January

New Year's Day. King's Day transfer of canes to new officials and various dances at all eight northern New Mexico pueblos. Turtle Dance at Taos Pueblo (no photography allowed). Call © 505/758-1028 for more information. January 1.

Tostitos Fiesta Bowl Football Classic, University of Phoenix Stadium, Glendale, AZ. This college bowl game usually sells out nearly a year in advance. Call © 800/635-5748 or 480/350 0911, or go to www.tostitos fiestabowl.com. Early January.

Wings over Willcox, Willcox, AZ. Birding tours, workshops, and, of course, watching the tens of thousands of sandhill cranes that gather in the Sulphur Springs Valley near Willcox. Call © 800/200-2272 or go to www. wingsoverwillcox.com. Mid-January.

FBR Open Golf Tournament, Scottsdale, AZ. Prestigious PGA golf tournament at the Tournament Players Club. Call © 602/870-0163 or go to www. fbropen.com. Late January.

February

Tubac Festival of the Arts, Tubac, AZ. Exhibits by North American artists and craftspcople. Call © 520/398-2704, or go to www.tubacaz.com/festival.asp. Early February.

World Championship Hoop Dance Contest, Phoenix, AZ. Native American dancers from around the nation take part in this colorful competition held at the Heard Museum. Call © 602/252-8848 or go to www.heard.org. Early February.

Arizona Renaissance Festival, Apache Junction, AZ. Patterned after a 16th-century English country fair, this festival features costumed participants and tournament jousting. Call © 520/463-2700 or go to www.royalfaires. com. Weekends from early February to early April.

Tucson Gem and Mineral Show, Tucson, AZ. This huge show at the Tucson Convention Center offers seminars, museum displays from around the world, and hundreds of dealers selling just about any kind of rock you can imagine. In addition, there are more than 40 other smaller shows in the weeks prior to the main show; for information on these smaller shows, visit www.tucsonshowguide.com. Call ✆ 520/322-5773 or go to www.tgms.org. Mid-February.

O'odham Tash, Casa Grande, AZ. One of the largest annual Native American festivals in the country, attracting dozens of tribes that participate in rodeos, arts-and-crafts exhibits, and dance performances. Call ✆ 520/836-4723. Mid-February.

Bryce Canyon Winter Festival, Bryce, UT. A winter celebration amid the colorful rock formations of the Bryce Canyon National Park area. Call ✆ 800/468-8660. Mid-February.

La Fiesta de los Vaqueros, Tucson, AZ. Cowboy festival and rodeo at the Tucson Rodeo Grounds, including the Tucson Rodeo Parade, which claims to be the world's largest nonmotorized parade. Call ✆ 800/964-5662 or 520/741-2233, or go to www.tucsonrodeo.com. Late February.

March

Heard Museum Guild Indian Fair and Market, Phoenix, AZ. Indian cultural and dance presentations and one of the greatest selections of Native American crafts in the Southwest make this a fascinating festival. Go early to avoid the crowds. Call ✆ 602/252-8848 or go to www.heard.org. Early March.

Parada del Sol Parade and Rodeo, Scottsdale, AZ. The state's longest horse-drawn parade, plus a street dance and rodeo. Call ✆ 480/990-3179 or go to www.scottsdalejaycees.com. Early March.

Rio Grande Arts and Crafts Festival, Albuquerque, NM. A juried show featuring 200 artists and craftspeople

from around the country takes place at the State Fairgrounds in Albuquerque during the second week of March. Call ✆ 505/292-7457 for more information.

Rockhound Roundup, Deming, NM. Gems, jewelry, tools, and crafted items are displayed and sold at the Southwest New Mexico State Fairgrounds. Call ✆ 505/267-4399. Mid-March.

Festival of the West, Chandler, AZ. A celebration of all things cowboy, from cowboy poetry to Western music to Western movies. There's a chuck-wagon cook-off, a mountain-man rendezvous, even horseback shooting contests. Call ✆ 602/996-4387 or go to www.festivalofthewest.com. Mid-March.

Ostrich Festival, Chandler, AZ. Although brief, these unusual races are something you ought to see at least once in your lifetime. Call ✆ 480/963-4571 or go to www.ostrichfestival.com. Mid-March.

Wa:k Pow Wow, Tucson, AZ. Tohono O'odham celebration at Mission San Xavier del Bac, featuring many Southwestern Native American groups. Call ✆ 520/294-5727. Second weekend in March.

Western Arts Festival, Cedar City, UT. Western lifestyle is the focus at this 4-day event featuring cowboy poetry, Western music, and food. Call ✆ 800/354-4849. Mid-March.

April

Easter Weekend Celebration, at most New Mexico pueblos celebrations including masses, parades, Corn Dances, and other dances, such as the Bow and Arrow Dance at Nambé. Call ✆ 505/843-7270 for information, or go to www.indianpueblo.org. Easter weekend.

St. George Art Festival, St. George, UT. This outdoors fine-arts festival draws artists and visitors from all over the American West. Call ℂ **435/634-5850.** Friday and Saturday of Easter weekend.

Gathering of Nations Powwow, University Arena, Albuquerque, NM. Dance competitions, arts-and-crafts exhibitions, and Miss Indian World contest. Call ℂ **505/836-2810** or visit www.gatheringofnations.com for more information. Late April.

Tour of Canyonlands, Moab, UT. This annual bike race brings riders from around the country and abroad for a spectacular weekend of racing. Call ℂ **303/432-1519.**

Tucson International Mariachi Conference, Tucson, AZ. Mariachi bands from all over the world come to compete before standing-room-only crowds. Call ℂ **520/838-3908** or go to www.tucsonmariachi.org. Mid- to late April.

May

Taos Spring Arts Festival, Taos, NM. Contemporary visual, performing, and literary arts are highlighted for 2 weeks at venues throughout Taos and Taos County. For dates and ticket info contact ℂ **800/732-TAOS** or 505/758-3873; www.taoschamber.com. Month of May.

Cinco de Mayo Fiestas, across the region. Celebrations of the restoration of the Mexican republic (from French occupation 1863–67) occur in, among other places, Phoenix, AZ (call ℂ **602/279-4669**); Tucson, AZ (ℂ **520/292-9326**); Las Cruces, NM, at Old Mesilla Plaza (ℂ **505/524-1968** or 505/541-2444); and Truth or Consequences, NM (ℂ **800/831-9487** or 505/894-3536). First weekend in May.

Taste of Santa Fe, Sweeney Convention Center, Santa Fe, NM. Sample Santa Fe's best chefs' recipes, including appetizers, entrees, and desserts. For information call ℂ **505/989-5328.** First Tuesday in May.

Phippen Western Art Show and Sale, Prescott, AZ. This is the state's premier Western-art sale. Call ℂ **928/778-1385** or go to www.phippenartmuseum.org. Memorial Day weekend.

Wyatt Earp Days, Tombstone, AZ. Gunfight reenactments in memory of the shootout at the O.K. Corral. Call ℂ **888/457-3929** or 520/457-3291, or go to www.tombstone.org. Late May.

Iron Horse Bicycle Classic, Durango, CO. Mountain bikers race against a steam train from Durango to Silverton. Call ℂ **970/259-4621** or visit the website at www.ironhorsebicycleclassic.com. Memorial Day weekend.

June

San Antonio Feast Day, NM. Corn Dances at many of the New Mexico pueblos. For information, call ℂ **505/843-7270** or go to www.indianpueblo.org. June 13.

Rodeo de Santa Fe, Santa Fe, NM. This 4-day event features a Western parade, a rodeo dance, and five rodeo performances. For tickets and information, call ℂ **505/471-4300** or go to www.rodeodesantafe.org. First weekend after Father's Day.

Telluride Bluegrass Festival, Telluride, CO. Features bluegrass, folk, and country music played among mountain splendor. Call ℂ **303/823-0848** or see www.planetbluegrass.com. Late June.

Groovefest, Cedar City, UT. Blues and bluegrass musicians entertain crowds at the Main Street Park. The daylong event includes barbecue and artisans selling their work. Call ℂ **435/867-9800** or visit www.groovefestutah.com. Late June.

Taos Solar Music Festival, Taos, NM. Sit on the grass at Kit Carson Municipal Park and listen to major players at this event celebrating the summer solstice. The event has a stage powered by a solar generator and educational displays within a "Solar Village." For information, call ☎ **505/758-9191** or go to www.solarmusic.com. Last weekend in June.

July

Santa Fe Opera, Santa Fe, NM. The world-class Santa Fe Opera season runs from the beginning of July to the end of August. Call ☎ **800/280-4654** or go to www.santafeopera.org for more information.

Hopi Festival of Arts and Culture, Flagstaff, AZ. Exhibition and sale at the Museum of Northern Arizona, including cultural events. Call ☎ **928/ 774-5213** or go to www.musnaz.org. Early July.

Fourth of July Celebrations. Parades, fireworks, and various other events are held all over the region. Call the chamber of commerce in each city or town for more information.

Prescott Frontier Days/World's Oldest Rodeo, Prescott, AZ. This is one of the state's two rodeos that claim to be the nation's oldest. Call ☎ **800/358-1888** or 928/445-3103, or go to www. worldsoldestrodeo.com. Early July.

Eight Northern Pueblos Artist and Craftsman Show, NM. More than 600 Native American artists exhibit their work at one of the eight northern pueblos. Traditional dances and food booths. Call ☎ **505/747-1593** or go to www.indianpueblo.org for exact dates and the location, which varies. Mid-July.

Fiestas de Santiago y Santa Ana, Taos, NM. The fiestas feature candlelight processions, special Masses, music, dancing, parades, crafts, and food booths. For information, contact the Taos Fiesta Council (☎ **800/732-8267;** www.fiestasdetaos.com). Third weekend in July.

The Spanish Markets, Santa Fe Plaza, Santa Fe, NM. More than 300 Hispanic artists from New Mexico and southern Colorado exhibit and sell their work in this lively community event. For information, contact the Spanish Colonial Arts Society (☎ **505/ 982-2226;** www.spanishcolonial.org). Last full weekend in July.

Navajo Festival of Arts and Culture, Flagstaff, AZ. Exhibition and sale at the Museum of Northern Arizona, including cultural events. Call ☎ **928/ 774-5213** or go to www.musnaz.org. Late July or early August.

August

Old Lincoln Days and Billy the Kid Pageant, Lincoln, NM. The main attraction is a reenactment of Billy the Kid's escape from the Lincoln jail. There's also a fiddling contest and living-history demonstrations (such as weaving and blacksmithing). Call ☎ **505/653-4025** for more information. First weekend in August.

Southwest Wings Birding and Nature Festival, Bisbee, AZ. Spotting hummingbirds and looking for owls and bats keep participants busy. Includes lectures and field trips throughout southeastern Arizona and Sonora, Mexico. Call ☎ **520/678-8237** or go to www.swwings.org. Early August.

Intertribal Indian Ceremonial, near Gallup, NM. Thirty tribes from the United States and Mexico participate in rodeos, parades, dances, athletic competitions, and an arts-and-crafts show at Red Rock State Park, east of Gallup. Contact ☎ **800/242-4282;** www.gallupnm.org. Second week in August.

Bat Flight Breakfast, Carlsbad Caverns National Park, NM. A buffet breakfast is served while participants watch the bats return to the cave in the early morning. Contact © 505/785-3012, or go to www.nps.gov/cave for details and exact date. Second Thursday of August.

Arizona Cowboy Poets' Gathering, Prescott, AZ. Not just traditional and contemporary poetry, but also storytelling that focuses on the cowboy lifestyle. Call © 928/445-3122 or go to www.sharlot.org. Third weekend in August.

The Indian Market, Santa Fe, NM. This is the largest all–Native American market in the country. About 1,200 artisans display their baskets, blankets, jewelry, pottery, and other arts. Sales are brisk. The market is free, but hotels are booked months in advance. Contact the Southwestern Association for Indian Art (© 505/983-5220; www.swaia.org). Third weekend after the first Thursday in August.

Great American Duck Race, Deming, NM. Devised in a bar in 1979, this event has grown to include a parade, tortilla toss, outhouse race, ballooning, dances, and, of course, the duck race. Takes place on the courthouse lawn ("Duck Downs"). Call © 888/345-1125 for details. Fourth weekend in August.

September

Navajo Nation Fair, Window Rock, AZ. A very large fair featuring traditional music and dancing, a fry bread contest, and more. Call © 928/871-7055 or go to www.navajonationfair.com. Early September.

New Mexico State Fair and Rodeo, State Fairgrounds, Albuquerque, NM. One of America's top state fairs, it features horse racing (with pari-mutuel betting), a nationally acclaimed rodeo,

entertainment by top country artists, Native American and Spanish villages, the requisite midway livestock shows, and arts and crafts. Call © 505/265-1791 or visit www.nmstatefair.com for more information. Early September.

Telluride Film Festival, Telluride, CO. This influential international festival celebrates the art of film and has featured the premieres of some of the finest independent films. Call © 970/728-4401 or see www.telluridefilmfestival.org. Labor Day weekend.

Chile Festival, Hatch, NM. New Mexicans celebrate their favorite fiery food item with a festival in the "Chile Capital of the World." Call © 505/267-5050. Labor Day weekend.

La Fiesta de Santa Fe, Santa Fe, NM. An exuberant combination of spirit, history, and general merrymaking, La Fiesta is the oldest community celebration in the United States. Zozobra, "Old Man Gloom," a 40-foot-tall effigy of wood, canvas, and paper, is burned at dusk on Thursday to revitalize the community. For information call © 505/988-7575. Weekend after Labor Day.

Moab Music Festival, Moab, UT. Live classical, jazz, bluegrass, and other types of music, presented in a stunning red-rock amphitheater and at other locations. Call © 435/259-7003. Early to mid-September.

Stone Lake Fiesta, Jicarilla Reservation, 19 miles south of Dulce, NM. Apache festival with rodeo, ceremonial dances, and footrace. Contact © 505/759-4276 or go to www.jicarillaonline.com for more information. Mid-September.

Grand Canyon Music Festival, Grand Canyon Village, AZ. For more than 20 years, this festival has been bringing classical music to the South Rim of the

Grand Canyon. Call ✆ 800/997-8285 or 928/638-9215, or go to www.grandcanyonmusicfest.org. Early to mid-September.

Taos Fall Festivals, Taos, NM. Events include the Fall Arts Festival, Old Taos Trade Fair, Wool Festival, and San Geronimo Day at Taos Pueblo. The arts-and-crafts festivals and cultural events are held throughout Taos and Taos County. Events, schedules, and tickets (where required) can be obtained from the Taos County Chamber of Commerce (✆ 800/732-8267 or 505/758-3873; www.taoschamber.com). Mid-September through late October.

Santa Fe Wine & Chile Fiesta, Santa Fe, NM. This lively celebration boasts five days of wine and food events. It takes place at many venues in downtown Santa Fe. Tickets go on sale in early July and sell out quickly. For information call ✆ 505/438-8060 or go to www.santafewineandchile.org. Last Wednesday through Sunday in September; the big event (Grand Food & Wine Tasting) is on the last Saturday.

Sedona Jazz on the Rocks, Sedona, AZ. Jazz festival held amid the red rocks of Sedona. Call ✆ 928/282-1985 or go to www.sedonajazz.com. Late September.

The Whole Enchilada Fiesta, Las Cruces, NM. The world's biggest enchilada (sometimes over 7 ft. wide) is created and eaten. Call ✆ 505/526-1968 or visit www.twefie.com for more information. Late September or early October.

October

Arizona State Fair, Phoenix, AZ. Rodeos, top-name entertainment, and ethnic food. Call ✆ 602/252-6771 or go to www.azstatefair.com. Mid-October to early November.

Shiprock Navajo Fair, Shiprock, NM. The oldest and most traditional Navajo fair, it features a rodeo, dancing and singing, a parade, and arts-and-crafts exhibits. Contact ✆ 800/448-1240 or go to www.farmingtonnm.org for details. Early October.

Albuquerque International Balloon Fiesta, Albuquerque, NM. The world's largest balloon rally, this 9-day festival brings together more than 750 colorful balloons and includes races and contests. Balloons lift off from Balloon Fiesta Park (at I-25 and Alameda Blvd. NE) on Albuquerque's northern city limits. For information, call ✆ 800/733-9918 or visit www.balloonfiesta.com. Second week in October.

Sedona Arts Festival, Sedona, AZ. One of the better arts festivals in the state. Call ✆ 928/204-9456 or go to www.sedonaartsfestival.org. Early to mid-October.

Fiesta de los Chiles, Tucson, AZ. Come for lots of hot chiles, served in dishes from around the world, along with crafts and music. Call ✆ 520/326-9686 or visit www.tucsonbotanical.org. Mid- to late October.

Helldorado Days, Tombstone, AZ. Fashion show of 1880s, beard contest, reenactments, and street entertainment. Call ✆ 888/457-3929 or 520/457-3291, or go to www.tombstone.org. Third full weekend in October.

Cowboy Artists of America Annual Sale & Exhibition, Phoenix, AZ. The Phoenix Art Museum hosts the most prestigious and best-known Western-art show in the region. Call ✆ 602/257-1222 or go to www.phxart.org. Late October to mid-November.

Canyonlands Fat Tire Festival, Moab, UT. Mountain-bike guided tours, hill climbs, and related events. Call ✆ 800/635-6622 or 435/259-1370. Late October to early November.

November

Festival of the Cranes, Bosque del Apache National Wildlife Refuge, near Socorro, NM. People come from all over the world to attend this bird-watching event just 1½ hours south of Albuquerque. Call ℂ **505/835-1828.** Weekend before Thanksgiving.

Christmas on the Pecos, Carlsbad, NM. Pontoon boat rides each evening take passengers past a fascinating display of Christmas lights on riverside homes and businesses. Contact ℂ **800/ 221-1224** or go to www.christmason thepecos.com for more information. Thanksgiving to New Year's Eve (except Christmas Eve).

December

Yuletide in Taos, Taos, NM. This holiday event emphasizes northern New Mexican traditions, cultures, and arts. The Taos County Chamber of Commerce (ℂ **800/732-8267;** www.taos chamber.com) stages events. Thanksgiving through January 1.

Pueblo Grande Museum Indian Market, Phoenix, AZ. Largest market of its kind in the state, with more than 450 Native American artisans. Call ℂ **877/706-4408** or 602/495-0901, or go to www.pueblogrande.com. Second full weekend in December.

Festival of Lights, Sedona, AZ. Thousands of luminarias are lit at dusk at the Tlaquepaque Arts and Crafts Village. Call ℂ **928/282-4838** or go to www.tlaq.com. Mid-December.

Sundown Torchlight Procession of the Virgin, various New Mexico pueblos. Vespers at San Juan, Picuris, Tesuque, Nambé, and Taos Pueblos;

Matachine Dances at Taos Pueblo; and Buffalo Dances at Nambé Pueblo. For more information, call ℂ **505/747-1593.** December 24.

Canyon Road Farolito Walk, Santa Fe, NM. Beginning at dusk, locals and visitors bundle up and stroll Canyon Road, where *farolitos* (candle lamps) line the streets and rooftops. Musicians play and carolers sing around *luminarias* (little fires) and sip cider. Though it's not responsible for the event, the Santa Fe Convention and Visitors Bureau (ℂ **800/777-2489** or 505/ 955-6200; www.santafe.org) can help direct you there. Or ask your hotel concierge. December 24.

Matachines Dances and Other Dances, various New Mexico pueblos. Many New Mexico pueblos celebrate Christmas with dances. The Matachines Dances take place at Picuris and San Juan Pueblos on Christmas morning. Contact ℂ **505/587-2519** for dance schedules for these and other pueblos. December 24 and 25.

Torchlight Procession, Taos Ski Valley, NM. Bold skiers carve down a steep run named Snakedance in the dark while carrying golden fire. For information, call ℂ **800/992-7669** or 505/776-2291, or go to www.skitaos. org. December 24 and December 31 (followed by fireworks on New Year's Eve).

Fiesta Bowl Parade, Phoenix, AZ area. Huge, nationally televised parade, featuring floats and marching bands. Call ℂ **800/635-5748** or 480/350-0911, or go to www.tostitosfiesta bowl.com. Late December.

5 Getting There

BY PLANE

Deciding where to touch down in the Southwest is a bit tricky. Where you land will depend on what part of the region you intend to focus on. For instance, Albuquerque is closest to the Four Corners region, but if you also intend to visit the Grand Canyon, you may be better off flying in and out of Phoenix, which would allow you to visit Sedona as well. However, if you intend to only visit the northernmost part of the region, you may want to fly into Las Vegas and possibly save on airfare. Meanwhile, if you want to experience some mountain country en route to the mostly desert attractions of the Southwest, you could fly into Durango. Your best bet is to take out a map, pinpoint where you want to focus your travel time, and find the closest airport. Alternatively, check out the suggested itineraries described in chapter 3. You'll find airlines listed below.

Many airlines flying to both Phoenix and Tucson serve Arizona from around the United States. The Phoenix **Sky Harbor Airport** (© **602/273-3300**) is the more centrally located of the two airports and is closer to the Grand Canyon. However, if you're planning to explore the southern part of the state or are going to visit both Phoenix and Tucson, you might want to fly into **Tucson International Airport** (© **520/573-8000**), which is smaller and charges lower taxes on its car rentals.

The following major airlines serve both Phoenix and Tucson:

- **Alaska Airlines** © 800/252-7522; www.alaskaair.com
- **American** © 800/433-7300; www.aa.com
- **Continental** © 800/523-3273; www.continental.com
- **Delta** © 800/221-1212; www.delta.com
- **Frontier** © 800/432-1359; www.flyfrontier.com
- **JetBlue Airways** © 800/538-2583; www.jetblue.com
- **Northwest/KLM** © 800/225-2525; www.nwa.com
- **Southwest** © 800/435-9792; www.southwest.com
- **United** © 800/864-8331; www.united.com

The following airlines serve Phoenix but not Tucson:

- **Aero México** © 800/237-6639; www.aeromexico.com
- **Air Canada** © 888/247-2262; www.aircanada.ca
- **British Airways** © 800/247-9297; www.ba.com
- **Ted** © 800/225-5833; www.flyted.com
- **US Airways** © 800/428-4322; www.usairways.com
- **WestJet** © 888/937-8538; www.westjet.com

The **Albuquerque International Sunport** (© **505/842-4366**) is the hub for travel to most parts of New Mexico. A secondary hub for southern New Mexico is **El Paso International Airport** (© **915/780-4700**) in western Texas. Both airports are served by **American, US Airways, Continental, Delta, Express Jet** (© 888/958-XJET), **Frontier,** and **Southwest.** Additional airlines serving Albuquerque include **Mesa** (© **800/637-2247**), **Northwest,** and **United.**

In conjunction with United Airlines, commuter flights are offered between Santa Fe and Denver by **Great Lakes Aviation** (© **800/554-5111**).

McCarran International Airport (© **702/261-5211;** www.mccarran.com) in Las Vegas, Nevada, is a good option if you plan to visit northern Arizona and southern Utah. Budget-conscious travelers may find good deals on airfares and rental cars from there.

Colorado Springs Airport (© 719/550-1900), in the southeast corner of Colorado Springs, handles over 100 flights each day, with connections to most major U.S. cities. The airport is served by **Allegiant** (© 702/505-8888), **American, US Airways, Continental, Delta, Express Jet, Mesa, Northwest,** and **United.** Even more convenient to the region is the **Durango/La Plata County Airport** (© 970/247-8143), with direct daily nonstop service from Denver, Phoenix, and, in winter, Dallas/Fort Worth. **America West Express, Delta,** and **United Express** serve Durango.

Those whose destination is western Colorado can make connections to Grand Junction's **Walker Field** (© 970/344-9100; www.walkerfield.com) from Denver, Phoenix, or Salt Lake City.

FLYING FOR LESS: TIPS FOR GETTING THE BEST AIRFARE

- Passengers who can book their tickers either **long in advance or at the last minute,** or who **fly midweek** or at **less-trafficked hours** may pay a fraction of the full fare. If your schedule is flexible, say so, and ask if you can secure a cheaper fare by changing your flight plans.
- Search **the Internet** for cheap fares. The most popular online travel agencies are **Travelocity.com** (www.travelocity.co.uk); **Expedia.com** (www.expedia.co.uk and www.expedia.ca); and **Orbitz.com.** In the U.K., go to **Travel supermarket** (© 0845/345-5708; www.travelsupermarket.com), a flight search engine that offers flight comparisons for the budget airlines whose seats often end up in bucket-shop sales. Other websites for booking airline tickets online include **Cheap flights.com, SmarterTravel.com, Priceline.com,** and **Opodo** (www.opodo.co.uk). Meta search sites

(which find and then direct you to airline and hotel websites for booking) include **Sidestep.com** and **Kayak.com**—the latter includes fares for budget carriers like JetBlue and Spirit as well as the major airlines. **Site59.com** is a great source for last-minute flights and getaways. In addition, most **airlines** offer online-only fares that even their phone agents know nothing about. British travelers should check **Flights International** (© 0800/0187050; www.flights-international.com) for deals on flights all over the world.

- Watch local newspapers for **promotional specials** or **fare wars,** when airlines lower prices on their most popular routes. Also keep an eye on price fluctuations and deals at websites such as **Airfarewatchdog.com** and **Farecast.com.**
- Try to book a ticket **in its country of origin.** If you're planning a one-way flight from Johannesburg to New York, a South Africa–based travel agent will probably have the lowest fares. For foreign travelers on multi-leg trips, book in the country of the first leg; for example, book New York–Chicago–Montréal–New York in the U.S.
- **Consolidators,** also known as bucket shops, are wholesale brokers in the airline-ticket game. Consolidators buy deeply discounted tickets ("distressed" inventories of unsold seats) from airlines and sell them to online ticket agencies, travel agents, tour operators, corporations, and, to a lesser degree, the general public. Consolidators advertise in Sunday newspaper travel sections (often in small ads with tiny type), both in the U.S. and the U.K. They can be great sources for cheap international tickets. On the down side, bucket shop tickets are often rigged with restrictions, such as stiff

cancellation penalties (as high as 50% to 75% of the ticket price). And keep in mind that most of what you see advertised is of limited availability. Several reliable consolidators are worldwide and available online. **STA Travel** (www.statravel.com) has been the world's leading consolidator for students since purchasing Council Travel, but their fares are competitive for travelers of all ages. **Flights.com** (© **800/TRAV-800;** www.flights. com) has excellent fares worldwide, particularly to Europe. They also have "local" websites in 12 countries. **Fly-Cheap** (© **800/FLY-CHEAP;** www. 1800flycheap.com) has especially good fares to sunny destinations. **Air Tickets Direct** (© **800/778-3447;** www.airticketsdirect.com) is based in Montréal and leverages the currently weak Canadian dollar for low fares; they also book trips to places that U.S. travel agents won't touch, such as Cuba.

• Join **frequent-flier clubs.** Frequent-flier membership doesn't cost a cent, but it does entitle you to free tickets or upgrades when you amass the airline's required number of frequent-flier points. You don't even have to fly to earn points; **frequent-flier credit cards** can earn you thousands of miles for doing your everyday shopping. But keep in mind that award seats are limited, seats on popular routes are hard to snag, and more and more major airlines are cutting their expiration periods for mileage points—so check your airline's frequent-flier program so you don't lose your miles before you use them. *Inside tip:* Award seats are offered almost a year in advance, but seats also open up at the last minute, so if your travel plans are flexible, you may strike gold. To play the frequent-flier game to your best advantage, consult the community bulletin boards on **FlyerTalk** (www.flyertalk.com) or go to Randy Petersen's **Inside Flyer** (www.insideflyer.com). Petersen and friends review all the programs in detail and post regular updates on changes in policies and trends.

ARRIVING AT THE AIRPORT

IMMIGRATION & CUSTOMS CLEARANCE Foreign visitors arriving by air, no matter what the port of entry, should cultivate patience and resignation before setting foot on U.S. soil. U.S. airports have considerably beefed up security clearances in the years since the terrorist attacks of 9/11, and clearing Customs and Immigration can take as long as 2 hours.

People traveling by air from Canada, Bermuda, and certain Caribbean countries can sometimes clear Customs and Immigration at the point of departure, which is much faster.

LONG-HAUL FLIGHTS: HOW TO STAY COMFORTABLE

• Your choice of airline and airplane will definitely affect your legroom. Find more details about U.S. airlines at **www.seatguru.com**. For international airlines, the research firm Skytrax has posted a list of average seat pitches at **www.airlinequality.com**.

• Emergency exit seats and bulkhead seats typically have the most legroom. Emergency exit seats are usually left unassigned until the day of a flight (to ensure that someone able-bodied fills the seats); it's worth getting to the ticket counter early to snag one of these spots for a long flight. Many passengers find that bulkhead seating (the row facing the wall at the front of the cabin) offers more legroom, but keep in mind that bulkhead seats have no storage space on the floor in front of you.

- To have two seats for yourself in a three-seat row, try for an aisle seat in a center section toward the back of coach. If you're traveling with a companion, book an aisle and a window seat. Middle seats are usually booked last, so chances are good you'll end up with three seats to yourselves. And in the event that a third passenger is assigned the middle seat, he or she will probably be more than happy to trade for a window or an aisle.
- Ask about entertainment options. Many airlines offer seatback video systems where you get to choose your movies or play video games—but only on some of their planes. (Boeing 777s are your best bet.)
- To sleep, avoid the last row of any section or the row in front of an emergency exit, as these seats are the least likely to recline. Avoid seats near highly trafficked toilet areas. Avoid seats in the back of many jets—these can be narrower than those in the rest of coach. Or reserve a window seat so you can rest your head and avoid being bumped in the aisle.
- Get up, walk around, and stretch every 60 to 90 minutes to keep your blood flowing. This helps avoid **deep vein thrombosis,** or "economy-class syndrome." See the box "Avoiding 'Economy Class Syndrome,'" p. 35.
- Drink water before, during, and after your flight to combat the lack of humidity in airplane cabins. Avoid caffeine and alcohol, which will dehydrate you.
- If you're flying with kids, don't forget to carry on toys, books, pacifiers, and snacks and chewing gum to help them relieve ear pressure buildup during ascent and descent.

BY CAR

Three interstate highways cross the Southwest. The north-south I-25 bisects New Mexico, passing through Albuquerque and Las Cruces. The east-west I-40 follows the path of the old Route 66 through Kingman and Flagstaff, in Arizona, and Gallup, Albuquerque, and Tucumcari in New Mexico. I-10 from San Diego crosses the southern part of the region, passing through Yuma and Tucson in Arizona, and intersecting I-25 at Las Cruces, New Mexico. I-15 crosses the region at the southwest corner of Utah. These major routes help provide easy access to the many sights in the region that are on much smaller state highways and roadways.

The distance to Phoenix from Los Angeles is approximately 369 miles; from San Francisco, 778 miles; from Albuquerque, 455 miles; from Salt Lake City, 660 miles; from Las Vegas, 287 miles; and from Santa Fe, 516 miles.

Your biggest concern is weather. In winter, be sure your car has front-wheel drive or four-wheel drive and good tires, because roads can become snowpacked and icy.

BY TRAIN

Amtrak has two routes through the region. The *Southwest Chief,* which runs between Chicago and Los Angeles, passes through the region once daily in each direction, with stops in Flagstaff, Gallup, Grants, Albuquerque, Lamy (for Santa Fe), Las Vegas, Raton, Trinidad, La Junta, and Lamar. A second train, the *Sunset Limited,* skims through the southern part of the region three times weekly in each direction between Los Angeles and New Orleans, with stops in Tucson, Benson, Lordsburg, Deming, and El Paso, Texas. Greyhound/Trailways bus lines provide through-ticketing for Amtrak between Albuquerque and El Paso.

You can get a copy of Amtrak's national timetable from any Amtrak station, from travel agents, or by contacting Amtrak (*©* **800/USA-RAIL;** www.amtrak.com).

6 Money & Costs

It's always advisable to bring money in a variety of forms on a vacation: a mix of cash, credit cards, and traveler's checks. You should also exchange enough petty cash to cover airport incidentals, tipping, and transportation to your hotel before you leave home, or withdraw money upon arrival at an airport ATM.

Prices in the Southwest vary greatly, which is good news for both moneybags and those with holes in their pockets. You can find world-class resorts if that's your bent, or a cheap roadside motel and a diner if you like to pinch pennies. If you come from a major city such as New York or London, you may find prices overall fairly inexpensive, though the major cities will be closer in price to what you're accustomed to. Exceptions are major tourist destinations such as the Grand Canyon, Zion National Park, and Carlsbad Caverns, where one or two concessionaires often have a monopoly and charge premium prices.

ATMs

Nationwide, the easiest and best way to get cash away from home is from an ATM (automated teller machine), sometimes referred to as a "cash machine," or "cashpoint." The **Cirrus** (© **800/424-7787;** www.mastercard.com) and **PLUS** (© **800/843-7587;** www.visa.com) networks span the country; you can find them even in remote regions. Go to your bank card's website to find ATM locations at your destination. Be sure you know your daily withdrawal limit before you depart.

Note: Many banks impose a fee every time you use a card at another bank's ATM, and that fee is often higher for international transactions (up to $5 or more) than for domestic ones (where they're rarely more than $2). In addition, the bank from which you withdraw cash may charge its own fee. To compare banks' ATM fees within the U.S., use **www.bankrate.com.** Visitors from outside the U.S. should also find out whether their bank assesses a 1% to 3% fee on charges incurred abroad.

CREDIT CARDS & DEBIT CARDS

Credit cards are the most widely used form of payment in the United States: **Visa** (Barclaycard in Britain), **MasterCard** (EuroCard in Europe, Access in Britain, Chargex in Canada), **American Express, Diners Club,** and **Discover.** They also provide a convenient record of all your expenses, and offer relatively good exchange rates. You can withdraw cash advances from your credit cards at banks or ATMs, but high fees make credit card cash advances a pricey way to get cash.

It's highly recommended that you travel with at least one major credit card. You must have a credit card to rent a car, and hotels and airlines usually require a credit card imprint as a deposit against expenses.

ATM cards with major credit card backing, known as **debit cards,** are now a commonly acceptable form of payment in most stores and restaurants. Debit cards draw money directly from your checking account. Some stores enable you to receive cash back on your debit-card purchases as well. The same is true at most U.S. post offices.

TRAVELER'S CHECKS

Though credit cards and debit cards are more often used, traveler's checks are still widely accepted in the U.S. Foreign visitors should make sure that traveler's checks are denominated in U.S. dollars; foreign-currency checks are often difficult to exchange.

You can buy traveler's checks at most banks. Most are offered in denominations of $20, $50, $100, $500, and sometimes $1,000. Generally, you'll pay a service charge ranging from 1% to 4%.

The most popular traveler's checks are offered by **American Express** (© **800/ 807-6233;** © 800/221-7282 for cardholders—this number accepts collect calls, offers service in several foreign languages, and exempts Amex gold and platinum cardholders from the 1% fee); **Visa** (© **800/732-1322**)—AAA members can obtain Visa checks for a $9.95 fee (for checks up to $1,500) at most AAA offices or by calling © **866/339-3378;** and **MasterCard** (© 800/223-9920).

Be sure to keep a copy of the traveler's checks serial numbers separate from your checks in the event that they are stolen or lost. You'll get a refund faster if you know the numbers.

Another option is the new **prepaid traveler's check cards,** reloadable cards that work much like debit cards but aren't linked to your checking account. The **American Express Travelers Cheque Card,** for example, requires a minimum deposit ($300), sets a maximum balance ($2,750), and has a one-time issuance fee of $15. You can withdraw money from an ATM ($2.50 per transaction, not including bank fees), and the funds can be purchased in dollars, euros, or pounds. If you lose the card, your available funds will be refunded within 24 hours.

7 Travel Insurance

The cost of travel insurance varies widely, depending on the cost and length of your trip, your age and health, and the type of trip you're taking, but expect to pay between 5% and 8% of the vacation itself. You can get estimates from various providers through **InsureMyTrip.com.** Enter your trip cost and dates, your age, and other information, for prices from more than a dozen companies.

For **U.K. citizens,** insurance is always advisable when traveling in the States. Travelers or families who make more than one trip abroad per year may find an annual travel insurance policy works out cheaper. Check **www.moneysupermarket. com,** which compares prices across a wide range of providers for single- and multi-trip policies.

Most big travel agents offer their own insurance and will probably try to sell you their package when you book a holiday. Think before you sign. **Britain's Consumers' Association** recommends that you insist on seeing the policy and reading the fine print before buying travel insurance. **The Association of British Insurers** (© **020/7600-3333;** www.abi. org.uk) gives advice by phone and publishes *Holiday Insurance,* a free guide to policy provisions and prices. You might also shop around for better deals: Try **Columbus Direct** (© **0870/033-9988;** www.columbusdirect.net).

TRIP-CANCELLATION INSURANCE

Trip-cancellation insurance will help retrieve your money if you have to back out of a trip or depart early, or if your travel supplier goes bankrupt. Trip cancellation traditionally covers such events as sickness, natural disasters, and State Department advisories. The latest news in trip-cancellation insurance is the availability of **expanded hurricane coverage** and the **"any-reason"** cancellation coverage—which costs more but covers cancellations made for any reason. You won't get back 100% of your prepaid trip cost, but you'll be refunded a substantial portion. **TravelSafe** (© **888/885-7233;** www.travelsafe.com) offers both types of coverage. Expedia also offers any-reason cancellation coverage for its air-hotel packages.

For details, contact one of the following recommended insurers: **Access America** (© 866/807-3982; www.access america.com); **Travel Guard International**

(© 800/826-4919; www.travelguard.com);
Travel Insured International (© 800/
243-3174; www.travelinsured.com); and
Travelex Insurance Services (© 888/
457-4602; www.travelex-insurance.com).

MEDICAL INSURANCE

Although it's not required of travelers,
health insurance is highly recommended.
Most health insurance policies cover you
if you get sick away from home—but
check your coverage before you leave.

International visitors should note that
unlike many European countries, the
United States does not usually offer free
or low-cost medical care to its citizens or
visitors. Doctors and hospitals are expensive, and in most cases will require
advance payment or proof of coverage
before they render their services. Good
policies will cover the costs of an accident, repatriation, or death. Packages
such as **Europ Assistance's "Worldwide
Healthcare Plan"** are sold by European
automobile clubs and travel agencies at
attractive rates. **Worldwide Assistance
Services, Inc.** (© 800/777-8710; www.
worldwideassistance.com) is the agent for
Europ Assistance in the United States.

Though lack of health insurance may
prevent you from being admitted to a
hospital in nonemergencies, don't worry
about being left on a street corner to die:
The American way is to fix you now and
bill the living daylights out of you later.

If you're ever hospitalized more than
150 miles from home, **MedjetAssist**
(© 800/527-7478; www.medjetassistance.

com) will pick you up and fly you to the
hospital of your choice in a medically
equipped and staffed aircraft 24 hours
day, 7 days a week. Annual memberships
are $225 individual, $350 family; you can
also purchase short-term memberships.

Canadians should check with their
provincial health plan offices or call
Health Canada (© 866/225-0709; www.
hc-sc.gc.ca) to find out the extent of their
coverage and what documentation and
receipts they must take home in case they
are treated in the United States.

LOST-LUGGAGE INSURANCE

On flights within the U.S., checked baggage is covered up to $2,500 per ticketed
passenger. On flights outside the U.S.
(and on U.S. portions of international
trips), baggage coverage is limited to
approximately $9.07 per pound, up to
approximately $635 per checked bag. If
you plan to check items more valuable
than what's covered by the standard lia-
bility, see if your homeowner's policy covers your valuables, get baggage insurance
as part of your comprehensive travel-
insurance package, or buy Travel Guard's
"BagTrak" product.

If your luggage is lost, immediately file
a lost-luggage claim at the airport, detail-
ing the luggage contents. Most airlines
require that you report delayed, damaged,
or lost baggage within 4 hours of arrival.
The airlines are required to deliver luggage, once found, directly to your house
or destination free of charge.

8 Health

STAYING HEALTHY

One thing that sets the Southwest apart
from most other regions is its elevation.
Much of the region is above 4,000 feet,
and many heavily traveled areas, including the Four Corners, Grand Canyon,
and Santa Fe, are at 7,000 feet or above.
Getting plenty of rest, avoiding large

meals, and drinking lots of nonalcoholic
fluids (especially water) can help make
the adjustment easier for flatlanders.

The reduced oxygen and humidity at
these altitudes can bring on some unique
problems, not the least of which is acute
mountain sickness. Characterized in its
early stages by headaches, shortness of

breath, appetite loss or nausea, tingling in the fingers or toes, lethargy, and insomnia, it ordinarily can be treated with aspirin and a slower pace. If it persists or worsens, you must descend to a lower altitude.

Sunburn is also a concern. No matter what time of year it is, the desert sun is strong and bright, and you can burn much faster at high elevations than at sea level, because the thinner atmosphere offers less protection from the sun. Use sunscreen even when driving in your car, and wear a hat and sunglasses.

Visitors from humid climates may find the Southwest's dryness pleasant—dry heat is not as oppressive, and sweat evaporates almost immediately, cooling the skin. This is a mixed blessing, however, because many people don't feel thirsty here until they're already significantly dehydrated. Early symptoms of **dehydration** include headache and lethargy, and the condition may progress to include impaired concentration and irregular heartbeat. If you feel any of these symptoms, immediately find a cool place to rest and drink plenty of water. Better yet, prevent dehydration by carrying some bottled water with you and sipping it throughout the day, whether or not you feel thirsty.

Other things to be wary of are **flash floods,** particularly in the narrow canyons of northern Arizona and southern Utah. These may occur without warning in the desert, when the sky above you is clear but it's raining upstream. Before entering any narrow canyons in the late summer or fall, be sure to check weather conditions with the local ranger station, and avoid crossing low-lying areas during rain showers.

Most people are surprised to learn that **exposure to cold** causes more injuries and deaths in the region than heat and dryness do. The same clear skies that bake the desert in sunlight all day allow heat to escape rapidly at night. Evening breezes add to this effect. Hikers, in particular, must be prepared for both heat and cold, especially in the northern mountains, where snow can fall at the highest elevations in June and even July.

Finally, if you're outdoors, be on the lookout for **desert creatures,** particularly snakes (rattlers), Gila monsters (black-and-orange lizards), scorpions, and tarantulas. If you do encounter any of these, slowly move away. Don't even get close enough to take a picture (unless you have a good zoom lens).

Refer to the "Fast Facts" section under each destination for the most reliable hospitals and pharmacies in each area.

Contact the **International Association for Medical Assistance to Travelers**

Avoiding "Economy Class Syndrome"

Deep vein thrombosis, or as it's know in the world of flying, "economy-class syndrome," is a blood clot that develops in a deep vein. It's a potentially deadly condition that can be caused by sitting in cramped conditions—such as an airplane cabin—for too long. During a flight (especially a long-haul flight), get up, walk around, and stretch your legs every 60 to 90 minutes to keep your blood flowing. Other preventative measures include frequent flexing of the legs while sitting, drinking lots of water, and avoiding alcohol and sleeping pills. If you have a history of deep vein thrombosis, heart disease, or another condition that puts you at high risk, some experts recommend wearing compression stockings or taking anticoagulants when you fly; always ask your physician about the best course for you. Symptoms of deep vein thrombosis include leg pain or swelling, or even shortness of breath.

Healthy Travels to You

The following government websites offer up-to-date health-related travel advice.

- **Australia:** www.dfat.gov.au/travel/
- **Canada:** www.hc-sc.gc.ca/index_e.html
- **U.K.:** www.dh.gov.uk/PolicyAndGuidance/HealthAdviceForTravellers/fs/en
- **U.S.:** www.cdc.gov/travel/

(IAMAT) (© 716/754-4883 or, in Canada, 416/652-0137; www.iamat.org) for tips on travel and health concerns in the countries you're visiting, and for lists of local, English-speaking doctors. The United States **Centers for Disease Control and Prevention** (© 800/311-3435; www.cdc.gov) provides up-to-date information on health hazards by region or country and offers tips on food safety. The website **www.tripprep.com**, sponsored by a consortium of travel medicine practitioners, **Travel Health Online,** may also offer helpful advice on traveling abroad. You can find listings of reliable clinics overseas at the **International Society of Travel Medicine** (www.istm.org).

WHAT TO DO IF YOU GET SICK AWAY FROM HOME

We list **hospitals** and **emergency numbers** under "Fast Facts," p. 49.

If you suffer from a chronic illness, consult your doctor before your departure. Pack prescription medications in your carry-on luggage, and carry them in their original containers, with pharmacy labels—otherwise they won't make it through airport security. Visitors from outside the U.S. should carry generic names of prescription drugs. For U.S. travelers, most reliable health-care plans provide coverage if you get sick away from home. Foreign visitors may have to pay all medical costs upfront and be reimbursed later. See "Medical Insurance," under "Travel Insurance," above.

9 Safety

STAYING SAFE

While tourist areas as a rule are safe, urban areas may not be at night. You should always stay alert. Check with your hotel's front desk staff if you are in doubt about which neighborhoods are safe. Avoid deserted areas, especially at night, and avoid public parks at night. Women should especially follow these guidelines. With purse snatchings a reality at tourist

spots in the country, it's best not to carry valuables.

Remember that hotels are open to the public, and in a large hotel, security may not be able to screen everyone who enters. Always lock your room door; don't assume that once inside your hotel you are automatically safe and no longer need to be aware of your surroundings.

10 Specialized Travel Resources

TRAVELERS WITH DISABILITIES

Most disabilities shouldn't stop anyone from traveling in the U.S. There are more options and resources out there than ever

before. Throughout the region, measures have been taken to provide access for travelers with disabilities. The chamber of commerce in each town will answer questions regarding accessibility in their areas. No matter what, it is advisable to call hotels, restaurants, and attractions in advance to be sure that they are fully accessible.

The **America the Beautiful—National Park and Federal Recreational Lands Pass—Access Pass** (formerly the **Golden Access Passport**) gives visually impaired or persons with permanent disabilities (regardless of age) free lifetime entrance to federal recreation sites administered by the National Park Service, including the Fish and Wildlife Service, the Forest Service, the Bureau of Land Management, and the Bureau of Reclamation. This may include national parks, monuments, historic sites, recreation areas, and national wildlife refuges.

The America the Beautiful Access Pass can only be obtained in person at any NPS facility that charges an entrance fee. You need to show proof of medically determined disability. Besides free entry, the pass also offers a 50% discount on some federal-use fees charged for such facilities as camping, swimming, parking, boat launching, and tours. For more information, go to www.nps.gov/fees passes.htm or call © **888/467-2757.**

Organizations that offer a vast range of resources and assistance to travelers with disabilities include **MossRehab** (© **800/ CALL-MOSS;** www.mossresourcenet. org); the **American Foundation for the Blind (AFB)** (© **800/232-5463;** www. afb.org); and **SATH (Society for Accessible Travel & Hospitality)** (© **212/447-7284;** www.sath.org). **AirAmbulanceCard.com** is now partnered with SATH and allows you to preselect top-notch hospitals in case of an emergency.

Access-Able Travel Source (© **303/ 232-2979;** www.access-able.com) offers a comprehensive database on travel agents from around the world with experience in accessible travel; destination-specific access information; and links to such

resources as service animals, equipment rentals, and access guides.

Many travel agencies offer customized tours and itineraries for travelers with disabilities. Among them are **Flying Wheels Travel** (© **507/451-5005;** www.flying wheelstravel.com), and **Accessible Journeys** (© **800/846-4537** or 610/521-0339; www.disabilitytravel.com).

Flying with Disability (www.flying-with-disability.org) is a comprehensive information source on airplane travel. **Avis Rent a Car** (© **888/879-4273**) has an "Avis Access" program that offers services for customers with special travel needs. These include specially outfitted vehicles with swivel seats, spinner knobs, and hand controls; mobility scooter rentals; and accessible bus service. Be sure to reserve well in advance.

Also check out the quarterly magazine *Emerging Horizons* (www.emerging horizons.com), available by subscription ($17 year U.S.; $22 outside U.S).

The "Accessible Travel" link at **Mobility-Advisor.com** (www.mobility-advisor.com) offers a variety of travel resources to persons with disabilities.

British travelers should contact **Holiday Care** (© **0845-124-9971** in UK only; www.holidaycare.org.uk) to access a wide range of travel information and resources for elderly people and travelers with disabilities.

GAY & LESBIAN TRAVELERS

In general, gay and lesbian travelers will find they are treated just like any other visitors in the Southwest. For information on gay- and lesbian-friendly businesses in the Phoenix metro area, contact the **Greater Phoenix Gay & Lesbian Chamber of Commerce** (© **888/4GP GLCC** or 602/266-5055; www.gpglcc. org). **Wingspan,** 425 E. Seventh St., Tucson (© **520/624-1779;** www.wingspan. org), is southern Arizona's lesbian, gay, bisexual, and transgender community center. *The Tucson Observer* (© 520/622-7176; www.tucsonobserver.com) is a local Tucson gay newspaper available at both Wingspan and **Antigone Bookstore,** 411 N. Fourth Ave. (© 520/792-3715; www.antigonebooks.com). At gay bars around Phoenix and Tucson, you can pick up various gay-oriented local publications, including *Echo Magazine* (© 602/266-0550; www.echomag.com). On the Web, check out **www.visitgayarizona.com,** which has links to gay and lesbian organizations all over the state.

Common Bond (© 505/891-3647) provides information and outreach services for Albuquerque's gay and lesbian community as well as referrals for other New Mexico cities. Another good New Mexico resource is **www.gaynm.com,** a website that provides news, resources, and lists of events. In Colorado, contact **Gay, Lesbian, and Bisexual Community Services Center of Colorado** (© 303/733-7743; www.coloradoglbt.org) in Denver; the organization provides information on services, events, and venues of interest to gay and lesbian visitors. The **Utah Pride Center,** 355 N. 300 West, 1st Floor, Salt Lake City (© 888/874-2743 or 801/539-8800; www.utahpridecenter.org), is a community center, coffeehouse, and information distribution point for Utah. In Las Vegas, head to **The Center,** 953 E. Sahara, Suite B-31 (© 702/733-9800; www.thecenter-lasvegas.com), for support and information. Another source is www.lasvegaspride.org, with lists of activities for the Las Vegas area.

The International Gay and Lesbian Travel Association (IGLTA) (© 800/448-8550 or 954/776-2626; www.iglta.org) is the trade association for the gay and lesbian travel industry, and offers an online directory of gay- and lesbian-friendly travel businesses and tour operators.

Many agencies offer tours and travel itineraries specifically for gay and lesbian travelers. **Above and Beyond Tours** (© 800/397-2681; www.abovebeyondtours.com) are gay Australia tour specialists. San Francisco–based **Now, Voyager** (© 800/255-6951; www.nowvoyager.com) offers worldwide trips and cruises, and **Olivia** (© 800/631-6277; www.olivia.com) offers lesbian cruises and resort vacations.

Gay.com Travel (© 800/929-2268 or 415/644-8044; www.gay.com/travel or www.outandabout.com) is an excellent online successor to the popular *Out & About* print magazine. It provides regularly updated information about gay-owned, gay-oriented, and gay-friendly lodging, dining, sightseeing, nightlife, and shopping establishments in every important destination worldwide. British travelers should click on the "Travel" link at **www.uk.gay.com** for advice and gay-friendly trip ideas.

The Canadian website **GayTraveler** (**gaytraveler.ca**) offers ideas and advice for gay travel all over the world.

The following travel guides are available at many bookstores, or you can order them from any online bookseller: *Spartacus International Gay Guide, 35th Edition* (Bruno Gmünder Verlag; www.spartacusworld.com/gayguide); *Odysseus: The International Gay Travel Planner, 17th Edition* (www.odyusa.com); and the *Damron* guides (www.damron.com), with separate, annual books for gay men and lesbians.

SENIOR TRAVEL

Senior travelers tend to enjoy the Southwest's mild climate. However, they are often more susceptible to changes in elevation and may experience heart or respiratory problems. Consult your physician before your trip.

Members of **AARP,** 601 E St. NW, Washington, DC 20049 (© 888/687-2277; www.aarp.org), get discounts on hotels, airfares, and car rentals. AARP offers members a wide range of benefits, including *AARP: The Magazine* and a monthly newsletter. Anyone over 50 can join.

The U.S. National Park Service offers an **America the Beautiful—National Park and Federal Recreational Lands Pass—Senior Pass** (formerly the **Golden Age Passport**), which gives seniors 62 years or older lifetime entrance to all properties administered by the National Park Service—national parks, monuments, historic sites, recreation areas, and national wildlife refuges—for a one-time processing fee of $10. The pass must be purchased in person at any NPS facility that charges an entrance fee. Besides free entry, the America the Beautiful Senior Pass also offers a 50% discount on some federal-use fees charged for such facilities as camping, swimming, parking, boat launching, and tours. For more information, go to www.nps.gov/fees_passes.htm or call © **888/467-2757.**

Many reliable agencies and organizations target the 50-plus market. **Elderhostel** (© **800/454-5768;** www.elderhostel.org) arranges worldwide study programs for those age 55 and over. **Elder-Treks** (© **800/741-7956** or 416/558-5000 outside North America; www.elder treks.com) offers small-group tours to off-the-beaten-path or adventure-travel locations, restricted to travelers 50 and older.

Recommended publications offering travel resources and discounts for seniors include: the quarterly magazine *Travel 50 & Beyond* (www.travel50andbeyond.com) and the bestselling paperback *Unbelievably Good Deals and Great Adventures That You Absolutely Can't Get Unless You're Over 50 2005–2006, 16th Edition* (McGraw-Hill), by Joann Rattner Heilman.

FAMILY TRAVEL

If you have enough trouble getting your kids out of the house in the morning,

dragging them thousands of miles away may seem like an insurmountable challenge. But family travel can be immensely rewarding, giving you new ways of seeing the world through smaller pairs of eyes.

With its robust mix of outdoorsy activities and cultural attractions, the Southwest lends itself to family vacations. That said, the drives between the activities and attractions can be rather long, and they don't always lead to the sort of juicy theme-park treats that you find in other states. Sure, you may stumble across a water park or a video arcade here and there, but the real attractions are the natural and cultural ones and the adventurous ways you can experience them: hiking along the Grand Canyon, white-water rafting down the Rio Grande, riding a horse through the cathedrals of Monument Valley, or climbing a wooden ladder up to a cliff dwelling, to name just a few.

If you're not traveling with an adventure-oriented brood, don't worry. Many of the hotels and resorts listed in this book have inviting pools around which you can sit, or on-site activities planned especially for kids. But keep in mind that the Southwest can truly offer your children a new perspective on life by exposing them to ancient ruins, zesty cuisine, and unique cultures.

To locate accommodations, restaurants, and attractions that are particularly kid-friendly, refer to the "Kids" icon throughout this guide.

Recommended family travel websites include **Family Travel Forum** (www.family travelforum.com), a comprehensive site that offers customized trip planning; **Family Travel Network** (www.familytravel network.com), an online magazine providing travel tips; **TravelWithYourKids. com** (www.travelwithyourkids.com), a comprehensive site written by parents for parents offering sound advice for long-distance and international travel with children.

For even more ideas, check out *Frommer's Las Vegas with Kids, Frommer's Family Vacations in the National Parks,* and *Frommer's 500 Places to Take Your Kids Before They Grow Up.*

AFRICAN-AMERICAN TRAVELERS

Black Travel Online (www.blacktravel online.com) posts news on upcoming events and includes links to articles and travel-booking sites. **Soul of America** (www.soulofamerica.com) is a comprehensive website with travel tips, event and family-reunion postings, and sections on historically black beach resorts and active vacations.

Agencies and organizations that provide resources for black travelers include: **Rodgers Travel** (© 800/825-1775; www. rodgerstravel.com); the **African American Association of Innkeepers International** (© 877/422-5777; www.african americaninns.com); and **Henderson Travel & Tours** (© 800/327-2309 or 301/650-5700; www.hendersontravel.com), which has specialized in trips to Africa since 1957.

Go Girl: The Black Woman's Guide to Travel & Adventure (Eighth Mountain Press) is a compilation of travel essays by writers including Jill Nelson and Audre Lorde. *The African-American Travel Guide* by Wayne C. Robinson (Hunter Publishing; www.hunterpublishing.com) was published in 1997, so it may be somewhat dated. *Travel and Enjoy Magazine* (© 866/266-6211; www.travel andenjoy.com) is a travel magazine and guide. The well-done *Pathfinders Magazine* (© 877/977-PATH; www.pathfinders travel.com) includes articles on everything from Rio de Janeiro to Ghana to upcoming ski, diving, golf, and tennis trips.

TRAVELING WITH PETS

If you're one of those soft hearts who just has to have Fido along, you're in luck. The Southwest is increasingly accepting of animals as travel companions. Many of the major chain hotels, such as Motel 6 and most Best Westerns, allow pets in the rooms (though restaurants still prohibit them). Your biggest concern when traveling with a pet in the region is the heat. In fact, if you're traveling during the warm months, you'd best leave your pet at home. Though some attractions, such as Carlsbad Caverns and the Grand Canyon, have kennels available, most do not. And with all the other times you'll need to leave your pet, the risk isn't worth the joy of having your companion there. Even leaving a pet in the car to run into a fast food restaurant can be harmful.

That said, during the cooler seasons, few places are more fun to bring a pet. Hiking abounds in the region, as does space to throw a stick. In accommodations listings throughout the book, look for the note that states whether the establishment allows pets and if it charges a fee. Some websites worth checking out include www.petswelcome.com, www.pet travel.com, and www.travelpets.com.

---

11 Sustainable Tourism/Ecotourism

Each time you take a flight or drive a car CO_2 is released into the atmosphere. You can help neutralize this danger to our planet through "carbon offsetting"—paying someone to reduce your CO_2 emissions by the same amount you've added. Carbon offsets can be purchased in the U.S. from companies such as **Carbonfund.org** (www. carbonfund.org) and **TerraPass** (www.terrapass.org), and from **Climate Care** (www. climatecare.org) in the U.K.

Frommers.com: The Complete Travel Resource

It should go without saying, but we highly recommend **Frommers.com**, voted Best Travel Site by *PC Magazine*. We think you'll find our expert advice and tips; independent reviews of hotels, restaurants, attractions, and preferred shopping and nightlife venues; vacation giveaways; and an online booking tool indispensable before, during, and after your travels. We publish the complete contents of over 128 travel guides in our **Destinations** section covering nearly 3,600 places worldwide to help you plan your trip. Each weekday, we publish original articles reporting on **Deals and News** via our free **Frommers.com Newsletter** to help you save time and money and travel smarter. We're betting you'll find our new **Events** listings (http://events.frommers.com) an invaluable resource; it's an up-to-the-minute roster of what's happening in cities everywhere—including concerts, festivals, lectures and more. We've also added weekly **Podcasts, interactive maps,** and hundreds of new images across the site. Check out our **Travel Talk** area featuring **Message Boards** where you can join in conversations with thousands of fellow Frommer's travelers and post your trip report once you return.

Although one could argue that any vacation that includes an airplane flight can't be truly "green," you can go on holiday and still contribute positively to the environment. In addition to purchasing carbon offsets from the companies mentioned above, you can take other steps toward responsible travel. Choose forward-looking companies that embrace responsible development practices, helping preserve destinations for the future by working alongside local people. An increasing number of sustainable tourism initiatives can help you plan a family trip and leave as small a "footprint" as possible on the places you visit.

In Arizona, one tour option is Vermont-based **Country Walkers** (© **800/464-9255** or 802/244-1387; www.countrywalkers.com), which offers a hiking-oriented trip that takes in the Grand Canyon and Sedona.

You'll find a few options in New Mexico. In Taos, **El Monte Sagrado,** a resort near the center of town, offers luxurious surroundings totally in tune with nature,

utilizing sustainable technologies throughout. Contact © **800/828-TAOS** or go online to www.elmontesagrado.com. In Santa Fe, **Santa Fe Mountain Adventures** (© **800/965-4010** or 505/988-4000; www.santafemountainadventures.com) leads programs that combine outdoor adventures with arts and cultural experiences, and spa treatments. A collaborative effort in conjunction with *Outside* magazine, the business is ecofriendly.

Other resources include **Responsible Travel** (www.responsibletravel.com), which is run by a spokesperson for responsible tourism in the travel industry, and contains a great source of sustainable travel ideas.

You can find eco-friendly travel tips, statistics, and touring companies and associations—listed by destination under "Travel Choice"—at the TIES website, **www.ecotourism.org.** Also check out **Conservation International** (www.conservation.org)—which, with *National Geographic Traveler,* annually presents **World Legacy Awards** (www.wlaward.org)

to those travel tour operators, businesses, organizations, and places that have made a significant contribution to sustainable tourism. **Ecotravel.com** is part online magazine and part ecodirectory that lets you search for touring companies in several categories (water-based, land-based, spiritually oriented, and so on).

In the U.K., **Tourism Concern** (www.tourismconcern.org.uk) works to reduce social and environmental problems connected to tourism and find ways of improving tourism so that local benefits are increased.

The **Association of British Travel Agents (ABTA)** (www.abtamembers.org/responsibletourism) acts as a focal point for the U.K. travel industry and is one of the leading groups spearheading responsible tourism.

The **Association of Independent Tour Operators (AITO)** (www.aito.co.uk) is a group of interesting specialist operators leading the field in making holidays sustainable.

12 Staying Connected

TELEPHONES

Generally, hotel surcharges on long-distance and local calls are astronomical, so you're better off using your **cellphone** or a **public pay telephone.** Many convenience groceries and packaging services sell **prepaid calling cards** in denominations up to $50; for international visitors these can be the least expensive way to call home. Many public pay phones at airports now accept American Express, MasterCard, and Visa credit cards. **Local calls** made from pay phones in most locales cost either 25¢ or 35¢ (no pennies, please).

Most long-distance and international calls can be dialed directly from any phone. **For calls within the United States and to Canada,** dial 1 followed by the area code and the seven-digit number. **For other international calls,** dial 011 followed by the country code, city code, and the number you are calling.

Calls to area codes **800, 888, 877,** and **866** are toll-free. However, calls to area codes **700** and **900** (chat lines, bulletin boards, "dating" services, and so on) can be very expensive—usually a charge of 95¢ to $3 or more per minute, and they sometimes have minimum charges that can run as high as $15 or more.

For **reversed-charge or collect calls,** and for person-to-person calls, dial the number 0 then the area code and number; an operator will come on the line, and you should specify whether you are calling collect, person-to-person, or both. If your operator-assisted call is international, ask for the overseas operator.

For **local directory assistance** ("information"), dial 411; for long-distance information, dial 1, then the appropriate area code and 555-1212.

CELLPHONES

Just because your cellphone works at home doesn't mean it'll work everywhere in the U.S. (thanks to our nation's fragmented cellphone system). It's a good bet that your phone will work in major cities, but take a look at your wireless company's coverage map on its website before heading out; T-Mobile, Sprint, and Nextel are particularly weak in rural areas. If you need to stay in touch at a destination where you know your phone won't work, **rent** a phone that does from **InTouch USA** (© **800/872-7626;** www.intouchglobal.com) or a rental car location, but beware that you'll pay $1 a minute or more for airtime.

If you're not from the U.S., you'll be appalled at the poor reach of our **GSM (Global System for Mobile Communications) wireless network,** which is used

Online Traveler's Toolbox

Veteran travelers usually carry some essential items to make their trips easier. Following is a selection of handy online tools to bookmark and use.

- **Airplane Food** (www.airlinemeals.net)
- **Airplane Seating** (www.seatguru.com; and www.airlinequality.com)
- **Foreign Languages for Travelers** (www.travlang.com)
- **Maps** (www.mapquest.com)
- **Subway Navigator** (www.subwaynavigator.com)
- **Time and Date** (www.timeanddate.com)
- **Travel Warnings** (http://travel.state.gov, www.fco.gov.uk/travel, www.voyage.gc.ca, www.dfat.gov.au/consular/advice)
- **Universal Currency Converter** (www.xe.com/ucc)
- **Visa ATM Locator** (www.visa.com), **MasterCard ATM Locator** (www.mastercard.com)
- **Weather** (www.intellicast.com; and www.weather.com)

by much of the rest of the world. Your phone will probably work in most major U.S. cities; it definitely won't work in many rural areas. To see where GSM phones work in the U.S., check out www.t-mobile.com/coverage/national_popup.asp. And you may or may not be able to send SMS (text messaging) home.

INTERNET/E-MAIL WITHOUT YOUR OWN COMPUTER

To find cybercafes in your destination check **www.cybercaptive.com** and **www.cybercafe.com**. Although you will find the occasional cybercafe around the region, they are not at all common. Your best bet, other than using access provided by your hotel or resort, is to head to the nearest public library or copy shop, such as FedEx Kinko's.

Most major airports have **Internet kiosks** that provide basic Web access for a per-minute fee that's usually higher than cybercafe prices. Check out copy shops like **Kinko's** (FedEx Kinkos), which offers computer stations with fully loaded software (as well as Wi-Fi).

WITH YOUR OWN COMPUTER

More and more hotels, resorts, airports, cafes, and retailers are going Wi-Fi (wireless fidelity), becoming "hotspots" that offer free high-speed Wi-Fi access or charge a small fee for usage. Wi-Fi is even found in campgrounds, RV parks, and even entire towns. Most laptops sold today have built-in wireless capability. To find public Wi-Fi hotspots at your destination, go to **www.jiwire.com**; its Hotspot Finder holds the world's largest directory of public wireless hotspots.

For dial-up access, most business-class hotels in the U.S. offer dataports for laptop modems, and a few thousand hotels in the U.S. and Europe now offer free high-speed Internet access.

Wherever you go, bring a **connection kit** of the right power and phone adapters, a spare phone cord, and a spare Ethernet network cable—or find out whether your hotel supplies them to guests.

For information on electrical currency conversions, see "Electricity," in the "Fast Facts" section at the end of this chapter.

13 Packages for the Independent Traveler

Package tours are simply a way to buy the airfare, accommodations, and other elements of your trip (such as car rentals, airport transfers, and sometimes even activities) at the same time and often at discounted prices.

One good source of package deals is the airlines themselves. Most major airlines offer air/land packages, including **American Airlines Vacations** (© 800/321-2121; www.aavacations.com), **Delta Vacations** (© 800/654-6559; www.deltavacations.com), **Continental Airlines Vacations** (© 800/301-3800; www.

covacations.com), and **United Vacations** (© 888/854-3899; www.unitedvacations.com). Several big **online travel agencies**—Expedia, Travelocity, Orbitz, Site59, and Lastminute.com—also do a brisk business in packages.

Travel packages are also listed in the travel section of your local Sunday newspaper. Or check ads in the national travel magazines such as *Arthur Frommer's Budget Travel Magazine, Travel + Leisure, National Geographic Traveler,* and *Condé Nast Traveler.*

14 Escorted General-Interest Tours

Escorted tours are structured group tours, with a group leader. The price usually includes everything from airfare to hotels, meals, tours, admission costs, and local transportation.

Despite the fact that escorted tours require big deposits and predetermine hotels, restaurants, and itineraries, many people derive security and peace of mind from the structure they offer. Escorted

tours—whether they're navigated by bus, motor coach, train, or boat—let travelers sit back and enjoy the trip without having to drive or worry about details. They take you to the maximum number of sights in the minimum amount of time with the least amount of hassle. They're particularly convenient for people with limited mobility and they can be a great way to make new friends.

Tips **Ask Before You Go**

Before you invest in a package deal or an escorted tour:

- Always ask about the **cancellation policy**. Can you get your money back? Is there a deposit required?
- Ask about the **accommodations choices and prices** for each. Then look up the hotels' reviews in a Frommer's guide and check their rates online for your specific dates of travel. Also find out what types of rooms are offered.
- Request a complete **schedule**. (Escorted tours only)
- Ask about the **size** and demographics of the group. (Escorted tours only)
- Discuss what is included in the **price** (transportation, meals, tips, airport transfers, and more). (Escorted tours only)
- Finally, look for **hidden expenses**. Ask whether airport departure fees and taxes, for example, are included in the total cost—they rarely are.

On the downside, you'll have little opportunity for serendipitous interactions with locals. The tours can be jam-packed with activities, leaving little room for individual sightseeing, whim, or adventure—plus they often focus on the heavily touristed sites, so you miss out on many a lesser-known gem.

Some reliable tours include **Gray Line Tours Phoenix** (© **800/777-3484** or 602/437-3484; www.graylinearizona.com), which offers a 3-day tour to the Grand Canyon by way of Sedona and Oak Creek Canyon.

Maupintour (© **800/255-4266;** www.maupintour.com), one of the largest tour operators in the world, offers an 8-day Arizona itinerary that covers the Grand Canyon, the Four Corners region, Phoenix, and Scottsdale.

Open Road Tours (© **800/766-7117;** www.openroadtours.com) offers a variety of 2- to 5-day tours around the state. Most of these focus on the Grand Canyon.

Detours (© **866/438-6877;** www.detoursaz.com) specializes in small-group

tours throughout Arizona and other parts of the Southwest. One of its tours, **Hillerman Country,** is a 5-day journey through northern Arizona with a focus on spots that have been mentioned in Tony Hillerman novels about Navajo Tribal Police officers Jim Chee and Joe Leaphorn.

The British tour company **Trek America** (© **800/221-0596,** or 973/983-1144 outside the U.S.; www.trekamerica.com) specializes in off-the-beaten-path, small-group adventure travel and offers lots of tours of the American Southwest; most include stops at the Grand Canyon and other scenic locations in Arizona.

Tauck World Discovery (© **800/788-7885;** www.tauck.com), 10 Norden Place, Norwalk, CT 06855, offers week-long cultural trips to New Mexico. **Destination Southwest, Inc.,** 20 First Plaza Galeria, Suite 212, Albuquerque, NM 87102 (© **800/999-3109** or 505/766-9068; www.destinationsouthwest.com), offers an escorted tour to the Albuquerque International Balloon Fiesta.

15 Getting Around the Southwest

BY CAR

The broad expanses of the American Southwest make driving the best means of getting around, and they also necessitate some precautions. If you plan to drive your own vehicle to and around the region, give it a thorough road check before starting out. There are lots of wide-open desert and wilderness spaces here, and it is not fun to be stranded in the heat or cold with a vehicle that doesn't run. Check your lights, windshield wipers, horn, tires, battery, drive belts, fluid levels, alignment, and other possible trouble spots. Make sure your driver's license, vehicle registration, safety-inspection sticker, and auto-club membership (if you have one) are valid. Check with your auto insurance company to make sure you're covered when out of state, or

when driving a rental car. A breakdown in the desert can be serious. Always carry water with you in the car.

Gasoline is readily available at service stations throughout the region. However, keep close tabs on your gauge, and in more remote areas fill up whenever you can. It's not unusual to drive 60 miles without seeing a gas station. Prices are cheapest in major cities and 10% to 15% more expensive in more isolated communities. All prices are subject to the same fluctuations as elsewhere in the United States.

If you're visiting from abroad and plan to rent a car in the United States, keep in mind that foreign driver's licenses are usually recognized in the U.S., but you should get an international one if your home license is not in English.

Check out **Breezenet.com**, which offers domestic car-rental discounts with some of the most competitive rates around.

CAR RENTALS   **Car rentals** are available in every sizable town and city in the region, always at the local airport, and usually also downtown. Major rental-car companies with offices in the Southwest include:

- **Alamo** ⓒ 800/327-9633; www.alamo.com
- **Avis** ⓒ 800/331-1212; www.avis.com
- **Budget** ⓒ 800/527-0700; www.budget.com
- **Dollar** ⓒ 800/800-4000; www.dollar.com
- **Enterprise** ⓒ 800/736-8222; www.enterprise.com
- **Hertz** ⓒ 800/654-3131; www.hertz.com
- **National** ⓒ 800/227-7368; www.nationalcar.com
- **Payless** ⓒ 800/237-2804; www.paylesscarrental.com
- **Thrifty** ⓒ 800/367-2277; www.thrifty.com

Drivers who need wheelchair-accessible transportation should call **Wheelchair Getaways of New Mexico** (ⓒ **800/408-2626** or 505/247-2626; www.wheelchairgetaways.com); the company rents vans by the day, week, or month.

DRIVING RULES   Unless otherwise posted, the **speed limits** on open roads are 65 mph to 75 mph on interstate highways, 65 mph on U.S. highways, and 55 mph on state highways. The minimum age for drivers is 16. Safety belts are required for drivers and all passengers age 5 and over; children under age 5 must be in an approved child seat secured by the seat belt.

Indian reservations are considered sovereign nations, and they enforce their own laws. For instance, the Navajo reservation

(the region's largest) prohibits transporting alcoholic beverages, leaving established roadways, and traveling without a seat belt. Motorcyclists must wear helmets.

EMERGENCIES   The New Mexico and Arizona State Highway and Transportation Departments provide up-to-the-hour information on road closures and conditions through their toll-free road-advisory hot lines (NM ⓒ **800/432-4269;** www.nmshtd.state.nm.us; AZ ⓒ **888/411-7623**).

Members of the **American Automobile Association (AAA)** can get free emergency road service by calling AAA's emergency number (ⓒ **800/AAA-HELP**).

MAPS   Excellent state highway maps are available from the **New Mexico Department of Tourism** and the **Arizona Department of Tourism** (see "Visitor Information & Maps," earlier in this chapter). The American Automobile Association (AAA) supplies detailed state and city maps free to members (see "Emergencies," above).

BY PLANE

This is a broad region, so if your time is short, you might want to consider flying between cities, though your options are limited. In Arizona, **US Airways** (ⓒ **800/428-4322;** www.usairways.com) serves Phoenix, Tucson, Flagstaff, Kingman, Prescott, Lake Havasu City, and Yuma. **Scenic Airlines** (ⓒ **800/634-6801;** www.scenic.com) flies between Las Vegas and the Grand Canyon.

In New Mexico, **Mesa Airlines** (ⓒ **800/637-2247;** www.mesa-air.com) flies between Albuquerque, Farmington, Carlsbad, Roswell, and Hobbs.

Overseas visitors can take advantage of the APEX (Advance Purchase Excursion) reductions offered by all major U.S. and European carriers. In addition, some large airlines offer transatlantic or transpacific passengers special discount tickets under the name **Visit USA,** which allows mostly one-way travel from one U.S. destination to another at very low prices. Unavailable in the U.S., these discount tickets must be purchased abroad in conjunction with your international fare. This system is the easiest, fastest, cheapest way to see the country.

BY TRAIN

Due to limited options, the train is not the best way of getting around the region. **Amtrak** has two routes. The *Southwest Chief,* which runs between Chicago and Los Angeles, passes through the region once daily in each direction, with stops in Flagstaff, Gallup, Grants, Albuquerque, Lamy (for Santa Fe), Las Vegas, Raton, Trinidad, La Junta, and Lamar. A second train, the *Sunset Limited,* crosses the southern part of the region three times weekly in each direction—between Los Angeles and New Orleans—with stops in Tucson, Benson, Lordsburg, Deming, and El Paso, Texas. Greyhound/Trailways bus lines provide through-ticketing for Amtrak between Albuquerque and El Paso.

If you're headed to the Grand Canyon, you can get to the town of Williams, 30 miles west of Flagstaff, on Amtrak, and transfer to the Grand Canyon Railway excursion train, which runs to Grand Canyon Village at the South Rim of the Grand Canyon. Be aware, however, that the Williams stop is on the outskirts of town; you'll have to arrange in advance to be picked up.

You can get a copy of Amtrak's national timetable from any Amtrak station, from travel agents, or by contacting Amtrak ((C) **800/USA-RAIL;** www.amtrak.com).

International visitors can buy a **USA Rail Pass,** good for 5, 15, or 30 days of unlimited travel on **Amtrak** ((C) **800/USA-RAIL;** www.amtrak.com). The pass is available online or through many overseas travel agents. See Amtrak's website for the cost of travel within the western, eastern, or northwestern United States. Reservations are generally required and should be made as early as possible. Regional rail passes are also available.

16 Tips on Accommodations

No two travelers are alike; fortunately, the Southwest has a broad enough range of accommodations to satisfy even the most eccentric adventurer. If you long to be pampered, you'll find swanky resorts, with a variety of the luxury options such as pool and exercise facilities, golf, tennis, horseback riding, and spa treatments. Of course none of it comes cheap. If you're looking to really savor the flavor of the region, you may want to opt for one of its historic hotels. They include hacienda-style inns—adobe one- or two-story structures often built around a courtyard. You'll also find some Victorian inns that have a frontier flavor. Amenities vary, from places with antique but workable plumbing and no television, to those with hot tubs and dataports in rooms.

When making your reservations during shoulder seasons, such as spring and fall, be sure to ask when hotel rates change (in the desert, for instance, they drop for the summer or go up in the fall), so you can schedule your trip to get the best rates. Remember, if you don't absolutely need all the amenities of a big resort, there are dozens of chain-motel options.

SURFING FOR HOTELS

In addition to the online travel booking sites **Travelocity, Expedia, Orbitz, Priceline,** and **Hotwire,** you can book hotels through **Hotels.com; Quikbook** (www.quikbook.com); and **Travelaxe** (www.travelaxe.net).

HotelChatter.com is a daily webzine offering smart coverage and critiques of hotels worldwide. Go to **TripAdvisor. com** or **HotelShark.com** for helpful independent consumer reviews of hotels and resort properties.

It's a good idea to **get a confirmation number** and **make a printout** of any online booking transaction.

SAVING ON YOUR HOTEL ROOM

The **rack rate** is the maximum rate that a hotel charges for a room. Hardly anybody pays this price, however, except in high season or on holidays. To lower the cost of your room:

- **Ask about special rates or other discounts.** You may qualify for corporate, student, military, senior, frequent flier, trade union, or other discounts.
- **Dial direct.** When booking a room in a chain hotel, you'll often get a better deal by calling the individual hotel's reservation desk rather than the chain's main number.
- **Book online.** Many hotels offer Internet-only discounts, or supply rooms to Priceline, Hotwire, or Expedia at rates much lower than the ones you can get through the hotel itself.
- **Remember the law of supply and demand.** Resort hotels are most crowded and therefore most expensive on weekends, so discounts are usually available for midweek stays. Business hotels in downtown locations are busiest during the week, so

you can expect big discounts over the weekend.

- **Look into group or long-stay discounts.** If you come as part of a large group, you should be able to negotiate a bargain rate. Likewise, if you're planning a long stay (at least 5 days), you might qualify for a discount. As a general rule, expect 1 night free after a 7-night stay.
- **Sidestep excess surcharges and hidden costs.** Many hotels have the unpleasant practice of nickel-and-diming their guests with opaque surcharges. When you book a room, ask what is included in the room rate, and what is extra. Avoid dialing direct from hotel phones, which can have exorbitant rates. And don't be tempted by the room's minibar offerings: Most hotels charge through the nose for water, soda, and snacks. Finally, ask about local taxes and service charges, which can increase the cost of a room by 15% or more.
- **Book an efficiency.** A room with a kitchenette allows you to shop for groceries and cook your own meals. This is a big money saver, especially for families on long stays.
- **Consider enrolling in hotel "frequent-stay" programs,** which are upping the ante lately to win the loyalty of repeat customers. Frequent guests can now accumulate points or credits to earn free hotel nights, airline miles, in-room amenities, merchandise, tickets

---

House-Swapping

House-swapping is becoming a more popular and viable means of travel; you stay in their place, they stay in yours, and you both get an authentic and personal view of the area, the opposite of the escapist retreat that many hotels offer. Try **HomeLink International** (Homelink.org), the largest and oldest home-swapping organization, founded in 1952, with over 11,000 listings worldwide ($75 for a yearly membership). **HomeExchange.org** ($50 for 6,000 listings) and **InterVac.com** ($69 for over 10,000 listings) are also reliable.

to concerts and events, discounts on sporting facilities—and even credit toward stock in the participating hotel, in the case of the Jameson Inn hotel group. Perks are awarded not only by many chain hotels and motels (Hilton HHonors, Marriott Rewards, Wyndham ByRequest, to name a few), but individual inns and B&Bs. Many chain hotels partner with other hotel chains, car-rental firms, airlines, and credit card companies to give consumers additional incentive to do repeat business.

LANDING THE BEST ROOM

Somebody has to get the best room in the house. It might as well be you. You can start by joining the hotel's frequent-guest program, which may make you eligible for upgrades. A hotel-branded credit card usually gives its owner "silver" or "gold" status in frequent-guest programs for free. Always ask about a corner room. They're often larger and quieter, with more windows and light, and they often cost the same as standard rooms. When you make your reservation, ask if the hotel is renovating; if it is, request a room away from the construction. If you're a light sleeper, request a quiet room away from vending or ice machines, elevators, restaurants, bars, and discos. Ask for a room that has most recently been renovated or redecorated.

If you aren't happy with your room when you arrive, ask for another one. Most lodgings will be willing to accommodate you.

FAST FACTS: The American Southwest

American Express There are offices or representatives in Phoenix, Scottsdale, and Albuquerque. For information, call © **800/528-4800.**

Area Codes The area code in Phoenix is 602. In Scottsdale, Tempe, Mesa, and the east valley, it's 480. In Glendale and the west valley, it's 623. The area code for Tucson and southeastern Arizona is 520. The rest of the state is area code 928. At press time the area code for all of New Mexico is 505, though in 2008 that code will apply only to central and northwestern New Mexico, while the rest of the state will use 575. The area code for southwestern Colorado is 719 and for southern Utah, 435. Las Vegas's code is 702.

ATM Networks See "Money & Costs," p. 32.

Automobile Organizations Auto clubs will supply maps, suggested routes, guidebooks, accident and bail-bond insurance, and emergency road service. The **American Automobile Association (AAA)** is the major auto club in the United States. If you belong to an auto club in your home country, inquire about AAA reciprocity before you leave. You may be able to join AAA even if you're not a member of a reciprocal club; to inquire, call AAA (© **800/222-4357**). AAA is actually an organization of regional auto clubs, so look under "AAA Automobile Club" in the White Pages of the telephone directory. AAA has a nationwide emergency road service telephone number (© 800/AAA-HELP).

Business Hours The following are general hours; specific establishments' hours may vary. Banks are open Monday through Friday from 9am to 5pm (some also on Sat 9am–noon). Stores are open Monday through Saturday from 10am to 6pm and Sunday from noon to 5pm (malls usually stay open until 8 or 9pm

Mon–Sat). Bars generally open around 11am and close between 1 and 2am, depending on the state.

Car Rentals See "Getting Around the Southwest," p. 45.

Cashpoints See "ATM Networks," above.

Currency The most common bills are the $1 (a "buck"), $5, $10, and $20 denominations. There are also $2 bills (seldom encountered), $50 bills, and $100 bills (the last two are usually not welcome as payment for small purchases).

Coins come in seven denominations: 1¢ (1 cent, or a penny); 5¢ (5 cents, or a nickel); 10¢ (10 cents, or a dime); 25¢ (25 cents, or a quarter); 50¢ (50 cents, or a half dollar); the gold-colored Sacagawea coin, worth $1; and the rare silver dollar.

For additional information see "Money & Costs," p. 32.

Customs **What You Can Bring Into the Southwest** Every visitor more than 21 years of age may bring in, free of duty, the following: (1) 1 liter of wine or hard liquor; (2) 200 cigarettes, 100 cigars (but not from Cuba), or 3 pounds of smoking tobacco; and (3) $100 worth of gifts. These exemptions are offered to travelers who spend at least 72 hours in the United States and who have not claimed them within the preceding 6 months. It is altogether forbidden to bring into the country foodstuffs (particularly fruit, cooked meats, and canned goods) and plants (vegetables, seeds, tropical plants, and the like). Foreign tourists may carry in or out up to $10,000 in U.S. or foreign currency with no formalities; larger sums must be declared to U.S. Customs on entering or leaving, which includes filing form CM 4790. For details regarding U.S. Customs and Border Protection, consult your nearest U.S. embassy or consulate, or **U.S. Customs** (© 202/927-1770; www.customs.ustreas.gov).

What You Can Take Home from the Southwest:

Canadian Citizens: For a clear summary of Canadian rules, write for the booklet *I Declare,* issued by the **Canada Border Services Agency** (© 800/461-9999 in Canada, or 204/983-3500; **www.cbsa-asfc.gc.ca**).

U.K. Citizens: For information, contact **HM Customs & Excise** at © 0845/010-9000 (from outside the U.K., 020/8929-0152), or consult their website at **www.hmce.gov.uk**.

Australian Citizens: A helpful brochure available from Australian consulates or Customs offices is *Know Before You Go.* For more information, call the **Australian Customs Service** at © 1300/363-263, or log on to **www.customs.gov.au**.

New Zealand Citizens: Most questions are answered in a free pamphlet available at New Zealand consulates and Customs offices: *New Zealand Customs Guide for Travellers, Notice no. 4.* For more information, contact **New Zealand Customs,** The Customhouse, 17–21 Whitmore St., Box 2218, Wellington (© 04/473-6099 or 0800/428-786; **www.customs.govt.nz**).

Drinking Laws The legal age for buying or consuming alcoholic beverages is 21. Each of the states in the region has its own restrictions on when and where you can buy alcohol. Arizona, New Mexico, and Colorado have pretty standard laws, which allow purchase from morning to 1 or 2am in licensed stores on most days, with some time restrictions on Sundays. Utah's laws are stricter; you can buy beer, wine, and hard liquor every day except Sunday, when the state-owned liquor stores are closed. You can buy 3.2% beer, which has less alcohol, 7 days a week. Note that some Indian reservations (including the Navajo reservation) prohibit alcohol within the reservation.

Do not carry open containers of alcohol in your car or any public area that isn't zoned for alcohol consumption. The police can fine you on the spot. And nothing will ruin your trip faster than getting a citation for DUI ("driving under the influence"), so don't even think about driving while intoxicated.

Driving Rules See "Getting Around the Southwest," p. 45.

Electricity Like Canada, the United States uses 110 to 120 volts AC (60 cycles), compared to 220 to 240 volts AC (50 cycles) in most of Europe, Australia, and New Zealand. Downward converters that change 220–240 volts to 110–120 volts are difficult to find in the United States, so bring one with you.

Embassies & Consulates All embassies are located in the nation's capital, Washington, D.C. Some consulates are located in major U.S. cities, and most nations have a mission to the United Nations in New York City. If your country isn't listed below, call for directory information in Washington, D.C. (© 202/555-1212) or log on to **www.embassy.org/embassies**.

The embassy of **Australia** is at 1601 Massachusetts Ave. NW, Washington, DC 20036 (© **202/797-3000;** www.austemb.org). There are consulates in New York, Honolulu, Houston, Los Angeles, and San Francisco.

The embassy of **Canada** is at 501 Pennsylvania Ave. NW, Washington, DC 20001 (© **202/682-1740;** www.canadianembassy.org). Other Canadian consulates are in Buffalo (New York), Detroit, Los Angeles, New York, and Seattle.

The embassy of **Ireland** is at 2234 Massachusetts Ave. NW, Washington, DC 20008 (© **202/462-3939;** www.irelandemb.org). Irish consulates are in Boston, Chicago, New York, San Francisco, and other cities. See website for complete listing.

The embassy of **New Zealand** is at 37 Observatory Circle NW, Washington, DC 20008 (© **202/328-4800;** www.nzemb.org). New Zealand consulates are in Los Angeles, Salt Lake City, San Francisco, and Seattle.

The embassy of the **United Kingdom** is at 3100 Massachusetts Ave. NW, Washington, DC 20008 (© **202/588-7800;** www.britainusa.com). Other British consulates are in Atlanta, Boston, Chicago, Cleveland, Houston, Los Angeles, New York, San Francisco, and Seattle.

Emergencies In most places in the region, call © **911** to report a fire, contact the police, or get an ambulance. A few small towns have not adopted the emergency phone number, so if 911 doesn't work, dial 0 (zero) for the operator and state the type of emergency.

Gasoline (Petrol) At press time, in the U.S., the cost of gasoline (also known as gas, but never petrol), is abnormally high. Taxes are already included in the printed price. One U.S. gallon equals 3.8 liters or .85 imperial gallons. Fill-up locations are known as gas or service stations.

Holidays Banks, government offices, post offices, and many stores, restaurants, and museums are closed on the following legal national holidays: January 1

(New Year's Day), the third Monday in January (Martin Luther King, Jr., Day), the third Monday in February (Presidents' Day), the last Monday in May (Memorial Day), July 4 (Independence Day), the first Monday in September (Labor Day), the second Monday in October (Columbus Day), November 11 (Veterans' Day/Armistice Day), the fourth Thursday in November (Thanksgiving Day), and December 25 (Christmas). The Tuesday after the first Monday in November is Election Day, a federal government holiday in presidential-election years (held every 4 years, and next in 2008).

For more information on holidays see "Calendar of Events," earlier in this chapter.

Hospitals See the "Fast Facts" sections in the city chapters throughout the book.

Internet Access Although you will find the occasional cybercafe around the region, they are not at all common. Your best bet, other than using access provided by your hotel or resort, is to head to the nearest public library or copy shop, such as FedEx Kinko's.

Laundromats Laundromats are available in all communities. Call the chamber of commerce or check the Yellow Pages of the phone book in your destination for names and addresses.

Legal Aid If you are "pulled over" for a minor infraction (such as speeding), never attempt to pay the fine directly to a police officer; this could be construed as attempted bribery, a much more serious crime. Pay fines by mail, or directly into the hands of the clerk of the court. If accused of a more serious offense, say and do nothing before consulting a lawyer. Here the burden is on the state to prove a person's guilt beyond a reasonable doubt, and everyone has the right to remain silent, whether he or she is suspected of a crime or actually arrested. Once arrested, a person can make one telephone call to a party of his or her choice. International visitors should call their embassy or consulate.

Lost & Found Be sure to tell all of your credit card companies the minute you discover your wallet has been lost or stolen and file a report at the nearest police precinct. Your credit card company or insurer may require a police report number or record of the loss. Most credit card companies have an emergency toll-free number to call if your card is lost or stolen; they may be able to wire you a cash advance immediately or deliver an emergency credit card in a day or two. Visa's U.S. emergency number is © 800/847-2911 or 410/581-9994. American Express cardholders and traveler's check holders should call © 800/221-7282. MasterCard holders should call © 800/307-7309 or 636/722-7111. For other credit cards, call the toll-free number directory at © 800/555-1212.

If you need emergency cash over the weekend when all banks and American Express offices are closed, you can have money wired to you via **Western Union** (© 800/325-6000; www.westernunion.com).

Mail At press time, domestic postage rates were 26¢ for a postcard and 41¢ for a letter. For international mail, a first-class letter of up to 1 ounce costs 90¢ (69¢ to Canada and Mexico); a first-class postcard costs 90¢ (69¢ to Canada and Mexico). For more information go to **www.usps.com** and click on "Calculate Postage."

If you aren't sure what your address will be in the United States, mail can be sent to you, in your name, c/o General Delivery at the main post office of the city or region where you expect to be. (Call ℂ **800/275-8777** for information on the nearest post office.) The addressee must pick up mail in person and must produce proof of identity (driver's license, passport, and so on). Most post offices will hold your mail for up to 1 month, and are open Monday to Friday from 8am to 6pm, and Saturday from 9am to 3pm.

Always include zip codes when mailing items in the U.S. If you don't know your zip code, visit www.usps.com/zip4.

Measurements See the chart on the inside front cover of this book for details on converting metric measurements to U.S. equivalents.

Newspapers & Magazines National newspapers include the *New York Times, USA Today,* and the *Wall Street Journal.* National newsweeklies include *Newsweek, Time,* and *U.S. News and World Report.* In large cities, most newsstands offer a small selection of the most popular foreign periodicals and newspapers, such as the *Economist* and *Le Monde.* The **El Paso Times** is favored in southern New Mexico. The state's favorite magazine is **New Mexico** (www.nm magazine.com), a high-quality monthly published by the State Tourism and Travel Division since 1923. Check out the "King of the Road" column in the magazine, for some interesting off-the-beaten-track destinations. The *Arizona Republic* is Arizona's largest daily newspaper and can be found throughout central and northern Arizona. In the southern part of the state, you are more likely to find Tucson's *Arizona Daily Star,* a morning daily. *Arizona Highways* is a beautiful and informative photo driven monthly magazine published by the Arizona Department of Transportation. Both Phoenix and Tucson have a number of glossy monthly lifestyle magazines that are worth picking up for their monthly events listings.

Passports **For Residents of Australia:** You can pick up an application from your local post office or any branch of Passports Australia, but you must schedule an interview at the passport office to present your application materials. Call the **Australian Passport Information Service** at ℂ **131-232,** or visit the government website at www.passports.gov.au.

For Residents of Canada: Passport applications are available at travel agencies throughout Canada or from the central **Passport Office,** Department of Foreign Affairs and International Trade, Ottawa, ON K1A 0G3 (ℂ **800/567-6868;** www.ppt.gc.ca). *Note:* Canadian children who travel must have their own passport. However, if you hold a valid Canadian passport issued before December 11, 2001, that bears the name of your child, the passport remains valid for you and your child until it expires.

For Residents of Ireland: You can apply for a 10-year passport at the **Passport Office,** Setanta Centre, Molesworth Street, Dublin 2 (ℂ **01/671-1633;** www.irl gov.ie/iveagh). Those under age 18 and over 65 must apply for a 3-year passport. You can also apply at 1A South Mall, Cork (ℂ **021/272-525**) or at most main post offices.

For Residents of New Zealand: You can pick up a passport application at any New Zealand Passports Office or download it from their website. Contact the

Passports Office at ✆ **0800/225-050** in New Zealand or 04/474-8100, or log on to www.passports.govt.nz.

For Residents of the United Kingdom: To pick up an application for a standard 10-year passport (5-yr. passport for children under 16), visit your nearest passport office, major post office, or travel agency or contact the **United Kingdom Passport Service** at ✆ **0870/521-0410** or search its website at www.ukpa.gov.uk.

Police In most places in the region, phone ✆ **911** for emergencies. A few small towns have not adopted the emergency number, so if 911 doesn't work, dial 0 (zero) for the operator and state your reason for calling.

Safety See "Safety," earlier in this chapter.

Smoking In much of the region, smoking is prohibited inside public buildings. In some places, rules are even stricter. Arizona and New Mexico prohibit smoking in all indoor public places, including restaurants and bars. In Utah smoking is prohibited in restaurants but not private clubs, lounges, or taverns. Colorado prohibits smoking in public places, but the southern area has no rules for restaurants, though most have designated smoking areas.

Taxes Combined city and state sales taxes vary from place to place but usually range from 6% to 9% for purchases, 9% to 13% for lodging. The United States has no value-added tax (VAT) or other indirect tax at the national level. Every state, county, and city may levy its own local tax on all purchases, including hotel and restaurant checks and airline tickets. These taxes will not appear on price tags.

Telegraph, Telex & Fax **Telegraph and telex services** are provided primarily by Western Union. You can telegraph money, or have it telegraphed to you, very quickly over the Western Union system, but this service can cost as much as 15 to 20 percent of the amount sent.

Most hotels have **fax machines** available for guest use (be sure to ask about the charge to use it). Many hotel rooms are even wired for guests' fax machines. A less expensive way to send and receive faxes may be at stores such as **The UPS Store** (formerly Mail Boxes Etc.).

Time The continental United States is divided into **four time zones:** Eastern Standard Time (EST), Central Standard Time (CST), Mountain Standard Time (MST), and Pacific Standard Time (PST). Alaska and Hawaii have their own zones. For example, when it's 9am in Los Angeles (PST), it's 7am in Honolulu (HST),10am in Denver (MST), 11am in Chicago (CST), noon in New York City (EST), 5pm in London (GMT), and 2am the next day in Sydney.

Daylight saving time is in effect from 1am on the second Sunday in March to 1am on the first Sunday in November, except in Arizona, Hawaii, the U.S. Virgin Islands, and Puerto Rico. Daylight saving time moves the clock 1 hour ahead of standard time.

The American Southwest is in the Mountain time zone, 1 hour ahead of the West Coast and 2 hours behind the East Coast. Note that Arizona does not observe daylight saving time, so time differences between Arizona and the rest of the country vary with the time of year. Meanwhile, the Navajo Reservation observes daylight saving time. However, the Hopi Reservation, which is completely surrounded by the Navajo Reservation, does not.

Tipping Tips are a very important part of certain workers' income, and gratuities are the standard way of showing appreciation for services provided. (Tipping is certainly not compulsory if the service is poor!) In hotels, tip **bellhops** at least $1 per bag ($2–$3 if you have a lot of luggage) and tip the **chamber staff** $1 to $2 per day (more if you've left a disaster area for him or her to clean up). Tip the **doorman** or **concierge** only if he or she has provided you with some specific service (for example, calling a cab for you or obtaining difficult-to-get theater tickets). Tip the **valet-parking attendant** $1 every time you get your car.

In restaurants, bars, and nightclubs, tip **service staff** 15% to 20% of the check, tip **bartenders** 10% to 15%, and tip **checkroom attendants** $1 per garment.

As for other service personnel, tip **cab drivers** 15% of the fare; tip **skycaps** at airports at least $1 per bag ($2–$3 if you have a lot of luggage); and tip **hairdressers** and **barbers** 15% to 20%.

Toilets You won't find public toilets or "restrooms" on the streets in most U.S. cities but they can be found in hotel lobbies, bars, restaurants, museums, department stores, railway and bus stations, and service stations. Large hotels and fast-food restaurants are often the best bets for clean facilities. If possible, avoid the toilets at parks and beaches, which tend to be dirty; some may be unsafe. Restaurants and bars in resorts or heavily visited areas may reserve their restrooms for patrons.

Useful Phone Numbers

U.S. Dept. of State Travel Advisory © **202/647-5225** (manned 24 hrs.)

U.S. Passport Agency © **202/647-0518**

U.S. Centers for Disease Control International Traveler's Hotline: © **404/332-4559**

Visas For information about U.S. Visas go to **http://travel.state.gov** and click on "Visas." Or go to one of the following websites:

Australian citizens can obtain up-to-date visa information from the **U.S. Embassy Canberra,** Moonah Place, Yarralumla, ACT 2600 (© **02/6214-5600**) or by checking the U.S. Diplomatic Mission's website at **http://usembassy-australia.state.gov/consular.**

British subjects can obtain up-to-date visa information by calling the **U.S. Embassy Visa Information Line** (© **0891/200-290**) or by visiting the "Visas to the U.S." section of the American Embassy London's website at **www.usembassy. org.uk.**

Irish citizens can obtain up-to-date visa information through the **Embassy of the USA Dublin,** 42 Elgin Rd., Dublin 4, Ireland (© **353/1-668-8777;** or by checking the "Consular Services" section of the website at **http://dublin.usembassy.gov.**

Citizens of **New Zealand** can obtain up-to-date visa information by contacting the **U.S. Embassy New Zealand,** 29 Fitzherbert Terrace, Thorndon, Wellington (© **644/472-2068**), or get the information directly from the website at **http://wellington.usembassy.gov.**

3

Suggested Southwest Itineraries

Because the Southwest is such an amazingly diverse region, planning a route through it can be overwhelming. The itineraries suggested here should help guide you to the highlights, and hopefully, your trip won't be too hectic. The most important thing to keep in mind when planning a trip to the Southwest is that this is a vast region. Distances always turn out to be much greater than they seem when you're scanning a map in the comfort of your living room. Be prepared to do a lot of driving, and you won't be too surprised by the number of miles you put on your rental car.

1 The Southwest in 1 Week

A week really isn't long enough to do justice to this vast and sprawling landscape, but if that's all the time you have, you can definitely hit the highlights. The following is just such an itinerary. You'll gaze in awe at the Grand Canyon, marvel at the play of light on the buttes and mesas of Monument Valley, ponder the mysterious cliff dwellings of Mesa Verde, and stroll the streets of Santa Fe. *Note:* If you take this trip in the summer, try to get an early start each day in order to avoid the heat. During the middle of the day, it's best to be in an air-conditioned car or hotel room.

Day ❶: Sedona 🐾🐾🐾
Fly into **Phoenix.** Before leaving town to head north to Sedona, stop at the **Desert Botanical Garden** (p. 427) or the **Heard Museum** (p. 427). Just be sure you make it to Sedona in time to watch the sunset from either **Airport Mesa** or **Crescent Moon Recreation Area** (p. 500).

Day ❷: Sedona to Grand Canyon National Park 🐾🐾🐾
In Sedona in the morning, do a **Jeep tour** (p. 503) or a hike. Then head north to the **Grand Canyon** by way of scenic **Oak Creek Canyon** (p. 501). Take US 89 from Flagstaff to the east entrance of Grand Canyon National Park. Be sure to stop at the **Cameron Trading Post** (p. 538) to see the gallery of Native American artifacts in the historic stone building. Stop at **Desert View,** just inside the park entrance, and also at **Lipan Point,** and catch the sunset over the Grand Canyon.

Day ❸: Canyon de Chelly National Monument 🐾🐾🐾
If you can, get up early enough to catch sunrise from one of the Grand Canyon overlooks. Then, head east out of the park to Cameron and go north to **Tuba City.** Be sure to check out the dinosaur footprints in the bedrock just west of Tuba City. Continue east through the villages

1 Sedona
2 Grand Canyon National Park
3 Canyon de Chelly National Monument
4 Monument Valley Navajo Tribal Park
5 Mesa Verde National Park
6–7 Santa Fe

of the Hopi mesas. Here, you can tour **Walpi village** (p. 99) with a guide and shop for Hopi crafts and jewelry at the many roadside crafts shops. When you reach **Canyon de Chelly National Monument** (p. 106), take one of the Rim Drives before it gets dark.

Day ❹: Canyon de Chelly to Monument Valley Navajo Tribal Park ✫✫✫

Do a half-day truck tour of Canyon de Chelly in the morning. After lunch, drive to **Monument Valley Navajo Tribal Park** (p. 112). Make sure that you get there in time to catch the sunset. If you arrive early enough in the day, do a Jeep tour of the valley. Alternatively, go for a horseback ride; there is no more scenic spot in the Southwest to connect with your inner cowboy or cowgirl. Whether at lunch or dinner, be sure to try some Navajo fry bread.

Day ❺: Monument Valley to Mesa Verde National Park ✫✫✫

Today, do a morning **Jeep tour** (p. 113) of Monument Valley before heading east to Mesa Verde. En route, be sure to stop at **Four Corners Monument Navajo Tribal Park** (p. 90), the only place in the country where four states meet. At **Mesa Verde National Park** (p. 87), sign up for a ranger-led tour so you can see Balcony House, Cliff Palace, and Long House. Spend the night in Cortez.

Days ❻–❼: Santa Fe ✫✫✫

After so many days in the desert, you'll find an oasis in Santa Fe. Spend a little time wandering the **plaza** and visiting the **Palace of the Governors** (p. 160). If you're interested in shopping for Southwestern jewelry, peruse the offerings under the Palace of the Governors portal. Next, head to the **St. Francis Cathedral** (p. 160) and, if you have time, the **Loretto Chapel Museum** (p. 163), with its "magical" staircase. If it's summer, take in a performance at the **Santa Fe Opera** or the **Santa Fe Chamber Music Festival**

(p. 179). The next day, start at the **Museum of International Folk Art** (p. 162), then visit the **Museum of Indian Arts & Culture** (p. 162). Have lunch at the **Museum Hill Café** (p. 162), and then see either the **Wheelwright Museum of the American Indian** (p. 163) or the **Museum of Spanish Colonial Art** (p. 163). Spend the late afternoon exploring and shopping along **Canyon Road** (p. 171), where you can also eat dinner.

2 The Southwest in 2 Weeks

If you have 2 weeks to explore the Southwest, consider yourself fortunate. You'll not only be able to hit the highlights, but you'll also be able to spend time getting to know such places as Tucson, Santa Fe, and the Grand Canyon. You'll also have time to visit some of the region's more out-of-the-way attractions, such as Carlsbad Caverns National Park and White Sands National Monument.

Days ❶–❷: Tucson 🏵🏵

Head straight for the pool at your resort—after all, lounging in the sun is one of the main reasons to visit Arizona. If you're a hiker, head to one of the trails in the foothills of the Santa Catalina Mountains. **Sabino Canyon** (p. 367) is just about the best place in the city for a quick hike. If you're more interested in culture, head to **Mission San Xavier del Bac** (p. 370), a Spanish mission church that is known as the "White Dove of the Desert." The next day, go west to the **Arizona–Sonora Desert Museum** (p. 366), which is more of a zoo than a museum. After you've hung out with the hummingbirds and communed with the coatis, drive a few miles to **Saguaro National Park** (p. 367). Be sure to check out the petroglyphs at Signal Hill.

Day ❸: White Sands National Monument 🏵🏵🏵

Spend the morning driving east across the Sonoran and Chihuahuan deserts. You'll see the lovely Chiricahua Mountains and the Gila National Forest en route. Stop

for lunch in Las Cruces on **Old Mesilla Plaza**. Spend the afternoon exploring **White Sands** (p. 296), the world's largest gypsum dune field, where you'll want to take the 16-mile Dunes Drive, stopping along the way to hike on the sand. Stay in the mountains at **The Lodge at Cloudcroft** (p. 296).

Day ❹: Carlsbad Caverns National Park 🏵🏵🏵

Today you'll drive farther, through forest and more Chihuahuan Desert to **Carlsbad Caverns National Park** (p. 311). Be sure to take the 1-mile self-guided walk down along the Natural Entrance route, following the original explorers' path deep into the earth. In the evening, visit the **Living Desert Zoo & Gardens State Park** (p. 308) to see some 50 species of (rescued) desert animals and 500 varieties of plants. Stay the night in Carlsbad.

Days ❺–❻: Santa Fe 🏵🏵🏵

It's a hearty drive to Santa Fe; once there, you'll enjoy the sophistication of the "City Different." See "The Southwest in 1 Week: Days 6–7," above.

1–2 Tucson
3 White Sands National Monument
4 Carlsbad Caverns National Park
5–6 Santa Fe
7 Mesa Verde National Park

8 Monument Valley Navajo Tribal Park
9 Canyon de Chelly National Monument
10–11 Grand Canyon National Park
12–13 Sedona
14a Phoenix
14b Las Vegas

Day 7: Mesa Verde National Park 🌟🌟🌟

Head north on one of the region's prettiest drives, US 84, to Pagosa Springs, Colorado, then across to Cortez. Spend the afternoon touring **Mesa Verde National Park** (p. 87), the largest archaeological preserve in the U.S. See "The Southwest in 1 Week: Day 5," above. Spend the night in Cortez.

Day 8: Monument Valley Navajo Tribal Park 🌟🌟🌟

From Mesa Verde, head to **Monument Valley Navajo Tribal Park** (p. 112). On the way, stop at **Four Corners Monument Navajo Tribal Park** (p. 90). Just be sure you reach Monument Valley early enough for a **Jeep tour** (p. 113) of the valley with a Navajo guide. Stick around

to take pictures of sunset on the Mitten Buttes. This is also the best place in Arizona to go for a horseback ride. You'll feel as if you've ridden into a scene from a John Ford movie.

Day 9: Canyon de Chelly National Monument 🌟🌟🌟

The next day, drive to **Canyon de Chelly National Monument** (p. 106), which Navajo families still inhabit in summer, farming and raising sheep in much the same way that their ancestors did. Make a reservation in advance for a half-day **"shake-and-bake" truck tour** (p. 110) of the canyon, or hire a Navajo guide to take you into the canyon by Jeep or on horseback. Alternatively, drive one of the rim drives. The **South Rim Drive** (p. 108) is our favorite because it provides the opportunity to hike down into the canyon on the **White House Ruins** trail (p. 109).

Days ⑩–⑪: Grand Canyon National Park 𝒜𝒜𝒜

From Canyon de Chelly, head south to Ganado and visit the historic **Hubbell Trading Post National Historic Site.** Then head west across the Hopi Reservation and stop in the village of **Walpi** (p. 99). You can take a guided tour of the ancient mesa-top pueblo. Also be sure to stop at the **Cameron Trading Post** (p. 538). At the Grand Canyon, stop at **Desert View,** just inside the park entrance, and at **Lipan Point,** and catch the sunset. The next day, get up for the sunrise, then do a day hike or **mule ride** (p. 535) down into the canyon. If you plan ahead, you can even spend the night down in the canyon at **Phantom Ranch.** If you're not a hiker, spend the day exploring along **Hermit Road,** where there are numerous overlooks.

Days ⑫–⑬: Sedona 𝒜𝒜𝒜

Sedona may be touristy, but the red-rock cliffs, buttes, and mesas that surround the city make it one of the most beautiful communities in America. To get out amid the red rocks, take a **Jeep tour** (p. 503) or hike the 4- to 5-mile loop trail around **Bell Rock** and **Courthouse Butte** (p. 499). Although this trail sees a lot of hikers, it is just about the best introduction to the area's amazing hiking. Head up on **Airport Mesa** for the sunset. If you arrive too late for a Jeep tour, plan to do one the next day. On your second day in Sedona, in the morning either take a Jeep tour or visit the fascinating **V Bar V petroglyph site** (p. 500). In the afternoon, head west of town to **Palatki Ruins** (p. 500) and go for a hike in the area, perhaps up **Boynton Canyon.** Head to the **Crescent Moon Recreation Area** (p. 500) for sunset.

Day ⑭ (Option 1): Phoenix 𝒜𝒜

Heading south from Sedona, you can stop at the cliff dwellings at **Montezuma Castle National Monument** (p. 495). Then spend the end of your trip lounging at a resort or playing a round of golf on one of the Phoenix area's many top-rated courses. Also, before catching your flight out of town, be sure to stop at the **Heard Museum** (p. 427) or the **Desert Botanical Garden** (p. 427).

Day ⑭ (Option 2): Las Vegas 𝒜𝒜

If your interests lean more toward casinos and neon lights, head west to Las Vegas, where you can marvel at the nation's foremost city of excess.

3 Family Time: The Southwest for Kids & the Young at Heart in 2 Weeks

Though the Southwest lacks the major theme-park variety of attractions, it makes up for it by offering experiences that have a deeper impact. This trip takes families to the region's most notable sights, including Grand Canyon National Park and White Sands National Monument, and offers some poolside lounging and a hike through an archaeological site. While you're planning this trip, keep in mind that in the Southwest, many miles can stretch between spectacular sights. Parents who like to drive with their kids (some we know actually do) can choose this journey. Those who find long drives with their kids difficult might want to vacation at a guest ranch or resort, or might want to focus in on one area with lots of family attractions.

The Southwest for Kids & the Young at Heart

1–3	Tucson	9	Chaco Culture National Historic Park
4	White Sands National Monument	10	Monument Valley Navajo Tribal Park
5	Carlsbad Caverns National Park	11–12	Grand Canyon National Park
6–8	Santa Fe	13–14	Sedona

Days ❶–❸: Tucson ⛄⛄

Spend your first couple of days in Tucson, where you can learn all about the desert and the kids can pet snakes and tarantulas at the **Arizona–Sonora Desert Museum** (p. 366). Spend the morning at this amazing place, then after lunch head to **Old Tucson Studios** (p. 371), a one-time movie set that is now a sort of Wild West amusement park, albeit without any thrill rides. On one of your nights in town, have dinner at a cowboy steak-house (p. 365). Alternatively, you could just spend a couple of days at a guest ranch (the Tucson area has three). On your third day in Tucson, do a day trip to **Tombstone** (p. 472). Yes, there is a Tombstone, and it's where Wyatt Earp and Doc Holliday shot it out with the

bad guys at the O.K. Corral. Sure, it's touristy, but you owe it to your kids to bring them to this icon of the American west. On the way back from Tombstone, be sure to head underground at **Kartchner Caverns State Park** (p. 468). The caverns here are second only to Carlsbad Caverns for impressiveness.

Day ❹: White Sands National Monument ⛄⛄⛄

Head east from Tucson, stopping at **Old Mesilla Plaza** in Las Cruces for lunch. **White Sands National Monument** (p. 296) is a kid's dream—a giant sand-box to play in all afternoon. The world's largest gypsum dune field supplies plenty of fun hiking and sand sliding for the kids and panoramic beauty for adults. Be sure to take the 16-mile **Dunes Drive.** In the afternoon, head up to Cloudcroft, where you can cool down in the forest and enjoy a lavish night at the **Lodge at Cloudcroft** (p. 296).

Day ❺: Carlsbad Caverns National Park 𝕲𝕲𝕲

Another kids' play land, **Carlsbad Caverns National Park** (p. 311) is especially appealing if you hike down into the caves from the Natural Entrance, the route the original spelunkers took. The late afternoon offers an opportunity to see gila monsters and bobcats at the **Living Desert Zoo & Gardens State Park** (p. 308). After dinner, take a stroll along or swim in the **Pecos River** (p. 308). Spend the night in Carlsbad.

Days ❻–❽: Santa Fe 𝕲𝕲𝕲

Head north, stopping to stretch your legs at the **International UFO Museum** (p. 306) in Roswell, which will challenge—or confirm—your belief in what's "out there." In the gift shop, your kids can stock up on the latest alien kitsch. Then head to Santa Fe, passing through the lovely Galisteo Basin. Wander the **Plaza** and explore the **Palace of the Governors** (p. 160) and **St. Francis Cathedral** (p. 160).

Begin your seventh day at the **Museum of International Folk Art** (p. 162), which displays works from over 100 countries. Kids enjoy the hundreds of toys on display. A morsel for the parents, the **Museum of Indian Arts & Culture** (p. 162) is like a journey into another world, with vivid displays of ancient Native American life. Alternatively, head to the **Santa Fe Children's Museum** (p. 167), where kids can rock climb and visit a horticulture garden. Spend the late afternoon wandering **Canyon Road** (p. 171), where parents will find world-class art and kids will find fun works such as mobiles and rocking horses. Take your last Santa Fe day to explore New Mexico's outdoors. If it's

winter, head up to **Ski Santa Fe** (p. 170). In spring or early summer, take a whitewater (or flat-water if you have small children) raft trip down the **Rio Grande** (p. 170) in Pilar. If it's summer or fall, hike in the Santa Fe National Forest. You can enjoy a **chairlift ride** (p. 170) to the Ski Santa Fe summit (panoramic views!) and then hike down.

Day ❾: Chaco Canyon National Historical Park 𝕲𝕲𝕲

There's plenty of space for kids to stretch their legs after the long drive to **Chaco Canyon National Historic Park** (p. 131). With its stunning desert setting and awesome ruins, the site offers opportunities to peek into dwellings and climb down into kivas. Be sure to hike up the **Pueblo Alto Trail** to see the ruins from above and get a view of the entire canyon. Spend the night in Farmington or Aztec.

Day ❿: Monument Valley Navajo Tribal Park 𝕲𝕲𝕲

From Farmington, head to **Monument Valley Navajo Tribal Park** (p. 112). On the way, be sure to stop at **Four Corners Monument Navajo Tribal Park** (p. 90), the only place in the country where four states meet. Because you can stand in Colorado, Utah, Arizona, and New Mexico at once, this is one of the Southwest's premier family photo ops. Just be sure you reach Monument Valley early enough to go for a horseback ride. We recommend **Diné Trail Ride Tours** (p. 114), which leads its rides from a point deep within the valley. Alternatively, do a **Jeep tour** (p. 113). Be sure to try some fry bread or a Navajo taco while you're here.

Days ⓫–⓬: Grand Canyon National Park 𝕲𝕲𝕲

From Monument Valley, head for the east entrance of **Grand Canyon National Park** (p. 522). En route, be sure to check out the cool **dinosaur footprints** (p. 102) just west of Tuba City. **Cameron Trading**

Post (p. 102) is a good place to stop for lunch. It has a huge selection of Native American crafts as well as souvenirs that will appeal to the kids. Just be sure you make it to the Grand Canyon in time for sunset. In the evening, you may be able to catch an interesting interpretive program. Spend the next day hiking a little way into the canyon, riding a mule down into the canyon (if your kids are old enough), or exploring along Hermit Road. The historic little Hermit's Rest is a good place to get cocoa and hang out by the fireplace.

Days ⑬–⑭: Grand Canyon to Sedona 𝒢𝒢𝒢

Head back out the east entrance of the park and then drive south toward Flagstaff and Sedona. You can dawdle along the way, perhaps by stopping at Wupatki National Monument (p. 554). From Flagstaff, drive down through Oak Creek Canyon and stop at Slide Rock State Park (p. 501), where you and the kids can cool off in the waters of Oak Creek and have a blast on the natural water slide. The next morning, do a Jeep tour so you can get out in the famous red rocks of Sedona. In the afternoon, head back to Slide Rock or to Grasshopper Point (p. 501), Oak Creek Canyon's other great swimming hole.

4 A Multisport Tour of the Southwest

Anyone who hikes, mountain bikes, or rafts knows that the Southwest's offerings for outdoors enthusiasts are unsurpassed. The Grand Canyon has the world's greatest rafting adventure, and Moab, Utah, is legendary among mountain bikers. Hikers are in awe of the canyonlands of southern Utah—not only for their bizarre and beautiful rock formations but also for their narrow slot canyons. In a 2-week adventure, you can take in the best this region has to offer. *Note:* Because Grand Canyon rafting trips are so popular and need to be booked up to a year in advance, this itinerary is workable only if you first book your raft trip.

Days ❶–❷: Zion National Park 𝒢𝒢

Fly into Las Vegas and immediately head out of Sin City bound for Zion National Park (p. 562), a sort of paradise amid the rugged cliffs of southwestern Utah. Hiking trails abound; weather permitting, plan a day hike up the spectacular Narrows. This route follows the Virgin River, and you will get your feet wet, but it's the perfect introduction to the slot canyons of the Southwest. You can hike as far up the canyon as your stamina allows. The next day, try the Lower Emerald Pools Trail or the Angel's Landing Trail. Stay at Zion Lodge (p. 566).

Day ❸: Bryce Canyon National Park 𝒢𝒢𝒢

From Zion, head north to Bryce Canyon National Park (p. 568), which is not a canyon but rather a series of bizarrely eroded natural amphitheaters. A maze of trails meanders amid the hoodoos and forests of the national park. Spend the night at Bryce Canyon Lodge (p. 571).

Days ❹–❺: Moab & Arches National Park 𝒢𝒢𝒢

After 3 days of hiking in Zion and Bryce Canyon, you'll probably appreciate the chance to sit for a while as you make the long drive to Moab, the mountain-biking capital of the Southwest. In Moab, rent a

A Multisport Tour of the Southwest

1–2	Zion National Park
3	Bryce Canyon National Park
4–5	Moab & Arches National Park
6	Monument Valley Navajo Tribal Park
7–9	Page, Lake Powell, Buckskin Gulch & Coyote Buttes
10–14	Grand Canyon National Park

bike, get your hands on a map, and head out on the slickrock trails of this wonderland of rock. In between bike rides, consider driving to **Arches National Park** (p. 577) to see some of its incredible sandstone arches.

Day ❻: Moab to Monument Valley

Get up early for one last bike ride in Moab. Then head south to **Monument Valley Navajo Tribal Park** (p. 112). Although this park isn't known specifically as an outdoor-sports destination, the scenery is too awesome to ignore. To burn off some calories, you can hike the 3.2-mile Wildcat Trail or hire a Navajo guide to take you on a hike deeper into the park. However, if you aren't already too saddle-sore from biking in Moab, you

should really saddle up a palomino and ride off into the sunset. No other place in the West will give you such a feeling of having ridden right into a classic Hollywood western. Stay at **Goulding's Lodge** (p. 115) just outside the park.

Day ❼: Page & Lake Powell 👣👣

The next day, drive west to Page. Just before you reach town, you can stop at **Antelope Canyon** (p. 119) and hike into one of the Southwest's most photographed slot canyons. It's beautiful but is also often crowded, which will give you a greater appreciation for the permit systems in effect at some of the region's other slot canyons. Now for something completely different: Although the Lake Powell reservoir is best known to houseboaters and water-skiers, it also offers the most spectacular **sea kayaking** in the Southwest. Rent a boat and head out to Antelope Canyon again. This time, you'll be paddling up from the mouth. If there isn't too much quicksand where the water gives way to land, you can even get out and hike up the slot canyon.

Days ❽–❾: Buckskin Gulch & Coyote Buttes ⭒⭒⭒

Using Page as a base, spend the next 2 days exploring some of the most famous slot canyons in the Southwest. The 37-mile **Paria Canyon** (p. 121) is a 3- to 4-day trip, but you can day hike into **Buckskin Gulch,** one of its tributaries. The hike starts at the Wire Pass Trailhead, about 30 miles west of Page. From this same trailhead, you can also hike into **Coyote Buttes** (p. 549), but only if you managed to get a permit, which can be difficult. If you have a permit, spend one day at Coyote Buttes and one day in Buckskin Gulch. Spend your second

night in Page or at Lees Ferry, depending on where your rafting trip starts.

Days ❿–⓮: Grand Canyon National Park ⭒⭒⭒

Rafting the Grand Canyon (p. 536) is the adventure of a lifetime. Although it's possible to spend less than a week rafting through a portion of the canyon, such trips are in big motorized rafts that detract from the wilderness experience of floating through the canyon. You owe it to yourself to make the most of the trip and go by oar-powered raft or dory. Talk about a thrill ride! If you opt for a trip that puts in at Lee's Ferry and ends at Phantom Ranch, you'll get to hike up out of the canyon at the end of your trip, adding one last great segment to an unforgettable two weeks in the Southwest. Spend your last night at one of the lodges on the park's South Rim, and the next day drive back to Las Vegas. You'll have to arrange through your rafting company to have your car shuttled to the national park.

5 Historical Delights: The Pueblo & Conquistador Trail in 2 Weeks

The Native American presence in the American Southwest stretches back as far as 3000 B.C. That history intersects with the Spanish conquistadors, whose culture has transformed over 4 centuries into its own unique way of life. Visitors encounter ancient ruins and artifacts, formidable mission churches, and poetic Spanish villages, set against the backdrop of stunning scenery. Those who want to travel back in time will find plenty of adventure here. Though you can take this trip anytime, it's best in spring, summer, or fall.

Day ❶: Albuquerque ⭒⭒

Enjoy a relaxing day. Stroll **Old Town** (p. 233), wandering some of the narrow back streets in search of shops displaying Native American and Spanish artifacts. Nearby is the **Indian Pueblo Cultural Center** (p. 240), where you can get acquainted with the cultures that you'll encounter throughout the New Mexico portion of your trip. If you have the

energy, head west of town to the **Petroglyph National Monument** (p. 243) to hike and watch the sunset.

Days ❷–❹: Santa Fe ⭒⭒⭒

In the morning of day 2, drive the **Turquoise Trail** (p. 259) to Santa Fe. You'll pass through old mining towns and hills where Native Americans and others once mined turquoise. See "The Southwest in

1 Week: Days 6–7" (p. 57) for pointers on how to spend days 2 and 3. On day 4, head north to explore **Bandelier National Monument** (p. 187), or take the **High Road to Taos** (p. 187) for a visit to **Taos Pueblo** (p. 213). Your choice will depend on whether you prefer to see ancient ruins or Native Americans' current lifestyles.

Day ❺: Acoma Pueblo 🕾🕾🕾

Today you'll head south and then west to **Acoma Pueblo** (p. 265). Take the bus and walking tour, but then hike down on your own to get a good sense of this mesa-top village, where people still live as their ancestors did hundreds of years ago. If you have energy and time afterward, visit **El Morro National Monument** (p. 268) to see inscriptions left by visitors for hundreds of years. Be sure to climb up to the Anasazi (ancestral Puebloan) ruins. Spend the night in Grants.

Day ❻: Chaco Culture National Historic Park 🕾🕾🕾

Though it's a long, dusty drive to **Chaco Culture National Historic Park** (p. 131), the combination of a stunning setting and expansive ruins makes the park worthwhile. Chaco is the Holy Grail for Southwest history buffs. Be sure to hike up the **Pueblo Alto Trail** to get a full view of the grand kivas and amazing network of dwellings. Spend the night in Farmington at **Casa Blanca** (p. 129).

Day ❼: Mesa Verde National Park & Monument Valley Navajo Tribal Park 🕾🕾🕾

Though similar to Chaco, **Mesa Verde** (p. 87) presents a whole different style of living and architecture. Sign up for a ranger-led tour to get a close-up view of some of the best ruins. When you've finished wandering, head for **Monument Valley Navajo Tribal Park** (p. 112), arriving in time to see the sun set on Mitten Buttes. Stay the night at **Goulding's Lodge** (p. 115).

Day ❽: Canyon de Chelly National Monument 🕾🕾🕾

Get an early start and drive to **Canyon de Chelly National Monument** (p. 106). See "The Southwest in 2 Weeks: Day 9."

Day ❾: The Hopi Mesas

After leaving Canyon de Chelly, head south to Ganado and visit the historic **Hubbell Trading Post National Historic Site**. Then head west across the Hopi Reservation and stop in the village of **Walpi** (p. 99), where you can take a guided tour of the ancient mesa-top pueblo. Also be sure to stop at **Tsakurshovi** (p. 101), a tiny crafts shop that specializes in traditional Hopi kachina dolls. Continue south to Winslow and stay at the historic **La Posada** hotel (p. 97).

Day ❿: Sedona 🕾🕾🕾

Although Sedona is best known for its red-rock scenery and art galleries, the area has several small Sinagua ruins and an impressive rock art site. Get an early start and head first to **Montezuma Castle National Monument** (p. 495), a Sinagua cliff dwelling. From there, head north to **Montezuma Well** (p. 495), then continue to the **V Bar V Petroglyph Site** (p. 500), which has a small rock wall covered with fascinating petroglyphs. After a picnic on the banks of Beaver Creek or lunch in Sedona, visit the remote cliff dwellings at **Palatki Ruins** (p. 500). If you have time, visit the partially reconstructed hilltop ruins at **Tuzigoot National Monument** (p. 496) in nearby Clarkdale.

Day ⓫: Phoenix 🕾🕾

Today, head south to Phoenix and visit the **Heard Museum** (p. 427), Arizona's foremost museum of Native American art and culture. This museum can help you make sense of what you've been seeing during your trip. If you want to see more petroglyphs, visit **Deer Valley Rock Art Center** (p. 427). Alternatively, you can see a partially reconstructed Hohokam

Historical Delights: The Pueblo & Conquistador Trail in 2 Weeks

village at **Pueblo Grande Museum and Archaeological Park** (p. 430). In the evening, stroll the grounds of the **Desert Botanical Garden** (p. 427), which has an ethnobotanical garden.

Day ⑫: Bisbee & Coronado National Memorial 🦌

Today, head south through Tucson to the historic copper-mining town of Bisbee. It makes a good base for exploring the nearby **Coronado National Memorial** (p. 469). This memorial commemorates the 16th-century expedition of Spanish explorer Francisco Vásquez de Coronado. As you drive south from Phoenix to Bisbee, detour to visit **Casa Grande Ruins National Monument** (p. 456), which

preserves a huge 650-year-old earth-walled Hohokam building that may have been an astronomical observatory.

Days ⑬–⑭: Tucson 🦌🦌

From Bisbee, head west on scenic back roads to the historic Spanish mission now preserved as **Tumacácori National Historical Park** (p. 460). Nearby you can tour more Spanish ruins at **Tubac Presidio State Historic Park** (p. 460). Be sure to stop at Wisdom's Café for a fruit burrito. As you drive north from Tubac, you'll come to **Mission San Xavier del Bac** (p. 370). This Spanish mission church, known as the White Dove of the Desert, is the most beautiful and best-preserved of all the Spanish churches in the

Southwest. The next day, stroll around the Barrio Viejo and El Presidio historic districts to get a feel for Spanish and Mexican days in Tucson. Several of the historic buildings in the Presidio neighborhood are part of the Tucson Museum of Art and are open to the public. Nearby, on the grounds of the Tucson Convention Center, you can visit the historic **Sosa-Carillo-Frémont House Museum** (p. 373).

4

The Active Vacation Planner

You may be pleasantly surprised at the range of outdoor fun available in the Southwest. From the deserts of the southern regions to the mountains and canyons of the north, diversity reigns. Whether you're interested in a short day hike or an overnight horse trip, groomed ski trails or backcountry adventures, you won't be disappointed.

For more in-depth coverage of the activities that follow, contact some of the local outfitters or organizations that appear in the "Getting Outside" sections, later in this book.

1 Bicycling

It's awesome to pedal out into the dry southwest air and see not only incredible terrain but also ancient history. Just about the entire region is conducive to the sport, making it one of the most popular places in the United States for avid cyclers, especially mountain bikers.

For road warriors, many miles of pavement traverse the area. Rides range greatly in length and difficulty; all provide beautiful scenery, and most have decent pavement with good shoulders. In northern New Mexico, try biking the Enchanted Circle (see chapter 7) and in southern New Mexico, try Silver City to Glenwood (see chapter 10). Road biking is highly recommended in Zion National Park as well (see chapter 16).

Few can think of mountain biking without Moab, Utah, coming to mind. Moab and many other parts of southern Utah hold hundreds of miles of trails, a wide variety of terrain, and spectacular scenery. In addition to the mountain-biking possibilities on four-wheel-drive roads in the national parks, abundant trails on Bureau of Land Management and national forest lands are much less trafficked than national park routes. Moab's most famous trail is undoubtedly the **Slickrock Bike Trail,** a scenic but challenging 9.6-mile loop that crosses a mesa of heavily eroded pale orange Navajo sandstone just a few minutes from downtown Moab (see chapter 16 for information about Moab).

In New Mexico, bikers will find excellent trails in **Albuquerque** at the base of the Sandia Mountains (see chapter 8). In **Santa Fe,** you'll find some very rugged and steep mountain trails, most accessed off the road to Ski Santa Fe (see chapter 6). **Taos** is a rider's paradise, with lots of extreme mountain trails, as well as some that are purely scenic, such as the west rim of the Rio Grande Gorge (see chapter 7). In northwestern New Mexico, you can ride around El Malpais National Monument in the **Grants** area (see chapter 9). You can also take your bike with you to Chaco Culture National Historical Park and tour the Anasazi ruins (see chapter 5). In the southwestern region, bikes are not allowed in the Gila Wilderness, but they are permitted in other parts of Gila National Forest; you'll find terrific trails that originate in **Silver City,** particularly the Continental Divide Trail (see chapter 10). In the southeast region, the **Cloudcroft** area has some excellent trails; there are a few that explore history as well as natural terrain, most notably the 17-mile Rim Trail (see chapter 10).

Some of the best biking in the area is in Arizona. With its wide range of climates, this sunny state offers good pedaling somewhere in the state every month of the year. In summer, the Kaibab National Forest (between Flagstaff and Grand Canyon National Park; see chapter 15) offers good mountain biking. There's also excellent biking at several Phoenix parks. Our favorite trail is the Desert Classic in South Mountain Park (see chapter 12). Tucson is one of the most bicycle-friendly cities in the country. Check out the Bajada Loop Drive in the Saguaro National Park (see chapter 11). One of the best spots in the region is Sedona; head to the Bell Rock Pathway (see chapter 14).

If you don't want to strike out on your own, **Mellow Velo Bikes,** Santa Fe (℃ **505/ 982-8986;** www.mellowbike.com), runs bike tours from April to October to some of the most spectacular spots in northern New Mexico. Trips range from easy, scenic jaunts to more mountainous technical rides. **Backroads** (℃ **800/462-2848** or 510/ 527-1555; www.backroads.com) offers a 6-day, inn-to-inn mountain-bike trip through the red-rock country of central Arizona. **Western Spirit Cycling** (℃ **800/845-2453** or 435/259-8732; www.westernspirit.com) offers a number of interesting mountain-bike tours, including trips to both the North and South rims of the Grand Canyon and through the desert south of Tucson. Each trip is 5 days in duration. **WomanTours** (℃ **800/247-1444;** www.womantours.com) offers a couple of different Arizona bike tours that are exclusively for women. In Utah, you can get information on trails and outfitters, as well as rent or repair bikes, at **Slickrock Cycles,** 415 N. Main St., Moab (℃ **800/825-9791** or 435/259-1134; www.slickrockcycles.com). **The World Outdoors** (℃ **800/488-8483** or 303/413-0938; www.theworldoutdoors.org) offers a variety of trips, including multi-sport adventures that include mountain biking, hiking, horseback riding, and rafting to the Canyonlands area, plus hiking/biking trips in the vicinities of Bryce Canyon, Zion, and the north rim of the Grand Canyon.

Some books to check out are *Mountain Biking Moab* (Falcon Press) and *Mountain Biking New Mexico* (Falcon Press). To research Arizona trails, pick up a copy of *Fat Tire Tales and Trails,* by Cosmic Ray.

2 Bird-Watching

Bird-watchers know that the Southwest is directly on the Central Flyway, which makes it a great spot for this activity all year long. Each region offers refuge to a wide variety of birds, including everything from doves, finches, bluebirds, and roadrunners (the New Mexico state bird) to the rare and wonderful whooping crane. The bald eagle is also frequently spotted during winter and spring migrations. A good place to pull out your binoculars is southeastern Arizona, where many species found primarily south of the border come to visit. Birding hot spots include **Ramsey Canyon Preserve** (known for its many species of hummingbirds), **Cave Creek Canyon** (nesting site for elegant trogons), **Patagonia–Sonoita Creek Preserve** (home to 22 species of flycatchers, kingbirds, and phoebes, as well as Montezuma quails), **Buenos Aires National Wildlife Refuge** (home to masked bobwhite quail and gray hawks), and the sewage ponds outside the town of **Willcox** (known for avocets and sandhill cranes). For further information on these birding spots, see chapter 13. If you're into eclectic bird-watching, head to the **Vermilion Cliffs** in northern Arizona, where you'll likely catch a glimpse of the noble California condor, which the California Condor Recovery Plan has brought to the area in the hope that it can flourish there (see chapter 15). To find out which birds have been spotted lately, call the **Tucson Audubon Society's Bird Report** (© **520/798-1005**).

Though not quite as renowned a birding spot as southern Arizona, New Mexico does host plenty of birds. Check out the wildlife refuge centers in New Mexico, most notably the **Bosque del Apache National Wildlife Refuge,** 93 miles south of Albuquerque (© **505/835-1828;** see chapter 10). Others include the **Las Vegas National Wildlife Refuge,** 5 miles southeast of Las Vegas (© **505/425-3581;** see chapter 9), and **Bitter Lake National Wildlife Refuge,** 13 miles northeast of Roswell (© **505/ 622-6755;** see chapter 10). Some common sightings at these areas might include sandhill cranes, snow geese, a wide variety of ducks, and falcons. New Mexico is also home to an amazing variety of hummingbirds. In fact, in early 1996, the state was able to add the Cinnamon Hummingbird to its list of birds. Its sighting in Santa Teresa marked only the second sighting in the United States. If you're interested in bird-watching during your trip to New Mexico, contact the state office of the **National Audubon Society** (© **505/983-4609**), P.O. Box 9314, Santa Fe, NM 87504.

In Utah, head to **Zion National Park,** where the rare peregrine falcon sometimes nests in the Weeping Rock area. Also in the park are golden eagles, hummingbirds, and roadrunners (see chapter 16).

Serious birders who want to be sure of adding lots of rare birds to their life lists may want to visit southeastern Arizona or New Mexico on a guided tour. Contact **High Lonesome Birdtours** (© **800/743-2668;** www.hilonesome.com), which runs trips in southern Arizona. **WestWing Bird Watching Tours** (© **800/583-6928** or 505/473-2780; http://home.earthlink.net/wingswestunn) offers customized birding tours in New Mexico and Sonora, Mexico.

3 Fishing

The variety of terrain in the Southwest, from deserts to canyons to mountains, makes for a diverse year-round fishing experience. In places such as Lees Ferry and Lake Powell, and the San Juan River and Navajo Lake, cold-water fishing and warm-water fishing are separated by yards rather than miles, thanks to dams set between these and many other rivers and lakes.

Warm-water lakes and streams are home to large- and small-mouth bass, walleye, stripers, catfish, crappie, and bluegill. In cold-water lakes and streams, look for the Rio Grande cutthroat, as well as kokanee salmon and rainbow, brown, lake, and brook trout.

Two of the best places for fishing in New Mexico are the San Juan River, near Farmington, and Elephant Butte Lake, not far from Truth or Consequences. The San Juan River offers excellent trout fishing and is extremely popular with fly fishers. Elephant Butte is great for bass fishing; in fact, it is considered one of the top 10 bass fishing locations in the United States.

Arizona offers good trout fishing on the Mogollon Rim and in the White Mountains there, as well as in the Grand Canyon and the more easily accessible sections of the free-running Colorado River between Glen Canyon Dam and Lees Ferry. In fact, this latter area is among the country's most fabled stretches of trout water. Near there, Lake Powell also offers abundant lake fishing within its many finger canyons.

Colorado has many cold-water species living in lakes and streams, including seven kinds of trout (native cutthroat, rainbow, brown, brook, lake, kokanee, and whitefish), walleye, yellow perch, northern pike, tiger muskie, and bluegill. Warm-water sport fish (especially in eastern Colorado and in large rivers) include catfish, crappie, and bass (largemouth, smallmouth, white, and wiper). Both lake and stream fishing are available in the Durango area.

We recommend Taylor Streit's *Fly Fishing New Mexico* (California Bill's Automotive Handbooks). It provides important details about 20 of the state's most notable waterways. Also of note are *49 Trout Streams in New Mexico* (University of New Mexico Press) and *Guide to Fly Fishing Arizona* (California Bill's Automotive Handbooks). They include information about regulations and descriptions of the types and varieties of fish you're likely to catch.

For information on obtaining fishing licensing, contact the **New Mexico Game and Fish Department** (℡ 505/476-8000; www.wildlife.state.nm.us), the **Arizona Game and Fish Department** (℡ 602/942-3000; www.gf.state.az.us), or the **Utah Division of Wildlife Resources** (℡ 877/592-5169 or 435/865-6100; http://wildlife. utah.gov/index.php). The **Colorado Division of Wildlife** (℡ 303/297-1192; http:// wildlife.state.co.us) can also help.

It is not necessary to have a fishing license in order to fish on Native American reservation land, but you must receive written permission and an official tribal document before setting out on any fishing trips. Phone numbers for individual tribes and pueblos are listed separately in the regional and city chapters later in this book.

4 Golf

Many come to this region specifically to play golf. The Southwest's hundreds of golf courses range from easy public layouts to PGA championship links that have challenged the best.

In Phoenix and Tucson, greens fees, like room rates, are seasonal. In the popular winter months, fees at resort courses range from about $90 to $250 for 18 holes, which usually includes mandatory cart rental. In summer, fees often drop more than 50%. Almost all resorts offer special golf packages as well. Municipal courses charge about $40, with cart rental an additional $20 or so. In New Mexico fees range from $20 to $145, with most averaging about $60, and with reduced rates in winter. (Cart rentals run about $15.)

North of Scottsdale in the town of Carefree, **The Boulders** (℡ 480/488-9028) offers some of the best playing and scenery in the state. Also in the valley, in Apache Junction, the **Gold Canyon Golf Resort** (℡ 480/982-9449) is an excellent course, with three of the best holes in the state. The **Wigwam Golf and Country Club** (℡ 800/ 909-4224) is legendary in the region. **The Phoenician** (℡ 800/888-8234) is another noteworthy resort course in the area, with a mix of traditional and desert-style holes. Though it's pricey, locals love the semiprivate **Troon North Golf Club** (℡ 480/585-7700), a course carved out of the raw desert. The pros head to the Stadium Course at the **Tournament Players Club (TPC) of Scottsdale** (℡ 888/400-4001), while the most popular municipal course is the **Papago Golf Course** (℡ 602/275-8428), which has an amazing 17th hole. For more information on these courses, see chapter 12.

In recent years, Tucson has gained a reputation for great golf. Among the city's resort courses, the Mountain Course at the **Ventana Canyon Golf and Racquet Club** (℡ 520/577-1400) is stellar. The Sunrise Course at **El Conquistador Country Club**

(© 520/544-1800) has some very memorable par-3 holes. The pros head to **Omni Tucson National Golf Resort and Spa** (© 520/575-7540), home of the Tucson Open. Tucson's best municipal course, **Randolph North** (© 520/791-4161), is the site of the city's annual LPGA tournament. The **Silverbell Municipal Course** (© 520/791-5235) boasts a bear of a par-5 17th hole, and at **Fred Enke Municipal Course** (© 520/791-2539), you'll find the city's only desert-style municipal golf course. For more information about all of these courses see chapter 11.

Options abound in other parts of Arizona as well. Check out the 18-hole course at **Los Caballeros Golf Club** (© 928/684-2704; see chapter 14), a luxury guest ranch outside Wickenburg. For spectacular scenery, few courses compare with the **Sedona Golf Resort** (© 928/284-9355; see chapter 14). Way up in the Four Corners region, in the town of Page, you'll find the 27-hole **Lake Powell National Golf Course** (© 928/645-2023), which is one of the most spectacular in the state. In western Arizona, along "Arizona's West Coast," check out Lake Havasu City's **London Bridge Golf Club** (© 928/855-2719), which offers a view of the London Bridge. The **Emerald Canyon Golf Course** (© 928/667-3366), a municipal course in Parker, offers unique terrain and even more dramatic views. See chapter 14 for both of these.

New Mexico provides the clear air and oft-cool climates that draw many golfers. The most challenging course in the state is the **Championship Golf Course at the University of New Mexico,** in Albuquerque (© 505/277-4546; see chapter 8). In the south, you can enjoy views, a challenging course, and cool climes (even in summer) at **The Links at Sierra Blanca,** in Ruidoso (© 800/854-6571 or 505/258-5330; see chapter 10). See individual chapters for many more suggestions.

If you can break away from the gambling tables long enough to play golf in Las Vegas, you'll be well rewarded. The city offers excellent courses. Three notable ones are **Bear's Best,** which offers dramatic views on a Jack Nicklaus–designed course, The **Las Vegas Paiute Golf Resort** has impeccable fairways on a challenging course, and **Dragon Ridge** offers play for many skill levels in natural desert mountain surroundings. Fees range from about $65 to $300, with summer and evening rates often half that. You can book any of these and see course overviews with photographs at www. opengolfteetimes.com, or call © 877/669-4653.

Utah's and Colorado's golf courses are known for their beautiful scenery and variety of challenging terrain. They range from mountain courses set among beautiful forests to desert courses with scenic views of red rock country. The warm climate of St. George, in Utah's southwest corner, makes it a perfect location for year-round golf, and it has become the premier destination for visiting golfers—**St. George's Sunbrook Golf Course** (© 435/634-5866) is probably Utah's best. Durango has two public courses worth checking out: **Hillcrest Golf Course** (© 970/247-1499) and **Dalton Ranch & Golf Club** (© 970/247-8774). These areas of Utah and Colorado are beyond the scope of this book, so call the numbers listed above for more information.

For more information on golfing in Arizona, contact the **Arizona Golf Association,** 7226 N. 16th St., Suite 200, Phoenix, AZ 85020 (© 800/458-8484 in Arizona, or 602/944-3035; www.azgolf.org), which publishes a directory listing all the courses in the state. In addition, you can pick up the *Tucson and Southern Arizona Golf Guide* or the *Official Arizona Golf Guide & Directory* at visitor bureaus, golf courses, and many hotels and resorts.

Golf New Mexico magazine is a good source of information, and the website lists all New Mexico golf courses (© 505/342-1563; www.golfnewmexico.com). For information on Colorado's major golf courses, contact the **Colorado Golf Resort Association** (✆ **303/680-9967;** www.coloradogolfresorts.com). Serious golfers may want to subscribe to *The Colorado Golfer,* available at the same source, which carries information on courses throughout the state. Contact the **Utah Office of Tourism** (✆ **800/200-1160** or 801/538-1030) for information on any of Utah's 100-plus courses.

5 Hiking

Everywhere you go in the region, you'll find opportunities for hiking. The terrain and climate vary from the heat and relative flatness of the desert to the cold, forested alpine areas. You can visit both (from 3,000–13,000 ft. in elevation) and anything in between in the same day without much trouble. Each part of the region is covered below. See later chapters for details about outfitters, guides, llama-trekking services, and whom to contact for maps and other information.

In the Santa Fe area, one of the most pleasant hikes is the **Aspen Vista Trail.** It's an easy hike through aspen forests that offers long views of New Mexico's broad eastern plains. See chapter 6 for details. If you're looking for something more challenging in the north-central region of the state, head up to Taos and give **Wheeler Peak** your best shot. The hike up New Mexico's highest peak is about 15 miles round-trip. If you want a much less difficult hike in the Taos area, try hiking down into **Rio Grande Gorge.** It's beautiful and can be hiked year-round. See chapter 7 for details on these two. In the northeastern region of New Mexico, try the 1-mile loop around **Capulin Volcano.** The crater rim offers stunning views, and you can look down into the dormant caldera (see chapter 9). If you're heading to the northwestern region of the state, try hiking the **Bisti/De-Na-Zin Wilderness,** 37 miles south of Farmington. Though there are no marked trails, the hiking is easy in this area of low, eroded hills and fanciful rock formations. See chapter 5 for details. This region is also home to **El Malpais National Monument,** where you can hike into great lava tubes (see chapter 9). In the southwestern region is the **Gila National Forest,** which has more than 1,400 miles of trails with varying ranges of length and difficulty. One favorite day hike in the forest is the **Catwalk,** a moderately strenuous hike along a series of steel bridges and walkways suspended over Whitewater Canyon. See chapter 10 for details. In the southeastern region, you'll find one of New Mexico's cherished places: **White Sands National Monument.** Hiking the white-sand dunes is easy, if sometimes awkward, and the magnificence of the view is unsurpassed. See chapter 10 for more information.

Arizona also has fascinating and challenging hiking. In northern Arizona, there are good day hikes in **Grand Canyon National Park** and in the **San Francisco Peaks** north of Flagstaff (see chapter 15). Hiking is the order of the day in Sedona, where such places as **Boynton Canyon** offer red-rock beauty and ancient ruins (see chapter 14). In the Phoenix area, popular day hikes include the trails up **Camelback Mountain** and **Squaw Peak** and the many trails in **South Mountain Park** (see chapter 12). In the Tucson area, there are good hikes on **Mount Lemmon** and in **Saguaro National Park, Sabino Canyon,** and **Catalina State Park** (see chapter 11). In the southern part of the state, there are good day hikes in Chiricahua National Monument, most notably the **Heart of Rocks Loop,** which meanders through formations that could have been created by Dr. Seuss. Also in the south are the **Coronado National Forest,** the Nature Conservancy's **Ramsey Canyon Preserve** and **Patagonia–Sonoita**

Creek Preserve, Cochise Stronghold, and Organ Pipe Cactus National Monument (see chapter 13).

The state's two most unforgettable overnight backpack trips are the hike down to Phantom Ranch at the bottom of the Grand Canyon and the hike into Havasu Canyon, a side canyon of the Grand Canyon. See chapter 15.

Hiking is the best—and sometimes the only—way to see many of Utah's most beautiful and exciting areas, and the state is interlaced with hiking trails. In particular, check out **Natural Bridges National Monument,** where numerous trails take hikers through magical stone formations (see chapter 5). At Zion, the **Lower Emerald Pools Trail** takes you along emerald-colored pools, and at Bryce, the **Navajo Loop/Queen's Garden Trail** is an intermediate trail that traverses the park's magical beauty. (See chapter 16.)

The **Continental Divide Trail Alliance (CDTA)** (© **888/909-2382** or 303/838-3760; www.cdtrail.org) is building a trail—using volunteers—along the mountains of the Great Divide, from Canada to Mexico, and that means right through the middle of Colorado and New Mexico. Each year, the CDTA publishes a project schedule for the next summer, complete with volunteer needs, project description, and difficulty rating.

Guided backpacking trips of different durations and levels of difficulty are offered by the **Grand Canyon Field Institute** (© 800/858-2808 or 928/638-2485; www. grandcanyon.org/fieldinstitute) and **Grand Canyon Trail Guides** (© 928/638-3194; www.grandcanyontrailguides.com). **Backroads** (© 800/462-2848 or 510/527-1555; www.backroads.com) offers a 6-day hiking/biking trip to Grand Canyon, Bryce Canyon, and Zion national parks. Vermont based **Country Walkers** (© 800/464-9255 or 802/244-1387; www.countrywalkers.com) has a hiking-oriented trip that takes in the Grand Canyon and Sedona. The highly respected **Colorado Mountain School** (© 800/836-4008; www.totalclimbing.com) leads climbs in various parts of Colorado. **The Colorado Trail Foundation** (© 303/384-3729; www.Colorado Trail.org) assembles volunteers to maintain the Colorado Trail, and offers supported treks and outdoor workshops on the Colorado Trail.

You can choose from hundreds of other hikes. Consider purchasing a hiking book or contacting the National Park Service, National Forest Service, Bureau of Land Management, or other appropriate agencies directly. The best guides for the region are *Hiking New Mexico* (Falcon), by Laurence Parent, which outlines 70 hikes throughout the state, and *75 Hikes in New Mexico*, by Craig Martin (The Mountaineers). *Hiking Arizona,* by Stewart Aitchison and Bruce Grubbs (Falcon), outlines many excellent excursions.

6 Horseback Riding

Adventurers come from all over the world to horseback ride in the Southwest. Some of the most notable Western historic moments took place here, and many Westerns have been filmed. There's a great variety in the types of riding a person can do in the Southwest, so do some research and choose carefully.

If you're content with a nose-to-tail kind of ride, you'll be happiest riding in the mountainous regions such as the White Mountains or in more controlled environments such as through Monument Valley. But if you'd prefer to really ride—to trot and canter your horse—you'll want to go to places where the terrain allows for such riding. The Wickenburg, Arizona, area offers plenty of open-trail riding. Check out the **Kay El Bar Guest Ranch** (© 800/684-7583 or 928/684-7593; www.kayelbar. com; see chapter 14). Among the more scenic spots for riding are the Grand Canyon (see chapter 15), Canyon de Chelly National Monument (see chapter 5), and the red-rock country around Sedona (see chapter 14).

Some of the most popular guided adventures in Arizona are mule rides down into the Grand Canyon. These trips vary in length from 1 to 2 days; for reservations and more information, contact **Xanterra Parks & Resorts** (© 303/297-2757; www. xanterra.com). Be advised, however, that you'll need to make mule-ride reservations many months in advance. If at the last minute (1 or 2 days before you want to ride) you decide you want to go on a mule trip into the Grand Canyon, contact the **Bright Angel Transportation Desk,** in Grand Canyon Village (© 928/638-3283), on the chance that there might be space available.

What's unique about much of New Mexico's horseback riding is its variety. You'll find a broad range of terrain, from open plains to high mountain wilderness. In the Santa Fe area, you can ride across the plains of the spectacular Galisteo Basin with the **Broken Saddle Riding Company** (© 505/424-7774; see chapter 6). In Taos, you can explore secluded Taos Pueblo land with the **Taos Indian Horse Ranch** (© 505/ 758-3212; see chapter 7). In the southeast, contact the **Inn of the Mountain Gods Resort & Casino,** in Carrizo Canyon (© 800/545-6040 or 505/464-4100; see chapter 10). If you're looking for a resort horseback riding experience, contact **Bishop's Lodge,** Bishop's Lodge Rd., Santa Fe (© 505/983-6377; see chapter 6). If you want an authentic cowpoke experience, call the **Double E Guest Ranch** (© 505/535-2048; see chapter 10) in the Silver City area.

Utah's most notable place to ride is Monument Valley Navajo Tribal Park. **Sacred Monument Tours** offers horseback trips ranging from 1 hour to overnight. For reservations and information, call © 435/727-3218. See chapter 5.

It's also possible to do overnight horseback rides in various locations around Arizona. For information on overnight rides into the Superstition Mountains east of Phoenix, contact **Don Donnelly Horseback Adventures** (© 602/810-7029; www. dondonnelly.com).

Want to kick it up a notch? At the **Arizona Cowboy College,** Lorill Equestrian Center, 30208 N. 152nd St., Scottsdale, AZ 85262 (© 888/330-8070 or 480/471-3151; www.cowboycollege.com), you can literally learn the ropes and the brands and how to say, "Git along little doggie" like you really mean it. This is no city slicker's staged roundup; this is the real thing. You actually learn how to be a real cowboy.

7 Hot-Air Ballooning

You can't hear about the Southwest without hearing about hot-air ballooning—the two seem to go hand in hand. In fact, one of the region's greatest attractions is the annual **Albuquerque International Balloon Fiesta** in early October (see the Calendar of Events, in chapter 2), which draws thousands of people from all over the world. It is possible to charter hot-air balloon rides in many parts of the region, particularly Taos and Albuquerque (see chapters 7 and 8) in New Mexico, and Tucson and Phoenix in Arizona (see chapters 11 and 12). One of the best spots for scenic floating is Sedona (see chapter 14). Most companies offer a variety of packages, from the standard flight to a more elaborate all-day affair that includes meals. For more information, see the individual chapters.

8 Houseboating

With the Colorado River turned into a long string of lakes, Arizona's "West Coast" provides excellent houseboat vacations. Although this doesn't have to be an active vacation, fishing, hiking, and swimming are usually part of a houseboat stay. Rentals are available on Lake Mead, Lake Mohave, and Lake Havasu (see chapter 14). The canyonlands scenery of Lake Powell makes it the best spot for a houseboat vacation— reserve well in advance for a summer trip. Houseboats provide all the comforts of home—toilets, showers, sleeping quarters, and full kitchens—but in somewhat tighter quarters. Some of the larger houseboats have facilities for up to a dozen people. You don't have to be an accomplished boater to drive one: Houseboats are easy to maneuver and can't go very fast. No boating license is required, but you'll need to reserve your houseboat well in advance, especially in summer, and send in a sizable deposit.

9 Skiing & Snowboarding

Believe it or not, the Southwest has some of the best snow skiing and snowboarding in the United States. With most alpine areas above 10,000 feet and many above 12,000 feet, several ski areas offer vertical drops of over 2,000 feet. Average annual snowfall ranges from 100 to 300 inches. Many areas, aided by vigorous snow-making efforts, open around Thanksgiving, and most open by mid-December, making this a popular vacation spot around the holidays. As a result, you'll see a definite rise in hotel room rates in and around ski areas during the holiday season. The ski season runs through March and often into the first week in April.

Some of the best skiing in the region is at **Taos Ski Valley** ((℃) **505/776-2291;** www.skitaos.org). Taos challenges skiers with plenty of vertical, and beginners can take advantage of one of the best ski schools in the country. Nearby, the resort town of **Angel Fire Resort** ((℃) **800/633-7463** or 505/377-6401; www.angelfireresort.com) offers interesting terrain and excellent facilities. **Red River Ski Area** ((℃) **800/331-7669** or 505/754-2223; www.redriverskiarea.com) is an excellent family mountain. See chapter 7.

Arizona has a couple of decent ski areas. The **Arizona Snowbowl** ((℃) **928/779-1951;** www.arizonasnowbowl.com; see chapter 15), outside Flagstaff, is most notable, with plenty of vertical feet. When it's a good snow year, Tucsonans head up to **Mount Lemmon Ski Valley** ((℃) **520/576-1321,** or 520/576-1400 for snow report; see chapter 11), the southernmost ski area in the United States. All ski areas in the region offer rentals and lessons. Prices for an adult all-day ticket range from about $32 to $50.

Some of the best **cross-country skiing** in the region can be found at the Enchanted Forest near Red River and in Chama, New Mexico (see chapter 9) and outside Flagstaff, Arizona (see chapter 15). Other great areas in Arizona include Sunrise Park outside the town of McNary, at the South Rim of the Grand Canyon, in the White Mountains around Greer and Alpine, outside Payson on the Mogollon Rim, and on Mount Lemmon outside Tucson (see chapter 11). In Utah, head to Bryce Canyon National Park to ski trails along the rim (see chapter 16).

10 Tennis

Tennis is one of the most popular winter sports in the desert, and resorts all over the region have courts. Although there may be better courts, none can match the views you'll have from those at **Enchantment Resort** ((℃) **800/826-4180** or 928/282-2900;

see chapter 14) outside Sedona. Other noteworthy tennis-oriented resorts include **The Lodge at Ventana Canyon** (© 800/WYNDHAM or 520/577-1400) and the **Hilton Tucson El Conquistador Golf & Tennis Resort** (© 800/325-7832 or 520/544-5000) in Tucson, and the **Phoenician** (© 800/888-8234 or 480/941-8200) in the Phoenix/Scottsdale area. See chapters 11 and 12 for more details.

Las Vegas is a nearly ideal spot to play tennis (except in the scorching heat of summer). One popular resort with a renowned spa and tennis facility is the **Flamingo Las Vegas** (© 800/732-2111 or 702/733-3111). The **Las Vegas Hilton** (© 888/732-7117 or 702/732-5111) also has good courts. See chapter 17.

Though New Mexico's high-and-dry climate is ideal for tennis much of the year, the sport is somewhat underdeveloped in the state. Certainly each of the major cities has municipal courts; you'll find information in the city and regional sections of this guide. If you're looking for a tennis resort experience, try **Bishop's Lodge** (© 505/983-6377), on Bishop's Lodge Road in Santa Fe (see chapter 6).

11 Watersports

Watersports in the Southwest? Absolutely! You'll find a variety of activities, ranging from white-water rafting to pleasure boating.

WHITE-WATER RAFTING   The most notable white-water rafting experience is down the Colorado River through the Grand Canyon. If it's one of your dreams, plan well ahead. Companies and trips are limited, and they tend to fill up early. For a discussion and list of companies that run trips down the canyon, see chapter 15, "The Grand Canyon & Northern Arizona." For 1-day rafting trips on the Colorado below the Grand Canyon, contact **Hualapai River Runners** (© 888/255-9550 or 928/769-2219; www.destinationgrandcanyon.com). For a half-day float on the Colorado above the Grand Canyon, contact **Colorado River Discovery** (© 888/522-6644; www.raftthecanyon.com), which runs trips between Glen Canyon Dam and Lees Ferry. Rafting trips are also available on the upper Salt River east of Phoenix. **Wilderness Aware Rafting** (© 800/462-7238 or 719/395-2112; www.inaraft.com), **Canyon Rio Rafting** (© 800/272-3353 or 928/774-4377; www.canyonrio.com), and **Mild to Wild Rafting** (© 800/567-6745; www.mild2wildrafting.com) all run trips of varying lengths down this river (conditions permitting).

In Utah, the town of Moab along the **Colorado River** is rapidly becoming a major boating center. You can travel down the river in a canoe, kayak, large or small rubber raft (with or without motor), or speedy, solid jet boat. A complete list of outfitters is available at the Moab Information Center or through the **Moab Area Travel Council** (© 800/635-6622 or 435/259-8825; www.discovermoab.com).

New Mexico offers good opportunities for white-water rafting and kayaking. The waters in the Chama River and the Rio Grande are generally at their best during the spring and summer (May–July). Most notable is the 1-day trip down the Taos Box Canyon, offering an almost nonstop series of class IV rapids. Many reputable companies run the Box, including **Los Rios River Runners** (© 800/544-1181 or 505/776-8854; www.losriosriverrunners.com) and **Native Sons Adventures** (© 800/753-7559 or 505/758-9342; www.nativesonsadventures.com). In addition to calling outfitters, you can contact the **Bureau of Land Management,** 226 Cruz Alta Rd., Taos, NM 87571 (© 505/758-8851), for information.

Opportunities for **pleasure boating** are available on many of the region's lakes and reservoirs. Lake Mead, Lake Mohave, and Lake Havasu, what many call Arizona's

"West Coast," offer plenty of water fun (see chapter 14). In New Mexico, Elephant Butte Lake is one of the best and most beautiful spots for boating (see chapter 10).

FLAT-WATER CANOEING & KAYAKING   Maybe these sports don't jump to mind when you think of the desert, but there are indeed calm rivers and lakes here—and they happen to be some of the best places to see wildlife. By far the most memorable place for a flat-water kayak tour is Lake Powell. **Wilderness Inquiry** (© 800/728-0719 or 612/676-9400; www.wildernessinquiry.org) offers several 6-day trips on the lake each spring and fall. Multiday kayak tours are also offered by **Hidden Canyon Kayak** (© 800/343-3121 or 928/645-8866; www.diamondriver.com/kayak).

A couple of companies rent canoes and offer trips on the Colorado River south of Lake Mead. See chapter 14.

12 Special-Interest Vacations

ARCHAEOLOGY   If you like time-traveling into ancient culture, contact the **Arizona State Museum,** P.O. Box 210026, Tucson, AZ 85721 (© **520/626-8381;** www.statemuseum.arizona.edu), which occasionally offers scholar-led archaeological tours, including a trip to Navajo and Hopi country.

The **Museum of Northern Arizona,** 3101 N. Fort Valley Rd., Flagstaff, AZ 86001 (© **928/774-5211,** ext. 220; www.musnaz.org), offers educational backpacking, river-rafting, and van tours primarily in the Colorado Plateau in northern Arizona in a program called Ventures. Trips range from several days to more than a week.

ARCHITECTURE   Architecture buffs can get their hands dirty with continued construction of **Arcosanti,** Paolo Soleri's dream of a city that merges architecture and ecology. Located 70 miles north of Phoenix, Arcosanti offers 5-week learning-by-doing workshops. Contact Arcosanti, Attn: Workshop Coordinator, H.C. 74, Box 4136, Mayer, AZ 86333 (© **928/632-7135;** www.arcosanti.org).

ART & COOKING TOURS   **Taos Art School** (© **505/758-0350;** www.taosartschool.org) offers a variety of imaginative art tours and hands-on courses. The Georgia O'Keeffe tour takes visitors to all the sites where the noted modern artist painted. The many hands-on experiences offer cultural bonuses, such as a potting course taught by relatives of the noted Pueblo potter Maria Martinez, as well as weaving and basketry courses. *Plein aire* (outdoor) painting and "Horses and Art" are two other popular courses.

For those interested in honing their Southwestern cooking skills, **Jane Butel's Cooking School** (© **800/472-8229** or 505/243-2622; www.janebutel.com) offers weekend and weeklong courses in Albuquerque.

CULTURAL TOURS   **Crossing Worlds Journeys & Retreats,** P.O. Box 623, Sedona, AZ 86339 (© **800/350-2693** or 928/203-0024; www.crossingworlds.com), offers tours in Sedona and throughout the Four Corners region, visiting the Hopi mesas as well as backcountry ruins on the Navajo Reservation.

NATURE   If you'd like to turn a trip to the Grand Canyon into an educational experience, contact the **Grand Canyon Field Institute,** P.O. Box 399, Grand Canyon, AZ 86023 (© **800/858-2808** or 928/638-2485; www.grandcanyon.org/fieldinstitute), which offers a variety of programs from early spring to late fall. Offerings include day hikes, photography and painting classes, backpacking trips for women, llama treks, archaeology trips, and plenty of guided hikes and backpacking trips with a natural-history or ecological slant.

The **Nature Conservancy,** 1510 E. Fort Lowell Rd., Tucson, AZ 85719 (© **520/ 622-3861;** www.nature.org), and 212 E. Marcy St., Suite 200, Santa Fe, NM 87501 (© **505/988-3867**), has preserved some of the Southwest's finest land, parts of which are open to the public for hiking, bird-watching, and nature study. The organization operates educational field trips.

If you have strong hands and a soft heart, and want to help with wilderness preservation, consider a Sierra Club service trip. These trips are for the purpose of building, restoring, and maintaining hiking trails in wilderness areas. Contact the **Sierra Club Outing Department,** 85 Second St., 2nd Floor, San Francisco, CA 94105 (© **415/ 977-5500;** www.sierraclub.org). The Sierra Club also offers hiking, camping, and other adventure trips to various destinations in the Southwest.

You can join a work crew organized by the **Arizona Trail Association** (© **602/ 252-4794;** www.aztrail.org). Crews spend 1 to 2 days building and maintaining various portions of the Arizona Trail, which will eventually stretch from the Utah state line to the Mexico border.

The National Park Service is also looking for help. Volunteers pick up trash left in Glen Canyon National Recreation Area. Helpers spend 5 days on a houseboat called the Trash Tracker, cruising through the canyonlands of Lake Powell. Volunteers must be at least 18 years old and must provide their own food, sleeping bag, and transportation to the marina. For information, contact **Glen Canyon National Recreation Area,** P.O. Box 1507, Page, AZ 86040 (© **928/608-6404** or 928/608-6352).

See also the "Hiking" section earlier in this chapter for information about the **Continental Divide Trail Alliance (CDTA)** trail-building project.

5

The Four Corners Area

The major archaeological center of the United States, the Four Corners area—where the borders of Colorado, New Mexico, Arizona, and Utah meet—is surrounded by a vast complex of ancient villages that dominated this entire region a thousand years ago. Here among the reddish-brown rocks, abandoned canyons, and flat mesas, you'll discover another world, once ruled by the Ancestral Puebloans (also known as Anasazi), and today largely the domain of the Navajo.

Wander among the scenic splendors of Monument Valley, where the Navajo still tend their sheep and weave their rugs, and then step back in time to discover a civilization that vanished more than 7 centuries ago, leaving behind more questions than answers. The single best place to explore this ancient culture is Mesa Verde National Park. Nearby, along the Colorado–Utah border, is one of America's newest national monuments, Canyon of the Ancients, created by presidential proclamation in June of 2000.

This region is sparsely populated, and you're not going to find your favorite chain motel, fast-food restaurant, or brand of gasoline right around every corner. That's assuming you can even *find* a corner. So, many travelers discover a place they like, rent a room or campsite for a few days, and take day trips. In this chapter, we've given you a gateway town for each state and also mentioned places to stay throughout the region.

1 Cortez: Colorado's Four Corners Gateway

45 miles W of Durango, 203 miles S of Grand Junction

An important archaeological center, Cortez is surrounded by a vast complex of ancient villages that dominated the Four Corners region—where Colorado, New Mexico, Arizona, and Utah meet—1,000 years ago. Mesa Verde National Park, 10 miles east, is certainly the most prominent nearby attraction, drawing hundreds of thousands of visitors annually. In addition, archaeological sites such as those at Canyons of the Ancients and Hovenweep national monuments as well as Ute Mountain Tribal Park are an easy drive from the city. Most visitors to Cortez won't be spending much time in the city, but will use it as a home base. Its elevation is 6,200 feet.

ESSENTIALS

GETTING THERE   By Car   Cortez is located at the junction of north–south US 491 and east–west US 160.

As it enters Cortez from the east, US 160 crosses Dolores Road (CO 145, which goes north to Telluride and Grand Junction), then runs due west through town for about 2 miles as Main Street. The city's main thoroughfare, Main Street intersects US 491 (Broadway) at the west end of town.

The Four Corners Region

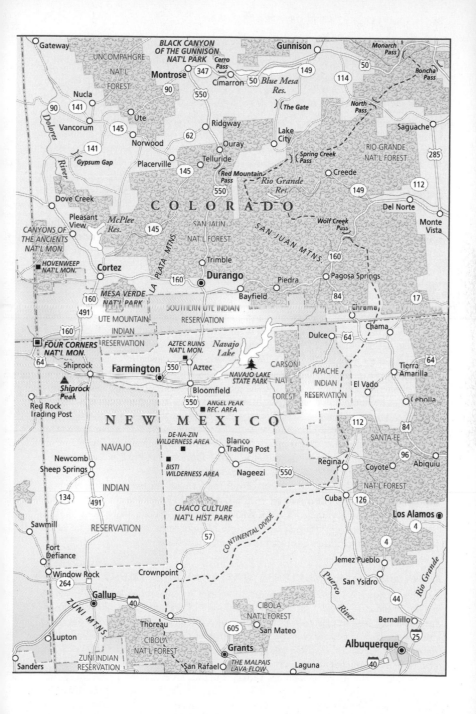

By Plane   Cortez Airport, off US 160 and 491, southwest of town (© **970/565-7458;** www.cityofcortez.com), is served by **Great Lakes Airlines** (© **800/554-5111** or 970/565-9510), with direct daily flights to Denver.

Budget (© **800/527-0700** or 970/564-9012) and **Enterprise** (© **800/325-8007** or 970/565-6824) provide car rentals at the airport.

VISITOR INFORMATION   Stop at the **Colorado Welcome Center at Cortez,** Cortez City Park, 928 E. Main St. (© **970/565-4048;** www.swcolo.org), open daily from 8am to 6pm in summer and from 8am to 5pm the rest of the year; or contact the **Mesa Verde Country Visitor Information Bureau,** P.O. Box HH, Cortez, CO 81321 (© **800/253-1616;** www.mesaverdecountry.com), or the **Cortez Area Chamber of Commerce,** P.O. Box 968, Cortez, CO 81321 (© **970/565-3414;** www.cortez chamber.org).

FAST FACTS   The local hospital is **Southwest Memorial Hospital,** 1311 N. Mildred Rd. (© **970/565-6666**), which has a 24-hour emergency room. The **post office** is at 35 S. Beech St.; contact the U.S. Postal Service (© **800/275-8777;** www.usps. com) for hours and additional information.

NEARBY ARCHAEOLOGICAL SITES
ANASAZI HERITAGE CENTER
When the Dolores River was dammed and the McPhee Reservoir was created in 1985, some 1,600 ancient archaeological sites were threatened. Four percent of the project costs were set aside for archaeological work, and over two million artifacts and other prehistoric items were rescued. Most are displayed in this museum. Located 10 miles north of Cortez, it is set into a hillside near the remains of 12th-century sites.

Operated by the Bureau of Land Management, the center emphasizes visitor involvement. Children and adults are invited to examine corn-grinding implements, a loom and other weaving materials, and a re-created pit house. You can touch artifacts 1,000 to 2,000 years old, examine samples through microscopes, use interactive computer programs, and engage in video lessons in archaeological techniques.

A half-mile trail leads from the museum to the **Dominguez Pueblo Ruins,** atop a low hill, with a beautiful view across the Montezuma Valley.

The center also serves as the visitor center for Canyons of the Ancients National Monument (see below). It is located at 27501 Colorado 184, Dolores (© **970/882-5600;** www.co.blm.gov/ahc). It's open March through October, daily from 9am to 5pm; November through February, daily from 10am to 4pm. An admission fee of $3 for adults is charged March through October only; admission is free for those 17 and under. Allow 2 hours.

CANYONS OF THE ANCIENTS NATIONAL MONUMENT
Among the country's newest national monuments, Canyons of the Ancients was created by presidential proclamation in June 2000. The 164,000-acre national monument, located west of Cortez, contains thousands of archaeological sites—what some claim is the highest density of archaeological sites in the United States—including the remains of villages, cliff dwellings, sweat lodges, and petroglyphs at least 700 years old, and possibly as much as 10,000 years old.

Canyons of the Ancients includes **Lowry Pueblo,** an excavated 12th-century village that is located 26 miles from Cortez via US 491, on C.R. CC, 9 miles west of Pleasant View. This pueblo, which was likely abandoned by 1200, is believed to have housed about 100 people. It has standing walls from 40 rooms plus 9 kivas (circular underground ceremonial chambers). A short, self-guided interpretive trail leads past a kiva and continues to the remains of a great kiva, which, at 54 feet in diameter, is among the largest ever found. The area offers a picnic area, drinking water, and toilets.

Canyons of the Ancients is overseen by the Bureau of Land Management, and as yet has no onsite visitor center or even a contact station. Those wishing to explore the monument are strongly advised to contact or preferably stop first at the visitor center located at **Anasazi Heritage Center** (see above) for information, especially current road conditions and directions. Information is also available online at www.co.blm.gov/canm, and from the welcome center in Cortez (see the Cortez section, above). Allow at least 2 hours.

CORTEZ CULTURAL CENTER

The center, 25 N. Market St., Cortez (✆ **970/565-1151;** www.cortezculturalcenter.org), includes a museum with exhibits on both prehistoric and modern American Indians, an art gallery with displays of regional art, and a good gift shop offering crafts by local tribal members. A variety of programs are offered year-round, ranging from guided kids' hikes to photo exhibits, and from late May through early September there are American Indian dances and cultural programs Monday through Saturday evenings starting at 7:30pm. The center is open Monday through Saturday from 10am to 10pm and Sunday from 10am to 2pm from late May through early September, with shorter hours the rest of the year. Admission is free and you should plan to spend at least an hour in the museum (more if there are dances or other programs).

UTE MOUNTAIN TRIBAL PARK ★★

Set aside by the Ute Mountain tribe to preserve its heritage, the 125,000-acre Ute Mountain Tribal Park, P.O. Box 109, Towaoc, CO 81334 (✆ **800/847-5485** or 970/565 3751 ext. 330; www.utemountainute.com/tribalpark.htm)—which abuts Mesa Verde National Park—includes wall paintings and ancient petroglyphs as well as hundreds of surface sites and cliff dwellings that are similar in size and complexity to those in Mesa Verde.

Access to the park is strictly limited to guided tours. Full- and half-day tours begin at the Ute Mountain Museum and Visitor Center at the junction of US 491 and US 160, 20 miles south of Cortez. Mountain-biking and backpacking trips are also offered. No food, water, lodging, gasoline, or other services are available within the park. Some climbing of ladders is necessary on the full-day tour. There's one primitive **campground** ($12 per vehicle; reservations required).

Charges for tours in your vehicle start at $22 per person for a half-day, $42 for a full day; it's $8 per person extra to go in the tour guide's vehicle, and reservations are required. Special private tours to remote sections of the park are also offered, with a minimum of four persons, at $60 per person per day.

HOVENWEEP NATIONAL MONUMENT

Preserving some of the most striking and isolated archaeological sites in the Four Corners area, this national monument straddles the Colorado-Utah border, 40 miles west of Cortez.

Hovenweep is the Ute word for "deserted valley," appropriate because its inhabitants apparently left around 1300. The monument contains six separate sites, and is noted for mysterious, 20-foot-high sandstone towers, some square, others oval, circular, or

D-shaped. Archaeologists have suggested their possible function as everything from guard or signal towers, celestial observatories, and ceremonial structures to water towers or granaries.

A ranger station, with exhibits, restrooms, and drinking water, is located at the **Square Tower Site,** in the Utah section of the monument, the most impressive and best preserved of the sites. The **Hovenweep Campground,** which contains 30 sites, is open year-round. Sites are fairly small—most appropriate for tents or small pickup-truck campers—but a few sites can accommodate RVs up to 36 feet long. The campground has flush toilets, drinking water, picnic tables, and fire pits, but no showers or RV hookups. Cost is $10 per night; reservations are not accepted, but the campground rarely fills.

From Cortez, take US 160 south to C.R. G (McElmo Canyon Rd.), and follow signs into Utah and the monument. The other five sites are difficult to find, and you'll need to obtain detailed driving directions and check on current road conditions before setting out. Summer temperatures can reach over 100°F (38°C), and water supplies are limited—so take your own and carry a canteen, even on short walks. Bug repellent is advised, as gnats can be a nuisance in late spring.

The visitor center/ranger station is open daily 8am to 6pm from April through September and 8am to 5pm the rest of the year; it's closed New Year's Day, Thanksgiving, and Christmas. Admission for up to a week costs $10 per vehicle or $5 per person on bike or foot. For advance information, contact Hovenweep National Monument, McElmo Route, Cortez, CO 81321 (© **970/562-4282;** www.nps.gov/hove).

WHERE TO STAY

Summer is the busy season here, and that's when you'll pay the highest lodging rates. Among the major chains providing comfortable, reasonably priced lodging (ranging from about $60–$160 double) in Cortez (zip code 81321) are **Best Western Turquoise Inn & Suites,** 535 E. Main St. (© 800/547-3376 or 970/565-3778); **Comfort Inn,** 2321 E. Main St. (© 800/424-6423 or 970/565-3400); **Econo Lodge,** 2020 E. Main St. (© 800/553-2666 or 970/565-3474); **Holiday Inn Express,** 2121 E. Main St. (© 888/465-4329 or 970/565-6000); **Super 8,** 505 E. Main St. (© 800/800-8000 or 970/565-8888); and **Travelodge,** 440 S. Broadway (© 800/578-7878 or 970/565-7778). Room tax adds about 8% to lodging bills.

Anasazi Motor Inn   This standard, well-kept motel offers spacious Southwest-decorated rooms with either one king-size bed or two queens; many of the ground-floor rooms have patios. There are also a sand volleyball court, horseshoe pits, a short walking trail, and free shuttle service to downtown.

640 S. Broadway, Cortez, CO 81321. (© **800/972-6232** or 970/565-3773. Fax 970/565-1027. www.anasazimotor inn.com. 87 units. $55–$75 double. AE, DC, DISC, MC, V. Pets accepted. **Amenities:** Restaurant (American); bar; pool (outdoor heated); hot tub; airport shuttle. *In room:* A/C, TV.

WHERE TO DINE

Homesteaders Restaurant ⊕ AMERICAN/MEXICAN   A rustic, Old West atmosphere pervades this popular family restaurant, which is decorated with historic photos and memorabilia. The menu has a good selection of home-style American basics, such as burgers, T-bones, and top sirloins. Those wanting a bit more zip might try the Southwestern steak—top sirloin smothered with salsa, green chile, and cheese. We also suggest the barbecued baby back ribs and the old-fashioned dinners, such as thin-sliced roast beef or deep-fried catfish filet. Several Mexican standards are also offered, as well as salads and vegetarian items.

45 E. Main St. ℂ **970/565-6253**. Fax 970/564-9217. www.thehomesteaders.com. Main courses $5–$9 lunch, $7–$19 dinner. AE, DISC, MC, V. Mon–Sat 11am–9:30pm; summer also Sun 4–9:30pm.

Main St. Brewery and Restaurant ⚅ AMERICAN   Fans slice the air under a stamped-tin ceiling, and fanciful murals splash color above subdued wood paneling. The pleasant contrasts found in the decor carry over to the menu. In addition to brewpub staples such as fish and chips, pizza, and bratwurst, this restaurant offers steaks and prime rib—dry aged Angus beef from its own herd of Angus cattle, raised with no artificial growth stimulants or antibiotics—plus a vegetarian stir-fry plate and Rocky Mountain trout. The beers brewed here go well with everything. We especially recommend the hoppy, slightly bitter Pale Export and the Munich-style Pale Bock.

21 E. Main St., Cortez. ℂ **970/564-9112**. Main courses $5.95–$23. AE, MC, V. Daily 3:30pm–close.

Nero's ⚅⚅ ITALIAN/AMERICAN   This is our top choice in this area when we're craving something unique. The innovative entrees, prepared by Culinary Institute of America chef Richard Gurd, include house specialties such as the Cowboy Steak (a charbroiled 12-ounce sirloin seasoned with a spicy rub and served with pasta or fries); our favorite, the mushroom ravioli served with an Alfredo sauce, sautéed spinach, sun dried tomatoes, and pecans; and shrimp Alfredo—sautéed shrimp with spinach served over fettuccine with Alfredo sauce and Romano cheese. There's an excellent selection of beef, plus seafood, fowl, pork, veal, and lots of homemade pasta. A small, homey restaurant with a Southwestern art-gallery decor, Nero's also offers pleasant outdoor seating in warm weather.

303 W. Main St. ℂ **970/565-7366**. www.subee.com/neros/home.html. Reservations recommended. Entrees $8.95–$21. AE, MC, V. Daily 5–9:30pm. Closed Sun in winter.

Pippo's Cafe AMERICAN   This friendly down-home cafe is great for those seeking a casual ambience, good basic American cooking, and reasonable prices. Located along busy Main Street, Pippo's serves only breakfast and lunch—the former, the restaurant's specialty, is served during all open hours. We especially like the omelets and the homemade hash browns, but then we wouldn't turn down the steak and eggs, either. The lunch menu includes the usual burger and fries, along with homemade soups, Navajo tacos, and fried chicken with mashed potatoes and gravy.

100 W. Main St. ℂ **970/565-6039**. Main courses $1.90–$5.90. MC, V. Mon–Sat 6:30am–3pm, Sun 6:30am–2pm.

2 Mesa Verde National Park

125 miles E of Bluff, 390 miles SE of Salt Lake City

Mesa Verde is the largest archaeological preserve in the United States, with some 4,000 known sites dating from A.D. 600 to 1300, including the most impressive cliff dwellings in the Southwest.

The earliest known inhabitants of Mesa Verde (Spanish for "green table") built subterranean pit houses on the mesa tops. During the 13th century they moved into shallow caves and constructed complex cliff dwellings. Despite being a massive construction project, these homes were only occupied for about a century; their residents left in about 1300 for reasons as yet undetermined.

The area was little known until ranchers Charles and Richard Wetherill chanced upon it in 1888. Looting of artifacts followed their discovery until a Denver newspaper reporter's stories aroused national interest in protecting the site. The 52,000-acre site was declared a national park in 1906—it's the only U.S. national park devoted entirely to the works of humans.

Fires have plagued the park in recent years, and burned trees and blackened ground are evident today. Two lightning-induced fires blackened about 40% of the park during the summer of 2000, closing the park for about 3 weeks. Officials said that although the park's piñon-juniper forests were severely burned, none of the major archaeological sites were damaged, and in fact the fires revealed some sites that they were not aware existed. Then a lightning-induced fire struck again in the summer of 2002, closing the park for about 10 days. It destroyed several employees' homes, a sewage treatment plant, and phone and power lines, and also damaged a water storage tank. Officials said that the only damage to archaeological sites was the scorching of the wall of one ruin.

ESSENTIALS

ENTRY   The park entrance is located on US 160, 10 miles east of Cortez and 6 miles west of Mancos.

FEES & REGULATIONS   Admission to the park for up to 1 week for private vehicles costs $15 from Memorial Day weekend through Labor Day weekend and $10 the rest of the year; rates for motorcyclists are $8 and $5, respectively. Tours of Cliff Palace, Balcony House, and Long House are $3; ranger-guided tours of other areas are free. To protect the many archaeological sites, the Park Service has outlawed backcountry camping and off-trail hiking. It's also illegal to enter cliff dwellings without a ranger present. The Wetherill Mesa Road cannot accommodate vehicles longer than 25 feet. Cyclists must have lights to pedal through the tunnel on the entrance road.

VISITOR CENTERS & INFORMATION   **Chapin Mesa,** site of the park headquarters, museum, and a post office, is 20 miles from the park entrance on US 160. The **Far View Visitor Center,** site of Far View Lodge, a restaurant, gift shop, and other facilities, is 15 miles off US 160. For a park brochure, contact Mesa Verde National Park, P.O. Box 8, Mesa Verde, CO 81330 (© **970/529-4465;** www.nps.gov/meve).

HOURS & SEASONS   The park is open daily year-round, but full interpretive services are available only from mid-June to Labor Day. In winter, the Mesa Top Road and museum remain open, but many other facilities are closed. The **Far View Visitor Center** is open from mid-April through mid-October only, from 8am to 5pm daily. The **Chapin Mesa Archeological Museum** is open daily from 8am to 6:30pm from early April through early October, daily from 8am to 5pm the rest of the year.

AVOIDING THE CROWDS   With close to half a million visitors annually, Mesa Verde seems packed at times, but the numbers are much lower just before and after the summer rush, usually from mid-June through mid-August. Another way to beat the crowds is to make the 12-mile drive to Wetherill Mesa, which attracts only a small percentage of park visitors.

RANGER PROGRAMS   In addition to guided tours to the cliff dwellings (see below), rangers give nightly campfire programs at Morefield Campground in summer.

Tips **Keeping Fido Safe & Happy**

While there's plenty to do for human visitors to Mesa Verde National Park, the U.S. Park Service is not very welcoming to our canine friends, and prohibits them on all trails (the only exceptions are for service dogs, such as Seeing Eye dogs). This means that if you want to explore the park you'll need to leave your dogs behind. Fortunately, there are several kennels in the area, including **The Dog Hotel**, 33350 CO 184, Mancos ((C) **970/882-5416**), which is a well-run facility, open seven days a week, that also offers accommodations for cats. Appointments are necessary, and pet owners must have proof of current vaccinations.

SEEING THE HIGHLIGHTS IN A DAY

If you have only a day to spend at the park, stop first at the Far View Visitor Center to buy tickets for a late-afternoon tour of either Cliff House or Balcony House—visitors are not allowed to tour both on the same day. Then travel to the Chapin Mesa archeological museum for a look at the history behind the sites you're about to see. From here, walk down the trail behind the museum to Spruce Tree House. Then drive the Mesa Top Loop Road. Cap your day with the guided tour.

EXPLORING THE PARK

Cliff Palace, the park's largest and best-known site, is a four-story apartment complex with stepped-back roofs forming porches for the dwellings above. Accessible by guided tour only, it is reached by a quarter-mile downhill path. Its towers, walls, and kivas (large circular rooms used for ceremonies) are all set back beneath the rim of a cliff. Another ranger-led tour takes visitors up a 32-foot ladder to explore the interior of **Balcony House.** Each of these tours is given only in summer and into fall (call for exact dates). Guided tours are also offered by Far View Lodge (see "Where to Stay & Dine," below).

Two other important sites—**Step House** and **Long House,** both on Wetherill Mesa—can be visited in summer only. Rangers lead free tours to **Spruce Tree House,** another of the major cliff-dwelling complexes, only in winter, when other park facilities are closed. Visitors can also explore Spruce Tree House on their own at any time.

Although none of the trails to the Mesa Verde sites are strenuous, the 7,000-foot elevation can make the treks tiring for visitors who aren't used to the altitude. For those who want to avoid hiking and climbing, the 12-mile **Mesa Top Road** makes a number of pit houses and cliff-side overlooks easily accessible by car. **Chapin Mesa Archeological Museum** houses artifacts and specimens related to the history of the area, including other nearby sites.

OUTDOOR ACTIVITIES   Though this isn't an outdoor recreation park per se— the reason to come here is to see the cliff dwellings and other archaeological sites— you'll find yourself hiking and climbing to get to the sites. Several longer hikes into scenic Spruce Canyon let you stretch your legs and get away from the crowds. Hikers must register at the ranger's office before setting out.

CAMPING   Open from early May to mid-October, **Morefield Campground** ((C) **800/449-2288** or 970/533-1944; www.visitmesaverde.com), 4 miles south of the park entrance, has 435 sites, including 15 with full RV hookups. The campground is set in rolling hills in a grassy area with scrub oak and brush. The attractive sites are fairly well spaced, and are mostly separated by trees and other foliage. Facilities include modern restrooms, coin-operated showers (not within easy walking distance of most campsites), picnic tables, grills, and an RV dump station. Programs on the area's human and natural history and other subjects are presented nightly at the campground amphitheater from Memorial Day weekend through Labor Day weekend. Campsites cost $20, $25 with hookups. If you're hoping to snare one of the 15 full hookup sites, try getting to the park by late morning; there are almost always non-hookup sites available. There are also several commercial campgrounds along US 160, just outside the park entrance.

WHERE TO STAY & DINE

There is only one lodging facility actually in the park, Far View Lodge (see below), which contains two restaurants and a bar. The company that runs the lodge also operates two other restaurants in the park—one near the campground and another near Chapin Mesa Museum. There are also numerous lodging and dining possibilities in nearby Cortez (see the previous section).

Far View Lodge   Located in the heart of Mesa Verde National Park, Far View Lodge offers not only the most convenient location for visiting the park but also the best views of any accommodations in the area. The facility lodges guests in 17 separate buildings spread across a hilltop. Rooms aren't fancy and some are a bit on the small side, but they are well maintained and more than adequate, with Southwestern decor. In fact, many of the units have recently been renovated and upgraded, and the "Kiva" rooms boast handcrafted furniture, one king- or two queen-size beds, bathrobes, CD players, and other upscale amenities. Most standard rooms have one queen-size bed or two doubles, although a variety of bed combinations are available. For a couple, we prefer the rooms with one bed—they seem less cramped than rooms with two beds. There are no TVs, but each unit has a private balcony, and the views are magnificent in all directions. All rooms are smoke-free.

The **lodge restaurants** serve three meals daily, and during the warmer months guided tours of the park are scheduled. Call for the current schedule and rates.

Mesa Verde National Park (P.O. Box 277), Mancos, CO 81328. © **800/449-2288** or 970-564-4300. Fax 970/564-4311. www.visitmesaverde.com. 150 units. Early May through Oct only. $118—$148 double. AE, DC, DISC, MC, V. Pets accepted w/$25 nonrefundable fee. **Amenities:** 2 restaurants. *In room:* Fridge (some), coffeemaker.

3 Four Corners Monument

This is the only place in the United States where you can stand in four states at once. There's a flat monument marking the spot where Utah, Colorado, New Mexico, and Arizona meet, on which visitors can perch for photos. Official seals of the four states are displayed, along with the motto FOUR STATES HERE MEET IN FREEDOM UNDER GOD. Surrounding the monument are the flags of the four states, the Navajo Nation and Ute tribes, and the United States.

There are often crafts demonstrations here, and jewelry, pottery, sand paintings, and other crafts are for sale, along with T-shirts and other souvenirs. In addition, traditional Navajo food, such as fry bread, is available, and there's a small visitor center with information on visiting the Navajo Nation.

Located a half-mile northwest of US 160, the monument is open daily from 7am to 8pm from May through September and 8am to 5pm the rest of the year. Entry costs

$3 per person. For information, contact the **Navajo Parks and Recreation Department,** P.O. Box 2520, Window Rock, AZ 86515 (© **928/871-6647;** www.navajo nationparks.org). Allow half an hour.

4 A Base Camp in Bluff: Utah's Four Corners Gateway

100 miles S of Moab, 338 miles SE of Salt Lake City

We particularly enjoy the tiny and friendly village of Bluff, which sits near the intersection of US 191 and US 163, with roads leading off toward all the attractions of the Four Corners. With a population of about 300, Bluff (elevation 4,320 ft.) is one of those comfortable little places with most basic services, but not a lot more. Founded by Mormon pioneers in 1880, the town's site had already been home to both Ancestral Puebloan and Navajo peoples. Local businesses distribute a free historic walking- and biking-tour guide that shows where ancient rock art and archaeological sites are located, as well as pointing out the locations of some of Bluff's handsome stone homes and other historic sites from the late 19th century.

For information on Bluff contact **The Business Owners of Bluff,** P.O. Box 220, Bluff, UT 84512 (www.bluffutah.org). You can also get information on Bluff, as well as on the other southeast Utah communities of Blanding, Monticello, Mexican Hat, and Monument Valley, from **Utah's Canyon Country,** 117 S. Main St. (P.O. Box 490), Monticello, UT 84535 (© **800/574-4386** or 435/587-3235 ext. 4139; www. utahscanyoncountry.com). There is no visitor center in Bluff.

WHITE-WATER RAFTING & OTHER ORGANIZED TOURS

Situated along the San Juan River, Bluff is a center for river rafting. **Wild Rivers Expeditions,** Box 118, Bluff, UT 84512 (© **800/422-7654** or 435/672-2244; www.riversandruins.com), offers river trips on the San Juan that are both fun and educational. Boaters see dozens of American Indian sites along the river, such as the spectacular Butler Wash Petroglyph Panel—a 250-yard-long wall of petroglyphs—plus spectacular rock formations. Trips, offered from March through October, range from a full day to more than a week, with rates starting at $150 per adult and $112 per child under 13, including lunch.

Guided tours to scenic areas and archaeological sites are offered by **Far Out Expeditions,** 7th East St. and Mulberry Ave. (P.O. Box 307), Bluff, UT 84512 (© **435/ 672-2294;** www.faroutexpeditions.com). The company also offers custom guided backpacking trips ranging from a half-day to several days. Trips start at $170 per person per day. Far Out Expeditions also offers lodging: The **Far Out Guest House,** 7th East St. and Mulberry Ave. (P.O. Box 307), Bluff, UT 84512 (© **435/672-2294;** www.faroutexpeditions.com), is a restored historic home with two bedrooms, decorated in Southwestern style. Each room has six bunk beds and a private bathroom (shower only). Both share a comfortable living room, screened porch, and fully equipped kitchen. Rates are $75 for a private room for one or two people, $85 for three or four people, $95 for five or six people, and $180 for the entire house.

Note that both of the above companies also collect per-person user fees charged by the Bureau of Land Management (BLM).

MORE TO SEE & DO

About 2 miles west of town is **Sand Island Recreation Site,** operated by the BLM. Located along the San Juan River among cottonwoods, Russian olives, and salt cedar, this area offers boating (there's a boat ramp) and fishing. Boaters must obtain river permits in advance, which are awarded through a lottery. Fees are charged, based on the time of year, section of river, and number of people in your party. To apply, as early as possible—preferably in December for the following summer—contact the Bureau of Land Management, 435 N. Main St. (P.O. Box 7), Monticello, UT 84535 (© **435/ 587-1500;** 435/587-1544, 8am–noon weekdays for permits and applications; www.ut.blm.gov). Nestled between the river and a high rock bluff are picnic tables, vault toilets, and graveled campsites; camping is $10 per night and drinking water is available. Head west from the boat launch to see a number of petroglyphs; some can be seen easily on foot, others are glimpsed only from a boat. Unfortunately, you must have your own boat with you, as there are no nearby rentals.

Goosenecks State Park, set on a rim high above the San Juan, offers spectacular views over the twisting, turning river some 1,000 feet below. It's named for the sharp turns in the river, which meanders more than 5 miles to progress just 1 linear mile, and provides a look straight down through 300 million years of geologic history. (The park also has some Hollywood history: It served as the location for the climactic scene in *Thelma & Louise.*) You'll find picnic tables, trash cans, vault toilets, and an observation shelter, but no drinking water, in a gravelly open area at the end of the paved road. The park is open around the clock and admission is free; primitive camping is permitted at no charge. The park is about 23½ miles from Bluff, just off the route to Monument Valley Navajo Tribal Park. Head west on US 163 for about 20 miles, turn north (right) on Utah 261 for about a mile, and then west (left) on Utah 316 for 2½ miles. For information, contact Goosenecks State Park, 600 W. 400 North, Blanding, UT 84511 (© **435/678-2238;** www.stateparks.utah.gov).

WHERE TO STAY

Lodging tax adds 9% to room bills in Bluff. Far Out Expeditions (see above) also offers accommodations in its guesthouse.

Desert Rose Inn and Cabins 🌟🌟   Built in 1999, this imposing log lodge-style building houses 30 attractively decorated motel rooms, all with air-conditioning, TVs, phones, coffeemakers, combination shower/tubs, and queen or king beds. Decor is Southwestern, with log headboards, pottery-style lamps, solid-wood furnishings, and signed prints by a Hopi artist. There is also an attractive suite with a wraparound porch, king bed, and separate living room. In addition there are five pleasant cabins, a bit more rustic in appearance, each with a large walk-in shower (no tubs), two queen beds, refrigerators and microwaves, porches, and cathedral ceilings with exposed beams.

701 W. Main St. (US 191), Bluff, UT 84512. © **888/475-7673** or 435/672-2303. Fax 435/672-2217. www.desert roseinn.com. 30 units, 1 suite, 6 cabins. Summer $79–$109 double; winter $69–$89 double. $125 suite. AE, DISC, MC, V. **Amenities:** Laundry service. *In room:* A/C, satellite TV, fridge (cabins only), coffeemaker, microwave, Wi-Fi.

Recapture Lodge *Value*   This property may be older, but we appreciate its quiet, clean, and inexpensive rooms. A well-kept motel located near the center of town, Recapture Lodge has an attractive Western decor and a nature trail that follows the San Juan River along the back of the property. Rooms contain two double beds or one queen, and combination shower/tubs; several budget units, with shower only and one double bed, are also available. Guests enjoy the heated pool and hot tub.

US 191 (P.O. Box 309), Bluff, UT 84512. © **435/672-2281.** Fax 435/672-2284. www.recapturelodge.com. 28 units. Summer $60 double; winter $40 double. Pets welcome. AE, DISC, MC, V. **Amenities:** Solar-heated outdoor pool; hot tub; coin-operated washers and dryers. *In room:* A/C, TV, Wi-Fi, no phone.

CAMPING

Campgrounds include **Cadillac Ranch RV Park,** US 191 (P.O. Box 157), Bluff, UT 84512 (✆ **800/538-6195** or 435/672-2262), a down-home sort of place on the east side of town with sites around a small fishing lake, where there's no license needed and no extra charge for fishing. There are 20 RV sites—all large pull-throughs—and 10 tent sites, as well as restrooms with showers. The campground is open year-round, but water is turned off in winter. Cost per site is $16 for tents and $21 to $23 for RVs; paddleboats can be rented at $4 per half hour. There is free Wi-Fi access.

WHERE TO DINE

Cottonwood Steakhouse ✮✮   Set up like the main street of an old tumbleweed

town, this Old West–style restaurant knows what to do with beef. The solid fare includes a 16-ounce T-bone steak, barbecued chicken or ribs, and 12-ounce rib-eye steak, accompanied by large salads and potatoes or baked beans; there's also a vegetarian plate. Diners sit at picnic tables, both inside the restaurant and outside under cottonwood trees. Beer (including Utah microbrew on tap) is available.

US 191 on the west side of Bluff. ✆ **435/672-2282.** Main courses $15–$25. MC, V. Daily from 5:30pm Mar to mid-Oct until close, usually around 10pm. Closed mid-Oct to Feb.

Twin Rocks Cafe   In the shadow of the prominent Twin Rocks formation, this cafe

has an open, airy dining room with large windows offering views of the surrounding red rock walls. The American and Southwest selections range from half-pound burgers to fried chicken and steaks. But the most popular items by far are the regional dishes—the sheepherder's sandwich (roast beef on fry bread with cheddar cheese), Navajo taco (available with meat or vegetarian), and Navajo fry bread. Microbrewed beers are available with meals. The cafe also serves the best breakfast in town. You can surf the Internet here, and check out the museum-quality American Indian arts and crafts at Twin Rocks Trading Post, under the same management, next door.

US 191 on the east end of Bluff. ✆ **435/672-2341.** www.twinrocks.com. Breakfast $4–$9; lunch and dinner main courses $7–$17. AE, DC, DISC, MC, V. Daily 7am–9pm in summer; reduced hours in winter.

5 Natural Bridges National Monument

60 miles NW of Bluff, 360 miles south of Salt Lake City

Utah's first National Park Service area—and the world's first "International Dark Sky Park"—Natural Bridges was designated primarily to show off and protect its three outstanding natural rock bridges, carved by streams and other forms of erosion beginning some 10,000 to 15,000 years ago. You can see the bridges from roadside viewpoints, take individual hikes to each one, or hike a loop trail that connects all three.

Giant **Sipapu Bridge** is considered a "mature" bridge. It's 220 feet high, with a span of 268 feet, and is believed to be the second-largest natural bridge in the world, after Rainbow Bridge in nearby Glen Canyon National Recreation Area. **Owachomo Bridge,** which appears to be on the brink of collapse (then again, it could stand for centuries), is the smallest of the three at 106 feet high, with a span of 180 feet. **Kachina Bridge,** 210 feet high with a span of 204 feet, is the thickest of the monument's bridges at 93 feet. All three bridges were given Hopi names: Sipapu means the "gateway to the spirit world" in Hopi legend; Owachomo is Hopi for "rock mound," so called for a rounded sandstone formation atop one side of the bridge; and Kachina was given its name because rock art on the bridge resembles decorations found on traditional Hopi kachina dolls.

ESSENTIALS

Natural Bridges National Monument is about 40 miles west of Blanding, 60 miles northwest of Bluff, 43 miles north of Mexican Hat, and about 50 miles east of Glen Canyon National Recreation Area's Hite or Halls Crossing marinas.

GETTING THERE   The national monument is located in southeast Utah, off scenic Utah 95 via Utah 275. From Monument Valley, follow US 163 north to Utah 261 (just past Mexican Hat); at Utah 95, go west to Utah 275 and the Monument. Beware, though—Utah 261, although a very pretty drive, has three miles with 10% grades and numerous steep switchbacks. It's not recommended for motor homes, those towing trailers, or anyone who's afraid of heights. The less adventurous and RV-bound should stick to approaching from the east, via Utah 95.

Make sure you have enough fuel for the trip to Natural Bridges; the closest gas stations are at least 40 miles away in Mexican Hat or Blanding. In fact, there are no services of any kind within 40 miles of the Monument.

INFORMATION/VISITOR CENTER   For a park brochure and other information, contact **Natural Bridges National Monument,** HC 60 Box 1, Lake Powell, UT 84533 (© **435/692-1234;** www.nps.gov/nabr).

A **visitor center** at the park entrance, open daily from 8am to 5pm with some seasonal variations, has exhibits and a video program on bridge formation, the human history of the area, and the monument's plants and wildlife. Rangers are available to advise you about hiking trails and scheduled activities. The visitor center is the only place in the monument where you can get drinking water.

FEES & REGULATIONS   Entry to the monument is $15 per vehicle or $7 per person on foot, bicycle, or motorcycle. Regulations are similar to those in most areas administered by the National Park Service, with an emphasis on protecting the natural resources. Be especially careful not to damage any of the fragile archaeological sites in the monument; climbing on the natural bridges is prohibited. Overnight backpacking is not permitted within the monument, and vehicles may not be left unattended overnight. Because parking at the overlooks and trailheads is limited, anyone towing trailers or extra vehicles is asked to leave them at the visitor center parking lot. Pets must be leashed and are not allowed on trails or in buildings.

RANGER PROGRAMS   Guided hikes and walks, evening campground programs, and talks at the visitor-center patio are presented from spring through fall. Schedules are posted at the visitor center.

SEEING THE HIGHLIGHTS

Natural Bridges National Monument probably won't be your major vacation destination, but you can easily spend a half- or full-day here (or possibly even 2 days). For those who want to take a quick look and get on to the other, larger national park lands in southern Utah, stop at the visitor center for a brief introduction, and then take the 9-mile (one-way) loop drive to the various natural bridge overlooks. Those with the time and the inclination might also take an easy hike down to Owachomo Bridge; it's a half-hour walk.

OUTDOOR PURSUITS

Hiking is the number-one activity here. From the trailheads, you can hike separately to each of the bridges, or start at one and do a loop hike to all three. Be prepared for summer afternoon thunderstorms that can cause flash flooding. Although the possibility of encountering a rattlesnake is very small, you should still watch carefully. During the hot summers, all hikers should wear hats and other protective clothing, use sunscreen, and carry a gallon of water per person for all but the shortest walks.

The easiest hike—more of a walk—leads to **Owachomo Bridge** (0.4 mile round-trip), with an elevation gain of 180 feet. Look toward the eastern horizon to see the twin buttes named Bear's Ears. Allow a half-hour.

The Sipapu and Kachina Bridge trails are both considered moderately strenuous—allocate about 1 hour for each. On the trek to **Sipapu Bridge,** you'll have a 500-foot elevation change, climbing two flights of stairs with three ladders and handrails on a 1.2-mile round-trip trail. This is the steepest trail in the park, and you'll have a splendid view of the bridge about halfway down. The hike takes about 1 hour.

The 1.5-mile round-trip hike to massive **Kachina Bridge** has a 400-foot elevation change, descending steep slickrock with handrails. Under the bridge, you'll notice a pile of rocks that fell in June 1992, slightly enlarging the bridge opening. Allow about 1 hour.

Those planning to hike the **loop to all three bridges** can start at any of the trailheads, although rangers recommend starting at Owachomo. The round-trip, including your walk back across the mesa, is 8.6 miles. Although the trails from the rim to the canyon bottom can be steep, the walk along the bottom is easy.

CAMPING

A primitive 13-site campground has pit toilets, tables, tent pads, and fire grates, but no drinking water, showers, or other facilities. It's limited to vehicles no more than 21 feet long, and only one vehicle is allowed per site. Cost is $10; sites are allotted on a first-come, first-served basis. (*Note:* Free drinking water is available from a spigot in the visitor center's parking lot, but there's a five-gallon limit.)

6 Winslow: Arizona's Four Corners Gateway

55 miles E of Flagstaff; 70 miles S of Second Mesa; 33 miles W of Holbrook

It's hard to imagine a town that could build its entire tourist fortunes on a mention in a pop song, but that is exactly what Winslow has done ever since the Eagles sang about "standin' on a corner in Winslow, Arizona," in their hit song "Take It Easy." On the corner of Second Street and Kinsley Avenue, the town has even built an official Standin' on the Corner Park (complete with a mural of a girl in a flatbed Ford).

Popular songs aside, Winslow can claim a couple of more significant attractions. Right in town is one of the Southwest's historic railroad hotels, La Posada, which, over recent years, has restored the building to its original glory. Twenty miles west of town is mile-wide Meteor Crater. And east of town is Homolovi Ruins State Park, which has ancient ruins as well as extensive petroglyphs.

Winslow makes a good home base for visiting some of Arizona's four corners attractions, but we've found some great places to stay scattered across the region; they're mentioned in the sections below. In particular, if you're hoping to spend some time at Canyon de Chelly National Monument, you should consider spending a night or two at one of the Chinle accommodations recommended in that section.

ESSENTIALS

GETTING THERE   Winslow is on I-40 at the junction with Arizona 87, which leads north to the Hopi mesas and south to Payson. **Amtrak** (© **800/872-7245**) trains stop in Winslow at La Posada hotel, 501 E. Second Street.

VISITOR INFORMATION   Contact the **Winslow Chamber of Commerce,** 101 E. Second St. (© **928/289-2434;** www.winslowarizona.org).

ONE BIG HOLE IN THE GROUND

Meteor Crater 𝕮𝕮   At 550 feet deep and 2½ miles in circumference, the Barringer Meteorite Crater is the best-preserved meteorite impact crater on earth. The meteorite, which estimates put at roughly 150 feet in diameter, was traveling at 40,000 mph when it slammed into the earth 50,000 years ago. Within seconds, more than 175 million tons of rock had been displaced, leaving a gaping crater and a devastated landscape. Today, you can stand on the rim of the crater (there are observation decks and a short trail) and marvel at the power, equivalent to 20 million tons of TNT, which created this otherworldly setting. In fact, so closely does this crater resemble craters on the surface of the moon that in the 1960s, NASA came here to train Apollo astronauts.

On the rim of the crater, there's a small museum that features exhibits on astrogeology and space exploration, as well as a film on meteorites. On display are a 1,400-pound meteorite and an Apollo space capsule. Throughout the day, there are 1-hour hiking tours along the rim of the crater.

20 miles west of Winslow at Exit 233 off I-40. © **800/289-5898** or 928/289-5898. www.meteorcrater.com. Admission $15 adults, $13 seniors, $6 children 6–17. Memorial Day to mid-Sept daily 7am–7pm; mid-Sept to Memorial Day daily 8am–5pm. Closed Christmas.

Fred Harvey & His Girls

Unless you grew up in the Southwest and can remember back to pre–World War II days, you may have never heard of Fred Harvey and the Harvey Girls. But if you spend much time in northern Arizona, you're likely to run into quite a few references to the Harvey Girls and their boss.

Fred Harvey was the Southwest's most famous mogul of railroad hospitality and an early promoter of tourism in the Grand Canyon State. Harvey, who was working for a railroad in the years shortly after the Civil War, developed a distaste for the food served at railroad stations. He decided he could do a better job and in 1876 opened his first Harvey House railway-station restaurant for the Santa Fe Railroad. By the time of his death in 1901, Harvey operated 47 restaurants, 30 diners, and 15 hotels across the West.

The women who worked as waitresses in the Harvey House restaurants came to be called Harvey Girls. Known for their distinctive black dresses, white aprons, and black bow ties, Harvey Girls had to adhere to very strict behavior codes and were the prim and proper women of the late-19th- and early-20th-century American West. In fact, in the late 19th century, they were considered the only real "ladies" in the West, aside from schoolteachers. So celebrated were they In their day that in the 1940s, Judy Garland starred in a Technicolor MGM musical called *The Harvey Girls.* Garland played a Harvey Girl who battles the evil town dance-hall queen (played by Angela Lansbury) for the soul of the local saloonkeeper.

OTHER AREA ATTRACTIONS

In downtown Winslow, near that famous corner, you'll find the little **Old Trails Museum,** 212 N. Kinsley Ave., at Second Street (© **928/289-5861**), which is something of a community attic and has exhibits on Route 66 and the Harvey Girls (who once worked in the nearby La Posada hotel; see the box, "Fred Harvey & His Girls," above). The museum is open Monday through Saturday from 9am to 5pm. Admission is free.

Even if you aren't planning on staying the night at the restored **La Posada,** 303 E. Second St. (© **928/289-4366**), be sure to stop by just to see this historic railway hotel. Self-guided tours are available for a $2 donation.

On the windswept plains north of Winslow, 1¼ miles north of I-40 at Exit 257, is **Homolovi Ruins State Park** (© **928/289-4106**; www.azstateparks.com), which preserves more than 300 Ancestral Puebloan archaeological sites, several of which have been partially excavated. Although these ruins are not nearly as impressive as those at Wupatki or Walnut Canyon, a visit here will give you a better understanding of the interrelationship of the many ancient pueblos of this region. Also in the park are numerous petroglyphs; ask for directions at the visitor center. Admission is $5 per vehicle. The ruins are open daily during daylight hours, but the visitor center is open only from 8am to 5pm. There's also a campground, charging $10 to $20 per site.

Continuing north from the state park, you'll find the little-known and little-visited **Little Painted Desert** ⚐ (© **928/524-4757**), a 660-acre county park. To reach the park and its viewpoint overlooking the painted hills of this stark yet colorful landscape, continue north on Arizona 87 from Homolovi Ruins State Park for another 12 miles.

If you're in the market for some Route 66 memorabilia, drop by **Roadworks Gifts & Souvenirs,** 101 W. Second St. (© **928/289-5423**; www.roadworksroute66.com). Also, be sure to check out the **SNOWDRIFT Art Space,** 120 W. Second St. (© **928/ 289-8201**; www.snowdriftart.com), an art gallery opened by artist Daniel Lutzick, who was one of the people who helped get the historic La Posada hotel up and running again.

WHERE TO STAY

In addition to the following historic hotel, you'll find lots of budget chain motels in Winslow.

La Posada ⚐⚐ *(Finds)*   What an unexpected beauty this place is! Designed by Mary Elizabeth Jane Colter, architect of many of the buildings on the South Rim of the Grand Canyon, this railroad hotel first opened in 1930. Colter gave La Posada the feel of an old Spanish hacienda and even created a fictitious history for the building. In the lobby are numerous pieces of original furniture as well as reproductions of pieces once found in the hotel. The nicest rooms are the large units named for famous guests—Albert Einstein, Howard Hughes, Harry Truman, Charles Lindbergh. The management's artistic flair comes across in these rooms, one of which (the Howard Hughes Room) has wide plank floors, murals, a fireplace, a rustic bed and armoire, Art Deco chairs, and a kilim rug. The bathroom is a classic of black-and-white tile and original fixtures. There are also rooms with whirlpool tubs. The hotel's Turquoise Room (see "Where to Dine," below) is by far the best restaurant in the entire Four Corners region. La Posada is in the process of being slowly but completely restored and is reason enough to overnight in Winslow.

303 E. Second St. (Rte. 66), Winslow, AZ 86047. (℃ **928/289-4366.** Fax 928/289-3873. www.laposada.org. 37 units. $99–$149 double; $175 suite. AE, DC, DISC, MC, V. Pets accepted ($10 fee). **Amenities:** Restaurant (New American/Southwestern); lounge; access to nearby health club; concierge; room service. In room: A/C, TV, hair dryer, iron, no phone.

WHERE TO DINE

The Turquoise Room ★★ (Value) NEW AMERICAN/SOUTHWESTERN Here, in La Posada's dining room, you'll get superb meals the likes of which you won't find anywhere else in northern Arizona. In summer, herbs and vegetables often come from the hotel's own gardens, and wild game is a specialty. Be sure to start your meal with the sweet-corn and black-bean soups, which are served side by side in the same bowl to create a sort of yin-yang symbol. On top of all this, you can watch the trains rolling by just outside the window.

At La Posada, 303 E. Second St. (℃ **928/289-2888.** www.theturquoiseroom.net. Reservations recommended. Main courses $8–$13 lunch, $16–$29 dinner. AE, DISC, MC, V. Daily 7am–2pm and 5–9pm.

7 The Hopi Reservation

67 miles N of Winslow; 250 miles NE of Phoenix; 100 miles SW of Canyon de Chelly; 140 miles SE of Page/Lake Powell

The Hopi Reservation, often referred to as Hopiland or just Hopi, is completely encircled by the Navajo Reservation and has at its center a grouping of mesas upon which the Hopi have lived for nearly 1,000 years. This remote region, with its flat-topped mesas and barren landscape, is the center of the universe for the Hopi people. Here the Hopi follow their ancient customs, and many aspects of pueblo culture remain intact. However, much of the culture is hidden from the view of visitors, and although the Hopi perform elaborate religious and social dances throughout the year, many of these dances are not open to outsiders.

The mesas are home to two of the oldest continuously inhabited villages in North America—Walpi and Old Oraibi. Although these two communities show their age and serve as a direct tie to the pueblos of the Ancestral Puebloan culture, most of the villages on the reservation are scattered collections of modern homes. These villages are not destinations unto themselves, but along Arizona 264 numerous crafts shops and studios sell kachinas, baskets, pottery, and silver jewelry. The chance to buy crafts directly from the Hopi is the main reason for a visit to this area, although you can also take a guided tour of Walpi village.

Important note: When visiting the Hopi pueblos, remember that you are a guest and your privileges can be revoked at any time. Respect all posted signs at village entrances, and remember that *photographing, sketching, and recording are prohibited in the villages and at ceremonies.* Also, kivas (ceremonial rooms) and ruins are off-limits.

ESSENTIALS

GETTING THERE This is one of the state's most remote regions. Distances are great, but highways are generally in good condition. Arizona 87 leads from Winslow to Second Mesa, and Arizona 264 runs from Tuba City in the west to the New Mexico state line in the east.

VISITOR INFORMATION For advance information, contact the **Office of Public Relations,** Hopi Tribe, P.O. Box 123, Kykotsmovi, AZ 86039 ((℃ **928/734-3283;** www.hopi.nsn.us); or the **Hopi Cultural Preservation Office** ((℃ **928/734-3612;** www.nau.edu/~hcpo-p).

THE VILLAGES

With the exception of Upper and Lower Moenkopi, which are near the Navajo town of Tuba City, and the recently settled Yuh Weh Loo Pah Ki community east of Keams Canyon, the Hopi villages are scattered along roughly 20 miles of Arizona 264. Although Old Oraibi is the oldest, there are no tours of this village, and visitors are not likely to feel very welcome here. Consequently, Walpi, the only village with organized tours, is the best place for visitors to learn more about life in the Hopi villages. We mention all of the Hopi villages below to provide a bit of history and perspective on this area, but for the most part, these villages (with the exception of Walpi and Old Oraibi) are not at all picturesque. However, most do have quite a few crafts galleries and stores selling silver jewelry.

FIRST MESA   At the top of First Mesa is the village of **Walpi,** which was located lower on the slopes of the mesa until the Pueblo Revolt of 1680 brought on fear of reprisal from the Spanish. The villagers moved Walpi to the very top of the mesa so that they could better defend themselves in the event of a Spanish attack. Parts of Walpi today still look much like the Ancestral Puebloan villages of the Arizona canyons. Small stone houses seem to grow directly from the rock of the mesa top, and ladders jut from the roofs of kivas. The view from here stretches for miles around.

Immediately adjacent to Walpi are the two villages of **Sichomovi,** which was founded in 1750 as a colony of Walpi, and **Hano,** which was founded by Tewa peoples who were most likely seeking refuge from the Spanish after the Pueblo Revolt. Neither of these villages has the ancient character of Walpi. At the foot of First Mesa is **Polacca,** a settlement founded in the late 1800s by Walpi villagers who wanted to be closer to the trading post and school.

SECOND MESA   Second Mesa is today the center of tourism in Hopiland, and this is where you'll find the Hopi Cultural Center. Villages on Second Mesa include **Shungopavi,** which was moved to its present site after Old Shungopavi was abandoned in 1680 following the Pueblo Revolt. Old Shungopavi is said to be the first Hopi village and was founded by the Bear Clan. Shungopavi is notable for its silver jewelry and its coiled plaques (flat baskets).

Mishongnovi, which means "place of the black man," is named for the leader of a clan that came here from the San Francisco Peaks around 1200. The original Mishongnovi village, located at the base of the mesa, was abandoned in the 1690s, and the village was reestablished at the current site atop the mesa. The Snake Dance is held here during odd-numbered years. It is doubtful that these dances will be open to non-Hopis.

Sipaulovi, which is located on the eastern edge of the mesa, was founded after the Pueblo Revolt of 1680.

THIRD MESA   **Oraibi,** which the Hopi claim is the oldest continuously occupied town in the United States, is located on Third Mesa. The village dates from 1150 and, according to legend, was founded by people from Old Shungopavi. A Spanish mission was established in Oraibi in 1629, and the ruins are still visible north of the village. Today, Oraibi is a mix of old stone houses and modern ones, usually of cinder block. Wander around Oraibi, and you'll likely be approached by village women and children offering to sell you various local crafts and the traditional blue-corn *piki* bread. You may also be invited into someone's home to see the crafts they have to offer. For this reason, Old Oraibi is the most interesting village in which to shop for local crafts.

For centuries, Oraibi was the largest of the Hopi villages, but in 1906, a schism arose due to Bureau of Indian Affairs policies, and many of the villagers left to form **Hotevilla.** This is considered the most conservative of the Hopi villages and has had frequent confrontations with the federal government. **Kykotsmovi,** also known as Lower Oraibi or New Oraibi, was founded in 1890 by villagers from Oraibi who wanted to be closer to the school and trading post. This village is the seat of the Hopi Tribal Government. **Bacavi** was founded in 1907 by villagers who had helped found Hotevilla but who later decided that they wanted to return to Oraibi. The people of Oraibi would not let them return, so they founded a new village.

MOENKOPI   This village is 40 miles to the west of the Hopi mesas. Founded in 1870 by people from Oraibi, Moenkopi sits in the center of a wide green valley where plentiful water makes farming more reliable. Moenkopi is only a few miles from Tuba City off US 160 and is divided into Upper Moenkopi and Lower Moenkopi.

EXPLORING THE WORLD OF THE HOPI

Start your visit to the Hopi pueblos at the **Hopi Cultural Center,** on Arizona 264 in Second Mesa (🕾 **928/734-6650**), a combination museum, motel, and restaurant. The museum is open Monday through Friday from 8am to 5pm; in summer, it's also open Saturday and Sunday from 9am to 3pm. The museum is sometimes open on Saturdays in spring and fall. Admission is $3 for adults and $1 for children 13 and under.

The most rewarding Hopi village to visit is **Walpi** 𐀪, on First Mesa. Guided tours of this tiny village are offered daily between 9:30am and 4pm (9am–5pm in summer). Admission is $8 for adults and $5 for youths 5 to 17. To sign up for a tour, drive to the top of First Mesa (in Polacca, take the road that says FIRST MESA VILLAGE) and continue through the village to **Ponsi Hall Visitor Center** (🕾 **928/737-2262**), where you'll see signs for the tours. The tours, which last 1 hour, are led by Hopis who will tell you the history of the village and explain a bit about the local culture. Similar tours are also offered by **Village of Walpi Tour Services** (🕾 **928/737-9556** or 928/737-9377). These tours are offered Monday through Friday from 8:30am to 4pm. The cost is $5.

CULTURAL TOURS

To get the most out of a visit to the Hopi mesas, it is best to book a guided tour. With a guide, you will probably learn much more about this rather insular culture than you ever could on your own. Tour companies frequently use local guides and stop at the homes of working artisans. This all adds up to a more in-depth and educational visit to one of the oldest cultures on the continent.

Bertram Tsavadawa at **Tsavadawa's Ancient Pathways** (🕾 **928/797-8145;** www. ancientpathwaystours.com) specializes in tours to Hopi petroglyph sites. These are sites that are not open to the public unless you are with a Hopi guide. Tours also visit Old Oraibi. The cost is $75 per person for a 3-hour tour and $165 for a 6-hour tour.

DANCES & CEREMONIES

The Hopi have developed the most complex religious ceremonies of any of the Southwest tribes. The masked kachina dances for which they are most famous are held from January to July. However, most kachina dances are closed to the non-Hopi public. Social dances (usually open to the public) are held August through February. If you're on the reservation during these months, ask if any dances are taking place. Who knows? You might get lucky. Snake Dances (usually closed to the non-Hopi public) are held August through December.

Kachinas, whether in the form of dolls or as masked dancers, are representative of the spirits of everything from plants and animals to ancestors and sacred places. According to legend, the kachinas lived with the Hopi long ago, but the Hopi people made the kachinas angry, causing them to leave. Before departing, though, the kachinas taught the Hopi how to perform their ceremonies.

Today, the kachina ceremonies, performed by men wearing elaborate costumes and masks, serve several purposes. Most important, they bring clouds and rain to water the all-important corn crop, but they also ensure health, happiness, long life, and harmony in the universe. As part of the kachina ceremonies, dancers often bring carved wooden kachina dolls to village children to introduce them to the various spirits.

The kachina season lasts from the winter solstice until shortly after the summer solstice. The actual dates for dances are determined by the position of the sun and usually are announced only shortly before the ceremonies are to be held.

Despite the importance of the kachina dances, it is the **Snake Dance** that has captured the attention of many non-Hopis. The Snake Dance is held every other year in Mishongnovi and Gray Spring and involves the handling of both poisonous and nonpoisonous snakes. The ceremony takes place over 16 days; the actual Snake Dance is performed on the last day. When all the snakes have been danced around the plaza, they are rushed down to their homes at the bottom of the mesa to carry the Hopi prayers for rain to the spirits of the underworld.

Due to the disrespectful attitude of some past visitors, many ceremonies and dances are now closed to non-Hopis. However, a couple of Hopi villages do allow visitors to attend some of their social dances.

SHOPPING

Most visitors come to the reservation to shop for Hopi crafts. Across the reservation, dozens of small shops sell crafts and jewelry of different quality, and some homes, especially at the foot of First Mesa, have signs indicating that they sell crafts. Shops often sell the work of only a few individuals, so you should stop at several to get an idea of the variety of work available. Also, if you tour Walpi or wander around in Oraibi, you will likely be approached by villagers selling various crafts, including kachina dolls. The quality is not usually as high as that in shops, but then, neither are the prices.

At Keams Canyon, almost 30 miles east of the cultural center, you'll find **McGee's Indian Art Gallery** (© **928/738-2295;** www.hopiart.com), which is the best place to shop for high-quality contemporary kachina dolls. This shop is adjacent to a grocery store and has been a trading post for more than 100 years.

If you're in the market for Hopi silver jewelry, stop in at **Hopi Fine Arts** (© **928/ 737-2222;** www.hopifinearts.net), which is at the foot of Second Mesa at the junction of Arizona 264 and Arizona 87. This shop also has a good selection of kachina dolls and some beautiful coil and wicker plaque baskets.

One of the best places to get a quick education in Hopi art and crafts is **Tsakurshovi** (© **928/734-2478**), a tiny shop 1½ miles east of the Hopi Cultural Center on Second Mesa. This shop has a huge selection of traditional kachina dolls and also has lots of jewelry. Janice and Joe Day, the owners, are very friendly and are always happy to share their expertise with visitors. This is also where you can buy a "Don't Worry Be Hopi" T-shirt.

If you're interested in kachina dolls, be sure to visit Oraibi's **Monongya Gallery** (© **928/734-2344**), a big building right on Arizona 264 outside of Oraibi. It usually has one of the largest selections of kachina dolls in the area. Also in Oraibi is **Hamana So-o's Arts & Crafts** (© **928/607-0176**), which is in an old stone house from which owner Sandra Hamana sells primarily artwork and crafts based on kachina images.

WHERE TO STAY & DINE

If you've brought your food along, you'll find picnic tables just east of Oraibi on top of the mesa. These tables have an amazing view!

Hopi Cultural Center Restaurant & Inn   Although it isn't much, this simple motel makes the best base for anyone planning to spend a couple of days shopping for crafts in the area. Because it is the only lodging for miles around, be sure you have a reservation before heading up for an overnight visit. Guest rooms are comfortable enough, though the grounds are quite desolate. The restaurant has a salad bar and serves American and traditional Hopi meals, including *piki* bread (a paper-thin bread made from blue corn) and Hopi stew with hominy, lamb, and green chile. There's also a museum.

P.O. Box 67, Second Mesa, AZ 86043. © **928/734-2401.** Fax 928/734-6651. www.hopiculturalcenter.com. 33 units. Mar 15–Oct 15 $95–$100 double; Oct 16–Mar 14 $70–$75 double. Children 12 and under stay free in parent's room. AE, DISC, MC, V. **Amenities:** Restaurant (American/Hopi); shopping arcade. *In room:* A/C, TV, coffeemaker, free local calls.

EN ROUTE TO OR FROM THE HOPI MESAS

On the west side of the reservation, in Tuba City, is the **Tuba City Trading Post,** Main Street and Moenave Avenue (© **928/283-5441**). This octagonal trading post was built in 1906 of local stone and is designed to resemble a Navajo hogan (there's also a real hogan on the grounds). The trading post sells Native American crafts, with an emphasis on books, music, and jewelry. Across the parking lot from the trading post you'll find **Hogan Espresso,** Main Street and Moenave Avenue (© **800/644-8383** or 928/283-4545), one of the few places on the reservation where you can get espresso. Behind the trading post, you'll find the new **Explore Navajo Interactive Museum,** Main Street and Moenave Avenue (© **928/283-4545**), a small museum in a giant tentlike structure that was used at the 2002 Salt Lake City Olympics. Although small, the museum provides a good introduction to Navajo culture. There is also a good Navajo code talkers exhibit here. The museum is open Monday through Saturday 10am to 8pm, and Sunday noon to 8pm. Admission is $9 for adults, $7 for seniors, and $6 for children ages 6 to 12.

On the western outskirts of Tuba City, on US 160, you'll find **Van's Trading Co.** (© **928/283-5343**), in the corner of a large grocery store. Van's has a dead-pawn auction on the 15th of each month at 3pm (any pawned item not reclaimed by the owner by a specified date is considered "dead pawn"). The auction provides opportunities to buy older pieces of Navajo silver-and-turquoise jewelry.

In mid-October, Tuba City is the site of the **Western Navajo Fair** (www.western navajofair.com), which sells Native American crafts.

West of Tuba City and just off US 160, you can see **dinosaur footprints** ⟨⟩ preserved in the stone surface of the desert. There are usually a few people waiting at the site to guide visitors to the best footprints (these guides will expect a tip of $1–$2). The scenery out your car window is some of the strangest in the region—red-rock sandstone formations that resemble petrified sand dunes.

The **Cameron Trading Post** ⟨⟩ (© **800/338-7385** or 928/679-2231; www. camerontradingpost.com), 16 miles south of the junction of US 160 and US 89, is well worth a visit. The main trading post is filled with souvenirs but has large selections of rugs and jewelry as well. In the adjacent stone-walled gallery are museum-quality Native American artifacts (with prices to match). The trading post includes a motel, convenience store, and gas station.

WHERE TO STAY

Quality Inn Navajo Nation   Located in the bustling Navajo community of Tuba City (where you'll find gas stations, fast-food restaurants, and grocery stores), this modern hotel is adjacent to the historic Tuba City Trading Post and is actually a more attractive place to stay in this region than the Hopi Cultural Center. The hotel offers comfortable rooms of average size, but the green lawns, shade trees, and old trading post (complete with hogan) are what really set this place apart. This hotel is also the site of the new Explore Navajo Interactive Museum and has an Internet cafe.

Main St. and Moenave Ave. (P.O. Box 247), Tuba City, AZ 86045. © 800/644-8383 or 928/283-4545. Fax 928/283-4144. www.qualityinntubacity.com. 80 units. Apr–Oct $105–$140 double; Nov–Mar $85–$115 double. Children 18 and under stay free in parent's room. AE, DC, DISC, MC, V. Pets accepted ($10 deposit). **Amenities:** Restaurant (American/Mexican/Navajo); business center; coin-op laundry. *In room:* A/C, TV, coffeemaker, hair dryer, iron, safe, microwave, high-speed Internet access, free local calls.

8 The Petrified Forest & Painted Desert ⋆

25 miles E of Holbrook; 90 miles E of Flagstaff; 118 miles S of Canyon de Chelly; 180 miles N of Phoenix

Petrified wood has long fascinated people, and although it can be found in almost every state, the "forest" of downed logs in northeastern Arizona is by far the most extensive. But don't head out this way expecting to see standing trees of stone with leaves and branches intact. Though there is enough petrified timber scattered across this landscape to fill a forest, it is, in fact, in the form of logs and not standing trees. Many a visitor has shown up expecting to find some sort of national forest of stone trees. The reality is much less impressive than the petrified forest of the imagination.

However, this area is still unique. When, in the 1850s, this vast treasure-trove of petrified wood was discovered scattered, enterprising people began exporting it to the East. Within 50 years, so much had been removed that in 1906 several areas were set aside as the Petrified Forest National Monument, which, in 1962, became a national park. A 27-mile scenic drive winds through the petrified forest and a corner of the Painted Desert, providing a fascinating high desert experience.

It may be hard to believe when you drive across this arid landscape, but at one time this area was a vast steamy swamp. That was 225 million years ago, when dinosaurs and huge amphibians ruled the earth and giant now-extinct trees grew on the high ground around the swamp. Fallen trees were washed downstream, gathered in piles in still backwaters, and eventually covered over with silt, mud, and volcanic ash. As water seeped through this soil, it dissolved the silica in the volcanic ash and redeposited this silica inside the cells of the logs. Eventually, the silica recrystallized into stone to form petrified wood.

This region was later inundated with water, and thick deposits of sediment buried the logs ever deeper. Eventually, the land was transformed yet again as a geologic upheaval thrust the lake bottom up above sea level. This upthrust of the land cracked the logs into the segments we see today. Wind and water gradually eroded the landscape to create the Painted Desert, and the petrified logs were once again exposed on the surface of the land.

ESSENTIALS

GETTING THERE The north entrance to Petrified Forest National Park is 25 miles east of Holbrook on I-40. The south entrance is 20 miles east of Holbrook on US 180.

FEES The entry fee is $10 per car. The park is open daily from 8am to 5pm (7am–7pm in summer).

VISITOR INFORMATION For further information on the Petrified Forest or the Painted Desert, contact **Petrified Forest National Park,** P.O. Box 2217, Petrified Forest, AZ 86028 (© **928/524-6228;** www.nps.gov/pefo). For information on Holbrook and the surrounding region, contact the **Holbrook Chamber of Commerce,** 100 E. Arizona St. (© **800/524-2459** or 928/524-6558; www.ci.holbrook.az.us).

EXPLORING A UNIQUE LANDSCAPE

Petrified Forest National Park has both a north and a south entrance. If you are coming from the west, it's better to start at the southern entrance and work your way north along the park's 27-mile scenic road, which has more than 20 overlooks. This way, you'll see the most impressive displays of petrified logs early in your visit and save the Painted Desert vistas for last. If you're coming from the east, start at the northern entrance and work your way south.

The **Rainbow Forest Museum** (© **928/524-6228**), just inside the south entrance to the park, is the best place to begin your tour. Here you can learn all about petrified wood, watch an introductory film, and otherwise get oriented. Exhibits chronicle the area's geologic and human history. There are also displays on the reptiles and dinosaurs that once inhabited this region. The museum sells maps and books and also issues free backpacking permits. It's open daily from 8am to 5pm.

The **Giant Logs self-guided trail** starts behind the museum. The trail winds across a hillside strewn with logs that are 4 to 5 feet in diameter. Almost directly across the parking lot from the museum is the entrance to the **Long Logs** and **Agate House** areas. On the 1.6-mile Long Logs trail, you can see more big trees, while at Agate House, a 2-mile round-trip hike will lead you to the ruins of a pueblo built from colorful petrified wood. These two trails can be combined into a 2.6-mile hike.

Heading north, you'll pass by the unusual formations known as **The Flattops.** These structures were caused by the erosion of softer mineral deposits from beneath a harder and more erosion-resistant layer of sandstone. The Flattops is one of the park's wilderness areas. The **Crystal Forest** is the next stop to the north, named for the beautiful amethyst and quartz crystals once found in the cracks of petrified logs. Concern over the removal of these crystals was what led to the protection of the petrified forest. A .75-mile loop trail winds past the logs that once held the crystals.

At the **Jasper Forest Overlook,** you can see logs that include petrified roots, and a little bit farther north, at the **Agate Bridge** stop, you can see a petrified log that forms a natural agate bridge. Continuing north, you'll reach **Blue Mesa,** where pieces of petrified wood form capstones over easily eroded clay soils. As wind and water wear away at the clay beneath a piece of stone, the balance of the stone becomes more and more precarious until it eventually comes toppling down. A 1-mile loop trail here leads into the park's badlands.

Erosion has played a major role in the formation of the Painted Desert, and to the north of Blue Mesa you'll see some of the most interesting erosional features of the area. It's quite evident why these hills of sandstone and clay are known as **The**

Teepees. The layers of different color are due to manganese, iron, and other minerals in the soil.

By this point, you've probably seen as much petrified wood as you'd ever care to see, so be sure to stop at **Newspaper Rock,** where instead of staring at more ancient logs, you can see a dense concentration of petroglyphs left by generations of Native Americans. At nearby **Puerco Pueblo,** the park's largest archaeological site, you can view the remains of homes built by the people who created the park's petroglyphs. This pueblo was probably occupied around A.D.1400. Don't miss the petroglyphs on its back side.

North of Puerco Pueblo, the road crosses I-40. From here to the Painted Desert Visitor Center, there are eight overlooks onto the southernmost edge of the **Painted Desert.** Named for the vivid colors of the soil and stone that cover the land here, the Painted Desert is a dreamscape of pastels washed across a barren expanse of eroded hills. The colors are created by minerals dissolved in sandstone and clay soils that were deposited during different geologic periods. There's a picnic area at Chinde Point overlook. At Kachina Point, you'll find the **Painted Desert Inn,** a renovated historic building that, unfortunately, does not offer overnight accommodations. From here, there's access to the park's other wilderness area. The inn, which was built in 1924 and expanded by the Civilian

> *Fun Fact* **Rock Talk**
>
> Gift shops throughout this region sell petrified wood in all sizes and colors, natural and polished. This petrified wood does not come from the national park, but is collected on private land in the area. No piece of petrified wood, no matter how small, may be removed from Petrified Forest National Park.

Conservation Corps, is noteworthy for both its architecture and the Fred Kabotie murals on the interior walls. Hours are 9am to 5pm daily. Between Kachina Point and Tawa Point, you can do an easy 1-mile round-trip hike along the rim of the Painted Desert. An even more interesting route leads down into the Painted Desert from behind the Painted Desert Inn.

Just inside the northern entrance to the park is the **Painted Desert Visitor Center** (© **928/524-6228**), open daily 8am to 5pm, where you can watch a short film that explains the process by which wood becomes fossilized. Adjacent to the visitor center are a cafeteria, a bookshop, and a gas station.

OTHER REASONS TO LINGER IN HOLBROOK

Although the Petrified Forest National Park is the main reason for visiting this area, you might want to stop by downtown Holbrook's **Old West Museum,** 100 E. Arizona St. (© **928/524-6558**), which also houses the Holbrook Chamber of Commerce visitor center. This old and dusty museum has exhibits on local history but is most interesting for its old jail cells. It's open Monday through Friday from 8am to 5pm (and Sat–Sun 8am–4pm in summer); admission is free. On weekday evenings between June and mid-August, there are Native American dances on the lawn in front.

Although it is against the law to collect petrified wood inside Petrified Forest National Park, there are several rock shops in Holbrook where you can buy pieces of petrified wood in all shapes and sizes. You'll find them lined up along the main street through town and out on US 180, the highway leading to the south entrance of Petrified Forest National Park. The biggest and best of these rock shops is **Jim Gray's**

Petrified Wood Co., 147 Hwy. 180 (© **928/524-1842;** www.petrifiedwoodco.com), which has everything from raw rocks to $24,000 petrified-wood coffee tables. This store also has a fascinating display of minerals and fossils. It's open daily from 8am to 6pm (longer hours in summer) and is well worth a stop.

In town on the north side of I-40 is **McGee's Gallery,** 2114 N. Navajo Blvd. (© **800/524-9183** or 928/524-1876; mcgeeshopitraders.com), a Native American crafts gallery with a wide selection of typical crafts at reasonable prices. There's a particularly good collection of kachina dolls here.

If you're interested in petroglyphs, you may want to schedule a visit to the **Rock Art Ranch** ⚜ (© **928/288-3260**), southwest of Holbrook on part of the old Hashknife Ranch, which was the largest ranch in the country during the late 19th century. Within the bounds of this ranch, pecked into the rock walls of Chevelon Canyon, are hundreds of Ancestral Puebloan petroglyphs. The setting, a narrow canyon that is almost invisible until you are right beside it, is enchanting, making this the finest place in the state to view petroglyphs. Tours (reservations required) are available Monday through Saturday year-round (call to get rate information and directions to the ranch).

WHERE TO STAY

Holbrook, the town nearest to Petrified Forest National Park, offers lots of budget chain motels charging very reasonable rates.

Wigwam Motel (Finds If you're willing to sleep on a saggy mattress for the sake of reliving a bit of Route 66 history, don't miss this collection of concrete wigwams (tepees, actually). This unique motel was built in the 1940s, when unusual architecture was springing up all along famous Route 66. The motel has been owned by the same family since it was built and still has the original rustic furniture. Old cars are kept in the parking lot for an added dose of Route 66 character.

811 W. Hopi Dr., Holbrook, AZ 86025. © **928/524-3048.** Fax 928/524-9335. www.galerie-kokopelli.com/wigwam. 15 units. $48–$54 double. MC, V. Pets accepted. *In room:* A/C, TV.

WHERE TO DINE

While there are plenty of inexpensive restaurants in Holbrook, none is particularly memorable or recommendable. Your best bet is to drive over to Winslow to the Turquoise Room at La Posada hotel.

9 Canyon de Chelly National Monument ⚜⚜⚜

68 miles NW of Window Rock; 222 miles NE of Flagstaff; 110 miles SE of Navajo National Monument; 110 miles SE of Monument Valley Navajo Tribal Park

It's hard to imagine narrow canyons less than 1,000 feet deep being more spectacular than the Grand Canyon, but in some ways Canyon de Chelly National Monument is just that. Gaze down from the rim at an ancient Ancestral Puebloan cliff dwelling as the whinnying of horses and clanging of goat bells drift up from far below, and you'll be struck by the continuity of human existence. For nearly 5,000 years, people have called these canyons home, and today there are not only the summer homes of Navajo farmers and sheepherders but also more than 100 prehistoric dwelling sites.

Canyon de Chelly National Monument consists of two major canyons—Canyon de Chelly (which is pronounced "canyon duh shay" and is derived from the Navajo word *tséyi,* meaning "rock canyon") and Canyon del Muerto (Spanish for "Canyon of the Dead")—and several smaller canyons. The canyons extend for more than 100 miles through the rugged slickrock landscape of northeastern Arizona, draining the seasonal snowmelt runoff from the Chuska Mountains.

In summer, Canyon de Chelly's smooth sandstone walls of rich reds and yellows contrast sharply with the deep greens of corn, pastures, and cottonwoods on the canyon floor. Vast stone amphitheaters form the caves in which the Ancestral Puebloans built their homes, and as you watch shadows and light paint an ever-changing canyon panorama, it's easy to see why the Navajo consider this sacred ground. With mysteriously abandoned cliff dwellings and breathtaking natural beauty, Canyon de Chelly is certainly as worthy of a visit as the Grand Canyon.

ESSENTIALS

GETTING THERE   From Flagstaff, the easiest route to Canyon de Chelly is I-40 to US 191 to Ganado. At Ganado, drive west on Arizona 264 and pick up US 191 N to Chinle. If you're coming down from Monument Valley or Navajo National Monument, Indian Route 59, which connects US 160 and US 191, is an excellent road with plenty of beautiful scenery.

FEES   Monument admission is free.

VISITOR INFORMATION   Before leaving home, you can contact **Canyon de Chelly National Monument,** P.O. Box 588, Chinle, AZ 86503 (© **928/674-5500;** www.nps.gov/cach), for information. The visitor center is open daily 8am to 5pm (MST, not Navajo Reservation time). The monument itself is open daily from sunrise to sunset.

SPECIAL EVENTS   The annual **Central Navajo Fair** is held in Chinle in August.

EXPLORING THE CANYON

Your first stop should be the **visitor center,** in front of which is an example of a traditional crib-style hogan, a hexagonal structure of logs and earth that Navajos use as both a home and a ceremonial center. Inside the visitor center, a small museum explores the history of Canyon de Chelly, and there's often a silversmith demonstrating Navajo jewelry-making techniques. Interpretive programs are offered at the monument Memorial Day to Labor Day. Check at the visitor center for daily activities, such as campfire programs and natural-history programs.

From the visitor center, most people tour the canyon by car. Very different views of the monument's system of canyons are provided by the 15-mile North Rim and 16-mile South Rim drives. The North Rim Drive overlooks Canyon del Muerto, while the South Rim Drive overlooks Canyon de Chelly. With stops, the drive along either rim road can easily take 2 to 3 hours. If you have time for only one, make it the South Rim Drive, which provides both a dramatic view of Spider Rock and the chance to hike down into the canyon on the only trail you can explore without hiring a guide. If, on the other hand, you're more interested in the history and prehistory of this area, opt for the North Rim Drive, which overlooks several historically significant sites within the canyon.

THE NORTH RIM DRIVE

The first stop on the North Rim is the **Ledge Ruin Overlook.** On the opposite wall, about 100 feet up from the canyon floor, you can see the Ledge Ruin. This site was occupied by the Ancestral Puebloans between 1050 and 1275. Nearby, at the unmarked Dekaa Kiva Viewpoint, you can see a lone kiva (circular ceremonial building). This structure was reached by means of toeholds cut into the soft sandstone cliff wall.

⌒Tips **Taking Photos on the Reservations**

Before taking a photograph of a Navajo, always ask permission. If it's granted, a tip of $1 or more is expected. Photography is not allowed at all in Hopi villages.

The second stop is the **Antelope House Overlook,** which is the all-around most interesting overlook in the monument. Not only do you get to hike .25 mile over the rugged rim-rock landscape, but you get to view ruins, rock art, and impressive cliff walls. The Antelope House ruin takes its name from the antelope paintings, believed to date back to the 1830s, on a nearby cliff wall. Beneath the ruins of Antelope House, archaeologists have found the remains of an earlier pit house dating from A.D. 693. Although most of the Ancestral Puebloan cliff dwellings were abandoned sometime after a drought began in 1276, Antelope House had already been abandoned by 1260, possibly because of damage caused by flooding. Across the wash from Antelope House, an ancient tomb, known as the Tomb of the Weaver, was discovered by archaeologists in the 1920s. The tomb contained the well-preserved body of an old man wrapped in a blanket of golden eagle feathers and accompanied by cornmeal, shelled and husked corn, pine nuts, beans, salt, and thick skeins of cotton. Also visible from this overlook is Navajo Fortress, a red-sandstone butte that the Navajo once used as a refuge from attackers. A steep trail once led to the top of Navajo Fortress, and by using log ladders that could be pulled up into the refuge, the Navajo were able to escape their attackers.

The third stop is **Mummy Cave Overlook,** named for two mummies found in burial urns below the ruins. Archaeological evidence indicates that this giant amphitheater consisting of two caves was occupied for 1,000 years, from A.D. 300 to 1300. In the two caves and on the shelf between are 80 rooms, including three kivas. The central structure between the two caves includes an interesting three-story building characteristic of the architecture in Mesa Verde in New Mexico. Archaeologists speculate that a group of Ancestral Puebloans migrated here from New Mexico. Much of the original plasterwork is still intact and indicates that the buildings were colorfully decorated.

The fourth and last stop on the North Rim is the **Massacre Cave Overlook,** which got its name after an 1805 Spanish military expedition killed more than 115 Navajo at this site. The Navajo at the time had been raiding Spanish settlements that were encroaching on their territory. Accounts of the battle at Massacre Cave differ. One version claims there were only women, children, and old men taking shelter in the cave, but the official Spanish records claim 90 warriors and 25 women and children were killed. Also visible from this overlook is Yucca Cave, which was occupied about 1,000 years ago.

THE SOUTH RIM DRIVE

The South Rim Drive climbs slowly but steadily, and at each stop you're a little bit higher above the canyon floor. Near the mouth of the canyon is the **Tunnel Overlook,** where a short narrow canyon feeds into Chinle Wash, a wash formed by the streams that cut through the canyons of the national monument. *Tsegi* is a Navajo word meaning "rock canyon," and at the nearby **Tsegi Overlook,** that's just what you'll see when you gaze down from the viewpoint.

The next stop is the **Junction Overlook,** so named because it overlooks the junction of Canyon del Muerto and Canyon de Chelly. Here you can see the Junction Ruin, which has 10 rooms and a kiva. Ancestral Puebloans occupied this ruin during the Great Pueblo Period, which lasted from around 1100 until shortly before 1300. First Ruin, which is perched precariously on a long narrow ledge, is also visible. In this ruin are 22 rooms and two kivas. Good luck picking out the two canyons in this maze of curving cliff walls.

The third stop is **White House Overlook,** from which you can see the 80-room White House Ruins, which are among the largest ruins in the canyon. These buildings were inhabited between 1040 and 1275. From this overlook, you have your only opportunity to descend into Canyon de Chelly without a guide or ranger. The **White House Ruins Trail** 𝄞𝄞 descends 600 feet to the canyon floor and crosses Chinle Wash before reaching the White House Ruins. The buildings of this ruin were constructed both on the canyon floor and 50 feet up the cliff wall in a small cave. Although you cannot enter the ruins, you can get close enough to get a good look. Do not wander off this trail, and please respect the privacy of the Navajo living here. The 2.5-mile round-trip hike takes about 2 hours. Be sure to carry water.

Notice the black streaks on the sandstone walls above the White House Ruins. These streaks, known as desert varnish, are formed by seeping water, which reacts with iron in the sandstone (iron is what gives the walls their reddish hue). To create the canyon's many petroglyphs, Ancestral Puebloan artists would chip away at the desert varnish. Later, the Navajo used paints to create pictographs of animals and historical events, such as the Spanish military expedition that killed 115 Navajo at Massacre Cave. Many of these petroglyphs and pictographs can be seen if you take a guided tour into the canyon.

The fifth stop is **Sliding House Overlook.** These ruins were built on a narrow shelf and appear to be sliding down into the canyon. Inhabited from about 900 until 1200, Sliding House contained between 30 and 50 rooms. This overlook is already more than 700 feet above the canyon floor, with sheer walls giving the narrow canyon a very foreboding appearance.

On the last access road to the canyon rim, you'll come to the **Face Rock Overlook,** which provides yet another dizzying glimpse of the ever-deepening canyon. Here you gaze 1,000 feet down to the bottom. However, it is the next stop—**Spider Rock Overlook**—that offers the monument's most spectacular view. This viewpoint overlooks the junction of Canyon de Chelly and Monument Canyon. The monolithic pinnacle known as Spider Rock rises 800 feet from the canyon floor, its two free-standing towers forming a natural monument. Across the canyon from Spider Rock stands the similarly striking **Speaking Rock,** which is connected to the far canyon wall.

OTHER WAYS TO SEE THE CANYON

Access to the floor of Canyon de Chelly is restricted; unless you're on the White House Ruins Trail (see "The South Rim Drive," above), you must be accompanied by an authorized guide in order to enter the canyon. **Navajo guides** usually charge $15 to $25 per hour with a 3-hour minimum and will lead you into the canyon on foot or in your own four-wheel-drive vehicle. **De Chelly Tours** (✆ 928/674-3772; www. dechellytours.com) charges $20 per hour, with a 3-hour minimum, to go out in your four-wheel-drive vehicle; if it supplies the vehicle, the cost goes up to $125 for three people for 3 hours. Similar tours are offered by **Canyon de Chelly Tours** (✆ 928/674-5433 or 928/349-1600; www.canyondechellytours.com), which will take you into the canyon in a jeep or a Unimog truck (a powerful four-wheel-drive off-road vehicle). Unimog tours are $50 to $52 for adults and $35 to $37 for children 12 and under. Tours depart from the Holiday Inn parking lot. Reservations are recommended. The monument visitor center also maintains a list of guides.

Another way to see Canyon de Chelly and Canyon del Muerto is on what locals call **shake-and-bake tours** 𝕏, via a six-wheel-drive truck. In summer, these excursions really live up to the name. (In winter, the truck is enclosed to keep out the elements.) The trucks operate out of **Thunderbird Lodge** (© 800/679-2473; www.tbirdlodge. com) and are equipped with seats in the bed. Tours make frequent stops for photographs and to visit ruins, Navajo farms, and rock art. Half-day trips cost around $41 per person ($32 for children 12 and under), while full-day tours cost around $67 for all ages. Full-day tours, offered spring through fall, leave at 9am and return at 5pm.

If you'd rather use a more traditional means of transportation, you can go on a guided horseback ride. To leave the crowds behind, drive east along South Rim Drive to **Totsonii Ranch** 𝕏 (© 928/755-6209; www.totsoniiranch.com), which is 1¼ miles past where the pavement ends. Rides from here visit a remote part of the canyon (including the Spider Rock area) and cost $15 per group per hour for the guide and $15 per person per hour. Totsonii Ranch also offers overnight rides for $335 per person and 2-night rides for $515 per person.

If you're physically fit and like hiking, consider hiring a guide to lead you down into the canyon. Hikes can start at the White House Ruin trail, near the Spider Rock overlook, or from near the Antelope House overlook. These latter two starting points are trails that are not open to the public without a guide and should be your top choices. The hike from Antelope House gets our vote for best option for a hike. Guides can be hired at the monument visitor center. Guides charge $15 per hour for up to 15 people.

SHOPPING

The **Thunderbird Lodge Gift Shop,** in Chinle (© 800/679-2473 or 928/674-5841), is well worth a stop while you're in the area. It has a huge collection of rugs, as well as good selections of pottery and plenty of souvenirs. In the canyon wherever visitors gather (at ruins and petroglyph sites), you're likely to encounter craftspeople selling jewelry and other types of handwork. These craftspeople, most of whom live in the canyon, accept cash, personal checks, traveler's checks, and sometimes credit cards.

WHERE TO STAY & DINE

Holiday Inn–Canyon de Chelly 𝕏𝕏   Located between the town of Chinle and the national monument entrance, this modern hotel is on the site of the old Garcia Trading Post, which has been incorporated into the restaurant and gift-shop building (although the building no longer has any historical character). All guest rooms have patios or balconies, and most face the cottonwood-shaded pool courtyard. Because Canyon de Chelly truck tours leave from the parking lot here and because the restaurant serves the best food in town, this should be your top choice for a room in Chinle.

Tips Forget About Wine with Dinner

Alcohol is prohibited on both the Navajo and the Hopi reservations. Unfortunately, however, despite this prohibition, drunk drivers are a problem on the reservation, so stay alert.

Indian Rte. 7 (P.O. Box 1889), Chinle, AZ 86503. © **800/465-4329** or 928/674-5000. Fax 928/674-8264. www. holiday-inn.com/chinle-garcia. 108 units. $69–$159 double. Children under 18 stay free in parent's room; children 12 and under eat for free. AE, DC, DISC, MC, V. **Amenities:** Restaurant (American/Navajo); outdoor pool; exercise room; concierge; room service; coin-op laundry. *In room:* A/C, TV, dataport, coffeemaker, hair dryer, iron, high-speed Internet access, Wi-Fi.

Thunderbird Lodge   Built on the site of an early trading post right at the mouth of Canyon de Chelly, the Thunderbird Lodge is the closest hotel to the national monument. The red-adobe construction of the lodge itself is reminiscent of ancient pueblos, and the presence on the property of an old stone-walled trading post gives this place lots of character. Guest rooms have both ceiling fans and air-conditioning. The old trading post now serves as a cafeteria, but there is a gift shop with a rug room on-site.

P.O. Box 548, Chinle, AZ 86503. © **800/679-2473** or 928/674-5841. Fax 928/674-5844. www.tblrdlodge.com. 74 units. Apr to mid-Nov $101–$106 double, $145 suite; mid-Nov to Mar $65 double, $91 suite. Children 2 and under stay free in parent's room. AE, DC, DISC, MC, V. Pets accepted. **Amenities:** Restaurant (American/Navajo); tour desk. *In room:* A/C, TV, Wi-Fi, free local calls.

CAMPGROUNDS

Adjacent to the Thunderbird Lodge is the free **Cottonwood Campground,** which has around 100 sites but does not take reservations. On South Rim Drive 10 miles east of the Canyon de Chelly visitor center is another option, the private **Spider Rock Campground** (© **928/674-8261;** www.spiderrockcampground.com), which has more than 30 spaces and charges $10 to $12 per night. This campground also has a couple of hogans for rent for $29 to $39 per night. The next nearest campgrounds are at **Tsaile Lake** and **Wheatfields Lake,** both south of the town of Tsaile on Indian Route 12. Tsaile is at the east end of the North Rim Drive.

10 Navajo National Monument ⌖

110 miles NW of Canyon de Chelly; 140 miles NE of Flagstaff; 60 miles SW of Monument Valley; 90 miles E of Page

Navajo National Monument, located 30 miles west of Kayenta and 60 miles northeast of Tuba City, encompasses three of the largest and best-preserved Ancestral Puebloan cliff dwellings in the region—Betatakin (Talastima), Keet Seel (Kawestima), and Inscription House. It's possible to visit both Betatakin and Keet Seel, but, due to its fragility, Inscription House is closed to the public. The name Navajo National Monument is a bit misleading. Although the Navajo do inhabit the area now, the cliff dwellings were built by Kayenta Ancestral Puebloans, who were the ancestral Hopi and Pueblo peoples. The Navajo did not arrive in this area until centuries after the cliff dwellings had been abandoned.

For reasons unknown, the well-constructed cliff dwellings here were abandoned around the middle of the 13th century. Tree rings suggest that a drought in the latter part of the 13th century prevented the Ancestral Puebloans from growing sufficient crops. In Tsegi Canyon, however, there's another theory for the abandonment. The canyon was usually flooded each year by spring and summer snowmelt, which made farming quite productive, but in the mid-1200s, weather patterns changed and streams began cutting deep into the soil, forming narrow little canyons called arroyos, which lowered the water table and made farming much more difficult.

ESSENTIALS

GETTING THERE   Navajo National Monument can be reached by taking US89 N to US 160 to Arizona 564 N.

FEES Monument admission is free.

VISITOR INFORMATION For information, contact **Navajo National Monument,** HC 71 Box 3, Tonalea, AZ 86044 (© **928/672-2700;** www.nps.gov/nava). Spring through fall, the visitor center is open daily from 8am to 7pm; in winter the visitor center is open daily from 9am to 5pm. The monument is open daily from sunrise to sunset.

EXPLORING THE MONUMENT

A visit to Navajo National Monument is definitely not a point-and-shoot experience. You're going to have to expend some energy if you want to see what this monument is all about. The shortest distance you'll have to walk is 1 mile, which is the round-trip from the visitor center to the Betatakin overlook. However, if you want to actually get close to these ruins, you're looking at strenuous day or overnight hikes.

Your first stop should be the **visitor center,** which has informative displays on the Ancestral Puebloan and Navajo cultures, including numerous artifacts from Tsegi Canyon. You can also watch a couple of short films or a slide show.

The only one of the monument's three ruins that can be seen easily is **Betatakin** ⊛, which means "ledge house" in Navajo. Built in a huge amphitheater-like alcove in the canyon wall, Betatakin was occupied only from 1250 to 1300 and may have housed 125 people. A 1-mile round-trip paved trail from the visitor center leads to overlooks of Betatakin. The strenuous 5-mile round-trip hike to Betatakin itself is led by a ranger, takes 3 to 5 hours, and involves descending more than 600 feet to the floor of Tsegi Canyon and later returning to the rim. Between late May and early September, these guided hikes are offered twice a day and leave the visitor center at 8:15 and 11am (MST, not Navajo Reservation time). Other months, tours leave weekends at 10am, but call to make sure the tour will be going out. These hikes are offered on a first-come, first-served basis. All participants should carry 1 to 2 quarts of water. This is a fascinating hike, and because the number of hikers is limited, you won't feel like you're shoulder to shoulder with a herd of tourists.

Keet Seel ⊛, which means "broken pieces of pottery" in Navajo, has a much longer history than Betatakin, with occupation beginning as early as A.D. 950 and continuing until 1300. At one point, Keet Seel may have housed 150 people. The 17-mile round-trip hike is quite strenuous. During the summer, hikers usually stay overnight at a primitive campground near the ruins, but in the winter, the hike is done as a day hike. You must carry enough water for your trip—up to 2 gallons in summer—because none is available along the trail. These hikes are offered daily between Memorial Day and Labor Day. You can apply for a permit 6 months in advance.

WHERE TO STAY

There is no lodge at the national monument, but there are two free campgrounds that have a total of 48 campsites. One is open year-round, and one is open April through September. The nearest reliable motels are 30 miles away in Kayenta. See the section on Monument Valley, below, for details.

11 Monument Valley Navajo Tribal Park ⊛⊛⊛

60 miles NE of Navajo National Monument; 110 miles NW of Canyon de Chelly; 200 miles NE of Flagstaff; 150 miles E of Page

In its role as sculptor, nature has, in the north central part of the Navajo Reservation, created a garden of monoliths and spires unequaled anywhere on earth. Whether you've ever been here or not, you've almost certainly seen Monument Valley before. This otherworldly landscape has been an object of fascination for years, and since Hollywood director John Ford first came here in the 1930s, it has served as backdrop for countless movies, TV shows, and commercials.

Located 30 miles north of Kayenta and straddling the Arizona-Utah state line (you actually go into Utah to get to the park entrance), Monument Valley is a vast flat plain punctuated by natural sandstone cathedrals. These huge monoliths rise up from the sagebrush with sheer walls that capture the light of the rising and setting sun and transform it into fiery hues. Evocative names including the Mittens, Three Sisters, Camel Butte, Elephant Butte, the Thumb, and Totem Pole reflect the shapes the sandstone has taken under the erosive forces of nature.

While it may at first seem as if this strange landscape is a barren wasteland, it is actually still home to a few hardy Navajo families. The Navajo have been living in the valley for generations, herding their sheep through the sagebrush scrublands, and some families continue to reside here today. In fact, human habitation in Monument Valley dates back hundreds of years. Within the park are more than 100 Ancestral Puebloan archaeological sites, ruins, and petroglyphs dating from before 1300.

ESSENTIALS

GETTING THERE   Monument Valley Navajo Tribal Park is 200 miles northeast of Flagstaff. Take US 89 north to US 160 to Kayenta, which is 23 miles south of Monument Valley and 29 miles east of Navajo National Monument. Then drive north on US 163.

FEES   Admission to the park is $5 per person (free for children 9 and under). *Note:* Because this is a tribal park and not a federal park, America the Beautiful passes are not valid here.

VISITOR INFORMATION   For information, contact **Monument Valley Navajo Tribal Park** (© 435/727-5874 or 435/727-5870; www.navajonationparks.org). May through September, the park is open daily from 6am to 8pm; between October and April, it's open daily from 8am to 5pm. The park is closed on Christmas and is open only from 8am to noon on Thanksgiving.

EXPLORING THE PARK

This is big country and, like the Grand Canyon, is primarily a point-and-shoot experience for most visitors. Because this is reservation land and people still live in Monument Valley, most backcountry and off-road travel are prohibited unless you're with a licensed guide. So basically, with one exception, your options for seeing the park are limited. You can take a few pictures from the overlook at the visitor center, drive the park's Valley Drive (a scenic but very rough 17-mile dirt road), take a jeep or van tour, or go on a guided hike or horseback ride. At the visitor center, you'll find a small museum, a great gift shop, and a restaurant with a knockout view. Adjacent to the visitor center is a campground, and a picnic area is a quarter-mile away.

Although Valley Drive is best driven in a high-clearance vehicle, plenty of people drive the loop in rental cars and other standard passenger vehicles. Take it slow, and you should do fine. However, if the first stretch of rocky, rutted road convinces you to change your mind about the drive, just return to the visitor center and book a jeep or van tour and let someone else pay the repair bills. Along the loop drive, you'll pass 11 very scenic viewpoints that provide ample opportunities for photographing the valley's many natural monuments. At many of these viewpoints, you'll also encounter

---

⌒Moments Monumental Sunsets

Be sure to save some film on your camera (or storage space in your digital camera) for sunset at Monument Valley. Sure these rocks are impressive at noon, but as the sun sets and the shadows lengthen, they are positively enchanting—one of the most spectacular sites in America.

Navajos selling jewelry and other crafts. At John Ford's Point, so named because it was a favorite shooting location for film director John Ford, you may even get the chance to photograph a Navajo on horseback posed in front of all that spectacular scenery. He'll expect a dollar.

Tip: If you're trying to decide whether to take a tour, here's some little-publicized information that might help you with your decision. Most tours don't just drive the 17-mile loop; they go off into a part of the valley that is closed to anyone who is not on a tour. This part of the valley is, in our opinion, the most beautiful. You'll get close-up looks at several natural arches and stop at some beautiful petroglyphs. Before booking a tour, make sure that the tour will go to this "closed" section of the valley. There are always plenty of jeep tour companies waiting for business in the park's main parking lot. If you've managed to get a room at Goulding's Lodge, which is our favorite hotel in the area and should be your first choice, then your best bet is to go out with **Goulding's Tours** (© 435/727-3231; www.gouldings.com), which has its office right at the lodge (see "Where to Stay & Dine," below), just a few miles from the park entrance. Goulding's offers 3½-hour tours ($42 for adults, $27 for children under 8) and full-day tours ($75 for adults, $57 for children). **Monument Valley Simpson's Trailhandler Tours** (© 435/727-3362; www.trailhandlertours.com), which charges $40 for a 2½-hour tour, is another reliable company to try, as is **Sacred Monument Tours** (© 435/727-3218 or 928/380-4527; www.monumentvalley.net), which charges $46 for a 2-hour jeep tour and $82 for a 4-hour sunrise or sunset tour.

The traditional way to explore this quintessentially Wild West landscape, however, is from the back of a horse, a la John Wayne. We recommend going out with **Diné Trail Ride Tours** (© 435/419-0135 or 928/697-3776), which starts its rides from John Ford's Point, about halfway around Valley Drive. Trail rides range in price from $35 for a half-hour ride to $95 for a half-day ride. Alternatively, try **Sacred Monument Tours** (© 435/727-3218 or 928/380-4527; www.monumentvalley.net), which charges from $50 for a 1-hour horseback ride up to $290 for an all-day ride.

Because the jeep and van tours are such a big business here, there's a steady stream of the vehicles on Valley Drive throughout the day. One way to get away from the rumble of engines is to go out on a guided hike. These are offered by **Sacred Monument Tours** (© 435/727-3218 or 928/380-4527; www.monumentvalley.net), which charges between $57 and $165 per person for hikes of different lengths. **Kéyah Hózhóní Tours** (© 928/309-7440; www.monumentvalley.com) also offers hiking tours and overnight camping trips; call for rates. Keep in mind that summers can be very hot here.

The exception to the no-traveling-off-road rule is the 3.25-mile **Wildcat Trail** 𝖆𝖆, a loop trail that circles West Mitten Butte and provides the only opportunity to get close to this picturesque butte. As you circle the butte, you'll get all kinds of different perspectives, even one that completely eliminates the "thumb." Because this is the park's only option for unguided hiking, it is a not-to-be-missed excursion and one of the most memorable hikes in the state. In summer, be sure to carry plenty of water.

ACTIVITIES OUTSIDE THE PARK

Before leaving the area, you might want to visit **Goulding's Museum & Trading Post,** at Goulding's Lodge (see "Where to Stay & Dine," below). This old trading post was the home of the Gouldings for many years and is set up as they had it back in the 1920s and 1930s. There are also displays about the many movies that have been shot here. The trading post hours vary with the seasons; admission is by $2 suggested donation.

Inside Kayenta's Burger King, which is next door to the Hampton Inn, there's an interesting exhibit on the Navajo code talkers of World War II. The code talkers were Navajo soldiers who used their own language to transmit military messages, primarily in the South Pacific.

WHERE TO STAY & DINE

In addition to the lodgings listed here, you'll find several budget motels north of Monument Valley in the Utah towns of Mexican Hat and Bluff. When it's time for a meal, try the View Restaurant, which is in the park's visitor center and more than lives up to its name. Alternatively, try the Stagecoach Dining Room at Goulding's. The Navajo steak, served atop fry bread, is great! If you need a latte to get you on down the road, stop by **Shepherd's Eyes** (© **928/697-3368**), an espresso bar and Internet cafe ¼ mile west of the junction of US 160 and US 163. This cafe also serves Navajo tea, which is made from a wild plant that grows in the area.

Best Western Wetherill Inn   Located in Kayenta a mile north of the junction of US 160 and US 163, and 20 miles south of Monument Valley, the Wetherill Inn offers neither the convenience of Goulding's Lodge nor the amenities of the nearby Holiday Inn or Hampton Inn. The rooms, however, are comfortable enough. A cafe next door serves Navajo and American food.

1000 Main St. (P.O. Box 175), Kayenta, AZ 86033. © **800/780-7234** or 928/697-3231. Fax 928/697-3233. www.best western.com/wetherillinn. 54 units. May 1–Oct 15 $125–$135 double; Oct 16–Nov 15 and Apr $80–$85 double; Nov 16–Mar 31 $65–$70 double. Children 12 and under stay free in parent's room. Rates include continental breakfast. AE, DC, DISC, MC, V. **Amenities:** Indoor pool; tour desk. *In room:* A/C, TV, dataport, coffeemaker, hair dryer, iron, free local calls.

Goulding's Lodge ☽   This is the only lodge actually located in Monument Valley and should be your first hotel choice in the area. Because this is the most popular hotel in the area, be sure to make your reservation well in advance. Goulding's offers superb views from the private balconies of its large guest rooms. The restaurant serves Navajo and American dishes, and its views are enough to make any meal an event. Unfortunately, although the setting is memorable, the service can be somewhat lacking. The lodge also has a museum and a video library that includes a few films that have been shot in Monument Valley.

P.O. Box 360001, Monument Valley, UT 84536. © **435/727-3231**. Fax 435/727-3344. www.gouldings.com. 62 units. Mar 15–Nov 15 $123–$175 double; Nov 16–Mar 14 $73–$83 double. Children 8 and under stay free in parent's room. AE, DC, DISC, MC, V. Pets accepted ($10 fee). **Amenities:** Restaurant (American/Navajo); indoor pool; exercise room; tour desk; coin-op laundry; grocery store; gas station. *In room:* A/C, TV/DVD, dataport, fridge, coffeemaker, hair dryer, iron, high-speed Internet access, Wi-Fi, free local calls.

Hampton Inn–Navajo Nation   In the center of Kayenta, this is the newest lodging in the area and, as such, should be your second choice after Goulding's. The hotel is built in a modern Santa Fe style and has spacious, comfortable guest rooms. It's adjacent to the Navajo Cultural Center and a Burger King that has an interesting display on the Navajo code talkers of World War II.

US 160 (P.O. Box 1219), Kayenta, AZ 86033. © 800/426-7866 or 928/697-3170. Fax 928/697-3189. www.hampton-inn.com. 73 units. $64–$137 double. Rates include continental breakfast. Children under 18 stay free in parent's room. AE, DC, DISC, MC, V. Pets accepted ($20 nonrefundable deposit). **Amenities:** Restaurant (American/Navajo); small outdoor pool; room service; coin-op laundry. In room: A/C, TV, dataport, coffeemaker, hair dryer, iron, high-speed Internet access.

Holiday Inn–Kayenta   This Holiday Inn, right in the center of Kayenta, is very popular with tour groups and is almost always crowded. Although the grounds are dusty and a bit run-down, the rooms are spacious and clean. We like the poolside units best. Part of the hotel's dining room is designed to look like an Ancestral Puebloan ruin, and the menu offers both American and Navajo cuisine.

US 160 and US 163 (P.O. Box 307), Kayenta, AZ 86033. © 888/465-4329 or 928/697-3221. Fax 928/697-3349. www.holiday-inn.com. 163 units. Nov–Apr $69–$999 double, $89–$119 suite; May–June $119–$149 double, $149–$179 suite; July–Oct $139–$169 double, $179–$209 suite. Children 18 and under stay free in parent's room; children 12 and under eat free. AE, DC, DISC, MC, V. **Amenities:** Restaurant (American/Navajo); small outdoor pool; exercise room; room service; coin-op laundry. In room: A/C, TV, dataport, coffeemaker, hair dryer, iron, high-speed Internet access.

CAMPGROUNDS

If you're headed to Monument Valley Navajo Tribal Park, you can camp in the park at the **Mitten View Campground** (© **435/727-5874** or 435/727-5870), which has 99 sites and charges $10 per night from April to September ($5 per night the rest of the year, when there are no facilities or running water). Another option, just outside the park, is **Goulding's Campground** (© **435/727-3231;** www.gouldings.com), which charges $22 to $36 per night. There are also small cabins that go for $69 per night. This campground is open year-round (limited services Nov to mid-Mar) and has an indoor pool, hot showers, a playground, and a coin-op laundry.

12 Lake Powell ⟨★⟨★ & Page

272 miles N of Phoenix; 130 miles E of Grand Canyon North Rim; 130 miles NE of Grand Canyon South Rim

Had the early Spanish explorers of Arizona suddenly come upon Lake Powell after traipsing for months across desolate desert, they would have either taken it for a mirage or fallen to their knees and rejoiced. Imagine the Grand Canyon filled with water, and you have a pretty good picture of Lake Powell. Surrounded by hundreds of miles of parched desert, this reservoir, created by the damming of the Colorado River at Glen Canyon, seems unreal when first glimpsed. Yet real it is, and it draws everyone in the region toward its promise of relief from the heat.

Construction of the Glen Canyon Dam came about despite the angry outcry of many who felt that this canyon was even more beautiful than the Grand Canyon and should be preserved in its natural state. Preservationists lost the battle, and construction of the dam began in 1960, with completion in 1963. It took another 17 years for Lake Powell to fill to capacity. Today, the lake is a watery powerboat playground, and houseboats and water-skiers cruise where birds and waterfalls once filled the canyon with their songs and sounds. These days most people seem to agree, though, that Lake Powell is as amazing a sight as the Grand Canyon, and it draws almost as many visitors each year as its downriver neighbor. In the past few years, however, Lake Powell has lost some of its luster as a prolonged drought in the Southwest has left the lake's

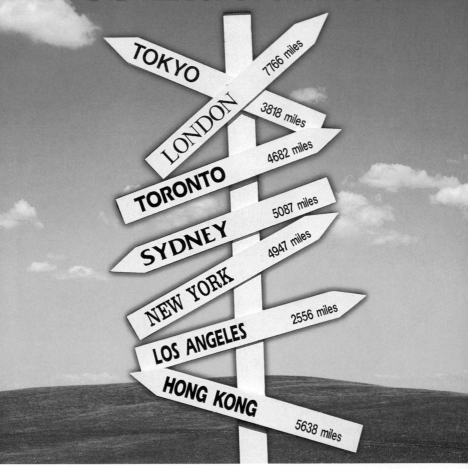

water level down by roughly 100 feet. Although this has left a bathtub-ring effect on the shores of the lake, it has also exposed wide expanses of beach in the Wahweap area.

While Lake Powell is something of a man-made wonder of the world, one of the natural wonders of the world—Rainbow Bridge—can also be found on the shores of the lake. Called *nonnozhoshi,* or "the rainbow turned to stone," by the Navajo, this is the largest natural bridge on Earth and stretches 275 feet across a side canyon off Lake Powell.

The town of Page, originally a camp constructed to house the workers who built the dam, has many motels and restaurants, and is the main base for many visitors who come to explore Lake Powell.

ESSENTIALS

GETTING THERE   Page is connected to Flagstaff by US 89. Arizona 98 leads southeast onto the Navajo Indian Reservation and connects with US 160 to Kayenta and Four Corners. The Page Airport is served by **Great Lakes Airlines** (© **800/554-5111** or 307/433-2899; www.greatlakesav.com), which flies from Phoenix. Round-trip airfares start around $200.

FEES   Admission to Glen Canyon National Recreation Area is $15 per car (good for 1 week). There is also a $16-per-week boat fee if you bring your own boat.

VISITOR INFORMATION   For further information on the Lake Powell area, contact the **Glen Canyon National Recreation Area** (© **928/608-6404;** www.nps.gov/glca); the **Page-Lake Powell Chamber of Commerce,** 608 Elm St., Page (© **888/261-7243** or 928/645-2741; www.pagelakepowellchamber.org); or the **John Wesley Powell Memorial Museum,** 6 N. Lake Powell Blvd., Page (© **888/597-6873** or 928/645-9496; www.powellmuseum.org). You can also go to www.powellguide.com.

GETTING AROUND   Rental cars are available at the Page Airport from **Avis** (© **800/331-1212** or 928/645-2024).

GLEN CANYON NATIONAL RECREATION AREA

Until the flooding of Glen Canyon formed Lake Powell, this area was one of the most remote regions in the contiguous 48 states. However, since the construction of Glen Canyon Dam at a spot where the canyon of the Colorado River was less than a third of a mile wide, this remote and rugged landscape has become one of the country's most popular national recreation areas. Today, the lake and much of the surrounding land is designated the Glen Canyon National Recreation Area and attracts around two million visitors each year. The otherworldly setting amid the slickrock canyons of northern Arizona and southern Utah is a tapestry of colors, the blues and greens of the lake contrasting with the reds and oranges of the surrounding sandstone cliffs. This interplay of colors and vast desert landscapes easily makes Lake Powell the most beautiful of Arizona's many reservoirs.

Built to provide water for the desert communities of the Southwest and West, **Glen Canyon Dam** stands 710 feet above the bedrock and contains almost 5 million cubic yards of concrete. The dam also provides hydroelectric power, and deep within its massive wall of concrete are huge power turbines. Although most Lake Powell visitors are more interested in water-skiing and powerboating than they are in drinking water and power production, there would be no lake without the dam, so any visit to this area ought to start at the **Carl Hayden Visitor Center** (© **928/608-6404**), which is located beside the dam on US 89 just north of Page. Here you can tour the dam and learn about its construction. Between mid-May and mid-September, the visitor center is open daily from 8am to 6pm; December to February, it's open daily 8am to 4pm; other months, it's open daily 8am to 5pm.

More than 500 feet deep in some places, and bounded by nearly 2,000 miles of shoreline, **Lake Powell** is a maze of convoluted canyons where rock walls often rise hundreds of feet straight out of the water. In places, the long, winding canyons are so narrow there isn't even room to turn a motorboat around. The only way to truly appreciate this lake is from a boat, whether a houseboat, a runabout, or a sea kayak. Water-skiing, riding personal watercrafts, and fishing have long been the most popular on-water activities, and consequently, you'll be hard-pressed to find a quiet corner of the lake if you happen to be a solitude-seeking sea kayaker. However, with so many miles of shoreline, you're bound to find someplace to get away from it all.

In addition to the Carl Hayden Visitor Center mentioned above, there's the **Bullfrog Visitor Center,** in Bullfrog, Utah (© **435/684-7423**). In April, it's open intermittently from 8am to 5pm; May through Labor Day, it's open daily from 8am to 5pm (closed Labor Day–Mar).

BOAT & AIR TOURS

There are few roads penetrating the Glen Canyon National Recreation Area, so the best way to appreciate this rugged region is by boat. If you don't have your own boat, you can at least see a small part of the lake on a boat tour. A variety of tours depart from **Wahweap Marina** (© **800/528-6154** or 928/645-2433; www.lakepowell.com). The **Canyon Princess** does a 1-hour tour ($14 for adults, $11 for children) that, unfortunately, doesn't really show you much more of the lake than you can see from shore. The *Canyon Princess* also offers sunset dinner cruises ($65). A better choice for those with limited time or finances would be the **Antelope Canyon Cruise** ($35 for adults, $28 for children). To see more of the lake, opt for the full-day tour to Rainbow Bridge (see below for details).

The Glen Canyon National Recreation Area covers an immense area, much of it only partially accessible by boat. If you'd like to see more of the area than is visible from car or boat, consider taking an air tour with **Westwind Scenic Air Tours** (© **800/245-8668** or 928/645-2494; www.westwindairservice.com), which offers several tours of northern Arizona and southern Utah, including flights over Rainbow Bridge and Monument Valley. Sample rates are $138 for a 35- to 45-minute flight over Rainbow Bridge ($124 for children 16 and under) and $245 for a 75-minute flight over Monument Valley ($221 for children). There are also tours that include a 2-hour jeep tour at Monument Valley. These tours are $280 for adults and $252 for children.

RAINBOW BRIDGE NATIONAL MONUMENT

Roughly 40 miles up Lake Powell from Wahweap Marina and Glen Canyon Dam, in a narrow side canyon of the lake, rises **Rainbow Bridge** ✦✦✦, the world's largest natural bridge and one of the most spectacular sights in the Southwest. Preserved in Rainbow Bridge National Monument, this natural arch of sandstone stands 290 feet high and spans 275 feet. Carved by wind and water over the ages, Rainbow Bridge is an awesome reminder of the powers of erosion that have sculpted this entire region into the spectacle it is today.

Rainbow Bridge is accessible only by boat or on foot (a hike of 14 miles minimum), and, of course, going by boat is by far the more popular method. **Lake Powell Resorts and Marinas** (© **800/528-6154** or 928/645-2433; www.lakepowell.com) offers full-day tours ($116 for adults, $81 for children) that not only get you to Rainbow Bridge in comfort, but also cruise through some of the most spectacular scenery on earth. Tours include a box lunch and a bit more exploring after visiting Rainbow Bridge. Currently, because the lake's water level is so low from years of drought, the boat must stop between 1 and 1¼ miles from Rainbow Bridge, so if you aren't able to walk this distance, you won't even be able to see the sandstone arch.

Rainbow Bridge National Monument (© 928/608-6200; www.nps.gov/rabr) is administered by Glen Canyon National Recreation Area. For information on hiking to Rainbow Bridge, contact the **Navajo Parks and Recreation Department, P.O.** Box 2520, Window Rock, AZ 86515 (© 928/871-6647; www.navajonationparks.org). The hike to Rainbow Bridge is about a 25-mile round-trip hike, should be done as an overnight backpacking trip, and requires a Navajo Nation permit. Permits are available through the Navajo Parks and Recreation Department, at the **Cameron Visitor Center** (© 928/679-2303), in the community of Cameron near the turnoff for the Grand Canyon, and at the **Antelope Canyon Park Office** (© 928/698-2808), 7 miles south of Page on Navajo Route 20 (beside the LeChee Chapter House).

ANTELOPE CANYON

If you've spent any time in Arizona, chances are you've noticed photos of a narrow sandstone canyon only a few feet wide. The walls of the canyon seem to glow with an inner light, and beams of sunlight slice the darkness of the deep slot canyon. Sound familiar? If you've seen such a photo, you were probably looking at Antelope Canyon (sometimes called Corkscrew Canyon). Located 2½ miles southeast of Page off Arizona 98 (at milepost 299), this photogenic canyon comprises the **Antelope Canyon Navajo Tribal Park** ✸✸✸ (© 928/698-2808), which is on the Navajo Indian Reservation and is divided into upper and lower canyons. The entry fee is $6 for adults, free for children 7 and under. April through October, Antelope Canyon is open daily from 8am to 5pm; November through March, hours vary and closures are common.

There are currently two options for visiting Antelope Canyon. The most convenient and reliable way is to take a 1½-hour tour with **Antelope Canyon Adventures** (© 866/645-5501 or 928/645-5501; www.jeeptour.com) or **Antelope Canyon Tours** (© 866/645-9102 or 928/645-9102; www.antelopecanyon.com), both of which charge $20 (plus Navajo permit fee) per adult for a basic tour. Photographic tours cost between $35 and $62. If you don't want to deal with crowds of tourists ogling the rocks and snapping pictures with their point-and-shoots, we recommend heading out with **Overland Canyon Tours** (© 928/608-4072; www.overlandcanyontours.com) to nearby Canyon X, which is much less visited than Antelope Canyon and is a good choice for serious photographers who want to avoid the crowds.

Alternatively, at both the upper and lower canyons, you'll find Navajo guides collecting park entry fees and fees for guide services. These guides charge $15 ($10 for children ages 6–12 at the lower section of the canyon). Upper Antelope Canyon is a short drive up a sandy stream bed from the highway, while Lower Antelope Canyon is a short walk from the parking area just off the highway. You'll get more out of your experience if you go on one of the guided tours mentioned above, but you'll save a little money by visiting the canyon on your own. For more information, contact **Antelope Canyon Navajo Tours** (© 928/698-3384; www.navajotours.com).

Just remember that if there is even the slightest chance of rain anywhere in the region, you should not venture into this canyon, which is subject to flash floods. In the past, people who have ignored bad weather predictions have been killed by such floods.

Fun Fact **So, What's with the Bathtub Ring?**
You'll notice that the red-rock cliff walls above the waters of Lake Powell are no longer red but are instead coated with what looks like a layer of white soap scum. Those are calcium carbonate deposits left on the rock over the past few years after a drought caused the lake level to drop more than 130 feet. Currently, the lake level is around 100 feet below what is known as full pool (when the reservoir is full).

WATERSPORTS

While simply exploring the lake's maze of canyons on a narrated tour is satisfying enough for many visitors, the most popular activities are houseboating, water-skiing, riding personal watercrafts, and fishing. Five marinas (only Wahweap is in Arizona) help boaters explore the lake. At the **Wahweap Marina** (② 800/528-6154 or 928/ 645-2433; www.lakepowell.com), you can rent powerboats, personal watercrafts, and water skis. Rates in summer range from about $330 to $473 per day, depending on the type of boat. Personal watercrafts go for $283 per day, and sea kayaks rent for $28 to $34 per day. For information on houseboats, see "Where to Stay," below.

If roaring engines aren't your speed, you might want to consider exploring Lake Powell by sea kayak. While afternoon winds can sometimes make paddling difficult, mornings are often quiet. With a narrow sea kayak, you can even explore canyons too small for powerboats. Rentals are available at **Twin Finn Diving,** 811 Vista Ave. (② 928/645-3114; www.twinfinn.com). Sea kayaks rent for $45 to $55 per day, and sit-on-top kayaks for $35 to $45. Multiday kayak tours are operated by **Hidden Canyon Kayak** (② 800/343-3121 or 928/645-8866; www.diamondriver.com/kayak), which charges $760 to $1,000 for 4- to 6-day trips. Guided kayak trips are also offered by **Kayak Powell** (② 888/854-7862; www.kayaklakepowell.com), which charges $85 for a half-day tour and $725 for a 4-day tour. Kayaks rent for $45 to $60 per day.

While most of Glen Canyon National Recreation Area consists of the impounded waters of Lake Powell, the recreation area also contains a short stretch of the Colorado River that still flows swift and free. If you'd like to see this stretch of river, try a float trip from Glen Canyon Dam to Lees Ferry, operated by **Colorado River Discovery** (② 888/522-6644; www.raftthecanyon.com) between March and November. Half-day trips cost $64 for adults and $54 for children ages 4 to 11. Try to reserve at least 2 weeks in advance.

If you have a boat (your own or a rental), avail yourself of some excellent year-round fishing. Smallmouth, largemouth, and striped bass, as well as walleye, catfish, crappie, and carp, are all plentiful. Because the lake lies within both Arizona and Utah, you'll need to know which state's waters you're fishing in whenever you cast your line out, and you'll need the appropriate license. (Be sure to pick up a copy of the Arizona and Utah state fishing regulations, or ask about applicable regulations at any of the marinas.) You can arrange licenses to fish the entire lake at **Lake Powell Resorts and Marinas** (② 928/645-2433), which also sells bait and tackle and can provide you with advice on fishing this massive reservoir. The best season is March through November, but walleye are most often caught during the cooler months. If you'd rather try your hand at catching enormous rainbow trout, try downstream of the Glen Canyon Dam, where cold waters provide ideal conditions for trophy trout. If you want a guide to take you where the fish are biting, contact Bill McBurney at **Ambassador Guide Service** (© **800/256-7596;** www.ambassadorguides.com).

If you're just looking for a good place for a swim near Lake Powell Resort, take the Coves Loop just west of the marina. Of the three coves, the third one, which has a sandy beach, is the best. The Chains area, another good place to jump off the rocks and otherwise lounge by the lake, is outside Page down a rough dirt road just before you reach Glen Canyon Dam. The view underwater at Lake Powell is as scenic as the view above it; to explore underwater, contact **Twin Finn Diving Center,** 811 Vista Ave. (© **928/645-3114;** www.twinfinn.com), which charges $45 a day for scuba gear.

OTHER OUTDOOR PURSUITS

If you're looking for a quick, easy hike with great views, head north on North Navajo Drive from downtown Page. At the end of this street is the main trail head for Page's **Rimview Trail.** This trail runs along the edge of Manson Mesa, upon which Page is built, and has views of Lake Powell and miles of red-rock country. The entire loop trail is 8 miles long, but if you want to do a shorter hike, we recommend the stretch of trail heading east (clockwise) from the trail head.

At Lees Ferry, a 39-mile drive from Page at the southern tip of the national recreation area, you'll find three short trails (Cathedral Wash, River, and Spencer). The 2-mile **Cathedral Wash Trail** is the most interesting of the three hikes and follows a dry wash through a narrow canyon with unusual rock formations. The trail head is at the second turnout after turning off US 89A. Be aware that this wash is subject to flash floods. The **River Trail** is a 2-mile round-trip hike along the river and starts at the boat ramp. The **Spencer Trail,** which begins along the River Trail, leads up to the top of a 1,700-foot cliff for spectacular views of Marble Canyon. Lees Ferry is also the southern trail head for famed **Paria Canyon** ⚑, a favorite of canyoneering backpackers. This trail is 38 to 47 miles long (depending on where you start) and follows the meandering route of a narrow slot canyon. Most hikers start from the northern trail head, which is in Utah on US 89. For more information on hiking in Paria Canyon, contact the **Arizona Strip Interpretive Association/Interagency Visitor Center,** 345 E. Riverside Dr., St. George, UT 84770 (© **435/688-3246;** www.az.blm.gov/asfo/asia.htm).

The 27-hole **Lake Powell National Golf Course** ⚑, 400 Clubhouse Dr. (© **928/645-2023;** www.golflakepowell.com), is one of the most spectacular in the state. The fairways wrap around the base of the red-sandstone bluff atop which sits the town of Page. The views stretch on forever, and in places, eroded sandstone walls come right down to the greens. Greens fees are $60.

OTHER AREA ATTRACTIONS

Between April and October, you can learn about Navajo culture at **Navajo Village Heritage Center** (© **928/660-0304;** www.navajo-village.com), a museum and living-history center on the northeast corner of Arizona 98 and Coppermine Road (on the south side of Page). Programs here include demonstrations by weavers, silversmiths, and other artisans. Prices range from $40 for a 2-hour tour ($30 for children) to $55 for a 4-hour tour ($40 for children). Both tours include dinner and traditional dances. Reservations are required. During the day, there are also 30-minute walk-through tours ($5). Although this is definitely a tourist attraction, you will come away with a better sense of Navajo culture.

John Wesley Powell Memorial Museum   In 1869, one-armed Civil War veteran John Wesley Powell and a small band of men spent more than 3 months fighting the rapids of the Green and Colorado rivers to become the first people to travel the length of the Grand Canyon. It is for this intrepid—some said crazy—adventurer that Lake Powell is named and to whom this small museum is dedicated. Besides documenting the Powell expedition with photographs, etchings, artifacts, and dioramas, the museum displays Native American artifacts ranging from Ancestral Puebloan pottery to contemporary Navajo and Hopi crafts. The museum also acts as an information center for Page, Lake Powell, and the surrounding region.

6 N. Lake Powell Blvd. © 888/597-6873 or 928/645-9496. www.powellmuseum.org. Admission $5 adults, $3 seniors, $1 children 5–12, free for children 4 and under. Mid-Feb to Nov Mon–Fri 9am–5pm (sometimes open on weekends in summer, but call to be sure). Closed Dec to mid-Feb.

WHERE TO STAY

HOUSEBOATS

Antelope Point Resort & Marina 🌟🌟 *Kids*   At this marina, you can rent some of the newest and most luxurious houseboats on the lake (the larger ones even have outdoor hot tubs). There are both 59-foot and 70-foot boats available, ranging in quality from deluxe to luxury. Speed boats ($295–$395 per day) and sea kayaks ($25 per day) can also be rented and are a great way to explore smaller waterways that your houseboat can't navigate. To reach the marina, head east out of Page on Arizona 98 and drive 5 miles to the signed Antelope Point Marina turnoff.

Antelope Point Marina, P.O. Box 4180, Page, AZ 86040. © 800/255-5561. Fax 480/998-7399. www.antelopepoint lakepowell.com. Early June to early Sept $7,494–$9,595 per week; lower rates other months. 3-, 4-, and 5-night rates also available. AE, DC, DISC, MC, V. *In room:* A/C, TV/DVD, kitchen, fridge, coffeemaker, no phone.

Lake Powell Resorts & Marinas 🌟 *Kids*   This is the original houseboat-rental operation on Lake Powell, and houseboats here range in size from 44 to 75 feet, sleep anywhere from 8 to 12 people, and come complete with showers and a fully equipped kitchen. The only things you really need to bring are bedding and towels. If you're coming in the summer, splurge on a boat with some sort of cooling system.

100 Lakeshore Dr., Page, AZ 86040. © 800/528-6154 or 602/278-8888. Fax 602/331-5258. www.lakepowell.com. Early June to late Sept $1,404–$11,545 per week; lower rates other months. 3-, 4-, 5-, and 6-night rates also available on most houseboats. AE, DISC, MC, V. Pets accepted. *In room:* Kitchen, fridge, no phone.

HOTELS & MOTELS

Best Western Arizonainn   Perched right at the edge of the mesa on which Page is built, this modern motel has a fine view across miles of desert, as do half of the guest rooms. The hotel's pool has a 100-mile view.

716 Rimview Dr., Page, AZ 86040. © 800/826-2718 or 928/645-2466. Fax 928/645-2053. www.bestwestern.com. 103 units. Mid-Apr to mid-May $79–$109 double; mid-May to mid-Oct $89–$109 double; mid-Oct to mid-Apr $49–$69 double. Rates include continental breakfast. Children under 18 stay free in parent's room. AE, DC, DISC, MC, V. Pets accepted ($10 fee). **Amenities:** Small outdoor pool; exercise room; Jacuzzi; courtesy airport shuttle; coin-op laundry; dry cleaning. *In room:* A/C, TV, dataport, coffeemaker, hair dryer, iron, high-speed Internet access, free local calls.

Courtyard by Marriott 🌟   Located at the foot of the mesa on which Page is built and adjacent to the Lake Powell National Golf Course, this is the top in-town choice. It's also the closest you'll come to a golf resort in this corner of the state. Although you'll pay a premium for views of the golf course or lake, it's a worthwhile investment. Guest rooms are larger than those at most area lodgings. Moderately priced meals are served in a casual restaurant that has a terrace overlooking the distant lake. The 18-hole golf course has great views of the surrounding landscape.

600 Clubhouse Dr. (P.O. Box 4150), Page, AZ 86040. ℂ 800/321-2211 or 928/645-5000. Fax 928/645-5004. www.courtyard.com. 153 units. $89–$149 double. Children under 18 stay free in parent's room. AE, DC, DISC, MC, V. **Amenities:** Restaurant (Southwestern/American); lounge; outdoor pool; 18-hole golf course; exercise room; Jacuzzi; room service; coin-op laundry; dry cleaning. *In room:* A/C, TV, dataport, coffeemaker, hair dryer, iron, high-speed Internet access, Wi-Fi.

Lake Powell Resort ✿   Simply because it is right on the lake, this hotel at the sprawling Wahweap Marina 5 miles north of Page should be your first lodging choice in the area. As the biggest and busiest hotel in the area, the Lake Powell Resort features many of the amenities and activities of a resort, but it is often overwhelmed by busloads of tour groups. Consequently, don't expect very good service. Guest rooms are arranged in several long two-story wings, and every unit has either a balcony or a patio. Half of the rooms have lake views; those in the west wing have the better vantage point, as the east wing overlooks a coal-fired power plant. The Rainbow Room (see "Where to Dine," below) offers fine dining. Because of all the tour groups that stay here, getting a reservation can be difficult.

100 Lakeshore Dr. (P.O. Box 1597), Page, AZ 86040. ℂ 800/528-6154 or 928/645-2433. Fax 928/645-1031. www. lakepowell.com. 348 units. May–Sept $119–$189 double, $217 suite; Oct–Apr $89–$139 double, $195 suite. Children under 18 stay free in parent's room. AE, DISC, MC, V. Pets accepted. **Amenities:** 2 restaurants (American/Southwestern, pizza); snack bar; lounge; 2 outdoor pools; exercise room; Jacuzzi; sauna; boat rentals; children's programs; tour desk; room service; coin-op laundry. *In room:* A/C, TV, fridge, coffeemaker, hair dryer, iron.

CAMPGROUNDS

There are campgrounds at **Wahweap** (ℂ **928/645-2433**) and **Lees Ferry** (ℂ **928/ 355-2320**) in Arizona, and at Bullfrog, Hite, and Halls Crossing in Utah. Some scrubby trees provide a bit of shade at the Wahweap site, but the wind and sun make this a rather bleak spot in summer. Nevertheless, because of the lake's popularity, these campgrounds stay packed for much of the year. Wahweap charges $19 to $34 per night and Lees Ferry charges $10; reservations are not accepted.

WHERE TO DINE

The Dam Bar & Grille AMERICAN   This theme restaurant is a warehouse-size space designed to conjure up images of the interior of Glen Canyon Dam. Inside, cement walls, hard hats, and a big transformer that sends out bolts of neon "electricity" will put you in a "dam" good mood. Sandwiches, pastas, and steaks dominate the menu, but the rotisserie chicken is our favorite dish. The lounge area is a popular local hangout, and next door is the affiliated Gunsmoke Saloon nightclub.

644 N. Navajo Dr. ℂ 928/645-2161. www.damplaza.com. Reservations recommended in summer. Main courses $7–$23. AE, DISC, MC, V. Mon–Sat 10am–10pm; Sun 4–10pm.

Rainbow Room AMERICAN/SOUTHWESTERN   With sweeping vistas of Lake Powell through the walls of glass, the Rainbow Room is both Page's top restaurant and its most touristy. Be prepared for a wait; this place regularly feeds busloads of tourists. The menu is short but usually includes a few dishes with Southwestern flavor.

At Lake Powell Resort, 100 Lakeshore Dr. ℂ 928/645-1162. Reservations recommended. Main courses $7–$15 lunch, $16–$26 dinner. AE, DISC, MC, V. Daily 6am–2pm and 5–9pm.

13 Farmington & Aztec: New Mexico's Four Corners Gateways

Farmington has historic and outdoor finds that can keep you occupied for at least a day or two. A town of 36,500 residents, it sits at the junction of the San Juan, Animas, and La Plata rivers. Adorned with arched globe willow trees, it's a lush place by New Mexico standards. A system of five parks along the San Juan River and its tributaries is its pride and joy. What's most notable for us, however, is the quaint downtown area, where century-old buildings still house thriving businesses and some trading posts with great prices. It's also an industrial center (coal, oil, natural gas, and hydroelectricity) and a shopping center for people within a 100-mile radius.

For visitors, Farmington is a takeoff point for explorations of the Navajo Reservation and Chaco Culture National Historical Park. For outdoor lovers, it's the spot to head for the Bisti/De-Na-Zin Wilderness, world-class fly-fishing on the San Juan River, lovely scenery at the Angel Peak Recreation Area, and even a trip up to Durango to enjoy some rafting, kayaking, skiing, and mountain biking. The nearby towns of Aztec and Bloomfield offer a variety of attractions as well.

ESSENTIALS

GETTING THERE   From Albuquerque, take US 550 (through Cuba) from the I-25 Bernalillo exit, then head west on US 64 at Bloomfield (45 min.). From Gallup, take US 491 north to Shiprock, and then head east on US 64 (2¼ hr.). From Taos, follow US 64 all the way (4½ hr.). From Durango, Colorado, take US 500 south (1 hr.).

All commercial flights arrive at busy **Four Corners Regional Airport** on West Navajo Drive (✆ **505/599-1395**). The principal carrier is **US Airways** (✆ **800/235-9292**).

Car-rental agencies at Four Corners Regional Airport include **Avis** (✆ **800/331-1212** or 505/327-9864), **Budget** (✆ **505/327-7304**), and **Hertz** (✆ **800/654-3131** or 505/327-6093).

VISITOR INFORMATION   The **Farmington Convention and Visitors Bureau,** 3041 E. Main St. (✆ **800/448-1240** or 505/326-7602; www.farmingtonnm.org), is the clearinghouse for tourist information for the Four Corners region. For more information, contact the **Farmington Chamber of Commerce,** 100 W. Broadway (✆ **505/325-0279;** www.gofarmington.com).

SEEING THE SIGHTS
IN FARMINGTON

Farmington Museum and Gateway Center   Small-town museums can be completely precious, and this one and its neighbor in Aztec (see below) typify a tiny part of the world, but the truths they reveal span continents. Here you get to see the everyday struggle of a people to support themselves within a fairly inhospitable part of the world, spanning boom and bust years of agriculture, oil and gas production, and tourism. Located in the slick Gateway Visitor Center, the museum's exhibits vary, utilizing over 7,000 objects. Excellent changing exhibits rotate through as well. While at the Gateway Center, ask about other local exhibits in other parts of the city, such as the Harvest Grove Farm and Orchards, the E3 Children's Museum and Science Center, and the Riverside Nature Center, all at Animas Park. A gift shop sells fun local art and some nice New Mexico–made treats.

3041 E. Main St. ✆ **505/599-1174.** Fax 505/326-7572. www.farmingtonmuseum.org. Free admission. Mon–Sat 8am–5pm.

IN NEARBY AZTEC

VISITOR INFORMATION   The **Aztec Chamber of Commerce,** 110 N. Ash St. (✆ **505/334-9551;** www.aztecchamber.com), is a friendly place with a wealth of information about the area.

Aztec Museum and Pioneer Village *(Kids)*   A real treat for kids, this museum and village transport visitors back a full century to a place populated by strangely ubiquitous mannequins. The museum is crammed with memorabilia, but the outer exhibit of replicas and real buildings, with all the trimmings, is what will hold interest. You'll walk through the actual 1912 Aztec jail—nowhere you'd want to live—into the sheriff's office, where a stuffed Andy of Mayberry look-alike is strangely lethargic. The blacksmith shop has an anvil and lots of dusty, uncomfortable-looking saddles, even some oddly shaped burro shoes. The Citizens Bank has a lovely oak cage and counter, and it's run by attentive mannequin women. You'll see an authentic 1906 church and a schoolhouse where mannequins Dick and Jane lead a possibly heated discussion.

125 N. Main Ave., Aztec. (C) 505/334-9829. www.aztecnm.com/museum/museum_index.htm. Admission $3 adults, $1 children 11–17, free for children 10 and under. Summer Mon–Sat 9am–5pm; winter Mon–Sat 10am–4pm.

Salmon Ruins *(R)* *(Kids)*   What really distinguishes the 150 rooms of these ruins, 11 miles west of Farmington near Bloomfield, is their setting on a hillside, surrounded by lush San Juan River bosque. You'll begin in the museum, though, where a number of informative displays range from one showing the variety of ancestral Puebloan vessels, from pitchers to canteens to wild plants. Like the ruins at Aztec, two strong architectural influences are visible here. First the Chacoan, who built the village around the 11th century, with walls of an intricate rubble-filled core with sandstone veneer. The more simple Mesa Verde masonry was added in the 13th century. A trail guide will lead you to each site.

Built in 1990, **Heritage Park,** on an adjoining plot of land, comprises a series of reconstructed ancient and historic dwellings representing the area's cultures, from a paleoarchaic sand-dune site to an Anasazi pit house, from Apache wickiups and tepees to Navajo hogans, and an original pioneer homestead. Visitors are encouraged to enter the re-creations.

In the visitor center, you'll find a gift shop and a scholarly research library.

6131 US 64 (P.O. Box 125), Bloomfield, NM 87413. (C) 505/632-2013. Fax 505/632-8633. www.salmonruins.com. Admission $3 adults, $1 children 6–16, $2 seniors, free for children under 6. Summer Mon–Fri 8am–5pm, Sat–Sun 9am–5pm; winter Mon–Fri 8am–5pm, Sat 9am–5pm, and Sun noon–5pm.

AZTEC RUINS NATIONAL MONUMENT *(R)*

These ruins offer an exciting and rare glimpse of a restored kiva, which visitors can enter and sit within, sensing the site's ancient history. The ruins of this 450-room Native American pueblo, left by the ancestral Puebloans 7 centuries ago, are 14 miles northeast of Farmington, in the town of Aztec on the Animas River. Early Anglo settlers, convinced that the ruins were of Aztec origin, misnamed the site. Despite the fact that this pueblo was built long before the Aztecs of central Mexico lived, the name persisted.

The influence of the Chaco culture is strong at Aztec, evidenced in the preplanned architecture, the open plaza, and the fine stone masonry in the old walls. But a later occupation shows the influence of Mesa Verde (which flourished 1200–75). This second group of settlers remodeled the old pueblo and built others nearby, using techniques less elaborate and decorative than those of the Chacoans. Aztec Ruins is best known for its Great Kiva, the only completely reconstructed Anasazi great kiva in existence. Visiting Aztec Ruins National Monument will take you approximately 1 hour, even if you take the .25-mile self-guided trail and spend some time in the visitor center, which displays some outstanding examples of Anasazi ceramics and basketry. Add another half-hour if you plan to watch the video that imaginatively documents the history of native cultures in the area.

ESSENTIALS

GETTING THERE   Aztec Ruins is approximately a half-mile north of US 550 on Ruins Road (C.R. 2900) on the north edge of the city of Aztec. The Ruins Road is the first street immediately west of the Animas River Bridge on Highway 516 in Aztec.

VISITOR INFORMATION   For more information, contact **Aztec Ruins National Monument,** 84 C.R. 2900, Aztec, NM 87410-0640 (© **505/334-6174,** ext. 30; www.nps.gov/azru).

ADMISSION FEES & HOURS   Admission is $5 for adults; children under 17 are admitted free. The monument is open daily from 8am to 6pm Memorial Day through Labor Day and 8am to 5pm the rest of the year; it's closed Thanksgiving, Christmas, and New Year's Day.

CAMPING

Camping is not permitted at the monument. Nearby, **Bloomfield KOA,** on Blanco Boulevard (© **800/562-8513** or 505/632-8339; www.koa.com), offers 83 sites, 73 full hookups, tenting, cabins, laundry and grocery facilities, picnic tables, grills, and firewood. The recreation room/area has coin games, a heated swimming pool, a basketball hoop, a playground, horseshoes, volleyball, and a hot tub.

Camping is also available at **Navajo Lake State Park** (© **505/632-2278**).

SHOPPING

Downtown Farmington shops are generally open from 10am to 6pm Monday through Saturday. Native American arts and crafts are best purchased at trading posts, either downtown on Main or Broadway streets, or west of Farmington on US 64 toward Shiprock. You may want to check out the following stores: **Bob French Navajo Rugs,** on US 64 18 miles west of Farmington (© **505/598-5621**), sells silver and turquoise jewelry and a range of antique and new rugs. **Hogback Trading Company,** 3221 US 64, Waterflow, 17 miles west of Farmington (© **505/598-5154**), has large displays of Indian jewelry, rugs, and folk art. And **Navajo Trading Company,** 126 E. Main St. (© **505/325-1685**), is an actual pawnshop, with lots of exquisite old jewelry. You can peruse bracelets and necklaces while listening to clerks speaking Navajo.

GETTING OUTSIDE: NEARBY PARKS & RECREATION AREAS
SHIPROCK PEAK

This distinctive landmark, on the Navajo Indian Reservation southwest of Shiprock, 29 miles west of Farmington via US 64, is known to the Navajo as *Tse bidá hi,* "Rock

---

Northwestern New Mexico through Artists' Eyes

Farmington's lush green fields and (mostly) mild climate are attracting more and more artists. A great place to sample some of the lively work is **Artifacts Gallery,** 302 E. Main St. (© **505/327-2907**). Set in a Victorian-style lumber building is a collection of art studios whose artists are often on hand to discuss their work. Look for the moody landscapes and still-life watercolors by Dwight Lawing, the whimsical ceramic plaques and masks of Mary Bruce, and contemporary landscapes by Allison Verlinich. Also on hand is a specialty-foods shop, where you can purchase such treats as Cibolo Junction Green Chile Pineapple Preserves or Besito Caliente Blackberry Habanero Marinade/Dipping Sauce.

with wings." Composed of igneous rock flanked by long upright walls of solidified lava, it rises 1,700 feet off the desert floor to an elevation of 7,178 feet. There are scenic viewing points off US 491, 6 to 7 miles south of the town of Shiprock. You can get closer by taking the tribal road to the community of Red Rock, but you must have permission to get any nearer to this sacred Navajo rock. Climbing is not permitted.

The town named after the rock is a gateway to the Navajo reservation and the Four Corners region. There's a tribal visitor center here.

From Shiprock, you may want to make the 32-mile drive west on US 64 to Teec Nos Pos, Arizona, and then north on US 160, to the **Four Corners Monument.** A concrete slab here sits astride the only point in the United States where four states meet: New Mexico, Colorado, Utah, and Arizona. Kids especially like the idea of standing at the center and occupying four states at once. There's no view here, but vendors sell crafts and food. Some people find a visit here not worth the trip or cost. For information, call © **928/871-6647.** The monument is open daily 7am to 7pm Memorial Day to Labor Day and 8am to 5pm the rest of the year. The cost is $3 per person for adults and $2 for kids under 7.

NAVAJO LAKE STATE PARK

The **San Juan River, Pine River,** and **Sims Mesa recreation sites,** all with camping, fishing, and boating, make this the most popular watersports destination for residents of northwestern New Mexico. Trout, northern pike, largemouth bass, and catfish are caught in lake and river waters, and the surrounding hills attract hunters seeking deer and elk. A visitor center at Pine River Recreation Area has interpretive displays on natural history and on the construction and purposes of the dam.

Navajo Lake, with an area of 15,000 acres, extends from the confluence of the San Juan and Los Pinos rivers 25 miles north into Colorado. Navajo Dam, an earthen embankment, is three-quarters of a mile long and 400 feet high. It provides Farmington-area cities, industries, and farms with their principal water supply. It's also the main storage reservoir for the Navajo Indian Irrigation Project, designed to irrigate 110,000 acres.

Anglers come from all over the world to fish the San Juan below the dam, a pastoral spot bordered by green hills, where golden light reflects off the water. Much of the water, designated "catch and release," is teeming with rainbow, brown, and cutthroat trout. Experts will be heartily challenged by these fish that are attuned to the best tricks, while amateurs may want to hire a guide. For more information, see "Fishing," in chapter 4. The park is 40 miles east of Farmington on NM 511. For more information, call © **505/632-2278.**

Not far from the park, **Wines of the San Juan,** 233 New Mexico 511 at Turley (© **505/632-0879**), offers wine tastings and sells bottles of wines ranging from cabernet sauvignon to muscat. Call ahead to find out about the Sunday programs offered spring through fall, which might include live jazz or flamenco guitar. The last weekend in September, the winery holds a festival with six bands and arts-and-crafts booths. The tasting room is open Monday to Saturday 10am to 6pm and Sunday noon to 6pm.

ANGEL PEAK RECREATION AREA

The distinctive pinnacle of 6,991-foot Angel Peak can often be spotted from the hillsides around Farmington. The area offers a short nature trail and a variety of unusual, colorful geological formations and canyons to explore on foot. The Bureau of Land

Management has developed a primitive campground with nine campsites and provided picnic tables in a few spots, but no drinking water is available here. The park is about 35 miles south of Farmington on US 550; the last 6 miles of access, after turning off US 550, are over a graded dirt road. For more information on the park, call ℂ 505/599-8900.

BISTI/DE-NA-ZIN WILDERNESS

Often referred to as Bisti Badlands (pronounced Bist-*eye*), this barren region may merit that name today, but it was once very different. Around 70 million years ago, large dinosaurs lived near what was then a coastal swamp, bordering a retreating inland sea. Today, their bones, and those of fish, turtles, lizards, and small mammals, are eroding slowly from the low shale hills.

Kirtland Shale, containing several bands of color, dominates the eastern part of the wilderness and caps the mushroom-shaped formations found there. Along with the spires and fanciful shapes of rock, hikers may find petrified wood sprinkled in small chips throughout the area, or even an occasional log. *Note:* Removing petrified wood, fossils, or anything else from the wilderness is prohibited.

Hiking in the Bisti is fairly easy; from the small parking lot, follow an arroyo east 2 or 3 miles into the heart of the formations, which you'll see on your right (aim for the two red hills). The De-Na-Zin Wilderness to the east requires more climbing and navigational skills. It has no designated trails, bikes and motorized vehicles are prohibited, and it has no water or significant shade. The hour just after sunset or, especially, just before sunrise is a pleasant and quite magical time to see this starkly beautiful landscape. Primitive camping is allowed, but bring plenty of water and other supplies.

Bisti/De-Na-Zin Wilderness is just off New Mexico 371, 37 miles south of Farmington. For more information, call the **Bureau of Land Management** at ℂ 505/599-8900.

WHERE TO STAY IN FARMINGTON & AZTEC

Courtyard by Marriott ☆ *Kids*   This property provides elegant rooms and all the amenities of a full-service hotel, with the consistency you'd expect from Marriott. The expansive lobby looking out over Riverwalk Park is decorated in a Southwestern style. Just off the lobby is a quiet lounge and a restaurant. The style carries into the rooms, which are spacious with comfortable beds and medium-size bathrooms with outer vanities. Southwestern landscape paintings adorn the walls. The suites are large and contain one bedroom and a living room with a sofa bed, wet bar, and microwave—a good choice for small families.

560 Scott Ave., Farmington, NM 87401. ℂ 800/228-9290 or 505/325-5111. Fax 505/325-5588. www.marriott.com. 125 units. $89–$99 double; $120–$125 suite. AE, DC, DISC, MC, V. **Amenities:** Restaurant; bar; indoor pool w/sun deck; exercise room; Jacuzzi; limited room service; coin-op laundry; same-day dry cleaning. *In room:* A/C, TV, coffeemaker, hair dryer, iron, high-speed Internet, Wi-Fi.

Soaring Eagle Lodge ☆ *Finds*   This lodge about 25 minutes from Farmington offers basic and clean cabins on a poetic bend of the San Juan River. It's mostly a place for fishing enthusiasts, who come to ply these world-renowned waters, but those seeking the quiet of a lovely river setting would like it, too. Each cabin has a kitchenette, partitioned-off bedroom space, and a front room with two easy chairs. Beds are comfortable and bathrooms very clean. A restaurant on-site serves tasty breakfasts and dinners. Be sure to reserve a cabin on the river edge, where the views couldn't be finer. The lodge can set you up with a guide, and you may fish for free from shore on the lodge's private waters.

48 C.R. 4370, off NM 511, Navajo Dam, NM, 87419. ℂ **800/866-2719** or 505/632-5621. www.soaringeagle lodge.net. 11 units. $120 per person, double. Price includes a full breakfast and fishing privileges. MC, V. **Amenities:** Restaurant; conference room w/Wi-Fi; private fishing waters; guide service. *In-room:* A/C, TV, fridge, coffeemaker, microwave.

Step Back Inn 🐾 This inn offers Victorian charm in a newer building with modern conveniences. Though it's a fair-size hotel, it has a cozy inn feel and plenty of amenities. The building was designed by the same architect who built the Inn of the Anasazi in Santa Fe (p. 138), and the tastefulness and functionality are apparent in the layout of the large rooms and good-size bathrooms, as well as in the quietness, which is due to good insulation. The rooms have pretty touches such as wallpaper and early American antique replica armoires, which hold the television. Each room is named after an early pioneer family of the area, some of whom are the ancestors of the hotel's owner, and each room includes a small booklet that tells their stories. The beds are comfortable, and the linens are good. Breakfast is a warm, delicious cinnamon roll as large as a plate, served in a quiet tearoom.

103 W. Aztec Blvd., Aztec, NM 87410 ℂ **800/334-1255** or 505/334-1200. 39 units. May 15–Nov 1 $78–$98 double; Nov 2–May 14 $68–$78 double. Rates include cinnamon roll, juice, and coffee. AE, MC, V. *In room:* A/C, TV, hair dryer, Wi-Fi in some rooms.

BED & BREAKFASTS

Casa Blanca 🐾🐾🐾 *Finds* A recent renovation has turned this B&B into a travel destination. In a quiet residential neighborhood just a few blocks from the shops and restaurants of Main Street, this inn, built in the 1940s, was once the home of a wealthy family that traded with the Navajos. In 2004, new owners expanded it, adding patios and fountains, and creating a lovely oasis. The large rooms, decorated in an elegant Southwestern style, have original artwork and plenty of amenities. Our favorite room is the Chaco, with red-brick floors, authentic Navajo rugs, and antique furnishings. Also of note is the Vista Grande, a large upstairs room with views in every direction. Travelers with disabilities are treated especially well here (there are two large suites especially for them), as are business travelers (there are high-speed Internet and Wi-Fi, a courtesy computer, and a meeting room). The full breakfast is always gourmet. In 2006, the inn added six extended-stay suites.

505 E. La Plata St., Farmington, NM 87401. ℂ **800/550-6503** or 505/327-6503. Fax 505/326-5680. www.casa blancanm.com. 15 units. $95–$185 double; $20 single-traveler discount. Rates include full breakfast. AE, MC, V. *In room:* A/C, TV, fridge, coffeemaker, hair dryer, iron, microwave, Wi-Fi.

Kokopelli's Cave 🐾🐾 Retired geologist Bruce Black wanted to build an office in a cave, so he gave some laid-off Grants miners $20,000 to bore as deeply as they could into the side of a cliff face. This luxury apartment was the result. Through time, it worked better as a living space than a work space, and that is what it remains. Built in a semicircle, both the entry hall and the bedroom have wide sliding glass doors leading to little balconies beyond which the cliff face drops hundreds of feet below. This really is a cliff dwelling, and you must hike a bit down to it, though good guardrails guide you. The apartment is laid out around a broad central pillar, and the ceilings and walls are thick, undulating stone. Golden eagles nest in the area, and ringtail cats tend to wander onto the balcony. A grill is outside, as are chairs where you can relax in the mornings and evenings. Fruit, juice, coffee, and pastries make up a self-serve breakfast.

3204 Crestridge Dr., Farmington, NM 87401. ℂ **505/326-2461.** Fax 505/325-9671. www.bbonline.com/nm/ kokopelli. 1 unit. $220 double; $260 for 3–4 people. Closed Dec–Feb. AE, MC, V. **Amenities:** Jacuzzi. *In room:* TV/VCR, kitchen, hair dryer, iron.

CAMPING

Downs RV Park (℃ **800/582-6427**) has 33 sites, 31 of them with full hookups. Tenting space is also available. The park has a playground, an arcade, and a game room. It's 5 miles west of Farmington on US 64. **Mom and Pop RV Park** (℃ **505/327-3200**) has 36 sites (35 with full hookups), tenting, a bathhouse, and a toy soldier shop. The sites are a bit desolate, around an asphalt central area, but a little grassy spot at the office has an incredible electric train set that Pop runs at certain times during the day. Mom and Pop RV Park is at 901 Illinois Ave., in Farmington (just off US 64).

WHERE TO DINE IN FARMINGTON & AZTEC

EXPENSIVE

The Bluffs 𝒜𝒜 *(Finds* SANDWICHES/SEAFOOD/STEAKS   Ten minutes east of town center, The Bluffs serves inventive food with attention to detail. A large room is sectioned off by wooden partitions crowned with elegantly glazed glass that's shaped like the bluffs prominent in the surrounding area. It's a comfortable atmosphere with roomy booths and stacked sandstone accents. Service is efficient. The outdoor patio is a nice spot on not-so-hot days. For lunch, our pick is the turkey-bacon club, served on ciabatta bread. The Thai beef salad is also tasty. At dinner, try your favorite steak cut of Angus beef or sesame-crusted ahi tuna. Dinners come with salad and a choice of vegetable or potato. There's a full bar here, but for a real treat, before dining, slip into the package store next door, owned by the same folks, where you'll find some very fine wines. In the restaurant, you'll pay a corking fee but still save a bundle.

3450 E. Main St. ℃ **505/325-8155**. Reservations recommended on weekend nights. Main courses $7–$11 lunch, $13–$35 dinner. AE, DISC, MC, V. Mon–Fri 11am–2pm, Mon–Thurs 5–9pm; Fri–Sat 4–10pm; lounge daily 3–9 or 10pm.

MODERATE

3 Rivers Eatery & Brewhouse 𝒜 *(Kids* AMERICAN   This brewpub on an elegant corner in the center of downtown serves some of the region's best food and beer. Our first sip of their Arroyo Amber Ale, we were sold. The restaurant is set in a big two-story brick building that once housed the Farmington Drug Store and the Farmington *Times-Hustler* newspaper. Hardwood floors and vintage items, such as period bottles and posters found in the renovation, complete the experience. It's a comfortable place where the owner might just sit down in one of the comfy booths with you and chat about his passion, beer brewing. We recommend the burgers, which come in a variety of flavors, from grilled onion and Swiss to jack and green chile. You'll also find barbecue pork ribs, steaks, and seafood. The taco salad is a masterpiece—greens, black beans, and chicken or beef, decorated with red, blue, and yellow corn chips. For dessert, try the brewmaster's root-beer float. Families enjoy the spacious booths in the back and a kid's menu.

101 E. Main St., Farmington. ℃ **505/324-2187**. www.threeriversbrewery.com. Main courses $5–$22. AE, DISC, MC, V. Mon–Thurs 11am–10pm; Fri–Sat 11am–11pm; Sun 11am–9pm.

INEXPENSIVE

Main Street Bistro 𝒜 BAKERY/CAFE   The place reels with imagination. The walls and floors are brightly colored, and the menu changes at the whim of the chefs. The service is friendly and decent, and the place bustles during peak hours; so if you want quiet time, go midmorning or later in the afternoon. You can't go wrong with the daily soup special, a salad, a sandwich (try the Ultimate—turkey, bacon, avocado, and sprouts), or the quiche, made fresh daily.

122 N. Main St., Aztec. ℃ **505/334-0109**. All menu items under $9. DISC, MC, V. Mon–Fri 7am–4pm; Sat 7am–noon.

FARMINGTON AFTER DARK

Sandstone Production's **Summer Outdoor Theater** ✸ stages two fun shows each year. Presented in the Lions Wilderness Park Amphitheater (off College Blvd.) against a sandstone backdrop, the offerings are usually a dramatic piece and a musical. Recent productions include *Cyrano de Bergerac* and the musical *Crazy for You.* For information and advance ticket sales, call © **505/599-1148,** log on to www.fmtn.org/sandstone, or purchase tickets at the gate. Shows are Wednesday through Saturday from mid-June through July, with dinner at 6:30pm and the performance at 8pm.

If you're looking for a pub, try **3 Rivers Tap & Game Room,** 113 E. Main St. (© **505/325-6605;** www.threeriversbrewery.com), a big hit with locals. This brewpub/game room has the feel of the bar from the television show *Cheers,* with wood floors, high ceilings, and lots of laughter and brew flowing. Pool tables, foosball, and shuffleboard are the draw for patrons in this smoke-free space; customers munch on popcorn and peanuts, and, some nights, listen to live music. You can order from the next-door brewpub/restaurant of the same name (see above).

14 Chaco Culture National Historical Park ✶✶✶

A combination of a stunning setting and well-preserved ruins makes the long drive to **Chaco Culture National Historic Park,** often referred to as Chaco Canyon, worth the trip. Whether you come from the north or the south, you drive in on a dusty (and sometimes muddy) road that seems to add to the authenticity and adventure of this remote New Mexico experience.

When you finally arrive, you walk through stark desert country that seems perhaps ill suited as a center of culture. However, the ancient Anasazi people successfully farmed the lowlands and built great masonry towns, which connected with other towns over a wide-ranging network of roads crossing this desolate place.

Its progress led to Chaco becoming the economic center of the San Juan Basin by A.D. 1000. As many as 5,000 people may have lived in some 400 settlements in and around Chaco. As masonry techniques advanced through the years, walls were raised more than four stories in height. Some of these are still visible today.

Chaco's decline after 1½ centuries of success coincided with a drought in the San Juan Basin between A.D. 1130 and 1180. Scientists still argue vehemently over why the site was abandoned and where the Chacoans went. Many believe that an influx of outsiders may have brought new rituals to the region, causing a schism among tribal members. Most agree, however, that the people drifted away to more hospitable places in the region and that their descendants live among the Pueblo people today.

This is an isolated area, and **no services** are available within or close to the park—no food, gas, auto repairs, firewood, lodging (besides the campground), or drinking water (other than at the visitor center) are available. Overnight camping is permitted year-round. If you're headed toward Santa Fe after a day at the park and need a place to spend the night, one nice option is the **Cañon del Rio–A Riverside Inn,** 16445 New Mexico 4, Jemez Springs, NM 87025 (© **505/829-4377;** www.canondelrio.com).

ESSENTIALS

GETTING THERE To get to Chaco from Santa Fe, take I-25 south to Bernalillo, then US 550 northwest. Turn off US 550 at C.R. 7900 (3 miles southeast of Nageezi and about 50 miles west of Cuba at mile 112.5). Follow the signs from US 550 to the park boundary (21 miles). This route includes 5 miles of paved road (C.R. 7900) and

16 miles of rough dirt road (C.R. 7950). This is the recommended route. Highway 57 from Blanco Trading Post is closed. The trip takes about 3½ to 4 hours. Farmington is the nearest population center, a 1½-hour drive away. The park can also be reached from Grants via I-40 west to New Mexico 371, then north on New Mexico 57 (with the final 19 miles ungraded dirt). This route is rough to impassable and is not recommended for RVs.

Whichever way you come, call ahead to inquire about **road conditions** (© 505/ **786-7014**) before leaving the paved highways. The dirt roads can get extremely muddy and dangerous after rain or snow, and afternoon thunderstorms are common in late summer. Roads often flood when it rains.

VISITOR INFORMATION   Ranger-guided walks and campfire talks are available in the summer at the visitor center where you can get self-guided trail brochures and permits for the overnight campground (see "Camping," below). If you want information before you leave home, write to the Superintendent, Chaco Culture National Historical Park, 1808 C.R. 7950, Nageezi, NM 87037 (© **505/786-7014;** www.nps. gov/chcu).

ADMISSION FEES & HOURS   Admission is $8 per car; a campsite is $10 extra. The visitor center is open daily 8am to 5pm. Trails are open from sunrise to sunset.

SEEING THE HIGHLIGHTS

Exploring the ruins and hiking are the most popular activities here. A series of pueblo ruins stand within 5 or 6 miles of each other on the broad, flat, treeless canyon floor. Plan to spend at least 3 to 4 hours here driving to and exploring the different pueblos. A one-way road from the visitor center loops up one side of the canyon and down the other. Parking lots are scattered along the road near the various pueblos; from most, it's only a short walk to the ruins.

You may want to focus your energy on seeing **Pueblo Bonito,** the largest prehistoric Southwest Native American dwelling ever excavated. It contains giant kivas and 800 rooms covering more than 3 acres. Also, the **Pueblo Alto Trail** is a nice hike that takes you up on the canyon rim so that you can see the ruins from above—in the afternoon, with thunderheads building, the views are spectacular. If you're a cyclist, stop at the visitor center to pick up a map outlining ridable trails.

Aerial photos show hundreds of miles of roads connecting these towns with the Chaco pueblos, one of the longest running 42 miles straight north to Salmon Ruins and the Aztec Ruins (see earlier in the chapter). It's this road network that leads some scholars to believe that Chaco was the center of a unified Anasazi society.

CAMPING

Gallo Campground, within the park, is quite popular with hikers. It's about 1 mile east of the visitor center; fees are $10 per night. The campground has 47 sites (group sites are also available), with fire grates (bring your own wood or charcoal), central toilets, and nonpotable water. Drinking water is available only at the visitor center. The campground cannot accommodate trailers over 30 feet.

Again, there's no place to stock up on supplies once you start the arduous drive to the canyon, so if you're planning to camp, make sure you come well supplied, especially with water.

6

Santa Fe

With its meandering streets, flat-topped adobe buildings, and dramatic clouds, Santa Fe—the "City Different"—has always had an exotic nature. The Native Americans enlighten the area with viewpoints and lifestyles deeply tied to nature and completely contrary to the American norm. Many of the Hispanics here still live in extended families and practice a devout Catholicism; they bring a slower pace to the city and an appreciation for deep-rooted ties. Meanwhile, a strong cosmopolitan element contributes cutting-edge cuisine, world-class opera, first-run art films, and some of the finest artwork in the world, seen easily while wandering on foot from gallery to gallery, museum to museum.

The city was originally named La Villa Real de la Santa Fe de San Francisco de Asis (The Royal City of the Holy Faith of St. Francis of Assisi) by its founder, Spanish governor Don Pedro de Peralta. He built the Palace of the Governors as his capitol on the central plaza; today it's an excellent museum of the city's 4 centuries of history and one of the major attractions in the Southwest. Under its portico,

Native Americans sell their crafts to eager tourists, as they have done for decades.

The plaza is the focus of numerous bustling art markets and Santa Fe's early-September fiesta, celebrated annually since 1770. The fiesta commemorates the time following the years of the Pueblo revolt, when Spanish governor Don Diego de Vargas reconquered the city in 1692. The plaza was also the terminus of the Santa Fe Trail from Missouri, and of the earlier Camino Real (Royal Road) from Mexico, when the city thrived on the wool and fur of the Chihuahua trade. Today, a new gazebo makes a fun venue for summer concerts.

The city's setting is captivating, backed by the rolling hills and the blue peaks of the Sangre de Cristo Mountains. In the summer, thunderheads build into giant swirling structures above those peaks and move over the city, dropping cool rain. In the winter, snow often covers the many flat-roofed adobe homes, creating a poetic abstraction that at every glance convinces you that the place itself is exotic art.

1 Orientation

Part of the charm of Santa Fe is that it's so easy to get around. Like most cities of Hispanic origin, it was built around a parklike central plaza. Centuries-old adobe buildings and churches still line the narrow streets; many of them house shops, restaurants, art galleries, and museums.

Santa Fe sits high and dry at the foot of the Sangre de Cristo range. Santa Fe Baldy rises to more than 12,600 feet, a mere 12 miles northeast of the plaza. The city's downtown straddles the Santa Fe River, a tiny tributary of the Rio Grande that is little more than a trickle for much of the year. North is the Española Valley and, about

70 miles beyond that, the village of Taos (see chapter 7). South are ancient Indian turquoise mines in the Cerrillos Hills; southwest is metropolitan Albuquerque, 58 miles away (see chapter 8). To the west, across the Caja del Rio Plateau, is the Rio Grande, and beyond that, the 11,000-foot Jemez Mountains and Valle Grande, an ancient and massive volcanic caldera. Native American pueblos dot the entire Rio Grande valley; they're an hour's drive in any direction.

ARRIVING

BY PLANE   Many people choose to fly into the Albuquerque International Sunport. However, if you want to save time and don't mind paying a bit more, you can fly into the **Santa Fe Municipal Airport** (© 505/955-2900), just outside the southwestern city limits on Airport Road. In conjunction with United Airlines, commuter flights are offered via Denver by **United Express** (© 800/241-6522; www.united. com), which is operated by **Great Lakes Aviation** (© 800/473-4118; www.greatlake sav.com).

If you do fly into Albuquerque, you can rent a car or take one of the bus services. See "Getting There," in chapter 2, for details.

From the Santa Fe Municipal Airport, **Roadrunner Shuttle** (© 505/424-3367) meets every flight and takes visitors anywhere in Santa Fe. From the Albuquerque Sunport to Santa Fe, **Santa Fe Shuttle** (© 888/833-2300 or 505/466-8500; www. shuttlesantafe.com) runs shuttles 8am to 8pm.

BY TRAIN & BUS   For detailed information about train and bus service to Santa Fe, see "Getting There," in chapter 2.

BY CAR   I-25 skims past Santa Fe's southern city limits, connecting it along one continuous highway from Billings, Montana, to El Paso, Texas. I-40, the state's major east-west thoroughfare, which bisects Albuquerque, affords coast-to-coast access to Santa Fe. (From the west, motorists leave I-40 in Albuquerque and take I-25 north; from the east, travelers exit I-40 at Clines Corners and continue 52 miles to Santa Fe on US 285. *Note:* Diesel is scarce on US 285, so be sure to fill up before you leave Clines Corners.) For those coming from the northwest, the most direct route is via Durango, Colorado, on US 160, entering Santa Fe on US 84.

For information on car rentals in Albuquerque, see "Getting Around the Southwest," in chapter 2; for agencies in Santa Fe, see "Getting Around," below.

VISITOR INFORMATION

The **Santa Fe Convention and Visitors Bureau** is at 125 Lincoln Ave. downtown (P.O. Box 909), Santa Fe, NM 87504-0909 (© 800/777-CITY or 505/955-6200). You can also log on to the bureau's website, at **www.santafe.org**. You might also try **www.visitsantafe.com** for more information.

CITY LAYOUT

MAIN ARTERIES & STREETS   The limits of downtown Santa Fe are demarcated on three sides by the horseshoe-shaped Paseo de Peralta and on the west by St. Francis Drive, otherwise known as US 84/285. Alameda Street follows the north side of the Santa Fe River through downtown, with the State Capitol and other government buildings on the south side of the river, and most buildings of historic and tourist interest on the north, east of Guadalupe Street.

The plaza is Santa Fe's universally accepted point of orientation. Its four diagonal walkways meet at a central fountain, around which a strange and wonderful assortment of people of all ages, nationalities, and lifestyles can be found at nearly any hour of the day or night.

If you stand in the center of the plaza looking north, you'll be gazing directly at the Palace of the Governors. In front of you is Palace Avenue; behind you, San Francisco Street. To your left is Lincoln Avenue, and to your right is Washington Avenue, which divides the downtown avenues into east and west. St. Francis Cathedral is the massive Romanesque structure a block east, down San Francisco Street. Alameda Street is 2 full blocks behind you.

Near the intersection of Alameda Street and Paseo de Peralta, you'll find Canyon Road running east toward the mountains. Much of this street is one-way. The best way to see it is to walk up or down, taking time to explore shops and galleries and even have lunch or dinner.

Running to the southwest from the downtown area, beginning opposite the state office buildings on Galisteo Avenue, is Cerrillos Road. Once the main north-south highway connecting New Mexico's state capital with its largest city, it is now a 6-mile-long motel and fast-food strip. St. Francis Drive, which crosses Cerrillos Road 3 blocks south of Guadalupe Street, is a far less tawdry byway, linking Santa Fe with I-25, 4 miles southwest of downtown. The Old Pecos Trail, on the east side of the city, also joins downtown and the freeway. St. Michael's Drive connects the three arteries.

FINDING AN ADDRESS   The city's layout makes it difficult to know exactly where to look for a particular address. It's best to call ahead for directions.

MAPS   Free city and state maps can be obtained at tourist information offices. An excellent state highway map is published by the **New Mexico Department of Tourism,** 491 Old Santa Fe Trail, Lamy Building, Santa Fe, NM 87503 (© **800/733-6396** or 505/827-7307; to receive a tourism guide call © **800/777-CITY**). There's also a Santa Fe visitor center in the same building. More specific county and city maps are available from the **State Highway and Transportation Department,** 1120 Cerrillos Rd., Santa Fe, NM 87504 (© **505/827-5100**). Members of the **American Automobile Association,** 1644 St. Michael's Dr. (© **505/471-6620**), can obtain free maps from the AAA office. Other good regional maps can be purchased at area bookstores.

2 Getting Around

The best way to see downtown Santa Fe is on foot. Free **walking-tour maps** are available at the **tourist information center,** 125 Lincoln Ave. (© **800/777-CITY** or 505/984-6760), and several guided tours are listed later in this chapter.

BY BUS

In 1993, Santa Fe opened **Santa Fe Trails** (© **505/955-2001;** http://santafetrails. santafenm.gov), its first public bus system. There are seven routes, and visitors can pick up a map from the Convention and Visitors Bureau. Some buses operate Monday to Friday 6am to 11pm and Saturday 8am to 8pm. There's some service on Sunday, as well as on holidays. Call or visit the website for a current schedule and fare information.

BY CAR

Cars can be rented from any of the following firms in Santa Fe: **Avis,** Santa Fe Airport (© **505/471-5892**); **Budget,** 1946 Cerrillos Rd. (© **505/984-1596**); **Enterprise,**

2641A Cerrillos Rd., 4450 Cerrillos Rd. (at the Auto Park), and Santa Fe Hilton, 100 Sandoval St. (© **505/473-3600**); and **Hertz,** Santa Fe Airport (© **505/471-7189**).

If Santa Fe is merely your base for an extended driving exploration of New Mexico, be sure to give the vehicle you rent a thorough road check before starting out. There are a lot of wide-open desert and wilderness spaces here, so if you break down, you could be stranded for hours before someone passes by, and cellphones don't tend to work in the state's remote areas.

Make sure your driver's license and auto club membership (if you have one) are valid before you leave home. Check with your auto-insurance company to make sure you're covered when out of state and/or when driving a rental car.

Note: In 2002, the Santa Fe City Council imposed a law prohibiting use of cellphones, except with a hands-free attachment, while driving within the city limits, with strict fines imposed. If you need to make a call, be sure to pull off the road.

Street parking is difficult to find during summer months. There's a metered parking lot near the federal courthouse, 2 blocks north of the plaza; a city lot behind Santa Fe Village, a block south of the plaza; and another city lot at Water and Sandoval streets. If you stop by the Santa Fe Convention and Visitors Bureau, at 125 Lincoln Ave., you can pick up a wallet-size guide to Santa Fe parking areas. The map shows both street and lot parking.

Unless otherwise posted, the speed limit on freeways is 75 mph; on most other two-lane open roads it's 60 to 65 mph. The minimum age for drivers is 16. Seat belts are required for drivers and all passengers ages 5 and over; children under 5 must use approved child seats.

Since Native American reservations enjoy a measure of self-rule, they can legally enforce certain designated laws. For instance, on the Navajo reservation, it is forbidden to transport alcoholic beverages, leave established roadways, or go without a seat belt. Motorcyclists must wear helmets. If you are caught breaking reservation laws, you are subject to reservation punishment—often stiff fines and, in some instances, detainment.

The **State Highway and Transportation Department** has a toll-free hot line (© **800/432-4269**) that provides up-to-the-hour information on road closures and conditions.

BY TAXI

Cabs are difficult to flag from the street, but you can call for one. Expect to pay a standard fee of $3.88 for the service and an average of about $2.50 per mile. **Capital City Cab** (© **505/438-0000**) is the main company in Santa Fe.

BY BICYCLE

Riding a bicycle is an excellent way to get around town. Check with **Sun Mountain Bike Company,** 102 E. Water St. (inside El Centro; © **505/982-8986**); **Bike-N-Sport,** 524 Cordova Rd. (© **505/820-0809**); or **Santa Fe Mountain Sports,** 607 Cerrillos Rd. (© **505/988-3337**), for rentals.

Driver's Warning

New Mexico has one of the highest per-capita rates of traffic deaths in the nation; although the number has actually been dropping in recent years, it's still a good idea to drive with extra care!

FAST FACTS

For physician and surgeon referral and information services, call the **American Board of Medical Specialties** (© 866/275-2267). The **Lovelace Clinic,** 440 St. Michaels Dr. (© 505/995-2400), is open Monday to Thursday 8am to 6pm, Friday 8am to 5pm, and Saturday 8am to 3pm. **St. Vincent Hospital,** 455 St. Michael's Dr. (© 505/ 983-3361 or 505/995-3934 for emergency services), is a 248-bed regional health center. Health services are also available at **Women's Health Services Family Care and Counseling Center** (© 505/988-8869). **Ultimed,** 707 Paseo de Peralta (© 505/ 989-8707), an urgent-care facility near the plaza, offers comprehensive health care. See also "Fast Facts: The American Southwest" in chapter 2.

3 Where to Stay

It's difficult to find a bad place to stay in Santa Fe. From downtown hotels to Cerrillos Road motels, ranch-style resorts to quaint bed-and-breakfasts, the standard of accommodations is almost universally high.

Be aware of the seasonal nature of the tourist industry in Santa Fe: Accommodations are often booked solid through the summer months, and most places raise their prices accordingly. Rates increase even more during Indian Market, the third weekend of August. During these periods, it's essential to make reservations well in advance.

DOWNTOWN

Everything within the horseshoe-shaped Paseo de Peralta and east a few blocks on either side of the Santa Fe River is considered downtown Santa Fe. All these accommodations are within walking distance of the plaza.

VERY EXPENSIVE

Eldorado Hotel & Spa ✶✶   Since opening in 1986, the Eldorado has been a model hotel for the city. In a large structure, the architects managed to meld pueblo revival style with an interesting cathedral feel, inside and out. The lobby has a high ceiling that continues into the court area and the cafe, all adorned with well over a million dollars' worth of Southwestern art. The spacious, quiet rooms received a makeover in 2006, maintaining an artistic motif, with a warm feel created by custom-made furniture and, in some units, kiva fireplaces. You'll find families, businesspeople, and conference-goers staying here. Most of the rooms have views of downtown Santa Fe, many from balconies. The recently opened Nidah Spa offers a full range of treatments worth sampling, including a turquoise gemstone therapy. The Eldorado also manages the nearby Zona Rosa condominiums, which are two-, three-, and four-bedroom suites with full kitchens. The hotel's innovative and elegant restaurant, the Old House (p. 154), serves creative American cuisine.

309 W. San Francisco St., Santa Fe, NM 87501. © 800/286-6755 or 505/988-4455. Fax 505/995-4544. www. eldoradohotel.com. 219 units. High season $169–$319 double; low season $119–$199 double. Ski and other package rates are available. AE, DC, DISC, MC, V. Valet parking $16 per night. Pets accepted. **Amenities:** 2 restaurants; bar; heated rooftop pool; medium-size health club (w/view); spa; Jacuzzi; his-and-hers saunas and steam baths; concierge; business center; salon; room service; massage; laundry service; dry cleaning. *In room:* A/C, TV, minibar, coffeemaker, hair dryer, iron, safe, high-speed Internet.

Hilton Santa Fe Historic Plaza ✶   With its landmark bell tower, the Hilton encompasses a full city block (1 block from the plaza) and incorporates most of the historic landholdings of the 350-year-old Ortiz family estate. Built around a lovely courtyard pool and patio area, it's a fine blend of ancient and modern styles. A

Reservations Services

Year-round reservation assistance is available from **Santa Fe Hotels.**com (© 800/ 745-9910), the **Accommodation Hot Line** (© 800/338-6877), **All Santa Fe Reservations** (© 877/737-7366), and **Santa Fe Stay,** which specializes in casitas (© 800/ 995-2272). **Emergency Lodging Assistance** is available free after 4pm daily (© 505/986-0038). All the above are private companies and therefore may have biases toward certain properties. Do your own research before calling.

renovation late in 2004 has brought more style to the rooms and common areas, with handcrafted furnishings and hip Southwestern decor. Rooms vary slightly in size; our favorites are a little smaller than some, but they have balconies opening onto the courtyard. The Hilton also has the Casa Ortiz de Santa Fe, luxury casitas with kitchens situated in a 1625 coach house adjacent to the hotel.

100 Sandoval St. (P.O. Box 25104), Santa Fe, NM 87501-2131. © 800/336-3676, 800/HILTONS, or 505/988-2811. Fax 505/986-6439. www.santafe.hilton.com. 157 units. $159–$299 double; $239–$549 suite; $419–$559 casita. Additional guest $20. AE, DC, DISC, MC, V. Parking $10 per night. **Amenities:** 2 restaurants; bar; outdoor pool; exercise room; Jacuzzi; concierge; car-rental desk; business center; room service; laundry service; dry cleaning. *In room:* A/C, TV, dataport, coffeemaker, hair dryer, iron, safe, Wi-Fi.

Inn of the Anasazi 🌟🌟🌟   The designers of this fine luxury hotel have crafted a feeling of grandness in a very limited space, and in 2006 a remodel added even finer touches, including new bedding and decor in the rooms, with bold splashes of color from indigenous rugs and handwoven fabrics. Flagstone floors and vigas create a warm and welcoming ambience that evokes the feeling of an Anasazi cliff dwelling. Oversize cactuses complete the look. Accents are appropriately Navajo, in a nod to the fact that the Navajo live in the area the Anasazi once inhabited. A half-block off the Santa Fe Plaza, this hotel was built in 1991 to cater to discerning travelers. Even the smallest rooms are spacious, with pearl-finished walls and decor in cream tones accented by novelties such as iron candle sconces, original art, four-poster beds, gaslit kiva fireplaces, and humidifiers. All the rooms are quiet and comfortable, though none have dramatic views. The Anasazi Restaurant (p. 151) serves creative Southwestern cuisine.

113 Washington Ave., Santa Fe, NM 87501. © 800/688-8100 or 505/988-3030. Fax 505/988-3277. www.innoftheanasazi.com. 56 units. Double Jan 5–Feb 26 $269–$469; Feb 27–Apr 28 $325–$525; Apr 29–June 23 $325–$525; June 24–Jan 4 $325–$525. AE, DC, DISC, MC, V. Valet parking $15 per day. **Amenities:** Restaurant; concierge; room service; in-room massage; laundry service; library/boardroom. *In room:* A/C, TV/DVD player, coffeemaker, hair dryer, iron, safe, Wi-Fi.

Inn of the Five Graces 🌟🌟 *Finds*   In the historic Barrio de Analco, just a few blocks from the Santa Fe Plaza, this inn holds true to its stated theme: "Here the Orient and the Old West meet, surprisingly at home in each other's arms." With floral-decked courtyards, elaborately decorated suites with kilim rugs, ornately carved beds, and often beautiful mosaic tile work in the bathrooms, this is truly a sheik place. All but a few suites are medium size, most with small bathrooms, and some with fireplaces. The lower-priced rooms are smaller. Request one of the suites in the buildings on the north side of East de Vargas Street; they're more spacious and substantially built. Travelers seeking an exotic stay will like this place, which is the same caliber as Inn of the Anasazi (above), but with more flair. And although the Five Graces doesn't have a full-service restaurant, a new kitchen now serves a variety of hot breakfasts and tapas (small

Downtown Santa Fe Accommodations & Dining

Santa Fe — DOWNTOWN

Church †
Information ⓘ
Post Office ✉

DINING ◆
Anasazi Restaurant **10**
Blue Corn Café **15**
Cafe Pasqual's **17**
Cowgirl Hall of Fame **13**
Coyote Café **14**
Fuego **25**
Guadalupe Café **36**
Il Piatto Cucina Italiano **3**
La Casa Sena **22**
Old House **6**
The Pink Adobe **35**
Plaza Café **19**
Railyard Restaurant & Saloon **27**
Santacafé **4**
The Shed **21**
Tomasita's Café **28**
Upper Crust Pizza **38**

ACCOMMODATIONS ■
Adobe Abode **2**
Don Gaspar Inn **33**
Eldorado Hotel & Spa **5**
El Farolito **31**
Garrett's Desert Inn **37**
Hacienda Nicholas **11**
Hilton Santa Fe
  Historic Plaza **12**
Hotel Plaza Real **8**
Hotel St. Francis **16**
Hotel Santa Fe **30**

Inn & Spa at Loretto **20**
Inn of the Anasazi **9**
Inn of the Five Graces **34**
Inn on the Alameda **23**
La Fonda **18**
La Posada de Santa Fe
  Resort & Spa **26**
The Lodge at Santa Fe **1**
The Madeleine **24**
Old Santa Fe Inn **32**
Santa Fe Motel and Inn **29**
Water Street Inn **7**

plates) as options for lunch and dinner. All rooms have robes, stocked fridges, patios, and CD players; some have kitchenettes.

150 E. de Vargas St., Santa Fe, NM 87501. *©* 505/992-0957. www.fivegraces.com. 23 units. $295–$750 double. Price includes extended breakfast and afternoon treats. AE, MC, V. Free parking. Pets welcome w/fee and deposit. **Amenities:** Concierge; Wi-Fi in the lobby. *In room:* A/C, TV, fridge, coffeemaker, hair dryer, iron, microwave, CD player.

Inn & Spa at Loretto *⋒*   This much-photographed hotel, just 2 blocks from the plaza, was built in 1975 to resemble Taos Pueblo. Light and shadow dance upon the five-level structure as the sun crosses the sky. With ongoing refinements, this hotel has become a comfortable and stylish place to stay. Decor is a Southwest/Montana ranch style, with faux painted walls and a moodily lit lobby lounge. The hotel's rooms and bathrooms are standard size, with the same decor as the rest of the hotel. Be aware that the Loretto likes convention traffic, so sometimes service lags for travelers. Overall, it is fairly quiet and has nice views—especially on the northeast side, where you'll see both the historic St. Francis Cathedral and the Loretto Chapel (with its "miraculous" spiral staircase; see "More Attractions," later in this chapter). The Spa Terre offers a range of treatments, from facials to massages, in intimate, Southwest-meets-Asia rooms.

211 Old Santa Fe Trail (P.O. Box 1417), Santa Fe, NM 87501. *©* 800/727-5531 or 505/988-5531. Fax 505/984-7968. www.innatloretto.com. 134 units. Double Jan–Mar $159–$275; Apr–June $185–$300; July–Oct $215–$499; Nov–Dec $185–$299. Additional person $25. Children 17 and under stay free in parent's room. AE, DC, DISC, MC, V. Valet parking $15 per night. **Amenities:** Restaurant; lounge; outdoor pool (heated year-round); spa; concierge; business center w/audiovisual conferencing equipment; room service; laundry service. *In room:* A/C, TV, fridge, coffeemaker, hair dryer, iron, Wi-Fi.

La Fonda *⋒*   Whether you stay in this hotel or not, it's worth strolling through just to get a sense of how Santa Fe once was—and in some ways still is. This was the inn at the end of the Santa Fe Trail; it saw trappers, traders, and merchants, as well as notables such as President Rutherford B. Hayes and General Ulysses S. Grant. The original inn was dying of old age in 1920 when it was razed and replaced by the current La Fonda. Its architecture is pueblo revival: imitation adobe with wooden balconies and beam ends protruding over the tops of windows. Inside, the lobby is rich and slightly dark, with people bustling about, sitting in the cafe, or buying jewelry from Native Americans.

The hotel has seen some renovation through the years, as well as a whole new wing recently completed to the east, where you'll find deluxe suites and new meeting spaces. If you want a feel of the real Santa Fe, this is the place to stay. Overall, however, this hotel isn't the model of refinement. For that, you'd best go to the Hotel Santa Fe (below) or one of the other newer places. No two rooms are the same here, and while each has its own funky touch, some are more kitsch than quaint. Some have refrigerators, fireplaces, and private balconies. A recently added spa offers a variety of treatments from massages to salt glows, as well as a sauna and Jacuzzi. La Plazuela serves some of the best new Southwestern cuisine in town, in a skylit garden patio. The Bell Tower Bar is the highest point in downtown Santa Fe—a great place for a cocktail and a view of the city.

100 E. San Francisco St. (P.O. Box 1209), Santa Fe, NM 87501. *©* 800/523-5002 or 505/982-5511. Fax 505/988-2952. www.lafondasantafe.com. 167 units. $219–$299 standard double; $239–$319 deluxe double; $349–$549 suite. Additional person $15. Children under 12 stay free in parent's room. AE, DC, DISC, MC, V. Parking $10 per day in a covered garage. **Amenities:** Restaurant; 2 bars; outdoor pool; exercise room; spa; 2 indoor Jacuzzis; concierge; tour desk; business center; room service; massage room and in-room massage; babysitting; laundry service; dry cleaning. *In room:* A/C, TV, dataport, coffeemaker, hair dryer, iron, safe, Wi-Fi.

La Posada de Santa Fe Resort & Spa 𝒢𝒢   If you're in the mood to stay in a little New Mexico adobe village, you'll enjoy this luxury hotel just 3 blocks from the plaza. The original main building is a Victorian mansion built in 1882 by Abraham Staab, a German immigrant, for his wife, Julia. Later an adobe structure was built around it, so now the Victorian features are present only within the charming bar (refurbished in 2006) and four rooms, which still maintain the original brick and high ceilings. If you like Victorian interiors more than Santa Fe style, these rooms are a good bet. It is said that Julia Staab, who died in 1896, continues to haunt the place; she is Santa Fe's best-known and most frequently witnessed ghost.

The rest of the hotel follows in the pueblo-style construction and is quaint; it's especially nice in the summer, when surrounded by acres of green grass. Here, you'll find squeaky maple floors, vigas and latillas, and, in many rooms, kiva fireplaces. Be aware that, notwithstanding the suites, most rooms tend to be fairly small. Fortunately, the hotel benefited from a $23-million face-lift completed in 1999, and all the bathrooms in historic rooms were renovated in 2004. In 2006, the hotel invested $1.5 million to improve its soft goods. Most notable are the Zen-Southwestern–style Avanyu spa and pool and spacious spa rooms, as well as a few "gallery suites," appointed with original artwork from some of the region's most prestigious artists. Travelers who are reluctant to trust the whims of older adobe construction should reserve one of the spa rooms or any of the other 40 new rooms. Most rooms don't have views but come with outdoor patios, and most are tucked back into the quiet compound. The top-notch on-site restaurant, **Fuego** (p. 153), serves artfully prepared international cuisine in a romantic, Spanish-colonial dining room.

330 E. Palace Ave., Santa Fe, NM 87501. © **800/727-5276** or 505/986-0000. Fax 505/982-6850. www.rockresorts. com. 157 units. $199–$359 double; suites $289 and way up, depending on the season. Various spa packages available. AE, DC, DISC, MC, V. Valet parking $15 per day. **Amenities:** 2 restaurants; bar; outdoor pool; exercise room; spa w/full treatments; Jacuzzi; bike rental; concierge; salon; room service; in-room massage; babysitting; dry cleaning; conference center. *In room:* A/C, TV, DVD player, minibar, coffeemaker, hair dryer, iron, safe, Wi-Fi, CD player.

EXPENSIVE

Don Gaspar Inn 𝒢𝒢 *(Finds*   If you'd like to pretend that you live in Santa Fe during your vacation—that you're blessed with your very own Southwestern-style home, in a historic neighborhood full of artful touches such as Native American tapestries and a kiva fireplace—this is your inn. A 10-minute walk from the plaza, the Don Gaspar comprises three homes connected by brilliant gardens and brick walkways. Rooms vary in size, though all are plenty spacious—most with patios, some with kitchenettes—and there's even a full house for rent. Though the rooms don't have views, all are quiet. The Courtyard Casita, with a kitchenette and a sleeper couch in its own room, is nice for a small family. All rooms include bathrobes and fireplaces. The friendly, dedicated staff serves a full breakfast, such as green chile stew with fresh baked items, on the patio or in the atrium.

623 Don Gaspar, Santa Fe, NM 87505. © **888/986-8664** or 505/986-8664. Fax 505/986-0696. www.dongaspar.com. 12 units. $115–$165 double; $165–$205 suite; $185–$245 casita; $295–$355 house. Rates include full breakfast. AE, MC, V. Free parking. **Amenities:** Babysitting; same-day laundry service. *In room:* A/C, TV/VCR, hair dryer, iron, high-speed Internet.

Hotel Plaza Real 𝒢 *(Value*   This New Orleans–meets–Santa Fe Territorial-style hotel, built in 1990, provides comfortable rooms near the central plaza. The construction and decor of the lobby are rustically elegant, built around a fireplace with balconies perched above. Clean and attractively decorated rooms have Southwestern-style furniture, many with French doors opening onto balconies or terraces that surround a quiet courtyard decorated with *ristras* (strung chiles). Beds are comfortably soft and bathrooms small but with an outer sink vanity. Junior suites have an especially nice layout, with a sitting area near a fireplace and good light from the north and south. The property could use some sprucing up, but such a low price this close to the plaza makes it a value.

125 Washington Ave., Santa Fe, NM 87501. © 877/901-7666 or 505/988-4900. Fax 505/983-9322. www.buynewmexico.com. 56 units. $119–$149 double; $149–$289 suite. Additional person $20. Children under 12 stay free in parent's room. AE, DC, DISC, MC, V. Parking $12 per day. Pets $50 per stay. **Amenities:** Lounge; laundry service; dry cleaning. *In room:* A/C, TV, dataport, coffeemaker, hair dryer, iron, Wi-Fi.

Hotel St. Francis ⚲   If you long for the rich fabrics, fine antiques, and slow pace of a European hotel, this is your place. The building was first constructed in the 1880s; it became fairly dilapidated but was renovated in 1986. Now elegantly redecorated, the lobby is crowned by a Victorian fireplace with hovering cherubs, a theme repeated throughout the hotel. European decor is also found in the rooms, each with a unique bent. You'll find a fishing room, a golf room, a garden room, and a music room, and each motif is evoked by the furnishings: a vintage set of golf clubs here, a sheet of music in a dry-flower arrangement there. The hotel, which attracts individual travelers as well as families and many Europeans, is well cared for by a concierge who speaks six languages. Enjoy high tea in the lobby 3 to 5:30pm daily. Request a room facing east, and you'll wake each day to a view of the mountains, seen through lovely lace. Larger rooms have coffeemakers and hair dryers.

210 Don Gaspar Ave., Santa Fe, NM 87501. © 800/529-5700 or 505/983-5700. Fax 505/989-7690. www.hotel stfrancis.com. 82 units. $99–$349 all rooms. Children under 12 stay free in parent's room. AE, DC, DISC, MC, V. Parking $5 per day. **Amenities:** Restaurant; bar; exercise room, access to nearby spa; concierge; room service; laundry service; dry cleaning; library; gaming tables. *In room:* A/C, TV, fridge, iron, safe, Wi-Fi.

Hotel Santa Fe ⚲ *Finds*   About a 10-minute walk south of the Santa Fe Plaza you'll find this newer three-story establishment, the only Native American–owned hotel in the city. Picuris Pueblo is the majority stockholder here, and part of the pleasure of staying here is the culture the Picuris bring to your visit. This is not to say that you'll get any sense of the rusticity of a pueblo in your accommodations—this sophisticated hotel, opened in 1991, is decorated in a contemporary Southwestern style. The rooms are medium size, with clean lines and comfortable beds, the decor accented with pine Taos-style furniture. Rooms on the north side get less street noise from Cerrillos Road, and have better views of the mountains, but they don't have the sun shining onto their balconies. You will get a strong sense of the Native American presence on the patio during the summer, when Picuris dancers come to perform and bread bakers uncover the *horno* (oven) and prepare loaves for sale.

1501 Paseo de Peralta, Santa Fe, NM 87501. © 800/825-9876 or 505/982-1200. Fax 505/984-2211. www.hotel santafe.com. 163 units. $99–$199 double; $129–$269 junior suite; Hacienda rooms and suites $199–$459. Children 17 and under stay free in parent's room. Additional person $20. AE, DC, DISC, MC, V. Free parking. Pets accepted with $20 fee. **Amenities:** Restaurant; outdoor pool; Jacuzzi; concierge; car-rental desk; room service; in-room massage; babysitting; dry cleaning. *In room:* A/C, TV, minibar, iron, safe, high-speed Internet.

Inn on the Alameda ⚲   Just across the street from the bosque-shaded Santa Fe River sits the Inn on the Alameda, a cozy stop for those who like the services of a hotel with the intimacy of an inn. Built in 1986, with additions over the years, it now rambles across four buildings. Lodgings include casita suites to the west, two three-story buildings at the center, and another one-story building that contains suites. All are pueblo-style adobe, ranging in age, but most were built in the late 1980s. Some of the tasteful rooms have refrigerators, CD players, safes, Jacuzzi tubs, and kiva fireplaces. The newer deluxe rooms and suites in the easternmost building are in the best shape. The traditional rooms are quaint, some with interesting angled bed configurations. The trees surrounding the inn—cottonwoods and aspens—make you feel as though you're in a treehouse when you step out on some of the balconies. If you're an art shopper, this is an ideal spot because it's a quick walk to Canyon Road. A full-service bar is open nightly.

303 E. Alameda St., Santa Fe, NM 87501. © 800/289-2122 or 505/984-2121. Fax 505/986-8325. www.innonthe alameda.com. 71 units. $120–$220 queen; $135–$235 king; $255–$375 suites; off season rates are available. Rates include breakfast, and afternoon wine-and-cheese reception. AE, DC, DISC, MC, V. Free parking. Pets under 30 pounds welcome. **Amenities:** Bar; medium-size fitness facility; 2 open-air Jacuzzis; concierge; massage; babysitting; coin-op laundry; same-day dry cleaning; pet amenities and a pet-walking map; Wi-Fi in lobby. *In room:* A/C, TV, hair dryer, iron.

MODERATE

Garrett's Desert Inn *(Value*   Completion of this hotel in 1957 prompted the Historic Design Review Board to implement zoning restrictions throughout downtown. Apparently, residents were appalled by the huge air conditioners adorning the roof. Though they're still unsightly, the hotel offers decent accommodations just 3 blocks from the plaza. It's a clean, two-story, concrete-block building around a broad parking lot. The hotel underwent a complete remodeling in 1994, with touch-ups through the years, though new carpet and updated furnishings are now needed. It has managed to maintain some '50s touches, such as Art Deco tile in the bathrooms and plenty of space in the rooms. If you're traveling in winter, ask for a south-facing room and you might be able to sunbathe under the portal. Minisuites have refrigerators and microwaves. The outdoor pool here is one of the nicest in town. Wi-Fi access is available in the restaurant.

311 Old Santa Fe Trail, Santa Fe, NM 87501. © 800/888-2145 or 505/982-1851. Fax 505/989-1647. www.garretts desertinn.com. 83 units. $89 $165, depending on season and type of room. AE, DISC, MC, V. **Amenities:** Restaurant; outdoor pool heated year-round. *In room:* A/C, TV, dataport, coffeemaker, hair dryer.

Old Santa Fe Inn ★ *(Finds*   Want to stay downtown and savor Santa Fe–style ambience without burning through your cash? This is your hotel. A multimillion-dollar renovation to this 1930s court motel created a comfortable, quiet inn just a few blocks from the plaza. Rooms verge on small but are decorated with such lovely handcrafted colonial-style furniture that you probably won't mind. All have small Mexican-tiled bathrooms with an outer vanity, and most units have gas fireplaces. You have a choice of king, queen, or twin bedrooms as well as suites. Breakfast is served in an atmospheric dining room next to a comfortable library. Note that this inn jacks prices *way* up during special event times such as the Indian Market.

320 Galisteo St., Santa Fe, NM 87501. © 800/745-9910 or 505/995-0800. Fax 505/995-0400. www.oldsantafe inn.com. 43 units. $80–$400 double. Rates include continental breakfast. AE, DC, DISC, MC, V. *In room:* A/C, TV/VCR, fridge, coffeemaker, Wi-Fi, CD player.

Santa Fe Motel and Inn ★   If you like walking to the plaza and restaurants but don't want to pay big bucks, this little compound is a good choice. Rooms here are larger than at the Old Santa Fe Inn (above) and have more personality than those at Garret's Desert Inn (above). Ask for one of the casitas in back—you'll pay more but get a little turn-of-the-20th-century charm, plus additional quiet and privacy. Some units have vigas; others have skylights, fireplaces, and patios. The main part of the motel, built in 1955, is two-story Territorial style, with upstairs rooms that open onto a portal with a bit of a view. Guest rooms are decorated with a Southwest motif and some have antique furnishings. All have medium-size bathrooms and comfortable beds. Some rooms have kitchenettes with refrigerators, microwaves, stoves, coffeemakers, and toasters. A full breakfast, including Sage Bakehouse bread, is served each morning in the Southwest-style dining room or on a quaint patio.

510 Cerrillos Rd., Santa Fe, NM 87501. ℰ 800/930-5002 or 505/982-1039. Fax 505/986-1275. www.santafemotel. com. 23 units. $69–$149 double. Rates include full breakfast. Additional person $10. AE, DC, MC, V. Free parking. *In room:* A/C, TV, hair dryer, iron, high-speed Internet.

INEXPENSIVE
Santa Fe Sage Inn *(Value* *(Kids*   If you're looking for a convenient, almost-downtown location at a reasonable price, this is one of your best bets. This two-story stucco adobe motel with portals is spread through three buildings and is about a 10-minute walk from the plaza. Built in 1985, the inn was remodeled in 2005. The smallish rooms have Southwestern furnishings, and contain comfortable beds and small bathrooms. There's a park in the back and an outdoor pool set in a secluded fenced area, a good place for kids. To avoid street noise, ask for a room at the back of the property.

725 Cerrillos Rd., Santa Fe, NM 87501. ℰ 866/433-0335 or 505/982-5952. Fax 505/984-8879. www.santafe sageinn.com. 160 units. $58–$72 double. Rate includes continental breakfast. Additional person $10. AE, DC, DISC, MC, V. Free parking. **Amenities:** Outdoor pool. *In room:* A/C, TV, dataport, coffeemaker, hair dryer, iron, Wi-Fi.

NORTHSIDE
Within easy reach of the Plaza, Northside encompasses the area that lies north of the loop of Paseo de Peralta.

VERY EXPENSIVE
Bishop's Lodge Ranch Resort & Spa *(Kids* *(Kids*   More than a century ago, when Archbishop Jean Baptiste Lamy was the spiritual leader of northern New Mexico's Roman Catholic population, he often escaped clerical politics by hiking into this valley called Little Tesuque. He built a retreat and a humble chapel (now on the National Register of Historic Places) with high-vaulted ceilings and a hand-built altar. Today, Lamy's 1,000-acre getaway has become Bishop's Lodge. In recent years, a $17-million renovation spruced up the place and added a spa and 10,000 square feet of meeting space. The guest rooms, spread through many buildings, feature handcrafted furniture and regional artwork. Standard rooms are spacious, and many have balconies, while deluxe rooms feature traditional kiva fireplaces, a combination bedroom/sitting room, and private decks or patios. The newest rooms are luxurious, and some have spectacular views of the Jemez Mountains. The Bishop's Lodge is an active resort three seasons of the year, with activities such as horseback riding, nature walks, and cookouts; in the winter, it becomes a romantic country retreat. A children's program keeps kids busy for much of the day.

Bishop's Lodge Rd. (P.O. Box 2367), Santa Fe, NM 87504. ℰ 505/983-6377. Fax 505/989-8939. www.bishopslodge. com. 111 units. Summer $399–$459 double; fall and spring $299–$399 double; midwinter $189–$269 double. Resort fee $15 per person per day. Children 3 and under stay free in parent's room. Additional person $15. Ask about packages that include meals. AE, DC, DISC, MC, V. Free parking. **Amenities:** Restaurant; outdoor pool; tennis courts; spa; Jacuzzi; concierge; courtesy shuttle; room service; in-room massage; babysitting; laundry service. *In room:* A/C, TV, coffeemaker, high-speed Internet.

EXPENSIVE
The Lodge at Santa Fe *(Kids* *(Kids*   The former Radisson Hotel has received a new name and complete multimillion-dollar face-lift. Set on a hill as you head north

toward the Santa Fe Opera, this three-story property is a convenient and relaxing place to stay. The new theme here is Native American, with Anasazi-style stacked sandstone throughout the lobby and dining room, a theme that carries into the guest rooms. Accommodations are medium size, decorated in earth tones with bold prints, and some have views of the mountains, while others overlook the pool. Premium rooms are more spacious—some have large living rooms and private balconies. Each parlor suite has a Murphy bed and kiva fireplace in the living room, a big dining area, a wet bar and refrigerator, and a jetted bathtub. The condo units nearby come with fully equipped kitchens, fireplaces, and private decks.

750 N. St. Francis Dr., Santa Fe, NM 87501. (C) 800/333-3333 or 505/992-5800. Fax 505/992-5856. www.thelodgeat santafe.com. 135 units. $89–$179 double; $129–$199 suite; $200–$300 condo. AE, DC, DISC, MC, V. Free parking. **Amenities:** Outdoor pool; free shuttle service to downtown. *In room:* A/C, TV, hair dryer, iron, high-speed Internet, Wi-Fi.

SOUTHSIDE

Santa Fe's major strip, Cerrillos Road, is US 85, the main route to and from Albuquerque and the I-25 freeway. It's about 5¼ miles from the Plaza to the Villa Linda Mall, which marks the southern boundary of the city. Most motels are on this strip, although several of them are to the east, closer to St. Francis Drive (US 84) or the Las Vegas Highway.

MODERATE

El Rey Inn *Finds Kids*   Staying at "The King" makes you feel as if you're traveling the old Route 66 through the Southwest. The white stucco buildings of this court motel are decorated with bright trim around the doors and hand-painted Mexican tiles on the walls. Opened in the 1930s, it received additions in the 1950s, and remodeling is ongoing. The lobby has vigas and tile floors, and it's decorated with Oriental rugs and dark Spanish furniture. No two rooms are alike. The oldest section, nearest the lobby, feels a bit cramped, though the rooms have style, with Art Deco tile in the bathrooms and vigas on the ceilings. Some units have little patios. Be sure to request a room as far back as possible from Cerrillos Road. The two stories of suites around the Spanish colonial courtyard are the best deal we've seen in all of Santa Fe. These rooms evoke a Spanish inn, with carved furniture and cozy couches. Some rooms have kitchenettes. To the north sit 10 deluxe units around the courtyard. These rooms offer more upscale amenities and gas log fireplaces, as well as distinctive furnishings and artwork. A complimentary continental breakfast is served in a sunny room or on a terrace in the warmer months. There's also a sitting room with a library and games tables, as well as a picnic area, a playground, and an exercise room. Wi-Fi access is available in the lobby.

1862 Cerrillos Rd. (P.O. Box 4759), Santa Fe, NM 87502. (C) 800/521-1349 or 505/982-1931. Fax 505/989-9249. www.elreyinnsantafe.com. 85 units. $95–$165 double; $120–$225 suite. Rates include continental breakfast. AE, DC, DISC, MC, V. Free parking. **Amenities:** Outdoor pool; exercise room; 2 Jacuzzis; sauna; coin-op laundry. Wi-Fi available in the lobby. *In room:* A/C, TV, dataport, fridge, coffeemaker, hair dryer, iron, safe.

INEXPENSIVE

La Quinta Inn *Value*   Though it's a good 15-minute drive from the plaza, this is our choice of economical Cerrillos Road chain hotels. Built in 1986, it has been fully remodeled in a very comfortable and tasteful way. The rooms within the three-story white-brick buildings have an unexpectedly elegant feel, with lots of deep colors and Art Deco tile in the bathrooms. There's plenty of space in these rooms, and they're lit

Greater Santa Fe

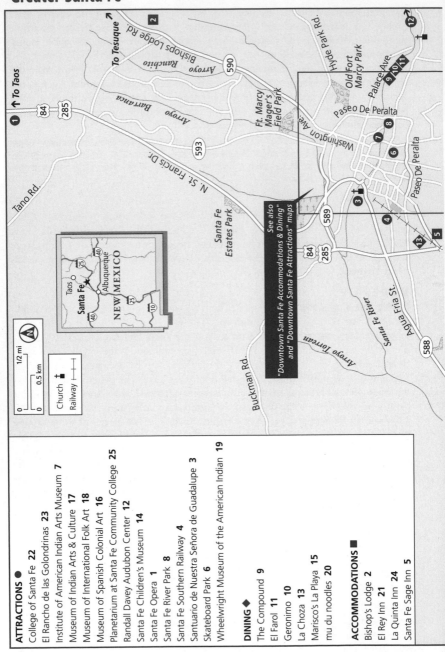

ATTRACTIONS ●

College of Santa Fe **22**
El Rancho de las Golondrinas **23**
Institute of American Indian Arts Museum **7**
Museum of Indian Arts & Culture **17**
Museum of International Folk Art **18**
Museum of Spanish Colonial Art **16**
Planetarium at Santa Fe Community College **25**
Randall Davey Audubon Center **12**
Santa Fe Children's Museum **14**
Santa Fe Opera **1**
Santa Fe River Park **8**
Santa Fe Southern Railway **4**
Santuario de Nuestra Señora de Guadalupe **3**
Skateboard Park **6**
Wheelwright Museum of the American Indian **19**

DINING ◆

The Compound **9**
El Farol **11**
Geronimo **10**
La Choza **13**
Marisco's La Playa **15**
mu du noodles **20**

ACCOMMODATIONS ■

Bishop's Lodge **2**
El Rey Inn **21**
La Quinta Inn **24**
Santa Fe Sage Inn **5**

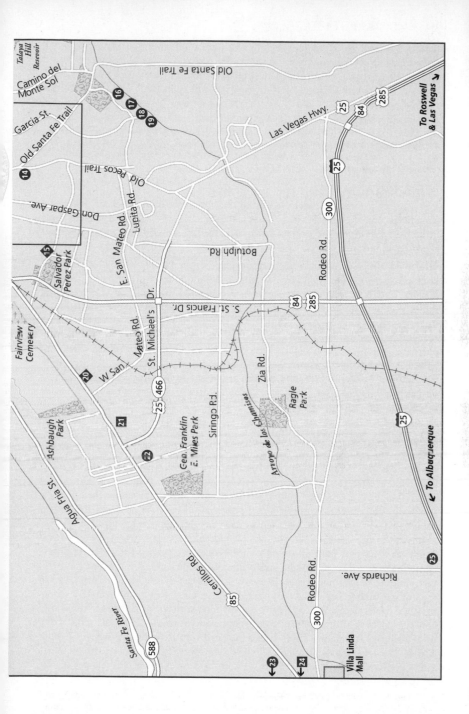

for mood as well as for reading. A complimentary continental breakfast is served in the intimate lobby. The outdoor kidney-shaped pool has a nice lounging area and is open and heated May to October. The hotel is just across a parking lot from the Santa Fe Place mall, which shoppers and movie-goers will appreciate. The Flying Tortilla coffee shop is adjacent.

4298 Cerrillos Rd., Santa Fe, NM 87507. © 800/531-5900 or 505/471-1142. Fax 505/438-7219. www.lq.com. 130 units. June to mid-Oct $89–$110 double; mid-Oct to May $60–$66 double. Rates include continental breakfast. Children 18 and under stay free in parent's room. Discount for AAA members. AE, DC, DISC, MC, V. Free parking. Maximum 2 pets stay free. **Amenities:** Outdoor heated pool; coin-op laundry; executive-level rooms. *In room:* A/C, TV, coffeemaker, hair dryer, iron, Wi-Fi.

BED & BREAKFASTS

If you prefer a homey, intimate setting to the sometimes-impersonal ambience of a large hotel, one of Santa Fe's bed-and-breakfast inns may be right for you. All those listed here are in or close to downtown and offer comfortable accommodations at expensive to moderate prices.

Adobe Abode ⊕   A short walk from the plaza, in the same quiet residential neighborhood as the Georgia O'Keeffe Museum, Adobe Abode is one of Santa Fe's most imaginative B&Bs. The cozy living room is decorated with folk art. The creativity shines in each of the guest rooms as well, some of which are in the main house, built in 1907. Others units, in back, are newer. The Galisteo Suite is decorated with Spanish colonial furniture and artwork, while the Bronco Room is filled with cowboy paraphernalia: hats, Pendleton blankets, pioneer chests, and an entire shelf lined with children's cowboy boots. Two rooms have fireplaces, and several have private patios. Complimentary sherry, fruit, and cookies are served daily in the living room. Every morning, a full breakfast of fresh fruit and a hot dish such as green chile corn soufflé is served in the country-style kitchen.

202 Chapelle St., Santa Fe, NM 87501. © 505/983-3133. Fax 505/983-3132. www.adobeabode.com. 6 units. $139–$179 double. Rates include breakfast and afternoon snacks. DISC, MC, V. Limited free parking. *In room:* A/C, TV, coffeemaker, hair dryer, iron, Wi-Fi.

El Farolito ⊕⊕   The owners of this inn, which is within walking distance of the plaza, have created an authentic theme experience for guests in each unit. The themes include the Native American Room, decorated with rugs and pottery; the South-of-the-Border Room, with Mexican folk art with a full-size sofa bed; and the elegant Santa Fe–style Opera Room, with hand-carved, lavishly upholstered furniture. A two-room suite has been added in the main building, with a queen-size iron bed and Southwestern decor. The walls of most of the rooms are rubbed with beeswax during plastering to give them a smooth, golden finish. All rooms have kiva fireplaces and private patios. The common area displays works by notable New Mexico artists. Part of the inn was built before 1912, and the rest is new, but the old-world elegance carries through. For breakfast, the focus is on healthy food with a little decadence thrown in. You'll enjoy fresh fruit and homebaked breads and pastries. Under the same stellar ownership (but a little less expensive) is the nearby **Four Kachinas Inn** ⊕ (© 888/634-8782; www.fourkachinas.com), where Southwestern-style rooms sit around a sunny courtyard. A little less lavish than those at El Farolito, these rooms are sparkly clean, all with patios.

514 Galisteo St., Santa Fe, NM 87501. © 888/634-8782 or 505/988-1631. Fax 505/988-4589. www.farolito.com. 8 units. $150–$280 casita. Rates include expanded continental breakfast. AE, DISC, MC, V. Free parking. **Amenities:** Babysitting; laundry service. *In room:* A/C, TV, coffeemaker, hair dryer, iron.

Hacienda Nicholas 𝒜𝒜   This inn, a few blocks from the plaza, has a delightful Southwest hacienda ambience. Rooms surround a sunny patio; our favorites are the bright Cottonwood, with a serene feel created by the sunshine-colored walls, wood floors, and a kiva fireplace. Even more luxurious, the Sunflower has French doors, plenty of space, and a fireplace. Units off the sitting room in the house are more modest but also have a warm "Southwest meets Provence" feel. All beds are comfortable and bathrooms range from small with showers only to larger with tub/showers. A full breakfast—including such delicacies as homemade granola and red-and-green breakfast burritos—and afternoon wine and cheese are served in the lovely Great Room or on the patio, both of which have fireplaces. Service here is excellent.

Under the same ownership, **Alexander's Inn** (© **888/321-5123** or 505/986-1431; www.alexanders-inn.com) rents out four casitas in the older district of Santa Fe. Each is a fully equipped home, with a kitchen, including fridge, stove, and microwave. All have unique Southwestern furnishings and plenty of charm.

320 E. Marcy St., Santa Fe, NM 87501. **888/284-3170** or 505/992-8385. Fax 505/982-8572. www.hacienda nicholas.com. 7 units. $110–$210 double. Rates include breakfast and afternoon wine and cheese. Additional person $25. AE, DISC, MC, V. Free parking. Pets accepted w/$20 deposit. **Amenities:** Concierge; activities desk. *In room:* A/C, TV, dataport, hair dryer.

The Madeleine 𝒜𝒜   Lace, flowery upholstery, and stained glass surround you at this 1886 Queen Anne–style inn just 5 blocks east of the plaza. All rooms have terry cloth robes and some have fireplaces. One of our favorites is the Morning Glory, with a king-size bed, a corner fireplace, and lots of sun. All rooms have comfortable beds and those in the main house have small bathrooms. An adjacent cottage, built in 1987, received an award for compatible architecture from the Santa Fe Historical Association. The two rooms in the cottage are larger than the other rooms, with king-size beds and bay windows, and are some of the nicest accommodations in the city. In the Victorian-cum-Asian lobby and out on a flagstone patio surrounded by flowers and fruit trees, visitors enjoy chai from the **Absolute Nirvana Spa, Tea Room & Gardens** (p. 172).

106 Faithway St., Santa Fe, NM 87501. (© **888/877-7622** or 505/982-3465. Fax 505/982-8572. www.madeleine inn.com. 7 units. $110–$210 double. Rates include full breakfast and afternoon wine and cheese. Additional person $25. AE, DISC, MC, V. Free parking. **Amenities:** Spa w/steam showers and soaking tubs; concierge. *In room:* A/C, TV/VCR, hair dryer, Wi-Fi.

Water Street Inn 𝒜𝒜   An award-winning adobe restoration 4 blocks from the plaza, this friendly inn features beautiful Mexican-tile bathrooms, several kiva fireplaces and wood stoves, and antique furnishings. Each room is packed with Southwestern art and books. All rooms are decorated in a Moroccan/Southwestern style. Room no. 3 provides a queen-size sofa bed to accommodate families. Room no. 4 features special regional touches in its decor and contains a chaise longue, a fur rug, built-in seating, and a corner fireplace. Four new suites have elegant contemporary Southwestern furnishings and outdoor private patios with fountains. Most rooms have balconies or terraces. In the afternoon, a happy hour, with quesadillas and margaritas, is offered in the living room or on the upstairs portal, where an extended continental breakfast is also served.

427 West Water St., Santa Fe, NM 87501. (© **800/646-6752** or 505/984-1193. Fax 505/984-6235. www.waterstreet inn.com. 12 units. $100–$250 double. Rates include continental breakfast and afternoon hors d'oeuvres and refreshments. AE, DISC, MC, V. Free parking. Children and pets welcome w/prior approval. **Amenities:** Jacuzzi; concierge; room service. *In room:* A/C, TV/VCR, hair dryer, Wi-Fi.

RV PARKS & CAMPGROUNDS

RV PARKS

At least four private camping areas, mainly for recreational vehicles, are within a few minutes' drive of downtown Santa Fe. Typical rates are $28 for full RV hookups, $18 for tents. Be sure to book ahead at busy times.

Los Campos RV Resort   The resort has 95 spaces with full hookups, picnic tables, and covered pavilion for use with reservation at no charge. It's 5 miles south of the plaza, so it's plenty convenient, but it is surrounded by the city. The campground honors a variety of discounts.

3574 Cerrillos Rd., Santa Fe, NM 87507. ② **800/852-8160.** Fax 505/471-9220. http://hometown.aol.com/los campossf. $28–$33 daily; $172–$212 weekly; $450 monthly/winter; $500 monthly/summer. MC, V. Pets welcome. **Amenities:** Outdoor pool; concierge; coin-op laundry; restrooms; showers; grills; vending machines; free cable TV; Wi-Fi in half of the park.

Rancheros de Santa Fe Campground ☞   Tents, motor homes, and trailers requiring full hookups are welcome here. The park's 127 sites are situated on 22 acres of piñon and juniper forest. Cabins are also available. About 6 miles southeast of Santa Fe, it's open March 15 to October 31.

736 Old Las Vegas Hwy. (exit 290 off I-25), Santa Fe, NM 87505. ② **800/426-9259** or 505/466-3482. www. rancheros.com. Tent site $18–$20; RV hookup $24–$36. AE, DISC, MC, V. **Amenities:** Outdoor pool; coin-op laundry; restrooms; showers; grills; cable-TV hookups; Wi-Fi; grocery store; recreation room; tables; fireplaces; nature trails; playground; free nightly movies May–Sept; public telephones; propane.

Santa Fe KOA   This campground, about 11 miles northeast of Santa Fe, sits among the foothills of the Sangre de Cristo Mountains, an excellent place to enjoy northern New Mexico's pine-filled high desert. It offers full hookups, pull-through sites, and tent sites.

934 Old Las Vegas Hwy. (exit 290 or 294 off I-25), Santa Fe, NM 87505. ② **800/KOA-1514** or 505/466-1419 for reservations. www.koa.com. Tent site $22–$25; RV hookup $26–$31. MC, V. **Amenities:** Coin-op laundry; restrooms; showers; store/gift shop; recreation room; playground; picnic tables; propane; dumping station; Wi-Fi.

CAMPGROUNDS

The forested sites along NM 475 on the way to Ski Santa Fe are open May to October. Overnight rates start at about $12.

Hyde Memorial State Park   About 8 miles from the city, this pine-surrounded park offers a quiet retreat. Seven RV pads with electrical pedestals and an RV dumping station are available. There are nature and hiking trails and a playground as well as a small winter ice-skating pond.

740 Hyde Park Rd., Santa Fe, NM 87501. ② **505/983-7175.** www.nmparks.com. **Amenities:** Shelters; water; tables; vault toilets.

Santa Fe National Forest ☞☞   Black Canyon campground, with 44 sites, is adjacent to Hyde Memorial State Park. It's one of the only campgrounds in the state for which you can make a reservation (② **877/444-6777;** www.reserveusa.com). The sites sit within thick forest, and there are hiking trails nearby. Big Tesuque, a first-come, first-served campground with 10 newly rehabilitated sites, is about 12 miles from town. The sites here are closer to the road and sit at the edge of aspen forests. Both Black Canyon and Big Tesuque campgrounds, along the Santa Fe Scenic Byway, NM 475, are equipped with vault toilets.

P.O. Box 1689, Santa Fe, NM 87504. ② **505/438-7840** or 505/753-7331. www.fs.fed.us/r3/sfe. **Amenities:** Water; vault toilets.

4 Where to Dine

Santa Fe abounds in dining options, with hundreds of restaurants of all categories. Competition is steep, and spots are continually opening and closing. Some chefs create dishes that incorporate traditional Southwestern foods with ingredients not indigenous to the region; these listings classify their restaurants as "creative Southwestern." Other options include standard regional New Mexican cuisine, excellent steak and seafood, continental, European, Asian, and, of course, Mexican menus.

Especially during peak tourist seasons, dinner reservations may be essential. Reservations are always recommended at better restaurants.

DOWNTOWN

This area includes the circle defined by the Paseo de Peralta and St. Francis Drive, as well as Canyon Road. See the map "Downtown Santa Fe Accommodations & Dining," p. 139.

EXPENSIVE

Anasazi Restaurant ✦✦✦ CREATIVE SOUTHWESTERN/NATIVE AMERICAN   Part of the Inn of the Anasazi (p. 138), this restaurant, named for the ancient people who once inhabited the area, offers one of Santa Fe's more interesting dining experiences. You dine surrounded by diamond-finished walls and stacked flagstone. There's no pretension here; the waitstaff is friendly but not overbearing, and tables are nicely spaced, making it a good place for a romantic dinner. The cuisine is inventive, especially now that Chef Martin Rios has come over from the Old House (p. 154). He made his mark there and now brings his bold and elegant palate to mostly organic meats and vegetables. For lunch, we've enjoyed the crispy ahi tuna tacos with mango salsa. Lunch portions are moderate size, so if you're hungry, order an appetizer as well. For dinner, try cinnamon-chili-rubbed beef tenderloin with potato bone-marrow puree, oyster mushrooms, and asparagus.

At the Inn of the Anasazi, 113 Washington Ave. ⓒ 505/988-3236. Reservations recommended. Main courses $7.50–$12 breakfast, $9.50–$15 lunch, $25–$36 dinner. AE, DISC, MC, V. Daily 7–10:30am, 11:30am–2:30pm, and 5:30–10pm.

Cafe Pasqual's ✦✦ CREATIVE SOUTHWESTERN/MEXICAN   "You have to become the food, erase the line between it as an object and you," says Pasqual's owner Katharine Kagel, who uses mostly organic ingredients in her dishes. Her attitude is apparent in this restaurant, where the walls are lined with murals depicting voluptuous villagers playing guitars, drinking, and even flying. A festive place with jovial, professional service, Cafe Pasqual is also excellent for a romantic dinner. Our favorite dish, for breakfast or lunch, is the *huevos motuleños* (two eggs over easy on blue-corn tortillas and black beans topped with sautéed bananas, feta cheese, salsa, and green chile). Soups and salads are also served for lunch, and there's a delectable grilled-salmon burrito with herbed goat cheese and cucumber salsa. The frequently changing dinner menu offers grilled meats and seafood, plus vegetarian specials. Start with the Iroquois corn tamale with roasted poblano, zucchini, and asadero cheese, and move on to the spinach, jack cheese, and red-onion enchiladas. There's a communal table for those who would like to meet new people over a meal. Pasqual's offers imported beers and wine by the bottle or glass. Try to go at a non-peak hour—late morning or afternoon—or make a reservation for dinner; otherwise, you'll have to wait.

121 Don Gaspar Ave. Ⓒ **505/983-9340**. Reservations recommended for dinner. Main courses $8–$15 breakfast, $9–$15 lunch, $19–$37 dinner. AE, MC, V. Mon–Sat 7am–3pm; Sun–Thurs 5:30–9:30pm; Fri–Sat 5:30–10pm; summer daily 5:30–10:30pm; brunch Sun 8am–2pm.

The Compound ⓇⓇⓇ NEW AMERICAN   This reincarnation of one of Santa Fe's classic restaurants serves some of the most flavorful and daring food in town. Inside, it's an elegant old adobe with white walls often offset by bold splashes of flowers. Outside, during warm months, a broad patio shelters diners from the city bustle. With friendly, efficient service, this is an excellent place for a romantic dinner or a relaxing lunch. Chef and owner Mark Kiffin, after nearly 8 years as chef at Coyote Café (see below), opened this place in 2000 as a venue where he could let his creativity soar. For lunch, monkfish chorizo with watercress is outrageously tasty. At dinner, you might start off with tuna tartare topped with Osetra caviar. For an entree, a signature dish is the grilled beef tenderloin with Italian potatoes and foie gras hollandaise. Finish with a bittersweet chocolate torte. A carefully selected beer and wine list accompanies the menu.

653 Canyon Rd. Ⓒ **505/982-4353**. Reservations recommended. Main courses $12–$20 lunch, $22–$44 dinner. AE, DC, DISC, MC, V. Mon–Fri noon–2pm; daily 6–9pm; bar opens nightly at 5pm.

Coyote Café ⓇⓇ CREATIVE SOUTHWESTERN/LATIN   World-renowned chef and cookbook author Mark Miller has been "charged with single-handedly elevating the chile to haute status." That statement from the *New York Times Magazine* sums up the experience of eating at this trendy nouveau Southwestern restaurant about a block from the plaza. The atmosphere is contemporary with an imaginative blend of warm colors and creative lighting. The waitstaff is efficient and friendly. It's the place to go for a fun night out, or you can sample the great food for lunch at a fraction of the price.

The menu changes seasonally. Start your meal with Coyote cocktails that might include a Brazilian daiquiri or margarita del Maguey. Then look for delights such as chipotle tiger prawns with griddled corn cakes or a duck tamale for appetizers. Move on to a braised-ancho lamb shank or horseradish-crusted Maine haddock. You can order drinks from the full bar or wine by the glass.

Coyote Café has an adjunct establishment. In summer, the place to be seen is the **Rooftop Cantina,** where light Latino/Cuban fare and cocktails are served on a festively painted terrace. (Try the chicken skewers on sugar cane.)

132 Water St. Ⓒ **505/983-1615**. Reservations highly recommended. Main courses $6–$16 (Rooftop Cantina), $19–$36 (Coyote Café). AE, DC, DISC, MC, V. Coyote Café daily 5:30–9pm; Rooftop Cantina daily 11:30am–9pm.

El Farol Ⓡ SPANISH   This is the place to head for local ambience and old-fashioned flavor. El Farol (The Lantern) is the original neighborhood bar in Canyon Road's artists' quarter. The restaurant has cozy low ceilings and hand-smoothed adobe walls. Thirty-five varieties of tapas are offered, including *gambas al ajillo* (shrimp with chile, garlic, Madeira, and lime) and *conejo y vino* (stewed rabbit). You can make a meal out of two or three tapas shared with your friends, or order a full dinner such as the paella or the grilled lamb chops with cranberry salsa. There's live entertainment 7 nights a week—including jazz/swing, folk, and Latin guitar music—starting at 9:30pm. In summer, two outdoor patios are open to diners.

808 Canyon Rd. Ⓒ **505/983-9912**. Reservations recommended. Tapas $4.50–$12; main courses $8–$15 lunch, $26–$32 dinner. AE, DC, DISC, MC, V. Daily 11:30am–3pm and 5:30–10pm (bar until 2am Mon–Sat, until midnight Sun).

Fuego ★★★ *Moments* INTERNATIONAL   A revamp of this restaurant has made it one of Santa Fe's most stylish and sophisticated dining experiences, though the change comes at a price. The restaurant offers the ambience of a traditional Southwestern hacienda, accented with colorful paintings from local galleries, grand iron chandeliers hanging from high ceilings, and comfortable couches, along with a broad dining patio that's one of Santa Fe's best. Service is excellent. Some locals consider the "Rancher's Brunch" one of the town's finest. Try the Southwestern omelet, which melds creamy goat cheese with toasted chilies, sun-dried tomatoes, ham, and avocado. For lunch, you might try the manchego and parsely stuffed calamari or the duck breast with a mole sauce. For dinner, the herb and salt crusted roast rack of lamb served with potatoes and black truffle juice is excellent. An award-winning wine list accompanies the menu. This is one of the most expensive spots in Santa Fe, but a worthwhile, memorable choice for special occasions.

330 E. Palace Ave. (at La Posada de Santa Fe Resort and Spa). (C) **800/727-5276** or 505/954-9670. Reservations recommended. $45 fixed-price brunch ($25 children under 12); $15–$28 lunch; $25–$45 dinner; prix-fixe tasting menus (dinner) $75–$125. AE, DC, DISC, MC, V. Breakfast daily 7–11am; lunch Mon–Sat 11:30am–2:30pm; brunch Sun 11:30am–2pm; dinner daily 6–9pm (summer 5:30–9pm).

Geronimo ★★★ CONTINENTAL   This elegant restaurant offers one of Santa's Fe's most delectable dining experiences. Occupying an old adobe structure known as the Borrego House—which was built by Geronimo Lopez in 1756 but has since been completely restored—it retains the feel of an old Santa Fe home. We especially recommend lunch here, when you can get a taste of this complex food for a fraction of the dinner price. Reserve a spot on the porch and watch the action on Canyon Road. For lunch, try the grilled mahimahi pineapple salad. For a dinner appetizer, the warm tomato tart with fresh goat cheese is delicious. If you want to try one of Santa Fe's most renowned entrees, order the peppery elk tenderloin, or, as a seafood alternative, the mesquite grilled lobster tails. For dessert, you won't be disappointed by the trio of brûlées—espresso chocolate, Chambord, and orange—or the Belgian chocolate Grand Marnier cake. The menu changes seasonally, and there's an excellent wine list.

724 Canyon Rd. (C) **505/982-1500.** Reservations recommended. Main courses $20–$29 lunch, $30–$50 dinner. AE, MC, V. Tues–Sun 11:30am–2pm; Sun–Thurs 5:45–9pm; Fri–Sat 5:45–9:30pm.

La Casa Sena ★★ CREATIVE SOUTHWESTERN   Combining alluring ambience and tasty food, this is one of Santa Fe's favorite restaurants, though the food here isn't as precise and flavorful as at Santacafé or Geronimo (below and above, respectively). La Casa Sena sits within the Sena compound, a prime example of a Spanish hacienda, in a Territorial-style adobe house built in 1867 by Civil War hero Major José Sena. The house, which surrounds a garden courtyard, is now a veritable art gallery, with museum-quality landscapes on the walls and Taos-style handcrafted furniture. The cuisine in the main dining room might be described as northern New Mexican with a continental flair. One of our favorite lunches is the flash-fried Baja sea bass fish tacos with mango salsa. In the evening, diners might start with a salad of garden greens and grilled mushrooms, then move to a grilled lamb rack marinated with Dijon and mint and accompanied by roasted root vegetables and green-peppercorn sauce.

In the adjacent **La Cantina,** waitstaff sing Broadway show tunes as they carry platters from the kitchen to the table. The more moderately priced Cantina menu offers the likes of cornmeal-breaded trout and grilled stuffed pork loin with peach-onion sauce. Both restaurants have exquisite desserts; try the black-and-white bittersweet chocolate terrine with raspberry sauce. The award-winning wine list features more than 850 selections. There's patio dining in summer. The patio here is Santa Fe's best.

125 E. Palace Ave. (C) 505/988-9232. Reservations recommended. La Casa Sena main courses $11–$19 lunch, $24–$42 dinner; 5-course chef's tasting menu $42, w/wine $58; La Cantina main courses $13–$28. AE, DC, DISC, MC, V. Mon–Sat 11:30am–3pm; Sun brunch 11am–3pm; daily 5:30–10pm.

Old House ✹✹✹ NEW AMERICAN/CONTINENTAL   Located within the Eldorado Hotel (p. 137), this restaurant consistently rates as Santa Fe's best eatery in local publications' polls. In a Southwestern atmosphere, rich with excellent Native American art, the Old House serves quality meats, poultry, and seafood in refined sauces. The menu changes seasonally, with some signature dishes that remain year-round. A must here, as either an appetizer or an entree, is the pan-seared Dungeness crab cakes with an organic watercress salad. For entrees, you might try the hand-harvested sea scallops with creamed corn or the wood-roasted tenderloin of beef with ancho chile grits and buttermilk onion rings. The mascarpone cheesecake here is excellent, but our favorite dessert is the warm Tanzanian chocolate cake. The wine list is a *Wine Spectator* award-winner.

309 W. San Francisco St. (in the Eldorado Hotel). (C) 505/988-4455, ext. 130. Reservations recommended. Main courses $12–$20 lunch, $24–$40 dinner. AE, DC, DISC, MC, V. Mon–Fri 11:30am–2pm; daily 5:30–9:30pm. Lounge daily 11:30am–closing.

The Pink Adobe ✹ CONTINENTAL/SOUTHWESTERN   More show than flavor? Probably. This restaurant, a few blocks off the plaza, offers a swirl of local old-timer gaiety and food that is more imaginative than flavorful. Nevertheless, the Pink Adobe has remained popular since it opened in 1944. The restaurant occupies an adobe home believed to be at least 350 years old. Guests enter through a narrow side door into a series of quaint, informal dining rooms with tile or hardwood floors. Stuccoed walls display original modern art and Priscilla Hoback pottery on built-in shelves. For lunch, we always have a chicken enchilada topped with an egg. At the dinner hour, the Pink Adobe offers the likes of escargot and shrimp rémoulade as appetizers. The local word here is that the steak Dunigan, with sautéed mushrooms and green chile, is "the thing" to order. You can't leave without trying the hot French apple pie.

   Under the same ownership, the charming bar (a real local scene) has its own menu, offering traditional New Mexican food. Locals come to eat hearty green-chile stew.

406 Old Santa Fe Trail. (C) 505/983-7712. Reservations recommended. Main courses $5–$9 lunch, $15–$28 dinner. AE, DC, DISC, MC, V. Mon–Fri 11:30am–2pm; daily 5:30pm–closing. Bar Mon–Fri 11:30am–midnight; Sat–Sun 5pm–midnight.

Santacafé ✹✹✹ (Moments) NEW AMERICAN/CREATIVE SOUTHWESTERN When you eat at this fine restaurant, be prepared for imaginative flavor adventures. The food combines the best of many cuisines, from Asian to Southwestern, served in an elegant setting with minimalist decor that accentuates the graceful architecture of the 18th-century Padre Gallegos House, 2 blocks from the plaza. The white walls are decorated only with deer antlers, and each room contains a fireplace. In warm months you can sit under elm trees in the charming courtyard. Beware that on busy nights the rooms are noisy. The dishes change to take advantage of seasonal specialties, each served with precision. For a starter, try the shiitake and cactus spring rolls with Southwestern ponzu. One of our favorite main courses is the Alaskan halibut with English peas and saffron couscous. A heartier eater might try the bacon-wrapped black-angus filet mignon with roasted-garlic mashed potatoes. There's an extensive wine list, with wine by the glass as well. Desserts, as elegant as the rest of the food, are made in-house; try the warm chocolate upside-down cake with vanilla ice cream.

231 Washington Ave. © 505/984-1788. Reservations recommended. Main courses $9–$15 lunch, $19–$40 dinner. AE, DISC, MC, V. Mon–Sat 11:30am–2pm; daily 5:30–10pm. Sun brunch served in summer, Easter Sun, and Mother's Day.

MODERATE

Cowgirl Hall of Fame ✿ REGIONAL AMERICAN/BARBECUE/CAJUN This raucous bar/restaurant serves decent food in a festive atmosphere. The main room is a bar—a hip hangout spot, and a good place to eat as well, with the quieter back room has wood floors and tables and plenty of cowgirl memorabilia. Best of all is sitting out on a brick patio lit with strings of white lights during the warm season. The service is sometimes brusque, and the quality of the food varies. In winter, our favorite dish is a big bowl of gumbo or crawfish étouffée, and the rest of the time, we order Jamaican jerk chicken or pork tenderloin when it's a special. Careful, both can be hot. The daily blue-plate special is a real buy, especially on Tuesday nights, when it's chile rellenos. There's even a special "kids' corral" that has horseshoes, a rocking horse, a horse-shaped rubber-tire swing, hay bales, and a beanbag toss. Happy hour is 3 to 6pm, and there's live music almost every night.

319 S. Guadalupe St. © 505/982-2565. Reservations recommended. Main courses $6–$12 lunch, $7–$22 dinner. AE, DISC, MC, V. Mon–Fri 11am–midnight; Sat 8:30am–midnight, Sun 8:30am–11pm. Bar Mon–Sat until 2am; Sun until midnight.

Il Piatto Cucina Italiano ✿✿ *Value* NORTHERN ITALIAN This simple Italian cafe brings innovative flavors to thinner wallets. It's simple and elegant, with contemporary art on the walls—nice for a romantic evening. Service here is efficient, though on a busy night the staff seem a bit overworked. The menu changes seasonally, complemented by a few perennial standards. For a starter, try the grilled calamari with shaved fennel and aioli. Among entrees, our favorite is the pancetta-wrapped trout with grilled polenta and wild mushrooms, though you can't go wrong with the jumbo scampi risotto with sweet peppers. The Gorgonzola-walnut ravioli is a favorite of many, though not quite enough food to fill us up. A full wine and beer menu is available.

95 W. Marcy St. © 505/984-1091. Reservations recommended. Main courses $13–$19. AE, DISC, MC, V. Mon–Fri 11:30am–2pm; daily 5:30–9pm. Closed July 4th.

Railyard Restaurant & Saloon ✿✿ *Finds* NEW AMERICAN Santa Fe locals' most talked-about new spot, the Railyard is a fun addition to the restaurant scene. Set in one of the city's old railroad buildings, the place offers a comfortable ambience and imaginative food at not-too-steep prices. The space has clean lines, with maroon walls and spacious booths and tables set under an industrial ceiling with visible ductwork. Service is friendly and knowledgeable. The Railyard is the creation of Louis Moskow, a well-known Santa Fe chef. Here, he's offering a slice of Americana, with dishes such as an outstanding rib-eye steak and tasty pan-fried pork chop, but also some less American fare, like sesame-and-panko-crusted tuna (our favorite). All menu items are a la carte, but the side portions you'll order separately are large enough to share. Select from a carefully considered wine list or from the full bar. An excellent but more limited selection of food is available all day at the bar.

530 S. Guadalupe St. (¼ block north of Paseo de Peralta). ℭ **505/989-3300.** www.railyardrestaurantandsaloon.com. Reservations recommended on weekend nights. Main courses $7.50–$23 lunch, $8–$23 dinner. Mon–Sat 11:30am–2:30pm; Sun–Thurs 5:30–9:30pm; Fri–Sat 5:30–10pm. Bar Mon–Thurs 11:30am–10pm; Fri–Sat 11:30am–11pm.

INEXPENSIVE

Blue Corn Café *(Kids* MICROBREWERY/NEW MEXICAN   If you're ready for a fun ambience and inexpensive New Mexican food, this is your place. Within a clean and breezy decor—wooden tables and abstract art—you'll find a raucous and buoyant atmosphere; it's a good place to bring kids. The overworked waitstaff may be slow, but they're friendly. We recommend sampling dishes from the combination menu. You can get two to five items served with your choice of rice, beans, or one of the best *posoles* (hominy and chile) that we've tasted. We had the chicken enchilada, which we recommend, and the chalupa, which we don't because it was soggy. You can have tacos, tamales, and rellenos, too. Kids have their own menu and crayons to keep them occupied. There are nightly specials—the shrimp fajitas are tasty, served with a nice guacamole and the usual toppings. Since this is also a brewery, you might want to sample the High Altitude Pale Ale or the Plaza Porter. The Spanish flan is tasty and large enough to share. **The Blue Corn Cafe & Brewery** (4056 Cerrillos Rd., Suite G; ℭ **505/438-1800**), on the south side at the corner of Cerrillos and Rodeo roads, has similar fare and atmosphere.

133 W. Water St. ℭ **505/984-1800.** Reservations accepted for parties of 6 or more. Main courses $9.50–$18. AE, DC, DISC, MC, V. Daily 11am–10pm.

Guadalupe Cafe ☆☆ NEW MEXICAN   When we want New Mexican food, we go to this restaurant. This casually elegant cafe is in a white stucco building that's warm and friendly and has a nice-size patio for dining in warmer months. Service is generally friendly and conscientious. For breakfast, try the spinach-mushroom burritos or huevos rancheros, and for lunch, the chalupas or stuffed *sopaipillas.* Any other time, we'd start with fresh roasted ancho chiles (filled with a combination of Montrachet and Monterey Jack cheeses and piñon nuts, and topped with your choice of chile) and move on to the sour-cream chicken enchilada or any of the other Southwestern dishes. Order both red and green chile ("Christmas") so that you can sample some of the best sauces in town. Beware, though: The chile here can be hot, and the chef won't put it on the side. Diners can order from a choice of delicious salads, such as a Caesar with chicken. Daily specials are available, and don't miss the famous chocolate-amaretto adobe pie for dessert. Beer and wine are served.

422 Old Santa Fe Trail. ℭ **505/982-9762.** Reservations not accepted. Breakfast $4.50–$8.75; lunch $6–$12; dinner $7–$15. DISC, MC, V. Tues–Fri 7am–2pm; Sat–Sun 8am–2pm; Tues–Sat 5:30–9pm.

La Choza ☆☆ NEW MEXICAN   This sister restaurant of the Shed (below) offers some of the best New Mexican food in town at a convenient location near the intersection of Cerrillos Road and St. Francis Drive. When other restaurants are packed, you'll only wait a little while here. It's a warm, casual eatery with vividly painted walls; it's especially popular on cold days, when diners gather around the wood-burning stove and fireplace. The patio is delightful in summer. Service is friendly and efficient. The menu offers enchiladas, tacos, and burritos on blue-corn tortillas, as well as green chile stew, chile con carne, and carne adovada. Our new favorite here is the blue-corn burritos (tortillas stuffed with beans and cheese) served with *posole;* the dish can be made vegetarian, too. For dessert, you can't leave without trying the mocha cake (chocolate cake with a mocha pudding filling, served with whipped cream). Vegetarians and children have their own menus. Beer and wine are available.

905 Alarid St. (C) **505/982-0909.** Reservations not accepted. Main courses $7.95–$10. AE, DISC, MC, V. Summer Mon–Sat 11am–9pm; winter Mon–Thurs 11am–8pm, Fri–Sat 11am–9pm.

Plaza Cafe ☆ AMERICAN/DELI/GREEK/NEW MEXICAN   Santa Fe's best example of diner-style eating, this cafe has excellent food in a bright and friendly atmosphere right on the plaza. We like to meet friends here, sit in a booth, eat, and laugh about life. A restaurant since the turn of the 20th century, it's been owned by the Razatos family since 1947. The decor has changed only enough to stay comfortable and clean, with red upholstered banquettes, Art Deco tile, and a soda fountain-style service counter. Service is always quick and conscientious, and only during the heavy tourist seasons will you have to wait long for a table. Breakfasts are excellent and large, and the hamburgers and sandwiches are good. We also like the soups and New Mexican dishes, such as the bowl of green chile stew, or, if you're more adventurous, the pumpkin *posole*. Beer and wine are available.

54 Lincoln Ave. (on the plaza). (C) **505/982-1664.** Reservations not accepted. Main courses $8–$15. AE, DISC, MC, V. Daily 7am–9pm.

The Shed ☆☆ NEW MEXICAN   This longtime locals' favorite is so popular that, during lunch, lines often form outside. Half a block east of the plaza, this luncheon institution since 1953 occupies several rooms and the patio of a rambling hacienda built in 1692. Festive folk art adorns the doorways and walls. The delicious food is some of the best in the state, and a compliment to traditional Hispanic and Pueblo cooking. The cheese enchilada is renowned in Santa Fe. Tacos and burritos are good, too, all served on blue-corn tortillas, with pinto beans on the side. The green chile soup is a local favorite. The Shed offers vegetarian and low-fat Mexican foods, as well as a variety of soups and salads and grilled chicken and steak. Don't leave without trying the mocha cake, possibly the best dessert you'll ever eat. In addition to wine and a number of beers, there's full bar service.

113½ E. Palace Ave. (C) **505/982-9030.** Reservations accepted at dinner. Lunch $5.75–$9.50; dinner $8–$17. AE, DC, DISC, MC, V. Mon–Sat 11am–2:30pm and 5:30–9pm.

Tomasita's Cafe ☆ NEW MEXICAN   Tomasita's is in a modern building near the train station, and its food has become renowned. The atmosphere is simple—hanging plants and wood accents—with lots of families sitting at booths or tables and a festive spillover from the bar, where many come to drink margaritas. Service is quick, even a little rushed, which is our biggest gripe about Tomasita's. Sure, the food is still tasty, but unless you go at some totally odd hour, you'll wait for a table, and once you're seated, you may eat and be out again in less than an hour. The burritos are still excellent, though you may want to try the chile rellenos, a house specialty. Vegetarian dishes, burgers, steaks, and daily specials are also offered. There's full bar service.

500 S. Guadalupe St. (C) **505/983-5721.** Reservations not accepted; large parties call ahead. Lunch $5.25–$14; dinner $5.75–$14. AE, DISC, MC, V. Mon–Sat 11am–10pm.

Upper Crust Pizza ☆ *Kids* PIZZA/ITALIAN   Upper Crust serves Santa Fe's best pizzas, in an adobe house near the old San Miguel Mission. The atmosphere is plain, with wooden tables; in summer, the outdoor patio overlooking Old Santa Fe Trail is more inviting. Meals-in-a-dish include the Grecian gourmet pizza (feta and olives) and the whole-wheat vegetarian pizza (topped with sesame seeds). You can either eat here or request free delivery (it takes about 30 min.) to your downtown hotel. Beer and wine are available, as are salads, calzones, sandwiches, and stromboli.

329 Old Santa Fe Trail. ⓒ 505/982-0000. Reservations not accepted. Pizzas $7.95–$16. DISC, MC, V. Summer daily 11am–midnight; winter Sun–Thurs 11am–10pm, Fri–Sat 11am–11pm.

SOUTHSIDE
Santa Fe's motel strip and other streets south of the Paseo de Peralta have their share of good, reasonably priced restaurants. See the "Greater Santa Fe" map (p. 146) for the location of the restaurants in this section.

MODERATE
mu du noodles ☞☞ PACIFIC RIM   If you're ready for a light, healthy meal with lots of flavor, head to this small restaurant about an 8-minute drive from downtown. There are two rooms, with plain pine tables and chairs and sparse Asian prints on the walls. The carpeted back room is cozier, and a woodsy-feeling patio is definitely worth requesting during the warmer months. The waitstaff is friendly and unimposing. We almost always order the Malaysian *laksa*, thick rice noodles in a blend of coconut milk, hazelnuts, onions, and red curry, stir-fried with chicken or tofu and julienned vegetables and sprouts. If you're eating with others, you may each want to order a different dish and share. The pad Thai is lighter and spicier than most, served with a chile/vinegar sauce. A list of beers, wines, and sakes is available, tailored to the menu. We're especially fond of the ginseng ginger ale. Menu items change seasonally.

1494 Cerrillos Rd. ⓒ 505/983-1411. Reservations for parties of 3 or larger only. Main courses $9–$18. AE, DC, DISC, MC, V. Mon–Sat 5:30–9pm (sometimes 10pm in summer).

INEXPENSIVE
Marisco's La Playa MEXICAN/SEAFOOD   What this Mexican seafood restaurant lacks in ambience it makes up for in *comida sabrosa* (tasty food). Set in a small shopping mall not far from St. Francis Drive, it has a beach scene mural on one wall and stark luminescent lighting from above. It was opened by two cousins who wanted to bring good Mexican *playa* (beach) food to the drylands, and judging from the crowds here (you may have to wait 15–20 min., but it's worth it), they've succeeded. Marisco's features such dishes as shrimp or fish tacos and *pescado a la plancha* (trout seasoned with butter, garlic, and paprika). Some locals complain that the place is too pricey, but we say for good fish it's a bargain. Our favorite dish is *caldo vuelve a la vida* (come-back-to-life soup), which is a huge bowl—even if you order the small—of shrimp, octopus, scallops, clams, crab legs, and calamari in a tasty broth. Wash it down with a domestic or imported beer. There's now a second location as well, at 2875 Cerrillos Rd. (ⓒ 505/473-4594).

537 Cordova Rd. ⓒ 505/982-2790. Main courses $8.95–$14. AE, DISC, MC, V. Fri–Wed 11am–9pm.

5 What to See & Do

One of the oldest cities in the United States, Santa Fe has long been a center for the creative and performing arts, so it's not surprising that most of the city's major sights are related to local history and the arts. The city's Museum of New Mexico, art galleries and studios, historic churches, and cultural sights associated with local Native American and Hispanic communities all merit a visit. It would be easy to spend a full week sightseeing in the city without ever heading out to any nearby attractions. Of special note is the recently opened Georgia O'Keeffe Museum.

Downtown Santa Fe Attractions

Barrio de Analco **9**

Georgia O'Keeffe Museum **2**

Institute of American Indian Arts Museum **6**

Loretto Chapel Museum **8**

Mission of San Miguel **11**

Museum of Fine Arts **3**

New Mexico State Capitol (Roundhouse) **10**

Padre Gallegos House **4**

Palace of the Governors **5**

Santuario de Nuestra Señora de Guadalupe **1**

St. Francis Cathedral **7**

THE TOP ATTRACTIONS

Museum of Fine Arts 🕉️   Located opposite the Palace of the Governors, this was one of the first pueblo revival–style buildings constructed in Santa Fe (in 1917). The museum's permanent collection of more than 20,000 works emphasizes regional art and includes landscapes and portraits by all the Taos masters, *los Cincos Pintores* (a 1920s organization of Santa Fe artists), and contemporary artists. The museum also has a collection of photographic works by such masters as Ansel Adams, Edward Weston, and Elliot Porter. Modern artists are featured in temporary exhibits throughout the year. Two sculpture gardens present a range of three-dimensional art, from the traditional to the abstract.

Graceful **St. Francis Auditorium,** patterned after the interiors of traditional Hispanic mission churches, adjoins the art museum (see "The Performing Arts," later in this chapter). A museum shop sells gifts, art books, prints, and postcards of the collection.

107 W. Palace (at Lincoln Ave.). ℂ 505/476-5072. www.museumofnewmexico.org. Admission $7 adults, free for seniors Wed, free for children 16 and under, free for all Fri 5–8pm. 4-day passes (good at all 4 branches of the Museum of New Mexico and the Museum of Spanish Colonial Art) $15 for adults. Tues–Sun 10am–5pm (Fri until 8pm). Closed New Year's Day, Easter, Thanksgiving, Christmas.

Palace of the Governors 🕉️🕉️   In order to fully appreciate this structure, it's important to know that this is where the only successful Native American uprising took place, in 1680. Prior to the uprising, this was the local seat of power, and after de Vargas reconquered the natives, it resumed that position. Built in 1610 as the original capitol of New Mexico, the palace has been in continuous public use longer than any other structure in the United States. Begin out front, where Native Americans sell jewelry, pottery, and some weavings under the protection of the portal. This is a good place to buy.

Inside, the museum illustrates 400 years of New Mexico history, from the 16th-century Spanish explorations through the frontier era and modern times. The museum focuses little on regional Native American culture. (Most Native American artifacts previously housed here have been moved to the Museum of Indian Arts & Culture.) The palace is the flagship of the Museum of New Mexico system; the main office is at 113 Lincoln Ave. (ℂ 505/476-5060). The system comprises five state monuments and four Santa Fe museums: the Palace of the Governors, the Museum of Fine Arts, the Museum of International Folk Art, and the Museum of Indian Arts & Culture.

North plaza. ℂ 505/476-5100. www.palaceofthegovernors.org. Admission $8 adults, free for children 16 and under, free for all 5–8pm Fri. 4-day passes (good at all 4 branches of the Museum of New Mexico and the Museum of Spanish Colonial Art) $15 for adults. Tues–Sun 10am–5pm. Closed New Year's Day, Thanksgiving, Christmas.

St. Francis Cathedral 🕉️   Santa Fe's grandest religious structure is an architectural anomaly in Santa Fe because its design is French. A block east of the plaza, it was built between 1869 and 1886 by Archbishop Jean Baptiste Lamy in the style of the great cathedrals of Europe. French architects designed the Romanesque building—named after Santa Fe's patron saint—and Italian masons assisted with its construction. The small adobe Our Lady of the Rosary chapel on the northeast side of the cathedral has a Spanish look. Built in 1807, it's the only portion that remains from Our Lady of the Assumption Church, founded along with Santa Fe in 1610. The new cathedral was built over and around the old church.

A wooden icon set in a niche in the wall of the north chapel, Our Lady of Peace, is the oldest representation of the Madonna in the United States. Rescued from the old

Value **Museum Binging**

If you're a museum buff, pick up one of Museum of New Mexico's 4-day passes. It's good at all four branches of the Museum of New Mexico: the Palace of the Governors, the Museum of Fine Arts, the Museum of International Folk Art, and the Museum of Indian Arts & Culture, with the Museum of Spanish Colonial Art thrown in for good measure. The cost is $15 for adults.

church during the 1680 Pueblo Rebellion, it was brought back by Don Diego de Vargas on his (mostly peaceful) reconquest 12 years later—thus, the name. Today, Our Lady of Peace plays an important part in the annual Feast of Corpus Christi in June and July.

The cathedral's front doors feature 16 carved panels of historic note and a plaque memorializing the 38 Franciscan friars who were martyred during New Mexico's early years. There's also a large bronze statue of Bishop Lamy himself; his grave is under the main altar of the cathedral.

Cathedral Place at San Francisco St. Ⓕ 505/982-5619. Donations appreciated. Daily. Visitors may attend Mass Mon–Sat 7am and 5:15pm; Sun 8am, 10am, noon, and 5:15pm. Free parking in city lot next to the cathedral to attend church services.

Santa Fe Plaza ★★ *Moments*   This square has been the heart and soul of Santa Fe, as well as its literal center, since its concurrent establishment with the city in 1610. Originally designed as a meeting place, it has been the site of innumerable festivals and other historical, cultural, and social events. Long ago the plaza was a dusty hive of activity as the staging ground and terminus of the Santa Fe Trail. Today, those who congregate around the central monument enjoy the best people-watching in New Mexico. Live music and dancing are often staged on the gazebo/bandstand in summer.

At the corner of San Francisco St. and Lincoln Ave. Daily 24 hours.

MORE ATTRACTIONS
MUSEUMS

Georgia O'Keeffe Museum ★★   The Georgia O'Keeffe museum, inaugurated in July 1997, contains the largest collection of O'Keeffes in the world: currently 117 oil paintings, drawings, watercolors, and pastels, and more than 50 works by other artists of note. It's the largest museum in the United States dedicated solely to one woman's work. You can see such remarkable O'Keeffes as *Jimson Weed,* painted in 1932, and *Evening Star No. VII,* from 1917. The rich and varied collection adorns the walls of a cathedral-like, 13,000-square-foot space—a former Baptist church with adobe walls. O'Keeffe's images are tied inextricably to local desert landscapes. She first visited New Mexico in 1917 and returned for extended periods from the '20s through the '40s.

217 Johnson St. Ⓒ 505/946-1000. www.okeeffemuseum.org. Admission $8, free for students, free for all Fri 5–8pm. July–Oct daily 10am–5pm (Fri until 8pm); Nov–June Thurs–Tues 10am–5pm (Fri until 8pm).

Institute of American Indian Arts Museum ★   A visit to this museum (the most comprehensive collection of contemporary Native American art in the world) offers a profound look into the lives of a people negotiating two worlds: traditional and

---

Cultural Chow

If you get hungry while visiting the Museum of Indian Arts & Culture, the Museum of International Folk Art, the Wheelwright Museum of the American Indian, and the Museum of Spanish Colonial Art (all located together, southeast of the plaza), you can feast on more than your fingernails. The **Museum Hill Café** ☆ (© **505/820-1776**) opens Tuesday through Saturday for beverages and snacks at 10am, and a tasty lunch from 11am to 3pm; it serves brunch on Sunday from 11am to 3pm.

---

contemporary. Here you'll see cutting-edge art that pushes the limits of many media, from creative writing to textile manufacturing to painting. Much of the work originates from artists from The Institute of American Indian Arts (IAIA), the nation's only congressionally chartered institute of higher education devoted solely to the study and practice of the artistic and cultural traditions of all American Indian and Alaskan native peoples.

108 Cathedral Place. © **505/983-8900.** www.iaiancad.org. Admission $4 adults, $2 seniors and students, free for children 16 and under. Oct–May Mon–Sat 10am–5pm, Sun noon–5pm; June–Sept daily 9am–5pm.

Museum of Indian Arts & Culture ☆☆   An interactive permanent exhibit here has made this one of the most exciting Native American museum experiences in the Southwest. "Here, Now and Always" takes visitors through thousands of years of Native American history. More than 70,000 pieces of basketry, pottery, clothing, carpets, and jewelry—much of it quite old—are on continual rotating display. You begin by entering through a tunnel that symbolizes the *sipapu,* the ancestral Puebloan (Anasazi) entrance into the upper worlds; you're greeted by the sounds of trickling water, drums, and Native American music. Videos show Native Americans telling creation stories. Visitors can reflect on the lives of modern-day Native Americans by juxtaposing a traditional Pueblo kitchen with a modern kitchen. You can step into a Navajo hogan and stroll through a trading post. The rest of the museum houses a lovely pottery collection as well as changing exhibits. There's always a contemporary show. Look for demonstrations of traditional skills by tribal artisans and regular programs in a 70-seat multimedia theater.

710 Camino Lejo. © **505/476-1250.** www.miaclab.org. Admission $7 adults, free for kids 16 and under. 4-day passes (good at all 4 branches of the Museum of New Mexico and the Museum of Spanish Colonial Art) $15 for adults. Tues–Sun 10am–5pm. Drive southeast on Old Santa Fe Trail (beware: Old Santa Fe Trail takes a left turn; if you find yourself on Old Pecos Trail, you missed the turn). Look for signs pointing right onto Camino Lejo.

Museum of International Folk Art ☆☆ *Kids*   This branch of the Museum of New Mexico may not seem quite as typically Southwestern as other Santa Fe museums, but it's the largest of its kind in the world. With a collection of some 130,000 objects from more than 100 countries, it's our favorite city museum, well worth an hour or two of perusing. It was founded in 1953 by the Chicago collector Florence Dibell Bartlett, who said, "If peoples of different countries could have the opportunity to study each other's cultures, it would be one avenue for a closer understanding between men." That's the basis on which the museum operates today. The special collections include Spanish colonial silver, traditional and contemporary New Mexican religious art, Mexican tribal costumes and majolica ceramics, Brazilian folk art, European glass, African sculptures, East Indian textiles, and the marvelous Morris Miniature Circus.

Children love to look at the hundreds of toys on display throughout the museum. The 80,000-square-foot museum also has a gift shop, where a variety of folk art is available for purchase.

706 Camino Lejo. (C) 505/476-1200. www.moifa.org. Admission $8 adults, free for kids 11 and under. 4-day passes (good at all 4 branches of the Museum of New Mexico) $15 for adults. Tues–Sun 10am–5pm. The museum is about 2 miles southeast of the plaza. Drive southeast on Old Santa Fe Trail (beware: Old Santa Fe Trail takes a left turn; if you find yourself on Old Pecos Trail, you missed the turn). Look for signs pointing right onto Camino Lejo.

Museum of Spanish Colonial Art &

Beauty often follows in the tragic wake of imperialism. A good example of this is Spanish colonial art, which has flourished from Europe across the Americas and even in the Philippines. This museum, set in the same compound as the Museum of International Folk Art, the Museum of Indian Arts & Culture, and the Wheelwright Museum of the American Indian, showcases a collection of 3,000 devotional and decorative works and utilitarian artifacts. Housed in a home built by noted architect John Gaw Meem, the museum displays *retablos* (religious paintings on wood), *bultos* (free-standing religious sculptures), furniture, metalwork, and textiles and, outside, an 18th-century wooden colonial house from Mexico. Plan to spend about an hour here.

750 Camino Lejo. (C) 505/982-2226. www.spanishcolonial.org. Admission $6 adults, free for kids 16 and under. 4-day passes (good at all 4 branches of the Museum of New Mexico and the Museum of Spanish Colonial Art) $15 for adults. Tues–Sun 10am–5pm. The museum is about 2 miles southeast of the plaza. Drive southeast on Old Santa Fe Trail (Old Santa Fe Trail takes a left turn—if you find yourself on Old Pecos Trail, you missed the turn). Look for signs pointing right onto Camino Lejo.

Wheelwright Museum of the American Indian & (Kids)

This museum resembles a Navajo hogan, with its doorway facing east (toward the rising sun) and its ceiling formed in the interlocking "whirling log" style. It was founded in 1937 by Boston scholar Mary Cabot Wheelwright, in collaboration with a Navajo medicine man, Hastiin Klah, to preserve and document Navajo ritual beliefs and practices. Klah took the designs of sand paintings used in healing ceremonies and adapted them into the woven pictographs that are a major part of the museum's treasure. In 1976, the museum's focus was altered to include the living arts of all Native American cultures. The museum offers three or four exhibits per year. You may see a basketry exhibit, mixed-media Navajo toys, or amazing contemporary Navajo rugs.

704 Camino Lejo. (C) 800/607-4636 or 505/982-4636. Fax 505/989-7386. www.wheelwright.org. Donations appreciated. Mon–Sat 10am–5pm; Sun 1–5pm. Closed New Year's Day, Thanksgiving, Christmas. Drive southeast on Old Santa Fe Trail (beware: Old Santa Fe Trail takes a left turn; if you find yourself on Old Pecos Trail, you missed the turn). Look for signs pointing right onto Camino Lejo.

CHURCHES

Loretto Chapel Museum &

Though no longer consecrated for worship, the Loretto Chapel is an important site in Santa Fe. Patterned after the famous Sainte-Chapelle church in Paris, it was constructed in 1873—by the same French architects and Italian masons who were building Archbishop Lamy's cathedral—as a chapel for the Sisters of Loretto, who had established a school for young women in Santa Fe in 1852.

The chapel is especially notable for its remarkable spiral staircase: It makes two complete 360-degree turns, with no central or other visible support. The structure is steeped in legend: The building was nearly finished in 1878, when workers realized the stairs to the choir loft wouldn't fit. Hoping for a solution more attractive than a ladder, the sisters made a novena to St. Joseph—and were rewarded when a mysterious carpenter appeared astride a donkey and offered to build a staircase. Armed with only a saw, a hammer, and a T-square, the master constructed this work of genius by soaking slats of wood in tubs of water to curve them and holding them together with wooden pegs. Then he disappeared without bothering to collect his fee.

207 Old Santa Fe Trail (between Alameda and Water sts.). © 505/982-0092. www.lorettochapel.com. Admission $2.50 adults, $2 children 7–12 and seniors over 65, free for children 6 and under. Mon–Sat 9am–5pm; Sun 10:30am–5pm.

Mission of San Miguel   If you really want to get the feel of colonial Catholicism, visit this church. Better yet, attend Mass here. You won't be disappointed. Built in 1610, the church has massive adobe walls, high windows, an elegant altar screen (erected in 1798), and a 780-pound San José bell (now found inside), which was cast in Spain in 1356. If that doesn't impress you, perhaps the buffalo-hide and deerskin Bible paintings, used in 1630 by Franciscan missionaries to teach the Native Americans, will. Anthropologists have excavated near the altar, down to the original floor that some claim to be part of a 12th-century pueblo. A small store just off the sanctuary sells religious articles.

401 Old Santa Fe Trail (at E. de Vargas St.). © 505/983-3974. Admission $1 adults, free for children under 6. Mon–Sat 9am–5pm; Sun 10am–4pm. Summer hours start earlier. Mass Sun 5pm.

Santuario de Nuestra Señora de Guadalupe ⋆   This church, built between 1776 and 1796 at the end of El Camino Real by Franciscan missionaries, is believed to be the oldest shrine in the United States honoring the Virgin of Guadalupe, the patron saint of Mexico. Better known as Santuario de Guadalupe, the shrine's adobe walls are almost 3 feet thick, and the deep-red plaster wall behind the altar was dyed with oxblood in traditional fashion when the church was restored early in the 20th century.

It is well worth a visit to see photographs of the transformation of the building over time; its styles have ranged from flat-topped pueblo to New England town meeting and today's northern New Mexico style. On one wall is a famous oil painting, *Our Lady of Guadalupe*, created in 1783 by the renowned Mexican artist José de Alzibar. Painted expressly for this church, it was brought from Mexico City by mule caravan.

100 S. Guadalupe St. © 505/988-2027. Donations appreciated. Mon–Sat 9am–4pm. Labor Day to Memorial Day 9am–6pm. Masses Mon–Fri 6:30am, Sat 8am, Sun noon.

OTHER ATTRACTIONS

El Rancho de las Golondrinas ⋆ *Kids*   This 200-acre ranch, about 15 miles south of the plaza via I-25, was once the last stopping place on the 1,000-mile El Camino Real from Mexico City to Santa Fe. Today, it's a living 18th- and 19th-century Spanish village, comprising a hacienda, a village store, a schoolhouse, and several chapels and kitchens. There are also a working molasses mill, wheelwright and blacksmith shops, shearing and weaving rooms, a threshing ground, a winery and vineyard, and four water mills, as well as dozens of farm animals. A walk around the entire property is 1¾ miles in length, with amazing scenery and plenty of room for the kids to romp.

334 Los Pinos Rd. © 505/471-2261. www.golondrinas.org. Admission $5 adults, $4 seniors and teens, $2 children 5–12, free for children under 5. Festival weekends $7 adults, $5 seniors and teens, $3 children 5–12. June–Sept Wed–Sun 10am–4pm; Apr–May and Oct open by advance arrangement. Closed Nov–Mar. From Santa Fe, drive south on I-25, taking exit 276; then go north on NM 599, turn left on W. Frontage Rd., drive half a mile, and turn right on Los Pinos Rd.; travel 3 miles to the museum.

New Mexico State Capitol (Roundhouse)   Some are surprised to learn that this is the only round capitol building in the U.S. Built in 1966, it's designed in the shape of a Zia Pueblo emblem (or sun sign, which is also the state symbol). It symbolizes the Circle of Life: four winds, four seasons, four directions, and four sacred obligations. Surrounding the capitol is a lush 6½-acre garden containing more than 100 varieties of plants, including roses, plums, almonds, nectarines, Russian olive trees, and sequoias. Inside you'll find standard functional offices, with New Mexican art hanging on the walls. Check out the Governor's Gallery and the Capitol Art Collection. Self-guided tours are available 8am to 5pm Monday through Friday year-round; Memorial Day to Labor Day guided tours are available Monday through Saturday at 10am and 2pm. All tours and self-guided brochures are free to the public.

Paseo de Peralta and Old Santa Fe Trail. (C) **505/986-4589.** www.legis.state.nm.us. Free admission. Mon–Sat 8am–5pm. Free parking.

Santa Fe Southern Railway (R   "Riding the old Santa Fe" always referred to riding the Atchison, Topeka & Santa Fe railroad. Ironically, the main route of the AT&SF bypassed Santa Fe, which probably forestalled some development for the capital city. A spur was run off the main line to Santa Fe in 1880, and today, an 18-mile ride along that spur offers views of some of New Mexico's most spectacular scenery.

Inside the restored coach, passengers are surrounded by aged mahogany and faded velvet seats. The train snakes through Santa Fe and into the Galisteo Basin, broad landscapes spotted with piñon and chamisa, with views of the Sandia and Ortiz mountains. Arriving in the small track town of Lamy, you get another glimpse of a Mission-style station, this one surrounded by spacious lawns where passengers picnic. Check out the sunset rides on weekends and specialty trains throughout the year.

410 S. Guadalupe St. (C) **888/989-8600** or 505/989-8600. Fax 505/983-7620. www.sfsr.com. Tickets from $18 (children 3–13), $28 (adults), $30–$80 Fri–Sat evening rides (Apr–Oct). Depending on the season, trains depart the Santa Fe Depot 9:30am–1pm Mon–Sat (call to check winter schedule). Rides also available Fri–Sat evening and Sun afternoon.

GETTING CLOSE TO NATURE: PARKS & REFUGES

Old Fort Marcy Park   Marking the 1846 site of the first U.S. military reservation in the Southwest, this park overlooks the northeast corner of downtown. Only a few mounds remain from the fort, but the Cross of the Martyrs, at the top of a winding brick walkway from Paseo de Peralta near Otero Street, is a popular spot for bird's-eye photographs. The cross was erected in 1920 by the Knights of Columbus and the Historical Society of New Mexico to commemorate the Franciscans killed during the Pueblo Rebellion of 1680. It has since played a role in numerous religious processions. The park is open daily 24 hours, though it's dark and not safe at night.

617 Paseo de Peralta (or travel 3 blocks up Artist Rd. and turn right).

Randall Davey Audubon Center (R   Named for the late Santa Fe artist who willed his home to the National Audubon Society, this wildlife refuge occupies 135 acres at the mouth of Santa Fe Canyon. Just a few minutes' drive from the plaza, it's an excellent escape. More than 100 species of birds and 120 types of plants live here, and varied mammals have been spotted—including black bears, mule deer, mountain lions, bobcats, raccoons, and coyotes. Trails winding through more than 100 acres of the nature sanctuary are open to day hikers, but not to dogs. There's also a natural history bookstore on site.

1800 Upper Canyon Rd. ℂ 505/983-4609. Trail admission $2 adults, $1 children. Daily 9am–5pm. House tours conducted 2pm Mon ($5 per person). Gift shop daily 10am–4pm (call for winter hours). Free 1-hr. guided bird walk every Sat at 8:30am.

Santa Fe River Park   This is a lovely spot for an early morning jog, a midday walk beneath the trees, or perhaps a sack lunch at a picnic table. The green strip follows the midtown stream for about 4 miles as it meanders along Alameda from St. Francis Drive upstream beyond Camino Cabra, near its source. It's open daily 24 hours, but it's not a safe place to linger at night.

Alameda St. ℂ 505/955-2103.

COOKING & ART CLASSES

If you're looking for something to do that's a little off the beaten tourist path, you might consider taking a class.

You can master the flavors of Santa Fe with an entertaining 3-hour demonstration cooking class at the **Santa Fe School of Cooking and Market** ✵, on the upper level of the Plaza Mercado, 116 W. San Francisco St. (ℂ **505/983-4511;** fax 505/983-7540; www.santafeschoolofcooking.com). The class teaches about the flavors and history of traditional New Mexican and contemporary Southwestern cuisines. "Cooking Light" classes are available as well. Prices range from $40 to $88 and include a meal; call for a class schedule. The adjoining market offers a variety of regional foods and cookbooks, with gift baskets available.

If Southwestern art has you hooked, take a drawing and painting class led by Santa Fe artist Jane Shoenfeld. Contact her at **Sketching Santa Fe,** P.O. Box 5912, Santa Fe, NM 87502 (ℂ **505/986-1108;** fax 505/986-3845; www.skyfields.net).

WINE TASTINGS

If you enjoy sampling regional wines, consider visiting the wineries within easy driving distance of Santa Fe: **Balagna Winery/Il Santo Cellars,** 223 Rio Bravo Dr., in Los Alamos (White Rock; ℂ **505/672-3678**), north on US 84/285 and then west on NM 502; **Santa Fe Vineyards,** with a retail outlet at 235 Don Gaspar Ave., in Santa Fe (ℂ **505/982-3474**), or the vineyard itself about 20 miles north of Santa Fe on US 84/285 (ℂ **505/753-8100**); **Madison Vineyards & Winery,** in Ribera (ℂ **505/421-8028**), about 45 miles east of Santa Fe on I-25 North; and the **Black Mesa Winery,** 1502 NM 68, in Velarde (ℂ **800/852-6372**), north on US 84/285 to NM 68. Be sure to call in advance to find out when the wineries are open for tastings and to get specific directions.

ESPECIALLY FOR KIDS

Don't miss taking the kids to the **Museum of International Folk Art** (p. 162), where they'll love the international dioramas and the toys. Also visit the tepee at the **Wheelwright Museum of the American Indian** (p. 163), where storyteller Joe Hayes spins traditional Spanish *cuentos,* Native American folk tales, and Wild West tall tales on weekend evenings. **The Bishop's Lodge** (p. 144) has extensive children's programs during the summer. These include horseback riding, swimming, arts-and-crafts programs, and special activities such as archery and tennis. Kids are sure to enjoy **El Rancho de las Golondrinas** (p. 164), a living 18th- and 19th-century Spanish village comprising a hacienda, a village store, a schoolhouse, and several chapels and kitchens.

The **Genoveva Chavez Community Center** is a full-service family recreation center on the south side of Santa Fe (3221 Rodeo Rd.). The complex includes a 50m pool, a leisure pool, a therapy pool, an ice-skating rink, three gyms, a workout room, racquetball courts, and an indoor running track, as well as a spa and sauna. For hours and more information, call ℭ **505/955-4001.**

Planetarium at Santa Fe Community College   The planetarium offers imaginative programs, combining star shows with storytelling and other interactive techniques. Among the planetarium's inventive programs: Rusty Rocket's Last Blast, in which kids launch a model rocket; and the Solar System Stakeout, in which kids build a solar system. There's also a 10-minute segment on the current night sky. Programs vary, from those designed for preschoolers to ones for high-school kids.

6401 Richards Ave. (south of Rodeo Rd.). ℭ **505/428-1677,** or 505/428-1777 for the information line. www.sfc cnm.edu. Admission $5 adults, $3 seniors and children 12 and under. Live lecture 1st Wed of month 7–8pm; Celestial Highlights (live program mapping the night sky for that particular month) 1st Thurs of month 7–8pm; prerecorded shows 2nd and 4th Thurs of month.

Santa Fe Children's Museum ⊛   This museum offers interactive exhibits and hands-on activities in the arts, humanities, and science. The most notable features include a 16-foot climbing wall that kids—outfitted with helmets and harnesses—can scale, and a 1-acre Southwestern horticulture garden, complete with animals, wetlands, and a greenhouse. This fascinating area serves as an outdoor classroom for ongoing environmental educational programs. Special performances and hands-on sessions with artists and scientists are regularly scheduled. In 2005, *Family Life* magazine named this one of the 10 hottest children's museums in the nation.

1050 Old Pecos Trail. ℭ **505/989-8359.** www.santafechildrensmuseum.org. Admission $4 New Mexico residents, $8 nonresidents; children under 12 must be accompanied by an adult. Wed–Sat 10am–5pm; Sun noon–5pm.

Skateboard Park   Split-level ramps for daredevils, park benches for onlookers, and climbing structures for youngsters are located at this park near downtown.

At the intersection of de Vargas and Sandoval sts. ℭ **505/955-2100.** Free admission. Daily 24 hr.

6 Organized Tours

BUS TOURS
LorettoLine   For an open-air tour of the city covering history and sights, contact this company that has been running tours for 18 years. Tours last 1¼ hours and are offered daily from April to October. They depart at 10am, noon, and 2pm—and sometimes more frequently in high summer.

At the Hotel Loretto, 211 Old Santa Fe Trail. Tours depart from the Loretto Chapel. ℭ **505/983-3701.** Tours $14 adults, $10 children 11 and under.

WALKING TOURS
Walking Tour of Santa Fe ⊛   One of Santa Fe's best walking tours begins under the T-shirt tree at Tees & Skis, 107 Washington Ave., near the northeast corner of the plaza (9:30am and 1:30pm daily May–Sept, by appointment Oct–Apr). It lasts about 2½ hours.

54½ E. San Francisco St. (tour meets at 107 Washington Ave.). ℭ **800/338-6877** or 505/983-6565. Tours $10 adults, free for children under 12.

MISCELLANEOUS TOURS
Pathways Customized Tours ⊛   Don Dietz offers several planned tours, including a downtown Santa Fe walking tour, a full city tour, a trip to the cliff dwellings and

native pueblos, a "Taos adventure," and a trip to Georgia O'Keeffe country (with a focus on the landscape that inspired the art now viewable in the O'Keeffe Museum). Don will try to accommodate any special requests you might have. These tours last from 2 to 9 hours, depending on the one you choose. With his extensive knowledge of the area's culture, history, geology, and flora and fauna, Don will help you make the most of your precious vacation time.

161-F Calle Ojo Feliz. ⓒ 505/982-5382. www.santafepathways.com. Tours $60–$200 (or more) per day per couple. Credit cards not accepted.

Rain Parrish ⓡ   A Navajo (or *Diné*) anthropologist, artist, and curator, Rain Parrish offers custom guide services focusing on cultural anthropology, Native American arts, and the history of the Native Americans of the Southwest. Some of these are true adventures to insider locations. Ms. Parrish includes visits to local Pueblo villages.

704 Kathryn St. ⓒ 505/984-8236. Tours $130 per couple for 4½ hr., $230 per couple for 7 hr.

Rojo Tours & Services   Customized and private tours are arranged to pueblos, cliff dwellings, ruins, hot-air ballooning, backpacking, or white-water rafting. Rojo also provides planning services for groups.

P.O. Box 15744. ⓒ 505/474-8333. Fax 505/474-2992. www.rojotours.com.

Santa Fe Detours ⓡ   Santa Fe's most extensive tour-booking agency accommodates almost all travelers' tastes, from bus and rail tours to river rafting, backpacking, and cross-country skiing. The agency can also facilitate hotel reservations, from budget to high end.

54½ E. San Francisco St. (summer tour desk, 107 Washington Ave.). ⓒ 800/338-6877 or 505/983-6565. www.sfde tours.com.

Southwest Safaris ⓡⓡ   This tour is one of the most interesting Southwestern experiences available. You'll fly in a small plane 1,000 feet off the ground to various destinations while pilot Bruce Adams explains millions of years of geologic history. Trips to many Southwestern destinations are available, including Monument Valley, Mesa Verde, Canyon de Chelly, Arches/Canyonlands, as well as a trip to Capulin Volcano and the ruins at Aztec, New Mexico. Tours depart from the Santa Fe Airport.

P.O. Box 945. ⓒ 800/842-4246 or 505/988-4246. Tours $149–$699 per person.

7 Getting Outside

Set between the granite peaks of the Sangre de Cristo Mountains and the subtler volcanic Jemez Mountains, and with the Rio Grande flowing through, the Santa Fe area offers outdoor enthusiasts many opportunities to play. This is the land of high desert, where temperatures vary with the elevation, allowing for a full range of activities throughout the year.

BIRD-WATCHING

Bird-watchers flock to the **Randall Davey Audubon Center** ⓡ (see "Parks & Refuges," above), 1800 Upper Canyon Rd. (ⓒ **505/983-4609**), to see more than 100 species of birds and many other animals. For guided bird-watching tours all over the region, contact **Wings West** at ⓒ **800/583-6928;** http://home.earthlink.net/~wings westnm. Bill West guides half-day tours to local spots such as the Santa Fe Mountains and Cochiti Lake ($95 for 1–2 people) and full-day ones farther afield ($175 for 1–2 people).

BIKING

You can cycle along main roadways and paved country roads year-round in Santa Fe, but be aware that traffic is particularly heavy around the plaza—and all over town, motorists are not particularly attentive to bicyclists, so you need to be especially alert. Mountain-biking interest has exploded here and is especially popular in the spring, summer, and fall; the high-desert terrain is rugged and challenging, but mountain bikers of all levels can find exhilarating rides. The Santa Fe Convention and Visitors Bureau (p. 134) can supply you with bike maps.

We recommend the following trails: West of Santa Fe, the **Caja del Rio** area has nice dirt roads and some light-to-moderate technical biking; the **railroad tracks south of Santa Fe** provide wide-open biking on beginner-to-intermediate technical trails; and the **Borrego Trail** up toward the Santa Fe Ski Area is a challenging technical ride that links in with the **Windsor Trail,** a nationally renowned technical romp with plenty of verticality.

Santa Fe Mountain Sports, 606 Cerrillos Rd. (© **505/988-3337**), rents hard-tail mountain bikes for $20 for a half-day and $25 for a full day, or full-suspension bikes for $35 for a full day. **Mellow Velo Bikes,** 102 E. Water St. (© **505/982-8986;** www.mellowbike.com), rents front-suspension mountain bikes for $23 per half-day and $30 per full day. Town cruisers run $23 for a half-day and $30 for a full day. Full-suspension bikes run $43 per day. Add $7, and Mellow Velo will deliver to and pick up from your hotel (in the Santa Fe area). Multiday rentals can be arranged. Both shops supply accessories such as helmets, locks, maps, and trail information, usually at an additional cost.

FISHING

In the lakes and waterways around Santa Fe, anglers typically catch trout (there are five varieties in the area). Other local fish include bass, perch, and kokanee salmon. The most popular fishing holes are Cochiti and Abiquiu lakes as well as the Rio Chama, Pecos River, and the Rio Grande. A world-renowned fly-fishing destination, the **San Juan River,** near Farmington, is worth a visit and can make for an exciting 2-day trip in combination with a tour around **Chaco Culture National Historic Park** (see chapter 5). Check with the **New Mexico Game and Fish Department** (© **505/476-8000**) for information (including maps of area waters), licenses, and fishing proclamations. **High Desert Angler,** 435 S. Guadalupe St. (© **505/988-7688**), specializes in fly-fishing gear and guide services.

GOLF

There are three courses in the Santa Fe area: the 18-hole **Santa Fe Country Club,** on Airport Road (© **505/471-2626**); the often-praised 18-hole **Cochiti Lake Golf Course,** 5200 Cochiti Hwy., Cochiti Lake, about 35 miles southwest of Santa Fe via I-25 and NM 16 and 22 (© **505/465-2239**); and Santa Fe's newest 18-hole course, **Marty Sanchez Links de Santa Fe,** 205 Caja del Rio (© **505/955-4400**). Both the Santa Fe Country Club and the Marty Sanchez Links offer driving ranges as well. North of Santa Fe on Pojoaque Pueblo land, the **Towa Golf Resort** (Cities of Gold Casino Resort, US 285/84; © **877/465-3489** or 505/455-9000; www.towagolf.com), offers 27 holes designed by Hale Irwin and William Phillips, set with views of the Jemez and Sangre de Cristo Mountains.

HIKING

It's hard to decide which of the 1,000 miles of nearby national forest trails to tackle. Four wilderness areas are nearby, most notably **Pecos Wilderness,** with 223,000 acres east of Santa Fe. Also visit the 58,000-acre **Jemez Mountain National Recreation Area.** Information on these and other wilderness areas is available from the **Santa Fe National Forest,** P.O. Box 1689 (1474 Rodeo Rd.), Santa Fe, NM 87504 (© 505/ 438-7840). If you're looking for company on your trek, contact the Santa Fe branch of the **Sierra Club,** 1472 S. St. Francis (© 505/983-2703). You can pick up a hiking schedule in the local newsletter outside the office. Some people enjoy taking a chair-lift ride to the summit of the **Santa Fe Ski Area** (© 505/982-4429; www.skisantafe. com) and hiking around up there during the summer. The most popular hiking trails are the **Borrego Trail,** a moderate 4-mile jaunt through aspens and ponderosa pines, ending at a creek; and **Aspen Vista,** an easy 1- to 5-mile hike through aspen forest with views to the east. Both are easy to find; simply head up Hyde Park Road toward Ski Santa Fe. The Borrego Trail is 8.5 miles up, while Aspen Vista is 10 miles.

HORSEBACK RIDING

Trips ranging in length from a few hours to overnight can be arranged by **Santa Fe Detours,** 54½ E. San Francisco St. (summer tour desk, 107 Washington Ave.; © 800/ 338-6877 or 505/983-6565). You'll ride with "experienced wranglers" and they can even arrange a trip that includes a cookout or brunch. Rides are also major activities at the **Bishop's Lodge** (p. 144). The **Broken Saddle Riding Company** (© 505/ 424-7774) offers rides through the stunning Galisteo Basin south of Santa Fe.

RIVER RAFTING & KAYAKING

Although Taos is the real rafting center of New Mexico, several companies serve Santa Fe during the April-to-October white-water season. They include **New Wave Rafting,** 70 County Rd. 84B, Santa Fe, NM 87506 (© 800/984-1444 or 505/984-1444) and **Santa Fe Rafting Co.,** 1000 Cerrillos Rd., Santa Fe, NM 87505 (© 888/988-4914 or 505/988-4914; www.santaferafting.com). You can expect the cost of a full-day trip to range from about $90 to $125 before tax and the 3% federal land use fee. The day of the week (weekdays are less expensive) and group size may also affect the price.

RUNNING

Despite its elevation, Santa Fe is popular with runners and hosts numerous competitions, including the annual **Old Santa Fe Trail Run** on Labor Day. Each Wednesday, Santa Fe runners gather at 6pm at the plaza and set out on foot for runs in the surrounding area. This is a great opportunity for travelers to find their way and to meet some locals. **Santa Fe Striders** (www.santafestriders.org) sponsors various runs during the year.

SKIING

There's something for every ability level at **Ski Santa Fe,** about 16 miles northeast of Santa Fe via Hyde Park (Ski Basin) Road. Lots of locals ski here, particularly on weekends; if you can, go on weekdays to avoid the crowds. It's a good family area and fairly small, so it's easy to split off from and later reconnect with your party. Built on the upper reaches of 12,000-foot Tesuque Peak, the area has an average annual snowfall of 225 inches and a vertical drop of 1,703 feet. Seven lifts, including a 5,000-foot triple chair and a new quad chair, serve 67 runs and 660 acres of terrain, with a total capacity of 7,800 riders an hour. Base facilities, at 10,350 feet, center around **La Casa Mall,** with a cafeteria, lounge, ski shop, and boutique. A restaurant, **Totemoff's,** has a mid-mountain patio.

The ski area is open daily from 9am to 4pm; the season often runs from Thanksgiving to early April, depending on snow conditions. Rates for all lifts are $51 for adults, $41 for teens (13–20 years), $37 for children and seniors; half-day am or pm tickets run $37. Tickets are free for kids less than 46 inches tall (in their ski boots), and for seniors 72 and older. For more information, contact **Ski Santa Fe,** 2209 Brothers Rd., Suite 220 (✆ **505/982-4429;** www.skisantafe.com). For 24-hour reports on snow conditions, call ✆ **505/983-9155. Ski New Mexico** (✆ **505/982-5300)** gives statewide reports. Ski packages are available through **santafehotels.com** (✆ **800/745-9910).**

Cross-country skiers find seemingly endless miles of snow to track in the **Santa Fe National Forest** (✆ **505/438-7840).** A favorite place to start is at the Black Canyon campground, about 9 miles from downtown en route to the Santa Fe Ski Area. In the same area are the **Borrego Trail** (high intermediate), **Aspen Vista Trail,** and the **Norski Trail,** all en route to Santa Fe Ski Area as well. Other popular activities at the ski area in winter include snowshoeing, snowboarding, sledding, and inner-tubing. Ski, snowboard, and snowshoe rentals are available at a number of downtown shops and the ski area.

SWIMMING

There's a public pool at the **Fort Marcy Complex** (✆ **505/955-2500)** on Camino Santiago, off Bishop's Lodge Road. Admission is $1.85 for adults, $1.50 for ages 13 to 18, 75¢ for ages 8 to 12, 30¢ for children 7 and under, and 75¢ for seniors.

TENNIS

Santa Fe has 44 public tennis courts and 4 major private facilities. The **City Recreation Department** (✆ **505/955-2100)** can help you locate indoor, outdoor, and lighted public courts.

8 Shopping

Santa Fe has a broad range of shopping, from traditional Native American crafts and Hispanic folk art to extremely innovative contemporary work. Some call Santa Fe one of the top art markets in the world. Galleries speckle the downtown area, and as an artists' thoroughfare, Canyon Road is preeminent. The greatest concentration of Native American crafts is displayed beneath the portal of the Palace of the Governors.

Any serious arts aficionado should try to attend one or more of the city's great arts festivals—the Spring Festival of the Arts in May, the Spanish Market in July, the Indian Market in August, and the Fall Festival of the Arts in October.

For a current listing of gallery openings, with recommendations for which ones to attend, purchase a copy of the monthly *Santa Fean* (444 Galisteo, Santa Fe, NM 87501; www.santafean.com). Also check in the Friday "Pasatiempo" section of the local newspaper, the *New Mexican* (www.santafenewmexican.com).

Business hours vary quite a bit, but most establishments are open at least weekdays from 10am to 5pm, with mall stores open until 8 or 9pm. Most shops are open similar hours on Saturday, and many also open on Sunday afternoon during the summer. Winter hours tend to be more limited.

Getting Pampered: The Spa Scene

If traveling, skiing, or other activities have left you weary, Santa Fe has a number of relaxation options. Newest to the city is the **Absolute Nirvana Spa, Tea Room & Gardens** ༈༈ (✆ 505/983-7942; www.absolutenirvana.com). This creation, voted one of the best three spas in town by the *Santa Fe Reporter,* offers imaginative Indo-Asian spa "experiences" as well as massages and facials. Their signature treatment, the Javanese Lulur, includes a full-body massage with jasmine oil, a sandlewood/rice powder exfoliation and yogurt/honey wrap, followed by a steam shower and decadent rose-petal bath—all accompanied by tea, fruit, and a housemade truffle. The tearoom is open daily 10am to 6pm, and the spa is open Sunday to Thursday 10am to 6pm and Friday and Saturday 10am to 8pm. Prices range from $95 to $220.

Another option with a more Japanese bent is **Ten Thousand Waves** ༈༈, a spa about 3 miles northeast of Santa Fe on Hyde Park Road (✆ 505/982-9304; www.tenthousandwaves.com). This serene retreat, nestled in a grove of piñons, offers hot tubs, saunas, and cold plunges, plus a variety of massage and other bodywork techniques. Bathing suits are optional in both the communal hot tub (during the day) and the women's communal tub, where you can stay as long as you want for $15. Nine private hot tubs cost $20 to $27 an hour, with discounts for seniors and children. A premium bath is offered at $59 for 85 minutes. You can also arrange for therapeutic massage, hot-oil massage, in-water *watsu* massage, herbal wraps, salt glows, facials, dry brush aromatherapy treatments, Ayurvedic treatments, and the much-praised Japanese Hot Stone Massage. If you call far enough in advance, you may be able to find lodging at **Ten Thousand Waves** as well. The spa is open Sunday, Monday, Wednesday, and Thursday from 10am to 10pm; Tuesday from 4:30 to 10pm; and Friday and Saturday from 10am to 11pm (winter hours are shorter, so be sure to call). Reservations are recommended, especially on weekends.

Decorated in Southwestern-cum-Asian style, with clean lines and lots of elegant stone, Santa Fe's chicest option is **Avanyu Spa** ༈༈, at the La Posada de Santa Fe Resort and Spa (✆ 505/986-0000). A full-service spa offering a range of treatments from massage to salt glows, this spot may initially seem expensive (about $120 for 60 min.), but treatments come with full use of the steam room, hot tub, and grass-surrounded pool.

THE TOP GALLERIES
CONTEMPORARY ART
Adieb Khadoure Fine Art   Featuring contemporary artists Steven Boone, Hal Larsen, Robert Anderson, and Barry Lee Darling, the works here are shown in the gallery daily from 10am to 6pm. Adieb Khadoure also sells elegant rugs, furniture, and pottery from around the world. 610 Canyon Rd. ✆ 505/820-2666.

Canyon Road Contemporary Art   This gallery represents some of the finest emerging U.S. contemporary artists as well as internationally known artists. You'll find figurative, landscape, and abstract paintings, as well as raku pottery. 403 Canyon Rd. ℭ 505/983-0433.

La Mesa of Santa Fe ℞ *(Finds*   Step into this gallery and let your senses dance. Dramatically colored ceramic plates, bowls, and other kitchen items fill one room. Contemporary kachinas by Gregory Lomayesva—a real buy—line the walls, accented by steel lamps and rag rugs. 225 Canyon Rd. ℭ 505/984-1688.

LewAllen Contemporary ℞℞ *(Finds*   This is one of Santa Fe's most prized galleries. You'll find bizarre and beautiful contemporary works in a range of media, from granite to clay to twigs. There are always exciting works on canvas. 129 W. Palace Ave. ℭ 505/988-8997.

Linda Durham Contemporary Art ℞   The opening of this broad and bright art space in summer 2004 marked the return of one of Santa Fe's best galleries. Longtime gallery owner Linda Durham had moved her gallery 25 miles south of town, but now she's returned, with a strong roster of talent including Greg Erf and Judy Tuwaletstiwa. 1101 Paseo de Peralta. ℭ 505/466-6600.

Peyton Wright Gallery ℞   Housed within the Historic Spiegelberg House (a refurbished Victorian adobe), this excellent gallery offers contemporary, American Modernism, Spanish Colonial, Russian, and 18th-century New Mexico *bultos* and *santos*. In addition to representing such artists as Orlando Leyba, Roni Stretch and Tim Murphy, the gallery features monthly exhibitions—including contemporary paintings, sculptures, and works on paper. 237 E. Palace Ave. ℭ 800/879-8898 or 505/989-9888.

Shidoni Foundry, Gallery, and Sculpture Gardens ℞℞ *(Moments*   Shidoni Foundry is one of the area's most exciting spots for sculptors and sculpture enthusiasts. At the foundry, visitors may take a tour through the facilities to view casting processes. In addition, Shidoni Foundry includes a 5,000-square-foot contemporary gallery, a bronze gallery, and a wonderful sculpture garden—a great place for a picnic. Bishop's Lodge Rd., Tesuque. ℭ 505/988-8001.

NATIVE AMERICAN & OTHER INDIGENOUS ART

Andrea Fisher Fine Pottery ℞   This expansive gallery is a wonderland of authentic Southwestern Indian pottery. You'll find real showpieces here, including the work of renowned San Ildefonso Pueblo potter Maria Martinez. 100 W. San Francisco St. ℭ 505/986-1234.

Frank Howell Gallery   If you've never seen the wonderful illustrative hand of the late Frank Howell, you'll want to visit this gallery. You'll find a variety of works by contemporary American Indian artists. The gallery also features sculpture, jewelry, and graphics. 103 Washington Ave. ℭ 505/984-1074.

Michael Smith Gallery ℞   This gallery's namesake has made his mark through the years by finding and displaying some of the region's most exciting rugs, baskets, jewelry, and paintings. It's a small shop with a big heart. 526 Canyon Rd. ℭ 505/995-1013.

Morning Star Gallery ℞℞ *(Finds*   This is one of our favorite places to browse. Throughout the rambling gallery are American Indian art masterpieces, all elegantly displayed. You'll see a broad range of works, from late-19th-century Navajo blankets to 1920s Zuni needlepoint jewelry. 513 Canyon Rd. ℭ 505/982-8187.

Ortega's on the Plaza   A hearty shopper could spend hours here, perusing inventive turquoise and silver jewelry and especially fine strung beadwork, as well as rugs and pottery. An adjacent room showcases a wide array of clothing, all with a hip Southwestern flair. 101 W. San Francisco St. ℂ **505/988-1866.**

Sherwoods ℱ   Set in the historic Bandelier House, this gallery features museum-quality Plains Indians antiquities such as an 1870 Nez Perce beaded dress and a Crow warshirt. Some paintings hang here as well, including works by Santa Fe masters such as J. H. Sharp and Gene Kloss. Firearm buffs will go ballistic over the gun room here. 1005 Paseo de Peralta. ℂ **505/988-1776.**

PHOTOGRAPHY

Andrew Smith Gallery ℱ   We're always amazed when we enter this gallery and notice works we've seen reprinted in major magazines. There they are, photographic prints, large and beautiful, hanging on the wall. Here you'll see famous works by Edward Curtis, Henri Cartier-Bresson, Ansel Adams, Annie Leibovitz, and others. 203 W. San Francisco St. ℂ **505/984-1234.**

Photo-Eye Gallery   You're bound to be surprised each time you step into this gallery, a few blocks off Canyon Road. Dealing in contemporary photography, the gallery represents both internationally renowned and emerging artists. 370 Garcia St. ℂ **505/988-5152.**

SPANISH & HISPANIC ART

Montez Gallery   This shop is rich with New Mexican (and Mexican) art, decorations, and furnishings such as *santos* (saints), *retablos* (paintings), *bultos* (sculptures), and *trasteros* (armoires). Sena Plaza Courtyard, 125 E. Palace Ave., Suite 33. ℂ **505/982-1828.**

TRADITIONAL ART

Altermann Galleries   This is a well of interesting traditional art, mostly 19th-, 20th-, and 21st-century American paintings and sculpture. The gallery represents Remington and Russell, in addition to Taos founders, Santa Fe artists, and members of the Cowboy Artists of America and the National Academy of Western Art. Stroll through the sculpture garden among whimsical bronzes of children and dogs. 225 Canyon Rd. ℂ **505/983-1590.**

Gerald Peters Gallery ℱℱ   Displayed throughout a graceful pueblo-style building, the works here are so fine you'll feel as though you're in a museum. You'll find 19th-, 20th-, and 21st-century American painting and sculpture, featuring the art of Georgia O'Keeffe, William Wegman, and the founders of the Santa Fe and Taos artist colonies, as well as more contemporary works. 1011 Paseo de Peralta. ℂ **505/954-5700.**

The Mayans Gallery Ltd.   Established in 1977, this is one of the oldest galleries in Santa Fe. You'll find 20th-century American and Latin American paintings, photography, prints, and sculpture. 601 Canyon Rd. ℂ **505/983-8068.**

Nedra Matteucci Galleries ℱ   As you approach this gallery, note the elaborately crafted stone and adobe wall that surrounds it, merely a taste of what's to come. The gallery specializes in 19th-, 20th-, and 21st-century American art. Inside, you'll find a lot of high-ticket works such as those of early Taos and Santa Fe painters, as well as classic American Impressionism, historical Western modernism, and contemporary Southwestern landscapes and sculpture. 1075 Paseo de Peralta. ℂ **505/982-4631.**

Arcade Shopping on the Plaza

Opened in 2004, the **Santa Fe Arcade,** 60 E. San Francisco St. (✆ **505/988-5792**), on the south side of the plaza, offers three stories of shops in a sleek, glassy European-style space. It's a far cry from the Woolworth's that once lived there. Showy Western wear, fine Indian jewelry, and hip clothing fill the display windows of some 60 spaces in the mall. If you like to pamper yourself with natural products, many made in New Mexico, step into **Sombria** (suite 222; ✆ **888/480-5554** or 505/982-7383). Look for their margarita salt glow, made with salt from Utah's Great Salt Lake. Prima Fine Jewelry's **Oro Fino** (suite 218; ✆ **505/983-9699**) sells contemporary and Southwestern inlaid jewelry in silver, gold, and platinum. After all the shopping, if you find yourself hungry, head to the **Rooftop Pizzeria** ✿ (top floor; ✆ **505/984-0008**) for some of the city's best pizza. Two types of crust, an "artisan" or a blue corn, are topped with imaginative concoctions such as smoked duck and roasted garlic or wild mushroom and Alfredo sauce. Salads and pasta dishes are available, as are beer and wine. It's open Sunday through Thursday 11am to 10pm and Friday and Saturday 11am to 11pm.

Owings-Dewey Fine Art ✿ These are treasure-filled rooms. You'll find 19th-, 20th-, and 21st-century American painting and sculpture, including works by Georgia O'Keeffe, Robert Henri, Maynard Dixon, Fremont Ellis, and Andrew Dasburg, as well as antique works such as Spanish colonial *retablos, bultos,* and tin works. 76 E. San Francisco St., upstairs. ✆ **505/982-6244.**

Zaplin Lampert Gallery ✿✿ Art aficionados as well as those who just like a nice landscape will enjoy this gallery, one of Santa Fe's classics. Hanging on old adobe walls are works by some of the region's early masters, including Bert Phillips, Gene Kloss, and Gustauve Baumann. 651 Canyon Rd. ✆ **505/982-6100.**

MORE SHOPPING A TO Z
ANTIQUES
El Paso Import Company ✿ Whenever we're in the vicinity of this shop, we stop in. It's packed—and we mean packed—with colorful, weathered colonial and ranchero furniture. The home furnishings and folk art here are imported from Mexico. 418 Sandoval St. ✆ **505/982-5698.**

Jackalope ✿ *(Kids* Spread over 7 acres of land, this is a wild place to spend a morning or an afternoon browsing through exotic furnishings from India and Mexico, as well as imported textiles, pottery, jewelry, and clothing. It's a great place to find gifts. Kids will love the prairie-dog village. 2820 Cerrillos Rd. ✆ **505/471-8539.**

BOOKS
Borders With close to 200 stores nationwide, this chain provides a broad range of books, music, and videos, and it hosts in-store appearances by authors, musicians, and artists. 500 Montezuma Ave. ✆ **505/954-4707.**

Collected Works Bookstore   This is a good downtown book source, with carefully recommended books upfront, in case you're not sure what you want, and shelves of Southwest, travel, nature, and other books. 208–B W. San Francisco St. ✆ 505/988-4226.

Nicholas Potter, Bookseller   This bookstore handles rare and used hardcover books, as well as tickets to many local events. 211 E. Palace Ave. ✆ 505/983-5434.

CRAFTS

Nambé ✿ *Finds*   The cooking, serving, and decorating pieces here are fashioned from an exquisite sand-cast and handcrafted alloy. These items are also available at the Nambe stores at 104 W. San Francisco St. (✆ 505/988-3574), and in Taos at 113A Paseo del Pueblo Norte (✆ 505/758-8221). 924 Paseo de Peralta. ✆ 505/988-5528.

FASHIONS

Back at the Ranch ✿   This shop has chic western wear and what it calls the "largest selection of handmade cowboy boots in the country." 209 E. Marcy St. ✆ 888/962-6687 or 505/989-8110. www.backattheranch.com.

Judy's Unique Apparel   Judy's has eclectic separates made locally and imported from around the globe. You'll find a wide variety of items here, many at surprisingly reasonable prices. 714 Canyon Rd. ✆ 505/988-5746.

Origins ✿ *Moments*   A little like a Guatemalan or Turkish marketplace, this store is packed with wearable art, folk art, and the work of local designers. Look for good buys on ethnic jewelry. Throughout the summer there are trunk shows, which offer opportunities to meet the artists. 135 W. San Francisco St. ✆ 505/988-2323.

Overland Sheepskin Company   The rich smell of leather will draw you in the door, and possibly hold onto you until you purchase a coat, blazer, hat, or other finely made leather item. 74 E. San Francisco St. ✆ 505/983-4727.

FOOD

The Chile Shop   This store has too many cheap trinketlike items for us, but many people find some novelty items to take back home. You'll find everything from salsas to cornmeal and tortilla chips. The shop also stocks cookbooks and pottery items. 109 E. Water St. ✆ 505/983-6080.

Señor Murphy Candy Maker   This is unlike any candy store you'll find in other parts of the country—everything here is made with local ingredients. The chile piñon-nut brittle is a taste sensation! Señor Murphy has another shop in the Santa Fe Place mall (✆ 505/471-8899). 100 E. San Francisco St. (La Fonda Hotel). ✆ 505/982-0461.

FURNITURE

Southwest Spanish Craftsmen   The Spanish colonial and Spanish provincial furniture, doors, and home accessories in this store are a bit too elaborate for our tastes, but if you find yourself dreaming of carved wood, this is your place. 314 S. Guadalupe St. ✆ 505/982-1767.

Taos Furniture   Here you'll find classic Southwestern furnishings handcrafted in solid ponderosa pine—both contemporary and traditional. Prices are a little better here than in downtown shops. 217 Galisteo St. ✆ 800/443-3448 or 505/988-1229.

GIFTS & SOUVENIRS

El Nicho *Value*   If you want to take a little piece of Santa Fe home with you, you'll likely find it at this shop. You'll find handcrafted Navajo folk art as well as jewelry and other items by local artisans, including woodcarvings (watch for the *santos!*) by the renowned Ortega family. 227 Don Gaspar Ave. ⓒ 505/984-2830.

JEWELRY

Packards 🎯   Opened by a notable trader, Al Packard, and later sold to new owners, this store on the plaza is worth checking out to see some of the best jewelry available. You'll also find exquisite rugs and pottery. 61 Old Santa Fe Trail. ⓒ 505/983-9241.

Tresa Vorenberg Goldsmiths   You'll find some wildly imaginative designs in this jewelry store, where more than 40 artisans are represented. All items are handcrafted, and custom commissions are welcomed. 656 Canyon Rd. ⓒ 505/988-7215.

MALLS & SHOPPING CENTERS

de Vargas Center   There are approximately 50 merchants and restaurants in this mall just northwest of downtown. This is Santa Fe's small, struggling mall. Though there are fewer shops than at Villa Linda, this is where we shop because we don't tend to get the "mall phobia" we get in the more massive places. Open Monday to Friday 10am to 7pm, Saturday 10am to 6pm, and Sunday noon to 5pm. N. Guadalupe St. and Paseo de Peralta. ⓒ 505/982-2655.

Sanbusco Market Center 🎯   Unique shops and restaurants occupy this remodeled warehouse near the old Santa Fe Railyard. Many of the shops are overpriced, but it's a fun place to window-shop. Open Monday to Saturday 10am to 6pm, Sunday noon to 5pm. 500 Montezuma St. ⓒ 505/989-9390.

Santa Fe Outlets   Outlet-shopping fans will enjoy this open-air mall on the south end of town. Anchors include Brooks Brothers, Jones New York, and Coach. Open Monday to Saturday 10am to 9pm, Sunday 11am to 6pm. 8380 Cerrillos Rd. ⓒ 505/474-4000.

Santa Fe Place   Santa Fe's largest mall is near the southwestern city limits, not far from the I-25 on-ramp. If you're from a major city, you'll probably find shopping here very provincial. Anchors include JC Penney, Sears, Dillard's, and Mervyn's. Open Monday to Saturday 10am to 9pm, Sunday noon to 6pm. 4250 Cerrillos Rd. (at Rodeo Rd.). ⓒ 505/473-4253.

MARKETS

Santa Fe Farmers Market 🎯🎯 *Finds*   This farmers market has everything from fruits, vegetables, and flowers to cheeses, cider, and salsas. Great local treats! If you're an early riser, stroll through and enjoy good coffee, excellent breakfast burritos, and music ranging from violin to fiddle. Open April to mid-November, Saturday and Tuesday 7am to noon. In winter, an abbreviated version takes place indoors. Look for the *Santa Fe Farmers Market Cookbook,* a compilation of farmer's recipes from the region, with vivid photography. In the Santa Fe Railyard, off Paseo de Peralta. ⓒ 505/983-4098.

Tesuque Flea Market 🎯 *Moments*   If you're a flea-market hound, you'll be happy to discover this one. More than 500 vendors here sell everything from used cowboy boots (you might find some real beauties) to clothing, jewelry, books, and furniture, all against a big northern New Mexico view. Open March to late November, Friday to Sunday. Vendors start selling at about 7:30am and stay open until about 6:30pm, weather permitting. US 84/285 (about 8 miles north of Santa Fe). No phone.

POTTERY & TILES

Artesanos Imports Company *✿* *(Moments*   Coming here is like taking a trip south of the border, with all the scents and colors you'd expect on such a journey. You'll find a wide selection of Talavera tile and pottery, as well as light fixtures and many other accessories for the home. There's even an outdoor market where you can buy fountains, sculpture items, and outdoor furniture. A second store is at 1414 Maclovia St. (*©* **505/471-8020**). 222 Galisteo St. *©* **505/983-1743**.

RUGS

Seret & Sons Rugs, Furnishings, and Architectural Pieces *✿*   If you're like us and find Middle Eastern decor irresistible, you'll want to wander through this shop. You'll find kilims and Persian and Turkish rugs, as well as some of the Moorish-style ancient doors and furnishings that you see around Santa Fe. 224 Galisteo St. *©* **505/988-9151** or 505/983-5008.

9 Santa Fe After Dark

Santa Fe is a city committed to the arts, so it's no surprise that the Santa Fe night scene is dominated by highbrow cultural events, beginning with the world-famous Santa Fe Opera. The club and popular-music scene runs a distant second.

Information on all major cultural events can be obtained from the **Santa Fe Convention and Visitors Bureau** (*©* **800/777-CITY** or 505/955-6200) or from the **City of Santa Fe Arts Commission** (*©* **505/955-6707**). Current listings are published each Friday in the "Pasatiempo" section of *The New Mexican* (www.santafenewmexican.com), the city's daily newspaper, and in the *Santa Fe Reporter* (www.sfreporter.com), published every Wednesday.

Nicholas Potter, Bookseller, 211 E. Palace Ave. (*©* **505/983-5434**); **Candyman,** 851 St. Michael's Dr. (*©* **505/983-5906**); and **CD Café,** 301 N. Guadalupe St. (*©* **505/986-0735**), sell tickets for many events. You can also order by phone from **Ticketmaster** (*©* **505/883-7800**). Discount tickets may be available on the night of a performance; for example, the opera offers standing-room tickets on the day of the performance. Sales start at 10am.

THE PERFORMING ARTS

At least two dozen performing-arts groups flourish in this city of 65,000. Many of them perform year-round, but some are seasonal. The acclaimed Santa Fe Opera, for instance, has just a 2-month summer season.

Note: Many companies below perform at locations other than their listed addresses—call or check the websites for details.

MAJOR PERFORMING ARTS COMPANIES

OPERA & CLASSICAL MUSIC

Santa Fe Opera *✿✿✿*   Many rank the Santa Fe Opera second only to the Metropolitan Opera of New York in the United States. Established in 1957, it consistently attracts famed conductors, directors, and singers. At the height of the season, the company is 500-people strong. It's noted for its performances of the classics, little-known works by classical European composers, and American premieres of 21st-century works. The theater, completed for the 1998 season, sits on a wooded hilltop 7 miles north of the city, off US 84/285. It's partially open-air, with open sides. The 8-week, 40-performance opera season runs from late June through late August. All performances begin at 9pm, until the end of July, when performances start at 8:30pm, and the last week of the season, when performances begin at 8pm. A small screen in front of each seat shows the libretto during the performance. A gift shop has been added, as has additional parking. The entire theater is wheelchair accessible. P.O. Box 2408. ℂ **800/280-4654** or 505/986-5900. www.santafeopera.org. Tickets $25–$160; standing room $10; Opening Night Gala $1,700–$3,000. Backstage tours July–Aug Mon–Sat at noon; $5 adults, free for children ages 5–17.

ORCHESTRAL & CHAMBER MUSIC

Santa Fe Pro Musica Chamber Orchestra & Ensemble   This chamber ensemble performs everything from Bach to Vivaldi to contemporary masters. During Holy Week, the Santa Fe Pro Musica presents its annual Mozart and Hayden Concert at the St. Francis Cathedral. Christmas brings candlelight chamber ensemble concerts. Pro Musica's season runs September to May. 430 Manhattan, Suite 10. ℂ **505/988-4640.** www.santafepromusica.com. Tickets $15–$50.

Santa Fe Symphony Orchestra and Chorus   This 60-piece professional symphony orchestra has grown rapidly in stature since its founding in 1984. Matinee and evening performances of classical and popular works are presented in a subscription series at the Lensic Performing Arts Center from October to May. There's a lecture before each performance. During the spring, the orchestra presents music festivals (call for details). P.O. Box 9692. ℂ **800/480-1319** or 505/983-1414. www.sf-symphony.org. Tickets $15–$55 (5 seating categories).

MUSIC FESTIVALS & CONCERT SERIES

Santa Fe Chamber Music Festival ⟨★★⟩   An extraordinary group of international artists comes to Santa Fe every summer for this festival. Its 6-week season runs mid-July to mid-August and is held in the St. Francis Auditorium and the Lensic Performing Arts Center. Each festival features chamber-music masterpieces, new music by a composer in residence, jazz, free youth concerts, preconcert lectures, and open rehearsals. Performances are Monday, Tuesday, Thursday, and Friday at 8pm; Saturday at various evening times; and Sunday at 6pm. Open rehearsals, youth concerts, and preconcert lectures are free to the public. 239 Johnson St., Suite B (P.O. Box 2227). ℂ **505/983-2075** or 505/982-1890 for box office (after June 22). www.sfcmf.org. Tickets $16–$125.

Santa Fe Concert Association   Founded in 1937, this oldest musical organization in northern New Mexico has a September-to-May season that includes approximately 17 annual events. Among them are a "Great Performances" series and an "Adventures" series, both featuring renowned instrumental and vocal soloists and chamber ensembles. The association also hosts special holiday concerts around Christmas. Performances are held at the Lensic Performing Arts Center and the St. Francis Auditorium; tickets are available at the Lensic box office at ℂ **505/988-1234,** and at 800/905-3315 (www.tickets.com) or 505/984-8759. 210 E. Marcy St. (P.O. Box 4626, 87502). Tickets $16–$75.

THEATER COMPANIES

Greer Garson Theater Center   In this graceful, intimate theater, the College of Santa Fe's Performing Arts Department produces four plays annually, with six presentations of each, given between October and May. Usually, the season consists of a comedy, a drama, a musical, and a classic. The college also sponsors studio productions and various contemporary music concerts. College of Santa Fe, 1600 St. Michael's Dr. ℂ **505/473-6511.** www.csf.edu. Tickets $10–$20 adults, $5 students.

Santa Fe Playhouse   Founded in the 1920s, this is the oldest active theater group in New Mexico. Still performing in a historic adobe theater in the Barrio de Analco, it attracts thousands for its dramas, avant-garde theater, and musical comedy. Its popular one-act melodramas call on the public to boo the sneering villain and swoon for the damsel in distress. 142 E. de Vargas St. © 505/988-4262. www.santafeplayhouse.org. Tickets are by donation, up to $20, depending on the show.

Theater Grottesco ⚜ *Finds*   This troupe combines the best of comedy, drama, and dance in its original productions performed each spring and summer. Expect to be romanced, shocked, intellectually stimulated, and, above all, struck silly with laughter. Look for upcoming winter shows as well. 551 W. Cordova Rd. #8400. © 505/474-8400. www.theatergrottesco.org. Tickets $10–$25.

Theaterwork Studio ⚜   A critic for the *Santa Fe New Mexican* called Theaterwork's performance of Chekhov's *Uncle Vanya* "the most rewarding experience I have yet had at a Santa Fe theater." That high praise is well deserved by this community theater that goes out of its way to present refreshing, at times risky, plays. Theaterwork offers seven main-stage productions a year, a broad variety including new plays and classics by regional and national playwrights. Expect to see works by such names as Brecht, Shakespeare, and Victor Hugo. 1336 Rufina Circle (mail: P.O. Box 842). © 505/471-1799. www.theaterwork.org. Tickets $10–$18. Call for performance times.

DANCE COMPANIES

Aspen Santa Fe Ballet ⚜   Founded in 1990, the Aspen Santa Fe Ballet brings classically trained dancers to Santa Fe and Aspen. Performances are an eclectic repertoire by some of the world's foremost choreographers. The season is year-round, with performances at the Lensic Performing Arts Center. 550-B St. Michael's Dr. © 505/983-5591. www.aspensantafeballet.com. Purchase tickets at the Lensic © 505/988-1234. Tickets $15–$52.

María Benitez Teatro Flamenco ⚜⚜ *Finds*   You won't want to miss this cultural treat. True flamenco is one of the most thrilling dance forms, displaying the inner spirit and verve of the gypsies of Spanish Andalusia, and María Benitez, trained in Spain, is a fabulous performer. The Benitez Company's "Estampa Flamenca" summer series is performed nightly except Tuesday from late June to early September. The María Benitez Theater at The Lodge at Santa Fe is modern and showy, yet it's intimate enough so you're immersed in the art. Institute for Spanish Arts, P.O. Box 8418. For tickets call © 888/435-2636, or the box office (June 16–Sept 3, © 505/982-1237). www.mariabenitez.com. Tickets $18–$50.

Major Concert Halls & All-Purpose Auditoriums

Center for Contemporary Arts and Cinematheque, 1050 Old Pecos Trail. © 505/982-1338. www.ccasantafe.org.
Lensic Performing Arts Center, 211 W. San Francisco St. © 505/988-7050. www.lensic.com.
St. Francis Auditorium, Museum of Fine Arts, Lincoln and Palace aves. © 505/476-5072.

Snub Out the Smokes

In 2006, smoking in Santa Fe bars and restaurants, including outdoor-dining areas, became illegal. The law was instituted mainly to protect entertainment and hospitality workers from secondhand smoke, but it will likely protect many others as well.

THE CLUB & MUSIC SCENE

In addition to the clubs and bars listed below, there are a number of hotels whose bars and lounges feature some type of entertainment (see "Where to Stay," earlier in this chapter).

COUNTRY, JAZZ & LATIN

Chispa! ⊛ A tapas bar with the *chispa* or "spark" of fun entertainment and dancing, this hot spot next to the dining room at El Meson draws locals of all types. Music ranges from guitar duos to jazz combos and Brazilian music, with flamenco dancers performing on some Saturday nights. On tango Tuesdays, locals turn out in their tightest dance clothes to party. The tapas are excellent. Open Tuesday to Saturday. 213 Washington Ave. ✆ 505/983-6756. Cover charge for select performances.

Cowgirl Hall of Fame It's difficult to categorize what goes on in this bar and restaurant, but there's live entertainment nightly. Some nights there's blues guitar, others folk music; you might also find "progressive rock," comedy, or cowboy poetry. In the summer, this is a great place to sit under the stars and listen to music. 319 S. Guadalupe St. ✆ 505/982-2565. Tues and Thurs–Sat $3 cover. Special performances $10.

Eldorado Hotel In a grand lobby-lounge full of fine art, classical guitarists and pianists perform nightly. 309 W. San Francisco St. ✆ 505/988-4455.

El Farol ⊛ This original neighborhood bar of the Canyon Road artists' quarter (its name means "the lantern") is the place to head for local ambience. Its low ceilings and dark brown walls are home to Santa Fe's largest and most unusual selection of tapas (bar snacks and appetizers). Jazz, swing, folk, and most notably, salsa and flamenco musicians (and dancers)—some of national note—perform most nights. 808 Canyon Rd. ✆ 505/983-9912. Cover $7.

La Fiesta Lounge ⊛ Set in the notable La Fonda hotel on the plaza, this nightclub offers excellent country bands on weekends, with old- and new-timers two-stepping across the floor. This lively lobby bar offers cocktails, an appetizer menu, and live entertainment nightly. It's a great authentic Santa Fe spot. La Fonda Hotel, 110 E. San Francisco St. ✆ 505/982-5511.

ROCK & DISCO

Catamount Bar and Grille The postcollege crowd hangs out at this bar, where there's live rock and blues music on weekends. Food is served until midnight, and there is also a billiards room. 125 E. Water St. ✆ 505/988-7222.

THE BAR SCENE

The Dragon Room ⊛ A number of years ago, *International Newsweek* named the Dragon Room at The Pink Adobe (p. 154) one of the top 20 bars in the world. The reason is its spirited but comfortable ambience, which draws students, artists, politicians, and even an occasional celebrity. The decor theme is dragons, which you'll find carved on the front doors as well as hanging from the ceiling, all within low-lit, aged elegance akin to the Pink Adobe's interior. Live trees also grow through the roof. In addition to the tempting lunch and bar menu, there's always a complimentary bowl of popcorn close at hand. 406 Old Santa Fe Trail. (C) 505/983-7712.

El Paseo Bar and Grill   You can almost always catch live music at this casual, unpretentious place (yet it's not a "sports bar"). The crowd here is somewhat younger than at most other downtown establishments, and on certain nights, the bar is completely packed. In addition to the open mic night on Tuesdays, a variety of local bands play here regularly—cranking out many types of music, from blues to rock to jazz to bluegrass. 208 Galisteo St. (C) 505/992-2848. Cover $3–$5 weekends.

Evangelo's   A popular downtown hangout with tropical decor and a mahogany bar, this place can get raucous at times. It's a bit seedy, but more than 60 varieties of imported beer are available, and pool tables are an added attraction. On Friday and Saturday at 9pm and Wednesday at 7:30pm, live bands play (jazz, rock, or reggae). Evangelo's is extremely popular with the local crowd. You'll find your share of businesspeople, artists, and even bikers here. Open Monday to Saturday noon to 1:30am and Sundays until midnight. 200 W. San Francisco St. (C) 505/982-9014. Cover for special performances only.

Swig ℛ *(Finds*   Santa Fe's most happening bar stirs a splash of '60s retro in with a good shot of contemporary chic. The result? A smooth sip of fun. Catering to a broad variety of clientele, this martini bar serves classic and cutting-edge drinks along with delectable small plates of Asian food. The lounge serves until 11pm on weekdays and midnight on weekends, making it one of the few Santa Fe spots for late-night food. A sushi bar, added in 2006, is a great bonus. Open Tuesday through Saturday from 5pm to 2am. 135 W. Palace Ave., level 3. (C) 505/955-0400.

Vanessie of Santa Fe ℛ   This is unquestionably Santa Fe's most popular piano bar. The talented Doug Montgomery and Charles Tichenor have a loyal local following. Their repertoire ranges from Bach to Billy Joel, Gershwin to Barry Manilow. They play nightly from 8pm until closing, which could be anywhere from midnight to 2am. There's an extra microphone, so if you're daring (or drunk), you can stand up and accompany the piano and vocals (though this is *not* a karaoke scene). National celebrities have even joined in—including Harry Connick, Jr. (and he wasn't even drunk). Vanessie's offers a great bar menu. 434 W. San Francisco St. (C) 505/982-9966.

10 Touring Some Pueblos Around Santa Fe

Of the eight northern pueblos, Tesuque, Pojoaque, Nambe, San Ildefonso, San Juan, and Santa Clara are within about 30 miles of Santa Fe. Picuris (San Lorenzo) is on the High Road to Taos (see "Taking the High Road to Taos," later in this chapter), and Taos Pueblo is just outside the town of Taos (p. 213).

The four pueblos described in this section can easily be visited in a single day's round-trip from Santa Fe, though we suggest visiting just the two that really give a feel of the ancient lifestyle: San Ildefonso, with its broad plaza, and San Juan, including its arts cooperative. In an easy day trip from Santa Fe you can take in both, with some delicious New Mexican food in Española en route. If you're in the area at a time when you can catch certain rituals, that's when you should see some of the other pueblos.

Excursions from Santa Fe

Pueblo Etiquette

When you visit pueblos, it is important to observe certain rules of etiquette. These are personal dwellings and/or important historic sites, and must be respected as such. Don't climb on the buildings or peek into doors or windows. Don't enter sacred grounds, such as cemeteries and kivas. If you attend a dance or ceremony, remain silent while it is taking place and refrain from applause when it's over. Many pueblos prohibit photography or sketches; others require you to pay a fee for a permit. If you don't respect the privacy of the Native Americans who live at the pueblo, you'll be asked to leave.

TESUQUE PUEBLO

Tesuque (Te-*soo*-keh) **Pueblo** is about 9 miles north of Santa Fe on US 84/285. You'll know that you're approaching the pueblo when you see a large store near the highway. If you're driving north and you get to the unusual Camel Rock and a large roadside casino, you've missed the pueblo entrance.

The 400 pueblo dwellers at Tesuque are faithful to their traditional religion, rituals, and ceremonies. Excavations confirm that a pueblo has existed here at least since the year A.D. 1200; accordingly, this pueblo is now on the National Register of Historic Places. When you come to the welcome sign at the pueblo, turn right, go a block, and park on the right. You'll see the plaza off to the left. There's not a lot to see; in recent years renovation has brought a new look to some of the homes around it. There's a big open area where dances are held, and the **San Diego Church,** completed in 2004 on the site of an 1888 structure that burned down recently. It's the fifth church on the pueblo's plaza since 1641. Visitors are asked to remain in this area.

Some Tesuque women are skilled potters; especially noteworthy are Ignacia Duran's black-and-white and red micaceous pottery, and Teresa Tapia's miniatures and pots with animal figures. You'll find many crafts at a gallery on the plaza's southeast corner. The **San Diego Feast Day,** which may feature harvest, buffalo, deer, flag, or Comanche dances, is November 12.

The Tesuque Pueblo's address is Route 5, Box 360-T, Santa Fe, NM 87501 (② **505/ 983-2667**). Admission to the pueblo is free; however, there is a $20 charge for use of still cameras; special permission is required for filming, sketching, and painting. The pueblo is open daily from 9am to 5pm. **Camel Rock Casino** (② **505/984-8414**) is open Sunday to Wednesday from 8am to 4am, and Thursday to Saturday for 24 hours; it has a snack bar on the premises.

SAN ILDEFONSO PUEBLO 🏵🏵

Pox Oge, as **San Ildefonso Pueblo** is called in its own Tewa language, means "place where the water cuts down through," possibly because of the way the Rio Grande cuts through the mountains nearby. Turn left on NM 502 at Pojoaque, and drive about 6 miles to the turnoff. This pueblo has a broad, dusty plaza, with a kiva on one side, ancient dwellings on the other, and a church at the far end. It's nationally famous for its matte-finish, black-on-black pottery, developed by tribeswoman María Martinez in the 1920s. One of the most visited pueblos in northern New Mexico, San Ildefonso attracts more than 20,000 visitors a year.

The San Ildefonsos could best be described as rebellious because this was one of the last pueblos to succumb to the reconquest spearheaded by Don Diego de Vargas in 1692. Within view of the pueblo is the volcanic Black Mesa, a symbol of the San Ildefonso people's strength. Through the years, each time San Ildefonso felt itself threatened by enemy forces, the residents, along with members of other pueblos, would hide out up on the butte, returning to the valley only when starvation set in. Today, a visit to the pueblo is valuable mainly in order to see or buy rich black pottery. A few shops surround the plaza, and there's the **San Ildefonso Pueblo Museum** tucked away in the governor's office beyond the plaza. We especially recommend visiting during ceremonial days. **San Ildefonso Feast Day,** on January 23, features the buffalo and Comanche dances in alternate years. **Corn dances,** held in late August or early September, commemorate a basic element in pueblo life, the importance of fertility in all creatures—humans as well as animals—and plants.

The pueblo has a 4½-acre fishing lake that is surrounded by *bosque* (Spanish for "forest"), open April to October. Picnicking is encouraged, though you may want to look at the sites before you decide to stay; some are nicer than others. Camping is not allowed.

The pueblo's address is Route 5, Box 315A, Santa Fe, NM 87506 (© 505/455-3549). Admission is $5 per car. The charge for taking photographs is $10; you'll pay $20 to film and $25 to sketch. The charge for fishing is $10 for adults and $5 for seniors and children under 12, but you'll want to call to be sure the lake is open. The pueblo is open in the summer, daily 8am to 5pm; call for weekend hours. In the winter, it's open Monday to Friday 8am to 4:30pm. It's closed for major holidays and tribal events.

OHKAY OWINGE (SAN JUAN PUEBLO) ☞

If you continue north on US 84/285, you will reach San Juan Pueblo, now renamed in Tewa language, Ohkay Owinge, via NM 74, a mile off NM 68, about 4 miles north of Española.

The largest (pop. 1,950) and northernmost of the Tewa-speaking pueblos, and headquarters of the Eight Northern Indian Pueblos Council, Ohkay Owinge is on the east side of the Rio Grande—opposite the 1598 site of San Gabriel, the first Spanish settlement west of the Mississippi River and the first capital of New Spain. In 1598, the Spanish, impressed with the openness and helpfulness of the people of San Juan, established a capital there (it was moved, 10 years later, to Santa Fe), making San Juan Pueblo the first pueblo to be subjected to Spanish colonization. The Indians were generous, providing food, clothing, shelter, and fuel—they even helped sustain the settlement when its leader, conquistador Juan de Oñate, became preoccupied with his search for gold and neglected the needs of his people.

The past and present cohabit here. Though many of the tribe members are Catholics, most of the Ohkay Owinge tribe still practice traditional religious rituals. Thus, two rectangular kivas flank the church in the main plaza, and *caciques* (pueblo priests) share power with civil authorities. The annual Ohkay Owinge **Fiesta** is held June 23 and 24; it features buffalo and Comanche dances. Another annual ceremony is the **turtle dance** on December 26. The **Matachine dance,** performed here Christmas day, vividly depicts the subjugation of the Native Americans by the Catholic Spaniards.

The address of the pueblo is P.O. Box 1099, Ohkay Owinge Pueblo, NM 87566 (© 505/852-4400 or 505/852-4210). Admission is free. Photography or sketching may be allowed with prior permission from the governor's office. The charge for fishing is $8 for adults, $5 for children and seniors. The pueblo is open every day during daylight hours.

The **Eight Northern Indian Pueblos Council** (© 505/747-1593) is a sort of chamber of commerce and social-service agency.

A crafts shop, Ohkay Owinge **Arts and Crafts Cooperative** (© 505/852-2372), specializes in local wares. This is a fine place to seek out San Juan's distinctive red pottery, a lustrous ceramic incised with traditional geometric symbols. Also displayed for sale are seed, turquoise, and silver jewelry; wood and stone carvings; indigenous clothing and weavings; embroidery; and paintings. Artisans often work on the premises, allowing visitors to watch. The co-op is open Monday through Saturday 9am to 4:30pm in winter, until 5pm in summer (but is closed San Juan Feast Day, June 24). **Sunrise Crafts,** another crafts shop, is to the right of the co-op. There, you'll find one-of-a-kind handcrafted pipes, beadwork, and burned and painted gourds.

Fishing and picnicking are encouraged at the **San Juan Tribal Lakes,** open year-round. **Ohkay Casino** (© 505/747-1668) offers table games and slot machines, as well as live music nightly Tuesday through Saturday. It's open 24 hours on weekends.

SANTA CLARA PUEBLO

Close to Española (on NM 5), Santa Clara has a population of about 1,800, making it one of the largest pueblos. You'll see the village sprawling across the river basin near the beautiful Black Mesa, rows of tract homes surrounding an adobe central area. Although it's in an incredible setting, the pueblo itself is not much to see; however, a trip through it will give a real feel for the contemporary lives of these people.

Follow the main route to the old village, where you come to the visitor center, also known as the neighborhood center. There you can get directions to small shops that sell distinctive black incised Santa Clara pottery, red burnished pottery, baskets, and other crafts. One stunning sight here is the cemetery. Stop on the west side of the church and look over the 4-foot wall. It's a primitive site, with plain wooden crosses and some graves adorned with plastic flowers.

There are corn and harvest dances on **Santa Clara Feast Day** (Aug 12); information on other special days (including the corn or harvest dances, as well as children's dances) can be obtained from the pueblo office.

The pueblo's address is P.O. Box 580, Española, NM 87532 (© 505/753-7326). Admission is free. The charge for taking photographs is $5; filming and sketching are not allowed. The pueblo is open every day from 9am to 4pm; the visitor center is open Monday to Friday from 8am to 4:30pm.

11 A Side Trip to Pecos National Historic Park

About 15 miles east of Santa Fe, I-25 meanders through **Glorieta Pass,** site of an important Civil War skirmish. In March 1862, volunteers from Colorado and New Mexico, along with Fort Union regulars, defeated a Confederate force marching on Santa Fe, thereby turning the tide of Southern encroachment in the West.

Follow NM 50 east to **Pecos** for about 7 miles. This quaint town, well off the beaten track since the interstate was constructed, is the site of a noted **Benedictine monastery.** About 26 miles north of here on NM 63 is the village of **Cowles,** gateway to the natural wonderland of the **Pecos Wilderness.** There are many camping, picnicking, and fishing locales en route.

Pecos National Historical Park 🏵🏵 (© 505/757-6414; www.nps.gov/peco), about 2 miles south of the town of Pecos off NM 63, contains the ruins of a 15th-century pueblo and 17th- and 18th-century missions that jut up spectacularly from a high meadow. Coronado mentioned Pecos Pueblo in 1540: "It is feared through the land," he wrote. The approximately 2,000 Native Americans here farmed in irrigated fields and hunted wild game. Their pueblo had 660 rooms and many kivas. By 1620, Franciscan monks had established a church and convent. Military and natural disasters took their toll on the pueblo, and in 1838, the 20 surviving Pecos went to live with relatives at the Jemez Pueblo.

The **E. E. Fogelson Visitor Center** tells the history of the Pecos people in a well-done, chronologically organized exhibit, complete with dioramas. A 1.5-mile loop trail begins at the center and continues through Pecos Pueblo and the **Misión de Nuestra Señora de Los Angeles de Porciuncula** (as the church was formerly called). This excavated structure—170 feet long and 90 feet wide at the transept—was once the most magnificent church north of Mexico City.

Pecos National Historical Park is open Memorial Day to Labor Day, daily 8am to 6pm; the rest of the year, daily 8am to 5pm. It's closed January 1 and December 25. Admission is $3 per person over age 16.

12 Los Alamos & the Ancient Cliff Dwellings of Bandelier National Monument

Los Alamos, a town of 18,000 residents, spreads over the colorful, fingerlike mesas of the Pajarito Plateau, between the Jemez Mountains and the Rio Grande Valley. It's the home of Los Alamos National Laboratory, established here during World War II, the origin of the first atomic bomb. Still the home of a world-renowned science laboratory, the town is about 35 miles west of Santa Fe and about 65 miles southwest of Taos. From Santa Fe, take US 84/285 north approximately 16 miles to the Pojoaque junction, then turn west on NM 502. Driving time is about 50 minutes. As NM 502 enters Los Alamos from Santa Fe, it follows Trinity Drive, where accommodations, restaurants, and other services are located.

A NEARBY ATTRACTION

Bandelier National Monument ♠♠♠   Less than 15 miles south of Los Alamos along NM 4, this National Park Service area contains stunningly preserved ruins of the ancient cliff-dwelling ancestral Puebloan (Anasazi) culture within 46 square miles of canyon-and-mesa wilderness. The national monument is named after the Swiss-American archaeologist Adolph Bandelier, who explored here in the 1880s. During busy summer months, head out early; there can be a waiting line for cars to park.

After an orientation stop at the visitor center and museum to learn about the culture that flourished here between 1100 and 1550, most visitors follow a trail along Frijoles Creek to the principal ruins. The pueblo site, including an underground kiva, has been stabilized. The biggest thrill for most folks is climbing hardy ponderosa pine ladders to visit an alcove—140 feet above the canyon floor—that was once home to prehistoric people. Tours are self-guided or led by a National Park Service ranger. Be aware that dogs are not allowed on trails.

NM 4 (HCR 1, Box 1, Suite 15, Los Alamos). ☎ **505/672-3861**, ext 517. www.nps.gov/band. Admission $12 per vehicle. Daily during daylight hours. No pets allowed on trails. Closed Christmas and New Year's Day.

13 Taking the High Road to Taos

Unless you're in a hurry to get from Santa Fe to Taos, the High Road—also called the Mountain Road or the King's Road—is by far the most fascinating route between the two cities. It begins in lowlands of mystically formed pink and yellow stone, passing by apple and peach orchards and chile farms in the weaving village of **Chimayo.** Then it

Home of the Atomic Bomb

Pueblo tribes lived in the rugged Los Alamos area for well over 1,000 years, and an exclusive boys' school operated atop the 7,300-foot plateau from 1918 to 1943. Then the **Los Alamos National Laboratory** was established here in secrecy, code-named Site Y of the Manhattan Project, the hush-hush wartime program that developed the world's first atomic bombs.

Project director J. Robert Oppenheimer, later succeeded by Norris E. Bradbury, worked along with thousands of scientists, engineers, and technicians in research, development, and production of those early weapons. Today, more than 10,000 people work at the Los Alamos National Laboratory, making it the largest employer in northern New Mexico. Operated by Los Alamos National Security, currently under a contract through the U.S. Department of Energy, its 2,800 individual facilities and 42 separate technical areas occupy 36 square miles of mesa-top land.

The lab is one of the world's foremost scientific institutions. It primarily focuses on nuclear weapons research—the Trident and Minuteman strategic warheads were designed here, for example—and has many other interdisciplinary research programs, including international nuclear safeguards and nonproliferation, space, and atmospheric studies; supercomputing; theoretical physics; biomedical and materials science; and environmental restoration.

Current plans call for Los Alamos National Laboratory to begin building a limited number of replacement plutonium pits for use in the enduring U.S. nuclear weapons stockpile. The lab has the only plutonium-processing facility in the United States that is capable of producing those components.

Bradbury Science Museum 🦅   This is a great place to get acquainted with what goes on at a weapons production facility after nuclear proliferation. Although the museum is run by Los Alamos National Laboratory, which definitely puts a positive spin on the business of producing weapons, it's a fascinating place to explore and it includes more than 35 hands-on exhibits. Begin in the History Gallery, where you'll learn about the evolution of the site from the Los Alamos Ranch School days through the Manhattan Project to the present. Meanwhile, listen for announcement of the film *The Town That Never Was*, an 18-minute presentation on this community that grew up shrouded in secrecy (shown in the auditorium). Further exploration will take you to the Defense Gallery, where you can test the heaviness of plutonium against that of other substances, see an actual 5-ton Little Boy nuclear bomb (like the one dropped on Hiroshima), and see firsthand how Los Alamos conducts worldwide surveillance of nuclear explosions.

15th St. and Central Ave., Los Alamos. Ⓒ 505/667-4444. Free admission. Tues–Sat 10am–5pm; Sun–Mon 1–5pm. Closed New Year's Day, Thanksgiving, and Christmas.

climbs toward the highlands to the village of **Cordova,** known for its woodcarvers, and higher still to **Truchas,** a renegade arts town where Hispanic traditions and ways of life continue much as they did a century ago. Though we've described this tour from south to north, the most scenic way to see it is from north to south, when you travel down off the mountains rather than up into them. This way, you see more expansive views.

CHIMAYO

About 28 miles north of Santa Fe on NM 76/285 is the historic weaving center of Chimayo. It's approximately 16 miles past the Pojoaque junction, at the junction of NM 520 and NM 76 via NM 503. In this small village, families still maintain the tradition of crafting hand-woven textiles initiated by their ancestors seven generations ago, in the early 1800s. One such family is the Ortegas, and **Ortega's Weaving Shop** (© 505/351-4215) and **Galeria Ortega** ⭐ (© 505/351-2288), both at the corner of NM 520 and NM 76, are fine places to take a close look at this ancient craft. A more humble spot is **Trujillo Weavings** (© 505/351-4457) on NM 76. If you're lucky enough to find the proprietors in, you might get a weaving history lesson. You can see an 80-year-old loom and a 100-year-old shuttle carved from apricot wood. The weavings you'll find are some of the best of the Rio Grande style, with rich patterns, many made from naturally dyed wool. Also on display are some fine Cordova woodcarvings. Near the Santuario de Chimayo, just off the plaza, look for the **High Road Marketplace** ⭐ (© 866/343-5381 or 505/351-1078; www.highroadnewmexico.com/marketplace.html), an artists' co-op gallery with a variety of offerings ranging from jewelry to landscape paintings to a broad range of crosses made from tin, rusted metal, and nails. Also check out **Centinela Traditional Arts,** 946 NM 76 (© 877/351-2180 or 505/351-2180), for a good selection of rugs made by weavers from up and down the Rio Grande Valley. Watch for the chenille shawls by Scarlet Rose.

One of the best places to shop in Chimayo, **Chimayo Trading and Mercantile** ⭐ (© 505/351-4566), on NM 76, is a richly cluttered store carrying local arts and crafts as well as select imports. It has a good selection of kachinas and Hopi corn maidens, as well as specialty items such as elaborately beaded cow skulls. Look for George Zarolinski's "smoked porcelain."

Many people come to Chimayo to visit **El Santuario de Nuestro Señor de Esquipulas (the Shrine of Our Lord of Esquipulas)** ⭐⭐, better known simply as El Santuario de Chimayo. Ascribed with miraculous powers of healing, this church has attracted thousands of pilgrims since its construction in 1814 to 1816. Up to 30,000 people participate in the annual Good Friday pilgrimage, many of them walking from as far away as Albuquerque.

Although only the earth in the anteroom beside the altar is presumed to have the gift of healing powers, the entire shrine radiates true serenity. A National Historic Landmark, the church has five beautiful *reredos* (panels of sacred paintings)—one behind the main altar and two on each side of the nave. Each year during the fourth weekend in July, the military exploits of the 9th-century Spanish saint Santiago are celebrated in a weekend fiesta, including the historic play *Los Moros y Los Cristianos (The Moors and the Christians).*

A good place to stop for a quick bite, **Leona's Restaurante de Chimayo** (© 505/351-4569) is right next door to the Santuario de Chimayo. Leona herself presides over this little taco and burrito stand with plastic tables inside and, during warm months, out. Leona has gained national fame for her flavored tortilla—such delicacies as raspberry and chocolate really are tasty. Burritos and soft tacos made with chicken, beef,

Inside a Volcano

While you're in the area, check out the **Valles Caldera National Preserve,** past Bandelier National Monument on NM 4, beginning about 15 miles from Los Alamos. The reserve is all that remains of a volcanic caldera created by a collapse after eruptions nearly a million years ago. When the mountain spewed ashes and dust as far away as Kansas and Nebraska, its underground magma chambers collapsed, forming this great valley—one of the largest volcanic calderas in the world. Lava domes that pushed up after the collapse obstruct a full view across the expanse, but the beauty of the place is still within grasp. Visitors have many guided options for exploring the preserve, from sleigh rides in winter to fly-fishing in summer. For more information, check out www.vallescaldera.gov.

or veggie-style with beans will definitely tide you over en route to Taos or Santa Fe. Leona's is open 11am to 5pm Thursday through Monday.

Nearby **Santa Cruz Lake** provides water for Chimayo Valley farms and also offers a recreation site for trout fishing and camping at the edge of the Pecos Wilderness. During busy summer months, trash might litter its shores. To reach the lake from Chimayo, drive 2 miles south on NM 520, then turn east on NM 503 and travel 4 miles.

WHERE TO STAY
Casa Escondida ⚑   Located on the outskirts of Chimayo, this inn offers a lovely retreat and a good home base for exploring the Sangre de Cristo Mountains and their many soulful farming villages. This hacienda-feeling place has a cozy living room with a large kiva fireplace. Decor is simple and classic, with Mission-style furniture lending a colonial feel. The breakfast room is a sunny atrium with French doors that open out in summer to a grassy yard spotted with apricot trees. The rooms are varied; all of our favorites are within the main house. The Sun Room catches all that passionate northern New Mexico sun upon its red-brick floors and on its private flagstone patio as well. It has an elegant feel and connects with a smaller room, so it's a good choice for families. The Vista is on the second story. Its dormer windows give it an oddly shaped roofline. It has a wrought-iron queen-size bed as well as a twin, and it opens out onto a large deck offering spectacular sunset views. The casita adjacent to the main house has a kiva fireplace, a stove, and a minifridge, as well as nice meadow views.

P.O. Box 142, Chimayo, NM 87522. © **800/643-7201** or 505/351-4805. Fax 505/351-2575. www.casaescondida. com. 8 units. $95–$155 double. Rates include full breakfast. MC, V. Pets welcome for a small fee; prearrangement required. **Amenities:** Jacuzzi; in-room massage.

WHERE TO DINE
Restaurante Rancho de Chimayo ⚑ NEW MEXICAN   Many of our friends' families have scheduled trips into northern New Mexico to coincide with lunch or dinner at this fun restaurant. Set in an adobe home built by Hermenegildo Jaramillo in the 1880s, it's now run as a restaurant by his descendants. Unfortunately, over the years the restaurant has become so famous that tour buses now stop here. But the food has suffered only a little. In the warmer months, request to dine on the terraced patio. During winter, you'll be seated in one of a number of cozy rooms with thick viga

ceilings. The food is native New Mexican, prepared from generations-old Jaramillo family recipes. You can't go wrong with the enchiladas, served layered, northern New Mexico style, rather than rolled. For variety you might want to try the *combinación picante* (carne adovada, tamale, enchilada, beans, and *posole*). Each plate comes with two *sopaipillas*. With a little honey, who needs dessert? The full bar serves delicious margaritas.

P.O. Box 11, Chimayo (CTR 98). © 505/351-4444. Reservations recommended. Lunch $7.50–$13; dinner $10–$18. AE, DC, DISC, MC, V. Daily May–Oct 11:30am–9pm; Sat–Sun breakfast 8:30–10:30am. Closed Mon Nov 1–Apr 30.

CORDOVA

Just as Chimayo is famous for its weaving, the village of Cordova, about 7 miles east on NM 76, is noted for its woodcarving. It's easy to whiz by this village, nestled below the High Road, but don't. Just a short way through this truly traditional northern New Mexico town is a gem: **The Castillo Gallery** ℛ (© 505/351-4067), a mile into the village of Cordova, carries moody and colorful acrylic paintings by Paula Castillo, as well as her metal welded sculptures. It also carries the work of Terry Enseñat Mulert, whose contemporary woodcarvings are treasures of the high country. En route to the Castillo, you may want to stop in at two other local carvers' galleries. The first you'll come to is that of **Sabinita Lopez Ortiz;** the second belongs to her cousin, **Gloria Ortiz.** Both are descendants of the well-noted José Dolores Lopez. Carved from cedarwood and aspen, the works range from simple statues of saints (*santos*) to elaborate scenes of birds.

TRUCHAS

Robert Redford's 1988 movie *The Milagro Beanfield War* featured the town of Truchas (which means "trout"). A former Spanish colonial outpost built on top of an 8,000-foot mesa, 4 miles east of Cordova, it was chosen as the site for the film in part because traditional Hispanic culture is still very much in evidence. Subsistence farming is prevalent here. The scenery is spectacular: 13,101-foot Truchas Peak dominates one side of the mesa, and the broad Rio Grande Valley dominates the other.

Be sure to find your way into **The Cordovas' Handweaving Workshop** (© 505/689-2437). In the center of town, this tiny shop is run by Harry Cordova, a fourth-generation weaver with a unique style. His works tend to be simpler than many Rio Grande weavings, utilizing mainly stripes in the designs.

Just down the road from the workshop is **Hand Artes Gallery** (© 800/689-2441 or 505/689-2443), a definite surprise in this remote region. Here you'll find an array of contemporary as well as representational art from noted regional artists. Look for Sheila Keeffe's worldly painted panels, and Norbert Voelkel's colorful paintings and monoprints.

About 6 miles east of Truchas on NM 76 is the small town of **Las Trampas,** noted for its 1780 **San José de Gracia Church,** which, with its thick walls and elegant lines, might possibly be the most beautiful of all New Mexico churches built during the Spanish colonial period.

PICURIS (SAN LORENZO) PUEBLO

Near the regional education center of Peñasco, about 24 miles from Chimayo, near the intersection of NM 75 and NM 76, is the Picuris (San Lorenzo) Pueblo (© 505/587-2519). The 375 citizens of this 15,000-acre mountain pueblo, native Tewa speakers, consider themselves a sovereign nation: Their forebears never made a treaty with any foreign country, including the United States. Thus, they observe a traditional form of tribal council government. A few of the original mud-and-stone houses still stand, as does a lovely church. A striking aboveground ceremonial kiva called "the Roundhouse," built at least 700 years ago, and some historic excavated kivas and storerooms are on a hill above the pueblo and are open to visitors. The **annual feast days** at San Lorenzo Church are August 9 and 10.

The people here are modern enough to have fully computerized their public showcase operations as Picuris Tribal Enterprises. Besides running the Hotel Santa Fe in the state capital, they own the **Picuris Pueblo Museum and Visitor's Center,** where weaving, beadwork, and distinctive reddish-brown clay cooking pottery are exhibited daily 9am to 6pm. Self-guided tours through the old village ruins begin at the museum and cost $5; the camera fee is $6; sketching and video camera fees are $25. There's also an information center, crafts shop, and restaurant. Fishing permits ($11 for adults, $8 for seniors, and $7 for children) are available, as are permits to camp ($8) at Tu-Tah Lake, which is regularly stocked with trout.

DIXON & EMBUDO

Taos is about 24 miles north of Peñasco via NM 518, but day-trippers from Santa Fe can loop back to the capital by taking NM 75 west from Picuris Pueblo. Dixon, approximately 12 miles west of Picuris, and its twin village Embudo, a mile farther on NM 68 at the Rio Grande, are home to many artists and craftspeople who exhibit their works during the annual **autumn show** sponsored by the Dixon Arts Association. If you get to Embudo at mealtime, stop in at **Embudo Station** (© 800/852-4707 or 505/852-4707), a restaurant right on the banks of the Rio Grande. From mid-April to October—the only time it's open—you can sit on the patio under giant cottonwoods and sip the restaurant's own microbrewed beer (try the green chile ale, its most celebrated) and signature wines while watching the peaceful Rio Grande flow by. The specialty here is Southwestern food, but you'll find other tantalizing tastes as well. Try the rainbow trout roasted on a cedar plank. The restaurant is generally open Tuesday to Sunday noon to 9pm, but call before making plans. It's especially known for its jazz on Sunday, an affair that PBS once featured.

To taste more of the local grape, follow signs to **La Chiripada Winery** (© 505/579-4437), whose product is surprisingly good, especially to those who don't know that New Mexico has a long winemaking history. Local pottery is also sold in the tasting room. The winery is open Monday to Saturday 10am to 5pm, Sunday noon to 5pm.

Two more small villages lie in the Rio Grande Valley at 6-mile intervals south of Embudo on NM 68. **Velarde** is a fruit-growing center; in season, the road here is lined with stands selling fresh fruit or crimson chile *ristras* and wreaths of native plants. **Alcalde** is the site of Los Luceros, an early-17th-century home that has been refurbished as an arts and history center. Also in the area, and worth checking out, is **Los Luceros** (© 505/852-1085), which makes wine in a straw-bale winery. The unique **Dance of the Matachines,** a Moorish-style ritual brought from Spain, is performed here on holidays and feast days.

ESPAÑOLA

The commercial center of Española (pop. 7,000) no longer has the railroad that led to its establishment in the 1880s, but it may have New Mexico's greatest concentration of **low riders.** These are late-model customized cars, so called because their suspension leaves them sitting quite close to the ground.

Georgia O'Keeffe & New Mexico: A Desert Romance

In June 1917, during a short visit to the Southwest, the painter Georgia O'Keeffe (born 1887) visited New Mexico for the first time. She was immediately enchanted by the stark scenery; even after her return to the energy and chaos of New York City, her mind wandered frequently to New Mexico's arid land and undulating mesas. However, not until the arts patron and "collector of people" Mabel Dodge Luhan coaxed her 12 years later did O'Keeffe return to the multihued desert of her daydreams.

O'Keeffe was reportedly ill, both physically and emotionally, when she arrived in Santa Fe in April 1929. New Mexico seemed to soothe her spirit and heal her physical ailments almost magically. Two days after her arrival, Mabel Dodge Luhan persuaded O'Keeffe to move into her home in Taos. There, she would be free to paint and socialize as she liked.

In Taos, O'Keeffe began painting what would become some of her best-known canvases—close-ups of desert flowers and objects such as cow and horse skulls. "The color up there is different . . . the blue-green of the sage and the mountains, the wildflowers in bloom," O'Keeffe once said of Taos. "It's a different kind of color from any I've ever seen—there's nothing like that in north Texas or even in Colorado." Taos transformed not only her art, but her personality as well. She bought a car and learned to drive. Sometimes, on warm days, she ran naked through the sage fields. That August, a new, rejuvenated O'Keeffe rejoined her husband, photographer Alfred Stieglitz, in New York.

The artist returned to New Mexico year after year, spending time with Mabel Dodge Luhan as well as staying at the isolated Ghost Ranch. She drove through the countryside in her snappy Ford, stopping to paint in her favorite spots along the way. Until 1949, O'Keeffe always returned to New York in the fall. Three years after Stieglitz's death, though, she relocated permanently to New Mexico, spending each winter and spring in Abiquiu and each summer and fall at Ghost Ranch. Georgia O'Keeffe died in Santa Fe in 1986.

A great way to see Ghost Ranch is on a hike that climbs above the mystical area. Take US 84 north from Española about 36 miles to Ghost Ranch and follow the road to the Ghost Ranch office. The ranch is owned by the Presbyterian Church, and the staff will supply you with a primitive map for the **Kitchen Mesa** and **Chimney Rock** hikes. If you hike there, be sure to check in at the front desk, which is open Monday to Saturday from 8am to 5pm. For more information, contact **Ghost Ranch,** 401 Old Taos Hwy., Santa Fe (© 505/685-4333; www.ghostranch.org).

Sights of interest in Española include the **Bond House Museum** (© 505/747-8535), a Victorian-era adobe home that exhibits local history and art; and the **Santa Cruz Church,** built in 1733 and renovated in 1979, which houses many fine examples of Spanish colonial religious art. The **Convento,** built to resemble a colonial cathedral, on the Española Plaza (at the junction of NM 30 and US 84), houses a variety of shops, including a trading post and an antiques gallery, as well as a display room for the Historical Society. Complete information on Española and the vicinity can be obtained from the **Española Valley Chamber of Commerce,** 710 Paseo de Onate, Española, NM 87532 (© **505/753-2831**).

If you admire the work of Georgia O'Keeffe, try to plan a short trip to **Abiquiu,** a tiny town at a bend of the Rio Chama, 14 miles south of Ghost Ranch and 22 miles north of Española on US 84. When you see the surrounding terrain, it will be clear that this was the inspiration for many of her startling landscapes. **O'Keeffe's adobe home** ⚘ (where she lived and painted) is open for public tours. Advance reservations are required; the fee for adults is $25 for a 1-hour tour. A number of tours are given each week—on Tuesday, Thursday, and Friday (Mar–Nov only)—and a limited number of people are accepted per tour. Visitors are not permitted to take pictures. Fortunately, O'Keeffe's home remains as it was when she lived there (until 1986). Call several months in advance for reservations (© **505/685-4539**).

WHERE TO DINE

El Paragua ⚘ NORTHERN NEW MEXICAN   This Española restaurant is a great place to stop en route to Taos, though some Santa Feans make a special trip here. Every time we enter El Paragua (which means "the umbrella"), with its red-tile floors and colorful Saltillo-tile trimmings, we feel as though we've stepped into Mexico. The restaurant opened in 1958 as a small taco stand owned by two brothers, and through the years it has flourished. It has received praise from many sources, including *Gourmet Magazine* and N. Scott Momaday, writing for the *New York Times*. You can't go wrong ordering the enchilada suprema, a chicken and cheese enchilada with onion and sour cream. Also on the menu are fajitas and a variety of seafood dishes and steaks. There's a full bar from which you may want to try Don Luis's Italian coffee, made with a coffee-flavored liquor called Tuaca. For equally excellent but faster food, skip next door to the kin restaurant **El Parasol** ⚘ and order a chicken taco—the best ever.

603 Santa Cruz Rd., Española (off the main drag; turn east at Long John Silver's). © **505/753-3211**. Reservations recommended. Main courses $11–$20. AE, DISC, MC, V. Daily 11am–9pm.

OJO CALIENTE

Many locals from the area like to rejuvenate at **Ojo Caliente Mineral Springs,** Ojo Caliente, NM 87549 (© **800/222-9162** or 505/583-2233); it's on US 285, 50 miles (a 1-hr. drive) northwest of Santa Fe and 50 miles southwest of Taos. This National Historic Site was considered sacred by prehistoric tribes. When Spanish explorer Cabeza de Vaca discovered and named the springs in the 16th century, he called them "the greatest treasure that I found these strange people to possess." No other hot spring in the world has Ojo Caliente's combination of iron, soda, lithium, sodium, and arsenic. If the weather is warm enough, the outdoor mud bath is a treat. The dressing rooms are in fairly good shape; the whole place, though, has an earthy feel. If you're a fastidious type, you won't be comfortable here. The resort offers herbal wraps and massages, lodging, and meals. It's open daily 8am to 8pm (to 9pm Fri–Sat). And if you get hungry on your way there or back, stop at **El Rito** (1212 Main St., El Rito, NM 87530; © **505/581-9509**) for a tasty taco or burrito.

7

Taos

New Mexico's favorite arts town sits in a masterpiece setting. It's wedged between the towering peaks of the Rocky Mountains and the plunging chasm of the Rio Grande Gorge.

Located just 40 miles south of the Colorado border, about 70 miles north of Santa Fe, and 135 miles from Albuquerque, this town of 5,000 residents combines 1960s hippiedom (thanks to communes set up in the hills back then) with the ancient culture of Taos Pueblo (some people still live without electricity and running water, as their ancestors did 1,000 years ago). It can be an odd place, where some completely eschew materialism and live "off the grid" in half-underground houses called earthships. But there are plenty of mainstream attractions as well—Taos boasts some of the best restaurants in the state, a hot and funky arts scene, and incredible outdoors action, including world-class skiing.

Taos's history is rich. Throughout the Taos valley, ruins and artifacts attest to a Native American presence dating back 5,000 years. The Spanish first visited this area in 1540, colonizing it in 1598. In the last 2 decades of the 17th century, they put down three rebellions at the Taos Pueblo. During the 18th and 19th centuries, Taos was an important trade center: New Mexico's annual caravan to Chihuahua, Mexico, couldn't leave until after the annual midsummer **Taos Fair.** French trappers began attending the fair in 1739. Even though the Plains tribes often attacked the pueblos at other times, they attended the market festival under a temporary annual truce. By the early 1800s, Taos had become a meeting place for American mountain men, the most famous of whom, Kit Carson, made his home in Taos from 1826 to 1868.

Taos remained loyal to Mexico during the Mexican War of 1846. The town rebelled against its new U.S. landlord in 1847, even killing newly appointed Governor Charles Bent in his Taos home. Nevertheless, the town was incorporated into the Territory of New Mexico in 1850. During the Civil War, Taos fell into Confederate hands for 6 weeks; afterward, Carson and two other men raised the Union flag over Taos Plaza and guarded it day and night. Since that time, Taos has had the honor of flying the flag 24 hours a day.

Taos's population declined when the railroad bypassed it in favor of Santa Fe. In 1898 two East Coast artists—Ernest Blumenschein and Bert Phillips—discovered the dramatic, varied effects of sunlight on the natural environment of the Taos valley and depicted them on canvas. By 1912, thanks to the growing influence of the **Taos Society of Artists,** the town had gained a worldwide reputation as a cultural center. Today, it is estimated that more than 15% of the population are painters, sculptors, writers, or musicians, or otherwise earn their income from artistic pursuits.

1 Orientation

ARRIVING

BY PLANE   The **Taos Municipal Airport** (© 505/758-4995) is about 8 miles northwest of town on US 64. Most people opt to fly into Albuquerque International Sunport, rent a car, and drive up to Taos from there. The drive takes approximately 2½ hours. If you'd rather be picked up at Albuquerque International Sunport, call **Faust's Transportation, Inc.** (© 505/758-3410), which offers charter bus service for $250 for 1 to 4 passengers, as well as taxi service between Taos and Taos Ski Valley.

BY BUS   The **Taos Bus Center** is 5 miles south of the plaza at 1386 Paseo del Pueblo Sur (© 505/758-1144). **TNM&O** arrives and departs from this depot several times a day. For more information on this and other bus services to and from Albuquerque and Santa Fe, see "Getting There," in chapter 2.

BY CAR   Most visitors arrive in Taos via either NM 68 or US 64. Northbound travelers should exit I-25 at Santa Fe, follow US 285 as far as Española, and then continue on the divided highway when it becomes NM 68. Taos is about 79 miles from the I-25 junction. Southbound travelers from Denver on I-25 should exit about 6 miles south of Raton at US 64 and then follow it about 95 miles to Taos. Another major route is US 64 from the west (214 miles from Farmington).

VISITOR INFORMATION

The **Taos County Chamber of Commerce,** at the junction of NM 68 and NM 585 (P.O. Drawer I), Taos, NM 87571 (© 800/732-TAOS or 505/758-3873; www.taos chamber.com), is open in summer daily 9am to 5pm. It's closed on major holidays. **Carson National Forest** also has an information center in the same building.

CITY LAYOUT

The **plaza** is a short block west of Taos's major intersection—where US 64 (Kit Carson Rd.) from the east joins NM 68, **Paseo del Pueblo Sur.** US 64 proceeds north from the intersection as **Paseo del Pueblo Norte. Camino de la Placita (Placitas Rd.)** circles the west side of downtown, passing within a block of the other side of the plaza. Many of the streets that join these thoroughfares are winding lanes lined by traditional adobe homes, some over 100 years old.

Most of the art galleries are on or near the plaza, which was paved over with bricks several years ago, and along neighboring streets. Others are in the **Ranchos de Taos** area, a few miles south of the plaza.

MAPS   To find your way around town, pick up a free Taos map from the **Chamber of Commerce at Taos Visitor Center,** 1139 Paseo del Pueblo Sur (© 505/758-3873). Good, detailed city maps can be found at area bookstores as well (see "Shopping," later in this chapter).

2 Getting Around

With offices at the Taos airport, **Enterprise** (© 505/369-4226) is reliable and efficient. Other car-rental agencies are available out of Albuquerque. See "Getting Around," in chapter 8, for details.

PARKING   Parking can be difficult during the summer rush, when the stream of tourists' cars moving north and south through town never ceases. If you can't find

Warning for Drivers

En route to many recreation sites, reliable paved roads often give way to poorer forest roads. When you get off the main roads, you don't find gas stations or cafes. **Four-wheel-drive vehicles** are recommended on snow and much of the unpaved terrain of the region. If you're doing some off-road adventuring, it's wise to go with a full gas tank, extra food and water, and warm clothing—just in case. At the higher-than-10,000-foot elevations of northern New Mexico, sudden summer snowstorms are not unheard of.

parking on the street or in the plaza, check out some of the nearby roads (Kit Carson Rd., for instance); there are plenty of metered and unmetered lots in Taos.

ROAD CONDITIONS   Information on highway conditions throughout the state can be obtained from the **State Highway Department** (✆ 800/432-4269).

BY BUS & TAXI

If you're in Taos without a car, you're in luck because there's local bus service, provided by **Chile Line Town of Taos Transit** (✆ 505/751-4459). It operates on the half-hour Monday to Saturday 7am to 7pm in summer, 7am to 6pm in winter, and on the hour Sunday 8am to 5pm. Two simultaneous routes run southbound from Taos Pueblo and northbound from the Ranchos de Taos Post Office. Each route makes stops at the casino and various hotels in town, as well as at Taos RV Park. Bus fares are 50¢ one-way, $1 round-trip, $5 for a 7-day pass, and $20 for a 31-day pass.

In addition, **Faust's Transportation** (✆ 505/758-3410) has a taxi service linking town hotels and Taos Ski Valley. Faust's Transportation also offers shuttle service and on-call taxi service daily from 7am to 8:30pm, with fares of about $10 anywhere within the city limits for up to two people ($2 per additional person).

BY BICYCLE

Bicycle rentals are available from **Gearing Up Bicycle Shop,** 129 Paseo del Pueblo Sur (✆ 505/751-0365); daily rentals run $35 for a full day and $25 for a half-day for a mountain bike with front suspension. From April to October, **Native Sons Adventures,** 1033-A Paseo del Pueblo Sur (✆ 800/753-7559 or 505/758-9342), rents no-suspension bikes for $15 for a half-day and $20 for a full day, front-suspension bikes for $25 per half-day and $35 per full day, and full-suspension bikes for $35 per half-day and $45 per full day. It also rents car racks for $5. Each shop supplies helmets and water bottles with rentals.

FAST FACTS

Members of the **Taos Medical Group,** on Weimer Road (✆ 505/758-2224), are highly respected. Also recommended are **Family Practice Associates of Taos,** 630 Paseo del Pueblo Sur, Suite 150 (✆ 505/758-3005). **Holy Cross Hospital,** 1397 Weimer Rd., off Paseo del Canyon (✆ 505/758-8883), has 24-hour emergency service. Serious cases are transferred to Santa Fe or Albuquerque.

Gross receipts tax for the city of Taos is 7%, and for Taos County it's 6.31%. There's an additional local bed tax of 4.5% in the city of Taos and 5% on hotel rooms in Taos County.

See also "Fast Facts: The American Southwest," in chapter 2.

3 Where to Stay

A tiny town with a big tourist market, Taos has thousands of rooms in hotels, motels, condominiums, and bed-and-breakfasts. Many new properties have recently opened, turning this into a buyer's market. In the slower seasons, January through early February and April through early May, when competition for travelers is steep, you may even want to try bargaining your room rate down. Book well ahead for ski holiday periods (especially Christmas) and for the annual arts festivals (late May to mid-June and late Sept to early Oct). Most of the hotels and motels are on Paseo del Pueblo Sur and Norte, with a few scattered just east of the town center, along Kit Carson Road. The condos and bed-and-breakfasts are generally scattered throughout Taos's back streets.

During peak seasons, visitors without reservations may have difficulty finding vacant rooms. **Taos Chamber of Commerce,** 1139 Paseo del Pueblo Sur (© **505/758-3873**), might be able to help. If you're looking to hook up to the Internet in this town, head for the plaza, which offers Wi-Fi access anywhere you sit.

Fifteen hundred or so of Taos County's beds are in condominiums and lodges at or near Taos Ski Valley. The **Taos Valley Resort Association,** P.O. Box 85, Taos Ski Valley, NM 87525 (© **800/776-1111** or 505/776-2233; fax 505/776-8842; www.visit newmexico.com), can book these, as well as rooms in Taos and all the rest of northern New Mexico, and it can book private home rentals.

Reservations of Taos, 1033-A Paseo del Pueblo Sur, Taos, NM 87571 (© **505/751-1292**), will help you find accommodations from bed-and-breakfasts to home rentals, hotels, RV parks, and cabins throughout Taos and the rest of northern New Mexico. It'll also help you arrange package prices for outdoor activities such as whitewater rafting, horseback riding, hot-air ballooning, snowmobiling, fishing, and skiing.

TAOS & VICINITY
EXPENSIVE
Hotels/Motels

El Monte Sagrado ★★★ *Moments*   New to Taos in 2003, this resort near the center of town offers a feast for the senses. Water running over falls, clear air, and delicious food and drink lull guests into a sweet samadhi, or state of relaxation, while the eyes luxuriate in the beauty of rooms impeccably decorated. These range in theme from the Caribbean Casita, a medium-size room with a medium-size bathroom, which evokes the feel of an African jungle; to the Argentina Global Suite, a huge two-bedroom unit decorated in cowboy-contemporary style with wood floors, leather furniture, iron and copper accents, and its own patio and outdoor hot tub; to the Kamasutra Suite, with suggestive carvings throughout, a room resort owner Tom Worrell describes as "the first honeymoon suite to come with instructions." All rooms are quiet and lovely, with patios or balconies and views. The rooms rim a grassy, cottonwood-shaded "Sacred Circle," which also has trout and koi ponds. The intimate spa, with a waiting area that resembles a greenhouse filled with light and large plants, offers a full range of excellent treatments. The **Anaconda Bar** (p. 229) and **De La Tierra** restaurant (p. 206) combine a contemporary feel with elegant Asian touches.

317 Kit Carson Rd., Taos, NM 87571. © **800/828-TAOS** or 505/758-3502. www.elmontesagrado.com. 36 units. $245–$299 historic 1-bedroom Casita; $349–$399 Native American suite; $549 Bali and Tibet Premier Suite; $699 2-bedroom Global Suite. AE, DC, DISC, MC, V. Valet parking $12. **Amenities:** Restaurant; bar; indoor pool; well-equipped health club and spa; Jacuzzi; concierge; babysitting; laundry service. *In room:* A/C, TV, hair dryer, safe, Wi-Fi, Ethernet cable, CD player.

Central Taos Accommodations & Dining

ACCOMMODATIONS ■

Adobe Sun God Lodge **15**
Best Western Kachina Lodge
  & Meeting Center **7**
Carson National Forest **3**
Casa de las Chimeneas **14**
Comfort Suites **16**
El Monte Sagrado **12**
Hacienda del Sol **2**
The Historic Taos Inn **10**
Hotel La Fonda de Taos **11**
Little Tree Bed & Breakfast **3**
Sagebrush Inn **16**

DINING ◆

The Apple Tree **9**
De La Tierra **12**
Doc Martin's **8**
Gutiz **4**
Gypsy 360° **3**
Joseph's Table **11**
Lambert's of Taos **13**
Michael's Kitchen **6**
Old Blinking Light **3**
Orlando's New Mexican Café **1**
Stakeout Grill & Bar **17**
Taos Cow **3**
Taos Pizza Out Back **5**
Trading Post Café **17**

The Historic Taos Inn ⓡ   It's rare to see a hotel that has withstood the years with grace, but the Historic Taos Inn has done just that. Here, you'll be surrounded by 20th-century luxury without ever forgetting that you're within the thick walls of a number of 19th-century Southwestern homes. Dr. Thomas Paul Martin, the town's first physician, purchased the complex in 1895. In 1936, a year after the doctor's death, his widow, Helen, enclosed the plaza—now the inn's darling two-story lobby—and turned it into a hotel. In 1981–82, the inn was restored; it's now listed on both the State and National Registers of Historic Places.

The lobby doubles as the **Adobe Bar,** a popular local gathering place, with adobe *bancos* (benches) and a sunken fireplace, all surrounding a wishing well that was once the old town well. A number of rooms open onto a balcony that overlooks this area. If you like community and don't mind the sound of jazz and flamenco drifting up toward your room, these rooms are for you. However, if you appreciate solitude and silence, request one of the courtyard rooms downstairs. All the rooms are unique and comfortable, decorated with Spanish colonial art, Taos-style furniture, and interesting touches such as hand-woven Oaxacan bedspreads and little niches decorated with Mexican pottery; many rooms have fireplaces.

In recent years we've had complaints from guests about the temperamental nature of these old buildings: You may encounter problems such as windows not staying open and some not having screens.

Doc Martin's, which serves nouveau Southwestern cuisine with a hint of Asia, is a good bet for dinner (p. 206).

125 Paseo del Pueblo Norte, Taos, NM 87571. ⓒ 800/TAOS-INN or 505/758-2233. Fax 505/758-5776. www.taosinn.com. 36 units. $70–$250, depending on the type of room and season. AE, DISC, MC, V. **Amenities:** Restaurant; bar; seasonal outdoor pool; Jacuzzi; room service; coffee or refreshments in lobby; Wi-Fi in lobby. *In room:* A/C, TV, VCR on request, hair dryer, iron.

Hotel La Fonda de Taos ⓡ   Finally, Taos has a recommendable hotel on the plaza. A $3-million renovation to this historic property built in 1880 has turned it into a comfortable, fun spot with a stellar location. The charismatic Taos figure Saki Kavaras put this hotel on the society map in the 1930s, when, most notably, British author D. H. Lawrence frequented it. His legacy is preserved in a unique D. H. Lawrence Forbidden Art Museum, where some of his risqué paintings hang—a must-see even if you don't stay here (free for guests; $3 for nonguests). Rooms are set off broad hallways, each styled in earth tones, Southwestern furnishings, and tile bathrooms. Standard units are small, each with a queen-size bed. Your better bet is to reserve a plaza or deluxe plaza room, or a suite. These are larger and have king beds. Our favorite rooms are nos. 201 and 301, which overlook the plaza. Groups can rent the whole top floor (or the whole hotel), which includes a full kitchen suite. **Joseph's Table** (p. 206), one of Taos's finest restaurants, is off the lobby.

108 South Plaza, Taos, NM 87571. ⓒ 800/833-2211 or 505/758-2211. Fax 505/758-8508. www.lafondataos.com. 24 units. $99–$149 standard double; $139–$209 plaza and deluxe plaza double; $189–$239 suite. AE, DC, DISC, MC, V. Free parking. **Amenities:** Restaurant; coffee shop; bar. *In room:* A/C, TV, hair dryer, iron, high-speed Internet.

Moderate
Best Western Kachina Lodge & Meeting Center ⓡ *Value* *Kids*   Built in the early 1960s, this lodge on the north end of town, within walking distance of the plaza, has a lot of charm despite the fact that it's a motor hotel. Remodeling is ongoing in the solidly built Southwestern-style rooms—some have couches and most have Taos-style *trasteros* (armoires) that hold the TVs. Beds are comfortable and bathrooms are small

but functional and very clean. Rooms sit around a grassy courtyard studded with huge blue spruce trees, allowing kids room to run. In the center is a stage where a family from Taos Pueblo builds a bonfire and dances nightly in the summer and explains the significance of the dances—a real treat for anyone baffled by the Pueblo rituals. A full, hot breakfast is served in a very retro kiva-shaped cafe.

413 Paseo del Pueblo Norte (P.O. Box NM), Taos, NM 87571. © 800/522-4462 or 505/758-2275. Fax 505/758-9207. www.kachinalodge.com. 118 units. $59–$139 double; includes full breakfast. Additional person $10. Children under 12 stay free in parent's room. AE, DC, DISC, MC, V. **Amenities:** 2 restaurants; lounge; outdoor pool; courtesy shuttle; salon; coin-op laundry. *In room:* A/C, TV, coffeemaker, hair dryer, iron, high-speed Internet.

Comfort Suites   New, clean, and predictable are what you'll get in this chain hotel about 5 minutes (by car) from the plaza. Each room has a small living/dining area, with a sleeper sofa, microwave, minifridge, and coffeemaker, and a bedroom with handcrafted wood furniture and a comfortable king- or queen-size bed. Bathrooms are medium-size. If you have kids, you might want a ground-floor poolside room. Though the pool isn't landscaped, it's warm, roomy, and accompanied by a hot tub. This hotel shares ownership with the Sagebrush Inn (below), so guests have easy access to its nightlife, hot breakfast (at an extra charge), and spacious grounds.

1500 Paseo del Pueblo Sur (P.O. Box 1268), Taos, NM 87571. © 888/751-1555 or 505/751-1555. Fax 505/751-1991. www.comfortsuites.com. 60 units. $69–$149 double. Rates include continental breakfast. AE, DC, DISC, MC, V. **Amenities:** Outdoor pool; Jacuzzi; in-room massage; same-day dry cleaning; Wi-Fi in lobby. *In room:* A/C, TV, fridge, coffeemaker, hair dryer, microwave, high speed Internet.

Sagebrush Inn   Three miles south of Taos, surrounded by acres of sage, this inn is housed in an adobe building that has been added on to decade after decade, creating an interesting mix of accommodations. The original structure was built in 1929, and the roof was held in place with hand-hewn vigas. Its three floors and 12 rooms, hand-sculpted from adobe, remain. The rooms are small and cozy and have the feel of old Taos—in fact, Georgia O'Keeffe lived and worked here for 10 months in the late 1930s. But for those more accustomed to refined style, it might feel dated.

The treasure of this place is the large grass courtyard dotted with elm trees, where visitors sit and read in the warm months. Be aware that some of the rooms added in the '50s through '70s have a tackiness not overcome by the vigas and tile work. The rooms are dark and need updating. More recent additions (to the west), away from the hotel proper, are spacious and full of amenities, but they, too, with their heavy Spanish colonial furnishings are too dark.

1508 Paseo del Pueblo Sur (P.O. Box 557), Taos, NM 87571. © 800/428-3626 or 505/758-2254. Fax 505/758-5077. www.sagebrushinn.com. 97 units. $70–$95 double; $95–$165 deluxe or small suite; $130–$185 executive suite. Rates include full breakfast. Children under 17 stay free in parent's room. Additional person $10. AE, DC, DISC, MC, V. Pets welcome, $7 per night fee. **Amenities:** 2 restaurants; bar; outdoor pool; tennis courts; Jacuzzi; courtesy shuttle; business center w/high-speed Internet connection; in-room massage; same-day dry cleaning; executive-level rooms. *In room:* A/C, TV, dataport, coffeemaker, hair dryer, iron.

Inexpensive
Adobe Sun God Lodge   For a comfortable, economical stay with a northern New Mexico ambience, this is a good choice. This hotel, a 5-minute drive from the plaza, has three distinct parts spread across 1½ acres of landscaped grounds. The oldest was solidly built in 1958 and has some court-motel charm, with a low ceiling and large windows. To update the rooms, the owners added tile sinks, Taos-style furniture, and new carpeting. To the south is a section built in 1988. The rooms are small but have little touches that make them feel cozy, such as little *nichos* (niches) and hand-carved

furnishings. In back to the east are the newest buildings, built in 1994. These are two-story structures with portal-style porches and balconies. Some rooms have kitchenettes, which include microwaves, refrigerators, and stoves; others have kiva fireplaces. The two suites on the northeast corner of the property are the quietest and have the best views.

919 Paseo del Pueblo Sur, Taos, NM 87571. © 800/821-2437 or 505/758-3162. Fax 505/758-1716. www.sungod lodge.com. 53 units. $49–$99 double; $69–$139 suite. AE, DISC, MC, V. Pets allowed for $10 per day. **Amenities:** Jacuzzi. *In room:* A/C, TV, coffeemaker, Wi-Fi.

Bed & Breakfasts

Casa de las Chimeneas 𝔊𝔊𝔊   This 1926 adobe home set on spacious grounds has, since its opening as a luxury inn in 1988, been a model of Southwestern elegance. Adding to its appeal is a spa with a small fitness room and sauna, as well as complete massage and facial treatments for an additional charge. We recommend the Rio Grande and Territorial rooms, which are spacious and air-conditioned. Both have heated Saltillo-tile floors, gas kiva fireplaces, and Jacuzzi tubs. If you prefer a more antique-feeling room, try the delightful older section, especially the Library Suite. Each room in the inn is decorated with original works of art and has elegant bedding, a private entrance, robes, and a minifridge stocked with complimentary soft drinks, juices, and mineral water. All rooms have kiva fireplaces, and most look out on flower and herb gardens. Breakfasts are delicious. Specialties include an artichoke-heart and mushroom omelet or ricotta cream-cheese blintz, plus innkeeper Susan Vernon's special fruit frappé. In the evenings she serves a full dinner, which may include corn-crusted tilapia or roasted chicken served with vegetables from a local organic farm. Smoking is not permitted.

405 Cordoba Rd., at Los Pandos Rd. (5303 NDCBU), Taos, NM 87571. © 877/758-4777 or 505/758-4777. Fax 505/758-3976. www.visittaos.com. 8 units. $180–$290 double; $325 suite. Rates include breakfast and evening supper. AE, DC, DISC, MC, V. **Amenities:** Small exercise room; spa; Jacuzzi; sauna; concierge; car-rental desk; courtesy computer; in-room massage; coin-op laundry; laundry service. *In room:* TV/VCR, free stocked minibar, coffeemaker, hair dryer, iron, Wi-Fi, free movies.

Hacienda del Sol 𝔊𝔊   What's unique about this bed-and-breakfast is its unobstructed view of Taos Mountain. Because the 1¼-acre property borders Taos Pueblo, the land is pristine. The inn also has a rich history. It was once owned by arts patron Mabel Dodge Luhan, and it was here that author Frank Waters wrote *The People of the Valley.* You'll find bold splashes of color in the gardens—where, in summer, tulips, pansies, and flax bloom—as well as in the rooms themselves, where woven bedspreads and original art evoke a Mexican ambience. The main house is more than 2 centuries old, so it has the wonderful curves of adobe as well as thick vigas. Some guest rooms are in this section. Others range from 7 to 25 years in age. The newer rooms are finely constructed, and we almost recommend them over the others because they're a little more private and the bathrooms are more refined. All rooms have robes and CD players, and most have fireplaces; three units have private Jacuzzis, four have private steam showers. Some have minifridges. A full and delicious breakfast, with favorites such as banana pancakes or scrambled eggs and turkey sausage, is served in the Spanish-hacienda-style dining area.

109 Mabel Dodge Lane (P.O. Box 177), Taos, NM 87571. © 505/758-0287. Fax 505/758-5895. www.taoshacien dadelsol.com. 11 units. $125–$325 double. Rates include full breakfast and evening sweets. AE, DISC, MC, V. **Amenities:** Jacuzzi; concierge; courtesy computer; in-room massage. *In room:* Minibar, hair dryer, Wi-Fi, CD player.

Little Tree Bed & Breakfast 🌟🌟 *(Finds)*   Little Tree is one of our favorite Taos bed-and-breakfasts, partly because it's in a beautiful, secluded setting, and partly because it's constructed with real adobe that's been left in its raw state, giving the place an authentic hacienda feel. Two miles down a country road, about midway between Taos and the ski area, it's surrounded by sage and piñon. The charming and cozy rooms have radiant heat under the floors, queen-size beds (one with a king-size), nice medium-size bathrooms (one with a Jacuzzi tub), and access to the portal and court-yard garden, at the center of which is the little tree for which the inn is named. The Piñon (our favorite) and Juniper rooms are equipped with fireplaces and private entrances. The Piñon and Aspen rooms offer sunset views. The Spruce Room, Victo-rian in ambience, is decorated with quilts. In the main building, the living room has a traditional viga-and-*latilla* ceiling and *tierra blanca* adobe (adobe that's naturally white; if you look closely, you can see little pieces of mica and straw). Visiting hum-mingbirds enchant guests who enjoy a scrumptious breakfast on the portal during warmer months. On arrival, guests are treated to refreshments. A courtesy computer with Internet is available for guest use.

County Road B-143 (P.O. Box 509), Taos, NM 87513. ℂ 800/334-8467 or 505/776-8467. www.littletreebandb.com. 4 units. $125–$185 double. Rates include breakfast and afternoon snack. MC, V. *In room:* TV/VCR.

TAOS SKI VALLEY

For information on skiing and the facilities at Taos Ski Valley, see "Skiing Taos," later in this chapter.

EXPENSIVE

Edelweiss Lodge & Spa 🌟🌟   Opened in 2005, this lodge at the base of the moun-tain took the place of a 1960s classic chalet. Now, it's a brand new condo-hotel. The condominiums are upscale, each with a flagstone fireplace and full kitchen with mar-ble countertops and stainless-steel appliances. Many units have nice views of the slopes, and all have luxury, earth-toned furnishings. The service here is less personal than, say, at the Powderhorn Suites and Condominiums (below). Hotel rooms have the same luxury as the condos. Rooms are medium-size with comfortable beds and medium-size bathrooms. Check the website for a glimpse of the rooms and other facil-ities. Underground parking, a full spa, an excellent restaurant, and—get this—valet service for your skis, add to the appeal.

106 Sutton Place, Taos Ski Valley, NM 87525. ℂ 800/I-LUV-SKI or 505/737-6900. Fax 505/737-6995. www.edel-weisslodgeandspa.com. 46 units. Hotel room winter $220–$440 double; summer $125 double; condo winter $275–$1,056 depending on the season; summer $198–$375 (ranges cover 1 bedroom/1 bathroom–3 bedrooms/3 bathrooms). AE, DISC, MC, V. Free parking. **Amenities:** Restaurant; bar; health club and full spa; 2 Jacuzzis; sauna; concierge; massage; ski shop; Wi-Fi in lobby. *In room:* TV, fridge, coffeemaker, hair dryer, high-speed Internet.

Powderhorn Suites and Condominiums 🌟🌟 *(Value)*   A cozy, homelike feel and Euro-Southwestern ambience make this inn one of the best deals in Taos Ski Valley, just a 2-minute walk from the lift. You'll find consistency and quality here, with impeccably clean medium-size rooms, mountain views, vaulted ceilings, spotless bath-rooms, and comfortable beds. The larger suites have stoves, balconies, and fireplaces. Adjoining rooms are perfect for families. You can expect conscientious and expert service as well. There's no elevator, so if stairs are a problem for you, make sure to ask for a room on the ground floor.

5 Ernie Blake Rd. (P.O. Box 69), Taos Ski Valley, NM 87525. ℂ 800/776-2346 or 505/776-2341. Fax 505/776-2341, ext. 103. www.taoswebb.com/powderhorn. 17 units. Ski season $99–$165 double, $130–$200 suite, $195–$400

condo; summer $69–$129 2- to 6-person occupancy. MC, V. Valet parking. **Amenities:** 2 Jacuzzis; massage. *In room:* TV, dataport, kitchenette.

Sierra del Sol Condominiums ⑱   The units of the Sierra del Sol, built in the 1960s, with additions through the years, have been well maintained. Though the condos are privately owned and therefore decorated at the whim of their owners, management does inspect them every year and make suggestions. They're smartly built and come in a few sizes: studio, one-bedroom, and two-bedroom. The one- and two-bedroom units have big living rooms with fireplaces and porches that look out on the ski runs. The bedrooms are spacious, and some have sleeping lofts. Each has a full kitchen, with a dishwasher, stove, oven, and refrigerator. Most units also have microwaves and humidifiers. Two-bedroom units sleep up to six. Grills and picnic tables on the grounds sit near a mountain river.

13 Thunderbird Rd. (P.O. Box 84), Taos Ski Valley, NM 87525. ⓒ **800/523-3954** or 505/776-2981. Fax 505/776-2347. www.sierrataos.com. 32 units. Prices range from $70 for studio in summer to $395 for 2-bedroom condo in high season. AE, DISC, MC, V. Free parking. **Amenities:** 2 Jacuzzis; 2 saunas; massage; babysitting; coin-op laundry. High-speed and Wi-Fi access. *In room:* TV/VCR, kitchen, hair dryer upon request, iron upon request, safe.

Snakedance Condominiums and Spa ⑱⑱   A recent $3.5-million renovation has transformed the rooms of this former hotel into comfortable condominiums. Skiers appreciate the inn's location, just steps from the lift, as well as amenities such as ski storage and boot dryers. The original structure that stood on this site (part of which has now been restored) was known as the Hondo Lodge. Before there was a Taos Ski Valley, Hondo Lodge served as a refuge for fishermen, hunters, and artists. Constructed from enormous pine timbers that had been cut for a copper-mining operation in the 1890s, it was literally nothing more than a place for the men to bed down for the night. The Snakedance Condominiums today are privately owned units, so each may differ some, though they seem consistent in quality. All have balconies with French doors and kitchens with granite counters and a range, fridge, dishwasher, and microwave. Many feature wood-burning fireplaces. The Hondo Restaurant and Bar, remodeled in 2006, offers dining and entertainment daily during the ski season (schedules vary off season) and also sponsors wine tastings and wine dinners. Grilled items, salads, and snacks are available on an outdoor deck. The hotel also offers shuttle service to and from nearby shops and restaurants. Smoking is prohibited on the property.

110 Sutton Place (P.O. Box 89), Taos Ski Valley, NM 87525. ⓒ **800/322-9815** or 505/776-2277. Fax 505/776-1410. www.snakedancecondos.com. 33 units. 1 bedroom condo $225–$475 double in winter, in summer $95; 2-bedroom condo $285–$600 for 4 people in winter, $120 in summer; 2-bedroom loft condo $345–$725 for 6 people in winter, $150 in summer. Extra person $30 in winter, $10 in summer. AE, DC, DISC, MC, V. Free parking at Taos Ski Valley parking lot. Closed mid-Apr to Memorial Day and mid-Oct to mid-Nov. **Amenities:** Restaurant; bar; exercise room; spa; Jacuzzi; sauna; massage; convenience store (w/food, sundries, video rental, and alcoholic beverages). *In room:* Satellite TV, kitchen, coffeemaker, hair dryer, Wi-Fi.

MODERATE

Alpine Village Suites ⑱   Alpine Village is a small village within Taos Ski Valley, a few steps from the lift. Owned by John and Barbara Cottam, the complex also houses a ski shop and bar/restaurant. The Cottams began with seven rooms, still nice rentals, above their ski shop. Each has a sleeping loft, for the agile who care to climb a ladder, as well as sunny windows. The newer section has nicely decorated rooms, with attractive touches such as Mexican furniture and inventive tile work done by locals. Like most other accommodations at Taos Ski Valley, the rooms are not especially soundproof. Fortunately, most skiers go to bed early. All rooms have VCRs and small kitchenettes equipped with stoves, microwaves, and minifridges. In the newer building, rooms have fireplaces and private balconies. Request a south-facing room for a view of the slopes. The Jacuzzi has a fireplace and a view of the slopes.

100 Thunderbird Rd. (P.O. Box 98), Taos Ski Valley, NM 87525. ℂ 800/576-2666 or 505/776-8540. Fax 505/776-8542. www.alpine-suites.com. 29 units. Ski season $70–$145 suite for 2, $265–$335 suite for up to 6; summer $80–$120 suite for 2 (includes continental breakfast). AE, DISC, MC, V. Covered valet parking $10 per night. **Amenities:** Jacuzzi; sauna; business center; massage. *In room:* TV/VCR, kitchenette; high-speed Internet & Wi-Fi access in all but 2 rooms.

Taos Mountain Lodge *(Value* These loft suites (which can each accommodate up to six) provide airy, comfortable accommodations for a good price. Built in 1990 about a mile west of Taos Ski Valley on the road from Taos, the place has undergone some renovation over the years. Don't expect a lot of privacy in these condominiums, but they're good for a romping ski vacation. The beds are comfortable and the small bathrooms are functional. Each unit has a small bedroom downstairs and a loft bedroom upstairs, as well as a foldout or futon couch in the living room. Regular rooms have kitchenettes with minifridges and stoves, and deluxe rooms have full kitchens, with full refrigerators, stoves, and ovens.

Taos Ski Valley Rd. (P.O. Box 202), Taos Ski Valley, NM 87525. ℂ 866/320-8267 or 505/776-2229. Fax 505/776-3982. www.taosmountainlodge.com. 10 units. Ski season $119–$280 suite; May–Oct $80–$100 suite. AE, DISC, MC, V. *In room:* Kitchen or kitchenette.

RV PARKS & CAMPGROUNDS

Carson National Forest   There are nine national-forest camping areas within 20 miles of Taos; these developed areas are open from Memorial Day to Labor Day. They range from woodsy, streamside sites on the road to Taos Ski Valley to open lowlands with lots of sage. Call the Forest Service to discuss the best location for your needs.

208 Cruz Alta Rd., Taos, NM 87571. ℂ 505/758-6200. www.fs.fed.us/r3/carson. $7–$15 per night. No credit cards.

Taos RV Park   This RV park, on the edge of town (and on a local bus line), offers a convenient location but a city atmosphere. It has very clean and nice bathrooms and showers. Two tepees rent for $25 each, but beware: They're right on the main drag and may be noisy. Senior discounts are available. Wi-Fi access is available throughout most of the park, and there's a high-speed Internet connection in the lobby.

1802 NM 68, Taos, NM 87557. ℂ 800/323-6009 or 505/758-1667. Fax 505/758-1989. www.taosbudgethost.com. 33 spaces. $17 w/no RV hookup; $25 w/RV hookup. DISC, MC, V.

Taos Valley RV Park and Campground   Just 2½ miles south of the plaza, this campground is surrounded by sage and offers views of the surrounding mountains. Each site has a picnic table and grill. The place has a small store, a laundry room, a playground, and tent shelters, as well as a dump station and very clean restrooms. Pets are welcome. Wi-Fi access is available throughout the park.

120 Este Rd., off NM 68 (7204 NDCBU), Taos, NM 87571. ℂ 800/999-7571 or 505/758-4469. Fax 505/758-4469. www.camptaos.com/rv. 92 spaces. $22 w/out RV hookup, $29–$35 w/RV hookup. MC, V.

4 Where to Dine

Taos is not a late-night place; most restaurants finish serving at about 9pm. For the locations of these restaurants, see the map "Central Taos Accommodations & Dining," on p. 199.

EXPENSIVE

De La Tierra 🦌🦌🦌 REGIONAL AMERICAN   Come here for artfully prepared American fare with an emphasis on wild game. Located in the ecoresort El Monte Sagrado (p. 198), this restaurant offers an old-world Orient ambience, with a high ceiling, comfortable black silk chairs, and notable contemporary art on the walls. Service is excellent, even down to the master sommelier overseeing the wine selections. The chef utilizes seasonal and local ingredients, including organic ones when he can. For starters, we recommend the Dungeness crab cake, or, for a more exotic treat, try the yak satay, the meat from the resort owner's high-mountain cattlelike animals. For a main course, we've enjoyed the venison medallions, served over garlic mashed potatoes and with roasted spring mushrooms. The Gardens, a more casual spot with lots of exotic plants and a lovely patio, serves tasty food during the day (try the yak-cheese frittata). The Anaconda Bar serves tapas.

In the El Monte Sagrado Hotel, 317 Kit Carson Rd. ℂ **800/828-TAOS** or 505/758-3502. Reservations recommended. The Gardens breakfast $7–$12; lunch $8–$16; De La Tierra dinner $27–$39. AE, DC, DISC, MC, V. The Gardens daily 7–10am and 11am–2:30pm; De La Tierra daily 5:30–10pm.

Doc Martin's 🦌 NEW AMERICAN   Doc Martin's serves innovative food in a historic setting. The restaurant comprises Dr. Thomas Paul Martin's former home, office, and delivery room. In 1912, painters Bert Philips (Doc's brother-in-law) and Ernest Blumenschein hatched the concept of the Taos Society of Artists in the dining room. Art still predominates here, in both the paintings that adorn the walls and the cuisine offered. The food is often good, but it can be inconsistent.

The wine list has received numerous "Awards of Excellence" from *Wine Spectator* magazine. In the rich atmosphere of a thick-walled adobe home with a kiva fireplace, diners feast on Southwestern breakfast fare such as huevos rancheros (fried eggs on a blue-corn tortilla smothered with chile and Jack cheese). Lunch might include the house specialty, the Doc Chile relleno or chipotle shrimp on corn cake. For dinner, a good bet is the piñon-encrusted salmon or the Southwest lacquered duck served with *posole* (hominy) and mango relish. If you still have room, there's always a nice selection of desserts—try the chocolate mousse cake or the *capirotada* (New Mexican bread pudding). The Adobe bar has live jazz with no cover charge. Brunch is served on Sundays from 7:30am to 2:30pm.

In the Historic Taos Inn, 125 Paseo del Pueblo Norte. ℂ **505/758-1977.** www.taosinn.com. Reservations recommended. Breakfast $5–$9; lunch $5.50–$11; dinner $14–$28; fixed-price menu $33. AE, DISC, MC, V. Daily 7:30–11am, 11:30am–2:30pm, and 5:30–9pm.

Joseph's Table 🦌🦌🦌 *Finds* MEDITERRANEAN/NEW AMERICAN   This notable eatery, in the Hotel La Fonda de Taos on the plaza, serves some of the most imaginative and precisely prepared food in northern New Mexico. The ambience feels like an Old West saloon blended with a sophisticated artist's home. Hand-painted pastel flowers decorate the walls and pussy-willow-and-iron chandeliers hang between hand-hewn vigas (beams) on the ceiling. There are hardwood floors and some Asian-style tables with pillow seating along the back. Chef/owner Joseph Wrede (once selected as one of the 10 "Best New Chefs" in America by *Food and Wine Magazine*) creates for lunch such delicacies as a juicy green chile buffalo burger served with homemade sweet potato chips, or Mediterranean mussels in a pesto broth. Dinner is equally inventive: It might start with tempura squash blossoms stuffed with goat cheese and green chiles, with fire-roasted tomato salsa, and move on to pepper-crusted elk tenderloin with creamed spinach, morel mushrooms, and truffle demi-glaze or the spice-rubbed grilled wild salmon with potato hash and sweet peas. There's typically a vegetarian option as well. An eclectic selection of beers and wines by the bottle and glass is available.

In the Hotel La Fonda de Taos, 108-A South Taos Plaza. © 505/751-4512. www.josephstable.com. Reservations recommended. Main courses $8–$18 lunch, $18–$35 dinner. AE, DISC, MC, V. May–Aug Mon–Sat 11:30am–2:30pm and daily 5:30–10pm; Sun brunch 10:30am–2:30pm. Hours are abbreviated in winter; call first.

Lambert's of Taos ☆☆ CONTEMPORARY AMERICAN Zeke Lambert, once the head chef at Doc Martin's (p. 206), opened this fine dining establishment in 1989 in the historic Randall Home near Los Pandos Road. It's a sparsely decorated hacienda with wood floors and lacey curtains—a nice spot for a romantic evening. The service ranges from good to begrudging. The food is well prepared and imaginative, though not quite of the caliber of Joseph's Table (above). You might start with a bowl of roasted corn chowder or duck dumplings. The spinach salad with sautéed mushrooms and bacon in a walnut-raspberry dressing is excellent. For an entree, the pepper-crusted lamb—very peppery—served with garlic pasta is a signature dish, but you might opt for one of the fresh fish specials, such as seared ahi tuna, or a game special such as buffalo tenderloin. For dessert, try the warm apple and almond crisp with white-chocolate ice cream, or Zeke's chocolate mousse with raspberry sauce. A full bar, with an interesting wine and beer list and espresso coffee, is available. Recently, the restaurant opened a cozy lounge with its own bar menu.

309 Paseo del Pueblo Sur. © 505/758-1009. Reservations recommended. Main courses $15–$32. AE, DC, DISC, MC, V. Daily 5pm–closing, usually 9pm or so.

Stakeout Grill & Bar ☆☆ CONTINENTAL/SEAFOOD/STEAKS This is one of northern New Mexico's most adventurous dining experiences. You drive about a mile up a dirt road toward the base of the Sangre de Cristo Mountains to reach the restaurant, and dine looking down on the Taos gorge while the sun sets over the Jemez Range. The warm, rustic decor of this sprawling hacienda with a broad patio (a great place to sit in summer) includes creaking hardwood floors—and a crackling fireplace in the winter. The fare, which focuses on steak and seafood, is fresh and thoughtfully prepared. Start with baked brie with sliced almonds and apples, or green chile crab cakes with citrus aioli. Move on to a filet mignon served with béarnaise sauce, or sample one of the chef's excellent pasta specials. Recently, we had shrimp over linguini with goat cheese that was a bowl of pure joy. This is also the place to come if you have a craving for lobster. Try to time your reservation so you can see the sunset. A full bar, an extensive wine list, and cigars are available.

101 Stakeout Dr. (9 miles south of Taos, just off Hwy. 68). © 505/758-2042. Reservations recommended. Main courses $20–$50. AE, DC, DISC, MC, V. Daily 5–9:30pm.

MODERATE

The Apple Tree ☆☆ AMERICAN/SOUTHWESTERN Eclectic music pervades the four adobe rooms of this hacienda, a block north of the plaza. Original paintings by Taos masters watch over the candlelit service indoors. Outside, diners sit at wooden tables beneath a sprawling apple tree. If you like comfort, both in your food and ambience, this is your place. For starters, the Apple Tree salad (greens sprinkled with dried cranberries and walnuts, tossed with honey–blue cheese dressing) is very good, as is the *calabasa* (squash) quesadilla. A local's favorite (and ours, too) is mango chicken enchiladas (chicken simmered with onions and spices, layered between blue-corn tortillas with mango chutney, sour cream, and salsa fresca, and smothered with green chile). Less adventuresome diners might prefer fresh rainbow trout with a citrus-piñon butter sauce, or roasted vegetable lasagna. The brunch offerings are worth sampling, even more so when eaten out on the lovely patio under the restaurant's namesake. Such standards as French toast and eggs Benedict are good, but the specials usually outshine them, especially the fresh-fruit crepes, such as blueberry or peach, served with whipped cream. The Apple Tree has an award-winning wine list, and the desserts are prepared fresh daily.

123 Bent St. © 505/758-1900. Reservations recommended. Main courses $5–$11 brunch, $6–$12 lunch, $12–$30 dinner. AE, DC, DISC, MC, V. Mon–Sat 11:30am–3pm; daily 5:30–9pm; brunch Sun 10:30am–3pm.

Old Blinking Light ⊛ AMERICAN   This restaurant on the Ski Valley Road provides tasty American food in a casual atmosphere. It's named for the blinking yellow light that was once the marker Taoseños used to give directions ("turn left at the blinking light," and so forth), now replaced by a stoplight. Decorated with Spanish colonial furniture and an excellent art collection, this restaurant is a good place to stop after skiing or for a romping night of music. The service is friendly and efficient. To accompany the free chips and homemade salsa, order a margarita—preferably their standard, made with Sauza Gold Tequila—and sip it next to the patio bonfire, open evenings year-round. The menu is broad, ranging from salads and burgers to steaks, seafood, and Mexican food. We say head straight for the fajitas, especially the jumbo shrimp wrapped in bacon and stuffed with poblano peppers and jack cheese. Leave room for the Old Blinking Light mud pie, made with local Taos Cow Ice Cream. Live music plays on Monday and Friday nights.

US 150, mile marker 1. © 505/776-8787. Reservations recommended weekends and Mon nights. Main courses $9–$26. AE, MC, V. Wine shop daily noon–10pm; restaurant daily 5–10pm.

Taos Pizza Out Back ⊛ ʀids GOURMET PIZZA/PASTA   Our kayaking buddies always go here after a day on the river. That will give you an idea of the level of informality (high), as well as the quality of the food and beer (great), and the size of the portions (large). It's a raucous old hippie-decorated adobe restaurant, with a friendly and eager waitstaff. What to order? *Pizza.* Sure, the spicy Greek pasta is good, as is the Veggie Zone (a calzone filled with stir-fried veggies and two cheeses). But the pizzas are incredible. All come with a delicious thin crust (no sogginess here) that's folded over on the edges and sprinkled with sesame seeds. The sauce is unimaginably tasty, and the variations are broad. There's Thai chicken pizza (pineapple, peanuts, and a spicy sauce); the Killer, with sun-dried tomatoes, Gorgonzola, green chile, and black olives; and our favorite, pizza Florentine (spinach, basil, sun-dried tomatoes, chicken breast, mushrooms, capers, and garlic sautéed in white wine). Check out the small selection of wines and large selection of microbrews.

712 Paseo del Pueblo Norte (just north of Allsup's). © 505/758-3112. Reservations recommended weekends and holidays. Pizzas $12–$26; pastas and calzones $7–$12. MC, V. Summer daily 11am–10pm; winter Sun–Thurs 11am–9pm, Fri–Sat 11am–10pm.

Trading Post Café ⊛⊛ ʀinds INTERNATIONAL/NORTHERN ITALIAN   One of our tastiest writing assignments was when we did a profile of this restaurant for the *New York Times.* Chef/owner René Mettler spent 3 hours serving course after course of dishes prepared especially for us. If you think this gastronomical orgy might color our opinion, just ask locals in town where they most like to eat. Even notables such as Dennis Hopper and Gene Hackman will likely name the Trading Post. What draws the crowds here is a gallery atmosphere, where rough plastered walls washed with an orange hue are set off by sculptures, paintings, and photographs. The meals are also artistically served. "You eat with your eyes," says Mettler. If you show up without reservations, be prepared to wait for a table, and don't expect quiet romance here: The place bustles. The outstanding Caesar salad has an interesting twist—garlic chips. If you like pasta, you'll find a nice variety on the menu. The fettuccine alla carbonara is tasty, as is the seafood pasta. Heartier appetites might like the New Zealand lamb chops with tomato-mint sauce. There's also a fresh fish of the day and usually some nice stews and soups at very reasonable prices. A good list of beers and wines rounds out the experience. For dessert, try the tarts.

4179 Paseo del Pueblo Sur, Ranchos de Taos. © 505/758-5089. Reservations recommended. Main courses $6–$28. AE, DC, DISC, MC, V. Tues–Sat 11:30am–9:30pm; Sun 5–9pm.

INEXPENSIVE

Gutiz *Finds* FRENCH/LATIN FUSION   Surrounded by lavender walls adorned with bright contemporary art, this new restaurant, the creation of chef Eduardo Gutiz, serves some of Taos's most unique and flavorful cuisine. Born in Spain, raised in France, he traveled in Peru and Bolivia. From these locales, he's combined flavors using organic greens and fresh meats and fish. Service is friendly and efficient. Breakfast brings delicacies such as a Tortilla Alicantina—a baked omelet with potatoes and onions, served with a green tampenade. The French toast is thick, made with home-baked bread, the best we've had since the old Super Chief luxury train days. Lunch might begin with fried calamari or chicken tenders served with an aji *amarillo* sauce. For an entree, the pork tenderloin with onion confit and garbanzo beans is delicious, as are the many sandwiches served on homemade bread. Alongside the great food, sip from a variety of coffees and chai tea. Eduardo hopes to open on weekend evenings; call to find out if he's done it yet.

812-B Paseo del Pueblo Norte. © 505/758-1226. Main courses $6.50–$15. Tues–Sun 7am–4pm.

Michael's Kitchen *Kids* AMERICAN/NEW MEXICAN   A couple of blocks north of the plaza, this eatery provides big portions of rib-sticking food in a relaxed atmosphere. Between its hardwood floor and viga ceiling are various knickknacks: an antique wood stove here, a Tiffany lamp there. Seating is at booths and tables. Breakfast is the meal to eat here, with a large selection of pancakes and egg preparations (with names like the "Moofy" and "Omelette Extraordinaire") served all day. Lunch features sandwiches, including a Philly cheesesteak, a tuna melt, and a veggie option. Some people like the generically (and facetiously) titled Health Food meal, a double order of fries with red or green chile and cheese. Dinners range from stuffed *sopaipillas* to chopped sirloin steak. If you're in a hurry, try one of the excellent doughnuts served from Michael's bakery.

304 C Paseo del Pueblo Norte. © 505/758-4178. Reservations not accepted. Main courses $3–$8 breakfast; $4–$9.50 lunch; $6–$14 dinner. AE, DISC, MC, V. Daily 7am–8:30pm (except major holidays).

Orlando's New Mexican Café *Kids* NEW MEXICAN   Festivity reigns in this spicy little cafe on the north end of town. Serving some of northern New Mexico's best chile, this place has colorful tables set around a bustling open kitchen and airy patio dining during warmer months. Service is friendly but minimal. Try the Los Colores, their most popular dish, with three enchiladas (chicken, beef, and cheese) smothered in chile and served with beans and *posole*. The taco salad is another favorite. Portions are big here, and you can order a Mexican or microbrew beer, or a New Mexican or California wine.

114 Don Juan Valdez Lane. (1¾ miles north of the plaza, off Paseo del Pueblo Norte). © **505/751-1450.** Reservations not accepted. Main courses under $10. No credit cards. Daily 10:30am–3pm and 5–9pm.

NORTH OF TOWN

Gypsy 360° ⊛ (Finds) AMERICAN/ASIAN   This funky cafe on a side street is as cute as the village of Arroyo Seco, where it's located. And the food is tasty and inventive. During the winter, diners sit in either a sunny atrium or a more enclosed space, all casual with lawn-style furnishings and bright colors. In warm months, a sunny patio opens up the place. Service is accommodating though at times overworked. The food ranges from sushi to Thai to sandwiches. The Berkley Bowl salad had lots of spring greens and crisp goodies such as carrots and jicama, and the chef accommodated our request for grilled salmon on top. The pesto dressing is now our all-time favorite. Other times we've enjoyed the noodle bowls, such as a Sri Lankan red curry or pad Thai. If you're staying in Taos, this spot makes for a great destination, with plenty of fun shops to peruse when your tummy's full.

480 NM 150, Seco Plaza, Arroyo Seco. © **505/776-3166.** Reservations not accepted. Main courses $7.50–$15. MC, V. Tues–Wed and Sat 8am–4pm; Thurs–Fri 8am–8pm; Sun 9am–3pm.

Taos Cow ⊛ (Kids) DELI/ICE CREAM   Set in one of our favorite villages, Taos Cow offers fun breakfast and lunch fare in a relaxed atmosphere—but the reason to come here is the ice cream! Our favorite this week is the cherry ristra, with piñon nuts and chocolate chunks. Kids love their shakes. On chillier afternoons, there's espresso, cappuccino, and hot chocolate to warm you after a day on the slopes.

485 NM 150, Arroyo Seco. © **505/776-5640.** Reservations not accepted. All menu items under $10. AE, DISC, MC, V. Daily 7am–7pm.

5 What to See & Do

With a history shaped by pre-Columbian civilization, Spanish colonialism, and the Wild West; outdoor activities that range from ballooning to world-class skiing; and a clustering of artists, writers, and musicians, Taos has something to offer almost everybody.

THE TOP ATTRACTIONS

Millicent Rogers Museum of Northern New Mexico ⊛   This museum will give you a glimpse of some of the finest Southwestern arts and crafts anywhere, but it's small enough to avoid being overwhelming. It was founded in 1953 by Millicent Rogers's family members after her death. Rogers was a wealthy Taos émigré who in 1947 began acquiring a magnificent collection of beautiful Native American arts and crafts. Included are Navajo and Pueblo jewelry, Navajo textiles, Pueblo pottery, Hopi and Zuni kachina dolls, paintings from the Rio Grande Pueblo people, and basketry from a wide variety of Southwestern tribes. The museum also presents exhibitions of Southwestern art, crafts, and design.

Since the 1970s, the scope of the museum's permanent collection has been expanded to include Anglo arts and crafts and Hispanic religious and secular arts and crafts, from Spanish and Mexican colonial to contemporary times. Included are *santos* (religious images), furniture, weavings, *colcha* embroideries, and decorative tinwork. Agricultural implements, domestic utensils, and craftspeople's tools dating from the 17th and 18th centuries are also displayed.

Taos Attractions

**Map labels:**

Taos
Santa Fe
Albuquerque
NEW MEXICO

CARSON NATIONAL FOREST

Hondo–Seco Rd.
Taos Ski Valley Rd.
Taos Municipal Airport
Millicent Rogers Rd.
Lucero Rd.
Blueberry Hill Rd.
Taos Mesa
Pueblo Creek
Upper Ranchitos Rd.
Camino de la Placita
Town Hall
Civic Center
Paseo del Pueblo Norte (North Santa Fe Rd.)
Ranchitos Rd.
Siler Rd.
Kit Carson Rd.
State Hwy. 240
Lower Ranchitos Rd.
Camino del Medio
Tewa Rd.
La Posta Rd.
Paseo del Pueblo Sur (South Santa Fe Rd.)
Los Pandos Rd.
Callejon
Camino de la Merced
Hardner Rd.
Santa Fe Rd.
Cruz Alta Rd.
Salazar Rd.
Arroyo de los Cayotes
Chamber of Commerce & Information Center
Paseo del Cañon
Roy Rd.
Gusdorf Rd.
Morgan Rd.
Estes Rd.
Sunshine Rd.
Chamisa Rd.
Camino de Abajo de la Llama
Cordillera Rd.
Espinosa Rd.
To Santa Fe
Weimer Rd.
Estes Rd.

0   1/2 mi
0   0.5 km

Airport ✈
Church ⍭
Information ⓘ
Post Office ✉

Legend:

Arroyo Seco **3**
D. H. Lawrence Ranch **2**
Ernest L. Blumenschein Home & Museum **10**
Harwood Museum of Art **9**
Martinez Hacienda **12**
Kit Carson Home and Museum **8**
Millicent Rogers Museum of Northern New Mexico **6**
Rio Grande Gorge Bridge **1**
San Francisco de Asis church **13**
Taos Art Museum **7**
Taos Plaza **11**
Taos Pueblo **5**
Taos Ski Valley **4**

Tips A Tip for Museumgoers

If you'd like to visit the Museum Association of Taos's five museums—Blumenschein Home, Martinez Hacienda, Harwood Museum, Millicent Rogers Museum, and Taos Art Museum—you'll save money by purchasing a combination ticket for $20. The fully transferable ticket allows one-time entry to each museum during a 1-year period. You may purchase the pass at any of the five museums. For more information, call © 505/758-0505.

The museum gift shop has a fine collection of superior regional art. Classes and workshops, lectures, and field trips are held throughout the year.

Off US 64, 4 miles north of Taos Plaza, on Millicent Rogers Rd. © 505/758-2462. www.millicentrogers.org. Admission $8 adults, $6 students, $7 seniors, $2 children 6–16, $18 family rate. Daily 10am–5pm. Closed Mon Nov–Mar, Easter, Thanksgiving, Christmas, New Year's Day.

San Francisco de Asis Church 🌟🌟   On NM 68, about 4 miles south of Taos, this famous church appears as a modern adobe sculpture with no doors or windows, an image that has often been photographed and painted, most notably by Georgia O'Keeffe. Visitors must walk through the garden on the east side to enter the two-story church and get a full perspective of its massive walls, authentic adobe plaster, and beauty.

A video presentation is given in the church office every hour on the half-hour. Also, displayed on the wall is an unusual painting, *The Shadow of the Cross,* by Henri Ault (1896). Under ordinary light, it portrays a barefoot Christ at the Sea of Galilee; in darkness, however, the portrait becomes luminescent, and the perfect shadow of a cross forms over the left shoulder of Jesus's silhouette. The artist reportedly was as shocked as everyone else to see this. The reason for the illusion remains a mystery. A few crafts shops surround the square.

Ranchos de Taos Plaza. © 505/758-2754. Admission $3 for video and mystery painting. Mon–Sat 9am–4pm. Visitors may attend Mass Mon–Fri 5pm, Sat 6pm (Mass rotates from this church to the 3 mission chapels); Sun 7 (Spanish), 9, and 11:30am. Closed to the public (except for services) 1st 2 weeks in June.

Taos Art Museum 🌟 *Finds*   Set in the home of Russian artist Nicolai Fechin (*Feh-shin*), this collection displays works of the Taos Society of Artists, which give a sense of what Taos was like in the late 19th and early 20th centuries. The works are rich and varied, including panoramas and images of the Native American and Hispanic villagers. The setting in what was Fechin's home from 1927 until 1933 is truly unique. The historic building commemorates his career. Born in Russia in 1881, Fechin came to the United States in 1923, already acclaimed as a master of painting, drawing, sculpture, architecture, and woodwork. In Taos, he renovated the home and embellished it with hand-carved doors, windows, gates, posts, fireplaces, and other features of a Russian country home. Fechin died in 1955.

227 Paseo del Pueblo Norte. © 505/758-2690. www.taosmuseums.org. Admission $8 adults, $4 children 6–12, free for children under 6. Summer Thurs–Sun 10am–5pm; call for winter hours.

Taos Historic Museums 🌟🌟   Two historical homes are operated as museums, affording visitors a glimpse of early Taos lifestyles. The Martinez Hacienda and Ernest Blumenschein home each has unique appeal.

The **Martinez Hacienda,** Lower Ranchitos Road, Highway 240 (℗ **505/758-1000**), is the only Spanish colonial hacienda in the United States that's open to the public year-round. This was the home of the merchant, trader, and *alcalde* (mayor) Don Antonio Severino Martinez, who bought it in 1804 and lived here until his death in 1827. His eldest son was Padre Antonio José Martinez, northern New Mexico's controversial spiritual leader from 1826 to 1867. On the west bank of the Rio Pueblo de Taos, about 2 miles southwest of the plaza, the museum is remarkably beautiful, with thick, raw adobe walls. The hacienda has no exterior windows—this was to protect against raids by Plains tribes. Exhibits tell the story of the Martinez family and life in Spanish Taos between 1598 and 1821, when Mexico gained control.

Taos Historic Museums has developed the Martinez Hacienda into a living museum with weavers, blacksmiths, and woodcarvers. Demonstrations are scheduled daily, and during the **Taos Trade Fair** (held in late Sept) they run virtually nonstop. The Trade Fair commemorates the era when Native Americans, Spanish settlers, and mountain men met here to trade with each other.

The **Ernest L. Blumenschein Home & Museum,** 222 Ledoux St. (℗ **505/758-0505**), 1½ blocks southwest of the plaza, re-creates the lifestyle of one of the founders of the Taos Society of Artists (founded 1915). An adobe home with garden walls and a courtyard, parts of which date from the 1790s, it became the home and studio of Blumenschein (1874–1960) and his family in 1919. Period furnishings include European antiques and handmade Taos furniture in Spanish-colonial style. An extensive collection of works by early-20th-century Taos artists, including some by Blumenschein's daughter, Helen, is on display in several rooms of the home.

222 Ledoux St. ℗ 505/758-0505 (information for both museums can be obtained at this number). www.taos historicmuseums.com. Admission for each museum $7 adults, $3 children ages 6–16, free for children 5 and under, $15 families. Summer daily 9am–5pm; call for winter hours.

Taos Pueblo ⊀⊀⊀   It's amazing that in our frenetic world, more than 100 Taos Pueblo residents still live much as their ancestors did 1,000 years ago. When you enter the pueblo, a World Heritage Site, you'll see two large buildings, both with rooms piled on top of each other, forming structures that echo the shape of Taos Mountain (to the northeast). Here, a portion of Taos residents live without electricity and running water; the remaining 4,000 residents of Taos Pueblo live in conventional homes on the pueblo's 95,000 acres.

The northernmost of New Mexico's 19 pueblos, Taos Pueblo has been home to the Tiwa tribes for more than 900 years. Many residents here still practice ancestral rituals. The center of their world is still nature; women use hornos to bake bread, and most still drink water that flows down from the sacred Blue Lake. Meanwhile, arts and crafts and other tourism-related businesses support the economy, along with government services, ranching, and farming.

The village looks much the same today as it did when a regiment from Coronado's expedition first came upon it in 1540. Though the Tiwa were essentially a peaceful agrarian people, they are perhaps best remembered for spearheading the only successful revolt by Native Americans in history. Launched by Popé (Poh-*pay*) in 1680, the uprising drove the Spanish from Santa Fe until 1692 and from Taos until 1698.

As you explore the pueblo, you can browse shops, visit the residents' studios, sample homemade bread, look into the **San Geronimo Chapel,** and wander past the fascinating ruins of the old church and cemetery. You're expected to ask permission from individuals before taking their photos; some will ask for a small payment. Do not trespass into kivas (ceremonial rooms) and other areas marked as restricted.

The **Feast of San Geronimo** (the patron saint of Taos Pueblo), on September 29 and 30, marks the end of the harvest season. Other annual events include a **turtle dance** on New Year's Day, **deer or buffalo dances** on Three Kings Day (Jan 6), and **corn dances** on Santa Cruz Day (May 3), San Antonio Day (June 13), San Juan Day (June 24), Santiago Day (July 25), and Santa Ana Day (July 26). The annual **Taos Pueblo Powwow,** a dance competition and parade that brings together tribes from throughout North America, is held the second weekend of July on tribal lands off NM 522 (see "Calendar of Events," in chapter 2). The pueblo Christmas celebration begins on Christmas Eve, with bonfires and a procession with children's dances. On Christmas day, the **deer** or **Matachine dances** take place.

During your visit to the pueblo you will have the opportunity to purchase traditional fried and oven-baked bread as well as a variety of arts and crafts. If you would like to try traditional feast-day meals, the **Tiwa Kitchen,** near the entrance to the pueblo, is a good place to stop. Close to Tiwa Kitchen is the **Oo-oonah Children's Art Center,** where you can see the creative works of Pueblo children.

Like many of the other pueblos in New Mexico, Taos Pueblo has opened a casino. **Taos Mountain Casino** (𝄪 **888/WIN-TAOS**) is on the main road to Taos Pueblo and features slot machines, blackjack, and poker.

Note: To learn more about the pueblo and its people, we highly recommend taking a 30-minute guided tour. Ask upon arrival when one will be given and where you should meet your guide.

Veterans Hwy. (P.O. Box 1846), Taos Pueblo. 𝄪 505/758-1028. www.taospueblo.com. Admission cost, as well as camera, video, and sketching fees, subject to change on a yearly basis; be sure to ask about telephoto lenses and digital cameras; photography not permitted on feast days. Daily 8am–4:30pm, w/a few exceptions. Guided tours available. Closed for 45 consecutive days every year late winter or early spring (call ahead). From Paseo del Pueblo Norte, travel north 2 miles on Veterans Hwy.

MORE ATTRACTIONS

D. H. Lawrence Ranch   A trip to this ranch north of Taos leads you into odd realms of devotion for the controversial author who lived and wrote in the area in the early 1920s. A short uphill walk from the ranch home (not open to visitors), is the D. H. Lawrence Memorial, a shedlike structure that's a bit of a forgotten place, where people have left a few mementos such as juniper berries and sticks of gum. The guest book is also interesting: One couple wrote of trying for 24 years to get here from England.

Lawrence lived in Taos on and off between 1922 and 1925. The ranch was a gift to his wife, Frieda, from the art patron Mabel Dodge Luhan. Lawrence repaid Luhan the favor by giving her the manuscript of *Sons and Lovers.* When Lawrence died in southern France in 1930 of tuberculosis, his ashes were returned here for burial. The grave of Frieda, who died in 1956, is outside the memorial. The memorial is the only public building at the ranch, which is operated today by the University of New Mexico as an educational and recreational retreat.

NM 522, San Cristobal. 𝄪 505/776-2245. Free admission. Daily 8am–5pm. Drive north from Taos about 15 miles on NM 522, then another 6 miles east into the forested Sangre de Cristo Range via a well-marked dirt road.

Harwood Museum of Art of the University of New Mexico 𝄪   With its high ceilings and broad wood floors, this museum is a lovely place to wander among New Mexico–inspired images. A cultural and community center since 1923, the museum

displays paintings, drawings, prints, sculpture, and photographs by Taos-area artists from 1800 to the present. Featured are paintings from the early days of the art colony by members of the Taos Society of Artists. Upstairs are 19th-century pounded-tin pieces and *retablos,* religious paintings of saints that have traditionally been used for decoration and inspiration in the homes and churches of New Mexico. The museum also schedules more than eight changing exhibitions a year, many of which feature works by celebrated artists currently living in Taos.

238 Ledoux St. ©️ 505/758-9826. www.harwoodmuseum.org. Admission $7, $6 seniors, free for children 11 and under. Tues–Sat 10am–5pm; Sun noon–5pm.

Kit Carson Home and Museum   If you want a glimpse into the modest lifestyle of Taos's frontiersmen, head to this three-room adobe home, a block east of the plaza. Built in 1825 and purchased in 1843 by Carson—the famous mountain man, Indian agent, and scout—it was a wedding gift for his young bride, Josefa Jaramillo. It remained their home for 25 years, until both died (exactly a month apart) in 1868. Rooms have sparse displays such as buffalo hide and sheepskin bedding, a wooden chest, basic kitchen utensils, and a cooking fireplace. The treasure of the museum is interpreter Natívidad Mascarenas-Gallegos, a distant relative of Carson, who can tell you plenty about the family. The museum also includes a film on Carson produced by the History Channel. The price of a visit here is a bit steep for what you see, but if you decide to come, plan on spending about a half-hour. If you'd like to see more of Carson's possessions, visit the Martinez Hacienda (above).

113 Kit Carson Rd. ©️ 505/758-4613. www.kitcarsonhome.com. Admission $5 adult, $4 seniors 65 years and older, $3 teens 13–18, $2 children 6–12. Daily 9am–6pm.

Kit Carson Park and Cemetery   Major community events are held in the park in summer. The cemetery, established in 1847, contains the graves of Carson, his wife, Governor Charles Bent, the Don Antonio Martinez family, Mabel Dodge Luhan, and many other noted historical figures and artists. Their lives are described briefly on plaques.

Paseo del Pueblo Norte. ©️ 505/758-8234. Free admission. Daily 24 hr.

Rio Grande Gorge Bridge ⊛ *Kids*   This impressive bridge, west of the Taos airport, spans the Southwest's greatest river. At 650 feet above the canyon floor, it's one of America's highest bridges. If you can withstand the vertigo, it's interesting to come more than once, at different times of day, to observe how the changing light plays tricks with the colors of the cliff walls. A curious aside is that the wedding scene in the movie *Natural Born Killers* was filmed here.

US 64, 10 miles west of Taos. Free admission. Daily 24 hr.

ORGANIZED TOURS

An excellent opportunity to explore the historic downtown area of Taos is offered by **Taos Historic Walking Tours** (©️ 505/758-4020). Tours cost $10 and take 1½ to 2 hours, leaving from the Mabel Dodge Luhan house at 10am Monday to Saturday (June–Aug). Call to make an appointment during the off season.

If you'd really like a taste of Taos history and drama, call **Enchantment Dreams Walking Tours** ⊛ (©️ 505/776-2562). Roberta Courtney Meyers, a theater artist, dramatist, and composer, will tour you through Taos's history while performing a number of characters, such as Georgia O'Keeffe and Kit Carson. Walking tours cost $20 per person.

6 Skiing Taos

DOWNHILL SKIING

Five alpine resorts are within an hour's drive of Taos; all offer complete facilities, including equipment rentals. Although exact opening and closing dates vary according to snow conditions, the season usually begins around Thanksgiving and continues into early April.

Ski clothing can be purchased, and ski equipment can be rented or bought, from several Taos outlets. Among them are **Cottam's Ski & Outdoor Shops,** with four locations (call ℂ **800/322-8267** or 505/758-2822 for the one nearest you), and **Taos Ski Valley Sportswear, Ski & Boot Co.,** in Taos Ski Valley (ℂ **505/776-2291**).

TAOS SKI VALLEY

Taos Ski Valley 🐸🐸🐸, P.O. Box 90, Taos Ski Valley, NM 87525 (ℂ **505/776-2291;** www.skitaos.org), is the preeminent ski resort in the southern Rocky Mountains. It was founded in 1955 by a Swiss-German immigrant, Ernie Blake. According to local legend, Blake searched for 2 years in a small plane for the perfect location for a ski resort comparable to what he was accustomed to in the Alps. He found it at the abandoned mining site of Twining, high above Taos. Today, under the management of two younger generations of Blakes, the resort has become internationally renowned for its light, dry powder (as much as 320 in. annually), its superb ski school, and its personal, friendly service.

Taos Ski Valley can best be appreciated by the more experienced skier. It offers steep, high-alpine, high-adventure skiing. The mountain is more intricate than it might seem at first glance, and it holds many surprises and challenges—even for the expert. The *London Times* called the valley "without any argument the best ski resort in the world. Small, intimate, and endlessly challenging, Taos simply has no equal." And, if you're sick of dealing with yahoos on snowboards, you will be pleased to know that they're not permitted on the slopes of Taos Ski Valley. The quality of the snow here (light and dry) is believed to be due to the dry Southwestern air and abundant sunshine.

Between the 11,819-foot summit and the 9,207-foot base, there are 72 trails and bowls, more than half of them designated for expert and advanced skiers. Most of the remaining trails are suitable for advanced intermediates; there's little flat terrain for novices to gain experience and mileage. However, many beginning skiers find that after spending time in lessons they can enjoy the **Kachina Bowl,** which offers spectacular views as well as wide-open slopes.

The area has an uphill capacity of 15,000 skiers per hour on its five double chairs, one triple, four quads, and one surface tow. Full-day lift tickets, depending on the season, cost $33 to $57 for adults, $21 to $35 for children 12 and under, $22 to $45 for teens ages 13 to 17, and $43 for seniors ages 65 to 79; free for seniors over 80 and for children 6 and under with an adult ticket purchase. Full rental packages are $20 for adults and $13 for children. Taos Ski Valley is open daily 9am to 4pm from Thanksgiving to around the second week of April. *Note:* Taos Ski Valley has one of the best ski schools in the country, specializing in teaching people how to negotiate steep and challenging runs.

Taos Ski Valley has many lodges and condominiums, with nearly 1,500 beds. (See "Taos Ski Valley," earlier in this chapter, for details on accommodations.) All offer ski-week packages; three of them have restaurants. There are three restaurants on the

---

(Kids) Skiing with Kids

With its children's ski school, Taos Ski Valley has always been an excellent choice for skiing families, but with the 1994 addition of an 18,000-square-foot children's center (Kinderkäfig Center), skiing with your children in Taos is even better. Kinderkäfig offers every service imaginable, from equipment rental for children to babysitting services. Call ahead for more information.

---

mountain in addition to the many facilities of Village Center at the base. For reservations, call the **Taos Valley Resort Association** (© **800/776-1111** or 505/776-2233).

RED RIVER SKI & SNOWBOARD AREA

Not far from Taos Ski Valley is **Red River Ski & Snowboard Area,** P.O. Box 900, Red River, NM 87558 (© **800/331-7669** for reservations; 505/754-2223 for information; www.redriverskiarea.com). One of the bonuses of this ski area is that lodgers at Red River can walk out their doors and be on the slopes. Two other factors make this 40-year-old, family-oriented area special: First, most of its 58 trails are geared toward the intermediate skier, though beginners and experts also have some trails; and second, good snow is guaranteed early and late in the year by snowmaking equipment that can work on 87% of the runs—more than any other in New Mexico. However, be aware that this human-made snow tends to be icy, and the mountain is full of inexperienced skiers, so you really have to watch your back. Locals in the area refer to this as "Little Texas" because it's so popular with Texans and other Southerners. A very friendly atmosphere, with a touch of redneck attitude, prevails.

There's a 1,600-foot vertical drop here to a base elevation of 8,750 feet. Lifts include four double chairs, two triple chairs, and a surface tow, with a capacity of 7,920 skiers per hour. The cost of a lift ticket for all lifts is $53 for adults for a full day, $39 half-day; $47 for teens 13 to 19 for a full day, $34 half-day; and $38 for children ages 4 to 12 and seniors 60 through 69 for a full day, $26 half-day. Free for seniors 70 and over. All rental packages start at $20 for adults, $13 for children. Lifts run daily 9am to 4pm Thanksgiving to about March 28. Ask about their lesson packages.

ANGEL FIRE RESORT

Also quite close to Taos is **Angel Fire Resort** ✦, P.O. Drawer B, Angel Fire, NM 87710 (© **800/633-7463** or 505/377-6401; www.angelfireresort.com). If you (or your kids) don't feel up to skiing steeper Taos Mountain, Angel Fire is a good choice. The 62 trails are heavily oriented to beginner and intermediate skiers and snowboarders, with a few runs for more advanced skiers and snowboarders. The mountain has received over $7 million in improvements in past years. This is not an old village like you'll find at Taos and Red River. Instead, it's a Vail-style resort, built in 1960, with a variety of activities besides skiing (see "Exploring the Enchanted Circle," later in this chapter). The snowmaking capabilities here are excellent, and the ski school is good, though we hear it's so crowded that it's difficult to get in during spring break. Two high-speed quad lifts whisk you to the top quickly. There are also three double lifts and one surface lift. A large snowboard park contains a banked slalom course, rails, jumps, and other obstacles. Cross-country skiing, snowshoeing, and snowbiking are also available. All-day lift tickets cost $48 for adults and $33 for children (ages 7–12).

Kids 6 and under and seniors 70 and over ski free. Angel Fire is open from approximately Thanksgiving to March 29 (depending on the weather) daily 9am to 4pm.

CROSS-COUNTRY SKIING

Just east of Red River, with 16 miles of groomed trails (in addition to 6 miles of trails strictly for snowshoers) in 400 acres of forestlands atop Bobcat Pass, is the **Enchanted Forest Cross Country Ski Area** ⟨ (© 505/754-6112; www.enchantedforestxc.com). Full-day trail passes, good 9am to 4:30pm, are $12 for adults; $9 for teens 13 to 17 and seniors 62 to 69; $5 for children ages 7 to 12; and free for seniors age 70 and over as well as for children 6 and under. In addition to cross-country ski and snowshoe rentals, Forest Cross also rents pulk sleds—high-tech devices in which children are pulled by their skiing parents. The ski area offers a full snack bar. Equipment rentals and lessons can be arranged either at Enchanted Forest or at **Miller's Crossing** ski shop, at 417 W. Main St. in Red River (© **505/754-2374**). Nordic skiers can get instruction in cross-country classic as well as freestyle skating. **Taos Mountain Outfitters**, 114 S. Plaza (© **505/758-9292**), offers telemark and cross-country sales, and rentals.

7 Getting Outside

Taos County's 2,200 square miles contain a great diversity of scenic beauty, from New Mexico's highest mountain, 13,161-foot **Wheeler Peak**, to the 650-foot-deep chasm of the **Rio Grande Gorge** ⟨⟨. Carson National Forest, which extends to the eastern city limits of Taos and cloaks a large part of the county, contains several major ski facilities as well as hundreds of miles of hiking trails through the Sangre de Cristo Range.

Recreation areas are mainly in the national forest, where pine and aspen provide refuge for abundant wildlife. Forty-eight areas are accessible by road, including 38 with campsites. There are also areas on the high desert mesa, carpeted by sagebrush, cactus, and, frequently, wildflowers. Two beautiful areas within a short drive of Taos are the **Valle Vidal Recreation Area,** north of Red River, and the **Wild Rivers Recreation Area,** near Questa. For complete information, contact **Carson National Forest,** 208 Cruz Alta Rd. (© **505/758-6200**), or the **Bureau of Land Management,** 226 Cruz Alta Rd. (© **505/758-8851**).

BALLOONING

As in many other towns throughout New Mexico, hot-air ballooning is a top attraction. Recreational trips over the Taos Valley and Rio Grande Gorge are offered by **Paradise Hot Air Balloon Adventure** (© **505/751-6098**). The company also offers ultralight rides.

The **Taos Mountain Balloon Rally,** P.O. Box 3096 (© **505/751-1000**), is held each year in late October. (See "Calendar of Events," in chapter 2.)

BIKING

Even if you're not an avid cyclist, it won't take long for you to realize that getting around Taos by bike is preferable to driving. You won't have the usual parking problems, and you won't have to sit in the line of traffic as it snakes through the center of town. If you feel like exploring the surrounding area, Carson National Forest rangers recommend several biking trails in the greater Taos area. Head to the **West Rim Trail** for a scenic and easy ride. To reach the trail, travel US 64 to the Taos Gorge Bridge, cross it, and find the trail head on your left. Or head south on NM 68 for 17 miles to Pilar; turn west onto NM 570. Travel along the river for 6¼ miles, cross the bridge, and drive to the top of the ridge. Watch for the trail marker on your right. For a more technical and challenging ride, go to **Devisadero Loop:** From Taos drive out of town on US 64 to your first pullout on the right, just as you enter the canyon at El Nogal Picnic Area. To ride the notorious **South Boundary Trail,** a 20-mile romp for advanced riders, contact Native Sons Adventures (below). Native Sons can arrange directions, a shuttle, and a guide, if necessary. The **U.S. Forest Service** office, 208 Cruz Alta Rd. (ⓒ **505/758-6200**), has excellent trail information. Also look for the *Taos Trails* map (created jointly by Carson National Forest, Native Sons Adventures, and Trails Illustrated) at area bookstores.

Bicycle rentals are available from the **Gearing Up Bicycle Shop,** 129 Paseo del Pueblo Sur (ⓒ **505/751-0365**); daily rentals run $35 for a mountain bike with front suspension.

Annual touring events include Red River's **Enchanted Circle Century Bike Tour** (ⓒ **505/754-2366**) on the weekend following Labor Day.

FISHING

In many of New Mexico's waters, fishing is possible year-round, though many high lakes and streams are fishable only during the warmer months. Overall, the best fishing is in the spring and fall. Naturally, the Rio Grande is a favorite fishing spot, but there's also excellent fishing in the streams around Taos. Taoseños favor the Rio Hondo, Rio Pueblo (near Tres Ritos), Rio Fernando (in Taos Canyon), Pot Creek, and Rio Chiquito. Rainbow, cutthroat, German brown trout, and kokanee (a freshwater salmon) are commonly stocked and caught. Pike and catfish have been caught in the Rio Grande as well. Jiggs, spinners, or woolly worms are recommended as lure, or worms, corn, or salmon eggs as bait; many experienced anglers prefer fly-fishing.

Licenses are required, of course, and are sold, along with tackle, at several Taos sporting-goods shops. For backcountry guides, try **Deep Creek Wilderness Outfitters and Guides,** P.O. Box 721, El Prado, NM 87529 (ⓒ **505/776-8423** or 505/776-5901), or **Taylor Streit Flyfishing Service,** 405 Camino de la Placita (ⓒ **505/751-1312;** www.streitflyfishing.com).

FITNESS FACILITIES

The **Taos Spa and Tennis Club,** 111 Dona Ana Dr. (across from Sagebrush Inn; ⓒ **505/758-1980;** www.taosspa.com), is a fully equipped fitness center that rivals any you'd find in a big city. It has a variety of cardiovascular machines, bikes, and weight-training machines, as well as saunas, indoor and outdoor Jacuzzis, a steam room, and indoor and outdoor pools. Classes range from yoga to Pilates to water fitness. In addition, it has tennis and racquetball courts. Therapeutic massage, facials, and physical therapy are available daily by appointment. Children's programs include a tennis camp and swimming lessons, and babysitting programs are available in the morning and evening. The spa is open Monday to Friday 4am to 9pm; Saturday and Sunday 7am to 8pm. Monthly memberships are available for individuals and families, as are summer memberships and punch cards. For visitors, the daily rate is $12.

The **Northside Health and Fitness Center,** at 1307 Paseo del Pueblo Norte (ⓒ **505/751-1242**), is also a full-service facility, featuring top-of-the-line Cybex equipment, free weights, and cardiovascular equipment. Aerobics classes are scheduled daily (Jazzercise classes weekly), and there are indoor/outdoor pools and four tennis courts, as well as children's and seniors' programs. It's open weekdays 6am to 9pm, weekends 8am to 8pm. The daily visitors' rate is $11.

GOLF

Since the summer of 1993, the 18-hole golf course at the **Taos Country Club,** 54 Golf Course Dr., Ranchos de Taos (℘ **800/758-7375** or 505/758-7300), has been open to the public. On Country Road 110, just 6 miles south of the plaza, it's a first-rate championship golf course designed for all levels of play. It has open fairways and no hidden greens. The club also features a driving range, practice putting and chipping green, and instruction by PGA professionals. Greens fees are seasonal and start at $49; cart and club rentals are available. The country club has also added a clubhouse, featuring a restaurant and full bar. It's always advisable to call ahead for tee times 1 week in advance, but it's not unusual for people to show up unannounced and still manage to find a time to tee off.

The par-72, 18-hole course at the **Angel Fire Resort Golf Course** (℘ **800/633-7463** or 505/377-3055) is PGA endorsed. Surrounded by stands of ponderosa pine, spruce, and aspen, at 8,500 feet, it's one of the highest regulation golf courses in the world. It also has a driving range and putting green. Carts and clubs can be rented at the course, and the club pro provides instruction. Greens fees range from $47 to $89.

HIKING

Hundreds of miles of hiking trails cross Taos County's mountain and high-mesa country. The trails are especially well traveled in the summer and fall, although nights turn chilly and mountain weather may be fickle by September.

Free materials and advice on all **Carson National Forest** trails and recreation areas can be obtained from the **Forest Service Building,** 208 Cruz Alta Rd. (℘ **505/758-6200**), open Monday to Friday 8am to 4:30pm. Detailed USGS topographical maps of backcountry areas can be purchased from **Taos Mountain Outfitters,** South Plaza (℘ **505/758-9292**).

One of the easiest hikes to access is the **West Rim Trail,** aptly named because it runs along the rim of the Rio Grande Gorge. Access this 9-mile-long trail by driving west from Taos on US 64, crossing the Rio Grande Gorge Bridge, and turning left into the picnic area. The 19,663-acre **Wheeler Peak Wilderness** is a wonderland of alpine tundra, encompassing New Mexico's highest peak (13,161 ft.). A favorite (though rigorous) hike to Wheeler Peak's summit (15 miles round-trip with a 3,700-ft. elevation gain) makes for a long but fun day. The trail head is at Taos Ski Valley. For year-round hiking, head to the **Wild Rivers Recreation Area** (℘ **505/770-1600**), near Questa (see "Exploring the Enchanted Circle," later in this chapter).

HORSEBACK RIDING

The sage meadows and pine-covered mountains around Taos make it one of the West's most romantic places to ride. **Taos Indian Horse Ranch**, on pueblo land off Ski Valley Road, just before **Arroyo Seco** (℘ **505/758-3212**), offers a variety of guided rides. Open by appointment, the ranch provides horses for all types of riders (English, Western, Australian, and bareback) and ability levels. Call ahead to reserve and for prices, which will likely run about $85 for a 2-hour trail ride.

Horseback riding is also offered by **Rio Grande Stables,** P.O. Box 2122, El Prado (℘ **505/776-5913;** www.lajitasstables.com/taos.htm), with rides taking place during the summer months at Taos Ski Valley. Most riding outfitters offer lunch trips and overnight trips. Call for prices and further details.

ICE-SKATING & SKATEBOARDING

If a latent Michelle Kwan or Brian Boitano dwells in you, try your blades at **Taos Youth Family Center,** 406 Paseo del Cañon, 2 miles south of the plaza and about ¾ mile off Paseo del Pueblo Sur (© **505/758-4160**). The rink is open daily from early November thorough mid-March. Call for hours. Skate rentals are available for adults and children. Admission is $4. Also at the center is an in-line-skate and skateboarding park, open when there's no snow or ice. Admission is free.

JOGGING

The paved paths and grass of Kit Carson Park (see "More Attractions," earlier in this chapter) provide a quiet place to stretch your legs.

LLAMA TREKKING

For a taste of the unusual, you might want to try letting a llama carry your gear and food while you—free of any heavy burdens—walk and explore. Llamas are friendly, gentle animals that have keen senses of sight and smell. Often, other animals, such as elk, deer, and mountain sheep, are attracted to the scent of the llamas and will venture closer to hikers if the llamas are present.

   Wild Earth Llama Adventures 𝒜𝒜 (© **800/758-LAMA [5262]** or 505/586-0174; www.llamaadventures.com) offers a "Take a Llama to Llunch" day hike—a full day of hiking into the Sangre de Cristo Mountains, complete with a gourmet lunch, for $89. Wild Earth also offers a variety of custom multiday wilderness adventures tailored to trekkers' needs and fitness levels for $125 per person per day. Children under 12 receive discounts. Camping gear and food are provided. On the trips, experienced guides provide information about native plants and local wildlife, as well as natural and regional history of the area. The head guide has doubled as a chef in the off season, so the meals on these treks are quite tasty.

   El Paseo Llama Expeditions 𝒜 (© **800/455-2627** or 505/758-3111; www.elpaseo llama.com) utilizes U.S. Forest Service maintained trails that wind through canyons and over mountain ridges. The llama expeditions are scheduled May to mid-October, and day hikes are scheduled year round. Gourmet meals are provided. Half day hikes cost $64, day hikes $84, and 2- to 8-day hikes run $249 to $989.

RIVER RAFTING

Half- or full-day white-water rafting trips down the Rio Grande and Rio Chama originate in Taos and can be booked through a variety of outfitters in the area. The wild **Taos Box** 𝒜𝒜𝒜, a steep-sided canyon south of the Wild Rivers Recreation Area, offers a series of class IV rapids that rarely let up for some 17 miles. The water drops up to 90 feet per mile, providing one of the most exciting 1-day white-water tours in the West. May and June, when the water is rising, is a good time to go. Experience is not required, but you will be required to wear a life jacket (which is provided), and you should be willing to get wet.

   Most of the companies listed run the **Taos Box** ($99–$112 per person) and **Pilar Racecourse** ($40–$52 per person for a half-day) on a daily basis.

   We highly recommend **Los Rios River Runners** 𝒜 in Taos, P.O. Box 2734 (© **800/ 544-1181** or 505/776-8854; www.losriosriverrunners.com). Other safe bets are **Native Sons Adventures,** 1033-A Paseo del Pueblo Sur (© **800/753-7559** or 505/758-9342; www.nativesonsadventures.com); and **Far Flung Adventures,** P.O. Box 707, El Prado (© **800/359-2627** or 505/758-2628; www.farflung.com).

Getting Pampered: The Spa Scene

Taos doesn't have the spa scene that Tucson and Phoenix do, but you can get pampered at **Taos Spa and Tennis Club** (see "Fitness Facilities," above). If you'd like to stay at a spa, consider **El Monte Sagrado,** 317 Kit Carson Rd. (© **800/828-TAOS** or 505/758-3502; www.elmontesagrado.com), or **Casa de las Chimeneas,** 405 Cordoba Rd. (© **877/758-4777** or 505/758-4777; www.visittaos.com), which offer a variety of treatments to their guests (see "Where to Stay," earlier in this chapter).

Safety warning: Taos is not the place to experiment if you're not an experienced rafter. Do yourself a favor and check with the **Bureau of Land Management** (© **505/758-8851**) to make sure that you're fully equipped to go white-water rafting without a guide. Have them check your gear to make sure that it's sturdy enough—this is serious rafting!

ROCK CLIMBING
Mountain Skills, P.O. Box 206, Arroyo Seco, NM 87514 (© **505/776-2222;** www.climbingschoolusa.com), offers rock-climbing instruction for all skill levels, from beginners to more advanced climbers who would like to fine-tune their skills or just find out about the best area climbs.

SNOWMOBILING & ATV RIDING
Native Sons Adventures, 1033-A Paseo del Pueblo Sur (© **800/753-7559** or 505/758-9342), runs fully guided tours in the Sangre de Cristo Mountains. Rates run $64 to $150. Advanced reservations required.

SWIMMING
The **Don Fernando Pool,** Civic Plaza Drive at Camino de la Placita, opposite the Convention Center (© **505/737-2622**), admits swimmers over age 8 without adult supervision.

TENNIS
Taos Spa and Tennis Club (see "Fitness Facilities," above) has four courts, and the **Northside Health and Fitness Center** (see "Fitness Facilities," above) has three tennis courts. In addition, there are four free public courts in Taos, two at **Kit Carson Park,** on Paseo del Pueblo Norte, and two at **Fred Baca Memorial Park,** on Camino del Medio, south of Ranchitos Road.

8 Shopping

Given the town's historical associations with the arts, it isn't surprising that many visitors come to Taos to buy fine art. Some 50-odd galleries are within walking distance of the plaza, and a couple of dozen more are just a short drive from downtown. Galleries and shops are generally open 7 days a week during summer and closed Sundays during winter. Hours vary but generally run from 10am to 5 or 6pm. Some artists show their work by appointment only.

The best-known artist in modern Taos is the late R. C. Gorman, a Navajo from Arizona who made his home in Taos for more than 2 decades. He was internationally acclaimed for his bright, somewhat surrealistic depictions of Navajo women. His **Navajo Gallery,** at 210 Ledoux St. (© **505/758-3250**), is a showcase for his widely varied work: acrylics, lithographs, silk screens, bronzes, tapestries, hand-cast ceramic vases, etched glass, and more.

Our favorite spot to shop is the village of **Arroyo Seco** ✺ on NM 150, about 5 miles north of Taos en route to Taos Ski Valley. Not only is there a lovely 1834 church, La Santísima Trinidad, but there are a few cute little shops lining the winding lane through town. Our favorites are the **Taos Sunflower** ✺ (© **505/776-5644**), selling specialty yarns and fibers, just off the highway near the Gypsy 360° cafe (p. 210), and **Arroyo Seco Mercantile** ✺ at 488 NM 150 (© **505/776-8806**), which is full of cowboy hats, antiques, and country home items.

ART

Act I Gallery This gallery has a broad range of works in a variety of media. You'll find watercolors, *retablos,* furniture, paintings, Hispanic folk art, pottery, jewelry, and sculpture. 218 Paseo del Pueblo Norte. © **800/666-2933** or 505/758-7831.

Farnsworth Gallery Taos This gallery sells works by painter John Farnsworth, known for his intimate images of horses often painted close up and at imaginative angles. Other painters are represented as well, all utilizing themes linked to nature. 133 Paseo del Pueblo Norte. © **877/319-7698** or 505/758-0776.

Fenix Gallery The Fenix Gallery focuses on Taos artists with national and/or international collections and reputations who live and work in Taos. The work is primarily nonobjective and very contemporary. Some "historic" artists are represented as well. 228A Ranchitos Rd. © **505/758-9120.**

Gallery A The oldest gallery in town, Gallery A has contemporary and traditional paintings and sculpture, including Gene Kloss etchings, watercolors, and oils, as well as regional and national collections. 105–107 Kit Carson Rd. © **505/758-2343.**

Inger Jirby Gallery ✺ *(Finds* The word *expressionist* could have been created to define the work of internationally known artist Inger Jirby. Full of bold color and passionate brush strokes, Jirby's oils record the lives and landscapes of villages from the Southwestern U.S. to Guatemala to Bali. This gallery, which meanders back through a 400-year-old adobe house, is a feast for the eyes and soul. 207 Ledoux St. © **505/758-7333.**

Lumina Contemporary Art ✺✺ *(Finds* North of Taos (about 8 min.) outside the village of Arroyo Seco, this gallery, a new version of the notable gallery that was in Taos, offers a tranquil museum-quality experience. Set within a 3-acre Japanese garden, it has a water cascade and Buddhist teahouse accented with large stone sculptures. Inside, works offer a refreshing look at the world through contemporary art. It's open in summer Thursday to Monday 11am to 6:30pm, winter Friday to Monday 11am to 5pm. 11 NM 230, Arroyo Seco. © **877/5LUMINA** or 505/758-7282.

Michael McCormick Gallery ✺ *(Finds* Nationally renowned artists dynamically play with Southwestern themes in the works hanging at this gallery, steps from the plaza. Especially notable are the bright portraits by Miguel Martinez. If the gallery's namesake is in, strike up a conversation about art or poetry. 106C Paseo del Pueblo Norte. © **800/279-0879** or 505/758-1372.

Nichols Taos Fine Art Gallery   Here you will find traditional works in all media, including Western and cowboy art. 403 Paseo del Pueblo Norte. ℰ **505/758-2475.**

Parks Gallery ℱ   Some of the region's finest contemporary art decks the walls of this gallery just off the plaza. Some of the top artists here include Melissa Zink, Jim Wagner, Susan Contreres, and Erin Currier. 127 Bent St. ℰ **505/751-0343.**

Philip Bareiss Gallery   The works of some 30 leading Taos artists, including sculptor and painter Ron Davis, sculptor Gray Mercer, and watercolorist Patricia Sanford, are exhibited here, along with early Taos modernists. 15 Rt. 150. ℰ **505/776-2284.** www.taosartappraisal.com.

R. B. Ravens   A trader for many years, including 23 on the Ranchos Plaza, R. B. Ravens is skilled at finding incredible period artwork. Here you'll see (and have the chance to buy) Navajo rugs, and pottery, all in the setting of an old home with raw pine floors and hand-sculpted adobe walls. 4146 NM 68 (across from the St. Francis Church Plaza), Ranchos de Taos. ℰ **505/758-7322.**

BOOKS

Brodsky Bookshop   Come here for the exceptional inventory of fiction, nonfiction, Southwestern and Native American–studies books, children's books, used books, cards, tapes, and CDs. 226 Paseo del Pueblo Norte. ℰ **888/223-8730 or 505/758-9468.**

Moby Dickens Bookshop ℱ   One of Taos's best bookstores, Moby Dickens has comfortable places to sit and read. You'll find children's and adults' collections of Southwest, Native American, and out-of-print books. 124A Bent St. ℰ **888/442-9980 or 505/758-3050.**

CRAFTS

Clay & Fiber Gallery   Clay & Fiber represents more than 150 artists from around the country. Merchandise changes frequently, but you should expect to see a variety of ceramics, fiber arts, jewelry, and wearables. 201 Paseo del Pueblo Sur. ℰ **505/758-8093.**

Taos Artisans Cooperative Gallery _Value_   This seven-member cooperative gallery, owned and operated by local artists, sells local handmade jewelry, wearables, clay work, glass, leather work, and garden sculpture. You'll always find an artist in the shop. 107C Bent St. ℰ **505/758-1558.**

Taos Blue   This gallery has fine Native American and contemporary handicrafts. 101A Bent St. ℰ **505/758-3561.**

Twining Weavers and Contemporary Crafts   Here, you'll find an interesting mix of hand-woven wool rugs and pillows by owner Sally Bachman, as well as creations by other gallery artists in fiber, basketry, and clay. 133 Kit Carson Rd. ℰ **505/758-9000.**

Weaving Southwest   Contemporary tapestries by New Mexico artists, as well as one-of-a-kind rugs, blankets, and pillows, are the woven specialties found here. 216B Paseo del Pueblo Norte. ℰ **505/758-0433.**

FASHIONS

Artemisia   Wearable art in bold colors defines this little shop a block from the plaza. Goods are pricey but unique, most hand-woven or hand-sewn, all for women. 115 Bent St. ℰ **505/737-9800.**

Mariposa Boutique What first caught our eyes in this little shop were bright chile-pepper-print overalls for kids. Closer scrutiny brought us to plenty of finds for adults, such as suede and rayon broomstick skirts and Mexican-style dresses, perfect for showing off turquoise jewelry. 120-F Bent St. ℂ 505/758-9028.

Overland Sheepskin Company ⋆ *Finds* You can't miss the romantically weathered barn sitting on a meadow north of town. Inside, you'll find anything you can imagine in leather: coats, gloves, hats, slippers. The coats here are exquisite, from oversize ranch styles to tailored blazers in a variety of leathers from sheepskin to buffalo hide. NM 522 (a few miles north of town). ℂ 505/758-8820.

FURNITURE

Country Furnishings of Taos Here you'll find unique hand-painted folk-art furniture. The pieces are as individual as the styles of the local folk artists who make them. There are also home accessories, unusual gifts, clothing, and jewelry. 534 Paseo del Pueblo Norte. ℂ 505/758-4633.

Lo Fino ⋆ Its name means "the refined," and this expansive showroom is worth taking time to wander through. You'll find a variety of home furnishings, from driftwood lamps and finely painted *trasteros* (armoires) to handcrafted traditional and contemporary Southwestern furniture. Lo Fino specializes in custom-built furniture. 201 Paseo del Pueblo Sur. ℂ 505/758-0298. lofino@newmex.com.

The Taos Company This interior-design showroom specializes in unique Southwestern and contemporary furniture and decorative accessories. Especially look for graceful stone fountains, iron-and-wood furniture, and custom jewelry. 124K John Dunn Plaza, Bent St. ℂ 800/548-1141 or 505/758-1141.

GIFTS & SOUVENIRS

Chimayo Trading del Norte Specializing in Navajo weavings, pueblo pottery, and other types of pottery, this is a fun spot to peruse on the Ranchos de Taos Plaza. Look especially for the Casas Grandes pottery from Mexico. #1 Ranchos de Taos Plaza. ℂ 505/758-0504.

El Rincón Trading Post *Finds* This shop has a real trading-post feel. It's a wonderful place to find turquoise jewelry, whether you're looking for contemporary or antique. In the back of the store is a museum's worth of Native American and Western artifacts. 114 Kit Carson Rd. ℂ 505/758-9188.

San Francisco de Asis Gift Shop Local devotional art fills this funky little shop behind the San Francisco de Asis church. *Retablos* (altar paintings), rosary beads, and hand-carved wooden crosses appeal to a range of visitors, from the deeply religious to the pagan power shopper. Ranchos de Taos Plaza. ℂ 505/758-2754.

JEWELRY

Artwares Contemporary Jewelry The gallery owners here call their contemporary jewelry "a departure from the traditional." True to this slogan, each piece here offers a new twist on traditional Southwestern and Native American design, by artists such as John Hardy, Diane Malouf, Judith Ripka, and Alex Sepkus. 129 N. Plaza. ℂ 800/527-8850 or 505/758-8850.

Taos Gems & Minerals In business for over 30 years, Taos Gems & Minerals is a fine lapidary showroom. This is a great place to explore; you can buy jewelry, carvings, and antique pieces at reasonable prices. 637 Paseo del Pueblo Sur. ℂ 505/758-3910.

MUSICAL INSTRUMENTS

Taos Drum Company 𝄞   Taos Drum has the largest selection of Native American log and hand drums in the world. In addition to drums, the showroom displays Southwestern and wrought-iron furniture, cowboy art, and more than 60 styles of rawhide lampshades. Ask about the tour that demonstrates the drum-making process. 5 miles south of Taos Plaza (off NM 68). (✆ **505/758-3796.**

POTTERY & TILES

Stephen Kilborn Pottery   Visiting this shop in town is a treat, but for a real adventure, go 17 miles south of Taos toward Santa Fe to Stephen Kilborn's studio in Pilar, open Monday to Saturday 11am to 5pm and noon to 4pm on Sunday. There, you'll see where the pottery is made. 136A Paseo del Pueblo Norte. (✆ **800/758-0136** or 505/758-5760. www.kilbornpottery.com.

Vargas Tile Co.   Vargas Tile has a great little collection of hand-painted Mexican tiles at good prices. You'll find beautiful pots with sunflowers on them and colorful cabinet doorknobs, as well as inventive sinks. South end of town on NM 68. (✆ **505/758-5986.**

9 Taos After Dark

For a small town, Taos has its share of top entertainment. The resort atmosphere and the arts community attract performers, and the city enjoys annual programs in music and literary arts. State troupes, such as the New Mexico Repertory Theater and New Mexico Symphony Orchestra, make regular visits.

Many events are scheduled by the **Taos Center for the Arts (TCA),** 133 Paseo del Pueblo Norte (✆ **505/758-2052;** www.taoscenterforthearts.org), at the **Taos Community Auditorium** (✆ **505/758-2052**). You can obtain information on current events in the *Taos News,* published every Thursday. The **Taos County Chamber of Commerce** (✆ **800/732-TAOS** or 505/758-3873; www.taoschamber.com) publishes semiannual listings of *Taos County Events,* as well as the annual *Taos Country Vacation Guide* that also lists events and happenings around town.

THE PERFORMING ARTS

Fort Burgwin   This historic site (of the 1,000-year-old Pot Creek Pueblo), about 10 miles south of Taos, is a summer campus of Dallas's Southern Methodist University. From mid-May through mid-August, the SMU-in-Taos curriculum (including studio arts, humanities, and sciences) includes courses in music and theater. There are regularly scheduled orchestral concerts, guitar and harpsichord recitals, and theater performances available to the community, without charge, throughout the summer. 6580 NM 518, Ranchos de Taos. (✆ **505/758-8322.**

The Major Concert & Performance Halls

Taos Civic Plaza and Convention Center, 121 Civic Plaza Dr. (✆ **505/758-5792**), has an exhibit center where presentations, lectures, and concerts are held.

Taos Community Auditorium, Kit Carson Memorial State Park (✆ **505/758-4677**), a comfortable, small-town space, is a nice venue for films, concerts, and lectures.

The Taos Area (Including Enchanted Circle)

D. H. Lawrence Ranch **1**
Kit Carson Park **4**
Rio Grande Gorge Bridge **2**
San Francisco de Asis church **5**
Taos Pueblo **3**
Vietnam Veterans Memorial
   State Park **6**

To Alamosa
Antonito
To Colorado Springs
159
COLORADO
NEW MEXICO
Costilla
Valle Vidal
196
Ski Rio
Costilla Lake
Latir Lakes
Rio Grande
522
378
285
Wild Rivers Recreation Area
Questa
Red River
38
Red River Ski
578
Elizabethtown
CARSON NATIONAL FOREST
Tres Piedras
To Farmington and Chama
64
522
San Cristobal
150
Taos Ski Valley
To Raton
Arroyo Hondo
Valdez
Eagle Nest
577
Arroyo Seco
Eagle Nest Lake
Taos Airport
TAOS
Angel Fire
Ranchos de Taos
64
Angel Fire Ski Resort
567
Talpa
434
285
68
Fort Burgwin Research Center
Ojo Caliente Hot Springs
Pilar
518
Rio Grande
Embudo
Vadito
Airport
Church
Ski Area
Enchanted Circle
Dixon
75
68
Las Trampas
Peñasco
518
Tres Ritos
Trampas Church
76
Sipapu Ski Area
To Santa Fe & Albuquerque
Truchas
CARSON NATIONAL FOREST
To Las Vegas, NM
Chimayo

Area of detail
Taos
Santa Fe
25
Albuquerque
NEW MEXICO
40
40
25
10

0   5 mi
0   5 km
N

Moments Exploring the Enchanted Circle

Longing for a little road trip? Few places offer more white-stripe adventure than the 90-mile loop around northern New Mexico's Enchanted Circle. The road leads through old Hispanic villages such as Arroyo Hondo and Questa. About 3 miles north of the latter, you can turn west of NM 522 onto NM 378 and travel 8 miles on a paved road to **Wild Rivers Recreation Area** (*(C)* **505/ 770-1600**), a great place to begin a hike into the Rio Grande Gorge. Next, the Enchanted Circle heads into a pass the Plains Indians once used, to the Wild West mining town of Red River, along the base of some of New Mexico's tallest peaks, to the resort village of Angel Fire, and back to Taos along the meandering Rio Fernando de Taos. Although you can drive the entire loop in 2 hours from Taos, most folks prefer to take a full day, and some take several days. If you get hungry along the way, stop for lunch at **Mountain Treasures** (212 W. Main St., Red River, NM 87558; *(C)* **505/754-2700**), a gallery, bistro, and espresso coffee bar that offers excellent sandwiches. To drive the loop, travel north on NM 522 10 miles to Arroyo Hondo. Then drive another 13 miles to Questa. Turn right on NM 38, traveling 12 miles to Red River. Stay on NM 38 and drive 16 miles to Eagle Nest. From there you come to US 64, which goes west for 12 miles to Angel Fire. The final leg is a lovely 21-mile jaunt on US 64 back to Taos.

Music from Angel Fire   This acclaimed program of chamber music begins in mid-August, with weekend concerts, and continues up to Labor Day. Based in the small resort community of Angel Fire (about 21 miles east of US 64), it also presents numerous concerts in Taos, Las Vegas, and Raton. P.O. Box 502, Angel Fire. *(C)* **505/377-3233** or 505/989-4772.

Taos School of Music   Founded in 1963, this music summer school at the Hotel St. Bernard in Taos Ski Valley offers excellent concerts by notable artists. From mid-June to mid-August there's an intensive 8-week study and performance program for advanced students of violin, viola, cello, and piano. The 8-week **Chamber Music Festival,** an important adjunct of the school, offers 16 concerts and seminars for the public. Performances have featured a variety of artists, including pianist Robert McDonald, the Miami Quartet, the Brentano String Quartet, Michael Tree, and the international young student artists. Performances are held at the Taos Community Auditorium and the Hotel St. Bernard. P.O. Box 1879. *(C)* **505/776-2388**. www.taosschoolof music.com. Tickets for chamber music concerts $15 for adults, $10 for children under 16.

THE CLUB & MUSIC SCENE

Adobe Bar ☆   A favorite gathering place for locals and visitors, the Adobe Bar is known for its live music series (nights vary) devoted to the eclectic talents of Taos musicians. The schedule offers a little of everything—classical, jazz, folk, Hispanic, and acoustic. The Adobe Bar features a wide selection of international beers, wines by the glass, light New Mexican dining, desserts, and an espresso menu. In the Historic Taos Inn, 125 Paseo del Pueblo Norte. *(C)* **505/758-2233**.

Alley Cantina *(* (*Moments*   This bar, which touts its location as the oldest house in Taos, has become the hot late-night spot. The focus is on interaction, as well as TV sports. Patrons playing shuffleboard, pool, chess, and backgammon listen to live music 4 to 5 nights a week. Burgers, fish and chips, and other informal dishes are served until 11pm. 121 Teresina Lane. *(*© 505/758-2121. Cover for live music only.

Anaconda Bar *(**(*   Set in the new ecoresort El Monte Sagrado (p. 198), this is a happening nightspot, with live entertainment—jazz, blues, Native American flute, or country—playing nightly. An anaconda sculpture snaking across the ceiling and an 11,000-gallon fish tank set the contemporary tone of the place, which serves a variety of delectable tapas. In the El Monte Sagrado hotel, 317 Kit Carson Rd. *(*© 505/758-3502.

Caffe Tazza *(*   This cozy three-room cafe, with a summer patio, attracts local community groups, artists, performers, and poets. Plays, films, comedy, and musical performances are given here on weekends (and some weeknights in summer). You can read one of the assorted periodicals available (including the *New York Times*) while sipping a cappuccino or *café Mexicano* (espresso with steamed milk and Mexican chocolate), made from organic coffee beans. The food—soups and sandwiches—is quite good. Pastries, which are imported from many bakeries around the region, are almost as big a draw here as the Taos Cow ice cream. Choose from 15 flavors. 122 Kit Carson Rd. *(*© 505/758-8706.

Sagebrush Inn *(*   This is a real hot spot for locals. The atmosphere is Old West, with a rustic wooden dance floor and plenty of smoke. Dancers generally two-step to country music nightly, year-round, starting at 9pm. Paseo del Pueblo Sur (P.O. Box 557). *(*© 505/758-2254.

8

Albuquerque

At first glance, New Mexico's largest city appears like one giant strip mall sandwiched between a spectacular mountain range, the Sandias, and the lifeblood of the state, the mighty Rio Grande. But this city offers much more than Walgreens and Wal-Mart. It's full of history, has many fun exhibits for kids and the young at heart, and boasts some of the best sunsets in the Southwest.

The railroad, which set up a major stop here in 1880, prompted much of Albuquerque's initial growth, but that economic explosion was nothing compared with what has happened since World War II. Designated a major national center for military research and production, Albuquerque became a trading center for New Mexico, whose populace spreads widely across the land. That's why the city may strike visitors as nothing more than one big strip mall. Look closely and you'll see ranchers, Native Americans, and Hispanic villagers stocking up on goods to take home.

Climbing out of the valley is **Route 66,** well worth a drive, if only to see the rust that time has left. Old court motels, many with funky '50s signage, still line the street. One enclave on this route is the **University of New Mexico district,** with a number of hippie-ish cafes and shops.

Farther downhill, you'll come to **downtown Albuquerque.** During the day, this area is all suits and heels, but at night it boasts a hip nightlife scene.

The **Old Town** section is worth a visit. Though it's the most touristy part of town, it's also a unique Southwestern village with a beautiful and intact plaza. Also in this area are Albuquerque's aquarium and botanical gardens, as well as its zoo.

Indian pueblos in the area welcome tourists, and they—along with other pueblos throughout the state—have worked together to create the Pueblo Cultural Center, a showplace of Indian crafts of both past and present. The country's longest aerial tramway takes visitors to the top of Sandia Peak, which protects the city's eastern flank. To the west runs a series of volcanoes; the Petroglyph National Monument there is an amazing tribute to the area's ancient Native American past.

1 Orientation

ARRIVING

Albuquerque is the transportation hub for New Mexico, so getting in and out of town is easy. For more detailed information, see "Getting There," in chapter 2.

BY PLANE The **Albuquerque International Sunport** (© **505/842-4366;** www.cabq.gov/airport) is in the southcentral part of the city, between I-25 on the west and Kirtland Air Force Base on the east, just south of Gibson Boulevard. Sleek and efficient, the airport is served by most national airlines and two local ones.

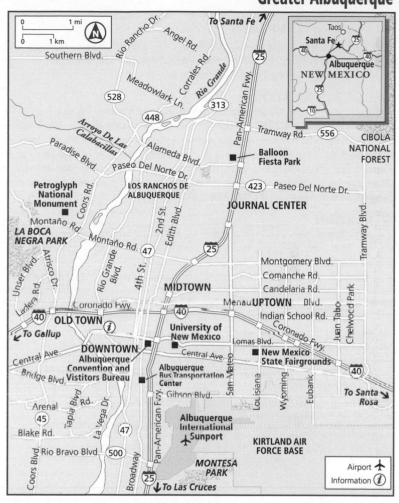

Most hotels have courtesy vans to meet their guests and take them to their respective destinations. In addition, **Checker Airport Express** (© 505/765-1234; www.airportshuttleabq.com) runs services to and from city hotels. **ABQ Ride** (© 505/243-7433; www.cabq.gov/transit/index.html), Albuquerque's public bus system, also makes airport stops. There is efficient taxi service to and from the airport, where you'll also find numerous car-rental agencies.

BY TRAIN Amtrak's *Southwest Chief* arrives and departs daily to and from Los Angeles and Chicago. The station is at 214 First St. SW, 2 blocks south of Central Avenue (© **800/USA-RAIL** or 505/842-9650; www.amtrak.com).

BY BUS Greyhound/Trailways (© **800/231-2222;** www.greyhound.com) and **TNM&O** (© **505/243-4435;** www.tnmo.com) arrive and depart from the

Albuquerque Bus Transportation Center, 300 Second St. SW (at the corner of Lead and Second, near the train station).

BY CAR   If you're driving, you'll probably arrive via either the east-west I-40 or the north-south I-25. Exits are well marked. For information and advice on driving in New Mexico, see "Getting There," in chapter 2.

VISITOR INFORMATION

The main office of the **Albuquerque Convention and Visitors Bureau** is at 20 First Plaza NW (℃ **800/284-2282** or 505/842-9918; www.itsatrip.org). It's open Monday to Friday 8am to 5pm. There are information centers at the airport, on the lower level at the bottom of the escalator, open daily 9:30am to 8pm; and in Old Town at 303 Romero St. NW (Suite 107), open daily 9am to 5pm. Tape-recorded information about current local events is available from the bureau after 5pm weekdays and all day Saturday and Sunday. Call ℃ **800/284-2282.**

CITY LAYOUT

The city's sprawl takes awhile to get used to. A visitor's first impression is of a grid of arteries lined with shopping malls and fast-food eateries, with residences tucked behind on side streets.

If you look at a map of Albuquerque, you'll notice that it lies at the crossroads of I-25 north-south and I-40 east-west. Focus your attention on the southwest quadrant: Here, you'll find both downtown Albuquerque and Old Town, site of many tourist attractions. Lomas Boulevard and Central Avenue, the old Route 66 (US 66), flank downtown on the north and south. They come together 2 miles west of downtown near Old Town Plaza, the historical and spiritual heart of the city. Lomas and Central continue east across I-25, staying about half a mile apart as they pass by the University of New Mexico and the New Mexico State Fairgrounds. The airport is directly south of the UNM campus, about 3 miles via Yale Boulevard. Kirtland Air Force Base—site of Sandia National Laboratories—is an equal distance south of the fairgrounds, on Louisiana Boulevard.

Roughly paralleling I-40 to the north is Menaul Boulevard, the focus of midtown and uptown shopping, as well as the hotel districts. As Albuquerque pushes northward, the Journal Center business park area, about 4½ miles north of the freeway interchange, is expanding. Near there is home to the Albuquerque International Balloon Fiesta and the new Balloon Museum. East of Eubank Boulevard lie the Sandia Foothills, where the alluvial plain slants a bit more steeply toward the mountains.

When looking for an address, it's helpful to know that Central Avenue divides the city into north and south, and the railroad tracks—which run just east of First Street downtown—are the east-west dividing line. Street names are followed by a directional: NE, NW, SE, or SW.

MAPS   The most comprehensive Albuquerque street map is distributed by the Convention and Visitors Bureau, 20 First Plaza NW (℃ **800/284-2282** or 505/842-9918).

2 Getting Around

Albuquerque is easy to get around, thanks to its wide thoroughfares, grid layout, and efficient transportation systems.

BY PUBLIC TRANSPORTATION   ABQ Ride (© 505/243-7433) cloaks the arterials with its city bus network. Call for information on routes and fares.

BY TAXI   Yellow Cab (© 505/247-8888) serves the city and surrounding area 24 hours a day.

BY CAR   The Yellow Pages list more than 30 car-rental agencies in Albuquerque. Among them are the following well-known national firms: **Alamo**, 3400 University Blvd. SE (© 505/842-4057; www.alamo.com); **Avis**, at the airport (© 505/842-4080; www.avis.com); **Budget**, at the airport (© 505/247-3443; www.budget.com); **Dollar**, at the airport (© 505/842-4224; www.dollar.com); **Hertz**, at the airport (© 505/842-4235; www.hertz.com); **Rent-A-Wreck**, 500 Yale Blvd. SE (© 505/232-7552; www.rentawreck.com/nm.htm); and **Thrifty**, 2039 Yale Blvd. SE (© 505/842-8733; www.thrifty.com). Those not located at the airport itself are close by and can provide rapid airport pickup and delivery service.

Parking is generally not difficult in Albuquerque. Meters operate weekdays 8am to 6pm and are not monitored at other times. Only the large downtown hotels charge for parking. Traffic is a problem only during rush hours. Avoid I-25 and I-40 at the center of town around 8am and 5pm.

FAST FACTS

Call the **Greater Albuquerque Medical Association**, at © 505/821-4583, for information. The major hospital facilities are **Presbyterian Hospital**, 1100 Central Ave. SE (© 505/841-1234, or 505/841-1111 for emergency services); and **University of New Mexico Hospital**, 2211 Lomas Blvd. NE (© 505/272-2111, or 505/272-2411 for emergency services).

In Albuquerque, the sales tax is 6.75%. An additional hotel tax of 6% will be added to your bill.

See also "Fast Facts: The American Southwest," in chapter 2.

3 Where to Stay

Albuquerque's hotel glut is good news for travelers looking for quality rooms at a reasonable cost. Except during peak periods—specifically, the New Mexico Arts and Crafts Fair (late June), the New Mexico State Fair (Sept), and the Albuquerque International Balloon Fiesta (early Oct)—most of the city's hotels have vacant rooms, so guests can frequently request and get lower room rates than the ones posted.

A tax of nearly 12.75% is added to every hotel bill. All hotels and bed-and-breakfasts listed offer rooms for nonsmokers and travelers with disabilities.

DOWNTOWN/OLD TOWN

This area is the best location to stay if you want to be close to many of the major sights and attractions.

Hotel Albuquerque at Old Town 🖈🖈   This completely renovated hotel just 5 minutes from Old Town offers artfully decorated rooms with views and excellent service. No Albuquerque hotel is closer to top tourist attractions than the Hotel Albuquerque. Constructed in 1975, it existed for years under the Sheraton banner. Now a Heritage Hotel, it has received a $16-million makeover. The cathedral-style lobby has Spanish-colonial furnishings and art, a theme that carries into the guest rooms. They're medium size, with comfortable beds and medium-size bathrooms with outer vanities. Request a southside room, and you'll get a balcony with a view over Old Town. A northside room has mountain views but no balconies (this is the side to request during the Balloon Fiesta). The lovely grounds have a long portal and a quaint chapel. The Q Bar is one of Albuquerque's chicest nightspots, with a good tapas menu and billiards.

800 Rio Grande Blvd. NW, Albuquerque, NM 87104. © 800/237-2133 reservations only, or 505/843-6300. Fax 505/842-8426. www.hotelabq.com. 188 units. $99–$209 double; $149–$350 junior suite double. Children stay free in parent's room. AE, DC, DISC, MC, V. Free parking. **Amenities:** 2 restaurants; lounge; outdoor pool open in summer; Jacuzzi; concierge; business center; limited room service; laundry service; same-day dry cleaning; executive-level rooms. *In room:* A/C, TV w/pay movies, coffeemaker, hair dryer, iron, Wi-Fi.

NEAR THE AIRPORT

Courtyard by Marriott ✯ This is one of Albuquerque's best airport-area hotels. Opened in 1990, the four-story member of the Marriott family is built around an attractively landscaped courtyard. Families appreciate the security system—access is only by key card between 11pm and 6am—though most of the hotel's clients are business travelers. The units are roomy and comfortable, with walnut furniture and firm beds. Ask for a balcony room on the courtyard.

1920 Yale Blvd. SE, Albuquerque, NM 87106. © 800/321-2211 or 505/843-6600. Fax 505/843-8740. www. marriott.com. 150 units. $139 double weekdays, $89–$99 weekends. AE, DC, DISC, MC, V. Free parking. **Amenities:** Restaurant; lounge; indoor pool; exercise room; Jacuzzi; laundry service; coin-op laundry. *In room:* A/C, TV, coffeemaker, hair dryer, iron, high-speed Internet.

JOURNAL CENTER/NORTH CITY

North of Montgomery Boulevard, the focal point is the I-25 interchange with Osuna Road and San Mateo Boulevard. On the west side of the freeway, the giant pyramid of the Crowne Plaza dominates the Journal Center business park. East of the freeway, at San Mateo and Academy boulevards, numerous hotels, restaurants, and shopping complexes dominate. This is the closest area to the Balloon Fiesta launch site.

Albuquerque Marriott Pyramid North ✯ About a 15-minute drive from Old Town and downtown, this Aztec pyramid–shaped structure provides well-appointed rooms in an interesting environment. The 10 guest floors are grouped around a hollow skylit atrium. Vines drape from planter boxes on the balconies, and water falls five stories to a pool between the two glass elevators. The rooms are spacious, though not extraordinary, all with picture windows and ample views. The third stage of a $10-million renovation was completed in 2005. Because the hotel contains lots of convention space, you're likely to encounter name-tagged conventioneers here. Overall, the service seems to be good enough to handle the crowds, but there are only two elevators, so guests often must wait.

5151 San Francisco Rd. NE, Albuquerque, NM 87109. © 800/262-2043 or 505/821-3333. Fax 505/822-8115. www.marriott.com/abqmc. 310 units. $159–$184 double; $169–$275 suite. Ask about special weekend and package rates. AE, DC, DISC, MC, V. Free parking. **Amenities:** Restaurant; lounge; indoor/outdoor pool; medium-size health club; Jacuzzi; concierge; business center; room service; laundry service, Wi-Fi. *In room:* A/C, TV, coffeemaker, hair dryer, iron, high-speed Internet.

La Quinta Inn La Quinta offers reliable, clean rooms at a decent price. Rooms are tastefully decorated, fairly spacious, and comfortable, each with a table and chairs and a shower-only bathroom big enough to move around in. Each king room has a recliner, and two-room suites are available. If you're headed to the Balloon Fiesta, this is a good choice because it's not far from the launch site, though you'll have to reserve as much as a year in advance.

Central Albuquerque Accommodations & Dining

ACCOMMODATIONS ■
Albuquerque Central KOA **13**
Albuquerque Marriott Pyramid North **4**
Albuquerque North Bernalillo KOA **1**
Böttger Mansion of Old Town **7**
Courtyard by Marriott **9**
Hotel Albuquerque at Old Town **6**
Hyatt Regency Tamaya Resort and Spa **1**
La Quinta Inn **3**

DINING ◆
Artichoke Cafe **8**
Flying Star Cafe **10**
La Crêpe Michel **7**
Range Café **2**
Sadie's **5**
Seasons Grill **7**
Scalo **12**
Zinc Wine Bar and Bistro **11**

There's another La Quinta near the airport (La Quinta Airport Inn, 2116 Yale Blvd. SE); you can make reservations for either branch at the toll-free number.

5241 San Antonio Dr. NE, Albuquerque, NM 87109. ☎ 800/531-5900 or 505/821-9000. Fax 505/821-2399. www.lq.com. 130 units. $70–$76 double (higher during Balloon Fiesta). Children stay free in parent's room. AE, DC, DISC, MC, V. Free parking. Pets welcome. Amenities: Heated outdoor pool open May–Oct. In room: A/C, TV, dataport, coffeemaker, hair dryer, iron, Wi-Fi.

A BED-&-BREAKFAST IN OLD TOWN

The Böttger Mansion of Old Town 🌴🌴   Decorated with antiques but not overdone with chintz, this Victorian inn situated right in Old Town is an excellent choice. It offers a sweet taste of a past era. Our favorite room is the Carole Rose, with a canopy bed and lots of sun; also lovely is the Rebecca Leah, with pink marble tile and a Jacuzzi tub. All rooms are medium size and have excellent beds; most have small bathrooms. The rooms facing south let in the most sun but pick up a bit of street noise from nearby Central Avenue and a nearby elementary school (both quiet down at night). Breakfast (such as green chile quiche) is elaborate enough to keep you going through the day, at the end of which you can enjoy treats from the guest snack bar (try the chocolate cookies with a little chile in them). During warm months, the patio is lovely.

110 San Felipe NW, Albuquerque, NM 87104. ☎ 800/758-3639 or 505/243-3639. www.bottger.com. 8 units. $110–$169 double. Rates include full breakfast and snack bar. AE, DISC, MC, V. In room: A/C, TV/VCR, hair dryer, Wi-Fi.

NEAR ALBUQUERQUE

Hyatt Regency Tamaya Resort and Spa 🌴🌴🌴   This is the spot for a get-away-from-it-all luxury vacation. Set in the hills above the lush Rio Grande Valley on the Santa Ana Pueblo, this pueblo-style resort offers a 16,000-square-foot full-service spa and fitness center, an 18-hole Twin Warriors Championship Golf Course designed by Gary Panks, and views of the Sandia Mountains. Rooms are spacious, with large tile bathrooms. Request one that faces the mountains for one of the state's more spectacular vistas. Other rooms look out across a large courtyard, where the pools and hot tub are. Though the resort is surrounded by acres of quiet countryside, it's only 20 minutes from Albuquerque and 50 minutes from Santa Fe. The concierge offers trips to attractions daily, as well as on-site activities such as hot-air balloon rides, horseback rides, and nature/cultural walks or carriage rides by the river. Plan at least one dinner at the innovative Corn Maiden.

1300 Tuyuna Trail, Santa Ana Pueblo, NM 87004. ☎ 800/55-HYATT or 505/867-1234. www.tamaya.hyatt.com. 350 units. May–Oct $245–$415; Nov–Apr $199–$305, depending on the type of room. Suite rates available upon request. Inquire about spa, horseback riding, golf, and family packages. AE, DC, DISC, MC, V. Free parking. From I-25 take exit 242, following US 550 west to Tamaya Blvd.; drive 1½ miles to the resort. Amenities: 2 restaurants; 2 snack bars; lounge; 3 pools (heated year-round); golf course; 2 tennis courts; health club and spa; children's programs; concierge; tour desk; elaborate business center; room service; laundry service; basketball court. In room: A/C, TV, fridge, coffeemaker, hair dryer, iron, safe, Wi-Fi.

RV PARKS

Albuquerque Central KOA   This RV park in the foothills east of Albuquerque is a good choice for those who want to be close to town. It offers lots of amenities and convenient freeway access. Cabins are available.

12400 Skyline Rd. NE, Albuquerque, NM 87123. ☎ 800/562-7781 or 505/296-2729. www.koa.com. $20–$36 tent site; $35–$51 RV site, depending on hookup; $38–$55 1-room cabin; $48–$65 2-room cabin. All prices valid for up to 2 people. Additional adult $5, child $3. AE, DISC, MC, V. Free parking. Pets welcome. Amenities: Outdoor pool (summer only); Jacuzzi; bike rentals; store; coin-op laundry; bathhouse; miniature golf; playground; accessible restroom; Wi-Fi access throughout the park.

Albuquerque North Bernalillo KOA *(ᴿ)* More than 1,000 cottonwood and pine trees shade this park, and you'll see many flowers in the warm months. At the foot of the mountains, 14 miles from Albuquerque, this campground has plenty of amenities. Guests enjoy a free pancake breakfast daily. Reservations are recommended. Six camping cabins are also available.

555 Hill Rd., Bernalillo, NM 87004. *(℗)* **800/562-3616** or 505/867-5227. www.koa.com. $20–$23 tent site; $30–$36 RV site, depending on hookup; $38 1-bedroom cabin; $48 2-bedroom cabin. Rates include pancake breakfast and are valid for up to 2 people. Children 5 and under free with parent. Additional person $4. AE, DISC, MC, V. Free parking. Pets welcome. **Amenities:** Restaurant; outdoor pool (summer only); store; coin-op laundry; playground; free outdoor movies; Wi-Fi access throughout the park.

4 Where to Dine

For the locations of these restaurants, see the map "Central Albuquerque Accommodations & Dining," on p. 235.

OLD TOWN & VICINITY

La Crêpe Michel *(ᴿᴿ)* FRENCH Locals love this small cafe tucked away in a secluded walkway not far from the plaza, where the food is fun and imaginatively prepared. Run by chef Claudie Zamet-Wilcox from France, it has a cozy, informal European feel, with checked table coverings and simple furnishings. Service is friendly and calm, which makes this a good place for a romantic meal. You can't miss with any of the crepes. The *crêpe aux fruits de mer* (blend of sea scallops, bay scallops, and shrimp in a velouté sauce with mushrooms) is especially nice, as is the *crêpe à la volaille* (chunks of chicken in a cream sauce with mushrooms and Madeira wine). For a heartier meal, try one of the specials listed on the board on the wall, such as the beef filet (tenderloin finished with either black peppercorn–brandy cream sauce or Roquefort-brandy cream sauce) or the *saumon au poivre vert* (filet of salmon with green peppercorn–brandy sauce). Both are served with vegetables cooked just enough to leave them crisp and tasty. Don't leave without having a *crêpe aux fraises* (strawberry crepe) for dessert. To accompany your meal, choose from a carefully planned beer and wine menu.

400 San Felipe #C2. *(℗)* **505/242-1251.** Reservations recommended. Main courses $6–$24. MC, V. Tues–Sun 11:30am–2pm; Tues–Sat 6–9pm.

Sadie's *(ᴿ) (Kids)* NEW MEXICAN Many New Mexicans lament the lost days when this restaurant was in a bowling alley. It's true that you can no longer hear the pins fall, and the main dining room is a little too big and the atmosphere a little too bright, but something is still drawing crowds: It's the food—simply some of the best in New Mexico, with tasty sauces and large portions. We recommend the enchilada, either chicken or beef. The stuffed *sopaipilla* dinner is also delicious and is one of the signature dishes. All meals come with chips and salsa, beans, and *sopaipillas*. There's a full bar, with excellent margaritas (and TV screens for you sports lovers). A casual atmosphere where kids can be themselves makes this a nice spot for families.

6230 Fourth St. NW. *(℗)* **505/345-5339.** Reservations accepted for 8 or more. Main courses $7–$15. AE, DC, DISC, MC, V. Mon–Sat 11am–10pm; Sun 10am–9pm.

Seasons Grill *(ᴿᴿ)* AMERICAN Between sunshine-colored walls and under an arched ceiling, this restaurant serves sophisticated flavors just steps from Old Town.

It's a sweet oasis at midday and a romantic spot in the evening. The upstairs cantina bustles at sundown, with folks drinking margaritas. Service is excellent. At lunch you can't go wrong with the Angus burger with lemon aioli and roasted poblano chiles and served with herb fries. For the lighter eater, a number of salads head the menu. Dinner brings more sophisticated offerings. The grilled pork chop with goat cheese and roasted potatoes is tasty, as is the hoisin-glazed Atlantic salmon with jasmine rice. A full bar and an imaginative wine and beer list accompany the menu. On Saturday and Sunday evenings in summer, live jazz plays.

2031 Mountain Rd. NW. ⓒ 505/766-5100. Reservations recommended at dinner. Main courses lunch $7–$14, dinner $16–$40. AE, DC, DISC, MC, V. Mon–Fri 11:30am–2:30pm; daily 5–10:30pm; cantina daily 4pm–midnight.

DOWNTOWN

Artichoke Cafe ⓡⓡ CONTINENTAL   An art gallery as well as a restaurant, this popular spot has modern paintings and sculptures set against azure walls, a hint at the innovative dining experience offered here. Set in three rooms, with dim lighting, this is a nice, romantic place. The staff is friendly and efficient, though a little slow on busy nights. We've been impressed with the list of special drinks available: a variety of interesting waters that included our favorite, Ame, as well as ginger beer, Jamaican iced coffee, microbrews, and an excellent list of California and French wines. You might start with an artichoke, steamed with three dipping sauces, or have roasted garlic with Montrachet goat cheese. For lunch, there are a number of salads and gourmet sandwiches, as well as dishes such as garlic and lime prawns with orzo. Check out the fresh fish specials; our favorite is wahoo on glass noodles with miso broth. From the menu, try the pumpkin ravioli with butternut squash, spinach, and ricotta filling with hazelnut-sage butter sauce.

424 Central Ave. SE. ⓒ 505/243-0200. Reservations recommended. Main courses $7–$12 lunch, $13–$24 dinner. AE, DC, DISC, MC, V. Mon–Fri 11am–2:30pm; Mon 5:30–9pm; Tues–Sat 5:30–10pm; Sun 5–9pm.

UNIVERSITY & NOB HILL

Flying Star Cafe CAFE/BAKERY   The Flying Star Cafe makes good on its promise of uptown food with down-home ingredients. It's a hip urban restaurant with excellent contemporary international food. But be aware that during mealtime, the university location on Central Avenue gets packed and rowdy. The selections range from 16 different breakfast options to homemade soups and salads to sandwiches and pasta (and pizza at the Juan Tabo and Rio Grande locations). Try the Rancher's Melt (New Zealand sirloin sautéed with green chile, provolone, and horseradish on sourdough), or the Buddha's Bowl (sautéed vegetables in ginger sauce with tofu over jasmine rice). Flying Star also has locations at 4501 Juan Tabo Blvd. NE (ⓒ **505/275-8311**), 8001 Menaul Blvd. NE (ⓒ **505/293-6911**), and 4026 Rio Grande Blvd. NW (ⓒ **505/344-6714**). They don't serve alcohol, but they brew up plenty of espresso and cappuccino. Though hours vary for each location, they are all open daily for breakfast, lunch, and dinner.

3416 Central Ave. SE. ⓒ 505/255-6633. Reservations not accepted. All menu items under $10. AE, DISC, MC, V. Daily 6am–11:30pm.

Scalo ⓡ INTERNATIONAL/ITALIAN   This Italian restaurant is a local favorite, so it's usually crowded, a good indication of the food's quality. The place has a simple, bistro-style elegance, with white-linen-clothed tables indoors, plus outdoor tables in a covered, temperature-controlled patio. Service is decent. The kitchen, which makes its own pasta and breads, offers an international menu with meals in small, medium, and large portions. Seasonal menus focus on New Mexico–grown produce. One signature dish is a risotto-fried calamari with a spicy marinara sauce. A hearty main dish is the double-cut pork chop with champagne-roasted peaches, kale, and fried shallots. The daily specials are big hits. Dessert selections change daily. There's a good wine list, from which you can sample 30 wines by the glass; or you may order from the full bar.

3500 Central Ave. SE. © 505/255-8781. Reservations recommended. Lunch $6–$10; dinner $8–$29. AE, DC, DISC, MC, V. Mon–Thurs 11:30am–10pm; Fri 11:30am–11pm; Sat 5–11pm; Sun 5–10pm.

Zinc Wine Bar and Bistro 🌟🌟 NEW AMERICAN   In a moody, urban atmosphere with wood floors and a high ceiling, this "in" place serves imaginative food meticulously prepared. The bi-level dining room with well-spaced tables can get crowded and noisy at peak hours (especially under the balcony, so avoid sitting there then). Service is congenial but inconsistent. Businesspeople and others fill the seats here, dining on such treats as a blackened flank steak over a Greek salad at lunch (our favorite), or portobello-crusted Alaskan halibut with chorizo sausage polenta at dinner. The restaurant offers other inventive elements, such as "wine flights," in which diners may sample a variety of wines from a particular region for a set and fairly reasonable price. Or, you may simply opt for an excellent martini from the full bar. In the lower level, a lounge serves less formally in a wine-cellar atmosphere with live music playing 2 to 3 nights a week (Mon–Sat 5pm–1am; food served to midnight).

3009 Central Ave. NE. © 505/254-ZINC. Reservations recommended. Main courses $8–$14 lunch, $17–$26 dinner. AE, DC, DISC, MC, V. Mon–Fri 11am–2:30pm; Mon–Thurs 5–10pm; Fri–Sat 5–11pm

OUTSIDE ALBUQUERQUE

Range Cafe 🌟 *(kids* NEW MEXICAN/AMERICAN   This cafe on the main drag of Bernalillo, about 20 minutes north of Albuquerque, is a perfect place to stop on your way out of town. Housed in what was once an old drugstore, the restaurant has a pressed tin ceiling and is decorated with Western touches, such as cowboy boots and whimsical art. The food ranges from enchiladas and burritos to chicken-fried steak to more elegantly prepared meals. The proprietors and chef here have come from such notable restaurants as Scalo in Albuquerque (p. 238) and Prairie Star at Santa Ana Pueblo, so you can count on great food. For breakfast, try the pancakes or the breakfast burrito. For lunch or dinner, we recommend Tom's meatloaf, served with roasted-garlic mashed potatoes, mushroom gravy, and sautéed vegetables. For dinner, you might try pan-seared trout with sun-dried tomato and caper butter sauce. In the same locale, the Range has opened the Lizard Rodeo Lounge, a smoke-free, hoppin' place with Wild West decor that offers live music many nights a week. Two other branches of the restaurant in Albuquerque have similar food offerings (4200 Wyoming Blvd. NE, © 505/293-2633; and 2200 Menaul Blvd. NE, © 505/888-1660).

925 Camino del Pueblo (P.O. Box 1780), Bernalillo. © 505/867-1700. Reservations accepted for 8 or more. Breakfast and lunch $5–$10; dinner $9–$25. AE, DISC, MC, V. Sun–Thurs 7:30am–9:30pm, Fri–Sat to 10pm (open a half-hour later in summer). Closed Thanksgiving and Christmas.

5 What to See & Do

Albuquerque's original town site, known today as Old Town, is the central point of interest for visitors. Here, grouped around the plaza, are the venerable Church of San Felipe de Neri and numerous restaurants, art galleries, and crafts shops. Several important museums are close by. Within a few blocks is the Albuquerque Biological Park (near Central Ave. and Tingley Dr. NW).

But don't get stuck in Old Town. Elsewhere you will find the Sandia Peak Tramway, the Petroglyphs National Monument, and a number of natural attractions. Within day-trip range are several pueblos and a trio of significant monuments (see "Touring the Jemez Mountain Trail," later in this chapter).

THE TOP ATTRACTIONS

Albuquerque Museum of Art and History ✸ *Kids*   Take an interesting journey down into the caverns of New Mexico's past in this museum on the outskirts of Old Town. Drawing on the largest U.S. collection of Spanish colonial artifacts, displays here include Don Quixote–style helmets, swords, and horse armor. You can wander through an 18th-century house compound with adobe floor and walls, and see gear used by *vaqueros,* the original cowboys who came to the area in the 16th century. A weaving exhibition allows kids to try spinning wool, and a trapping section provides them with pelts to touch. In an old-style theater, two films on Albuquerque history are shown. In the History Hopscotch area, kids can explore an old trunk or play with antique blocks and other toys. An Old Town walking tour originates here at 11am Tuesday to Sunday during spring, summer, and fall. The upper floors house permanent art collections and, best of all, a huge exhibit space (recently expanded), where you'll find some extraordinary shows. A gift shop sells books and jewelry and has a nice selection of Navajo dolls. Plan to spend 1 to 2 hours.

2000 Mountain Rd. NW. ℭ 505/243-7255. www.albuquerquemuseum.com. Admission $4 adults, $2 seniors 65 and older and $1 children 4–12. Tues–Sun 9am–5pm. Closed major holidays.

Balloon Museum ✸✸ *Kids*   With the Albuquerque International Balloon Fiesta drawing hundreds of brilliantly colored and imaginatively shaped balloons to the city each October (p. 26), this museum's time has come. It tells the history of ballooning, from the first flight in France in 1783, with a rooster, sheep, and duck as passengers, to the use of balloons in military, science, and aerospace research. Most poignant are displays of Albuquerque balloonists Maxie Anderson and Ben Abruzzo, who, with Larry Newman, completed the first manned crossing of the Atlantic Ocean in 1978. Originals and replicas of various historic crafts dot the three-story-tall space, and windows look out at the Sandia Mountains and Rio Grande Valley. Kids will enjoy the flight simulator, which tests their ability to fly and land a balloon on target. Plan on spending at least an hour here.

9201 Balloon Museum Dr. NE. ℭ **505/768-6020.** www.balloonmuseum.com. Admission $4 adults, $2 seniors 65 and older, $1 children 4–12, free for children 3 and under. Tues–Sun 9am–5pm.

Indian Pueblo Cultural Center ✸ *Kids*   Owned and operated as a nonprofit organization by the 19 pueblos of New Mexico, this is a fine place to begin an exploration of Native American culture. About a mile northeast of Old Town, this museum—modeled after Pueblo Bonito, a spectacular 9th-century ruin in Chaco Culture National Historic Park—consists of several parts.

You'll want to spend 1 to 2 hours here. Begin in the basement, where a permanent exhibit depicts the **evolution of the various pueblos** from prehistory to present, including displays of the distinctive handicrafts of each community. Note especially how pottery differs in concept and design from pueblo to pueblo. The **Pueblo House Children's Museum,** in a separate building, is a hands-on experience that gives children the opportunity to learn about and understand the evolution of Pueblo culture. There they can touch pot shards, play with *heishi* (shell) drills, and even don fox tails and dance.

Central Albuquerque Attractions

Albuquerque Biological Park: Aquarium and Botanic Garden **5**

Albuquerque Museum of Art and History **7**

American International Rattlesnake Museum **6**

Balloon Museum **2**

iExploral Science Center and Children's Museum **7**

Indian Pueblo Cultural Center **4**

National Hispanic Cultural Center **9**

New Mexico Museum of Natural History and Science **7**

Petroglyph National Monument **3**

Rio Grande Zoo **8**

Sandia Peak Tramway **1**

Upstairs in the main building is an enormous (10,000-sq.-ft.) **gift shop** featuring fine pottery, rugs, sand paintings, kachinas, drums, and jewelry, among other things. Southwestern clothing and souvenirs are also available. Prices here are quite reasonable. Every weekend throughout the year, **Native American dancers** perform at 11am and 2pm in an outdoor arena surrounded by original murals. Often, artisans demonstrate their crafts there as well. During certain weeks of the year, such as the Balloon Fiesta, dances are performed daily.

A restaurant serves traditional Native American foods. It's a good place for some Indian fry bread and a bowl of *posole*.

2401 12th St. NW. © 800/766-4405 or 505/843-7270. www.indianpueblo.org. Admission $6 adults, $5 seniors, $3 students, free for children 4 and under. AE, DISC, MC, V. Daily 9am–5:30pm; restaurant 8am–3pm. Closed New Year's Day, Memorial Day, July 4th, Labor Day, Thanksgiving, and Christmas.

National Hispanic Cultural Center ⏣   In the historic Barelas neighborhood on the Camino Real, this gem of Albuquerque museums offers a rich cultural journey through hundreds of years of history and across the globe. It explores Hispanic arts and lifeways with visual arts, drama, music, dance, and other programs. We most enjoyed the 11,000-square-foot gallery space, which exhibits exciting contemporary and traditional works. Look for photographs by Miguel Gandert. A restaurant offers New Mexican and American food. It's a good spot to sample authentic regional dishes such as tacos and enchiladas, either from a buffet or by ordering from the menu. Our favorite is the tortilla burger (a burger served in a flour tortilla, with all the fixin's). Plans are to incorporate a cultural cooking component into the center, which would allow visitors to sample Hispanic foods from all over the world. Plan to spend 1 to 2 hours here.

1701 Fourth St. SW (corner of Fourth St. and Avenida César Chávez). © 505/246-2261. Fax 505/246-2613. www.nhccnm.org. Admission Tues–Sat $3 adults, $2 seniors 60 and over, free for children 16 and under; Sun $1 adults and seniors. AE, DISC, MC, V. Tues–Sun 10am–5pm; restaurant 8am–3pm. Closed New Year's Day, Easter, Memorial Day, Labor Day, and Christmas.

Old Town ⏣⏣   A maze of cobbled courtyard walkways leads to hidden patios and gardens, where many of Old Town's 150 galleries and shops are located. Adobe buildings, many refurbished in the pueblo-revival style of the 1950s, are grouped around the tree-shaded plaza, created in 1780. Pueblo and Navajo artisans often display their pottery, blankets, and silver jewelry on the sidewalks lining the plaza.

The buildings of Old Town once served as mercantile shops, grocery stores, and government offices, but the importance of Old Town as Albuquerque's commercial center declined after 1880, when the railroad came through 1¼ miles east of the plaza and businesses relocated to be closer to the trains. Old Town clung to its historical and sentimental roots, but the quarter fell into disrepair until the 1930s and 1940s, when artisans and other shop owners rediscovered it and the tourism industry burgeoned.

When Albuquerque was established in 1706, the first building erected by the settlers was the **Church of San Felipe de Neri,** which faces the plaza on its north side. It's a cozy church with wonderful stained-glass windows and vivid *retablos* (religious paintings). This house of worship has been in almost continuous use for nearly 300 years.

Though you'll wade through a few trinket and T-shirt shops on the plaza, don't be fooled: Old Town is an excellent place to shop. Look for good buys from the Native Americans selling jewelry on the plaza, especially silver bracelets and strung turquoise. If you want to take something fun home and spend very little money, buy a dyed corn necklace. Your best bet when wandering around Old Town is to just peek into shops, but there are a few places you'll definitely want to spend time in. See "Shopping," later in this chapter, for a list of recommendations. An excellent Old Town historic walking tour originates at the Albuquerque Museum of Art and History (above) at 11am Tuesday to Sunday during spring, summer, and fall. Plan to spend 2 to 3 hours strolling around.

Northeast of Central Ave. and Rio Grande Blvd. NW. Old Town Visitor Center: 303 Romero St. NW, Albuquerque, NM 87104 (across the street from the Church of San Felipe de Neri). (C) 505/243-3215. Visitor center daily 9am–5pm summer; daily 9:30am–4:30pm rest of the year.

Petroglyph National Monument *Kids* These lava flows were once a hunting and gathering area for prehistoric Native Americans, who left a chronicle of their beliefs etched on the dark basalt boulders. Some 25,000 petroglyphs provide a nice outdoor adventure after a morning in a museum. You'll want to stop at the visitor center to get a map, check out the interactive computer, and, in summer, hook up with a ranger-led tour. From there, you can drive north to the Boca Negra area, where you'll have a choice of three trails. Take the Mesa Point Trail (30 min.) that climbs quickly up the side of a hill, offering many petroglyph sightings as well as an outstanding view of the Sandia Mountains. If you're traveling with your dog, you can bring it along on the Rinconada Trail. Hikers can have fun searching the rocks for more petroglyphs; there are many yet to be found. This trail (a few miles south of the visitor center) runs for miles around a huge *rincón* (corner) at the base of the lava flow. Camping is not permitted in the park; it's strictly for day use, with picnic areas, drinking water, and restrooms provided.

6001 Unser Blvd. NW (3 miles north of I-40 at Unser and Western Trail). (C) 505/899-0205. Fax 505/899-0207. www.nps.gov/petr. Admission $1 per vehicle weekdays, $2 weekends. DISC, MC, V. Visitor center and Boca Negra area daily 8am–5pm. Closed New Year's Day, Thanksgiving, and Christmas.

Sandia Peak Tramway *Kids* This fun and exciting half-day or evening outing allows incredible views of the Albuquerque landscape and wildlife. The Sandia Peak Tram is a "jigback"; in other words, as one car approaches the top, the other nears the bottom. The two pass halfway through the trip, in the midst of a 1½-mile "clear span" of unsupported cable between the second tower and the upper terminal.

Several hiking trails are available on Sandia Peak, and one of them—La Luz Trail—takes you on a steep and rigorous trek from the base to the summit. The views in all directions are extraordinary. *Note:* The trails on Sandia may not be suitable for

Cooking School

If you've fallen in love with New Mexican and Southwestern cooking during your stay (or if you did even before you arrived), you might like to sign up for cooking classes with Jane Butel, a leading Southwest cooking authority, author of 18 cookbooks, and host of the national TV show *Jane Butel's Southwestern Kitchen*. At **Jane Butel Cooking School**, 2655 Pan American NE, Suite F ((C) **800/473-8226** or 505/243-2622; fax 505/243-8296; www.jane butel.com or www.pecosvalley.com), you'll learn the history and techniques of Southwestern cuisine and have ample opportunity for hands-on preparation.

children. There's a decent restaurant at Sandia's summit. Special tram rates apply with dinner reservations. Note that the tram does not operate on very windy days.

10 Tramway Loop NE. ⓒ **505/856-7325.** Fax 505/856-6335. www.sandiapeak.com. Admission $15 adults, $13 seniors, $10 children 5–12, free for children under 5. Memorial Day to Labor Day daily 9am–9pm; spring and fall Thurs–Tues 9am–8pm, Wed 5–8pm; ski season Thurs–Tues 9am–8pm, Wed noon–8pm. Closed 2 weeks each spring and fall for maintenance; check the website for details. Parking $1 daily. AE, DISC, MC, V. To reach the base of the tram, take I-25 north to Tramway Rd. (exit 234), then proceed east about 5 miles on Tramway Rd. (NM 556); or take Tramway Blvd., exit 167 (NM 556), north of I-40 approximately 8½ miles.

6 Especially for Kids

Albuquerque Biological Park: Aquarium and Botanic Garden 🌟 *Kids*   For those of us born and raised in the desert, this attraction quenches years of soul thirst. The self-guided aquarium tour begins with a beautifully produced 9-minute film that describes the course of the Rio Grande from its origin to the Gulf Coast. Then you move on to the touch pool, where at certain times of day you can gently touch hermit crabs and starfish. Next are the eel tank, an arched aquarium you get to walk through, and a colorful coral-reef exhibit, as well as the culminating show, in a 285,000-gallon shark tank.

In a state-of-the-art, 10,000-square-foot conservatory, you'll find the botanical garden, split into two sections. The smaller one houses the desert collection and features plants from the lower Chihuahuan and Sonoran deserts, including unique species from Baja California. The larger pavilion exhibits the Mediterranean collection and includes many exotic species native to the Mediterranean climates of southern California, South Africa, Australia, and the Mediterranean Basin. Allow at least 2 hours to see both parks. There is a restaurant on the premises. May to September, the new PNM Butterfly Pavilion fills with the colors of several hundred North American butterflies.

In December, you can see the River of Lights holiday light display Tuesday through Sunday; and June through August you can attend Thursday evening concerts.

2601 Central Ave. NW. ⓒ **505/764-6200.** www.cabq.gov/biopark. Admission $7 adults ($12 with Rio Grande Zoo admission), $3 seniors 65 and over and children 12 and under ($5 with Rio Grande Zoo admission). Ticket sales stop a half-hour before closing. MC, V. Tues–Sun 9am–5pm (June–Aug Sat–Sun until 6pm) Closed New Year's Day, Thanksgiving, and Christmas.

American International Rattlesnake Museum *Finds* *Kids*   This unique museum, just off Old Town Plaza, has living specimens of common, uncommon, and very rare rattlesnakes of North, Central, and South America in naturally landscaped habitats. Oddities such as albino and patternless rattlesnakes are included, as is a display popular with youngsters: baby rattlesnakes. More than 30 species can be seen, followed by a 7-minute film on this contributor to the ecological balance of our hemisphere. Throughout the museum are rattlesnake artifacts from early American history, Native American culture, medicine, the arts, and advertising. You'll also find a gift shop that specializes in Native American jewelry, T-shirts, and other memorabilia related to the natural world and the Southwest, all with an emphasis on rattlesnakes.

202 San Felipe St. NW. ⓒ **505/242-6569.** www.rattlesnakes.com. Admission $3.50 adults, $3 seniors, $2.50 children. AE, DISC, MC, V. Mon–Sat 10am–6pm; Sun noon–5pm.

¡Explora! Science Center and Children's Museum 🌟 *Kids*   A center for lifelong learning, ¡Explora! houses more than 250 hands-on scientific exhibits for visitors of all ages, on topics as diverse as water, the Rio Grande, light and optics, biological perception, and energy. It features exhibits utilizing technology that is creatively accessible to the public and exhibits that engage visitors in creating all kinds of art. You could spend an hour and a half to a full day here.

1701 Mountain Rd. NW. © 505/224-8300. Fax 505/224-8325. www.explora.mus.nm.us. Admission $7 adults ages 12–64, $5 seniors 65 and over and $3 children 1–11, free for children under 1. Mon–Sat 10am–6pm; Sun noon–6pm.

New Mexico Museum of Natural History and Science 🌟🌟 *(Kids)* This museum takes you through 12 billion years of natural history, from the formation of the universe to the present day. Begin by looking at a display of stones and gems, then stroll through the "Age of Giants" display, where you'll find dinosaur skeletons cast from the real bones. You can ride the Evolator (kids love this!), a simulated time-travel experience that moves and rumbles, taking you 1¼ miles up (or down) and through 38 million years of history. Be sure to check out the newest addition to the museum, the LodeStar Astronomy Center, a sophisticated planetarium with the Virtual Voyages Simulation theater. Those exhibits, as well as the DynaTheater, which surrounds you with images and sound, cost an additional fee. A gift shop on the ground floor sells imaginative nature games and other curios. This museum has good access for people with disabilities, including scripts for people with impaired hearing and exhibit text written in Braille. Plan to spend 1 to 2 hours here—more if you take in extra attractions.

1801 Mountain Rd. NW. © 505/841-2800. www.nmnaturalhistory.org. Admission $6 adults, $5 seniors, $3 children 3–12, free for children under 3. Extra charge (about $6 adults, $3 children) for DynaTheater, planetarium, and Virtual Voyages. Discounted ticket combinations available. Daily 9am–5pm. Jan and Sept closed Mon except major holidays; also closed Thanksgiving and Christmas.

Rio Grande Zoo 🌟 *(Kids)* More than 1,200 animals from 300 species live on 60 acres of riverside bosque among ancient cottonwoods. Open-moat exhibits with animals in naturalized habitats are a treat for zoo goers. Major exhibits include polar bears, giraffes, sea lions (with underwater viewing), the catwalk, the bird show, and ape country, with gorillas and orangutans. The zoo has an especially fine collection of elephants, mountain lions, koalas, reptiles, and native Southwestern species. A children's petting zoo is open during the summer. There are numerous snack bars on the zoo grounds, and La Ventana Gift Shop carries film and souvenirs. Also check out the seal and sea-lion feeding at 10:30am and 3:30pm daily and the summer Zoo Music Concert Series.

903 10th St. SW. © 505/764-6200. www.cabq.gov/biopark/zoo. Admission $7 adults ($10 w/Aquarium and Botanic Garden admission), $3 seniors and children 3–12 ($5 w/Aquarium and Botanic Garden admission), free for children 2 and under. Daily 9am–5pm (6pm summer weekends). Closed New Year's Day, Thanksgiving, and Christmas.

7 Getting Outside
BALLOONING

Visitors have a choice of several hot-air balloon operators; rates start at about $150 per person per hour. Call **Rainbow Ryders,** 11520 San Bernardino NE (© **505/823-1111**), or **World Balloon Corporation,** 1103 La Poblana NW (© **505/293-6800**).

If you'd rather just watch, go to the annual **Albuquerque International Balloon Fiesta** 🌟🌟, which is held the first through second weekends of October (see "Calendar of Events," in chapter 2, for details).

BIKING

Albuquerque is a major bicycling hub in the summer, for both road racers and mountain bikers. For an excellent map of Albuquerque bicycle routes, call the **Albuquerque Parks & Recreation Department** (© 505/768-3550) or visit www.cabq.gov/recreation/bicycle.html. (You can also find links to many recreation opportunities for adults and kids at www.cabq.gov/recreation/index.html.) A great place to bike is **Sandia Peak** (© 505/242-9133; www.sandiapeak.com) in Cíbola National Forest. You can't take your bike on the tram, but chairlift no. 1 is available for up- or downhill transportation with a bike. Bike rentals are available at the top and bottom of the chairlift. They cost $40 for adult bikes, $30 for junior ones. The lift costs $16 and runs on Saturday and Sunday, with Friday added in July and August, though you'll want to call ahead to verify. Helmets are mandatory. Bike maps are available; the clearly marked trails range from easy to very difficult.

Down in the valley, the **bosque trail** runs along the Rio Grande, accessed through the Rio Grande Nature Center (see "Especially for Kids," above). To the east, the **Foothills Trail** runs along the base of the mountains. It's a fun 7-mile-long trail that offers excellent views. Access it by driving east from downtown on Montgomery Boulevard, past the intersection with Tramway Boulevard. Go left on Glenwood Hills Drive and head north about ½ mile before turning right onto a short road that leads to the Embudito trail head.

Northeast Cyclery, 8305 Menaul Blvd. NE (© 505/299-1210), rents bikes for $25 per day for front-suspension mountain bikes, $35 per day for road bikes. Multi-day discounts are available. Unfortunately, the shop doesn't rent children's bikes. Rentals come with helmets.

BIRD-WATCHING

Bosque del Apache National Wildlife Refuge 𝒜𝒜 (© 505/835-1828) is a haven for migratory waterfowl such as snow geese and cranes. It's 90 miles south of Albuquerque on I-25, and it's well worth the drive. See chapter 10 for more details. Closer to town, check out the **Rio Grande Nature Center State Park** (see "Especially for Kids," above).

FISHING

There are no real fishing opportunities in Albuquerque, but there is a nearby fishing area known as **Shady Lakes** (© 505/898-2568). Nestled among cottonwood trees, it's near I-25 on Albuquerque's north side. The most common catches are rainbow trout, black bass, bluegill, and channel catfish. To reach Shady Lakes, take I-25 north to the Tramway exit. Follow Tramway Road west for a mile and then go right on NM 313 for half a mile. **Sandia Lakes Recreational Area** (© 505/897-3971), also on NM 313, is another popular fishing spot. There is a bait-and-tackle shop there.

GOLF

There are quite a few public courses in the Albuquerque area. The **Championship Golf Course at the University of New Mexico,** 3601 University Blvd. SE (© 505/277-4546), is one of the best in the Southwest and was rated one of the country's top 25 public links by *Golf Digest*. **Paradise Hills Golf Course,** 10035 Country Club Lane NW (© 505/898-7001), is a popular 18-hole golf course on the west side of town.

Other Albuquerque courses to check with for tee times are **Ladera,** 3401 Ladera Dr. NW (© **505/836-4449**); **Los Altos,** 9717 Copper Ave. NE (© **505/298-1897**); **Puerto del Sol,** 1800 Girard Blvd. SE (© **505/265-5636**); and **Arroyo del Oso,** 7001 Osuna Rd. NE (© **505/884-7505**).

If you're willing to drive a short distance just outside Albuquerque, you can play at the **Santa Ana Golf Club at Santa Ana Pueblo,** 288 Prairie Star Rd., Bernalillo, NM 87004 (© **505/867-9464**), which the *New York Times* rated as one of the best public courses in the country. Club rentals are available (call for information). In addition, **Isleta Pueblo,** 4001 NM 47 (© **505/869-0950**), south of Albuquerque, has an 18-hole course.

HIKING

The 1.5-million-acre **Cíbola National Forest** offers ample hiking opportunities. The best hike in town is the **Embudito Trail,** which heads up into the foothills and has spectacular views down across Albuquerque. The 5.5-mile one-way hike is moderate to difficult. Allow 1 to 8 hours, depending on how far you want to go. Access it by driving east from downtown on Montgomery Boulevard past the intersection with Tramway Boulevard. Go left on Glenwood Hills Drive and head north about a half-mile before turning right onto a short road that leads to the trail head. The premier Sandia Mountain hike is **La Luz Trail,** a very strenuous journey from the Sandia foothills to the top of the Crest. It's a 15-mile round-trip jaunt, and it's half that if you take the Sandia Peak Tramway (see "The Top Attractions," earlier in this chapter) either up or down. Allow a full day for this hike. Access is off Tramway Boulevard and Forest Service Road 333. For more details contact **Sandia Ranger Station,** NM 337 south toward Tijeras (© **505/281-3304**).

HORSEBACK RIDING

If you want to get in a saddle and eat some trail dust, call the **Hyatt Regency Tamaya Resort and Spa,** 1300 Tuyuna Trail, Santa Ana Pueblo (© **505/771-6037**). The resort offers 2½-hour-long rides near the Rio Grande for $75 per person. Children must be over 7 years of age and over 4 feet tall. The resort is about 15 miles north of Albuquerque. From I-25, take exit 242, following US 550 west to Tamaya Boulevard, and drive 1½ miles to the resort.

SKIING

Sandia Peak Ski Area is a good place for family skiing. There are plenty of beginner and intermediate runs. (If you're looking for more challenge or more variety, you'd better head north to Santa Fe or Taos.) The ski area has twin base-to-summit chairlifts to its upper slopes at around 10,378 feet and a 1,700-foot vertical drop. There are 30 runs (35% beginner, 55% intermediate, 10% advanced) above the day lodge and ski-rental shop. Four chairs and two pomas accommodate 3,400 skiers an hour. All-day lift tickets are $43 for adults, $35 for teens ages 13 to 20, $32 for children ages 6 to 12 and seniors (ages 62–71), and free for children 46 inches tall or less in ski boots and seniors ages 72 and over; rental packages are available. The season runs mid-December to mid-March. Contact the ski area, 10 Tramway Loop NE (© **505/242-9133**), for more information, or call the hot line for ski conditions (© **505/857-8977**).

Cross-country skiers can enjoy the trails of the Sandia Wilderness from the ski area, or they can go an hour north to the remote Jemez Wilderness and its hot springs.

TENNIS

Albuquerque has 29 public parks with tennis courts. Because of the city's size, your best bet is to call the **Albuquerque Convention and Visitors Bureau** (© 800/ 284-2282) to find out which park is closest to your hotel.

8 Spectator Sports

BASEBALL

The **Albuquerque Isotopes** (© 505/924-2255; www.albuquerquebaseball.com) play 72 home games as part of the Pacific Coast League in their new stadium, Isotopes Park. Tickets range in price from $5 to $10. Isotopes Park is at 1601 Avenida César Chávez SE. Take I-25 south of town to Avenida César Chávez and go east; the stadium is at the intersection with University Boulevard.

BASKETBALL

The University of New Mexico team, **The Lobos,** plays an average of 16 home games from late November to early March. Capacity crowds cheer the team at the 17,121-seat University Arena (fondly called "The Pit") at University and Stadium boulevards. For tickets and information, call © 505/925-LOBO (www.golobos.com).

FOOTBALL

The **UNM Lobos** football team plays from September to November, usually with five home games, at the 30,000-seat University of New Mexico Stadium, opposite both Albuquerque Sports Stadium and University Arena at University and Stadium boulevards. For tickets and information call © 505/925-LOBO (www.golobos.com).

HOCKEY

The **New Mexico Scorpions** play in the Western Professional Hockey League. Their home is at the **Rio Rancho Events Center,** Rio Rancho (© 505/881-7825; www.scorpionshockey.com).

9 Shopping

Visitors seeking regional specialties will find many **local artists** and **galleries** of interest in Albuquerque, although not as many as in Santa Fe and Taos. The galleries and regional fashion designers around the plaza in Old Town comprise a kind of a shopping center for travelers, with more than 40 merchants represented. The Sandia Pueblo runs its own **crafts market** at the reservation, off I-25 at Tramway Road, just beyond Albuquerque's northern city limits.

Albuquerque has three of the largest **shopping malls** in New Mexico, two within 2 blocks of each other on Louisiana Boulevard just north of I-40—Coronado Center and Winrock Center. The other is the Cottonwood Mall on the west mesa, at 10000 Coors Blvd. NW (© 505/899-SHOP).

Business hours vary, but shops are generally open Monday to Saturday 10am to 6pm; many have extended hours; some have reduced hours; and a few, especially in shopping malls or during the high tourist season, are open on Sunday.

In Albuquerque the sales tax is 6.75%.

BEST BUYS

The best buys in Albuquerque are Southwestern regional items, including **arts and crafts** of all kinds—traditional Native American and Hispanic as well as contemporary

Desert Shopping

While cruising the remote desert lands between Albuquerque and Santa Fe, you may want to stop in at **Traditions! A Festival Marketplace,** on I-25, exit 257 (𝄐 **505/867-9700**). The open-air mall offers shoppers the chance to sample many forms of New Mexico culture, from art to jewelry to food to entertainment. It's open 10am to 5pm; closed Tuesday and Wednesday.

works. In local Native American art, look for silver and turquoise jewelry, pottery, weavings, baskets, sand paintings, and Hopi kachina dolls. Hispanic folk art—handcrafted furniture, tinwork and *retablos,* and religious paintings—is worth seeking out. The best contemporary art is in paintings, sculpture, jewelry, ceramics, and fiber art, including weaving.

Other items of potential interest are Southwestern fashions, gourmet foods, and unique local Native American and Hispanic creations.

By far, the most **galleries** are in Old Town; others are spread around the city, with smaller groupings in the university district and the northeast heights.

ARTS & CRAFTS

Amapola Gallery 𝄐   Fifty artists and craftspeople show their talents at this lovely cooperative gallery off a cobbled courtyard. You'll find pottery, paintings, textiles, carvings, baskets, jewelry, and other items. 205 Romero St. 𝄐 **505/242-4311.**

Bien Mur Indian Market Center 𝄐   Sandia Pueblo's crafts market, on the reservation, sells turquoise and silver jewelry, pottery, baskets, kachina dolls, hand-woven rugs, sand paintings, and other arts and crafts. The market is open Monday through Saturday from 9am to 5:30pm and Sunday from 11am to 5pm. I-25 at Tramway Rd. NE. 𝄐 **800/365-5400** or **505/821-5400.**

Dartmouth Street Gallery 𝄐   This gallery features vapor mirage works of Larry Bell, tapestries by Nancy Kozikowski, and a variety of work by 40 other contemporary artists, most from New Mexico. 3011 Monte Vista NE. 𝄐 **800/474-7751** or **505/266-7751.** www.dsg-art.com.

Gallery One   This gallery features folk art, jewelry, contemporary crafts, cards and paper, and natural-fiber clothing. In the Nob Hill Shopping Center, 3500 Central Ave. SE. 𝄐 **505/268-7449.**

La Piñata   This shop features—what else?—piñatas, in shapes from dinosaurs to parrots to pigs, as well as paper flowers, puppets, toys, and crushable bolero hats decorated with ribbons. 2 Patio Market (Old Town). 𝄐 **505/242-2400.**

Mariposa Gallery 𝄐𝄐 (Value)   Eclectic contemporary art, jewelry, blown glass, and sculpture fill this Nob Hill shop, with prices that even a travel writer can afford. In the Nob Hill Shopping Center, 3500 Central Ave. SE. 𝄐 **505/268-6828.**

Ortega's Indian Arts and Crafts   An institution in Gallup, adjacent to the Navajo Reservation, Ortega's now has this Albuquerque store. It sells, repairs, and appraises silver and turquoise jewelry. 6600 Menaul Blvd. NE, no. 359. 𝄐 **505/881-1231.**

The Pueblo Loft (at Gallery One)   Owner Kitty Trask takes pride in the fact that all items featured at The Pueblo Loft are crafted by Native Americans. For almost 15 years, her slogan has been, "Every purchase is an American Indian work of art." In the Nob Hill Shopping Center, 3500 Central Ave. SE. 𝄐 **505/268-8764.**

R. C. Gorman Nizhoni Gallery Old Town ✸   The painting and sculpture of the late Navajo artist Gorman, who was a resident of Taos, are shown here. Most works are available in limited-edition lithographs. 323 Romero NW, Suite 1. ℂ 505/843-7666.

Skip Maisel's ⦿Value   If you want a real bargain in Native American arts and crafts, this is the place to shop. You'll find a broad range of quality and price here in goods such as pottery, weavings, and kachinas. *Take note:* Adorning the outside of the store are murals painted in 1933 by notable Navajo painter Harrison Begay and Pueblo painter Pablita Velarde. 510 Central Ave. SW. ℂ 505/242-6526.

Tanner Chaney Galleries ✸   In business since 1875, this gallery has fine jewelry, pottery, rugs, and more. 323 Romero NW, No. 4 (Old Town). ℂ 800/444-2242 or 505/247-2242.

Wright's Collection of Indian Art   This gallery, opened in 1907, features a free private museum and carries fine handmade Native American arts and crafts, both contemporary and traditional. 1100 San Mateo Blvd. NE. ℂ 505/266-0120.

BOOKS

Barnes & Noble   On the west side, just north of Cottonwood Mall, this huge bookstore offers plenty of browsing room and a Starbucks Cafe for lounging. The store is known for its large children's section and weekly story-time readings. 3701 Ellison Dr. NW #A. ℂ 505/792-4234. Or at the Coronado Center, 6600 Menaul Blvd. NE. ℂ 505/883-8200.

Bookworks ✸   This store stocks both new and used books and has one of the most complete Southwestern nonfiction and fiction sections in the region. A good place to linger, the store has a coffee bar and a stage area for readings. It also carries CDs, cassettes, and books on tape. 4022 Rio Grande Blvd. NW. ℂ 505/344-8139.

Borders   This branch of the popular chain provides a broad range of books, music, and videos, and hosts in-store appearances by authors, musicians, and artists. Winrock Center, 2100 Louisiana Blvd. NE. ℂ 505/884-7711.

FOOD

The Candy Lady   Having made chocolate for over 20 years, the Candy Lady is especially known for 21 varieties of fudge, including jalapeño flavor. 524 Romero NW (Old Town). ℂ 800/214-7731 or 505/243-6239.

La Mexicana   This is a great place to shop if you're a diehard fan of Mexican food. Many items at La Mexicana are imported directly from Mexico, and others, such as

---

A Taste of the Grape

In addition to everything else New Mexico has to offer, wineries are springing up all over the state. Wineries in Albuquerque or within a short driving distance of the city include **Anderson Valley Vineyards,** 4920 Rio Grande Blvd. NW, Albuquerque NM 87107 (ℂ 505/344-7266); **Sandia Shadows Vineyard and Winery,** 11704 Coronado NE, Albuquerque NM 87122 (ℂ 505/856-1006; www.nmwine.com/wineries/sandiashadows.htm); and **Gruet Winery,** 8400 Pan-American Hwy. NE, Albuquerque 87113 (ℂ 505/821-0055; www.gruetwinery.com). Call ahead for hours.

> ### *Moments* **All that Glitters Is on Gold**
>
> For years, downtown Albuquerque has been reinventing itself, and nowhere is the luster more brilliant than on Gold Avenue. A funky boutique street, it's the home of many unique shops and restaurants, well worth a morning or afternoon perusal. Look for "fine, fun, and funky" functional art at **Patrician Design,** 216 Gold Ave. SW (✆ **505/242-7646).** Nearby, you'll find kitschy shoes and clothing at **Ruby Shoesday,** 228 Gold Ave. SW (✆ **505/848-RUBY).** Down the street, step into **Ooh! Aah! Jewelry,** 311 Gold Ave. SW (✆ **505/242-7101),** to find a wide selection of contemporary jewelry and handbags. If you work up an appetite, head to **Gold Street Caffè,** 218 Gold Ave. SW (✆ **505/765-1633),** or for a creamy snack, try **Cold Stone Creamery,** 101 Gold Ave. SW (✆ **505/843-9456),** for a serious selection of ice cream flavors made in-house.

tortillas, tamales, and Mexican pastries, are made fresh daily. 423 Atlantic Ave. SW. ✆ 505/243-0391.

FURNITURE

Ernest Thompson Furniture *✿* Original-design, handcrafted furniture is exhibited in the factory showroom. Thompson is a fifth-generation furniture maker who still uses traditional production techniques. 4531 Osuna Rd. NE (1/4 block west of I-25 and 1/2 block north of Osuna Rd.). ✆ 800/568-2344 or 505/344-1994.

Strictly Southwestern You'll find nice, solid pine and oak Southwestern-style furniture here. Lighting, art, pottery, and other interior items are also available. 1321 Eubank Blvd. NE. ✆ 505/292-7337.

GIFTS/SOUVENIRS

Jackalope International *✿✿* Wandering through this vast shopping area is like an adventure in another land—to many lands, really. You'll find Mexican *trasteros* (armoires) next to Balinese puppets. The store sells sculpture, pottery, and Christmas ornaments as well. 834 US 550, Bernalillo. ✆ 505/867-9813.

MARKETS

Flea Market Every Saturday and Sunday, year-round, the fairgrounds host this market from 8am to 5pm. It's a great place to browse for turquoise and silver jewelry and locally made crafts, as well as newly manufactured, inexpensive goods such as socks and T-shirts. The place has the atmosphere of a fair. There's no admission charge. New Mexico State Fairgrounds. For information, call the Albuquerque Convention and Visitors Bureau, ✆ 800/284-2282.

SOUTHWESTERN APPAREL

Albuquerque Pendleton Cuddle up in a large selection of blankets and shawls, and haul them away in a handbag. 1100 San Mateo NE, Suites 2 and 4. ✆ 505/255-6444.

10 Albuquerque After Dark

Albuquerque has an active performing-arts and nightlife scene, as befits a city of half a million people. The performing arts are multicultural, with Hispanic and (to a lesser extent) Native American productions sharing stage space with Anglo works, including

The Major Concert & Performance Halls

Journal Pavilion, 5601 University Blvd. NE (© **505/452-5100**).

Keller Hall, University of New Mexico, Cornell Street at Redondo Drive South NE (© **505/277-4569**).

KiMo Theatre, 423 Central Ave. NW (© **505/768-3544**).

Popejoy Hall, University of New Mexico, Cornell Street at Redondo Drive South NE (© **505/277-3824**).

South Broadway Cultural Center, 1025 Broadway Blvd. SE (© **505/848-1320**).

theater, opera, symphony, and dance. Albuquerque also attracts many national touring companies. Nightclubs music varies, with rock, jazz, and country predominant.

Complete information on all major cultural events can be obtained from the **Albuquerque Convention and Visitors Bureau** (© **800/284-2282** for recorded information after 5pm). Current listings appear in the two daily newspapers; detailed weekend arts calendars can be found in the Thursday evening *Tribune* and the Friday morning *Journal.* The monthly *On the Scene* also carries entertainment listings.

Tickets for nearly all major entertainment and sporting events can be obtained from **Ticketmaster,** 4004 Carlisle Blvd. NE (© **505/883-7800**). Discount tickets are often available for midweek and matinee performances; check with individual theater or concert hall box offices.

THE PERFORMING ARTS
CLASSICAL MUSIC
New Mexico Symphony Orchestra ⊛   The NMSO first played in 1932 and remains a strong cultural force. The symphony performs classics and pops, as well as family and neighborhood concerts. Each season a few notable artists visit; recent guests include Yo Yo Ma and Guillermo and Ivonne Figueroa. We recommend going to one of the outdoor concerts at the band shell at the Rio Grande Zoo. 3301 Menaul Blvd. NE, Suite 4. © **800/251-6676** for tickets and information, or 505/881-9590. www.nmso.org. Ticket prices vary with concert; call for details.

DANCE
New Mexico Ballet Company   Founded in 1972, the state's oldest ballet company holds most of its performances at Popejoy Hall. Typically there's a fall production such as *Dracula,* a holiday one such as *The Nutcracker* or *A Christmas Carol,* and a contemporary spring production. 4200 Wyoming Blvd. NE, Suite B2 Albuquerque, NM 87154-1518. © **505/292-4245**. www.nmballet.org. Tickets $20–$25 adults, $10–$20 children 12 and under.

THEATER
Albuquerque Little Theatre   The Albuquerque Little Theatre has been offering a variety of productions ranging from comedies to dramas to musicals since 1930. Seven plays are presented here annually during an August-to-May season. Located across from Old Town, Albuquerque Little Theatre offers plenty of free parking. 224 San Pasquale Ave. SW. © **505/242-4750**. www.swcp.com/~alt. Tickets $18, $16 students, $13 seniors. Box office Mon–Fri noon–6pm.

La Compañía de Teatro de Albuquerque *(Finds* Productions given by the company can provide a focused view into New Mexico culture. One of the few major professional Hispanic companies in the United States and Puerto Rico, La Compañía stages a series of bilingual productions (most original New Mexican works) every year, late September to May. Comedies, dramas, and musicals are offered, along with an occasional Spanish-language play. Performances take place in the National Hispanic Cultural Center, the South Broadway Cultural Center (1025 Broadway Blvd. SE), and other venues regionally. P.O. Box 884. (C) 505/242-7929. Tickets $12 adults, $8 students ages 18 and above and seniors, $7 children under 18.

Musical Theatre Southwest From February to January, this theater presents six major Broadway musicals, in addition to several smaller productions, at either Popejoy Hall or the MTS's own 890-seat Hiland Theater. Most productions are staged for three consecutive weekends, including some Sunday matinees. 2401 Ross. SE. (C) 505/262-9301. www.musicaltheatresw.com. Tickets $15–$30 adults; $2 discount students and seniors.

Vortex Theatre (C) A 30-year-old community theater known for its innovative productions, the Vortex is Albuquerque's "Off-Broadway" theater, presenting a range of plays from classic to original. You'll see such plays as *One Flew Over the Cuckoo's Nest* and *Wait Until Dark* by Frederick Knott. Performances are Friday and Saturday at 8pm and on Sunday at 6pm. The black-box theater seats 90. 2004½ Central Ave. SE. (C) 505/247-8600. Tickets $10 adults, $8 students and seniors, $8 for everyone on Sun.

THE CLUB & MUSIC SCENE
COMEDY CLUBS/DINNER THEATER

Laffs Comedy Cafe This club offers top acts from each coast, including comedians who have appeared on *The Late Show with David Letterman* and HBO. Shows Wednesday through Sunday night. Call for times. San Mateo Blvd. and Osuna Rd., in the Fiesta del Norte Shopping Center. (C) 505/296-5653. www.laffscomedy.com. $8 per person, with a 2-drink/menu-item minimum purchase.

Mystery Cafe *(Finds* If you're in the mood for a little interactive dinner theater, the Mystery Cafe might be just the ticket. You'll help the characters in this ever-popular, delightfully funny show solve the mystery as they serve you a four-course meal. Reservations are a must. Performances Friday and Saturday at 7:30pm; doors open at 7pm. P.O. Box 11433. Performances held at Sheraton Uptown (at Menaul Blvd. and Louisiana Blvd.). (C) 505/237-1385. www.abqmystery.com. Approximately $39.

ROCK/JAZZ

Burt's Tiki Lounge This club won the weekly paper *Alibi's* award for best variety of drinks. Live music is Thursday to Sunday and there's no cover. 313 Gold Ave. (C) 505/243-BURT.

Kelly's BYOB Near the university, Kelly's is a local brewpub in a renovated autobody shop. The place has tasty pub fare, excellent brew specials, and live music Thursday to Saturday, usually with no cover. 3222 Central SE. (C) 505/262-2739.

Martini Grille (C) On the eastern side of the Nob Hill district, this is the place for young professionals, who lush out on more than 30 flavors of martinis within a seductive Batman-cave atmosphere. Live entertainment plays most weekends and some weeknights. 4200 Central SE. (C) 505/255-4111.

MORE ENTERTAINMENT

Albuquerque's best nighttime attraction is the **Sandia Peak Tramway** (see "What to See & Do," earlier in this chapter). You can enjoy a view nonpareil of the Rio Grande Valley and the city lights.

Many travelers like to include a little dice-throw and slot-machine play in their trip to New Mexico. Those who do are in luck, with the expansive **Sandia Casino,** north of I-25 and a quarter-mile east on Tramway Boulevard (© 800/526-9366; www. sandiacasino.com). The $80-million structure sits on Sandia Pueblo land and has outstanding views of the Sandia Mountains. Built in pueblo architectural style, the graceful casino has a 3,650-seat outdoor amphitheater, three restaurants (one, **Bien Shur,** has excellent food), a lounge, more than 1,350 slot and video poker machines, the largest poker room in the state, and blackjack, roulette, and craps tables. It's open from 8am to 4am Sunday to Wednesday and 24 hours Thursday to Saturday. The **Isleta Gaming Palace,** 11000 Broadway SE (© 800/460-5686 or 505/724-3800; www.isletacasinoresort.com), is a luxurious, air-conditioned casino (featuring blackjack, poker, slots, bingo, and keno) with a full-service restaurant, smoke-free section, and free bus transportation on request. It's open Monday to Thursday 8am to 4am, Friday to Sunday 24 hours a day.

11 Touring the Jemez Mountain Trail ⟨⋆

Ten Native American pueblos are within an hour's drive of central Albuquerque. One of them, Acoma, is discussed in chapter 9. If you'd like to combine a tour of the archaeological sites and inhabited pueblos, consider driving the **Jemez Mountain Trail.** Head north on Interstate 25 to Bernalillo, where you can visit the Coronado State Monument. Continue west on US 550 to Zia Pueblo. Six miles farther on US 550 you reach NM 4, where you'll turn north and drive through orchards and along narrow cornfields of Jemez Pueblo. Farther north on NM 4, you'll find another archaeological site, the Jemez State Monument. You'll also find Jemez Springs, where you can stop for a hot soak. The road continues to the Los Alamos area, where you can see the spectacular ruins at Bandelier National Monument. From there you have the option of returning the way you came or via Santa Fe.

ZIA PUEBLO

Zia Pueblo, 135 Capitol Square Dr., Zia Pueblo, NM, 87053 (© 505/867-3304), which has 720 inhabitants, blends in so perfectly with the soft tans of the stone and sand of the desertlike land around it that it's very hard to see—it's like a chameleon on a tree trunk. The pueblo is best known for its famous sun symbol—now the official symbol of the state of New Mexico—adapted from a pottery design showing three rays going in each of the four directions from a sun, or circle. It is hailed in the pledge to the state flag as "a symbol of perfect friendship among united cultures."

Zia has a reputation for excellence in pottery making. Its pottery is identified by its unglazed terra-cotta coloring, traditional geometric designs, and plant and animal motifs painted on a white slip. Paintings, weaving, and sculptures are also prized products of the artists of the Zia community. Their work can be viewed at the **Zia Cultural Center** located at the pueblo. Our Lady of the Assumption, the patron saint, is given a celebratory corn dance on her day, August 15.

The pueblo is about 17 miles northwest of Bernalillo, just off US 550. It's open to visitors daily during daylight hours, and admission is free. Photography is not permitted.

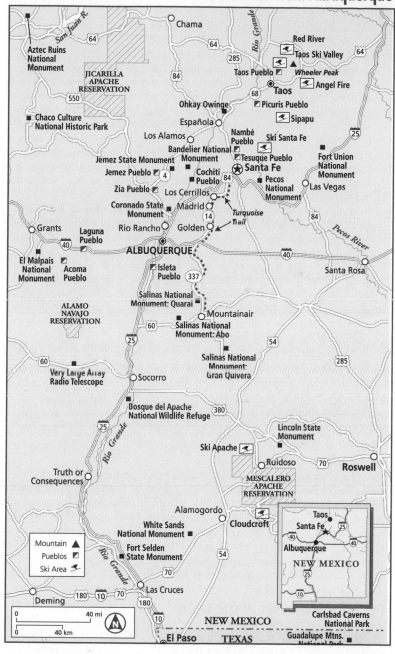

Excursions from Albuquerque

Aztec Ruins
National
Monument

San Juan R.

Chama

64

64

285

Red River

Taos Ski Valley

Wheeler Peak

64

JICARILLA
APACHE
RESERVATION

84

Taos Pueblo

Angel Fire

550

Taos

68

Chaco Culture
National Historic Park

Ohkay Owinge

Picuris Pueblo

Sipapu

Española

Los Alamos

Nambé
Pueblo

Ski Santa Fe

25

Bandelier National
Monument

Jemez State Monument

Tesuque Pueblo

Fort Union
National
Monument

Jemez Pueblo

4

Cochiti
Pueblo

Santa Fe

Zia Pueblo

Los Cerrillos

Pecos
National
Monument

Las Vegas

Coronado State
Monument

Madrid

84

Grants

Laguna
Pueblo

Rio Rancho

Golden

14

Turquoise
Trail

Pecos River

40

ALBUQUERQUE

40

Santa Rosa

El Malpais
National
Monument

Acoma
Pueblo

Isleta
Pueblo

337

ALAMO
NAVAJO
RESERVATION

Salinas National
Monument: Quarai

Mountainair

60

Salinas National
Monument: Abo

54

25

60

Very Large Array
Radio Telescope

Socorro

Salinas National
Monument:
Gran Quivera

285

Rio Grande

Bosque del Apache
National Wildlife Refuge

380

25

Lincoln State
Monument

Ski Apache

70

Roswell

Truth or
Consequences

Rio Grande

Ruidoso

MESCALERO
APACHE
RESERVATION

Alamogordo

White Sands
National Monument

Cloudcroft

Mountain

Pueblos

Ski Area

Fort Selden
State Monument

54

70

Deming

180

10

70

Las Cruces

180

0   40 mi

0   40 km

10

NEW MEXICO

Taos

Santa Fe

25

40

Albuquerque

40

NEW MEXICO

25

10

Carlsbad Caverns
National Park

El Paso

TEXAS

Guadalupe Mtns.
National Park

Tips   Pueblo Etiquette: Dos & Don'ts

Those who are not Native American are welcome to visit Indian pueblos and reservations; as a guest on tribal land, you should follow some guidelines.

Native American reservations and pueblos have their own systems of government and, therefore, their own laws and regulations. If you don't follow their laws, you will be subject to punishment as outlined by the American Indian government. The best thing that could happen is that you'd simply be asked to leave.

Stay out of cemeteries and ceremonial rooms, such as kivas, which are sacred grounds. Remember, these are not museums or tourist attractions in their own right; they are people's homes. Don't peek into doors and windows, and don't climb on top of buildings.

Most pueblos require a permit to carry a camera or to sketch or paint on location, and many prohibit photography at any time. If you want to take pictures, make a video, or sketch anything on pueblo or reservation land, find out about permits and fees in advance.

Do not wander around on your own if the residents have asked that you visit the pueblo only by guided tour. If, on a guided tour, you are asked not to take pictures of something, or are asked to stay out of a certain area, follow the guidelines. If you don't have to visit by guided tour, don't go into private buildings without being escorted by someone who lives there or who has the authority to take you inside.

Be respectful of ceremonial dances. Do not speak during dances or ceremonies, and don't applaud at the end—the participants aren't dancing for your amusement; they are dancing as part of their ceremony.

In short, be respectful and courteous and don't do anything you wouldn't do in your own mother's house.

JEMEZ PUEBLO

The more than 3,400 **Jemez Pueblo** natives—including descendants of the Pecos Pueblo, east of Santa Fe, abandoned in 1838—are the only remaining people to speak the Towa dialect of the Tanoan group. The Jemez are famous for their excellent dancing and feast-making; their feast days attract residents from other pueblos, turning the celebrations into multitribal fairs. Two rectangular kivas are central points for groups of dancers. However, in recent years the pueblo has been closed to visitors. Though they are allowed to visit on dance days, the pueblo has become close-mouthed about when dances occur. However, visitors can partake of the crafts at local shops along NM 4 and at the Walatowa Visitor Center (see box below). The primary craft is Jemez pottery.

A STATE MONUMENT IN THE AREA

Coronado State Monument *(★)*   When the Spanish explorer Coronado traveled through this region in 1540–41 while searching for the Seven Cities of Cíbola, he wintered at a village on the west bank of the Rio Grande—probably one on the ruins of the ancient Anasazi Pueblo known as Kuaua. Those excavated ruins have been preserved in this state monument.

Historic Culture with a Hint of Honey

Jemez Pueblo, home to more than 3,000, no longer welcomes visitors except on selected days. But visitors can get a taste of the Jemez culture at the **Walatowa Visitor Center**, on NM 4, 8 miles north of the junction with US 550 (✆ **877/733-5687** or 505/834-7235; www.jemezpueblo.org). A museum and shop highlight the center, which also offers information about hiking and scenic tour routes. While in the area, you may encounter Jemez people sitting under ramadas (thatch-roofed lean-tos) selling home-baked bread, cookies, and pies. If you're lucky, they may also be making fry bread, which you can smother with honey for one of New Mexico's more delectable treats.

Hundreds of rooms can be seen, and a kiva has been restored so that visitors can descend a ladder into the enclosed space, once the site of sacred rites. Unique multicolored murals, depicting human and animal forms, were found on successive layers of wall plaster in this and other kivas here; some examples are displayed in the monument's small archaeological museum.

485 Kuana Rd., Bernalillo. ✆ **505/867-5351.** Admission $3 adults, free for children under 17. Wed–Mon 8am–5pm. Closed New Year's Day, Easter, Thanksgiving, and Christmas. To get to the site (20 miles north of Albuquerque), take I-25 to Bernalillo and US 550 west for 1 mile.

JEMEZ SPRINGS

Getting to this village along the Jemez River is half the fun. You'll drive the **Jemez Mountain Trail** 🞳 into the Jemez Mountains, a trip that can provide a relaxing retreat and/or an exhilarating adventure. In the area are historic sites and relaxing hot springs, as well as excellent stream fishing, hiking, and cross country skiing. You may want to combine a drive through this area with a visit to Los Alamos and Bandelier National Monument (see chapter 6).

North of town you'll come to the **Soda Dam,** a strange and beautiful mineral mass formed by travertine deposits—minerals that precipitate out of geothermal springs. Considered a sacred site by Native Americans, it has a gushing waterfall and caves. During the warm months, it's a popular swimming hole.

Jemez State Monument 🞳 A stop at this small monument takes you on a journey through the history of the Jemez people. The journey begins in the museum, which tells the tale of Giusewa, "place of boiling waters," the original Tewa name of the area. Then it moves out into the mission ruins, whose story is told on small plaques that juxtapose the first impressions of the missionaries against the reality of the Jemez life. The missionaries saw the Jemez people as barbaric and tried to settle them. Part of the process involved hauling up river stones and erecting 6-foot-thick walls of the Mission of San José de los Jemez (founded in 1621). Excavations in 1921–22 and 1935–37 unearthed this massive complex through which you may wander. You enter through a broad doorway to a room that once held elaborate fresco paintings, the room tapering back to the nave, with a giant bell tower above. The setting is startling next to a creek, with steep mountains rising behind.

18160 NM 4 (P.O. Box 143), Jemez Springs. ✆ **505/829-3530.** Admission $3 adults, free for children under 18. Wed–Mon 8:30am–5pm. Closed New Year's Day, Easter, Thanksgiving, and Christmas. From Albuquerque, take NM 550 (NM 44) to NM 4 and then continue on NM 4 for about 18 miles.

Moments **Bath Time**

The waters running through the Jemez area are high in mineral content. In fact, the owner of **Jemez Springs Bath House,** 62 NM 4, on the Jemez Springs Plaza (✆ **505/829-3303;** www.jemezspringsbathhouse.com), says they are so healing, more than once she's had to run after visitors who walked off without their canes. This bathhouse was one of the first structures to be built in what is now Jemez Springs. Built of river rock and mud from 1870 to 1878, it has thick walls and a richly herbal scent. You soak in individual tubs. In back is a series of massage rooms, and outside is a hot tub within a wooden fence—not the most romantic setting. In front is a gift shop packed with interesting soaps and soulful gifts. Jemez Springs Bath House is open daily 10am to 8pm.

WHERE TO STAY & DINE

Cañon del Rio–Riverside Inn ☆ "Eventually the watcher joined the river, and there was only one of us. I believe it was the river," wrote Norman Maclean in *A River Runs Through It.* That was our experience while sitting on a cottonwood-shaded bench at Cañon del Rio, on a long bow of the Jemez River, a small, fast-flowing stream. Built in 1994, the inn has clean lines and comfortable rooms, each named after a Native American tribe. They're not large but are well planned, with built-in drawers and functional bathrooms. Each has a sliding glass door that opens out to a patio where there's a fountain. The beds are comfortable and the place is very quiet. The Great Room has a cozy, welcoming feel, with a big-screen TV, as well as a large table where breakfast is served family style. A separate house is available for rent, the only option for children at the inn. Smoking is not allowed.

16445 NM 4, Jemez Springs, NM 87025. ✆ 505/829-4377. www.canondelrio.com. 7 units. $89–$109 double; house $125–$150. Rates include full breakfast w/inn room. AE, DISC, MC, V. **Amenities:** Jacuzzi. *In room:* A/C, hair dryer, Wi-Fi, no phone.

The Laughing Lizard Inn & Cafe ☆ AMERICAN This place has thick adobe walls, wood floors, and a wood-burning stove. Added touches are the brightly painted walls and funky old tables, and in summer, an airy porch and shaded patio. The menu is eclectic—most dishes have a bit of an imaginative flair. The burritos come in a variety of types, such as fresh spinach with black beans, mushrooms, jack cheese, salsa, and guacamole. The homemade pizzas, made with blue-corn crusts, feature ingredients such as pesto, sun-dried tomatoes, and feta, or more basic ones with red sauce as well. Our favorite dish is the chicken quesadilla, with jack cheese, corn, and fresh herbs. Beer and wine are served, and there are daily dessert treats such as piñon pie, chocolate mousse, and berry cobbler. The staff is friendly and accommodating. A small inn attached to the cafe provides inexpensive rooms that are clean but a bit time-worn.

17526 NM 4, Jemez Springs, NM 87025. ✆ 505/829-3108. www.thelaughinglizard.com. Main courses lunch $5–$10, dinner $6–$13. DISC, MC, V. May–Nov Tues–Sat 11am–8pm, Sun 11am–6pm; Dec–Apr Thurs–Sat 11am–8pm, Sun 11am–6pm.

12 En Route to Santa Fe: Along the Turquoise Trail

Known as "The Turquoise Trail," NM 14 begins about 16 miles east of downtown Albuquerque, at I-40's Cedar Crest exit, and winds some 46 miles to Santa Fe along the east side of the Sandia Mountains. This state-designated scenic and historic route traverses the revived ghost towns of Golden, Madrid, and Cerrillos, where gold, silver, coal, and turquoise were once mined in great quantities. Modern-day settlers, mostly artists and craftspeople, have brought a renewed frontier spirit to the old mining towns.

MADRID   Madrid (pronounced *Mah*-drid) is about 12 miles north of Golden. This town and neighboring Cerrillos were in a fabled turquoise-mining area dating back to prehistory. Gold and silver mines followed, and when they faltered, there was coal. The Turquoise Trail towns supplied fuel for the locomotives of the Santa Fe Railroad until the 1950s, when the railroad converted to diesel fuel. Madrid used to produce 100,000 tons of coal a year and was a true "company town," but the mine closed in 1956. Today, this is a village of artists and craftspeople seemingly stuck in the 1960s: Its funky, ramshackle houses have many counterculture residents who operate several crafts stores and import shops.

The **Old Coal Mine Museum and Old West Photography** (© 505/438-3780) invites visitors to peek into a mine that was saved when the town was abandoned. You can see the old mine's offices, steam engines, machines, and tools. It's open daily; admission is $4 for adults, $3 for seniors, $1 for children 6 to 12, and free for children under 6. You might want to have a picture taken in one of the 1,000 costumes at Old West Photography, $3 per person and $25 for one 8×10 photo or two 5×7s.

Next door, the **Mine Shaft Tavern** (© 505/473-0743) continues its colorful career by offering a variety of burgers (try the green chile cheeseburger) and presenting live music Saturday nights and Sunday afternoons; it's open for meals in summer Monday to Thursday 11am to 6pm and Friday to Sunday 11am to 8pm. In winter, meals are served Monday to Thursday from noon to 4pm and Friday to Sunday noon to 8pm. The bar is open in summer Sunday to Thursday 11am to 11pm and Friday to Saturday 11am to 1am. In winter the bar is open from Sunday to Thursday noon to 10pm and Friday to Saturday noon to 1am. Next door is the **Madrid Engine House Theater** (© 505/438-3780), offering melodrama during the summer. Its back doors open out so a steam locomotive can take center stage. The place to eat is **Mama Lisa's Café** ✪, 2859 NM 14 (© 505/471-5769), which offers salads, sandwiches, and New Mexican specialties, all prepared with fresh ingredients. During the summer, it's open Wednesday to Monday 11am to 4:30pm. In winter, it's open intermittently, so call ahead.

CERRILLOS & GALISTEO   Cerrillos, about 3 miles north of Madrid, is a village of dirt roads that sprawls along Galisteo Creek. It appears to have changed very little since it was founded during a lead strike in 1879; the old hotel, the saloon, and even the sheriff's office look very much like parts of an Old West movie set. You may want to stop in at **Casa Grande Trading Post,** 17 Waldo St. (© 505/436-3005), a shop that was featured on PBS's *Antiques Roadshow.* You'll find lots of jewelry and rocks, as well as the **Cerrillos Turquoise Mining Museum,** full of artifacts from this region's mining era.

It's another 15 miles to Santa Fe and I-25. If, like us, you're enchanted by the Galisteo Basin, you might want to stay a night or two in nearby Galisteo at the **Galisteo**

Inn ⭐⭐ (© **866/404-8200** or 505/466-4000; www.galisteoinn.com). Set on grassy grounds under towering cottonwood trees, this 300-year-old hacienda has thick adobe walls and all the quiet a person could want. Rooms, all remodeled in 2004, are decorated with brightly painted walls and fun, bold-colored art. In their La Mancha restaurant, May through October, the inn serves Sunday brunch, lunch Friday and Saturday, and dinner Tuesday to Saturday; some nights live music plays on the lovely patio; in winter, hours are more limited. There's a lovely pool large enough to swim laps, a hot tub, and guided horseback riding with **Galarosa Stables** (© **505/466-465;** www. galarosastables.com). The inn is on NM 41, 15 miles from Cerrillos via the dirt County Road 42. For another good horseback-riding outfitter in this beautiful area, try **Broken Saddle Riding Company** (© **505/424-7774** for recorded message; www.brokensaddle.com). A 1½-hour ride is $55 a person, and riders are grouped according to skill level.

9

Pueblos, Reservations & the Best of Northern New Mexico

If the humdrum of contemporary American life has you longing for excitement, this is the place to get your adrenaline flowing. Not only can you travel to a "foreign land"—namely Gallup, what locals call "Indian Country"—but you can also sample a history of Wild West shootouts and exploding volcanoes.

The biggest presence in the northwest is Native American culture, old and new. The Pueblo, Navajo, and Apache inhabit the area. They are the majority and set the pace and tone of the place. The Zuni, Acoma, and Laguna pueblos are within a short distance of I-40. Acoma's "Sky City" has been continually occupied for more than 9 centuries. Part of the Navajo Reservation—the largest in America—takes up a huge chunk of the northwest, and the Jicarilla Apache Reservation stretches 65 miles south from the Colorado border.

Three main towns provide launching points for adventures. **Grants** (pop. 8,900) is a boom-and-bust town on Route 66, and **Gallup** (pop. 20,000) is a mecca for silver jewelry shoppers. Outdoor adventurers head to **Chama** (pop. 1,000), where many enjoy a ride on the Cumbres & Toltec Railroad.

Two other national monuments in northwestern New Mexico also speak of the region's history. **El Morro** is a sandstone monolith known as "Inscription Rock," where travelers and explorers

documented their journeys for centuries, and **El Malpais** is a volcanic badland with spectacular cinder cones, ice caves, and lava tubes.

Meanwhile, the northeast is a place of wide-open plains once traversed by wagon trains on the Santa Fe Trail—a 19th-century trade route that ran from Missouri to Santa Fe. In **Cimarron** you'll see evidence of the holdings of cattle baron Lucien Maxwell, who controlled most of these prairies as his private empire in the latter half of the 19th century. Cimarron attracted nearly every gunslinger of the era, from Butch Cassidy to Clay Allison, Black Jack Ketchum to Jesse James.

Established long before its Nevada namesake, **Las Vegas** was the largest city in New Mexico at the turn of the 20th century, with a fast-growing, cosmopolitan population. Doc Holliday, Bat Masterson, and Wyatt Earp walked its wild streets in the 1880s. A decade later, it was the headquarters of Teddy Roosevelt's Rough Riders, and early in the 20th century, it was a silent film capital. Today, with a population of approximately 17,000, it is the region's largest city and the proud home of 900 historic properties. **Raton** (pop. 7,500), on I-25 in the Sangre de Cristo foothills, is the gateway to New Mexico from the north. **Clayton** (pop. 2,500), **Tucumcari** (pop. 6,831), and **Santa Rosa** (pop. 2,500) are all transportation hubs and ranching centers.

Two national monuments are particular points of interest. **Fort Union,** 24 miles north of Las Vegas, was the largest military installation in the Southwest in the 1860s and 1870s. **Capulin Volcano,** 33 miles east of Raton, last erupted 60,000 years ago; visitors can now walk inside the crater.

Drained by the Pecos and Canadian rivers, northeastern New Mexico is notable for the number of small lakes that afford opportunities for fishing, hunting, boating, camping—even scuba diving. Eleven state parks and about a half dozen designated wildlife areas are within the region.

1 Getting Outside in Northern New Mexico

BIKING   Some of the best biking is in Farmington, where the "Durangatangs" come during the winter to train and ride (Durango is a mountain-biking mecca). **Bicycle Express,** 103 N. Main Ave. (© **505/334-4354**), in Aztec, will give trail directions, as will **Cottonwood Cycles,** 4370 E. Main (© **505/326-0429;** www.cotton woodcycles.com), in Farmington. Cottonwood also rents bikes. Be sure to check out the **Lions Wilderness Park,** where you'll find its renowned **Road Apple Trail** on the north end of town. Bikers are also welcome at the **Bureau of Land Management Conservation Area,** just off NM 117 near **El Malpais National Monument** (see "Acoma Pueblo," below). At Chaco Canyon, check out the Wijiji Ruin trail—nice and easy through beautiful country leading to an Anasazi ruin.

BIRD-WATCHING   **Las Vegas National Wildlife Refuge** (© **505/425-3581**), 5 miles southeast of Las Vegas, is a great place for bird-watching. Species spotted year-round include prairie falcons and hawks; during late fall and early winter, migratory birds such as sandhill cranes, snow geese, Canada geese, and bald and golden eagles frequent the refuge. In all, more than 240 species can be sighted in the area. The **Maxwell National Wildlife Refuge** (© **505/375-2331**), near Raton, also boasts a rich population of resident and migratory birds, including raptors and bald eagles.

BOATING   If you're towing a boat, good places to stop are **Bluewater Lake State Park** (© **505/876-2391**), a reservoir between Gallup and Grants, and **Navajo Lake State Park** (© **505/632-2278**), about 25 miles east of Bloomfield. Both of these state parks have boat ramps, and Navajo Lake has several marinas (from which visitors can rent boats), picnic areas, a visitor center, and groceries for those who plan to make a day of it. (To find information on New Mexico state parks, go to **www.nmparks.com.**) **Zuni Lakes,** six bodies of water operated by the Zuni tribe, also offers opportunities for boating, although you're not allowed to use gasoline motors and you must receive a permit (© **505/782-5851**) before setting out. You'll find opportunities for boating, windsurfing, and swimming throughout this northeastern region. Two of the most popular boating areas are **Storrie Lake State Park** (© **505/425-7278**), 6 miles north of Las Vegas, and **Conchas Lake State Park** (© **505/868-2270**), near Tucumcari. Storrie Lake is especially popular among **windsurfers,** who favor its consistent winds.

FISHING   **Bluewater Lake State Park** (see "Boating," above) is one of the best fishing places in the area. In fact, some people believe it has the highest catch rate of all New Mexico lakes. Look to catch trout here. A world-renowned fishing destination, the **San Juan River** ♠♠, just below Navajo Dam, was recently named the best fishing spot in the United States by *Field & Stream.* The scenery is outstanding and excellent guides in the area can help you find the choicest spots. **Navajo Lake State Park** (see "Boating," above) features about 150 miles of shoreline where fishers go to catch trout, bass,

Northwestern New Mexico

catfish, and pike. Navajo Lake is one of the largest lakes in New Mexico, and the park is very heavily trafficked, so if crowds aren't your thing, look for another fishing hole. Just 4 miles south of Kirtland is **Morgan Lake,** a quiet spot for largemouth bass and catfish. If you need fishing gear or want to hire a guide while in the area, contact **Abe's Motel and Fly Shop,** 1791 US 173, Navajo Dam (© **505/632-2194**). In Farmington, contact **Dad's Boat Parts and Backyard Boutique,** 210 E. Piñon St. (© **505/326-1870**), or **Zia Sporting Goods,** 500 E. Main (© **505/327-6004;** www.ziasportingoods. com). Isolated and primitive **Morphy Lake State Park** is a favorite destination for serious anglers. The lake is regularly stocked with rainbow trout. **Cimarron Canyon State Park** is also popular with fishers. Lake Alice in **Sugarite Canyon State Park,** just north of Raton at the Colorado border, is a good spot for fly-fishing.

GOLF   In this region, greens fees range from $20 to $55, with most averaging about $25; winter rates are lower. Cart rentals run about $15. In 2002, *Golf Digest* rated **Piñon Hills Golf Course,** 2101 Sunrise Pkwy., in Farmington (© **505/326-6066**), the "best municipal course" in the United States. Also in Farmington is the **Civitan Golf Course,** 2100 N. Dustin (© **505/599-1194**). In Kirtland (approximately 7 miles west of Farmington), your golf option is **Riverview Golf Course,** on US 64 (© **505/598-0140**). Duffers in the northeast can get in a few holes in or near virtually every town covered in this section. We recommend the following courses: **Raton Municipal Golf Course,** 510 Country Club Rd., Raton NM 87740 (© **505/445-8113**); **Pendaries Village Mountain Resort,** in Rociada (© **505/425-3561;** www.pendaries.net), 13 miles south of Mora and 27 miles northwest of Las Vegas; and **Tucumcari Municipal Golf Course,** Route 66 Boulevard, Tucumcari, NM 88401 (© **505/461-1849**).

HIKING   This part of the state has some great hiking trails. You'll see ancient archaeological ruins in places such as Aztec Ruins and Chaco Canyon. In **Cíbola National Forest** (© **505/287-8833;** www.fs.fed.us/r3/cibola), the hike to the summit of Mount Taylor is excellent. In cooler months, but not winter, try hiking around **El Malpais National Monument** (© **505/285-4641;** www.nps.gov/elma). Two good hikes to try in El Malpais are the Zuni–Acoma Trail (this one is extremely taxing, so if you're not in shape, don't expect to make the 15-mile round-trip hike) and the Big Lava Tubes Trail (1 mile round-trip). For quiet hiking in state parks, head to **Bluewater Lake State Park** (© **505/876-2391**), **Red Rock State Park** (© **505/722-3839**), or **Angel Peak Recreation Area** (© **505/599-8900**).

Sporting-goods stores where you can get hiking gear include **REI-Albuquerque,** 1550 Mercantile Ave. NE in Albuquerque (© **505/247-1191;** www.rei.com); **Frontier Sports,** 300 NE Aztec Blvd. in Aztec (© **505/334-0009**); and **Zia Sporting Goods,** 500 E. Main in Farmington (© **505/327-6004;** www.ziasportinggoods.com).

Northeastern New Mexico abounds in great places to hike, including the trails at Capulin Volcano; but the best places are in the mountains to the north of Las Vegas and west of Santa Fe and Taos. **Clayton Lake, Coyote Creek, Morphy Lake, Santa Rosa Lake, Sugarite Canyon,** and **Villanueva state parks** all have hiking trails, which range from fairly informal to clearly marked. For information about them, contact © **888/NM-PARKS** or 505/476-3355 (www.nmparks.com). The region's premier hike takes you to the top of **Hermit's Peak,** a lovely but strenuous 8-mile round-trip foray onto a stunning precipice. Take NM 65 about 15 miles northwest of Las Vegas to the El Porvenir Campground. It's probably best to acquire equipment and supplies in Albuquerque before you set out. Try REI-Albuquerque (listed above).

SCUBA DIVING   There couldn't possibly be scuba diving in this dry, landlocked state, could there? Yes, there is, with the best at Santa Rosa, where you'll find the **Blue Hole,** an 81-foot-deep artesian well that's a favorite of divers from around the world. The best place to rent equipment is at the **Santa Rosa Dive Center** on Blue Hole Road, open only on weekends (© **505/472-3370**).

SKIING   Some of the best cross-country skiing in the state is in the Chama area. Lots of broad bowls make the area a favorite of backcountry skiers as well as day-touring skiers. If you're up for an overnight adventure, contact **Southwest Nordic Center** (© **505/758-4761;** www.southwestnordiccenter.com), a company that rents five yurts (Russian-style huts), four of which are in the Rio Grande National Forest near Chama. Some like to ski the old logging roads of Mount Taylor in **Cíbola National Forest,** near Grants. Contact the Ranger Station in Grants (© **505/287-8833**) for more information. If you need to rent ski equipment, try **Chama Ski Service** (© **505/756-2492**), which also offers snow reports and trail information.

SWIMMING   Good swimming is available at **Navajo Lake State Park** (© **505/ 632-2278**). Before diving in at other lakes in state parks, make sure swimming is permitted. Swimming is best (although chilly) at **Clayton, Conchas, Morphy, Storrie,** and **Ute lakes.** (You can find directions to and specifics about these lakes later in this chapter.) In addition, though it's an indoor rather than outdoor experience, the **Las Vegas Recreation Center**'s (© **505/426-1739**) swimming pool, at 1751 N. Grand Ave., is an especially good place to take kids. It's Olympic-size and has an incredible slide that will keep kids busy for hours. Call for more information.

2 Acoma Pueblo

30 miles SE of Grants, 90 miles SE of Gallup, 150 miles SE of Farmington

Your best base for exploring the Acoma Pueblo, as well as the El Malpais and El Morro National Monuments (see section 3, below), is the town of Grants, 1¼ hours west of Albuquerque on I-40. Places to stay and dine in Grants, as well as details on the interesting New Mexico Mining Museum in Grants, appear below.

ACOMA PUEBLO ✸✸✸

The spectacular Acoma Sky City, a walled adobe village perched high atop a sheer rock mesa 367 feet above the 6,600-foot valley floor, is said to have been inhabited at least since the 11th century—it's the longest continuously occupied community in the United States. Native history says it has been inhabited since before the time of Christ. Both the pueblo and its mission church of **San Esteban del Rey** are National Historic Landmarks. When Coronado visited in 1540, he suggested that Acoma was "the greatest stronghold in the world"; those who attempt to follow the cliffside footpath down after their guided tour, rather than take the bus back down, may agree.

About 50 to 75 Keresan-speaking Acoma (pronounced *Ack*-oo-mah) reside year-round on the 70-acre mesa top. Many others maintain ancestral homes and occupy them during ceremonial periods. The terraced three-story buildings face south for maximum exposure to the winter sun. Most of Sky City's permanent residents make their living off the throngs of tourists who flock here to see the magnificent church, built in 1639 and containing numerous masterpieces of Spanish colonial art, and to purchase the thin-walled white pottery with brown-and-black designs for which the pueblo is famous.

Many Acomas work in Grants, 15 miles west of the pueblo; in Albuquerque; or for one of Acoma's business enterprises, such as Sky City Casino. Others are cattle ranchers and farm individual family gardens.

ESSENTIALS

GETTING THERE   To reach Acoma from Grants, drive east 15 miles on I-40 to McCartys, then south 13 miles on paved tribal roads to the visitor center. From Albuquerque, drive west 65 miles to the Acoma–Sky City exit (102), then 15 miles southwest.

VISITOR INFORMATION   For additional information before you leave home, contact the pueblo at P.O. Box 309, Acoma, NM 87034 (© **800/747-0181** or 505/522-6604; www.skycity.com).

ADMISSION FEES & HOURS   Admission is $10 for adults, $9 for seniors 60 and over, $7 for children 6 to 17, and free for children under 6. Group discounts apply to parties of 15 or more, and there's also a discount for Native American visitors. The photography charge is $10; no filming, sketching, or painting is allowed except by special permission. The pueblo is open daily in the summer from 8am to 6pm and daily the rest of the year from 8am to 4pm.

SEEING THE HIGHLIGHTS

You absolutely cannot wander freely around Acoma Pueblo, but you can start your tour there at the new 40,000-square-foot museum and peruse their gallery, offering art and crafts for sale, and have a meal at the Yaak'a Café. One-hour tours begin every 30 minutes, depending on the demand; the last tour is scheduled 1 hour before closing. The pueblo is closed to visitors on Easter weekend (some years), June 24 and 29, July 10 to 13, and the first or second weekend in October. It's best to call ahead to make sure that the tour is available when you're visiting.

You'll board the tour bus, which climbs through a rock garden of 50-foot sandstone monoliths and past precipitously dangling outhouses to the mesa's summit. With no running water or electricity in this medieval-looking village, it's a truly unique place. A small reservoir collects rainwater for most uses, and drinking water is transported up from below. Wood-hole ladders and mica windows are prevalent among the 300-odd adobe structures. As you tour the village, you'll have many opportunities to buy pottery and other pueblo treasures. Pottery is expensive here, but you're not going to find it any cheaper anywhere else, and you'll be guaranteed that it's authentic if you buy it directly from the craftsperson. Along the way, be sure to sample some Indian fry bread topped with honey.

DANCES & CEREMONIES

The annual San Esteban del Rey feast day is September 2, when the pueblo's patron saint is honored with a mid-morning Mass, a procession, an afternoon corn dance, and an arts-and-crafts fair. The Governor's Feast is held annually in February; and 4 days of Christmas festivals run from December 25 to 28. Still cameras are allowed for a $10 fee, and guided tours do not operate on the mesa during feast days.

Other **celebrations** are held in low-lying pueblo villages at Easter (in Acomita), the first weekend in May (Santa Maria feast at McCartys), and August 10 (San Lorenzo Day in Acomita).

GRANTS

If you've ever wondered what a "boom-and-bust town" looks like, come to Grants. It first boomed with the coming of the railroad in the late 19th century, when 4,000 workers descended on the tiny farm town. When the railroad was completed, the workers left, and the town went bust. Next, Grants saw high times in the 1940s, growing carrots and sending them to the East Coast, but when packaging became more advanced, Grants lost its foothold in the market and busted again. Then came the 1950s, when a Navajo sheep rancher named Paddy Martinez discovered some strange yellow rocks near Haystack Mountain, northwest of town. The United States was in need of uranium, and his find led to the biggest boom in the area. By the early 1980s, demand for uranium had dropped, and so went the big wages and big spenders that the ore's popularity had produced. Today, the city on a segment of Route 66 is a jumping-off point for outdoor adventures.

The city is the seat of expansive Cíbola County, which stretches from the Arizona border nearly to the Albuquerque area. For more information, contact the **Grants/Cíbola County Chamber of Commerce** at 100 N. Iron Ave. (P.O. Box 297), Grants, NM 87020 (✆ **800/748-2142** or 505/287-4802; www.grants.org). It's in the same building as the Mining Museum (see below).

WHAT TO SEE IN GRANTS

New Mexico Mining Museum ✦ *Kids*   This enormously interesting little museum primes you for the underground adventure of traveling into a re-creation of a mine shaft by showing you, on ground level, some geology, such as a fossilized dinosaur leg bone and a piece of Malpais lava. The world's only underground uranium-mining museum also gives you a sense of the context within which uranium was mined, through photos of the uranium-mining pioneers. Thus, the stage is set for your walk into a mine shaft–like doorway adorned with rusty metal hats. An elevator takes you down into a spooky, low-lit place with stone walls. You begin in the station, where uranium was loaded and unloaded, and travel down into the earth to places defined on wall plaques. While exploring, you get a sense of the dark and dirty work that mining can be. Those with claustrophobia may have to content themselves with visiting the exhibits *above* ground.

100 N. Iron Ave., at Santa Fe Ave. ✆ 800/748-2142 or 505/287-4802. Fax 505/287-8224. www.grants.org. Admission $3 adults, $2 seniors over age 60 and children 7–18; free for children 6 and under. Mon–Sat 9am–4pm.

Northwest New Mexico Visitor Center ✦   East of Grants, this new center sits within an expansive Pueblo-style building with a broad atrium showing off views of the Malpais. It offers fliers and films on the region's parks, forests, and Indian country. A real treat here is a series of suggested driving tours displayed with large color photos and free cards describing the routes. One tour takes visitors along the volcanoes of the Malpais, another through the abandoned logging communities of the Zuni Mountains Historical Loop, and another to the stunning geologic formations of the Cabezon and Rio Puerco area. A fun shelf of Southwest book titles is worth perusing.

1900 Santa Fe Ave. ✆ 505/876-2783. Fax 505/876-2791. Free admission. Daily 9am–6pm during daylight saving time; 8am–5pm during Mountain Standard Time.

WHERE TO STAY IN GRANTS

Grants hotels are all on or near Route 66, with major properties near I-40 interchanges, and smaller or older motels nearer downtown. Lodger's tax is 5%, which is added to the gross receipts tax of 7.50%, for a total room tax of 12.5%. Parking is usually free.

Holiday Inn Express   This two-story motel, just off the interstate, provides large, well-conceived rooms with a comfortable atmosphere. Ground-floor rooms open both off an inner corridor and from an outside door that faces the parking lot. Rooms are spacious, with high ceilings, comfortable beds, and large bathrooms.

1496 E. Santa Fe Ave., Grants, NM 87020. ℂ 800/HOLIDAY or 505/285-4676. Fax 505/285-6998. www.hiexpress.com. 58 units. $101 double. Rates include continental breakfast. AE, DC, DISC, MC, V. Pets are welcome. **Amenities:** Small indoor pool; Jacuzzi. *In room:* A/C, TV, dataport, coffeemaker, hair dryer, iron.

CAMPING

Grants has three decent campgrounds with both tent and RV facilities. All range in price from $9 to $14 for tent camping and $13 to $19 for full hookups. **Blue Spruce RV Park** (ℂ **505/287-2560**), which has 25 sites and 16 full hookups, is open year-round. The park has enough trees to block the wind and some grass, and the roads and parking spaces are gravel, so dust is minimized. Cable television hookups are available, as are laundry facilities and a recreation room. To reach the park, take I-40 to exit 81 and then go a quarter mile south on NM 53.

Lavaland RV Park (ℂ **505/287-8665;** www.lavalandrvpark.com), the closest site to Grants, has 51 sites and 39 full hookups. Near a lava outcropping, the site is clean, though a little desolate and dusty, with a few pine trees to block the wind. Air-conditioning and heating hookups are available, as are some free cable and telephone hookups. In addition, you'll find cabins, laundry, limited grocery facilities, picnic tables and grills, and recreation facilities. Lavaland is open year-round. From I-40, get off at exit 85 and continue 100 yards south on Access Road.

WHERE TO DINE IN GRANTS

In general, you won't find places to eat at pueblos or national monuments, so you're best off looking for a restaurant in Grants.

El Cafecito *(Value (Kids* AMERICAN/MEXICAN   This real locals' spot serves up tasty food in a relaxed atmosphere. At mealtime, the brightly lit space with Saltillo tile floors bustles with families eating huevos rancheros (eggs over tortillas, smothered in chile) for breakfast, and enchiladas, stuffed *sopaipillas,* and burgers for lunch and dinner. All meals are large and inexpensive. Kids enjoy their own menu selections.

820 E. Santa Fe Ave. ℂ **505/285-6229.** Main courses $3–$7 breakfast, $5–$10 lunch or dinner. AE, DISC, MC, V. Mon–Fri 7am–9pm; Sat 7am–8pm.

La Ventana NEW MEXICAN/STEAKS   Grants locals come here for a big dinner or lunch out. With one large room that seats about 50 people, the restaurant is done in a cheesy Southwestern decor, with a two-horse sculpture and some dancing kachinas. The place is dark, with few windows, so if you can catch Grants on a nonwindy day, opt for the patio. Service is friendly and varies in its efficiency. You can't go wrong with one of the salads, such as the chicken fajita, or with the prime rib. You'll also find sandwiches such as turkey and guacamole served on seven-grain bread. There's a full bar.

110½ Geis St., Hillcrest Center. ℂ **505/287-9393.** Reservations recommended. Main courses $5–$10 lunch, $8–$20 dinner. AE, DC, DISC, MC, V. Mon–Sat 11am–11pm.

3 El Malpais & El Morro National Monuments

El Malpais: 15 miles S of Grants, 75 miles SE of Gallup, 135 miles S of Farmington; El Morro: 30 miles SW of Grants, 45 miles SE of Gallup, 149 miles S of Farmington

Northwestern New Mexico has two national monuments that are must-sees for anyone touring this region: El Malpais and El Morro.

EL MALPAIS: EXPLORING THE BADLANDS ⟨ͬ⟩

Designated a national monument in 1987, El Malpais (Spanish for "badlands") is considered one of the outstanding examples of volcanic landscapes in the United States. El Malpais contains 115,000 acres of cinder cones, vast lava flows, hundreds of lava tubes, ice caves, sandstone cliffs, natural bridges and arches, Anasazi (ancestral Puebloan) ruins, ancient Native American trails, and Spanish and Anglo homesteads.

ESSENTIALS

GETTING THERE   You can take one of two approaches to El Malpais, via NM 117 or NM 53. NM 117 exits I-40 7 miles east of Grants.

VISITOR INFORMATION   Admission to El Malpais is free (unless you're visiting the privately owned Ice Caves), and it's open to visitors year-round. The **visitor center,** off Route 53 between mile markers 63 and 64, is open daily from 8:30am to 4:30pm. Here you can pick up maps of the park, leaflets on specific trails, and other details about exploring the monument. For more information, contact **El Malpais National Monument,** NPS, P.O. Box 939, Grants, NM 87020 (② **505/285-4641;** www.nps.gov/elma).

SEEING THE HIGHLIGHTS

From **Sandstone Bluffs Overlook** (10 miles south of I-40 off NM 117), many craters are visible in the lava flow, which extends for miles along the eastern flank of the Continental Divide. The most recent flows are only 1,000 years old; Native American legends tell of rivers of "fire rock." Seventeen miles south of I-40 is **La Ventana Natural Arch,** the largest accessible natural arch in New Mexico.

From NM 53, which exits I-40 just west of Grants, visitors have access to the **Zuni–Acoma Trail,** an ancient Pueblo trade route that crosses four major lava flows in a 7½-mile (one-way) hike. A printed trail guide is available. **El Calderon,** a forested area 20 miles south of I-40, is a trail head for exploring a cinder cone, lava tubes, and a bat cave. (*Warning:* Hikers should not enter the bat cave or otherwise disturb the bats.)

The largest of all Malpais cinder cones, **Bandera Crater** is on private property 25 miles south of I-40. The National Park Service has laid plans to absorb this commercial operation, known as **Ice Caves Resort** (② **888/ICE-CAVE** or 505/783-4303; www.icecaves.com). For a fee ($8 for adults and $4 for children 5–12), visitors hike up the crater or walk to the edge of an ice cave. It's open daily from 8am to 7pm in summer and from 8am to 4pm in winter (generally closing 1 hr. before sunset).

Perhaps the most fascinating phenomenon of El Malpais is the lava tubes, formed when the outer surface of a lava flow cooled and solidified. When the lava river drained, tunnel-like caves were left. Ice caves within some of the tubes have delicate ice-crystal ceilings, ice stalactites, and floors like ice rinks.

HIKING & CAMPING

El Malpais has several hiking trails, including the above-mentioned Zuni–Acoma Trail. Most are marked with rock cairns; some are dirt trails. The best times to hike this area are during spring and fall, when it's not too hot. You're pretty much on your own when you explore this area, so prepare accordingly. Carry plenty of water with you; do not drink surface water. Carrying first-aid gear is always a good idea, too; the lava rocks can be extremely sharp and inflict nasty cuts. Never go into a cave alone. The park service advises wearing hard hats, boots, protective clothing, and gloves, and carrying three sources of light when entering lava tubes. The weather can change suddenly, so be prepared; if lightning is around, move off the lava as quickly as possible.

Primitive camping is allowed in the park, but you must first obtain a free backcountry permit from the visitor center.

EL MORRO NATIONAL MONUMENT &

Travelers who like to look history straight in the eye are fascinated by "Inscription Rock," 43 miles west of Grants along NM 53. Looming up out of the sand and sagebrush is a bluff 200 feet high, holding some of the most captivating messages in North America. Its sandstone face displays a written record of the many who inhabited and traveled through this land, beginning with the ancestral Puebloans, who lived atop the formation around 1200. Carved with steel points are the signatures and comments of almost every explorer, conquistador, missionary, army officer, surveyor, and pioneer emigrant who passed this way from 1605, when Gov. Don Juan de Oñate carved the first inscription, to 1906, when it was preserved by the National Park Service. Oñate's inscription, dated April 16, 1605, was perhaps the first graffiti any European left in America.

A paved walkway makes it easy to walk to the writings, and a stone stairway leads up to other treasures. One entry reads: "Year of 1716 on the 26th of August passed by here Don Feliz Martinez, Governor and Captain General of this realm to the reduction and conquest of the Moqui." Confident of success as he was, Martinez actually got nowhere with any "conquest of the Moqui," or Hopi, peoples. After a 2-month battle, they chased him back to Santa Fe.

Another special group to pass by was the U.S. Camel Corps, on their way from Texas to California in 1857. The camels worked out fine in mountains and deserts, outlasting horses and mules 10 to 1, but the Civil War ended the experiment. When Peachy Breckinridge, fresh out of the Virginia Military Academy, came by with 25 camels, he noted the fact on the stone here.

El Morro was at one time as famous as the Blarney Stone of Ireland: Everybody had to stop by and make a mark. But when the Santa Fe Railroad was laid 25 miles to the north, El Morro was no longer on the main route to California, and from the 1870s, the tradition began to die out.

Atop Inscription Rock via a short, steep trail, Anasazi ruins occupy an area 200 by 300 feet. Inscription Rock's name, Atsinna, suggests that carving one's name here is a very old custom indeed: The word, in Zuni, means "writing on rock."

ESSENTIALS
GETTING THERE   El Morro is 43 miles west of Grants on NM 53.

VISITOR INFORMATION   For information, contact **El Morro National Monument,** Route 2, Box 43, Ramah, NM 87321-9603 (© **505/783-4226;** www.nps.gov/ elmo). Admission to El Morro is $3 adults, free for children under 17. Self-guided trail booklets are available at the visitor center (turn off NM 53 at the El Morro sign and travel approximately a half-mile), open year-round from 9am to 5pm. Trails are also open year-round; check with the **visitor center** for hours. A **museum** at the visitor center features exhibits on the 700 years of human activity at El Morro. A 15-minute video gives a good introduction to the park. Also within the visitor center is a **bookstore** where you can pick up souvenirs and informational books. It takes from 2 to 4 hours to visit the museum and to hike a couple of trails. The park is closed on Christmas and New Year's Day.

CAMPING & LODGING
Though it isn't necessary to camp here in order to see most of the park, a nine-site campground at El Morro is open from around Memorial Day to Labor Day, and it

costs $5 per night. No supplies are available within the park, so if you're planning on spending a night or two, be sure to arrive well equipped.

One nearby private enterprise, **El Morro RV Park,** HC 61, Box 44, Ramah, NM 87321 (© **505/783-4612;** www.elmorro-nm.com), has cabins, RV and tent camping, and a cafe. If you'd like a week to months-long extended stay in the area, contact **Oso Vista Ranch,** P.O. Box 700, Ramah, NM 87321 (© **888/214-7493** or 602/614-5618; www.osovistaranch.com). Set on the side of a valley, it has spectacular views of some of the region's exotic rock formations.

4 Gallup: Gateway to Indian Country ★

62 miles NW of Grants; 118 miles NW of Albuquerque; 164 miles W of Santa Fe

Gallup has always been a mysterious place—home to many Native Americans, with dust left from its Wild West days, and with an unmistakable Route 66 architectural presence, it just doesn't seem to exist in this era. The best way to get a sense of Gallup is by walking around downtown, through the trading posts and pawnshops and by the historic buildings. In doing so you'll get a real feel for the "Heart of Indian Country."

Gallup started when the railroad from Arizona reached this spot in 1881. At that time, the town consisted of a stagecoach stop and a saloon. Within 2 years, coal mining had created a boom, and some 22 saloons and an opera house filled the town, most of which was inhabited by immigrants from mining areas in eastern Europe, England, Wales, Germany, and Italy.

When the popularity of the railroads declined, Gallup turned briefly to the movie business. The area's red-rock canyons and lonely deserts were perfect for Westerns of the era such as *Big Carnival,* with Kirk Douglas; *Four Faces West,* with Joel McCrea; and *The Bad Man,* starring Wallace Beery, Lionel Barrymore, and Ronald Reagan. These stars and many others stayed in a Route 66 hotel built by R. E. Griffith in 1937. Today, the El Rancho Hotel and Motel is one of Gallup's most notable landmarks; it's worth strolling through (see "Where to Stay," below). Gallup's next income generator was trade and tourism. Its central location between the Navajo Reservation and the Zuni lands, as well as its proximity to the ancient ruins at Chaco, make it a crossroads for trade and travel.

Gallup's most notable special event is the **Inter-Tribal Indian Ceremonial** held every August. Native Americans converge on the town for a parade, dances, and an all-Indian rodeo east of town at Red Rock State Park. It's a busy time in Gallup, and reservations must be made way in advance. If you're not in town for the Ceremonial, try hitting Gallup on a Saturday. Many Native Americans come to town to trade, and the place gets busy. Best of all on this day is the **Flea Market,** north of town just off U.S. 666. Here you can sample fry bread, Zuni bread, and Acoma bread; eat real mutton stew; and shop for anything from jewelry to underwear. After the Flea Market, most Gallup-area residents—native and nonnative alike—go to Earl's (see "Where to Dine," below) to eat and then to Wal-Mart to shop.

ESSENTIALS

GETTING THERE   From Albuquerque, take I-40 west (2½ hr.). From Farmington, take US 64 west to Shiprock, then US 491 south (2½ hr.). From Flagstaff, Arizona, take I-40 east (3 hr.). Gallup is not served by any commercial airlines at this time.

VISITOR INFORMATION   The **Gallup–McKinley County Chamber of Commerce,** 103 W. US 66, Gallup, NM 87301 (© **800/242-4282** or 505/722-2228;

www.thegallupchamber.com), is just south of the main I-40 interchange for downtown Gallup.

WHAT TO SEE & DO
EXPLORING GALLUP

Gallup has 20 buildings that are either listed on or have been nominated to the National Register of Historic Places. Some hold trading posts worth visiting. A good place to start is at the **Santa Fe Railroad Depot,** which also houses the **Gallup Cultural Center** (for details, see "Sunset Dances," below) at East 66 Avenue and Strong Street. Built in 1923 in modified Mission style, it has been renovated into a community transportation and cultural center, with a small museum worth visiting, as well as a gift shop and diner. Across the street, the **Drake Hotel** (later the Turquoise Club but now abandoned), built of blond brick in 1919, had the Prohibition-era reputation of being controlled by bootleggers, with wine running in the faucets in place of water.

The 1928 **White Cafe,** 100 W. 66 Ave., is an elaborate decorative brick structure that catered to the early auto tourist traffic. Now it's a jewelry store. Down the street, the **Eagle Café,** 220 W. 66 Ave. (© **505/722-3220**), an 80-year-old establishment, serves diner food in an authentic atmosphere. A few doors down, **Richardson's Trading Company,** 222 W. 66 Ave. (© **505/722-4762**), has been selling good Native American arts and crafts since 1913.

The **Rex Hotel,** 300 W. 66 Ave., constructed of locally quarried sandstone, was once known for its "ladies of the night." It's now the **Rex Museum** (© **505/863-1363**), a somewhat random display of items from the Gallup Historical Society Collection, but fun for history buffs. It's open daily, though with unpredictable hours. Call before setting out.

Gallup's architectural gems include the **Chief Theater,** 228 W. Coal Ave. This structure was built in 1920; in 1936, it was completely redesigned in Pueblo-Deco style, with zigzag relief and geometric form, by R. E. "Griff" Griffith (who also built the El Rancho Hotel), brother of Hollywood producer D. W. Griffith. Now this is **City Electric Shoe Shop** (© **505/863-5252**), where the Native Americans go to buy feathers, leather, and other goods to make ceremonial clothing. It's known to locals simply as City Electric, so called because it was the first shop in town to have an automated shoe-repair machine. Also visit the 1928 **El Morro Theater,** 207 W. Coal Ave., built in Spanish colonial revival style with Spanish baroque plaster carving and bright polychromatic painting; it's where locals come to see movies and dance performances.

SHOPPING: BEST BUYS ON JEWELRY & CRAFTS

Nowhere are the jewelry and crafts of Navajo, Zuni, and Hopi tribes less expensive than in Gallup. The most intriguing places to shop are the trading posts and pawnshops, which provide a surprising range of services for their largely Native American clientele and have little in common with the pawnshops of large U.S. cities.

Navajoland **pawnbrokers** in essence are bankers, at least from the Navajo and Zuni viewpoint. Pawnshops provide safekeeping of valuable personal goods and make small-collateral loans. The trader will hold on to an item for months or even years before deeming it "dead" and putting it up for sale. Less than 5% of items ever go unredeemed, but over the years traders do accumulate a selection, so the shops are worth perusing.

If you're shopping for jewelry, look for silver concho belts, worn with jeans and Southwestern skirts; cuff bracelets; and necklaces, from traditional squash blossoms to silver beads to *heishi,* which are very fine beads worn in several strands. Earrings may be only silver, or they may be decorated with stones.

Also be on the lookout for bolo ties and belt buckles of silver or turquoise. Silver concho hatbands go great on Stetson hats. Silver or gold handcrafted earrings, sometimes decorated with turquoise, are big sellers.

Hand-woven Native American rugs may be draped on couches, hung on walls, or used on floors. Also look for pottery, kachinas, and sculpture.

Most shops are open Monday through Saturday from 9am to 5pm. For a look at everything from pawn jewelry to Pendleton robes and shawls to enamel and cast-iron kitchenware, visit **Ellis Tanner Trading Company** (© 505/863-4434), Highway 602 Bypass, south from I-40 on Highway 602 about 2 miles; it's at the corner of Nizhoni Boulevard. Also try **Perry Null-Tobe Turpen's Indian Trading Company,** 1710 S. Second St. (© **505/722-3806**), farther out on Second Street; it's a big free-standing brick building full of jewelry, rugs, kachinas, and pottery.

SUNSET DANCES

Every evening Memorial Day to Labor Day, dancers from a variety of area tribes sing, drum, and twirl in a stunning display of ritual from 7 to 8pm. The dances take place at the **Gallup Cultural Center** on East 66 Avenue and Strong Street (© **505/863-4131**). The center is open weekdays from 9am to 5pm, often with extended hours in the summer. Also at the center are a gift shop, a cafe, and a museum with a permanent exhibit on regional history, and other changing art exhibits. Admission to the center and dances is free.

WHERE TO STAY IN GALLUP

Virtually every accommodation in Gallup is somewhere along Route 66, either near the I-40 interchanges or on the highway through downtown.

MODERATE

El Rancho Hotel and Motel 🐾 This historic hotel owes as much to Hollywood as to Gallup. Built in 1937 by R. E. "Griff" Griffith, brother of movie mogul D. W. Griffith, it became the place for film companies to set up headquarters when filming here. Between the 1940s and 1960s, a who's who of Hollywood stayed here. Their autographed photos line the walls of the hotel's cafe. Spencer Tracy and Katharine Hepburn stayed here during production of *The Sea of Grass;* Burt Lancaster and Lee Remick were guests when they made *The Hallelujah Trail.* The list goes on and on: Gene Autry, Lucille Ball, Jack Benny, Humphrey Bogart, James Cagney, Errol Flynn, Henry Fonda, the Marx Brothers, Ronald Reagan, Rosalind Russell, James Stewart, John Wayne, and Mae West all stayed here.

In 1986, Gallup businessman Armand Ortega, a longtime jewelry merchant, bought the run-down El Rancho and restored it to its earlier elegance. The lobby staircase rises to the mezzanine on either side of an enormous stone fireplace, and heavy ceiling beams and railings made of tree limbs give the room a hunting-lodge ambience. The hotel is on the National Register of Historic Places.

Rooms in El Rancho differ from one to the next and are named for the stars that stayed in them. Most are long and medium-size, with wagon-wheel headboards and heavy, dark-stained pine furniture. Bathrooms are small, some with showers, others with shower/tub combos. All have lovely small white hexagonal tiles. Many rooms have balconies. Two suites with kitchenettes are also available. Light sleepers should be aware that the train can be heard from all rooms in the hotel.

1000 E. 66 Ave., Gallup, NM 87301. ✆ 800/543-6351 or 505/863-9311. Fax 505/722-5917. www.elranchohotel.com. 100 units. $52–$86 double; $105 suite. AE, DISC, MC, V. Pets are welcome. **Amenities:** Restaurant (below); lounge; seasonal outdoor pool; coin-op laundry. *In room:* A/C, TV.

La Quinta 🎯   The challenge in Gallup is to find a quiet place to sleep. With trains running right through town, most accommodations stay noisy through the night. Sitting east of town, this is one of the quietest places we've found, but you'll have to reserve carefully. New medium-size room have high ceilings and the calming green decor for which this chain is known, as well as comfortable beds and fairly spacious bathrooms. A hot breakfast adds to the appeal. Ask for a room on the side of the hotel that faces *away* from the tracks and you'll get a good night's sleep.

675 Scott Ave., Gallup, NM 87401. ✆ 800/531-5900 or 505/327-4706. Fax 505/325-6583. www.laquinta.com. 66 units. $99 double; $134 suite. Rates include hot breakfast. AE, DC, DISC, MC, V. **Amenities:** Outdoor pool; Jacuzzi; guest laundry. *In room:* A/C, TV, fridge, coffeemaker, hair dryer, iron, microwave, high-speed Internet.

CAMPING

As in the rest of the state, the Gallup area offers plenty of places to pitch a tent or hook up your RV. **USA RV Park** (✆ 505/863-5021) has 145 sites, 50 full hookups (cable TV costs extra), and cabins, as well as grocery and laundry facilities. Recreation facilities include coin games, a seasonal heated swimming pool, and a playground. An outdoor breakfast and dinner are served at an extra cost. Sites range from $21 for tents to $27 for full hookups. Cabins are $35. To reach the campground, take I-40 to the US 66/Business I-40 junction (exit 16); go 1 mile east on US 66/Business I-40.

  Red Rock State Park campground (✆ 505/863-9330) has 106 sites—50 with no hookups and 56 with water and electricity. Tent sites are available. The campground offers dry camping for $15 and camping with water and electrical hookups for $20. The sites are right against the buttes; in the spring, they will surely be dusty because there is little protection from the wind. Also accessible are a convenience store, picnic tables, and grills.

WHERE TO DINE IN GALLUP

Earl's *Finds* *Kids* AMERICAN/NEW MEXICAN   This is where the locals come to eat, particularly on weekends, en route to and from trading in Gallup. The place fills up with a variety of clientele, from college students to Navajo grandmothers. A Denny's-style diner, with comfortable booths and chairs, the restaurant allows Native Americans to sell their wares to you while you eat; however, you have the option of putting up a sign asking not to be disturbed. Often on weekends, vendors set up tables out front, so the whole place takes on a bustling bazaar atmosphere. And the food is good. We recommend the New Mexican dishes such as huevos rancheros, the enchilada plate, or the smothered grande burrito. Earl's offers a kids' menu and half-portion items for smaller appetites, as well as some salads and a "baked potato meal." Open since 1947, Earl's continues to please.

1400 E. 66 Ave. ✆ 505/863-4201. Reservations not accepted Fri–Sat. Most menu items under $10. AE, MC, V. Mon–Sat 6am–9pm; Sun 7am–9pm.

El Rancho 🎯 *Moments* *Kids* AMERICAN/NEW MEXICAN   Set in the historic El Rancho Hotel (see above), this restaurant has fans all across the Southwest. They come to experience the Old West decor—with well-spaced, heavy wooden furniture and movie memorabilia on the walls—and the sense of the many movie stars who once ate here. The food is fine-diner-style, with dishes such as steak and eggs or hot cakes for breakfast, as well as regional delights, such as *atole* (hot blue-corn cereal) or a break-fast taco. At lunch you can always count on a good burger here or select from a cast of sandwiches, such as the Doris Day (sirloin steak on French bread), or salads. At dinner, steaks are a big hit, as is the grilled salmon, both served with soup or salad, vegetable, and your choice of potato or rice. The New Mexican food is also good. Kids can select from the "little buckaroos" menu. A full bar is available.

In the El Rancho Hotel and Motel, 1000 E. 66 Ave. ℭ **800/543-6351** or 505/863-9311. Reservations not accepted. Main courses $4–$10 breakfast, $7–$9 lunch, $8–$16 dinner. AE, DISC, MC, V. Daily 6:30am–10pm.

5 Chama: Home of the Cumbres & Toltec Scenic Railroad

59 miles NW of Taos; 91 miles NW of Santa Fe; 95 miles E of Farmington

This pioneer village of 1,250 people at the base of the 10,000-foot Cumbres Pass is New Mexico's undiscovered play land. Now, with some new additions, the town is really looking up. A park, clock-tower, and—drumroll, please—sidewalks (!) give it a friendlier tone.

Bordered by three wilderness areas, the Carson, Rio Grande, and Santa Fe national forests, the area is indeed prime for hunting, fishing, cross-country skiing, snowmobiling, snowshoeing, and hiking.

Another highlight is America's longest and highest narrow-gauge coal-fired steam line, the **Cumbres & Toltec Scenic Railroad,** which winds through valleys and mountain meadows 64 miles between Chama and Antonito, Colorado. The village of Chama boomed when the railroad arrived in 1881. A rough-and-ready frontier town, the place still maintains that flavor, with lumber and ranching making up a big part of the economy.

Landmarks to watch for are the **Brazos Cliffs** and waterfall and **Heron and El Vado lakes.** Tierra Amarilla, the Rio Arriba County seat, is 14 miles south, and is at the center—along with Los Ojos and Los Brazos—of a wool-raising and weaving tradition. Local craftspeople still weave masterpieces. Dulce, governmental seat of the Jicarilla Apache Indian Reservation, is 27 miles west.

ESSENTIALS

GETTING THERE   From Santa Fe, take US 84 north (2 hr.). From Taos, take US 64 west (2½ hr.). From Farmington, take US 64 east (2¼ hr.).

VISITOR INFORMATION   The **New Mexico Visitor Information Center,** P.O. Box 697, Chama, NM 87520 (ℭ **505/756-2235**), is at 2372 NM 17. It's open daily from 8am to 6pm in the summer, from 8am to 5pm in the winter. At the same address is the **Chama Valley Chamber of Commerce** (ℭ **800/477-0149** or 505/756-2306).

ALL ABOARD THE HISTORIC C&T RAILROAD

Cumbres & Toltec Scenic Railroad ☆☆ *Moments*   If you have a passion for the past and for incredible scenery, climb aboard America's longest and highest narrow-gauge steam railroad, the historic C&T. It operates on a 64-mile track between Chama and Antonito, Colorado. Built in 1880 as an extension of the Denver and Rio Grande line to serve the mining camps of the San Juan Mountains, it is perhaps the finest surviving example of what once was a vast network of remote Rocky Mountain railways.

The C&T passes through forests of pine and aspen, past striking rock formations, and over the magnificent Toltec Gorge of the Rio de los Pinos. It crests at the 10,015-foot Cumbres Pass, the highest in the United States used by scheduled passenger trains.

Steam Power Shopping

After sitting on the steam train, you may want to stroll awhile, hitting a few of the shops in Chama. One of note is the **Local Color Gallery**, 567 Terrace Ave. (© **888/756-2604** or 505/756-2604), in the center of town. You'll find all kinds of locally made arts and crafts, from pottery to moody candles painted with petroglyph symbols to picturesque watercolors of the Chama area.

Halfway through the route, at Osier, Colorado, the *New Mexico Express* from Chama meets the *Colorado Limited* from Antonito. They stop to exchange greetings, engines, and through passengers. Round-trip day passengers return to their starting point, while through passengers continue on to Antonito and return by van. Both enjoy a lunch of turkey and all the fixin's at a big dining hall beside the old water tank and stock pens in Osier. Note that both trips are nearly full-day events. Those who find it uncomfortable to sit for long periods may instead want to opt for hiking or skiing in the area. Ask about their Parlor Car, a more luxurious alternative to coach seating.

A walking-tour brochure, describing 23 points of interest in the Chama railroad yards, can be picked up at the 1899 depot in Chama. A registered National Historic Site, the C&T is owned by the states of Colorado and New Mexico. Special cars with lifts for people with disabilities are available with a 7-day advance reservation.

P.O. Box 789, Chama. © **888/CUMBRES** or 505/756-2151. Fax 505/756-2694. www.cumbresandtoltec.com. Lunch is included with all fares. Round-trip to Osier: adults $70, children under $37. Through trip to Antonito, return by van (or to Antonito by van, return by train): adults $65, children $35. Reservations highly recommended. Memorial Day to mid-Oct trains leave Chama daily at 10am; vans depart for Antonito at 8am.

WHERE TO STAY IN CHAMA

Most accommodations in this area are on NM 17 or south of the US 64/84 junction, known as the "Y."

Chama Trails Inn ⊛ This stucco building, adorned with chile *ristras* (decorative strung chiles), has homey motel-style rooms at a reasonable price. The place is impeccably kept, and the medium-size rooms feature custom-made pine furnishings and minifridges. Note that the rooms are a bit dark because of stucco-colored walls. A few rooms have ceiling fans, gas fireplaces, and/or Mexican-tile bathroom floors. A new gazebo in the front grassy area provides a great place for a picnic lunch or dinner. Most noteworthy: The owners take great care of this place and are on hand to make your stay pleasant.

2362 Hwy. 17 (P.O. Box 975), Chama, NM 87520. © **800/289-1421** or 505/756-2156. Fax 505/756-2855. www. chamatrailsinn.com. 15 units. $50–$85 double, depending on the season. AE, DC, DISC, MC, V. Pets accepted w/$10 fee. **Amenities:** Exercise room; Jacuzzi; sauna. *In room:* TV, fridge, coffeemaker, iron, Wi-Fi.

River Bend Lodge Set on a bend of the Chama River, this lodge offers the best cabins in town and clean motel rooms. Though they're prefab cabins, they're better than some of the more authentic and overly rustic ones at nearby lodgings. If you can reserve cabin 40, 50, or 60, at the back of the property, you'll have a sweet riverside stay. Some of these are split-level, with a queen-size sleeping loft and a bedroom—not great for privacy but good for a family that doesn't mind sharing space. Others are similar, but without the loft. Every cabin has a foldout futon in the living room, an efficient little kitchen, and a small bathroom. The motel rooms are medium-size, with basic furnishing and a long portal to relax on in the afternoons.

2625 US 84/64, Chama, NM 87520. © 800/288-1371 or 505/756-2264. Fax 505/756-2664. www.chamariverbend lodge.com. 20 units. Motel rooms $65–$78 double; cabins $89–$129 double. Additional person $10. Children under 13 stay free in parent's room. AE, DC, DISC, MC, V. Pets accepted w/$10 fee. **Amenities:** Jacuzzi; river for fishing and wading. *In room:* A/C, TV, fridge, coffeemaker (upon request), microwave (upon request).

CAMPING

At **Rio Chama RV Campground** (© 505/756-2303), you're within easy walking distance of the Cumbres & Toltec Scenic Railroad depot. This shady campground with 94 sites along the Rio Chama is ideal for RVers and tenters who plan to take train rides. The campground also offers great photo opportunities of the old steam trains leaving the depot. Hot showers, a dump station, and complete hookups are available. It's only open May to mid-October. The campground is 2¼ miles north of the US 84/64 junction on NM 17.

Twin Rivers Trailer Park (© 505/756-2218; www.twinriversonline.net) has 50 sites and 40 full hookups; phone hookups are offered. Tenting is available, as are laundry facilities and ice and picnic tables. River swimming and fishing are popular activities; other sports facilities include basketball, volleyball, badminton, and horseshoes. Twin Rivers, 100 yards west of the junction of NM 17 and US 84/64, is open April 15 to November 15.

WHERE TO DINE IN CHAMA

Cookin' Books *Finds* AMERICAN/DELI   This is Chama's new gem, a fun community-style cafe serving creative, delectable food. The main room has a vaulted ceiling with bookshelves on one side and lots of windows. Diners order at a counter and serve themselves water and coffee, while the food is made fresh and brought to them. The menu ranges broadly. You might start with shrimp ceviche or a chicken quesadilla. For an entree, the tastiest sandwich is the roast turkey, goat cheese, and pesto served on a fresh ciabatta roll. Lighter appetites may select from a few salad options such as a grilled salmon steak on organic greens. During a recent visit, we had the daily special: a stellar chicken *putanesca* (chicken cooked with olives, tomatoes, and onions), served with a salad. While you wait for your food, be sure to peruse the community room/gallery in back, displaying local art including "found" pieces by Bruce McIntosh. Beer and wine accompany the menu.

2449 U.S. 84/64, at the Y, Chama. © 505/756-1717. All menu items under $9. MC, V. Thurs–Mon 10am–8pm.

High Country Restaurant and Saloon NEW MEXICAN/SEAFOOD/STEAKS This is definitely a country place, with functional furniture, orange vinyl chairs, brown carpet, and a big stone fireplace. But it's *the* place innkeepers recommend, and one traveling couple we spoke to had eaten lunch and dinner here every day of their weeklong stay. The steaks are a big draw. More sophisticated appetites may like the *trucha con piñon,* trout dusted in flour and cooked with pine nuts, garlic, and shallots. Meals are served with a salad and choice of potato. The New Mexican food is also good. The attached saloon has a full bar and bustles with people eating peanuts and throwing the shells on the floor. Breakfast on Sunday is country-style, with offerings such as steak and eggs, and biscuits and gravy topping the menu, as well as omelets, pancakes, and huevos rancheros.

Main St. (⅒ mile north of the Y), Chama. © 505/756-2384. Sun $8.95 breakfast buffet; $6–$12 lunch; $6–$20 dinner. AE, DISC, MC, V. Mon–Sat 11am–10pm; Sun 8am–10pm. Closed Easter, Thanksgiving, and Christmas.

ON THE ROAD: WHAT TO SEE & DO ON US 84 SOUTH

Note: For a map of this area, see "Excursions from Santa Fe," in chapter 6.

Distinctive yellow earth provided a name for the town of **Tierra Amarilla,** 14 miles south of Chama at the junction of US 84 and US 64. Throughout New Mexico, this name is synonymous with a continuing controversy over the land-grant rights of the descendants of the original Hispanic settlers. But the economy of this community of 1,000 is dyed in the wool—literally.

The organization *Ganados del Valle* (Livestock Growers of the Valley) is at work to save the longhaired Spanish churro sheep from extinction, to introduce other unusual wool breeds to the valley, and to perpetuate a 200-year-old tradition of shepherding, spinning, weaving, and dyeing. Many of the craftspeople work in conjunction with **Tierra Wools** ⍟, P.O. Box 229, Los Ojos, NM 87551 (ℭ **505/588-7231;** www.hand weavers.com), which has a showroom and workshop in a century-old mercantile building just north of Tierra Amarilla. One-of-a-kind blankets and men's and women's apparel are among the products displayed and sold.

Just down the street, across from the Los Ojos General Store, is an interesting little art studio worth checking out. **Yellow Earth Studio** (ℭ **505/588-7807**), the passion of Paul Trachtman, the resident artist, is a great place to see and purchase enchanting scenes of the Los Ojos area in the form of paintings and monotype, woodcut, and metal engraving prints.

Two state parks are a short drive west from Tierra Amarilla. **El Vado Lake State Park,** 14 miles southwest on NM 112 (ℭ **505/588-7247**), offers boating and water-skiing, fishing, and camping in summer; cross-country skiing and ice fishing in winter. **Heron Lake State Park,** 11 miles west on US 64 and NM 95 (ℭ **505/588-7470**), has a no-wake speed limit for motor vessels, adding to its appeal for fishing, sailing, wind-surfing, canoeing, and swimming. The park has an interpretive center, plus camping, picnic sites, hiking trails, and cross-country skiing in the winter. The 5½-mile Rio Chama trail connects the two lakes.

East of Tierra Amarilla, the Rio Brazos cuts a canyon through the Tusas Mountains and around 11,403-foot Brazos Peak. Just north of Los Ojos, NM 512 heads east 7½ miles up the **Brazos Box Canyon.** High cliffs that rise straight from the valley floor give it a Yosemite-like appearance—which is even more apparent from an overlook on US 64, 18 miles east of Tierra Amarilla en route to Taos. **El Chorro,** an impressive waterfall at the mouth of the canyon, usually flows only from early May to mid-June. Several resort lodges are in the area.

About 37 miles south of Tierra Amarilla on US 84, and 3 miles north of Ghost Ranch, is **Echo Canyon Amphitheater** (ℭ **505/684-2486**), a U.S. Forest Service campground and picnic area. The "theater," hollowed out of sandstone by thousands of years of erosion, is a natural work of art with layers of stone ranging from pearl-color to blood red. The walls send back eerie echoes and even clips of conversations. It's just a 10-minute walk from the parking area. The fee is $2 per car. Some 13 miles west of here, via the dirt Forest Service Road 151 into the Chama River Canyon Wilderness, is the isolated **Monastery of Christ in the Desert** (www.christdesert.org), built in 1964 by Benedictine monks. The chapel is a graceful structure set against bold cliffs, worth visiting if you like a taste of solemnity. The brothers produce crafts, sold at a small gift shop, and operate a guesthouse.

Along the same road (F.S. 151) is access to the Chama River, a good place to hike, mountain bike, raft, kayak, and camp. The **Rim Vista Trail** will take you to the top of the rim, with vast views out across Abiquiu Lake and Ghost Ranch. Primitive camp-sites can be found all along the river.

A 3-mile drive from there is **Ghost Ranch,** a collection of adobe buildings that make up an adult study center maintained by the United Presbyterian Church. A number of hauntingly memorable hikes originate from this place, which gets its name from the *brujas,* or witches, said to inhabit the canyons. Most notable among the hikes is **Kitchen Mesa,** directions for which can be obtained at the visitor center. World-renowned painter Georgia O'Keeffe spent time at Ghost Ranch painting these canyons and other land formations. Eventually she bought a portion of the ranch and lived in a humble adobe house there. The ranch now offers seminars on a variety of topics, ranging from art to literature to religion, that are open to all. For information, contact **Ghost Ranch,** 401 Old Taos Hwy., Santa Fe (© **505/982-8539;** www.ghostranch.org).

The **Florence Hawley Ellis Museum of Anthropology** has interpretative exhibits of a Spanish ranch house and Native American anthropology, and the **Ruth Hall Paleontology Museum** (both museums © **505/685-4333;** www.ghostranch.org) displays fossils of the early dinosaur, named coelophysis, found on the ranch. A lightly built creature, it was very fast when chasing prey. It roamed the area 250 million years ago, making it the oldest dinosaur found in New Mexico.

Georgia O'Keeffe spent most of her adult life in **Abiquiu,** a tiny town in a bend of the Rio Chama 14 miles south of the Ghost Ranch, and 22 miles north of Española, on US 84. The inspiration for O'Keeffe's startling landscapes (many of which can now be seen in the Georgia O'Keeffe Museum; p. 161) is clear in the surrounding terrain. **O'Keeffe's adobe home,** where she lived and painted until her death in 1986, is open for public tours, but reservations are required 1 to 2 months in advance (call © **505/685-4539).** The charge is $22 for a 1-hour tour. A number of tours are given each week—on Tuesday, Thursday, and Friday—and a limited number of people are accepted per tour. Visitors are not permitted to take pictures. Fortunately, O'Keeffe's home remains as it was when she lived there. Abiquiu is on the High Road between Santa Fe and Taos (p. 187).

Many dinosaur skeletons have been found in rocks along the base of cliffs near **Abiquiu Reservoir** (© **505/685-4371),** a popular boating and fishing spot formed by the Abiquiu Dam.

A good place to stay in the area is the **Abiquiu Inn,** a small country inn, restaurant, art gallery, and gift shop, half a mile north of the village of Abiquiu (© **505/685-4378).** The casitas are especially nice. Rates are $109 to $189.

A GREAT NEARBY PLACE TO STAY & DINE

Rancho de San Juan ★★ *(Moments*   Just 38 miles from Santa Fe, set between Española and Ojo Caliente, this inn provides an authentic northern New Mexico desert experience with the comforts of a luxury hotel and the ease of staying with friends. In 2006, this hot spot was listed on the *Condé Nast Traveler* Gold List and named as one of the top six inns in the United States by *Executive Traveler.* It's the passion of architect and chef John Johnson, responsible for the design and cuisine, and interior designer David Heath, responsible for the elegant interiors. The original part of the inn comprises four recently renovated and enlarged rooms around a central courtyard. Additional casitas with kitchens are in the outlying hills. Rooms here are open, bright, and very elegant—stylishly decorated with a creative mix from the owners' personal art collections including contemporary paintings, tribal masks, and European antiques. From private patios, you'll have spectacular views of desert landscapes and distant, snow-capped peaks. The Kiva suite is the most innovative, with a round bedroom and a skylight just above the bed, perfect for stargazing.

A few minutes' hike from the inn is **"Windows in the Earth,"** an impressive shrine that the innkeepers commissioned to be carved into a sandstone outcropping, where weddings and other festivities are held. With a key, you can unlock the structure and go inside for a don't-miss experience—it feels like you're standing in a life-size sandcastle.

US 285 (en route to Ojo Caliente), P.O. Box 4140, Fairview Station, Española, NM 87533. © 505/753-6818. www. ranchodesanjuan.com. 12 units. $275–$550 double. AE, MC, V. **Amenities:** Restaurant; concierge; in-room massage and other spa treatments; laundry service. *In room:* A/C, fridge w/stocked beverages, coffeemaker, hair dryer, dial-up Internet access, CD player, fireplace.

6 Las Vegas & Environs

21 miles E of Santa Fe; 59 miles SE of Taos; 141 miles NE of Albuquerque

Once known as the "gateway to New Mexico," **Las Vegas** ⟨★★⟩, a pleasant town in the foothills of the Sangre de Cristo Mountains, was founded by a land grant from the Mexican government in 1835. A group of 29 Spanish colonists planted crops in the area and built a central plaza, which started out as a meeting place and a defense against Indian attack but soon became a main trading center on the Santa Fe Trail. Las Vegas boomed with the advent of the Atchison, Topeka, and Santa Fe Railway in 1879; almost overnight, the town became the most important trading center and gathering place in the state. It was one of the largest towns in the Rocky Mountain West, rivaling Denver, Tucson, and El Paso in size.

Settlers who arrived by train in the late 19th century shunned the indigenous adobe architecture, favoring building styles more typical of the Midwest or New England. They put up scores of fancy Queen Anne and Victorian-style houses and hotels, and the town is noted to this day for its dazzling diversity of architectural styles. Some 900 buildings in Las Vegas are on the National Register of Historic Places.

ESSENTIALS
GETTING THERE   From Santa Fe, take I-25 northeast 60 miles (1¼ hr.); from Raton, take I-25 south 105 miles (1¾ hr.); from Taos, follow NM 518 southeast 78 miles through Mora (2 hr.); from Tucumcari, follow NM 104 west 112 miles (2 hr.). **Las Vegas Municipal Airport** handles private flights and charters but has no regularly scheduled commercial service.

VISITOR INFORMATION   The **Las Vegas & San Miguel County Chamber of Commerce** is at 701 Grand Ave. (P.O. Box 128), Las Vegas, NM 87701 (© **800/832-5947** or 505/425-8631; www.lasvegasnm.org). It's open weekdays from 9am to 5pm.

EXPLORING LAS VEGAS
THE HISTORIC DISTRICT
The chamber of commerce (see "Essentials," above) has a map of a self-guided tour of this area. What's most notable is the town's early Spanish history; some adobe buildings date from the first Spanish visits in the 16th century. In addition, you'll rarely see such a well-preserved collection of Territorial-style buildings. Most of the interesting structures are in the Plaza–Bridge Street area. In particular, don't miss the **Plaza Hotel,** 230 Old Town Plaza, the finest hotel in the New Mexico Territory in 1881. (See "Where to Stay in Las Vegas," below.)

Housed in a 1940s-era Work Projects Administration (WPA) building, the **Las Vegas City Museum and Rough Riders Memorial Collection,** 727 Grand Ave. (© **505/454-1401,** ext. 283), is a fun spot to spend about an hour. The largest contingent of Rough Riders was recruited from New Mexico to fight in the 1898 Spanish–American War. This museum chronicles their contribution to U.S. history and also contains artifacts relating to the history of the city. Another exhibit documents the history of Las Vegas. Admission is free. The museum is open Tuesday to Sunday 10am to 4pm, and by appointment.

In the plaza area, the **Santa Fe Trail Interpretive Center,** 127 Bridge St. (© **505/ 425-8803;** www.lasvegasnmcchp.com), offers a glimpse into efforts to restore the town's 918 historic buildings as well as information about the Santa Fe Trail. Set in the 1890s Winternitz Building, it's a fun stop, if you find it open. Volunteers staff the center, so hours vary.

EXPLORING THE AREA

La Cueva National Historic Site and Salman Ranch *(Finds*   Each fall, we make a bit of a pilgrimage to this spot in a lush valley along the Mora River. Its history is

---

Value Weaving Magic

You can watch weavers at work at **Tapetes de Lana** on the Las Vegas Plaza. Appropriately set in a late-1800s textile shop, this fun shop and weavers' studio offers a peek into the art as well as lovely works to buy. Hanging from antique stone walls are scarves, shawls, and Rio Grande–style rugs woven as part of a job-training program for people with low income, many of whom have mastered the art beautifully. It's located at 1814 Plaza (© **505/426-8638; www.tapetesdelana.com**) and is open Monday through Friday 8am to 5pm and Saturday 10am to 5pm. Prices are uncommonly reasonable.

---

rich, dating from the early 1800s, when a man named Vicente Romero began farming and raising sheep here. He completed an elegant two-story northern New Mexico home that still stands, as well as a mill that ground flour and supplied electricity for the area (the real draw). Just north of these historic sites is the San Rafael Mission Church, with exquisite French Gothic windows. Recently restored by local people, it's now painted blue and white. The trip through these sites is worth the time during any season, but in the fall, the raspberries ripen and turn this into a must-do trip. The ranch's current owner, Frances Salman, planted 20 acres of the delectable fruit and now sells it by the basket or crate, as well as in jams and over soft vanilla ice cream. Delicious.

NM 518, 6 miles east of Mora, Buena Vista, NM 87712. © 505/387-2900. Free admission. Summer Mon–Sat 9am–5pm, Sun 10am–5pm; winter hours limited (call first).

FORT UNION NATIONAL MONUMENT 🌟

Established in 1851 to defend the Santa Fe Trail against attacks from Plains Indians, Fort Union was expanded in 1861 in anticipation of a Confederate invasion, which was subsequently thwarted at Glorieta Pass, 20 miles southeast of Santa Fe. Fort Union's location on the Santa Fe Trail made it a welcome way station for travelers, but when the railroad replaced the trail in 1879, the fort was on its way out. It was abandoned in 1891. Today, Fort Union, the largest military installation in the 19th-century Southwest, is in ruins. Though it offers little to see but adobe walls and chimneys, the very scope of the fort is impressive. Santa Fe Trail wagon ruts can still be seen nearby. Follow the 1½-mile self-guided interpretive trail that wanders through the ruins and imagine yourself a weary 19th-century wagon traveler stopping for rest and supplies.

The national monument has a small visitor center and museum with exhibits and booklets on the fort's history. Visitors should allow 2 hours to tour the ruins.

JUST THE FACTS   To reach the site from Las Vegas, drive 18 miles north on I-25 to the Watrous exit, and then another 8 miles northwest on NM 161. Admission is $3 per person. Fort Union National Monument is open Memorial Day to Labor Day daily 8am to 6pm; during the rest of the year, it is open daily 8am to 4pm. It's closed Thanksgiving, Christmas, and New Year's Day.

A gift shop carries a wide selection of books on New Mexico history and women's history, and frontier military books. Camping is not available at the monument, but facilities are available in nearby Las Vegas.

For more information on the monument, contact Fort Union National Monument, P.O. Box 127, Watrous, NM 87753 (© **505/425-8025;** www.nps.gov/foun).

WHERE TO STAY IN LAS VEGAS

Most motels are on US 85 (Grand Ave.), the main north-south highway through downtown Las Vegas. (An exception is the Plaza Hotel, below.)

Inn on the Santa Fe Trail ℛ   Built in the 1920s as a court motel, this inn has been remodeled in a hacienda style, with all rooms facing the central courtyard, creating a quiet, intimate, and sophisticated retreat just off busy Grand Avenue. Although it's not as historical as the Plaza Hotel (see below), the rooms are a bit more up-to-date and functional, and you can park your car right outside. Rooms are medium-size with nice accents, such as handcrafted iron light fixtures, towel racks, and hand-carved pine furniture—even *trasteros* (armoires) to conceal the televisions. The beds are comfortably firm, and each room has a table with two chairs and a desk. The bathrooms are small but very clean. Suites have sofa beds and minifridges. The inn's restaurant, Blackjack's Grill (see "Where to Dine," below), is one of Las Vegas's fanciest. The heated outdoor pool, open seasonally, is lovely. Ask about the regional cultural events that the inn helps organize.

1133 Grand Ave., Las Vegas, NM 87701. ℂ 888/448-8438 or 505/425-6791. www.innonthesantafetrail.com. 42 units. $79 double. Rates include continental breakfast. Extra person $5. AE, DISC, MC, V. Pets permitted for $5 fee. **Amenities:** Restaurant (p. 284); outdoor heated pool. *In room:* A/C, TV, coffeemaker, Wi-Fi.

Plaza Hotel ℛ   A stay in this hotel offers a romantic peek into the past, with a view of the plaza. The windows look out on the spot where, in 1846, a ceremony led by Gen. Stephen Kearny marked the takeover of New Mexico by the United States. The inn was built in Italianate bracketed style in 1882, in the days when Western towns, newly connected with the East by train, vied with one another in constructing fancy "railroad hotels," as they were known. Considered the finest hotel in the New Mexico Territory when it was built, it underwent a $2-million renovation exactly 100 years later. Stately walnut staircases frame the lobby and conservatory (with its piano); throughout the hotel, the architecture is true to its era.

As with most renovations in northern New Mexico, don't expect to see the elegance of the Ritz. Instead, expect a more frontier style, with Old West antiques. Rooms vary in size, but most are average size, with elegantly high ceilings, antique furnishings, comfortably firm beds, and armoires concealing the televisions. The bathrooms also range in size; most are small, with lots of original tile but up-to-date fixtures. The rooms either have windows facing outward toward the plaza and surrounding streets or inward toward an atrium. The inward-facing rooms are quieter but a bit claustrophobic. All rooms open onto spacious hallways with casual seating areas.

The hotel offers limited room service from its **Landmark Grill,** which has good food, especially the New Mexican dishes, in a period setting. On Friday nights, be sure to sample their prime rib. Notice the walls of the Landmark: The original 19th-century stenciling has been restored. The restaurant is open for lunch and dinner. Byron T's 19th-century saloon often features live music on Friday and Saturday evenings.

230 Plaza, Las Vegas, NM 87701. ℂ 800/328-1882 or 505/425-3591. Fax 505/425-9659. www.plazahotel-nm.com. 36 units. $99–$129 double; $154–$176 suite. Rates include hot cooked-to-order breakfast. AE, DC, DISC, MC, V. **Amenities:** Restaurant; bar. *In room:* A/C, TV, coffeemaker, Wi-Fi.

CAMPING

There's plenty of camping available in and around Las Vegas. We recommend the **Las Vegas KOA** (ℂ 800/562-3423 or 505/454-0180; www.koa.com), which has 65 sites,

15 with full hookups, 26 with water and electricity. Laundry, grocery, ice, and recreational facilities (including a pool) are available, as is a large gift shop. Seasonal cookouts are offered. From I-25, go 1 block southeast on US 84, then half a mile southwest on Frontage Road (also called Sheridan Rd.).

WHERE TO DINE IN LAS VEGAS

Blackjack's Grill ✷✷ SEAFOOD/STEAKS   The main dining room at Blackjack's is small and cozy, done in brilliant colors with mood lighting. In the warmer months, diners can sit on a patio under white cloth umbrellas. As befits the area, it's a fairly informal restaurant that does fill up, so try to make reservations. Each night the chef serves some special dishes, most of which are fairly traditional. We've enjoyed beef medallions in wine sauce served with garlic mashed potatoes. The pasta dishes, such as fettuccine Alfredo, can also be good. Most meals come with bread, a choice of salad or soup, and a vegetable. A variety of dessert specials are available. Beer and wine are served.

At the Inn on the Santa Fe Trail, 1133 Grand Ave. ⊘ **888/448-8438** or 505/425-6791. Reservations recommended. Main courses $13–$20. AE, MC, V. Daily 5–8:30pm.

El Rialto Restaurant & Lounge ✷ *Kids* NEW MEXICAN   This has been a favorite restaurant for years. The food is excellent. It's a locals' place, full of families, old Hispanic farmers, and students from the United World College. The decor is cheesy pastels, but it can be overlooked for the comfort, especially of the booths. The lounge still retains the original red upholstery, which is more to our liking. Service is friendly and efficient. The chile, especially the green, is outstanding here (order anything smothered with it). Our favorite is the chicken enchilada plate. The beef enchilada is good, too, and the rellenos are quite tasty. There are a variety of stuffed *sopaipillas,* and steaks, too, as well as sandwiches and a kids' menu. For dessert, we usually smother a *sopaipilla* with honey, though you can order pie or flan. There's a full bar and outdoor patio here.

141 Bridge St. ⊘ **505/454-0037.** Reservations recommended. Main courses $5–$10 lunch, $7–$23 dinner. AE, DC, DISC, MC, V. Mon–Sat 10:30am–8:30pm.

7 Cimarron & Raton: Historic Towns on the Santa Fe Trail

Cimarron: 35 miles E of Taos, 23 miles NE of Las Vegas, 76 miles NE of Santa Fe; Raton: 67 miles NE of Taos, 93 miles NE of Las Vegas, 111 miles NE of Santa Fe

CIMARRON ✷

Few towns in the American West have as much lore or legend attached to them as Cimarron, 41 miles southwest of Raton on US 64. Nestled against the eastern slope of the Sangre de Cristo Mountains, the town (its name is Spanish for "wild" or "untamed") achieved its greatest fame as a wild and woolly outpost on the Santa Fe Trail from the 1850s to 1880s. It was a gathering place for area ranchers, traders, gamblers, gunslingers, and other characters. Frontier personalities such as Kit Carson and Wyatt Earp, Buffalo Bill Cody and Annie Oakley, Bat Masterson and Doc Holliday, Butch Cassidy and Jesse James, painter Frederic Remington and novelist Zane Grey all passed through and stayed in Cimarron—most of them at the **St. James Hotel,** 17th Street and Collison (⊘ **866/472-5019** or 505/376-2664). Even if you're not planning an overnight stay, it's a fun place to visit for an hour or two. The **Old Mill Museum** (⊘ **505/376-2417**), a grand, three-story stone structure that's well worth visiting, houses an interesting collection of early photos as well as memorabilia. It's open in May and September, Saturday from 9am to 5pm and Sunday from 1 to 5pm; Memorial Day to Labor Day, Friday through Wednesday from 9am to 5pm. It's closed October through April. Admission is $2 for adults, $1 for seniors and children. The **Cimarron Chamber of Commerce**, 104 N. Lincoln Ave. (P.O. Box 604), Cimarron, NM 87714 (© **505/376-2417;** www.cimarronnm.com), has complete information on the region. It is open in summer Thursday through Monday from 8:30am to 4:30pm; in winter Monday through Friday from 10am to 3pm.

RATON

Raton was founded in 1879 at the site of Willow Springs, a watering stop on the Santa Fe Trail. Mountain man "Uncle Dick" Wooton, a closet entrepreneur, had blasted a pass through the Rocky Mountains just north of the spring, and he began charging tolls. When the railroad bought Wooton's road, Raton developed as the railroad, mining, and ranching center for this part of the New Mexico Territory. Today it has a well-preserved historic district. The tourist information center is at the **Raton Chamber and Economic Development Council,** 100 Clayton Rd., at the corner of 2nd Street (P.O. Box 1211), Raton, NM 87740 (© **800/638-6161** or 505/445-3689; www.raton.info). The center is open daily from Memorial Day to Labor Day, 8am to 6pm, 8am to 5pm the rest of the year.

East of Raton is Capulin Mountain, home to **Capulin Volcano National Monument** (★★), which offers visitors the rare opportunity to walk inside a volcanic crater. A 2-mile road spirals up from the visitor center more than 600 feet to the crater of the 8,182-foot peak. Two self-guided trails leave from the parking area: an energetic and spectacular 1-mile hike around the crater rim, and a 100-foot descent into the crater to the ancient volcanic vent. One of the most interesting features here is the symmetry of the main cinder cone. The volcano was last active about 60,000 years ago, when it sent out the last of four lava flows. The monument is 30 miles east of Raton; take US 64/87 and go north 3 miles on NM 325. The visitor center, located at the base of the western side of the volcano, is open daily Memorial Day to Labor Day from 7:30am to 6:30pm, the rest of the year daily 8am to 4pm. An audiovisual program discusses volcanism, and park personnel will answer questions. Admission is $5 per car. For more information, contact **Capulin Volcano National Monument,** P.O. Box 40, Capulin, NM 88414 (© **505/278-2201;** www.nps.gov/cavo).

8 The I-40 Corridor

The 216 freeway miles on I-40 from Albuquerque to the Texas border cross featureless prairie and very few towns. But the valleys of the Pecos River (site of Santa Rosa) and the Canadian River (Tucumcari is on its banks) have several attractions, including natural lakes. There's not a lot to explore here unless you're a bird-watcher or a fisher, but both towns can make a day's stopover worthwhile.

ESSENTIALS

GETTING THERE   Travel time from Albuquerque to Tucumcari via I-40 is 2 hours, 40 minutes; to Santa Rosa, 1 hour, 45 minutes. There's no regularly scheduled commercial-airline service into either Tucumcari or Santa Rosa. Private planes can land at **Tucumcari Municipal Airport** (© 505/461-3229).

VISITOR INFORMATION   Contact the **Tucumcari–Quay County Chamber of Commerce,** 404 W. Rte. 66 Blvd. (P.O. Drawer E), Tucumcari, NM 88401 (© **888/ 664-7255** or 505/461-1694; www.tucumcarinm.com), or the **Santa Rosa City Information Center,** 486 Historic Rte. 66, Santa Rosa, NM 88435 (© **505/472-3763**).

WHERE TO STAY

Major chain hotels are at I-40 interchanges in both Tucumcari and Santa Rosa. Smaller "ma and pa" motels lie along the main streets that were once segments of legendary Route 66—Tucumcari Boulevard in Tucumcari, and Will Rogers Drive in Santa Rosa.

IN TUCUMCARI

Best Western Discovery Inn   This pink Mission-style motel has large quiet rooms and provides an oasis in the somewhat barren eastern part of the state. It's located off the strip, but near I-40; take exit 332. Opened in 1985, remodeling is ongoing. Rooms are decorated in earth tones, with comfortable beds. Bathrooms are small but each has an outer sink/vanity and dressing room. Everything is very clean. Complimentary morning coffee is an added touch, and K-Bob's restaurant is right next door.

200 E. Estrella Ave. (at I-40 exit 332), Tucumcari, NM 88401. © 800/528-1234 or 505/461-4884. Fax 505/461-2463. www.bestwestern.com/discoveryinn. 107 units. May–Oct $79 double; Nov–Apr $65 double. AE, DC, DISC, MC, V. Pets additional $5 per day. **Amenities:** Seasonal outdoor pool; fitness center; Jacuzzi; coin-op laundry. *In room:* A/C, TV, Wi-Fi.

Camping Near Tucumcari

A good campground near Tucumcari is **Tucumcari KOA** (© **800/562-1871** or 505/ 461-1841; www.koa.com) with 111 sites, laundry and grocery facilities, RV supplies, picnic tables, and grills. It also offers a recreation hall with video games, a heated swimming pool, a basketball hoop, a playground, horseshoes, and shuffleboard, along with lots of elm trees for shade. To get there from I-40, get off the interstate at exit 335, and then go a quarter-mile east on South Frontage Road.

IN SANTA ROSA

La Quinta 🐕   Perched on a hill above Santa Rosa, this newer whitewashed chain hotel offers clean and very functional rooms. All are medium-size, decorated in tasteful earth tones. Each has a small bathroom with an outer sink/vanity. Beds are comfy and rooms include a table and chairs. The place is inventively landscaped with a rock grotto patio where the hot tub sits.

1701 Will Rogers Dr., Santa Rosa, NM 88435. © 800/531-5900 or 505/472-4800. Fax 505/472-4809. www.laquinta. com. 60 units. $75–$90 double. Rates include continental breakfast. AE, DC, DISC, MC, V. **Amenities:** Indoor pool; outdoor Jacuzzi. *In room:* A/C, TV, coffeemaker, hair dryer, safe, high-speed Internet, Wi-Fi.

Camping near Santa Rosa

The **Santa Rosa Campground** (© **505/472-3126**) offers 94 sites, 33 full hookups, laundry and grocery facilities, fire rings, grills, a heated swimming pool, and a playground for the kids. Situated in a piñon and juniper forest near town, the campground has a few small elm trees on the grounds. Coming from the east on I-40, take exit 277 and go 1 mile west on Business Loop; coming from the west on I-40, take exit 275 and go ¼ mile east on Business Loop.

Also in the area is **Santa Rosa Lake State Park** (© **505/472-3110**), with year-round camping at 75 sites (about a third with electric hookups) as well as grills, boating, fishing, and hiking trails. Swimming is permitted but not encouraged because of the lake's uneven bottom and lack of beaches; children are safer swimming in Park Lake in Santa Rosa.

Moments Route 66 Revisited: Rediscovering New Mexico's Stretch of the Mother Road

As the old Bobby Troupe hit suggests: *Get your kicks on Route 66.* The highway that once stretched from Chicago to California was hailed as the road to freedom. During the Great Depression, it was the way west for farmers escaping Dust Bowl poverty out on the plains. And if you found yourself in a rut in the postwar late 1940s and early '50s, all you had to do was hop in the car and head west on Route 66.

The road existed long before it gained such widespread fascination. Built in the late 1920s and paved in 1937, it was the lifeblood of communities in eight states. Nowadays, however, US 66 is as elusive as the fantasies that once carried hundreds of thousands west in search of a better life. Replaced by other roads, covered up by interstates (mostly I-40), and just plain out of use, Route 66 still exists in New Mexico, but you'll have to do a little searching and take some extra time to find it.

Motorists driving west from Texas can take a spin (make that a slow spin) on a 20-mile gravel stretch of the original highway running from Glenrio (Texas) to San Jon. From San Jon to Tucumcari, you can enjoy nearly 24 continuous paved miles of vintage 66. In Tucumcari, the historic route sliced through the center of town along what is now Tucumcari Boulevard. Santa Rosa's Will Rogers Drive is that city's 4-mile claim to the Mother Road. In Albuquerque, US 66 follows Central Avenue for 18 miles, from the 1936 State Fairgrounds, past original 1930s motels and the historic Nob Hill district, west through downtown.

One of the best spots to pretend you are a 1950s road warrior crossing the desert—whizzing past rattlesnakes, tepees, and tumbleweeds—is along NM 124, which winds 25 miles from Mesita to Acoma in northwestern New Mexico. You can next pick up old Route 66 in Grants, along 6-mile Santa Fe Avenue. In Gallup, a 9-mile segment of US 66 is lined with restaurants and hotels reminiscent of the city's days as a Western film capital from 1929 to 1964. Just outside Gallup, the historic route continues west to the Arizona border as NM 118.

For more information about Route 66, contact the **Grants/Cíbola County Chamber of Commerce** (© 800/748-2142) or the **New Mexico Department of Tourism** (© 800/545-2040).

WHERE TO DINE

Del's Family Restaurant AMERICAN/NEW MEXICAN   The big cow atop the neon sign is not only a Route 66 landmark, but it also points to the fine steaks inside. The restaurant has big windows along almost every wall, letting in plenty of daylight or neon light at night. Del's is a casual, diner-style eatery with lots of plants. Breakfast is big plates of dishes such as scrambled eggs and pancakes. At lunch, sample sandwiches and salads. The roast beef, a big seller here at dinnertime, is served with a scoop of mashed potatoes and a trip to the salad bar. You can also order a grilled chicken breast. The New Mexican food is good but not great. Del's is not licensed for alcoholic beverages.

1202 E. Route 66, Tucumcari. © 505/461-1740. Reservations not accepted. Main courses $4–$7 breakfast, $5–$9 lunch, $8–$15 dinner. MC, V. Mon–Sat 7am–9pm.

Joseph's Restaurant & Cantina ☆ AMERICAN/NEW MEXICAN   You may want to plan your drive so that you can eat a meal at "Joe's." In business since 1956, it's a real Route 66 diner, with linoleum tables, comfortable booths, and plenty of memorabilia, from license plates to vintage RC Cola posters. The locals all eat here: You'll see Hispanic grandmothers, skinny cowboys in straw hats, and dusty farmhands just in from the fields. The varied menu offers excellent fare. Breakfast is eggs and bacon or omelets. At lunch, we've enjoyed a salad topped with juicy grilled chicken. The New Mexican dishes are large and chile-smothered, and the burgers are juicy, with a variety of toppings, from the Rio Pecos, topped with green chile, to the Acapulco, with guacamole. Reasonably priced steaks are also a big seller. For dessert, try a piece of pie or a shake. Also on the premises are a bakery, a full-service bar, and a gift shop.

865 Will Rogers Dr., Santa Rosa. © 505/472-3361. Reservations not accepted. Main courses $4–$8 breakfast, $6–$9 lunch, $6–$12 dinner. AE, DC, DISC, MC, V. Summer daily 7am–10pm; winter daily 7am–9pm.

UFOs & Carlsbad Caverns: Southern New Mexico from Top to Bottom

If your idea of fun is road-tripping across exotic landscapes, delving into ancient cultures, peering into outer space, and chatting up an alien or two, southern New Mexico is your destination. Here you'll find an astonishing array of singular landscapes and unusual attractions, from the rolling gypsum sand dunes of White Sands National Monument to the underground natural cathedrals of Carlsbad Caverns National Park.

Wildness abounds at places such as the Bosque del Apache National Wildlife Refuge and the 3.3-million-acre Gila National Forest, both known for great bird-watching. Within the forest lies Gila Cliff Dwellings National Monument, home to the Mogollon people 1,000 years ago. The final frontier is also present in this region, at places such as the International UFO Museum and Research Center in Roswell, the area where aliens may have landed, and the Very Large Array, the world's most powerful radio telescope.

Between the sights lie more miles of open country than most people can imagine. Though on first glance it may appear desolate, it's actually filled with petroglyphs and lava fields, hot springs and ghost towns, places where legends such as Geronimo and Billy the Kid once roamed.

The big city in the area is Las Cruces, New Mexico's second largest, with a population of 73,600. Set at the foot of the dramatic Organ Mountains, it is an agricultural and education center. To the east lies Ruidoso, a booming resort town with good skiing in winter. To the west is Silver City, a charming mining town that's been revived in recent years. The Rio Grande slices a green swath through the center of the region, nourishing many communities along its banks.

With such long distances to cover, you'll need a reliable car to get around. Flip on the tunes, keep a close eye on the gas gauge, and enjoy the ride.

1 Getting Outside in Southern New Mexico

BIKING Several forest roads and single-track trails in this region are favorites with mountain bikers. In the Ruidoso area, near Cloudcroft, the **Rim Trail,** a 17-mile intermediate trail that offers views of the White Sands, is considered one of the top ten trails in the nation. To reach the trail, take NM 130 from Cloudcroft to NM 6563, turn right, and look for the Rim Trail signs. The Cloudcroft area offers three other good trails: La Luz Canyon, Silver Springs Loop, and Pumphouse Canyon. For directions, contact the Cloudcroft Ranger Station (© **505/682-2551**). A popular cycling area is in the Socorro area, at **Bosque del Apache National Wildlife Refuge** (© 505/835-1828), where cyclists enjoy the 12-mile loop tour. Bikes are not allowed in the Gila Wilderness, but they are permitted on trails in other parts of **Gila National Forest** (© 505/388-8201; www.fs.fed.us/r3/gila). See "Other Adventures in Gila National Forest," later in this chapter, for some specific ride suggestions, and contact **Gila Hike and Bike** (© 505/388-3222) in Silver City for rentals and guidebooks to riding in the Gila National Forest.

BIRD-WATCHING   Bitter Lake National Wildlife Refuge (© 505/622-6755), northeast of Roswell, is particularly good for watching migratory waterfowl, and **Bluff Springs** (© 505/682-2551), south of Cloudcroft, is popular with turkeys and hummingbirds. If you find turkey vultures particularly fascinating, **Rattlesnake Springs** (© 505/785-2232), south of Carlsbad, is the place to go. **Bosque del Apache National Wildlife Refuge** (© 505/835-1828) is a refuge for migratory waterfowl such as snow geese and cranes. It's 16 miles south of Socorro. The **Gila National Forest** (© 505/ 388-8201) has become quite popular with birders. Guests at the **Bear Mountain Lodge** (© 877/620-2327 or 505/538-2538; www.bearmountainlodge.com) benefit from an on-site naturalist and occasional birding tours. In the Gila National Forest, a favorite birding spot is **Lake Roberts,** where hummingbirds abound.

BOATING   Boating, water-skiing, jet-skiing, and sailing are permitted at **Carlsbad Municipal Park,** which runs through town for just over a mile along the west bank of Lake Carlsbad. The lake also has a beach that's open to swimmers. **Brantley Lake State Park** (© 505/457-2384), 15 miles north of Carlsbad, is popular with windsurfers who favor its consistent desert winds. In the Gila National Forest, both **Lake Roberts** (© 505/536-2250), about 40 miles north of Silver City on NM 15, and **Snow Lake** (© 505/533-6231), north on US 180 from Silver City and then east on NM 159, allow boating. Lake Roberts features motorboat rentals, whereas Snow Lake only permits canoes, rowboats, and other boats without gas motors. **Elephant Butte Lake State Park** (© 505/744-5923) has the largest body of water in New Mexico; the lake is 43 miles long and popular with boating enthusiasts. Three ramps provide boating access to the lake, and there are launching areas for smaller vessels. To find information on New Mexico state parks, go to **www.nmparks.com.**

FISHING   Bonito Lake and Rio Ruidoso are popular destinations for trout fishing. Guide service and fly-fishing lessons are available in Ruidoso at **Fly's Etc.,** 2801 Sudderth Dr., Suite F (© 505/257-4968 or 505/336-1684; www.flys-etc.com). The scenic **Oasis State Park** (© 505/356-5331), just north of Portales, also offers fishing. **Caballo Lake State Park** (© 505/743-3942), about 18 miles south of Truth or Consequences, offers smallmouth and largemouth bass, stripers, bluegill, crappie, catfish, and walleye fishing in its 11,500-acre lake. **Elephant Butte Lake State Park** (© 505/ 744-5923), also near Truth or Consequences, is another great fishing location. Look to catch white bass, black bass, catfish, walleye, crappie, and stripers here. **Lake Roberts** (© 505/536-2250), about 40 miles north of Silver City in the Gila National Forest, is prime rainbow trout fishing waters. A fishing license and habitat stamp are both required. You'll find fly-fishing in the **Gila River** year-round, but the best seasons are spring and fall. Mainly rainbow trout swim these waters, with catfish on the lower Gila. For more information, contact the **New Mexico Game and Fish Department** (© 505/476-8000; www.wildlife.state.nm.us).

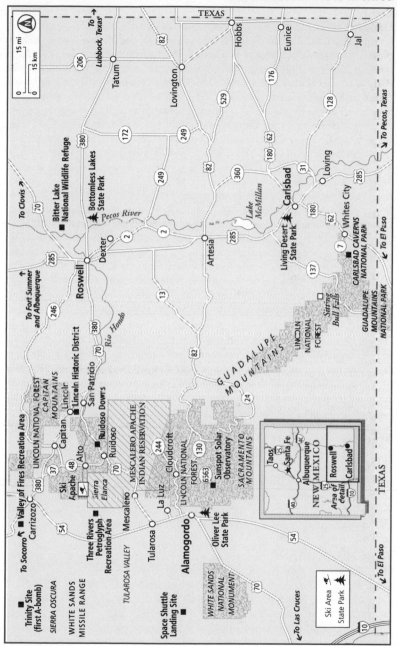

Southeastern New Mexico

TEXAS

To Lubbock, Texas

82

Hobbs

Eunice

Jal

206

Tatum

Lovington

176

128

529

To Clovis

70

172

249

249

380

Bitter Lake
National Wildlife Refuge

82

360

180

62

Bottomless Lakes
State Park

Pecos River

Lake
McMillan

Carlsbad

31

Loving

285

2

2

285

Whites City

Dexter

180

62

To El Paso

285

Artesia

Living Desert
State Park

CARLSBAD CAVERNS
NATIONAL PARK

7

To Fort Sumner
and Albuquerque

Roswell

13

137

246

380

Sierra
Bull Falls

GUADALUPE
MOUNTAINS
NATIONAL PARK

Rio Hondo

82

70

GUADALUPE MOUNTAINS

LINCOLN
NATIONAL
FOREST

San Patricio

Lincoln Historic District

Lincoln

24

Capitan

Ruidoso Downs

LINCOLN NATIONAL FOREST

CAPITAN
MOUNTAINS

Ruidoso

Alto

MESCALERO APACHE
INDIAN RESERVATION

244

Cloudcroft

130

Sunspot Solar
Observatory

To Socorro

Valley of Fires Recreation Area

Carrizozo

37

48

Ski
Apache

70

LINCOLN NATIONAL
FOREST

6563

SACRAMENTO
MOUNTAINS

380

Sierra
Blanca

Mescalero

La Luz

54

Three Rivers
Petroglyph
Recreation Area

Tularosa

Alamogordo

Oliver Lee
State Park

TULAROSA VALLEY

Trinity Site
(first A-bomb)

SIERRA OSCURA

WHITE SANDS
MISSILE RANGE

Space Shuttle
Landing Site

WHITE SANDS
NATIONAL
MONUMENT

70

To Las Cruces

To El Paso

54

10

NEW MEXICO

Taos

25

Santa Fe

Albuquerque

Roswell

Carlsbad

Area of
detail

40

25

10

TEXAS

Ski Area

State Park

15 mi

15 km

0

0

291

GOLF   This region has plenty of golfing opportunities. In Ruidoso, **Cree Meadows Country Club,** Country Club Drive off Sudderth Drive (© 505/257-5815), is an 18-hole public course. Also public in the Ruidoso area are the 18-hole courses at the **Inn of the Mountain Gods Resort & Casino,** 287 Carrizo Canyon Rd. (© 800/545-6040 or 505/464-4100; www.innofthemountaingods.com); and **The Links at Sierra Blanca,** 105 Sierra Blanca Dr. (© 505/258-5330). In Cloudcroft, the 9-hole **Lodge at Cloudcroft Golf Course** (© 800/395-6343 or 505/682-2566; www.thelodge resort.com) has an elevation of 9,200 feet; it's one of the highest courses in the world and one of the oldest in the United States. Alamogordo's **Desert Lakes Golf Course** (© 505/437-0290; www.desertlakesgolf.com) has views of Sierra Blanca and the Sacramento Mountains. In Socorro, the 18-hole **New Mexico Tech Golf Course** (© 505/835-5335) offers tree-lined fairways and water on more than half of its holes. The **Truth or Consequences Golf Course** (© 505/894-2603) offers 9 fairly traditional holes in a desert setting. A more contemporary course is in Las Cruces, at the 18-hole **Sonoma Ranch Golf Course** (© 505/521-1818; www.sonomaranchgolf.com), which opened in 2000. Las Cruces also has the **New Mexico State University Golf Course** (© 505/646-3219; www.nmsu.edu/~golf), built with collegiate golf in mind. With wide-spanning views and undulating terrain, this Cal Olsen–designed course has much to offer. Deming has the 18-hole **Rio Mimbres Country Club** (© 505/546-9481), while Silver City golfers go to the 18-hole **Silver City Golf Course** (© 505/538-5041), home to the annual Billy Casper Golf Tournament, where the legend himself returns each year in September (usually Labor Day) to participate.

HIKING   More than 225 miles of trails weave a web through the Smokey Bear Ranger District of the **Lincoln National Forest.** From Ruidoso, a favorite destination of hikers is the White Mountain Wilderness, with nine trails, and the Capitan Mountains Wilderness, with 11 trails. **Smokey Bear Ranger District office,** 901 Mechem Dr., Ruidoso (© **505/257-4095**), has excellent and inexpensive maps of each wilderness area. Monjeau Lookout is a popular destination off Ski Run Road (NM 532). **Carlsbad Caverns National Park** has an extensive trail system as well (outside the caves, of course). There's great hiking in the **Gila National Forest** (© **505/388-8201**), which has approximately 1,500 miles of trails, ranging in length and difficulty. Your best bet for hiking in the area is to purchase a guidebook devoted entirely to hiking the Gila National Forest. Popular areas include the Crest Trail, the West Fork Trail, and the Aldo Leopold Wilderness. One favorite day hike in the forest is the Catwalk, a moderately strenuous hike along a series of steel bridges and walkways suspended over Whitewater Canyon. See "Other Adventures in Gila National Forest," later in this chapter, for more hiking suggestions. Whenever and wherever you go hiking, be sure to carry plenty of water.

HORSEBACK RIDING   Horseback riding is popular in Ruidoso. Try the **Inn of the Mountain Gods Resort & Casino** (© **800/545-6040** or 505/464-4100; www.innofthemountaingods.com) or **Cowboy Stables** (© **505/378-8217**). The **Double E Guest Ranch** (© **505/535-2048;** www.doubleeranch.com) offers authentic ranch riding in the southwestern New Mexico desert and forest lands. Because it's also a working cattle ranch, the Double E has an authentic feel, and a guest capacity of only 12 adds to the atmosphere. Trail rides and cattle drives range across 30,000 acres, which adjoin the legendary 3-million-acre Gila Wilderness.

SKIING   Southern New Mexico's premier ski resort is **Ski Apache** (© **505/257-9001** for snow reports, 505/336-4356 for information), only 20 miles northwest of

Ruidoso in the Mescalero Apache Indian Reservation. Situated on an 11,500-foot ridge of the 12,003-foot Sierra Blanca, the resort has a gondola, two quad chairs, five triple chairs, one double chair, a day lodge, a sport shop, a rental shop, a ski school, a first-aid center, four snack bars, and a lounge. Ski Apache has 55 trails and slopes (20% beginner, 35% intermediate, and 45% advanced), with a vertical drop of 1,900 feet and a total skier capacity of 16,500 an hour. Though its location seems remote, a lot of skiers fill this mountain during weekends and holidays. Because the mountain is owned and run by the Apaches, you can experience another culture while skiing. All-day lift tickets range in price from $42 to $56 for adults and $30 to $37 for children under 13, depending on the time of week and the season. Seniors 70 and over ski free. The mountain is open Thanksgiving to Easter daily from 8:45am to 4pm. Lift-and-lodging packages can be booked through the **Inn of the Mountain Gods Resort & Casino** (© **800/545-6040** or 505/464-4100; www.innofthemountaingods.com).

SWIMMING   Swimming is permitted at **Elephant Butte Lake State Park** (© **505/744-5923**) and **Caballo Lake State Park** (© **505/743-3942**), but not at some others. Be sure to ask first.

2 Alamogordo

60 miles NE of Las Cruces; 83 miles SW of Roswell; 146 miles SE of Albuquerque

Famous for its leading role in America's space research and military technology industries, **Alamogordo** (pop. 35,582) achieved worldwide fame on July 16, 1945, when the first atomic bomb was exploded at nearby Trinity Site. Today, it is home of the New Mexico Museum of Space History, White Sands National Monument, and Holloman Air Force Base. While traveling in this area, we came to jokingly call it "Alamageddon," mostly because the town itself is fairly desolate, without many amenities, although it is improving. Twenty miles east and twice as high, the resort village of **Cloudcroft** (elevation 8,650 ft.) attracts vacationers to the forested heights of the Sacramento Mountains.

ESSENTIALS

GETTING THERE   From Albuquerque, take I-25 south 87 miles to San Antonio; turn east on US 380, go 66 miles to Carrizozo; then head south on US 54 for 58 miles (4 hr.). From Las Cruces, take US 70 northeast (1½ hr.). (Note that US 70 may be closed for up to 2 hr. during tests on White Sands Missile Range.) From El Paso, take US 54 north (1½ hr.).

The nearest major airport is **El Paso International.** The local airport, **Alamogordo–White Sands Regional Airport** (© **505/439-4110**) does not offer commercial service.

VISITOR INFORMATION   The **Alamogordo Chamber of Commerce** and visitor center is at 1301 N. White Sands Blvd., Alamogordo, NM 88311 (© **800/826-0294** or 505/437-6120; www.alamogordo.com).

CITY LAYOUT   Alamogordo is on the eastern edge of the Tularosa Valley, at the foot of the Sacramento Mountains. US 54 (White Sands Blvd.) is the main street, extending several miles north and south. The downtown district is actually a few blocks east of White Sands Boulevard, off 10th Street.

WHAT TO SEE & DO

In addition to the attractions in Alamogordo itself, also enjoyable is the small, historic village of **La Luz,** 3 miles north of Alamogordo. It has attracted a number of resident artists and craftspeople who live, work, and display some of their products for sale. Worth seeing are the old adobe corral and the small Our Lady of Light Church.

New Mexico Museum of Space History ⭐ The New Mexico Museum of Space History comes in two parts: the International Space Hall of Fame and the Clyde W. Tombaugh IMAX Dome Theater. Both are on the lower slopes of the Sacramento Mountains, 2 miles east of US 54, and just above New Mexico State University's Alamogordo branch campus.

The Space Hall of Fame occupies the "Golden Cube," a five-story building with walls of golden glass. Visitors are encouraged to start on the top floor and work their way down. En route, they recall the accomplishments of the first astronauts and cosmonauts, including America's Mercury, Gemini, and Apollo programs, and the early Soviet orbital flights. Spacecraft and a lunar exploration module are exhibited. Displays tell the history and purposes of rocketry, missiles, and satellites, and provide an orientation to astronomy and other planets.

At Tombaugh Theater, IMAX projection and Spitz 512 Planetarium Systems create earthly and cosmic experiences on a 2,700-square-foot dome screen.

Located at the top of NM 2001. ℂ 877/333-6589 outside New Mexico, or 505/437-2840. Fax 505/434-2245. www. spacefame.org. Admission to International Space Hall of Fame $3 adults, $2.75 seniors (60 and older) and military, $2.50 children 4–12, free for children under 4. IMAX Theater $6 adults, $5.50 seniors, $4.50 children, free for children under 4; additional charge for double feature. Prices subject to change w/no notice. Daily 9am–5pm.

TRINITY SITE

The world's first atomic bomb was exploded in this desert never-never land on July 16, 1945. It is strictly off-limits to civilians—except twice a year, on the first Saturday of April and October. A small lava monument commemorates the explosion, which left a crater a quarter-mile across and 8 feet deep, and transformed the desert sand into a jade-green glaze called "Trinitite" that remains today. The McDonald House, where the bomb's plutonium core was assembled 2 miles from ground zero, has been restored to its 1945 condition. The site is on the west slope of Sierra Oscura, 90 air miles northwest of Alamogordo. For more information, call the public affairs office of **White Sands Missile Range** (ℂ **505/678-1134**).

EXPLORING THE SURROUNDING AREA

Cloudcroft ⭐ is a picturesque mountain village of 765 people high in the Sacramento Mountains, surrounded by Lincoln National Forest. Though only about 20 miles east of Alamogordo via US 82, it is twice as high, overlooking the Tularosa Valley from a dizzying elevation of almost 9,000 feet. It was founded in 1899 when railroad surveyors reached the mountain summit and built a lodge for Southern Pacific Railroad workers. Today, The Lodge is Cloudcroft's biggest attraction and biggest employer (see "Nearby Places to Stay & Dine," below). Other accommodations are also available in town, as are lots of recreational opportunities and community festivals. For information, contact the **Cloudcroft Chamber of Commerce,** P.O. Box 1290, Cloudcroft, NM 88317 (ℂ **505/682-2733;** www.cloudcroft.net). It's in a log cabin in the center of town, on the south side of US 82.

If you'd like a tasty meal in this mountain town, head to where the locals eat, **Dave's Café,** 300 Burro Ave. (ℂ **505/682-2127**). You can order from an array of sandwiches and salads. Try the Coney-style burger with grilled onions or the grilled chicken salad with lots of veggies and bacon. For dessert, pick up truffles or ice cream from the attached sweets shop. An excellent treat is the Amazon Storm: white-chocolate ice cream with peanuts and chocolate chips. Dave's is open Sunday to Thursday 6:30am to 5pm and Friday and Saturday 6:30am to 8pm.

WHERE TO STAY IN ALAMOGORDO

All accommodations in Alamogordo are along White Sands Boulevard, the north-south highway through town.

Holiday Inn Express ☆   This new hotel on the south end of town provides what you'd expect from this chain—clean, comfortable rooms with a bit of flair. The hotel is steps above most of the other accommodations in town. Rooms are medium size, with high ceilings and come in standards and suites. All are spacious, decorated in natural hues, and have comfortable beds, while the bathrooms are medium size with granite countertops.

100 Kerry Ave. ℂ **800/465-4329** or 505/434-9773. Fax 505/434-3279. www.hiexpress.com. 80 units. $99 double; $119–$129 suite. Rates include continental breakfast. AE, DC, DISC, MC, V. **Amenities:** Indoor pool; exercise room. *In room:* A/C, TV, fridge, coffeemaker, hair dryer, iron, microwave, high-speed Internet.

CAMPING

Alamogordo Roadrunner (ℂ **877/437-3003** or 505/437-3003; www.roadrunner campground.com) offers clean and partly shaded campgrounds. It has laundry and grocery facilities as well as a recreation room, swimming pool, playground, shuffleboard, and planned group activities in winter. The campground is on 24th Street in Alamogordo, just east of the US 54/70/82 junction. **Oliver Lee State Park,** 15 miles southeast of Alamogordo via US 54 and Dog Canyon Road (ℂ **505/437-8284**), is another good choice; it has 44 sites, 10 full hookups, picnic tables, grills, tenting availability, a playground, and hiking trails.

WHERE TO DINE IN ALAMOGORDO

Memories Restaurant ☆ *(Finds* AMERICAN   Set in a 1907 Victorian home in a residential neighborhood right on the edge of historic downtown, this restaurant serves excellent food in an old-world setting. Functional tables sit on Brazilian oak floors within what was once the living room and den, creating a casual, comfortable atmosphere—which is a good thing because the service is overworked and therefore slow. Many of the clients here at lunch are women, who come to sample salads and croissant sandwiches; dinner customers include a more even mix of genders. Basically, the place is packed nonstop while it's open. We recommend the crab salad served over avocado, or the turkey and avocado croissant sandwich. For dinner, a big seller is the prime rib, which comes with salad or soup, bread, a side dish, and vegetable. The grilled shrimp is also good. Beer and wine are available.

1223 New York Ave. (corner of 13th St.). ℂ **505/437-0077.** Reservations recommended. Main courses $5–$10 lunch, $11–$17 dinner. AE, DISC, MC, V. Mon–Sat 11am–9pm.

NEARBY PLACES TO STAY & DINE

Casa de Sueños ☆ *(Kids* NEW MEXICAN   For tasty New Mexican fare, with a good dose of the whimsy of Mexico, check out this fun restaurant about 15 miles north of Alamogordo, outside Tularosa. Decorated with Mexican folk paintings and a country home mural, it exudes a fiesta atmosphere. Outside, the broad patio is lit with little Christmas lights and has chile peppers printed on the tablecloths. For breakfast, try the huevos rancheros (eggs over tortillas smothered in chile). A lunch buffet provides a good sampling of enchiladas and beans. To start your meal, order the guacamole, made with red onions. For an entree, order anything with the green chile sauce, made with fresh chiles and well seasoned. Otherwise, you might try the chicken *adovado*—marinated chicken breast that's charbroiled—or sample a stuffed *sopaipilla*. Vegetarian and children's selections round out the menu. You can order from a variety of beers and wines.

35 St. Francis Dr., Tularosa, NM. © 505/585-3494. Reservations recommended on weekends. Main courses $5–$8 breakfast, $7–$13 lunch and dinner. AE, DISC, MC, V. Mon–Fri and Sun 11am–8:30pm; Sat 10:30am–8:30pm.

The Lodge at Cloudcroft 𝕮𝕮 This lodge is an antique jewel, a well-preserved relic of another era. From the grand fireplace in the lobby to the homey Victorian decor in the guest rooms, it exudes gentility and class. Its 9-hole golf course, one of the nation's highest, challenges golfers across rolling hills between 8,600 and 9,200 feet above sea level. Most rooms in The Lodge have views and all are filled with antiques, from sideboards and lamps to mirrors and steam radiators. The standard rooms are small, so you may want to reserve one of the suites, which have a bedroom and a sitting room with a foldout couch. Some suites have Jacuzzi tubs. Guests are greeted by a stuffed bear sitting on their bed with a sampler of homemade fudge from The Mercantile gift shop. In 1991, more rooms were added in the form of The Pavilion and The Retreat, which were built adjacent to The Lodge. These are most often rented out in blocks and are less desirable than those in the main hotel. The hotel's new Spirit of the Mountain Spa offers a variety of massage treatments.

Rebecca's (© **505/682-2566**), the lodge's restaurant, is named for the resident ghost, believed to have been a chambermaid in the 1930s who was killed by her lumberjack lover. Three meals, plus a midday snack menu, are served daily. The champagne Sunday brunch is a must here, offering a prime-rib serving station and an array of side selections.

1 Corona Place (P.O. Box 497), Cloudcroft, NM 88317. © **800/395-6343** or 505/682-2566. Fax 505/682-2715. www. thelodgeresort.com. 59 units. $109–$159 double; $169–$329 suite. AE, DC, DISC, MC, V. Free parking. **Amenities:** Restaurant; bar; outdoor heated pool; golf course; access to nearby tennis courts; exercise room; spa; Jacuzzi; sauna; fax and photocopying services; babysitting. *In room:* A/C, TV, coffeemaker, hair dryer (upon request), iron (upon request), Wi-Fi.

---

3 White Sands National Monument 𝕶𝕶𝕶

15 miles SW of Alamogordo; 46 miles NE of Las Cruces; 150 miles S of Albuquerque

Arguably the most memorable natural area in this part of the Southwest, **White Sands National Monument** preserves the best part of the world's largest gypsum dune field, an area of 275 square miles of pure white gypsum sand extending over the floor of the Tularosa Basin in wavelike dunes. Plants and animals have evolved in special ways to adapt to the bright white environment here. Some creatures have a bleached coloration to match the whiteness all around them, and some plants have evolved means for surviving against the smothering pressures of the blowing sands.

The surrounding mountains—the Sacramentos to the east, with their forested slopes, and the serene San Andres to the west—are composed of sandstone, limestone, sedimentary rocks, and pockets of gypsum. Over millions of years, rains and melting snows dissolved the gypsum and carried it down into Lake Lucero. Here the hot sun and dry winds evaporate the water, leaving the pure white gypsum to crystallize. Then the persistent winds blow these crystals, in the form of minuscule bits of sand, in a northeastern direction, adding them to growing dunes. As each dune grows and moves farther from the lake, new ones form, rank after rank, in what seems an endless procession.

The dunes are especially enchanting at sunrise and under the light of a full moon, but you'll have to camp here to experience this extraordinary sight (see "Camping," below).

If you're not camping, you'll probably want to spend only a couple of hours here. Refreshments and snacks can be purchased at the visitor center, along with books, maps, posters, and other souvenirs; however, no dining or grocery facilities are available here.

ESSENTIALS

GETTING THERE   The visitor center is 15 miles southwest of Alamogordo on US 70/82. (*Note:* Due to missile testing on the adjacent White Sands Missile Range, this road is sometimes closed for up to 2 hr. at a time.) The nearest major airport is **El Paso International,** 90 miles away (see "Essentials," under "Alamogordo," earlier in this chapter).

VISITOR INFORMATION   For more information, contact **White Sands National Monument,** P.O. Box 1086, Holloman AFB, NM 88330-1086 (*©* **505/ 479-6124;** www.nps.gov/whsa). When driving near or in the monument, tune your radio to 1610 AM for information on what's happening.

ADMISSION FEES & HOURS   Admission is $3 for adults 17 and over (free for children 16 and under). Memorial Day to Labor Day, the visitor center is open daily from 8am to 7pm, and Dunes Drive is open daily from 7am to 9pm. Ranger talks and sunset strolls are given nightly at 7 and 8:30pm during summer. During the rest of the year, the visitor center is open daily from 8am to 5pm, and Dunes Drive is open daily from 7am to sunset.

SEEING THE HIGHLIGHTS

The 16-mile **Dunes Drive** loops through the "heart of sands" from the visitor center. Information available at the center tells you what to look for on your drive. Sometimes the winds blow the dunes over the road, which must then be rerouted. All the dunes are in fact moving slowly to the northeast, pushed by prevailing southwest winds, some at the rate of as much as 20 feet per year.

In the center of the monument, the road itself is made of hard-packed gypsum (*Note:* It can be especially slick after an afternoon thunderstorm, so drive cautiously!) Visitors are invited to get out of their cars at established parking areas and explore a bit; some like to climb a dune for a better view of the endless sea of sand. If you'd rather experience the park by hiking than on the long drive, try the Big Dune Trail, a good trail right near the entrance. It takes you on a 45-minute loop along the edges of the dunes and then into their whiteness, ending atop a 60-foot-tall one.

In summer, nature walks and evening programs take place in the dunes. Ranger-guided activities include orientation talks and nature walks.

Tips Safety Warnings

The National Park Service emphasizes that:

- Tunneling in this sand can be dangerous, because it collapses easily and could suffocate a person.
- Sand-surfing down the dune slopes, although permitted, can also be hazardous. Undertake it with care, and never near an auto road.
- Hikers can get lost in a sudden sandstorm if they stray from marked trails or areas.

CAMPING

We recommend camping here, especially to see the dunes at sunrise or under a full moon. The park closes at dusk, and you'll have to leave if you're not camping. It doesn't reopen until after dawn, so you'll have no way to see the sunrise unless you camp. White Sands has no campgrounds or facilities, however, so this is strictly a backcountry adventure. Only tent camping is allowed, and you'll hike three-quarters of a mile to the campsite where you can pitch a tent. On a full moon, the campsites go quickly; you may want to arrive early in the morning. At other times, availability shouldn't be a problem. You must register at the visitor center, get clearance, and pay a small fee. Call ℂ 505/479-6124 for information.

If backcountry camping isn't your speed, try one of the other campgrounds in nearby Alamogordo and Las Cruces (see the "Where to Stay" sections under "Alamogordo," earlier in this chapter).

---

4 Ruidoso ⊛ & the Mescalero Apache Indian Reservation

33 miles NE of Alamogordo; 62 miles W of Roswell; 125 miles SE of Albuquerque

Ruidoso (most New Mexicans pronounce it "Ree-uh-*do*-so") is situated at 6,900 feet in the timbered Sacramento Mountains, the southernmost finger of the Rockies. It is a mountain resort town named for its site on a noisy stream and is most famous for the nearby Ruidoso Downs racetrack, where the world's richest quarter-horse race is run for a $2.5 million purse. Outdoors lovers, hikers, horseback riders, fishers, and hunters are drawn to the surrounding Lincoln National Forest. Southern New Mexico's most important ski resort, Ski Apache, is just out of town. The nearby **Mescalero Apache Indian Reservation** includes the Inn of the Mountain Gods Resort & Casino. Not far away, the historic village of **Lincoln** recalls the Wild West days of Billy the Kid. Be aware that during those busiest of months, Ruidoso seems to live up to its Spanish name—which translates as "noisy," although, the name originally referred to the sound of the river running through town.

ESSENTIALS

GETTING THERE   From Albuquerque, take I-25 south 87 miles to San Antonio; turn east on US 380 and travel 74 miles; then head south on NM 37/48 (4 hr.). From Alamogordo, take US 70 northeast via Tularosa (1 hr.). From Roswell, take US 70 west (1½ hr.). No commercial service is available to **Sierra Blanca Regional Airport** (ℂ 505/336-8111), 17 miles north, near Alto.

VISITOR INFORMATION   The **Ruidoso Valley Chamber of Commerce** and visitor center are at 720 Sudderth Dr. For information, contact P.O. Box 698, Ruidoso, NM 88345 (ℂ 800/253-2255 or 505/257-7395; www.ruidosonow.com).

EXPLORING RUIDOSO

GALLERY HOPPING

Many noted artists—among them Peter Hurd, Henriette Wyeth, and Gordon Snidow—have made their homes in Ruidoso and the surrounding Lincoln County. Dozens of other art-world hopefuls have followed them here, resulting in a proliferation of galleries in town. Most are open daily from 10am to 6pm, except where noted. Among our favorites are **De Carol Designs,** 2616 Sudderth Dr. (ℂ 505/257-5024); **Stampede Leather,** 2331 E. Sudderth Dr. (ℂ 505/258-4029); **McGary Studios,** a bronze foundry at 2002 Sudderth Dr. (ℂ 505/257-1000); and **Hurd–La Rinconada**

(© 505/653-4331), in San Patricio, 20 miles east of Ruidoso on US 70 (see "A Scenic Drive Around the Lincoln Loop," later in this chapter), open Monday through Saturday from 9am to 5pm.

Ruidoso's best shopping is at 2801 Sudderth Dr., where a cluster of shops fulfill many desires. Slip on sassy sandals and other contemporary shoes at **Steppin' Out** (© 505/257-5924). Next door, tots and teens can find upscale duds at **Klassy Kids** (© 505/257-3857). Meanwhile, wine lovers may want to sample the grape and artisanal cheeses at **End of the Vine** (© 505/630-WINE). And finally, foodies will like the kitchen selection at **House of Kelham** (© 505/257-2492).

RUIDOSO DOWNS

In a stunning setting surrounded by green grass and pine trees, the famous **Ruidoso Downs racetrack** and **Billy the Kid Casino** (© 505/378-4431; www.ruidosodowns racing.com), 2 miles east of Ruidoso on US 70, is home to the world's richest quarter-horse race, the $2.5 million **All American Futurity,** run each year on Labor Day. Many other days of quarter-horse and thoroughbred racing lead up to the big one, beginning in May and running to Labor Day. Post time is 1pm Thursday through Sunday. Grandstand admission is free; call about reserved seating prices, which range from $6.50 to $42.

The on-site casino has all the neon, noise, and smoke gamblers love. Though you'll find only slots at this casino (for more variety, head to Inn of the Mountain Gods Resort & Casino, p. 302), bonuses here include simulcast racing on big-screen TVs in the bar and a well-priced buffet with tables overlooking the track. It's open Saturday through Thursday from 11am to 11pm, and Friday from noon to midnight.

AN INTERESTING MUSEUM

The Hubbard Museum of the American West ⋆   This museum contains a collection of thousands of horse-related items, including saddles from all over the world, a Russian sleigh, a horse-drawn "fire engine," and an 1860 stagecoach. Several great American artists, including Frederic Remington and Charles M. Russell, are represented in the museum's permanent collection. A gift shop has some interesting books and curios.

841 W. US 70, Ruidoso Downs, NM 88346. © 505/378-4142. Fax 505/378-4166. www.hubbardmuseum.org. Admission $8 adults, $6 seniors and military, $3 children 6–16, free for children under 6. Mon–Fri 10am–5pm. Closed Thanksgiving and Christmas.

RUIDOSO AFTER DARK: SPENCER THEATER FOR THE PERFORMING ARTS ⋆⋆

The dream of Alto, New Mexico, residents Dr. A. N. and Jackie Spencer, the 514-seat Spencer Theater, on Sierra Blanca Airport Highway 220, 4½ miles east of NM 48 (© 888/818-7872 or 505/336-4800; www.spencertheater.com), is a model performance space that cost more than $20 million to construct. Opened in 1997, the theater has

---

⟨*Kids*⟩ Family Fun

Families crave the excitement at **Funtrackers Family Fun Center,** 101 Carrizo Canyon Rd. (© 505/257-3275), which offers go-kart courses, bumper boats, bull riding, and miniature golf. *Beware:* It can be crammed with people midsummer. It's open Memorial Day to Labor Day from 10am to 10pm; from September to May it's open weekends only, with limited hours.

drawn such talents as the Paul Taylor Dance Company and Marvin Hamlisch. In recent years top billings included country singer-songwriter Michelle Wright and the 1950s four-part harmony group, the Platters. Free tours are offered at 10am Tuesday and Thursday. Performances take place weekends and weekdays. The theater runs two seasons year-round, and tickets cost from $25 to $60.

MESCALERO APACHE INDIAN RESERVATION

Immediately south and west of Ruidoso, the Mescalero Apache Indian Reservation covers over 460,000 acres (719 sq. miles) and is home to about 2,800 members of the Mescalero, Chiricahua, and Lipan bands of Apaches. Established by order of Pres. Ulysses S. Grant in 1873, it sustains a profitable cattle-ranching industry and the Apache-run logging firm of Mescalero Forest Products.

SEEING THE HIGHLIGHTS

Even if you're not staying or dining here, visit the **Inn of the Mountain Gods Resort & Casino,** a luxury resort owned and operated by the tribe (p. 302); it's the crowning achievement of Wendell Chino, former president of the Mescalero Apache tribe.

Also on the reservation, on US 70 about 17 miles southwest of Ruidoso, is the **Mescalero Cultural Center** (© 505/671-4494), open weekdays from 8am to 4:30pm. Photos, artifacts, clothing, crafts, and other exhibits demonstrate the history and culture of the tribe.

St. Joseph's Apache Mission ⊛ (© 505/464-4473), just off US 70 in Mescalero, on a hill overlooking the reservation, is a grand, stone Romanesque-style structure that stands 103-feet tall and has walls 4 feet thick. Built from 1920 to 1939, the mission church also contains an icon of the Apache Christ, with Christ depicted as a Mescalero holy man, as well as other Apache religious art. Local arts and crafts and religious items are for sale at the parish office. The church is open daily during daylight hours.

LINCOLN HISTORIC DISTRICT: A WALK IN THE FOOTSTEPS OF BILLY THE KID ⊛⊛

One of the last historic yet uncommercialized 19th-century towns remaining in the American West, the tiny community of Lincoln lies 37 miles northeast of Ruidoso on US 380, in the valley of the Rio Bonito. Only 70 people live here today, but it was once the seat of the largest county in the United States, and the focal point of the notorious Lincoln County War of 1878–1879.

Various ranching and merchant factions fought the bloody Lincoln County War over the issue of beef contracts for nearby Fort Stanton. A sharpshooting teenager named William Bonney—soon to be known as Billy the Kid—sided with "the good guys," escaping from the burning McSween House after his employer and colleague were shot and killed. Three years later, after shooting down a sheriff, he was captured in Lincoln and sentenced to be hanged. But he shot his way out of his jail cell in the **Old Courthouse,** now a state museum that still has a hole made by a bullet from the Kid's gun. Visitors can hear a talk on this famous escape, by request, at the Old Courthouse.

Many of the original structures from that era have been preserved and restored by the Museum of New Mexico, the Lincoln County Historical Society, and an organization called **Historic Lincoln** (© 505/653-4025), a subsidiary of the Hubbard Museum of the American West.

JUST THE FACTS   At the **Visitor Center,** on NM 380 on the east side of town (© 505/653-4025), exhibits explain the role in Lincoln's history of Apaches, Hispanics,

Anglo cowboys, and the black Buffalo Soldiers, and detail the Lincoln County War. A brief slide show on Lincoln history is presented in an old-fashioned theater. Start your visit here and join a tour, included in the admission cost. Across the courtyard is the **Luna Museum Store.**

An annual **folk pageant,** *The Last Escape of Billy the Kid,* has been presented outdoors since 1949 as a highly romanticized version of the Lincoln County War. It's staged Friday and Saturday night and Sunday afternoon during the first full weekend in August as part of the **Old Lincoln Days** celebration. The festival also includes living-history demonstrations of traditional crafts, musical programs, and food booths throughout the village.

ESSENTIALS   The historic district is open year-round daily from 9am to 4:30pm. Admission is $5 for adults (includes entry to six buildings). It's free for children 16 and under. For more information, write to P.O. Box 36, Lincoln, NM 88338, or call 🕾 **505/653-4372.**

You can jostle your way back to the 1800s on a ride in the four-horse-drawn **Lincoln County Overland Stage** ℛ, NM 380, mile markers 91–92, west of Lincoln (🕾 **505/653-4954;** www.stagecoach.bz). Morning and afternoon rides from about March to November take 2 hours to cover 5½ miles of an old stagecoach route from near Lincoln to Old Fort Stanton cemetery. The ride costs $35 for adults, $22 for children 3 to 16, and free for children under 3.

WHERE TO STAY IN & AROUND RUIDOSO

If you're looking for a budget stay in Ruidoso, the **Motel 6** on the outskirts of town has clean, reliable rooms. Call 🕾 **800/466-8356** for reservations.

IN ALTO

Scarborough House ℛℛ *(Finds*   On a ridge 15 minutes northeast of Ruidoso, this B&B offers rustic elegance and spectacular views. Created by a couple from Austin, Texas, the inn has a bit of city flair. It is timber-frame construction, with high Douglas fir beams above a stacked flagstone fireplace in the great room. Guest rooms offer tasteful, imaginative accommodations, with an eye for detail. Our favorite is the East Meets West room, which has Old West rusticity and old East Coast elegance. All rooms have fine touches; one might have a locally made cedar bed or a marble bathroom sink. All have pillow-top mattresses, fine linens, and signature soaps, as well as robes, spa towels, and slippers—handy when you're heading out to the hot tub, which occupies part of the 2,000 square feet of deck space. Those decks offer views of Sierra Blanca Peak and the Capitan Mountains. Breakfast includes such delights as eggs Benedict, made with roast duck confit instead of Canadian bacon, and home-baked croissants. Smoking is not allowed.

110 Great View Court, Alto, NM 88312. 🕾 **866/875-2592** or 505/336-4500. www.scarboroughhousebandb.com. 4 units. $119–$189 double; ask about discount packages. Rates include full breakfast and afternoon snacks. AE, DISC, MC, V. Children not allowed. **Amenities:** Jacuzzi; courtesy computer. *In room:* A/C, TV/CD player, hair dryer, Wi-Fi.

IN TOWN

Hawthorn Suites Conference and Golf Resort ℛℛ   Surrounded by a golf course, this most refined hotel in town is a good choice. However, if you find convention traffic daunting, you'll want to ask what's scheduled at the next-door convention center before reserving. When we visited, the hotel was quiet and serene. The grand lobby centers on an Anasazi-style stacked sandstone fireplace, creating an elegance that carries into the rooms. The rooms are medium-size, decorated in a contemporary Southwestern style, with comfortable earth tones and plenty of amenities. The suites, which are large, have sofa beds, fireplaces, and balconies. Many of the rooms have two-person Jacuzzi tubs. The hotel offers golf packages that are worth checking out.

107 Sierra Blanca Dr., Ruidoso, NM 88345. ℂ 866/211-7727 or 505/258-5500. Fax 505/258-2419. www.ruidoso hawthorn.com. 120 units. $119–$189 double; $139–$299 suite. Rates include full breakfast. AE, DISC, MC, V. Take Mechem Dr. 5 min. north of Sudderth. Pets allowed. **Amenities:** Indoor pool; golf course; exercise room; Jacuzzi; massage; courtesy computer. *In room:* A/C, TV, fridge, coffeemaker, iron, microwave, Wi-Fi.

Inn of the Mountain Gods Resort & Casino ☆☆   What's most impressive about this resort is its location, set on a grassy slope above a mountain lake on the Mescalero Apache Indian Reservation, 3½ miles southwest of Ruidoso. It was the brainchild of former tribal president Wendell Chino, who wanted to help his people get into the recreation and tourism business. In 2004, the original resort was leveled and a new one built, much of it in the style of a Lake Tahoe casino, with glossy gaming rooms, a variety of restaurants, and a golf course. Though the architecture has a cold modernity, the rooms are comfortable with luxurious touches. You're greeted outside by an impressive Crown Dancer fountain, and inside by banks of windows looking out on the lake. The rooms come in a few sizes, though standard ones are pretty spacious, all with quality bedding, very comfortable mattresses, and medium-size bathrooms. We recommend paying a little more for a lakeside view. The hotel is still working out some kinks—the hot water in our room didn't work, but the problem was remedied by a repairman, and we noticed the wall coverings in the pool area were peeling because of moisture.

Wendell's restaurant, with a mountain and lake view, features steak and seafood, and has extensive wine offerings. The resort also has a sports bar, a nightclub where a variety of types of live music play Thursday to Saturday nights, and a casino with more than 1,000 slot machines and 45 table games. Fishing is offered in the lake, though you must purchase a permit at the inn.

287 Carrizo Canyon Rd., Mescalero, NM 88340. ℂ 800/545-9011 or 505/464-7777. www.innofthemountaingods.com. 273 units. $119–$209 forest-view double, $149–$269 lake-view double; $249–$329 suite, depending on the season and type of room. Golf and ski packages available. AE, DC, DISC, MC, V. **Amenities:** 3 restaurants; 2 bars; indoor pool; golf course; Jacuzzi; watersports equipment/rentals; tour/activities desk; limited room service. *In room:* A/C, TV, coffeemaker, hair dryer, iron, safe, Wi-Fi.

IN LINCOLN: A HISTORIC B&B
Ellis Store and Co. Country Inn ☆   With part of this house dating from 1850, this is believed to be the oldest existing residence in Lincoln County, and as a B&B,

---

A Silver Dollar Dinner

One of the region's most cherished relics has recently been restored. **Tinnie Silver Dollar Steakhouse and Saloon,** on US 70, 43 miles west of Roswell and 28 miles east of Ruidoso (ℂ **505/653-4177;** www.tinniesilverdollar.com) offers excellent food and fine accommodations. The elegant 1870s Victorian structure provides a perfect backdrop for frontier-style dining.

The same location has a deli offering packaged liquor sales, a gift shop and two suites for overnight guests. The suites range in price from $89 to $175, depending on the season. The steakhouse is open Monday to Thursday from 5 to 9pm, and Friday and Saturday from 5 to 10pm, with the saloon opening at 4pm. While eating, enjoy the view of the gardens and water fountain from the veranda and the original Peter Hurd paintings that hang in each room of the restaurant.

it gives visitors a real taste of 19th-century living but with most of today's luxuries. The house has plenty of history. Billy the Kid spent several weeks here, although somewhat unwillingly, according to court records that show payment of $64 for 2 weeks' food and lodging for The Kid and a companion held under house arrest.

Three rooms in the main house are a step back into the 1800s, with wood-burning fireplaces or stoves providing heat, antique furnishings, and handmade quilts. The separate Mill House, built of adobe and hand-hewn lumber in the 1880s, isn't quite as cozy as the main house, but it definitely offers an Old West feel. Two suites are good for families and those seeking solitude. Be aware that service here has become less consistent in recent years.

US 380 (P.O. Box 15), Lincoln, NM 88338. (𝒞 **800/653-6460** or 505/653-4609. www.ellisstore.com. 8 units, 4 w/private bathrooms. $89–$119 double. Rates include gourmet breakfast. AE, DISC, MC, V. Pets not allowed inside, but kennels are available. **Amenities:** Restaurant by reservation only. *In room:* Wi-Fi, no phone.

CAMPING

Lincoln National Forest has more than a dozen campgrounds in the region; four of them are within the immediate area. The **Smokey Bear Ranger Station,** 901 Mechem Dr., Ruidoso (𝒞 **505/257-4095**), is open Memorial Day to Labor Day from 7:30am to 4:30pm Monday through Saturday, and the same hours Monday through Friday the rest of the year.

WHERE TO DINE IN & AROUND RUIDOSO
IN TOWN

Casa Blanca *Kids* NEW MEXICAN   This is a real locals' favorite for the margaritas and fun New Mexican food. You can count on a decent meal here, though it's not at the level of what you can find in Santa Fe or Albuquerque. The decor is casual—four rooms in a sprawling house on a hill within town, each with orange-washed walls. The garden room and patio are our top choices. All of them can get a little noisy from the many kids who like the menu selections here. Your efficient and friendly server will start you out with complimentary chips and salsa. The best bet here is the chicken enchiladas with sour cream, or the beef or chicken fajitas. For dessert? What else but *sopaipillas* smothered in honey.

501 Mechem Dr. (𝒞 **505/257-2495**. Main courses $5–$10. AE, MC, V. Mon–Sat 11am–10pm; Sun 11am–8pm. Closed Thanksgiving and Christmas.

Cattle Baron Steak House ⚓ SEAFOOD/STEAK   This is the place to go if you really have an appetite. It's a casually elegant restaurant, part of a chain with six locations around the Southwest, that may not serve the best steaks and seafood you've tasted, but still provides good-quality food. Decorated in an opulent Western style with lots of burgundy upholstery and brass, the restaurant is often busy and festive, so it's not ideal for a romantic getaway. Service is efficient and friendly. For lunch, try the turkey and avocado sandwich or the teriyaki kabob. For dinner, we usually order the filet mignon or the shrimp scampi. A large salad bar dominates the main dining room, and a comfortable lounge sits near the entryway.

657 Sudderth Dr. (𝒞 **505/257-9355**. Reservations recommended for 6 or more. Main courses $8–$12 lunch, $12–$22 dinner. AE, DC, DISC, MC, V. Mon–Thurs and Sun 11am–10pm; Fri–Sat 11am–10:30pm.

A NEARBY PLACE TO DINE

Flying J Ranch *Kids* CHUCK WAGON   This ranch is like a Western village, complete with staged gunfights and pony rides for the kids. Gates open at 6pm; a hearty

⌒Moments   A Scenic Drive Around the Lincoln Loop

An enjoyable way to see many of the sights of the Ruidoso area is a 1- or 2-day 162-mile loop tour. Heading east from Ruidoso on US 70, about 18 miles past Ruidoso Downs, is the small community of **San Patricio,** where you'll find (watch for signs) the **Hurd–La Rinconada Gallery** (© **505/653-4331;** www.wyethartists.com). Late artist Peter Hurd, a Roswell native, flunked out of West Point before studying with artist N. C. Wyeth, marrying Wyeth's daughter Henriette, and eventually returning with her to New Mexico. This gallery shows and sells works by Peter Hurd, Henriette Wyeth, their son Michael Hurd, Andrew Wyeth, and N. C. Wyeth. Many of the works capture the ambience of the landscape in the San Patricio area. In addition to original works, signed reproductions are available. The gallery is open Monday through Saturday from 9am to 5pm and Sunday from 10am to 4pm.

From San Patricio, continue east on US 70 for 4 miles to the community of Hondo, at the confluence of the Rio Hondo and Rio Bonito, and turn west onto US 380. From here it's about 10 miles to **Lincoln,** a fascinating little town that is also a National Historic Landmark (see "Lincoln Historic District: A Walk in the Footsteps of Billy the Kid," p. 300). Heading west takes you to **Carrizozo,** the Lincoln County seat since 1912. The **Outpost,** 415 Central Ave. (© **505/648-9994**), serves one of the best green-chile cheeseburgers in the Southwest. To continue the loop tour, turn south onto US 54 and go about 28 miles to the turnoff to **Three Rivers Petroglyph National Recreation Area** (© **505/525-4300**), about 5 miles east on a paved road. Some 20,000 individual rock art images are here, carved by Mogollon peoples who lived in the area centuries ago. A trail about .75 mile long links many of the most interesting petroglyphs, and the view surrounding the area, with mountains to the east and White Sands to the southwest, is outstanding. The day use fee is $2 per vehicle. Overnight camping is $10. The U.S. Forest Service also has a campground in the area, about 5 miles east on a gravel road.

Continuing south on US 54, drive about 2 miles to Tularosa and turn east onto US 70, which you take for about 16 miles to the village of **Mescalero** on the Mescalero Apache Indian Reservation. From US 70, take the exit for the Bureau of Indian Affairs and follow the signs to the imposing **St. Joseph's Apache Mission** (see "Mescalero Apache Indian Reservation," p. 298). After you return to US 70, it's about 19 miles back to Ruidoso.

chuck-wagon dinner of barbecue beef or chicken, baked potato, beans, biscuits, applesauce cake, and coffee or lemonade is served promptly at 7:30. Then, at 8:20pm, the Flying J Wranglers present a fast-paced stage show with Western music and a world-champion yodeler.

NM 48, 1 mile north of Alto. © **888/458-3595** or 505/336-4330. Reservations highly recommended. $19 ages 13 and up, $10 children 4–12, free for children under 4. DISC, MC, V. May–Labor Day Mon–Sat (Labor Day to mid-Oct Sat only) doors open at 6pm, dinner served at 7:30pm.

NORTH OF TOWN

Greenhouse Café ⋆⋆ *(Moments* NEW AMERICAN   A complete novelty, this little gem in Capitan, about 25 minutes from Ruidoso, serves fresh dishes highlighted by vegetables grown in Tom and Gail Histen's greenhouse just up the hill. Veggies always vary, with heirloom lettuces the top stars. The setting is eclectic, a gallery displaying lovely jewelry and other art, accented by tile-topped tables and lots of plants, with a patio out back. Food ranges from vegan offerings to meatier options. Our favorite is a sun-dried tomato–spinach cream sauce with shrimp over angel-hair pasta. The breaded chicken with apple, pear, and cranberry compote is also nice. Soups, sandwiches, and salads are delicious, as are desserts such as carrot cake and a float made with local Sierra Blanca Brewery Root Beer. Sunday brunch might include a salmon omelet with cream cheese and caper filling. The menu is enhanced by select wines and beers.

103 S. Lincoln, Capitan. ⓒ 505/354-0373. Reservations recommended. Main courses $8–$12 lunch, $14–$30 dinner. MC, V. Wed–Sat 11am–2pm and 5–9pm; Sun 9am–1pm. Hours may be abbreviated in winter, so call first.

5 Roswell

62 miles E of Ruidoso; 83 miles NE of Alamagordo; 158 miles SE of Albuquerque

Best known as a destination for UFO enthusiasts and conspiracy theorists, Roswell has become a household name thanks to old Mulder and Scully. And even if you're not glued to your set for reruns of *The X-Files,* you may remember Roswell as the setting for major scenes from the 1996 blockbuster *Independence Day.* Government cover-ups, alien autopsies, and cigarette-smoking feds . . . come along as we venture into the UFO capital of the world.

ESSENTIALS

GETTING THERE   From Albuquerque, take I-40 east 59 miles to Clines Corners; turn south on US 285, and travel 140 miles to Roswell (4 hr.). From Las Cruces, take US 70 east (4 hr.). From Carlsbad, follow US 285 north (1½ hr.).

   Roswell Airport, at Roswell Industrial Air Center on South Main Street (ⓒ 505/347-5703), is served commercially by **Mesa Airlines** (ⓒ 800/MESA-AIR; www.mesa-air.com), which flies to Albuquerque almost hourly throughout the day and directly to Dallas twice daily.

VISITOR INFORMATION   The **Roswell Chamber of Commerce** is at 131 W. 2nd St. (P.O. Box 70), Roswell, NM 88202 (ⓒ **505/623-5695;** www.roswellnm.org). The **Roswell Convention and Visitors Bureau** is at 912 N. Main (ⓒ **888/ROSWELL** or 505/624-0860).

SEEING THE SIGHTS

Roswell Museum and Art Center ⋆   This highly acclaimed small museum is a good place to get a sense of this area before heading out to explore. Established in the 1930s through the efforts of city government, local archaeological and historical societies, and the Works Progress Administration (WPA), the museum proclaims this city's role as a center for the arts and a cradle of America's space industry.

   The art center contains the world's finest collection of works by Peter Hurd and his wife, Henriette Wyeth, many of which depict the gentry-ranching lifestyle in this area. You'll also find works by Georgia O'Keeffe, Ernest Blumenschein, Joseph Sharp, and others famed from the early-20th-century Taos and Santa Fe art colonies. The museum has an early-historical section, but its pride and joy is the **Robert Goddard Collection,**

Fun Fact   The Incident at Roswell

by Su Hudson

In 1947, something "happened" in Roswell. What was it? Debate still rages. On July 8, a local rancher named MacBrazel found unusual debris scattered across his property. The U.S. military released a statement saying the debris was wreckage from a spaceship crash. Four hours later, however, the military retracted the statement, claiming what fell from the sky was "only a weather balloon." Most of the community didn't believe the story, although some did suspect that the military was somehow involved—Robert Goddard had been working on rockets in this area since the 1930s, and the Roswell Air Base was nearby. Eyewitnesses to the account, however, maintain the debris "was not of this world."

Theorists believe that the crash actually involved two spacecraft. One disintegrated, hence the debris across the MacBrazel ranch, and the other crash-landed, hence the four alien bodies that were also claimed to have been discovered.

UFO believers have remained dissatisfied with the U.S. Air Force's weather balloon story and have insisted on an explanation for the "alien bodies." The most recent comment from the Air Force came in 1997, 2 weeks before the 50th anniversary of the "crash." The Air Force said that the most likely explanation for the unverified alien reports was that people were simply remembering and misplacing in time a number of life-size dummies dropped from the sky during a series of experiments in the 1950s.

The main place to go in Roswell to learn more about the incident is the **International UFO Museum and Research Center** (© 505/625-9495; www.iufomrc.org), in the old Plains Theater on Main Street. Staffers will be more than happy to discuss the crash and the alleged military cover-up. In addition to displaying an hour-by-hour timeline of the "incident," the museum has photographs of bizarre and elaborate crop circles, and a videotape in which an alleged witness tells his account. The museum is open daily from 9am to 5pm; admission is $2 for adults, $1 for those 18 and under, and infants are free.

If you want to see one of the two possible crash sites, call Bruce Rhodes at © 505/622-0628. The short tour is 53 miles, takes 3 hours, and costs $75 for one to three people. The long tour covers approximately 123 miles (including the debris site), takes about 5 hours, and costs $125 for one to three people. Call to set up your own private tour.

Roswell hosts a **UFO Festival** every year during the first week in July. Some of the special events include guest speakers, the Crash and Burn Expo Race, concerts, out-of-this-world food, a laser-light show, and an alien invasion at the Bottomless Lakes recreation area. For details on the event, call © 505/625-8607.

which presents actual engines, rocket assemblies, and specialized parts developed by Goddard in the 1930s, when he lived and worked in Roswell. Goddard's workshop has been re-created for the exhibit. A special display commemorates Apollo 17, which undertook the last manned lunar landing in 1972. The Goddard Planetarium is used as a science classroom for local students and for special programs.

100 W. 11th St., Roswell, NM 88201. ☎ 505/624-6744. Fax 505/624-6765. www.roswellmuseum.org. Free admission. Mon–Sat 9am–5pm; Sun and holidays 1–5pm. Closed Thanksgiving, Christmas Eve, Christmas Day, and New Year's Day.

WHERE TO STAY IN ROSWELL

Fairfield Inn & Suites by Marriott ⚝   This inn at the center of town offers bright new rooms with plenty of amenities. The lobby and breakfast area have a living-room feel, and the whole place offers the convenience and good prices one expects from a Fairfield. Elements such as marble and tile in the bathrooms and a nice pool are welcome enhancements. The suites offer an interesting angled two-room configuration, with a big TV and a CD player, and the standard rooms are medium size, each with a desk. All rooms have comfortable beds.

1201 N. Main St., Roswell, NM 88201. ☎ 800/228-2800 or 505/624-1300. www.marriott.com. 67 units. $84–$109 double. Rates include continental breakfast. AE, DC, DISC, MC, V. **Amenities:** Outdoor pool; exercise room; business center; guest laundry; Wi-Fi. **In room:** A/C, TV, coffeemaker, hair dryer, iron, microwave, high-speed Internet.

CAMPING

Town and Country RV Park (☎ **800/499-4364** or 505/624-1833; www.roswell-USA. com/tandcrv), south of Roswell, is your best bet for camping, with some grass and cottonwood and elm trees for shade. The campground has 75 sites, most with full hookups. Prices range from $21 to $23. Tent campers can set up here as well. Bathrooms are clean and convenient, as is the large pool. The campground is at 331 W. Brasher Rd. Head south on Main Street for 3 miles, then turn west on West Brasher Road.

WHERE TO DINE IN ROSWELL

Tia Juana's Mexican Grille & Cantina ⚝ *(Kids* NEW MEXICAN   On the north end of town, this spot serves tasty New Mexican fare in a festive Mexican cantina ambience. Red-chile lights and photos of Oaxaca accent the large dining area, which is made intimate with booths and tables nicely spaced. Service is friendly and on the mark. The food is prepared with fresh ingredients and good chile—the restaurant even makes its own tortillas daily. You can't go wrong with the enchiladas, served rolled or stacked, or the tacos, served soft or crisp. We order tacos topped with guacamole. More sophisticated offerings such as a chile-rubbed rib-eye or the shrimp del fuego (shrimp stuffed with jalapeño and wrapped in bacon and mesquite broiled) are also excellent choices. Finish your meal with the Kahlúa sombrero cake, made with liqueur and topped with toffee whipped cream. Kids have plenty of menu options, and adults can enjoy a full bar.

3601 N. Main St. ☎ **505/627-6113**. www.tiajuanas.net. Main courses $6–$19. AE, DC, DISC, MC, V. Mon–Thurs 11am–9:30pm; Fri–Sat 11am–10pm; Sun 11am–9pm.

6 Carlsbad & Environs

65 miles S of Roswell; 98 miles SE of Alamogordo; 139 miles E of Las Cruces

Carlsbad is a city of 27,800 on the Pecos River. Founded in the late 1800s, its area was controlled by Apaches and Comanches until just a little over a century ago. Besides getting a good tourist business from Carlsbad Caverns, the town, named for the spa in Bohemia (Czech Republic), thrives on farming, with irrigated crops of cotton, hay, and pecans. The area is the largest producer of potash in the United States.

The caverns (see "Carlsbad Caverns National Park," below) are the big attraction, having drawn more than 33 million visitors since opening in 1923. A satellite community, White's City (www.whitescity.com), was created 20 miles south of Carlsbad at the park entrance junction. The family of Jack White, Jr., owns all its motels, restaurants, gift shops, and other attractions.

ESSENTIALS

GETTING THERE   From Albuquerque, take 1-40 east 59 miles to Clines Corners; turn south on US 285, and travel 216 miles to Carlsbad via Roswell (6 hr.). From El Paso, take US 62/180 east (3 hr.).

Mesa Airlines (© 800/MESA-AIR or 505/885-0245; www.mesa-air.com) provides commercial service, with four flights daily between Albuquerque and **Cavern City Air Terminal** (© 505/887-3060), 4 miles south of the city via National Parks Highway (US 62/180). You can rent a car at the airport from **Enterprise** (© 505/887-3039).

VISITOR INFORMATION   The **Carlsbad Chamber of Commerce** and the **Carlsbad Convention and Visitors Bureau,** both at 302 S. Canal St. (US 285), P.O. Box 910, Carlsbad, NM 88220 (© 800/221-1224 or 505/887-6516; www.carlsbadchamber.com), are open Monday from 9am to 5pm and Tuesday through Friday from 8am to 5pm.

SEEING THE SIGHTS

Carlsbad's pride and joy is the broad Pecos River, with a 3.5-mile **riverwalk** along the tree-shaded banks, beginning near the north end of Riverside Drive. This is a lovely place for a picnic, and if you'd like to cool off, a municipal beach at the north end has changing rooms and showers. Annual **Christmas on the Pecos** ⊛ pontoon boat rides take place each evening from Thanksgiving to New Year's Eve (except Christmas Eve), past a fascinating display of Christmas lights on riverside homes and businesses. Advance reservations, available from the chamber of commerce, are required.

The **Carlsbad Museum and Art Center,** 418 W. Fox St., 1 block west of Canal Street (© 505/887-0276), contains Apache relics, pioneer artifacts, and an impressive art collection. The museum's store has a small but fine selection of jewelry at reasonable prices. The museum is open Monday through Saturday from 10am to 5pm; admission is free, although donations are welcome.

GETTING OUTSIDE

Recreational facilities in the Carlsbad area include some two dozen parks, several golf courses, numerous tennis courts and swimming pools, a municipal beach, and a shooting and archery range. Contact the **City of Carlsbad Recreation Department** (© 505/887-1191).

Living Desert Zoo & Gardens State Park ⊛ (Kids)   Situated within 1,200 acres of authentic Chihuahuan Desert, this park contains more than 50 species of desert mammals, birds, and reptiles, and almost 500 varieties of plants. Even for people who cringe at the thought of zoos, this is a pleasant 1.3-mile walk. You pass through displays with plaques pointing out vegetation such as mountain mahogany, and geologic formations such as gypsum sinkholes. In addition to a new nocturnal exhibit, you're likely to see lizards and other wild creatures, as well as captive ones.

Rehabilitation programs provide for the park's animals, which have been sick or injured and are no longer able to survive in the wild. You'll see golden eagles and great horned owls among the birds of prey in the aviary, and large animals such as deer and elk in outdoor pastures. The view from the park, high atop the Ocotillo Hills on the northwest side of Carlsbad, is superb.

1504 Miehls Dr. (P.O. Box 100), Carlsbad, NM 88221-0100. (C) **505/887-5516.** www.emnrd.state.nm.us/PRD/Living Desert.htm. Admission $5 adults, $3 children 7–12, free for children 6 and under. Group rates are available. Memorial Day weekend to Labor Day 8am–8pm, last park entry by 6:30pm; rest of year 9am–5pm, last park entry by 3:30pm. Gift shop closes 45 min. prior to zoo. Closed Christmas. Take Miehls Dr. off US 285 west of town and proceed just over a mile.

WHERE TO STAY IN & AROUND CARLSBAD

Most properties are along the highway south toward Carlsbad Caverns National Park (see "Carlsbad Caverns National Park," below). Only the Best Western Cavern Inn is near the National Park. The downside to staying there is that your restaurant and activity options are limited.

Best Western Cavern Inn   If you'd like to be close to the caverns, this is the place to stay. The lobby is within an Old West storefront, and the accommodations are across the street. The staff here seems to be overworked, so you may not get the service you would in Carlsbad. The motel has two main sections. The best is the Guadalupe Inn, which is built around a courtyard; rooms have a rich feel, with vigas on the ceilings and nice Southwestern pine furniture. Bathrooms are roomy enough, and the beds are comfortably firm. In back is a big pool surrounded by greenery. Next door, the two-story Cavern Inn provides 1970s rooms that are large, though the small bathrooms with jetted tubs could use sprucing up.

The White's City arcade contains a post office, a grocery store, a gift shop, the Million Dollar Museum of various antiques and paraphernalia, and Granny's Opera House, a theater for weekend melodramas scheduled intermittently.

17 Carlsbad Cavern Hwy. at NM 7 (P.O. Box 128), White's City, NM 88268. ⒸⒷ 800/CAVERNS or 505/785-2291. Fax 505/785-2283. www.bestwestern.com. 63 units. May 15–Sept 15 $65–$115 double; Sept 16–May 14 $50–$93 double. Rates include breakfast. AE, DC, DISC, MC, V. Pets welcome w/$10 fee. **Amenities:** 2 restaurants; 2 outdoor pools; tennis court; Jacuzzi; game room; shopping arcade; courtesy computer; volleyball; basketball. *In room:* A/C, TV, coffeemaker, hair dryer, iron, Wi-Fi.

Best Western Stevens Inn   This is a comfortable and welcoming place after the rigor of traveling in this part of the state, where there are miles between stops. The grounds are carefully landscaped, and the inn offers numerous types of rooms built in different eras. Some need to be upgraded, so be sure to request a remodeled one or, better yet, request one of the brand-new rooms at the south end of the property, which are large and have spacious bathrooms; each of these units has a fridge and microwave, and some have full kitchens. All the rest of the rooms are medium size, decorated in a Southwestern print, and have firm beds. Bathrooms are small but have outer double-sink vanities. The **Flume** is one of the better restaurants in town.

1829 S. Canal St., Carlsbad, NM 88220. ⒸⒷ 800/730-2851, 800/528-1234, or 505/887-2851. Fax 505/887-6338. www.bestwestern.com. 221 units. $59–$89 double; $69–$99 suite. Rates include breakfast buffet. AE, DISC, MC, V. Small pets allowed, w/$25 deposit. **Amenities:** 2 restaurants; bar; large outdoor pool; exercise room; playground; airport shuttle; business center; limited room service; coin-op laundry; laundry service; same-day dry cleaning; executive-level rooms available; courtesy computer. *In room:* A/C, TV, fridge, coffeemaker, hair dryer, iron, microwave, Wi-Fi.

CAMPING

Brantley Lake State Park (Ⓒ 505/457-2384) in Carlsbad has RV hookups as well as tent campsites. Picnic tables, grills, and recreational facilities are available. Boating and lake fishing are popular here. **Carlsbad RV Park and Campground,** on the south end of town at 4301 National Parks Hwy. (Ⓒ 888/878-7275 or 505/885-6333; www.carlsbad rvpark.com), is a large, full-service campground with a swimming pool and playground.

WHERE TO DINE IN & AROUND CARLSBAD

Blue House Ⓖ *Finds* BAKERY/CAFE   On a quiet residential street just north of historic downtown is this gem, set in a Queen Anne–style blue house with morning-glory vines adorning the front fence. Inside, Parisian colors warm the walls, contrasting with brightly painted chairs and small round tables. The fare is simple, fresh, and imaginative, with espresso, lattes, and Italian sodas the biggest draws, along with special sandwiches and soups daily. Excellent baked goods top the breakfast menu. For lunch, try the feta spinach croissant, a deli sandwich on French country bread, or, for something sweeter, the cream cheese–raspberry coffee cake.

609 N. Canyon Rd. Ⓒ 505/628-0555. All menu items under $8. No credit cards. Mon–Sat 6am–3pm. Hours may vary, so call before setting out. Take Canal St. to Church St. east, then south on Canyon Rd.

Lucy's Ⓖ MEXICAN   When you walk in the door of this busy restaurant with festive Mexican decor, Lucy is likely to wave you toward the dining room and tell you to find a seat. Such is the casual nature of the place—and a sign of the good home-style food to come. Since 1974, Lucy and Justo Yanez's restaurant has been dedicated to the words of a Mexican proverb printed on the menu: *El hambre es un fuego, y la comida*

Finds Dining on the Oil Fields

If you're cruising through the town of Artesia en route to Carlsbad, this is the place to eat. In a stroke of brilliance, Artesia oil man Frank Yates, Jr., conceived **The Wellhead** (ℱ, 32 W. Main St. ((℃ **505/746-0640**), a brewpub designed around the notion of oil wells. It's open Sunday through Thursday from 11am to 11pm and Friday and Saturday from 11am to midnight. Reservations are recommended on weekends and holidays. Main courses range from $6 to $20, and most major credit cards are accepted.

---

es fresca (Hunger is a burning, and eating is a coolness). You'll probably want to start with a margarita or Mexican beer. The food is tasty, with Lucy's personal adaptations of old favorites, often invented by requests from regulars. We recommend the chicken fajita burrito or the combination plate. Finish with a dessert of *buñelos* (fritters), sprinkled with cinnamon sugar. Children's plates are available. A second Lucy's restaurant is in Hobbs, at 4428 Lovington Hwy. ((℃ **505/392-1802**).

701 S. Canal St. (℃ 505/887-7714. Reservations recommended on weekends. Main courses $4–$13. AE, DC, DISC, MC, V. Mon–Sat 11am–9:30pm.

Velvet Garter Saloon and Restaurant AMERICAN This is the only restaurant in the Carlsbad Caverns area, besides the one in the base of the caverns. Despite this monopoly, the place does a pretty amazing job of preparing tasty food for a mass of travelers that pass through. The steaks are good quality and come with a trip to the salad bar, baked potato, vegetable, and bread. Your best bet may be one of the pasta dishes. Try the shrimp fettuccini Alfredo or the lasagna. In the same building, Fat Jack's serves breakfast and lunch in a setting heavy with linoleum. Standards such as eggs and bacon, sandwiches, and burgers are some of the only offerings near the caverns, so the place fills up. If possible, plan to eat in Carlsbad instead. The saloon is unmistakable, with longhorns mounted over the door.

26 Carlsbad Cavern Hwy., White's City. (℃ 505/785-2291. Reservations recommended in summer. Main courses $10–$20 (Velvet Garter); $5.50–$10 breakfast or lunch (Fat Jack's). AE, DC, DISC, MC, V. Velvet Garter daily 4–9pm (last seating at 8:30pm); Fat Jack's daily 7am–4pm; Saloon daily 4–9pm.

CARLSBAD AFTER DARK

Fairly recently Carlsbad has sprung a night scene. You have two options. The **Silver Spur,** 1829 S. Canal St. ((℃ **505/887-2851**), offers live country-and-western music most nights and free hors d'oeuvres during happy hour, as well as a big-screen TV. The **Post Time Saloon,** 313 W. Fox St. ((℃ **505/628-1977**), is a huge place with pool tables, three bars, and a dance floor. The club offers a range of DJ mixes, including country, Tejano, and karaoke.

---

7 Carlsbad Caverns National Park ★★★

23 miles SW of Carlsbad; 81 miles S of Roswell; 150 miles NE of El Paso

One of the largest and most spectacular cave systems in the world, **Carlsbad Caverns** comprise some 100 known caves that snake through the porous limestone reef of the Guadalupe Mountains. Fantastic and grotesque formations fascinate visitors, who find every shape imaginable (and unimaginable) naturally sculpted in the underground world—from frozen waterfalls to strands of pearls, from soda straws to miniature castles, from draperies to ice-cream cones.

Although Native Americans had known of the caverns for centuries, they were not discovered by Anglos until about a century ago, when settlers were attracted by sunset flights of bats from the cave. Jim White, a guano miner, began to explore the main cave in the early 1900s and to share its wonders with tourists. By 1923, the caverns had become a national monument, upgraded to national park status in 1930.

ESSENTIALS

GETTING THERE   Take US 62/180 from either Carlsbad (see "Essentials," under "Carlsbad & Environs," above), which is 23 miles to the northeast, or El Paso, Texas, which is 150 miles to the west. The scenic entrance road to the park is 7 miles long and originates at the park gate at White's City. Van service to Carlsbad Caverns National Park from White's City, south of Carlsbad, is provided by **Sun Country Tours/White's City Services** (© **505/785-2291**).

VISITOR INFORMATION   For more information about the park, contact **Carlsbad Caverns National Park,** 3225 National Parks Hwy., Carlsbad, NM 88220 (© **800/ 967-CAVE** for tour reservations, 505/785-2232 for information about guided tours, and 505/785-3012 for bat flight information; www.nps.gov/cave).

ADMISSION FEES & HOURS   General admission to the park is $6 for adults, $3 for children 6 to 15, and free for children under 6. Admission is good for 3 days and includes entry to the two self-guided walking tours. Guided tours range in price from $7 to $20, depending on the type of tour, and reservations are required. The visitor center and park are open daily from Memorial Day to mid-August from 8am to 7pm; the rest of the year they are open 8am to 5pm, except Christmas, when they are closed.

TOURING THE CAVES

Two caves, **Carlsbad Cavern** and **Slaughter Canyon Cave,** are open to the public. The National Park Service has provided facilities, including elevators, to make it easy for everyone to visit the cavern, and a kennel for pets is available. Visitors in wheelchairs are common.

In addition to the tours described below, inquire at the visitor center information desk about other ranger-guided tours, including climbing and crawling "wild" cave tours. Be sure to call days in advance because some tours are offered only 1 day per week. Spelunkers who seek access to the park's undeveloped caves require special permission from the park superintendent.

CARLSBAD CAVERN TOURS

You can tour Carlsbad Cavern in one of three ways, depending on your time, interest, and level of ability. The first, and least difficult, option is to take the elevator from the

---

Carlsbad Cavern Tour Tips

Wear flat shoes with rubber soles and heels for the cavern's slippery paths. A light sweater or jacket feels good in the constant temperature of 56°F (13°C), especially when it's 100°F (38°C) outside in the sun. The cavern is well lit, but you may want to bring along a flashlight as well. Rangers are stationed in the cave to answer questions.

visitor center down 750 feet to the start of the self-guided tour of the Big Room. More difficult and time-consuming, but vastly more rewarding, is the 1-mile self-guided tour along the Natural Entrance route, which follows the traditional explorer's route, entering the cavern through the large historic natural entrance. The paved walkway through the natural entrance winds into the depths of the cavern and leads through a series of underground rooms; this tour takes about an hour. Parts of it are steep. At its lowest point, the trail reaches 750 feet below the surface, ending finally at an underground rest area.

Visitors who take either the elevator or the Natural Entrance route begin the self-guided tour of the spectacular Big Room near the rest area. The floor of this room covers 14 acres; the tour, over a relatively level path, is 1.25 miles long and takes about an hour.

The third option is the 1½-hour ranger-guided Kings Palace tour, which also departs from the underground rest area. This tour descends 830 feet beneath the surface of the desert to the deepest portion of the cavern open to the public. Reservations are required, and an additional fee is charged.

OTHER GUIDED TOURS

Be sure to ask about the Slaughter Canyon Cave, Left Hand Tunnel, Lower Cave, Hall of the White Giant, and Spider Cave tours. These vary in degree of difficulty and adventure, from Left Hand, which is an easy half-mile lantern tour, to Spider Cave, where you can expect tight crawlways and canyonlike passages, to Hall of the White Giant, a strenuous tour in which you're required to crawl long distances, squeeze through tight crevices, and climb up slippery flow-stone-lined passages. Call in advance for times of each tour. All these tours depart from the visitor center.

BAT FLIGHTS

Every sunset from May to October, a crowd gathers at the natural entrance of the cave to watch a quarter-million bats take flight for a night of insect feasting. (The bats winter in Mexico.) All day long, the Mexican free-tailed bats sleep in the cavern; at night, they strike out on an insect hunt. A ranger program is offered around 7:30pm (verify the time at the visitor center) at the outdoor Bat Flight Amphitheater. On the second Thursday in August (usually), the park sponsors a **Bat Flight Breakfast** from 5 to 7am, during which visitors watch the bats return to the cavern. The cost is $7 for adults and $3 for children 12 and under. For information, call © **505/785-2232,** ext. 0.

OTHER PARK ACTIVITIES

Aside from the caves, the park offers a 10-mile one-way scenic loop drive through the Chihuahuan Desert to view Rattlesnake and Upper Walnut canyons. Picnickers can head for Rattlesnake Springs Picnic Area, on County Road 418 near Slaughter Canyon Cave, a water source for hundreds of years for the Native Americans, and a prime birding spot. Backcountry hikers must register at the visitor center before going out on any of the trails in the park's 46,766 acres.

8 Socorro: Gateway to Bosque del Apache & the VLA

62 miles NE of Truth or Consequences; 69 miles S of Albuquerque; 112 miles N of Las Cruces

Socorro, a quiet, pleasant town of about 9,000 residents, is an unusual mix of the 19th, 20th, and 21st centuries. Established as a mining settlement and ranching center, its downtown area is dominated by numerous mid-1800s buildings and the 17th-century San Miguel Mission. **The New Mexico Institute of Mining and Technology** (New Mexico Tech) is a major research center. Socorro is also the gateway to a vast and varied two-county region that includes the **Bosque del Apache National Wildlife Refuge,** the **Very Large Array National Radio Astronomy Observatory (VLA),** and three national forests.

ESSENTIALS

GETTING THERE   From Albuquerque, take I-25 south (1¼ hr.). From Las Cruces, take I-25 north (2¾ hr.).

VISITOR INFORMATION   The **Socorro County Chamber of Commerce,** which is also the visitor information headquarters, is at 101 Plaza (P.O. Box 743), Socorro, NM 87801 (© **505/835-0424;** www.socorro-nm.com).

EXPLORING SOCORRO

The best introduction to Socorro is a walking tour of the historic district. A brochure with a map and guidebook, available at the chamber of commerce on the **plaza,** where the tour begins, points out several historic buildings, many on the National Register of Historic Places.

You'll definitely want to check out the old **Val Verde Hotel** at the corner of Manzanares and 6th streets. The horseshoe-shaped Val Verde, a National Historic Landmark, was built in 1919 in California Mission style. It's been converted to apartments.

OTHER ATTRACTIONS

El Camino Real International Heritage Center ⊛   This museum, which opened in 2005, tells the story of El Camino Real, the 1,500-mile international trade route from Mexico to San Juan Pueblo, near Santa Fe. An impressive $5-million, 20,000-square-foot structure set in the middle of the desert, it's an award-winning building perched like a ship above Sheep Canyon, between Socorro and Truth or Consequences. In fact, the center is designed with ship elements, including a bowsprit on the helm. "The journey across the Jornada del Muerto reminded travelers of crossing the sea, with its tufts of grass, mirages and overwhelming silence," says Monument Ranger Dave Wunker. The real fun starts in the exhibit hall, where visitors get to travel the trail themselves, beginning at Zacatecas Plaza in Mexico, one of many stops along the road. Artifacts from the Camino days—a *caja fuerte* (strong box), and an Apache water jug—help tell the story, though our one complaint about the museum is that it's a bit short on artifacts, which may be remedied as the facility matures. Excellent period photos and some high-tech displays help fill the gap.

C.R. 1598, 30 miles south of Socorro. From I-25 take exit 115 and follow the signs. © **505/854-3600.** www.camino realheritage.org. Admission $5 adults; free for children under 16. Daily 8:30am–5pm.

Old San Miguel Mission ⊛⊛   Built during the period from 1615 to 1626 but abandoned during the Pueblo Revolt of 1680, this graceful church was subsequently restored, and a new wing was built in 1853. It boasts thick adobe walls, large carved vigas (rafters), and supporting corbel arches. English-language Masses are Saturday at 6pm and Sunday at 9:30 and 11am.

403 El Camino Real NW, 2 blocks north of the plaza. © **505/835-1620.** Free admission. Summer Mon–Fri 8am– 7:30pm; winter Mon–Fri 8am–6:30pm.

SEEING THE SIGHTS NEAR SOCORRO

SOUTH OF SOCORRO   The village of **San Antonio,** the boyhood home of Conrad Hilton, is 10 miles from Socorro via I-25. During the financial panic of 1907, his merchant father, Augustus Hilton, converted part of his store into a rooming house.

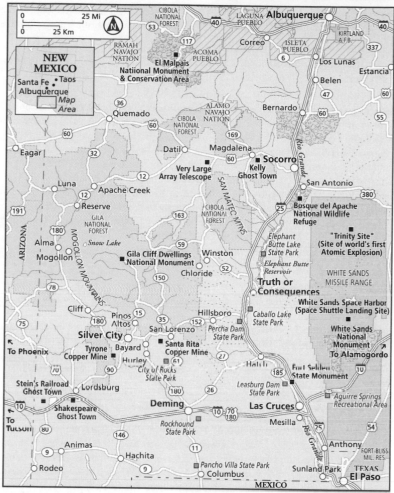

This gave Conrad his first exposure to the hospitality industry, and he went on to worldwide fame as a hotelier. Only ruins of the store/boardinghouse remain.

WEST OF SOCORRO Fifty-four miles west of Socorro via US 60 is the **Very Large Array National Radio Astronomy Observatory (VLA).** (The Socorro office is at 1003 Lopezville Rd. NW; ☎ 505/835-7000; www.nrao.edu.) Here, 27 dish-shaped antennas, each 82 feet in diameter, are spread across the plains of San Agustin, forming a single gigantic radio telescope. Many recognize the site from the 1997 movie *Contact,* starring Jodie Foster. Photographs taken with this apparatus are similar to those taken with the largest optical telescopes, except that radio telescopes are sensitive to low-frequency radio waves. All types of celestial objects are photographed, including the sun and its planets, stars, quasars, galaxies, and even the faint remains of the "big bang" that scientists believe occurred some 10 billion years ago. On the outdoor, self-guided walking tour, you'll have a chance to get a closer look at the massive antennas. Admission is free, and visitors are welcome daily from 8:30am to sunset.

WHERE TO STAY IN THE SOCORRO AREA

Most accommodations are along California Street, the main highway through town, or the adjacent I-25 frontage road. Most lodgings provide free parking.

Casa Blanca   The ideal situation in this part of the world is to be just a few minutes away from the Bosque del Apache. That way, you only have to get out of bed a half-hour or so before sunrise in order to get to the wildlife refuge and see the morning flight (see "Oasis in the Desert: Bosque del Apache National Wildlife Refuge," below). Casa Blanca is the place to stay for this reason. It's a cozy Victorian farmhouse and home to proprietor Phoebe Wood, a former schoolteacher. The place has a genuine homelike quality—comfortable and well maintained. The best room is the Heron with a queen-size bed and private bathroom with a whirlpool tub. An early-morning snack and coffee are offered for those leaving early to the Bosque, and later, upon your return, a full breakfast is available. Fruit, cereals, eggs, and home-baked muffins are served in a homey kitchen. Smoking is not permitted.

13 Montoya St. (P.O. Box 31), San Antonio, NM 87832. ✆ 505/835-3027. www.casablancabedandbreakfast.com. 3 units. $80–$100 double. Rates include generous breakfast. MC, V. Closed June–Sept. Children and pets welcome.

Holiday Inn Express   Like most of the accommodations of this newer chain of hotels, this two-story inn offers clean, functional rooms and plenty of amenities. Guests can select from two types of rooms here: hotel-style ones opening off corridors or motel-style ones in which you park your car near your door. All rooms are medium-size with medium-firm beds and standard-size bathrooms.

1100 California Ave. NE, Socorro, NM 87801. ✆ 888/526-4567 or 505/838-0556. Fax 505/838-0598. www.hiexpress.com. 120 units. $105 double. Rates include continental breakfast. AE, DISC, MC, V. Pets are welcome for a $10 1-time fee. **Amenities:** Indoor pool; 2 exercise rooms; indoor/outdoor Jacuzzis. *In room:* A/C, TV, fridge, coffeemaker, hair dryer, iron, microwave, high-speed Internet, Wi-Fi.

CAMPING

Casey's Socorro RV Park (✆ 800/674-2234 or 505/835-2234) offers mountain and valley views and plenty of shade, as well as 100 sites and 30 full hookups. Tenting is available, as are picnic tables, grills, and ice. A playground and swimming pool are open year-round. To reach Casey's, take I-25 to exit 147, go 1 block west on Business I-25, and then proceed 1 block south on West Frontage Road.

WHERE TO DINE IN THE SOCORRO AREA

Manny's Buckhorn Tavern 🎯🎯 AMERICAN   For years, the cafe across the street, the Owl Bar, held the state's title for the best green-chile cheeseburger. More recently, however, Manny's has assumed that role. *GQ* magazine named Manny's burgers as one of the 20 best in the country. *Travel + Leisure* and the *New York Times* have also written about this charming place that's full of local color. It has hardwood floors, neon beer signs, and memorabilia on the walls—a Christ crucifix, antelope antlers—set above cozy booths. Order their specialty, a Buckhorn Burger, made with hand-patted 80-percent-lean beef, topped with green chile and cheese. On the side, choose fries or onion rings, both good and crispy. If you're not a burger fan, try the tacos or tamales. Wash your meal down with a beer or margarita from the full bar.

Building 68, NM 380, San Antonio (10 miles south of Socorro). ✆ 505/835-4423. All menu items under $6. MC, V. Mon–Sat 11am–8pm.

Socorro Springs Brewing Company ⭐⭐ AMERICAN/PIZZA   This little pocket of sophistication is a nice addition to small-town Socorro. On most any day, the place is full of happy diners sampling the brew and eating tasty wood-oven cuisine. It's a casual place with a refined brewpub atmosphere, with wooden tables and colorful walls. The service is congenial, though not quick. You may choose from salads and sandwiches, calzones and pizzas, and more upscale dishes. A good pizza choice is the Bandido, topped with pepperoni, Italian sausage, prosciutto, and jalapeños, or the Vigilante, covered with artichoke hearts, chicken, and kalamata olives. We often order the grilled salmon served with a red-pepper sauce. The beer, which has a bit of a smoky taste, is good.

1012 W. California St., Socorro. ⓒ 505/838-0650. Reservations accepted. Main courses $5–$12. AE, DISC, MC, V. Daily 7am–10pm.

9 Oasis in the Desert: Bosque del Apache National Wildlife Refuge ⭐⭐

16 miles S of Socorro; 85 miles S of Albuquerque; 100 miles N of Las Cruces

by Ian Wilker

The barren lands on either side of I-25 south of Albuquerque hardly seem fit for rattlesnakes, much less for one of the Southwest's greatest concentrations of wildlife. The plants that do find purchase in the parched washes and small canyons along the road—forbiddingly named hardies such as creosote bush, tarbush, and white thorn serve notice that you are within the northernmost reaches of the great Chihuahuan Desert, which covers southern New Mexico and southwestern Texas and runs deep into Mexico.

To the east of the interstate is the green-margined Rio Grande. In the midst of such a blasted landscape, the river stands out as an inviting beacon to wildlife, and nowhere does it shine more brightly than at Bosque del Apache's 7,000 acres of carefully managed riparian habitat, which includes marshlands, meadows, agricultural fields, arrowweed thickets on the riverbanks, and big old-growth cottonwoods lining what were once the oxbows of the river. The refuge supports a riot of wildlife, including all the characteristic mammals and reptiles of the Southwest (mule deer, jackrabbits, and coyotes are common) and some 377 species of birds.

A visit here during the peak winter season—November to March—is one of the most consistently thrilling wildlife spectacles in the lower 48 states, especially if you're an avid bird-watcher. You might call Bosque del Apache the LAX of the Central Flyway, one of four paths that migratory birds follow every year between their summer breeding grounds in the tundral north and wintering grounds in the southern United States, Mexico, and even as far away as South America. Many of these birds stop over here to recharge their batteries or to settle down for the winter.

It is not enough to say that hundreds of species of birds are on hand; the wonder is in the sheer numbers. In early December, the refuge may harbor as many as 45,000 snow geese, 57,000 ducks of many different species, and 18,000 sandhill cranes. The huge, ungainly birds have a special majesty in flight, pinkish in the sun at dawn or dusk. Plenty of raptors are also about—numerous red-tailed hawks and northern harriers (sometimes called marsh hawks), Cooper's hawks and kestrels, and even bald and golden eagles—as well as Bosque del Apache's many year-round avian residents: pheasants and quail, wild turkeys, and much-mythologized roadrunners (*El Paisano,* in Mexican folklore). The interest of experienced birders will be whetted by the presence of Mexican mallards, Chihuahuan ravens, burrowing owls, rare grebes, beautiful long-billed American avocets, and especially whooping cranes (a very few remain from an experiment to imprint the migratory path of sandhills on whoopers). Everyone will be mesmerized by the huge societies of sandhills, ducks, and geese, going about their daily business of feeding, gabbling, quarreling, honking, and otherwise making an immense racket.

The refuge has a 12-mile auto-tour loop, which you should drive very slowly; the south half of the loop travels past numerous water impoundments, where the majority of the ducks and geese hang out, and the north half has the meadows and farmland, where you'll see the roadrunners and other land birds, and where the cranes and geese feed from midmorning through the afternoon.

A few special experiences bear further explanation. Dawn is definitely the best time to be here—songbirds are far more active in the first hours of the day, and the cranes and geese take flight en masse. This last event is not to be missed. Dusk, when the birds return to the water, is also a good time. At either dawn or dusk, find your way to one of the observation decks and wait for what birders call the "fly out" (off the water to the fields) or "fly in" (from the fields to the water).

Don't despair if you can't be at the Bosque del Apache during the prime winter months; it's a special place any time of year. By April, the geese and ducks have flown north, and the refuge drains the water impoundments to allow the marsh plants to regenerate; the resulting mud flats are an ideal feeding ground for the migrating shorebirds that arrive in April and May.

If you'd like to stretch your legs a bit, check out the **Chupadera Peak Trail,** which follows a 2-mile loop or a 9.5-mile loop to a high point overlooking the refuge. Ask for directions at the visitor center.

JUST THE FACTS   The Bosque del Apache National Wildlife Refuge is about a 1½-hour drive from Albuquerque. Follow I-25 for 9 miles south of Socorro, then take the San Antonio exit. At the main intersection of San Antonio, turn south onto NM 1. In 3 miles, you'll be on refuge lands, and another 4 miles will bring you to the excellent visitor center, which has a small museum with interpretive displays and a large shelf of field guides, natural histories, and other books of interest for visitors to New Mexico. The visitor center is open from 7:30am to 4pm weekdays, and from 8am to 4:30pm weekends. The refuge is open daily year-round from 1 hour before sunrise to 1 hour after sunset. Admission is $3 per vehicle. For more information, contact **Bosque del Apache National Wildlife Refuge,** P.O. Box 1246, Socorro, NM 87801 (© **505/835-1828;** www.fws.gov/southwest/refuges/newmex/bosque).

10 Truth or Consequences

58 miles N of Las Cruces; 62 miles SW of Socorro; 131 miles S of Albuquerque

Originally known as Hot Springs, after the therapeutic mineral springs bubbling up near the river, the town took the name Truth or Consequences—usually shortened to "T or C"—in 1950. That was the year that Ralph Edwards, producer of the popular radio and television program *Truth or Consequences,* began his weekly broadcast with these words: "I wish that some town in the United States liked and respected our show so much that it would like to change its name to Truth or Consequences." The reward to any city willing to do so was to become the site of the 10th-anniversary broadcast of the program, which would put it on the national map in a big way. The locals voted for the name change, which has survived three protest elections over the years.

Fun Fact **Next Stop: Space**

Fasten your seat belt and settle back for an orbit or two of Earth—that's what space-minded folks, such as New Mexico Governor Bill Richardson and British tycoon Richard Branson foresee as a reality soon. **Space tourists** would take off from the proposed $225-million Airport America, near Truth or Consequences. In its embryonic stages now, the spaceport will include one or more runways, hangars, a control building, and launch pads. Test flights started in 2007, while the completion date for the spaceport is 2010.

When it's finished, Branson plans to headquarter Virgin Galactic here. Currently Virgin is selling tickets for $200,000 each for a 2.5-hour flight, including 5 minutes of weightlessness. The first of these flights will likely fly out of the Mojave Airport, in California, where SpaceShipOne became the first privately manned rocket to reach space in 2004. Virgin Galactic has contracted to build a fleet of rockets called SpaceShipTwo, with hopes of initiating tourist flights in 2008 or 2009. For updates, log onto **www.virgingalactic.com** or **www.edd.state.nm.us.**

Although the TV program was canceled decades ago, Ralph Edwards continued to return for the annual **Truth or Consequences Fiesta,** the first weekend of May. He died in 2005. Another popular annual festival is **Geronimo Days,** the second weekend of October. Despite its festive roots, T or C seems to have an identity crisis—perhaps a consequence of giving up your name for the fame and fortune of television. The city displays a forlorn quality, possibly owing to the struggling economy. However, in recent years, a few of the bathhouses have undergone renovation, so there may be hope. Overall, you'll want to visit here to explore the strangeness of a town that traded away its identity.

ESSENTIALS

GETTING THERE   From Albuquerque, take I-25 south (2½ hr.). From Las Cruces, take I-25 north (1¼ hr.). Though no commercial flight service exists, those who fly themselves may contact the **Truth or Consequences Municipal Airport,** Old North Highway 85 (© **505/894-6199**).

VISITOR INFORMATION   The **visitor information center** is at the corner of Main (Business Loop 25) and Foch streets in downtown Truth or Consequences. Also there is the **Truth or Consequences & Sierra County Chamber of Commerce,** P.O. Drawer 31, Truth or Consequences, NM 87901 (© **505/894-3536;** www.truthor consequencesnm.net).

CITY LAYOUT   This year-round resort town and retirement community of 7,500 is spread along the Rio Grande between the Elephant Butte and Caballo reservoirs, two of the three largest bodies of water in the state. Business Loop 25 branches off from I-25 to wind through the city, splitting into Main Street (one-way west) and South Broadway (one-way east) in the downtown area. Third Avenue connects T or C with the Elephant Butte resort community, 5 miles east.

TAKING THE WATERS AT THE HISTORIC HOT SPRINGS

The town's "original" attraction is its hot springs. The entire downtown area is located over a table of odorless hot mineral water, 98°F to 115°F (37°C–46°C), that bubbles to the surface through wells or pools. The first bathhouse was built in the 1880s; most of the half-dozen historic spas operating today date from the 1930s. Generally open from morning to early evening, these spas welcome visitors for soaks and massages. Baths of 20 minutes or longer start at $5 per person.

The chamber of commerce has information on all the local spas (see "Essentials," above). Among them is **Sierra Grande Lodge & Spa** , 501 McAdoo St. (© 505/894-6976; www.sierragrandelodge.com), where Geronimo himself is rumored to have taken a break. (See "Where to Stay in & Around Truth or Consequences," below.) **Artesian Bath House,** 312 Marr St. (© 505/894-2684), is quite clean and has an RV park on the premises.

We highly recommend the **Hay-Yo-Kay Hot Springs** , 300 Austin St. (©505/894-2228; www.hay-yo-kay.com). It has natural-flow pools (vs. tubs filled with spring water). The tub rooms are private and gracefully tiled. The Long House, a cooler tub, is the largest in town and can hold up to 20 people. Hay-Yo-Kay is open in the summer Wednesday through Friday 4 to 8pm, weekends from noon to 8pm. Winter hours (Sept–May) are Wednesday through Friday 10am to 7pm, weekends from noon to 7pm. Hours on Monday holidays are from noon to 7pm. Massages and reflexology are also available.

A MUSEUM IN TRUTH OR CONSEQUENCES

Geronimo Springs Museum Outside this museum is Geronimo's Spring, where the great Apache shaman is said to have taken his warriors to bathe their battle wounds. Turtleback Mountain, looming over the Rio Grande east of the city, is believed to have been sacred to Native Americans.

Exhibits include prehistoric Mimbres pottery (A.D. 950–1250); the Spanish Heritage Room, updated and renovated, featuring artifacts of the first families of Sierra County; and artists' work, including historical murals and sculptured bronzes. An authentic miner's cabin has been moved here from the nearby mountains. The Ralph Edwards Wing contains the history and highlights of the annual fiestas and celebrates the city's name change, including television footage from the shows filmed in T or C. The museum is geothermally heated.

211 Main St. © 505/894-6600. Admission $3 adults, $1.50 students; family rates available. DISC, MC, V. Mon–Sat 9am–5pm; Sun 11am–4pm.

SOUTH OF TRUTH OR CONSEQUENCES Thirty-two miles from Truth or Consequences, via I-25 south to NM 152, then west, is **Hillsboro** , another ghost town that's fast losing its ghosts to a small invasion of artists and craftspeople, antiques shops, and galleries. This town boomed after an 1877 gold strike nearby, and during its heyday it produced $6 million in silver and gold. It was the county seat from 1884 to 1938. Hillsboro's Labor Day weekend **Apple Festival** is famous throughout the state.

WHERE TO STAY IN & AROUND TRUTH OR CONSEQUENCES

Elephant Butte Inn For a comfortable stay and a unique experience, try Elephant Butte Inn. It sits above Elephant Butte Lake and has panoramic views as well as a relaxing resortlike feel. Recent years have brought a complete face-lift to the whole place. It caters to boaters, fishers, and other relaxation lovers. Rooms are standard size, furnished with medium-firm king- or queen-size beds. Bathrooms are small but functional. We recommend the lakeside view, where a big grassy lawn stretches down to tennis courts. The pool was recently remodeled and is now heated. For golfers, packages are available that include greens fees at the nearby Truth or Consequences Golf Course. A courtesy computer with Internet is available in the lobby.

NM 195 (P.O. Box 996), Elephant Butte, NM 87935. ℭ 505/744-5431. Fax 505/744-5044. www.elephantbutteinn.com. 48 units. Mid-Sept to Apr $70–$100 double; May to mid-Sept $79–$109 double. AE, DC, DISC, MC, V. Amenities: Restaurant; outdoor pool; limited room service. *In room:* A/C, TV, coffeemaker, hair dryer, iron, Wi-Fi.

Sierra Grande Lodge & Spa 𝒦   Prepare yourself for a sensual oasis at this resort in southern New Mexico. The biggest draw is the springs. Nowhere else in the state can you stay in luxury while partaking of warm, healing waters rich in minerals. The medium-size rooms in this renovated 1920s lodge have refined, handcrafted furnishings, and many have balconies. Suites have in-room Jacuzzis. A special casita with its own outdoor tub is so popular it's reserved months in advance. When it opened, *Condé Nast Traveler* placed the lodge's restaurant (unfortunately open only intermittently) on its list of the world's 50 top new restaurants. It serves a light spa menu.

501 McAdoo St., Truth or Consequences, NM 87901. ℭ 505/894-6976. www.sierragrandelodge.com. 17 units. $65–$95 double Tues–Thurs; $95–$125 double Fri–Mon; $215 suite. AE, DISC, MC, V. Amenities: Restaurant; spa; massage; 4 hot mineral baths; Wi-Fi. *In room:* A/C, TV, DVD player upon request, hair dryer.

CAMPING

Elephant Butte Lake State Park (ℭ 505/744-5923) welcomes backpackers and RVs alike, with 200 developed campsites, 150 RV hookups, picnic tables, and access points for swimming, hiking, boating, and fishing. Kids love the playground.

Not far from Elephant Butte Lake is **Monticello Point RV Park** (ℭ 505/894-6468), which offers tenting and 69 sites with full hookups. Laundry and grocery facilities are also on the premises, as are restrooms with showers. To reach Monticello Point, take I-25 to exit 89, and proceed 5½ miles east on the paved road—follow the signs.

Lakeside RV Park and Lodging (ℭ 505/744-5996), also near Elephant Butte, has 50 sites, two overflow sites (all 52 are full hookups), as well as a recreation room with cable and laundry facilities. When you are headed south on I-25, the RV park is 4 miles southeast of the I-25 and NM 195 junction (exit 83) on NM 195. To reach the RV park when you're headed north on I-25, take exit 79, go half a mile east on the paved road, 1½ miles north on NM 181, then 1½ miles east on NM 171, and finally a quarter-mile south on NM 195.

Camping is also available at **Caballo Lake State Park** and **Percha Dam State Park.** For information on either park, call ℭ 505/743-3942 or visit **www.nmparks.com**.

WHERE TO DINE IN & AROUND TRUTH OR CONSEQUENCES

La Cocina *(Kids* AMERICAN/NEW MEXICAN   A real locals' place, this restaurant serves decent New Mexican food in a festive atmosphere. The *tostadas* (crispy tortillas covered with beans and meat) and chile rellenos are tasty, but our favorite is the cheese enchiladas. Even better are the huge *sopaipillas*. Kids like the big booths and their own quesadillas and tacos.

1 Lakeview Dr. (at Date St.). ℭ 505/894-6499. Reservations recommended on weekends. Main courses $7–$19 lunch and dinner. DISC, MC, V. Mon–Thurs 10:30am–10pm in summer; Mon–Thurs 10:30am–9pm in winter; Fri–Sun 10:30am–10pm year-round.

Los Arcos Steak & Lobster 𝒦 AMERICAN   This spacious hacienda-style restaurant fronted by a lovely desert garden is intimate and friendly, as if you're at an old friend's home. Its steaks are regionally famous; our choice is always the filet mignon, served with salad and a choice of potato or rice. The fish dishes are also good. You may want to try a fresh catch, such as walleye pike or catfish, served on the weekends. The restaurant also has a fine dessert list and cordial selection. During warmer months, diners enjoy the outdoor patio.

1400 Date St. (C) 505/894-6200. Main courses $10–$40. AE, DC, DISC, MC, V. Sun–Thurs 5–9:30pm; Fri–Sat 5–10:30pm.

11 Las Cruces

60 miles SW of Alamogordo; 112 miles S of Socorro; 180 miles S of Albuquerque

Picture a valley full of weathered wooden crosses marking graves of settlers brutally murdered by Apaches, and behind them mountains with peaks so jagged they resemble organ pipes. Such was the scene that caused people to begin calling this city Las Cruces, meaning "the crosses." Even today, the place has a mysterious presence, its rich history haunting it still. Reminders of characters such as Billy the Kid, who was sentenced to death in this area, and Pancho Villa, who spent time here, are present throughout the region.

Established in 1849 on El Camino Real, the "royal highway" between Santa Fe and Mexico City, Las Cruces became a supply center for miners prospecting the Organ Mountains and soldiers stationed at nearby Fort Selden. Today, it's New Mexico's second-largest urban area, with 73,600 people. It's noted as an agricultural center, especially for its cotton, pecans, and chiles; as a regional transportation hub; and as the gateway to the White Sands Missile Range and other defense installations.

Las Cruces manages to survive within a desert landscape that gets only 8 inches of moisture a year, pulling enough moisture from the Rio Grande, which runs through, to irrigate a broad swath of valley.

ESSENTIALS

GETTING THERE   From Albuquerque, take I-25 south (4 hr.). From El Paso, take I-10 north (¾ hr.). From Tucson, take I-25 east (5 hr.).

Las Cruces International Airport ((C) **505/524-2762;** www.las-cruces.org/airport), 8 miles west of the city, has service several times daily to and from Albuquerque on **Mesa Airlines** ((C) **800/MESA-AIR** or 505/326-3338; www.mesa-air.com). **El Paso International Airport** ((C) **915/772-4271;** www.elpasointernationalairport.com), 47 miles south, has daily flights to Albuquerque, Phoenix, Dallas, and Houston, among other cities. The **Las Cruces Shuttle Service,** P.O. Box 3172, Las Cruces, NM 88003 ((C) **800/288-1784** or 505/525-1784; www.lascrucesshuttle.com), provides service between the El Paso airport and Las Cruces. It leaves Las Cruces 12 times daily between 5am and 9:30pm for a charge of $30 one-way or $46 round-trip per person, with large discounts for additional passengers traveling together. A $7 charge is added for pickup or drop-off at places other than its regular stops at major hotels. Connections can also be made three times a day from Las Cruces to Deming and Silver City.

VISITOR INFORMATION   The **Las Cruces Convention and Visitors Bureau** is at 211 N. Water St., Las Cruces, NM 88001 ((C) **877/266-8252** or 505/541-2444; www.lascrucescvb.org). The **Greater Las Cruces Chamber of Commerce,** 760 W. Picacho St., can be reached by writing P.O. Drawer 519, Las Cruces, NM 88004 ((C) **505/524-1968;** www.lascruces.org).

WHAT TO SEE & DO IN LAS CRUCES

On a hot day, when the church bells are ringing and you're wandering the brick streets of **Mesilla** (★★, you may for a moment slip back into the late 16th century—or certainly feel as though you have. This village on Las Cruces's southwestern flank was established in the late 1500s by Mexican colonists. It became the crossroads of El Camino Real and the Butterfield Overland Mail route. The Gadsden Purchase, which annexed Mesilla to the United States and fixed the current international boundaries of New Mexico and Arizona, was signed here in 1854.

Mesilla's most notorious resident, William Bonney, otherwise known as Billy the Kid, was sentenced to death at the county courthouse here. He was sent back to Lincoln, New Mexico, to be hanged, but escaped before the sentence was carried out. Legendary hero Pat Garrett eventually tracked down and killed the Kid at Fort Sumner; later, Garrett was mysteriously murdered in an arroyo just outside Las Cruces. He is buried in the local Masonic cemetery.

Thick-walled adobe buildings, which once protected residents against Apache attacks, now house art galleries, restaurants, museums, and gift shops. Throughout Mesilla, colorful red chile *ristras* decorate homes and businesses. On Sunday during the summer locals sell crafts and baked goods, and mariachi bands play.

PLACES OF NOTE IN MESILLA

At the **J. Paul Taylor Visitor Center** in the new Mesilla Town Hall, 2231 Avenida de Mesilla (© **505/524-3262**, ext. 117), you'll find period photos and plenty of brochures on the area, as well as clean public restrooms. Nearby is the **Gadsden Museum,** a grand old house full of memorabilia that's open only intermittently. In the back of the museum parking lot is a replica of the old Mesilla jail, a dismal storage shed with original jail doors that once helped to incarcerate Billy the Kid.

OTHER ATTRACTIONS

Las Cruces Museum of Natural History *(Kids)*   This small city-funded museum offers a variety of exhibits, changed quarterly, that emphasize science and natural history. The museum features live animals of the Chihuahuan Desert, hands-on science activities, and a small native plant garden. The Cenozoic Shop offers scientific toys and books about the region. Exhibits, such as "Insects and Bugs," change every few months. In summer 2006, the museum hosted an exhibit titled "Wild Weather."

Mesilla Valley Mall, 700 S. Telshor Blvd. (© **505/522-3120.** Free admission. Mon–Thurs and Sat 10am–5pm; Fri 10am–8pm; Sun 1–5pm.

New Mexico Farm and Ranch Heritage Museum *&*   This 47-acre interactive museum brings to life the 3,000-year history of farming, ranching, and rural living in New Mexico. It's housed within a huge structure that's well designed to look like a hacienda-style barn, with a U-shaped courtyard in back and exhibits surrounding it on expansive grounds. The museum displays such relics as a 1937 John Deere tractor and a number of examples of how ranchers "make do," ingeniously combining tools such as a tractor seat with a milk barrel to come up with a chair. Visitors can watch a cow being milked, stroll along corrals filled with livestock, enjoy several gardens, and drop by the blacksmith shop. Annual events at the museum are the La Fiesta de San Ysidro in May and the Cowboy Days on the third weekend in October.

4100 Dripping Springs Rd. (follow University Ave. east beyond the edge of town). (© **505/522-4100.** www.frhm.org. Admission $5 adults, $3 seniors 60 and over, $2 children 5–17; free for children 4 and under. Mon–Sat 9am–5pm; Sunday noon–5pm.

San Albino Church *&&*   This is one of the oldest churches in the Mesilla valley. The present structure was built in 1906 on the foundation of the original church, constructed in 1851. It was named for St. Albin, a medieval English bishop of North

Africa, on whose day an important irrigation ditch from the Rio Grande was completed. The church bells date from the early 1870s; the pews were made in Taos of Philippine mahogany.

North side of Old Mesilla Plaza. © 505/526-9349. Free admission; donations appreciated. Usually Mon–Sat 1–3pm (call ahead). English-language Mass Sat 5:30pm and Sun 11am; Spanish Mass Sun 8am, weekdays 7am.

SHOPPING
Shoppers should be aware that in Las Cruces, Monday is a notoriously quiet day—some stores are closed then, so it's best to call ahead before traveling to a specific store.

For art, visit **Lundeen's Inn of the Arts** *✦*, 618 S. Alameda Blvd. (© **505/526-3326**), which displays the works of about 30 Southwest painters, sculptors, and potters; **Rising Sky Artworks,** 415 E. Foster (© **505/525-8454**), which features works in clay by local and Western artists; and the **William Bonney Gallery,** 2060 Calle de Parian, just off the southeast corner of Old Mesilla Plaza (© **505/526-8275**), which contains a variety of Southwestern art.

For books, try **Mesilla Book Center,** in an 1856 mercantile building on the west side of Old Mesilla Plaza (© **505/526-6220**).

For native crafts and jewelry, check out **Silver Assets** *✦*, 1948 Calle de Santiago (© **505/523-8747**), 1½ blocks east of San Albino Church in Mesilla.

Mesilla Valley Mall is a full-service shopping center at 700 S. Telshor Blvd., just off the I-25 interchange with Lohman Avenue (© **505/522-1001**), with well over 100 stores. The mall is open Monday through Saturday from 10am to 9pm and Sunday from noon to 6pm.

LAS CRUCES AFTER DARK
National recording artists frequently perform at NMSU's **Pan Am Center** (© **505/646-1420**). The **NMSU Music Department** (© **505/646-2421**) offers free jazz, classical, and pop concerts from August to May, and the **Las Cruces Symphony Orchestra** (© **505/646-3709;** www.lascrucessymphony.com) often performs here as well.

Hershel Zohn Theater (© **505/646-4515**), at NMSU, presents plays of the professional/student **American Southwest Theatre Company** from September to May, featuring dramas, comedies, musicals, and original works. Visit **http://theatre.nmsu.edu/astc** for information.

The **Las Cruces Community Theatre** (© **505/523-1200;** www.lcctnm.org) has six productions a year at its own facility on the downtown mall.

The **Mesilla Valley Film Society** (© **505/524-8287**) runs a good selection of contemporary and vintage art films at the Fountain Theatre (www.fountaintheatre.org), 2469 Calle de Guadalupe, a half-block south of the plaza in Mesilla, nightly at 7:30pm and sometimes 9:45pm, and Sunday at 2:30pm and sometimes 5pm.

EXPLORING THE AREA
NORTH OF LAS CRUCES   The town of **Hatch,** 39 miles north via I-25 or 34 miles north via NM 185, calls itself the "chile capital of the world." It's the center of a 22,000-acre agricultural belt that grows and processes more chiles than anywhere else in the world. The annual Hatch Chile Festival over Labor Day weekend celebrates the harvest. For information, call the **Hatch Chamber of Commerce** (© **505/267-5050**).

SOUTH OF LAS CRUCES   **Stahmann Farms,** 10 miles south of Mesilla on NM 28, is one of the world's largest single producers of pecans. Several million pounds are harvested, mostly during November, from orchards in the bed of an ancient lake.

Stahmann's Country Store (© 800/654-6887 or 505/526-8974; www.stahmanns. com) sells pecans, pecan candy, and other specialty foods, and it has a small cafe. It's open Monday through Saturday from 9am to 6pm, Sunday from 11am to 5pm.

War Eagles Air Museum ⨍ (© 505/589-2000; www.war-eagles-air-museum.com), at the Santa Teresa Airport, about 35 miles south of Las Cruces via I-10 (call or check the website for directions), has an extensive collection of historic aircraft from World War II and the Korean War, plus automobiles and a tank. The museum is open Tuesday through Sunday from 10am to 4pm; admission is $5 for adults, $4 for senior citizens age 65 and over, and free for children under 12.

EAST OF LAS CRUCES The **Organ Mountains,** so-called because they resemble the pipes of a church organ, draw inevitable comparisons to Wyoming's Grand Tetons. Organ Peak, at 9,119 feet, is the highest point in Doña Ana County.

The **Aguirre Springs Recreation Area** (© 505/525-4300), off US 70 on the western slope of the Organ Mountains, is one of the most spectacular places we've ever camped. Operated by the Bureau of Land Management, the camping and picnic sites sit at the base of the jagged Organ Mountains. Visitors to the area can hike, camp, picnic, or ride horseback (no horse rentals on site). If you'd like to hike, don't miss the **Baylor Pass** trail, which crosses along the base of the Organ peaks, up through a pass, and over to the Las Cruces side. Though the hike is 6 miles one-way, just over 2 miles will get you to the pass, where there's a meadow with amazing views.

WHERE TO STAY IN & AROUND LAS CRUCES

Hotel Encanto de Las Cruces ⨍   Built in 1986 as the Las Cruces Hilton, this hotel's new owner has remodeled the property, bringing a Spanish Colonial theme to the lobby and guest rooms. At seven stories on the east side of town, about a 15-minute drive from Mesilla, it has an incredible view of the city and the Organ Mountains. Rooms are spacious, with comfortable beds and plenty of amenities. Bathrooms are medium-size and very clean. Some rooms flank the pool and have little patios.

705 S. Telshor Blvd., Las Cruces, NM 88011. © 877/901-ROOM or 505/522-4300. Fax 505/521-4707. www. buynm.com. 205 units. $99–$149 double; $179–$199 suite. AE, DC, DISC, MC, V. **Amenities:** Restaurant; lounge; heated outdoor pool; exercise room; Jacuzzi; car rental; courtesy van; limited room service; valet laundry. In room: A/C, TV, coffeemaker, hair dryer, iron, Wi-Fi.

La Quinta ⨍   Five minutes from Old Mesilla, this chain hotel provides relatively quiet and very comfortable rooms with plenty of amenities. The clean, well-designed rooms range from medium to large, all with desks and medium-size bathrooms. Within a comfortable courtyard is an outdoor pool—an important addition in this warm climate. Guests eat their continental breakfast in a bright garden room off the lobby. When you reserve here ask for one of the "annex" rooms, which are the largest. Also, be aware that trains pass near this area at night. A new **Village Inn** restaurant just opened across the street.

790 Avenida de Mesilla, Las Cruces, NM 88005. © 800/531-5900 or 505/524-0331. Fax 505/525-8360. www.laquinta.com. $75–$85 double. Rates include continental breakfast. AE, DISC, MC, V. Pets welcome. **Amenities:** Outdoor pool; small fitness room. In room: A/C, TV, coffeemaker, hair dryer, iron, Wi-Fi.

A BED & BREAKFAST

The Lundeen Inn of the Arts ⨍⨍   This inn is a late-1890s adobe home, with whitewashed walls, narrow alleys, and arched doorways. It's a composite of rooms stretching across 10,000 square feet of floor space. There's a wide range of rooms, each named for an artist. Our favorites are in the main part of the house, set around a two-story garden room, with elegant antiques and arched windows. Most rooms are medium-size with comfortably firm beds dressed in fine linens. Bathrooms are generally small and simple but clean. Our favorite rooms are the Georgia O'Keeffe, which has a balcony, and the Olaf Wieghorst, which has a romantic red bathtub. The inn is also an art gallery displaying the works of about 300 Southwestern painters, sculptors, and potters. Breakfast includes fresh fruit and such specialties as vanilla almond pancakes and huevos rancheros.

618 S. Alameda Blvd., Las Cruces, NM 88005. (✆ 888/526-3326 or 505/526-3326. Fax 505/647-1334. www.innofthe arts.com. 7 units. $79–$85 double; $85–$105 suite. Rates include full breakfast. AE, DC, DISC, MC, V. Pets welcome. **Amenities:** Secretarial service; babysitting. *In room:* A/C, TV, hair dryer, iron.

CAMPING

Quite a few campgrounds are in or near Las Cruces. All the ones listed here include full hookups for RVs, tenting areas, and recreation areas. **Best View RV Park** (✆ 505/526-6555) also offers cabins and laundry and grocery facilities. From the junction of I-10 and US 70 (exit 135), go 1½ miles east on US 70, then half a block south on Weinrich Road.

Another option is **Dalmont's RV Park** (✆ 505/523-2992). If you're coming from the west, when you reach the junction of I-25 and I-10, go 2½ miles northwest on I-10 to the Main Street exit, then go 2 blocks west on Valley Drive. If you're coming from the east, at the junction of I-10 and Main Street, go ¼ mile north on Main Street and then 1 block west on Valley Drive. To reach **Siesta RV Park** (✆ 505/523-6816), at the junction of I-10 and NM 28, take exit 140 and go half a mile south on NM 28. **Leasburg Dam State Park** (✆ 505/524-4068) is a smaller park that also offers RV and tent camping, but it has no laundry or grocery facilities. A general country store is about 1 mile down the road, and hiking and fishing are available.

WHERE TO DINE IN & AROUND LAS CRUCES

EXPENSIVE

Double Eagle 👧👧 CONTINENTAL   This 150-year-old Territorial-style hacienda that was once the governor's mansion is on the National Register of Historic Places. Built around a central courtyard, it has numerous rooms, one of which is said to be frequented by a ghost. The menu is quite varied and includes pasta, chicken, fish, and steak dishes. Our favorite is the filet mignon bordelaise, served on a French rusk with a rich red-wine sauce. The Columbia River salmon, served with a triple citrus-chipotle chile sauce, is also delicious. All entrees come with salad, vegetable, and choice of potato or pasta. There's a full bar. A more casual restaurant under the same ownership, **Peppers,** occupies the courtyard.

2355 Calle de Guadalupe, on the east side of Old Mesilla Plaza. (✆ 505/523-6700. Reservations recommended. Main courses $5.25–$12 lunch, $11–$27 dinner. AE, DC, DISC, MC, V. Mon–Sat 11am–10pm; Sun 11am–9pm.

MODERATE

La Posta de Mesilla 👧*Kids* NEW MEXICAN/STEAKS   If you're on the Old Mesilla Plaza and want to eat New Mexican food for not much money, walk in here. The restaurant occupies a mid-18th-century adobe building that is the only surviving stagecoach station of the Butterfield Overland Mail route from Tipton, Missouri, to San Francisco. Kit Carson, Pancho Villa, General Douglas MacArthur, and Billy the Kid were all here at one time. The entrance leads through a jungle of tall plants beneath a Plexiglas roof, past a tank of piranhas and a noisy aviary of macaws and

Amazon parrots, to nine dining rooms with bright, festive decor. (Kids love this and their own menu selections.) The tables are basic, with vinyl and metal chairs. Try the enchiladas, which come with a nice chile sauce. Avoid the dry rellenos and the soggy tacos. The tostadas (tortilla cups filled with beans and topped with chile and cheese) are a house specialty. There's a full-service bar.

2410 Calle de San Albino (southeast corner of Old Mesilla Plaza). ⓒ 505/524-3524. Reservations recommended. Main courses $4–$13. AE, DC, DISC, MC, V. Sun and Tues–Thurs 11am–9pm; Fri–Sat 11am–9:30pm.

Lemongrass 🎇🎇 *Finds* THAI   This new addition to the Las Cruces dining scene offers delicious flavors in a comfortably elegant atmosphere. It's set in an open room accented with Thai tapestries on the tables and Thai village scenes on the walls. Service is congenial, though be prepared to wait a bit for the food. Chef Kimberly Miag uses very fresh ingredients and brings her own touch to traditional Thai dishes such as pad Thai. We've also enjoyed a delicious pad pong kari—broccoli, bell pepper, straw mushrooms, and chicken or shrimp in a yellow curry and coconut-milk sauce. The chef is open to dialing the spice way down so even tender stomachs can enjoy eating here. Enjoy beer and wine with your meal.

2540 El Paseo Rd. ⓒ 505/523-8778. Reservations recommended on weekends in summer. Main courses $6–$11 lunch, $13–$19 dinner. AE, DISC, DC, MC, V. Mon–Fri 11am–2pm; Sat–Sun 5–9pm.

Lorenzo's Restaurante Italiano de Old Mesilla 🎇 SICILIAN   In a spirited building with lots of brick and with tile murals depicting rural scenes on the walls, this restaurant offers the feel of a Sicilian village cafe, a good indication of the quality of the food here. Rather than fancy Italian food like you find in many cities, this restaurant serves traditional Sicilian meals, with lots of red sauces and homemade pasta. It's big with locals, and it fills up, so you may want to make reservations. The atmosphere is jovial and the service is good, though it can be a bit slow because all the food is cooked in-house. You can't go wrong with standards such as spaghetti marinara or lasagna, or for something more adventurous, try the linguini and clams. Wash it down with a carafe of Chianti or your favorite beer.

1750 Calle de Mercado #4 (Onate Plaza, a block from Old Mesilla Plaza). ⓒ 505/525-3174. Reservations recommended. Main courses $8–$16. AE, DISC, MC, V. Mon–Thurs 11am–9pm; Fri–Sat 11am–9:30pm; Sun 11–8:30pm.

12 Deming & Lordsburg

Deming: 44 miles SE of Silver City, 52 miles W of Las Cruces, 193 miles SW of Albuquerque; Lordsburg: 52 miles W of Deming, 36 miles SW of Silver City

This is New Mexico's least populated corner, which includes the "boot heel" of the Gadsden Purchase, poking 40 miles down toward Mexico (a great place for backpacking). These two railroad towns, an hour apart on I-10, see a lot of traffic, but whereas **Deming** (pop. 14,500) is thriving as a ranching and retirement center, **Lordsburg** has had a steady population of about 3,000 for years. This is a popular area for rockhounds, aficionados of ghost towns, and history buffs: **Columbus,** 32 miles south of Deming, was attacked by the Mexican bandit-revolutionary Pancho Villa in 1916. The U.S. military retaliated by sending 10,000 troops into Mexico to find him, but to no avail.

ESSENTIALS

GETTING THERE   From Las Cruces, take I-10 west (1 hr. to Deming, 2 hr. to Lordsburg). From Tucson, take I-10 east (3 hr. to Lordsburg, 4 hr. to Deming).

The **Grant County Airport** (© **505/388-4554**), 15 miles south of Silver City, is served by **Mesa Airlines** (© **800/MESA-AIR** or 505/326-3338; www.mesa-air.com), with daily flights to Albuquerque. The **Las Cruces Shuttle Service,** P.O. Box 3172, Las Cruces, NM 88003 (© **800/288-1784** or 505/525-1784; www.lascrucesshuttle. com), runs several times daily between Deming and the El Paso airport by way of Las Cruces.

VISITOR INFORMATION   The **Deming–Luna County Chamber of Commerce** is at 800 E. Pine St., Deming (© **800/848-4955** or 505/546-2674; www.deming chamber.com). You can write to them at P.O. Box 8, Deming, NM 88031. The **Lordsburg–Hidalgo County Chamber of Commerce** is at 117 E. 2nd St., Lordsburg, NM 88045 (© **505/542-9864;** www.hidalgocounty.org/lordsburgcoc).

WHAT TO SEE & DO NEAR DEMING
GETTING OUTSIDE
At **Rockhound State Park** ⊛, 14 miles southeast of Deming via NM 11, visitors are encouraged to pick up and take home with them as much as 15 pounds of minerals— jasper, agate, quartz crystal, flow-banded rhyolite, and others. At the base of the Little Florida Mountains, the park is a lovely, arid, cactus-covered land with paths leading down into dry gullies and canyons. (You may have to walk a bit, as the more accessible minerals have been largely picked out.)

The campground ($10 for nonelectric hookup; $14 with electric hookup), which has shelters, restrooms, and showers, offers a distant view of mountain ranges all the way to the U.S.–Mexico border. The park also has one marked hiking trail and a playground. Admission is $5 per vehicle, and the park is open year-round from dawn to dusk. For more information, call © **505/546-6182.**

Some 35 miles south of Deming is the tiny border town of **Columbus,** which looks across to Mexico. The **Pancho Villa State Park** here marks the last foreign invasion of American soil. A temporary fort, where a tiny garrison was housed in tents, was attacked in 1916 by 600 Mexican revolutionaries, who cut through the boundary fence at Columbus. Eighteen Americans were killed, 12 wounded; an estimated 200 Mexicans died. The Mexicans immediately retreated across their border. An American punitive expedition, headed by Gen. John J. Pershing, was launched into Mexico but got nowhere. Villa restricted his banditry to Mexico after that, until his assassination in 1923.

The state park includes ruins of the old fort and a new visitor center and 7,000-square-foot museum offering exhibits and a film. The park also has a strikingly beautiful desert botanical garden (worth the trip alone), plus campsites, restrooms, showers, an RV dump station, and a playground. There's a $5-per-vehicle entrance fee; the park is staffed from 8am to 5pm daily. For more information, call © **505/531-2711.**

Across the street from the state park is the old Southern Pacific Railroad Depot, which has been restored by the Columbus Historical Society and now houses the **Columbus Historical Museum** (© **505/531-2620**), which contains railroad memorabilia and exhibits on local history. Call for hours, which vary.

Three miles south across the border in Mexico is **Las Palomas, Chihuahua** (pop. 1,500). The port of entry is open 24 hours. A few desirable restaurants and tourist-oriented businesses are in Las Palomas. Mostly, though, it's a drug-trafficking town. Beware of barhopping in Palomas at night, which can be dangerous.

WHAT TO SEE & DO NEAR LORDSBURG

Visitors to Lordsburg can go **rockhounding** in this area rich in minerals of many kinds. Desert roses can be found near Summit, and agate is known to exist in many abandoned mines locally. Mine dumps, southwest of Hachita, contain lead, zinc, and gold; the Animas Mountains have manganese. Volcanic glass can be picked up in Coronado National Forest, and you can pan for gold in Gold Gulch.

Rodeo, 30 miles southwest via I-10 and NM 80, is the home of the **Chiricahua Gallery** (© 505/557-2225), open Monday through Saturday from 10am to 4pm. Regional artists have joined in a nonprofit, cooperative venture to exhibit works and offer classes in a variety of media. Many choose to live on the high-desert slopes of the Chiricahua Range. The gallery is on NM 80 en route to Douglas, Arizona.

Shakespeare Ghost Town *(Kids)*   A national historic site, Shakespeare was once the home of 3,000 miners, promoters, and dealers of various kinds. Under the name Ralston, it enjoyed a silver boom in 1870. This was followed by a notorious diamond fraud in 1872, in which a mine was salted with diamonds in order to raise prices on mining stock; many notables were sucked in, particularly William Ralston, founder of the Bank of California. It enjoyed a mining revival in 1879 under its new name, Shakespeare. It was a town with no church, no newspaper, and no local law. Some serious fights resulted in hangings from the roof timbers in the Stage Station. Since 1935, it's been privately owned by the Hill family, which has kept it uncommercialized, with no souvenir hype or gift shops. Six original buildings and two reconstructed buildings survive in various stages of repair. Two-hour guided tours are offered on a limited basis, and reenactments and living history are staged on the fourth weekends of April, June, August, and October, if performers are available. Phone to confirm the performances.

2½ miles south of Lordsburg (no street address), P.O. Box 253, Lordsburg, NM 88045. © 505/542-9034. www. shakespeareghostown.com. Admission $4 adults, $3 children 6–12; for shoot-outs and special events $5 adults, $4 children. 10am–2pm on the 2nd Sun and preceding Sat of each month. Special tours by appointment. To reach Shakespeare, drive 1½ miles south from I-10 on Main St. Just before the town cemetery, turn right, proceed ½-mile, and turn right again. Follow the dirt road another ½-mile into Shakespeare.

Stein's Railroad Ghost Town *(Kids)*   This settlement 19 miles west of Lordsburg started as a Butterfield Stage stop and then was a railroad town of about 1,000 residents from 1880 to 1955. It was so isolated that water, hauled from Doubtful Canyon, cost $1 a barrel!

Today there remain 12 buildings, with 16 rooms filled with artifacts and furnishings from the 19th and early 20th centuries. There's also a petting zoo for kids and the Steins Mercantile shop.

Exit 3, I-10 (P.O. Box 2185), Road Forks, NM 88045. © 505/542-9791. Admission $4; free for children under 12. Fri–Wed 9am–dusk.

WHERE TO STAY

IN DEMING

La Quinta Inn *(⚘)*   True to its origins, this new whitewashed hotel provides consistent and comfortable rooms at a decent price. Each unit is medium-size with high ceilings, red-wood furniture and earth-tone decor. The beds are comfortable and the bathrooms, which have granite countertops, are adequately spacious. This La Quinta is a good option if you prefer a newer style hotel than the Holiday Inn next door.

4300 E. Pine St., Deming, NM 88030. ⓒ 800/531-5900 or 505/546-0600. Fax 505/544-8207. www.laquinta.com. 58 units. $69–$99 double. Rates include continental breakfast. AE, DISC, DC, MC, V. **Amenities:** Outdoor heated pool; exercise room; business center. *In room:* A/C, TV, fridge, coffeemaker, hair dryer, iron, microwave, Wi-Fi.

IN LORDSBURG

Holiday Inn Express ⓐ   This hotel remains true to the Holiday Inn Express name, providing clean and comfortable rooms at a reasonable price. This is a motel-style property, allowing you to park right outside your room. All accommodations are medium-size with earth-tone-colored decor and comfortable beds. The bathrooms are small but have an outer sink vanity. A newer property than the Best Western, it provides more up-to-date accommodations in a quiet location in the center of town. Four of the rooms offer a fridge and microwave.

1408 S. Main St. Lordsburg, NM 88045. ⓒ 800/HOLIDAY or 505/542-3666. Fax 505/542-3665. www.hiexpress.com. 40 units. $85 double. Rates include continental breakfast. AE, DC, DISC, MC, V. Pets $20 fee. **Amenities:** Outdoor pool; business center. *In room:* A/C, TV, coffeemaker, hair dryer, iron, Wi-Fi.

CAMPING IN & AROUND DEMING & LORDSBURG

City of Rocks State Park, in Deming (ⓒ **505/536-2800**), has 52 campsites, 10 with electric hookups; tenting is available, and picnic tables and a hiking trail are nearby. **Dreamcatcher RV Park** (ⓒ **505/544-4004**), also in Deming (take exit 85, Motel Dr., off I-10 and go 1 block south on Business I-10), has 92 sites, all with full hookups. It also offers free access to a nearby swimming pool and on-site laundry facilities. **Little Vineyard RV Park** (ⓒ **505/546-3560**) in Deming (from I-10 take exit 85 and go 1 mile southwest on Business I-10 toward Deming) is larger than those mentioned above. It offers the same facilities as Dreamcatcher RV Park, with the addition of limited groceries, an indoor pool and hot tub, cable TV hookups, e-mail access, and a small RV parts store. The campground at **Rockhound State Park** (ⓒ **505/546-6182**) is picturesque and great for rockhounds who can't get enough of their hobby. RV sites with hookups and tenting are both available, as are shelters, restrooms, and showers.

If you'd rather camp near Lordsburg, try **Lordsburg KOA** (ⓒ **800/562-5772** or 505/542-8003; www.koa.com). It's in a desert setting but with shade trees, and tenting is permitted. Grocery and laundry facilities are available, in addition to a recreation room/area, a swimming pool, a playground, and horseshoes. To reach the campground, take I-10 to exit 22 and then go 1 block south; next, turn right at the Chevron station and follow the signs to the campground.

WHERE TO DINE
IN DEMING

Si Señor ⓐ NEW MEXICAN   Locals crowd this basic downtown cafe to eat platters full of tasty New Mexican food. The plain interior has functional furniture and a few woodcarved pictures on the wall. At breakfast, try the huevos rancheros (eggs over corn tortillas, smothered in chiles). The big seller here for lunch and dinner is the deluxe combination, with a chile relleno, a tamale, a cheese enchilada, a taco, refried beans, Spanish rice, and red or green chiles. The menu also includes salads, hamburgers, and chicken and fish dishes. All come with chips and salsa, and wine and beer are served.

200 E. Pine, Deming. ⓒ **505/546-3938.** Main courses $4–$8 breakfast, $5–$10 lunch and dinner. DISC, MC, V. Mon–Sat 9am–8:30pm; Sun 1–10pm.

IN LORDSBURG

Kranberry's Family Restaurant AMERICAN/MEXICAN A friendly, casual Denny's-style family restaurant decorated with Southwestern art, Kranberry's offers American favorites, including eggs and pancakes for breakfast; and burgers, chicken, beef, and salads, as well as Mexican selections for lunch and dinner. Baked goods are made on the premises daily. Our favorite is the corn bread, served with the soup special.

1405 S. Main St., Lordsburg. (C) **505/542-9400.** Main courses $3–$6 breakfast, $5–$15 lunch and dinner. AE, DC, DISC, MC, V. Daily 6am–10pm.

---

13 Silver City: Gateway to the Gila Cliff Dwellings ★★

44 miles NW of Deming; 57 miles SW of Truth or Consequences; 170 miles SW of Albuquerque

Silver City (pop. 10,545) is an old mining town, in the foothills of the Pinos Altos Range of the Mogollon Mountains, and gateway to the Gila Wilderness and the Gila Cliff Dwellings. Early Native Americans mined turquoise from these hills, and by 1804, Spanish settlers were digging for copper. In 1870, a group of prospectors discovered silver, and the rush was on. In 10 short months, newly christened Silver City grew from a single cabin to more than 80 buildings. Early visitors included Billy the Kid, Judge Roy Bean, and William Randolph Hearst.

This comparatively isolated community kept pace with every modern convenience: telephones in 1883, electric lights in 1884 (only 2 years after New York City installed its lighting), and a water system in 1887. The town should have busted with the crash of silver prices in 1893. But unlike many Western towns, Silver City did not become a picturesque memory. It capitalized on its high, dry climate to become today's county seat and trade center. Copper mining and processing are still the major industry. Silver City also can boast a famous son: The late Harrison (Jack) Schmitt, the first civilian geologist to visit the moon, and later a U.S. senator, was born and raised in nearby Santa Rita.

ESSENTIALS

GETTING THERE From Albuquerque, take I-25 south, 15 miles past Truth or Consequences; then west on NM 152 and US 180 (5 hr.). From Las Cruces, take I-10 west to Deming, then north on US 180 (2 hr.).

Great Lakes Airlines ((C) **505/388-4115**) flies daily to **Grant County Airport** ((C) **505/388-4554**), 15 miles south of Silver City near Hurley. **Silver Stage Lines** ((C) **800/522-0162**) offers daily shuttle service to the El Paso airport, and charter service to Tucson. The **Las Cruces Shuttle Service** ((C) **800/288-1784** or 505/525-1784; www.lascrucesshuttle.com) runs several times daily from Silver City to the El Paso airport, by way of Las Cruces.

VISITOR INFORMATION The **Murray Ryan Visitor Center** at 201 N. Hudson St., Silver City, NM 88061 ((C) **800/548-9378** or 505/538-3785; www.silvercity.org), also houses the Silver City Grant County Chamber of Commerce and is a good source of information. The chamber produces extremely useful tourist publications. Also of note at this site is a replica 1870s log cabin donated to the city by movie producer Ron Howard. It was built for the filming of the 2005 movie *The Missing*. A plaque on it says that Billy the Kid likely lived in one similar to it when he was a young resident of this town.

WHAT TO SEE & DO IN SILVER CITY

Silver City's downtown **Historic District** ★, the first such district to receive National Register recognition, is a must-see for visitors. The downtown core is marked by the

Way Beyond Silver

Silver City has become an artists' mecca, as creative people retreat to the small town for the peace it offers. You can spend a fun day wandering the streets. Some of our favorite shops and galleries include **Silver City Trading Company's Antique Mall,** 205 W. Broadway ((℃) **505/388-8989**), which is packed with a range of items, from fun junk to Western antiques. **Bloomin' Gourdworks,** 211-A N. Texas St. ((℃) **505/534-1071**), offers fabulous folk art, much of it made from gourds. Imaginative art adorns the walls at **Luna Gallery,** 108 W. Yankie St. ((℃) **505/534-4702**); look for still-life paintings and haunting masks. Meanwhile **Eklekticas,** 104 W. Yankie St. ((℃) **505/538-8081**), offers contemporary sculpture and glass work.

extensive use of brick in construction: Brick clay was discovered in the area soon after the town's founding in 1870, and an 1880 ordinance prohibited frame construction within the town limits. Mansard-roofed Victorian houses, Queen Anne and Italianate residences, and commercial buildings show off the cast-iron architecture of the period. Some are still undergoing restoration.

An 1895 flood washed out Main Street and turned it into a gaping chasm, which was eventually bridged over; finally, the **Big Ditch,** as it's called, was made into a green park in the center of town. Facing downtown, in the 500 block of North Hudson Street, was a famous red-light district from the turn of the 20th century until the late 1960s.

Billy the Kid lived in Silver City as a youth. You can see his cabin site a block north of the Broadway Bridge, on the east side of the Big Ditch. The Kid (William Bonney) waited tables at the Star Hotel, at Hudson Street and Broadway. He was jailed (at 304 N. Hudson St.) in 1875 at the age of 15, after being convicted of stealing from a Chinese laundry, but he escaped—a first for the Kid. The grave of Bonney's mother, Catherine McCarty, is in Silver City Cemetery, east of town on Memory Lane, off US 180. She died of tuberculosis about a year after the family moved here in 1873.

Silver City Museum ⊕ This well-presented museum of city and regional history contains collections relating to southwestern New Mexico history, mining, Native American pottery, and early photographs. Exhibits include a southwestern New Mexico history timeline; a parlor displaying Victorian decorative arts; and a chronicle of commerce in early Silver City. A local history research library is also available to visitors. The main gallery features changing exhibits. The museum is lodged in the 1881 H. B. Ailman House, a former city hall and fire station, remarkable for its cupola and Victorian mansard roof. Ailman came to Silver City penniless in 1871, made a fortune in mining, and went on to start the Meredith and Ailman Bank. Guided historic-district walking tours are offered on Memorial Day and Labor Day. There's also a museum store.

312 W. Broadway. (℃) **505/538-5921.** Fax 505/388-1096. Free admission. Tues–Fri 9am–4:30pm; Sat–Sun 10am–4pm. Closed Mon except Memorial Day and Labor Day.

SILVER CITY AFTER DARK

Some of southwestern New Mexico's most passionate performances are held at the **Pinos Altos Melodrama Theater,** 30 Main St., Pinos Altos (in the Pinos Altos Opera House, next to the Buckhorn Saloon; (℃) **505/388-3848**). Friday and Saturday nights from February to November, local actors fight the forces of good and evil in such productions as *The Legend of Billy the Kid* or *It's Just a Little Gun Play.*

EXPLORING THE AREA

NORTH OF SILVER CITY   The virtual ghost town of **Pinos Altos** ⊛, straddling the Continental Divide, is 6 miles north of Silver City on NM 15. Dubbed "Tall Pines" when it was founded in the gold- and silver-rush era, Apache attacks and mine failures took their toll.

The adobe **Methodist-Episcopal Church** was built with William Randolph Hearst's money in 1898 and now houses the Grant County Art Guild. The town also has the **Log Cabin Curio Shop and Museum,** set in an 1866 cabin (© **505/388-1882**), and the **Buckhorn Saloon and Opera House** (p. 334).

SOUTH OF SILVER CITY   **City of Rocks State Park** ⊛ (© **505/536-2800**), 25 miles from Silver City via US 180 and NM 61, is an area of fantastically shaped volcanic rock formations, formed in ancient times from thick blankets of ash that hardened into tuff. This soft stone, eroded by wind and rain, was shaped into monolithic blocks reminiscent of Stonehenge. Day use is allowed from 6am to 9pm for $5 per vehicle; a campsite costs $8 to $18. The visitor center is typically open from 10am to 4pm, but hours vary, depending on volunteer staffing.

WEST OF SILVER CITY   US 180, heading northwest from Silver City, is the gateway to Catron County and most of the Gila National Forest, including the villages of Glenwood, Reserve, and Quemado. For details on this area, see "Other Adventures in Gila National Forest," below.

WHERE TO STAY IN & AROUND SILVER CITY

Silver City now offers a full range of chain hotels, many with reasonable prices, so if you have a favorite, call their 800 number to see if it's represented. Most lodgings in town provide free parking.

Holiday Inn Express ⊛ *Kids*   East of downtown, this hotel offers clean and quiet rooms with standards you expect from the brand name. Rooms are medium-size, decorated with earth tones, and have high ceilings and large windows letting in lots of sunlight. Beds are comfortable, too. The medium-size bathrooms are very clean. Be sure *not* to book room no. 121, which has noisy pipes that will keep you awake through the night.

1103 Superior St., Silver City, NM 88061. © **800/HOLIDAY** or 505/538-2525. Fax 505/538-2525. 60 units. $95 double. AE, DC, DISC, MC, V. Pets allowed in some rooms. **Amenities:** Jacuzzi; exercise room; business center; coin-up laundry; dry cleaning, Wi-Fi. *In room:* A/C, TV, coffeemaker, hair dryer, iron, high-speed Internet.

SMALLER INNS

Bear Mountain Lodge ⊛⊛   Set on 160 acres just 3½ miles northwest of downtown Silver City, this lodge, owned and operated by the Nature Conservancy, is ideal for outdoors enthusiasts, from birders to bikers. The 1920s guesthouse offers large rooms with maple floors and high ceilings. Each is equipped with modern amenities, including country-inn Southwestern decor and comfortable beds. Four rooms have private balconies. This is a nature lover's delight. On-site naturalist Nature Conservancy staff members are on hand to inform visitors about the flora and fauna of the area, and they also conduct guided trips. Dinner is served for guests nightly for an extra fee. It's a gourmet buffet-style affair that changes seasonally with such offerings as poached salmon and a Thai dinner. A guest computer provides Internet access. What's best here is that you can count on complete quiet.

2251 Cottage San Rd., Silver City, NM 88061. (P.O. Box 1163, Silver City, NM 88062). © **877/620-BEAR (2327)** or 505/538-2538. www.bearmountainlodge.com. 11 units. $125–$185 double. 2-night minimum stay. Rates include full breakfast. Box lunches available for an extra charge. Horse boarding $15/night. AE, MC, V. Turn north off US 180 on Alabama St. (½-mile west of NM 90 intersection). Proceed 3 miles (Alabama becomes Cottage San Rd.) to dirt road turnoff to left; the lodge is another ½-mile. No children under 10. **Amenities:** Mountain-bike rental; conference and event spaces; hiking trails; free naturalist activities and guided hikes. *In room:* A/C, dataport, hair dryer.

Casitas de Gila 𝒢𝒢★　If you're looking for a remote and peaceful stay in the quintessential southern New Mexico terrain, this inn is for you. Set on a little bluff above Bear Creek, about a half-hour from Silver City, these five casitas offer the epitome of Southwestern style. The adobe-style dwellings are decorated with Spanish-style furniture and Mexican rugs. The medium-size bedrooms and bathrooms come well equipped with comfortably firm beds, bath supplies, and bathrobes. Each also has a kiva fireplace and a small porch with a *chiminea* (Mexican ceramic fireplace) and a grill. On hand is a hot tub with a view of the creek, canyon, and sky. The area is great for birding and hiking, and horseback riding can be arranged. Also on the property are 90 acres of hiking trails, an art gallery, and a courtyard.

50 Casita Flats Rd. (P.O. Box 325), Gila, NM 88038. ℂ **877/923-4827** or 505/535-4455. Fax 505/535-4456. www.casitasdegila.com. 5 casitas. $120–$190 double. Rates include continental breakfast. AE, DISC, MC, V. **Amenities:** Jacuzzi; activities desk; telescopes. *In room:* Kitchen, hair dryer, iron, Wi-Fi.

CAMPING

Silver City KOA (ℂ **800/562-7623** or 505/388-3351; www.koa.com) has 82 sites and 42 full hookups, and it offers groceries, laundry facilities, and a pool. The campground is 5 miles east of the NM 90/US 180 junction on US 180. **Silver City RV Park** (ℂ **505/538-2239;** www.silvercityrv.com) has 48 sites (45 with full hookups), showers, laundry facilities, and picnic tables. It's downtown on Bennett Street, behind Food Basket supermarket. Camping is also available at the Gila Cliff Dwellings (see "Gila Cliff Dwellings National Monument," below).

WHERE TO DINE IN & AROUND SILVER CITY

Buckhorn Saloon and Opera House★ BURGERS/SEAFOOD/STEAKS　Seven miles north of Silver City in Pinos Altos, the Buckhorn offers fine dining in 1860s decor. It's completely authentic, with vigas on the ceiling and thick adobe walls, but be aware that the dining room has very low light. The restaurant is noted for its Western-style steaks, seafood, homemade desserts, and excellent wine list. If you've got a big appetite, try the New York strip with green chile and cheese. We like the shrimp and chicken kabobs. Entrees are served with a salad (try the blue-cheese dressing) or soup and choice of potatoes or rice. Live entertainment is offered nightly. The high-personality saloon offers big round tables and a great wooden bar. Many come to this saloon to have excellent burgers and hear live music on selected nights. Enjoy a drink from the full bar.

32 Main St., Pinos Altos. ℂ **505/538-9911.** Reservations highly recommended. Main courses $7–$46. MC, V. Mon–Sat 6–10pm; saloon Mon–Sat 3–10pm.

Diane's Bakery & Cafe 𝒢𝒢 NEW AMERICAN　This is a wonderful find in such a small town. Diane Barrett, who was once a pastry chef at La Traviata and Eldorado in Santa Fe, has brought refined city food to this small town. At lunch, the atmosphere is bustling, usually with a slight wait for a table. At dinner, the tone is more romantic and low key, with more nouveau specialties. The service is friendly and adequate. You can't go wrong with any of the baked goods here. At brunch, try the hatch Benedict, a version of eggs Benedict made with home-baked chile cheddar toast. At lunch we suggest the *spano,* a baked spinach pastry, served with a salad; the quiche of the day is also delicious. At dinner, you may want to opt for one of the night's specials, such as grilled lamb with wild mushroom demiglace or the chef's choice lasagna. Diane's also serves great steaks. There's a small but creative wine and beer menu.

510 N. Bullard St., Silver City. © 505/538-8722. Reservations recommended for dinner. Main courses $5–$7 lunch, $14–$25 dinner. MC, V. Tues–Sat 11am–2pm and 5:30–9pm; brunch Sat–Sun 9am–2pm.

Jalisco's *Kids* NEW MEXICAN   Set within an enchanting brick building in the historic district, this festive, nonsmoking restaurant serves big portions of good food. Three dining rooms fill the old structure, which has been Latinized with arched doorways and bold Mexican street-scene calendars on the walls. The combination plates are large and popular, as are the enchiladas. There are also burgers and a children's menu. Whatever you do, be sure to order a *sopaipilla* for dessert, which is delicious and huge. Beer and wine are served here.

103 S. Bullard St., Silver City. © 505/388-2060. Reservations not accepted. Main courses $5–$10. DISC, MC, V. Mon–Sat 11am–8:30pm.

14 Gila Cliff Dwellings National Monument ★/★

44 miles N of Silver City

It takes 1½ to 2 hours to reach the **Gila Cliff Dwellings** from Silver City, but it's definitely worth the trip. First-time visitors are inevitably awed by the remains of an ancient civilization set in the mouths of caves, abandoned for 7 centuries. You reach the dwellings on a 1-mile moderate hike along which you catch first glimpses of the ruins. This walk is an elaborate journey into the past. It winds its way into a narrow canyon, from which you first spot the poetic ruins perched in six caves 180 feet up on the canyon wall, stone shiny and hard as porcelain. Then the ascent begins up innumerable steps and rocks until you're standing face-to-face with these ancient relics, which offer a glimpse into the lives of Native Americans who lived here from the late 1270s through the early 1300s. Tree-ring dating indicates their residence didn't last longer than 30 to 40 years.

However, the earliest ruin that has been found within the monument is a pit house dated between A.D. 100 and 400. This dwelling below ground level was an earlier type of home occupied by the Mogollon people who grew corn and beans, hunted, and gathered wild plant food.

What's remarkable about the journey through the cliff dwellings is the depth of some of the caves. At one point, you'll climb a ladder and pass from one cave into the next, viewing the intricate little rooms (42 total) and walls that once made up a community dwelling. Probably not more than 10 to 15 families (about 40–50 people) lived in the cliff dwellings at any one time. The inhabitants were excellent weavers and skilled potters.

The cliff dwellings were discovered by Anglo settlers in the early 1870s, near where the three forks of the Gila River rise. Once you leave the last cave, you'll head down again traversing some steep steps to the canyon floor. Pets are not allowed within the monument, but they can be taken on trails within the Gila Wilderness. Be sure to pick up a trail guide at the visitor center.

ESSENTIALS

GETTING THERE   From Silver City, take NM 15 north 44 miles to the Gila Cliff Dwellings. Travel time from Silver City is approximately 2 hours. You won't find any gas stations between Silver City and Gila Cliff Dwellings, so plan accordingly. Also know that at the monument, vehicles are permitted on paved roads only.

VISITOR INFORMATION   For more information, contact **Gila Cliff Dwellings National Monument,** HC 68, Box 100, Silver City, NM 88061 (© **505/536-9461;** www.nps.gov/gicl).

ADMISSION FEES & HOURS   Admission to the monument is $3 per person, with children under 13 admitted free. The visitor center, where you can pick up detailed brochures, is open from 8am to 5pm Memorial Day to Labor Day and from 8am to 4:30pm the rest of the year. The cliff dwellings are open from 8am to 6pm in the summer and from 9am to 4pm the rest of the year.

SEEING THE HIGHLIGHTS

Today, the dwellings allow a rare glimpse inside the homes and lives of prehistoric Native Americans. About 75% of what is seen is original, although the walls have been capped and the foundations strengthened to prevent further deterioration. It took a great deal of effort to build these homes: The stones were held in place by mortar, and all the clay and water for the mortar had to be carried by hand up from the stream, as the Mogollon did not have any pack animals. The vigas for the roof were cut and shaped with stone axes or fire.

The people who lived here were farmers, as shown by the remains of beans, squash, and corn in their homes. The fields were along the valley of the west fork of the Gila River and on the mesa across the canyon. No signs of irrigation have been found.

A 1-mile loop trail, rising 175 feet from the canyon floor, provides access to the dwellings.

Near the visitor center, about a mile away, the remains of an earlier pit house (A.D. 100–400), built below ground level, and later pit houses (up to A.D. 1000), above-ground structures of adobe or wattle, have been found.

CAMPING

Camping and picnicking are encouraged in the national monument, which has four developed campgrounds. Camping is free and some sites are RV accessible, though there are no hookups. Overnight lodging can be found in Silver City and in the nearby town of Gila Hot Springs, which also has a grocery store, horse rentals, and guided pack trips. For information, contact the visitor center (© **505/536-9461**).

15 Other Adventures in Gila National Forest

Gila National Forest, which offers some of the most spectacular mountain scenery in the Southwest, comprises 3.3 million acres in four counties. Nearly one-fourth of that acreage (790,000 acres) is the **Gila, Aldo Leopold,** and **Blue Range wildernesses.** Its highest peak is Whitewater Baldy, at 10,892 feet. The forest encompasses six out of seven life zones, so the range of plant and wildlife is broad. You may see mule deer, elk, antelope, black bear, mountain lion, and bighorn sheep. Nearly 400 miles of streams and a few small lakes sustain populations of trout as well as bass, bluegill, and catfish. Anglers can head to Lake Roberts, Snow Lake, and Quemado Lake.

JUST THE FACTS   For more information on the national forest, contact the **U.S. Forest Service,** Forest Supervisor's Office, 3005 East Camino del Bosque, Silver City, NM 88061 (© **505/388-8201;** www.fs.fed.us).

The national forest has 29 campgrounds, all with toilets and six with drinking water. Car and backpack camping are also permitted throughout the forest.

GETTING OUTSIDE

The forest has 1,490 miles of trails for hiking and horseback riding, and, in winter, cross-country skiing. Outside the wilderness areas, trail bikes and off-road vehicles are permitted. Hiking trails in the Gila Wilderness, especially the 41-mile Middle Fork Trail, with its east end near Gila Cliff Dwellings, are among the most popular in the state and can sometimes be crowded. If you are more interested in communing with nature than with fellow hikers, you will find plenty of trails to suit you, both in and out of the officially designated wilderness areas.

Most of the trails are maintained and easy to follow. Trails along river bottoms have many stream crossings (so be prepared for hiking with wet feet) and may be washed out by summer flash floods. It's best to inquire about trail conditions before you set out. More than 50 trail heads provide roadside parking.

Some of the best hikes in the area are the Frisco Box, Pueblo Creek, Whitewater Baldy, the Catwalk and Beyond, the Middle Fork/Little Bear Loop, and the Black Range Crest Trail. The Gila National Forest contains several wilderness areas that are off-limits to mountain bikes, including the Gila, Aldo Leopold, and the Blue Range Primitive Area. However, cyclists can use quite a few trails. Some to look for are the Cleveland Mine trail, Silver City Loop, Continental Divide, Signal Peak, Pinos Altos Loop, Fort Bayard Historical Trails, and Forest Trail 100.

The Catwalk National Recreation Trail ⚐ (☏ **505/539-2481**), 68 miles north of Silver City on US 180, then 5 miles east of Glenwood via NM 174, is a great break after a long drive. Kids are especially thrilled with this hike. It follows the route of a pipeline built in 1897 to carry water to the now-defunct town of Graham and its electric generator. About a quarter-mile above the parking area is the beginning of a striking 250-foot metal causeway clinging to the sides of the boulder-choked Whitewater Canyon, which in spots is 20 feet wide and 250 feet deep. Along the way, you'll find water pouring through caves and waterfalls spitting off the cliff side. Farther up the canyon, a suspension bridge spans the chasm. Picnic facilities are near the parking area. There's a $3 fee per car.

11

Tucson

Encircled by mountain ranges and book-ended by the two units of Saguaro National Park, Tucson is Arizona's second-largest city, and for the vacationer it has everything that Phoenix has to offer, plus a bit more. There are world-class golf resorts, excellent restaurants, art museums and galleries, an active cultural life, and, of course, plenty of great weather. Tucson also has a long history that melds Native American, Hispanic, and Anglo roots. And with a national park, a national forest, and other natural areas just beyond the city limits, Tucson is a city that celebrates its Sonoran Desert setting.

Founded by the Spanish in 1775, Tucson was built on the site of a much older Native American village, and the city's name comes from the Pima Indian word *chukeson,* which means "spring at the base of black mountain," a reference to the peak now known simply as "A Mountain." From 1867 to 1877, Tucson was the territorial capital of Arizona, but eventually the capital was moved to Phoenix. Consequently, Tucson did not develop as quickly as Phoenix and still holds fast to its Hispanic and Western heritage.

Back in the days when urban renewal meant out with the old and in with the new, Tucson's citizens turned back the bulldozers and managed to preserve at least some of the city's old Mexican character. Likewise, today, in the face of the sort of sprawl that has given Phoenix the feel of a landlocked Los Angeles, advocates for controlled growth are fighting hard to preserve both Tucson's desert environment and the city's unique character.

The struggle to retain an identity distinct from other Southwestern cities is ongoing, and despite long, drawn-out attempts to breathe life into the city's core, the past few years have seen the loss of downtown's vibrancy as shops, galleries, and restaurants have moved out to the suburbs. However, downtown Tucson still has its art museum, convention center, and historic neighborhoods.

Despite this minor shortcoming, Tucson remains Arizona's most beautiful and most livable city. With the Santa Catalina Mountains for a backdrop, Tucson boasts one of the most dramatic settings in the Southwest, and whether you're taking in the mountain vistas from the saddle of a palomino or a table for two, we're sure you'll agree that Tucson makes a superb vacation destination.

1 Orientation

ARRIVING

BY PLANE Located 6 miles south of downtown, **Tucson International Airport** (© 520/573-8000; www.tucsonairport.org) is served by the following major airlines: **Alaska/Horizon** (© 800/252-7522; www.alaskaair.com), **American** (© 800/433-7300; www.aa.com), **Continental** (© 800/523-3273; www.continental.com), **Delta**

(© 800/221-1212; www.delta.com), **Frontier** (© 800/432-1359; www.flyfrontier.
com), **JetBlue Airways** (© 800/538-2583; www.jetblue.com), **Northwest/KLM**
(© 800/225-2525; www.nwa.com), **Southwest** (© 800/435-9792; www.southwest.
com), **United** (© 800/864-8331; www.ual.com), and **US Airways** (© 800/428-4322;
www.usairways.com).

Visitor centers in both baggage-claim areas can give you brochures and reserve a
hotel room if you haven't done so already.

Many resorts and hotels in Tucson provide free or competitively priced airport shuttle service. **Arizona Stagecoach** (© 520/889-1000; www.azstagecoach.com) operates
24-hour van service to downtown Tucson and the foothills resorts. Fares to downtown
are around $20 one-way and $38 round-trip ($23 and $44 for a couple), and to the
foothills resorts around $36 one-way and $62 round-trip ($42 and $74 for a couple).
It takes between 45 minutes and 1 hour to reach the foothills resorts. To return to the
airport, it's best to call at least a day before your scheduled departure.

You'll also find taxis waiting outside baggage claim, or you can call **Yellow Cab**
(© 520/624-6611) or **Allstate Cab** (© 520/881-2227). The flag-drop rate at the airport is $4.50, and then $2 per mile. A taxi to downtown costs around $23, to the
foothills resorts about $26 to $46.

Sun Tran (© 520/792-9222; www.suntran.com), the local public transit system,
operates bus service to and from the airport. The fare is $1. Route no. 6, to down-
town, runs Monday through Friday from about 4:50am to 7:20pm, Saturday from
about 7:15am to 6:15pm, and Sunday from about 6:20am to 5:20pm. Departures are
every 30 minutes on weekdays and every hour on weekends. It takes 40 to 50 minutes
to reach downtown. Route no. 11 operates on a similar schedule and travels along
Alvernon Road to the midtown area.

BY CAR   I-10, the main east-west interstate across the southern United States,
passes through Tucson and connects to Phoenix. **I-19** connects Tucson with the Mexican border at Nogales. **Arizona 86** heads southwest into the Tohono O'odham Indian
Reservation, and **Arizona 79** leads north toward Florence and eventually connects
with **US 60** into Phoenix.

If you're headed downtown, take the Congress Street exit off I-10. If you're coming
from the north and going to one of the foothills resorts north of downtown, you'll
probably want to take the Ina Road exit off I-10.

BY TRAIN   Tucson is served by **Amtrak** (© 800/872-7245; www.amtrak.com) passenger rail service. The *Sunset Limited*, which runs between Orlando and Los Angeles,
stops in Tucson. The **train station** is at 400 E. Toole Ave. (© 520/623-4442), in the
heart of downtown and within walking distance of the Tucson Convention Center, El
Presidio Historic District, and a few hotels. You'll see taxis waiting to meet the train.

BY BUS   **Greyhound** (© 800/231-2222 or 520/792-3475; www.greyhound.com)
connects Tucson to the rest of the United States through its extensive system. The bus
station is currently at 471 W. Congress St., but this is a temporary location. Call at
the time you are traveling to confirm the station location.

VISITOR INFORMATION

The **Metropolitan Tucson Convention & Visitors Bureau (MTCVB),** 100 S.
Church Ave. (at Broadway), Suite 7199 (© 800/638-8350 or 520/624-1817;
www.visittucson.org), is an excellent source of information on Tucson and environs.

The visitor center is open Monday through Friday from 8am to 5pm, Saturday and Sunday from 9am to 4pm.

CITY LAYOUT

MAIN ARTERIES & STREETS   Tucson is laid out on a grid that's fairly regular in the downtown areas but becomes less orderly the farther you go from the city center. In the flatlands, major thoroughfares are spaced at 1-mile intervals, with smaller streets filling in the squares created by the major roads. In the foothills, the grid system breaks down completely because of the hilly terrain.

The main **east-west roads** are (from south to north) 22nd Street, Broadway Boulevard, Speedway Boulevard, Grant Road (with Tanque Verde Rd. as an extension), and Ina Road/Skyline Drive/Sunrise Road. The main **north-south roads** are (from west to east) Miracle Mile/Oracle Road, Stone/Sixth Avenue, Campbell Avenue, Country Club Road, Alvernon Road, and Swan Road. **I-10** cuts diagonally across the Tucson metropolitan area from northwest to southeast.

In **downtown Tucson,** Congress Street and Broadway Boulevard are the main east-west streets; Stone Avenue, Sixth Avenue, and Fourth Avenue are the main north-south streets.

FINDING AN ADDRESS   Because Tucson is laid out on a grid, finding an address is relatively easy. The zero (or starting) point for all Tucson addresses is the corner of Stone Avenue, which runs north and south, and Congress Street, which runs east and west. From this point, streets are designated either north, south, east, or west. Addresses usually, but not always, increase by 100 with each block, so that an address of 4321 E. Broadway Blvd. should be 43 blocks east of Stone Avenue. In the downtown area, many of the streets and avenues are numbered, with numbered streets running east and west, and numbered avenues running north and south.

2 Getting Around

BY CAR

Unless you plan to stay by the pool or on the golf course, you'll want to rent a car. Luckily, rates are fairly economical. At press time, Dollar was charging $133 per week ($171 with taxes and surcharges included) for a compact car with unlimited mileage in Tucson. See "Getting Around the Southwest" in chapter 2 for general tips on car rentals in Arizona.

The following agencies have offices at Tucson International Airport as well as other locations in the area. Because taxes and surcharges add up to 30% or more on car rentals at the airport, you may want to consider renting at some other location, where you can avoid paying some of these fees. Among the Tucson car-rental agencies are **Alamo** (✆ 800/462-5266 or 520/573-4740), **Avis** (✆ 800/331-1212 or 520/294-1494), **Budget** (✆ 800/527-0700 or 520/573-8476), **Dollar** (✆ 800/800-3665), **Enterprise** (✆ 800/261-7331 or 520/573-5250), **Hertz** (✆ 800/654-3131 or 520/573-5201), and **National** (✆ 800/227-7368 or 520/573-8050).

Downtown Tucson is still a relatively easy place to find a parking space, and parking fees are low. There are two huge parking lots at the south side of the Tucson Convention Center, a couple of small lots on either side of the Tucson Museum of Art (one at Main Ave. and Paseo Redondo, south of El Presidio Historic District, and one at the corner of Council St. and Court Ave.), and parking garages beneath the main library (101 N. Stone Ave.) and El Presidio Park (on Alameda St.). You'll find plenty of metered parking on the smaller downtown streets. Almost all Tucson hotels and resorts provide free parking.

Lanes on several major avenues in Tucson change direction at rush hour to facilitate traffic flow, so pay attention to signs that tell you the time and direction of traffic.

BY PUBLIC TRANSPORTATION

BY BUS   Covering much of the Tucson metropolitan area, **Sun Tran** (© 520/792-9222; www.suntran.com) public buses are $1 for adults and students, 40¢ for seniors, and free for children 5 and under. Day passes are available on buses for $2.

The **Ronstadt Transit Center,** at Congress Street and Sixth Avenue, is served by about 30 regular and express bus routes to all parts of Tucson. The bus system does *not* extend to such tourist attractions as the Arizona–Sonora Desert Museum, Old Tucson, Saguaro National Park, or the foothills resorts, and thus is of limited use to visitors. However, Sun Tran does provide a shuttle for sports games and special events. Call the above phone number for information.

BY TROLLEY   Although they don't go very far, the restored electric streetcars of **Old Pueblo Trolley** (© 520/792-1802; www.oldpueblotrolley.org) are a fun way to get from the Fourth Avenue shopping district to the University of Arizona. The trolleys operate on Friday from 6 to 10pm, Saturday from noon to midnight, and Sunday from noon to 6pm. The fare is $1 for adults and 50¢ for children 6 to 12. The fare on Sunday is only 25¢ for all riders. Friday and Saturday all day passes are $2.50 for adults and $1.25 for children.

T.I.C.E.T., or Tucson Inner City Express Transit (© 520/747-3778), operates five free downtown-area shuttles, only two of which are of much use to visitors. The Orange Route, which has stops near the visitor center, the Tucson Convention Center, the Tucson Children's Museum, Old Town Artisans, and the Tucson Museum of Art, operates Monday through Friday and runs every 20 minutes between 6am and 6pm. The Red Route, which links downtown with the numerous museums at the University of Arizona, operates Monday through Friday every 20 minutes between 6:30am and 5:30pm.

BY TAXI

If you need a taxi, you'll have to phone for one. **Yellow Cab** (© 520/624-6611) and **Discount Cab** (© 520/388-9000) provide service throughout the city. The flag-drop rate is between $2.25 and $2.50, and after that it's $1.75 to $1.80 per mile. Although distances in Tucson are not as great as those in Phoenix, it's still a good 10 or more miles from the foothills resorts to downtown Tucson, so expect to pay at least $10 for a taxi. Most resorts have shuttle vans or can arrange taxi service to major attractions.

ON FOOT

Downtown Tucson is compact and easily explored on foot, and many old streets in the downtown historic neighborhoods are narrow and much easier to appreciate if you leave your car in a parking lot. Also, although several major attractions—including the Arizona–Sonora Desert Museum, Old Tucson Studios, Saguaro National Park, and Sabino Canyon—can be reached only by car, they require quite a bit of walking once you arrive. These attractions often have uneven footing, so be sure to bring a good pair of walking shoes.

FAST FACTS

For a doctor referral, ask at your hotel or call University Medical Center (© 520/694-8888). For a dentist referral, call the Arizona Dental Association (© 800/866-2732).

Local hospitals are the **Tucson Medical Center** at 5301 E. Grant Rd. (℃ **520/ 327-5461**) and the **University Medical Center** is at 1501 N. Campbell Ave. (℃ **520/ 694-0111**).

In addition to the 5.6% sales tax levied by the state, Tucson levies a 2% city sales tax. Car-rental taxes, surcharges, and fees add up to around 30%. The hotel tax in the Tucson area is usually 11.5% to 12%.

3 Where to Stay

Although Phoenix still holds the title of Resort Capital of Arizona, Tucson is not far behind, and this city's resorts boast much more spectacular settings than most comparable properties in Phoenix and Scottsdale. As far as nonresort accommodations go, Tucson has a wider variety than Phoenix—partly because several historic neighborhoods have become home to bed-and-breakfast inns. The presence of several guest ranches within a 20-minute drive of Tucson also adds to the city's diversity of accommodations.

At the more expensive hotels and resorts, summer rates, usually in effect from May to September or October, are often less than half what they are in winter. Surprisingly, temperatures usually aren't unbearable in May or September, which makes these good times to visit if you're looking to save money. When making late spring or early fall reservations, always be sure to ask when rates are scheduled to go up or down. If you aren't coming to Tucson specifically for the winter gem and mineral shows, then you'll save quite a bit if you avoid the last week in January and the first 2 weeks in February, when hotels around town generally charge exorbitant rates.

Most hotels offer special packages, weekend rates, various discounts (such as for AARP or AAA members), and free accommodations for children, so it helps to ask when you reserve. Nearly all hotels have smoke-free and wheelchair-accessible rooms.

BED & BREAKFASTS   If you're looking to stay in a B&B, several agencies can help. The **Arizona Association of Bed and Breakfast Inns** (www.arizona-bed-breakfast. com) has several members in Tucson. **Mi Casa Su Casa** (℃ **800/456-0682** or 480/ 990-0682; www.azres.com) will book you into one of its many home-stays (informal B&Bs) in the Tucson area or elsewhere in the state, as will **Arizona Trails Travel Services** (℃ **888/799-4284** or 480/837-4284; www.arizonatrails.com).

DOWNTOWN & THE UNIVERSITY AREA
VERY EXPENSIVE

Arizona Inn 𝄞𝄞𝄞   With its pink-stucco buildings and immaculately tended flower gardens, the Arizona Inn is a 14-acre oasis of tranquility in central Tucson. Gracious, welcoming, and comfortable, it's an unforgettable place to spend a vacation. Originally opened in 1930 by Isabella Greenway, Arizona's first congresswoman, the inn is still family owned and operated, and is imbued with a gracious character and Old Arizona charm you won't find elsewhere in the state. Playing a game of croquet, taking high tea in the library (complimentary), or lounging by the pool, we always feel as if this were a second home. Guest rooms vary in size and decor, but most have a mix of reproduction antiques and original pieces custom made for the inn years ago by disabled World War I veterans. Guest rooms also have such modern amenities as DVD players (and access to a library of films featuring actors and actresses who were once inn guests). Some units have gas fireplaces, and most suites have private patios or enclosed sun porches. The inn's main dining room (p. 355) is a casually elegant space.

2200 E. Elm St., Tucson, AZ 85719. 🕾 **800/933-1093** or 520/325-1541. Fax 520/881-5830. www.arizonainn.com. 95 units. Mid-Jan to mid-Apr from $319 double, from $469 suite; mid-Apr to May from $229 double, from $369 suite; June to mid-Sept from $179 double, from $289 suite; mid-Sept to mid-Dec from $229 double, from $369 suite; mid-Dec to mid-Jan $259 double, from $359 suite. Summer rates include full breakfast and complimentary evening ice-cream fountain. Children 12 and under stay free in parent's room. AE, DC, MC, V. **Amenities:** 3 restaurants (Continental/American, International); 2 lounges; heated outdoor pool; 2 Har-Tru clay tennis courts; well-equipped exercise room; saunas; bikes; concierge; business center; room service; massage; babysitting; laundry service; dry cleaning; croquet; table tennis; badminton. *In room:* A/C, TV/DVD, dataport, fridge, coffeemaker, hair dryer, iron, safe, high-speed Internet access, free local calls.

EXPENSIVE

Doubletree Hotel Tucson at Reid Park ✶✶   This in-town high-rise hotel, with its pleasant orange-tree-shaded pool area, is midway between the airport and downtown Tucson, and is something of an in-town budget resort (the Randolph Park municipal golf course is right across the street). Guest rooms boast bright colors and bold contemporary designs, and there's a big exercise room by the pool. Although the hotel does a lot of convention business and sometimes feels crowded, the gardens, with their citrus trees (feel free to pick the fruit) and lawns, are always tranquil. Guest rooms are divided between a nine-story tower that offers views of the valley and a two-story building with patio rooms overlooking the garden and pool area.

445 S. Alvernon Way, Tucson, AZ 85711. 🕾 **800/222-TREE** or 520/881-4200. Fax 520/323-5225. www. dtreidpark.com. 295 units. Jan–May $199–$314 double, $349–$439 suite; June–Aug $99–$124 double, $199–$309 suite; Sept–Dec $155–$184 double, $255–$309 suite. Children under 18 stay free in parent's room. AE, DC, DISC, MC, V. Pets accepted ($25 fee). **Amenities:** 2 restaurants (Southwestern, American); 2 lounges; outdoor pool; 3 tennis courts; exercise room; Jacuzzi; concierge; car-rental desk; business center; room service; laundry service; dry cleaning. *In room:* A/C, TV, dataport, coffeemaker, hair dryer, iron, high-speed Internet access.

The Lodge on the Desert ✶✶   Dating from 1936 and set amid neatly manicured lawns and gardens, The Lodge on the Desert is a classic old Arizona resort. The lush and relaxing retreat looks a lot like the Arizona Inn (though not nearly as deluxe, and without the superb service). Guest rooms are in hacienda-style adobe buildings tucked amid cacti and orange trees. Rooms feature a mix of contemporary and Southwestern furnishings; many units have beamed ceilings or fireplaces, and some have tile floors and also patios. The small pool has a good view of the Catalinas.

306 N. Alvernon Way, Tucson, AZ 85711. 🕾 **800/456-5634** or 520/325-3366. Fax 520/327-5834. www.lodgeon thedesert.com. 35 units. Mid-Jan to mid-Apr $189–$299 double; mid-Apr to mid-May and mid-Sept to mid-Jan $129–$204 double; mid-May to mid-Sept $89–$154 double. Rates include full breakfast. Children under 6 stay free in parent's room. AE, DC, DISC, MC, V. Pets accepted ($50 deposit plus $20 per night). **Amenities:** Restaurant (American/Continental); lounge; small outdoor pool; access to nearby health club; concierge; laundry service; dry cleaning. *In room:* A/C, TV, coffeemaker, hair dryer, iron, Wi-Fi.

MODERATE

Catalina Park Inn ✶✶   Close to downtown and overlooking a shady park, this 1927 home has been lovingly restored by owners Mark Hall and Paul Richard. From the outside, the inn has the look of a Mediterranean villa, while many interesting and playful touches enliven the classic interior. The huge Catalina Room in the basement is one of our favorites. Not only does it conjure up the inside of an adobe, but it has a whirlpool tub in a former cedar closet. Two upstairs rooms have balconies, while two units in a separate cottage across the garden feature more contemporary styling.

309 E. First St., Tucson, AZ 85705. 🕾 **800/792-4885** or 520/792-4541. www.catalinaparkinn.com. 6 units. $136–$166 double (lower rates late spring through fall). Rates include full breakfast. AE, DISC, MC, V. No children under 10. **Amenities:** Concierge. *In room:* A/C, TV/DVD, dataport, hair dryer, iron, high-speed Internet access, Wi-Fi, free local calls.

Tucson Accommodations

The Royal Elizabeth 👁👁 A block from the Temple of Music and Art, The Royal Elizabeth is an 1878 Victorian adobe home that features an unusual combination of architectural styles that makes for a uniquely Southwestern-style inn. In classic 19th-century Tucson fashion, the old home looks thoroughly unpretentious from the outside, but inside you'll find beautiful woodwork and gorgeous Victorian-era antique furnishings. Guest rooms open off a large, high-ceilinged central hall. The immediate neighborhood isn't as attractive as the nearby El Presidio neighborhood, but art galleries, the Tucson Museum of Art, and several good restaurants are within walking distance.

204 S. Scott Ave., Tucson, AZ 85701. (©) 877/670-9022 or 520/670-9022. Fax 928/833-9974. www.royalelizabeth.com. 6 units. Aug–May $155–$245 double; June–July $115–$205 double. Rates include full breakfast. Children under 10 stay free in parent's room. AE, DISC, MC, V. **Amenities:** Outdoor heated pool; access to nearby health club; Jacuzzi; concierge; business center; massage. *In room:* A/C, TV/VCR/DVD, dataport, fridge, hair dryer, iron, safe, Wi-Fi, free local and long-distance calls.

INEXPENSIVE

In addition to the hotel listed below, you'll find dozens of budget chain motels along I-10 as it passes through downtown. Among the better ones are **Days Inn Tucson,** 222 S. Freeway, Exit 258 (© **520/791-7511**); **Motel 6–Tucson/Congress Street,** 960 S. Freeway, Exit 258 (© **520/628-1339**); **Motel 6–Tucson/22nd Street,** 1222 S. Freeway, Exit 259 (© **520/624-2516**); and **Super 8–Tucson/Downtown,** 1248 N. Stone St., Exit 257 (© **520/622-6446**).

Hotel Congress *Finds* Located in the heart of downtown Tucson, the Hotel Congress, built in 1919 to serve railroad passengers, once hosted John Dillinger. Today, it operates as a budget hotel and youth hostel. Although the place is utterly basic, the lobby has loads of Southwestern elegance. Guest rooms remain true to their historical character, with antique telephones and old radios, so don't expect anything fancy (like TVs). Most bathrooms have tubs or showers, but a few have both. There's the classic little Cup Cafe off the lobby (think Edward Hopper meets Gen X), as well as a tiny Western Tap Room bar. At night, the Club Congress (p. 388) is a popular (and loud) dance club (pick up earplugs at the front desk).

311 E. Congress St., Tucson, AZ 85701. (©) 800/722-8848 or 520/622-8848. Fax 520/792-6366. www.hotelcongress.com. 40 units. $59–$109 double. AE, DC, DISC, MC, V. Pets accepted ($10 per night). **Amenities:** Restaurant; lounge; nightclub. *In room:* Wi-Fi.

EAST TUCSON
MODERATE

Comfort Suites at Sabino Canyon 👁 Although it looks rather stark from the outside and shares a parking lot with a shopping center, this Comfort Suites is surprisingly pleasant inside. Built around four tranquil and lushly planted garden courtyards, the hotel has (for the most part) large rooms, some of which have kitchenettes. This is a good economical choice close to Sabino Canyon, the Mount Lemmon Highway, and Saguaro National Park's east unit.

7007 E. Tanque Verde Rd., Tucson, AZ 85715. (©) 800/424-6423 or 520/298-2300. Fax 520/298-6756. www.choice hotels.com. 90 units. Jan to mid-Apr $99–$179 double; mid-Apr to mid-May and late Sept to Dec $89–$169 double; mid-May to late Sept $72–$95 double. Rates include continental breakfast and evening social hour Mon–Fri. Children 18 and under stay free in parent's room. AE, DC, DISC, MC, V. Pets accepted ($15 per night). **Amenities:** Small outdoor pool; access to nearby health club; Jacuzzi; coin-op laundry; dry cleaning. *In room:* A/C, TV, dataport, fridge, coffeemaker, hair dryer, iron, microwave, Wi-Fi, free local calls.

Radisson Suites Tucson 👁👁 *Value* With large and very attractive rooms, this all-suite hotel is a good choice for both those who need plenty of space and those who want to be in the east-side business corridor. The five-story brick building is arranged around two long garden courtyards, one of which has a large pool and whirlpool. In fact, the pool and gardens are among the nicest at any nonresort hotel in Tucson and are the best reasons to stay here. Some rooms have Sleep Number® beds, and rooms on the fourth and fifth floors on the east side have nice mountain views.

6555 E. Speedway Blvd., Tucson, AZ 85710. © **888/201-1718** or 520/721-7100. Fax 520/721-1991. www.radisson. com/suites_tucson. 299 suites. Oct–May $159–$219 double; June–Sept $124–$149 double. Children under 18 stay free in parent's room. AE, DC, DISC, MC, V. Pets accepted ($50 fee). **Amenities:** Restaurant (international); lounge; outdoor pool; exercise room; access to nearby health club; Jacuzzi; concierge; courtesy shopping shuttle; business center; room service; coin-op laundry; laundry service; dry cleaning. *In room:* A/C, TV, dataport, fridge, coffeemaker, hair dryer, iron, microwave, high-speed Internet access, Wi-Fi.

INEXPENSIVE

Extended StayAmerica Tucson ⓕ   With no pool or exercise room and maid service only if you pay extra or stay for more than a week, this eastside hotel is pretty basic, but the rooms are clean and the rates are low. Guest rooms also have full kitchens, so you can save even more money on your Tucson stay by doing a little cooking in your room.

5050 E. Grant Rd., Tucson, AZ 85712. © **800/804-3724** or 520/795-9510. Fax 520/795-9504. www.extendedstay america.com. 120 units. $75–$100 double (lower weekly rates). Children under 18 stay free in parent's room. AE, DISC, MC, V. Pets accepted ($25 per night, $75 maximum). **Amenities:** Coin-op laundry. *In room:* A/C, TV, dataport, kitchen, fridge, coffeemaker, iron, microwave, Wi-Fi, free local calls.

THE FOOTHILLS

VERY EXPENSIVE

Loews Ventana Canyon Resort ⭐⭐⭐ *(Kids*   For breathtaking scenery, fascinating architecture, and superb resort facilities (including two Tom Fazio golf courses, a full-service spa, and lots of options for kids), no other Tucson resort can compare. The Santa Catalina Mountains rise behind the property, and flagstone floors in the lobby lend a rugged but luxurious appeal. Guest rooms have balconies that overlook city lights or mountains. Bathrooms include tubs for two, and some rooms have fireplaces. Both the Ventana Room (p. 361) and the Flying V Bar & Grill are among the best restaurants in Tucson, and both have great views. The lobby lounge serves afternoon tea before becoming an evening piano bar. In addition to numerous other amenities, there are jogging and nature trails and a playground.

7000 N. Resort Dr., Tucson, AZ 85750. © **800/234-5117** or 520/299-2020. Fax 520/299-6832. www.loewshotels.com/ hotels/tucson. 398 units. Early Jan to late May from $365 double, from $750 suite; late May to early Sept from $150 double, from $295 suite; early Sept to early Jan from $325 double, from $700 suite. Children under 18 stay free in parent's room. AE, DC, DISC, MC, V. **Amenities:** 5 restaurants (New American, steakhouse, American); 2 lounges; 2 outdoor pools; 2 acclaimed 18-hole golf courses; 8 tennis courts; croquet court; exercise room; full-service spa; 2 Jacuzzis; saunas; bike rentals; children's programs; concierge; tour desk; courtesy shuttle; business center; 24-hr. room service; massage; babysitting; laundry service; dry cleaning. *In room:* A/C, TV, dataport, minibar, fridge, hair dryer, iron, safe, high-speed Internet access.

EXPENSIVE

Hacienda del Sol Guest Ranch Resort ⭐⭐ *(Finds*   With its colorful Southwest styling, historical character, mature desert gardens, and ridgetop setting, Hacienda del Sol is one of Tucson's most distinctive hotels. The lodge's basic rooms, set around flower-filled courtyards, are evocative of old Mexican inns and have rustic and colorful character, with a decidedly artistic flair. If you prefer more modern, spacious accommodations, ask for a suite; if you want loads of space and the chance to stay where Katharine Hepburn and Spencer Tracy may have stayed, ask for a casita. With large terraces for alfresco dining, The Grill (p. 361) is one of Tucson's best restaurants.

5601 N. Hacienda del Sol Rd., Tucson, AZ 85718. ℂ **800/728-6514** or 520/299-1501. www.haciendadelsol.com. 30 units. Early Jan to May $175–$280 double, $345–$355 suite, $395–$495 casita; June–Sept $99–$154 double, $165–$185 suite, $185–$300 casita; Oct to early Jan $155–$250 double, $320–$330 suite, $360–$485 casita. 2-night minimum stay weekends and holidays. Children under 12 stay free in parent's room. AE, DC, DISC, MC, V. Pets accepted ($50). **Amenities:** Restaurant (regional American); lounge; small outdoor pool; access to nearby health club; Jacuzzi; room service; massage; dry cleaning; horseback riding. *In room:* A/C, TV, dataport, minibar, fridge, coffeemaker, hair dryer, iron, high-speed Internet access, Wi-Fi.

Hilton Tucson El Conquistador Golf & Tennis Resort ✦✦✦

Although this large resort is a bit out-of-the-way, the view of the Santa Catalina Mountains rising behind El Conquistador makes this northern foothills resort one of our favorites in Tucson. Sunsets are truly spectacular! Most guest rooms are built around a central courtyard with manicured lawns and a large oasis of swimming pools, one of which has a long water slide. Consequently, this place is a great choice for families. All rooms feature Southwestern-influenced contemporary furniture, spacious marble bathrooms, and balconies or patios. Be sure to ask for a mountain-view room. While golf on the resort's three courses is the favorite pastime, nongolfers have plenty of options, too.

10000 N. Oracle Rd., Tucson, AZ 85704. ℂ **800/325-7832** or 520/544-5000. Fax 520/544-1222. www.hiltonel conquistador.com. 428 units. Jan to late May $209–$319 double, from $359 suite; late May to early Sept $119–$209 double, from $179 suite; early Sept to Dec $149–$259 double, from $239 suite. Rates do not include $10 daily service fee. Children under 18 stay free in parent's room. AE, DC, DISC, MC, V. Valet parking $11. Pets accepted ($50 deposit). **Amenities:** 5 restaurants (Southwestern, steakhouse, Mexican, American); 2 lounges; 4 pools; 1 9-hole and 2 18-hole golf courses; 31 tennis courts; 7 racquetball courts; basketball court; volleyball court; 2 exercise rooms; spa; 5 Jacuzzis; saunas; bike rentals; children's programs; concierge; tour desk; business center; shopping arcade; room service; massage; babysitting; laundry service; dry cleaning; horseback riding. *In room:* A/C, TV, dataport, minibar, coffeemaker, hair dryer, iron, safe, high-speed Internet access, Wi-Fi.

The Lodge at Ventana Canyon ✦✦✦

Golf is the name of the game at this boutique resort set within a gated country-club community at the base of the Santa Catalina Mountains. The third hole of the resort's Tom Fazio–designed Mountain Course plays across a deep ravine, which makes it one of the most photographed holes in Tucson. Though small, this exclusive lodge offers plenty of big-resort amenities and places an emphasis on personal service. The accommodations are in spacious suites, most of which have walls of windows facing the Catalinas, modern mission-style furnishings, small kitchens, and large bathrooms with oversize tubs (some are even old-fashioned footed tubs).

6200 N. Clubhouse Lane, Tucson, AZ 85750. ℂ **800/828-5701** or 520/577-1400. Fax 520/577-4065. www.the lodgeatventanacanyon.com. 50 units. Jan to early Apr $279–$549 1-bedroom suite, $449–$729 2-bedroom suite; early Apr to mid-May $189–$419 1-bedroom suite, $359–$619 2-bedroom suite; mid-May to early Sept $99–$175 1-bedroom suite, $189–$275 2-bedroom suite; early Sept to Dec $179–$399 1-bedroom suite, $349–$599 2-bedroom suite. Rates do not include $20 nightly service charge. Children under 18 stay free in parent's room. AE, DC, DISC, MC, V. Pets accepted ($50 fee). **Amenities:** Restaurant (New American); lounge; snack bar; outdoor pool; 2 acclaimed 18-hole golf courses; 12 tennis courts; exercise room; full-service spa; concierge; room service; massage; coin-op laundry; laundry service; dry cleaning. *In room:* A/C, TV, dataport, kitchen, coffeemaker, hair dryer, iron, microwave, high-speed Internet access.

Omni Tucson National Golf Resort & Spa ✦✦✦

As the name implies, golf is the driving force at this boutique resort, which for many years was the site of the annual Tucson Open PGA golf tournament. So, if you don't have your own clubs, you might feel out of place. Then again, you could just avail yourself of the superb full-service spa. Most of the spacious guest rooms cling to the edges of the golf course and have their own patios or balconies. At press time, this resort was undergoing a major renovation and only a limited number of rooms were available. The renovation is expected to continue until late 2008, and by then, the rooms here should be some of the best and most luxurious in town.

2727 W. Club Dr. (off Magee Rd.), Tucson, AZ 85742. (©) 800/THE-OMNI or 520/297-2271. Fax 520/297-7544. www. omnitucsonnational.com. 167 units. Jan–Apr $279–$459 double, $309–$499 suite; May and Sept–Dec $169–$299 double, $209–$359 suite; June–Aug $109–$209 double, $139–$299 suite. Rates do not include $12 nightly service charge. Children under 18 stay free in parent's room. AE, DC, DISC, MC, V. Pets accepted ($50 nonrefundable deposit). **Amenities:** 2 restaurants (American, Southwestern); lounge; 2 large pools; 2 18-hole golf courses; 4 tennis courts; basketball court; health club; full-service spa; 3 Jacuzzis; children's programs; concierge; business center; 24-hr. room service; massage; laundry service. In room: A/C, TV, dataport, minibar, coffeemaker, hair dryer, iron, safe, high-speed Internet access.

The Westin La Paloma Resort & Spa (kids) (Kids) If grand scale is what you're looking for, this is the place. Everything about The Westin La Paloma is big—big portico, big lobby, big pool area—and from the resort's sunset-pink mission-revival buildings, there are big views. While adults will appreciate the resort's tennis courts, exercise facilities, and poolside lounge chairs, kids will love the 177-foot water slide. Guest rooms are in 27 low-rise buildings surrounded by desert landscaping. Couples should opt for the king rooms (ask for a mountain or golf-course view if you don't mind spending a bit more). French-inspired Southwestern cuisine is the specialty at Janos (p. 360), which is one of Tucson's finest restaurants.

3800 E. Sunrise Dr., Tucson, AZ 85718. (©) 800/WESTIN-1 or 520/742-6000. Fax 520/577-5878. www.westinlapaloma resort.com. 487 units. Jan to late May $249–$479 double, from $445 suite; late May to mid-Sept $119–$169 double, from $245 suite; mid-Sept to Dec $209–$279 double, from $375 suite. Rates do not include $11 daily service fee. Children under 18 stay free in parent's room. AE, DC, DISC, MC, V. Valet parking $12. Pets accepted. **Amenities:** 5 restaurants (Southwestern, American, swim-up bar and grill); 2 lounges; 5 pools (1 for adults only); 27-hole golf course; 10 tennis courts; racquetball court; volleyball court; health club; full-service Red Door Spa by Elizabeth Arden; 4 Jacuzzis; children's programs, concierge; car-rental desk; business center; shopping arcade; salon; 24-hr. room service; massage; babysitting; laundry service; dry cleaning. In room: A/C, TV, dataport, minibar, coffeemaker, hair dryer, iron, safe, high-speed Internet access, Wi-Fi.

Westward Look Resort (★★) (Value) This reasonably priced resort, with the desert at its doorstep and a nature trail through the cacti, is a favorite of ours. Built in 1912 as a private estate, Westward Look is the oldest resort in Tucson, and although it doesn't have a golf course, it has riding stables, an excellent spa, and plenty of tennis courts. The large guest rooms have a Southwestern flavor and private patios or balconies with city views. For the ultimate in Southwest luxury, opt for one of the stargazer spa suites, which have outdoor hot tubs. The Gold Room (p. 361) serves excellent Continental and Southwestern cuisine and utilizes herbs and vegetables grown on-site. If you aren't a golfer but do enjoy resort amenities, this is one of your best bets in Tucson.

245 E. Ina Rd., Tucson, AZ 85704. (©) 800/722-2500 or 520/297-1151. Fax 520/297-9023. www.westwardlook.com. 244 units. Jan–Apr $179–$395 double; May $149–$199 double; June–Sept $89–$189 double; Oct–Dec $169–$295 double. Rates do not include $12 daily resort fee. Children under 18 stay free in parent's room. AE, DC, DISC, MC, V. Pets accepted ($75 fee). **Amenities:** 2 restaurants (Continental/Southwestern, American); lounge; 3 pools; 8 tennis courts; exercise room; full-service spa; 3 Jacuzzis; bike rentals; concierge; tour desk; car-rental desk; business center; room service; massage; laundry service; dry cleaning, executive-level rooms; horseback riding. In room: A/C, TV, dataport, minibar, coffeemaker, hair dryer, iron, high-speed Internet access, Wi-Fi.

MODERATE
Windmill Suites at St. Philip's Plaza (★) (Value) Located on the edge of the foothills in the St. Philip's Plaza shopping center, this hotel offers both a good location and good value. There are good restaurants and upscale shops right across the parking lot.

Bikes are available to guests, and out the hotel's back door is a paved pathway along the Rillito River (which is usually bone dry). Accommodations are spacious and have double vanities, wet bars, and two TVs—basically, everything you need for a long, comfortable stay.

4250 N. Campbell Ave., Tucson, AZ 85718. © 800/547-4747 or 520/577-0007. Fax 520/577-0045. www.wind millinns.com. 122 units. Feb–Mar $165–$185 double; Apr–May and Oct–Jan $115–$159 double; June–Sept $89–$130 double. Rates include continental breakfast. Children under 18 stay free in parent's room. AE, DC, DISC, MC, V. Pets accepted. **Amenities:** Outdoor pool; exercise room; access to nearby health club; Jacuzzi; bikes; business center; coin-op laundry; laundry service; dry cleaning. *In room:* A/C, TV, fridge, hair dryer, iron, microwave, free local calls.

INEXPENSIVE

La Posada Lodge and Casitas 𝒢𝒢   Although this hotel fronts busy Oracle Road, once you check in and park yourself on your patio overlooking the pool or the grassy courtyard, you'll forget all about the traffic out front. There are several different types of rooms here, but our favorites are the "Western" style rooms, which have a sort of retro south-of-the-border decor that includes headboards painted with classic Mexican scenes. Casitas, which are the largest and most expensive rooms here, have a similar decor. There are also some fun rooms with a 1950s retro feel. The attractive rooms, pleasant pool area, and on-site Mexican restaurant together make this an excellent and economical choice.

5900 N. Oracle Rd., Tucson, AZ 85704. © 800/810-2808 or 520/887-4800. Fax 520/293-7543. www.laposada lodge.com. 72 units. $89–$149 double. Rates include continental breakfast. Children under 18 stay free in parent's room. AE, DC, DISC, MC, V. Pets accepted ($50 fee). **Amenities:** Restaurant (Mexican); lounge; outdoor pool; exercise room; Jacuzzi; laundry service; dry cleaning. *In room:* A/C, TV, dataport, fridge, coffeemaker, hair dryer, iron, microwave, high-speed Internet access, free local calls.

WEST OF DOWNTOWN
EXPENSIVE

La Zarzuela 𝒢𝒢   Some people come to the desert wanting to be *in* the desert, not in the middle of the city. That's why we love this modern B&B. It sits high on a hill surrounded by saguaros and is just down a dirt road from Tucson Mountain Park, which is every bit as beautiful as Saguaro National Park. La Zarzuela has four colorfully decorated guest rooms spread around this sprawling modern Santa Fe–style building. The pool and hot tub are built on the edge of the desert, while courtyards and patios have splashes of colorful flowers in their landscaping. It's all very Southwestern, the perfect place to stay if you want to explore the desert. For all this seclusion, the inn is surprisingly close to downtown Tucson.

455 N. Camino de Oeste (P.O. Box 86030), Tucson, AZ 85754. © 888/848-8225. www.zarzuela-az.com. 5 units. $275–$325 double. Rates include full breakfast and evening wine and hors d'oeuvres. 2-night minimum. MC, V. Closed June 15–Sept 15. No children under 18. **Amenities:** Outdoor pool; access to nearby health club; Jacuzzi; concierge; massage; laundry service. *In room:* A/C, TV/DVD, fridge, coffeemaker, hair dryer, iron, high-speed Internet access, free local calls.

MODERATE

Casa Tierra Adobe Bed & Breakfast Inn 𝒢   If you've come to Tucson to be in the desert, then this secluded B&B west of Saguaro National Park is well worth considering. Built to look as if it has been here since Spanish colonial days, the modern adobe home is surrounded by cactus and palo verde trees. There are great views across a landscape full of saguaros to the mountains, and sunsets are enough to take your breath away. Guest rooms, which have wrought-iron sleigh beds, open onto a central courtyard surrounded by a covered seating area. The two outdoor hot tubs make perfect stargazing spots, and there are a couple of telescopes on the property.

11155 W. Calle Pima, Tucson, AZ 85743. (©) **866/254-0006** or 520/578-3058. www.casatierratucson.com. 4 units. $135–$195 double, $200–$325 suite. Rates include full breakfast. 2-night minimum stay. AE, DISC, MC, V. Closed June 16–Aug 14. **Amenities:** Exercise room; Jacuzzi; concierge; massage. *In room:* A/C, dataport, fridge, hair dryer, iron, microwave, Wi-Fi, free local calls.

NEAR THE AIRPORT
MODERATE

Hyatt Place Tucson Airport   Okay, we know the airport location is none too appealing and that this is primarily a business-travelers' hotel, but it's just so pretty and well-designed that you should consider it. The suites all have separate sitting and sleeping areas with 42-inch wall-hung flat-panel TVs that can be angled to either area. Unusual features include electronic self-service check-in kiosks, continental (free) or hot (charge) breakfasts, and a tiny lounge area to one side of the lobby. You can even get a light meal here if you don't feel like going out to a restaurant for dinner.

6885 S. Tucson Blvd., Tucson, AZ 85709. (©) **800/492-8847** or 520/295-0405. Fax 520/295-9140. www.hyattplace.com. 120 units. $99–$249 double. Rates include continental breakfast. Children under 18 stay free in parent's room. AE, DC, DISC, MC, V. **Amenities:** Restaurant (American); lounge; outdoor pool; exercise room; business center; coin-op laundry; laundry service; dry cleaning. *In room:* A/C, TV, dataport, fridge, coffeemaker, hair dryer, iron, high-speed Internet access, Wi-Fi.

Starr Pass Golf Suites ★★   Located 3 miles west of I-10, Starr Pass is the most economically priced golf resort in the city. It's a condominium resort, however, which means you won't find the sort of service you get at other resorts. Accommodations are in privately owned Santa Fe–style casitas rented as two-bedroom units, master suites, or standard hotel-style rooms. The small hotel-style rooms are a bit cramped and not nearly as lavishly appointed as the master suites, which are more comfortable and have fireplaces, full kitchens, balconies, and a Southwestern style throughout. The desert-style 27-hole golf course is one of the best courses in the city. There are also hiking/biking trails on the property.

3645 W. Starr Pass Blvd., Tucson, AZ 85745. (©) **800/503-2898** or 520/670-0500. Fax 520/670-0427. www.shell hospitality.com. 80 units. Jan to late May $179 double, $309 suite, $429 casita; late May to Sept $89 double, $139 suite, $199 casita; Oct–Dec $119 double, $179 suite, $249 casita. Children under 18 stay free in parent's room. AE, DC, DISC, MC, V. **Amenities:** 2 restaurants (steakhouse, American); lounge; outdoor pool; 27-hole golf course; 2 tennis courts; exercise room; Jacuzzi. *In room:* A/C, TV, fridge, coffeemaker, hair dryer, microwave, high-speed Internet access.

INEXPENSIVE

There are numerous budget motels near the Tucson Airport. These include **Motel 6**, 1031 E. Benson Hwy., Exit 262 off I-10 ((©) **520/628-1264**), which charges $43 to $62 double, and **Super 8–Tucson/East**, 1990 S. Craycroft Rd., Exit 265 off I-10 ((©) **520/790-6021**), which charges $50 to $94 double.

Clarion Hotel Airport   Located just outside the airport exit, this hotel provides convenience and some great amenities, including a complimentary nightly cocktail reception and midnight snacks. Accommodations are generally quite large. King rooms are particularly comfortable, while poolside units are convenient for swimming and lounging.

6801 S. Tucson Blvd., Tucson, AZ 85706. (©) **800/424-6423** or 520/746-3932. Fax 520/889-9934. www.clarionhotel.com. 188 units. Jan–Feb $109–$189 double; Mar–May $89–$119 double; June–Aug $69–$99 double; Sept–Dec $79–$119 double. Rates include full breakfast and cocktail hour. Children 18 and under stay free in parent's room. AE, DC, DISC, MC, V. **Amenities:** Restaurant (American); lounge; outdoor pool; exercise room; Jacuzzi; courtesy airport shuttle; room service; coin-op laundry; laundry service; dry cleaning. *In room:* A/C, TV, dataport, fridge, coffeemaker, hair dryer, iron, high-speed Internet access.

OUTLYING AREAS
NORTH OF TUCSON
Across the Creek at Aravaipa Farms 🏶🏶 *Finds*   Located 60 miles north of Tucson on Aravaipa Creek, this B&B is a romantic getaway near one of the state's most spectacular desert wilderness areas. Because the inn is 3 miles up a gravel road and then across a stream (high-clearance vehicles recommended), it's a long way to a restaurant. Consequently, innkeeper Carol Steele provides all meals. Guests entertain themselves hiking in the Aravaipa Canyon Wilderness, bird-watching, and cooling off in the creek. The casitas are eclectically decorated with a mix of folk art and rustic Mexican furnishings, and have tile floors, stone-walled showers, and shady verandas. For a romantic weekend or a vigorous vacation, this inn makes an ideal base.

89395 Aravaipa Rd., Winkelman, AZ 85292. ℂ 520/357-6901. www.aravaipafarms.com. 5 units. Mar–May $325 double; June–Feb $285 double. Rates include all meals. 2-night minimum stay weekends and holidays. No credit cards. Children by prior arrangement. **Amenities:** Dining room; outdoor swimming pool. *In room:* Fridge, coffeemaker, no phone.

SOUTH OF TUCSON
Chuparosa Inn 🏶   Tucked amid the shady trees of Madera Canyon, this rustic inn is built of stone and wood, and, with its tower at the front entrance, looks a bit like a miniature castle or a chalet. In other words, this place is beautiful and is a delightful place to stay if you have come up the canyon to do some bird-watching, which is the objective of many of the inn's guests. The inn's name is Spanish for "hummingbird," and in the warmer months, you're likely to see plenty of hummers (14 species have been spotted here). There are also hummingbird banding programs here.

1300 W. Madera Canyon Rd., Madera Canyon, AZ 85614. ℂ 520/393-7370. www.chuparosainn.com. 3 units. $130 double; $150 suite. Rates include continental breakfast. 2-night minimum on weekends, holidays, and Mar–May. MC, V. Children over 12 are welcome. *In room:* A/C, kitchenette, fridge, coffeemaker, hair dryer, iron, microwave, no phone.

Santa Rita Lodge Nature Resort   This lodge in the shady depths of Madera Canyon is used almost exclusively by bird-watchers and hikers, and getting a room in late spring, when the birds are out, can be difficult. March through August, the lodge even offers guided bird walks ($20 per person). The rooms and cabins are large and comfortable. The nearest restaurants are 13 miles away, so bring food for your stay.

1218 S. Madera Canyon Rd., Madera Canyon, AZ 85614. ℂ 520/625-8746. Fax 520/625-1956. www.santarita lodge.com. 12 units. $85–$98 double. MC, V. Pets accepted June–Feb ($25 per day). *In room:* A/C, TV/DVD, kitchen, fridge, coffeemaker, microwave.

SPAS
Canyon Ranch Health Resort 🏶🏶🏶   Canyon Ranch, one of America's premier health spas, offers the sort of complete spa experience that's available at only a handful of places around the country. On staff are doctors, nurses, psychotherapists and counselors, fitness instructors, massage therapists, and tennis and golf pros. Services offered include health and fitness assessments; health, nutrition, exercise, and stress-management evaluations; fitness classes; massage therapy; therapeutic body treatments; facials, manicures, pedicures, and haircuts; makeup consultations; cooking demonstrations; and art classes. Guests stay in a variety of spacious and very comfortable accommodations. Three gourmet, low-calorie meals are served daily.

8600 E. Rockcliff Rd., Tucson, AZ 85750. ℂ 800/742-9000 or 520/749-9000. Fax 520/239-8535. www.canyon ranch.com. 185 units. Sept to early June 4-night packages from $3,280 double; early June to Aug 4-night packages from $2,450 double. Rates include all meals and a variety of spa services and programs. AE, DC, DISC, MC, V. Pets accepted. No children under 14 (with exception of infants in the care of personal nannies). **Amenities:** 2 dining rooms; 11,000-sq.-ft. aquatic center and 3 outdoor pools; 7 tennis courts; racquetball and squash courts; 7 exercise rooms; 80,000-sq.-ft. spa complex; 8 Jacuzzis; saunas; steam rooms; bikes; concierge; courtesy airport shuttle; salon; room service; massage; guest laundry; laundry service; dry cleaning. *In room:* A/C, TV/DVD, dataport, hair dryer, iron, safe, high-speed Internet access, free local calls.

Miraval Life in Balance Resort and Spa 🏆🏆🏆 Focusing on what it calls "life balancing," Miraval emphasizes stress management, self-discovery, and relaxation rather than facials and mud baths. To this end, activities at the all-inclusive resort include meditation, tai chi, Pilates, and yoga; more active types can go hiking, mountain biking, rock climbing, and horseback riding. Miraval offers lifestyle-management workshops, fitness/nutrition consultations, exercise classes, an "equine experience" program, massage, and skin care and facials. The spa's main pool is a gorgeous three-tiered leisure pool surrounded by waterfalls and desert landscaping. Guest rooms, many of which have views of the Santa Catalina Mountains, are done in a Southwestern style. Most of the bathrooms have showers but no tubs.

5000 E. Via Estancia Miraval, Catalina, AZ 85739. © **800/232-3969.** Fax 520/825-5163. www.miravalresorts.com. 102 units. Jan to late May and mid-Oct to Dec $1,260–$1,300 double; late May to mid-Oct $940 double. Rates do not include 17.5% service charge. Rates include all meals, classes, and a $110 per-person per-day credit for spa service, a round of golf, or private consultation. AE, DC, DISC, MC, V. No children. **Amenities:** 2 restaurants; lounge; 2 snack areas; 4 pools; 2 tennis courts; croquet lawn; superbly equipped exercise room; spa; 5 Jacuzzis; saunas; steam rooms; concierge; car-rental desk; courtesy airport shuttle; business center; massage; laundry service; dry cleaning; horseback riding. *In room:* A/C, TV/DVD, dataport, fridge, coffeemaker, hair dryer, iron, safe, high-speed Internet access, Wi-Fi, free local calls.

GUEST RANCHES

Lazy K Bar Guest Ranch 🏆 In operation as a guest ranch since 1936, the Lazy K Bar Ranch covers more than 200 acres and is adjacent to Saguaro National Park's west unit. Ranch activities include trail rides, guest rodeos, cookouts, and wagon rides, as well as nature talks, guided hikes, rappelling, and stargazing. Guest rooms vary in size and comfort level (some have fireplaces and private patios); try for one of the newest units, which are absolutely gorgeous. Family-style meals consist of hearty American ranch food, with cookouts offered twice a week.

8401 N. Scenic Dr., Tucson, AZ 85743. © **800/321-7018** or 520/744-3050. Fax 520/744-7628. www.lazykbar.com. 24 units. Oct to mid-Dec $340–$445 double; mid-Dec to Apr $360–$505 double; May and Sept $250–$345 double. Rates include all meals and horseback riding. Children under 3 stay free in parent's room. AE, DISC, MC, V. Closed June–Aug. **Amenities:** Dining room; lounge; small outdoor pool; access to nearby health club; Jacuzzi; game room; courtesy airport shuttle (limited hours); massage; coin-op laundry; horseback riding. *In room:* A/C, no phone.

Tanque Verde Ranch 🏆🏆 Want to spend long days in the saddle but don't want to give up resort luxuries? Then Tanque Verde Ranch, which was founded in 1868 and still has some of its original buildings, is for you. This is far and away the most luxurious guest ranch in Tucson. The ranch borders Saguaro National Park and the Coronado National Forest, so there's plenty of room for horseback riding. There are also nature trails and a nature center, and at the end of the day, the spa provides ample opportunities to recover from too many hours in the saddle. Guest rooms are spacious and comfortable, with fireplaces and patios in many units. Some casitas are quite large and are among the most luxurious accommodations in the state.

14301 E. Speedway Blvd., Tucson, AZ 85748. © **800/234-DUDE** or 520/296-6275. Fax 520/721-9426. www.tanque verderanch.com. 74 units. Mid-Dec to Apr $420–$640 double; May–Sept $330–$440 double; Oct to mid-Dec $370–$515 double. Rates include all meals and ranch activities. Children 3 and under $15 extra. AE, DC, DISC, MC, V. **Amenities:** Dining room; lounge; 3 pools (indoor and outdoor); 5 tennis courts; exercise room; small full-service spa; 2 Jacuzzis; saunas; bike rentals; children's programs; courtesy airport shuttle with 4-night stay; massage; babysitting; coin-op laundry; laundry service; dry cleaning; horseback riding; children's playground. *In room:* A/C, dataport, fridge, coffeemaker, hair dryer, iron.

White Stallion Ranch *(Kids)* Set on 3,000 acres of desert, the White Stallion Ranch is perfect for those who crave wide-open spaces. Operated since 1965 by the True family, this spread has a more authentic feel than any other guest ranch in the area. A variety of horseback rides are offered Monday through Saturday, and a petting zoo keeps kids entertained. There are also nature trails, guided nature walks and hikes, hayrides, weekly rodeos, and team cattle penning. Guest rooms vary considerably in size and comfort, from tiny, spartan single units to deluxe two-bedroom suites. Renovated rooms are worth requesting.

9251 W. Twin Peaks Rd., Tucson, AZ 85743. *(©)* **888/977-2624** or 520/297-0252. Fax 520/744-2786. www.wsranch.com. 42 units. Sept $234–$272 double, $292–$332 suite; Oct to mid-Dec, Jan, and late Apr to mid-June $286–$332 double, $352–$404 suite; mid-Dec to Jan 1 and Feb to late Apr $324–$392 double, $414–$476 suite. Rates do not include 15% service charge. Rates include all meals. 4- to 6-night minimum stay in winter. Children under 3 stay free in parent's room. No credit cards. Closed mid-June to Aug 31. **Amenities:** Dining room; lounge; small outdoor pool; tennis court; exercise room; small spa; Jacuzzi; sauna; bikes; children's programs; concierge; courtesy airport shuttle; business center; massage; coin-op laundry; horseback riding. *In room:* A/C, hair dryer, no phone.

4 Where to Dine

Variety, they say, is the spice of life, and Tucson certainly dishes up plenty of variety (and spice) when it comes to eating out. Tucson is a city that lives for spice, and in the realm of fiery foods, Mexican reigns supreme. There's historical Mexican at El Charro Café, *nuevo* Mexican at Café Poca Cosa and J Bar, and family-style Mexican at Casa Molina. So if you like Mexican food, you'll find plenty of places in Tucson to get all fired up.

On the other hand, if Mexican leaves you cold, don't despair—there are plenty of other restaurants serving everything from the finest French cuisine to innovative American, Italian, and Southwestern food. The latter is almost as prevalent in Tucson as Mexican food, and you should be sure to dine at a Southwestern restaurant early in your visit. This cuisine can be brilliantly creative, and after trying it, you may want *all* your meals to be Southwestern.

Foodies fond of the latest culinary trends will find plenty of spots to satisfy their cravings. Concentrations of creative restaurants can be found along East Tanque Verde Road and at foothills resorts and shopping plazas. On the other hand, if you're on a tight dining budget, look for early-bird dinners, which are quite popular with retirees.

DOWNTOWN
MODERATE
Café Poca Cosa *(Value)* NUEVO MEXICAN The cuisine served at this stylish downtown restaurant is the creation of owner/chef Suzana Davila and has been compared to the dishes dreamed up in *Like Water for Chocolate*. Although ostensibly Mexican, this food is not just *any* Mexican food; it's imaginative and different and is served in a bold and angular space that belies the location on the ground floor of a parking garage. Expect such creations as grilled beef with a jalapeño chile and tomatillo sauce, and chicken with a dark mole sauce made with Kahlúa, chocolate, almonds, and chiles. However, we always opt for the *plato* Poca Cosa, a trio of dishes chosen by the chef. This lively restaurant is an excellent value.

110 E. Pennington St. *(©)* **520/622-6400.** www.cafepocacosainc.com. Reservations highly recommended. Main courses $12–$13 lunch, $18–$23 dinner. MC, V. Tues–Thurs 11am–9pm; Fri–Sat 11am–10pm.

El Charro Café ✿ SONORAN MEXICAN   El Charro, housed in an old stone building in El Presidio Historic District, is Tucson's oldest family-operated Mexican restaurant and is legendary around these parts for its unusual *carne seca*, a traditional air-dried beef that is a bit like shredded beef jerky. To see how they make *carne seca*, just glance up at the restaurant's roof as you approach. The large metal cage up there is filled with beef drying in the desert sun. You'll rarely find *carne seca* on a Mexican menu outside of Tucson, so indulge while you're here.

The adjacent ¡Toma! (p. 389), a colorful bar/cantina, is under the same ownership. There are other El Charro locations at 6310 E. Broadway (✆ **520/745-1922**), 4699 E. Speedway Blvd. (✆ **520/325-1922**), and 100 W. Orange Grove (✆ **520/615-1922**).

311 N. Court Ave. ✆ **520/622-1922**. www.elcharrocafe.com. Reservations recommended for dinner. Main courses $6–$19. AE, DC, DISC, MC, V. Sun–Thurs 11am–9pm; Fri–Sat 11am–10pm.

INEXPENSIVE
Café à la C'Art SALADS/SANDWICHES   Located in the courtyard on the grounds of the Tucson Museum of Art, this cafe serves up tasty sandwiches and makes a good lunch spot if you're downtown wandering the Presidio neighborhood or touring the museum. Try the gingered apricot-almond chicken-salad croissant or the Cuban sandwich, which is made with roasted pork and ham. Wash it all down with some fresh lemonade, and be sure to save room for dessert.

150 N. Main Ave. ✆ **520/628-8533**. Reservations not accepted. Sandwiches and salads $7.25–$9.25. DISC, MC, V. Mon–Fri 11am–3pm.

CENTRAL TUCSON & THE UNIVERSITY AREA
EXPENSIVE
Arizona Inn ✿✿ FRENCH/AMERICAN   The dining room at the Arizona Inn, one of the state's first resorts, is consistently excellent. The pink-stucco pueblo-style buildings are surrounded by neatly manicured gardens that have matured gracefully, and it's romantic to dine in the courtyard or on the bar patio overlooking the colorful gardens. The menu changes regularly, but includes a good balance of classics such as vichyssoise and bouillabaisse and Southwestern-inspired dishes such as a grilled shrimp "martini" with watermelon salsa and salmon with a chile-scallion glaze. Presentation is artistic, and fresh ingredients are emphasized.

2200 E. Elm St. ✆ **520/325-1541**. www.arizonainn.com. Reservations recommended. Main courses $10–$19 lunch, $27–$37 dinner; tasting menu $45–$60 ($60–$80 with wine). AE, DC, MC, V. Daily 6:15–10am, 11:30am–2pm, and 6–10pm.

The Dish Bistro & Wine Bar ✿✿ NEW AMERICAN   Located in the rear of the Rumrunner Wine and Cheese Co., this tiny, minimalist restaurant is brimming with urban chic. On a busy night, the space could be construed as either cozy or crowded, so if you like it more on the quiet side, come early or late. The chef has a well-deserved reputation for daring dishes such as chorizo-stuffed veal chops with trumpet mushrooms; and lamb loin with a glaze made from star anise, allspice, sassafras, and maple syrup. Naturally, because this place is associated with a wine shop, the wine list is great; the well-informed servers will be happy to help you choose a bottle.

3200 E. Speedway Blvd. ✆ **520/326-1714**. www.dishbistro.com. Reservations highly recommended. Main courses $17–$34. AE, MC, V. Tues–Thurs 5–9pm; Fri–Sat 5–10pm.

MODERATE
Cuvée World Bistro ✿✿ *Value* INTERNATIONAL   This stylish restaurant in a shopping center on busy Speedway Boulevard affects a sort of Moroccan-palace decor,

Tucson Dining

University Blvd.
N. 6th Ave.
N. Stone Ave.
N. Court Ave.
N. Main St.
Granada Ave.
6th St.
N. 4th Ave.
N. Euclid Ave.
Blvd.
La Cholla
Toole
Ave.
Alameda St.
E. 9th St.
S. Scott Ave.
E. Congress St.
E. Broadway Blvd.

Sunset Rd.
El Camino de Cerro
Ruthrauff Rd.
SAGUARO NATIONAL PARK
Sweetwater Dr.
Camino de Oeste
To Saguaro National Park (West),
Arizona–Sonora Desert Museum
& Old Tucson
Ironwood Hill Dr.
Tucson Mountain Park
Speedway Blvd.
Gates Pass Rd.
Anklam Rd.
Kinney Rd.
Silverlake Rd.
Bopp Rd.
Ajo Way
Valencia Rd.
86
15
ARIZONA
40
40
17
Phoenix
10
8
Tucson
19
10
Mission Rd.
SAN XAVIER
INDIAN RESERVATION

and if you take a seat in the lounge, you can sprawl on a banquette covered with plush pillows for a thoroughly romantic and hedonistic experience. The menu travels all over the globe for inspiration and then blends flavors and textures in deliciously creative ways. The menu changes regularly, but if you see something (perhaps wild-mushroom cakes) served over avocado pesto, order it. This pesto is so creamy and rich it ought to be made into a spa treatment! Almost everything on the menu here sounds utterly tempting, and with prices so reasonable, you might want to come back a few times.

3352 E. Speedway Blvd. © 520/881-7577. www.cuveebistro.com. Reservations recommended. Main courses $9–$15 lunch, $16–$22 dinner. AE, DC, DISC, MC, V. Mon–Thurs 11am–10pm; Fri 11am–midnight; Sat 4:30pm–midnight.

Kingfisher Bar & Grill ✇ SEAFOOD   If you're serious about seafood, Kingfisher is definitely one of your best bets. The freshest seafood, artfully blended with bright flavors and imaginative ingredients, is deftly prepared as appetizers, sandwiches, and main dishes. You may have difficulty deciding whether to begin with Hama Hama oysters, house-smoked trout, or scallop *ceviche*—so why not tackle them all and call it a meal? Meat eaters and vegetarians will also find items on the menu, and the warm cabbage salad is a must. The atmosphere is upscale and lively, the bar and late-night menu are a hit with night owls, and there's live jazz and blues on Monday and Saturday nights.

2564 E. Grant Rd. © 520/323-7739. www.kingfisherbarandgrill.com. Reservations recommended. Main courses $8–$12 lunch, $16–$23 dinner. AE, DC, DISC, MC, V. Mon–Fri 11am–midnight; Sat–Sun 5pm–midnight.

Pastiche Modern Eatery ✇✇ NEW AMERICAN   Located in a little shopping plaza that has lots of Tucson character, this high-energy bistro has for several years now been one of *the* hip places to dine in Tucson. The colorful artwork and vibrant contemporary food fairly shout *trendy,* but the restaurant manages to appeal to a broad spectrum of the population. From thyme-crusted sea bass to pumpkin ravioli with sage brown butter, there's enough here to keep everyone at the table happy. Light eaters can get half-orders of entrees and desserts. The crowded bar is a popular watering hole that turns out tasty margaritas. There's also an adjacent wine-and-gift shop that has interesting picnic fare and free wine tastings on Friday evenings from 5 to 6:30pm.

3025 N. Campbell Ave. © 520/325-3333. www.pasticheme.com. Reservations recommended. Main courses $7–$28. AE, DC, DISC, MC, V. Mon–Fri 11:30am–midnight; Sat–Sun 4:30pm–midnight.

INEXPENSIVE

Beyond Bread ✇ AMERICAN/BAKERY   Although ostensibly a bakery, this place is really a bustling sandwich shop that also sells great breads and pastries. You can even get hot breakfasts here, but we much prefer a latte and a selection from the pastry case. The sandwich list is long, with both hot and cold varieties, and they all come on the great bread that's baked here on the premises. Most of the sandwiches are so big that you could split them between two people if you weren't too hungry.

There's another Beyond Bread over on the east side of town at Monterey Village, 6260 E. Speedway Blvd. (© 520/747-7477).

3026 N. Campbell Ave. © 520/322-9965. www.beyondbread.com. Reservations not accepted. Main dishes $4.25–$9.25. AE, MC, V. Mon–Fri 6:30am–8pm; Sat 7am–8pm; Sun 7am–6pm.

El Guero Canelo *Finds* MEXICAN   The first time we stopped in at El Guero Canelo for one of their famous Sonoran hot dogs, a teenage mariachi band started playing *La Bamba* just as we ordered the meal. It was a Sunday afternoon, and the place was packed with local Hispanic families. The sun was shining in through 20-foot-tall walls of glass, and just about everything in the restaurant was painted in the colors of the Mexican flag (green, white, and red). The hot dog, wrapped in bacon and slathered with beans and salsa, was good, but it wasn't nearly as memorable as the restaurant scene itself. For a slice of authentic Tucson culture, this place is not to be missed. The original El Guero Canelo is at 5201 S. 12th Ave. (© **520/295-9005**).

2480 N. Oracle Rd. © **520/882-8977**. www.elguerocanelo.com. Main courses $1.25–$6.50. No credit cards. Mon–Sat 6:30am–midnight; Sun 7am–midnight.

Feast *★ finds* INTERNATIONAL   This place is not only a casual sit-down restaurant, but also a gourmet to-go place; it's the perfect place to pick up food for a sunset picnic dinner at Sabino Canyon Recreation Area or Saguaro National Park. The menu changes regularly, but you may find a sandwich made with roast pork and quince paste. Other possibilities are gnocchi with house-made sausage or white seafood lasagna.

4122 E. Speedway Blvd. © **520/326-9363** or 520/326-6500. www.eatatfeast.com. Reservations not accepted. Main courses $8–$15. AE, DISC, MC, V. Tues–Sun 11am–9pm.

Lovin' Spoonfuls *★* VEGETARIAN   Chili dogs, turkey sandwiches, tuna melts, bacon cheeseburgers. The menu at this casual little place may not sound too interesting until you realize that not one of those dishes actually has meat in it. This is a vegan restaurant, so there are no eggs or dairy products to be seen (or tasted), either. If you're already a vegetarian or vegan, you may not want to eat anywhere else while you're in Tucson.

2990 N. Campbell Ave., Suite 120. © **520/325-7766**. www.lovinspoonfuls.com. Main courses $6.25–$11. DISC, MC, V. Mon–Sat 9:30am–9pm; Sun 10am–3pm.

Yoshimatsu Healthy Japanese Food & Café *★* JAPANESE   We found out about this unusual place from a friend who had recently been to Japan and raved about this restaurant's authenticity. However, that's only part of the story. Not only is there a long menu of health-conscious Japanese dishes, but the decor in this ultra-casual place is truly outrageous, with little glass cases displaying all manner of Japanese toys and action figures. The *okonomiyaki*, sort of a Japanese pizza, is one of our favorite dishes here, and for a truly bizarre treat, try the green-tea milkshake. There's also a stylish little sushi bar attached to the restaurant.

2660 N. Campbell Ave. © **520/320-1574**. Reservations not accepted. Main dishes $6.50–$17. MC, V. Sat–Thurs 11:30am–2:30pm and 5–8:45pm; Fri 11:30am–2:30pm and 5–9:45pm.

EAST TUCSON
MODERATE
Le Delice *★★* FRENCH   We know that desert hiking and French food go together about as well as the Eiffel Tower and enchiladas, but if you've been out hiking in Sabino Canyon all morning and you're starving, you don't have a whole lot of decent choices near the canyon. That's why Le Delice is such a delicious option. You can duck in for a pastry or a quick pick from the to-go case, or you can sit down and savor a classic quiche Lorraine, salad Lyonnaise, or steak frite. If its dinner time, you might want to pull on a clean shirt and change out of your hiking boots before dining on sweetbreads, coq au vin, or duck a l'orange.

7245 E. Tanque Verde Rd. © **520/290-9714**. www.le-delice.com. Reservations recommended at dinner. Main courses $7–$15 lunch, $8.75–$35 dinner. AE, DC, MC, V. Tues–Sat 7am–8:30pm; Sun–Mon 7am–2:30pm.

Sky Blue Wasabi *★ finds* JAPANESE   The same old friend who first took us to Yoshimatsu (see above) also brought us to this little out-of-the-way Japanese restaurant on Tucson's east side. With lots of blue lights and a contemporary feel, this place feels as though it ought to be in some upscale shopping center in the foothills; instead you'll find it tucked amid office buildings and shopping plazas just south of Broadway. While you can get a show at one of the teppanyaki tables, the real reason to eat here is the special sushi rolls. Do not miss, we repeat, do not miss, the Sky Blue Wasabi ultimate roll, which is made with lobster, shrimp, and 24-karat gold leaf! Likewise, try the Sky Blue Wasabi roll, which is made with eel and topped with fresh strawberries. Trust us, it works.

250 S. Craycroft Rd., no. 100. ℂ 520/747-0228. Reservations recommended on weekends. Main courses $5–$14 lunch, $12–$30 dinner; sushi $4–$15. MC, V. Mon–Thurs 11am–2pm and 5–10pm; Fri 11am–2pm and 5–11pm; Sat 5–11pm; Sun 5–9pm.

INEXPENSIVE

Casa Molina MEXICAN   Casa Molina, which sports a festive atmosphere, has been Tucson's favorite family-run Mexican restaurant for many years and is usually abuzz with families, groups, and couples. The margaritas are inexpensive yet tasty, and the *carne seca* shouldn't be missed. Light eaters will enjoy a layered *topopo* salad made with tortillas, refried beans, chicken, lettuce, celery, avocado, tomato, and jalapeños. The food is good, and the service efficient.

Other locations include 3001 N. Campbell Ave. (ℂ **520/795-7593**) and 4240 E. Grant Rd. (ℂ **520/326-6663**).

6225 E. Speedway Blvd. (near Wilmot Rd.). ℂ **520/886-5468**. www.casamolina.com. Reservations recommended. Dinners $6.50–$18. AE, DC, DISC, MC, V. Daily 11am–10pm.

Little Anthony's Diner (Kids) AMERICAN   This place is primarily for kids, although lots of big kids enjoy the 1950s music and decor. The menu includes such offerings as a Jailhouse Rock burger and Chubby Checker triple-decker club sandwich. Daily specials and bottomless soft drinks make feeding the family fairly inexpensive. A video-game room will keep your kids entertained while you finish your milkshake. If you want to make a night of it (and you make a reservation far enough in advance), you can take in an old-fashioned melodrama next door at the Gaslight Theatre. Together, these two places make for a fun night out with the family.

7010 E. Broadway Blvd. (in back of the Gaslight Plaza). ℂ **520/296-0456**. Burgers and sandwiches $4.75–$9. MC, V. Mon 11am–9pm; Tues–Thurs 11am–10pm; Fri 11am–11pm; Sat 10:30am–11pm; Sun 10:30am–10pm.

THE FOOTHILLS
VERY EXPENSIVE

Anthony's in the Catalinas 𝄢𝄢 NEW AMERICAN/CONTINENTAL   From the moment you drive up and let the valet park your car, Anthony's, housed in a modern Italianate building overlooking the city, exudes Southwestern elegance. The waiters are smartly attired in tuxedos, and guests (the cigar-and-single-malt foothills set) are nearly as well dressed. In such a rarefied atmosphere, you'd expect only the finest meal and service, and that's exactly what you get. The house-smoked salmon and oysters Rockefeller are both fitting beginnings, followed by the likes of chateaubriand with béarnaise sauce. Wine is not just an accompaniment, but also a reason for dining out at Anthony's; at more than 100 pages, the wine list may be the most extensive in the city. Don't miss out on the next best part of a meal here (after the wine)—the day's soufflé (order early).

6440 N. Campbell Ave. ℂ 520/299-1771. www.anthonyscatalinas.com. Reservations highly recommended. Main courses $24–$41 dinner. AE, DC, DISC, MC, V. Daily 5:30–10pm.

Janos 𝄢𝄢𝄢 SOUTHWESTERN/REGIONAL AMERICAN   Janos Wilder, Tucson's most celebrated chef, is not only a world-class chef; he's a real sweetheart, too.

Should you happen to bump into him while dining here, he'll make you feel as though you've been a regular at his restaurant for years. It is this conviviality—which spills over into all aspects of a meal here—that makes Janos one of our favorite restaurants in the entire state. Consequently, this luxuriously appointed restaurant, which is just outside the front door of The Westin La Paloma, is our top choice for a special-occasion dinner while in Tucson. The menu changes both daily and seasonally, with such complex offerings as beef tournedos with foie gras butter and truffle sauce and lamb chops with a complex spicy Southwestern rub.

At The Westin La Paloma, 3770 E. Sunrise Dr. ℂ 520/615-6100. www.janos.com. Reservations highly recommended. Main courses $28–$45; 5-course tasting menu $80 ($115 with wine). AE, DC, MC, V. Mon–Thurs 5:30–9pm; Fri–Sat 5:30–9:30pm.

Ventana Room ⟨★★★ NEW AMERICAN   The Ventana Room is Tucson's poshest and most classically elegant restaurant, as you'll immediately guess from the wall of wine bottles just inside the door. *Ventana* means "window" in Spanish, and the views through the windows of this restaurant are every bit as memorable as the food. Be sure you make an early dinner reservation so that you can catch the sunset. The tasting menus are designed to provide you with a delicious variety of flavors and textures. In the restaurant's rarefied atmosphere, you'll be pampered by a bevy of waiters providing professional and unobtrusive service. For superb French-inspired cuisine and gorgeous views, this restaurant just can't be beat.

At Loews Ventana Canyon Resort, 7000 N. Resort Dr. ℂ 520/615-5494. www.ventanaroom.com. Reservations highly recommended. Jackets recommended for men. Prix-fixe menus $75–$105. AE, DC, DISC, MC, V. Tues–Thurs 6–9:30pm; Fri–Sat 6–10pm. Closed mid-Aug to mid-Sept.

EXPENSIVE

The Gold Room ⟨★★ SOUTHWESTERN/CONTINENTAL   With its contemporary Southwestern decor, menu of creative contemporary fare and updated comfort foods, superb views of the city far below, and expansive terrace for alfresco dining, The Gold Room is one of the best places in Tucson for a memorable Southwestern dining experience. Think jerked chicken with prickly pear–jalapeño glaze, sugar and spice scallops with truffle risotto, and beef tenderloin served with house-made green-chile tater tots. The length of the wine list is staggering, and there's a welcome range of prices. Desserts are decadently rich, so be sure to save room. Although you can eat here on the cheap at lunch, the restaurant is most remarkable at night, when the cityscape of Tucson twinkles in the distance.

At the Westward Look Resort, 245 E. Ina Rd. ℂ 520/917-2930. Reservations recommended. Main courses $10–$16 lunch, $19–$29 dinner; Sun brunch $25. AE, DISC, MC, V. Mon–Sat 7–11am, 11:30am–2pm, and 5:30–10pm; Sun 11am–1:30pm and 5:30–10pm.

The Grill ⟨★★ REGIONAL AMERICAN   Great food, historical Southwest character, views, live jazz—this place has it all. Located in a 1920s hacienda-style building at a former foothills dude ranch, The Grill is one of Tucson's best restaurants, so don't leave town without having at least one meal here. For openers, try the grilled andouille sausage with cornbread and prickly-pear chorizo sauce. Despite the price, the dry-aged New York strip steak is deservedly the most popular entree on the menu and is big enough for two people to share. Sunday brunch here is a real treat. The main patio overlooks the Catalinas and the fairways of The Westin La Paloma's golf course. Thursday through Sunday, the restaurant's Terraza del Sol bar has live music.

At the Hacienda del Sol Guest Ranch Resort, 5601 N. Hacienda del Sol Rd. ℂ 520/529-3500. www.haciendadelsol.com. Reservations recommended. Main courses $23–$38; Sun brunch $32. AE, DC, DISC, MC, V. Mon–Sat 5:30–10pm; Sun 10am–1:30pm and 5:30–10pm.

McMahon's Prime Steakhouse ℛℛ STEAKHOUSE/SEAFOOD   If a perfectly done steak is what you're craving, then McMahon's is the place. This restaurant serves some of the best steaks in Tucson, and with a decidedly modern opulence, McMahon's boasts an atmosphere calculated to impress (a large glass-walled wine room dominates the main dining room). You can drop a bundle on dinner here, but no more than you'd spend at such high-end restaurants as Janos or the Ventana Room. The main difference is that your choices at McMahon's are simpler: steak, seafood, or steak and seafood. You'd be wasting a night out, though, if you didn't order a steak. There's a separate piano lounge and cigar bar.

2959 N. Swan Rd. ℂ 520/327-7463. www.metrorestaurants.com. Reservations recommended. Main courses $9–$20 lunch, $18–$50 dinner. AE, DC, DISC, MC, V. Mon–Fri 11:30am–10pm; Sat–Sun 5–10pm.

Miguel's ℛℛ NUEVO LATINO   If you're staying at one of the foothills resorts and just can't get enough south-of-the-border cuisine, this is another good bet. Be sure to start your meal with the guacamole and the lobster "cigars" with a reduction of guava and serrano chiles. The bacon-wrapped Guaymas shrimp and the seafood-stuffed chile relleno are favorites of mine, but there are also flavorful steaks and lots of seafood dishes. The tequila selection here is one of the best in Tucson, and the margaritas are delicious. If you can, eat before the sun goes down; there are views of the Santa Catalinas and the city.

At La Posada, 5900 N. Oracle Rd. ℂ 520/887-3777. www.miguelstucson.com. Reservations recommended. Main courses $14–$29. AE, DISC, MC, V. Oct–May Sun–Thurs 11am–3pm and 5–10pm, Fri–Sat 11am–3pm and 5–11pm; June–Sept Sun–Thurs 5–10pm, Fri–Sat 5–11pm.

MODERATE
Bistro Zin ℛℛ REGIONAL AMERICAN   Sophisticated and urbane, Bistro Zin, Tucson's premier wine bar/restaurant, affects an urban feel with its wine-colored walls decorated with black-and-white photos of jazz greats. It's all very classy and cool, and with more than 20 different wine flights available on any given day, this is the perfect place to sample wines from around the world. There's also plenty of good food to accompany the many wines. The duck breast with seasonal fruit-flavored sauce is always a good bet.

At Joesler Village, 1865 E. River Rd., Suite 101. ℂ 520/299-7799. www.foxrestaurantconcepts.com. Reservations recommended. Main courses $8–$13 lunch, $14–$29 dinner. AE, DISC, MC, V. Mon–Thurs 11am–10pm; Fri–Sat 4–11:30pm; Sun 5–9pm.

Bluefin Seafood Bistro ℛ SEAFOOD   Sure, this is the middle of the desert, but there's only so much beef you can eat on a week's vacation. If you've had enough steak to start your own ranch and are craving a nice bouillabaisse, this is a good choice. Adopting a sort of New Orleans styling, Bluefin is a sister restaurant to the ever-popular and always-reliable Kingfisher in central Tucson (p. 358). The menu is extensive; in addition to that bouillabaisse, you can get simply prepared grilled fish served with a choice of sauces. We go for the rock shrimp–chipotle salsa.

In Casas Adobes Shopping Center, 7053 N. Oracle Rd. ℂ 520/531-8500. www.bluefinseafoodbistro.com. Reservations recommended. Main courses $8.50–$12 lunch, $16–$28 dinner. AE, DISC, MC. V. Sun–Wed 11am–9:30pm; Thurs–Sat 11am–midnight.

Candela Restaurant ℛ (Finds) PERUVIAN/LATIN AMERICAN   It's easy to miss this nondescript little restaurant, which is tucked into an older shopping plaza on

Oracle Road south of Ina. However, keep looking. When you find it, you're in for a real treat if you enjoy trying new cuisines. As soon as you sit down, you'll be brought a basket of salty banana chips and a spicy dipping sauce. Make sure you order at least one dish with quinoa, a tiny South American grain. We love the quinoa salad, which is made with avocados, olive oil, and balsamic vinegar. Another must-have is the *pescado sudado* (steamed fish). If you see *chicha morada* on the menu, try it. It's an unusual purple corn drink that tastes much better than it sounds.

5845 N. Oracle Rd. (C) 520/407-0111. Reservations recommended on weekends. Main courses $6–$8 lunch, $14–$25 dinner. AE, DISC, MC, V. Mon–Fri 11am–2:30pm and 5–9pm; Sat–Sun noon–9pm.

Firecracker Bistro (★ PAN-ASIAN With a menu that knows no boundaries and wild architectural touches that include flames issuing from torches atop the building and faux tree trunks in the bar, Firecracker is one of Tucson's liveliest restaurants. Hip decor aside, it's the large portions and reasonable prices that keep people coming back. The spicy vegetarian lettuce-cup appetizers (sort of roll-your-own burritos) are a fun finger-food starter. Seafood is definitely the strong suit here, and the wok-charred chunks of salmon covered with cilantro pesto are just about the best thing on the menu.

2990 N. Swan Rd. (at Fort Lowell). (C) 520/318-1118. www.metrorestaurants.com. Reservations recommended. Main courses $9–$23 lunch, $11–$23 dinner. AE, DC, DISC, MC, V. Mon–Thurs 11am–10pm; Fri 11am–10:30pm; Sat 4–10:30pm; Sun 4–10pm.

HiFalutin Rapid Fire Western Grill (★ AMERICAN The first time we walked into this lively Western grill, we were absolutely hooked. The smell of burning juniper filled the restaurant, and we could almost taste the steaks. It wasn't until our second visit that we discovered the aroma was actually incense. Still, this place knows how to set the mood, and they come through with tasty comfort food with a Western twist. Get anything with the marinated flank steak, and you won't be disappointed. You can get it tossed with pasta, in a salad, or just plain straight up. Wash it all down with one of the great margaritas they serve, and you definitely have a highfalutin kind of meal.

6780 N. Oracle Rd. (C) 520/297-0518. www.hifalutintucson.com. Reservations recommended. Main courses $9–$25. AE, DC, DISC, MC, V. Daily 11am–9pm.

J Bar (★★★ SOUTHWESTERN The mouthwatering culinary creations of celebrity chef Janos Wilder at half-price? Sounds impossible, but that's pretty much what you'll find at this casual bar and grill adjacent to the famed foothills restaurant. Ask for a seat out on the heated patio, and with the lights of Tucson twinkling in the distance, dig into the best nachos you'll ever taste—here made with chorizo sausage and chili con queso. No matter what you order, you'll likely find that the ingredients and flavor combinations are most memorable. Who can forget spicy jerked pork with cranberry–habañero chutney or Yucatán-style plantain-crusted chicken with green coconut-milk curry? You won't want to miss sampling one of the *postres* (desserts). The dark chocolate–jalapeño sundae may sound unusual, but it's delicious.

At The Westin La Paloma, 3770 E. Sunrise Dr. (C) 520/615-6100. www.janos.com. Reservations highly recommended. Main courses $15–$28. AE, DC, MC, V. Mon–Sat 5–9:30pm.

Tavolino Ristorante Italiano (★ ITALIAN Located in a shopping center at the corner of Oracle and Ina roads, this is not the Italian restaurant of your youth. Forget the red-and-white checked tablecloths; Tavolino Ristorante Italiano has a hip urban trattoria personality. Because it's small, it stays packed and boisterous. Sure, there's a nice antipasto plate, but we'd opt for the eggplant stuffed with salmon mousse. For an entree, we like the lamb chops, which are pounded thin and tender.

In La Toscana Village Shopping Center, 7090 N. Oracle Rd. ℂ 520/531-1913. Reservations recommended. Main courses $15–$22. AE, DC, MC, V. Mon–Sat 5:30–10pm.

Terra Cotta ℛℛ REGIONAL AMERICAN/SOUTHWESTERN   Terra Cotta is Arizona's original Southwestern restaurant and is one of our favorite places to eat in Tucson. The combination of reasonably priced creative Southwestern cooking, a casual atmosphere with loads of contemporary Southwestern appeal, and lots of local artwork makes Terra Cotta truly distinctive and an Arizona classic. We always start our meals here with the rich-and-creamy garlic custard, which is served with warm salsa vinaigrette and herbed hazelnuts. The poblano chiles rellenos stuffed with either shrimp or adobo pork are another of our must-haves, as is the chutney-stuffed pork chop. A large brick oven turns out creative pizzas, while salads, sandwiches, and small plates flesh out the long menu.

3500 E. Sunrise Dr. ℂ 520/577-8100. www.dineterracotta.com. Reservations recommended. Main courses $9–$14 lunch, $14–$27 dinner. AE, DC, DISC, MC, V. Daily 4–10pm (call for seasonal lunch hours).

Vivace Restaurant ℛℛ NORTHERN ITALIAN   With a beautiful Tuscan-inspired setting, this restaurant serves reasonably priced, creative dishes. The atmosphere is lively and the food down-to-earth. For starters, consider indulging in the luscious antipasto platter for two, containing marinated artichokes, prosciutto, roasted red peppers, grilled asparagus, and herbed goat cheese. Pasta dishes, such as penne with sausage and roasted-pepper sauce, come nicely presented and in generous portions. But it's the crab-filled chicken breast that is most memorable. The wine list has plenty of selections, many fairly reasonably priced.

At St. Philip's Plaza, 4310 N. Campbell Ave. ℂ 520/795-7221. Reservations recommended. Main courses $9–$17 lunch, $15–$29 dinner. AE, DC, DISC, MC, V. Mon–Thurs 11:30am–9pm; Fri–Sat 11:30am–10pm.

Wildflower ℛℛ NEW AMERICAN   Stylish comfort food in large portions is the order of the day at this chic and casually elegant north Tucson bistro. A huge wall of glass creates minimalist drama, and large flower photographs on the walls enhance the bright and airy decor. The heaping plate of fried calamari with mizuna greens is a good bet for a starter, and entrees run the gamut from a comforting meatloaf to herb-crusted rack of lamb. Pasta and salmon also both show up in reliable guises. With so many tempting, reasonably priced dishes to sample, Wildflower is a foodie's delight.

At Casas Adobes Shopping Plaza, 7037 N. Oracle Rd. (at Ina Rd.). ℂ 520/219-4230. www.foxrestaurantconcepts.com. Reservations recommended. Main courses $8–$15 lunch, $15–$29 dinner. AE, DC, DISC, MC, V. Mon–Thurs 11am–3pm and 5–9pm; Fri 11am–3pm and 5–10pm; Sat 5–10pm; Sun 5–9pm.

INEXPENSIVE

Tohono Chul Tea Room REGIONAL AMERICAN   Located in a brick territorial-style building in 49-acre Tohono Chul Park (p. 370), this is one of the most tranquil restaurants in the city, and the garden setting provides a wonderful opportunity to experience the desert. Before or after lunching on grilled raspberry-chipotle chicken or tortilla soup, you can wander through the park's desert landscaping and admire the many species of cacti. The patios, surrounded by natural vegetation and plenty of potted flowers, are frequented by many species of birds. The adjacent gift shop offers Mexican folk art, nature-themed toys, household items, T-shirts, and books.

7366 N. Paseo del Norte (1 block west of the corner of Ina and Oracle roads in Tohono Chul Park). © **520/797-1222.**
www.tohonochulpark.org. Reservations accepted only for parties of 6 or more. Main courses $7–$11. AE, MC, V. Daily
8am–5pm.

Zona 78 ⟨★ ⟨*Finds* PIZZA   We're suckers for good pizza, and the pizza here is the best
in Tucson. Maybe it's the big stone oven they use or maybe it's all the locally grown
organic produce, but whatever it is, this place does it right. Try the Tuscany, an oval
pizza covered with Italian sausage, mozzarella, kalamata olives, fennel, garlic, onions,
and mushrooms. This pie is just bursting with flavors. To really get the most out of a
visit to Zona 78, you need to bring enough people so that you can order the big
antipasto plate or the cheese-and-fruit plate, which has lots of great imported cheeses.
If you're not that hungry, try the Tuscan bean-and-spinach soup.

78 W. River Rd. © **520/888-7878.** www.zona78.com. Reservations accepted only for parties of 8 or more. Main
courses $7.50–$19. AE, DISC, MC, V. Mon–Thurs 11am–10pm; Fri–Sat 11am–11pm; Sun 4–9pm.

WEST TUCSON
INEXPENSIVE
Teresa's Mosaic Café ⟨★ ⟨*Finds* MEXICAN   A mile or so west of I-10, this casual
Mexican restaurant, with colorful mosaic tile tables, mirror frames, and kitchen
counter, is hidden behind a McDonald's on the corner of Grant and Silverbell roads
but is well worth finding for breakfast or lunch. Try the *chilaquiles* or chorizo and eggs
for breakfast, and don't pass up the fresh lemonade or *horchata* (spiced rice milk). This
is an especially good spot for a meal if you're on your way to the Arizona–Sonora
Desert Museum, Old Tucson, or Saguaro National Park's west unit.

⟨*Kids* Cowboy Steakhouses

Cowboy steakhouses are family restaurants that generally provide big portions
of grilled steaks and barbecued ribs, as well as entertainment such as live country music. They tend to be touristy, but they're generally a big hit with the kids.

Located in Trail Dust Town (p. 375), a Wild West–themed shopping, dining, and family entertainment center, **Pinnacle Peak Steakhouse**, 6541 E.
Tanque Verde Rd. (© **520/296-0911**), specializes in family dining in a fun
cowboy atmosphere. Stroll the wooden sidewalks past the opera house and
saloon to the grand old dining rooms of the restaurant. Once through the
doors, you'll be surprised at the authenticity of the place, which really does
resemble a dining room in Old Tombstone or Dodge City. Be prepared for
crowds—this place is very popular with tour buses. Oh, and by the way, wear
a necktie into this place and it will be cut off! Main courses run $8 to $19.

Owned by the same folks who run Tucson's Pinnacle Peak Steakhouse, **El
Corral Restaurant**, at 2201 E. River Rd. (© **520/299-6092**), is another inexpensive and atmospheric steakhouse. Good prime rib and cheap prices have made
this place hugely popular with retirees and families. The restaurant doesn't
accept reservations, so expect long lines. Inside, the hacienda building has a
genuine old-timey feeling, with flagstone floors and wood paneling that
make it dark and cozy. You'll pay $9 to $19 for a complete dinner here.

2456 N. Silver Mosaic Rd. ℭ 520/624-4512. Reservations recommended. Main courses $4.75–$16. DC, DISC, MC, V. Mon–Sat 7:30am–9pm; Sun 7:30am–2pm.

5 Seeing the Sights

Go west, young man (and woman). That's what you'll need to do if you're visiting Tucson and want to immerse yourself in the desert Southwest or the cinematic Wild West. Out past the western outskirts of Tucson, where the cactus grows and the tumbleweed blows, you'll find not only the west unit of Saguaro National Park (with the biggest and best stands of saguaro cactus), but also the Arizona–Sonora Desert Museum (one of the nation's top zoological parks) and Old Tucson Studios (film site over the years for hundreds of Westerns). Put these three attractions together for one long day of getting to know Tucson, and you have the city's best family outing (and you can bet the kids will be beat by the end of the day).

TUCSON AREA'S (MOSTLY) NATURAL WONDERS

Arizona–Sonora Desert Museum ☆☆☆ *Kids*   Don't be fooled by the name. This is a zoo, and it's one of the best in the country. The Sonoran Desert of central and southern Arizona and parts of northern Mexico contains within its boundaries not only arid lands, but also forested mountains, springs, rivers, and streams. To reflect this diversity, exhibits here encompass the full spectrum of Sonoran Desert life—from plants to insects to fish to reptiles to mammals—and all are on display in very natural settings. Coyotes and javelinas (peccaries) seem very much at home in their compounds, which are surrounded by fences that are nearly invisible and that make it seem as though there is nothing between you and the animals. You'll also see black bears and mountain lions, tarantulas and scorpions, prairie dogs and desert bighorn sheep. However, our favorite exhibit is the walk-in hummingbird aviary.

The grounds here are quite extensive, so wear good walking shoes; a sun hat of some sort is also advisable. Don't be surprised if you end up staying here hours longer than you had intended. If you get hungry, there are two excellent dining options. You'll find this zoological park 14 miles west of downtown.

2021 N. Kinney Rd. ℭ 520/883-2702. www.desertmuseum.org. Admission Sept–May $12 adults, $4 children 6–12; June–Aug $9 adults, $2 children 6–12. Oct–Feb daily 8:30am–5pm; Mar–Sept daily 7:30am–5pm. From downtown Tucson, go west on Speedway Blvd., which becomes Gates Pass Rd., and follow the signs.

Moments Driving the Catalina Highway

Within a span of only 25 miles, the Catalina Highway climbs roughly 1 mile in elevation from the lowland desert landscape of cacti and ocotillo bushes to forests of ponderosa pines. Passing through several different life zones, this route is the equivalent of driving from Mexico to Canada. When you look at it this way, the $5 use fee is small compared to what a flight to Canada would cost (and that fee will also get you into Sabino Canyon). Along the way, there are numerous overlooks, some of which are nauseatingly vertiginous. Other spots are particularly popular with rock climbers. There are numerous hiking trails, picnic areas, and campgrounds along the route. For more information, contact the **Coronado National Forest Santa Catalina Ranger District,** 5700 N. Sabino Canyon Rd. (ℭ 520/749-8700; www.fs.fed.us/r3/coronado).

Moments **Sunset on Signal Hill**

A hike to Signal Hill, located off the Bajada Loop Drive in Saguaro National Park's west unit and only a quarter-mile walk from the parking area, will reward you with not only a grand sunset vista away from the crowds at Gates Pass, but also the sight of dozens of petroglyphs.

Sabino Canyon Recreation Area ★★ Located at the base of the Santa Catalina Mountains on the northeastern edge of the city, Sabino Canyon is a desert oasis and, with its impressive desert scenery, hiking trails, and stream, is a fabulous place to commune with the desert for a morning or an afternoon. The chance to splash in the canyon's waterfalls and swim in natural pools (water conditions permitting) attracts many visitors, but it is just as enjoyable simply to gaze at the beauty of crystal-clear water flowing through a rocky canyon guarded by saguaro cacti. There are numerous picnic tables in the canyon, and many miles of hiking trails wind their way into the mountains from here, making it one of the best places in the city for a day hike.

A narrated tram shuttles visitors up and down the lower canyon, and between April and November (but not July or Aug), there are moonlight tram rides three times each month (usually the nights before the full moon). The Bear Canyon tram is used by hikers heading to the picturesque Seven Falls, which are at the end of a 2.5-mile trail.

Another good way to experience the park is by bicycling up the paved road during the limited hours when bikes are allowed: Sunday through Tuesday, Thursday, and Friday before 9am and after 5pm. This is a strenuous uphill ride for most of the way, but the scenery is beautiful.

5900 N. Sabino Canyon Rd. ✆ 520/749-8700, 520/749-2861 for shuttle information, or 520/749-2327 for moonlight shuttle reservations. www.fs.fed.us/r3/coronado or www.sabinocanyon.com. Parking $5 (also good for driving the Catalina Hwy.). Sabino Canyon tram ride $7.50 adults, $3 children 3–12; Bear Canyon tram ride $3 adults, $1 children 3–12. Park daily dawn–dusk. Sabino Canyon tram rides daily 9am–4:30pm (July to mid-Dec Mon–Fri 9am–4pm, Sat–Sun 9am–4:30pm); Bear Canyon tram rides daily 9am–4:30pm. Take Grant Rd. east to Tanque Verde Rd., continuing east; at Sabino Canyon Rd., turn north and watch for the sign.

Saguaro National Park ★★★ Saguaro cacti are the quintessential symbol of the American desert and occur naturally only here in the Sonoran Desert. Sensitive to fire and frost, and exceedingly slow to mature, these massive, treelike cacti grow in great profusion around Tucson but have long been threatened by both development and plant collectors. In 1933, to protect these desert giants, the federal government set aside two large tracts of land as a saguaro preserve. This preserve eventually became Saguaro National Park. The two units of the park, one on the east side of the city (Rincon Mountain District) and one on the west (Tucson Mountain District), preserve not only dense stands of saguaros, but also the many other wild inhabitants of this part of the Sonoran Desert. Both units have loop roads, nature trails, hiking trails, and picnic grounds.

The west unit of the park, because of its proximity to both the Arizona–Sonora Desert Museum and Old Tucson Studios, is the more popular area to visit (and your best choice if you're trying to do a lot in a short amount of time). This also happens to be where you'll see the most impressive stands of saguaros. Be sure to take the scenic Bajada Loop Drive, where you'll find good views and several hiking trails (the Hugh Morris Trail involves a long, steep climb, but great views are the reward). To reach the west unit of the park, follow Speedway Boulevard west from downtown Tucson.

Tucson Attractions

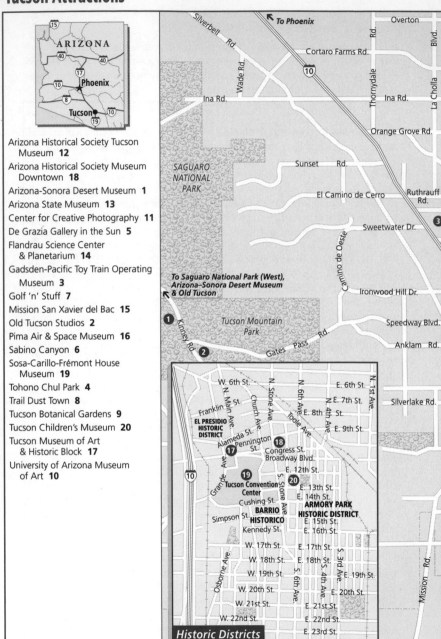

Arizona Historical Society Tucson Museum **12**

Arizona Historical Society Museum Downtown **18**

Arizona-Sonora Desert Museum **1**

Arizona State Museum **13**

Center for Creative Photography **11**

De Grazia Gallery in the Sun **5**

Flandrau Science Center & Planetarium **14**

Gadsden-Pacific Toy Train Operating Museum **3**

Golf 'n' Stuff **7**

Mission San Xavier del Bac **15**

Old Tucson Studios **2**

Pima Air & Space Museum **16**

Sabino Canyon **6**

Sosa-Carillo-Frémont House Museum **19**

Tohono Chul Park **4**

Trail Dust Town **8**

Tucson Botanical Gardens **9**

Tucson Children's Museum **20**

Tucson Museum of Art & Historic Block **17**

University of Arizona Museum of Art **10**

The east section of the park contains an older area of saguaro "forest" at the foot of the Rincon Mountains. This section is popular with hikers because most of it has no roads. It has a visitor center, a loop scenic drive, a picnic area, and a trail open to mountain bikes (the paved loop drive is a great road-bike ride). To reach the east unit of the park, take Speedway Boulevard east, then head south on Freeman Road to Old Spanish Trail.

Rincon Mountain District visitor center: 3693 S. Old Spanish Trail. $\mathcal{C}$ 520/733-5153. Tucson Mountain District visitor center: 2700 N. Kinney Rd. $\mathcal{C}$ 520/733-5158. www.nps.gov/sagu. Entry fee $10 per car, $5 per hiker or biker. Daily 7am–sunset; visitor centers daily 9am–5pm; open to hikers 24 hr. a day. Visitor centers closed Christmas.

Tohono Chul Park ⚘⚘   Although this park covers fewer than 50 acres, it provides an excellent introduction to the plant and animal life of the desert. You'll see a forest of cholla cacti as well as a garden of small pincushion cacti. From mid-February to April, the wildflower displays here are gorgeous (if enough rain has fallen in the previous months). The park also includes an ethnobotanical garden; a garden for children that encourages them to touch, listen, and smell; a demonstration garden; natural areas; an exhibit house for art displays; a tearoom (p. 364) that's great for breakfast, lunch, or afternoon tea; and two very good gift shops. Park docents lead guided tours throughout the day.

7366 N. Paseo del Norte (off Ina Rd. west of the intersection with Oracle Rd.). $\mathcal{C}$ 520/742-6455. www.tohonochul park.org. Admission $5 adults, $4 seniors, $3 students, $2 children ages 5–12; free for all on 1st Tues of every month. Grounds daily 8am–5pm (visitors may remain until sunset). Exhibit house daily 9am–5pm. Tearoom daily 8am–5pm. Buildings closed New Year's Day, July 4th, Thanksgiving, and Christmas (free admission to grounds on these days).

Tucson Botanical Gardens   Set amid residential neighborhoods in midtown Tucson, these gardens are an oasis of greenery and, though small, are well worth a visit if you happen to be interested in desert plant life, landscaping, or gardening. On the 5½-acre grounds, there are a dozen different gardens that not only have visual appeal, but are also educational. You can learn about creating a garden for birds or for butterflies, and then see what sort of crops the Native Americans of this region have traditionally grown. A sensory garden stimulates all five senses. In past years, there has been a tropical butterfly house here from fall through spring.

2150 N. Alvernon Way. $\mathcal{C}$ 520/326-9686. www.tucsonbotanical.org. Admission $5 adults, $2.50 children 6–12. Daily 8:30am–4:30pm. Closed New Year's Day, July 4th, Thanksgiving, and Dec 24–25. Bus: 11.

HISTORIC ATTRACTIONS BOTH REAL & REEL

Mission San Xavier del Bac ⚘   Called the White Dove of the Desert, Mission San Xavier del Bac, an active Roman Catholic church serving the San Xavier Indian Reservation, is a blindingly white adobe building that rises from a sere, brown landscape. Considered the finest example of mission architecture in the Southwest, the beautiful church was built between 1783 and 1797, and incorporates Moorish, Byzantine, and Mexican Renaissance architectural styles. The church, however, was never actually completed, which only becomes apparent when the two bell towers are compared. One is topped with a dome, while the other has none.

Colorful murals cover the interior walls, and behind the altar are elaborate decorations. To the left of the main altar, in a glass sarcophagus, is a statue of St. Francis Xavier, the mission's patron saint, who is believed to answer the prayers of the faithful. A visit to San Xavier's little museum provides a bit of historical perspective and a chance to explore more of the mission. To the east of the church, atop a small hill, you'll find a replica of the famous grotto in Lourdes, France. There are often food stalls selling fry bread in the parking lot in front of the church.

1950 W. San Xavier Rd. © 520/294-2624. www.sanxaviermission.org. Free admission; donations accepted. Daily
8am–5pm. Take I-19 S 9 miles to Exit 92 and turn right.

Old Tucson Studios *(Kids* **Kids*** Despite the name, this is not the historical location
of the old city of Tucson—it's a Western town originally built as the set for the 1939
movie *Arizona*. In the years since, Old Tucson has been used during the filming of
John Wayne's *Rio Lobo, Rio Bravo,* and *El Dorado;* Clint Eastwood's *The Outlaw Josey
Wales;* Kirk Douglas's *Gunfight at the O.K. Corral;* Paul Newman's *The Life and Times
of Judge Roy Bean;* and, more recently, *Tombstone* and *Geronimo.*

Today, however, Old Tucson is far more than just a movie set. In addition to serving as a site for film, TV, and advertising productions (call ahead to find out if any
filming is scheduled), it has become a Wild West theme park with diverse family-oriented activities and entertainment. Throughout the day, there are staged shootouts in
the streets, stunt demonstrations, a cancan musical revue, and other performances.
Train and kiddie rides, restaurants, and gift shops round out the experience.

201 S. Kinney Rd. © 520/883-0100. www.oldtucson.com. Admission $17 adults, $11 children 4–11. Daily 10am–
4pm. Closed Thanksgiving, Dec 24–25, and occasional special events. Take Speedway Blvd. west, continuing in the
same direction when it becomes Gates Pass Blvd., and turn left on S. Kinney Rd.

ART MUSEUMS

Center for Creative Photography Have you ever wished you could see an original Ansel Adams print up close, or perhaps an Edward Weston or a Richard Avedon?
You can at the Center for Creative Photography. Originally conceived by Ansel
Adams, the center now holds more than 60,000 master prints by more than 2,000 of
the world's best photographers, making it one of the best and largest collections in the
world. The center mounts fascinating exhibits year-round and is also a research facility that preserves the photographic archives of more than 60 photographers, including Adams. While the main gallery is open on a regular basis, you must make an
appointment to view images from the archives.

University of Arizona campus, 1030 N. Olive Rd. (east of Park Ave. and Speedway Blvd.). © 520/621-7968. www.creative
photography.org. Admission by donation. Mon–Fri 9am–5pm; Sat–Sun noon–5pm. Closed major holidays. Bus: 1, 4, 5, or 6.

De Grazia Gallery in the Sun Southwestern artist Ettore "Ted" De Grazia was a
Tucson favorite son, and his home, a sprawling, funky adobe building in the foothills,
is a city landmark and now serves as a museum for this prolific artist. De Grazia is said
to be the most reproduced artist in the world because many of his images of big-eyed
children were used as greeting cards during the 1950s and 1960s. Today De Grazia's
images seem trite and maudlin, but in his day he was a very successful artist. This
gallery is packed with original paintings, so it may surprise you to learn that, near the
end of his life, De Grazia burned several hundred thousand dollars' worth of his paintings in a protest of IRS inheritance taxes.

6300 N. Swan Rd. © 800/545-2185 or 520/299-9191. www.degrazia.org. Free admission. Daily 10am–4pm. Closed
New Year's Day, Easter, Thanksgiving, and Christmas.

Tucson Museum of Art & Historic Block *(* This museum complex is one of the
two best reasons to venture into downtown Tucson (the other is El Charro Café). The
museum includes galleries housed in historic adobe homes, a courtyard frequently
used to display sculptures, and a large modern building that frequently mounts the
most interesting exhibits in town. The *Palice Pavilion—Art of the Americas* exhibit is a
highlight of the museum. This exhibit consists of a large collection of pre-Columbian

---

Finds The Conley Museum of the West

Although little more than a room at the back of the **Mark Sublette Medicine Man Gallery,** 7000 E. Tanque Verde Rd. (© 520/722-7798; www.medicineman gallery.com), the **Conley Museum of the West** packs a lot into a tiny space. You can see not only 19th- and 20th-century pieces by some of the biggest names in Western art, but also Indian artifacts and art, Spanish colonial antiquities, and historical maps dating back to 1739. This place is a must for fans of Western art. The museum is open Monday through Saturday from 10am to 5pm and Sunday from 1 to 4pm. Admission is free.

---

art that represents 3,000 years of life in Mexico and Central and South America. This collection is housed in the historic Stevens/Duffield House, which also contains Spanish colonial artifacts and Latin American folk art. The noteworthy Goodman Pavilion of Western Art comprises an extensive collection that depicts cowboys, horses, and the wide-open spaces of the American West. The museum has also preserved five historic homes on this same block, all open to the public. See "History Museums & Landmark Buildings," below, for details.

140 N. Main Ave. © 520/624-2333. www.tucsonarts.com. Admission $8 adults, $6 seniors, $3 students, free for children 12 and under; free on 1st Sun of each month. Tues–Sat 10am–4pm; Sun noon–4pm. Closed major holidays. All downtown-bound buses.

The University of Arizona Museum of Art 🎯🎯   With European and American works from the Renaissance to the 20th century, the art collections at this museum are even more extensive and diverse than those of the Tucson Museum of Art. Tintoretto, Rembrandt, Picasso, O'Keeffe, Warhol, and Rothko are all represented. Another attraction, the *Retablo of Ciudad Rodrigo,* consists of 26 paintings from 15th-century Spain that were originally placed above a cathedral altar. The museum also has an extensive collection of 20th-century sculpture that includes more than 60 clay and plaster models and sketches by Jacques Lipchitz.

University of Arizona campus, Park Ave. and Speedway Blvd. © 520/621-7567. www.artmuseum.arizona.edu. Free admission. Tues–Fri 9am–5pm; Sat–Sun noon–4pm. Closed major holidays. Bus: 1, 4, 5, or 6.

HISTORY MUSEUMS & LANDMARK BUILDINGS

In addition to the attractions listed below, downtown Tucson has a couple of historic neighborhoods that are described in the box "Architectural Highlights," below. Among the more interesting buildings are those maintained by the Tucson Museum of Art and located on the block surrounding the museum. A map and brochures are available at the museum's front desk, and free (with admission to the museum) guided tours of the historic block and Corbett House are available.

Arizona Historical Society Downtown Museum   If you want to learn more about the history of Tucson, this is the museum to visit. Exhibits cover Spanish presidio days, American army days, merchants, and schools. Through the use of artifacts and old photos, these exhibits help bring the city's past to life. One of the most curious exhibits focuses on the gangster John Dillinger, who was arrested here in Tucson.

140 N. Stone Ave. © 520/770-1473. www.arizonahistoricalsociety.org. Admission $3 adults, $2 seniors and students ages 12–18, free for children under 12; free on 1st Fri of each month. Mon–Fri 10am–4pm. Closed major holidays. All downtown-bound buses.

Arizona Historical Society Tucson Main Museum   As the state's oldest historical museum, this repository of all things Arizonan is a treasure-trove for the history buff. If you've never explored a real mine, you can do the next best thing by exploring the museum's full-scale reproduction of an underground mine tunnel. You'll see an assayer's office, miner's tent, stamp mill, and blacksmith's shop in the mining exhibit. A transportation exhibit displays stagecoaches and the horseless carriages that revolutionized life in the Southwest, while temporary other exhibits also give a pretty good idea of what it was like back then.

949 E. Second St. (© 520/628-5774. www.arizonahistoricalsociety.org. Admission $5 adults, $4 seniors and students ages 12–18, free for children under 12; free for all on the 1st Sat of each month. Mon–Sat 10am–4pm. Closed major holidays. Bus: 1, 4, 5, or 6.

Arizona State Museum   This museum, which is the oldest anthropological museum in the Southwest, houses *Paths of Life: American Indians of the Southwest,* one of the state's most interesting exhibits on prehistoric and contemporary Native American cultures of the Southwest. The exhibit focuses on 10 different tribes from around the Southwest and northern Mexico, not only displaying a wide range of artifacts, but also exploring the lifestyles and cultural traditions of Indians living in the region today. In addition, the museum showcases a collection of some 20,000 ceramic pieces. This pottery spans 2,000 years of life in the desert Southwest.

University of Arizona campus, 1013 E. University Blvd. at Park Ave. (© 520/621-6302. www.statemuseum. arizona.edu. Admission $3 suggested donation. Mon–Sat 10am–5pm. Sun noon–5pm. Closed major holidays. Bus: 1, 4, 5, or 6.

Sosa-Carillo-Frémont House Museum   Located on the shady grounds of the modern Tucson Convention Center, the Sosa-Carillo-Frémont House is a classic example of Sonoran-style adobe architecture. Originally built in the 1870s, the house was rented in 1878 to territorial governor John Charles Frémont, who had led a distinguished military career as an explorer of the West. The building has been restored in the style of this period, and all rooms are decorated with period antiques. The flat roof is made of pine beams called *vigas,* which were traditionally covered with saguaro cactus ribs and topped by a layer of hard-packed mud. From November through mid-April, this museum offers six different tours of historic Tucson ($10 for adults, free for children under 12) on Thursday and Saturday mornings at 10am.

151 S. Granada Ave. (in the Tucson Convention Center complex). (© 520/622-0956. Admission $3 adults, $2 seniors and students ages 12–18, free for children under 12; free on 1st Sat of each month. Wed–Sat 10am–4pm. Closed major holidays. All downtown-bound buses.

Value **Passport to Tucson**

The **Tucson Attractions Passport** is a great way to save money on admissions to many of the city's top attractions. The passport, available at the downtown Visitors Center, 100 S. Church St. ((© **800/638-8350** or 520/624-1817; www.tucson passport.com), costs $15 and gets you two-for-one admissions to the Arizona–Sonora Desert Museum, Old Tucson Studios, Biosphere 2, the Pima Air & Space Museum, Tohono Chul Park, the Tucson Museum of Art, Kartchner Caverns State Park, and many other attractions in Tucson and across southern Arizona.

SCIENCE & TECHNOLOGY MUSEUMS

Biosphere 2 *Overrated*   For 2 years, beginning in September 1991, four men and four women were locked inside this airtight, 3-acre greenhouse in the desert 35 miles north of Tucson near the town of Oracle. During their tenure in Biosphere 2 (earth is considered Biosphere 1), they conducted experiments on how the earth, basically a giant greenhouse, manages to support all the planet's life forms. Today there are no longer any people living in Biosphere 2, and the former research facility is operated more as a tourist attraction than as a science center. Tours take visitors inside the giant greenhouse and into the mechanisms that helped keep this sealed environment going for 2 years. The strangest sight is the giant "lung" that allowed for the expansion and contraction of the air within Biosphere 2. Although the building, which sits in the middle of desert hill country, is an impressive sight, the tours are something of a letdown.

32540 S. Biosphere Rd. (off Ariz. 77 at mile marker 96.5). © 520/838-6200. www.bio2.com. Admission $20 ages 13 and older, $13 children 6–12. Daily 9am–4pm. Closed Thanksgiving and Christmas. Take Oracle Rd. north out of Tucson and continue north on Ariz. 77 until you see the sign.

Flandrau Science Center & Planetarium   Located on the University of Arizona campus, Flandrau Planetarium is the most convenient place in Arizona to do a little stargazing through a professional telescope. As such, it should be on the itinerary of anyone coming to Tucson (unless it happens to be cloudy). The planetarium theater presents a variety of programs on the stars, and the exhibit halls contain a large mineral collection and hands-on science exhibits. However, the best reason to visit is to gaze through the planetarium's 16-inch telescope.

University of Arizona campus, 1601 E. University Blvd., at Cherry Ave. © 520/621-STAR. www.flandrau.org. Telescope viewing free. $2.50 per person. Wed 6–9pm; Thurs–Fri 9am–3pm and 6–9pm; Sat noon–9pm; Sun noon–5pm. Telescope viewing (weather permitting) Wed–Sat 7–10pm. Closed major holidays. Bus: 1, 3, 4, 5, 9, or 15.

The International Wildlife Museum   This castlelike building (modeled after a French Foreign Legion fort), located on the road that leads to the Arizona–Sonora Desert Museum, is a natural-history museum filled with stuffed animals in lifelike poses and surroundings. Animals from all over the world are displayed, and there are exhibits of extinct animals, including the Irish elk and the woolly mammoth. Among the more lifelike displays are the predator-and-prey exhibits. There are also fascinating exhibits of butterflies and other unusual insects.

4800 W. Gates Pass Rd. © 520/629-0100. www.thewildlifemuseum.org. Admission $7 adults, $5.50 seniors and students, $2.50 children 4–12. Mon–Fri 9am–5pm; Sat–Sun 9am–6pm. Closed Thanksgiving and Christmas. Take Speedway Blvd. W., continuing in the same direction when it becomes Gates Pass Blvd. The museum is 5 miles west of I-10.

Pima Air & Space Museum *⚔*   Located just south of Davis Monthan Air Force Base, the Pima Air & Space Museum houses one of the largest collections of historic aircraft in the world. On display are more than 250 aircraft, including an X-15 (the world's fastest aircraft), an SR-71 Blackbird, several Russian MiGs, a "Superguppy," and a B-17G "Flying Fortress." Tours are available.

The museum also offers guided tours of Davis Monthan's AMARC (Arizona Maintenance and Regeneration Center) facility, which goes by the name of the Boneyard. Here, thousands of mothballed military planes are lined up in neat rows under the Arizona sun. Tours last just under an hour and cost $6 for adults and $3 for children 12 and under. Tour reservations (© 520/574-0462) should be made about a week in advance.

6000 E. Valencia Rd. ℭ 520/574-0462. www.pimaair.org. Admission Nov–May $14 adults, $11 seniors and military, $9 children 7–12; June–Oct $12 adults, $9.75 seniors and military, $8 children 7–12. Daily 9am–5pm. Closed Thanksgiving and Christmas. Take the Valencia Rd. exit from I-10 and drive east 2 miles to the museum.

Titan Missile Museum ℛ   If you've ever wondered what it would be like to have your finger on the button of a nuclear missile, here's your opportunity to find out. This deactivated intercontinental ballistic missile (ICBM) silo is now a museum—and is the only museum in the country that allows visitors to descend into a former missile silo. There's a huge Titan missile on display, and, even without its nuclear warhead, it is a terrifying sight. The guided tours do a great job of explaining not only the ICBM system, but also what life was like for the people who worked here. Operated by the Pima Air & Space Museum, this museum is located 25 miles south of Tucson near the community of Green Valley. On the first Saturday of each month, there is a special reservation-only "Beyond the Blast Doors" tour that takes visitors into areas not on the normal tour. There are also special tours on Tuesdays at 2pm. Other special tours are also available, and it is even possible to spend the night in the silo. Contact the museum for details.

1580 W. Duval Mine Rd., Sahuarita (Exit 69 off I-19). ℭ 520/625-7736. Admission $8.50 adults, $7.50 seniors, $5 children 7–12; Beyond the Blast Door Tour $18 adults, $16 seniors, $9.95 children 8–12. Daily 9am–5pm. Closed Thanksgiving and Christmas. Take I-19 south to Green Valley; take Exit 69 W a half-mile to main entrance.

ESPECIALLY FOR KIDS

In addition to the museums listed below, two of the greatest places to take kids in the Tucson area are the Arizona–Sonora Desert Museum and Old Tucson Studios. Kids will also get a kick out of the Sabino Canyon tram ride, the Reid Park Zoo, Flandrau Science Center & Planetarium, and the Pima Air & Space Museum. All are described in detail earlier in this chapter.

They'll also enjoy **Trail Dust Town,** 6541 E. Tanque Verde Rd. (ℭ **520/296-5442;** www.traildusttown.com), a Wild West–themed shopping and dining center. It has a full-size carousel, a scaled-down train to ride, shootout shows, and miniature golf next door. Basically, it's a sort of scaled-down Old Tucson. If the kids are into miniature golf, take them to **Golf n' Stuff,** 6503 E. Tanque Verde Rd. (ℭ **520/296-2366;** www.golfnstuff.com), which is right next door to Trail Dust Town. Not only is there a miniature golf course, there are bumper boats, go-karts, batting cages, laser tag, a climbing wall, and a video-game arcade.

T Rex Museum ℛ   If you've got kids who are crazy for dinosaurs, be sure to bring them to this little homegrown private museum that likes to make learning about

---

Kids All Aboard!

If you've got kids who idolize Thomas the Tank Engine, then you'd better schedule your Tucson visit for the second or fourth Sunday of the month. On those days (with a few exceptions), the **Gadsden-Pacific Division Toy Train Operating Museum,** 3975 N. Miller Ave. (ℭ **520/888-2222;** http://hometown. aol.com/ienglish), sends out little engines that think they can. The trains chug around a variety of layouts built in different model railroad gauges. The museum is open from 12:30 to 4:30pm 2 days each month. Admission is free. In July and August, the museum is closed.

dinosaurs fun. There are exhibits of live insects and reptiles to give context to the fossils that are on display, and videos about dinosaurs are screened throughout the day.

100 E. Drachman St. (℃ 520/792-2884. www.trexmuseum.org. Admission $5 per person. Mon–Sat 10am–5pm; Sun noon–5pm. Closed Easter, July 4th, Thanksgiving, and Christmas. Bus: 10 or 16.

Tucson Children's Museum   This museum, in the historic Carnegie Library in downtown Tucson, is filled with fun and educational hands-on activities. Exhibits include a bakery and farmers' market and an electricity gallery. Expect to find such perennial kid favorites as a fire truck, a toy train, and dinosaur sculptures. Activities are featured daily.

200 S. Sixth Ave. (℃ 520/792-9985. www.tucsonchildrensmuseum.org. Admission $7 adults, $5 seniors, $3.50 children 2–16; free 1 day each month (call for date). Tues–Sat 10am–5pm; Sun noon–5pm. Closed Thanksgiving and Christmas. All downtown-bound buses.

6 Organized Tours

For a look at a completely different sort of excavation, head 15 miles south of Tucson to the **ASARCO Mineral Discovery Center,** 1421 W. Pima Mine Rd., Sahuarita (℃ 520/625-7513; www.mineraldiscovery.com), where you can tour a huge open-pit copper mine and learn about copper mining past and present. The center is open Tuesday through Saturday from 9am to 5pm; admission is free. November through April, 1-hour mine tours are offered five times a day. These tours cost $6 for adults, $5 for seniors, and $4 for children 5 to 12. To get here, drive south from Tucson on I-19 and take Exit 80. You might want to combine this tour with a visit to the nearby Titan Missile Museum.

Want to taste raw cactus, learn about cholla-extraction devices, and hold a live tarantula or snake? Call **Sunshine Jeep Tours** (℃ 520/742-1943; www.sunshinejeep tours.com), which has a two-person minimum and charges $130 for the first two people and then, after the minimum is met, charges $50 for adults, $35 for children 11 to 15, and $25 for children 6 to 10. On these tours, you'll pass through some of the densest stands of saguaro cacti in the state.

Balloon America (℃ 520/299-7744; www.balloonridesusa.com) offers flights over the desert ($225) or a more adventurous trip over the foothills of the Santa Catalina Mountains ($475). **Fleur de Tucson Balloon Tours** (℃ 520/529-1025; www.fleurde tucson.net) offers rides over the Tucson Mountains, Saguaro National Park, and the Avra Valley. Rates are $225 to $250 per person, including brunch and a champagne toast.

7 Getting Outside

BICYCLING   Tucson is one of the best bicycling cities in the country, and the dirt roads and trails of the surrounding national forest and desert are perfect for mountain biking. Rentals at **Fair Wheel Bikes,** 1110 E. Sixth St. (℃ 520/884-9018), go for $40 per day for road bikes and $30 per day for mountain bikes.

If you'd rather confine your pedaling to paved surfaces, there are some great options around town. The number-one choice in town for cyclists in halfway decent shape is the road up **Sabino Canyon** (p. 367). Keep in mind, however, that bicycles are allowed on this road only 5 days a week and then only before 9am and after 5pm (the road is closed to bikes all day Wed and Sat). For a much easier ride, try the **Rillito**

Architectural Highlights

Tucson has a long and varied cultural history, which is most easily seen by strolling through the downtown historic neighborhoods. Start your explorations in El Presidio Historic District, which is named for the Presidio of San Augustín del Tucson (1775), the Spanish garrison built here to protect the San Xavier del Bac Mission from the Apaches. For many years the presidio was the heart of Tucson, and although no original buildings are still standing, there are numerous structures from the mid–19th century. Some of our favorites are listed below.

- **La Casa Cordova,** at 175 N. Meyer Ave., dates from about 1848 and is one of the oldest buildings in Tucson. It's been restored to look as it might have in the late 1800s. Each year from November to March, this building exhibits a very elaborate *nacimiento,* a Mexican folk-art nativity scene.

- **Corbett House,** a restored Mission Revival–style building located at 180 N. Main Ave., was built in 1907. The house, which is set back behind a green lawn, is strikingly different from the older, Sonoran-style adobe homes on this block. On Tuesdays at 11am, the Tucson Museum of Art offers a guided tour.

- **Fish House,** at 120 N. Main Ave., was built in 1867 on the site of old Mexican barracks. Named for Edward Nye Fish, a local merchant, it now houses the art museum's Western-art collection.

- **Julius Kruttschnidt House,** at 297 N. Main Ave., dates from 1886 and now houses a bed-and-breakfast inn. Victorian trappings, including a long veranda, disguise the adobe origins of this unique and beautifully restored home.

- **Steinfeld House,** at 300 N. Main Ave., was built in 1900 in California Mission Revival style and was designed by Henry Trost, Tucson's most noted architect. It served as the original Owl's Club, a gentlemen's club for some of Tucson's most eligible turn-of-the-20th-century bachelors.

- **Owl's Club Mansion,** at 378 N. Main Ave., was built in 1902 and designed by Henry Trost in the Mission Revival style, albeit with a great deal of ornamentation. It replaced the Steinfeld House as home to the bachelors of the Owl's Club.

- Built in 1928, the **Pima County Courthouse,** located at 115 N. Church Ave., incorporates Moorish, Spanish, and Southwestern architectural features, including a colorful tiled dome.

- **Sosa-Carillo-Frémont House,** located at 151 S. Granada Ave., was built in the 1850s and later served as the home of territorial governor John C. Frémont. The restored building is open to the public and is furnished in the style of the period.

- **The Barrio Histórico District** is another worthwhile area to explore, especially the northern (and more restored) section. With 150 adobe row houses, this neighborhood contains the largest collection of 19th-century Sonoran-style adobe buildings in the United States.

River Park path, which has a 1-mile paved section between Swan and Craycroft roads and a 6-mile paved section between Campbell Avenue and I-10. The trail parallels River Road and the usually dry bed of the Rillito River.

If mountain biking is more your speed, there are lots of great rides in the Tucson area. For an easy and very scenic dirt-road loop through forests of saguaros, head to the west unit of Saguaro National Park (p. 367) and ride the 6-mile **Bajada Loop Drive.** You can turn this into a 12-mile ride by starting at the Red Hills Visitor Center.

BIRD-WATCHING   Southern Arizona has some of the best bird-watching in the country, and although the best spots are south of Tucson, there are a few places around the city that birders will enjoy seeking out. Call the **Tucson Audubon Society's Rare Bird Alert** (© 520/798-1005) for a list of recent sightings.

The city's premier birding spot is the **Sweetwater Wetland,** a man-made wetland just west of I-10 and north of Prince Road. These wetlands are part of a wastewater treatment facility and have an extensive network of trails that wind past numerous ponds and canals. There are enough different types of wildlife habitat that the area attracts a wide variety of bird species. To find the wetlands, take I-10 south to the Prince Road exit, and at the end of the exit ramp, turn right onto Sweetwater Drive. If you're driving west on Prince Road, go to the end of the road, turn right on Business Center Drive, turn left on River Park Road (which becomes Commerce Dr.), take the first left (probably unmarked), and then turn left again on Sweetwater Drive. The wetlands are closed on Monday mornings late March to mid-November.

Roy P. Drachman Agua Caliente Park, 12325 E. Roger Rd. (off N. Soldier Trail), in the northeast corner of the city, is just about the best place in Tucson to see birds. The year-round warm springs here are a magnet for dozens of species, including waterfowl, great blue herons, black phoebes, soras, and vermilion flycatchers. To find the park, follow Tanque Verde Road east 6 miles from the intersection with Sabino Canyon Road and turn left onto Soldier Trail. Watch for signs.

The best area for bird-watching is **Madera Canyon National Forest Recreation Area** ℱ (© 520/281-2296; www.fs.fed.us/r3/coronado), about 40 miles south of the city in the Coronado National Forest. Because of the year-round water here, Madera Canyon attracts a surprising variety of bird life. Avid birders flock to this canyon from around the country in hopes of spotting more than a dozen species of hummingbirds and an equal number of flycatchers, warblers, tanagers, buntings, and grosbeaks. If you're heading out for the day, arrive early—parking is very limited. To reach Madera Canyon, take the Continental Road/Madera Canyon exit off I-19; from the exit, it's another 12 miles southeast. The canyon is open daily from dawn to dusk; there is a $5 day-use fee. For information on the canyon's Santa Rita Lodge and Chuparosa Inn, see p. 352.

GOLF   Although there aren't quite as many golf courses in Tucson as in Phoenix, this is still a golfer's town. For last-minute tee-time reservations, contact **Standby Golf** (© 800/655-5345; www.discountteetimes.com). No fee is charged for this service.

In addition to public and municipal links, numerous resort courses allow nonguests to play. Perhaps the most famous of these are the two 18-hole courses at **Ventana Canyon Golf and Racquet Club** ℱ, 6200 N. Clubhouse Lane (© 520/577-4015). These Tom Fazio–designed courses offer challenging desert target-style play that is nearly legendary. The 3rd hole on the Mountain Course is one of the most photographed holes in the West. In winter, greens fees are $115 to $195 (slightly less if you are staying at Loews Ventana Canyon Resort or The Lodge at Ventana Canyon).

As famous as the Ventana Canyon courses is the 27-hole **Omni Tucson National Golf Resort and Spa** ⚔, 2727 W. Club Dr. (© **520/575-7540** or 520/297-2271; www.tucsonnational.com), a traditional course that is perhaps more familiar to golfers due to the fact that it was for many years the site of the annual Tucson Open. One of the 9-hole courses here was rebuilt as a desert-style target course in 2005, which makes this a good place for an introduction to desert golfing. If you are not staying at the resort, greens fees are $185 in winter, $70 in summer.

El Conquistador Country Club, 10555 N. La Cañada Dr., Oro Valley (© **520/544-1800;** www.elconquistadorcc.com), with two 18-hole courses and a 9-hole course, offers stunning (and very distracting) views of the Santa Catalina Mountains. Greens fees are $55 to $125 in winter.

At **Starr Pass Country Club & Spa,** 3645 W. Starr Pass Blvd. (© **800/503-2898** or 520/670-0400; www.starrpasstucson.com), the fairways play up to the narrow Starr Pass, which was once a stagecoach route. Greens fees are $199 in winter.

There are many public courses around town. The **Arizona National,** 9777 E. Sabino Greens Dr. (© **520/749-3636;** www.arizonanationalgolfclub.com), incorporates stands of cacti and rocky outcroppings into the course layout. Greens fees are $135 to $165 in winter. **The Golf Club at Vistoso,** 955 W. Vistoso Highlands Dr. (© **877/548-1110** or 520/797-9900; www.vistosogolf.com), has a championship desert course, with fees of $129 to $175 in winter. **Heritage Highlands Golf & Country Club,** 4949 W. Heritage Club Blvd., Marana (© **520/579-7000;** www.heritagehighlands. com), is a championship desert course at the foot of the Tortolita Mountains; greens fees are $115 in winter.

Tucson Parks and Recreation operates five municipal golf courses, of which the **Randolph** and **Dell Urich,** 600 S. Alvernon Way (© **520/791-4161**), are the premier courses. The former has been the site of Tucson's LPGA tournament. Greens fees for 18 holes at these two courses are $42 to $56 in winter. Other municipal courses include **El Rio,** 1400 W. Speedway Blvd. (© **520/791-4229**); **Silverbell,** 3600 N. Silverbell Rd. (© **520/791-5235**); and **Fred Enke,** 8251 E. Irvington Rd. (© **520/791-2539**). This latter course is the city's only desert-style golf course. Greens fees for 18 holes at these three courses are $36 to $50 in winter. For general information and tee-time reservations for any of the municipal courses, visit **www.tucsoncitygolf.com**.

HIKING   Tucson is nearly surrounded by mountains, most of which are protected as city and state parks, national forest, or national park, and within these public areas are hundreds of miles of hiking trails.

Saguaro National Park (© **520/733-5153**) flanks Tucson on both the east and west, with units accessible off Old Spanish Trail east of Tucson and past the end of Speedway Boulevard west of the city. In these areas, you can observe Sonoran Desert vegetation and wildlife, and hike among the huge saguaro cacti for which the park is named. For saguaro-spotting, the west unit is the better choice. See p. 367 for details.

Tucson Mountain Park, at the west end of Speedway Boulevard, is adjacent to Saguaro National Park and preserves a similar landscape. The parking area at Gates Pass, on Speedway, is a favorite sunset spot.

Sabino Canyon (p. 367), off Sabino Canyon Road, is one of Tucson's best hiking areas, but is also the city's most popular recreation area. A cold mountain stream here cascades over waterfalls and forms pools that make great swimming holes. The 5-mile round-trip **Seven Falls Trail,** which follows Bear Canyon deep into the mountains, is the most popular hike in the recreation area. You can take a tram to the trail head or add extra miles by hiking from the main parking lot.

With the city limits pushing right to the boundary of the Coronado National Forest, there are some convenient hiking options in Tucson's northern foothills. The **Ventana Canyon Trail** begins at a parking area adjacent to the Loews Ventana Canyon Resort (off Sunrise Dr. west of Sabino Canyon Rd.) and leads into the Ventana Canyon Wilderness. A few miles west, there's the **Finger Rock Trail,** which starts at the top of the section of Alvernon Road accessed from Skyline Drive. There are actually a couple of trails starting here, so you can hike for miles into the desert. Over near the Westward Look Resort is the **Pima Canyon Trail,** which leads into the Ventana Canyon Wilderness and is reached off Ina Road just east of Oracle Road. Both of these trails provide desert canyon hikes of whatever length you feel like doing. Just south of the Hilton Tucson El Conquistador Golf & Tennis Resort, you'll find the **Linda Vista Trail,** which begins just off Oracle Road on Linda Vista Boulevard. This trail lies at the foot of Pusch Ridge and winds through dense stands of prickly-pear cactus. Because this trail is shaded by Pusch Ridge in the morning, it's a good choice for an early hike on a hot day.

Catalina State Park, 11570 N. Oracle Rd. (© **520/628-5798;** www.azparks.gov/ Parks/parkhtml/catalina.html), is set on the rugged northwest face of the Santa Catalina Mountains, between 2,500 and 3,000 feet high. Hiking trails here lead into the Pusch Ridge Wilderness; however, the park's best day hike is the 5.5-mile round-trip to **Romero Pools,** where small natural pools of water set amid the rocks are a refreshing destination on a hot day (expect plenty of other people on a weekend). This hike involves about 1,000 feet of elevation gain. Admission to the park is $6 per vehicle ($3 between Memorial Day weekend and Labor Day weekend). Within the park is an ancient Hohokam ruin.

One of the reasons Tucson is such a livable city is the presence of the cool (and, in winter, snow-covered) pine forests of 8,250-foot Mount Lemmon. Within the **Mount Lemmon Recreation Area,** at the end of the Catalina Highway, are many miles of trails. There is a $5-per-vehicle charge to use any of the sites within this recreation area. Even if you plan to only pull off at a roadside parking spot and ogle the view of the desert far below, you'll need to stop at the roadside ticket kiosk at the base of the mountain and pay your fee. For more information, contact the **Coronado National Forest Santa Catalina Ranger District,** 5700 N. Sabino Canyon Rd. (© **520/749-8700;** www.fs.fed.us/r3/coronado).

HORSEBACK RIDING   If you want to play cowboy or just go for a leisurely ride through the desert, there are plenty of stables around Tucson where you can saddle up. In addition to renting horses and providing guided trail rides, some of the stables below offer sunset rides with cookouts. Although reservations are not always required, they're a good idea. If you stay at a guest ranch, you can do as much riding as your muscles can stand.

Pusch Ridge Stables, 13700 N. Oracle Rd. (© **520/825-1664;** www.puschridge stables.com), is adjacent to Catalina State Park and Coronado National Forest. Rates are $30 for 1 hour, $50 for 2 hours, and $40 for a sunset ride.

Over on the east side of Tucson, there's **Spanish Trail Outfitters** (© **520/749-0167;** www.spanishtrailoutfitters.com), which leads rides into the foothills of the Santa Catalina Mountains off Sabino Canyon Road. Rates are $35 for a 1-hour ride, $55 for a 2-hour or sunset ride.

WILDFLOWER-VIEWING   Bloom time varies from year to year, but April and May are good times to view native wildflowers in the Tucson area. While the crowns of white blossoms worn by saguaro cacti are among the most visible blooms in the area, other cacti are far more colorful. **Saguaro National Park** (p. 367) and **Sabino Canyon** (p. 367) are among the best local spots to see saguaros, other cactus species, and various wildflowers in bloom. If you feel like heading farther afield, the wildflower displays at **Picacho Peak State Park** (p. 456), between Tucson and Casa Grande, are the most impressive in the state.

8 Spectator Sports

BASEBALL   The **Colorado Rockies** (✆ 520/327-9467) pitch spring-training camp in March at Hi Corbett Field, 3400 E. Camino Campestre, in Reid Park (at Randolph Way and E. Broadway). Tickets are $2 to $15. Both the **Chicago White Sox** and the **Arizona Diamondbacks** have their spring-training camps and exhibition games at Tucson Electric Park, 2500 E. Ajo Way (✆ 866/672-1343 or 520/434-1367; www.kinosportscomplex.com), on the south side of the city near the airport. Tickets range from $5 to $16.

Tucson Electric Park is also where you can watch the **Tucson Sidewinders** (✆ 520/434-1021; www.tucsonsidewinders.com), the AAA affiliate team of the Arizona Diamondbacks. The season runs April through early September; tickets are $6 to $9.

FOOTBALL   The **University of Arizona Wildcats** (✆ 800/452-2287 or 520/621-2287; www.arizonaathletics.com), a Pac-10 team, play at UA's Arizona Stadium.

GOLF TOURNAMENTS   The **World Golf Championships–Accenture Match Play Championship** (✆ 866/942-2672; www.pgatour.com), Tucson's main PGA tournament, is held in late February at The Gallery Golf Club at Dove Mountain. Daily tickets are $30 to $50.

HORSE/GREYHOUND RACING   **Rillito Park Race Track,** 4502 N. First Ave. (✆ 520/293-5011), the birthplace of both the photo finish and organized quarter-horse and Arabian racing, hosts quarter-horse and thoroughbred racing for one month each winter. The ponies run on weekends from mid-February to early March, and admission is $3 to $5.

Greyhounds race year-round at **Tucson Greyhound Park,** 2601 S. Third Ave. (✆ 520/884-7576; www.tucdogtrak.com). Grandstand admission is $1.25. Races are held Monday through Saturday from 7:40pm. To reach the track, take Exit 261 off I-10.

9 Day Spas

If you'd prefer a massage to a round on the links, consider spending a few hours at a spa. While full-service health spas can cost $400 to $500 or more per day, for under $100 you can avail yourself of a spa treatment or two (massages, facials, seaweed wraps, loofah scrubs, and the like) and maybe even get to spend the day lounging by the pool at some exclusive resort. Spas are also great places (for both men and women) to while away an afternoon if you couldn't get a tee time at that golf course you wanted to play or if it happens to be raining.

The **Elizabeth Arden Red Door Spa,** at The Westin La Paloma Resort & Spa, 3666 E. Sunrise Dr. (✆ 520/742-7866, ext. 7890; www.reddoorspas.com), focuses on skin-care services, but there are plenty of body wraps and massages available as well. With a 50-minute treatment (mostly $110–$130), you can use the spa's facilities for the day. However, unlike other spas in town, the Red Door is more about relaxation than staying fit, so you won't find aerobics classes or a pool here. Spa packages range in price from $199 to $552.

For a variety of services and a gorgeous location, you just can't beat **The Lakeside Spa & Tennis Center at Loews Ventana Canyon Resort,** 7000 N. Resort Dr. (© **520/529-7830;** www.loewshotels.com), which is wedged between the rugged Catalinas and manicured fairways of one of the most fabled golf courses in the state. Soothed by the scent of aromatherapy, you can treat yourself to herbal wraps, mud treatments, different styles of massage, specialized facials, complete salon services, and much more. Fifty-minute treatments run $100 to $125. With any 50-minute body treatment, you get use of the spa's facilities and pool and can attend any fitness classes being held that day.

With six locations around the Tucson area, **Gadabout Day Spa** (www.gadabout. com) offers the opportunity to slip a relaxing visit to a spa into a busy schedule. Mud baths, facials, and massages as well as hair and nail services are available, and body treatments and massages range from about $40 for a quick massage to $364 for a full day at the spa. You'll find Gadabout at the following locations: St. Philip's Plaza, 1990 E. River Rd. (© **520/577-2000**); 6393 E. Grant Rd. (© **520/885-0000**); 3207 E. Speedway Blvd. (© **520/325-0000**); Sunrise-Kolb, 6960 E. Sunrise Dr. (© **520/615-9700**); and 8303 N. Oracle Rd. (© **520/742-0000**). The sixth location is Gadabout Man, 2951 N. Swan Rd. (© **520/325-3300**).

10 Shopping

Although the Tucson shopping scene is overshadowed by that of Scottsdale and Phoenix, Tucson does provide a respectable diversity of merchants. Tucsonans have a strong sense of their place in the Southwest, and this is reflected in the city's shopping opportunities. Southwestern clothing, food, crafts, furniture, and art abound (and often at reasonable prices), as do shopping centers built in a Southwestern architectural style.

The city's population center has moved steadily northward, so it is in the northern foothills that you'll find most of the city's large enclosed shopping malls as well as the more tasteful small shopping plazas specializing in boutiques and galleries.

In downtown Tucson, on Fourth Avenue, between Congress Street and Speedway Boulevard, more than 50 shops, galleries, and restaurants make up the **Fourth Avenue historic shopping and entertainment district.** The buildings here were constructed in the early 1900s, and the proximity to the University of Arizona helps keep this district bustling. Many of the shops cater primarily to student needs and interests. Through the underpass at the south end of Fourth Avenue is Congress Street, the heart of the **Downtown Arts District,** where there are still a few art galleries (most, however, have moved to the foothills). Both areas are primarily hangouts for college students.

El Presidio Historic District around the Tucson Museum of Art is the city's center for crafts shops. This area is home to Old Town Artisans and the Tucson Museum of Art museum shop. The city's **"Lost Barrio"** section, on the corner of Southwest Park Avenue and 12th Street (a block off Broadway), is a good place to look for Mexican imports and Southwestern-style home furnishings at good prices.

ANTIQUES & COLLECTIBLES

In addition to the places listed below, a great concentration of antiques shops can be found along Grant Road between Campbell Avenue and Alvernon Way.

American Antique Mall This antiques mall has 100 dealers and is one of the largest such places in southern Arizona. For sale are all manner of collectibles and a few antiques. 3130 E. Grant Rd. ℂ 520/326-3070. www.americanantiquemall.com.

Eric Firestone Gallery 𝓡𝓡 Collectors of Stickley and other Arts and Crafts furniture will not want to miss this impressive gallery, which is located in one of the historic buildings at Joesler Village shopping plaza. In addition to the furniture, there are period paintings and accessories. At Joesler Village, 4425 N. Campbell Ave. ℂ 520/577-7711. www.ericfirestonegallery.com.

Michael D. Higgins & Son Located next door to the Eric Firestone Gallery, this little shop specializes in pre-Columbian artifacts but also carries African, Asian, and even ancient Greek and Roman pieces. At Joesler Village, 4429 N. Campbell Ave. ℂ 520/577-8330. www.mhiggins.com.

Morning Star Antiques In a shop that adjoins Morning Star Traders (see "Native American Art, Crafts & Jewelry," below), Morning Star Antiques carries an excellent selection of antique Spanish and Mexican furniture, as well as other unusual and rustic pieces. 2000 E. Speedway Blvd. ℂ 520/881-3060. www.morningstartraders.com.

Primitive Arts Gallery This is the best gallery in Tucson for pre-Columbian art, with an eclectic mix of ancient artifacts focusing on ceramics. You'll also find a smattering of other artifacts, from Greek urns to contemporary Argentine *mate* gourds. At Broadway Village, 3026 E. Broadway. ℂ 520/326-4852.

ART

Tucson's gallery scene is not as concentrated as that in many other cities. Most Tucson galleries have in the past few years abandoned downtown in favor of the foothills and other more affluent suburbs. The current art hot spot is the corner of Campbell Avenue and Skyline Drive, where you'll find **El Cortijo,** a stylishly modern Southwestern shopping plaza that has several contemporary art galleries and an upscale restaurant. Behind this complex, at 6420 N. Campbell Ave., is a small courtyard complex that is home to **Sanders Galleries** (ℂ 520/299-1763; www.sandersgalleries.com) and **Settlers West Galleries** (ℂ 520/299-2607; www.settlerswest.com), both of which specialize in Western art, as well as **Gallery West** (see below).

Davis Dominguez Gallery Located just a couple of blocks off Fourth Avenue in downtown Tucson, this huge gallery features some of the best and most creative contemporary art in the city. A couple of other contemporary art galleries on the same block make this the best place in Tucson to see cutting-edge art. 154 E. Sixth St. ℂ 866/629-9759 or 520/629-9759. www.davisdominguez.com.

El Presidio Gallery Long one of Tucson's premier galleries, El Presidio deals primarily in traditional and contemporary paintings of the Southwest, and is located in a large, modern space in El Cortijo Arts Annex. Contemporary works tend toward the large and bright, and are favorites for decorating foothills homes. At El Cortijo Arts Annex, 3001 E. Skyline Dr. ℂ 800/487-7069 or 520/299-1414. www.elpresidiogallery.com.

Etherton Gallery For more than 25 years, this gallery has been presenting some of the most distinctive art to be found in Tucson, including contemporary and historical photographs. A favorite of museums and serious collectors, Etherton Gallery isn't afraid to present work with strong themes. 135 S. Sixth Ave. ℂ 520/624-7370. www.etherton gallery.com. Also a smaller location at the Temple of Music and Art, 330 S. Scott Ave. (ℂ 520/624-7370).

Jane Hamilton Fine Art   This gallery's boldly colored contemporary art really stands out, and much of the artwork reflects a desert aesthetic. At Joesler Village, 1825 E. River Rd., Suite 111. ⓒ 800/555-3051 or 520/529-4886. www.janehamiltonfineart.com.

Mark Sublette Medicine Man Gallery 𝒦𝒦𝒦   This gallery has the finest and most tasteful traditional Western art you'll find just about anywhere in Arizona. Artists represented include Ed Mell, Maynard Dixon, and Howard Post, and most of the gallery's artists have received national attention. There's an excellent selection of Native American crafts as well; see "Native American Art, Crafts & Jewelry," below, for more details. The gallery is also the site of the Conley Museum of the West, a small collection of Western art and old maps. There's another Mark Sublette Gallery in the foothills at 2890 E. Skyline Dr., Suite 190 (ⓒ **520/299-7798**). At Santa Fe Sq., 7000 E. Tanque Verde Rd. ⓒ 800/422-9382 or 520/722-7798. www.medicinemangallery.com.

Philabaum Contemporary Art Glass   For more than 25 years, this gallery has been exposing Tucson to the latest trends in contemporary glass art. The gallery is full of lovely and colorful pieces by Tucson's own Tom Philabaum and more than 100 other artists from around the country. In St. Philip's Plaza, 4280 N. Campbell Ave., Suite 105. ⓒ **520/299-1939**. www.philabaumglass.com.

BOOKS

Chain bookstores in the Tucson area include **Barnes & Noble,** 5130 E. Broadway Blvd. (ⓒ **520/512-1166**) and 7325 N. La Cholla Blvd., Suite 100, in the Foothills Mall (ⓒ **520/742-6402**); and **Borders,** 4235 N. Oracle Rd. (ⓒ **520/292-1331**) and 5870 E. Broadway Blvd., at the Park Place Mall (ⓒ **520/584-0111**).

Bookman's   This big bookstore, housed in a former supermarket, is crammed full of used books and recordings, and has long been a favorite of Tucsonans. There are other Bookman's stores at 6230 E. Speedway Blvd. (ⓒ **520/748-9555**) and 3733 W. Ina Rd. (ⓒ **520/579-0303**). 1930 E. Grant Rd. ⓒ 520/325-5767. www.bookmans.com.

Clues Unlimited   If you forgot to pack your vacation reading, drop by this fun little store. Not only can you shop for the latest Carl Hiassen or other mystery, but you can say hi to Sophie, the resident pot-bellied pig. Broadway Village, 123 S. Eastbourne St. ⓒ 520/326-8533. www.cluesunlimited.com.

CRAFTS

Details Art & Design   If you enjoy highly imaginative and colorful crafts with a sense of humor, you'll get a kick out of this place. Unexpected objets d'art turn up in the forms of clocks, ceramics, glass, and other media. At El Cortijo Gallery Row, 3001 E. Skyline Dr., no. 103. ⓒ 520/577-1995. www.detailsart.com.

Obsidian Gallery   Contemporary crafts by nationally recognized artists fill this gallery. You'll find luminous glass art, unique and daring jewelry, imaginative ceramics, and much more. At St. Philip's Plaza, 4320 N. Campbell Ave. (at River Rd.). ⓒ **520/577-3598**. www.obsidian-gallery.com.

Old Town Artisans 𝒦   Housed in a restored 1850s adobe building covering an entire city block of El Presidio Historic District, this unique shopping plaza houses half a dozen different shops brimming with traditional and contemporary Southwestern designs. There's also free Wi-Fi in the courtyard here. 201 N. Court Ave. ⓒ 800/782-8072 or 520/623-6024. www.oldtownartisans.com.

Tucson Museum of Art Shop   The museum's gift shop offers a colorful and changing selection of Southwestern crafts, mostly by local and regional artists. 140 N. Main Ave. C 520/624-2333. www.tucsonarts.com.

FASHION

See also the listing for the Beth Friedman Collection under "Jewelry," below. For cowboy and cowgirl attire, see "Western Wear," below.

Dark Star Leather   If you're in the market for a distinctive leather jacket, belt, or purse, be sure to stop by this little locally owned shop in Plaza Palomino. Exotic leathers are used in the one-of-a-kind designs. You can sometimes find great deals on sale items. At Plaza Palomino, 2940 N. Swan Rd. C 520/881-4700. www.darkstarleather.com.

Maya Palace   This shop features ethnic-inspired but sophisticated women's clothing in natural fabrics. The friendly staff helps customers of all ages put together a Southwestern chic look, from casual to dressy. Shops can also be found at El Mercado, 6332 E. Broadway Blvd. (C 520/748-0817), and at Casas Adobes Plaza, 7057 N. Oracle Rd. (C 520/575-8028). At Plaza Palomino, 2960 N. Swan Rd. C 520/325-6411. www. mayapalacetucson.com.

Rochelle K Fine Women's Apparel   With everything from the latest in the little black dress to drapey silks and casual linens, Rochelle K attracts a well-heeled clientele. You'll also find beautiful accessories and jewelry here. At Casas Adobes Plaza, 7039 N. Oracle Rd. (C 520/797-2279. www.rochellek.com.

GIFTS & SOUVENIRS

Native Seeds/SEARCH *Finds*   Gardeners, cooks, and just about anyone in search of an unusual gift will likely be fascinated by this tiny shop, which is operated by a nonprofit organization dedicated to preserving the biodiversity offered by native Southwest seeds. The shelves are full of heirloom beans, corn, chiles, and other seeds from a wide variety of native desert plants. There are also gourds and inexpensive Tarahumara Indian baskets, bottled sauces and salsas made from native plants, and books about native agriculture. 526 N. Fourth Ave. C 866/622-5561 or 520/622-5561. www.nativeseeds.org.

Picánte Designs   The plethora of Hispanic-themed icons and accessories here include *milagros,* Day of the Dead skeletons, Mexican crosses, jewelry, greeting cards, and folk art from around the world. This is a great place to shop for distinctive south-of-the-border kitschy gifts. 2932 E. Broadway. C 520/320-5699.

Tohono Chul Museum Shops *Finds*   The two shops here are packed with Mexican folk art, nature-themed toys, household items, T-shirts, and books. These shops are an absolute must after a visit to surrounding Tohono Chul Park, which is landscaped with desert plants. Add a meal at the park's tearoom, and you've got a good afternoon's outing. For a description of the park, see p. 370. 7366 N. Paseo del Norte (1 block west of the corner of Ina and Oracle roads in Tohono Chul Park). C 520/742-6455. www.tohonochulpark.org.

JEWELRY

In addition to the stores mentioned below, see the listing for the Obsidian Gallery under "Crafts," above.

Beth Friedman Collection   This shop sells a well-chosen collection of jewelry by Native American craftspeople and international designers. It also carries some extravagant cowgirl get-ups in velvet and lace, as well as contemporary women's fashions. At Joesler Village, 1865 E. River Rd., Suite 121. ℂ 520/577-6858. www.bethfriedmanonline.com.

Turquoise Door   The contemporary Southwestern jewelry here is among the most stunning in the city, made with opals, diamonds, lapis lazuli, amethysts, and the ubiquitous turquoise. At St. Philip's Plaza, 4330 N. Campbell Ave. (at River Rd.). ℂ 520/299-7787. www. turquoisedoorjewelry.com.

MALLS & SHOPPING CENTERS

Plaza Palomino   Built in the style of a Spanish hacienda with a courtyard and fountains, this little shopping center is home to some of Tucson's most interesting specialty shops, as well as galleries and restaurants. There's a farmers' market here on Saturday mornings. Southeast corner of North Swan and Fort Lowell roads. ℂ 520/320-6344. www.plaza palomino.com.

St. Philip's Plaza   This upscale Southwestern-style shopping center contains a couple of good restaurants, a luxury beauty salon/day spa, and numerous shops and galleries, including Bahti Indian Arts and Turquoise Door jewelry. On Sunday mornings, there is a farmers' market. Makes a great one-stop Tucson shopping outing. 4280 N. Campbell Ave. (at River Rd.). ℂ 520/529-2775. www.stphilipsplaza.com.

Tucson Mall   The foothills of northern Tucson have become shopping-center central, and this is the largest of the malls. You'll find more than 200 retailers in this busy, two-story skylit complex. 4500 N. Oracle Rd. ℂ 520/293-7330. www.shoptucsonmall.com.

NATIVE AMERICAN ART, CRAFTS & JEWELRY

Bahti Indian Arts   Family-owned for more than 50 years, this store sells exquisitely made Native American crafts—jewelry, baskets, sculpture, paintings, books, weavings, kachina dolls, Zuni fetishes, and much more. At St. Philip's Plaza, 4280 N. Campbell Ave., Suite 100. ℂ 520/577-0290. www.bahti.com.

Gallery West   Located right below Anthony's in the Catalinas restaurant, this tiny shop specializes in very expensive Native American artifacts (mostly pre-1940s) such as New Mexico Pueblo pots, Apache and Pima baskets, 19th-century Plains Indian beadwork, Navajo weavings, and kachinas. There is also plenty of both contemporary and vintage jewelry. 6420 N. Campbell Ave. (at Skyline Dr.). ℂ 520/529-7002. www.indianartwest.com.

Kaibab Courtyard Shops ♠   In business since 1945, this store offers one of the best selections of Native American art and crafts in Tucson. You can find high-quality jewelry, Mexican pottery and folk arts, home furnishings, glassware, kachinas, and rugs. 2837–2841 N. Campbell Ave. ℂ 520/795-6905.

Mark Sublette Medicine Man Gallery   This shop has the best and biggest selection of old Navajo rugs in the city, and perhaps even in the entire state. There are also Mexican and other Hispanic textiles, Acoma pottery, basketry, and other Indian crafts, as well as artwork by cowboy artists. The gallery is the site of the Conley Museum of the West. There's another Mark Sublette Gallery in the foothills at 2890 E. Skyline Dr., Suite 190 (ℂ 520/299-7798). At Santa Fe Sq., 7000 E. Tanque Verde Rd. ℂ 800/422-9382 or 520/722-7798. www.medicinemangallery.com.

Morning Star Traders ♠♠♠   With hardwood floors and a museum-like atmosphere, this store features museum-quality goods: antique Navajo rugs, kachinas, furniture, and a huge selection of old Native American jewelry. This just may be the best store of its type in the entire state. An adjoining shop, Morning Star Antiques, carries an impressive selection of antique furniture (see "Antiques & Collectibles," above). 2020 E. Speedway Blvd. ℂ 520/881-2112. www.morningstartraders.com.

Silverbell Trading   Not your run-of-the-mill crafts store, Silverbell specializes in regional Native American artwork, such as baskets and pottery, and carries unique pieces that the shop owner handpicks. Items such as stone Navajo corn maidens, Zuni fetishes, and figures carved from sandstone are among the highlights. At Casas Adobes Plaza, 7119 N. Oracle Rd. ℂ 520/797-6852. www.silverbelltrader.com.

WESTERN WEAR

Arizona Hatters   Arizona Hatters carries the best names in cowboy hats, from Stetson to Bailey to Resistol, and the shop specializes in custom-fitting hats to the customer's head and face. You'll also find bolo ties, belts, and other accessories here. 2790 N. Campbell Ave. ℂ 520/292-1320. www.azhatters.com.

Stewart Boot Manufacturing Co.   Boots that fit so well you don't even need socks. That's how a Tucson friend described the custom-made cowboy boots turned out by this South Tucson bootmaker. You'll have to wait for your boots, though, since all the boots sold here are made to order. 30 W. 28th St. ℂ 520/622-2706.

11 Tucson After Dark

The **Downtown Arts District** is the center of the action, with the Temple of Music and Art, the Tucson Convention Center Music Hall, and several nightclubs. The **University of Arizona campus,** a mile away, is another hot spot for entertainment.

The free *Tucson Weekly* contains thorough listings of concerts, theater and dance performances, and club offerings. The entertainment section of the *Arizona Daily Star* ("Caliente") and the *Tucson Citizen*'s "Calendar" both come out each Thursday and are good sources of information for what's going on around town.

THE CLUB & MUSIC SCENE
COUNTRY

Cactus Moon Café   A 20- to 40-something crowd frequents this large and glitzy nightclub, which features primarily country music (with dance lessons several nights each week). Keep in mind, though, that some nights of the week may have rock instead of country. Check the schedule before putting on your boots. 5470 E. Broadway Blvd. (at Craycroft Rd.). ℂ 520/748-0049. www.cactusmoon.net. Cover $2–$5.

The Maverick: King of Clubs   The Maverick, in different incarnations and different locations around town, has been Tucson's favorite country music dance club since 1962. Currently it's located in a modern space out in east Tucson and is open Tuesday through Sunday nights, with live country music Thursday through Saturday nights. 6622 E. Tanque Verde Rd. ℂ 520/298-0430. mavericktucson.com. No cover to $5.

DANCE CLUB

El Parador Restaurant   Tropical decor and an abundance of potted plants set the mood for live Latin dance music and salsa lessons on Friday nights. The music starts at 9:30pm and dance lessons start at 10:15pm. On Saturday, DJs spin more salsa music, and every other Saturday night there's a live band. Customers of this "all ages" club range from 20- to 60-somethings. 2744 E. Broadway. ℂ 520/881-2808. www.elparador tucson.com. Cover $6.

JAZZ

To find out what's happening on the local jazz scene, contact the **Tucson Jazz Society** ((C) **520/903-1265;** www.tucsonjazz.org). This organization's website lists various jazz nights at restaurants all over Tucson. Some of those restaurants include **Old Pueblo Grill,** 60 N. Alvernon Way ((C) **520/326-6000**), with live jazz on Sunday nights; and **Acacia at St. Philip's Plaza,** 4340 N. Campbell Ave. ((C) **520/232-0101**), with live jazz Thursday through Saturday nights, plus a jazz brunch on Sunday.

The Grill 𝄐𝄐   No other jazz venue in Tucson has more flavor of the Southwest than this restaurant lounge, perched high on a ridge-top overlooking the city. There's live music (mostly jazz) Thursday through Sunday nights. At Hacienda del Sol Guest Ranch Resort, 5601 N. Hacienda del Sol Rd. (C) 520/529-3500. www.haciendadelsol.com.

MARIACHI

Tucson is the mariachi capital of the United States, and no one should visit without spending at least one evening listening to some of these strolling minstrels.

La Fuente 𝄐𝄐   La Fuente is one of the largest Mexican restaurants in Tucson and serves up good food, but what really draws the crowds is the live mariachi music. If you just want to listen and not have dinner, you can hang out in the lounge. The mariachis perform Wednesday through Sunday nights. 1749 N. Oracle Rd. (C) 520/623-8659. www.lafuenterestaurant.com.

ROCK, BLUES & REGGAE

Chicago Bar   Transplanted Chicagoans love to watch their home teams on the TVs at this neighborhood bar, but there's also live music nightly. Sure, blues gets played a lot, but so do reggae and rock and about everything in between. 5954 E. Speedway Blvd. (C) 520/748-8169. www.chicagobartucson.com. No cover to $5.

Club Congress   Just off the lobby of the restored Hotel Congress (now a budget hotel catering to younger travelers), Club Congress is Tucson's main alternative-music venue. There are usually a couple of nights of live music each week, and over the years such bands as Nirvana, Dick Dale, and the Goo Goo Dolls have played here, although more recently, the club has tended to book primarily local and regional acts. 311 E. Congress St. (C) 520/622-8848. www.hotelcongress.com. Cover $4–$15.

The Rialto Theatre   This renovated 1919 vaudeville theater, although not a nightclub, is now Tucson's main venue for performances by bands that are too big to play across the street at Club Congress (Shawn Colvin, Los Lobos, Beck). 318 E. Congress St. (C) 520/740-1000. www.rialtotheatre.com. Tickets $10–$35.

THE BAR, LOUNGE & PUB SCENE

Arizona Inn   If you're looking for a quiet, comfortable scene, the piano music in the Audubon Lounge at the Arizona Inn is sure to soothe your soul. The lounge, which has been restored to its original appearance, has a classic feel, and the resort's gardens are beautiful. 2200 E. Elm St. (C) 520/325-1541.

Cascade Lounge 𝄐   This is Tucson's ultimate piano bar. With a view of the Catalinas, the plush lounge is perfect for romance or relaxation at the start or end of a night on the town. Tuesday through Sunday nights, there's live piano music or a jazz band, and on Fridays and Saturdays, there's a DJ and dancing. At Loews Ventana Canyon Resort, 7000 N. Resort Dr. (C) 520/299-2020.

Cushing Street Bar & Restaurant   Located on the edge of the Barrio Histórico district just south of the Tucson Convention Center, this restaurant/bar is in a historic adobe building and has loads of old Tucson character. There's also live music on weekends. 198 W. Cushing St. (✆ 520/622-7984. www.cushingstreet.com.

58° & Holding   This combination wine shop and wine bar in east Tucson is a good bet for a glass or two of wine in a relaxing setting. There are Wednesday-night wine tastings as well. There's a second wine bar in the foothills at St. Philip's Plaza, 4280 Campbell Rd., Suite 27 & 55 (✆ **520/299-5804**). 5340 E. Broadway Blvd. (✆ **520/747-5858**. www.58degrees.com.

Gentle Ben's Brewing Co.   Located just off the UA campus, Gentle Ben's, a big, modern place with plenty of outdoor seating, is Tucson's favorite microbrewery and, not surprisingly, attracts primarily a college crowd. 865 E. University Blvd. (✆ 520/624-4177. www.gentlebens.com.

Nimbus Brewing ✪   Located in a warehouse district on the south side of Tucson, this brewpub is basically the front room of Nimbus's brewing and bottling facility. The beer is good, and there's live bluegrass, rock, or jazz on a regular basis. Hard to find, and definitely a local scene. 3850 E. 44th St. (2 blocks east of Palo Verde Rd.). (✆ **520/745-9175**. www.nimbusbeer.com.

Thunder Canyon Brewery   This big brewpub is your best bet in Tucson for handcrafted ales and is the most convenient brewpub for anyone staying at a foothills resort. At Foothills Mall, 7401 N. La Cholla Blvd. (at Ina Rd.). (✆ **520/797-2652**. www.thundercanyon brewery.com.

¡Toma! ✪   This bar, set in El Presidio Historic District and owned by the family that operates El Charro Café next door, has a fun and festive atmosphere complete with a Mexican hat fountain/sculpture in the courtyard. Drop by for cheap margaritas during happy hour (daily 3–6pm). 311 N. Court Ave. (✆ **520/622-1922**.

COCKTAILS WITH A VIEW

Most of the best views in town are at foothills resorts; luckily, they don't mind sharing with nonguests. The lounge at **Anthony's in the Catalinas** also has a great view.

Desert Garden Lounge   If you'd like a close-up view of the Santa Catalina Mountains, drop by the Desert Garden Lounge (at sunset, perhaps). The large lounge has live piano music several nights a week. At The Westin La Paloma, 3800 E. Sunrise Dr. (✆ 520/742-6000.

SPORTS BARS

Famous Sam's   With nearly a dozen branches around the city, Famous Sam's (www.famoussams.com) keeps a lot of Tucson's sports fans happy with its cheap prices and large portions. Other convenient locations include 7930 E. Speedway Blvd. (✆ **520/290-9666**) and 2320 N. Silverbell Rd. (✆ **520/884-7267**). 1830 E. Broadway Blvd. (✆ **520/884-0119**.

GAY & LESBIAN BARS & CLUBS

To find out about other gay bars around town, keep an eye out for the *Observer*, Tucson's newspaper for the gay, lesbian, and bisexual community. You'll find it at **Antigone Books**, 411 N. Fourth Ave. (✆ **520/792-3715;** www.antigonebooks.com), as well as at the bars listed here.

Ain't Nobody's Bizness   Located in a small shopping plaza in midtown, this bar has long been *the* lesbian gathering spot in Tucson. There are pool tables, a dance floor, and a quiet, smoke-free room where you can duck out of the noise. Lately, this bar has also been doing nights for gay men as well, so check the schedule. 2900 E. Broadway Blvd., Suite 118. ℭ 520/318-4838. www.aintnobodysbizness-az.com.

IBT's   Located on funky Fourth Avenue, IBT's has long been the most popular gay men's dance bar in town. The music ranges from 1980s retro to hip-hop, and regular drag shows add to the fun. There's always an interesting crowd. 616 N. Fourth Ave. ℭ 520/882-3053. www.ibts.net.

THE PERFORMING ARTS

To a certain extent, Tucson is a clone of Phoenix when it comes to the performing arts. Three of Tucson's major companies—the Arizona Opera Company, Ballet Arizona, and the Arizona Theatre Company—spend half their time in Phoenix. This means that whatever gets staged in Phoenix also gets staged in Tucson. This city does, however, have its own symphony and manages to sustain a diversified theater scene as well.

Usually, the best way to purchase tickets is directly from the company's box office. Tickets to Tucson Convention Center events (but not the symphony or the opera) and other venues around town may be available by calling **Ticketmaster** (ℭ **520/321-1000;** www.ticketmaster.com) or by stopping by the **TCC box office,** 250 S. Church Ave. (ℭ **520/791-4101;** www.cityoftucson.org/tcc).

OUTDOOR VENUES & SERIES

Weather permitting, Tucsonans head to Reid Park's **DeMeester Outdoor Performance Center,** at Country Club Road and East 22nd Street (ℭ **520/791-4873**), for performances under the stars. This amphitheater stages live theater performances, as well as frequent concerts.

Performing-Arts Centers & Concert Halls

Tucson's largest performance venue is the **Tucson Convention Center (TCC) Music Hall,** 260 S. Church Ave. (ℭ **520/791-4101;** www.cityoftucson.org/tcc). It's the home of the Tucson Symphony Orchestra and where the Arizona Opera Company usually performs when it's in town.

The centerpiece of the Tucson theater scene is the **Temple of Music and Art,** 330 S. Scott Ave. (ℭ **520/622-2823**), a restored historic theater dating from 1927. The 605-seat Alice Holsclaw Theatre is the Temple's main stage, but there's also the 90-seat Cabaret Theatre.

University of Arizona Centennial Hall, 1020 E. University Blvd. at Park Avenue (ℭ **520/621-3341;** www.uapresents.org), on the UA campus, is Tucson's other main performance hall. It stages performances by touring national musical acts, international companies, and Broadway shows.

The **Center for the Arts Proscenium Theatre,** Pima Community College (West Campus), 2202 W. Anklam Rd. (ℭ **520/206-6986**), is another good place to check for classical music performances. It offers a wide variety of shows.

The **Tucson Jazz Society** (© 520/903-1265; www.tucsonjazz.org), which manages to book a few well-known jazz musicians each year, sponsors different series at various locations around the city. Tickets are usually between $15 and $30.

CLASSICAL MUSIC, OPERA & DANCE

Both the **Tucson Symphony Orchestra** (© 520/882-8585 or 520/792-9155; www.tucsonsymphony.org), which is the oldest continuously performing symphony in the Southwest, and the **Arizona Opera Company** (© 520/293-4336 or 520/321-1000; www.azopera.com), the state's premier opera company, perform at the Tucson Convention Center Music Hall. Symphony tickets run $18 to $47; opera tickets are $35 to $140.

THEATER

Arizona Theatre Company (ATC; © 520/622-2823; www.aztheatreco.org), which performs at the Temple of Music and Art, splits its time between Tucson, Phoenix, and Mesa, and is the state's top professional theater company. Each season sees a mix of comedy, drama, and Broadway-style musical shows; tickets cost $27 to $48.

The **Invisible Theatre,** 1400 N. First Ave. (© 520/882-9721; www.invisible theatre.com), a tiny theater in a converted laundry building, has been home to Tucson's most experimental theater for more than 35 years (it does off-Broadway shows and musicals). Tickets go for about $22 to $25.

The West just wouldn't be the West without good old-fashioned melodramas, and the **Gaslight Theatre,** 7010 E. Broadway Blvd. (© 520/886-9428; www.grand matonyspizza.com), is where evil villains, stalwart heroes, and defenseless heroines pound the boards. You can boo and hiss, cheer and sigh as the predictable stories unfold on stage. It's all great fun for kids and adults, with plenty of pop-culture references thrown into the mix. Tickets are $16 for adults, $14 for students and seniors, and $7 for children 12 and under. Performances are held Tuesday through Sunday, with two shows nightly Tuesday through Saturday, plus a Sunday matinee. Tickets sell out a month in advance, so get them as soon as possible. On Monday nights, you can catch interesting live music performances.

12

Phoenix, Scottsdale & the Valley of the Sun

Forget the stately cacti and cowboys riding off into the sunset; think Los Angeles without the Pacific. While the nation has carefully nurtured its image of Phoenix as a desert cow town, this city in the Sonoran Desert has rocketed into the 21st century and become the fifth-largest city in the country. Sprawling across more than 500 square miles of what once was cactus and creosote bushes, the greater Phoenix metropolitan area, also known as the Valley of the Sun (or, more commonly, just the Valley), is now a major metropolitan area replete with dozens of resort hotels, fabulous restaurants, excellent museums, hundreds of golf courses, world-class shopping, four pro sports teams, and a red-hot nightlife scene.

Sure, it also has traffic jams and smog, but at the end of the day, it can usually claim to have had beautiful sunny weather. Sunshine and blue skies, day after day after day, have made this one of the most popular winter destinations in the country. When Chicago weather forecasts call for snow and subzero temperatures, you can have a hard time getting a tee time on a Phoenix-area golf course. Phoenicians may get the summertime blues when temperatures hit the triple digits, but from September to May, the climate here can verge on perfect—warm enough in the daytime for lounging by the pool, cool enough at night to require a jacket.

With green lawns, orange groves, swimming pools, and palm trees, it's easy to forget that Phoenix is in the middle of the desert. Water channeled in from distant reservoirs has allowed this city to flourish like a desert oasis. However, if you find yourself wondering where the desert is, you need only lift your eyes to one of the many mountains that rise amid the suburban sprawl. South Mountain, Camelback Mountain, Mummy Mountain, Piestewa Peak, Papago Buttes, Pinnacle Peak—these rugged, rocky summits have been preserved in their natural states, and it is to these cactus-covered uplands that the city's citizens retreat when they've had enough asphalt and air-conditioning. From almost anywhere in the Valley, you're no more than a 15- or 20-minute drive from a natural area where you can commune with cacti while gazing out across a bustling, modern city.

Best of all, at the end of the day, you can retreat to a comfortable bed at one of the country's top resorts.

1 Orientation

ARRIVING

BY PLANE Centrally located 3 miles east of downtown Phoenix, **Sky Harbor International Airport,** 3400 E. Sky Harbor Blvd. (© **602/273-3300;** www.phxsky harbor.com), has three terminals, with a free 24-hour shuttle bus offering frequent

---

Tips **A Name Change**

In 2003, the official name of Phoenix's Squaw Peak was changed to Piestewa Peak (pronounced Pie-ess-too-uh) to honor Pfc. Lori Ann Piestewa, a member of the Hopi tribe and the first female soldier killed in the Iraq War. The peak in north Phoenix has long been a popular hiking destination. If you hear people referring to both Squaw Peak and Piestewa Peak, it's one and the same place. Ditto for the Squaw Peak Parkway, which is now Piestewa Freeway.

---

service between them. For lost and found, call $\textcircled{C}$ 602/273-3307. For information on airlines serving Phoenix, see chapter 2.

There are two entrances to the airport. The west entrance can be accessed from either the Papago Freeway (I-10) or 24th Street, while the east entrance can be accessed from the Hohokam Expressway (Ariz. 143) or the Sky Harbor Expressway (Ariz. 153), which is an extension of 44th Street. If you're headed to downtown Phoenix, leave by way of the 24th Street exit and continue west on Washington Street. If you're headed to Scottsdale, Tempe, or Mesa, head east out of the airport and follow signs for Arizona 202 Loop.

SuperShuttle ($\textcircled{C}$ 800/BLUE-VAN or 602/244-9000; www.supershuttle.com) offers 24-hour door-to door van service between Sky Harbor Airport and resorts, hotels, and homes throughout the Valley. Per-person fares average $7 to $12 to the downtown and Tempe area, $16 to downtown Scottsdale, and $30 to $35 to north Scottsdale.

Taxis can be found outside all three terminals and cost only slightly more than shuttle vans. You can also call **AAA Cab** ($\textcircled{C}$ 602/437-4000), **Discount Cab** ($\textcircled{C}$ 602/200-2000), or **Allstate Cab** ($\textcircled{C}$ 602/275-8888). A taxi from the airport to downtown Phoenix will cost around $16; to Scottsdale, between $20 and $35.

Valley Metro ($\textcircled{C}$ 602/253-5000; www.valleymetro.org) provides public bus service throughout the Valley, with the Red Line operating between the airport and downtown Phoenix, Tempe, and Mesa. The Red Line runs daily starting between 3:30 and 5:30am and continues operating until between 10:30pm and 1am, depending on the day of the week and whether you are traveling east or west. The ride from the airport to downtown takes about 20 minutes and costs $1.25. There is no direct bus to Scottsdale, so you would first need to go to Tempe and then transfer to a northbound bus. You can pick up a copy of the *Bus Book,* a guide and route map for the Valley Metro bus system, at airport information desks or at Central Station, which is at the corner of Central Avenue and Van Buren Street.

BY CAR   Phoenix is connected to Los Angeles and Tucson by I-10 and to Flagstaff via I-17. If you're headed to Scottsdale, the easiest route is to take the Red Mountain Freeway (Ariz. 202) east to US 101 N. US 101 loops all the way around the east, north, and west sides of the Valley. The Superstition Freeway (US 60) leads to Tempe, Mesa, and Chandler.

BY TRAIN   There is no passenger rail service to Phoenix. **Amtrak** ($\textcircled{C}$ 800/872-7245; www.amtrak.com) will sell you a ticket to Phoenix, but you'll have to take a shuttle bus from either Flagstaff or Tucson. The scheduling is so horrible on these routes that you'd have to be a total masochist to opt for Amtrak service to Phoenix.

VISITOR INFORMATION

You'll find **tourist information desks** in all three terminals at Sky Harbor Airport. The city's main visitor center is the **Greater Phoenix Convention & Visitors Bureau,** 50 N. Second St. (© **877/225-5749** or 602/452-6282; www.visitphoenix.com), on the corner of Adams Street in downtown Phoenix. There's also a small visitor information center at the Biltmore Fashion Park shopping center, at Camelback Road and 24th Street (© **602/957-0380**).

The **Visitor Information Line** (© **602/252-5588**) has recorded information about current events in Phoenix and is updated weekly.

If you're staying in Scottsdale, you can get information at the **Scottsdale Convention & Visitors Bureau Visitor Center,** Galleria Corporate Center, 4343 N. Scottsdale Rd., Suite 170 (© **800/782-1117** or 480/421-1004; www.scottsdalecvb.com).

CITY LAYOUT

MAIN ARTERIES & STREETS   **US Loop 101** forms a loop around the east, north, and west sides of the Valley, providing freeway access to Scottsdale from I-17 on the north side of Phoenix and from US 60 in Tempe.

I-17 (Black Canyon Fwy.), which connects Phoenix with Flagstaff, is the city's main north-south freeway. This freeway curves to the east just south of downtown (where it is renamed the **Maricopa Fwy.** and merges with I-10). **I-10,** which connects Phoenix with Los Angeles and Tucson, is called the **Papago Freeway** on the west side of the Valley and as it passes north of downtown; as it curves around to pass to the west and south of the airport, it merges with I-17 and is renamed the Maricopa Freeway. At Tempe, this freeway curves to the south and heads out of the Valley.

North of the airport, **Arizona 202 (Red Mountain Fwy.)** heads east from I-10 and passes along the north side of Tempe, providing access to downtown Tempe, Arizona State University, Mesa, and Scottsdale (via US Loop 101). On the east side of the airport, **Arizona 143 (Hohokam Expwy.)** connects Arizona 202 with I-10.

At the interchange of I-10 and Arizona 202, northwest of Sky Harbor Airport, **Arizona 51 (Piestewa Fwy.)** heads north through the center of Phoenix to US Loop 101 and is the best north-south route in the city.

South of the airport off I-10, **US 60 (Superstition Fwy.)** heads east to Tempe, Chandler, Mesa, and Gilbert. **US Loop 101** leads north from US 60 (and Ariz. 202) through Scottsdale and across the north side of Phoenix to connect with I-17. US 60 and US 101 provide the best route from the airport to the Scottsdale resorts. US Loop 101 also heads south through Chandler to connect with I-10. This section is called the Price Freeway. The section of this freeway north through Scottsdale is called the Pima Freeway.

Secondary highways in the Valley include the **Beeline Highway (Ariz. 87),** which starts at the east end of Arizona 202 (Red Mountain Fwy.) in Mesa and leads to Payson, and **Grand Avenue (US 60),** which starts downtown and leads west to Sun City and Wickenburg.

Phoenix and the surrounding cities of Mesa, Tempe, Scottsdale, and Chandler, and even those cities farther out in the Valley, are laid out in a grid pattern with major avenues and roads about every mile. For traveling east to west across Phoenix, your best choices (other than the above-mentioned freeways) are Camelback Road, Indian School Road, and McDowell Road. For traveling north and south, 44th Street, 24th Street, and Central Avenue are good choices. Hayden Road is a north-south alternative to Scottsdale Road, which gets jammed at rush hours.

FINDING AN ADDRESS   Central Avenue, which runs north to south through downtown Phoenix, is the starting point for all east-and-west street numbering. **Washington Street** is the starting point for north and south numbering. North-to-south numbered *streets* are to be found on the east side of the city, while north-to-south numbered *avenues* will be found on the west. For the most part, street numbers advance by 100 with each block. Odd-numbered addresses are on the south and east sides of streets, while even-numbered addresses are on the north and west sides of streets.

For example, if you're looking for 4454 E. Camelback Rd., you'll find it 44 blocks east of Central Avenue between 44th and 45th streets on the north side of the street. If you're looking for 2905 N. 35th Ave., you'll find it 35 blocks west of Central Avenue and 29 blocks north of Washington Street on the east side of the street. Just for general reference, Camelback Road marks the 5000 block north. Also, whenever getting directions, ask for the cross street closest to where you're going.

2 Getting Around
BY CAR

Phoenix and the surrounding cities that together make up the Valley of the Sun sprawl across more than 400 square miles, so if you want to make the best use of your time, it's essential to have a car. Outside downtown Phoenix, there's almost always plenty of free parking wherever you go (although finding a parking space can be time-consuming in Old Scottsdale and at some of the more popular malls and shopping plazas). If you want to feel like a local, opt for the ubiquitous valet parking (just be sure to keep plenty of small bills on hand for tipping the parking attendants).

Because Phoenix is a major tourist destination, good car-rental rates are often available. However, taxes and surcharges on rentals at Sky Harbor Airport now run 50% or more, which pretty much negates any deal you might get on your rate. Expect to pay anywhere from $160 to $250 per week ($225–$370 with taxes) for a compact car in the high season. See chapter 2 for general tips on car rentals.

All major rental-car companies have desks at Sky Harbor Airport's Rental Car Center, which is separate from the airport terminals and is served by a free shuttle bus. Be sure to leave time in your schedule to get from the Rental Car Center to the correct terminal for your flight. There are also plenty of other car-rental offices in Phoenix and Scottsdale. Rental-car companies at the airport include the following: **Advantage** (© 800/777-5500 or 602/244-0450), **Alamo** ((© 800/462-5266 or 602/244-0897), **Avis** (© 800/331-1212 or 602/261-5900), **Budget** (© 800/527-0700 or 602/261-5950), **Dollar** (© 800/800-3665 or 866/434-2226), **Enterprise** (© 800/261-7331 or 602/225-0588), **Hertz** (© 800/654-3131 or 602/267-8822), **National** (© 800/227-7368 or 602/275-4771), **Payless** (© 800/729-5377 or 602/681-9589), and **Thrifty** (© 800/847-4389 or 877/283-0898).

BY PUBLIC TRANSPORTATION

The free **Downtown Area Shuttle (DASH)** provides bus service within the downtown area Monday through Friday from 6:30am to 11pm. These buses serve regular stops every 6 to 18 minutes; they're primarily for downtown workers, but attractions along the route include the state capitol and Heritage and Science Park. In Tempe, **Free Local Area Shuttle (FLASH)** buses provide a similar service on a loop around Arizona State University. The route includes Mill Avenue and Sun Devil Stadium. For information on both DASH and FLASH, call © **602/253-5000.**

In Scottsdale, you can ride the **Scottsdale Trolley** (© 480/421-1004; www.valley metro.org) shuttle buses between Scottsdale Fashion Square, the Fifth Avenue shops, the Main Street Arts district, and the Old Town district. These buses run Monday through Saturday from 11am to 9pm. Between mid-January and mid-April, free shuttles serve many of the area's resorts, including, among others, Camelback Inn, Sanctuary on Camelback, Hyatt Regency Scottsdale Resort and Spa at Gainey Ranch, and Renaissance Scottsdale Resort. These trolleys operate Tuesday through Sunday and will take you to Scottsdale Fashion Square. From there you can take the Scottsdale Trolley to other shopping districts.

BY TAXI

Because distances in Phoenix are so great, the price of an average taxi ride can be quite high. However, if you don't have your own wheels or had too much to drink and the bus isn't running because it's late at night or the weekend, you won't have any choice but to call a cab. **Yellow Cab** (© 602/252-5252) charges $2.50 for the first mile and $1.80 per mile thereafter. **Discount Cab** (© 602/200-2000) charges $1.80 for the first mile and $2.95 per mile after that.

FAST FACTS

The Banner Good Samaritan Medical Center, 1111 E. McDowell Rd., Phoenix (© 602/239-2000), is one of the largest hospitals in the valley. For a doctor referral, call the Banner Health Physician & Resource Line (© 602/230-2273); for a dentist referral, call the Dental Referral Service (© 800/428-8774).

State sales tax is 5.6% (plus variable local taxes, so expect to pay around 8%). Hotel room taxes vary considerably by city but are mostly between 10% and 11%. The total taxes and surcharges when renting a car at Sky Harbor Airport add up to more than 50%.

See also "Fast Facts: The American Southwest" in chapter 2.

3 Where to Stay

The Phoenix area has the greatest concentration of resorts in the continental United States. However, sunshine and spring training combine to make it hard to find a room on short notice between February and April. If you're planning to visit during these months, make your reservations as far in advance as possible. Also keep in mind that in winter, the Phoenix metro area has some of the highest room rates in the country.

With the exception of valet-parking services and parking garages at downtown convention hotels, parking is free at almost all Phoenix hotels. If there is a parking charge, we have noted it. You'll find that all hotels have nonsmoking rooms and all but the cheapest have wheelchair-accessible rooms.

Most resorts offer a variety of weekend, golf, and tennis packages, as well as off-season discounts and corporate rates (which you can often get just by asking). We've given only the official "rack rates," or walk-in rates, below, but it always pays to ask about special discounts or packages. Don't forget your AAA or AARP discounts if you belong to one of these organizations. Business hotels downtown and near the airport often lower their rates on weekends, and many hotels offer website-only specials.

BED & BREAKFASTS   While most people dreaming of a Phoenix vacation have visions of luxury resorts dancing in their heads, there are plenty of bed-and-breakfast inns around the Valley. **Mi Casa Su Casa** (© 800/456-0682 or 480/990-0682; www. azres.com) can book you into dozens of different homes in the Valley of the Sun, as can **Arizona Trails Bed & Breakfast Reservation Service** (© **888/799-4284** or 480/ 837-4284; www.arizonatrails.com), which also books tour and hotel reservations.

SCOTTSDALE

Scottsdale is the center of the Valley's resort scene. Because Scottsdale is also the Valley's prime shopping and dining district, this is the most convenient place to stay if you're here to eat and shop. However, traffic in Scottsdale is bad, the landscape at most resorts is flat, and you don't get much of a feel for the desert.

VERY EXPENSIVE

Camelback Inn, A JW Marriott Resort & Spa ✯✯✯   Set at the foot of Mummy Mountain and overlooking Camelback Mountain, the Camelback Inn, which opened in 1936, is one of the grande dames of the Phoenix hotel scene and abounds in traditional Southwestern character. Although the two 18-hole golf courses are the main attractions for many guests, the spa is among the finest in the state. There's also an extensive pool complex that appeals to families. Guest rooms, which are spread over the sloping grounds, are decorated with Southwestern furnishings and art, and all have balconies or patios. Some rooms even have their own private pools. This is an old-money sort of place that seamlessly melds tradition with modern amenities.

5402 E. Lincoln Dr., Scottsdale, AZ 85253. © 800/24-CAMEL or 480/948-1700. Fax 480/951-8469. www.camelback inn.com. 453 units. Jan to early June $299–$549 double, $570–$2,500 suite; early June to early Sept $179–$199 double, $260–$900 suite; early Sept to Dec $349–$459 double, $595–$1,700 suite. Children under 18 stay free in parent's room. AE, DC, DISC, MC, V. Small pets accepted. **Amenities:** 7 restaurants (American, Mexican, healthy); 2 lounges; 3 pools; 2 outstanding 18-hole golf courses; 6 tennis courts; exercise room; full-service spa; 6 Jacuzzis; bike rentals; children's programs and playground; concierge; car-rental desk; seasonal courtesy shopping shuttle; business center; 24-hr. room service; massage; babysitting; guest laundry and laundry service; dry cleaning. *In room:* A/C, TV, dataport, minibar, coffeemaker, hair dryer, iron, safe, high-speed Internet access.

Doubletree Paradise Valley Resort ✯✯ *Value*   With its distinctive styling and convenient location, this is an excellent choice. Its low-rise design and textured-block construction gives a bow to the pioneering architectural style of Frank Lloyd Wright and thus stands out from comparable resorts in the area. Built around several courtyards containing swimming pools, bubbling fountains, palm trees, and gardens with desert landscaping, the property has much the look and feel of the nearby Hyatt Regency Scottsdale (although on a less grandiose scale and at more bearable room rates). Accommodations have a very contemporary feel, with lots of blond wood and, in some cases, high ceilings that make the rooms feel particularly spacious.

5401 N. Scottsdale Rd., Scottsdale, AZ 85250. © 877/445-6677 or 480/947-5400. Fax 480/946-1524. www.paradise valley.doubletree.com. 387 units. Jan–Mar $329–$359 double; Apr–May and Sept $139–$199 double; Oct–Dec $249–$289 double; June–Aug $119–$159 double. Children under 18 stay free in parent's room. AE, DC, DISC, MC, V. Pets accepted ($50 fee). **Amenities:** Restaurant (Southwestern); lounge; poolside snack bar; 2 outdoor pools; putting green; 2 tennis courts; 2 racquetball courts; health club; 2 Jacuzzis; seasonal children's programs; concierge; car-rental desk; business center; room service; massage; laundry service; dry cleaning. *In room:* A/C, TV, dataport, minibar, coffeemaker, hair dryer, iron, high-speed Internet access.

Hotel Valley Ho ✯✯   This Scottsdale classic dates back to the 1950s, but in 2005, the hotel got a complete face-lift. The Valley Ho has become one of our favorite Scottsdale hotels; it's hip and convenient, and has loads of outdoor space for soaking up the sun. We just love the big rooms, which are done in a bold contemporary style. The studio rooms are our favorites; they have curtains to partition off the vanity area and an ultracool free-standing tub. Big balconies and patios provide plenty of space for lounging outdoors. Back in the day when midcentury modern was fresh and not

Phoenix, Scottsdale & the Valley of the Sun Accommodations

retro, this hotel was a favorite hangout of Hollywood stars. For that totally retro experience, there's even a Trader Vic's here.

6850 E. Main St., Scottsdale, AZ 85251. (C) 866/882-4484 or 480/248-2000. Fax 480/248-2002. www.hotelvalleyho. com. 194 units. Jan–Apr $319–$359 double, $419–$569 suite; May and Sept $199–$259 double, $299–$449 suite; June–Aug $149–$179 double, $249–$399 suite; Oct–Dec $259–$299 double, $359–$509 suite. Children under 18 stay free in parent's room. AE, DC, DISC, MC, V. Valet parking $12. Pets accepted. **Amenities:** 2 restaurants (American, Polynesian); 3 lounges; pool; exercise room; access to nearby health club; full-service spa; 2 Jacuzzis; bike rental; children's programs; concierge; business center; 24-hr. room service; massage; babysitting; laundry service; dry cleaning. *In room:* A/C, TV, dataport, minibar, coffeemaker/espresso maker, hair dryer, iron, safe, high-speed Internet access, Wi-Fi.

Hyatt Regency Scottsdale Resort & Spa at Gainey Ranch ⭐⭐⭐ (Kids)
From the colonnades of palm trees to the lobby walls that slide away, this luxurious resort is designed to impress and continues to be our favorite Scottsdale resort. It's relatively close to downtown Scottsdale and has interesting architecture, beautiful grounds, and a large spa. What's not to love? A 2½-acre water playground serves as the resort's focal point, and the extravagant complex of 10 swimming pools includes a water slide and a huge whirlpool spa. Guest rooms are luxurious and are designed to reflect the desert location. The resort's Native American and Environmental Learning Center provides a glimpse into Sonoran Desert culture and ecology. Children's programs make this a super choice for families.

7500 E. Doubletree Ranch Rd., Scottsdale, AZ 85258. (C) 800/55-HYATT or 480/444-1234. Fax 480/483-5550. www. scottsdale.hyatt.com. 490 units. Jan to late May $419 double, from $629 suite and casita; late May to early Sept $195 double, from $289 suite and casita; early Sept to Dec $315 double, from $479 suite and casita. Children under 18 stay free in parent's room. AE, DC, DISC, MC, V. Valet parking $20. **Amenities:** 3 restaurants (American, Italian); snack bar; lounge; coffee bar; juice bar; 10 pools; 27-hole golf course (w/lots of water hazards); 4 tennis courts; access to nearby health club; health club; full-service spa; 3 Jacuzzis; bikes; children's programs; concierge; car-rental desk; business center; room service; massage; babysitting; laundry service; dry cleaning; concierge-level rooms. *In room:* A/C, TV, dataport, minibar, coffeemaker, hair dryer, iron, safe, high-speed Internet access, Wi-Fi, free local calls.

The Phoenician ⭐⭐⭐ (Kids)
Situated on 250 acres at the foot of Camelback Mountain, this palatial resort is one of the finest resorts in the world. So, if you must stay at the very best, this is it. Polished marble and sparkling crystal abound in the lobby, but the valley view through a long wall of glass is what commands most guests' attention when they first arrive. Service here is second to none, and the character is very international. The pool complex, which has a water slide for the kids, is irresistibly seductive, and the resort's Centre for Well Being offers all the spa pampering anyone could ever want. There are also 27 challenging holes of golf. Mary Elaine's (p. 421) is Phoenix's ultimate special-occasion restaurant. The luxurious guest rooms have large patios and sunken tubs for two.

6000 E. Camelback Rd., Scottsdale, AZ 85251. (C) 800/888-8234 or 480/941-8200. Fax 480/947-4311. www.the phoenician.com. 654 units. Jan–May $625 double, from $1,550 suite; June to mid-Sept $295 double, from $995 suite; mid-Sept to Dec $525 double, from $1,450 suite. Children under 12 stay free in parent's room. AE, DC, DISC, MC, V. Valet parking $26. Pets under 40 lb. accepted. **Amenities:** 3 restaurants (Modern French, Southwestern, American); 4 snack bars/cafes; lounge; 9 pools; 27-hole golf course; putting green; 12 tennis courts; health club and spa; Jacuzzi; bike rentals; children's programs; concierge; car-rental desk; business center; shopping arcade; salon; 24-hr. room service; massage; babysitting; laundry service; dry cleaning; executive-level rooms; lawn games. *In room:* A/C, TV, dataport, minibar, hair dryer, iron, safe, high-speed Internet access.

Sanctuary on Camelback Mountain ⭐⭐⭐
This visually breathtaking place did the W Hotel thing first here in Scottsdale, and we still like the contemporary rooms here better than those at other area hip hotels. Located high on the northern flanks of Camelback Mountain, the lushly landscaped property has unforgettable views across

the valley, especially from the restaurant and lounge. The extremely spacious guest rooms are divided between the more conservative deluxe casitas and the boldly contemporary spa casitas. With their dyed-cement floors, kidney-shape daybeds, and streamline-moderne cabinetry, these latter units are absolutely stunning. Bathrooms are huge, and some have private outdoor soaking tubs. The resort's spa is gorgeous!

5700 E. McDonald Dr., Paradise Valley, AZ 85253. © **800/245-2051** or 480/948-2100. Fax 480/483-7314. www. sanctuaryoncamelback.com. 98 units. Early Jan to late May and late Dec $495–$690 double, $620–$1,505 suite; late May to mid-Sept and mid-Dec $225–$395 double, $325–$890 suite; mid-Sept to mid-Dec $395–$590 double, $520–$1,305 suite. Children under 17 stay free in parent's room. AE, DC, DISC, MC, V. Pets accepted. **Amenities:** Restaurant (New American); lounge; 4 pools; 5 tennis courts; fitness center; full-service spa; 2 Jacuzzis; bike rentals; concierge; business center; 24-hr. room service; massage; babysitting; laundry service; dry cleaning. *In room:* A/C, TV/DVD, dataport, minibar, coffeemaker, hair dryer, iron, safe, high-speed Internet access.

EXPENSIVE

FireSky Resort & Spa ☆☆   An exceptional location in the heart of the Scottsdale shopping district, a dramatic Southwestern/Moroccan styling (the focal point of the lobby is a massive sandstone fireplace), and a small but well-designed pool area are the main reasons we like this little resort. Set in a lushly planted courtyard are a small lagoon-style pool, complete with sand beach and short water slide, and a second pool with flame-topped columnar waterfalls. An artificial stream and faux sandstone ruins all add up to a fun desert fantasy landscape (although not on the grand scale to be found at some area resorts). The guest rooms are quite comfortable, and there's a pretty little spa on the premises.

4925 N. Scottsdale Rd., Scottsdale, AZ 85251. © **800/528-7867** or 480/945-7666. Fax 480/946-4056. www.firesky resort.com. 204 units. Jan to late May $289 double, $599 suite; late May to early Sept $149 double, $299 suite; early Sept to Dec $239 double, $549 suite. Children under 18 stay free in parent's room. AE, DISC, MC, V. Pets accepted. **Amenities:** Restaurant (Italian); lounge; snack bar; 2 pools; exercise room; access to nearby health club; full-service spa; Jacuzzi; concierge; courtesy shopping shuttle; business center; room service; massage; laundry service; dry cleaning. *In room:* A/C, TV, dataport, minibar, coffeemaker, hair dryer, iron, safe, high-speed Internet access, Wi-Fi.

Hotel Indigo ☆☆   Located in the heart of downtown Scottsdale's nightlife district, this stylish hotel is a great choice for anyone in town to party. Guest rooms are distinctively different from most hotels in that they have wood floors and area rugs. The rooms are designed in a Scandinavian-modern aesthetic and have absolutely gorgeous bathrooms. Clock radios have MP3 jacks, and the beds have halogen reading lamps. Seasonal fragrances scent the air; and photo-murals make the Indigo a feast for the senses.

4415 N. Civic Center Plaza, Scottsdale, AZ 85251. © **866/2-INDIGO** or 480/941-9400. Fax 480/675-5240. scottsdale hiphotel.com. 126 units. Jan–Apr $259–$279 double; May and Oct–Dec $174–$199 double; June–Sept $79–$105 double. Children under 18 stay free in parent's room. AE, DC, DISC, MC, V. **Amenities:** Restaurant (American); lounge; small outdoor pool; exercise room; concierge; courtesy shopping shuttle; business center; room service; laundry service; dry cleaning. *In room:* A/C, TV, dataport, hair dryer, iron, safe, Wi-Fi.

Renaissance Scottsdale Resort ☆☆ *(Value)*   If coming to Scottsdale for a romantic getaway, we would stay here. Located adjacent to the upscale Borgata shopping center (which is designed to resemble Tuscany's San Gimignano), this casual yet luxurious boutique resort feels like an isolated hideaway and is designed to resemble a Spanish oasis. Set amid shady lawns, the Renaissance Scottsdale consists of spacious, comfortable casita-style rooms and suites that are done in a Southwestern style. More than 100 of the suites have their own private outdoor hot tubs (very romantic). Several excellent restaurants are within walking distance.

6160 N. Scottsdale Rd., Scottsdale, AZ 85253. Ⓒ 800/309-8138 or 480/991-1414. Fax 480/951-3350. www.renaissance scottsdale.com. 171 units. Jan–May $259–$319 double, $279–$369 suite; June to early Sept $129 double, $149–$159 suite; early Sept to Dec $219 double, $269–$319 suite. Children under 16 stay free in parent's room. AE, DC, DISC, MC, V. Pets accepted ($50 deposit). **Amenities:** 3 restaurants (Mediterranean, Spanish, American); lounge; 2 pools; putting green; 4 tennis courts; croquet court; access to nearby health club; 2 Jacuzzis; bike rentals; concierge; courtesy shopping shuttle; business center; room service; massage; babysitting; laundry service; dry cleaning. *In room:* A/C, TV, dataport, minibar, coffeemaker, hair dryer, iron, safe, high-speed Internet access, Wi-Fi.

Scottsdale Resort & Athletic Club 𝒞𝒞 Fitness fanatics rejoice; this club's for you. If you can't stand the thought of giving up your workout just because you're on vacation, book a stay at this little boutique hotel (and timeshare resort) just off busy Scottsdale Road and adjacent to the Silverado Golf Course. With standard rooms and huge one- and two-bedroom "villas," this place is plenty comfortable, but the main reason we like this hotel is that it's affiliated with the Scottsdale Athletic Club, a large workout facility that emphasizes its tennis program. The basic rooms are a real steal for Scottsdale. On top of all this, you get a view of Camelback Mountain.

8235 E. Indian Bend Rd., Scottsdale, AZ 85250. Ⓒ 877/343-0033 or 480/344-0600. Fax 480/344-0650. www.scottsdale resortandathleticclub.com. 85 units. Late Dec to Apr $249 double, $359–$1,100 suite or villa; May–Sept $119 double, $179–$549 suite or villa; Oct–late Dec $149 double, $219–$669 suite or villa. Rates include continental breakfast. Children under 12 stay free in parent's room. AE, DISC, MC, V. **Amenities:** Restaurant (American); lounge; 3 pools; 11 tennis courts; health club; full-service spa; Jacuzzi; sauna; children's programs; concierge; car-rental desk; business center; room service; massage; babysitting; coin-op laundry. *In room:* A/C, TV/DVD, dataport, fridge, coffeemaker, hair dryer, iron, high-speed Internet access, free local calls.

Westin Kierland Resort & Spa 𝒞★★ 𝑲𝒊𝒅𝒔 A convenient location and distinct sense of place make this one of our favorite Phoenix-area resorts. Located just off Scottsdale Road adjacent to the Kierland Commons shopping center, the resort features artwork by Arizona artists, numerous interpretive plaques, and historical photos that provide insight into Arizona's cultural and natural history. Guest rooms all have balconies or patios, and although the bathrooms aren't all that large, this minor inconvenience is compensated for by Westin's Heavenly Beds, which are incredibly comfortable pillow-top beds. Excellent Nuevo Latino cuisine is served at deseo, and there's a great cowboy-style bar as well. The main pool area includes a long tubing river, a water slide, and a beach area.

6902 E. Greenway Pkwy., Scottsdale, AZ 85254. Ⓒ 800/WESTIN-1 or 480/624-1000. Fax 480/624-1001. www.kierland resort.com. 735 units. Jan–Apr $279–$529 double; May–June $189–$369 double; July to mid-Sept $149–$269 double; mid-Sept to Dec $189–$489 double. Children under 16 stay free in parent's room. AE, DC, DISC, MC, V. Valet parking $21. Pets accepted ($100 refundable deposit). **Amenities:** 5 restaurants (Nuevo Latino, American, Southwestern); poolside snack bar; espresso bar/ice-cream parlor; 4 lounges; 4 pools; 3 9-hole golf courses; 2 tennis courts; health club; full-service spa; 3 Jacuzzis; children's programs; concierge; car-rental desk; courtesy shopping shuttle; business center; 24-hr. room service; massage; babysitting; laundry service; dry cleaning; executive-level rooms. *In room:* A/C, TV, dataport, minibar, coffeemaker, hair dryer, iron, safe, high-speed Internet access, Wi-Fi, free local calls.

MODERATE

Hyatt Place Scottsdale Old Town 𝒞𝒞 With a great location in the heart of downtown Scottsdale, this hip business hotel is well worth choosing even if you're in town on vacation. The guest rooms are all spacious suites done in a homey, contemporary style with separate sitting and sleeping areas and 42-inch wall-hung flat-panel TVs that can be angled to either area. Unusual features include electronic self-service check-in kiosks, continental (free) or hot (charge) breakfasts, and a tiny lounge area to one side of the lobby. You can even get a light meal here if you don't feel like going out to a restaurant for dinner.

7300 E. Third Ave., Scottsdale, AZ 85251. © **888/492-8847** or 480/423-9944. Fax 480/423-2991. www.hyattplace. com. 127 units. $159–$229 double. Rates include continental breakfast. Children under 18 stay free in parent's room. AE, DC, DISC, MC, V. **Amenities:** Restaurant (American); lounge; outdoor pool; exercise room; courtesy shopping shuttle; business center. *In room:* A/C, TV, dataport, fridge, coffeemaker, hair dryer, iron, high-speed Internet access, Wi-Fi.

INEXPENSIVE

Despite the high-priced real estate, Scottsdale does have a few relatively inexpensive chain motels, although during the winter season, prices are higher than you might expect. For location alone, your best choice would be the **Motel 6–Scottsdale,** 6848 E. Camelback Rd. (© **480/946-2280**), which has doubles for $76 to $86 during the high season.

Days Inn Scottsdale Resort at Fashion Square Mall 🎈 *Kids* *Value*   This is one of the last economical hotels in the Old Town Scottsdale area, and its location adjacent to the Scottsdale Fashion Square mall makes it a great choice for shopaholics. This may be just an aging chain motel, but green lawns, tall palm trees, and a convenient location all make it worth recommending.

4710 N. Scottsdale Rd., Scottsdale, AZ 85251. © **800/DAYS-INN** or 480/947-5411. Fax 480/946-1324. www.scottsdale daysinn.com. 167 units. Jan–Mar $101–$199 double; Apr–Dec $59–$199 double. Rates include continental breakfast. Children under 18 stay free in parent's room. AE, DC, DISC, MC, V. **Amenities:** Seasonal poolside bar; small outdoor pool; tennis court; Jacuzzi; car-rental desk; courtesy shopping shuttle; coin-op laundry; dry cleaning service. *In room:* A/C, TV, dataport, fridge, coffeemaker, hair dryer, iron.

Ramada Limited Scottsdale on 5th Avenue *Value*   For convenience and price, this motel can't be beat. Located at the west end of the Fifth Avenue shopping district, the Ramada Limited is within walking distance of some of the best shopping and dining in Scottsdale. The three-story building is arranged around a central courtyard, where you'll find the small pool. Guest rooms are large.

6935 Fifth Ave., Scottsdale, AZ 85251. © **800/528-7396** or 480/994-9461. Fax 480/947-1695. www.ramadascottsdale com. 92 units. Jan–Apr $89–$159 double; Oct–Dec $79–$89 double; May–Sept $59 double. Rates include continental breakfast. Children 18 and under stay free in parent's room. AE, DISC, MC, V. Small pets accepted ($15 fee). **Amenities:** Small outdoor pool; exercise room; coin-op laundry; laundry service. *In room:* A/C, TV, dataport, fridge, coffeemaker, hair dryer, iron, free local calls.

NORTH SCOTTSDALE, CAREFREE & CAVE CREEK

Situated at least a 30-minute drive from downtown Scottsdale, this area boasts the newest resorts, the most spectacular hillside settings, and the best golf courses.

VERY EXPENSIVE

The Boulders Resort and Golden Door Spa 🎈🎈🎈   Set amid a jumble of giant boulders 45 minutes north of Old Town Scottsdale, this was the first luxury golf resort in the north Valley's rugged foothills. When not golfing, you can relax around the small pool, play tennis, relax at the resort's Golden Door Spa, or try your hand at rock climbing. The lobby is in a Santa Fe–style building with tree-trunk pillars and a flagstone floor, and the guest rooms continue the pueblo styling with stucco walls, beehive fireplaces, and beamed ceilings. For the best views, ask for one of the second-floor units. Bathrooms are large and luxuriously appointed, with tubs for two and separate showers.

34631 N. Tom Darlington Dr. (P.O. Box 2090), Carefree, AZ 85377. © **866/397-6520** or 480/488-9009. Fax 480/ 488-4118. www.theboulders.com. 215 units. Late Dec to May $599 double, from $1,099 villa; June to early Sept $199 double, from $499 villa; early Sept to early Dec $349 double, from $799 villa; early to late Dec $299 double, from $699 villa. (For all rates there is an additional $29–$33 nightly service charge.) Children under 17 stay free in parent's room. AE, DC, DISC, MC, V. Pets accepted ($100). **Amenities:** 6 restaurants (regional American, Southwestern, Mexican, spa cuisine, bakery/deli); lounge; 4 pools; 2 18-hole golf courses; 8 tennis courts; exercise room; full-service spa; 3 Jacuzzis; bike rentals; concierge; business center; shopping arcade; room service; massage; babysitting; laundry service; dry cleaning; rock climbing. *In room:* A/C, TV, dataport, minibar, coffeemaker, hair dryer, iron, safe, high-speed Internet access, Wi-Fi.

Copperwynd Resort and Club ★★ *Value*

Although it's a ways from Old Town Scottsdale, this boutique hotel, high on a ridge overlooking the town of Fountain Hills, is one of the most luxurious resorts in the area. The hotel boasts some of the most picturesque mountain vistas in the Valley, which is one of the reasons we like it so much. The resort has a fabulous tennis facility, an impressive health club, and a spa. The resort's Jacuzzi, tucked into a rocky hillside, is as romantic as they come. All guest rooms have great views and feature a European deluxe decor. Balconies provide plenty of room for taking in the vista. There's an excellent restaurant on the premises.

13225 N. Eagle Ridge Dr., Fountain Hills, AZ 85268. *©* **877/707-7760** or 480/333-1900. Fax 480/333-1901. www. copperwynd.com. 40 units. Late Dec to late Apr $379–$425 double, $825–$925 villa; late Apr to mid-May and late Sept to late Dec $229–$269 double, $750–$900 villa; mid-May to late Sept $129–$189 double, $550–$650 villa. Children under 18 stay free in parent's room. AE, DC, DISC, MC, V. **Amenities:** 2 restaurants (New American, American); 2 lounges; 2 pools; 9 tennis courts; health club and full-service spa; 3 Jacuzzis; saunas; children's game room; concierge; business center; room service; massage; babysitting; laundry service; dry cleaning. *In room:* A/C, TV, dataport, fridge, coffeemaker, hair dryer, iron, safe, high-speed Internet access, Wi-Fi, free local calls.

Four Seasons Resort Scottsdale at Troon North ★★★

Located in the foothills of north Scottsdale adjacent to (and with privileges at) the legendary Troon North golf course, the Four Seasons is even more impressive than the nearby Boulders resort. With casita accommodations scattered across a boulder-strewn hillside, the Four Seasons boasts one of the Valley's most dramatic settings, and with a hiking trail to the nearby Pinnacle Peak Park, the resort is a good choice for anyone who wants to explore the desert on foot. Guest rooms and suites are among the most lavish you'll find in Arizona. If you can afford it, opt for one with a private plunge pool and an outdoor shower—a luxury usually found only in tropical resorts.

10600 E. Crescent Moon Dr., Scottsdale, AZ 85262. *©* **888/207-9696** or 480/515-5700. Fax 480/515-5599. www. fourseasons.com/scottsdale. 210 units. Jan–May $525–$725 double, $845–$5,000 suite; June–Aug $195–$270 double, $450–$2,650 suite; Sept–Dec $475–$715 double, $845–$5,000 suite. Children under 18 stay free in parent's room. AE, DC, DISC, MC, V. Small pets accepted. **Amenities:** 4 restaurants (Southwest, contemporary steakhouse, American); lounge; 2 pools (including large 2-level pool); 2 18-hole golf courses; 2 tennis courts; large exercise room; health club; spa; Jacuzzi; children's programs; concierge; car-rental desk; business center; 24-hr. room service; massage; laundry service; dry cleaning. *In room:* A/C, TV/DVD, dataport, minibar, coffeemaker, hair dryer, iron, safe, high-speed Internet access.

EXPENSIVE

The Fairmont Scottsdale Princess ★★★

We know this faux Moorish palace belongs in Spain, not Arizona, but we still love it. With its royal palms, tiled fountains, and waterfalls, the Princess offers an exotic atmosphere unmatched in the area and will delight anyone in search of a romantic hideaway. A water playground (with two water slides) and a kids' fishing pond also make this resort a hit with families. The resort is located a 20-minute drive from Old Town Scottsdale and is home to the FBR Open golf tournament (a stop on the PGA Tour), which means the fairways here are top-notch. There's also the Willow Stream spa. Guest rooms, which have just been renovated, are done in an elegant Southwestern style, and bathrooms have double vanities and separate showers and tubs. All units have private balconies.

7575 E. Princess Dr., Scottsdale, AZ 85255. © 800/441-1414 or 480/585-4848. Fax 480/585-0091. www.fairmont. com/scottsdale. 651 units. $159–$589 double; $319–$3,800 suite. Children 12 and under stay free in parent's room. AE, DC, DISC, MC, V. Pets accepted ($25 per night). **Amenities:** 3 restaurants (Mexican, steakhouse, American); 3 lounges; 5 pools; 2 18-hole golf courses; 7 tennis courts; exercise room; full-service spa; Jacuzzi; concierge; car-rental desk; business center; golf and tennis pro shops; shopping arcade; salon; 24-hr. room service; massage; babysitting; laundry service; dry cleaning. *In room:* A/C, TV, dataport, minibar, coffeemaker, hair dryer, iron, safe.

Radisson Fort McDowell Resort & Casino ✮✮✮   In the Scottsdale area, you just can't stay any closer to the desert than at this beautiful new resort northeast of Fountain Hills. Although the Radisson is a 30-minute drive from downtown Scottsdale, the location is hard to beat if you've come to the area to experience the desert. The resort is on the Fort McDowell Yavapai Nation and, consequently, the tribe's Fort McDowell Casino is a big draw for many guests. However, the two 18-hole courses at the adjacent We-Ko-Pa Golf Club are also a major draw here. We like the resort best for its creative Native American styling and its great desert and mountain views.

10438 N. Fort McDowell Rd., Scottsdale/Fountain Hills, AZ 85264. © 800/333-3333 or 480/789-5300. Fax 480/789-5333. www.radisson.com/ftmcdowellaz. 246 units. Jan–Mar $269–$299 double; Apr $199–$210 double; May, Sept, and Dec $169–$189 double; June–Aug $109–$139 double; Oct–Nov $219–$239 double. Children under 12 stay free in parent's room. AE, DC, DISC, MC, V. Pets accepted. **Amenities:** 2 restaurants (Southwestern, American); 2 lounges; casino; 2 outdoor pools; 2 18-hole golf courses; exercise room; full-service spa; 2 Jacuzzis; concierge; car-rental desk; courtesy shopping shuttle; business center; room service; massage; babysitting; dry cleaning; executive-level rooms; horseback riding. *In room:* A/C, TV, dataport, minibar, coffeemaker, hair dryer, safe, high-speed Internet access, Wi-Fi.

CENTRAL PHOENIX & THE CAMELBACK CORRIDOR

This area is the heart of the upscale Phoenix shopping and restaurant scene. Old money and new money rub shoulders along the avenues here, and valet parking is de rigueur. Located roughly midway between Old Scottsdale and downtown Phoenix, this area is a good bet for those intending to split their time between the downtown Phoenix cultural and sports district and the world-class shopping and dining in Scottsdale.

VERY EXPENSIVE

Arizona Biltmore Resort & Spa ✮✮✮   For decades this resort has been the favored Phoenix address of celebrities, politicians, and old money, and the distinctive cast-cement blocks inspired by a Frank Lloyd Wright design make it a unique architectural gem. It's the historical character and timeless elegance that really set this place apart. With wide lawns, colorful flower gardens, and views of Piestewa Peak, this is a resort for outdoor lounging. While the two golf courses and expansive spa are the main draws, the children's activities center also makes this a popular choice for families. The "resort rooms" are quite comfortable and have balconies or patios, and those rooms in the Arizona Wing are also good choices.

2400 E. Missouri Ave., Phoenix, AZ 85016. © 800/950-0086 or 602/955-6600. Fax 602/381-7600. www.arizonabiltmore. com. 738 units. Jan to mid-May $465–$675 double, from $730 suite; mid-May to early Sept $205–$310 double, from $340 suite; early Sept to Dec $394–$604 double, from $709 suite. Rates do not include the $25 daily service fee. Children under 18 stay free in parent's room. AE, DC, DISC, MC, V. Pets under 50 lb. accepted in cottage rooms ($100 deposit, $50 non-refundable). **Amenities:** 4 restaurants (American, Southwestern); lounge; 8 pools; 2 18-hole golf courses; 7 tennis courts; health club and full-service spa; 2 Jacuzzis; saunas; bike rentals; lawn games children's programs; concierge; car-rental desk; courtesy shopping shuttle; business center; 24-hr. room service; massage; laundry service; dry cleaning. *In room:* A/C, TV, dataport, minibar, hair dryer, iron, safe, high-speed Internet access, free local calls.

Hermosa Inn ✮✮   This luxurious boutique hotel, once a guest ranch, is one of the few hotels in the Valley to offer any Old Southwest atmosphere, and because the

Hermosa Inn is all about getting a little peace and quiet, we breathe a big sigh of relief every time we arrive here. Built in 1930 by cowboy artist Lon Megargee, the inn is situated on more than 6 acres of attractive gardens in an upscale residential neighborhood. The inn provides luxury, yet is completely removed from Scottsdale's hectic pace. The only other nearby place this tranquil is the Royal Palms, which is more service oriented. Rooms vary from cozy to spacious and are decorated in contemporary Western decor.

5532 N. Palo Cristi Rd., Paradise Valley, AZ 85253. ℂ 800/241-1210 or 602/955-8614. Fax 602/955-8299. www. hermosainn.com. 35 units. Jan–May $299–$369 double, $399–$709 suite; June–Aug $159–$189 double, $159–$469 suite; Sept–Dec $219–$349 double, $219–$639 suite. Rates do not include daily hospitality fee of $12. Rates include full breakfast. AE, DC, DISC, MC, V. Take 32nd St. north from Camelback Rd., turn right on Stanford Rd., and turn left on N. Palo Cristi Rd. From Lincoln Dr., turn south on N. Palo Cristi Rd. (east of 32nd St.). Pets accepted ($50 fee). **Amenities:** Restaurant (New American); lounge; outdoor pool; tennis court; access to nearby health club; 2 Jacuzzis; concierge; room service; massage; babysitting; laundry service; dry cleaning. *In room:* A/C, TV, dataport, minibar, coffeemaker, hair dryer, iron, safe, high-speed Internet access, Wi-Fi, free local calls.

Royal Palms Resort and Spa 𝒢𝒢𝒢

This romantic, beautiful resort is located midway between Old Town Scottsdale and Biltmore Fashion Park. It was constructed more than 50 years ago by Cunard Steamship executive Delos Cooke and is done in Spanish mission style. Giving the resort the tranquil feel of a Mediterranean monastery are lush walled gardens where antique water fountains splash. The most memorable guest rooms are the deluxe casitas, each with a distinctive decor ranging from opulent contemporary to classic European. The Alvadora Spa provides a place to be pampered. This gorgeous little hideaway has the feel of a Spanish villa that was transported to Arizona. A real gem!

5200 E. Camelback Rd., Phoenix, AZ 85018. ℂ 800/672-6011 or 602/840-3610. Fax 602/840-6927. www.royal palmsresortandspa.com. 119 units. Jan–May $429–$609 double, $459–$2,600 suite; June to mid-Sept $199–$329 double, $229–$1,600 suite; mid-Sept to Dec $389–$559 double, $429–$2,400 suite. Rates do not include daily service fee of $22. Children under 18 stay free in parent's room. AE, DC, DISC, MC, V. Pets accepted ($300 deposit, $100 nonrefundable). **Amenities:** Restaurant (Mediterranean); poolside grill; lounge; outdoor pool w/cabanas; exercise room; full-service spa; Jacuzzi; bike rentals; concierge; business center; 24-hr. room service; massage; babysitting; laundry service; dry cleaning. *In room:* A/C, TV, dataport, minibar, coffeemaker, hair dryer, iron, safe, Wi-Fi.

EXPENSIVE

Embassy Suites Biltmore 𝒢𝒢

Located across the parking lot from the Biltmore Fashion Park shopping center, this hotel makes a great base if you want to be within walking distance of half a dozen good restaurants. The atrium is filled with interesting tile work, tropical greenery, waterfalls, and ponds filled with koi (colorful Japanese carp). In the atrium, you'll also find a romantic lounge with huge banquettes shaded by palm trees. With a major renovation planned at press time, this place should look better than ever in 2008. All in all, this hotel is a good value.

2630 E. Camelback Rd., Phoenix, AZ 85016. ℂ 800/EMBASSY or 602/955-3992. Fax 602/955-6479. www.phoenix biltmore.embassysuites.com. 232 units. Jan to late May $239–$409 double; late May to early Sept $109–$219 double; early Sept to Dec $239–$329 double. Rates include full breakfast and afternoon drinks. Children under 18 stay free in parent's room. AE, DC, DISC, MC, V. Valet parking $8. Pets accepted ($25). **Amenities:** Restaurant (steakhouse); lounge; outdoor pool; exercise room; access to nearby health club; Jacuzzi; concierge; courtesy shopping shuttle; business center; room service; massage; coin-op laundry; laundry service; dry cleaning; executive-level rooms. *In room:* A/C, TV, dataport, fridge, coffeemaker, hair dryer, iron, microwave, high-speed Internet access, Wi-Fi.

Maricopa Manor 𝒢

Centrally located between downtown Phoenix and Scottsdale, Maricopa Manor is just a block off busy Camelback Road and has long been

Phoenix's best B&B. The inn's main building, designed to resemble a Spanish manor house, was built in 1928, and the orange trees, palms, and large yard all lend an Old Phoenix atmosphere. All guest rooms are large, comfortable suites, many with Arts and Crafts touches. One suite has a sunroom and kitchen, while another has two separate sleeping areas. You can eat your breakfast at tables in the garden.

15 W. Pasadena Ave., Phoenix, AZ 85013. ℰ 800/292-6403 or 602/274-6302. Fax 602/266-3904. www.maricopa manor.com. 7 units. Late Dec to Apr $179–$229 double; May–June and Nov to late Dec $139–$179 double; mid-Sept to Oct $129–$169 double; July to mid-Sept $99–$129 double. Rates include extended continental breakfast. Children under 13 stay free in parent's room. AE, DC, DISC, MC, V. **Amenities:** Outdoor pool; access to nearby health club; Jacuzzi; massage. *In room:* A/C, TV/VCR/DVD, dataport, fridge, coffeemaker, hair dryer, iron, high-speed Internet access, Wi-Fi, free local calls.

INEXPENSIVE

Extended Stay Deluxe Phoenix-Biltmore   Billing itself as a temporary residence and offering discounts for stays of 7 days or more, this hotel consists of studio-style apartments located just north of Camelback Road and not far from Biltmore Fashion Park. Although designed primarily for corporate business travelers on temporary assignment in the area, this lodging makes a good choice for families as well. All units have full kitchens, big bathrooms, and separate sitting areas.

5235 N. 16th St., Phoenix, AZ 85016. ℰ 800/804-3724 or 602/265-6800. Fax 602/265-4111. www.extendedstaydeluxe. com. 112 units. $55–$130 double. Children under 17 stay free in parent's room. AE, DC, DISC, MC, V. Pets accepted ($25 per night, $75 maximum). **Amenities:** Small outdoor pool; exercise room; Jacuzzi; coin-op laundry; dry cleaning. *In room:* A/C, TV, dataport, kitchen, coffeemaker, hair dryer, iron, high-speed Internet access.

NORTH PHOENIX

Some of the Valley's best scenery is to be found in north Phoenix, where several small mountains have been protected as parks and preserves; the two Pointe Hilton resorts claim great locations close to these parks. However, the Valley's best shopping and dining, as well as most major attractions, are all at least a 30-minute drive away.

VERY EXPENSIVE

JW Marriott Desert Ridge Resort & Spa ✿✿✿   This is the largest resort in the state and stays crowded with conference and convention groups. Because it is miles from any other resorts, high-end shopping areas, or concentrations of good restaurants, Desert Ridge is primarily a place to stay put and spend your days sitting in the sun drinking margaritas by the pool. To this end, there are 4 acres of water features and pools (including a tubing "river"). The Revive Spa, where the focus is on indigenous ingredients such as turquoise, has its own lap pool and plans to unveil a new services menu this year. At the resort's grand entrance, desert landscaping and rows of palm trees give the resort a sense of place, and the lobby's roll-up walls let plenty of balmy desert air in during the cooler months. Guest rooms have balconies and hints of Mediterranean styling. Be sure to ask for a room with a view to the south.

5350 E. Marriott Blvd., Phoenix, AZ 85054. ℰ 800/835-6206 or 480/293-5000. Fax 480/293-3600. www.jwdesert ridgeresort.com. 950 units. Jan to early May $449–$569 double; early May to mid-June and early Sept to Dec $349–$489 double; mid-June to early Sept $169–$249 double; $319–$1,999 suite year-round. Children under 18 stay free in parent's room. AE, DC, DISC, MC, V. **Amenities:** 5 restaurants (Southwestern, Hawaiian fusion, Italian, steakhouse, healthful); 2 snack bars/cafes; 3 lounges; 5 pools; 2 18-hole golf courses; 8 tennis courts; health club; full-service spa; 3 Jacuzzis; children's programs; concierge; car-rental desk; business center; 24-hr. room service; massage; babysitting; guest laundry; laundry service; dry cleaning. *In room:* A/C, TV, dataport, minibar, coffeemaker, hair dryer, iron, safe, high-speed Internet access.

EXPENSIVE

Pointe Hilton Squaw Peak Resort *★★★ (Kids* At the foot of the Phoenix Mountains, this lushly landscaped resort makes a big splash with its 4-acre Hole-in-the-Wall River Ranch aquatic playground, which features a tubing "river," water slide, waterfall, sports pool, and lagoon pool. An 18-hole putting course and shopping arcade also help make it a great family vacation spot. The resort is done in the Spanish villa style, and most of the guest rooms are large suites. For a family vacation, this place is hard to beat. However, we prefer the nearby Pointe Hilton Tapatio Cliffs Resort for its dramatic hillside setting and location adjacent to the North Mountain Recreation Area.

7677 N. 16th St., Phoenix, AZ 85020. (℗ 800/876-4683 or 602/997-2626. Fax 602/997-2391. www.pointehilton. com. 563 units. Jan to mid-Apr $159–$379 double; mid-Apr to mid-Sept $89–$199 double; mid-Sept to Dec $99–$299 double, year-round $1,500 grande suite. Rates do not include daily resort fee of $9. Children under 18 stay free in parent's room. AE, DC, DISC, MC, V. Pets accepted ($75–$100 deposit). **Amenities:** 3 restaurants (American, Southwestern, Western); 2 snack bars; 5 lounges; 8 pools; 18-hole golf course (4 miles away by shuttle); 4 tennis courts; health club (extra charge) and small spa; 6 Jacuzzis; saunas; children's programs; concierge; car-rental desk; business center; shopping arcade; room service; massage; babysitting; coin-op laundry; laundry service; dry cleaning. *In room:* A/C, TV, dataport, minibar, coffeemaker, hair dryer, iron, high-speed Internet access.

Pointe Hilton Tapatio Cliffs Resort *★★★ (Value* If you love to lounge by the pool, then this resort is a great choice. The Falls, a 3½-acre water playground, includes two pools, a 138-foot water slide, 40-foot cascades, a whirlpool tucked into an artificial grotto, and rental cabanas. If you're a hiker, you can head out on the trails of the adjacent North Mountain Recreation Area. All rooms are spacious suites with Southwest-inspired furnishings; corner units are particularly bright. This resort has steep walkways, so you need to be in good shape to stay here. At the top of the property is Different Pointe of View, a restaurant with one of the best views in the city.

11111 N. Seventh St., Phoenix, AZ 85020. (℗ 800/876-4683 or 602/866-7500. Fax 602/993-0276. www.pointehilton. com. 585 units. Jan to mid-May $159–$379 double; mid-May to mid-Sept $89–$199 double; mid-Sept to Dec $99–$299 double; year-round $1,500 grande suite. Rates do not include $9 daily resort fee. Children under 18 stay free in parent's room. AE, DC, DISC, MC, V. Pets accepted ($75–$100 deposit). **Amenities:** 5 restaurants (Continental, Tuscan, American, Mexican); 2 poolside cafes; 5 lounges; 8 pools; golf course; 2 tennis courts; fitness center (extra charge); small full-service spa; 8 Jacuzzis; sauna; steam room; seasonal children's programs; concierge; business center; shopping arcade; room service; massage; babysitting; coin-op laundry; laundry service; dry cleaning. *In room:* A/C, TV, dataport, minibar, coffeemaker, hair dryer, iron, high-speed Internet access.

MODERATE/INEXPENSIVE

Among the better moderately priced chain motels in north Phoenix are the **Best Western Inn Suites Hotel Phoenix,** 1615 E. Northern Ave., at 16th Street (℗ **800/752-2204** or 602/997-6285; www.bestwestern.com), charging high-season rates of $99 to $199 double; and the **Best Western Bell Hotel,** 17211 N. Black Canyon Hwy. (℗ **877/263-1290** or 602/993-8300; www.bestwestern.com), charging $89 to $149 in the high season.

DOWNTOWN, SOUTH PHOENIX & THE AIRPORT AREA

Unless you're a sports fan or are in town for a convention, there's not much to recommend downtown Phoenix. This 9-to-5 area can feel like a ghost town at night. For the most part, south Phoenix is one of the poorest parts of the city. However, it does have a couple of wealthy enclaves that are home to exceptional resorts, and Phoenix South Mountain Park is one of the best places in the city to experience the desert.

VERY EXPENSIVE

Sheraton Wild Horse Pass Resort & Spa ☆☆☆   Named for the area's wild horses, this resort is located 20 minutes south of Phoenix Sky Harbor International Airport on the Gila River Indian Reservation, and because the resort looks out across miles of desert, it has a pleasantly remote feel. Throw in horseback riding, a full-service spa featuring desert-inspired treatments, two golf courses, a nature trail along a 2½-mile-long artificial river, a pool with a water slide, the Rawhide wild-west theme park, and a nearby casino, and you'll find plenty to keep you busy. The resort is owned by the Maricopa and Pima tribes, who go out of their way to share their culture with resort guests. Guest rooms have great beds, small patios, and large bathrooms with separate tubs and showers. The menu in Kai, the main dining room, focuses on indigenous Southwestern flavors.

5594 W. Wild Horse Pass Blvd., Chandler, AZ 85226. ℂ **888/218-8989** or 602/225-0100. Fax 602/225-0300. www.wildhorsepassresort.com. 500 units. Early Jan to late May $329–$495 double, $650–$1,400 suite; late May to mid-Sept $189–$289 double, $600–$950 suite; mid-Sept to early Jan $289–$495 double, $650–$1,400 suite. Children stay free in parent's room. AE, DC, DISC, MC, V. Pets accepted. **Amenities:** 5 restaurants (Native American, Southwestern, American); 3 lounges; 4 outdoor pools; 2 18-hole golf courses; 2 tennis courts; health club; full-service spa; 6 Jacuzzis; bike rentals; concierge; car-rental desk; business center; shopping arcade; 24-hr. room service; massage; babysitting; laundry service; dry cleaning; horseback riding. *In room:* A/C, TV, dataport, minibar, coffeemaker, hair dryer, iron, safe, high-speed Internet access.

EXPENSIVE

The Buttes, A Marriott Resort ☆☆   Just 3 miles from Sky Harbor Airport, this resort makes the most of its craggy hilltop location, and although some people complain that the nearby freeway ruins the view, the rocky setting is quintessentially Southwestern. The only other resorts in the area with as much desert character are the far more expensive Boulders and Four Seasons. From the cactus garden and waterfall *inside* the lobby to the circular restaurant and free-form swimming pools, this resort is calculated to take your breath away. Guest rooms are stylishly elegant. The city-view rooms are a bit larger than the hillside-view rooms, but second-floor hillside-view rooms have patios. Unfortunately, most bathrooms have only three-quarter-size tubs. The Top of the Rock restaurant has great views.

2000 Westcourt Way, Tempe, AZ 85282. ℂ **888/867-7492** or 602/225-9000. Fax 602/438-8622. www.marriott.com/phxtm. 353 units. Jan to mid-Apr $199–$329 double, from $475 suite; mid-Apr to mid-May $189–$289 double, from $475 suite; mid-May to early Sept $99–$199 double, from $375 suite; early Sept to Dec $159–$279 double, from $475 suite. Children 18 and under stay free in parent's room. AE, DC, DISC, MC, V. **Amenities:** 3 restaurants (New American/Southwestern, American, bar and grill); 3 lounges; 2 pools; 4 tennis courts; volleyball courts; exercise room; health club; full-service spa; 4 Jacuzzis; sauna; bike rentals; concierge; business center; room service; massage; babysitting; dry cleaning; executive-level rooms. *In room:* A/C, TV, dataport, minibar, coffeemaker, hair dryer, iron, high-speed Internet access.

Pointe South Mountain Resort ☆☆☆ *Kids*   This sprawling resort abuts the 17,000-acre South Mountain Park, and is one of the best choices in the Valley for families. Kids will love the wave pool, tubing "river," twisty water slide, and two free-fall-style water slides. Stables at the resort allow you and the kids to ride into the sunset on South Mountain, and there are numerous children's programs, plus a kid-friendly cowboy steakhouse (Rustler's Rooste, p. 419). The guest rooms, all suites, feature contemporary Southwestern furnishings and lots of space. At press time, there were plans to double the size of the resort's spa.

7777 S. Pointe Pkwy., Phoenix, AZ 85044. ℂ **866/267-1321** or 602/438-9000. Fax 602/431-6535. www.pointesouthmtn.com. 640 units. Jan–Apr from $279 double; May to early Sept from $139 double; early Sept to Dec from $159

double. Rates do not include $16 daily resort fee. Children under 18 stay free in parent's room. AE, DC, DISC, MC, V.
Amenities: 6 restaurants (steakhouse, Mexican, Southwestern, international); 3 lounges; 11 outdoor pools (including 6-acre water park); 18-hole golf course; 5 tennis courts; racquetball court; health club; full-service spa; 9 Jacuzzis; bike rentals; children's programs; concierge; business center; room service; massage; babysitting; coin-op laundry; laundry service; dry cleaning; executive-level rooms; horseback riding. *In room:* A/C, TV, dataport, minibar, coffeemaker, hair dryer, iron, high-speed Internet access, Wi-Fi, free local calls.

TEMPE, MESA & THE EAST VALLEY

Tempe, which lies just a few miles east of the airport, is home to Arizona State University and consequently supports a lively nightlife scene. Along Tempe's Mill Avenue, you'll find one of the only neighborhoods in the Valley where locals actually get out of their cars and walk the streets. Tempe is also convenient to Papago Park, which is home to the Phoenix Zoo, the Desert Botanical Garden, a municipal golf course, and hiking and mountain-biking trails.

EXPENSIVE

Tempe Mission Palms Hotel 𝒢𝒢   With a great location on Tempe's lively Mill Avenue and guest rooms decorated in a wild combination of bold colors and modern geometric patterns, this is the perfect choice for a fun-filled weekend in Tempe. Sure, this is a business hotel (ergonomic desk chairs), but with a rooftop pool, tennis court, and Mill Avenue's nightlife right out the front door, it's also a great choice for active travelers. Come in the spring and you won't want to leave the courtyard, which is scented by the flowers of citrus trees.

60 E. Fifth St., Tempe, AZ 85281. © 800/547-8705 or 480/894-1400. Fax 480/968-7677. www.missionpalms.com. 303 units. Jan–Apr $189–$259 double, $359 suite; May–June $129–$179 double, $279 suite; July–Aug $99–$169 double, $269 suite; Sept–Dec $149–$209 double, $309 suite. Rates do not include $9.75 daily hospitality fee. Children under 18 stay free in parent's room. AE, DC, DISC, MC, V. Pets accepted ($100 deposit, $25 nonrefundable). **Amenities:** 2 restaurants (Southwestern); 2 lounges; outdoor pool; tennis court; exercise room; access to nearby health club; 2 Jacuzzis; bike rentals; concierge; car-rental desk; courtesy airport shuttle; business center; room service; massage; laundry service; dry cleaning. *In room:* A/C, TV, dataport, coffeemaker, hair dryer, iron, high-speed Internet access, Wi-Fi, free local calls.

MODERATE

Best Western Dobson Ranch Inn & Resort 𝒢   This aging budget resort may not be very luxurious, but it has just about everything a sun-starved winter visitor could ask for—green lawns, flower gardens, palm trees, and a big pool surrounded by lounge chairs. The location right off US 60 at the junction with US 101 also makes this resort relatively convenient for exploring the valley. Guest rooms are functional, not fancy, and are certainly dated, but the grounds more than make up for the unremarkable rooms. Oh, and by the way, this is the spring training home of the Chicago Cubs.

1666 S. Dobson Rd., Mesa, AZ 85202. © 800/528-1356 or 480/831-7000. Fax 480/831-7000. www.dobsonranch inn.com. 213 units. Mid-Sept to Feb and Apr $105–$185 double; Mar $160–$200 double; May to mid-Sept $80–$130 double. Rates include full breakfast. Children 12 and under stay free in parent's room. AE, DC, DISC, MC, V. Pets accepted. **Amenities:** Restaurant (American); lounge; large outdoor pool; exercise room; 2 Jacuzzis; business center; room service; massage; free self-service laundry; laundry service; dry cleaning. *In room:* A/C, TV, dataport, fridge, coffeemaker, hair dryer, iron, high-speed Internet access, free local calls.

Crowne Plaza San Marcos Golf Resort 𝒢   Built in 1912, the San Marcos is the oldest golf resort in Arizona and has a classic mission-revival styling. We love the timeless feel of this resort's palm-shaded courtyards, and we're sure you will, too. Downtown Chandler, where the San Marcos is located, has been undergoing something of a renaissance in recent years. There are now art galleries and some decent restaurants on the plaza just outside the resort's front door. Guest rooms are simply furnished, nothing special, but they have been kept up-to-date. You'll want to spend your time splashing around in the pool when you aren't playing tennis or golf.

One San Marcos Place, Chandler, AZ 85225. (C) **800/528-8071** or 480/812-0900. Fax 480/963-6777. www.sanmarcos resort.com. 295 units. $124–$250 double; $176–$300 suite (lower rates in summer). Children under 18 stay free in parent's room. AE, DC, DISC, MC, V. Pets accepted ($50 nonrefundable deposit). **Amenities:** 2 restaurants (American); 2 lounges; outdoor pool; 18-hole golf course; 2 tennis courts; exercise room; Jacuzzi; concierge; business center; salon; room service; laundry service; dry cleaning. *In room:* A/C, TV, dataport, coffeemaker, hair dryer, high-speed Internet access, free local calls.

Fiesta Inn Resort 🦶 *Value*   Reasonable rates, green lawns, palm- and eucalyptus-shaded grounds, and a location close to the airport, ASU, and Tempe's Mill Avenue make this older, casual resort one of the best deals in the Valley. Okay, so it doesn't have the desert character of The Buttes resort across the freeway, and it isn't as stylish as the resorts in Scottsdale, but you can't argue with the rates. The large guest rooms, although a bit dark, have an appealing retro mission styling.

2100 S. Priest Dr., Tempe, AZ 85282. (C) **800/528-6481** or 480/967-1441. Fax 480/967-0224. www.fiestainnresort. com. 270 units. Nov to late May $109–$250 double; late May to Oct $100–$124 double. Children under 15 stay free in parent's room. AE, DC, DISC, MC, V. **Amenities:** 2 restaurants (American/Southwestern); lounge; pool; exercise room; Jacuzzi; concierge; courtesy airport shuttle; business center; room service; laundry service; dry cleaning. *In room:* A/C, TV, dataport, fridge, coffeemaker, hair dryer, iron, high-speed Internet access, free local calls.

Gold Canyon Golf Resort 🦶🦶 *Value*   Golfers willing to stay way out on the eastern outskirts of the Valley of the Sun (a 30- to 45-min. drive from the airport) should be thrilled by the economical room rates and great golf at this resort. Located at the foot of the Superstition Mountains, Gold Canyon is a favorite of golfers for its exceedingly scenic holes. The spacious guest rooms are housed in blindingly white pueblo-inspired buildings; some have fireplaces, while others have whirlpools. The deluxe golf-course rooms are definitely worth the higher rates. If you're here primarily to play golf and don't have a fortune to spend, this is *the* place to stay.

6100 S. Kings Ranch Rd., Gold Canyon, AZ 85218. (C) **800/624-6445** or 480/982-9090. Fax 480/983-9554. www. qcgr.com. 101 units. $135–$260 double. Children under 16 stay free in parent's room. AE, DISC, MC, V. Pets accepted ($75 fee). **Amenities:** 2 restaurants (American); lounge; pool; 2 18-hole golf courses; exercise room; small full-service spa; Jacuzzi; bike rentals; concierge; room service; massage; laundry service; dry cleaning. *In room:* A/C, TV, dataport, minibar, coffeemaker, hair dryer, iron, free local calls.

INEXPENSIVE

Apache Boulevard in Tempe becomes Main Street in Mesa, and along this stretch of road there are numerous old motels charging some of the lowest rates in the Valley. However, these motels are very hit-or-miss. If you're used to staying at nonchain motels, you might want to cruise this strip and check out a few places. Otherwise, try the chain motels in the area (which tend to charge $20–$40 more per night than nonchain motels).

Chain options in the Tempe area include the **Days Inn–Tempe,** 1221 E. Apache Blvd. ((C) **480/968-7793**), charging $55 to $110 double; and **Super 8–Tempe,** 1020 E. Apache Blvd. ((C) **480/967-8891**), charging $54 to $129 double.

Chain options in the Mesa area include the **Motel 6–Mesa,** 336 W. Hampton Ave. ((C) **480/844-8899**), charging $48 to $68 double; and **Super 8–Mesa,** 6733 E. Main St. ((C) **480/981-6181**), charging $65 to $96 double.

WEST VALLEY

The Wigwam Golf Resort & Spa 𝒢𝒢   Located 20 minutes west of downtown Phoenix, this property opened its doors to the public in 1929 and remains one of the nation's premier golf resorts. It's a classic, with old-school gentility, but when the money all headed to Scottsdale, this place became an elegant oasis surrounded by tract houses. Like the Arizona Biltmore and the Camelback Inn, The Wigwam Golf Resort & Spa is an old-money sort of place, and the traditional-style golf courses are the main attraction. Most of the guest rooms are in adobe-style buildings, surrounded by green lawns and colorful gardens, and all of the spacious units feature contemporary Southwestern furniture, plush new beds, and flat-screen TVs. Some units have fireplaces, but the rooms to request are those along the golf course.

300 Wigwam Blvd., Litchfield Park, AZ 85340. (℃) **800/327-0396** or 623/935-3811. Fax 623/935-3737. www.wigwam resort.com. 331 units. Early Jan to mid-May $269–$799 double, from $329 suite; mid-May to early Sept $119–$259 double, from $159 suite; early Sept to early Jan $199–$449 double, from $249 suite. Children under 17 stay free in parent's room. AE, DC, DISC, MC, V. Pets accepted ($50 deposit, $25 nonrefundable). **Amenities:** 3 restaurants (Southwestern, American, steakhouse); 3 lounges; 2 pools; 3 18-hole golf courses; 9 tennis courts; croquet court; health club; full-service spa; 2 Jacuzzis; bikes; children's programs; concierge; car-rental desk; business center; 24-hr. room service; massage; babysitting; laundry service; dry cleaning; executive-level rooms. *In room:* A/C, TV, dataport, minibar, coffeemaker, hair dryer, iron, safe, high-speed Internet access.

4 Where to Dine

The Valley of the Sun boasts hundreds of excellent restaurants, with most of the best dining options concentrated in the Scottsdale Road, north Scottsdale, and Biltmore Corridor areas. If you want to splurge on only one expensive meal while you're here, consider a resort restaurant that offers a view of the city lights. Other meals not to be missed are the cowboy dinners served amid Wild West decor at the area's "cowboy" steakhouses.

Good places to go trolling for a place to eat include the trendy Biltmore Fashion Park shopping center, at Camelback Road and 24th Street (℃ **602/955-1963**), and Old Town Scottsdale. At the former, you'll find nearly a dozen restaurants. In downtown Scottsdale, within an area of roughly 4 square blocks, you'll also find about a dozen good restaurants. A few of our favorites in both places are listed in the following pages.

Phoenix is a sprawling city, and it can be a real pain to have to drive around in search of a good lunch spot. If you happen to be visiting the Phoenix Art Museum, the Heard Museum, or the Desert Botanical Garden anytime around lunch, stay put for your noon meal. All three of these attractions have cafes serving decent, if limited, menus.

SCOTTSDALE
EXPENSIVE

Cowboy Ciao 𝒢 SOUTHWESTERN/FUSION   Yee-ha, bambino, the food at this place is great! A fun, "cowboy chic" atmosphere and delicious food with a global influence make a meal here unforgettable. You absolutely have to start your meal with the Stetson chopped salad; it's both a work of art and an explosion of flavors and textures once it passes your lips. Other not-to-be-missed dishes include the exotic mushroom pan-fry and the daily soup. Whatever you decide on for an entree, think small; you want to save room for one of pastry chef Tracy Dempsey's legendary desserts. Cowboy

Ciao is also notable for its wine list and bar. Located in downtown Scottsdale, the restaurant attracts a diverse crowd.

7133 E. Stetson Dr. (at Sixth Ave.). © 480/WINE-111. www.cowboyciao.com. Reservations recommended. Main courses $8–$32 lunch, $22–$32 dinner. AE, DC, DISC, MC, V. Sun–Thurs 11:30am–2:30pm and 5–10pm; Fri–Sat 11:30am–2:30pm and 5–11pm.

El Chorro Lodge ✸ CONTINENTAL   Built in 1934 as a girls' school, El Chorro is a Valley landmark and one of the area's last traditional establishments. Even if the interior is a little dowdy, at nighttime the lights twinkle on the saguaro cactus and the restaurant takes on a timeless tranquility. The adobe building houses several dining rooms, but the patio is the place to be, especially on cool evenings when a fire crackles in the fireplace. The menu features such classics as chateaubriand and rack of lamb, as well as such seldom-seen dishes as shad roe on toast. Save room for the legendary sticky buns.

5550 E. Lincoln Dr., Paradise Valley. © 480/948-5170. www.elchorro.com. Reservations recommended. Main courses $12–$21 lunch, $15–$65 dinner. AE, DC, DISC, MC, V. Mon–Fri 11am–2pm and 5:30–10pm; Sat 5:30–10pm; Sun 9am–2pm and 5:30–9pm. Sun brunch served only Oct–May.

Rancho Pinot ✸✸ NEW AMERICAN   Rancho Pinot, hidden at the back of a nondescript shopping center adjacent to the upscale Borgata shopping plaza, combines a homey cowboy-chic decor with nonthreatening contemporary American cuisine, and has long been a favorite with Scottsdale and Phoenix residents. Look elsewhere if you crave wildly creative flavor combinations, but if you like simple, well-prepared food, Rancho Pinot is a great choice. Our favorite starter is the grilled squid salad with preserved lemon; for a entree, you can always count on the handmade pasta or Nonni's chicken, braised with white wine, mushrooms, and herbs.

6208 N. Scottsdale Rd., in Lincoln Village Shops (southwest corner of Scottsdale Rd. and Lincoln Dr.). © 480/367-8030. www.ranchopinot.com. Reservations recommended. Main courses $18–$29. AE, MC, V. Mon–Sat 5:30–10pm. Summer hours may vary.

Roaring Fork ✸✸ SOUTHWESTERN   This restaurant serves some of the most creative Southwestern fare in the Valley. While no meal here is complete without a side of the green-chile macaroni and cheese, you'll probably also want an entree. Try the excellent duck breast with onion jam and sour-cherry mustard or the beef tenderloin (which just happens to come with the green-chile macaroni). If you can't get a table, dine in the saloon or the saloon patio. Happy hour (Mon–Sat 4–7pm) is a good time for an early meal from the saloon menu, actually worth eating from just so you can order the "big ass burger," a 12-ounce patty with roasted green chiles. Wash it all down with a huckleberry margarita.

4800 N. Scottsdale Rd. (in the Finova Building at the corner of Chaparral Rd.). © 480/947-0795. www.roaringfork.com. Reservations highly recommended. Main courses $17–$35. AE, DISC, MC, V. Mon–Sat 5–10pm; Sun 5–9pm.

Sea Saw ✸✸ JAPANESE   You'd never guess that this unpretentious hole-in-the-wall with seating for only 28 people is home to chef Nobuo Fukuda, considered one of the best chefs in the country. The menu lists barely more than a dozen dishes, so it's almost impossible to go wrong here. Not one of these dishes can really be considered sushi, so don't expect items such as California rolls. Instead, consider the seared tuna *tataki* or warm white-fish carpaccio. For the full treatment from Nobuo, order the multicourse *omakase* dinner. The restaurant is affiliated with the adjacent Cowboy Ciao and has an overwhelmingly long wine list that includes lots of premium sakes. By press time, Sea Saw will have moved to its new location at Scottsdale's South

Phoenix, Scottsdale & the Valley of the Sun Dining

Waterfront (call for address), and this space will be home to pastry chef Tracey Dempsey's French tea room.

7133 E. Stetson Dr. (480/481-9463. www.seasaw.net. Reservations not accepted. All plates $6–$16; tasting menu $90 ($125 w/wine). AE, DC, DISC, MC, V. Sun–Thurs 5:30–10pm; Fri–Sat 5:30–11pm.

MODERATE

Arcadia Farms ⚐ NEW AMERICAN   Long a favorite of the Scottsdale ladies-who-lunch crowd, this Old Town restaurant features a romantic setting and well-prepared contemporary fare. Try the delicious raspberry goat cheese salad with jicama and candied pecans. The warm mushroom, spinach, and goat cheese tart is another winner. Try to get a seat on the shady patio. This restaurant also operates cafes at the Heard Museum, the new Heard Museum North, and the Phoenix Art Museum.

7014 E. First Ave. (480/941-5665. www.arcadiafarmscafe.com. Reservations recommended. Main courses $12–$15. MC, V. Daily 11am–3pm.

Bandera ⚐ (Value) AMERICAN   Once you've gotten a whiff of the wood-roasted chickens turning on the rotisseries in Bandera's back-of-the-building, open-air stone oven, you'll know exactly what to order when you finally get seated at this perennially popular spot in Old Town. What an aroma! The succulent spit-roasted chicken is the meal to have here, and make sure you get it with some of Bandera's great mashed potatoes or cornbread. Sure, you could order prime rib or clams, but you'd be a fool if you did. Stick with the chicken or maybe the barbecued ribs, and you won't go wrong.

3821 N. Scottsdale Rd. (480/994-3524. Reservations recommended. Main courses $14–$29. AE, DC, DISC, MC, V. Sun–Thurs 4:30–10pm; Fri–Sat 4:30–11pm.

Bloom ⚐⚐ (Value) NEW AMERICAN   Located in the upscale Shops at Gainey Village, Bloom is part of a regional chain that includes several great Phoenix area restaurants and a couple of our favorite Tucson restaurants—Wildflower and Bistro Zin. The minimalist decor emphasizes flowers, an elegant wine bar serves a wide range of flights (tasting assortments), and the bistro-style menu has lots of great dishes in a wide range of prices. Opt for one of the wonderfully creative salads, such as fresh artichoke hearts with shaved Parmesan and white-truffle oil; there are also enough interesting appetizers to create a very satisfying dinner. The roast duck with drunken cherry sauce is excellent. This place is big and always buzzing with energy.

8877 N. Scottsdale Rd. (480/922-5666. Reservations recommended. Main courses $9–$15 lunch, $15–$29 dinner. AE, DC, DISC, MC, V. Mon–Thurs 11am–3pm and 5–10pm; Fri–Sat 11am–3pm and 5–10:30pm; Sun 5–9pm.

Carlsbad Tavern ⚐ NEW MEXICAN   Carlsbad Tavern blends the fiery tastes of New Mexican cuisine with a hip and humorous bat-theme atmosphere (a reference to Carlsbad Caverns). The menu lists traditional New Mexican dishes such as *carne adovada* (pork simmered in a fiery red-chile sauce), as well as contemporary Southwestern specialties such as poblano chiles stuffed with crab and pasta with an unusual chipotle stroganoff. Cool off your taste buds with a prickly-pear margarita. A lagoon makes this place feel like a beach bar, while the patio fireplace is cozy on a cold night.

3313 N. Hayden Rd. (south of Osborn). (480/970-8164. www.carlsbadtavern.com. Reservations accepted for 5 or more. Main courses $9–$23. AE, DISC, MC, V. Daily 11am–2am (limited menu daily 10 or 11pm–2am).

Old Town Tortilla Factory ⚐ MEXICAN   Located in an old house surrounded by attractive patios and citrus trees that bloom in winter and spring, this moderately priced Mexican restaurant has a great atmosphere, great food, and a lively bar scene (more than 80 premium tequilas). As you enter the restaurant grounds, you might even see someone making fresh tortillas, which come in a dozen different flavors. The rich tortilla soup and the tequila-lime salad make good starters. For an entree, try the pork chops crusted with ancho chile powder and raspberry sauce.

6910 E. Main St. Ⓒ 480/945-4567. www.oldtowntortillafactory.com. Reservations accepted only for parties of 6 or more. Main courses $9.25–$33. AE, DC, DISC, MC, V. Sun–Thurs 4:30–9:30pm; Fri–Sat 4:30–10:30pm.

Thaifoon ☆ THAI   This may not be traditional Thai food, but it sure is good. Thaifoon merges a hip upscale setting with flavorful food at economical prices. In fact, the dishes here are so good you'll likely find yourself coming back repeatedly to try others. The *tom kha gai* (Thai-style coconut-mushroom soup) is the best we've ever had, and the many shrimp dishes are packed with lively flavors. Don't miss the great tropical cocktails.

At The Shops at Gainey Village, 8777 N. Scottsdale Rd. Ⓒ 480/998-0011. www.thaifoon.com. Reservations recommended. Main courses $8–$16. AE, DISC, MC, V. Mon–Fri 11am–10pm; Sat noon–10pm; Sun 1–10pm.

Veneto Trattoria Italiana ☆ VENETIAN ITALIAN   This pleasantly low-key bistro, specializing in the cuisine of Venice, serves satisfying "peasant food," including traditional pork-and-garlic sausages served with grilled polenta and braised savoy cabbage. *Baccala mantecato* (creamy fish mousse on grilled polenta, made with dried salt cod soaked overnight in milk) may sound unusual, but it's absolutely heavenly. Other good bets include the salad of thinly sliced smoked beef, shaved Parmesan, and arugula. For a finale, try the *semifreddo con frutta secca,* a partially frozen meringue with dried fruits in a pool of raspberry sauce. There's a welcoming bistro ambience and outdoor seating on the patio.

6137 N. Scottsdale Rd., in Hilton Village. Ⓒf 480/948-9928. www.venetotrattoria.com. Reservations recommended. Main courses $8.50–$20 lunch, $14–$25 dinner. AE, DC, DISC, MC, V. Mon–Sat 11:30am–2:30pm and 5–10pm.

Zinc Bistro ☆☆ *Finds* FRENCH   It may seem incongruous to find a French bistro in sunny Scottsdale, and in a modern outdoor shopping center at that, but here it is. This place is a perfect reproduction of the sort of bistro you may have loved on your last trip to Paris. Everything is authentic, from the zinc bar to the sidewalk cafe seating to the hooks under the bar for ladies' purses. Try the Provençal-style ahi tuna, the omelet piled high with shoestring potatoes, or anything that comes with the fabulous bistro fries. For dessert, try the Zinc chocolate soufflé.

In Kierland Commons, 15034 N. Scottsdale Rd. Ⓒ 480/603-0922. www.zincbistroaz.com. Reservations accepted only for parties of 6 or more. Main courses $12–$15 lunch, $8–$43 dinner. AE, DC, MC, V. Daily 11am–10pm.

INEXPENSIVE

El Molino Mexican Café ☆ *Finds* MEXICAN   Located a bit out of the Old Town Scottsdale mainstream, this small Mexican joint is little more than a fast-food place, but it serves the best chimichangas in town. If you're among the few people in this country still not familiar with what a chimichanga is, it's a deep-fried burrito. That said, the chimis here have crispy, light shells and are packed with tasty fillings. Try one with *machaca* (shredded and spiced beef) or green chile, and we're sure you'll become a convert. If fried food just doesn't do it for you, opt for a couple of green corn tamales, an Arizona specialty.

3554 N. Goldwater Blvd. Ⓒ 480/994-3566. www.elmolinocafe.com. Reservations not accepted. Main courses $2–$9.50. DISC, MC, V. Mon–Sat 9am–8pm.

El Paso Barbeque Company ☆ BARBECUE   This is Scottsdale-style barbecue, which means you'll be licking your fingers amid upscale cowboy decor. If you're in the mood for raucous good times, this place is worth the trip. The barbecue runs the gamut from ribs to smoked chicken to more uptown dishes such as barbecued salmon and prime rib. The pulled pork with a smoky sauce and fresh coleslaw is scrumptious. There's also a wide variety of sandwiches, making this a good lunch or takeout spot. The roll of paper towels on your table should give you an idea of how messy a meal here will be.

8220 N. Hayden Rd. ℂ 480/998-2626. www.elpasobarbeque.com. Reservations accepted for parties of 8 or more. Main courses $8–$24. AE, DISC, MC, V. Sun–Thurs 11am–10pm; Fri–Sat 11am–11pm.

Grazie ☆ (Finds PIZZA   This little neighborhood pizzeria and wine bar is in downtown Scottsdale at the west end of Main Street near the Valley Ho resort and is a little gem of a place—sophisticated and full of contemporary art. It's also very popular on weekends, and the noise level can be deafening. Come on a weeknight or for lunch if you want to carry on a conversation without shouting. The weekend buzz aside, this is a great place to sip Italian wines and share a couple of designer pizzas from the wood-fired oven. Start your meal with the carpaccio, which is served with arugula, parmigiano-reggiano cheese, and a lemon vinaigrette; or a salad made with arugula, baby greens, parmigiano-reggiano, red onions, red bell peppers, and pine nuts. The pizzas here have paper-thin crusts, so don't worry about filling up before it's time to order the signature ice cream calzone.

6952 E. Main St. ℂ 480/663-9797. www.grazie.us. Reservations recommended Fri–Sat nights. Main courses $9–$15. AE, MC, V. Mon–Sat 11am–2pm and 5–10pm; Sun 5–10pm.

Los Olivos ☆ MEXICAN   Los Olivos is a Scottsdale institution, one of the last restaurants in Old Town that dates to the days when cowboys tied up their horses on Main Street. Although the food is just standard Mexican fare, the building is a fascinating folk-art construction. The entrance is a bit like a cement cave, with strange figures rising from the roof. Amazingly, this throwback to slower times is only steps away from the Scottsdale Museum of Contemporary Art. On Friday and Saturday nights, there's Latin dancing from 9pm until 1am.

There's another Los Olivos up in north Scottsdale at 15544 N. Pima Rd. (ℂ 480/596-9787).

7328 Second St. ℂ 480/946-2256. www.losolivosrestaurant.com. Reservations recommended. Main courses $6.50–$16. AE, DISC, MC, V. Sun–Thurs 11am–10pm; Fri–Sat 11am–11pm.

Los Sombreros ☆ (Finds MEXICAN   Although this casual Mexican restaurant is in an attractive old house, it doesn't look all that special from the outside. However, the menu is surprisingly creative and veers from the standard dishes served at most Mexican restaurants. Start with the chunky homemade guacamole, which is some of the best in the city. Be sure to order the *puerco en chipotle,* succulent, slow-roasted pork in tomatillo-chipotle sauce. Finish it all off with the flan, which will spoil you for flan anywhere else. For a real treat, get it with almond-flavored tequila.

2534 N. Scottsdale Rd. (at McKellips Rd.), Scottsdale. ℂ 480/994-1799. www.lossombreros.com. Reservations accepted for 5 or more. Main courses $14–$17. AE, DC, MC, V. Sun and Tues–Thurs 5–9pm; Fri–Sat 5–10pm.

NORTH SCOTTSDALE, CAREFREE & CAVE CREEK
EXPENSIVE
La Hacienda ☆☆ GOURMET MEXICAN   As you may guess from the price range below, this is not your average taco joint. La Hacienda serves gourmet Mexican cuisine

Cowboy Steakhouses

Cowboy steakhouses are family restaurants that generally provide big portions of grilled steaks and barbecued ribs, outdoor and "saloon" dining, live country music, and various other sorts of entertainment.

At **Rustler's Rooste** 👁 you can start your meal by scooting down a big slide from the bar to the main dining room. While the view north across Phoenix is entertainment enough for most people, there are also cowboy bands playing for those who like to kick up their heels. If you've got the appetite of a hardworking cowpoke, try the enormous cowboy "stuff" platter consisting of, among other things, steak kebabs, barbecued ribs, cowboy beans, fried shrimp, barbecued chicken, and skewered swordfish. You'll find Rustler's at the Pointe South Mountain Resort, 8383 S. 48th St., in Phoenix (© **602/431-6474**; www.rustlersrooste.com). Entrees range from $15 to $30.

Of the many cowboy steakhouses around the valley, this is by far your best bet for a family dinner. Not only are the steaks some of the best you'll find at a family steakhouse, but there's an entire Western town mock-up surrounding the restaurant, so there's plenty to keep you and your kids entertained before and after dinner. If you feel adventurous, start your meal with some rattlesnake or "Rocky Mountain oysters" (bull's testicles). Cowboy bands keep the crowds entertained during dinner. From February to June, there are also sundown cookouts ($45 adults, $19 children) that include a hayride, chuck-wagon dinner, live country music, and lots of other traditional Wild West entertainment.

in an upscale, glamorous, but rustic setting reminiscent of an early 1900s hacienda (stone-tiled floor, Mexican glassware and crockery, a beehive fireplace). Be sure to start with the *antojitos* (appetizers) platter, which might include pork flautas (a rolled-up fried tortilla), baked shrimp, crabmeat enchiladas, and a red-corn quesadilla made with squash blossoms, wild mushrooms, and goat cheese. Roasted whole suckling pig carved tableside is the house specialty and should not be missed. However, the rack of lamb crusted with pumpkin seeds has long been a local favorite. Live music lends a party atmosphere.

At The Fairmont Scottsdale Princess, 7575 E. Princess Dr. (about 12 miles north of downtown Scottsdale). © **480/585-4848**. Reservations recommended. Main courses $25–$42. AE, DC, DISC, MC, V. Thurs–Tues 5:30–10pm.

Michael's 👁👁 NEW AMERICAN/INTERNATIONAL   Located in the classy little Citadel shopping/business plaza in north Scottsdale, this restaurant is one of the Valley's best. The setting is simple yet elegant, which allows the drama of food presentation to come to the fore. To start things off, do not miss the "silver spoons" hors d'oeuvres—tablespoons each containing three or four ingredients that burst with flavor. From there, it's on to main courses such as duck and foie gras with a sweet-potato ravioli in sage-balsamic butter. For drinks with or without a light meal, head upstairs to the bar.

8700 E. Pinnacle Peak Rd., N. Scottsdale. © **480/515-2575**. www.michaelsrestaurant.com. Reservations recommended. Main courses $8–$18 lunch, $25–$36 dinner; prix-fixe menu $55 ($90–$100 w/wine). AE, DC, DISC, MC, V. Mon–Fri 11am–2pm and 6–10pm; Sat 6–10pm; Sun 10am–2pm (brunch) and 6–10pm.

Mosaic ☆☆☆ *Finds* NEW AMERICAN   The Pinnacle Peak area of north Scottsdale boasts one of the Valley's greatest concentrations of excellent, high-end restaurants, and this just may be the best of a very good bunch. Okay, so dinner here is going to set you back quite a bit, but the food is superb, and if you come before the sun goes down, you can soak up some of the best desert views in the Valley. Chef/owner Deborah Knight is one of the best chefs around and likes to show off her culinary creativity with a menu that changes regularly and is always provocative and daring. How about Sri Lankan–spiced prime rib or crispy duck in Tanzanian peanut curry to start things out? For an entree, you might order a lamb rack crusted with almonds and walnuts or pork loin dusted with four peppercorns. You get the picture; this is a foodie's nirvana.

10600 E. Jomax Rd., N. Scottsdale. ☎ 480/563-9600. www.mosaic-restaurant.com. Reservations recommended. Main courses $26–$40; tasting menu $65–$85 ($100–$120 w/wine). AE, DC, DISC, MC, V. Tues–Sat 5:30–9 or 10pm. Closed mid-Aug to mid-Sept.

Sassi ☆☆ ITALIAN   If you've had to forego this year's vacation in Italy, then don't miss an opportunity to have a meal at this Tuscan villa transplanted to the Arizona desert. Every room in this beautiful, sprawling building is gorgeous and has a distinctive character of its own. You just might have to eat here a few times before you decide which room you like the best. The menu is not your standard southern Italian menu, so don't go looking for spaghetti and meatballs (although you might find an excellent spaghetti primavera). Instead, try the wood-oven shrimp with asparagus, lemon, roasted garlic, and prosciutto broth, or a dish with the house-made sausage or house-made mortadella. In fact, the best thing to do here is order a bunch of dishes and then share everything, as any good Italian family would.

10455 E. Pinnacle Peak Pkwy., Scottsdale. ☎ 480/502-9095. www.sassi.biz. Reservations highly recommended. Primi $12–$20; secondi $18–$38. AE, DC, DISC, MC, V. Tues–Sun 5:30–9 or 10pm.

MODERATE

Bodega Bistro & Tapas Bar ☆☆ SPANISH   This tiny Spanish tapas restaurant, tucked away in a courtyard in downtown Carefree's Spanish Village shopping center, is well worth searching out. Not only will you find the best tapas in the Phoenix area, but an excellent wine list (try some of the Argentine wine). The friendly owner and staff make this a fun, casual place for a light meal after cowboying up in adjacent Cave Creek. Try the Catalan flatbread (sort of like pizza), the *banderillas* (skewers of meat, olives, and red and yellow peppers), or paella.

In Spanish Village, 7208 Ho Rd., Carefree. ☎ 480/488-4166. www.bodegabistroaz.com. Reservations recommended. Main courses $8–$38. AE, MC, V. Sun–Thurs 5–9pm; Fri–Sat 5–10pm.

The Original Crazy Ed's Satisfied Frog Saloon & Restaurant *Finds* AMERICAN/BARBECUE   Cave Creek is the Phoenix area's favorite cow-town hangout and is filled with Wild West–themed saloons and restaurants. Crazy Ed's—affiliated with the Black Mountain Brewing Company, which produces Cave Creek Chili Beer—is our favorite. This place is just plain fun, with big covered porches and sawdust on the floor. Stick to steaks and barbecue. You'll find Crazy Ed's in the tourist-trap Frontier Town.

At Frontier Town, 6245 E. Cave Creek Rd., Cave Creek. ☎ 480/488-3317. www.satisfiedfrog.com. Reservations recommended on weekends. Main courses $9–$29. AE, DC, DISC, MC, V. Daily 11am–10pm.

INEXPENSIVE

Greasewood Flat ☆ *Finds* AMERICAN   Burgers and beer are the mainstays at this rustic open-air restaurant in the Pinnacle Peak area of north Scottsdale. Located down a potholed gravel road behind Reata Pass steakhouse, Greasewood Flat is a desert party spot where families, motorcycle clubs, cyclists, and horseback riders all rub shoulders. Place your order at the window and grab a seat at one of the picnic tables. While you wait for your meal, you can check out the old farm equipment. This place is the antithesis of Scottsdale posh, and that's exactly why we love it. Only in Arizona could you find a place like this.

27375 N. Alma School Pkwy. ℭ 480/585-9430. www.greasewoodflat.net. Main courses $3.75–$8. No credit cards. Daily 11am–1am.

CENTRAL PHOENIX & THE CAMELBACK CORRIDOR
VERY EXPENSIVE

Mary Elaine's 𝒢𝒢𝒢 FRENCH   There quite simply is no place else in Arizona to compare with Mary Elaine's, and if you happen to be in town for a major wedding anniversary or milestone birthday, this is the place to celebrate. At least once in your life you should splurge on the sort of dining experience provided here. Situated atop the posh Phoenician resort, this elegant restaurant is the pinnacle of Arizona dining not only for its haute cuisine, but also for its award-winning wine list (and master sommelier), exemplary service, and superb table settings. The menu focuses on classic French cuisine with an emphasis on impeccably fresh ingredients; foie gras, truffles, lobster, and caviar all make frequent appearances. Menus change seasonally, and there are also themed tasting menus. Try to make a reservation that allows you to take in the sunset.

At The Phoenician, 6000 E. Camelback Rd. ℭ 480/423-2530. Reservations highly recommended. Jackets suggested for men. Main courses $45–$48; 7-course tasting menu $125 (plus $85 for matched wines). AE, DC, DISC, MC, V. Tues–Thurs 5:30–9:30pm; Fri–Sat 5:30–10pm.

EXPENSIVE

Coup des Tartes 𝒢 *Finds* COUNTRY FRENCH   Chain restaurants, theme restaurants, restaurants that are all style and little substance: Sometimes in Phoenix it seems impossible to find a genuinely homey little hole-in-the-wall that serves good food. Don't despair; Coup des Tartes is just the ticket. With barely a dozen tables and no liquor license (bring your own wine; $8 corkage fee), it's about as removed from the standard Phoenix glitz as you can get without boarding a plane and leaving town. Start your meal with pâté de campagne or the scrumptious brie brûlée, which is covered with caramelized apples. The entree menu changes regularly, but the Moroccan lamb shank with couscous is so good that it's always available. The filet mignon, with the sauce of the moment, is another good choice. Of course, for dessert, you absolutely must have a tart.

4626 N. 16th St. (a couple blocks south of Camelback Rd.). ℭ 602/212-1082. www.nicetartes.com. Reservations recommended. Main courses $18–$36. AE, MC, V. Wed–Sat 5:30–10pm.

LON'S at the hermosa 𝒢𝒢 NEW AMERICAN   Located in a beautiful old adobe hacienda built by cowboy artist Lon Megargee and surrounded by colorful gardens, this restaurant is one of the most classically Arizonan places in the Phoenix area, and the patio, with its views of Camelback Mountain, is blissfully tranquil. Lunch on the patio is the meal to have here. Entrees are reliable, and if you peruse the menu closely, you'll turn up some interesting Southwestern ingredients, including prickly pear and Arizona-farmed shrimp. Basically, you eat here more for the atmosphere than for gustatory epiphanies. The bar has a cozy and romantic Wild West feel.

At the Hermosa Inn, 5532 N. Palo Cristi Rd. ℭ 602/955-7878. www.lons.com. Reservations recommended. Main courses $11–$15 lunch, $23–$34 dinner. AE, DC, DISC, MC, V. Mon–Fri 11:30am–2pm and 6–10pm; Sat 6–10pm; Sun 10am–2pm (brunch) and 6–10pm.

T. Cook's 𝒢𝒢𝒢 MEDITERRANEAN   Ready to pop the question? On your honeymoon? Celebrating an anniversary? This is the place for you. There just isn't a more romantic restaurant in the Valley. Located within the walls of the Mediterranean-inspired Royal Palms Resort and Spa, it's surrounded by decades-old gardens and even has palm trees growing right through the roof of the dining room. The focal point of the open kitchen is a wood-fired oven that turns out a fabulous spit-roasted chicken as well as an impressive platter of paella. T. Cook's continues to make big impressions right through to the dessert course.

At the Royal Palms Resort and Spa, 5200 E. Camelback Rd. Ⓒ **866/579-3636** or 602/808-0766. www.royal palmshotel.com. Reservations highly recommended. Main courses $11–$16 lunch, $25–$36 dinner. AE, DC, DISC, MC, V. Mon–Sat 6–10am, 11am–2pm, and 5:30–10pm; Sun 6–10am, 10am–2pm (brunch), and 5:30–10pm.

Vincent's on Camelback 𝒢𝒢 SOUTHWESTERN   Vincent's is a Phoenix bastion of Southwestern cuisine and has long enjoyed a devoted local following. The menu blends Southwestern influences with classic European dishes. You could order a delicious lobster salad or sautéed beef tenderloins with pinot noir glaze, but if you're from outside the region, you should try the Southwestern dishes. Don't miss the duck tamale or the tequila soufflé, and for an entree, the veal sweetbreads with blue cornmeal are an enduring favorite. For a casual breakfast or lunch, try the attached Vincent's Market Bistro (see below), which is affiliated with the restaurant's Saturday farmers' market.

3930 E. Camelback Rd. Ⓒ 602/224-0225. www.vincentsoncamelback.com. Reservations highly recommended. Main courses $11–$16 lunch, $29–$32 dinner. AE, DC, DISC, MC, V. Mon–Fri 11:30am–2pm and 5–10pm; Sat 5–10pm.

MODERATE

Chelsea's Kitchen 𝒢 NEW AMERICAN   Although this restaurant can seem a bit expensive for what you get, the setting, on the banks of a canal just a block off Camelback Road, is gorgeous. The patio, with a wood-burning fireplace, is nearly as large as the dining room and is where you should try to get a table. The sunsets can be absolutely unforgettable. Separating the dining room and patio is a fun indoor-outdoor bar. Under the same ownership as the nearby La Grande Orange Pizzeria and Postino wine bar, Chelsea's Kitchen features a menu of familiar comfort foods with a few more creative dishes thrown into the mix. The seasonal salads are usually a good choice, as are the ahi tuna tacos. Be sure to try the fried chicken and the short-rib hash.

5040 N. 40th St. Ⓒ 602/957-2555. www.chelseaskitchenaz.com. Main courses $10–$27. AE, MC, V. Mon–Fri 11am–10pm; Sat–Sun 4–10pm.

Delux 𝒢 BURGERS   With a sleek and stylish decor, a very limited menu (you'd better like burgers), and one of the best selections of draft beers in the Valley, this is the ultimate ultra-hip burger-and-beer joint. The burgers get our vote for best burgers in the city, but it's the cute Barbie-size shopping carts full of crispy french fries that are the real reason to dine here. Talk about your guilty pleasures—it just doesn't get much better than a cart of fries and a pint of Old Rasputin imperial stout. If you're not a burger-meister, don't despair; there are great salads and a few nonbeef sandwiches.

In the Biltmore Plaza, 3146 E. Camelback Rd. Ⓒ 602/522-2288. www.deluxburger.com. Reservations not accepted. Main courses $6–$10. AE, DC, DISC, MC, V. Daily 11am–2am.

Sierra Bonita 𝒢 SOUTHWESTERN   This neighborhood restaurant is the sort of place you dream about finding—flavorful food, big portions, moderate prices. What's not to like? Well, it is a bit out-of-the-way if you're just visiting Phoenix, but don't let that scare you off. Start with the guacamole and the bacon-wrapped shrimp, and then maybe order the same thing again. Next, order whatever's being served with the mashed sweet potatoes (they're heavenly). If you're really hungry, opt for the pork *osso buco* (pork shank) with green chile sauce. Did somebody say Oaxacan chocolate soufflé for dessert?

6933 N. Seventh St. ✆ 602/264-0700. www.sierrabonitagrill.com. Reservations recommended. Main courses $8–$26. AE, MC, V. Sun–Thurs 11am–10pm; Fri–Sat 11am–11pm.

Vincent's Market Bistro 🎇 FRENCH   Located in back of the ever-popular Vincent's restaurant, this casual place does a respectable job of conjuring up a casual backstreet bistro in Paris. It's utterly quaint without being froufrou. Tables have cast-iron bases, and chairs have woven-reed seats. You can sit down and have a meal here (try the coq au vin), or get some gourmet food to go. This place stays packed on Saturday mornings when Vincent's farmers' market attracts crowds of shoppers in search of gourmet snacks and fresh produce.

3930 E. Camelback Rd. ✆ 602/224-3727. www.vincentsoncamelback.com. Main courses $7–$13. AE, DC, DISC, MC, V. Mon–Fri 7am–8pm; Sat–Sun 7am–2pm.

INEXPENSIVE

5 & Diner AMERICAN   If it's 2am and you just have to have a big, greasy burger and a side of fries, head for the 24-hour 5 & Diner. You can't miss it—it's the classic streamliner diner that looks as if it just materialized from New Jersey.

Other locations are in Paradise Valley, 12802 N. Tatum Blvd. (✆ **602/996-0033**); and in Scottsdale at Scottsdale Pavilions, 9069 E. Indian Bend Rd. (✆ **480/949-1957**).

5220 N. 16th St. ✆ 602/264-5220. www.5anddiner.com. Reservations not accepted. Sandwiches/plates $5.50–$15. AE, DC, DISC, MC, V. Daily 24 hr.

La Grande Orange Pizzeria 🎇 PIZZA   Good pizza and an off-the-beaten-tourist-path neighborhood location make this casual restaurant a good place to feel like a local. Best of all, La Grande Orange is convenient to both downtown Scottsdale and the pricey Camelback corridor. Gourmet pizzas are what this place is all about, but you should start with the orange-fennel salad or one of the other great salads. While you're here, check out the adjacent La Grande Orange gourmet grocery (great for stocking a picnic) and gelateria (delightful on a hot day).

4410 N. 40th St. (at Campbell St.). ✆ 602/840-7777. www.lagrandeorangepizzeria.com. Reservations not accepted. Main courses $10–$14. AE, MC, V. Daily 4–10pm.

Pane Bianco 🎇 *Finds* BAKERY/SANDWICHES   Chris Bianco, owner of downtown's immensely popular Pizzeria Bianco (see below), has another winner on his hands with this casual counter-service bakery and sandwich shop not far from the Heard Museum. The menu consists of only four sandwiches and a couple of salads, but all the breads are baked on the premises in a wood-fired oven. The house-made mozzarella is exquisitely fresh and is served both as a caprese salad with tomatoes and basil and in a focaccia sandwich with the same ingredients. And that focaccia? The best in Phoenix.

4404 N. Central Ave. ✆ 602/234-2100. Reservations not accepted. Main courses $8. AE, MC, V. Tues–Sat 11am–3pm.

DOWNTOWN, SOUTH PHOENIX & THE AIRPORT AREA
EXPENSIVE

Quiessence 🎇 *Finds* NEW AMERICAN   This place is as far from a typical Phoenix/Scottsdale dining experience as you can get without going to the airport and getting on a plane. Set at the back of a shady pecan grove not far from South Mountain Park, Quiessence is surrounded by organic vegetable gardens. It is these gardens, and the freshness of the ingredients they provide, that makes the food here so wonderful, but it is the delightfully rural setting that makes Quiessence truly special. The herbed chicken here is so good you'll forget that it's actually good for you. Don't pass it up if it's on the menu. Oh, and by the way, the desserts are outrageous!

6106 S. 32nd St. © 602/276-0601. www.quiessencerestaurant.com. Reservations recommended. Main courses $19–$24. AE, DC, MC, V. Tues–Sat 5–9pm.

MODERATE

Alice Cooper'stown 𝄢 BARBECUE   Owned by Alice Cooper himself, this sports-and-rock-themed restaurant/bar is downtown's premier eat-o-tainment center. Sixteen video screens (usually showing sporting events) are the centerpiece, but there's also an abundance of memorabilia, including guitars once used by the likes of Fleetwood Mac and Eric Clapton. The waitstaff even wears Alice Cooper makeup. Barbecue is served in various permutations, including a huge barbecue sandwich. If you're an Alice Cooper fan, or hope to spot some local pro athletes, this place is a must.

101 E. Jackson St. © 602/253-7337. www.alicecooperstown.com. Reservations accepted for only parties of 7 or more. Sandwiches/barbecue $8–$19. AE, MC, V. Sun–Thurs 11am–8 or 9pm; Fri–Sat 11am–9 or 10pm.

Pizzeria Bianco 𝄢 PIZZA   Even though this historic brick building is in the heart of downtown Phoenix, the atmosphere is so cozy it feels like your neighborhood local, and the wood-burning oven turns out delicious rustic pizzas. One of our favorites is made with red onion, Parmesan, rosemary, and crushed pistachios. Don't miss the fresh mozzarella, either: Pizzeria Bianco makes its own, and it can be ordered as an appetizer or on a pizza.

At Heritage Sq., 623 E. Adams St. © 602/258-8300. www.pizzeriabianco.com. Reservations accepted for 6–10 people. Pizzas $10–$14. AE, MC, V. Tues–Sat 5–10pm.

INEXPENSIVE

Carolina's (Finds MEXICAN   Located in a somewhat run-down neighborhood south of the US Airways Center and Chase Field, Carolina's is a Phoenix institution. As such you'll find everyone from Hispanic construction workers to downtown corporate-types (men in suits, women in high heels and pearls). Everyone enjoys the down-home Mexican cooking here, but Carolina's flour tortillas are what really set this place apart. Order a burrito, perhaps with shredded beef in a spicy green sauce, and you'll be handed what feels like a down-filled pillow, so soft you'll want to lay your head on it. Or get the tortillas to go and use them as the basis for a fun Phoenician picnic.

There's a second Carolina's in north Phoenix at 2126 E. Cactus Rd. (© 602/275-8231).

1202 E. Mohave St. © 602/252-1503. www.carolinasmex.com. Main dishes $3–$5.75. AE, DISC, MC, V. Mon–Fri 7am–7:30pm; Sat 7am–6pm.

The Farm at South Mountain/The Farm Kitchen & Morning Glory Café 𝄢 (Finds (Kids SANDWICHES/SALADS   If being in the desert has you dreaming of shady trees and green grass, you'll enjoy The Farm Kitchen, an oasis reminiscent of a Deep South pecan orchard. A rustic outbuilding has been converted to a counter-service lunch restaurant where you can order a filling sandwich or a delicious pecan turkey Waldorf salad. Breakfast means baked goods such as muffins and scones. The grassy lawn, shaded by pecan trees, is ideal for a picnic. And you can let the kids run all over while you enjoy your salad or sandwich. At the back of the farm, you'll find the **Morning Glory Café** (© **602/276-8804**), a cozy little breakfast place.

6106 S. 32nd St. © 602/276-7288. www.thefarmatsouthmountain.com. Sandwiches and salads $9.95. AE, DC, MC, V. Mid-Sept to May Tues–Sun 8am–4pm. (If weather is inclement, call to be sure it's open.) Closed June to mid-Sept. Take Exit 151A off I-10 and go south on 32nd St.

Fry Bread House *Finds* NATIVE AMERICAN   Fry bread is just what it sounds like—fried bread—and it's a mainstay on Indian reservations throughout the West. Although you can eat these thick, chewy slabs of fried bread plain, salted, or with honey, they also serve as the wrappers for Indian tacos, which are made with meat, beans, and lettuce. If you've already visited the Four Corners region of Arizona, then you've probably had an Indian taco. Forget them—the ones here are the best in the state. Try one with green chile. If you still have room for dessert, do not miss the fry bread with chocolate and butter.

4140 N. Seventh Ave. © 602/351-2345. Reservations not accepted. Main courses $3–$6.50. DISC, MC, V. Mon–Thurs 10am–7pm; Fri–Sat 10am–8pm.

Los Dos Molinos ✿ MEXICAN   You better travel with a fire extinguisher, because you're gonna need it if you eat at this legendary hot spot in south Phoenix. The food here is New Mexican–style, which means that everything, with the exception of the margaritas, is incendiary. Actually, there are a few dishes for the timid, but people who don't like their food fiery know enough to stay away from this place. So popular is the food at Los Dos Molinos that there's even one in New York. Here in the Phoenix area, there's another at 260 S. Alma School Rd., Mesa (© 480/969-7475). Expect a 2- to 3-hour wait for a table on weekends.

8646 S. Central Ave. © 602/243-9113. Reservations not accepted. Main courses $3.50–$13. AE, DC, DISC, MC, V. Tues–Fri 11am–2:30pm and 5–9pm; Sat 11am–9pm.

MacAlpine's Restaurant and Soda Fountain *Finds* AMERICAN   This is the oldest operating soda fountain in the Southwest, and it hasn't changed much since its opening in 1928. Wooden booths and worn countertops show the patina of age. Big burgers and sandwiches make up the lunch offerings and should be washed down with a root beer float, chocolate malted, or egg cream.

2303 N. Seventh St. © 602/262-5545. Reservations not accepted. Sandwiches/specials $4–$6.75. AE, DISC, MC, V. Sun–Thurs 11am–7pm; Fri–Sat 11am–8pm.

TEMPE & MESA
EXPENSIVE
House of Tricks ✿✿ NEW AMERICAN   Despite the name, you'll find far more treats here than tricks. Housed in a pair of old Craftsman bungalows surrounded by a garden of shady trees, this restaurant seems a world away from the bustle on nearby Mill Avenue. This is a nice spot for a romantic evening and a good place to try some innovative cuisine. The garlicky Caesar salad and house-smoked salmon with avocado, capers, and lemon cream are good bets for starters. Among the entrees, the seared ahi tuna is a good choice. Try to get a seat on the grape-arbor–covered patio.

114 E. Seventh St., Tempe. © 480/968-1114. www.houseoftricks.com. Reservations recommended. Main courses $7.25–$12 lunch, $22–$34 dinner. AE, DISC, MC, V. Mon–Sat 11am–10pm.

MODERATE
Blue Adobe Grille ✿✿ *Finds* MEXICAN   This restaurant looks like the sort of place you should drive right past. Don't! Despite appearances, this New Mexican–style

Moments **Dining with a View**

When you've got one of the best views around and some of the best patio dining, do you really have to serve good food? Probably not, but luckily **elements,** the stylish restaurant at the Sanctuary on Camelback Mountain resort, doesn't try to slide by on looks alone. That said, the view is a big part of dinner here, so try to make a reservation so that you can catch the sunset light on Mummy Mountain. The menu changes regularly and includes influences from around the world. The restaurant is located at Sanctuary on Camelback, 5700 E. McDonald Dr., in Paradise Valley (② **480/607-2300;** www. elementsrestaurant.com). Main courses range from $12 to $21 at lunch and from $27 to $36 at dinner.

restaurant serves deliciously creative Southwestern fare at very economical prices. To get an idea of what the food here is all about, order the Tres Santa Fe combination plate and request a tenderloin burrito, a shrimp enchilada, and *carne adovada.* Of course, there are great margaritas, but there's also a surprisingly good wine list. This place is a hangout for Chicago Cubs fans and makes a good dinner stop on the way back from driving the Apache Trail. There's a second Blue Adobe at 10885 N. Frank Lloyd Wright Blvd., Scottsdale (② **480/314-0550**).

144 N. Country Club Dr., Mesa. ② **480/962-1000.** www.blueadobegrille.com. Reservations recommended. Main courses $9–$24. AE, DC, DISC, MC, V. Sun–Thurs 11am–9pm; Fri–Sat 11am–10pm.

Monti's La Casa Vieja ❀ AMERICAN   If you're tired of the Scottsdale glitz and are looking for Old Arizona, try this place. The adobe building was constructed in 1873 (*casa vieja* means "old house" in Spanish) on the site of the Salt River ferry, which operated in the days when the river flowed year-round. Today, local families know Monti's well and rely on the restaurant for solid meals and low prices—you can get a filet mignon for as little as $12. The dark dining rooms are filled with memorabilia of the Old West.

100 S. Mill Ave. (at Rio Salado Pkwy.), Tempe. ② **480/967-7594.** www.montis.com. Reservations recommended for dinner. Main courses $10–$33. AE, DC, DISC, MC, V. Sun–Thurs 11am–10pm; Fri–Sat 11am–11pm.

INEXPENSIVE

Organ Stop Pizza ❀ *Kids* PIZZA   The pizza here may not be the best in town, but the mighty Wurlitzer theater organ, the largest in the world, sure is memorable. This massive instrument, which contains more than 5,500 pipes, has four turbine blowers to provide the wind to create the sound, and with 40-foot ceilings in the restaurant, the acoustics are great. As you marvel at the skill of the organist, who performs songs ranging from the latest pop tunes to *The Phantom of the Opera,* you can enjoy simple pizzas, pastas, or snacks.

1149 E. Southern Ave. (at Stapley Dr.), Mesa. ② **480/813-5700.** www.organstoppizza.com. Reservations for large groups only. Pizzas and pastas $5–$17. No credit cards. Thanksgiving to mid-Apr Sun–Thurs 4–9pm, Fri–Sat 4–10pm; mid-Apr to Thanksgiving Sun–Thurs 5–9pm, Fri–Sat 5–10pm.

5 Seeing the Sights

THE DESERT & ITS NATIVE CULTURES

Deer Valley Rock Art Center ✿   Located in the Hedgepeth Hills in the northwest corner of the Valley of the Sun, the Deer Valley Rock Art Center preserves an amazing concentration of Native American petroglyphs, some of which date back 5,000 years. Although these petroglyphs may not at first seem as impressive as those at more famous sites, the sheer numbers make this a fascinating spot. The drawings, which range from simple spirals to much more complex renderings of herds of deer, are on volcanic boulders along a quarter-mile trail. An interpretive center provides background information on this site and on rock art in general. From October through early May, there are guided tours Saturday at 10am.

3711 W. Deer Valley Rd. ✆ 623/582-8007. www.asu.edu/clas/anthropology/dvrac. Admission $5 adults, $3 seniors and students, $2 children 6–12. Oct–Apr Tues–Sat 9am–5pm, Sun noon–5pm; May–Sept Tues–Fri 8am–2pm, Sat 9am–5pm, Sun noon–5pm. Closed major holidays. Take the Loop 101 highway west to 27th Ave., go north to Deer Valley Rd., and go west 2½ miles to just past 35th Ave.

Desert Botanical Garden ✿✿✿   Located in Papago Park adjacent to the Phoenix Zoo, this botanic garden displays more than 20,000 desert plants from around the world, and its Plants and People of the Sonoran Desert Trail is the state's best introduction to Southwestern ethnobotany (human use of plants). On the Desert Wildflower Trail, you'll find colorful wildflowers throughout much of the year. Each spring, there's usually a butterfly pavilion filled with live butterflies. If you come late in the day, you can stay until after dark and see night-blooming flowers and dramatically lit cacti. A cafe on the grounds makes a great lunch spot. From late November through late December, during *Las Noches de las Luminarias*, the gardens are lit at night by *luminarias* (candles inside small bags).

In Papago Park, 1201 N. Galvin Pkwy. ✆ 480/941-1225. www.dbg.org. Admission $10 adults, $9 seniors, $5 students 13–18, $4 children 3–12. Oct–Apr daily 8am–8pm; May–Sept daily 7am–8pm. Closed July 4th, Thanksgiving, and Christmas. Bus: 3.

Heard Museum ✿✿✿   The Heard Museum is one of the nation's finest museums dealing exclusively with Native American cultures and is an ideal introduction to the indigenous peoples of Arizona. From pre-Columbian to contemporary, if it's art created by Native Americans, you'll find it here. If you're interested in the native cultures of Arizona, this should be your very first stop in the state. The museum is an invaluable introduction to the state's many tribes. The **Home: Native Peoples of the Southwest** exhibit examines the culture of each of the major tribes of the region and is the heart and soul of the museum. Included in this exhibit are more than 500 kachina dolls. In another gallery, you'll find fascinating exhibits of contemporary Native American art. Guided tours are offered daily.

The museum also operates the new **Heard Museum North,** 32633 N. Scottsdale Rd. (✆ **480/488-9817**), in Carefree. This gallery is open Monday through Saturday from 10am to 5:30pm, and Sunday from noon to 5pm. Admission is $3 for adults and is free for children under 6. A third museum—**Heard Museum West**—is located in the city of Surprise at 16126 N. Civic Center Plaza (✆ **623/344-2200**). This museum is open Tuesday through Sunday from 9:30am to 5pm. Admission is $5 for adults, $4 for seniors, $2 for students, and free for children under 6. Both of these satellite museums are free for all on the second Sunday of each month.

Phoenix, Scottsdale & the Valley of the Sun Attractions

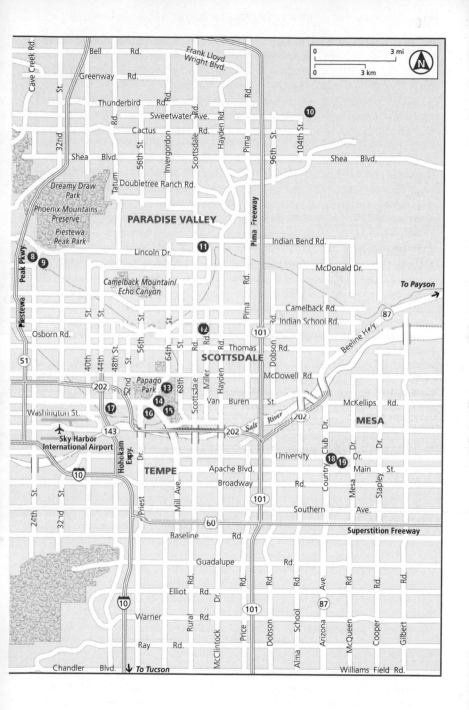

2301 N. Central Ave. $\mathcal{C}$ 602/252-8848. www.heard.org. Admission $10 adults, $9 seniors, $5 students, $3 children 6–12. Daily 9:30am–5pm. Closed major holidays. Bus: Blue (B), Red (R), or O.

Pueblo Grande Museum and Archaeological Park Located near Sky Harbor Airport, the Pueblo Grande Museum and Archaeological Park houses the ruins of an ancient Hohokam village that was one of several villages along the Salt River between A.D. 300 and 1400. Sometime around 1450, this and other villages were mysteriously abandoned. Some speculate that drought and a buildup of salts from irrigation water reduced the fertility of the soil and forced the people to seek more fertile lands. The small museum here displays many of the artifacts that have been dug up on the site. Furnished replicas of Hohokam-style houses give a good idea of how the Hohokam lived. The museum sponsors workshops, demonstrations, and petroglyph hikes.

4619 E. Washington St. (between 44th and 48th sts.). $\mathcal{C}$ 877/706-4408 or 602/495-0901. www.pueblogrande.com. Admission $2 adults, $1.50 seniors, $1 children 6–17; free on Sun. Mon–Sat 9am–4:45pm; Sun 1–4:45pm. Closed major holidays. Bus: 1.

ART MUSEUMS

Arizona State University Art Museum at Nelson Fine Arts Center ✸ Although it isn't very large, this museum is memorable for its innovative architecture and excellent temporary exhibitions. With its purplish-gray stucco facade and pyramidal shape, the stark, angular building conjures up images of sunsets on desert mountains. The entrance is down a flight of stairs that leads to a cool underground garden area. Inside are galleries for crafts, prints, contemporary art, and Latin American art, along with outdoor sculpture courts and a gift shop. The collection of American art includes works by Georgia O'Keeffe, Edward Hopper, and John James Audubon. Definitely a must for both art and architecture fans. Across the street is the **Ceramics Research Center,** 10th Street and Mill Avenue ($\mathcal{C}$ **480/965-2787**), a gallery that showcases the university's extensive collection of fine-art ceramics. The latter gallery is open Tuesday through Saturday from 10am to 5pm and is another place not to miss. You just won't believe the amazing creativity on display.

10th St. and Mill Ave., Tempe. $\mathcal{C}$ 480/965-2787. asuartmuseum.asu.edu. Free admission. Tues 10am–9pm (10am–5pm in summer); Wed–Sat 10am–5pm. Closed major holidays. Bus: Red (R), 1, 66, or 72.

Phoenix Art Museum ✸✸ This is one of the largest art museums in the Southwest, and within its labyrinth of halls and galleries is a respectable collection that spans the major artistic movements from the Renaissance to the present. Exhibits cover decorative arts, historical fashions, Spanish colonial furnishings and religious art, and, of course, works by members of the Cowboy Artists of America. The collection of modern and contemporary art is particularly good, with works by Diego Rivera, Frida Kahlo, Pablo Picasso, Alexander Calder, Henry Moore, Georgia O'Keeffe, Henri Rousseau, and Auguste Rodin. The popular Thorne Miniature Collection consists of tiny rooms on a scale of 1 inch to 1 foot. Because this museum is so large, it frequently mounts traveling blockbuster exhibits. The cafe here is a good spot for lunch.

1625 N. Central Ave. (at McDowell Rd.). $\mathcal{C}$ 602/257-1222. www.phxart.org. Admission $10 adults, $8 seniors and students, $4 children 6–17; free on Tues 3–9pm. Tues 10am–9pm; Wed–Sun 10am–5pm. Closed major holidays. Bus: Blue (B), Red (R), or O.

Scottsdale Museum of Contemporary Art ✸✸ Scottsdale may be obsessed with art featuring lonesome cowboys and solemn Indians, but this boldly designed museum makes it clear that patrons of contemporary art are also welcome here. Cutting-edge art, from the abstract to the absurd, fills the galleries, with exhibits rotating every few months. In addition to the main building, there are several galleries in the adjacent Scottsdale Center for the Arts. Don't miss James Turrell's skyspace *Knight Rise*, which can be visited for free.

7374 E. Second St., Scottsdale. ℂ 480/994-ARTS. www.smoca.org. Admission $7 adults, $5 students, free for children under 15; free on Thurs. Early Sept to early June Tues–Wed and Fri–Sat 10am–5pm, Thurs 10am–8pm, Sun noon–5pm; early June to early Sept Wed noon–5pm, Thurs 10am–8pm, Fri–Sat 10am–5pm, Sun noon–5pm. Closed major holidays. Bus: 41, 50, or 72. Also accessible via Scottsdale Trolley shuttle bus.

HISTORY MUSEUMS & HISTORIC LANDMARKS

Arizona Capitol Museum   In the years before Arizona became a state, the territorial capital moved from Prescott to Tucson, then back to Prescott, before finally settling in Phoenix. In 1898, a stately territorial capitol building was erected (with a copper roof to remind the local citizenry of the importance of that metal in the Arizona economy). Atop this copper roof was placed the statue *Winged Victory*, which still graces the old capitol building today. This building no longer serves as the actual state capitol, but has been restored to the way it appeared in 1912, the year Arizona became a state. There are free guided tours at 10am and 2pm.

1700 W. Washington St. ℂ 602/542-4675. www.lib.az.us/museum. Free admission. Mon–Fri 8am–5pm. Closed state holidays. Bus: 1 or DASH downtown shuttle.

Arizona Historical Society Museum in Papago Park   This museum, at the headquarters of the Arizona Historical Society, focuses its well-designed exhibits on the history of central Arizona. Temporary exhibits on the lives and works of the people who helped shape this region are always the highlights of a visit. An interesting permanent exhibit features life-size statues of everyday people from Arizona's past (a Mexican miner, a Chinese laborer, and so on). Quotes relate their individual stories, while props reveal what items they might have traveled with during their days in the desert.

1300 N. College Ave. (just off Curry Rd.), Tempe. ℂ 480/929-0292. www.arizonahistoricalsociety.org. Admission $5 adults, $4 seniors and students 12–18, free for children under 12; free on 1st Sat of each month. Tues–Sat 10am–4pm; Sun noon–4pm. Bus. 66.

Historic Heritage Square   The city of Phoenix was founded in 1870, but today few of the city's early homes remain. However, if you have an appreciation for old houses and want a glimpse of how Phoenix once looked, stroll around this collection of historic homes, which stand on the original town site. All of the buildings are listed on the National Register of Historic Places, and although most are modest buildings from the early 20th century, one impressive Victorian home was built in 1895. Today, the buildings house museums, restaurants, and gift shops. The Eastlake Victorian Rosson House, furnished with period antiques, is open for tours. The Stevens House features the Arizona Doll & Toy Museum. The Teeter House (ℂ 602/252-4682; www. theteeterhouse.com) now serves as a Victorian tearoom (with cocktails and live jazz in the evening), the old Baird Machine Shop contains Pizzeria Bianco (see "Where to Dine," earlier in this chapter), and the Thomas House is home to Bar Bianco (see "Phoenix & Scottsdale After Dark," later in this chapter).

115 N. Sixth St., at Monroe. ℂ 602/262-5029. www.rossonhousemuseum.org. Rosson House tours $5 adults, $4 seniors and students, $2 children 6–12. Wed–Sat 10am–4pm; Sun noon–4pm. Hours vary for other buildings; call for information. Closed Easter, Thanksgiving, Christmas Eve, Christmas, and New Year's. Bus: Red (R), 0, 1, or DASH downtown shuttle.

Architectural Highlights

Architecture buffs will find plenty to gape at in Phoenix. Here's a list of our favorite buildings.

- **Arizona Biltmore** This resort hotel, although not designed by Frank Lloyd Wright, shows the famed architect's hand in its distinctive cast-cement blocks. It also displays sculptures, furniture, and stained glass designed by Wright. To learn more about the building, reserve ahead for a tour ($10 for non-guests, free for guests). The Biltmore is located at 2400 E. Missouri Ave. (© 602/955-6600).

- **Burton Barr Library** This library is among the most daring pieces of public architecture in the city, and no fan of futuristic art or science fiction should miss it. The five-story cube is partially clad in enough ribbed copper sheeting to produce roughly 17,500,000 pennies. It's located at 1221 N. Central Ave. (© 602/262-4636; www.phoenixpubliclibrary.org). Free admission.

- **Mystery Castle** 𝒜 Built for a daughter who longed for a castle more permanent than those built in sand at the beach, Mystery Castle is a wondrous work of folk-art architecture. The 18-room fantasy has 13 fireplaces, parapets, and many other unusual touches. It's located at 800 E. Mineral Rd. (© 602/268-1581). Admission $5 adults, $3 children 5–15. Closed June–Sept.

- **Taliesin West** 𝒜𝒜𝒜 Frank Lloyd Wright fell in love with the Arizona desert and, in 1937, built Taliesin West as a winter camp that served as his home, office, and school. Today, the buildings of Taliesin West are the headquarters of the Frank Lloyd Wright Foundation and School of Architecture. Basic tours cost $18 to $19 adults, $16 students and seniors, and $5 to $10 for children (ages 4–12). Prices vary by season. Expanded Insight Tours ($19–$23), behind-the-scenes tours ($35–$45), guided desert walks ($25), apprentice shelter tours ($30), and night hikes ($25–$30) are available at certain times of year. Call ahead for schedule information. Taliesen West is located at 12621 Frank Lloyd Wright Blvd. (at Cactus/114th St.), Scottsdale (© 480/860-8810 for information or 480/860-2700, ext. 494 or 495, for reservations; www.franklloydwright.org).

Phoenix Museum of History 𝒜 Located in the Heritage and Science Park in downtown Phoenix, this modern museum presents an interesting look at the history of a city that, to the casual visitor, might not seem to *have* any history. The modern design and interactive exhibits make this place much more interesting than your average local history museum. One unusual exhibit explores how "lungers" (tuberculosis sufferers) inadvertently helped originate the tourism industry in Arizona, while another exhibit looks at the once-popular occupation of ostrich farming.

105 N. Fifth St. © 602/253-2734. www.pmoh.org. Admission $6 adults, $4 seniors and students, $3 children 7–12, free for children 6 and under. Tues–Sat 10am–5pm. Closed major holidays. Bus: Red (R), 0, 1, or DASH downtown shuttle.

Wells Fargo History Museum 🎯 *Finds*   Yes, this museum is small, and, yes, it's run by the Wells Fargo Bank, but the collection of artifacts here goes a long way toward conjuring up the Wild West so familiar from Hollywood movies. Not only is there an original Wells Fargo stagecoach on display, but there are also gold nuggets to ogle, old photos from the *real* Wild West, and plenty of artifacts and memorabilia from the days of stagecoach travel. There are also original paintings by N. C. Wyeth and bronze sculptures by Frederic Remington and Charles Russell.

100 W. Washington St. 📞 **602/378-1852.** www.wellsfargohistory.com. Free admission. Mon–Fri 9am–5pm. Closed major holidays. Bus: Red (R), 0, 1, or DASH downtown shuttle.

SCIENCE & INDUSTRY MUSEUMS

Arizona Science Center 🎯 *Kids*   So, the kids weren't impressed with the botanical garden or the Native American artifacts at the Heard Museum. Bring 'em here. They can spend the afternoon pushing buttons, turning knobs, and interacting with all kinds of cool science exhibits. In the end, they might even learn something in spite of all the fun they have. The science center also includes a planetarium and a large-screen theater, both of which carry additional charges.

600 E. Washington St. 📞 **602/716-2000.** www.azscience.org. Admission $9 adults, $7 seniors and children 3–12. Planetarium and film combination tickets also available. Daily 10am–5pm. Closed Thanksgiving and Christmas. Bus: Red (R), 0, 1, or DASH downtown shuttle.

Mesa Southwest Museum 🎯🎯 *Kids*   This is one of the best museums in the Valley, and its wide variety of exhibits appeals to people with a range of interests. For the kids, there are animated dinosaurs on an indoor "cliff" with a roaring waterfall. Of course, there are also plenty of dinosaur skeletons. Also of interest are an exhibit on movies that have been filmed in the state, a display on Arizona mammoth kill sites, some old jail cells, and a walk-through mine mock-up with exhibits on the Lost Dutchman Mine. There's also a mock-up of a Hohokam village and an artificial cave filled with beautiful mineral specimens.

53 N. MacDonald St. (at First St.), Mesa. 📞 **480/644-2230.** www.mesasouthwestmuseum.com. Admission $8 adults, $7 seniors and students, $4 children 3–12. Tues–Fri 10am–3pm; Sat 11am–5pm; Sun 1–5pm. Closed major holidays. Bus: Red (R) or 30.

PARKS & ZOOS

Perhaps the most unusual park in the Phoenix metro area centers on **Tempe Town Lake,** 620 N. Mill Ave., Tempe (📞 **480/350-8625;** www.tempe.gov/rio), which was created in 1999 by damming the Salt River with inflatable dams. Tempe's 2-mile-long lake is lined with parks and bike baths on both the north and south shores. The best lake access is at Tempe Town Beach, at the foot of the Mill Avenue Bridge. Here you can rent kayaks and other small boats. Tempe Town Lake is the focus of a grand development plan that includes the new Tempe Center for the Arts.

Among the city's most popular parks are its natural areas and preserves. These include Phoenix South Mountain Park, Papago Park, Phoenix Mountains Preserve (site of Piestewa Peak), North Mountain Preserve, North Mountain Recreation Area, and Camelback Mountain–Echo Canyon Recreation Area. For more information on these parks, see "Hiking," "Bicycling," and "Horseback Riding" under "Getting Outside," below.

Phoenix Zoo 🎯 *Kids*   Forget about polar bears and other cold-climate creatures; this zoo focuses its attention primarily on animals that come from climates similar to that of the Phoenix area (the rainforest exhibit is an exception). Most impressive of the displays are the African savanna and the baboon colony. The Southwestern exhibits are also of interest, as are the giant Galápagos tortoises and the exhibit featuring monkeys from Central and South America. All animals are kept in naturalistic enclosures, and what with all the palm trees and tropical vegetation, the zoo sometimes manages to make you forget you're in the desert. Families will enjoy *Zoolights,* an after-hours holiday light display held late November to early January.

At Papago Park, 455 N. Galvin Pkwy. © 602/273-1341. www.phoenixzoo.org. Admission $14 adults, $9 seniors, $6 children 3–12. Oct to early Nov and early Jan to May daily 8am–5pm; early Nov to early Jan daily 8am–4pm; June–Sept Mon–Fri 7am–2pm, Sat–Sun 7am–4pm. Closed Christmas. Bus: 3.

ESPECIALLY FOR KIDS

In addition to the following suggestions, kids are likely to enjoy the Arizona Science Center, the Mesa Southwest Museum, the Hall of Flame Firefighting Museum, and the Phoenix Zoo—all described in detail earlier in this chapter.

Arizona Museum for Youth   Using both traditional displays and participatory activities, this museum allows children to explore the fine arts and their own creativity. It's housed in a refurbished grocery store, and the highlight is Artville, an arts-driven kid-size town. Exhibits are geared mainly to toddlers through 12-year-olds, but all ages can work together to experience the activities.

35 N. Robson St. (between Main and First sts.), Mesa. © 480/644-2467. www.arizonamuseumforyouth.com. Admission $5, free for children under 1. Tues–Sat 10am–4pm; Sun noon–4pm. Closed all government holidays. Bus: Red (R) or 30.

Goldfield Ghost Town 🌟 *Kids*   Over on the east side of the Valley, just 4 miles northeast of Apache Junction, you'll find a reconstructed 1890s gold-mining town. Although it's a bit of a tourist trap—gift shops, an ice-cream parlor, and the like—it's also home to the **Goldfield Superstition Museum** (© 480/677-6463), which has interesting exhibits on the history of the area. Of particular note is the exhibit on the Lost Dutchman gold mine, perhaps the most famous mine in the country, despite the fact that no one knows where it is. Goldfield Mine Tours provides guided tours of the gold mine beneath the town. The Superstition Scenic Narrow Gauge Railroad circles the town, and the **Goldfield Livery** (© 480/982-0133) offers horseback riding and carriage rides. If you're here at lunchtime, you can get a meal at the steakhouse/saloon.

Ariz. 88, 4 miles northeast of Apache Junction. © 480/983-0333. www.goldfieldghosttown.com. Museum admission $4 adults, $3 seniors, $1 children ages 5–12; train rides $5 adults, $4 seniors, $3 children 5–12; mine tours $6 adults, $5 seniors, $3 children 6–12; horseback rides $30 for 1 hr., $50 for 2 hr. Town daily 10am–5pm; museum, tour, and ride hours vary. Closed Christmas.

Hall of Flame Firefighting Museum 🌟 *Kids*   The world's largest firefighting museum houses a fascinating collection of vintage fire trucks. The displays date from a 1725 English hand pumper to several classic engines from the 20th century. All are beautifully restored and, mostly, fire-engine red. In all, more than 90 vehicles are on display.

At Papago Park, 6101 E. Van Buren St. © 602/275-3473. www.hallofflame.org. Admission $6 adults, $5 seniors, $4 students 6–17, $1.50 children 3–5, free for children under 3. Mon–Sat 9am–5pm; Sun noon–4pm. Closed New Year's Day, Thanksgiving, and Christmas. Bus: 3.

McCormick-Stillman Railroad Park   If you or your kids happen to like trains, you won't want to miss this park. On the grounds are restored railroad cars and engines, two old railway depots, model railroad layouts, and, best of all, a 5⁄12-scale model railroad that takes visitors around the park. There's also a 1929 carousel and a general store.

7301 E. Indian Bend Rd. (at Scottsdale Rd.), Scottsdale. ℂ 480/312-2312. www.therailroadpark.com. Train and carousel rides $1; museum admission $1 adults, free for children 12 and under. Hours vary with the season; call for schedule. Closed Thanksgiving and Christmas. Bus: 72.

Rawhide at Wild Horse Pass *Kids*   This fake cow town is so much fun and such a quintessentially Phoenician experience that no family should get out of town without first moseying down the dusty streets of Rawhide. Those streets are lined with lots of tourist shops and plenty of places for refreshments, including a steakhouse. Rawhide is run like other amusement parks; you buy a bunch of $1 tickets and then trade various numbers of those tickets for performances (stunt shows, gunfights, trick-roping demonstrations) and activities and attractions (stagecoach, camel, and train rides; a mechanical bull; gold panning). There are also Saturday-night sundown cookouts ($45 adults, $19 children) with hayrides, live music, and storytellers.

5700 W. North Loop Rd., Chandler. ℂ 480/502-5600. www.rawhide.com. Free admission (individual shows and rides priced separately). Hours vary with the seasons; call for details.

6 Organized Tours & Excursions

The Valley of the Sun is a sprawling, often congested place, and if you're unfamiliar with the area, you may be surprised at how great the distances are. If map reading and urban navigation are not your strong points, consider taking a guided tour. Numerous companies offer tours of both the Valley of the Sun and the rest of Arizona. However, tours of the Valley tend to include only brief stops at highlights.

BUS TOURS   **Gray Line Tours Phoenix** (ℂ 800/777-3484 or 602/437-3484; www.graylinearizona.com) is one of the largest tour companies in the Valley. It offers a 4-hour tour of Phoenix and the Valley of the Sun for $52; reservations are necessary. The tour points out such local landmarks as the state capitol, Heritage Square, Arizona State University, and Old Town Scottsdale.

HOT-AIR BALLOON RIDES   The still morning air of the Valley of the Sun is perfect for hot-air ballooning, and because of the stiff competition, prices are among the lowest in the country—between $135 and $195 per person for a 1- to 1½-hour ride. Companies to try include **Over the Rainbow** (ℂ 602/225-5666; www.letsgoballooning.com) and **Adventures Out West** (ℂ 800/755-0935 or 480/991-3666; www.adventuresoutwest.com).

JEEP TOURS   After spending a few days in Scottsdale, you'll likely start wondering where the desert is. Well, it's out there, and the easiest way to explore it is to book a jeep tour. Most hotels and resorts work with particular companies, so start by asking your concierge. Alternatively, you can contact one of the following companies. Most will pick you up at your hotel, take you off through the desert, and maybe even let you pan for gold or shoot a six-gun. Depending on how many people there are in your party and where you're staying, rates range from $65 to $100 for a 3-hour tour. Companies include **Arizona Desert Mountain Jeep Tours** (ℂ 800/567-3619; www.azdesertmountain.com) and **Arizona Bound Tours** (ℂ 480/962-6620; www.arizonabound.com).

If you want to really impress your friends when you get home, you'll need to try something a little different. How about a Hummer tour? Sure, a Hummer is nothing but a jeep on steroids, but these military-issue off-road vehicles still turn heads. Contact **Desert Storm Hummer Tours** (© 866/374-8637 or 480/922-0020; www.ds hummer.com), which charges $95 for a 4-hour tour; or **Stellar Adventures** (© 877/ 878-3552 or 602/402-0584; www.stellaradventures.com), which charges $125 for a basic 4-hour tour and $155 for its extreme tour. Both companies also offer night tours ($125–$130) that let you spot wildlife with night-vision equipment.

7 Getting Outside

BICYCLING   Although the Valley of the Sun is a sprawling place, it's mostly flat and has numerous paved bike paths, which makes bicycling a breeze as long as it isn't windy or, in the summer, too hot. In Scottsdale, **Arizona Outback Adventures,** 16447 N. 91st St. (© 866/455-1601 or 480/945-2881; www.azoutbackadventures.com) rents hybrid bikes for $35 per day and mountain bikes for $35 to $85 per day. Mountain-biking trail maps are also available. This company also does half-day and full-day guided mountain-bike tours.

Among the best mountain-biking spots in the city are Papago Park (at Van Buren St. and Galvin Pkwy.), Phoenix South Mountain Park (use the entrance off Baseline Rd. on 48th St.), and North Mountain Preserve (off Seventh St. between Dunlap Ave. and Thunderbird Rd.). With its rolling topography and wide dirt trails, Papago Park is the best place for novice mountain-bikers to get in some desert riding (and the scenery here is great). For hard-core pedalers, Phoenix South Mountain Park is the place to go. The National Trail is the ultimate death-defying ride here, but there are lots of trails for intermediate riders, including the Desert Classic Trail and the short loop trails just north of the parking area at the 48th Street entrance. North Mountain is another good place for intermediate riders.

There's also plenty of good road biking and mountain biking up in the Cave Creek area, where you can rent a bike for $40 to $50 a day at **Flat Tire Bike Shop,** 6149 Cave Creek Rd. (© 480/488-5261). This shop also offers guided mountain-bike tours for $75 per person. If you'd like a guide for some of the best biking in the desert, contact **Desert Biking Adventures** (© 888/249-BIKE or 602/320-4602; www.desert bikingadventures.com), which leads 2-, 3-, and 4-hour tours (and specializes in downhill rides). Prices range from $70 to $97.

If you'd rather confine your cycling to a paved surface, there's no better route than Scottsdale's **Indian Bend Wash greenbelt,** a paved path that extends for more than 10 miles along Hayden Road (from north of Shea Blvd. to Tempe). The Indian Bend Wash pathway can be accessed at many points along Hayden Road. At the south end, the path connects to paved paths on the shores of Tempe Town Lake and provides easy access to Tempe's Mill Avenue shopping district.

GOLF   With roughly 200 courses in the Valley of the Sun, golf is just about the most popular sport in Phoenix and one of the main reasons people flock here in winter. Sunshine, spectacular views, and the company of coyotes, quails, and doves make playing a round of golf here a truly memorable experience.

However, despite the number of courses, it can be difficult to get a tee time on any of the more popular courses (especially during the months of Feb, Mar, and Apr). If you're staying at a resort with a course, be sure to make your tee-time reservations at the same time you make your room reservations. If you aren't staying at a resort, you might still be able to play a round on a resort course if you can get a last-minute tee time. Try one of the tee-time reservations services below.

The only thing harder than getting a winter or spring tee time in the Valley is facing the bill at the end of your 18 holes. Greens fees at most public and resort courses range from $90 to $170, with the top courses often charging $200 to $250 or more. Municipal courses, on the other hand, charge less than $50. You can save money on many courses by opting for twilight play, which usually begins between 1 and 3pm.

You can get more information on Valley of the Sun golf courses from the **Greater Phoenix Convention & Visitors Bureau,** 50 N. Second St. (© **877/225-5749** or 602/452-6282; www.visitphoenix.com).

It's a good idea to make reservations well in advance. You can avoid the hassle of booking tee times yourself by contacting **Golf Xpress** (© **888/679-8246** or 602/404-GOLF; www.azgolfxpress.com), which can make reservations farther in advance than you could if you called the golf course directly, and can sometimes get you lower greens fees as well. This company also makes hotel reservations, rents golf clubs, and provides other assistance to golfers visiting the Valley. For last-minute reservations, call **Stand-by Golf** (© **800/655-5345;** www.discountteetimes.com).

The many resort courses are the favored fairways of valley visitors. Some of our favorites are listed below:

- **The Boulders** ✦✦ For spectacular scenery, the two Jay Morrish–designed 18-hole courses at The Boulders, 34631 N. Tom Darlington Dr., Carefree (© **480/488-9028;** www.thebouldersclub.com), just can't be beat. Given the option, play the South Course, and watch out as you approach the tee box on the 7th hole—it's a real heart-stopper. You'll pay $165 to $285 for a round in winter.

- **Wigwam Golf and Country Club** ✦ Wigwam has, count 'em, three championship 18-hole courses. The Gold Course is legendary, but even the Blue and Red courses are worth playing. The club is at Litchfield Park, on the far west side of the valley, 300 Wigwam Blvd. (© **800/909-4224** or 623/935-9414). In high season, greens fees are $162 for any of the three courses.

- **Gold Canyon Golf Resort** ✦ This course, way over on the east side of the valley at the foot of the Superstition Mountains, has been rated the best public course in the state. It's located at 6100 S. Kings Ranch Rd., Gold Canyon (© **480/982-9449;** www.gcgr.com). Greens fees on the Dinosaur Mountain course range from $164 to $189 in winter. The Sidewinder course is more traditional and less dramatic, but much more economical. Greens fees are $89 to $104 in winter.

- **Phoenician Golf Club** Set at the base of Camelback Mountain (6000 E. Camelback Rd.; © **800/888-8234** or 480/423-2450; www.thephoenician.com), this club has 27 holes that mix traditional and desert styles. Greens fees for non-resort guests are $139 to $199 in winter and spring, and reservations can be made up to 30 days in advance.

- **Troon North Golf Club** ✦✦✦ Of the valley's many daily-fee courses, the two 18-hole courses at this club garner the most local accolades. This is the finest example of a desert course that you'll find anywhere in the state. It's located at 10320 E. Dynamite Blvd., Scottsdale (© **480/585-7700;** www.troonnorthgolf. com). Greens fees are $195 to $295 in winter and spring.

- **Tournament Players Club (TPC) of Scottsdale** ✦✦ If you want to swing where the pros do, beg, borrow, or steal a tee time on the Tom Weiskopf and Jay Morrish–designed Stadium Course. The TPC's second 18, the Desert Course, is actually a municipal course. It's located at 17020 N. Hayden Rd. (© **888/400-4001** or 480/585-4334; www.playatpc.com). Stadium course fees top out at $249 in winter and spring, while Desert Course fees are a reasonable $63 in winter and spring.

- **Legacy Golf Resort**   If you're looking for good value in traditional or links-style courses, try the Legacy Golf Resort, Stonecreek Golf Club (6808 S. 32nd St.; © 888/828-FORE or 602/305-5555; www.legacygolfresort.com), which is a fairly forgiving course on the south side of the valley. Greens fees are $89 to $149 in winter.

- **Dove Valley Ranch Golf Club**   If you want to take a crack at a desert-style course or two but don't want to take out a second mortgage, try this club at 33750 N. Dove Lakes Dr., Cave Creek (© 480/488-0009; www.dovevalleyranch.com). Designed by Robert Trent Jones Jr., it was voted Arizona's best new public course when it opened in 1998. Greens fees are $120 to $140 in winter.

- **We-Ko-Pa Golf Club**   This course is on the Fort McDowell Yavapai Nation, and the name is Yavapai for "Four Peaks," which is the mountain range you'll be marveling at as you play. Unlike at other area courses, fairways are bounded by desert, not luxury homes, so make sure you keep your ball on the grass. The course is located off the Beeline Highway (Ariz. 87) in the northeast corner of the valley (18200 East Toh Vee Circle, Fort McDowell; © 480/836-9000; www.wekopa. com). Greens fees are $170 to $195 in winter. Reservations are taken up to 90 days in advance.

- **Papago Golf Course**   One of the municipal courses in Phoenix, Papago offers fine views and a killer 17th hole. This is such a great course that it's used for Phoenix Open qualifying. It's located at 5595 E. Moreland St. (© 602/275-8428), at the foot of the red sandstone Papago Buttes. In winter, greens fees are $18 to $38 to walk ($12 extra for a golf cart).

HIKING   Several mountains around Phoenix, including Camelback Mountain and Piestewa Peak, have been set aside as parks and nature preserves, and these natural areas are among the city's most popular hiking spots. The city's largest nature preserve, **South Mountain Park/Preserve** (© 602/534-6324; www.phoenix.gov/PARKS/southmnt.html), covers 16,000 acres and is one of the largest city parks in the world. This park contains around 50 miles of hiking, mountain-biking, and horseback-riding trails, and the views of Phoenix (whether from along the National Trail or from the parking lot at the Buena Vista Lookout) are spectacular, especially at sunset. To reach the park's main entrance, drive south on Central Avenue, which leads right into the park. Once inside the park, turn left on Summit Road and follow it to the Buena Vista Lookout, which provides a great view of the city and is the trail head for the National Trail. If you hike east on this trail for 2 miles, you'll come to an unusual little tunnel that makes a good turnaround point.

Another place to get in some relatively easy and convenient hiking is **Papago Park,** Galvin Parkway and Van Buren Street (© 602/256-3220), home to the Desert Botanical Garden, the Phoenix Zoo, and the fascinating Hole in the Rock (a red-rock butte with a large natural opening in it). There are both paved and dirt trails within the park; the most popular hikes are around the Papago Buttes (park on W. Park Dr.) and up onto the rocks at Hole in the Rock (park past the zoo at the information center). During World War II, there was a German POW camp here.

Perhaps the most popular hike in the city is the trail to the top of **Camelback Mountain,** in the **Echo Canyon Recreation Area** (© 602/262-6862; www.phoenix. gov/PARKS/hikecmlb.html), near the boundary between Phoenix and Scottsdale. At

2,704 feet high, this is the highest mountain in Phoenix and boasts the finest mountaintop views in the city. The 1.2-mile Summit Trail that leads to the top of Camelback Mountain is outrageously steep and gains 1,200 feet from trail head to summit. Yet on any given day there will be ironmen and ironwomen nonchalantly jogging up and down to stay fit. At times, it almost feels like a health-club singles scene. To reach the trail head, drive up 44th Street until it becomes McDonald Drive, turn right on East Echo Canyon Drive, and continue up the hill until the road ends at a parking lot, which is often full. Don't attempt this one in the heat of the day, and bring at least a quart of water.

At the east end of Camelback Mountain is the Cholla Trail, which, at 1.75 miles in length, isn't as steep as the Summit Trail (at least, not until you get close to the summit, where the route gets steep, rocky, and quite difficult). The only parking for this trail is along Invergordon Road at Chaparral Road, just north of Camelback Road (along the east boundary of The Phoenician resort). Be sure to park in a legal parking space and watch the hours that parking is allowed. There's a good turnaround point about 1.5 miles up the trail, and great views down onto the fairways of the golf course at The Phoenician.

The 2,608-foot-tall **Piestewa Peak,** in the **Phoenix Mountains Park and Recreation Area/Dreamy Draw Park** (② 602/262-7901; www.phoenix.gov/PARKS/hike phx.html), offers another aerobic workout of a hike and has views almost as spectacular as those from Camelback Mountain. The round-trip to the summit is 2.4 miles and gains almost 1,200 feet. Piestewa Peak is reached from Squaw Peak Drive off Lincoln Drive between 22nd and 23rd streets. Another section of this park, with much easier trails, can be reached by taking the Northern Avenue exit of Arizona 51 and then driving east into Dreamy Draw Park.

Of all the popular mountain trails in the Phoenix area, the trail through **Pinnacle Peak Park,** 26802 N. 102nd Way (② **480/312-0990;** www.scottsdaleaz.gov/parks/ pinnacle), in north Scottsdale, is our favorite. The trail through the park is a 3.5-mile round-trip hike and is immensely popular with the local fitness crowd. Forget about stopping to smell the desert penstemon; if you don't keep up the pace, someone's liable to knock you off the trail into a prickly pear. If you can find a parking space (arrive before 9am on weekends) and can ignore the crowds, you'll be treated to views of rugged desert mountains (and posh desert suburbs). November through April, there are guided hikes Tuesday through Sunday at 10am. There are also wildflower walks, full-moon hikes, and astronomy evenings here. To find the park from central Scottsdale, go north on Pima Road, east on Happy Valley Road, and north on Alma School Parkway, and turn left at the sign for Pinnacle Peak Patio restaurant.

For much less vigorous hiking (without the crowds), try **North Mountain Park** (② 602/262-7901; www.phoenix.gov/PARKS/nmvc.html), in North Mountain Preserve. This natural area, located on either side of Seventh Street between Dunlap Avenue and Thunderbird Road, has more flat hiking than Camelback Mountain or Piestewa Peak. To orient yourself and get trail maps, stop by the **North Mountain Visitor Center,** 12950 N. Seventh St. (② **602/495-5540**).

The **Peralta Trail** in the impossibly steep and jagged Superstition Mountains just might be our favorite hike in the entire state. Unfortunately, a lot of other people feel the same way, and on weekends, the trail is almost always packed with people. However, if you come early on a weekday, you can have this trail almost all to yourself. The route climbs steadily, though not too steeply, past huge old saguaros to a saddle with a view that will take your breath away (or was it the hike up from the trail head that's left you gasping?). The view is an in-your-face look at Weaver's Needle, the Superstition Mountains' most famous pinnacle. The hike to the view at Fremont Saddle is a 4.6-mile round-trip hike. To reach the trail head, drive east from Phoenix on US 60 past Apache Junction to Peralta Road, and then drive 8 miles north, mostly on gravel road, to the trail head. For information, contact the **Tonto National Forest's Mesa Ranger District,** 5140 E. Ingram St., Mesa (© **480/610-3300;** www.fs.fed.us/r3/tonto).

Another great place to go for a hike in the desert is north Scottsdale's **McDowell Sonoran Preserve** (© **480/998-7971;** www.mcdowellsonoran.org), where you'll find miles of relatively easy and uncrowded trails. The best place to access these trails is at the Lost Dog Trailhead at 124th Street north of Via Linda. To reach this trail head, drive east on Shea Boulevard, turn north on 124th Street, and watch for the parking lot after you pass Via Linda. The 2.5-mile Ringtail Loop Trail is a good choice for an hour's hike.

HORSEBACK RIDING   Even in the urban confines of the Phoenix metro area, people like to play at being cowboys, and there are plenty of places around the Valley to saddle up your palomino. Because any guided ride is going to lead you through interesting desert scenery, your best bet is to pick a stable close to where you're staying. Keep in mind that most stables require or prefer reservations.

On the south side of the city, try **Ponderosa Stables,** 10215 S. Central Ave. (© **602/268-1261;** www.arizona-horses.com), which leads rides into South Mountain Park and charges $25 for a 1-hour ride or $45 for a 2-hour ride. These stables also offer fun dinner rides ($34) to the T-Bone Steakhouse, where you buy your own dinner before riding back under the stars. If you have time for only one horseback ride while you're in Phoenix, make it this latter ride.

On the north side of the Valley, **Cave Creek Outfitters,** off Dynamite Boulevard at 31313 N. 144th St. (© **888/921-0040** or 480/471-4635; www.cavecreekoutfitters. com), offers 2-hour rides for $65 to $80.

On the east side of the Valley, on the southern slopes of the Superstitions, you'll find **D-Spur Ranch/Preservation of the Cowboy Way Society,** 15371 Ojo Rd. (off Peralta Rd.), Apache Junction (© **602/810-7029;** www.cowboywaysociety.org), which charges $26 for a 1-hour ride, $50 for a 2-hour ride, and $190 per person for an overnight trip.

WATER PARKS   At **Phoenix Waterworld Safari,** 4243 W. Pinnacle Peak Rd. (© **623/ 581-8446;** www.golfland.com), you can free-fall down the Kilimanjaro speed slide or catch a gnarly wave in the wave pool. **Mesa Golfland Sunsplash,** 155 W. Hampton Ave., Mesa (© **480/834-8319;** www.golfland.com), has a wave pool and a water roller coaster. **Big Surf,** 1500 N. McClintock Rd., Tempe (© **480/947-2477;** www.golf land.com), has the country's original wave pool and all kinds of wild water slides.

All three of these parks charge $24 for anyone taller than 48 inches, $20 for seniors and anyone under 48 inches, and $3 for children 2 and under. Phoenix Waterworld Safari is open from Memorial Day weekend to Labor Day weekend Monday through Saturday from 10am to 8pm and Sunday from 11am to 7pm. Mesa Golfland/Sunsplash is open from Memorial Day weekend to Labor Day weekend Monday through Saturday from 10am to 8pm and Sunday from noon to 8pm. Big Surf is open from around Memorial Day to Labor Day Monday through Saturday from 10am to 6pm and Sunday from 11am to 7pm. Mesa Golfland also has three slides that open at the start of spring break and are open Saturday and Sunday from noon to 6pm. After Memorial Day, these slides are open the same hours as Sunsplash.

WHITE-WATER RAFTING & TUBING   The desert may not seem like the place for white-water rafting, but up in the mountains to the northeast of Phoenix, the **Upper Salt River** still flows wild and free and offers some exciting rafting. Most years from about late February to late May, snowmelt from the White Mountains floods the river and fills it with exciting Class III and IV rapids (sometimes, however, there just isn't enough water). Companies operating full-day, overnight, and multiday rafting trips on the Upper Salt River (conditions permitting) include **Wilderness Aware Rafting** (© 800/462-7238; www.inaraft.com), **Canyon Rio Rafting** (© 800/272-3353; www.canyonrio.com), and **Mild to Wild Rafting** (© 800/567-6745; www. mild2wildrafting.com). Prices range from $99 to $115 for a day trip.

Tamer river trips can be had from **Salt River Tubing & Recreation** (© 480/984-3305; www.saltrivertubing.com), which has its headquarters 20 miles northeast of Phoenix on Power Road at the intersection of Usery Pass Road in Tonto National Forest. For $13, the company will rent you a large inner tube and shuttle you by bus upriver for the float down. The inner-tubing season runs from mid-May to September.

8 Spectator Sports

Phoenix is nuts for pro sports and is one of the few cities in the country with teams for all four of the major sports (baseball, basketball, football, and hockey). Add to this baseball's spring training, professional women's basketball, golf and tennis tournaments, the annual Fiesta Bowl college football classic, and ASU football, basketball, and baseball, and you have enough action to keep even the most rabid sports fans happy. The all-around best month to visit is March, when you could feasibly catch baseball's spring training, the Suns, the Coyotes, and ASU basketball and baseball, as well as the Safeway International LPGA Tournament.

Call **Ticketmaster** (© 480/784-4444; www.ticketmaster.com) for tickets to most of the events below. For sold-out events, try **Tickets Unlimited** (© 800/289-8497 or 602/840-2340; www.ticketsunlimitedinc.com) or **Ticket Exchange** (© 800/800-9811; ticketexchangeusa.com).

BASEBALL   Although the **Arizona Diamondbacks** (© 888/777-4664 or 602/514-8400; www.diamondbacks.com) haven't put in as impressive a showing in the years since they won the 2001 World Series, they still have a devoted fan base and regularly pack downtown Phoenix's impressive Chase Field. The ballpark's retractable roof allows for comfortable play during the blistering summers and makes this one of only a few enclosed baseball stadiums with natural grass. Tickets to ballgames are available through the Chase Field ticket office and cost between $5 and $185. The best seats are in sections J and Q. If you'd like to get a behind-the-scenes look at Chase Field, you can take a guided tour. Tours cost $6 for adults, $4 for seniors and children ages 7 to 12, and $2 for children ages 4 to 6.

For decades, baseball's spring-training season has been immensely popular, especially with fans from northern teams, and don't think that the Cactus League's preseason exhibition games are any less popular just because the Diamondbacks play all summer. **Spring-training games** may rank second only to golf in popularity with winter visitors to the Valley. Nine major-league baseball teams have spring-training camps around the Valley in the month of March, and exhibition games are scheduled at seven different stadiums. Tickets cost $5 to $24. Get a schedule from a visitor center, check the *Arizona Republic* while you're in town, check the website of the Cactus League (www.cactusleague.com), or visit www.cactusleagueinfo.com. Games often sell out, especially on weekends, so be sure to order tickets in advance. The spring-training schedule for 2008 should be out by November 2007.

Teams training in the Valley include the **Los Angeles Angels of Anaheim,** Tempe Diablo Stadium, 2200 W. Alameda Dr. (48th St. and Broadway Rd.), Tempe (© 480/350-5205 or 480/784-4444 for tickets; www.angelsbaseball.com); the **Chicago Cubs,** HoHoKam Park, 1235 N. Center St., Mesa (© 800/905-3315 for tickets or 480/964-4467; www.chicagocubs.com); the **Kansas City Royals,** Surprise Stadium, 15754 N. Bullard Ave., Surprise (© 623/594-5600 or 480/784-4444 for tickets; www.kcroyals.com); the **Milwaukee Brewers,** Maryvale Baseball Park, 3600 N. 51st Ave., Phoenix (© 623/245-5500; www.milwaukeebrewers.com); the **Oakland Athletics,** Phoenix Municipal Stadium, 5999 E. Van Buren St., Phoenix (© 602/392-0217 or 877/493-BALL for tickets; www.oaklandathletics.com); the **San Diego Padres,** Peoria Sports Complex, 16101 N. 83rd Ave., Peoria (© 800/409-1511, 623/878-4337, or 480/784-4444 for tickets; www.padres.com); the **San Francisco Giants,** Scottsdale Stadium, 7408 E. Osborn Rd., Scottsdale (© 480/312-2586 or 800/225-2277 for tickets; www.sfgiants.com); the **Seattle Mariners,** Peoria Sports Complex, 16101 N. 83rd Ave., Peoria (© 800/409-1511, 623/878-4337, or 480/784-4444 for tickets; www.seattlemariners.com); and the **Texas Rangers,** Surprise Stadium, 15850 N. Bullard Ave., Surprise (© 623/594-5600 or 480/784-4444 for tickets; www.texasrangers.com).

BASKETBALL   The NBA's **Phoenix Suns** play at the US Airways Center, 201 E. Jefferson St. (© **800/4-NBA-TIX** or 602/379-SUNS; www.suns.com). Most tickets cost between $10 and $200. Suns tickets are hard to come by; if you haven't planned ahead, try contacting the box office the day before or the day of a game to see if tickets have been returned. Otherwise, you'll have to try a ticket agency and pay a premium.

Phoenix also has a WNBA team, the **Phoenix Mercury** (© **602/252-9622** or 602/514-8333; www.phoenixmercury.com), which plays at the US Airways Center between late May and mid-August. Tickets cost $10 to $146.

FOOTBALL   The **Arizona Cardinals** (© **800/999-1402** or 602/379-0102; www.azcardinals.com) play at the $450-million state-of-the-art University of Phoenix Stadium in the west valley city of Glendale. This stadium has a retractable roof made of translucent fabric that lets lots of light in when the roof is closed. However, the stadium's most distinctive feature is its moveable playing field, which is rolled out into the sun outside the stadium until a game is scheduled. This 2-acre, grass-covered tray is the first of its kind in North America. Most tickets cost $15 to $67, and single-game tickets for the entire season go on sale around mid-July. Of course, if you're a football fan, you know that the 2008 Superbowl is being played here.

GOLF TOURNAMENTS   It's not surprising that, with more than 200 golf courses and ideal golfing weather throughout the fall, winter, and spring, the Valley of the Sun hosts some major golf tournaments. Late January's **FBR Open Golf Tournament** (© **602/870-0163;** www.fbropen.com) is by far the biggest. Held at the Tournament Players Club (TPC) of Scottsdale, it attracts more spectators than any other golf tournament in the world (more than 500,000 each year). The 18th hole has standing room for 40,000. Tickets start at $25 and are available through Ticketmaster (see above).

A Day at the Spa

If you can't or don't want to spend the money to stay at a top resort and avail yourself of the spa, you may still be able to indulge. Most resorts open their spas to the public, and for the cost of a body treatment or massage, you can spend the day at the spa, taking classes, working out in an exercise room, or lounging by the pool.

If you want truly spectacular surroundings and bragging rights, head north to the **Golden Door Spa at the Boulders,** 34631 N. Tom Darlington Dr., Carefree (© **480/595-3500;** www.goldendoorspas.com). This spa has tremendous name recognition, but it's not our favorite. The turquoise wrap, the spa's signature treatment, is a real desert experience.

Willow Stream–The Spa at Fairmont, 7575 E. Princess Dr. (© **800/908-9540** or 480/585-2732; www.fairmont.com), is our favorite valley spa. Designed to conjure up images of the journey to northern Arizona's Havasu Canyon, it includes a rooftop swimming pool and a large hot tub in a grotto below the pool.

Located high on the flanks of Mummy Mountain, the **Spa at Camelback Inn,** 5402 E. Lincoln Dr., Scottsdale (© **800/922-2635** or 480/596-7040; www.camelbackspa.com), is a deliciously tranquil place and has long been one of the valley's premiere spas. You just can't beat this spa for convenience and variety of treatments.

The **Centre for Well Being,** at the Phoenician, 6000 E. Camelback Rd., Scottsdale (© **800/843-2392** or 480/423-2452; www.centreforwellbeing.com), is one of the valley's most prestigious spas. Treatments include a botanical hydrating wrap and an aromatherapy tranquility scrub.

The historic setting and convenient location of the **Arizona Biltmore Spa,** 2400 E. Missouri Ave. (© **602/381-7632;** www.arizonabiltmore.com), make this facility an excellent choice if you're spending time along the Camelback Corridor. The spa menu includes dozens of different treatments, such as massages with lavender and a cactus flower body wrap.

Each March, the **Safeway International LPGA Tournament** (© **877/983-3300** or 602/495-4653; www.safewaygolf.com), held at the Superstition Mountain Golf & Country Club, 800 E. Club Village Dr., lures nearly 100 of the top women golfers from around the world. Daily tickets are $20; weekly tickets are $50.

RODEOS, POLO & HORSE SHOWS   Cowboys, cowgirls, and other horsey types will find plenty of the four-legged critters going through their paces most weeks at **WestWorld of Scottsdale,** 16601 N. Pima Rd., Scottsdale (© **480/312-6802;** www.scottsdaleaz.gov/westworld). With its hundreds of stables, numerous equestrian arenas, and a polo field, this complex provides an amazing variety of entertainment and sporting events. There are rodeos, polo matches, horse shows, horseback rides, and horseback-riding instruction.

9 Shopping

For the most part, shopping in the Phoenix area means malls. They're everywhere, and they're air-conditioned, which, we're sure you'll agree, makes shopping in the desert far more enjoyable when it's 110°F (43°C) outside.

Scottsdale and the Biltmore District of Phoenix (along Camelback Rd.) are the Valley's main upscale shopping areas, with several high-end shopping centers and malls. The various distinct shopping districts of downtown Scottsdale are among the few outdoor shopping areas in the Valley and are home to hundreds of boutiques, galleries, jewelry stores, Native American crafts stores, and souvenir shops. The Western atmosphere of Old Town Scottsdale is partly real and partly a figment of the local merchants' imaginations, but nevertheless it's the most popular tourist shopping area in the Valley. With dozens of galleries in the Main Street Arts and Antiques District and the nearby Marshall Way Contemporary Arts District, it also happens to be the heart of the Valley's art market.

For locals, Scottsdale's shopping scene has been moving steadily northward over the past decade. Kierland Commons and the Shops at Gainey Village are both north of Old Town Scottsdale on North Scottsdale Road and are packed with women's fashion boutiques.

Shopping hours are usually Monday through Saturday from 10am to 6pm and Sunday from noon to 5pm; malls usually stay open until 9pm Monday through Saturday.

ANTIQUES & COLLECTIBLES

With more than 80 antiques shops and specialty stores, downtown Glendale (northwest of downtown Phoenix) is the Valley's main antiques district. You'll find the greatest concentration of antiques stores just off Grand Avenue between 56th and 59th avenues. A half dozen times each year, the **Arizona Antique Shows** (© 602/717-7337; www.azantiqueshow.com), Arizona's largest collectors' shows, are held at the Arizona State Fairgrounds, 19th Avenue and McDowell Road.

Antique Trove   If you love browsing through packed antiques malls searching for your favorite collectibles, then this should be your first stop in the Valley. With more than 100 dealers, it's one of the biggest antiques malls in the area. 2020 N. Scottsdale Rd., Scottsdale. © 480/947-6074. www.antiquetrove.com.

Arizona West Galleries ✸✸   Nowhere else in Scottsdale will you find such an amazing collection of cowboy collectibles and Western antiques. There are antique saddles and chaps, old rifles and six-shooters, sheriffs' badges, spurs, and the like. 7149 E. Main St., Scottsdale. © 480/994-3752.

Bishop Gallery for Art & Antiques ✸   This cramped shop is wonderfully eclectic, featuring everything from Asian antiques to unusual original art. Definitely worth a browse. 7164 Main St., Scottsdale. © 480/949-9062.

ART

In the Southwest, only Santa Fe is a more important art market than Scottsdale, and along the streets of Scottsdale's Main Street Arts and Antiques District and the Marshall Way Contemporary Arts District, you'll see dozens of galleries selling everything from monumental bronzes to contemporary art created from found objects. On Main Street, you'll find cowboy art, both traditional and contemporary, while on North Marshall Way, you'll discover more imaginative and daring contemporary art.

In addition to the galleries listed here, you'll usually find a huge tent full of art along Scottsdale Road in north Scottsdale. The annual **Celebration of Fine Art** (ⓒ 480/443-7695; www.celebrateart.com) takes place each year between mid-January and late March. Not only will you get to see the work of 100 artists, but on any given day, you'll also find dozens of the artists at work on the premises. Admission is $8 for adults and $7 for seniors. Call or check the website for this year's location.

Bentley Projects   Housed in a huge old warehouse south of Chase Field in downtown Phoenix, this massive gallery is one the city's most cutting-edge contemporary-art spaces. You probably aren't in the market for a 12-foot-tall Jim Dine bronze statue of Venus, but if you'd like to see one, stop by this gallery. There's a second gallery in Scottsdale at 4161 N. Marshall Way (ⓒ **480/946-6060**). 215 E. Grant St., Phoenix. ⓒ 602/340-9200. www.bentleygallery.com.

Cervini Haas Gallery   This is Scottsdale's premier gallery of fine contemporary crafts, including furniture, ceramics, and jewelry. The works on display here often push the envelope of what's possible in any given medium. 4222 N. Marshall Way, Scottsdale. ⓒ 480/429-6116. www.cervinihaas.com.

Lisa Sette Gallery   If you aren't a fan of cowboy or Native American art, don't despair. Instead, drop by this gallery, which always mounts eclectic and fascinating shows, often melding 19th- and 21st-century aesthetics. 4142 N. Marshall Way, Scottsdale. ⓒ 480/990-7342. www.lisasettegallery.com.

Overland Gallery of Fine Art ★★   Traditional Western and Russian Impressionist paintings form the backbone of this gallery's fine collection. These are museum-quality works (prices sometimes approach $100,000) definitely worth a look. The gallery also shows the angular Southwest landscapes of Ed Mell, one of our favorite Southwest artists. 7155 Main St., Scottsdale. ⓒ 800/920-0220 or 480/947-1934. www.overlandgallery.com.

Roberts Gallery   The feathered masks and sculptures of Virgil Walker are high lights, and if you have an appreciation for fine detail work, you'll likely be fascinated by these pieces. Walker's annual show is held on Thanksgiving weekend. El Pedregal Festival Marketplace, 34505 N. Scottsdale Rd., Carefree. ⓒ 480/488 1088.

Wilde Meyer Gallery   Brightly colored and playful are the norm at this gallery, which represents Linda Carter-Holman, a Southwestern favorite who does cowgirl-inspired paintings. There are also Wilde Meyer galleries at 7100 E. Main St., Scottsdale (ⓒ **480/947-1489**) and in the Shops at Gainey Village, 8777 N. Scottsdale Rd. (ⓒ **480/488-3200**). 4142 N. Marshall Way, Scottsdale. ⓒ 480/945-2323. www.wildemeyer.com.

BOOKS

Major chain bookstores in the area include **Borders,** at Biltmore Fashion Park, 2402 E. Camelback Rd., Phoenix (ⓒ **602/957-6660**), 699 S. Mill Ave., Tempe (ⓒ **480/921-8659**), and 4555 E. Cactus Rd., Phoenix (ⓒ **602/953-9699**); and **Barnes & Noble,** 10235 N. Metro Parkway E., Phoenix (ⓒ **602/678-0088**), in Kierland Commons, N. Scottsdale Rd. and Greenway Rd., Scottsdale (ⓒ **480/948-8551**), and 10500 N. 90th St., Scottsdale (ⓒ **480/391-0048**).

Guidon Books   Whether you're already a student of Western and Civil War history or have only recently developed an interest in the past, this cramped little bookshop in Old Town Scottsdale should not be missed. Rare and out-of-print books are a specialty, but there are plenty of new books as well. Western Americana and the Civil War are the main focus here. 7117 W. Main St., Scottsdale. ⓒ 480/945-8811. www.guidon.com.

FASHION

In addition to the options mentioned below, there are lots of great shops in malls all over the city. Favorite destinations for upscale fashions include Biltmore Fashion Park, The Borgata of Scottsdale, el Pedregal Festival Marketplace, and Scottsdale Fashion Square. See "Malls & Shopping Centers," below, for details.

For cowboy and cowgirl attire, see "Western Wear," below.

Barbwire Western Couture   If you, or perhaps your daughter, are looking for the latest in over-the-top cowgirl chic fashions, look no further. Barbwire is, well, cutting edge when it comes to clothes and accessories inspired by both the Wild West and rock 'n' roll. 15425 N. Scottsdale Rd., Suite 230, Scottsdale. ⓒ 866/929-9473 or 480/443-9473. www.barbwire.com.

Conrad Leather Boutique   It may be hot when you visit Arizona, but remember, you have to go home where it's probably a whole lot cooler. If you need a new leather jacket or belt, there's no better place in the Valley to look than this north Scottsdale boutique. Beautiful leather jackets for both men and women fill the shop. In el Pedregal, 34505 N. Scottsdale Rd., Suite E-7, Scottsdale. ⓒ 480/488-2190.

Objects   This eclectic shop carries hand-painted, wearable art—both casual and dressy—along with unique artist-made jewelry, contemporary furnishings, and all kinds of delightful and unusual items for the home. In The Shops at Gainey Village, 8787 N. Scottsdale Rd., Scottsdale. ⓒ 480/994-4720. www.objectsgallery.com.

Scottsdale Jean Company   If you're searching for the latest high-fashion jeans, don't leave town without dropping by this shop in north Scottsdale. It has the biggest and best selection of jeans in the city. 14747 N. Northsight Blvd. (at Raintree Dr., on the NE corner), Scottsdale. ⓒ 480/905-9300. www.scottsdalejc.com.

Stefan Mann   Purses, purses, purses. Gorgeous leather purses, wallets, and luggage are to be had here at Stefan Mann, which has been in business for more than 25 years. If you're constantly on the prowl for a standout handbag, you'll certainly find something here. In el Pedregal, 34505 N. Scottsdale Rd., Suite J-6, Scottsdale. ⓒ 480/488-3371. www.stefanmann.com.

GIFTS & SOUVENIRS

The Store @ Scottsdale Center for the Performing Arts 🌟   This gift shop on the downtown Scottsdale mall has a wonderful selection of fun, contemporary, and artistic gifts, including lots of jewelry. There's another gift shop next door at the Scottsdale Museum of Contemporary Art. 7380 E. Second St., Scottsdale. ⓒ 480/874-4644. www.scottsdaleperformingarts.com.

Two Plates Full   We love wandering through this shop just to marvel at all the bright colors and fun designs. Featuring functional art and crafts, home accessories, and jewelry, this is a great place to shop for unique gifts. In The Borgata, 6166 N. Scottsdale Rd., Suite 402, Scottsdale. ⓒ 480/443-3241. www.twoplatesfull.com.

JEWELRY

Cornelis Hollander   Although this shop is much smaller and not nearly as dramatic as the nearby Jewelry by Gauthier store (see below), the designs are just as cutting edge. Whether you're looking for classic chic or trendy modern designs, you'll find plenty to interest you here. There's a second store in north Scottsdale at 36207

N. Scottsdale Rd. (© **480/575-5583**). 4151 N. Marshall Way, Scottsdale. © **480/423-5000**. www.cornelishollander.com.

Jewelry by Gauthier   This elegant store sells the designs of the phenomenally talented Scott Gauthier. The stylishly modern pieces use precious stones and are miniature works of art. There's a second, much smaller shop in Kierland Commons, 15034 N. Scottsdale Rd., Suite 120 (© **480/443-4030**). 4211 N. Marshall Way, Scottsdale. © **888/ 411-3232** or 480/941-1707. www.jewelrybygauthier.com.

Sami   This little jewelry store northeast of Scottsdale in the town of Fountain Hills specializes in amethyst from a mine in the nearby Four Peaks Mountains. The mine has been producing gemstones since Spanish colonial times, and the very best of the stones wind up at this shop. You'll also find Arizona peridot and "anthill" garnet jewelry here. 16704 Avenue of the Fountains, Suite 100, Fountain Hills. © **877/376-6323** or 480/837- 8168. www.arizonagems.com.

MALLS & SHOPPING CENTERS

The **Scottsdale Waterfront,** is a mixed-use development along a canal at the corner of Camelback and Scottsdale roads. There are shops, most of which are either national chains or satellites of popular local boutiques, and restaurants (once again national and local chains). The only real difference between the Scottsdale Waterfront and the attached Scottsdale Fashion Square is that at the waterfront you actually have to (get to?) walk around outside. Unfortunately, Scottsdale's canal, a cement-lined trough, is not exactly a romantic water course. Still, the Scottsdale Waterfront is the prettiest new shopping and dining destination in town.

Biltmore Fashion Park ⊛   This open-air shopping plaza with garden courtyards is one of the most pleasant places to shop in Phoenix. Saks Fifth Avenue and Macy's are the two anchors, while smaller storefronts bear familiar names including Tommy Bahama, Victoria's Secret, Ralph Lauren, and The Sharper Image. There are also nearly a dozen moderately priced restaurants here. 2502 E. Camelback Rd. (at 24th St.). © 602/955-8400 or 602/955-1963. www.shopbiltmore.com.

The Borgata of Scottsdale ⊛⊛   Designed to resemble the medieval Italian village of San Gimignano, complete with turrets, stone walls, and ramparts, The Borgata is far and away the most architecturally interesting mall in the Valley. Within its walls, you'll find about 50 upscale boutiques, galleries, and restaurants. On Friday evenings, there's live jazz. This shopping center has just undergone an extensive remodeling and is looking better than ever. 6166 N. Scottsdale Rd. © 602/953-6311. www.borgata.com.

el Pedregal Shops & Dining at The Boulders ⊛⊛   Adjacent to The Boulders resort 30 minutes north of Old Scottsdale, el Pedregal is the most self-consciously Southwestern shopping center in the Valley, and it's worth the long drive out just to see the neo–Santa Fe/Moroccan architecture. The shops offer high-end merchandise, fashions, and art. The Heard Museum also has a branch here. 34505 N. Scottsdale Rd., Carefree. © 480/488-1072. www.elpedregal.com.

Kierland Commons ⊛⊛   The urban-village concept of a shopping center—narrow streets, sidewalks, and residences mixed in with retail space—has taken off all over the country, and here in Scottsdale, the concept has taken on Texas-size proportions. However, despite the grand scale of this shopping center, it has a great feel. You'll find Tommy Bahama, Ann Taylor Loft, Crate & Barrel, and even a few local boutiques, including favorites Mahsa and 42 Saint, which stock fashions not found elsewhere. N. Scottsdale and Greenway roads (C) 480/348-1577. www.kierlandcommons.com.

Scottsdale Fashion Square   Scottsdale has long been the Valley's shopping mecca, and for years this huge mall has been the reason why. It now houses four major department stores—Nordstrom, Dillard's, Neiman Marcus, and Macy's—and smaller stores such as Coach, Eddie Bauer, J. Crew, and Louis Vuitton. 7014-590 E. Camelback Rd. (at Scottsdale Rd.), Scottsdale. (C) 480/949-0202. www.westcor.com.

The Shops at Gainey Village   This upscale shopping center is much smaller than Kierland Commons farther up Scottsdale Road, but is no less impressive, especially after dark when lights illuminate the tall palm trees. There may not be a more impressive concentration of women's clothing stores anywhere in Scottsdale. 8777–8989 N. Scottsdale Rd. (at Doubletree Ranch Rd.). (C) 858/622-0858. www.theshopsgaineyvillage.com.

NATIVE AMERICAN ARTS, CRAFTS & JEWELRY

Bischoff's at the Park 🌶🌶   This museum-like store and gallery is affiliated with another Bischoff's right across the street (see "Gifts & Souvenirs," above). However, this outpost carries higher-end jewelry, Western-style home furnishings, and clothing, ceramics, sculptures, contemporary paintings, and books and music with a regional theme. 3925 N. Brown Ave., Scottsdale. (C) 480/946-6155.

Faust Gallery 🌶   Old Native American baskets and pottery, as well as old and new Navajo rugs, are the specialties at this interesting shop. It also sells Native American and Southwestern art, including ceramics, paintings, bronzes, and unusual sculptures. 7103 E. Main St., Scottsdale. (C) 480/946-6345. www.faustgallery.com.

Gilbert Ortega Gallery & Museum   You'll find Gilbert Ortega shops all over the Valley, but this is the biggest and best. As the name implies, there are museum displays throughout the store. Jewelry is the main attraction, but there are also baskets, sculptures, pottery, rugs, paintings, and kachina dolls. 3925 N. Scottsdale Rd. (C) 480/990-1808. www.gilbertortega.com.

Heard Museum Gift Shop   The Heard Museum (see "Seeing the Sights," earlier in this chapter) has an astonishing collection of well-crafted and very Native American jewelry, art, and crafts of all kinds. This is the best place in the Valley to shop for Native American arts and crafts; you can be absolutely assured of the quality. Because the store doesn't have to charge sales tax, you'll save a bit of money. At the Heard Museum, 2301 N. Central Ave. (C) 602/252-8344. www.heard.org.

John C. Hill Antique Indian Art 🌶🌶   While shops selling Native American art and artifacts abound in Scottsdale, few offer the high quality available in this tiny shop. Not only does the store have one of the finest selections of Navajo rugs in the Valley, including quite a few older rugs, but there are kachina dolls, superb pieces of Navajo and Zuni silver-and-turquoise jewelry, baskets, and pottery. 6962 E. First Ave., Suite 104, Scottsdale. (C) 480/946-2910. www.johnhillgallery.com.

Old Territorial Shop 🌶🌶   Owned and operated by Alston and Deborah Neal, this is the oldest Indian arts-and-crafts store on Main Street and offers good values on jewelry, concho belts, kachina dolls, fetishes, pottery, and Navajo rugs. 7077 E. Main St., Suite 7, Scottsdale. (C) 480/945-5432. www.oldterritorialshop.com.

River Trading Post   If you are interested in getting into collecting Native American art or artifacts, this is a good place to get in on the ground floor. Quality is high and prices are relatively low. Not only are there high-quality Navajo rugs, but there are also museum-quality pieces of ancient Southwestern pottery. 7140 E. First Ave., Scottsdale. ⓒ 866/426-6901 or 480/444-0001. www.rivertradingpost.com.

WESTERN WEAR

Az-Tex Hat Company   If you're looking to bring home a cowboy hat, this is the best place in Scottsdale to do your shopping. The small shop in Old Scottsdale offers custom shaping and fitting of both felt and woven hats. 3903 N. Scottsdale Rd., Scottsdale. ⓒ 800/972-2116 or 480/481-9900. www.aztexhats.com.

Out West ⓐ   If the revival of 1950s cowboy fashions and interior decor has hit your nostalgia button, then you'll want to high-tail it up to this eclectic shop. All things Western are available, and the fashions are both beautiful and fun (although fancy and pricey). 7003 E. Cave Creek Rd., Cave Creek. ⓒ 480/488-0180. www.outwestmercantile.com.

Saba's Western Stores   Since 1927, this store has been outfitting Scottsdale's cowboys and cowgirls, visiting dude ranchers, and anyone else who wants to adopt the look of the Wild West. Call or check the website for other locations around Phoenix. 7254 Main St., Scottsdale. ⓒ 877/342-1835 or 480/949-7404. www.sabaswesternwear.com.

Sheplers Western Wear   Although it isn't the largest Western-wear store in the Valley, Sheplers is still sort of a department store of cowboy duds. If you can't find it here, it just ain't available in these parts. Other locations include 8999 E. Indian Bend Rd., Scottsdale (ⓒ 480/948-1933), and 2643 E. Broadway Rd., Mesa (ⓒ 480/827-8244). 9201 N. 29th Ave., Suite 39. ⓒ 602/870-8085. www.sheplers.com.

10 Phoenix & Scottsdale After Dark

If you're looking for nightlife in the Valley of the Sun, you won't have to look hard, but you may have to drive quite a ways. Although much of the nightlife scene is centered on Old Town Scottsdale, Tempe's Mill Avenue, and downtown Phoenix, you'll find things going on all over.

The weekly *Phoenix New Times* tends to have the most comprehensive listings for clubs and concert halls. "Calendar" in the Thursday edition of the *Arizona Republic* also lists upcoming events and performances. *Get Out,* published by the *Tribune,* is another tabloid-format arts-and-entertainment publication that is available free around Scottsdale, Phoenix, and Tempe. Other publications to check for abbreviated listings are *Valley Guide, Arizona Key,* and *Where Phoenix/Scottsdale,* all of which are free and can usually be found at hotels and resorts.

Tickets to many concerts, theater performances, and sporting events are available through **Ticketmaster** (ⓒ 480/784-4444; www.ticketmaster.com), which has outlets at Macy's department stores and Fry's Marketplace grocery stores.

THE CLUB & MUSIC SCENE

Packed into a couple of dozen blocks surrounding Old Town Scottsdale, near the corner of Camelback and Scottsdale roads, there are dozens of trendy dance clubs and chic bars. This is where the wealthy fashionistas (and the wannabes) come to party. The crowd is young, affluent, and attractive. Cruise along **Stetson Drive,** which is divided into two sections (east and west of Scottsdale Rd.) to find the latest hot spots.

Although Scottsdale is the nexus of nightclubbing for the fashion conscious, the Valley has plenty of other clubs and bars for those who don't wear Prada. Other nightlife districts include Tempe's Mill Avenue and downtown Phoenix.

Mill Avenue in Tempe is a good place to wander around until you hear your favorite type of music. Because Tempe is a college town, the crowd tends to be young and rowdy.

Downtown Phoenix is home to Symphony Hall, the Herberger Theater Center, and several sports bars. However, much of the action revolves around sports events and concerts at US Airways Center and Chase Field.

Clubs come and go quickly, so to find out what's hot, get a copy of the *New Times*. Bars and clubs are allowed to serve alcohol until 2am.

COUNTRY

Buffalo Chip Saloon & Steakhouse   Cave Creek is the Valley's last Wild West town and is full of cowboy bars. This barnlike place is a local favorite, especially with fans of the Green Bay Packers. There's live country music Thursday through Sunday nights, all-you-can-eat fish fries featuring walleye, and s'mores on the dessert menu. 6811 E. Cave Creek Rd., Cave Creek. ℂ 480/488-9118. www.buffalochipsaloon.com.

Handlebar-J   This Scottsdale landmark is about as genuine a cowboy bar as you'll find in Phoenix. You'll hear live two-steppin' nightly; free dance lessons given Wednesday, Thursday, and Sunday at 7pm. 7116 Becker Lane (1 block N of the NW corner of Scottsdale Rd. and Shea Blvd.), Scottsdale. ℂ 480/948-0110. www.handlebarj.com. No cover to $5.

Rusty Spur Saloon   A small, rowdy, drinkin'-and-dancin' place frequented by tourists, this bar is loads of fun, with peanut shells all over the floor, dollar bills stapled to the walls, and live country music afternoons and evenings. If you're a cowboy or cowgirl at heart, this is the place to party when you're in Scottsdale. 7245 E. Main St., Old Scottsdale. ℂ 480/425-7787. www.rustyspursaloon.com.

DANCE CLUBS & DISCOS

Axis/Radius   If you're looking to do a bit of celebrity-spotting, Axis is one of the best places in town to keep your eye on. For several years now, this has been one of Scottsdale's hottest dance clubs and liveliest singles scenes. The two-story glass box is a bold contemporary space with an awesome sound system. 7340 E. Indian Plaza (2 blocks east of Scottsdale Rd. and 1 block south of Camelback Rd.), Scottsdale. ℂ 480/970-1112. www.axis-radius. com. No cover to $10.

Barcelona   It's big, it's beautiful, and it's busy. This is Scottsdale's premier supper club, and after the dinner crowd gives up its tables Thursday through Saturday nights, Barcelona becomes one of the city's top dance spots. The well-heeled crowd ranges primarily from their 30s to 50s. 15440 Greenway-Hayden Loop. ℂ 480/603-0370. www.barcelona dining.com. No cover to $10.

e4   Taking its design theme from the four elements—earth, air, fire, and water—this stylish nightclub provides the four coolest club spaces in Scottsdale. There's the sexy red light and dance floor of the fire room, the cool blue and bubbly liquid room (a dance space), the space-age air patio, and the earth lounge for chilling out. 4282 N. Drinkwater Blvd., Scottsdale. ℂ 480/970-3325. www.e4-az.com. No cover to $10.

Myst   Always packed to the walls with the Valley's beautiful people, Myst is currently *the* place to see and be seen. The atmosphere is lavishly ostentatious, with various themed rooms. The club is open Wednesday, Friday, and Saturday. 7340 E. Shoeman Lane, Scottsdale. ℂ 480/970-5000. www.mystaz.com. Cover $5–$20.

Pepin   Friday and Saturday starting at 10pm and Sunday beginning at 9pm, a DJ plays Latin dance music at this small Spanish restaurant located in the Scottsdale Mall.

Friday and Saturday evenings, there are also live flamenco performances. 7363 Scottsdale Mall, Scottsdale. © 480/990-9026. www.pepinrestaurant.com. Cover $8.

ROCK, JAZZ & BLUES

Geordie's at the Wrigley Mansion   Open only on Friday and Saturday nights, this lounge is inside the historic Wrigley Mansion, which was built between 1929 and 1931 by chewing gum magnate William Wrigley, Jr. The sprawling mansion is located on a hilltop adjacent to the Arizona Biltmore resort. 2501 E. Telawa Trail. © 602/955-4079. www.wrigleymansionclub.com. No cover.

Char's Has the Blues   You wouldn't think to look at this little cottage, but it really does have those mean-and-dirty, low-down blues. All of the best blues brothers and sisters from around the city and around the country make the scene here. 4631 N. Seventh Ave., 4 blocks south of Camelback Rd. © 602/230-0205. www.charshastheblues.com. No cover to $10.

The Rhythm Room   This blues club, long the Valley's most popular, books quite a few national acts as well as the best of the local scene, and has a dance floor if you want to move to the beat. 1019 E. Indian School Rd. © 602/265-4842. www.rhythmroom.com. No cover to $25.

THE BAR, LOUNGE & PUB SCENE

AZ88   Located across the park from the Scottsdale Center for the Arts, this sophisticated bar/restaurant has a cool, contemporary ambience that's just right for a cocktail (try a martini) or a basket of waffle fries before or after a performance. There's also a great patio area. 7353 Scottsdale Mall, Scottsdale. © 480/994-5576. www.az88.com.

Bar Bianco ⊛   Located downtown on Heritage Square, this little wine bar is in a restored historic home and is affiliated with Pizzeria Bianco, the tiny and ever-popular designer pizza place right next door. This is a very romantic place for a drink. 609 E. Adams St. © 602/528-3699.

Four Peaks Brewing Company   Consistently voted the best brewpub in Phoenix, this Tempe establishment brews good beers and serves decent pub grub. It's a favorite of ASU students. You'll find this pub south of East University Drive between South Rural Road and South McClintock Drive. There's a second brewpub in north Scottsdale at the corner of Hayden Road and Frank Lloyd Wright Boulevard (© **480/991-1795**). 1340 E. Eighth St., Tempe. © 480/303-9967. www.fourpeaks.com.

Hyatt Regency Scottsdale Lobby Bar ⊛⊛   The open-air lounge just below the main lobby of this posh Scottsdale resort sets a romantic stage for nightly live music (often flamenco or Caribbean steel drum music). Wood fires burn in patio fire pits, and the terraced gardens offer plenty of dark spots for a bit of romance. 7500 E. Doubletree Ranch Rd., Scottsdale. © 480/444-1234. www.scottsdale.hyatt.com.

Six ⊛   There are those who frequent this posh bar just to see the look on newcomers' faces when they see the high-tech unisex bathrooms—the glass is transparent until you go inside! Regardless of why you come, you'll find one of the coolest and most stylish drinking establishments in the state. Popular with visiting celebrities. 7316 E. Stetson Dr., Scottsdale. © 480/663-6620. www.6az.com.

T. Cook's ⊛⊛   If you aren't planning on having dinner at this opulent Mediterranean restaurant, at least stop by for a cocktail in the bar. With its mix of Spanish colonial and 1950s tropical furnishings, this is as romantic a lounge as you'll find anywhere in the Valley. At the Royal Palms Resort & Spa, 5200 E. Camelback Rd. © 602/840-3610. www.royalpalmshotel.com.

WINE BARS

Cave Creek Coffee Co. & Wine Purveyors   Located way up north in the cow town of Cave Creek, this hip coffeehouse doubles as a lively wine bar that also happens to book some great music. Past performers have included Kelly Joe Phelps, Michelle Shocked, Richie Havens, and Leo Kottke. 6033 E. Cave Creek Rd., Cave Creek. (C) **480/488-0603.** www.cavecreekcoffee.com. Cover $15–$38.

Kazimierz World Wine Bar (R)   Sort of a speak-easy crossed with a wine cellar, this place offers the same wide selection of wines available at the affiliated Cowboy Ciao restaurant. There are dozens of wines by the glass and live jazz ($5 cover after 8pm) several nights each week. The entrance is hard to find (look for the big wood door with a sign that says THE TRUTH IS INSIDE), but it's worth seeking out. 7137 E. Stetson Dr., Scottsdale. (C) **480/946-3004.** www.kazbar.net.

Postino (RR)   This immensely popular wine bar south of Camelback Road is housed in a former post office. Casual yet stylish, the bar has garage-style doors that roll up to expose the restaurant to the outdoors. Choose from a great selection of wines by the glass. 3939 E. Campbell Ave. (C) **602/852-3939.** www.postinowinecafe.com.

COCKTAILS WITH A VIEW

The Valley of the Sun has more than its fair share of spectacular views. Unfortunately, most of them are from expensive restaurants. All these restaurants have lounges, though, where, for the price of a drink (and perhaps valet parking), you can sit back and ogle a crimson sunset and the purple mountains' majesty. Among the best choices are **Different Pointe of View,** at the Pointe Hilton Tapatio Cliffs Resort, and **jade bar,** at The Sanctuary on Camelback Mountain.

Thirsty Camel   Whether you've already made your millions or are still working your way up the corporate ladder, you owe it to yourself to spend a little time in the lap of luxury. You may never drink in more ostentatious surroundings. The view is one of the best in the city. At The Phoenician, 6000 E. Camelback Rd. (C) **480/941-8200.**

Wright Bar & Squaw Peak Terrace   Can't afford the lifestyles of the rich and famous? For the cost of a couple of drinks, you can sink into a seat here at the Biltmore's main lounge and watch the sunset test its color palette on Piestewa Peak. At the Arizona Biltmore Resort & Spa, 2400 E. Missouri Ave. (C) **602/381-7632.** www.arizonabiltmore.com.

SPORTS BARS

Alice Cooper'stown   Sports and rock mix it up at this downtown restaurant/bar run by, you guessed it, Alice Cooper. Chase Field, where the Arizona Diamondbacks play ball, is only a block away. See p. 441 for more information. 101 E. Jackson St. (C) 602/253-7337. www.alicecooperstown.com.

Don & Charlie's   Although this is primarily a steakhouse, it also has the best sports bar in Scottsdale. What makes Don & Charlie's such a great sports bar is not the size or number of its TVs, but rather all the sports memorabilia on the walls. 7501 E. Camelback Rd. (C) **480/990-0900.** www.donandcharlies.com.

Majerle's Sports Grill   If you're a Phoenix Suns fan, you won't want to miss this sports bar only a couple of blocks from US Airways Center, where the Suns play. Suns memorabilia covers the walls, and who knows, you just might bump into a team member while you're here. 24 N. Second St. (C) **602/253-0118.** www.majerles.com.

GAY & LESBIAN BARS & CLUBS

Ain't Nobody's Bizness   Located in a small shopping plaza, this is the city's most popular lesbian bar. The music here is primarily hip-hop, and on weekends, the dance floor is usually packed. 3031 E. Indian School Rd., Suite 7. © 602/224-9977. www.aintnobodys bizness-az.com.

Amsterdam/Club Miami/Malibu Beach Bar   This downtown Phoenix nightclub complex may not look like much from the outside, but through the doors, you'll find a classy spot that's known across the Valley for its great martinis. There's usually a female impersonator one night of the week, and other nights, there's live music or DJ dance music. 718 N. Central Ave. © 602/258-6122. www.amsterdambar.com.

THE PERFORMING ARTS

Downtown Phoenix claims the Valley's greatest concentration of performance halls, but there are major performing-arts venues scattered across the Valley. Calling these many valley venues home are such major companies as the Phoenix Symphony, Scottsdale Symphony Orchestra, Arizona Opera Company, Ballet Arizona, Center Dance Ensemble, Actors Theatre of Phoenix, and Arizona Theatre Company. A wide variety of touring companies also stop in the Valley.

OUTDOOR VENUES & SERIES

The **Cricket Pavilion,** 2121 N. 83rd Ave., Phoenix (© 602/254-7200; www. cricket-pavilion.com), west of downtown and ½-mile north of I-10 between 75th and

---

Major Performing-Arts Centers

Symphony Hall, 225 E. Adams St. (© 602/262-7272), is home to the Phoenix Symphony and the Arizona Opera Company. It also hosts touring Broadway shows and various other concerts and theatrical productions.

The **Orpheum Theatre,** 203 W. Adams St. (© 602/262-7272), is an elegant, historic Spanish-colonial baroque theater built in 1929.

Celebrity Theatre, 440 N. 32nd St. (© 602/267-1600; www.celebritytheatre. com), seems to be booking lots of great acts these days, such as Carole King, Chris Isaak, and Joe Satriani.

The **Dodge Theatre,** 400 W. Washington St. (© 602/379-2800; www. dodgetheatre.com), which seats from 2,000 to 5,000 people, books top names in entertainment as well as Broadway shows and international touring companies.

The Frank Lloyd Wright–designed **Grady Gammage Auditorium,** Mill Avenue and Apache Boulevard, Tempe (© 480/965-3434; www.asugammage. com), on the Arizona State University campus, hosts everything from barbershop quartets to touring Broadway shows.

The **Scottsdale Center for the Arts,** 7380 E. Second St., Scottsdale (© 480/994-2787; www.scottsdaleperformingarts.org), hosts a variety of performances and series, ranging from alternative dance to classical music.

83rd avenues, is the city's top outdoor venue. This 20,000-seat amphitheater is open year-round and hosts everything from Broadway musicals to rock concerts.

The **Mesa Amphitheater,** at University Drive and Center Street, Mesa (© **480/ 644-2560;** www.mesaamp.com), is a much smaller amphitheater that holds a wide variety of concerts in spring and summer, and occasionally other times of year as well.

Throughout the year, the **Scottsdale Center for the Arts,** 7380 E. Second St., Scottsdale (© **480/994-2787;** www.scottsdaleperformingarts.org), stages outdoor performances in the adjacent Scottsdale Amphitheater on the Scottsdale Civic Center Mall. The Sunday A'fair series runs from October to April, with free concerts from noon to 4:30pm on selected Sundays. Performances range from blues to zydeco.

Two perennial favorites of Valley residents take place in particularly attractive surroundings. The Music in the Garden concerts at the **Desert Botanical Garden,** 1201 N. Galvin Pkwy. in Papago Park (© **480/941-1225;** www.dbg.org), are held on Sundays between January and March. The season always includes an eclectic array of musical styles. Tickets are $16 and include admission to the gardens. Sunday brunch is served for an additional charge. Between late March and late June, there are also Friday-night jazz concerts. Up on the north side of the Valley, just outside Carefree, **el Pedregal Shops & Dining at The Boulders,** 34505 N. Scottsdale Rd., Scottsdale (© **480/488-1072;** www.elpedregal.com), stages occasional jazz, blues, and rock concerts, and sometimes has free live music on weekends.

CLASSICAL MUSIC, OPERA & DANCE

The **Phoenix Symphony** (© **800/776-9080** or 602/495-1999; www.phoenixsymphony. org), the Southwest's leading symphony orchestra, performs at Symphony Hall (tickets mostly run $18–$67).

Opera buffs will want to see what the **Arizona Opera Company** (© **602/266-7464;** www.azopera.org) has scheduled. Each season, this company stages up to five operas, both familiar and more obscure, and splits its time between Phoenix and Tucson. Tickets cost $30 to $125. Performances are held at Symphony Hall.

Ballet Arizona (© **888/3-BALLET** or 602/381-1096; www.balletaz.org) performs at both the Orpheum Theatre and stages both classical and contemporary ballets; tickets run $10 to $104. The **Center Dance Ensemble** (© **602/252-8497;** www.center dance.com), the city's contemporary dance company performs at the Herberger Theater Center. Tickets cost $21. Between September and April, **Southwest Arts & Entertainment** (© **602/482-6410;** www.southwestae.com) brings acclaimed dance companies and music acts to Phoenix, with performances staged primarily at the Orpheum. Tickets are usually around $30.

THEATER

Downtown, the **Herberger Theater Center,** 222 E. Monroe St. (© **602/254-7399;** www.herbergertheater.org) is the city's main venue for live theater. Its two Broadway-style theaters together host hundreds of performances each year, including productions by the **Actors Theatre of Phoenix (ATP)** and the **Arizona Theatre Company (ATC).** ATP (© **602/253-6701;** www.atphx.org) tends to stage smaller, lesser-known off-Broadway-type works; tickets go for $24 to $49. ATC (© **602/256-6995;** www. arizonatheatre.org) is the state theater company of Arizona. Productions range from world premieres to Tony award–winners to classics. Tickets run $21 to $62.

The **Phoenix Theatre,** 100 E. McDowell Rd. (© **602/254-2151;** www.phxtheatre. org), is located in the Phoenix Art Museum building. Musicals are the mainstays here;

tickets are $24 to $39. The **Broadway in Arizona** series (© 480/965-3434; www.broadwayacrossamerica.com/tempe), focusing mostly on comedies and musicals, is held at the Gammage Auditorium in Tempe. Tickets cost roughly $20 to $70, with the occasional higher prices for a real blockbuster show.

11 A Side Trip from Phoenix: The Apache Trail ★★

There isn't a whole lot of desert or history left in Phoenix, but only an hour's drive to the east you'll find quite a bit of both. The **Apache Trail,** a narrow, winding, partially gravel road that snakes its way around the north side of the Superstition Mountains, offers some of the most scenic desert driving in central Arizona. Along the way are ghost towns and ancient ruins, saguaros and century plants, reservoirs and hiking trails. Pick and choose the stops that appeal to you, and be sure to get an early start. The gravel section of the road is well graded and is passable for regular passenger cars.

If you'd rather leave the driving to someone else, **Apache Trail Tours** (© 480/982-7661; www.apachetrailtours.com) offers guided half-day and full-day tours along the Apache Trail. Tours range in price from $70 to $145.

To start this drive, head east on US 60 to the town of Apache Junction, and then go north on Arizona 88. About 4 miles out of town is **Goldfield Ghost Town,** a reconstructed gold-mining town (see "Especially for Kids" under "Seeing the Sights," earlier in this chapter). Allow plenty of time if you plan to stop here.

Not far from Goldfield is **Lost Dutchman State Park,** 6109 N. Apache Trail (© 480/982-4485), where you can hike into the rugged Superstition Mountains. Springtime wildflower displays here can be absolutely gorgeous. Park admission is $5 per vehicle ($3 during the summer); a campground charges $12 to $25 per site.

Continuing northeast, you'll reach **Canyon Lake,** set in a deep canyon flanked by colorful cliffs and rugged rock formations. At Canyon Lake, you can swim at the Acacia Picnic Area or the nearby Boulder Picnic Area, which is in a pretty side cove. You can also take a cruise on the *Dolly* steamboat (© 480/827-9144; www.dollysteamboat.com). A 90-minute jaunt on this reproduction paddle-wheeler costs $18 for adults and $10 for children 5 to 12. Lunch and dinner cruises ($34–$52) are also available, and there's a lakeside restaurant at the boat landing. But if you're at all hungry, try to hold out for nearby **Tortilla Flat** (© 480/984-1776; www.tortillaflataz.com), an old stagecoach stop with a restaurant, saloon, and general store. Don't miss the prickly-pear ice cream (guaranteed spineless).

A few miles past Tortilla Flat, the pavement ends and the truly spectacular desert scenery begins. Among the rocky ridges, arroyos, and canyons of this stretch of road, you'll see saguaro cacti and century plants (a type of agave that dies after sending up its flower stalk, which can reach heights of 15 ft.).

Shortly before reaching pavement again, you'll see **Theodore Roosevelt Dam.** This dam, built in 1911, forms Roosevelt Lake and is the largest masonry dam in the world. However, a face-lift a few years ago hid the original masonry construction; it now looks much like any other concrete dam in the state.

Continuing on Arizona 88, you'll next come to **Tonto National Monument** ★ (© 928/467-2241; www.nps.gov/tont), which preserves some of the southernmost cliff dwellings in Arizona. These pueblos were occupied between about 1300 and 1450 by the Salado people and are some of the few remaining traces of this tribe. The lower ruins are a half-mile up a steep trail, and getting to the upper ruins requires a 3-mile round-trip hike. The lower ruins are open daily year-round; the upper ruins are

En Route to Tucson

Driving southeast from Phoenix for about 60 miles will bring you to the Casa Grande and Coolidge area, where you can learn about the Hohokam people who once inhabited this region, and, in spring, see desert wildflowers.

Casa Grande Ruins National Monument ★★, located outside Coolidge, preserves one of the most unusual Indian ruins in the state; an earth-walled structure built 650 years ago by the Hohokam people. Instead of using adobe bricks or stones, the people who built this structure used layers of hard-packed soil. Located 1 mile north of Coolidge on Arizona 87 (© 520/723-3172; www.nps.gov/cagr). Admission is $5.

Alternatively, if you're heading to Tucson by way of I-10, consider a stop at **Picacho Peak State Park** ★★, 35 miles northwest of Tucson at exit 219 (© 520/466-3183; www.pr.state.az.us). Picacho Peak, which rises 1,500 feet above the desert, is a visual landmark for miles around. Hiking trails around the peak and up to the summit are especially popular in spring, when the wildflowers bloom. Admission is $6 per car ($3 in summer) for up to 4 adults; campsites in the park cost $10 to $22.

open November through April on guided tours (reserve at least 2 weeks in advance). The park is open daily from 8am to 5pm (you must begin the lower ruin trail by 4pm); admission is $3.

Keep going on Arizona 88 to the copper-mining town of **Globe.** Be sure to visit **Besh-Ba-Gowah Archaeological Park** ★ (© 928/425-0320), on the eastern outskirts of town. Several rooms at this Salado Indian pueblo site are set up to reflect the way they might have looked when they were first occupied about 700 years ago. The ruins are open daily from 9am to 5pm (admission $3 adults, $2 seniors, free children 12 and under). To get here, head out of Globe on South Broad Street to Jesse Hayes Road.

From Globe, head west on US 60. Three miles west of Superior, you'll come to **Boyce Thompson Arboretum** ★★, 37615 US 60 (© 520/689-2811; arboretum.ag. arizona.edu), dedicated to researching and propagating desert plants. As you hike the nature trails of this 320-acre garden, watch for the two bizarre boojum trees. The arboretum is open daily from 8am to 5pm (May through August daily 6am to 3pm); admission is $7.50 for adults and $3 for children 5 to 12.

13

The Deserts, High Plains & Sky Islands of Southern Arizona

In the southeastern corner of Arizona, the mile-high grasslands, punctuated by forested mountain ranges, have long supported vast ranches where cattle range across wide-open plains. It was also here that much of America's now-legendary Western history took place. Wyatt Earp and the Clantons shot it out at Tombstone's O.K. Corral, Doc Holliday played his cards, and Cochise and Geronimo staged the last Indian rebellions. Cavalries charged, and prospectors wandered the wilderness in search of the mother lode. Today, ghost towns litter the landscape of southeastern Arizona, but the past is kept alive by people searching for a glimpse of the Wild West.

The combination of low deserts, high plains, and even higher mountains has given this region a fascinating diversity of landscapes. Giant saguaros cover the slopes of the Sonoran Desert throughout much of southern Arizona, and in the western parts of this region, organ pipe cacti reach the northern limit of their range. In the cool mountains, cacti give way to pines, and passing clouds bring snow and rain. Narrow canyons and broad valleys, fed by the rain and snowmelt, provide habitat for hundreds of species of birds and other wildlife. This is the northernmost range for many birds usually found only south of the border. Consequently, southeastern Arizona has become one of the nation's most important bird-watching spots.

1 Organ Pipe Cactus National Monument ★★

135 miles S of Phoenix; 140 miles W of Tucson; 185 miles SE of Yuma

Located roughly midway between Yuma and Tucson, Organ Pipe Cactus National Monument is a preserve for the rare cactus for which the monument is named. The organ pipe cactus resembles the saguaro cactus in many ways, but instead of forming a single main trunk, organ pipes have many trunks, some 20 feet tall, that resemble—you guessed it—organ pipes.

This is a rugged region with few towns or services. To the west lie the inaccessible Cabeza Prieta National Wildlife Refuge and the Barry M. Goldwater Air Force Range (a bombing range), and to the east is the large Tohono O'odham Indian Reservation. The only motels in the area are in the small town of Ajo, a former company town that was built to house the workers at a now-abandoned copper mine. The downtown plaza, with its tall palm trees and arched and covered walkways, has the look and feel of a Mexican town square. Be sure to gas up your car before leaving Ajo.

ESSENTIALS

GETTING THERE   From Tucson, take Arizona 86 W to Why and turn south on Arizona 85. From Yuma, take I-8 E to Gila Bend and drive south on Arizona 85.

FEES   The park entry fee is $8 per car.

VISITOR INFORMATION   For information, contact **Organ Pipe Cactus National Monument** (© 520/387-6849; www.nps.gov/orpi). The visitor center is open daily from 8am to 5pm, although the park itself is open 24 hours a day. The visitor center is closed Thanksgiving, Christmas, and all federal holidays during the summer.

EXPLORING THE MONUMENT

Two well-graded gravel roads lead through different sections of this large national monument. Puerto Blanco Drive, formerly a long loop drive, is currently a 5-mile route leading only to the Red Tanks trail head, while Ajo Mountain Drive is a 21-mile one-way loop. Guides available at the park's visitor center explain natural features of the landscape along both drives. There are also a number of hiking trails along the roads, but many of these trails are now closed to the public due to safety concerns surrounding the use of this area by illegal immigrants crossing the border from Mexico. Be sure to check with the national monument before planning any hikes. In the winter, there are guided tours of Ajo Mountain Drive.

WHERE TO STAY

There are two campgrounds within the park. Campsites are $8 in primitive **Alamo Campground** and $12 in more developed **Twin Peaks Campground.** The nearest lodgings are in Ajo, with several old and very basic motels as well as a B&B. There are also plenty of budget chain motels in the town of Gila Bend, 70 miles north of the monument.

Guest House Inn Bed & Breakfast   Built in 1925 as a guesthouse for mining executives, this B&B has attractive gardens in the front yard, a mesquite thicket off to one side, and a modern Southwestern feel to its interior decor. Guest rooms are simply furnished with reproduction antique and Southwestern furnishings. There are sunrooms on both the north and the south sides of the house.

700 Guest House Rd., Ajo, AZ 85321. © 520/387-6133. www.guesthouseinn.biz. 4 units. $89 double. Rates include full breakfast. DC, MC, V. *In room:* A/C, fridge, hair dryer, iron, microwave, Wi-Fi, no phone.

2 Tubac ⟨★★ & Buenos Aires National Wildlife Refuge ⟨★

45 miles S of Tucson; 21 miles N of Nogales; 84 miles W of Sierra Vista

Located in the fertile valley of the Santa Cruz River 45 miles south of Tucson, Tubac is one of Arizona's largest arts communities and home to a developing retirement community. The town's old buildings house more than 80 shops selling fine arts, crafts, unusual gifts, and lots of Southwest souvenirs, making Tubac one of southern Arizona's most popular destinations.

After visiting Tubac Presidio State Historic Park and Tumacacori National Historical Park to learn about the area's history, you'll probably want to spend some time browsing through the shops. Keep in mind, however, that many of the local artists leave town in summer, prompting many local shops to close on weekdays in the summer. The shops are open daily during the busy season of October through May.

Southern Arizona

Chiricahua National Monument **10**

Cochise Stronghold **8**

Coronado National Memorial **6**

For. Bowie National Historic Site **9**

Kartchner Caverns State Park **4**

Las Cienegas National Conservation Area **3**

Ramsey Canyon Preserve **5**

San Pedro Riparian National Conservation Area **7**

Tubac Presidio State Historic Park **1**

Tumacacori National Historical Park **2**

ESSENTIALS

GETTING THERE   The Santa Cruz Valley towns of Amado, Tubac, and Tumacácori are all due south of Tucson on I-19.

VISITOR INFORMATION   For information on Tubac and Tumacácori, contact the **Tubac Chamber of Commerce** (© 520/398-2704; www.tubacaz.com); or the **Tubac-Santa Cruz Visitor Center**, 4 Plaza Rd. (© 520/398-0007; www.toursanta cruz.com).

ART & HISTORY IN THE SANTA CRUZ VALLEY

Tubac Center of the Arts ⊛   Tubac is an arts community, and this Spanish colonial building serves as its center for cultural activities. Throughout the season, the center features workshops, traveling exhibitions, juried shows, an annual crafts show, and theater and music performances. The quality of the art at these shows is generally better than what's found in most of the surrounding stores. There is also a good little gift shop here.

9 Plaza Rd. © 520/398-2371. www.tubacarts.org. Admission by donation. Mon–Sat 10am–4:30pm; Sun 1–4:30pm. Closed mid-May to Labor Day and major holidays.

Tubac Presidio State Historic Park   Although little remains of the old presidio (fort) but buried foundation walls, this small park does a good job of presenting the region's Spanish colonial history. The nearby Tumacácori mission (see below) was founded in 1691, but it was not until 1752 that Tubac Presidio was established in response to a Pima Indian uprising. Park exhibits focus on the Spanish soldiers, Native Americans, religion, and contemporary Hispanic culture in southern Arizona. Also on the grounds is the old Tubac School, built in 1885 and the oldest schoolhouse in the state. Living-history presentations are staged October through March on Sundays between 1 and 4pm. Among the characters you'll meet are Spanish soldiers, settlers, and friars.

Presidio Dr. © 520/398-2252. www.azstateparks.com. Admission $3 adults ($2 between Memorial Day and Labor Day), free for children under 14. Daily 8am–5pm. Closed Christmas.

Tumacácori National Historical Park ⊛   Founded in 1691 by Jesuit missionary and explorer Father Eusebio Francisco Kino, San José de Tumacácori mission was one of the first Anglo settlements in what is today Arizona. Father Kino's mission was to convert the Pima Indians, and for the first 60 years, the mission was successful. However, in 1751, during the Pima Revolt, the mission was destroyed. For the next 70 years, this mission struggled to survive, but during the 1820s, an adobe mission church was constructed. Today, the mission ruins are a haunting reminder of the role that Spanish missionaries played in settling the Southwest. Much of the old adobe mission church still stands. On weekends between October and April, Native American and Mexican craftspeople give demonstrations of indigenous arts. On the second Wednesday of the month from October to March, there are special living-history tours to the nearby ruins of San Cayetano de Calabazas mission. These tours are by reservation and cost $10 per person.

1891 E. Frontage Rd. © 520/398-2341. www.nps.gov/tuma. Admission $3 adults, free for children under 16. Daily 8am–5pm. Closed Thanksgiving and Christmas. Take I-19 to Exit 29; Tumacácori is 3 miles south of Tubac.

SHOPPING

While tourist brochures like to tout Tubac as an artists' community, the town is more of a Southwest souvenir mecca. There are a few genuine art galleries here, but you have to look hard amid the many tourist shops to find the real gems.

Some of the better fine art in the area is found at the **Karin Newby Gallery,** Mercado de Baca, 19 Tubac Rd. (© **888/398-9662** or 520/398-9662; www.karinnewby gallery.com). For traditional Western art, some by members of the prestigious Cowboy Artists of America, visit the **Big Horn Galleries,** 37 Tubac Rd. (© **520/398-9209;** www.bighorngalleries.com).

If you're in the market for jewelry, be sure to visit **Blackstar,** E. Frontage Road (© **520/398-0451**), in nearby Amado (at Exit 48 off I-19). This small jewelry store specializes in locally mined opal and other exotic gemstones.

Near Tumacacori National Historical Park, you'll find all things hot (chiles, hot sauces, salsas, spices) arranged on the shelves of the **Santa Cruz Chile and Spice Company,** 1868 E. Frontage Rd. (© **520/398-2591;** www.santacruzchili.com). The shop is open Monday through Saturday from 8am to 5pm.

BUENOS AIRES NATIONAL WILDLIFE REFUGE ⌖

If you're a bird-watcher, you'll definitely want to make the trip to **Buenos Aires National Wildlife Refuge,** P.O. Box 109, Sasabe, AZ 85633 (© **520/823-4251;** www. fws.gov/southwest/refuges/arizona/buenosaires/index.html), about 28 miles from Tubac. To get here, head north from Tubac on I-19 to Arivaca Junction, then drive west on a winding two-lane road. The refuge begins just outside the small community of Arivaca.

Your first stop should be **Arivaca Cienega,** a quarter of a mile east of Arivaca. *Cienega* is Spanish for "marsh," and that is exactly what you'll find here. A boardwalk leads across this marsh, which is fed by seven springs that provide year-round water and consequently attract an amazing variety of bird life. This is one of the few places in the United States where you can see a gray hawk, and vermilion flycatchers are quite common. Other good birding spots within the refuge include **Arivaca Creek,** 2 miles west of Arivaca, and **Aguirre Lake,** a half-mile north of the refuge headquarters and visitor center, which is off Arizona 286 north of Sasabe.

The **visitor center** is a good place to spot one of the refuge's rarest birds, the masked bobwhite quail. These quail disappeared from Arizona in the late 19th century, but have been reintroduced in the refuge. Other birds you might spot outside the visitor center include Bendire's thrashers, Chihuahuan ravens, canyon towhees, and green-tailed towhees. The visitor center is open daily from 7:30am to 4pm (closed Thanksgiving, Christmas, New Year's Day, and summer weekends).

Other wildlife in the refuge includes pronghorn antelopes, javelinas, coatimundis, white-tailed deer, mule deer, and coyotes. Guided birding and other tours are offered weekends November through April. Call for details; some walks require reservations.

If you're looking for a strenuous hike, try the **Mustang Trail,** which has its trail head 2 miles west of Arivaca. The trail climbs from Arivaca Creek into the surrounding dry hills and makes for a 5-mile round-trip hike.

GETTING OUTSIDE

Linking Tubac with Tumacácori is the 8-mile **de Anza Trail,** which follows the Santa Cruz River for much of its route and passes through forests and grasslands. This trail is part of the **Juan Bautista de Anza National Historic Trail,** which stretches from Nogales to San Francisco and commemorates the overland journey of the Spanish captain who, in 1775 and 1776, led a small band of colonists overland to California. These settlers founded what is now the city of San Francisco. Today, bird-watching is the most popular activity along the trail. The most convenient trail head is beside

Tubac Presidio State Historic Park. **Rex Ranch** (© **800/547-2696** or 520/398-2914; www.rexranch.com) offers horseback rides for $35 per hour.

If golf is more your speed, you can play a round at the **Tubac Golf Resort** (© **520/ 398-2211;** www.tubacgolfresort.com), just north of Tubac off East Frontage Road. Greens fees range from $39 to $109 in the winter.

WHERE TO STAY
IN AMADO
The Inn at Amado Territory Ranch ⚑   This modern inn just off I-19 at the crossroads of Amado is built in the territorial style and captures the feel of an old Arizona ranch house. Guest rooms are outfitted in a mix of Mexican rustic furnishings and reproduction East Coast antiques, much in the style that homes would have been furnished in Arizona 100 years ago. Rooms on the second floor feature balconies with views across the farm fields of the Santa Cruz Valley, while those on the ground floor have patios. The Amado Café is right next door.

3001 E. Frontage Rd. (P.O. Box 81), Amado, AZ 85645. © 888/398-8684 or 520/398-8684. Fax 520/398-8186. www. amado-territory-inn.com. 9 units. Nov–June $130–$145 double; July–Oct $105–$115 double. Rates include full breakfast. AE, DISC, MC, V. Pets accepted. **Amenities:** Restaurant (American/Greek); massage. *In room:* A/C, hair dryer, Wi-Fi, no phone.

The Rex Ranch ⚑ *Finds*   With its classic Southwestern styling and location adjacent to the de Anza Trail, this place is truly a hidden getaway. Just getting to this remote property is something of an adventure, since you have to drive *through* the Santa Cruz River to reach it. When you see the pink-walled mission-revival building in the middle of the desert, you'll know you've arrived someplace distinctly different. Although not all of the guest rooms are as attractively decorated as the public areas, the new rooms and the more recently renovated rooms are quite comfortable. The ranch offers a wide variety of spa treatments and massages. The dining room here is one of this area's best restaurants.

131 Amado Montosa Rd. (P.O. Box 636), Amado, AZ 85645. © 800/547-2696 or 520/398-2914. www.rexranch.com. 30 units. Oct to mid-Dec $115–$125 double, $160 suite; mid-Dec to May $135–$175 double, $205 suite; June–Sept $95–$105 double, $125 suite. Rates include continental breakfast. AE, DISC, MC, V. 2-night minimum stay. **Amenities:** Restaurant (Southwestern/New American); outdoor pool; spa; Jacuzzi; mountain-bike rentals; concierge; massage; horseback riding. *In room:* A/C, fridge, coffeemaker, Wi-Fi, no phone.

IN TUBAC
Tubac Golf Resort ⚑⚑ *Value*   This economical golf resort is built on the Otero Ranch, which dates back to 1789 and is the oldest Spanish land-grant ranch in the Southwest. With its green fairways, the resort is a lush oasis amid the dry hills of the Santa Cruz Valley. The ranch is both a secluded hideaway and a modern golf resort with a more classic Southwestern ambience than at most Tucson golf resorts. This golf resort also has a more low-key feel. The red-tile roofs and brick archways throughout the resort conjure up the Spanish heritage, while guest rooms are spacious and modern and set amid expansive lawns. Casitas have patios and beehive fireplaces; newer rooms are worth requesting. Watch out for cows grazing on the golf course.

1 Otero Rd. (P.O. Box 1297), Tubac, AZ 85646. © 800/848-7893 or 520/398-2211. Fax 520/398-9261. www.tubac golfresort.com. 98 units. $109–$229 double; $139–$359 suite. Children under 12 stay free in parent's room. AE, DISC, MC, V. Pets accepted ($25 fee). **Amenities:** 3 restaurants (Continental, Mexican); lounge; outdoor pool; 27-hole golf course; tennis court; exercise room; spa; Jacuzzi; bike rental; business center; shopping arcade; room service; massage; babysitting; coin-op laundry; laundry service. *In room:* A/C, TV, dataport, fridge, coffeemaker, hair dryer, iron, safe.

Starry, Starry Nights

Southern Arizona's clear skies and the absence of lights in the surrounding desert make the night sky here as brilliant as anywhere on earth. This fact has not gone unnoticed by the world's astronomers—southern Arizona has come to be known as the Astronomy Capital of the World.

Many observatories are open to the public, but you'll need to make tour reservations well in advance. In addition to the ones listed below, the **Flandrau Science Center & Planetarium** (p. 374) in Tucson offers public viewings. In Flagstaff, there are public viewing programs at the **Lowell Observatory** (p. 553).

The **Smithsonian Institution Fred Lawrence Whipple Observatory,** located atop 8,550-foot Mount Hopkins, is the largest observatory operated by the Smithsonian Astrophysical Observatory. Tours last about 6 hours. No food is available here, so be sure to bring a picnic lunch. It's located on Mount Hopkins Road, near Amado (© **520/670-5707**). Six-hour tours of the observatory are offered mid-March through November Monday, Wednesday, and Friday, and cost $7 for adults, $2.50 for children 6 to 12; no children under 6 allowed. Reservations are required and should be made 4 to 6 weeks in advance.

Located in the Quinlan Mountains atop 6,875-foot Kitt Peak, **Kitt Peak National Observatory** ⓐ is the largest and most famous astronomical observatory in the region. This is the area's only major observatory to offer public nighttime viewing. Day visitors must be content with a visitor center (open daily 9am to 3:45pm), museum, and guided tour. Tours are held at 10am, 11:30am, and 1:30pm. Suggested donation is $2 per person, and tours are $3.50 for adults and $2 for children ages 6 to 12. The observatory is 56 miles southwest of Tucson off Arizona 86 (© **520/318-8726**; www.noao.edu/kpno). Nighttime stargazing (reservations required; call 4–8 weeks in advance) costs $39 adults; $34 students, seniors, and children under 18.

The **Mount Graham International Observatory** near the town of Safford offers 7-hour tours that include lunch but do not include viewing through the observatory's telescopes. Tours are arranged through **Eastern Arizona College's Discovery Park Campus,** 1651 W. Discovery Park Blvd., Safford (© **928/428-6260**; www.discoverypark.com). The tours are held on Saturdays between early May and mid-November, and cost $40 (reservations required).

Situated on the grounds of the privately owned Vega-Bray Observatory, an amateur observatory with six telescopes and a planetarium, the **Astronomer's Inn** ⓐ, 1311 S. Astronomer's Rd., Benson, AZ 85602 (© **520/586-7906**; www.astronomersinn.com), is one of the most unusual lodgings in the state. The inn provides guests with not only a bed for the night, but a chance to observe the night sky and the sun through the observatory's telescopes. Viewing programs range from $59 to $130 per night. The inn is located 4 miles outside Benson; call for directions. Rates are $85 to $129 double.

WHERE TO DINE

In addition to the restaurants mentioned below, the **Tubac Golf Resort** (see "Where to Stay," above) has two good restaurants.

IN AMADO

Amado Café MEDITERRANEAN/AMERICAN   There aren't a lot of dining options out here, making this restaurant, in a handsome territorial-style building just off I-19, a good bet for lunch or dinner. The best part of the experience is sitting out back on the rustic flagstone patio, listening to the gurgling fountain, and contemplating the view of the mountains in the distance. The menu includes sandwiches, salads, and more filling fare such as prime rib. The Greek dishes, including a Greek salad and stuffed grape leaves, are good bets.

3001 E. Frontage Rd. (Exit 48 off I–19), Amado. 𝒞 **520/398-9211.** Reservations not necessary. Main courses $7.50–$11 lunch, $11–$22 dinner. AE, DISC, MC, V. Tues–Sat 11:30am–2pm and 5–8pm; Sun 11:30am–2pm.

IN TUBAC & TUMACACORI

Nob Hill Gourmet Market and Fine Dining 𝒢 NEW AMERICAN   In the past few years, there has been an explosion of upscale retirement communities in and around Tubac, but until this restaurant opened, there was nowhere right in Tubac for the new well-heeled residents to enjoy a white-tablecloth dinner. Actually, this is much more than someplace to sit down to trout stuffed with lemon and fennel or a filet mignon with truffle-port demi-glaze.

In Plaza de Anza, 10 Avenida Goya, Suite B. 𝒞 **520/398-1010.** www.nobhilltubac.com. Main courses $7.50–$13 lunch, $17–$32 dinner. AE, MC, V. Daily 11am–3pm and 5–8:30pm.

Shelby's Bistro AMERICAN   Located behind a small shopping plaza and across a little foot bridge, this casual place has a very pleasant patio and is a great spot for lunch. The lunch menu is a mix of pastas, salads, sandwiches, and pizzas; in the evening, there's prime rib, lobster, and steaks. Try the Sonoran spice-rubbed chicken breast.

In Mercado de Baca, 19 Tubac Rd. 𝒞 **520/398-8075.** Reservations not necessary. Main courses $9.25–$33 dinner. MC, V. Sun–Tues 11am–4pm; Wed–Sat 11am–4pm and 5–9pm.

Wisdom's Cafe *(Finds* MEXICAN   Located between Tubac and Tumacácori (look for the giant chicken statues out front), this roadside diner is a Santa Cruz Valley institution, in business since 1944. With a cement floor and walls hung with old cowboy stuff, it feels a bit like a cross between a cave and an old barn. The menu is short but includes some twists on standard Mexican fare, including tostadas, tacos, and enchiladas made with turkey. Don't eat too much, though, or you won't have room for this restaurant's main draw—huge fruit burritos that are basically Mexican fruit pies.

1931 E. Frontage Rd., Tumacácori. 𝒞 **520/398-2397.** www.wisdomscafe.com. Reservations not necessary. Main dishes $4.50–$15. AE, DISC, MC, V. Mon–Sat 11am–3pm and 5–8pm.

3 Patagonia 𝒢𝒢 & Sonoita 𝒢

Patagonia: 18 miles NW of Nogales; 60 miles SE of Tucson; 171 miles SE of Phoenix; 50 miles SW of Tombstone

A mild climate, numerous good restaurants, bed-and-breakfast inns, and a handful of wineries have turned the small communities of Patagonia and Sonoita into a favorite weekend getaway for Tucsonans. Sonoita Creek, one of the only perennial streams in southern Arizona, attracts an amazing variety of bird life.

Patagonia and Sonoita are only about 12 miles apart, but they have decidedly different characters. Patagonia is a sleepy little hamlet with tree-shaded streets, quite a few old adobe buildings, and a big park in the middle of town. The Nature Conservancy preserve on the edge of town makes Patagonia popular with bird-watchers. Sonoita, on the other hand, sits out on the windswept high plains and is really just a highway crossroads, not a real town. The landscape around Sonoita, however, is filled with expensive new homes on small ranches, and not far away are the vineyards of Arizona's wine country.

ESSENTIALS

GETTING THERE   Sonoita is at the junction of Arizona 83 and Arizona 82. Patagonia is 12 miles southwest of Sonoita on Arizona 82.

VISITOR INFORMATION   The **Patagonia Area Business Association Visitor's Center,** 307 McKeown Ave. (℃ **888/794-0060** or 520/394-9186; www.patagonia az.com), inside Mariposa Books in the center of Patagonia, is open Monday through Saturday from 10am to 5pm and Sunday from 11am to 4pm.

BIRD-WATCHING & WINE TASTING

Patagonia Lake State Park (℃ **520/287-6965;** www.azstateparks.com), about 7 miles south of Patagonia off Arizona 82, is a popular boating and fishing lake that was formed by the damming of Sonoita Creek. The lake is 2½ miles long and stocked in winter with rainbow trout. Other times of year, people fish for bass, crappie, bluegill, and catfish. Park facilities include a picnic ground, campground, and swimming beach. There is also good bird-watching here—elegant trogons, which are among the most beautiful of southern Arizona's rare birds, have been spotted. The park day-use fee is $7 ($8 holidays and summer weekends). Campsites are $12 to $25. Adjacent to the park, you'll find the **Sonoita Creek State Natural Area** (℃ **520/287-2791**), a 5,000-acre preserve along the banks of Sonoita Creek. During much of the year, the natural area operates boat tours several mornings each week. These tours focus on the birds and history of the area. There are also guided hikes and guided bird watching outings.

The **Patagonia–Sonoita Creek Preserve** (℃ **520/394-2400;** www.nature.org) is owned by the Nature Conservancy and protects 2 miles of Sonoita Creek riparian (riverside) habitat, which is important to migratory birds. More than 300 species of birds have been spotted at the preserve. Among the rare birds that can be seen are 22 species of flycatchers, kingbirds, and phoebes, plus the Montezuma quail. A forest of cottonwood trees, some of which are 100 feet tall, lines the creek and is one of the best remaining examples of such a forest in southern Arizona. To reach the preserve, turn west on Fourth Avenue and then south on Pennsylvania Street, and continue about 1 mile. From April to September, hours are Wednesday through Sunday from 6:30am to 4pm; from October to March, hours are Wednesday through Sunday from 7:30am to 4pm. Admission is $5 ($3 for Nature Conservancy members). On Saturday at 9am, there are naturalist-guided walks through the preserve; reservations are not required.

On your way to or from the Nature Conservancy Preserve, be sure to drop by **Paton's Birder's Haven,** which is basically the backyard of Marion Paton. Numerous hummingbird feeders and a variety of other feeders attract an amazing range of birds to the yard, making this a favorite stop of avid birders who are touring the region. If you're heading out to the Nature Conservancy preserve, just watch for the BIRDER'S HAVEN sign at 477 Pennsylvania Rd. after you cross the creek.

Avid birders will also want to visit **Las Cienegas National Conservation Area** (© **520/258-7200;** www.az.blm.gov/nca/lascienegas/lascieneg.htm), which has grasslands, wetlands, and oak forests. This is a good place to look for the rarely seen gray hawk. Access is off the east side of Arizona 83, about 7 miles north of Sonoita.

Sonoita proper is little more than a crossroads with a few shops and restaurants, but surrounding the community are miles of rolling grasslands that are a mix of luxury-home "ranchettes" and actual cattle ranches, all of which have spectacular big-sky views. Out on those high plains, vineyards have made Sonoita Arizona's own little wine country. Most of the wineries are located in or near the village of Elgin, which is 10 miles east of Sonoita. Right in Sonoita, you'll find **Dos Cabezas Wine Works** (© **602/622-0399;** www.doscabezaswinery.com), which is located on Arizona 82 in the middle of town. The winery's tasting room is open Friday through Sunday from 10:30am to 4:30pm. Just west of Elgin, you'll find **Callaghan Vineyards,** 336 Elgin Rd. (© **520/455-5322;** www.callaghanvineyards.com), which is open for tastings Friday through Sunday from 11am to 3pm. This winery produces by far the best wines in the region and, perhaps, the best wines in the state. The two other area wineries don't do nearly as good a job, but you can be the judge yourself. In the ghost town of Elgin, there's the **Village of Elgin Winery** (© **520/455-9309;** www.elginwines.com), which is open daily from 10am to 5pm. Three miles south of Elgin, you'll find **Sonoita Vineyards,** on Elgin-Canelo Road (© **520/455-5893;** www.sonoitavineyards. com), which is open daily from 10am to 4pm. The above tasting-room hours are subject to change, so you might want to call ahead.

WHERE TO STAY
IN PATAGONIA
Duquesne House B&B ⊛   This old adobe building 1 block off Patagonia's main street was built in 1898 as miners' apartments. The unusual little building, with its shady front porch, is your best choice for overnight accommodations in Patagonia. Each unit has its own entrance, sitting room, and bedroom, and is decorated in quintessentially Southwestern style. Our favorite room has an ornate woodstove and clawfoot tub. At the back of the house, an enclosed porch overlooks the garden.

357 Duquesne Ave. (P.O. Box 162), Patagonia, AZ 85624. © **520/394-2732.** 4 units. $99 double. Rate includes full breakfast. No credit cards. *In room:* A/C, no phone.

IN SONOITA
La Hacienda de Sonoita ⊛   Located on the east side of Sonoita and not too far out of town, this hacienda-style B&B has unobstructed views that stretch to the distant mountain ranges surrounding these high plains. The inn is built around a central courtyard, which has a bubbling fountain and covered porches. There's also another covered porch that looks out to the eastern views. The decor in the guest rooms ranges from rancho deluxe to cowboy chic. Our is the Grand Canyon Room.

34 Swanson Rd. (P.O. Box 408), Sonoita, AZ 85637. © **520/455-5308.** Fax 520/455-5309. www.haciendasonoita. com. 4 units. $115–$140 double. Children under 12 stay free in parent's room. AE, MC, V. *In room:* A/C, no phone.

Sonoita Inn   Housed in a barnlike building, the Sonoita Inn plays up the area's ranching history. The building was originally constructed by the owner of the famed Triple Crown–winning thoroughbred Secretariat, and in 1999 it was converted into an inn. The lobby, with its wooden floors, huge fireplace, and ranch brands for decoration, is cool and dark (a welcome escape on hot summer days). Guest rooms feature Indian rugs and 1950s-inspired bedspreads for a retro cowboy touch. Although it's right on Sonoita's main road, the fascinating decor more than makes up for the less-than-quiet location. The Mountain View Room on the second floor has the best view. A popular steakhouse is adjacent to the inn.

At intersection of Ariz. 82 and Ariz. 83, P.O. Box 99, Sonoita, AZ 85637. © 800/696-1006 or 520/455-5935. www. sonoitainn.com. 18 units. $99–$149 double. Rates include deluxe continental breakfast. Children under 18 stay free in parent's room. AE, DISC, MC, V. Pets accepted ($25 per night). *In room:* A/C, TV/VCR, free local calls.

WHERE TO DINE
IN PATAGONIA

For good coffee and pastries, check out **Gathering Grounds,** 319 McKeown Ave. (© **520/394-2097**), which also serves ice cream and has a deli. Looking for a bit of night life? Don't miss **La Mision de San Miguel,** 335 McKeown St. (© **520/394-0123;** www.lamisionpatagonia.com), a Mexican-inspired bar with live music and dancing on Saturday nights.

Velvet Elvis Pizza Company ITALIAN   This casual hangout sums up the unusual character of Patagonia's residents. Faux-finished walls ooze artiness, while paeans to pop culture include shrines to both the Virgin Mary and Elvis. The menu features a variety of pizzas heaped with veggies, cheeses, and meats, but if you can remember to plan a day in advance, you should call in an order for the Inca pizza (made with a quinoa-flour crust). Add an organic salad and accompany it with some fresh juice, microbrew, espresso, or wine.

292 Naugle Ave. © **520/394-2102.** www.velvetelvispizza.com. Reservations not accepted. Pizzas $12–$45; other dishes $6.50–$16. MC, V. Thurs–Sun 11:30am–8:30pm.

IN SONOITA

Grab good breads and pastries, hot breakfasts, and sandwiches at the **Grasslands Bakery/Café,** 3119 Arizona 83 (© **520/455-4770;** www.grasslandsbakery.com), which is an outpost of organic foods. The bakery is open Thursday through Sunday from 8am to 3pm.

Café Sonoita ☞ AMERICAN   A tiny place with just a handful of tables, this cafe serves some of the best food in the area and has long been a favorite with locals. The menu, which changes daily and is limited to a handful of dishes that are listed on a blackboard, is surprisingly creative. Ingredients are always fresh, which is why the menu changes all the time, and there are local wines to accompany the meals. Although you can get straightforward traditional fare such as steaks and prime rib, the best reason to eat here is the more creative dishes.

3280 Ariz. 82 (at the east end of town). © **520/455-5278.** www.cafesonoita.com. Reservations accepted only for parties of 4 or more. Main courses $5.50–$8.75 lunch; $8.50–$18 dinner. DISC, MC, V. Wed–Thurs 5–8pm; Fri–Sat 11am–2:30pm and 5–8pm.

Canela ☞ SOUTHWESTERN   This little restaurant at the crossroads of Sonoita is the most upscale restaurant in the area and was an instant hit when it opened. The menu changes frequently to take advantage of what's fresh and seasonal, but may include Hubbard squash soup flavored with Indian spices and pumpkin seeds, mussels in a green-chile–white-wine broth, or fennel-crusted venison flank steak served with pecan cous-cous. If you're looking for the quintessential Arizona wine-country restaurant, this is it.

3252 Ariz. 82. © **520/455-5873.** Reservations recommended. Main courses $15–$21. AE, DISC, MC, V. Thurs–Sun 5–10pm.

The Steak Out ⚐ STEAKHOUSE   This is ranch country, and this big barn of a place is where the ranchers and everyone else for miles around head when they want a good steak. A classic cowboy atmosphere prevails—there's even a mounted buffalo head just inside the front door. The restaurant's name and the scent of a mesquite fire should be all the hints you need about what to order—a grilled steak, preferably the exceedingly tender filet mignon. Wash it down with a margarita, and you've got the perfect cowboy dinner.

At intersection of Ariz. 82 and Ariz. 83. ℂ **520/455-5205.** Reservations recommended. Main courses $10–$35. AE, DISC, MC, V. Mon–Thurs 5–9pm; Fri 5–10pm; Sat and Sun 11am–10pm.

4 Sierra Vista & the San Pedro Valley ⚐

70 miles SE of Tucson; 189 miles SE of Phoenix; 33 miles SW of Tombstone; 33 miles W of Bisbee

Located at an elevation of 4,620 feet above sea level, Sierra Vista is blessed with the perfect climate—never too hot, never too cold. This fact more than anything else has contributed in recent years to Sierra Vista becoming one of the fastest-growing cities in Arizona. The city is wedged between the Huachuca Mountains and the valley of the San Pedro River, making it a good base for exploring the region's natural attractions.

Within a few miles' drive of town are the San Pedro Riparian National Conservation Area, Coronado National Memorial, and the Nature Conservancy's Ramsey Canyon Preserve. No other area of the United States attracts more attention from birders, who come in hopes of spotting some of the 300 species that have been sighted in southeastern Arizona. About 25 miles north of town (9 miles south of Benson) is Kartchner Caverns State Park, the region's biggest attraction,.

ESSENTIALS

GETTING THERE   Sierra Vista is at the junction of Arizona 90 and Arizona 92 about 35 miles south of I-10. Sierra Vista Municipal Airport is served by **Great Lakes Airlines** (ℂ **800/554-5111;** www.greatlakesav.com) from Phoenix.

VISITOR INFORMATION   The **Sierra Vista Convention & Visitors Bureau,** 3020 Tacoma St. (ℂ **800/288-3861** or 520/417-6960; www.visitsierravista.com), can provide information on the area. To find the visitor center if you're coming from the north, take the Arizona 90 Bypass, turn right on Coronado Drive, turn left on Tacoma Street, and continue to the Oscar Yrun Community Center.

ATTRACTIONS AROUND BENSON

The Western town movie set of **Mescal** (ℂ **520/883-0100**) is operated by Old Tucson Studios and has been used for years in the making of Westerns, as well as TV shows and commercials. Hour-long walking tours of Mescal provide a feel for the many movies that have been shot here. For fans of old Westerns, this is a must. Tours are available Tuesday, Thursday, and Saturday between 10am and 2pm and cost $8. Roughly 35 miles east of Tucson, take Exit 297 off I-10, then head north for 3 miles on Mescal Road. When the pavement ends, head west for ½ mile on the dirt road to the town, which is visible on the hill ahead.

Kartchner Caverns State Park ⚐⚐   These caverns are among the largest and most beautiful in the country, and because they are wet caverns, stalactites, stalagmites, soda straws, and other cave formations are still growing. Within the caverns are two huge rooms, each larger than a football field with ceilings more than 100 feet high. These two rooms can be visited on two separate tours. On the shorter Rotunda/Throne Room

Tour, you will see, in the Rotunda Room, thousands of delicate soda straws. The highlight, though, is the Throne Room, at the center of which is a 58-foot-tall column. The second, and longer, tour visits the Big Room and leads past many strange and rare cave formations. Within the park are several miles of aboveground hiking trails. A campground charging $22 per night provides a convenient place to stay in the area.

Because the caverns are a popular attraction and tours are limited, try to make a reservation in advance, especially if you want to visit on a weekend. However, it is sometimes possible to get same-day tickets if you happen to be passing by.

Off Ariz. 90, 9 miles south of Benson. © 520/586-CAVE. www.azstateparks.com. Admission $5 per car; Rotunda/ Throne Room Tour $19 adults, $9.95 children 7–13, free for children under 7; Big Room Tour $23 adults, $13 children 7–13, children under 7 not allowed. Park daily 7:30am–6pm; cave tours approximately every 20 min. 8am–5pm. Closed Christmas.

BIRDING HOT SPOTS & OTHER NATURAL AREAS

Bird-watching is big business in these parts, with birders' B&Bs, bird refuges, and even birding festivals. The **Southwest Wings Birding Festival** (© 520/678-8237; www.swwings.org), one of southern Arizona's biggest annual birding events, is held each year in early August in Sierra Vista.

If you'd like to join a guided bird walk along the San Pedro River or up Carr Canyon in the Huachuca Mountains, an owl-watching night hike, or a hummingbird banding session, contact the **Southeastern Arizona Bird Observatory** (© 520/432-1388; www.sabo.org), which also has a public bird-viewing area at its headquarters 2 miles north of the Mule Mountain Tunnel on Arizona 80 north of Bisbee (watch for Hidden Meadow Lane). Most activities take place between April and September, and cost $15 to $65. Workshops and tours are also offered.

Serious birders who want to be sure to add lots of rare birds to their life lists might want to visit this area on a guided tour. Your best bet is **Mark Pretti Nature Tours** (© 520/803-6889; www.markprettinaturetours.com), run by the former resident naturalist at Ramsey Canyon Preserve. A half-day birding tour costs $120 and a full-day tour costs $200 to $220. Three-day ($625) and 8-day ($1,250) trips are also offered. Other reliable area guides include Wezil Walraven of **Wezil Walraven Bird Tours** (© 520/234-0123; www.wrensandravens.com) and Melody Kehl of **Melody's Outdoor Adventures** (© 888/296-9437 or 520/296-9437; www.ebiz.netopia.com/ outdoor). **High Lonesome Birdtours** (© 800/743-2668 or 520/458-9446; www.hi lonesome.com), another local tour company, charges about $975 per person for a 4-day birding trip. You can also attend birding-oriented seminars offered by **Sky Island Field Seminars** (© 866/900-1146 or 520/558-1146; www.skyislandfieldseminars.com).

Coronado National Memorial   About 20 miles south of Sierra Vista is a 5,000-acre preserve dedicated to Francisco Vásquez de Coronado, the first European to

---

Moments Hummingbird Heaven

In summer, hummingbird lovers should take a drive up Miller Canyon (south of Ramsey Canyon) to **Beatty's Miller Canyon Guest Ranch and Orchard,** 2173 E. Miller Canyon Rd., Hereford (© 520/378-2728; www.beattysguestranch.com), where a public hummingbird-viewing area is set up. Fifteen species of hummers have been sighted here.

explore this region. In 1540, Coronado, leading more than 700 people, left Compostela, Mexico, in search of the fabled Seven Cities of Cíbola, said to be rich in gold and jewels. Sometime between 1540 and 1542, Coronado led his band of weary men and women up the valley of the San Pedro River, which this monument overlooks. At the visitor center, you can learn about Coronado's fruitless quest for riches and check out the wildlife observation area. After stopping at the visitor center, drive up to 6,575-foot Montezuma Pass, which provides far-reaching views of Mexico to the south, the San Pedro River to the east, and several mountain ranges and valleys to the west. Along the .75-mile round-trip Coronado Peak Trail, you'll also have good views of the valley and can read quotations from the journals of Coronado's followers. There are also some longer trails where you'll see few other hikers.

4101 E. Montezuma Canyon Rd., Hereford. (② 520/366-5515. www.nps.gov/coro. Free admission. Daily 9am–5pm. Closed Thanksgiving and Christmas. Take Ariz. 92 south from Sierra Vista to S. Coronado Memorial Drive and continue 5 miles to the visitor center.

Ramsey Canyon Preserve ⊘   Each year, beginning in late spring, a buzzing fills the air in Ramsey Canyon, but it's not the buzzing of the bees. This preserve is home to 14 species of hummingbirds, and it is the whirring of these diminutive birds' wings that fills the air. Situated in a wooded gorge in the Huachuca Mountains, this Nature Conservancy preserve covers only 380 acres. However, because Ramsey Creek, which flows through the canyon, is a year-round stream, it attracts a wide variety of wildlife, including nearly 200 species of birds. April and May are the busiest times here, while May and August are the best times to see hummingbirds. Guided walks are offered March through October.

27 Ramsey Canyon Rd., off Ariz. 92, 5 miles south of Sierra Vista. (② 520/378-2785. www.nature.org. Admission $5 ($3 for Nature Conservancy members); free on 1st Sat of each month. Feb–Oct daily 8am–5pm; Nov–Jan Thurs–Mon 9am–4pm. Closed New Year's Day, Thanksgiving, and Christmas.

San Pedro Riparian National Conservation Area ⊘   Located 8 miles east of Sierra Vista, this conservation area is one of Arizona's rare examples of a natural riverside habitat. Over the past 100 years, 90% of the region's free-flowing year-round rivers and streams have disappeared due to human use of desert waters. These rivers and streams once provided water and protection to myriad plants, animals, and even humans. Fossil findings from this area indicate that people were living along this river 11,000 years ago. At that time, this area was a swamp, not a desert, but today, the San Pedro River is all that remains of this ancient wetland. Although much of the San Pedro now flows underground, the river attracts wildlife, including more than 300 species of birds.

For bird-watching, the best place is the system of trails at the Arizona 90 crossing of the San Pedro. Here you will find the **San Pedro House** ((② **520/508-4445**), a 1930s ranch that is operated as a visitor center and bookstore. It's open daily from 9:30am to 4:30pm. Throughout the year, there are guided walks and hikes, bird walks, bird-banding sessions, and other events. Check with the San Pedro House for a calendar.

Ariz. 90. (② 520/458-3559. www.az.blm.gov/nca/spnca/spnca-info.htm. Free admission. Parking areas open sunrise–sunset.

WHERE TO STAY
IN BENSON
Holiday Inn Express ⊘   If you're looking for lodging close to Kartchner Caverns, try this off-ramp budget hotel in Benson. The hotel's lobby is done in Santa Fe style

with flagstone floors and rustic Southwestern furniture. Guest rooms are strictly hotel modern, but they are roomy and reliable.

630 South Village Loop, Benson, AZ 85602. © **888/465-4329** or 520/586-8800. Fax 520/586-1370. www.benson az.hiexpress.com. 62 units. $93–$229 double. Rates include continental breakfast. Children under 18 stay free in parent's room. AE, DC, DISC, MC, V. **Amenities:** Outdoor pool; exercise room; access to nearby health club; coin-op laundry. *In room:* A/C, TV, dataport, fridge, coffeemaker, hair dryer, iron, high-speed Internet access, Wi-Fi, free local calls.

IN HEREFORD

Casa de San Pedro *ⵀ*   Built with bird-watching tour groups in mind, this modern inn is set on the west side of the San Pedro River on 10 acres of land. While the setting doesn't have the historical character of the San Pedro River Inn (see below), it is much more up-to-date, with large, comfortable hotel-style guest rooms. Built in the territorial style around a courtyard garden, the inn has a large common room where birders gather to swap tales of the day's sightings. The inn also offers birding, cultural, and history tours. This is by far the most upscale inn in the region, and our favorite.

8933 S. Yell Lane, Hereford, AZ 85615. © **888/257-2050** or 520/366-1300. Fax 520/366-0701. www.bedandbirds. com. 10 units. $149–$175 double. Rates include full breakfast. AE, DISC, MC, V. No children under 12. **Amenities:** Outdoor pool; Jacuzzi; concierge; business center; guest laundry. *In room:* A/C, hair dryer, high-speed Internet access, Wi-Fi, free local calls.

Ramsey Canyon Inn Bed & Breakfast *ⵀ*   Adjacent to the Nature Conservancy's Ramsey Canyon Preserve, this inn is the most convenient choice in the area for avid birders to see the canyon's famous hummingbirds. The property straddles Ramsey Creek, with guest rooms in the main house and apartments reached by a footbridge over the creek. A large country breakfast is served in the morning. Book early.

29 Ramsey Canyon Dr., Hereford, AZ 85615. © **520/378-3010.** www.ramseycanyoninn.com. 9 units. $130–$150 double; $150–$225 suite. Room rates include full breakfast (accept in suites). MC, V. No children under 16 in inn, but children over 12 accepted in suites. *In room:* No phone.

WHERE TO DINE

Adobe Southwestern Cuisine *ⵀⵀ* SOUTHWESTERN   The fact that Bisbee residents are willing to drive to Sierra Vista to eat dinner is a sure sign that the food at this southwestern restaurant is some of the best in the region. Rivaling Cafe Roka (see below) in creativity, Adobe specializes in south-of-the-border flavors. There's adobo-rubbed pork tenderloin with chipotle-spiced sweet potatoes and bourbon-pecan glaze, chile-crusted rack of lamb with prickly-pear sauce, and halibut encrusted with fresh cilantro and coriander seeds. To start things off, try the scallop-and-mango ceviche. You'll find this restaurant near the turnoff for Ramsey Canyon.

5043 S. Hwy. 92. © **520/378-2762.** Reservations recommended. Main courses $16–$26. AE, DISC, MC, V. Wed–Mon 5–9pm.

The Mesquite Tree STEAKHOUSE   This casual steakhouse south of town (and not far from the mouth of Ramsey Canyon) has long been a favorite of locals. It's funky and dark, and the prices can't be beat. Although you can get chicken and fish dishes done in a variety of traditional Continental styles, most people come here for the steaks. Try the Vargas rib-eye, which is smothered with green chiles, jack cheese, and enchilada sauce—a real border-country original. When the weather is warm, try to get a seat on the patio.

S. Ariz. 92 and Carr Canyon Rd. © **520/378-2758.** Reservations recommended. Main courses $9–$22. AE, DISC, MC, V. Tues–Sat 5–9pm; Sun 5–8pm.

The Outside Inn (✿ STEAKHOUSE/SEAFOOD/ITALIAN   Much more formal than the nearby Mesquite Tree, The Outside Inn has long been Sierra Vista's top special-occasion restaurant. Housed in a cottagelike building south of town and just north of the turnoff for Ramsey Canyon, The Outside Inn may not be in the most picturesque of surroundings, but the food is definitely among the best you'll find in the area. In the main dining room or out on the patio, you can enjoy such fare as blackened mahimahi or crab-stuffed giant Guaymas shrimp.

4907 S. Ariz. 92. (✆ 520/378-4645. Reservations recommended. Main courses $8–$12 lunch, $16–$34 dinner. AE, MC, V. Mon–Fri 11am–1:30pm and 5–9pm; Sat 5–9pm.

5 Tombstone (✿

70 miles SE of Tucson; 181 miles SE of Phoenix; 24 miles N of Bisbee

It was on these very streets, outside a livery stable known as the O.K. Corral, that Wyatt Earp, his brothers Virgil and Morgan, and their friend Doc Holliday took on the outlaws Ike Clanton and Frank and Tom McLaury on October 26, 1881. Today, Tombstone, "the town too tough to die," is one of Arizona's most popular attractions.

Tombstone got its start as a mining town, and between 1880 and 1887, an estimated $37 million worth of silver was mined here. Such wealth created a sturdy little town, and as the Cochise County seat of the time, Tombstone boasted a number of imposing buildings, including the county courthouse, which is now a state park. In 1887, an underground river flooded the silver mines, which were never reopened. With the demise of the mines, the boom came to an end and the population rapidly dwindled.

Today, Tombstone's historic district consists of both original buildings that went up after the town's second fire and newer structures built in keeping with the architectural styles of the late 19th century. Most house souvenir shops and restaurants, which should give you some indication that this place is a classic tourist trap, but kids (and adults raised on Louis L'Amour and John Wayne) love it, especially when the famous shootout is reenacted.

ESSENTIALS

GETTING THERE   From Tucson, take I-10 E to Benson and then Arizona 80 S to Tombstone. From Sierra Vista, take Arizona 90 north to Arizona 82, heading east.

VISITOR INFORMATION   The **Tombstone Chamber of Commerce** ((✆ 888/457-3929 or 520/457-3929; www.tombstone.org) operates a visitor center at the corner of Allen and Fourth streets.

GUNSLINGERS & SALOONS: IN SEARCH OF THE WILD WEST

As portrayed in novels, movies, and TV shows, the shootout has come to epitomize the Wild West, and nowhere is this great American phenomenon more glorified than in Tombstone, where the star attraction is the famous **O.K. Corral,** 308 E. Allen St. ((✆ 520/457-3456; www.ok-corral.com), site of a 30-second gun battle that has taken on mythic proportions over the years. Inside the corral, you'll find not only displays on the shootout, but also an exhibit on Tombstone prostitutes and another focusing on local photographer C. S. Fly, who ran the boardinghouse where Doc Holliday was staying at the time of the shootout. The O.K. Corral is open daily from 9am to 5pm, and admission is $5.50.

When the smoke cleared in 1881, three men lay dead. They were later carted off to the **Boot Hill Graveyard** ((✆ 520/457-3300) on the north edge of town. The graves

of Clanton and the McLaury brothers, as well as those of others who died in gunfights or by hanging, are well marked. Entertaining epitaphs grace the grave markers; among the most famous is that of Lester Moore—"Here lies Lester Moore, 4 slugs from a 44, No Les, no more." The cemetery is open to the public Monday through Thursday from 9am to 5pm and Friday through Sunday from 9am to 6pm; admission is by suggested $2 donation. Enter through a gift shop on Arizona 80.

When the residents of Tombstone weren't shooting each other in the streets, they were likely to be found in the saloons and bawdy houses that lined Allen Street. Most famous was the **Bird Cage Theatre,** Allen and Sixth Streets (© 520/457-3421), so named for the cagelike cribs (what most people would think of as box seats) suspended from the ceiling. These velvet-draped cages were used by prostitutes to ply their trade. For old Tombstone atmosphere, this place is hard to beat. Admission is $8 for adults, $7.50 for seniors, $6 for children 8 to 18, or $22 for a family; the theater is open daily from 8am to 6pm.

For a cold beer, Tombstone has a couple of very lively saloons. The **Crystal Palace Saloon,** at Allen and Fifth streets (© 520/457-3611; www.crystalpalacesaloon.com), was built in 1879 and has been completely restored. This is one of the favorite hangouts of the town's costumed actors and other would-be cowboys and cowgirls. **Big Nose Kate's,** 417 E. Allen St. (© 520/457-3107; www.bignosekate.com), is an equally entertaining spot full of Wild West character and characters.

Tombstone has long been a tourist town, and its streets are lined with souvenir shops. There are also several small museums scattered around town. At the **Rose Tree Inn Museum,** at Fourth and Toughnut streets (© 520/457-3326), you can see the world's largest rose tree. Inside are antique furnishings from Tombstone's heyday in the 1880s. The museum is open daily from 9am to 5pm (closed Thanksgiving and Christmas). Admission is $3 (free for children under 14).

Tombstone Courthouse State Park, at 223 Toughnut St. (© 520/457-3311; www.azstateparks.com), is the most imposing building in town and provides a much less sensationalized version of local history. Built in 1882, the courthouse is now a state historic park and museum that chronicles Tombstone's lively past. In the courtyard, you can still see the gallows that once ended the lives of outlaws. The courthouse is open daily from 8am to 5pm (closed on Christmas); the entrance fee is $4 ($3 between Memorial Day and Labor Day) and children under 14 are free.

Don't leave town without visiting the **Tombstone Western Heritage Museum,** Arizona 80 and Sixth St. (© 520/457-3800; www.thetombstonemuseum.com), a privately owned museum that is filled with Tombstone artifacts. Included in this impressive collection are artifacts that once belonged to Wyatt and Virgil Earp, plus rare photos of the Earps and the outlaws of Tombstone. The museum is open Monday, Tuesday, and Thursday through Saturday from 9am to 6pm and Sunday from 12:30 to 6pm; admission is $5 for adults and $3 for children 12 to 18 ($13 for families).

WHERE TO STAY

Holiday Inn Express ☆   On the northern outskirts of Tombstone, right next door to the older Best Western, this is the newest and most reliable hotel in Tombstone. The decor draws on a bit of Southwestern and Spanish colonial styling, but basically this is just a modern motel.

580 W. Randolph Way, Tombstone, AZ 85638. © 888/465-4329 or 520/457-9507. Fax 520/457-9506. www.hiexpress.com. 60 units. $75–$125 double. Rates include continental breakfast. Children under 18 stay free in parent's

room. AE, DISC, MC, V. **Amenities:** Outdoor pool; Jacuzzi; concierge; coin-op laundry. *In room:* A/C, TV, dataport, coffeemaker, hair dryer, iron, high-speed Internet access, free local calls.

Tombstone Boarding House   Housed in two whitewashed 1880s adobe buildings with green trim, this inn is in a quiet residential neighborhood only 2 blocks from busy Allen Street. The main house was originally the home of Tombstone's first bank manager. Guest rooms are in an old boardinghouse. Accommodations are comfortable and clean, with country decor. Hardwood floors and antiques lend a period feel.

108 N. Fourth St. (P. O. Box 1700), Tombstone, AZ 85638. ✆ **877/225-1319** or 520/457-3716. www.tombstone boardinghouse.com. 5 units. $89–$109 double. Rates include full breakfast. DISC, MC, V. Pets accepted ($10 per night). **Amenities:** Restaurant (Continental). *In room:* No phone.

WHERE TO DINE

Big Nose Kate's Saloon SANDWICHES   Okay, so the food here isn't all that memorable, but the atmosphere sure is. Big Nose Kate's dates back to 1880 and is primarily a saloon. As such, it stays packed with visitors who have come to revel in Tombstone's outlaw past. So, while you sip your beer, why not order a sandwich and call it lunch? You might even catch some live country music.

417 E. Allen St. ✆ **520/457-3107.** www.bignosekate.com. Reservations not accepted. Sandwiches $6.50–$8. AE, MC, V. Mon–Fri 11am–8pm; Sat–Sun 9am–8pm.

The Lamplight Room ⊛ CONTINENTAL   Located a few blocks off busy Allen Street, this restaurant serves the best food in Tombstone. The Lamplight Room is in the living room of an old 1880s home, which also lends this place more character than that of any of the other restaurants in town. The menu is short and includes such dishes as chicken cordon *bleu* and roasted pork loin. On Friday and Saturday nights, there's live classical guitar music.

At the Tombstone Boarding House, 108 N. Fourth St. ✆ **520/457-3716.** Reservations recommended. Main courses $6–$17. DISC, MC, V. Mon–Sat 11:30am–8pm; Sun 11:30am–7pm.

6 Bisbee ⊛⊛

94 miles SE of Tucson; 205 miles SE of Phoenix; 24 miles NW of Douglas

Arizona has a wealth of ghost towns that boomed on mining profits and then quickly went bust when the mines played out, but none is as impressive as Bisbee, which is built into the steep slopes of Tombstone Canyon on the south side of the Mule Mountains. Between 1880 and 1975, Bisbee's mines produced more than $6 billion worth of metals. When the Phelps Dodge Company shut down its copper mines here, Bisbee nearly went the way of other abandoned mining towns, but because it's the Cochise County seat, it was saved from disappearing into the desert dust.

Bisbee's glory days date from the late 19th and early 20th centuries, and because the town stopped growing in the early part of the 20th century, it is now one of the best-preserved historic towns anywhere in the Southwest. Old brick buildings line narrow winding streets, and miners' shacks sprawl across the hillsides above downtown. Many artists call the town home, and aging hippies and other urban refugees have for many years been dropping out of the rat race to restore Bisbee's old buildings and open small inns, restaurants, and galleries. Between the rough edges left over from its mining days and this new cosmopolitan atmosphere, Bisbee is one of Arizona's most interesting towns. However, be aware that Bisbee is not for everyone. It appeals mostly to young, hip travelers who don't expect much from their accommodations and who like to stay up late partying. The rumble of motorcycles is a constant on Bisbee's streets, especially on weekends.

ESSENTIALS

GETTING THERE   Bisbee is on Arizona 80, which begins at I-10 in the town of Benson, 45 miles east of Tucson.

VISITOR INFORMATION   Contact the **Bisbee Visitor Center,** 2 Copper Queen Plaza (© **866/2-BISBEE** or 520/432-3554; www.discoverbisbee.com).

EXPLORING THE TOWN

At the Bisbee Chamber of Commerce visitor center, right in the middle of town, pick up walking-tour brochures that will lead you past the most important buildings and sites.

Don't miss the **Bisbee Mining and Historical Museum** ⊛, 5 Copper Queen Plaza (© **520/432-7071;** www.bisbeemuseum.org), housed in the 1897 Copper Queen Consolidated Mining Company office building. This small but comprehensive museum features exhibits on the history of Bisbee. It's open daily from 10am to 4pm; admission is $7.50 for adults, $6.50 for seniors, and $3 children 16 and under.

For another look at early life in Bisbee, visit the **Muheim Heritage House,** 207 Youngblood Hill (© **520/432-7698**), which is reached by walking up Brewery Gulch. The house was built between 1902 and 1915 and has an unusual semicircular porch. The interior is decorated with period furniture. It's open Friday through Tuesday from 10am to 4pm; admission is by $4 suggested donation for adults.

O.K. Street, which parallels Brewery Gulch but is high on the hill on the southern edge of town, is a good place to walk for views of Bisbee. At the top of O.K. Street, there's a path that takes you up to a hill above town for an even better panorama of Bisbee's jumble of old buildings. Atop this hill are numerous small, colorfully painted shrines built into the rocks and filled with candles, plastic flowers, and pictures of the Virgin Mary. It's a steep climb on a rocky, very uneven path, but the views and the fascinating little shrines make it worth the effort.

Mining made this town what it is, so you should be sure to head underground on a tour to find out what it was like to be a miner here in Bisbee. **Queen Mine Tours** ⊛ (© **866/432-2071** or 520/432-2071; www.queenminetour.com) takes visitors down into one of the town's old copper mines. Tours are offered daily between 9am and 3:30pm and cost $12 for adults and $5 for children 4 to 15. The ticket office and mine are just south of the Old Bisbee business district at the Arizona 80 interchange.

For an exploration of some of the steeper and narrower streets of Bisbee, take a 90-minute tour ($35) of old Bisbee with **Lavender Jeep Tours** (© **520/432-5369**). Several other tours are also available. For a walk on the dark side, sign up for the **Old Bisbee Ghost Tour** (© **520/432-3308;** www.oldbisbeeghosttour.com). These 90-minute tours are offered Friday through Sunday nights at 7pm (and occasionally at 9pm as well) and cost $12 for adults and $7 for children under 12.

If it's art you're after, check out some of the local galleries. At the **Johnson Gallery,** 28 Main St. (© **520/432-2126**), you'll find an outstanding selection of Native American crafts, including Navajo rugs and jewelry, Hopi kachinas and pottery, and lots of Zuni fetishes. **Bisbee Clay,** 30 Main St. (© **520/432-1916**), has beautiful pottery, both functional and decorative, in unusual designs and colors. For fine contemporary crafts that will fit in a suitcase, visit **Twist,** 51 Main St. (© **520/432-3046**).

To protect your face from the burning rays of the sun (and make a fashion statement), visit **Optimo Custom Hat Works,** 47 Main St. (© **888/FINE-HAT** or 520/ 432-4544; www.optimohatworks.com), which sells and custom-fits Panama straw hats as well as felt hats. (By the way, Panama hats actually come from Ecuador.)

WHERE TO STAY

Canyon Rose Suites *(★ (Value* Located on the second floor of a commercial building just off Bisbee's main street, this property offers spacious suites with full kitchens, which makes it a good bet for longer stays. All units have hardwood floors and high ceilings, and the works by local artists and the mix of contemporary and rustic furnishings give the place plenty of Bisbee character. Constructed on a steep, narrow street, the building housing this lodging has an unusual covered sidewalk, making it one of the more distinctive commercial buildings in town.

27 Subway at Shearer St. (P.O. Box 1915), Bisbee, AZ 85603. © **866/296-7673** or 520/432-5098. www.canyonrose. com. 7 units. $89–$220 double. Children under 12 stay free in parent's room. AE, MC, V. **Amenities:** Access to nearby health club; guest laundry. *In room:* A/C, TV/DVD, kitchen, fridge, coffeemaker, hair dryer, iron, Wi-Fi, free local calls.

Copper City Inn *(★ (Finds* This inn is operated by Fred Miller, who has been the bartender at Bisbee's Cafe Roka for more than a decade. The inn boasts some of the best and most attractive rooms in Bisbee these days. One room is done up with French antiques, while the other room has a modern Art Deco styling and is dedicated to early-20th-century hotel designer Mary Jane Colter. The suite has modern mission-style furnishings, tile floors, and a full kitchen. All the rooms have balconies overlooking Bisbee, and there is a pleasant deck at the back of the inn. The Copper City Inn is a "self-service" sort of place; when you make your reservation, you'll be given the key code for the door of your suite and allowed to check yourself in.

99 Main St., Bisbee, AZ 85603. © **520/432-1418** or 520/456-4254. www.coppercityinn.com. 3 units. $110 double; $135 suite. AE, DC, DISC, MC, V. *In room:* TV/DVD, fridge, coffeemaker, hair dryer, Wi-Fi, no phone.

Copper Queen Hotel Built in 1902 by the Copper Queen Mining Company and right at the center of town, this is Bisbee's grande dame. The atmosphere is casual yet quite authentic. Behind the check-in desk, there's an old oak roll-top desk and a safe that has been here for years. Spacious halls lead to guest rooms furnished with antiques but that vary considerably in size (the smallest being quite cramped). The hotel has been undergoing renovations for several years; be sure to ask for one of the renovated units, which are up-to-date and attractively furnished. The restaurant serves decent food, and out front is a terrace for alfresco dining.

11 Howell Ave. (P.O. Drawer CQ), Bisbee, AZ 85603. © **520/432-2216.** Fax 520/432-3819. www.copperqueen.com. 52 units. $87–$177 double. Children under 17 stay free in parent's room. AE, MC, V. **Amenities:** Restaurant (American); lounge; small outdoor pool. *In room:* A/C, TV.

Letson Loft Hotel *(★★* Located up a flight of stairs, the Letson Loft Hotel feels a bit like an old Italian villa and has the prettiest rooms in town. High ceilings, old wood floors, Asian antiques, and plush beds with great linens all add up to comforts and class rarely seen in this funky town. Book one of the front rooms and you'll have a front row seat for watching the Main Street action through bay windows. If you're a light sleeper, ask for a room at the back of the hotel or avail yourself of the bedside earplugs; Bisbee can be a bit noisy at times. One of our favorite rooms has a huge skylight and another has a claw-foot tub. There's even a suite with a kitchen.

26 Main St. (P.O. Box 623), Bisbee, AZ 85603. © 877/432-3210 or 520/432-3210. www.letsonlofthotel.com. 8 units. $110–$145 double; $135–$165 suite. Rates include continental breakfast. AE, DISC, MC, V. No children under 12. **Amenities:** Concierge; business center; massage. *In room:* A/C, TV/DVD, hair dryer, iron, Wi-Fi.

Shady Dell RV Park *(Finds* Yes, this really is an RV park, but you'll find neither shade nor dell at the Shady Dell's roadside location just south of the Lavender Pit mine. What you will find are nine vintage trailers, a 1947 Airporter bus done in retro-Tiki style, and a 1947 Chris Craft yacht. All have been lovingly restored. Although the trailers don't have their own private bathrooms (a bathhouse is in the middle of the RV park), they do have all kinds of vintage decor and furnishings—even tapes and records of period music and radio shows. In the trailers that have vintage TVs, there are VCRs and videotapes of old movies. After numerous write-ups in national publications, the Shady Dell has become so famous that reservations need to be made far in advance.

1 Old Douglas Rd., Bisbee, AZ 85603. © 520/432-3567. www.theshadydell.com. 11 units. $45–$145 per trailer (for 1–2 people). MC, V. No children under 10. **Amenities:** Restaurant; coin-op laundry. *In room:* A/C, kitchen, fridge, coffeemaker, no phone.

WHERE TO DINE

Café Cornucopia, 14 Main St. (© **520/432-4820**), offers fresh juices, smoothies, and sandwiches. It's open Thursday through Monday from 10am to 5pm. For good coffee and a mining theme, check out the **Bisbee Coffee Co.,** Copper Queen Plaza, Main Street (© **520/432-7879**). For gourmet picnic supplies, peruse the shelves of the **High Desert Market,** 203 Tombstone Canyon Rd. (© **520/432-6775**), which has organic produce, imported cheeses, wine, and other assorted goodies for a great picnic.

Bisbee Breakfast Club *(Finds* AMERICAN Located in the Lowell district on the far side of the Lavender Pit from old Bisbee, this huge diner is a locals' favorite. Big breakfasts (served all day) are the specialty here, and the cinnamon rolls are legendary around town. At lunch, try the coffee-charred breast of chicken salad; it'll really wake up your taste buds. The owners, Pat and Heather Grimm, are the couple who originally put Bisbee's diminutive Dot's Diner on the map.

75A Erie St. © 520/432-5885. www.bisbeebreakfastclub.com. Main courses $4–$7. AE, MC, V. Thurs–Mon 7am–3pm.

Cafe Roka *(Finds* CONTEMPORARY Wow! The food at Cafe Roka is reason enough to visit Bisbee. Casual and hip, this place is a real find in such an out-of-the-way town and offers good value as well as delicious and imaginatively prepared food. Meals include salad, soup, sorbet intermezzo, and entree. The grilled salmon with a Gorgonzola crust and artichoke-and-portobello lasagna are two of our favorites. Flourless chocolate cake with raspberry sauce is an exquisite ending. Local artists display their works, and on some evenings jazz musicians perform.

35 Main St. © 520/432-5153. www.caferoka.com. Reservations highly recommended. Main courses $14–$24. AE, MC, V. Summer Fri–Sat 5–9pm; spring and fall Wed–Sat 5–9pm; winter Thurs–Sat 5–9pm.

Dot's Diner *(Finds* AMERICAN At Dot's Diner, an original 1957 Valentine diner, you can take a step back into the Eisenhower years. This tiny diner has barely a half-dozen stools at the counter, which overlooks the kitchen and soda fountain area. As in the old days, meals are simple—filling breakfasts, basic sandwiches, fresh house-made burgers, and foot-long hot dogs. However, there are daily specials that may include grits so good they could call them polenta and charge twice as much for them.

At Shady Dell RV Resort, 1 Old Douglas Rd. © 520/432-1112. www.theshadydell.com. Reservations not accepted. Main courses $5–$6.25. No credit cards. Wed–Sun 7am–3pm.

7 Exploring the Rest of Cochise County (★

Willcox: 81 miles E of Tucson; 192 miles SE of Phoenix; 74 miles N of Douglas

Although the towns of Bisbee, Tombstone, and Sierra Vista all lie within Cochise County, much of the county is taken up by the vast Sulphur Springs Valley, which is bounded by multiple mountain ranges. It is across this wide-open landscape that Apache chiefs Cochise and Geronimo once rode. Gazing out across this country today, it is easy to understand why the Apaches fought so hard to keep white settlers out.

While the Chiricahua and Dragoon mountains, which flank the Sulphur Springs Valley on the east and west respectively, are relatively unknown outside the region, they offer some of the Southwest's most spectacular scenery. Massive boulders litter the mountainsides, creating fascinating landscapes. The Chiricahua Mountains are also a favorite destination of bird-watchers, for it is here that the colorfully plumed elegant trogon reaches the northern limit of its range.

ESSENTIALS

GETTING THERE   Willcox is on I-10, with Arizona 186 heading southeast toward Chiricahua National Monument.

VISITOR INFORMATION   The **Willcox Chamber of Commerce and Agriculture,** 1500 N. Circle I Rd. (© **800/200-2272** or 520/384-2272; www.willcoxchamber. com), can provide information.

SOUTHWEST OF WILLCOX
SCENIC LANDSCAPES

South of the community of Dragoon, which is now known for its pistachio farms, lies a much less accessible area of the Dragoon Mountains known as **Cochise Stronghold** (★ (www.cochisestronghold.com). During the Apache uprisings of the late 19th century, the Apache leader Cochise used this rugged section of the Dragoon Mountains as his hide-out and managed to elude capture for years. The granite boulders and pine forests made it impossible for the army to track him and his followers. Cochise eventually died and was buried at an unknown spot somewhere within the area. This rugged jumble of giant boulders is reached by a rough gravel road, at the end of which you'll find a campground, a picnic area, and hiking trails. For a short, easy walk, follow the .4-mile Nature Trail. For a longer and more strenuous hike, head up the Cochise Trail. The Stronghold Divide makes a good destination for a 6-mile round-trip hike. For more information, contact the **Coronado National Forest Douglas Ranger District,** 1192 W. Saddleview Rd., Douglas (© **520/364-3468;** www.fs.fed. us/r3/coronado).

A MEMORABLE MUSEUM IN AN UNLIKELY LOCALE

Amerind Foundation Museum (★★   This museum is well worth seeking out. Established in 1937, the Amerind Foundation is dedicated to the study, preservation, and interpretation of prehistoric and historical Indian cultures. To that end, the foundation has compiled the nation's finest private collection of archaeological artifacts and contemporary pieces. There are exhibits on the dances and religious ceremonies of the major Southwestern tribes and cases full of archaeological artifacts. Fascinating ethnology exhibits include intricate beadwork from the Plains tribes, old Zuni fetishes, Pima baskets, old kachina dolls, pottery, and Navajo weavings. The art gallery displays works by 19th- and 20th-century American artists, such as Frederic Remington, whose paintings focused on the West.

2100 N. Amerind Rd., Dragoon. ℂ 520/586-3666. www.amerind.org. Admission $5 adults, $4 seniors, $3 college students and children 12–18, free for children under 12. Tues–Sun 10am–4pm. Closed major holidays. Located 64 miles east of Tucson between Benson and Willcox; take the Dragoon Rd. exit (Exit 318) from I-10 and continue 1 mile east.

EAST OF WILLCOX

Chiricahua National Monument 𝄐𝄐   These gravity-defying rock formations—called "the land of the standing-up rocks" by the Apache and the "wonderland of rocks" by the pioneers—are the equal of any of Arizona's many amazing rocky landmarks. Rank upon rank of monolithic giants seem to have been turned to stone as they marched across the forested Chiricahua Mountains. If you're in good physical condition, don't miss the chance to hike the 7.5-mile round-trip **Heart of Rocks Trail** 𝄐𝄐, which can be accessed from the visitor center or the Echo Canyon or Massai Point parking areas. This trail leads through the most spectacular scenery in the monument. A shorter loop is also possible. Within the monument are a visitor center, a campground, a picnic area, miles of hiking trails, and a scenic drive with views of many of the most unusual rock formations.

Ariz. 186, 36 miles southeast of Willcox. ℂ 520/824-3560. www.nps.gov/chir. Admission $5 adults. Visitor center daily 8am–4:30pm. Closed Christmas.

Fort Bowie National Historic Site 𝄐   Fort Bowie was established in 1862 to ensure the passage of slow-moving stagecoaches traversing Apache Pass. Later, it was from Fort Bowie that federal troops battled Geronimo until the Apache chief finally surrendered in 1886. Today, there's little left of Fort Bowie but some crumbling adobe walls, but the hike along the old stage route to the ruins conjures up the ghosts of Geronimo and the Indian Wars.

3203 S. Old Fort Bowie Rd. (off Ariz. 186). ℂ 520/847-2500. www.nps.gov/fobo. Free admission. Visitor center daily 8am–4:30pm; grounds daily dawn–dusk. Closed Christmas. From Willcox, drive southeast on Ariz. 186; after about 20 miles, watch for signs; it's another 8 miles up a dirt road to the trail head. Alternatively, drive east from Willcox to Bowie and go 13 miles south on Apache Pass Rd. From the trail head, it's a 1.5-mile hike to the fort.

NEAR DOUGLAS

Slaughter Ranch Museum 𝄐 *Finds*   Down a dusty gravel road outside the town of Douglas lies a little-known Southwestern landmark: the Slaughter Ranch. In 1884, former Texas Ranger John Slaughter bought the San Bernardino Valley and turned it into one of the finest cattle ranches in the West. Slaughter later went on to become the sheriff of Cochise County and helped rid the region of unsavory characters. Today, the ranch is a National Historic Landmark and has been restored to its late-19th-century appearance. Surrounding the ranch buildings are wide lawns and a large pond that together attract a variety of birds, making this one of Arizona's best winter birding spots.

6153 Geronimo Trail, about 14 miles east of Douglas. ℂ 520/558-2474. www.slaughterranch.com. Admission $5 adults, free for children under 14. Wed–Sun 10am–3pm. Closed Christmas and New Year's Day. From Douglas, go east on 15th St., which runs into Geronimo Trail; continue east 14 miles.

BIRDING HOT SPOTS

At the **Willcox Chamber of Commerce,** 1500 N. Circle I Rd. (ℂ **800/200-2272** or 520/384-2272; www.willcoxchamber.com), you can pick up several birding maps and checklists for the region.

To the east of Chiricahua National Monument, on the far side of the Chiricahuas, lies **Cave Creek Canyon** ⟨⟩, one of the most important bird-watching spots in the United States. It's here that the colorful elegant trogon reaches the northern limit of its range. Other rare birds that have been spotted here include sulfur-bellied flycatchers and Lucy's, Virginia's, and black-throated gray warblers. Stop by the visitor center for information on the best birding spots in the area. Cave Creek Canyon is just outside the community of Portal.

The **Cochise Lakes** ⟨⟩ (actually, the Willcox sewage ponds) are another great bird-watching spot. Birders can see a wide variety of waterfowl and shorebirds, including avocets and ibises. To find the ponds, head south out of Willcox on Arizona 186, turn right onto Rex Allen, Jr., Drive at the sign for the Twin Lakes golf course, and go past the golf course.

Between October and March, as many as 30,000 sandhill cranes gather in the Sulphur Springs Valley south of Willcox, and in January, the town holds the **Wings Over Willcox** festival, a celebration of these majestic birds. During these months, you can see these majestic birds at the **Apache Station Wildlife Viewing Area** southwest of Willcox on US 191 near the Apache Station electric generating plant and the community of Cochise. The Sulphur Springs Valley is also well known for its large wintering population of raptors.

Near Douglas, the **Slaughter Ranch,** which has a large pond, and the adjacent **San Bernardino National Wildlife Refuge** are good birding spots in both summer and winter. (See the description of the Slaughter Ranch Museum, above, for directions.)

WHERE TO STAY
NEAR WILLCOX

Cochise Stronghold B&B ⟨⟩ *(Finds)*   Set on 15 acres of private land within Coronado National Forest's Cochise Stronghold area, this remote and beautiful B&B is one of our favorites in the state. The inn is an energy-efficient, passive solar home with two housekeeping suites. It makes a superb base for hikes amid the area's fascinating rock formations and for excursions farther afield in Cochise County. Owners John and Nancy Yates are a great source of information both on solar-home design and on the preservation of desert. For a more adventurous experience, book the tipi or yurt.

2126 W. Windancer Trail (P.O. Box 232), Pearce, AZ 85625. ℂ 877/426-4141 or 520/826-4141. www.cochisestronghold bb.com. $179–$209 double; $99 tipi; $119 yurt. Rates include full breakfast. 2-night minimum stay. AE, DISC, MC, V. **Amenities:** Jacuzzi; massage. *In room (but not in tipi):* A/C, TV/VCR, kitchenette, fridge, coffeemaker, microwave, free local calls.

Sunglow Guest Ranch ⟨⟩ *(Value)*   Located in the western foothills of the Chiricahua Mountains roughly 40 miles southeast of Willcox, this remote ranch is surrounded by Coronado National Forest and is one of the most idyllic spots in the state. Rising behind a small lake are the peaks of the Chiricahuas. The guest rooms are quite large, and decor includes rustic Mexican furnishings. More than half the units have wood-burning fireplaces. This guest ranch is different from others around the state, in that it doesn't offer horseback riding, but there is a stable just down the road that will bring its horses to the ranch.

14066 S. Sunglow Rd., Pearce, AZ 85625. ℂ 866/786-4569 or 520/824-3334. www.sunglowranch.com. 9 units. $250–$350 double. Rates include breakfast and dinner. Children 5 and under stay free in parent's room. AE, DC, DISC, MC, V. Pets accepted ($25 per night). **Amenities:** Dining room; bikes. *In room:* Fridge, coffeemaker, microwave, no phone.

IN PORTAL

Portal Peak Lodge, Portal Store & Cafe   This motel-like lodge, located behind the general store/cafe in the hamlet of Portal, has fairly modern guest rooms that face one another across a wooden deck. Meals are available in the adjacent cafe. If you're seeking predictable accommodations in a remote location, you'll find them here.

2358 Rock House Rd. (P.O. Box 16282), Portal, AZ 85632. ℂ **520/558-2223.** Fax 520/558-2473. www.portalpeak lodge.com. 16 units. $75–$85 double. AE, DISC, MC, V. **Amenities:** Restaurant (American). *In room:* A/C, TV, coffeemaker, no phone.

Southwestern Research Station, The American Museum of Natural History *(Finds)*   Located far up in Cave Creek Canyon, this is a field research station that takes guests when the accommodations are not filled by scientists doing research. As such, it is the best place in the area for serious bird-watchers, who will find the company of researchers a fascinating addition to a visit. Guests stay in simply furnished cabins scattered around the research center. Spring and fall are the easiest times to get reservations and the best times for bird-watching.

P.O. Box 16553, Portal, AZ 85632. ℂ **520/558-2396.** Fax 520/558-2018. www.research.amnh.org/swrs. 12 units. Mar–Oct $150 double (rate includes all meals); Nov–Feb $60–$80 double (no meals provided). Children under 4 stay free in parent's room. DISC, MC, V. **Amenities:** Dining room; outdoor pool; volleyball court; guest laundry. *In room:* No phone.

CAMPGROUNDS

A 22-site campground charges $12 per night at **Chiricahua National Monument** (described above), on Arizona 186 (ℂ **520/824-3560**). At **Cochise Stronghold,** 35 miles southwest of Willcox off US 191, a 10-site campground charges $10 per night. For information on the national forest campgrounds, contact the Coronado National Forest Douglas Ranger District, 1192 W. Saddleview Rd., Douglas (ℂ **520/364-3468;** www.fs.fed.us/r3/coronado).

14

Sedona & the Colorado River: The Best of Central & Western Arizona

Between Phoenix and the Grand Canyon lies one of the most beautiful landscapes on earth—the red-rock country of Sedona. Decades ago, Hollywood came to Sedona to shoot Westerns; then came the artists and the retirees and the New Agers. Now it seems Hollywood is back, but this time the stars are building huge homes in the hills.

Central Arizona isn't just red rock and retirees, though. It also has the former territorial capital of Prescott, historic sites, ancient Indian ruins, an old mining town turned artists' community, even a few good old-fashioned dude ranches (now called "guest ranches") out Wickenburg way. There are, of course, thousands of acres of cactus-studded desert, but there are also high mountains, cool pine forests, and a fertile river valley. And north of Sedona's red rocks is Oak Creek

Canyon, a tree-shaded cleft in the rocks with one of the state's most scenic stretches of highway running through it.

Also included in this chapter is Arizona's "west coast," 340 miles of Colorado River waters, most of which are impounded in three huge reservoirs—Lake Mead, Lake Mohave, and Lake Havasu—that provide water and electricity to sprawling Southwestern boomtowns like Phoenix and Las Vegas.

As with any warm coastline, Arizona's West Coast is lined with lakefront resorts, hotels, RV parks, and campgrounds. Of course, watersports of all types are extremely popular here. For the most part, however, it's a destination for desert residents, so you won't find any hotels or resorts even remotely as upscale or expensive as those in Phoenix, Tucson, or Sedona.

1 Wickenburg

53 miles NW of Phoenix; 61 miles S of Prescott; 128 miles SE of Kingman

Once known as the dude-ranch capital of the world, the town of Wickenburg, located in the desert northwest of Phoenix, attracted celebrities and families from all over the country. Today, although the area has only a handful of dude (or guest) ranches still in business, Wickenburg clings to its Wild West image. If you've come to the Southwest searching for the West the way it used to be, Wickenburg is a good place to look.

ESSENTIALS
GETTING THERE From Phoenix, take I-17 N to Arizona 74 W and then continue west on US 60. From Prescott, take Arizona 89. If you're coming from the west, take US 60 from I-10. US 93 comes down from I-40 in northwestern Arizona.

Central Arizona

Seligman

Ash Fork

KAIBAB

Williams

Parks

Bellemont

Flagstaff

40

NATIONAL

FOREST

89

17

0 — 20 mi
0 — 20 km

N

Munds
Park

Mormon
Lake

10
9

PRESCOTT
NATIONAL
FOREST

Paulden

Sedona

8

Mormon
Lake

Clarkdale

5

6 **7**

Oak Creek

COCONINO

Chino
Valley

Jerome

4

89A

Cottonwood

179

Cornville

NATIONAL FOREST

89A

260

3

260

Prescott Valley

69

169

Camp
Verde

2

Skull Valley

Prescott

Dewey

Humboldt

Strawberry

87

Kirkland

Wilhoit

Pine

Hillside

Kirkland Jct.

Mayer

88

PRESCOTT
NATIONAL
FOREST

Bumble
Bee

Cordes Junction

Verde River

TONTO
NATIONAL
FOREST

Peeples
Valley

Congress

Yarnell

Crown
King

Aqua Fria
National
Monument

93 89

Black Canyon City
Rock Springs

Wickenburg

1

River

Lake
Pleasant

17

New River

VULTURE MTNS.

HIEROGLYPHIC MTNS.

Morristown

Circle City

74

Cave
Creek

Sunflower

Wittman

60

Agua Fria

Carefree

87

Beardsley
Surprise

↓ To Phoenix

Ft. McDowell

15

ARIZONA

40 40

Area of
detail

Flagstaff

17

10

Phoenix

8

Tucson

10

19

VISITOR INFORMATION   Contact the **Wickenburg Chamber of Commerce,** 216 N. Frontier St. (© **928/684-5479;** www.outwickenburgway.com). The visitor center is open Monday through Friday from 9am to 5pm, Saturday and Sunday from 10am to 2pm.

EXPLORING THE AREA
A WALK AROUND TOWN

While Wickenburg's main attractions remain the guest ranches outside of town, a walk around downtown also provides a glimpse of the Old West. Most of the buildings here were built between 1890 and the 1920s (although a few are older), and although not all of them look their age, there is just enough Western character to make a stroll worthwhile (if it's not too hot).

Two of the town's most unusual attractions aren't buildings at all. The **Jail Tree,** behind the convenience store at the corner of Wickenburg Way and Tegner Street, is an old mesquite tree that served as the local hoosegow. Outlaws were simply chained to the tree. Their families would often come to visit and have a picnic in the shade of the tree. The second, equally curious, town attraction is the **Wishing Well,** which stands beside the bridge over the Hassayampa. Legend has it that anyone who drinks from the Hassayampa River will never tell the truth again. How the well adjacent to the river became a wishing well is unclear.

MUSEUMS & MINES
Desert Caballeros Western Museum ★★   Wickenburg thrives on its Western heritage, and inside this museum you'll find an outstanding collection of Western art depicting life on the range, including works by Albert Bierstadt, Charles Russell, Thomas Moran, Frederick Remington, Maynard Dixon, and other members of the Cowboy Artists of America. The Hays "Spirit of the Cowboy" collection is an impressive display of historical cowboy gear that alone makes this museum worth a stop.

21 N. Frontier St. © **928/684-2272.** www.westernmuseum.org. Admission $7.50 adults, $6 seniors, $1 children 6–16, free for children under 6. Mon–Sat 10am–5pm; Sun noon–4pm. Closed Mon July–Aug, New Year's Day, Easter, July 4th, Thanksgiving, and Christmas.

Robson's Arizona Mining World   Boasting the world's largest collection of antique mining equipment, this private museum is a must for anyone fascinated by Arizona's rich mining history. Located on the site of an old mining camp and with the feel of a ghost town, this museum consists of more than 30 buildings filled with antiques and displays. You can pan for gold or hike through the desert to see ancient petroglyphs. Also on the property, you'll find Litsch's Bed & Breakfast (charging $90–$110 double; no credit cards accepted) and a restaurant.

Ariz. 71, 28 miles west of Wickenburg. © **928/685-2609.** www.robsonsminingworld.com. Admission $5.50 adults, $5 seniors, free for children under 10. Oct–Apr Mon–Fri 9:30am–4pm, Sat–Sun 9:30am–5pm. Closed May–Sept. Head west out of Wickenburg on US 60 and, after 20 miles, turn north on Ariz. 71.

A BIRDER'S PARADISE
Hassayampa River Preserve ★   At one time the Arizona desert was laced with rivers that flowed for most, if not all, of the year. In the past 100 years, however, these rivers, and the riparian habitats they once supported, have disappeared at an alarming rate. Riparian areas support trees and plants that require more water than is usually available in the desert, and this lush growth provides food and shelter for hundreds of

species of birds, mammals, and reptiles. The Hassayampa River Preserve is one of central Arizona's finest examples of a riparian forest.

The Nature Conservancy owns and manages this preserve, which is one of the state's most important bird-watching sites (more than 230 species of birds have been spotted here). Nature trails lead along the river beneath cottonwoods and willows and past the spring-fed Palm Lake.

49614 US 60 (3 miles southeast of Wickenburg on US 60). ℂ 928/684-2772. www.nature.org. Suggested donation $5 ($3 for Nature Conservancy members). Mid-Sept to mid-May Wed–Sun 8am–5pm; mid-May to mid-Sept Fri–Sun 7–11am. Closed Thanksgiving, day after Thanksgiving, Christmas Eve, Christmas Day, New Year's Eve, and New Year's Day.

GETTING OUTSIDE

If you're in the area for more than a day or just can't spend another minute in the saddle, you can go out on a jeep tour and explore the desert backcountry, visit Vulture Peak, see some petroglyphs, or check out old mines. Call **B.C. Jeep Tours** (ℂ **928/ 684-7901** or 928/231-1010; www.bcjeeptours.com), which charges $50. However, if you've got time for only one jeep tour on your Southwest vacation, make it in Sedona.

Los Caballeros Golf Club, 1551 S. Vulture Mine Rd. (ℂ **928/684-2704**), has been rated one of the best courses in the state. Greens fees are $135 in the cooler months.

Hikers have a couple of interesting options. Southwest of town at the end of Vulture Mine Road (off US 60), you can climb Vulture Peak, a steep climb best done in the cooler months. The views from up top (or even just the saddle near the top) are well worth the effort.

WHERE TO STAY

Flying E Ranch 🌟 (Kids   This is a working cattle ranch with 20,000 high, wide, and handsome acres for you and the cattle to roam. Family-owned since 1952, the Flying E attracts plenty of repeat business, with families finding it a particularly appealing and down-home kind of place. The main lodge features a spacious lounge where guests like to gather by the fireplace. Accommodations vary in size, but all have Western-style furnishings and either twin or king-size beds. There's no bar, so you'll need to bring your own liquor. There are also breakfast cookouts, lunch rides, and evening chuck-wagon dinners.

2801 W. Wickenburg Way, Wickenburg, AZ 85390. ℂ 888/684-2650 or 928/684-2690. Fax 928/684-5304. www.flying eranch.com. 17 units. $285–$363 double. Rates include all meals. 2- to 4-night minimum stay. MC, V. Closed May–Oct. Drive 4 miles west of town on US 60. **Amenities:** Dining room; outdoor pool; tennis court; exercise room; Jacuzzi; sauna; horseback riding ($35–$50 per person per day); horseshoes; lawn games; hayrides; guest rodeos. In room: A/C, TV, fridge.

Kay El Bar Guest Ranch 🌟   This is the smallest and oldest of the Wickenburg guest ranches, and its adobe buildings, built between 1914 and 1925, are listed on the National Register of Historic Places. The well-maintained ranch is quintessentially Wild West in style, and the setting, on the bank of the (usually dry) Hassayampa River, lends the ranch a surprisingly lush feel compared with the arid surrounding landscape. While the cottage and the Casa Grande room are the most spacious, the smaller rooms in the adobe main lodge have original Monterey-style furnishings and classic 1950s dude-ranch decor. We like this place because you feel as though you're on a friend's ranch.

Rincon Rd., off US 93 (P.O. Box 2480), Wickenburg, AZ 85358. ℂ 800/684-7583 or 928/684-7593. Fax 928/684-4497. www.kayelbar.com. 11 units. $340–$425 double; $725–$815 cottage for 4. Rates do not include 15% service charge. Rates include all meals and horseback riding. 2- to 4-night minimum stay. Children 3 and under stay free in parent's room. MC, V. Closed May to mid-Oct. **Amenities:** Dining room; lounge; small outdoor pool; access to nearby health club; Jacuzzi; massage; laundry service; horseback riding. *In room:* Hair dryer, no phone.

Rancho de los Caballeros 🌟🌟   Located on 20,000 acres 2 miles west of Wickenburg, Rancho de los Caballeros is part of an exclusive country club–resort community and, as such, feels more like a resort than a guest ranch. However, the main lodge itself, with its flagstone floor, copper fireplace, and colorfully painted furniture, has a very Southwestern feel. Peace and quiet are the keynotes of a visit here, and most guests focus on golf (the golf course is one of the best in the state) and horseback riding. In addition, the ranch has a new spa called the Ranch House and offers skeet and trap shooting and guided nature walks. Bedrooms are filled with handcrafted furnishings, exposed-beam ceilings, Indian rugs, and, in some, tile floors and fireplaces. Dinner here is quite formal, with proper attire required.

1551 S. Vulture Mine Rd. (off US 60 west of town), Wickenburg, AZ 85390. ℂ **800/684-5030** or 928/684-5484. Fax 928/684-9565. www.sunc.com. 79 units. Mid-Oct to mid-Dec and late Apr to early May $386–$412 double; $452–$490 suite; mid-Dec to late Apr $446–$486 double, $526–$596 suite. Rates do not include 15% gratuity charge. Rates include all meals. Riding, golf, and spa packages available. Children under 5 stay free in parent's room. MC, V. Closed early May to mid-Oct. **Amenities:** Dining room; 2 lounges; small outdoor pool; 18-hole golf course; 4 tennis courts; exercise room; access to nearby health club; full-service spa; bike rentals; children's programs; concierge; business center; massage; babysitting; coin-op laundry; laundry service; dry cleaning; horseback riding ($35–$60 per ride). *In room:* A/C, TV, dataport, fridge, coffeemaker, hair dryer, iron, microwave.

WHERE TO DINE
House of Berlin GERMAN/CONTINENTAL   Wickenburg may seem like an unusual place for an authentic German restaurant, but that's exactly what you'll find right downtown. The place is small and casual, and serves a mix of German and other Continental dishes. Local favorites include the Wiener schnitzel and *sauerbraten.*

169 E. Wickenburg Way. ℂ **928/684-5044.** Reservations recommended. Main courses $6.50–$15 lunch, $12–$18 dinner. MC, V. Tues 5–9pm; Wed–Sun 11:30am–2pm and 5–9pm.

---

2 Prescott

100 miles N of Phoenix; 60 miles SW of Sedona; 87 miles SW of Flagstaff

Prescott, the former territorial capital, is an anomaly; it doesn't seem like Arizona at all. With its stately courthouse on a tree-shaded square, its well-preserved historic downtown business district, and its old Victorian homes, Prescott wears the air of the quintessential American small town. Prescott has just about everything a small town should have: an 1890s saloon (The Palace), an old cattlemen's hotel (Hassayampa Inn), a burger shop (Kendall's), and a brewpub (Prescott Brewing Company). Add to this several small museums, a couple of other historic hotels, the strange and beautiful landscape of the Granite Dells, and the nearby Prescott National Forest, and you have a town that appeals to visitors with a diverse range of interests.

Prescott has become an upscale retirement community, as much for its historic heritage as for its mild year-round climate. In summer, Prescott is also a popular weekend getaway for Phoenicians; it is usually 20° cooler here than it is in Phoenix.

ESSENTIALS
GETTING THERE   Prescott is at the junction of Arizona 89, Arizona 89A, and Arizona 69. If you're coming from Phoenix, take the Cordes Junction exit (Exit 262) from I-17. From Flagstaff, the most direct route is I-17 to Arizona 169 to Arizona 69. From Sedona, just take Arizona 89A all the way.

Great Lakes Airlines (© 800/554-5111; www.greatlakesav.com) flies between Prescott's Ernest A. Love Airport, on US 89, and both Phoenix and Kingman. **Shuttle "U"** (© 800/304-6114 or 928/442-1000; www.shuttleu.com) provides service to Prescott from Sky Harbor Airport for $31 one-way, $52 round-trip.

VISITOR INFORMATION   The **Prescott Chamber of Commerce** is at 117 W. Goodwin St. (© 800/266-7534 or 928/445-2000; www.prescott.org). The visitor center is open Monday through Friday from 9am to 5pm, and Saturday and Sunday from 10am to 2pm.

GETTING AROUND   For car rentals, call **Enterprise** (© 800/261-7331) or **Hertz** (© 800/654-3131).

EXPLORING THE TOWN

A walk around **Courthouse Plaza** should be your first introduction to Prescott. The stately old courthouse in the middle of the tree-shaded plaza sets the tone for the whole town. The building, far too large for a small regional town such as this, dates from the days when Prescott was the capital of the Arizona territory. Under the big shade trees, you'll find several bronze statues of cowboys and soldiers.

Surrounding the courthouse and extending north for a block is Prescott's **historic business district.** Stroll around admiring the brick buildings, and you'll realize that Prescott was once a very important place. Duck into an old saloon or the lobby of one of the historic hotels, and you'll understand that the town was also part of the Wild West.

Fort Whipple Museum   Located north of town off US 89 on the grounds of what is now a Veterans Administration hospital, this museum focuses on the history of this fort, which was active from 1863 to 1922 and has many stately officers' homes. Don't miss the display about Fiorello LaGuardia's time at the fort.

Veterans Administration campus, Building 11, 500 N. Hwy. 89. © 928/445-3122. Free admission. Thurs–Sat 10am–4pm.

Phippen Museum 🖈   If you're a fan of classic Western art, you won't want to miss this small museum. Located on a hill a few miles north of town, the Phippen is named after the first president of the prestigious Cowboy Artists of America organization and exhibits works by both established Western artists and newcomers. Also on display are artifacts and photos that help place the artwork in the context of the region's history. More than 100 Arizona artists are represented in the museum store. The **Phippen Western Art Show & Sale** is held each year on Memorial Day weekend.

4701 US 89 N. © 928/778-1385. www.phippenartmuseum.org. Admission $5 adults, $4 seniors and students, free for children under 12. Tues–Sat 10am–4pm; Sun 1–4pm.

Sharlot Hall Museum 🖈   Opened in 1928 in a log home that once served as the governor's mansion of the Arizona territory, this museum was founded by Sharlot Hall, who served as the territorial historian from 1909 to 1911. In addition to the governor's "mansion," which is furnished much as it might have been when it was built, several other interesting buildings can be toured. With its traditional wood-frame construction, the Frémont House, which was built in 1875 for the fifth territorial governor, shows how quickly Prescott grew from a remote logging and mining camp into a civilized little town. The 1877 Bashford House reflects the Victorian architecture that was popular throughout the country around the end of the 19th century. The Sharlot Hall Building houses exhibits on Native American cultures and territorial Arizona. Every year in early summer, artisans, craftspeople, and costumed exhibitors participate in the **Folk Arts Fair.**

415 W. Gurley St. ℂ **928/445-3122.** www.sharlot.org. Admission $5 adults. May–Sept Mon–Sat 10am–5pm, Sun noon–4pm; Oct–Apr Mon–Sat 10am–4pm, Sun noon–4pm.

The Smoki Museum This interesting little museum, which houses a collection of Native American artifacts in a historic stone building, is named for the fictitious Smoki tribe. The tribe was dreamed up in 1921 by a group of non-Indians who wanted to inject some new life into Prescott's July 4th celebrations. Despite its phony origins, the museum contains genuine artifacts and basketry from many different tribes, mainly Southwestern. The museum also sponsors interesting lectures on Native American topics.

147 N. Arizona St. ℂ **928/445-1230.** www.smokimuseum.org. Admission $5 adults, $4 seniors, $3 students. Mon–Sat 10am–4pm; Sun 1–4pm. Closed Easter, Thanksgiving, Christmas, Jan 1–15.

GETTING OUTSIDE

Prescott is situated on the edge of a wide expanse of high plains with the pine forests of **Prescott National Forest** at its back. Within the national forest are lakes, camp-grounds, and many miles of hiking and mountain-biking trails. Our favorite hiking and biking areas are Thumb Butte (west of town) and the Granite Mountain Wilderness (northwest of town).

Thumb Butte, a rocky outcropping that towers over the forest just west of town, is Prescott's most readily recognizable natural landmark. A 1.2-mile trail leads nearly to the top of this butte, and from the saddle near the summit, there's a panoramic vista of the entire region. The trail itself is very steep but paved much of the way. The summit of the butte is a popular rock-climbing spot. An alternative return trail makes a loop hike possible. To reach the trail head, drive west out of town on Gurley Street, which becomes Thumb Butte Road. Follow the road until you see the National Forest signs, after which there's a parking lot, picnic area, and trail head. The parking fee is $2.

The Granite Basin Recreation Area provides access to the **Granite Mountain Wilderness.** Trails lead beneath the cliffs of Granite Mountain, where you might spot peregrine falcons. For the best views, hike 1.5 miles to Blair Pass and then on up the Granite Mountain trail as far as you feel like going. To reach this area, take Gurley Street west from downtown, turn right on Grove Avenue, and follow it around to Iron Springs Road, which will take you northwest out of town to the signed road for the Granite Basin Recreation Area (less than 8 miles from downtown). There is a $2 parking fee here.

Both of the above areas also offer mountain-biking trails. You can rent a bike and get maps and trail recommendations at **Ironclad Bicycles,** 710 White Spar Rd. (ℂ **928/776-1755;** www.ironcladbicycles.com), which charges $24 to $48 per day for mountain bikes. This shop also rents bikes at **Encore Performance & Fabrication,** 2929 N. Arizona 89 (ℂ **928/778-7910**), near the Peavine Trail (see below).

For maps and information on these and other hikes and bike rides in the area, stop by the **Bradshaw Ranger Station,** 344 S. Cortez St. (ℂ **928/443-8000;** www.fs.fed.us/r3/prescott).

North of town 5 miles on Arizona 89 is an unusual and scenic area known as the **Granite Dells.** Jumbled hills of rounded granite suddenly jut from the landscape, creating a maze of huge boulders and smooth rock. In the middle of this dramatic landscape lies **Watson Lake,** the waters of which push their way in among the boulders to create one of the prettiest lakes in the state. On the highway side of the lake, you'll find **Watson Lake Park,** which has picnic tables and great views. Spring through fall (weather permitting) on Saturday and Sunday between 10am and 4pm, you can rent **canoes and kayaks** ($10–$15 per hr.) at the lake. Call **Prescott Outdoors** (✆ **928/ 925-1410;** www.prescottoutdoors.com) to make sure they'll be at the lake with their boats.

For hiking in the Watson Lake area, we recommend heading to the scenic **Peavine Trail,** which is one of the most gratifying easy hikes in the state, To find the trail head, turn east onto Prescott Lake Parkway, which is between Prescott and the Granite Dells, and then turn left onto Sun Dog Ranch Road. This rails-to-trails path extends for several miles through the middle of the Granite Dells and is the best way to fully appreciate the Dells. Although this is a fascinating, easy hike, it also makes a great, equally easy, mountain-bike ride that can be extended 7.5 miles on the Iron King Trail.

A couple of miles west of Watson Lake on Willow Creek Road, you can hike in **Willow Creek Park,** where several miles of trails lead through grasslands and groves of huge cottonwood trees adjacent to Willow Lake. The trails eventually lead to the edge of the Granite Dells. There's great bird-watching in the trees in this park, and there are even great blue heron and cormorant rookeries.

If you want to explore the area on horseback, try **Granite Mountain Stables,** 2400 Shane Dr. (✆ **928/771-9551;** www.granitemountainstables.com), which offers guided trail rides in the Prescott National Forest. A 1-hour ride is $35.

Reasonably priced golf is available at the 36-hole **Antelope Hills Golf Course,** 1 Perkins Dr. (✆ **800/972-6818** or 928/776 7888; www.antelopehillsgolf.com). Greens fees range from $38 to $55.

SHOPPING

Downtown Prescott is filled with antiques stores, especially along North Cortez Street, and is the best place in Arizona to do some antiques shopping. For Native American crafts and Old West memorabilia, be sure to stop in at **Ogg's Hogan,** 111 N. Cortez St. (✆ **928/443-9856).** In the Hotel St. Michael's shopping arcade, check out **The Hotel Trading Post,** 110 S. Montezuma St. (✆ **928/778-7276),** which carries some genuine Native American artifacts at reasonable prices. Owner Ernie Lister also makes silver jewelry in the 19th-century Navajo style. On the same block are both the **Arts Prescott Gallery,** 134 S. Montezuma St. (✆ **928/776-7717;** www.artsprescott.com), a cooperative of local artists; and **Van Gogh's Ear,** 156B S. Montezuma St (✆ **928/ 776-1080;** www.vgegallery.com), which was founded by a splinter group from the co-op and actually has higher-quality art and crafts. Also on this block you'll find the **Newman Gallery,** 106-A S. Montezuma St. (✆ **928/442-9167;** www.newmangallery. net), which features the colorful Western-inspired pop-culture imagery of artist Dave Newman.

WHERE TO STAY
EXPENSIVE
Hassayampa Inn 🦋   Built as a luxury hotel in 1927, the Hassayampa Inn, which is listed on the National Register of Historic Places, evokes the time when Prescott was the bustling territorial capital. In the lobby, exposed ceiling beams, wrought-iron chandeliers, and arched doorways all reflect the place's Southwestern heritage. Although guest rooms tend to be very small, each is unique and features either original furnishings or antiques. Some suites are very oddly configured; you might find the

shower in one closet and the commode in another. One room is said to be haunted; any hotel employee will be happy to tell you the story of the ill-fated honeymooners whose ghosts supposedly reside here.

122 E. Gurley St., Prescott, AZ 86301. © 800/322-1927 or 928/778-9434. www.hassayampainn.com. 68 units. $109–$159 double; $160–$249 suite. Children under 12 stay free in parent's room. AE, DC, DISC, MC, V. **Amenities:** Restaurant; lounge; exercise room; room service; laundry service; dry cleaning. *In room:* A/C, TV, dataport, hair dryer, iron, Wi-Fi.

MODERATE
Hotel Vendome ☞   Not quite as luxurious as the Hassayampa, yet not as basic as the St. Michael, the Vendome is a good middle-price choice for those who want to stay in a historic hotel. Built in 1917 as a lodging house, the restored brick building is only 2 blocks from the action of Whiskey Row, but far enough away that you can get a good night's sleep. Guest rooms are outfitted with new furnishings, but some of the bathrooms still contain original claw-foot tubs. Naturally, this hotel, like several others in town, has its own resident ghost.

230 S. Cortez St., Prescott, AZ 86303. © 888/468-3583 or 928/776-0900. www.vendomehotel.com. 20 units. $99–$139 double; $139–$179 2-bedroom unit. Rates include continental breakfast. AE, DISC, MC, V. **Amenities:** Lounge; concierge. *In room:* A/C, TV, dataport, hair dryer, iron, free local calls.

Rocamadour Bed & Breakfast for (Rock) Lovers ☆☆   The Granite Dells, just north of Prescott, is the area's most unforgettable feature. Should you wish to stay amid these jumbled boulders, there's no better choice than Rocamadour. Mike and Twila Coffey honed their innkeeping skills as owners of a 40-room château in France, and antique furnishings from that château can now be found throughout this inn. The most elegant pieces are in the Chambre Trucy, which also boasts an amazing underlit whirlpool tub. One cottage is built into the boulders and has a large whirlpool tub on its deck. The unique setting, engaging innkeepers, and thoughtful details everywhere you turn make this one of the state's must-stay inns.

3386 N. Hwy. 89, Prescott, AZ 86301. © 888/771-1933 or 928/771-1933. 3 units. $149–$169 double; $219 suite. Rates include full breakfast. AE, DC, DISC, MC, V. *In room:* A/C, TV/VCR.

INEXPENSIVE
Hotel St. Michael *(Value*   Located right on Whiskey Row, this restored hotel, complete with resident ghost and the oldest elevator in Prescott, offers a historic setting at budget prices (don't expect the most stylish furnishings). All rooms are different; some have bathtubs but no showers. The casual Caffe St. Michael, where breakfast is served, overlooks Courthouse Plaza.

205 W. Gurley St., Prescott, AZ 86301. © 800/678-3757 or 928/776-1999. Fax 928/776-7318. www.hotelstmichael. net. 72 units. $59–$99 double; $89–$119 suite. Rates include full breakfast. AE, DISC, MC, V. **Amenities:** Restaurant; access to nearby health club; shopping arcade. *In room:* A/C, TV, free local calls.

WHERE TO DINE
MODERATE
129½ ☞ NEW AMERICAN   Prescott, a classic small-town-America sort of place, may seem an odd location for a classic New York–style jazz club, but this restaurant has it down. It may not be in a basement and it isn't smoky, but everything else has just the right feel. Best of all, the restaurant has great food. Steaks are the specialty and can be had with an assortment of delicious sauces, such as rosemary cream, mushroom

ragout, and pinot and green peppercorn (our personal favorite). Money-saving early dinners are served Tuesday through Thursday between 4 and 6pm.

129½ N. Cortez St. ℂ 928/443-9292. www.fourcornersrestaurants.com. Reservations recommended. Main courses $6–$11 lunch, $16–$28 dinner. AE, DISC, MC, V. Tues–Thurs 11am–2pm and 4–9:30pm; Fri 11am–2pm and 5–10pm; Sat 5–10pm.

The Palace 🏵 SOUTHWESTERN/STEAKHOUSE/SEAFOOD   The Palace is the oldest saloon in Arizona (in business for more than 120 years) and looks just the way it might have at the start of the 20th century. While the front of The Palace is centered on the old bar, most of the cavernous space is dedicated to a bustling dining room. The generous steaks are your best bet here. If you bump into someone carrying a shotgun, don't panic! It's probably the owner, who likes to dress the part of a Wild West saloon-keeper. There's live music Friday and Saturday nights, and on Sunday afternoons there's a honky-tonk piano player. Dinner shows are held a couple of times each month.

120 S. Montezuma St. ℂ 928/541-1996. www.historicpalace.com. Reservations suggested on weekends. Main courses $7–$11 lunch, $11–$27 dinner. AE, DISC, MC, V. Sun–Thurs 11am–3:30pm and 4:30–9pm; Fri–Sat 11am–3:30pm and 4:30–10pm.

The Rose Restaurant 🏵🏵 CONTINENTAL   This is Prescott's best restaurant and is a must for anyone staying in town. Year after year, The Rose, which is housed in a building that was constructed around 1900, continues to satisfy locals and visitors alike. Veal dishes can also be outstanding, and the pasta with scallops and Italian sausage is a curious combination of flavors that works well. The wine list includes plenty of reasonably priced options.

234 S. Cortez St. ℂ 928/777-8308. www.theroserestaurant.com. Reservations recommended. Main courses $20–$38. AE, DC, DISC, MC, V. Wed–Sat 5–9pm; Sun 10am–2pm (Apr to mid-Dec) and 5–9pm.

INEXPENSIVE

Prescott Brewing Company AMERICAN/PUB FARE   Popular primarily with a younger crowd, this brewpub keeps a good selection of its own beers on tap, but its cheap and filling meals are just as sought after. Fajitas are a specialty, along with such pub standards as fish and chips, bangers and mash, and not-so-standard spent-grain beer-dough pizzas and vegetarian dishes. The Caesar salad with chipotle dressing packs a wallop.

130 W. Gurley St. ℂ 928/771-2795. www.prescottbrewingcompany.com. Main courses $7.50–$19. AE, DISC, MC, V. Sun–Thurs 11am–10pm; Fri–Sat 11am–11pm (pub stays open 2 hr. after kitchen closes).

Sweet Tart 🏵 (Finds) EUROPEAN/PASTRIES   This little hole-in-the-wall makes the best pastries in Arizona. Not only that, we once had a chicken panini here that was the best we've ever had; the bread had a biscuitlike texture and was slathered with pesto. Before you walk through the door, make sure you're hungry enough for dessert because the pastry case here is absolutely irresistible. At breakfast, they have, among other treats, a variety of brioches, including blueberry and mixed-fruit. Currently, Sweet Tart is doing four-course dinners every Saturday night; call for reservations.

123 N. Cortez St. ℂ 928/443-8587. Reservations required for dinner. Main courses $7–$10; prix-fixe dinners $45. AE, DISC, MC, V. Tues–Sat 7am–4pm; Sun 8am–3pm.

PRESCOTT AFTER DARK

Back in the days when Prescott was the territorial capital and a booming mining town, it supported dozens of rowdy saloons, most of which were concentrated along Montezuma Street on the west side of Courthouse Plaza. This section of town was known as **Whiskey Row,** and legend has it there was a tunnel from the courthouse to one of the saloons so lawmakers wouldn't have to be seen ducking into the saloons during regular business hours. On July 14, 1900, a fire consumed most of Whiskey Row. However, concerned cowboys and miners managed to drag the tremendously heavy bar of The Palace saloon across the street before it was damaged.

Today, Whiskey Row still has a few noisy saloons with genuine Wild West flavor. However, within a few blocks of Whiskey Row, you can hear country, folk, jazz, and rock at a surprisingly diverse assortment of bars, restaurants, and clubs.

If you want to see what this street's saloons looked like back in the old days, drop by **The Palace,** 120 S. Montezuma St. (© 928/541-1996; www.historicpalace.com), which still has a classic bar up front.

If you want to drink where the ranchers drink and not where the hired hands carouse, head upstairs to the **Jersey Lilly Saloon,** 116 S. Montezuma St. (© 928/ 541-7854), which attracts a more well-heeled clientele than the street-level saloons. On weekends, there is live music in a wide range of styles.

Two blocks away you'll find the **Raven Café,** 142 N. Cortez St. (© 928/717- 0009), which is the most artsy and eclectic nightlife venue in town. Not only does the Raven have the best beer list in Prescott (with an emphasis on Belgian beers and American microbrews), but the entertainment lineup ranges from vintage movies on Tuesday nights to live jazz and salsa dancing.

3 Jerome

35 miles NE of Prescott; 28 miles W of Sedona; 130 miles N of Phoenix

Few towns anywhere in Arizona make more of an impression on visitors than Jerome, a historic mining town that clings to the slopes of Cleopatra Hill high on Mingus Mountain. The town is divided into two sections that are separated by an elevation change of 1,500 vertical feet, with the upper part of town 2,000 feet above the Verde Valley. On a clear day, the view from Jerome is stupendous—it's possible to see for more than 50 miles, with the red rocks of Sedona, the Mogollon Rim, and the San Francisco Peaks all visible in the distance. Add to the unforgettable views the abundance of interesting shops and galleries and the winding narrow streets, and you have a town that should not be missed.

ESSENTIALS
GETTING THERE   Jerome is on Arizona 89A roughly halfway between Sedona and Prescott. Coming from Phoenix, take Arizona 260 from Camp Verde.

VISITOR INFORMATION   Contact the **Jerome Chamber of Commerce** (© 928/ 634-2900; www.jeromechamber.com) for information.

EXPLORING THE TOWN
Wandering the streets, soaking up the atmosphere, and shopping are the main pastimes in Jerome. But before you launch yourself on a shopping tour, you can learn about the town's past at the **Jerome State Historic Park,** off Arizona 89A on Douglas Road in the lower section of town (© 928/634-5381). Located in a mansion built in 1916 as a home for mine owner "Rawhide Jimmy" Douglas and as a hotel for visiting mining executives, the Jerome State Historic Park contains exhibits on mining as well as a few of the mansion's original furnishings. From its perch on a hill above Douglas's Little Daisy Mine, the mansion overlooks Jerome and, dizzyingly far below, the Verde

Valley. The mansion was constructed of adobe bricks and once contained a wine cellar, billiards room, marble shower, steam heat, and central vacuum system. Admission is $3, and the park is open daily (except Christmas) from 8am to 5pm.

To learn more about Jerome's history, stop in at the **Jerome Historical Society's Mine Museum,** 200 Main St. (© **928/634-5477;** www.jeromehistoricalsociety.org), which has some small and old-fashioned displays on mining. It's open daily from 9am to 5pm; admission is $2 for adults, $1 for seniors, and free for children 12 and under. For that classic mining-town tourist-trap experience, follow the signs up the hill from downtown Jerome to the **Gold King Mine** (© **928/634-0053),** where you can see lots of old, rusting mining equipment and maybe even catch a demonstration. The mine is open 9am to 5pm daily, and admission is $4 for adults, $3 for seniors, and $2 for children ages 6 to 12.

Most visitors come to Jerome for the shops, which offer an eclectic blend of contemporary art, chic jewelry, one-of-a-kind handmade fashions, and unusual imports. Of course, there are now also the inevitable ice cream parlors and shops full of tacky souvenirs.

WHERE TO STAY

Connor Hotel of Jerome   Housed in a renovated historic hotel, this lodging has spacious rooms with large windows; views of the valley, however, are limited. Although a few of the rooms are located directly above the hotel's popular bar, which can be quite noisy on weekends, most rooms are quiet enough to provide a good night's rest. Better yet, come on a weekday when the Harley-Davidson poseur crowd from the Scottsdale area isn't thundering through the streets on their hogs.

164 Main St. (P.O. Box 1177), Jerome, AZ 86331. © **800/523-3554** or 928/634-5006. Fax 928/649-0981. www.connor hotel.com. 12 units. $90–$165 double. Children under 12 stay free in parent's room. AE, DISC, MC, V. Pets accepted. **Amenities:** Bar. *In room:* A/C, TV, dataport, fridge, coffeemaker, hair dryer, iron, free local calls.

Ghost City Inn   With its long verandas on both floors, this restored old house is hard to miss as you drive into town from Clarkdale. It manages to capture the spirit of Jerome, with a mix of Victorian and Southwestern decor. Most bedrooms have great views across the Verde Valley (and these are definitely worth requesting). Two units feature antique brass beds. The rooms are on the small side, so if space is a priority, opt for the suite.

541 Main St. (P.O. Box T), Jerome, AZ 86331. © **888/634-4678.** www.ghostcityinn.com. 6 units. $95–$120 double; $145 suite. Rates include full breakfast. AE, DISC, MC, V. Pets accepted ($20 nonrefundable deposit). No children under 14. **Amenities:** Jacuzzi. *In room:* TV/VCR, no phone.

WHERE TO DINE

The Asylum *(Finds* ECLECTIC   As the name would imply, this restaurant (inside a former hospital building high above downtown Jerome) is a bit out of the ordinary. The bedpan full of candy at the front desk and the odd little notes in the menu will also make it absolutely clear that this place doesn't take much, other than good food, seriously. We like the distinctly Southwestern dishes, including the prickly-pear barbecued pork tenderloin with tomatillo salsa, and an unusual butternut-squash soup made with a cinnamon-lime cream sauce. Cocktails all get wacky loony-bin names, and there's also a superb, award-winning wine list.

200 Hill St. © **928/639-3197.** www.theasylum.biz. Reservations recommended. Main courses $9–$13 lunch, $17–$28 dinner. AE, DISC, MC, V. Daily 11am–3:30pm and 5–9pm.

Flatiron Café BREAKFAST/LIGHT MEALS   The tiny Flatiron Café is a simple breakfast-and-lunch spot in, you guessed it, Jerome's version of a flatiron building. The limited menu includes the likes of lox and bagels, a breakfast quesadilla, black-bean hummus, smoked-salmon quesadillas, fresh juices, and espresso drinks. It looks as though you could hardly squeeze in here, but there's more seating across the street. Definitely not your usual ghost-town lunch counter.

416 Main St. (at Hull Ave.). © **928/634-2733.** Reservations not accepted. Most items $7–$10. MC, V. Thurs–Mon 8:30am–3:30pm.

4 The Verde Valley

Camp Verde: 20 miles E of Jerome; 30 miles S of Sedona; 95 miles N of Phoenix

Named by early Spanish explorers who were impressed by the sight of such a verdant valley in an otherwise brown desert landscape, the Verde Valley has long been a magnet for both wildlife and people. Today, the valley is one of Arizona's richest agricultural and ranching regions and is quickly gaining popularity with retirees. Cottonwood and Clarkdale, the valley's two largest towns, are old copper-smelting towns, while Camp Verde was an army post back in the days of the Indian Wars. All three towns have some interesting historic buildings, but it is the valley's two national monuments—Tuzigoot and Montezuma Castle—that are the main attractions.

These two national monuments preserve the ruins of Sinagua pueblos. Long before the first European explorers entered the Verde Valley, the Sinagua people were living by the river and irrigating their fields with its waters. By the time the first pioneers began settling in this region, the Sinaguas had long since moved on, and Apaches had claimed the valley as part of their territory. When settlers came into conflict with the Apaches, Fort Verde, now a state park, was established. Between this state park and the two national monuments, hundreds of years of Verde Valley history and prehistory can be explored. This valley is also the site of the state's most scenic railroad excursion.

ESSENTIALS

GETTING THERE   Camp Verde is just off I-17 at the junction with Arizona 260. The latter highway leads northwest through the Verde Valley for 12 miles to Cottonwood.

VISITOR INFORMATION   Contact the **Cottonwood Chamber of Commerce,** 1010 S. Main St., Cottonwood (© **928/634-7593;** www.cottonwood.verdevalley.com).

A RAILWAY EXCURSION

Verde Canyon Railroad 🎈🎈   When the town of Jerome was busily mining copper, a railway was built to link the booming town with the territorial capital at nearby Prescott. Because of the rugged mountains between Jerome and Prescott, the railroad was forced to take a longer but less difficult route north along the Verde River before turning south toward Prescott. Today, you can ride these same tracks aboard the Verde Canyon Railroad. The route through the canyon traverses both the remains of a copper smelter and unspoiled desert that is inaccessible by car and is part of Prescott National Forest. The views of the rocky canyon walls and green waters of the Verde River are quite dramatic, and if you look closely along the way, you'll see ancient Sinagua cliff dwellings. In late winter and early spring, nesting bald eagles can also be spotted. Of the two excursion train rides in Arizona, this is by far the more scenic (although the Grand Canyon Railway certainly has a more impressive destination). Live music and a very informative narration make the ride entertaining as well.

300 N. Broadway, Clarkdale. © 800/320-0718. www.verdecanyonrr.com. Tickets $55 adults, $50 seniors, $35 children 2–12; 1st-class tickets $80. Call or visit the website for schedule and reservations.

NATIONAL MONUMENTS & STATE PARKS

Fort Verde State Historic Park   Just south of Montezuma Castle and Montezuma Well, in the town of Camp Verde, you'll find Fort Verde State Historic Park. Established in 1871, Fort Verde was the third military post in the Verde Valley and was occupied until 1891. The military had first come to the Verde Valley in 1865 at the request of settlers who wanted protection from the local Tonto Apache and Yavapai. The tribes, traditionally hunters and gatherers, had been forced to raid the settlers' fields for food after their normal economy was disrupted by the sudden influx of whites and Mexicans into the area.

The state park preserves three officers' quarters, an administration building, and some ruins. The buildings that have been fully restored house exhibits on the history of the fort and what life was like here in the 19th century.

125 E. Holloman St., Camp Verde. © 928/567-3275. www.pr.state.az.us. Admission $2 adults, free for children under 14. Daily 8am–5pm. Closed Christmas.

Montezuma Castle National Monument ⚑   This Sinagua ruin is one of the best-preserved cliff dwellings in Arizona. The site consists of two impressive stone pueblos that were, for some unknown reason, abandoned by the Sinagua people when they disappeared in the early 14th century.

The more intriguing of the two ruins is set in a shallow cave 100 feet up a cliff overlooking Beaver Creek. Construction on this five-story, 20-room village began in the early 12th century. Another structure, containing 45 rooms on a total of six levels, stands at the base of the cliff. This latter dwelling, which has been subjected to rains and floods over the years, is not nearly as well preserved as the cliff dwelling.

Montezuma Well, located 11 miles north of Montezuma Castle (although still part of the national monument), is a spring-fed sinkhole that was a true oasis in the desert for native peoples. This sunken pond was formed when a cavern in the area's porous limestone bedrock collapsed. Underground springs quickly filled the sinkhole, which today contains a pond measuring over 360 feet across and 65 feet deep. Sinagua structures are clustered in and near the sinkhole.

Exit 289 off I-17. © 928/567-3322. www.nps.gov/moca. Admission $5 adults ($8 w/Tuzigoot National Monument admission), free for children 16 and under; no charge to visit Montezuma Well. Memorial Day weekend to Labor Day weekend daily 8am–6pm; rest of year daily 8am–5pm.

Out of Africa Wildlife Park ⚑ *(Kids)*   Lions and tigers and bears, oh my. And zebras and giraffes and wildebeests, oh yes. That's what you'll encounter at this sprawling wildlife park between Camp Verde and Cottonwood. The park includes both a "wildlife preserve" of large fenced predator enclosures and a "Serengeti Safari" area. In this latter area, you ride on a rugged safari vehicle through a vast enclosure populated by giraffes, zebras, ostriches, wildebeests, and other animals of the Serengeti. You may even get to feed a giraffe or zebra. The other half of the park is home to numerous lions, tigers, wolves, panthers, hyenas, and other large predators. All these carnivores are fed on Sunday, Wednesday, and Friday at 3pm, and following the feeders is a highlight of a visit to the park.

Verde Valley Justice Rd., Camp Verde. © 928/567-2840. www.outofafricapark.com. Admission $28 adults, $26 seniors, $20 children ages 3–12, free for children under 3. Wed–Sun 9:30am–5pm. Also open on many holiday Mon. Closed Thanksgiving, Christmas, and July 4th.

Tuzigoot National Monument   Perched atop a hill overlooking the Verde River, this small, stone-walled pueblo was built by the Sinagua people and was inhabited between 1125 and 1400. The Sinagua, whose name is Spanish for "without water," were traditionally dry-land farmers relying entirely on rainfall to water their crops.

An interpretive trail leads through the Tuzigoot ruins, explaining different aspects of Sinaguan life, and inside the visitor center is a small museum displaying many of the artifacts unearthed here. Desert plants, many of which were used by the Sinagua, are identified along the trail.

Just outside Clarkdale off Ariz. 89A. (℃ **928/634-5564**. www.nps.gov/tuzi. Admission $5 adults ($8 w/Montezuma Castle National Monument admission), free for children 16 and under. Memorial Day weekend to Labor Day weekend daily 8am–6pm; rest of year daily 8am–5pm. Closed Christmas.

WHERE TO STAY

Hacienda de la Mariposa ★★ *Finds*   This modern Santa Fe–style inn is set on the banks of Beaver Creek and is just up the road from Montezuma Castle National Monument. Guest rooms contain rustic Mexican furnishings, gas beehive-style fireplaces, small private patios, and lots of character. Bathrooms feature skylights and whirlpool tubs. With a patio overlooking the creek, the Mariposa Creekside room is our favorite. The little Casita de Milagros, a sort of cottage/massage room that serves as a gathering spot for guests, has a huge amethyst geode set into the ceiling. In a walled garden out back, you'll find a swimming pool only steps from the creek.

3875 Stagecoach Rd. (P.O. Box 310), Camp Verde, AZ 86322. (℃ **888/520-9095** or 928/567-1490. www.lamariposa-az. com. 5 units. $195–$225 double. AE, DISC, MC, V. No children. **Amenities:** Outdoor pool; Jacuzzi; massage. *In room:* A/C, TV/VCR, coffeemaker, hair dryer, free local calls.

WHERE TO DINE

Blazin' M Ranch Chuckwagon Suppers *Kids* AMERICAN   Located adjacent to Dead Horse Ranch State Park, the Blazin' M Ranch is classic Arizona-style family entertainment—steaks and beans accompanied by cowboy music and comedy. This place is geared primarily toward the young 'uns, with pony rides, farm animals, and a little cow town for the kids to explore. If you're young at heart, you might enjoy the Blazin' M, but it's definitely more fun if you bring the whole family. One of the highlights is the gallery of animated woodcarvings, which features humorous Western scenes.

Off 10th St., Cottonwood. (℃ **800/937-8643** or 928/634-0334. www.blazinm.com. Reservations recommended. Dinner $35 adults, $33 seniors, $25 children ages 3–12. AE, DISC, MC, V. Mon–Sat gates open at 5pm, dinner at 6:30pm, show at 7:30pm. Closed Jan.

Old Town Café *Finds* CAFE   The almond croissants at this European-style cafe in downtown Cottonwood are among the best we've ever had. If that isn't recommendation enough for you, there are also good salads and sandwiches, such as a grilled panini of smoked turkey, spinach, and tomatoes.

1025 "A" N. Main St., Cottonwood. (℃ **928/634-5980**. Reservations not accepted. Salads and sandwiches $6–$9. MC, V. Tues–Sat 8am–3pm.

5 Sedona & Oak Creek Canyon ★★

56 miles NE of Prescott; 116 miles N of Phoenix; 106 miles S of the Grand Canyon

There is not a town anywhere in the Southwest with a more beautiful setting than Sedona. On the outskirts of town, red-rock buttes, eroded canyon walls, and mesas rise into blue skies. Off in the distance, the Mogollon Rim looms, its forests of juniper

Sedona & Vicinity

To Boynton Canyon & Enchantment Resort

To Flagstaff/ Slide Rock State Park

Dry Creek Rd.

Steamboat Rock

Coffee Pot Rock

SEDONA CITY LIMITS

89A

Capitol Butte

Oak Creek Canyon Rd.

Soldiers Pass Rd.

UPTOWN SEDONA

Chimney Rock

89A

Schnebly Hill Rd.

Cottonwood-Sedona Hwy.

Snoopy Rock

89A

660 Rd.

Airport Rd.

To Jerome

Sedona-Oak Creek Airport

Airport Mesa

179

Upper Red Rock Loop Rd.

SEDONA CITY LIMITS

Chapel Spire Rock

Submarine Rock

Chapel Rd.

Bell Rock

Courthouse Butte

Oak Creek

Village of Oak Creek

Cathedral Rock

179

0   1/2 mi
0   0.5 km

N

To 17 / Phoenix

RED ROCK STATE PARK

ARIZONA

15

40   Flagstaff

Sedona   40

17

10   Phoenix

8

10

Tucson   10

19

Airport Mesa **2**

Chapel of the Holy Cross **4**

Crescent Moon Recreation Area **5**

Red Rock State Park **6**

Sedona-Oak Creek Visitor Center **1**

Tlaquepaque **3**

and ponderosa pine dark against the rocks. With a wide band of rosy sandstone predominating in this area, Sedona has come to be known as red-rock country, and each evening at sunset, the rocks put on an unforgettable light show that is reason enough for a visit. All this may sound perfectly idyllic, but if you lower your eyes from the red rocks, you'll see the flip side of Sedona—a sprawl of housing developments and strip malls. However, not even the proliferation of timeshare sales offices disguised as "visitor information centers" can mar the beauty of the backdrop.

With national forest surrounding the city (and even fingers of forest extending into what would otherwise be the city limits), Sedona also has some of the best outdoor access of any city in the Southwest. All around town, alongside highways and down side streets in suburban neighborhoods, there are trail heads. Trek down any one of these trails and you leave the city behind and enter the world of the red rocks.

Located at the mouth of Oak Creek Canyon, Sedona was first settled by pioneers in 1877 and named for the first postmaster's wife. Word of Sedona's beauty did not begin to spread until Hollywood filmmakers began using the region's red rock as backdrop to their Western films. Next came artists, lured by the landscapes and desert light (it was here in Sedona that the Cowboy Artists of America organization was formed). Although still much touted as an artists' community, Sedona's art scene these days is geared more toward tourists than toward collectors of fine art.

With its drop-dead gorgeous scenery, dozens of motels and resorts, and plethora of good restaurants, Sedona makes an excellent base for exploring central Arizona. Several ancient Indian ruins (including an impressive cliff dwelling), the "ghost town" of Jerome, and the scenic Verde Canyon Railroad are all within easy driving distance, and even the Grand Canyon is but a long day trip away.

ESSENTIALS

GETTING THERE   Sedona is on Arizona 179 at the mouth of Oak Creek Canyon. From Phoenix, take I-17 to Arizona 179 N. From Flagstaff, head south on I-17 until you see the turnoff for Arizona 89A and Sedona. Arizona 89A also connects Sedona with Prescott.

Sedona Phoenix Shuttle (✆ **800/448-7988** in Arizona, or 928/282-2066; www.sedona-phoenix-shuttle.com) operates several trips daily between Phoenix's Sky Harbor Airport and Sedona. The fare is $45 one-way, $85 round-trip.

VISITOR INFORMATION   The **Sedona–Oak Creek Canyon Chamber of Commerce Visitor Center/Uptown Gateway Visitor Center,** 331 Forest Rd. (✆ **800/288-7336** or 928/282-7722; www.visitsedona.com), operates a visitor center at the corner of Arizona 89A and Forest Road near uptown Sedona. The visitor center is open Monday through Saturday from 8:30am to 5pm, and Sunday and holidays from 9am to 3pm.

You can also get information, as well as a Red Rock Pass for parking at area trail heads, at the **South Gateway Visitor Center,** Tequa Shopping Plaza, 7000 Ariz. 179, Village of Oak Creek (✆ **928/284-5324**), which is open daily from 8:30am to 5pm; or the **North Gateway Visitor Center,** Oak Creek Vista Overlook, Arizona 89A (✆ **928/282-4119**), which is open March 1 through November 1, weather permitting, daily from 9am to 4:30pm.

GETTING AROUND   Whether traveling by car or on foot, you'll need to cultivate patience when trying to cross major roads in Sedona. Traffic here, especially on weekends, is some of the worst in the state. Also be prepared for slow traffic on roads that have good views; drivers are often distracted by the red rocks. You may hear or see references to the **"Y,"** which refers to the intersection of Arizona 179 and Arizona 89A between the Tlaquepaque shopping plaza and uptown Sedona.

Rental cars are available through **Enterprise** (✆ **800/261-7331**). You can also rent a jeep from **Farabee Jeep Rentals of Sedona** (✆ **928/282-8700;** www.farabeejeep rentals.com), which charges $125 for 4 hours and $185 for 8 hours. Or you can get around Sedona on the **Sedona Roadrunner,** a free shuttle bus that operates every 8 to 15 minutes between uptown, Tlaquepaque, and the Hillside Shops.

EXPLORING RED-ROCK COUNTRY

The Grand Canyon may be Arizona's biggest attraction, but there's actually far more to do in Sedona. If you aren't an active type, there's the option of just gazing in awe at the rugged cliffs, needlelike pinnacles, and isolated buttes that rise from the green forest floor at the mouth of Oak Creek Canyon. Want to see more? Head out into the red rocks on a jeep tour or drift over the red rocks in a hot-air balloon. Want a closer look? Go for a hike, rent a mountain bike, go horseback riding. (See "Organized Tours," below, and "Getting Outside," later in this chapter, for details.)

Although **Schnebly Hill Road,** which climbs into the red rocks east of Sedona, is a rough dirt road, it's a must for superb views. This road is best driven in a high-clearance vehicle or SUV, but depending on how recently it has been maintained, it can be passable in a regular car. To reach this scenic road, head south out of Sedona on Arizona 179, turn left after you cross the bridge over Oak Creek, and head up the road, which starts out paved but soon turns to dirt. As this road climbs to the top of the Mogollon Rim, each switchback and cliff-edged bend in the road yields a new and more astonishing view. At the rim is the Schnebly Hill overlook, offering a view that just begs to be savored over a long picnic. If you don't feel comfortable doing this drive in your own vehicle, consider booking a jeep tour that heads up this way.

Just south of Sedona, on the east side of Arizona 179, you'll see the aptly named **Bell Rock.** There's a parking area at the foot of this formation, and trails lead up to the top. Adjacent to Bell Rock is **Courthouse Butte,** and to the west stands **Cathedral Rock.** From the Chapel of the Holy Cross (see "Attractions & Activities Around Town," below) on Chapel Road, you can see **Eagle Head Rock** (from the front door of the chapel, look three-quarters of the way up the mountain to see the eagle's head), the **Twin Nuns** (two pinnacles standing side by side), and **Mother and Child Rock** (to the left of the Twin Nuns).

If you head west out of Sedona on Arizona 89A and turn left onto Airport Road, you'll drive up onto **Airport Mesa,** which commands an unobstructed panorama of Sedona and the red rocks. About halfway up the mesa is a small parking area from which trails radiate. The views from here are among the best in the region, and the trails are very easy.

Boynton Canyon, located 8 miles west of the "Y," is a narrow red-rock canyon and is one of the most beautiful spots in the Sedona area. This canyon is also the site of the deluxe Enchantment resort, but hundreds of years before there were luxury casita suites here, there were Sinagua cliff dwellings. Several of these cliff dwellings can still be spotted high on the canyon walls. **Boynton Canyon Trail** leads 3 miles up into this canyon from a trail head parking area just outside the gates of Enchantment. To get to the trail head, drive west out of Sedona on Arizona 89A, turn right on Dry Creek Road, take a left at the first T intersection, and a right at the second T.

On the way to Boynton Canyon, look north from Arizona 89A, and you'll see **Coffee Pot Rock,** also known as Rooster Rock, rising 1,800 feet above Sedona. Three pinnacles, known as the **Three Golden Chiefs** by the Yavapai tribe, stand beside Coffee Pot Rock. As you drive up Dry Creek Road, on your right you'll see **Capitol Butte,** which resembles the U.S. Capitol.

To the west of Boynton Canyon, you can visit the well-preserved Sinagua cliff dwellings at **Palatki Heritage Site** (© **928/282-3854**). These small ruins, tucked under the red cliffs, are the best place in the area to get a feel for the ancient Native American cultures that once lived in this region. Among the ruins, you'll see numerous pictographs (paintings) created by the past residents of Palatki. Before heading out to these ruins, be sure you make a reservation by calling the number above. To reach the ruins, follow the directions to Boynton Canyon, but instead of turning right at the

Value **The High Cost of Red-Rock Views**

A Red Rock Pass will allow you to visit Palatki Ruins and the V Bar V Heritage Site (site of petroglyphs) and park at any national forest trailhead parking areas. The cost is $5 for a 1-day pass, $15 for a 7-day pass, and $20 for a 12-month pass. Passes are good for everyone in your vehicle. If you plan to be in the area for more than a week and also want to visit Grasshopper Point (a swimming hole), Banjo Bill (a picnic area), Call of the Canyon (the West Fork Oak Creek trail head), and Crescent Moon (Sedona's top photo-op site), you'll want to buy a Red Rock Grand Pass, for $40. These sites each charge a $5 to $7 admission, so if you aren't planning on going to all of them, the pass won't save you anything. For more information on the Red Rock Pass, visit www.redrockcountry.org.

second T intersection, turn left onto unpaved Boynton Pass Road (Forest Rd., or FR, 152), which is one of the most scenic roads in the area. Follow this road to another T intersection and go right onto FR 525, then veer right onto FR 795, which dead-ends at the ruins. You can also get here by taking Arizona 89A W from Sedona to FR 525, a gravel road leading north to FR 795. To visit Palatki, you'll need a Red Rock Pass (see "The High Cost of Red-Rock Views," below); ruins are usually open daily from 9:30am to 3pm. The dirt roads around here become impassable to regular cars when they're wet, so don't try coming out here if the roads are at all muddy.

South of Arizona 89A and a bit west of the turnoff for Boynton Canyon is Upper Red Rock Loop Road, which leads to **Crescent Moon Recreation Area,** a National Forest Service recreation area that has become a must-see for visitors to Sedona. Its popularity stems from a beautiful photograph of Oak Creek with **Cathedral Rock** in the background—an image that has been reproduced countless times in Sedona promotional literature and on postcards. Hiking trails lead up to Cathedral Rock. Admission is $7 per vehicle (unless you have previously purchased a Red Rock Grand Annual Pass; see "The High Cost of Red-Rock Views," below). For more information, contact the Red Rock Ranger Station (© **928/282-4119;** www.fs.fed.us/r3/coconino).

If you continue on Red Rock Loop Road, you will come to **Red Rock State Park,** 4050 Red Rock Loop Rd. (© **928/282-6907**), which flanks Oak Creek. The views here take in many of the rocks listed above, and you have the bonus of being right on the creek (though swimming and wading are prohibited). Park admission is $6 per car. The park offers lots of guided walks and interpretive programs.

South of Sedona, near the junction of I-17 and Arizona 179, you can visit one of the premier petroglyph sites in Arizona. The rock art at the **V Bar V Heritage Site** covers a small cliff face and includes images of herons and turtles. To get here, take the dirt road that leads east for 2⅔ miles from the junction of I-17 and Arizona 179 to the Beaver Creek Campground. The entrance to the petroglyph site is just past the campground. From the parking area, it's about a half-mile walk to the petroglyphs, which are open Friday through Monday from 9:30am to 3:30pm. To visit this site, you'll need a Red Rock Pass or other valid pass. For information, contact the **Red Rock Ranger District** (© **928/282-4119;** www.fs.fed.us/r3/coconino).

OAK CREEK CANYON

The **Mogollon Rim** (pronounced "*mug*-ee-un" by the locals) is a 2,000-foot escarpment cutting diagonally across central Arizona and on into New Mexico. At the top of the Mogollon Rim are the ponderosa pine forests of the high mountains, while at the bottom the lowland deserts begin. Of the many canyons cutting down from the rim, Oak Creek Canyon is the most beautiful (and one of the few that has a paved road down through it). Arizona 89A runs through the canyon from Flagstaff to Sedona, winding its way down from the rim and paralleling Oak Creek. Along the way are overlooks, parks, picnic areas, campgrounds, cabin resorts, and small inns.

If you have a choice of how first to view Oak Creek Canyon, approach it from the north. Your first stop after traveling south from Flagstaff will be the **Oak Creek Canyon Vista,** which provides a view far down the valley to Sedona and beyond. The overlook is at the edge of the Mogollon Rim, and the road suddenly drops in tight switchbacks just south of here.

Although the top of the Mogollon Rim is a ponderosa pine forest and the bottom a desert, Oak Creek Canyon supports a forest of sycamores and other deciduous trees. There is no better time to drive scenic Arizona 89A than between late September and mid-October, when the canyon is ablaze with red and yellow leaves.

In the desert, swimming holes are powerful magnets during the hot summer months, and consequently, **Slide Rock State Park,** 6871 N. US 89A (© **928/282-3034; www.pr.state.az.us),** located 7 miles north of Sedona on the site of an old homestead, is the most popular spot in all of Oak Creek Canyon. What pulls in the crowds of families and teenagers is the park's natural water slide and great little swimming hole. On hot days, the park is jammed with people splashing in the water and sliding over the algae-covered sandstone bottom of Oak Creek. Sunbathing and fishing are other popular pastimes. The park is open daily; admission is $8 per vehicle ($10 during the summer). There's another popular swimming area at **Grasshopper Point,** several miles closer to Sedona. Admission is $7 per vehicle, unless you have previously purchased a Red Rock Grand Annual Pass (see "The High Cost of Red-Rock Views," above, for details).

Within Oak Creek Canyon, several hikes of different lengths are possible. By far the most spectacular and popular is the 6-mile round-trip up the **West Fork of Oak Creek.** This is a classic canyon-country hike with steep canyon walls rising from the creek. At some points, the canyon is no more than 20 feet wide, with walls rising up more than 200 feet. You can also extend the hike many more miles up the canyon for an overnight backpacking trip. The trail head for the West Fork of Oak Creek hike is 9.5 miles up Oak Creek Canyon from Sedona at the Call of the Canyon Recreation Area, which charges a $7 day-use fee per vehicle unless you have already purchased a Red Rock Grand Annual Pass.

Stop by the Sedona–Oak Creek Chamber of Commerce for a free map of area hikes. The **Coconino National Forest's Red Rock Ranger Station,** which, at press time, was in a temporary space 2 miles east of I-17 at Exit 298 (Beaver Creek Rd.), is an even better source of hiking information. It's open Monday through Friday from 8am to 4:30pm. Sometime in 2008, the ranger station will relocate to a new facility on Arizona 179 south of the Village of Oak Creek.

ATTRACTIONS & ACTIVITIES AROUND TOWN

Sedona's most notable architectural landmark is the **Chapel of the Holy Cross,** 780 Chapel Rd. (© **928/282-4069**), a small church built right into the red rock on the south side of town. If you're driving up from Phoenix, you can't miss it—the chapel sits high above the road just off Arizona 179. With its contemporary styling, it is one of the most architecturally important modern churches in the country. Marguerite Brunswig Staude, a devout Catholic painter, sculptor, and designer, had the inspiration for the chapel in 1932, but it wasn't until 1957 that her dream was finally realized. The chapel's design is dominated by a simple cross forming the wall that faces the street. The cross and the starkly beautiful chapel seem to grow directly from the rock, allowing the natural beauty of the red rock to speak for itself. It's open Monday through Saturday from 9am to 6pm and Sunday from 10am to 6pm.

The **Sedona Arts Center,** 15 Art Barn Rd. at Arizona 89A (© **888/954-4442** or 928/282-3809; www.sedonaartscenter.com), near the north end of uptown Sedona, has a gallery that specializes in works by local and regional artists.

To learn a bit about the local history, stop by the **Sedona Heritage Museum,** 735 Jordan Rd. (© **928/282-7038;** www.sedonamuseum.org), in Jordan Historical Park. The museum, which is housed in a historic home, is furnished with antiques and contains exhibits on the many movies that have been filmed in the area. The farm was once an apple orchard, and there's still apple-processing equipment in the barn. Hours are daily from 11am to 3pm; admission is $3.

While Sedona isn't yet a resort spa destination on par with Phoenix or Tucson, it does have a few spas that might add just the right bit of pampering to your vacation. **Therapy on the Rocks,** 676 N. Hwy. 89A (© **928/282-3002;** www.myofascialrelease. com), with its creekside setting, is a longtime local favorite that offers massage, myofascial release, and great views of the red rocks. For personal attention, try the little **Red Rock Healing Arts Center,** Creekside Plaza, 251 Hwy. 179 (© **888/31-9033** or 928/203-9933; www.redrockhealing.com), which is just up the hill from the Tlaquepaque shopping plaza and offers a variety of massages, wraps, scrubs, and facials. In the Village of Oak Creek, there's the **Hilton Spa,** at the Hilton Sedona Resort & Spa, 10 Ridge View Dr. (© **928/284-6900;** www.hiltonsedonaspa.com), offering a variety of treatments. There are also exercise and yoga classes, and a pool. Prices for 60-minute treatments range from $129 to $139.

It may be a bit premature to start calling Sedona the next Napa Valley, but there are a few wineries in the nearby community of Page Springs, 20 minutes west of Sedona. To reach these wineries, drive west from Sedona on Arizona 89A, and turn south on Page Springs Road. You'll first come to **Oak Creek Vineyards and Winery,** Page Springs Road (© **928/649-0290;** www.oakcreekvineyards.net). The tasting room is open Wednesday through Sunday from 11am to 5pm. **Page Springs Vineyards & Cellars,** 1500 N. Page Springs Rd. (© **928/639-3004;** www.pagespringscellars.com), is the more impressive and reliable of the two wineries. Rhone varietals are the specialty here. The tasting room is open Thursday through Sunday from 11am to 6pm. **Echo Canyon Vineyard & Winery,** our favorite local winery, can be visited on Jeep tours operated by Sun Country Adventures (© **877/783-6000;** www.scadventures. net). The 2½-hour tours cost $95 per person.

ORGANIZED TOURS

For an overview of Sedona, take a tour on the **Sedona Trolley** (© **928/282-4211;** www.sedonatrolley.com), which leaves several times daily on two separate tours. One tour visits the Tlaquepaque shopping plaza, the Chapel of the Holy Cross, and several art galleries, while the other goes out through west Sedona to Boynton Canyon and Enchantment Resort. Tours are $10 for adults ($19 for both tours) and $5 for children 12 and under ($9 for both tours).

The red-rock country surrounding Sedona is the city's greatest natural attraction, and there's no better way to explore it than by four-wheel-drive vehicle. These tours will get you out onto rugged roads and 4×4 trails with spectacular views. The unchallenged leader in Sedona jeep tours is **Pink Jeep Tours,** 204 N. Hwy. 89A (℗ **800/ 873-3662** or 928/282-5000; www.pinkjeep.com), which has been heading deep into the Coconino National Forest since 1958. It offers tours ranging in length from 1½ to 4 hours, however, the 2-hour "Broken Arrow" tour ($72 adults, $54 children 12 and under) is the most adventurous and is the tour we recommend.

If a jeep just isn't manly enough for you, how about a Hummer? Better yet, how about a Hummer that runs on enviro-friendly bio-diesel? **Hummer Affair,** 273 N. Hwy. 89A, Suite C (℗ **928/282-6656;** www.hummeraffair.com), will take you out in the red rocks in the ultimate off-road vehicle. One-hour tours run $40 to $69 ($29–$59 for children), but the 2-hour "Jeep Eater Tour" for $89 ($79 for children) is the most fun.

How about a chance to play cowboy? **A Day in the West,** 252 N. Hwy. 89A (℗ **800/973-3663** or 928/282-4320; www.adayinthewest.com), has its own private ranch for some of its jeep tours and horseback rides. There are cowboy cookouts, too. Prices range from $45 to $165.

If you'd like to have a very knowledgeable local tour guide show you around places you're interested in seeing at your own pace, We recommend getting in touch with Steve "Benny" Benedict at **Touch the Earth Adventures** (℗ **928/203-9132;** www.earthtours.com). Benny likes to take clients to spots that even many locals don't know about. Half-day excursions run $125 per person, and full-day outings are $225 per person.

For a tour of the Sedona area from a Native American perspective, contact **Way of the Ancients** (℗ **866/204-9243;** www.wayoftheancients.com), which offers 5-hour tours that cost $69 for adults and $59 for children. There are also excursions to the Hopi mesas ($139 for adults and $129 for children).

Just because it's too dark to see the red rocks doesn't mean there's nothing to see and do in Sedona at night. How about a tour of the heavens? **Evening Sky Tours** (℗ **866/701-0398** or 928/203-0006; www.eveningskytours.com) takes advantage of the dark night skies over Sedona to lead people on astronomy tours of the stars and planets. Tours cost $60 for adults and $20 for children.

As spectacular as Sedona is from the ground, it is even more so from the air. **Arizona Helicopter Adventures** (℗ **800/282-5141** or 928/282-0904; www.azhcli. com) offers short flights to different parts of this colorful region. Prices start at $58 per person for a 12-minute flight. **Sky Safari Air Tours** (℗ **888/TOO-RIDE** or 928/ 204-5939; www.sedonaairtours.com) offers a variety of flights in small planes. A 15-minute air tour will run you $49 per person, while a 45-minute tour will cost $99. Flights as far afield as the Grand Canyon and Canyon de Chelly can also be arranged.

Our favorite Sedona air tours are those offered by **Red Rock Biplane Tours** (℗ **888/TOO-RIDE** or 928/204-5939; www.sedonaairtours.com), which operates modern Waco open-cockpit biplanes. With the wind in your hair, you'll feel as though you've entered the world of Snoopy and the Red Baron. Tours lasting 20 to 60 minutes are offered; a 20-minute tour costs $89 per person with a two-person minimum.

If something a bit slower is more your speed, how about drifting over the sculpted red buttes of Sedona in a hot-air balloon? **Northern Light Balloon Expeditions** (℗ **800/230-6222** or 928/282-2274; www.northernlightballoon.com) charges $190 per person; **Red Rock Balloon Adventures** (© 800/258-3754; www.redrock balloons.com) charges $195 per person; while **Sky High Balloon Adventures** (© 800/ 551-7597; www.skyhighballoons.com), which floats over the Verde Valley and includes a "splash-and-dash" descent to the river, charges $180 per person.

GETTING OUTSIDE

Hiking is the most popular outdoor activity in the Sedona area, with dozens of trails leading off into the red rocks. The most convenient trail is along the **Bell Rock Pathway,** which begins alongside Ariz. 179 just north of the Village of Oak Creek. The trail winds around the base of Bell Rock and accesses many other trails that lead up its sloping sides. It's about 5 miles to go all the way around Bell Rock. Unfortunately, it's a very popular hiking area and is always crowded.

You'll see fewer tourists if you head to the ¾-mile **Cathedral Rock Trail,** which is also located between the Village of Oak Creek and uptown Sedona. The trail follows cairns (piles of rocks) up the slickrock slopes on the north side of Cathedral Rock. To reach this trail, turn off Arizona 179 at the sign for the Back o' Beyond housing development and watch for the trail head at the end of the paved road. For convenience and solitude, you can't beat the **Mystic Trail,** which begins at an unmarked roadside pull-off on Chapel Road halfway between Arizona 179 and the Chapel of the Holy Cross. This is an easy out-and-back trail that runs between a couple of housing developments, but once you're on the trail, you'll feel all alone.

Among the most popular trails in the Sedona area are those that lead into **Boynton Canyon** (site of Enchantment Resort). Here you'll glimpse ancient Native American ruins built into the red-rock cliffs. Although the scenery is indeed stupendous, the great numbers of other hikers on the trail detract considerably from the experience, and the parking lot usually fills up early in the day. The 1.5-mile **Vultee Arch Trail,** which leads to an impressive sandstone arch, is another great hike. The turnoff for the trail head is 2 miles up Dry Creek Road and then another 3½ miles on a very rough dirt road. The **Devil's Bridge Trail,** which starts on the same dirt road, is a little easier to get to and leads to the largest natural sandstone arch in the area. This one is a 1.8-mile round-trip hike.

For the hands-down best views in Sedona, hike all or part of the **Airport Mesa Trail,** a 3.5-mile loop that circles Airport Mesa. With virtually no elevation gain, this is an easy hike. You'll find the trail head about halfway to the top of Airport Mesa on Airport Road. Try this one as early in the day as possible; by midday, the parking lot is usually full and it stays that way right through sunset.

For more information on hiking in Oak Creek Canyon (site of the famous West Fork Oak Creek Trail), see "Oak Creek Canyon," above. For more information on all these hikes, contact the **Coconino National Forest's Red Rock Ranger Station** (© 928/282-4119; www.fs.fed.us/r3/coconino), which, at press time, was in a temporary space 2 miles east of I-17 at Exit 298 (Beaver Creek Rd.). The ranger district has plans to relocate to a site on Arizona 179 south of the Village of Oak Creek.

Sedona is rapidly becoming one of the Southwest's meccas for mountain biking. One of our favorite places to ride is around the base of Bell Rock. Starting at the trail head parking area just north of the Village of Oak Creek, you'll find the easy Bell Rock Path but also numerous more challenging trails.

Another great ride starts above uptown Sedona, where you can take the Jim Thompson Trail to Midgely Bridge or the network of trails that head toward Soldier Pass. The riding here is moderate and the views are superb. To reach these trails, take

Jordan Road to a left onto Park Ridge Road, and follow this road to where it ends at a dirt trail head parking area. You can rent bikes from **Sedona Sports,** Creekside Plaza (below the "Y"), 251 N. Hwy. 179 (℗ **866/204-2377** or 928/282-1317; www.sedona sports.com), or **Mountain Bike Heaven,** 1695 W. Hwy. 89A (℗ **928/282-1312;** www.mountainbikeheaven.com). Rates are around $35 to $50 per day. **Sedona Bike & Bean,** 6020 Hwy. 179, Village of Oak Creek (℗ **928/284-0210;** www.bike-bean.com), across the street from the popular Bell Rock Pathway and its adjacent mountain-bike trails, rents bikes (and serves coffee). Bikes go for $40 to $50 for a full day. If you'd prefer to have a guide take you out on either a mountain-bike or a road-bike tour, contact **Sedona MTB Adventures** (℗ **888/984-1246** or 928/284-1246; www.sedonamtbadventures.com).

Trail Horse Adventures (℗ **800/723-3538;** www.trailhorseadventures.com) offers guided horseback trail rides. A 2-hour ride (that includes creek crossings) will cost you $75. There are also lunch and dinner rides. **Sedona Red Rock Jeep Tours,** 270 N. Hwy. 89A (℗ **800/848-7728** or 928/282-6826; www.redrockjeep.com), offers horse-back rides ($85 for 2 hr.) that include transportation by jeep to the ranch where the rides are held.

Surprisingly, Sedona has not yet been ringed with golf courses. However, what few courses there are offer superb views to distract you from your game. The **Oakcreek Country Club,** 690 Bell Rock Blvd. (℗ **888/703-9489** or 928/284-1660; www.oak creekcountryclub.com), south of town off Arizona 179, has stunning views from the course. Greens fees are $69 to $125. The **Sedona Golf Resort** 🏵🏵, 35 Ridge Trail Dr. (℗ **877/733-9885** or 928/284-9355; www.sedonagolfresort.com), south of town on Arizona 179, offers equally breathtaking views of the red rocks. Greens fees are $59 to $105.

SHOPPING

Ever since the Cowboy Artists of America organization was founded in Sedona back in 1965 (at what is now the Cowboy Club restaurant), this town has had a reputation as an artists' community. Today, with dozens of galleries around town, it's obvious that art is one of the driving forces behind the local economy. Most of Sedona's galleries specialize in traditional Western, contemporary Southwestern, and Native American art, and in some galleries, you'll see works by members of the Cowboy Artists of Amer-ica. You'll find the greatest concentration of galleries and shops in the uptown area of Sedona (along Ariz. 89A just north of the "Y") and at Tlaquepaque.

With more than 40 stores and restaurants, **Tlaquepaque** (℗ **928/282-4838;** www.tlaq.com), on Arizona 179 at the bridge over Oak Creek on the south side of Sedona, bills itself as Sedona's arts-and-crafts village and is designed to resemble a Mexican village. (It was named after a famous arts-and-crafts neighborhood in the suburbs of Guadalajara.) The maze of narrow alleys, courtyards, fountains, and even a chapel and a bell tower are worth a visit even if you aren't in a buying mood. Many of the shops here are high-end art galleries. We wish all shopping centers were such fascinating places. **Hillside Sedona,** just south of Tlaquepaque, is another shopping center dedicated to art galleries and upscale retail shops. It's at 671 Hwy. 179 (℗ **928/ 282-4500;** www.hillsidesedona.net).

WHERE TO STAY

Sedona is one of the most popular destinations in the Southwest, with dozens of hotels and motels around town. However, across the board, accommodations here tend to be a bit overpriced for what you get. Our advice is to save money elsewhere on your trip so you can afford a room with a view here in Sedona.

VERY EXPENSIVE

El Portal Sedona ✹✹   You just can't help but fall in love with this amazing inn. Owners Steve and Connie Segner and Lynda Bourgeois have done everything right, and the overall experience here makes this one of the very best lodgings in the state. Located adjacent to the Tlaquepaque shopping center and built of hand-formed adobe blocks, El Portal, with its pleasant central courtyard, is designed to resemble a 200-year-old hacienda and is a monument to fine craftsmanship. The inn is filled with Arts-and-Crafts–period antiques, including not only the furniture, but also the door knobs, hinges, and even air-conditioning vents. In the living room, the huge ceiling beams were salvaged from a railroad bridge over the Great Salt Lake. Each of the large guest rooms has its own distinctive character, from Arts and Crafts to cowboy chic (rustic log furniture). All but two rooms have whirlpool tubs, and many rooms have private balconies with red-rock views. Exquisite breakfasts and dinners are served.

95 Portal Lane, Sedona, AZ 86336. © 800/313-0017 or 928/203-9405. Fax 928/203-9401. www.elportal sedona.com. 12 units. $259–$550 double. Rates include afternoon hors d'oeuvres. 2-night minimum on weekends and holidays. AE, DC, DISC, MC, V. Pets accepted. Children under 6 discouraged. **Amenities:** Restaurant (New American); access to nearby health club and adjacent resort pools; concierge; massage; laundry service; guided hikes and Jeep tours. *In room:* A/C, TV/DVD, dataport, minibar, fridge, hair dryer, iron, high-speed Internet access, Wi-Fi, free local calls.

Enchantment Resort ✹✹✹   Located at the mouth of Boynton Canyon, this resort more than lives up to its name. The setting is breathtaking, the pueblo-style architecture blends in with the landscape, and the affiliated Mii amo spa is one of the finest in the state. The individual casitas can be booked as two-bedroom suites, one-bedroom suites, or single rooms, but it's worth reserving a suite just so you can enjoy the casita living rooms, which feature high beamed ceilings and beehive fireplaces. All the rooms, however, have patios with dramatic views. The Yavapai Restaurant (p. 512) and a less formal bar and grill offer tables outdoors; don't miss lunch on the terrace.

The Mii amo spa is actually a separate entity within the resort and has its own restaurant, guest rooms, and rates (see separate review, below). Enchantment Resort guests do, however, have access to the spa facilities and can book treatments.

525 Boynton Canyon Rd., Sedona, AZ 86336. © 800/826-4180 or 928/282-2900. Fax 928/282-9249. www. enchantmentresort.com. 220 units. $350–$450 double; $450–$550 junior suite; $750–$950 1-bedroom suite; $1,125–$1,525 2-bedroom suite. Rates do not include $22 resort fee. Children 12 and under stay free in parent's room. AE, DC, DISC, MC, V. **Amenities:** 3 restaurants (New American, Southwestern, spa cuisine); lounge; 7 pools; par-3 golf course; putting green; 7 tennis courts; croquet lawn; health club; full-service spa; Jacuzzi; bikes; children's programs; concierge; business center; room service; massage; babysitting; guest laundry; laundry service; dry cleaning. *In room:* A/C, TV/VCR, dataport, minibar, coffeemaker, hair dryer, iron, safe, high-speed Internet access, Wi-Fi.

Mii amo, a destination spa at Enchantment ✹✹✹   This full-service health spa inside the gates of the exclusive Enchantment Resort easily claims the best location in the state. Designed to resemble a modern Santa Fe–style pueblo from the outside, the spa backs up to red-rock cliffs and is shaded by cottonwood trees. Mii amo is beautifully designed, with indoor and outdoor pools, a crystal grotto, and outdoor massage cabanas at the foot of the cliffs. Guest rooms have a bold, contemporary styling (mixed with Indonesian art and artifacts) that makes them some of the finest accommodations in the state. All units have private patios and gas fireplaces. Mii amo is a world unto itself, and no other spa in Arizona has a more Southwestern feel.

525 Boynton Canyon Rd., Sedona, AZ 86336. ℂ **888/749-2137** or 928/203-8500. Fax 928/203-8599. www.miiamo. com. 16 units. 3-night packages: Apr–May and Sept–Oct $2,640–$4,440 double; Dec–Jan $2,040–$3,840 double; Feb–Mar, June–Aug, and Nov $2,340–$4,140 double. Rates include 3 meals per day and 6 spa treatments. AE, DC, DISC, MC, V. **Amenities:** Restaurant (New American/spa cuisine); 2 pools (indoor and outdoor); exercise room; full-service spa with 24 treatment rooms and wide variety of body treatments; 3 Jacuzzis; bikes; concierge; room service; laundry service; dry cleaning. *In room:* A/C, TV, dataport, minibar, coffeemaker, hair dryer, iron, safe, high-speed Internet access, Wi-Fi.

EXPENSIVE

Adobe Village Graham Inn 𝒜𝒜   A garden full of bronze statues of children greets you when you pull up to this luxurious inn in the Village of Oak Creek, 6 miles south of uptown Sedona. The inn lies almost at the foot of Bell Rock and features a variety of themed accommodations. The villas, the Sundance room, and the Sedona suite are the most impressive rooms here. Our favorite is the Purple Lizard villa, which opts for a colorful Taos-style interior and an amazing rustic canopy bed. The Wilderness villa resembles a luxurious log cabin. The Lonesome Dove villa is an upscale cowboy cabin with a fireplace, potbellied stove, and hot tub in a "barrel."

150 Canyon Circle Dr., Sedona, AZ 86351. ℂ **866/846-1425** or 928/284-1425. Fax 928/284-0767. www.sedonas finest.com. 11 units. $199–$329 double; $389–$409 suite; $349–$479 villa. Rates include full breakfast. 2-night minimum weekends; 3-night minimum holidays. AE, DISC, MC, V. **Amenities:** Outdoor pool; Jacuzzi; concierge; room service; massage and spa services. *In room:* A/C, TV/VCR, dataport, coffeemaker, hair dryer, iron, free local calls.

Briar Patch Inn 𝒜𝒜 *Value*   If you're searching for tranquillity or a romantic retreat amid the cool shade of Oak Creek Canyon, this is the place. Located 3 miles north of Sedona on the banks of Oak Creek, this inn's cottages are surrounded by beautiful grounds where bird songs and the babbling creek set the mood. The cottages date from the 1940s, but have been attractively updated (some with flagstone floors), and a Western/rustic Mexican style now predominates. Most units have fireplaces and kitchenettes. There are also swimming holes and a stone gazebo for massages. The only drawback is the lack of red-rock views from the tree-shaded location.

3190 N. Hwy. 89A, Sedona, AZ 86336. ℂ **888/809-3030** or 928/282-2342. Fax 928/282-2399. www.briar patchInn.com. 18 units. $195–$385 double. Rates include full breakfast. Children under 4 stay free in parent's room. AE, MC, V. **Amenities:** Access to nearby health club; concierge; massage and spa services. *In room:* A/C, kitchen, fridge, coffeemaker, hair dryer, iron, no phone.

Canyon Villa 𝒜𝒜   Located in the Village of Oak Creek, 6 miles south of Sedona, this bed-and-breakfast offers luxurious accommodations and spectacular views of the red rocks. All rooms but one have views, as do the pool area, living room, and dining room. Guest rooms are varied in style—Victorian, Santa Fe, country, rustic—but no matter what the decor, the furnishings are impeccable. All rooms have balconies or patios, and several have fireplaces. Breakfast is a lavish affair meant to be lingered over, and in the afternoon there's an elaborate spread of appetizers.

40 Canyon Circle Dr., Sedona, AZ 86351. ℂ **800/453-1166** or 928/284-1226. Fax 928/284-2114. www.canyon villa.com. 11 units. $189–$304 double. Rates include full breakfast. AE, DC, DISC, MC, V. No children under 11. **Amenities:** Outdoor saltwater pool; concierge. *In room:* A/C, TV, hair dryer, iron, Wi-Fi, free local calls.

Garland's Oak Creek Lodge 𝒜 *Finds*   Located 8 miles north of Sedona in the heart of Oak Creek Canyon, this may be the hardest place in the area to book a room. People have been coming here for so many years and like it so much that they reserve a year in advance (last-minute cancellations do occur, so don't despair). What makes the lodge so special? Maybe it's that you have to drive *through* Oak Creek to get to your log cabin. Maybe it's the beautiful gardens or the slow, relaxing atmosphere of an old-time summer getaway. The well-maintained cabins, most of which have air-conditioning, are rustic but comfortable; the larger ones have their own fireplaces. Meals include organic fruits and vegetables grown on the property.

P.O. Box 152, Sedona, AZ 86339. (Ⓒ 928/282-3343. www.garlandslodge.com. 16 units. $225–$275 double (plus 15% service charge). Rates include breakfast and dinner. 2-night minimum. Children under 2 stay free in parent's room. MC, V. Closed mid-Nov to Mar and Sun year-round. **Amenities:** Dining room; lounge; tennis court; concierge; massage; babysitting. *In room:* No phone.

L'Auberge de Sedona 🏨🏨   If you had to forgo your vacation in France this year, consider a stay at this luxurious boutique resort on the banks of Oak Creek. Shaded by towering sycamore trees and with colorful flower gardens surrounding its many cottages, the resort is a sort of French country retreat in the middle of the desert. L'Auberge's cottages, which look like rustic log cabins from the outside, have a classic styling worthy of a luxury French country inn (leather couches, gorgeous beds, plush towels, wood-burning fireplaces). Although there are rooms in the main lodge, the much larger cottages are definitely worth the extra cost. The restaurant, which carries on the French theme in its decor and menu, has a creekside terrace during the summer.

301 L'Auberge Lane, Sedona, AZ 86336. (Ⓒ 800/272-6777 or 928/282-1661. Fax 928/282-2885. www.lauberge.com. 56 units. $175–$375 double; $275–$525 cottage; $500–$800 2-bedroom cottage. Children under 18 stay free in parent's room. AE, DC, DISC, MC, V. Pets accepted ($35 fee). **Amenities:** Restaurant (French); lounge; access to nearby health club; small full-service spa; Jacuzzi; concierge; courtesy shopping shuttle; business center; babysitting; laundry service; dry cleaning. *In room:* A/C, TV, fridge, coffeemaker, hair dryer, iron, safe, high-speed Internet access, Wi-Fi.

The Lodge at Sedona 🏨🏨   Set amid pine trees a block off Arizona 89A in west Sedona, this large inn is decorated in the Arts and Crafts style, which makes it one of the more distinctive inns in Sedona. The best rooms are those on the ground floor. These tend to be large, and several are suites. Second-floor rooms are more economical and tend to be fairly small. Suites are only slightly more expensive than deluxe rooms, which makes the suites the best choices here. If you want views, book one of the small upstairs rooms or the Desert Trail, Copper Canyon, or Whispering Winds suite. Breakfasts are five-course affairs that will often tide you over until dinner.

125 Kallof Place, Sedona, AZ 86336. (Ⓒ 800/619-4467 or 928/204-1942. Fax 928/204-2128. www.lodgeat sedona.com. 14 units. $170–$339 double. Rates include full breakfast. 2-night minimum on weekends. AE, DISC, MC, V. Dogs accepted ($35 per night). No children under 11. **Amenities:** Access to nearby health club; concierge; massage. *In room:* A/C, hair dryer, iron, Wi-Fi, no phone.

Saddle Rock Ranch 🏨   The stunning views alone make this one of Sedona's top lodging choices, but in addition, you get classic Western ranch styling in a 1926-vintage home that once belonged to Barry Goldwater. Walls of stone and adobe, huge exposed beams, and plenty of windows to take in the scenery are enough to enchant guests even before they reach their rooms. In one room you'll find Victorian elegance, in another an English canopy bed and stone fireplace. Dressing areas and private gardens add to the charm. The third room is a separate little cottage with a pine bed, flagstone floors, and a beamed ceiling. The pool area has one of the best views in town.

255 Rock Ridge Dr., Sedona, AZ 86336. (Ⓒ 866/282-7640 or 928/282-7640. Fax 928/282-7640. www.saddlerock ranch.com. 3 units. $159–$229 double. Rates include full breakfast. MC, V. No children under 14. **Amenities:** Small outdoor pool; access to nearby health club; Jacuzzi; concierge; massage; laundry service; dry cleaning. *In room:* A/C, TV/VCR, fridge, coffeemaker, hair dryer, iron, Wi-Fi, free local calls.

Sedona Rouge Hotel & Spa 🏨🏨   This stylish boutique hotel is the newest luxury hotel in Sedona, and though it is located right on busy US 89A in west Sedona, it has a very distinctive character that we like. Merging contemporary styling with North African details, the hotel manages to create an ambience that is very international in feel. Antique wrought-iron window grates from Tunisia decorate hallways, and guest rooms hold Moroccan-inspired tables. Bathrooms, with dual-head rain-type showers, are a real highlight. If you can, try to get a room on the third floor; these have vaulted ceilings that make the rooms seem larger. The tiny lobby is just off an enclosed courtyard with a splashing fountain. A rooftop patio has the best view at the hotel. This is a good pick for couples in a romantic mood.

2250 W. Hwy. 89A, Sedona, AZ 86336. (℃) 866/312-4111 or 928/203-4111. Fax 928/203-9094. www.sedonarouge. com. 77 units. Jan–Feb $169–$259 double; Mar–May and Sept–Oct $189–$289 double; June–Aug and Nov–Dec $179–$269 double. AE, DC, DISC, MC, V. Pets accepted ($100 refundable deposit, $50 fee). **Amenities:** Restaurant (New American); lounge; outdoor pool; exercise room; full-service spa; Jacuzzi; concierge; room service; massage; babysitting; laundry service; dry cleaning. In room: A/C, TV, dataport, fridge, coffeemaker, hair dryer, iron, high-speed Internet access, Wi-Fi, free local calls.

MODERATE

Amara Resort and Spa 𝄒𝄒 This stylish boutique hotel offers the best of both worlds here in Sedona. This hip resort may seem like an odd fit for a town that has long boasted of its cowboy heritage, but the minimalist decor and Zen-inspired style are a welcome addition to the Sedona hotel scene. From the outside, the hotel fits right in with the red-rock surroundings, while inside, bold splashes of color contrast with black-and-white photos. Guest rooms all have balconies or patios, wonderful pillow-top beds, and furnishings in black and red. The resort's dining room draws on interesting flavor influences from around the globe. The resort recently added a spa.

310 N. Hwy. 89A, Sedona, AZ 86336. (℃) 866/455-6610 or 928/282-4828. Fax 928/282-4825. www.amararesort. com. 100 units. $139–$248 double; $249–$500 suite. Children under 12 stay free in parent's room. AE, DC, DISC, MC, V. Pets accepted ($75). **Amenities:** 3 restaurants (New American, Mexican, American); 3 lounges; outdoor saltwater pool; exercise room; health club; full-service spa; Jacuzzi; sauna; concierge; courtesy shopping shuttle; business center; room service; massage; babysitting; laundry service; dry cleaning. In room: A/C, TV/DVD, dataport, minibar, fridge, coffeemaker, hair dryer, iron, high-speed Internet access, Wi-Fi, free local calls.

Best Western Inn of Sedona 𝄒 Located about midway between uptown and west Sedona, this hotel has great views of the red rocks from its wide terraces and outdoor pool. Unfortunately, although the guest rooms are comfortable enough, not all of them have views. However, the modern Southwestern decor and the setting, surrounded by native landscaping and located beyond the tourist mainstream, make this an appealing choice.

1200 W. Hwy. 89A, Sedona, AZ 86336. (℃) 800/292-6344 or 928/282-3072. Fax 928/282-7218. www.innof sedona.com. 110 units. Mar–Oct $131–$209 double; Nov–Feb $115–$189 double. Rates include continental breakfast. Children 12 and under stay free in parent's room. AE, DC, DISC, MC, V. Pets accepted ($20 fee). **Amenities:** Small outdoor pool; Jacuzzi; concierge. In room: A/C, TV, dataport, fridge, coffeemaker, hair dryer, iron, high-speed Internet access.

The Orchards Inn of Sedona 𝄒𝄒 Located in the heart of uptown Sedona and affiliated with L'Auberge de Sedona, the adjacent French country inn/resort (see review, above), this hotel claims an enviable location on a hillside above Oak Creek. The views from the hillside setting are spectacular and are some of the best in Sedona. Despite the name, this is much more of a hotel than an inn, though the rooms have a very tasteful and comfortable classic style. Don't be discouraged when you drive up to the front door; though the hotel is located amid the uptown tourist crowds, it seems miles away once you check into your room and gaze out at the red rocks.

254 Hwy. 89A, Sedona, AZ 86336. ℂ 877/700-2944 or 928/282-2405. Fax 928/282-7818. www.orchardsinn.com. 41 units. $110–$220 double. Children under 12 stay free in parent's room. AE, DC, DISC, MC, V. **Amenities:** Restaurant (Regional American); small outdoor pool; access to nearby health club; Jacuzzi; concierge; room service; massage; babysitting; laundry service; dry cleaning. *In room:* A/C, TV, dataport, fridge, coffeemaker, hair dryer, iron, safe, high-speed Internet access.

INEXPENSIVE

Cedars Resort on Oak Creek   Located right at the "Y" and set atop a 100-foot cliff, this motel has fabulous views across Oak Creek to the towering red rocks. Guest rooms are large and have been fairly recently refurbished. Creekside rooms have private balconies, but for the best views, ask for a king-size room. A long stairway leads down to the creek, and the shops of uptown Sedona are just a short walk away.

20 W. Hwy. 89A (P.O. Box 292), Sedona, AZ 86339. ℂ 800/874-2072 or 928/282-7010. Fax 928/282-5372. www. sedonacedarsresort.com. 38 units. $99–$149 double. Rates include continental breakfast. Children 12 and under stay free in parent's room. AE, DC, DISC, MC, V. **Amenities:** Small outdoor pool; exercise room; Jacuzzi; concierge; business center; massage. *In room:* A/C, TV, dataport, fridge, coffeemaker, hair dryer, iron, Wi-Fi, free local calls.

Forest Houses 🌟 *(Finds*   Set at the upper end of Oak Creek Canyon and built right on the banks of the creek, these rustic houses and apartments date back to the 1940s. Built by a stone sculptor, they feature artistic touches that set them apart from your average cabins. About half of the houses are built right on the creek, and some seem to grow straight from the rocks in the streambed. Terraces let you fully enjoy the setting. One of our favorite units is the two-bedroom Cloud House, with stone floors, peeled-log woodwork, and a loft. This property is certainly not for everyone (no phones, no TVs, and you have to drive through the creek to get here), but those who discover the Forest Houses often come back year after year.

9275 N. Hwy. 89A, Sedona, AZ 86336. ℂ 928/282-2999. www.foresthousesresort.com. 15 units. $90–$145 double. 2- to 4-night minimum stay. AE, MC, V. Pets accepted ($20 deposit). Closed Jan to mid-Mar. *In room:* Kitchen, fridge, coffeemaker, no phone.

Matterhorn Inn   Located in the heart of the uptown shopping district, this choice is convenient to restaurants and shops, and all of the attractively furnished guest rooms have excellent views of the red-rock canyon walls. Although the Matterhorn is set above a row of shops fronting busy Arizona 89A, if you lie in bed and keep your eyes on the rocks, you'd never know there was so much going on below you. This place is a great value for Sedona.

230 Apple Ave., Sedona, AZ 86336. ℂ 800/372-8207 or 928/282-7176. www.matterhorninn.com. 23 units. Mar–Nov $99–$169 double; Dec–Feb $79–$149 double. Children under 5 stay free in parent's room. AE, MC, V. Pets accepted ($10 per day). **Amenities:** Small outdoor pool; access to nearby health club; Jacuzzi. *In room:* A/C, TV, dataport, fridge, coffeemaker, hair dryer, iron, Wi-Fi, free local calls.

Rose Tree Inn *(Finds*   This little inn, only a block from Sedona's uptown shopping district, is tucked amid pretty gardens (yes, there are lots of roses) on a quiet street. The property consists of an eclectic cluster of older buildings that have all been renovated. Each unit is furnished differently—one Victorian, one Southwestern, two with gas fireplaces. Four guest rooms have kitchenettes, making them good choices for families or for longer stays. The Rose Tree Inn also handles bookings for a pair of modern little apartments a block away. Called the Rooms Upstairs, these apartments are upstairs from and owned by a local architectural firm.

376 Cedar St., Sedona, AZ 86336. © 888/282-2065 or 928/282-2065. www.rosetreeinn.com. 5 units. $98–$139 double. Children under 16 stay free in parent's room. AE, MC, V. **Amenities:** Access to nearby health club; concierge; laundry service. *In room:* A/C, TV/VCR, kitchen, fridge, coffeemaker, hair dryer, iron, microwave, Wi-Fi.

Sky Ranch Lodge   This motel is located atop Airport Mesa and has the most stupendous vista in town. From here you can see the entire red-rock country, with Sedona filling the valley below. Although the rooms are fairly standard motel issue, some have such features as gas fireplaces, barn-wood walls, and balconies. Only the nonview units fall into the inexpensive category, but those great views are just steps away.

Airport Rd. (P.O. Box 2579), Sedona, AZ 86339. © 888/708-6400 or 928/282-6400. Fax 928/282-7682. www.skyranchlodge.com. 94 units. $75–$189 double. AE, MC, V. Pets accepted ($10 per night). **Amenities:** Small outdoor pool; Jacuzzi; coin-op laundry. *In room:* A/C, TV, dataport, coffeemaker.

CAMPGROUNDS

Within Oak Creek Canyon along Arizona 89A, there are five National Forest Service campgrounds. **Manzanita,** 6 miles north of town, is both the largest and the most pleasant (and the only one open in winter). Other Oak Creek Canyon campgrounds include **Bootlegger,** 9 miles north of town; **Cave Springs,** 13 miles north of town; and **Pine Flat,** 12 miles north of town. All of these campgrounds charge $18 per night. The **Beaver Creek Campground,** 3 miles east of I-17 on FR 618, which is an extension of Arizona 179 (take Exit 298 off I 17), is a pleasant spot near the V Bar V Heritage petroglyph site. Campsites here are $14 per night. For more information on area campgrounds, contact the **Coconino National Forest's Red Rock Ranger Station** (© 928/282-4119; www.fs.fed.us/r3/coconino), which, at press time, was in a temporary space 2 miles east of I-17 at Exit 298 (Beaver Creek Rd.). The ranger district has plans to relocate to a site on Arizona 179 south of the Village of Oak Creek. Reservations can be made for Manzanita, Pine Flat, and Cave Springs campgrounds by contacting the **National Recreation Reservation Center** (© 877/444-6777 or 518/885-3639; www.reserveusa.com).

WHERE TO DINE
EXPENSIVE

El Portal Sedona 𝑅𝑅 NEW AMERICAN/SOUTHWESTERN   Although El Portal is primarily a deluxe inn, it also serves superb dinners on Wednesday through Saturday nights. While many of the diners are guests at the inn, the meals are open to the public by reservation. These dinners provide anyone who is not staying at this inn a chance to lounge around in the courtyard and living room/dining room, and get a sense for what it's like to stay here. The menu is short and usually includes less than a half-dozen entrees and an equal number of appetizers and salads. If the baked brie with roasted garlic and raspberry chipotle sauce is on the menu, don't even think of resisting. This dish is heavenly! Crab- and lobster-filled ravioli in a Manchego cheese sauce and spice-encrusted duck breast with shallot/cherry/pinot noir sauce are just two examples of the sorts of entrees you can expect.

95 Portal Lane. © 928/203-4942. www.innsedona.com. Reservations required. Main courses $20–$45. AE, DC, DISC, MC, V. Wed–Sat 5:30–8pm.

The Heartline Café 𝑅𝑅 SOUTHWESTERN/INTERNATIONAL   The heart line, from Zuni mythology, is a symbol of health and longevity; it is also a symbol for the healthful, creative food served here. To start with, don't miss the tea-smoked chicken dumplings with spicy peanut sauce or the Gorgonzola torte with caramelized pear. Memorable entrees include pecan-crusted local trout with Dijon cream sauce. Those searching out variety in vegetarian choices will find it here. The beautiful courtyard and traditionally elegant interior are good places to savor a meal accompanied by a selection from the reasonably priced wine list. The Heartline Café also has a takeout restaurant next door.

1610 W. Hwy. 89A. ℭ **928/282-0785.** www.heartlinecafe.com. Reservations recommended. Main courses $8.25–$15 lunch, $16–$28 dinner. AE, DC, DISC, MC, V. Wed–Mon 11am–3pm and 5–9:30pm (no lunch on Tues in summer).

René at Tlaquepaque ⟨𝔯⟩𝔯 CONTINENTAL/AMERICAN   Although a formal dining experience and traditional French fare may seem out of place in a town that celebrates its cowboy heritage, René's makes fine dining seem as natural as mesquite-grilled steak and cowboy beans. Located in Tlaquepaque, the city's upscale south-of-the-border-themed shopping center, this restaurant is the best place in Sedona for a special meal. The house specialty here is rack of lamb, and if you like lamb, this dish should not be missed. More adventurous diners may want to try the excellent tenderloin of venison with whiskey–juniper berry sauce. Finish with a flambéed dessert and selections from the after-dinner drink cart.

At Tlaquepaque, 336 Ariz. 179, Suite 118. ℭ **928/282-9225.** www.rene-sedona.com. Reservations recommended. Main courses $9–$16 lunch, $20–$42 dinner. AE, MC, V. Sun–Thurs 11:30am–2pm and 5:30–8:30pm; Fri–Sat 11:30am–2pm and 5:30–9pm.

Shugrue's Hillside Grill ⟨𝔯⟩𝔯 NEW AMERICAN/CONTINENTAL   Located at the back of the Hillside Sedona shopping plaza, this is the most upscale outpost in a small chain of popular Arizona restaurants. Although the prices are high at dinner, if you come before the sun sets, you'll be treated to unforgettable views through the walls of glass. The extensive menu includes influences from around the world. For a starter, try the blackened shrimp saganaki. There are plenty of good steak and fish entrees, too.

671 Hwy. 179. ℭ **928/282-5300.** www.shugrues.com. Reservations highly recommended. Main courses $8–$18 lunch, $21–$30 dinner. AE, DC, MC, V. Sun–Thurs 11:30am–3pm and 5–9pm; Fri–Sat 11:30am–3pm and 5–10pm.

Yavapai Restaurant ⟨𝔯⟩𝔯 SOUTHWESTERN   The Yavapai Restaurant, at the exclusive Enchantment Resort, has the best views and most memorable setting of any restaurant in Sedona. It is also one of the town's most formal restaurants (no blue jeans allowed), which doesn't quite fit with the rugged setting but is in keeping with Enchantment's exclusive character. The menu changes regularly to take advantage of seasonal ingredients, but keep an eye out for venison dishes and veal chops with the sauce of the moment. Because the scenery is every bit as important as the food here, make sure you make dinner reservations to take in the sunset on the red rocks. You can also soak up the views at breakfast and lunch and save quite a bit of money.

At Enchantment Resort, 525 Boynton Canyon Rd. ℭ **928/204-6000.** www.enchantmentresort.com. Reservations required. Main courses $15–$19 lunch, $27–$42 dinner; Sun brunch $40 for adults, $20 for children ages 5–11. AE, DISC, MC, V. Mon–Sat 6:30am–2:15pm, and 5:30–9:15pm; Sun 10:30am–2:15pm.

MODERATE

Cowboy Club Grille & Spirits 𝔯 SOUTHWESTERN   With its big booths, huge steer horns over the bar, and cowboy gear adorning the walls, this restaurant looks like a glorified cowboy steakhouse—but this is big flavor country, and the menu isn't the sort any real cowboy would likely have anything to do with. Start out with fried cactus strips with black-bean gravy or perhaps a rattlesnake brochette. For an entree, be sure to try the buffalo sirloin, which is served with some flavorful sauce of the moment. At lunch, try the buffalo burger. Service is relaxed and friendly. The adjacent Silver Saddle Room is a more upscale spin on the same concept. It was in this building in 1965 that the Cowboy Artists of America organization was formed.

241 N. Hwy. 89A. ℂ 928/282-4200. www.cowboyclub.com. Reservations recommended. Main courses $7–$24 lunch, $10–$43 dinner. AE, DC, DISC, MC, V. Daily 11am–4pm and 5–10pm.

Cucina Rústica 🌶🌶 MEDITERRANEAN/SOUTHWESTERN   With its various distinct dining rooms and numerous antique doors, this sister restaurant to west Sedona's wonderful Dahl & DiLuca (see below) feels like a luxurious villa. One dining room has a central dome that is lit by what appear to be thousands of stars. For a genuine starlit dinner, ask for a seat on the patio. Start with the *bruschetta pomodoro*, a tomato-and-basil appetizer that tastes like a bite of summer; then, when it comes time to order an entree, just ask for the *gamberi del capitano*. These grilled prawns, wrapped in radicchio and prosciutto, are among the best we've ever had—positively ambrosial.

7000 Hwy. 179, Village of Oak Creek. ℂ 928/284-3010. www.cucinarustica.com. Reservations recommended. Main courses $12–$28. AE, DC, MC, V. Sun–Thurs 5–9; Fri–Sat 5–10pm.

Dahl & DiLuca 🌶🌶 ROMAN ITALIAN   A faux-Tuscan villa interior, complete with a bar in a grotto, makes this the most romantic restaurant in Sedona, and the excellent Italian food makes it that much more unforgettable. Be sure to start with some of the *pane romano*, which, as far as we're concerned, is the best garlic bread west of New York's Little Italy. Pasta predominates here, and portions are big. We like the linguine Siciliana with calamari and mushrooms. The kitchen also serves up a panoply of deftly prepared seafood, chicken, and vegetarian dishes. The eggplant Parmesan and portobello *alla griglia* are real standouts. Genial and efficient service, reasonably priced wines, and nightly live music make this place even more enjoyable.

2321 W. Hwy. 89A (in west Sedona diagonally across from the Safeway Plaza). ℂ 928/282-5219. www.dahl-diluca.com. Reservations recommended. Main courses $11–$28. AE, DISC, MC, V. Daily 5–10pm.

Fournos Restaurant 🌶 *(Finds* MEDITERRANEAN   Fournos is a refreshingly casual place run by the husband-and-wife team of Shirley and Demetrios Fournos. Step through the front door, and you almost have to walk through the kitchen to get to the handful of tables in the dining room. In the kitchen, chef Demetrios cooks up a storm, preparing such dishes as shrimp flambéed in ouzo and baked with feta; Cephalonian-style lamb shanks with herbs and potatoes; and Mykonos-style poached fish with a sauce of yogurt, onions, mayonnaise, and butter. Other specialties are rack of lamb and lamb Wellington.

3000 W. Hwy. 89A. ℂ 928/282-3331. www.fournosrestaurant.com. Reservations highly recommended. Main courses $16–$21. AE, DISC, MC, V. Thurs–Sat seatings at 6 and 8pm.

INEXPENSIVE

The Hideaway Restaurant ITALIAN/DELI   This casual family restaurant is as popular with locals as it is with visitors. Basic pizzas, subs, sandwiches, salads, and pastas are the choices here, and both the salad dressings and sausages are made on the premises. However, most people come for the knockout views. From the shady porch, you can see the creek below and the red rocks rising across the canyon. Lunch or an early sunset dinner is your best bet. The *paisano* (Sicilian sausage soup and a sandwich) lunch and antipasto salad are both good choices.

Country Sq., 251 Ariz. 179. ℂ 928/282-4204. Reservations accepted only for parties of 10 or more. Main courses $6–$16. AE, DISC, MC, V. Daily 11am–9pm.

Javelina Cantina ℛ MEXICAN   Although Javelina Cantina is part of a chain of Arizona restaurants, the formula works, and few diners leave disappointed. Sure, the restaurant is touristy, but what it has going for it is good Mexican food, a lively atmosphere, decent views, and a convenient location in the Hillside shops. The grilled fish tacos are tasty, as is the pork adobo sandwich. Other dishes worth trying include the salmon tostadas. There are also plenty of different margaritas and tequilas to accompany your meal. Expect a wait.

At Hillside Sedona shopping plaza, 671 Hwy. 179. ℂ 928/203-9514. www.javelinacantina.com. Reservations recommended. Main courses $8–$19. AE, DISC, MC, V. Daily 11:30am–9:30pm.

Picazzo's ℛ PIZZA   For down-home pizza in an upscale setting, nothing in Sedona can compare with this artistic pizza place. Throw in an attractive walled patio dining area and a view of Coffee Pot Rock, and you have one of the best values in town. There are good by-the-slice lunch specials, and during happy hour, there are half-price appetizers. Try the Southwestern pizza, which is made with salsa, spicy chicken or beef, pepper jack cheese, and black beans. Or how about a bacon cheeseburger pizza? Great setting, great view, great pizza, and best of all, by eating here you can avoid the crowds in uptown Sedona.

1855 W. Hwy. 89A. ℂ 928/282-4140. www.picazzos.com. Reservations not accepted. Pizzas $11–$23. AE, DC, MC, V. Sun–Thurs 11am–10pm; Fri–Sat 11am–11pm.

Red Planet Diner ℛ (Kids) INTERNATIONAL   With its flying saucer fountain out front and its totally cosmic decor, this casual diner is a UFO-spotter's dream come true. You can sip a mother-ship "vorttini" while you wait for your food, but most people come here for the milk shakes. Those shakes are best accompanied by a Roswell burger or maybe some Flash Gordon chili. The walls are plastered with photos of UFOs and images from old sci-fi movies. Unfortunately, you may sometimes feel as if aliens have kidnapped your waitress.

1655 W. Hwy. 89A. ℂ 928/282-6070. Main courses $8–$16. AE, DISC, MC, V. Daily 10am–11pm.

SEDONA AFTER DARK

If you're searching for good microbrewed beer, head to the **Oak Creek Brewing Co.,** 2050 Yavapai Dr. (ℂ **928/204-1300;** www.oakcreekbrew.com), north of Arizona 89A off Coffee Pot Drive. There's also the affiliated **Oak Creek Brewery and Grill** (ℂ **928/282-3300;** www.oakcreekpub.com) in the Tlaquepaque shopping complex. If you're looking for some live music, check out **Olde Sedona Bar & Grille,** 1405 W. Hwy. 89A (ℂ **928/282-5670;** www.oldesedona.com). Down in the Village of Oak Creek, you can do a little dancing at the **Full Moon Saloon,** 7000 Hwy. 179 (ℂ **928/ 284-1872;** www.thefullmoonsaloon.com), which is located in the Tequa Plaza shopping center and has live music several nights a week.

6 Lake Mead National Recreation Area

70 miles NW of Kingman; 256 miles NW of Phoenix; 30 miles SE of Las Vegas, NV

This watersports playground straddles the border between Arizona and Nevada, boasting two reservoirs and a scenic, free-flowing stretch of the Colorado River. Throughout the year, anglers fish for striped bass, rainbow trout, channel catfish, and other

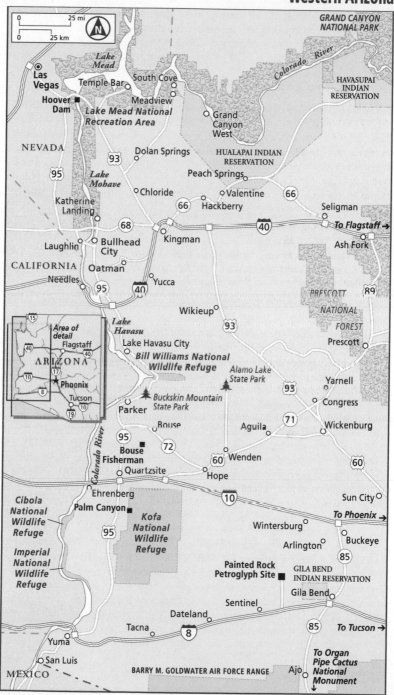

Western Arizona

sport fish, while during the hot summer months, lakes Mead and Mohave attract tens of thousands of water-skiers and personal watercraft riders.

The larger reservoir, Lake Mead, was created by the Hoover Dam, which was constructed between 1931 and 1935. By supplying huge amounts of electricity and water to Arizona and California, the dam set the stage for the phenomenal growth the region experienced in the second half of the 20th century.

ESSENTIALS

GETTING THERE   US 93, which runs between Las Vegas and Kingman, crosses over Hoover Dam, and traffic backups at the dam have in the past been absolutely horrendous. However, now that trucks are prohibited from crossing the dam, the traffic jams have lessened somewhat. Several small secondary roads lead to various marinas on the lake. There are also many miles of unpaved roads within the recreation area. If you have a high-clearance or four-wheel-drive vehicle, these roads can take you to some of the least visited shores of the two lakes.

VISITOR INFORMATION   For information, contact the **Lake Mead National Recreation Area,** 601 Nevada Way, Boulder City, NV 89005 (© **702/293-8906;** www.nps.gov/lame), or stop by the **Alan Bible Visitor Center** (© **702/293-8990**), between Hoover Dam and Boulder City. The visitor center is open daily from 8:30am to 4:30pm (closed New Year's Day, Thanksgiving, and Christmas).

DAM, LAKE & RIVER TOURS

Standing 726 feet tall, from bedrock to the roadway atop it, and tapering from a thickness of 660 feet at its base to only 45 feet at the top, **Hoover Dam** (© **866/730-9097** or 702/494-2517; www.usbr.gov/lc/hooverdam) is the tallest concrete dam in the Western Hemisphere. Behind this massive dam lie the waters of **Lake Mead,** which at 110 miles long and with a shoreline of more than 550 miles is the largest artificial lake in the United States. To learn about the construction of Hoover Dam, stop in at the visitor center, which is open daily from 9am to 5pm (closed Thanksgiving and Christmas). Guided tours cost $11 for adults, $9 for seniors, and $6 for children 7 to 16. Parking is an additional $7. Including a tour, it takes about 2 hours to visit the dam.

If you'd like to tour the lake, call **Lake Mead Cruises** (© **702/293-6180;** www.lakemeadcruises.com) to book passage on the *Desert Princess* or *Desert Princess Too* paddle-wheeler. These cruises leave from Lake Mead Cruises Landing, off Lakeshore Drive on the Nevada side of Hoover Dam. Day tours, which go to the dam, last 1½ hours and cost $22 for adults and $10 for children 2 to 11. Other options include dinner cruises ($46 for adults, $25 for children), brunch cruises ($37 for adults, $18 for children), and weekend dinner-and-dancing cruises ($58).

One of the most interesting ways to see remote parts of Lake Mohave is by sea kayak. **Desert River Outfitters** (© **888/KAYAK-33;** www.desertriveroutfitters.com) will rent you a boat and shuttle you and your gear to and from put-ins and take-outs. The trip through Black Canyon ($55 per person with a four-person minimum) starts at the base of Hoover Dam and is the most interesting route. (*Note:* This trip requires advance planning because a permit is necessary.) You can also paddle past the casinos in Laughlin ($25), through the Topock Gorge ($45), or around Lake Mohave ($35). Raft trips through Black Canyon are offered by **Black Canyon River Adventures** (© **800/455-3490;** www.blackcanyonadventures.com). The 1-day rafting trips, on big motorized rafts, are an easy float through a scenic canyon and cost $83 for adults,

$80 for children ages 13 to 15, and $51 for children ages 5 to 12. This is a great way to see this remote stretch of river

GETTING OUTSIDE

Swimming, fishing, water-skiing, and powerboating are the most popular activities in Lake Mead National Recreation Area. On Arizona shores, there are swimming beaches at Lake Mohave's Katherine Landing (outside Bullhead City) and Lake Mead's Temple Bar (north of Kingman off US 93). Picnic areas can be found at these two areas as well as Willow Beach on Lake Mohave and more than half a dozen spots on the Nevada side of Lake Mead.

In Arizona, marinas can be found at Katherine Landing on Lake Mohave (just outside Bullhead City), near the north end of Lake Mohave at Willow Beach (best access for trout angling), and at Temple Bar on Lake Mead. There's also a boat ramp at South Cove, north of the community of Meadview at the east end of Lake Mead. On the Nevada side of Lake Mohave, there's a marina at Cottonwood Cove, and on the Nevada side of Lake Mead, you'll find marinas at Boulder Beach, Las Vegas Bay, Callville Bay, and Echo Bay. These marinas offer motels, restaurants, general stores, campgrounds, and boat rentals. At **Temple Bar Resort & Marina** (© 800/255-5561 or 928/767-3211), you can rent speedboats for $250 to $350 per day. At **Lake Mohave Resort** (© 800/752-9669 or 928/754-3245), you can rent ski boats, fishing boats, and patio boats for between $90 and $260 per day. Personal watercraft go for $285 per day.

WHERE TO STAY

Seven Crown Resorts rents houseboats (see below) and runs a motel on Lake Mohave. For more information, contact **Seven Crown Resorts** (© 800/752-9669; www.seven crown.com). **Lake Mohave Resort** has huge rooms that are great for families ($60–$125 double). **Temple Bar Resort**, on Lake Mead, although really just a motel, has a wonderful remote setting with a beach right in front, great fishing nearby, and 40 miles of prime skiing waters extending from the resort. Rooms go for $70 to $125 double. For more information, contact Temple Bar Resort (© 800/255-5561 or 928/767-3211; www.templebarlakemead.com).

HOUSEBOATS

Seven Crown Resorts 🛶 *(Kids)*   Why pay extra for a lake-view room when you can rent a houseboat that always has a 360-degree water view? There's no better way to explore Lake Mead than on one of these floating vacation homes. You can cruise for miles, tie up at a deserted cove, and enjoy a wilderness adventure with all the comforts of home. Houseboats come complete with full kitchens, air-conditioning, and space to sleep up to 13 people. Bear in mind that the scenery here on Lake Mead isn't nearly as spectacular as that on Lake Powell, Arizona's other major houseboating lake.

P.O. Box 16247, Irvine, CA 92623-6247. © 800/752-9669. www.sevencrown.com. $1,250–$4,250 per week. DISC, MC, V. Pets accepted. *In room:* A/C, kitchen, fridge, coffeemaker, microwave, no phone.

CAMPING

In Arizona, there are campgrounds at Katherine Landing on Lake Mohave and at Temple Bar on Lake Mead. Both of these campgrounds have been heavily planted with trees, so they provide some semblance of shade during the hot, but popular, summer months. In Nevada, you'll find campgrounds at Cottonwood Cove on Lake Mohave and at Boulder Beach, Las Vegas Bay, Callville Bay, and Echo Bay on Lake

Mead. Campsites at all campgrounds are $10 per night. For more information, contact **Lake Mead National Recreation Area** (© **702/293-8906** or 702/293-8990; www.nps.gov/lame).

7 Lake Havasu & the London Bridge

60 miles S of Bullhead City; 150 miles S of Las Vegas, NV; 200 miles NW of Phoenix

London Bridge is falling down, falling down, falling down. At least it was, until Robert McCulloch, founder of Lake Havasu City, hit upon the brilliant idea of buying the bridge and having it shipped to his undertouristed little planned community in the Arizona desert. Some 35 years later, London Bridge attracts tourists by the millions.

Lake Havasu was formed in 1938 by the building of the Parker Dam, but it wasn't until 1963 that McCulloch founded the town of Lake Havasu City. In the town's early years, not too many people were keen on spending time in this remote corner of the desert, where summer temperatures are often over 110°F (43°C). It was then that McCulloch began looking for ways to attract more people to his little "city" on the lake. His solution proved to be a stroke of genius.

Today, Lake Havasu City attracts an odd mix of visitors. In winter, the town is filled with retirees. On weekends, during the summer, and over spring break, however, Lake Havasu City is popular with Arizona college students and the water-ski and personal-watercraft crowds. Expect lots of noise on weekends and holidays.

ESSENTIALS

GETTING THERE   From Phoenix, take I-10 W to Arizona 95 N. From Las Vegas, take US 95 S to I-40 E to Arizona 95 S.

US Airways (© **800/428-4322**) has regular flights to Lake Havasu City from Phoenix. The **Havasu/Vegas Express** (© **800/459-4884** or 928/453-4884; www. havasuvegasexpress.com) operates a shuttle van between Lake Havasu City and Las Vegas. Fares are $55 one-way and $95 round-trip ($51 and $86 for seniors).

VISITOR INFORMATION   For more information on this area, contact the **Lake Havasu Convention & Visitors Bureau,** English Village, 314 London Bridge Rd. (© **800/242-8278** or 928/453-3444; golakehavasu.com), which is at the foot of the London Bridge.

GETTING AROUND   For car rentals, try **Avis** (© **800/331-1212** or 928/764-3001), **Enterprise** (© **800/261-7331** or 928/453-0033), or **Hertz** (© **800/654-3131** or 928/764-3994).

LONDON BRIDGE

Back in the mid-1960s, when London Bridge was sinking into the Thames River due to heavy car and truck traffic, the British government decided to sell the bridge. Robert McCulloch and his partner paid nearly $2.5 million for it and had it shipped 10,000 miles to Lake Havasu City. Reconstruction of the bridge was begun in 1968, and the grand reopening was held in 1971.

At the base of the bridge sits **English Village,** which is done up in proper English style and has shops, restaurants, and a waterfront promenade. You'll find several cruise boats and boat-rental docks here, as well as the chamber of commerce's visitor center.

Unfortunately, the London Bridge is not very impressive as bridges go, and the tacky commercialization of its surroundings makes it something of a letdown for

Moments **Canoeing the Colorado**

Paddling down a desert river is an unusual and unforgettable experience. Both outfitters listed here provide boats, paddles, life jackets, maps, and shuttles to put-in and take-out points, but usually no guide. **Western Arizona Canoe and Kayak Outfitter** (© **888/881-5038** or 928/715-6414; www.azwacko.com) offers self-guided kayak or canoe trips through the beautiful and rugged Topock Gorge, where you can see ancient petroglyphs and possibly bighorn sheep. Trips take 5 to 6 hours, and the cost is $45 per person. **Jerkwater Canoe & Kayak Company** (© **800/421-7803** or 928/768-7753; www.jerkwater.com) offers a similar Topock Gorge excursion and also arranges other canoe and kayak trips of varying lengths. Jerkwater's Topock Gorge self-guided 5- to 6-hour trip is $40 per person in a canoe or $55 per person in a kayak.

many visitors. On top of that, over the years the jolly olde England styling that once predominated around here has been supplanted by a Mexican beach-bar aesthetic designed to appeal to partying college students on spring break.

LAND, LAKE & RIVER TOURS

Several companies offer different types of boat tours on Lake Havasu. **Bluewater Jet-boat Tours** (© **888/855-7171** or 928/855-7171; www.coloradoriverjetboattours. com) runs jet-boat tours that leave from the London Bridge and spend 2½ hours cruising up the Colorado River to the Topock Gorge, a scenic area 25 miles from Lake Havasu City. The cost is $38 for adults, $35 for seniors, and $20 for children 5 to 12. You can also go out on the *Dixie Belle* (© **928/453-6776** or 928/855-0888), a small replica paddle-wheel riverboat or the even smaller *Kontiki.* Cruises are $15 for adults and $8 for children 5 to 12. The *Kontiki* goes to Copper Canyon, the narrow cliff-ringed cove that is the destination for college-age partiers each year during spring break.

To explore the desert surrounding Lake Havasu City, arrange an off-road adventure in a six-wheel-drive Pinzgauer truck with **Outback Off-Road Adventures** (© **928/680-6151;** www.outbackadventures.us), which charges $65 to $80 for a half-day tour and $165 for a full-day tour.

GETTING OUTSIDE

GOLF **London Bridge Golf Club,** 2400 Club House Dr. (© **928/855-2719;** www.americangolf.com), with two 18-hole courses, is the area's premier course. High-season greens fees (with cart) top out at $75 on the West Course and $65 on the East Course. The **Havasu Island Golf Course,** 1040 McCulloch Blvd. (© **928/855-5585**), is a 4,012-yard, par-61 executive course with lots of water hazards. Greens fees are $25 if you walk and $35 if you ride. The 9-hole **Bridgewater Links,** 1477 Queen's Bay Rd. (© **928/855-4777;** www.londonbridgeresort.com), at the London Bridge Resort, is the most accessible and easiest of the area courses. Greens fees for 9 holes are $18 if you walk and $24 if you ride.

Golfers won't want to miss the **Emerald Canyon Golf Course** ✦, 7351 Riverside Dr., Parker (© **928/667-3366;** www.emeraldcanyongolf.com), about 30 miles south of Lake Havasu City. This municipal course is the most spectacular in the region and plays through rugged canyons and past red-rock cliffs, from which there are views of the Colorado River. One hole even has you hitting your ball off a cliff to a green 200 feet below! Expect to pay $35 to $55 for greens fees in the cooler months. Also in Parker is the golf course at the **Havasu Springs Resort,** 2581 Arizona 95 (© **928/ 667-3361**), which some people claim is the hardest little 9-hole, par-3 course in the state. It's atop a rocky outcropping with steep drop-offs all around. If you aren't staying here, greens fees are only $10 for 9 holes and $15 for 18 holes.

WATERSPORTS   While the London Bridge is what made Lake Havasu City, these days watersports on 45-mile-long Lake Havasu are the area's real draw.

London Bridge Beach, the best in-town beach, is located in a county park behind the Island Inn, off West McCulloch Boulevard. It features a sandy beach and lots of palm trees. Just south of the London Bridge on the "mainland" side, you'll find the large **Rotary Community Park** and the **Lake Havasu Aquatic Center,** 100 Park Ave. (© **928/453-2687**), which has an indoor pool and 254-foot water slide. There are more beaches at **Lake Havasu State Park** (© **928/855-2784** www.azstateparks. com/Parks/parkhtml/havasu.html), 2 miles north of the London Bridge, and **Cattail Cove State Park** (© **928/855-1223**), 15 miles south of Lake Havasu City. Both state parks charge a $9 day-use fee.

At the **Adventure Center,** in English Village (© **928/453-4386**), you can rent pedal boats for $20 an hour. In this same area, you can also go for a ride on the **London Bridge Gondola** (© **928/486-1891**; www.londonbridgegondola.com); the gondolier even sings in Italian as you cruise beneath the London Bridge. Ride prices range from $15 to $35.

If you didn't bring your own boat, you can rent one from **Fun Time Boat Rentals,** 1685 Industrial Blvd. (© **800/680-1003** or 928/680-1003; www.funtimerentals. com). Pontoon boats and ski boats equipped with water skis or knee boards both rent for $300 per day.

WHERE TO STAY
HOTELS & MOTELS

Agave Inn *(kids) (Finds)*   Located at the foot of the London Bridge, this stylish boutique hotel is by far the hippest hotel between Scottsdale and Las Vegas. Guest rooms are reminiscent of those at W hotels, although here you get much more room at a much lower price. Rooms are large and have balconies, and most overlook the bridge or the water. Platform beds, stylish lamps, and a sort of Scandinavian modern aesthetic make this the most distinctive hotel on this side of the state. One caveat: the open-air bar across the channel plays loud music until 2am on warm nights.

1420 McCulloch Blvd N., Lake Havasu City, AZ 86403. © 866/854-2833 or 928/854-2833. Fax 928/854-1130. www.agaveinn.com. 23 units. $119–$429 suite. Children under 18 stay free in parent's room. AE, DISC, MC, V. **Amenities:** Exercise room; concierge; massage; dry cleaning. *In room:* A/C, TV/DVD, dataport, coffeemaker, hair dryer, iron, microwave, high-speed Internet access, Wi-Fi, free local calls.

London Bridge Resort *(kids)*   Merry Olde England has given way to the Tropics and the desert as this resort strives to please its young, partying clientele (who tend to make a lot of noise and leave the hotel looking much the worse for wear). Although the bridge is just out the hotel's back door, and a replica of Britain's gold State Coach is inside the lobby, guests are more interested in the three pools and the tropical-theme outdoor nightclub. The one- and two-bedroom units are spacious, comfortable, and attractive, and those on the ground floor have double whirlpool tubs.

1477 Queens Bay, Lake Havasu City, AZ 86403. ℂ 866/331-9231 or 928/855-0888. Fax 928/855-5404. www. londonbridgeresort.com. 122 units. $179–$259 1-bedroom condo. AE, MC, V. **Amenities:** Restaurant (American); 2 lounges; 3 pools; 9-hole executive golf course; tennis court; exercise room; spa; Jacuzzi; babysitting; coin-op laundry. *In room:* A/C, TV/VCR, dataport, kitchen, coffeemaker, hair dryer, iron, high-speed Internet access.

CAMPING

There are two state park campgrounds in the Lake Havasu City area. **Lake Havasu State Park** (ℂ **928/855-2784**) is 2 miles north of the London Bridge on London Bridge Road, while **Cattail Cove State Park** (ℂ **928/855-1223**) is 15 miles south of Lake Havasu City off Arizona 95. The former campground charges $14 to $25 per night per vehicle, while the latter charges $19 to $25 per site. Reservations are not accepted. In addition to sites in these campgrounds, there are boat-in campsites within Lake Havasu and Cattail Cove state parks.

WHERE TO DINE

Javelina Cantina MEXICAN   At the foot of the London Bridge on the island side, this large Mexican restaurant is affiliated with Shugrue's. As at Shugrue's, there is a great view of the bridge. In this case, it is from a large patio area that is kept heated during the cooler winter months. The bar has an excellent selection of tequilas, and margaritas are a specialty here. Accompany your libations with tortilla soup, fish tacos, or a salad made with blackened scallops, papaya, pecans, and blue cheese.

1420 McCulloch Blvd. (ℂ **928/855-8226**. www.javelinacantina.com. Reservations not accepted. Main courses $7.50–$16. AE, DISC, MC, V. Sun–Thurs 11am–8:30 or 9pm; Fri–Sat 11am–10 or 11pm.

Shugrue's (Kids STEAKHOUSE/SEAFOOD   Just across the London Bridge from English Village, Shugrue's seems to be popular as much for its view of the bridge as for its food. Offerings include seafood, prime rib, burgers, sandwiches, and a short list of pastas. This place is a favorite of vacationing retirees and families, especially for its inexpensive sunset dinners, which are served Sunday through Thursday from 5 to 6:30pm. The adjacent affiliated Barley Brothers Brewpub has the same good view of the bridge and serves a menu calculated to appeal to a younger clientele.

At the Island Mall, 1425 McCulloch Blvd. (ℂ **928/453-1400**. www.shugrues.com. Reservations recommended. Main courses $7–$12 lunch, $11–$25 dinner. AE, DC, DISC, MC, V. Sun–Thurs 11am–3pm and 4:30–9pm; Fri–Sat 11am–3pm and 4:30–10pm.

15

The Grand Canyon & Northern Arizona

The Grand Canyon attracts millions of visitors from all over the world each year. The pastel layers of rock weaving through the canyon's rugged ramparts, the interplay of shadows and light, the wind in the pines, and the croaking of ravens on the rim—these are the sights and sounds that transfix the hordes of visitors who gaze awestruck into the canyon's seemingly infinite depths.

Yet other parts of northern Arizona contain worthwhile, and less crowded, attractions. Only 60 miles south of the canyon stand the San Francisco Peaks, the tallest of which, Humphreys Peak, rises to 12,643 feet. These peaks, sacred to the Hopi and Navajo, are ancient volcanoes that today are popular with skiers, hikers, and mountain bikers.

Amid northern Arizona's miles of windswept plains and ponderosa pine forests stands the city of Flagstaff, home to Northern Arizona University. Born of the railroads and named for a flagpole, Flagstaff is now the main jumping-off point for trips to the Grand Canyon.

1 The Grand Canyon South Rim ★★★

60 miles N of Williams; 80 miles NE of Flagstaff; 230 miles N of Phoenix; 340 miles N of Tucson

Whether you merely stand on the rim gazing in awe, spend several days hiking deep in the canyon, or ride the roller-coaster rapids of the Colorado River, a trip to the Grand Canyon is an unforgettable experience. A mile deep, 277 miles long, and up to 18 miles wide, the canyon is so large that it is positively overwhelming in its grandeur, truly one of the great wonders of the world.

Layers of sandstone, limestone, shale, and schist give the canyon its colors, and the interplay of shadows and light from dawn to dusk creates an ever-changing palette of hues and textures. Written in these bands of stone are more than 2 billion years of geologic history. According to geologists, it has taken between 3 million and 6 million years for the Colorado River to carve the Grand Canyon, but the canyon's history extends much further back in time.

Millions of years ago, vast seas covered this region. Sediments carried by sea water were deposited and, over millions of years, turned into limestone and sandstone. According to one theory, when the ancient seabed was thrust upward to form the Kaibab Plateau, the Colorado River began its work of cutting through the plateau. Today, 21 sedimentary layers, the oldest of which is more than a billion years old, can be seen in the canyon. Beneath all these layers, at the very bottom, is a stratum of rock so old that it has metamorphosed, under great pressure and heat, from soft shale to a much harder stone. Called Vishnu schist, this layer is the oldest rock in the Grand Canyon and dates from 2 billion years ago.

The Grand Canyon & Northern Arizona

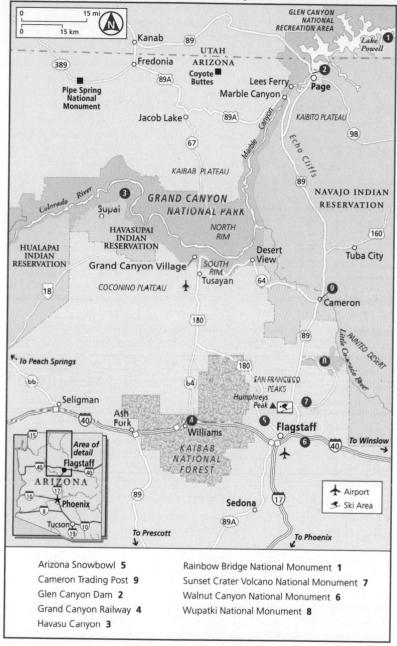

Arizona Snowbowl **5**
Cameron Trading Post **9**
Glen Canyon Dam **2**
Grand Canyon Railway **4**
Havasu Canyon **3**

Rainbow Bridge National Monument **1**
Sunset Crater Volcano National Monument **7**
Walnut Canyon National Monument **6**
Wupatki National Monument **8**

In the more recent past, the Grand Canyon has been home to several Native American cultures, including the Ancestral Puebloans (Anasazi), who are best known for their cliff dwellings in the Four Corners region. About 150 years after the Ancestral Puebloans and Coconino peoples abandoned the canyon in the 13th century, another tribe, the Cerbat, moved into the area. Today, the Hualapai and Havasupai tribes, descendants of the Cerbat people, still live in and near the Grand Canyon on the south side of the Colorado River. On the North Rim lived the Southern Paiute, and in the east, the Navajo.

However, there have been those in the recent past who regarded the canyon as mere wasted space, suitable only for filling with water. Upstream of the Grand Canyon stands Glen Canyon Dam, which forms Lake Powell, while downstream lies Lake Mead, created by Hoover Dam. The same thing could have happened to the Grand Canyon, but luckily the forces for preservation prevailed. Today, the Grand Canyon is the last major undammed stretch of the Colorado River.

All this popularity has taken its toll; with roughly four million people visiting the park each year, traffic during the summer months has become almost as bad at the South Rim as it is during rush hour in any major city, and finding a parking space is a challenge. But don't let these inconveniences dissuade you from visiting. Despite the crowds, the Grand Canyon still more than lives up to its name and is one of the most memorable sights on earth.

ESSENTIALS
GETTING THERE
BY CAR   The South Rim of the Grand Canyon is 60 miles north of Williams and I-40 on Arizona 64 and US 180. Flagstaff, the nearest city of any size, is 80 miles away. From Flagstaff, it's possible to take US 180 directly to the South Rim or US 89 to Arizona 64 and the east entrance to the park. This latter route is our preferred way of getting to the canyon since it sees slightly less traffic. Be sure you have plenty of gasoline in your car before setting out for the canyon; there are few service stations in this remote part of the state and what gas stations there are charge exorbitant prices.

Long waits at the entrance gates, parking problems, and traffic congestion have become the norm at the canyon during the popular summer months, and even during the spring and fall there can be backups at the entrance gates and visitors can have a hard time finding a parking space. However, in 2007, extra ticketing lanes were added at the south entrance to the park, and the park service was even experimenting with hand-held ticketing machines that help speed visitors on their way.

BY PLANE   The Grand Canyon Airport is in Tusayan, 6 miles south of Grand Canyon Village. **Scenic Airlines** (© **800/634-6801;** www.scenic.com) flies from the North Las Vegas Airport and charges $218 to $318 round-trip. Alternatively, you can fly into Flagstaff and then arrange another mode of transportation the rest of the way to the national park (see "Flagstaff," later in this chapter, for details).

BY TRAIN   The **Grand Canyon Railway** operates excursion trains between Williams and the South Rim of the Grand Canyon. See "Williams," later in this chapter, for details.

For long-distance connections, **Amtrak** (© **800/872-7245;** www.amtrak.com) provides service to Flagstaff and Williams. From Flagstaff, it's then possible to take a bus directly to Grand Canyon Village. From Williams, you can take the Grand Canyon Railway excursion train to Grand Canyon Village. *Note:* The Amtrak stop in Williams

Grand Canyon South Rim

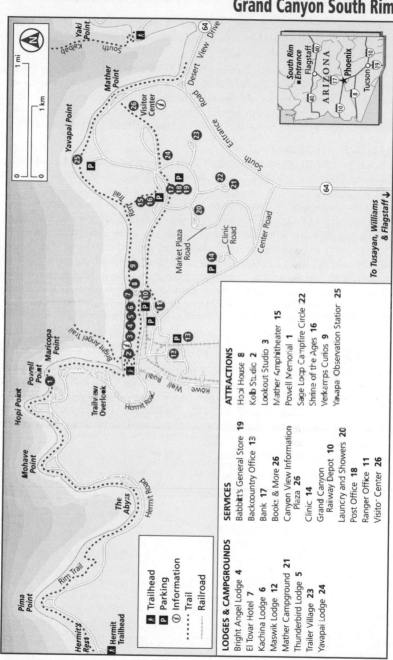

LODGES & CAMPGROUNDS
Bright Angel Lodge **4**
El Tovar Hotel **7**
Kachina Lodge **6**
Maswik Lodge **12**
Mather Campground **21**
Thunderbird Lodge **5**
Trailer Village **23**
Yavapai Lodge **24**

SERVICES
Babbitt's General Store **19**
Backcountry Office **13**
Bank **17**
Books & More **26**
Canyon View Information
Plaza **26**
Clinic **14**
Grand Canyon
Railway Depot **10**
Laundry and Showers **20**
Post Office **18**
Ranger Office **11**
Visitor Center **26**

ATTRACTIONS
Hopi House **8**
Kolb Studio **2**
Lookout Studio **3**
Mather Amphitheater **15**
Powell Memorial **1**
Sage Loop Campfire Circle **22**
Shrine of the Ages **16**
Verkamps Curios **9**
Yavapa Observation Station **25**

To Tusayan, Williams & Flagstaff

is undeveloped and is on the outskirts of town. If you plan to take an Amtrak train to Williams, a shuttle from the Grand Canyon Railway Hotel will pick you up where the Amtrak train drops you off.

BY BUS   Bus service between Phoenix, Flagstaff, Williams, and Grand Canyon Village is provided by **Open Road Tours** (© **800/766-7117** or 602/997-6474; www.openroad tours.com). Between Phoenix and Flagstaff, adult fares are $42 one-way and $76 round-trip ($30 and $52 for children); between Flagstaff and the Grand Canyon (by way of Williams), fares are $27 one-way and $54 round-trip ($19 and $38 for children).

VISITOR INFORMATION

You can get advance information on the Grand Canyon by contacting **Grand Canyon National Park,** P.O. Box 129, Grand Canyon, AZ 86023 (© **928/638-7888;** www. nps.gov/grca).

When you arrive at the park, stop by the **Canyon View Visitor Center,** at Canyon View Information Plaza, 6 miles from the south entrance. Here you'll find exhibits, an information desk, and a shop selling maps, books, and videos. The center is open daily 8am to 5pm. Unfortunately, the information plaza, which is well designed for handling large crowds, has no adjacent parking, so you'll have to park where you can and then walk or take a free shuttle bus. The nearest places to park are at Mather Point, Market Plaza, park headquarters, and Yavapai Observation Station. If you're parked anywhere in Grand Canyon Village, you'll want to catch the Village Route bus. If you park at Yaki Point, you can take the Kaibab Trail Route bus. *The Guide,* a small newspaper full of useful information about the park, is available at both South Rim park entrances.

ORIENTATION

Grand Canyon Village is built on the South Rim of the canyon and divided roughly into two sections. At the east end of the village are the Canyon View Information Plaza, Yavapai Lodge, Trailer Village, and Mather Campground. At the west end are El Tovar Hotel and Bright Angel, Kachina, Thunderbird, and Maswik lodges, as well as several restaurants, the train depot, and the trail head for the Bright Angel Trail.

FEES

The entry fee for Grand Canyon National Park is $25 per car (or $12 per person if you happen to be coming in on foot or by bicycle). Your admission ticket is good for 7 days (don't lose it, or you'll have to pay again).

GETTING AROUND

As mentioned earlier, the Grand Canyon Village area can be extremely congested, especially in summer. If possible, you may want to use one of the transportation options below to avoid the park's traffic jams and parking problems. To give you an idea, in summer you can expect at least a 20- to 30-minute wait at the South Rim entrance gate just to get into the park. You can cut the waiting time here by acquiring an America the Beautiful–National Parks & Federal Recreational Lands Pass, before arriving. These passes are available as an Annual Pass ($80), a lifetime Senior Pass (available to U.S. citizens and permanent residents 62 or older for $10), and a lifetime Access Pass (available free to U.S. citizens and permanent residents with permanent disabilities). With pass in hand, you can use the express lane.

For **accessibility information,** check *The Guide* for park programs, services, and facilities that are partially or fully accessible. You can also get *The Grand Canyon*

National Park Accessibility Guide at park entrances, Canyon View Center, Yavapai Observation Station, Kolb Studio, Tusayan Museum, and Desert View Information Center. Temporary accessibility permits are available at the park entrances, Canyon View Information Plaza, Yavapai Observation Station, Kolb Studio, El Tovar concierge desk, and Bright Angel Lodge transportation desk. The national park has wheelchairs available at no charge for temporary use inside the park. You can usually find one of these wheelchairs at the Canyon View Information Plaza. Wheelchair-accessible shuttle buses can be arranged a day in advance by calling the national park (© **928/638-0591**). Accessible tours can also be arranged by contacting any lodge transportation desk or by calling **Grand Canyon National Park Lodges** (© **928/638-2631**).

BY BUS   Free shuttle buses operate on four routes within the park. The **Village Route** bus circles through Grand Canyon Village throughout the day with frequent stops at the Canyon View Information Plaza, Market Plaza (site of a general store, bank, laundry, and showers), hotels, campgrounds, restaurants, and other facilities. The **Hermit's Rest Route** bus takes visitors to eight canyon overlooks west of Bright Angel Lodge (this bus does not operate Dec–Feb.). The **Kaibab Trail Route** bus stops at the Canyon View Information Plaza, Pipe Creek Vista, the South Kaibab trail head, and Yaki Point. This latter stop is the trail head for the South Kaibab Trail to the bottom of the canyon. The **Canyon View/Mather Point Route** is specifically for visitors who need mobility assistance and shuttles between the Mather Point parking lot and the Canyon View Information Center. There's also a Hikers' Express bus to Yaki Point. This bus stops at Bright Angel Lodge and the Back Country Information Office. Hikers needing transportation to or from Yaki Point when the bus is not running can use a taxi (© **928/638-2822** or 928/638-2631, ext. 6563).

Between mid-May and mid-October, **Trans Canyon** (© **928/638-2820**) offers shuttle-bus service between the South Rim and the North Rim. The vans leave the South Rim at 1:30pm and arrive at the North Rim at 6pm. The return trip leaves the North Rim at 7am, arriving back at the South Rim at 11:30am. The fare is $70 one-way and $130 round-trip; reservations are required.

BY CAR   Service stations are outside the south entrance to the park in Tusayan, at Desert View near the east entrance (this station is seasonal), and east of the park at Cameron. Because of the long distances within the park and to towns outside the park, fill up before setting out on a drive. Gas at the canyon is very expensive.

If you want to avoid **parking** headaches, try using the lot in front of the Market Plaza (the general store), which is up a side road near Yavapai Lodge and the Canyon View Information Plaza. From this large parking area, a paved hiking trail leads to the historic section of the village in less than 1.5 miles, and most of the route is along the rim. Another option is to park at the Maswik Transportation Center parking lot, which is served by the Village Route shuttle bus.

BY TAXI   Taxi service is available to and from the airport, trail heads, and other destinations (© **928/638-2822** or 928/638-2631, ext. 6563). The fare from the airport to Grand Canyon Village is $10 for up to two adults ($5 for each additional person).

FAST FACTS

There's an ATM at the **Chase** bank (© **928/638-2437**) at Market Plaza, which is near Yavapai Lodge. The bank is open Monday through Thursday from 9am to 5pm and Friday from 9am to 6pm.

The **North County Community Health Center** (© 928/638-2551) is on Clinic Drive, off Center Road (the road that runs past the National Park Service ranger office). The clinic is open daily from 8am to 6pm (shorter hours in winter). It provides 24-hour emergency service as well.

The **climate** at the Grand Canyon is dramatically different from that of Phoenix, and between the rim and the canyon floor there's also a pronounced difference. Winter temperatures at the South Rim can be below 0°F (-18°C) at night, with daytime highs in the 20s or 30s (minus single digits to single digits Celsius). Summer temperatures at the rim range from highs in the 80s (20s Celsius) to lows in the 50s (teens Celsius). The North Rim is slightly higher than the South Rim and stays a bit cooler. On the canyon floor, temperatures are considerably higher. In summer, the mercury can reach 120°F (49°C) with lows in the 70s (20s Celsius), while in winter, temperatures are quite pleasant with highs in the 50s (teens Celsius) and lows in the 30s (single digits Celsius).

DESERT VIEW DRIVE

The vast majority of visitors to the Grand Canyon enter through the south entrance, head straight for Grand Canyon Village, and proceed to get caught up in traffic jams. You can avoid much of this congestion and have a much more enjoyable experience if you enter the park through the east entrance. To reach the east entrance from Flagstaff, take US 89 to Arizona 64. Even before you reach the park, you can stop and take in views of the canyon of the Little Colorado River. These viewpoints are on the Navajo Reservation, and at every stop you'll have opportunities to shop for Native American crafts and souvenirs at the numerous vendors' stalls that can be found at virtually every scenic viewpoint on the Navajo Reservation.

Desert View Drive, the park's only scenic road open to cars year-round, extends for 25 miles from Desert View, which is just inside the park's east entrance, to Grand Canyon Village, the site of all the park's hotels and most of its other commercial establishments. Along Desert View Drive, you'll find not only good viewpoints, but several picnic areas. Much of this drive is through forests, and canyon views are limited, but where there are viewpoints, they are among the best in the park.

Desert View, with its trading post, general store, snack bar, service station, information center, bookstore, and historic watchtower, is the first stop on this scenic drive. From anywhere at Desert View, the scenery is breathtaking but the very best perspective here is from atop the **Desert View Watchtower.** Architect Mary Elizabeth Jane Colter, who is responsible for much of the park's historic architecture, designed it to resemble the prehistoric towers that dot the Southwestern landscape, but the tower actually dates from 1932. Built as an observation tower and rest stop for tourists, the watchtower incorporates Native American designs and art. The curio shop on the ground floor is a replica of a kiva (sacred ceremonial chamber) and has lots of interesting souvenirs, regional crafts, and books. The tower's second floor features work by Hopi artist Fred Kabotie. Covering the walls are pictographs incorporating traditional designs. On the walls and ceiling of the upper two floors are more traditional images by artist Fred Geary, this time reproductions of petroglyphs from throughout the Southwest. From the roof, which, at 7,522 feet above sea level, is the highest point on the South Rim, it's possible to see the Colorado River, the Painted Desert to the northeast, the San Francisco Peaks to the south, and Marble Canyon to the north. Several black-mirror "reflectoscopes" provide interesting darkened views of some of the most spectacular sections of the canyon. The gift shop offers a pamphlet describing the watchtower in detail.

At **Navajo Point,** the next stop along the rim, the Colorado River and Escalante Butte are both visible, and there's a good view of the Desert View Watchtower. However, we suggest heading straight to **Lipan Point** ✪✪, where you get what we think is the South Rim's best view of the Colorado River. You can actually see several stretches of the river, including a couple of major rapids. From here you can also view the Grand Canyon supergroup: several strata of rock tilted at an angle to the other layers of rock in the canyon. The red, white, and black rocks of the supergroup are composed of sedimentary rock and layers of lava.

The **Tusayan Museum** (daily 9am–5pm) is the next stop along Desert View Drive. This small museum is dedicated to the Hopi tribe and the Ancestral Puebloan people who inhabited the region 800 years ago; inside are artfully displayed exhibits on various aspects of Ancestral Puebloan life. Outside is a short self-guided trail through the ruins of an Ancestral Puebloan village. Free guided tours are available.

Next along the drive is **Moran Point,** from which you can see a bright-red layer of shale in the canyon walls. This point is named for 19th-century landscape painter Thomas Moran, who is known for his paintings of the Grand Canyon.

The next stop, **Grandview Point,** affords a view of Horseshoe Mesa, another interesting feature of the canyon landscape. The mesa was the site of the Last Chance Copper Mine in the early 1890s. Later that same decade, the Grandview Hotel was built and served canyon visitors until its close in 1908. The steep, unmaintained Grandview Trail leads down to Horseshoe Mesa from here. This trail makes a good less-traveled alternative to the South Kaibab Trail, although it is somewhat steeper.

The last stop along Desert View Drive is **Yaki Point,** which is no longer open to private vehicles. The park service would prefer it if you parked your car in Grand Canyon Village and took the Kaibab Trail Route shuttle bus from the Canyon View Information Plaza to Yaki Point. The reality is that people passing by in cars want to see what this viewpoint is all about and now park their cars alongside the main road and walk up the Yaki Point access road. The spectacular view from here encompasses a wide section of the central canyon. The large, flat-topped butte to the northeast is Wotan's Throne, one of the canyon's most readily recognizable features. Yaki Point is the site of the trail head for the South Kaibab Trail and consequently is frequented by hikers headed down to Phantom Ranch at the bottom of the canyon. The South Kaibab Trail is the preferred downhill hiking route to Phantom Ranch and is a more scenic route than the Bright Angel Trail. If you're planning a day hike into the canyon, this should be your number-one choice. Be sure to bring plenty of water.

GRAND CANYON VILLAGE & VICINITY

Grand Canyon Village is the first stop for the vast majority of the nearly four million people who visit the Grand Canyon every year (though we recommend coming in from the east entrance and avoiding the crowds). Consequently, it is the most crowded area in the park, but it also has the most overlooks and visitor services. Its many historic buildings add to the popularity of the village, which, if it weren't so crowded all the time, would have a pleasant atmosphere.

For visitors who have entered the park through the south entrance, that unforgettable initial gasp-inducing glimpse of the canyon comes at **Mather Point.** From this overlook, there's a short paved path to the Canyon View Information Plaza, but because you're allowed to park at Mather Point only for a maximum of 1 hour, you'll have to hurry if you want to take in the views and gather some park information.

Continuing west toward the village proper, you next come to **Yavapai Point,** which has the best view from anywhere in the vicinity of Grand Canyon Village. From here you can see the Bright Angel Trail, Indian Gardens, Phantom Ranch, and even the suspension bridge that hikers and mule riders use to cross the Colorado River near Phantom Ranch. Oh, yes, and of course you can also see the Colorado River. This viewpoint is a particularly great spot to take sunrise and sunset photos. Here you'll also find the historic **Yavapai Observation Station,** which houses a small museum and has big walls of glass to take in those extraordinary vistas. A paved pathway extends west from Yavapai Point for 3 miles, passing through Grand Canyon Village along the way. This trail also continues 2.5 miles east to the Pipe Creek Vista.

Continuing west from Yavapai Point, you'll come to a parking lot at park headquarters and a side road that leads to parking at the Market Plaza, which is one of the closest parking lots to the Canyon View Information Plaza.

West of these parking areas is Grand Canyon Village proper, where a paved pathway leads along the rim providing lots of good (though crowded) spots for taking pictures. The village is also the site of such historic buildings as **El Tovar Hotel** and **Bright Angel Lodge,** both of which are worth brief visits to take in the lodge ambience of their lobbies. Inside Bright Angel Lodge you'll find the **Bright Angel History Room,** which has displays on Mary Elizabeth Jane Colter and the Harvey Girls. Be sure to check out this room's fireplace, which is designed with all the same geologic layers that appear in the canyon. Adjacent to El Tovar are two historic souvenir and curio shops. **Hopi House Gift Store and Art Gallery,** the first shop in the park, was built in 1905 to resemble a Hopi pueblo and to serve as a place for Hopi artisans to work and sell their crafts. Today, it's full of Hopi and Navajo arts and crafts, including expensive kachina dolls, rugs, jewelry, and pottery. The nearby **Verkamps Curios** originally opened in a tent in 1898, but John Verkamp soon went out of business. The store reopened in 1905 and ever since has been the main place to look for souvenirs and crafts. Just inside the door is a 535-pound meteorite. Both shops are open daily; hours vary seasonally.

To the west of Bright Angel Lodge, two buildings cling precariously to the rim of the canyon. These are the Kolb and Lookout studios, both of which are listed on the National Register of Historic Places. **Kolb Studio** is named for Ellsworth and Emory Kolb, two brothers who set up a photographic studio on the rim of the Grand Canyon in 1904. The construction of this studio generated one of the Grand Canyon's first controversies—over whether buildings should be allowed on the canyon rim. Because the Kolbs had friends in high places, their sprawling studio and movie theater remained. Emory Kolb lived here until his death in 1976, by which time the studio had been listed as a historic building. It now serves as a bookstore, while the auditorium houses special exhibits. **Lookout Studio,** built in 1914 from a design by Mary Elizabeth Jane Colter, was the Fred Harvey Company's answer to the Kolb brothers' studio and incorporates architectural styles of the Hopi and the Ancestral Puebloans. The use of native limestone and an uneven roofline allow the studio to blend in with the canyon walls and give it the look of an old ruin. It now houses a souvenir store and two lookouts. The Kolb and Lookout studios are open daily; hours vary seasonally.

HERMIT ROAD

Hermit Road leads 8 miles west from Grand Canyon Village to Hermit's Rest, and mile for mile, it has the greatest concentration of breathtaking viewpoints in the park. Because it is closed to private vehicles March through November, it is also one of the most pleasant places to do a little canyon viewing or easy hiking during the busiest times of year: no traffic jams, no parking problems, and plenty of free shuttle buses operating along the route. Westbound buses stop at eight overlooks (Trailview, Maricopa Point, Powell Point, Hopi Point, Mohave Point, The Abyss, Pima Point, and Hermit's Rest); eastbound buses stop only at Mohave and Hopi points. From December to February, you can drive your own vehicle along this road, but keep in mind that winters usually mean a lot of snow, and the road can sometimes be closed due to hazardous driving conditions.

Because you probably won't want to stop at every viewpoint along this route, here are some tips to help you get the most out of an excursion along Hermit Road. First of all, keep in mind that the earlier you catch a shuttle bus, the more likely you are to avoid the crowds (buses start 1 hr. before sunrise, so photographers can get good shots of the canyon in dawn light). Second, remember that the closer you are to Grand Canyon Village, the larger the crowds will be. So, head out early and get a couple of miles between you and the village before getting off the shuttle bus.

The first two stops are **Trailview Overlook** and **Maricopa Point,** both on the paved section of the Rim Trail and within 1½ miles of the village, thus usually pretty crowded. If you just want to do a short, easy walk on pavement, get out at Maricopa Point and walk back to the village. From either overlook, you have a view of the Bright Angel Trail winding down into the canyon from Grand Canyon Village. The trail, which leads to the bottom of the canyon, crosses the Tonto Plateau about 3,000 feet below the rim. This plateau is the site of Indian Garden, where there's a campground in a grove of cottonwood trees. Because the views from these two overlooks are not significantly different from those in the village, we suggest skipping these stops if you've already spent time gazing into the canyon from the village.

Powell Point, the third stop, is the site of a memorial to John Wesley Powell, who, in 1869 with a party of nine men, became the first person to navigate the Colorado River through the Grand Canyon. Visible at Powell Point are the remains of the Orphan Mine, a copper mine that began operation in 1893. The mine went out of business because transporting the copper to a city where it could be sold was too expensive. Uranium was discovered here in 1954, but in 1966 the mine was shut down, and the land became part of Grand Canyon National Park. Again, we recommend continuing on to the more spectacular vistas that lie ahead.

The next stop is **Hopi Point,** which is one of the three best stops along this route. From here you can see a long section of the Colorado River far below you. Because of the great distance, the river seems to be a tiny, quiet stream, but in reality the section you see is more than 100 yards wide and races through Granite Rapids. Because Hopi Point juts into the canyon, it is one of the best spots in the park for taking sunrise and sunset photos; shuttle buses operate from 1 hour before sunrise to 1 hour after sunset.

The view is even more spectacular at the next stop, **Mohave Point.** Here you can see the river in two directions. Three rapids are visible from this overlook, and on a quiet day, you can sometimes even hear Hermit Rapids. As with almost all rapids in the canyon, Hermit Rapids are at the mouth of a side canyon where boulders loosened by storms and carried by flooded streams are deposited in the Colorado River. Don't miss this stop; it's got the best view on Hermit Road.

Next you come to **The Abyss,** the appropriately named 3,000-foot drop created by the Great Mojave Wall. This vertiginous view is one of the most awe-inspiring in the park. The walls of The Abyss are red sandstone that's more resistant to erosion than the softer shale in the layer below. Other layers of erosion-resistant sandstone have formed the free-standing pillars that are visible from here. The largest of these pillars is called the Monument. If you're looking for a good hike along this road, get out here and walk westward to either Pima Point (3 miles distant) or Hermit's Rest (4 miles away).

The **Pima Point** overlook, because it is set back from the road, is another good place to get off the bus. From here, the Rim Trail leads through the forest near the canyon rim, providing good views undisturbed by traffic on Hermit Road. From this overlook, it's also possible to see the remains of Hermit Camp on the Tonto Plateau. Built by the Santa Fe Railroad, Hermit Camp was a popular tourist destination between 1911 and 1930 and provided cabins and tents. Only foundations remain.

The final stop on Hermit Road is at **Hermit's Rest,** which was named for Louis Boucher, a prospector who came to the canyon in the 1890s and was known as the Hermit. The log-and-stone Hermit's Rest building, designed by Mary Elizabeth Jane Colter and built in 1914, is on the National Register of Historic Places and is one of the most fascinating structures in the park. With its snack bar, it makes a great place to linger while you soak up a bit of park history. The steep Hermit Trail, which leads down into the canyon, begins just past Hermit's Rest.

HIKING THE CANYON

No visit to the canyon is complete without journeying below the rim on one of the park's hiking trails. Gazing up at all those thousands of feet of vertical rock walls provides a very different perspective than that from atop the rim. Should you venture far below the rim, you also stand a chance of seeing fossils, old mines, petroglyphs, wildflowers, and wildlife. However, because of the Grand Canyon's popularity, the park's main hiking trails are usually crowded.

That said, there is no better way to see the canyon than on foot (our apologies to the mules), and a hike down into the canyon will likely be the highlight of your visit. The Grand Canyon offers some of the most rugged and strenuous hiking anywhere in the United States, and for this reason anyone attempting even a short walk should be well prepared. Each year, injuries and fatalities are suffered by day hikers who set out without sturdy footgear or without food and adequate amounts of water. Even a 30-minute hike in summer can dehydrate you, and a long hike in the heat can necessitate drinking more than a gallon of water. So, carry and drink at least 2 quarts (2 liters) of water if you go for a day hike during the summer. Don't attempt to hike from the rim to the Colorado River and back in a day; there are plenty of hikers who have tried this and died. Also remember that mules have the right of way.

DAY HIKES

There are no loop trails on the South Rim, but the vastly different scenery in every direction makes out-and-back hikes here as interesting as any loop trail could be. The only problem is that instead of starting out by slogging up a steep mountain, you let gravity assist you in hiking down into the canyon. With little negative reinforcement and few natural turnaround destinations, it is easy to hike so far that the return trip back up the trail becomes an arduous death march. Turn around *before* you become tired. On the canyon rim, the only hiking trail is the Rim Trail, while the Bright Angel, South Kaibab, Grandview, and Hermit trails all head down into the canyon.

For an easy, flat hike, your only option is the **Rim Trail,** which stretches from Pipe Creek Vista east of Grand Canyon Village to Hermit's Rest, 8 miles west of the village. Around 5 miles of this trail are paved, and the portion that passes through Grand

Canyon Village is always the most crowded stretch of trail in the park. To the west of the village, after the pavement ends, the Rim Trail leads another 6.75 miles out to Hermit's Rest. For most of this distance, the trail follows Hermit Road, which means you'll have to deal with traffic noise (mostly from shuttle buses). To get the most enjoyment out of a hike along this stretch, head out as early in the morning as possible (to avoid the crowds) and get off at The Abyss shuttle stop. From here it's a 4-mile hike to Hermit's Rest; for more than half of this distance, the trail isn't as close to the road as it is at the Grand Canyon Village end of the route. Plus, Hermit's Rest makes a great place to rest, and from here you can catch a shuttle bus back to the village. Alternatively, you could start hiking from Grand Canyon Village (it's just more than 8 miles from the west end of the village to Hermit's Rest) or any of the seven shuttle-bus stops en route, or take the shuttle all the way to Hermit's Rest and then hike back.

The **Bright Angel Trail,** which starts just west of Bright Angel Lodge in Grand Canyon Village, is the most popular trail into the canyon because it starts right where the greatest number of park visitors tend to congregate (near the ice-cream parlor and the hotels). It is also the route used by mule riders headed down into the canyon. Bear in mind that this trail follows a narrow side canyon for several miles down into the Grand Canyon and thus has somewhat limited views. For these reasons, this trail is worth avoiding if you're on foot. On the other hand, it's the only maintained trail into the canyon that has potable water, and there are four destinations along the trail that make good turnaround points. Both 1½ Mile Resthouse (1,131 ft. below the rim) and 3 Mile Resthouse (2,112 ft. below the rim) have water (except in winter, when the water is turned off). Keep in mind that these rest houses take their names from their distance from the rim; if you hike to 3 Mile Resthouse, you still have a 3-mile hike back up. Destinations for longer day hikes include Indian Garden (9 miles round-trip) and Plateau Point (12 miles round-trip), which are both just more than 3,000 feet below the rim. There is year-round water at Indian Garden.

The **South Kaibab Trail** ☆☆☆ begins near Yaki Point east of Grand Canyon Village and is the preferred route down to Phantom Ranch. This trail also offers the best views of any of the day hikes into the canyon, so should you have time for only one day hike, make it this trail. From the trail head, it's 3 miles round-trip to Cedar Ridge and 6 miles round-trip to Skeleton Point. The hike is very strenuous, and no water is available along the trail.

If you're looking to escape the crowds and are an experienced mountain or desert hiker with good, sturdy boots, consider the unmaintained **Hermit Trail,** which begins at Hermit's Rest, 8 miles west of Grand Canyon Village at the end of Hermit Road. It's a 5-mile round-trip hike to Santa Maria Spring on a trail that loses almost all of its elevation (1,600–1,700 ft.) in the first 1.5 miles. Beyond Santa Maria Spring, the Hermit Trail descends to the Colorado River, but it is a 17-mile hike, one-way, from the trail head. Alternatively, you can do a 7-mile round-trip hike to Dripping Springs. Water from either of these two springs must be treated with a water filter, iodine, or purification tablets, or by boiling for at least 10 minutes, so you're better off just carrying sufficient water for your hike. Hermit Road is closed to private vehicles from March to November, so chances are, you'll need to take the free shuttle bus out to the trail head. If you take the first bus of the day, you'll probably have the trail almost all to yourself.

The **Grandview Trail,** which begins at Grandview Point 12 miles east of Grand Canyon Village, is another steep and unmaintained trail that's a good choice for physically fit hikers. A strenuous 6-mile round-trip hike leads down to Horseshoe Mesa,

2,600 feet below the rim-top trail head. No water is available, so carry at least 2 quarts. Allow at least 7 hours for this rugged hike. Just to give you an idea of how steep this trail is, you'll lose more than 2,000 feet of elevation in the first .75 mile down to Coconino Saddle.

BACKPACKING

Backpacking the Grand Canyon is an unforgettable experience. Although most people are content to simply hike down to Phantom Ranch and back, there are many miles of trails deep in the canyon. Keep in mind, however, that to backpack the canyon, you'll need to do a lot of planning. A **Backcountry Use Permit** is required of all hikers planning to overnight in the canyon, unless you'll be staying at Phantom Ranch in one of the cabins or a dormitory.

Because a limited number of hikers are allowed into the canyon on any given day, it's important to make reservations as soon as it is possible to do so. Reservations are taken in person, by mail, by fax (but not by phone), and online. Contact the **Backcountry Information Center,** Grand Canyon National Park, P.O. Box 129, Grand Canyon, AZ 86023 (© **928/638-7875** Mon–Fri 1–5pm for information; fax 928/638-2125; www.nps.gov/grca). The office begins accepting reservations on the first of every month for the following 5 months. Holiday periods are the most popular—if you want to hike over the Labor Day weekend, be sure you make your reservation on May 1. If you show up without a reservation, go to the Backcountry Information Center (daily 8am–noon and 1–5pm), adjacent to the Maswik Lodge, and put your name on the waiting list. When applying for a permit, you must specify your exact itinerary, and once in the canyon, you must stick to this itinerary. Backpacking fees include a nonrefundable $10 backcountry permit fee and a $5 per-person per-night backcountry camping fee. American Express, Diners Club, Discover, MasterCard, and Visa are accepted for permit fees. Keep in mind that you'll still have to pay the park entry fee when you arrive at the Grand Canyon.

There are **campgrounds** at Indian Garden, Bright Angel Campground (near Phantom Ranch), and Cottonwood, but hikers are limited to 2 nights per trip at each of these campgrounds (except Nov 15–Feb 28, when 4 nights are allowed at each campground). Other nights can be spent camping at undesignated sites in certain regions of the park.

The *Backcountry Trip Planner* contains information to help you plan your itinerary. It's available through the Backcountry Information Center (see contact information, above). Maps are available through the **Grand Canyon Association,** P.O. Box 399, Grand Canyon, AZ 86023 (© **800/858-2808** or 928/638-2481; www.grandcanyon. org), and at bookstores and gift shops within the national park, including Canyon View Information Plaza, Kolb Studio, Desert View Information Center, Yavapai Observation Station, Tusayan Museum, and, on the North Rim, Grand Canyon Lodge.

The best times of year to backpack are spring and fall. In summer, temperatures at the bottom of the canyon are frequently above 100°F (38°C), while in winter, ice and snow at higher elevations make footing on trails precarious (crampons are recommended). Plan to carry at least 2 quarts, and preferably 1 gallon, of water whenever backpacking in the canyon.

The Grand Canyon is an unforgiving landscape and, as such, many people might want a professional guide while backpacking through this rugged corner of the Southwest. To arrange a guided backpacking trip into the canyon, contact **Discovery Treks,** 28248 N. Tatum Blvd. Suite B1-414, Cave Creek, AZ 85331 (© **888/256-8731** or

480/247-9266; www.discoverytreks.com), which offers 3- to 5-day all-inclusive hikes into the canyon with rates ranging from $975 to $1,395 per person.

OTHER WAYS OF SEEING THE CANYON
BUS TOURS
If you'd rather leave the driving to someone else and enjoy more of the scenery, opt for a bus or van tour of one or more sections of the park. **Grand Canyon National Park Lodges** (© 928/638-2631; www.grandcanyonlodges.com) offers several tours within the park. These can be booked by calling or stopping at one of the transportation desks, which are at Bright Angel, Maswik, and Yavapai lodges (see "Where to Stay," below). Prices range from around $15 for a 1½-hour sunrise or sunset tour to around $40 for a combination tour to both Hermit's Rest and Desert View.

MULE RIDES 𝄢
Mule rides into the canyon have been popular since the beginning of the 20th century, when the Bright Angel Trail was a toll road. After having a look at the steep drop-offs and narrow path of the Bright Angel Trail, you might decide this isn't exactly the place to trust your life to a mule. Never fear: Wranglers will be quick to reassure you they haven't lost a rider yet. Trips of various lengths and to different destinations are offered. The 1-day trip descends to Plateau Point, where there's a view of the Colorado River 1,300 feet below. This grueling trip requires riders to spend 6 hours in the saddle. Those who want to spend a night down in the canyon can choose an overnight trip to Phantom Ranch, where cabins and dormitories are available at the only lodge actually in the canyon. From November to March, a 3-day trip to Phantom Ranch is offered; other times of year, you'll ride down one day and back up the next. Mule trips range in price from $148 for a 1-day ride to $401 for an overnight ride to $566 for the 2-night ride. Couples get discounts on overnight rides.

Riders must weigh less than 200 pounds fully dressed; stand at least 4 feet, 7 inches tall; and speak fluent English. Pregnant women are not allowed on mule trips.

Because these trail rides are very popular (especially in summer), they often book up 6 months or more in advance (reservations are taken up to 13 months in advance). For more information or to make a reservation, contact **Xanterra Parks & Resorts** (© 888/297-2757 or 303/297-2757; www.grandcanyonlodges.com). If at the last minute (5 days or fewer from the day you want to ride) you decide you want to go on a mule trip, contact **Grand Canyon National Park Lodges** at its Arizona phone number (© 928/638-2631) for the remote possibility that there may be space available. If you arrive at the canyon without a reservation and decide that you'd like to go on a mule ride, stop by the Bright Angel Transportation Desk to get your name put on the next day's waiting list.

THE GRAND CANYON RAILWAY 𝄢𝄢
In the early 20th century, most visitors to the Grand Canyon arrived by train, and it's still possible to travel to the canyon along the steel rails. The **Grand Canyon Railway** (© 800/843-8724 or 928/773-1976; www.thetrain.com), which runs from Williams to Grand Canyon Village, uses both 1950s-vintage diesel engines and, between Memorial Day and Labor Day, early-20th-century steam engines to pull 1920s and 1950s passenger cars. Trains depart from the Williams Depot, which is housed in the historic 1908 Fray Marcos Hotel and also contains a railroad museum, gift shop, and cafe. (Grand Canyon Railway also operates the adjacent Grand Canyon Railway Hotel.) At Grand Canyon Village, the trains use a 1910 log railway terminal.

Passengers have the choice of five classes of service: coach (which includes both Pullman and Budd cars), club class, first class, observation dome (upstairs in the dome car), and luxury parlor class. Actors posing as cowboys provide entertainment, including musical performances, aboard the train. The round-trip takes 8 hours, including a 3¼- to 3¾-hour layover at the canyon. Fares range from $65 to $170 for adults, $40 to $145 for children 11 to 16, and $30 to $95 for children 2 to 10 (not including tax or the park entry fee).

A BIRD'S-EYE VIEW

Despite controversies over noise and safety (there have been a few crashes over the years), airplane and helicopter flights over the Grand Canyon remain one of the most popular ways to see this natural wonder. If you want to join the crowds buzzing the canyon, you'll find several companies operating out of Grand Canyon Airport in Tusayan. Air tours last anywhere from 30 minutes to about 2 hours.

Companies offering tours by small plane include **Air Grand Canyon** (② 800/247-4726 or 928/638-2686; www.airgrandcanyon.com) and **Grand Canyon Airlines** (② 866/235-9422 or 928/638-2359; www.grandcanyonairlines.com). This latter company has been offering air tours since 1927 and is the oldest scenic airline at the canyon. Fifty-minute flights cost $99 to $119 for adults and $79 to $89 for children (including current $10 per person fuel surcharge).

Helicopter tours are available from **Maverick Airstar Helicopters** (② 888/261-4414 or 702/261-0007; www.airstar.com), **Grand Canyon Helicopters** (② 800/541-4537 or 928/638-2764; www.grandcanyonhelicoptersaz.com), and **Papillon Grand Canyon Helicopters** (② 800/528-2418 or 928/638-2419; www.papillon. com). Rates range from $145 to $175 for a 30-minute flight and from $205 to $235 for a 45- to 55-minute flight. Children sometimes receive a discount (usually around $20), and discounts can also be found on the various tour company websites.

THE GRAND CANYON FIELD INSTITUTE

If you're the active type or would like to turn your visit to the Grand Canyon into more of an educational experience, you may want to consider doing a trip with the **Grand Canyon Field Institute** (② 866/471-4435 or 928/638-2485; www.grand canyon.org/fieldinstitute). Cosponsored by Grand Canyon National Park and the Grand Canyon Association, the Field Institute schedules an amazing variety of guided, educational trips, such as challenging backpacking trips through the canyon (some for women only) and programs lasting anywhere from 1 to 18 days. Subjects covered include wilderness studies, geology, natural history, human history, photography, and art.

JEEP TOURS

If you'd like to explore parts of Grand Canyon National Park that most visitors never see, contact **Grand Canyon Jeep Tours & Safaris** (② 800/320-5337 or 928/638-5337; www.grandcanyonjeeptours.com), which offers three different tours that visit the park as well as the adjacent Kaibab National Forest. One tour stops at a lookout tower that affords an elevated view of the canyon, while another visits an Indian ruin and site of petroglyphs and cave paintings. Prices range from $45 to $104 for adults and $35 to $84 for children 12 and under.

RAFTING THE COLORADO RIVER ✦✦✦

Rafting down the Colorado River as it roars and tumbles through the mile-deep gorge of the Grand Canyon is the adventure of a lifetime. Ever since John Wesley Powell ignored everyone who knew better and proved that it was possible to travel by boat down the tumultuous Colorado, running the big river has become a passion and an obsession with adventurers. Today, anyone from grade-schoolers to grandmothers can join the elite group of people who have made the run. However, be prepared for some of the most furious white water in the world.

Most trips start from Lees Ferry near Page and Lake Powell. It's also possible to start (or finish) a trip at Phantom Ranch, hiking in or out from either the North or South Rim. The main rafting season is April through October, but some companies operate year-round. Rafting trips tend to book up more than a year in advance, and most companies begin taking reservations between March and May for the following year's trips. Expect to pay between $220 and $280 per day for your white-water adventure, depending on the length of the trip and the type of boat used.

The following are some of the companies we recommend checking out when you start planning your Grand Canyon rafting adventure:

- **Arizona Raft Adventures,** 4050 E. Huntington Rd., Flagstaff, AZ 86004 (© **800/ 786-7238;** www.azraft.com); 6- to 16-day motor, oar, and paddle trips. Although this is not one of the larger companies operating on the river, it offers lots of different trips, including those that focus on natural history and photography. They also do trips in paddle rafts that allow you to help navigate and provide the power while shooting the canyon's many rapids.

- **Canyoneers,** P.O. Box 2997, Flagstaff, AZ 86003 (© **800/525-0924** or 928/326-0924; www.canyoneers.com); 3- to 7-day motorized-raft trips and 5- to 14-day oar-powered trips. Way back in 1938, this was the first company to take paying customers down the Colorado, and Canyoneers is still one of the top companies on the river. In 2007, Canyoneers' oar-powered trips were accompanied by a restored 1947 Grand Canyon cataract boat.

- **Diamond River Adventures,** P.O. Box 1300, Page, AZ 86040 (© **800/343-3121** or 928/645-8866; www.diamondriver.com); 4- to 8-day motorized-raft trips and 5- to 13-day oar trips. This is the only women-owned and -managed rafting company operating in the Grand Canyon.

- **Grand Canyon Expeditions Company,** P.O. Box O, Kanab, UT 84741 (© **800/ 544-2691** or 435/644-2691; www.gcex.com); 8-day motorized trips and 14- and 16-day dory trips. If you've got the time, we highly recommend these dory trips as among the most thrilling adventures in the world.

- **Hatch River Expeditions,** HC 67 Box 35, Marble Canyon, AZ 86036 (© **800/ 856-8966;** www.hatchriverexpeditions.com); 4- and 7-day motorized trips. The 4-day trips involve hiking either into the canyon or out of the canyon. On the 7-day trip, a helicopter lifts you out of the canyon at the end of the trip. This company has been in business since 1929 and claims to be the oldest commercial rafting company in the U.S. With so much experience, you can count on Hatch to provide you with a great trip.

- **Outdoors Unlimited,** 6900 Townsend Winona Rd., Flagstaff, AZ 86004 (© **800/ 637-7238** or 928/526-4511; www.outdoorsunlimited.com); 5- to 13-day oar and paddle trips. This company has been taking people through the canyon for nearly 40 years and usually sends them home very happy.

- **Wilderness River Adventures,** P.O. Box 717, Page, AZ 86040 (© **800/992- 8022** or 928/645-3296; www.riveradventures.com); 4- to 8-day motorized-raft trips and 6-, 7-, 12-, and 14-day oar trips. The 4-day trips (actually 3½ days)

A Shopping Break

Outside the east entrance to the park, the Cameron Trading Post (© 800/338-7385 or 928/679-2231; www.camerontradingpost.com), at the crossroads of Cameron where Arizona 64 branches off US 89, is the best trading post in the state. The original stone trading post, a historic building, now houses a gallery of Indian artifacts, clothing, and jewelry. The main trading post is a more modern building. Don't miss the beautiful terraced gardens in back of the original trading post.

involve hiking out from Phantom Ranch. This is one of the bigger companies operating on the canyon, and it offers a wide variety of trips, which makes it a good one to check with if you're not sure which type of trip you want to do.

For information on 1-day rafting trips at the west end of the Grand Canyon, see "Havasu Canyon & Grand Canyon West," later in this chapter.

WHERE TO STAY

Hotel rooms both within and just outside the park are in high demand. Make reservations as far in advance as possible, and don't expect to find a room if you head up here in summer without a reservation. There, is, however, one long-shot option. See "Inside the Park," below, for details.

INSIDE THE PARK

All hotels inside the park are operated by **Xanterra Parks & Resorts.** Reservations are taken up to 13 months in advance, beginning on the first of the month. If you want to stay in one of the historic rim cabins at Bright Angel Lodge, reserve at least a year in advance. However, rooms with shared bathrooms at Bright Angel Lodge are often the last in the park to book up, and although they're small and very basic, they're your best bet if you're trying to get a last-minute reservation.

To make reservations at any of the in-park hotels listed below, contact **Grand Canyon National Park Lodges/Xanterra Parks & Resorts,** 6312 S. Fiddlers Green Circle, Suite 600N, Greenwood Village, CO 80111 (© **888/297-2757** or 303/297-2757; www.xanterra.com or www.grandcanyonlodges.com). It is sometimes possible, due to cancellations and no-shows, to get a same-day reservation; it's a long shot, but it happens. Same-day reservations can be made by calling © **928/638-2631.** Xanterra accepts American Express, Diners Club, Discover, MasterCard, and Visa. Children 16 and under stay for free in their parent's room.

Moderate

El Tovar Hotel 🏨🏨   El Tovar Hotel, which first opened its doors in 1905 and was completely renovated in 2005, is the park's premier lodge. Built of local rock and Oregon pine by Hopi craftsmen, it's a rustic yet luxurious mountain lodge that perches on the edge of the canyon (although with views from only a few rooms). The lobby, entered from a veranda set with rustic furniture, has a small fireplace, cathedral ceiling, and log walls on which moose, deer, and antelope heads are displayed. Although guest rooms are comfortable and attractively decorated, the standard units are rather small, as are the bathrooms. For more leg room, book a deluxe unit. Suites, with private terraces and stunning views, are extremely spacious. El Tovar Dining Room (see

"Where to Dine," below) is the best restaurant in the village. Just off the lobby is a cocktail lounge with a view.

78 units. $142–$205 double; $258–$322 suite. **Amenities:** Restaurant (Continental/Southwestern); lounge; concierge; tour desk; room service. In room: A/C, TV, dataport, fridge, hair dryer, iron, safe.

Thunderbird & Kachina Lodges   If you want great views, these hotels are your best bets—but only if you get a room with a view. These two side-by-side hotels date from the 1960s and, with their dated styling, are a far cry from what you might imagine a national park hotel would look like. They do, however, have a couple of things going for them. They have the biggest windows of any of the four hotels right on the canyon rim, and major renovations a few years ago extensively modernized them. Try to get a second-story room on the canyon side of either hotel (these rooms at the Kachina Lodge get the nod for having *the* best views). Book early—these two lodges are some of the park's most popular accommodations. Just remember, if it's not a view room, you'll be staring at the parking lot. Unfortunately, when making reservations, you cannot request a view room. Good luck.

104 units. $139–$152 double. In room: TV, dataport, fridge, coffeemaker, hair dryer, iron, safe.

Inexpensive

Bright Angel Lodge & Cabins ✿   Bright Angel Lodge, which began operation in 1896 as a collection of tents and cabins on the edge of the canyon, is the most affordable lodge in the park, and, with its flagstone floor lobby and huge fireplace, it has a genuine, if crowded, mountain-lodge atmosphere. It offers the greatest variety of accommodations in the park. The best and most popular units are the rim cabins, which should be booked a year in advance for summer. Outside the winter months, other rooms should be booked at least 6 months in advance. Most of the rooms and cabins feature rustic furnishings. The Buckey Suite, the oldest structure on the canyon rim, is arguably the best room in the park, with a canyon view, gas fireplace, and king-size bed. The tour desk, fireplace, museum, and restrooms account for the constant crowds in the lobby. This lodge was completely renovated in 2007.

86 units, 20 w/shared bathrooms. $52 double w/sink only; $58 double w/sink and toilet; $70–$143 double w/private bathroom; $92–$239 cabin. **Amenities:** 2 restaurants (American, steakhouse/Southwestern); lounge; ice-cream parlor; tour desk. In room: No phone.

Maswik Lodge   Set back ¼ mile or so from the rim, the Maswik Lodge offers spacious rooms and cabins that have been comfortably modernized without losing their appealing rustic character. If you don't mind roughing it a bit, the 28 old cabins, which are available only in summer, have lots of character. These cabins have high ceilings and ceiling fans, and are our top choice away from the rim. If you crave modern appointments, lots of space, and predictably comfortable air-conditioned accommodations, opt for one of the large Maswik North rooms, all of which were renovated in 2006. Second-floor rooms have high ceilings and balconies, which makes them your other best bet away from the rim.

278 units. $77–$138 double (winter discounts available); $77 cabin. **Amenities:** Cafeteria; lounge; tour desk. In room: A/C, TV, fridge, coffeemaker, safe.

Phantom Ranch ✿   Built in 1922, Phantom Ranch is the only lodge at the bottom of the Grand Canyon and has a classic ranch atmosphere. Accommodations are in rustic stone-walled cabins or 10-bed gender-segregated dormitories. Evaporative coolers keep both the cabins and the dorms cool in summer. Make reservations as early as possible, and don't forget to reconfirm. It's also sometimes possible to get a room on the day of departure if there are any last-minute cancellations. To attempt this, you must put your name on the waiting list at the Bright Angel Lodge transportation desk the day before you want to stay at Phantom Ranch.

Family-style meals must be reserved in advance. The menu consists of beef-and-vegetable stew ($23), a vegetarian dinner ($23), and steak ($36). Breakfasts ($18) are hearty, and sack lunches ($10) are available as well. Between meals, the dining hall becomes a canteen selling snacks, drinks, gifts, and necessities. After dinner, it serves as a beer hall. There's a public phone here, and mule-back duffel transfer ($61) between Grand Canyon Village and Phantom Ranch can be arranged.

℃ **928/638-3283** for reconfirmations. 11 cabins, 40 dorm beds. $93 double in cabin; $34 dormitory bed. Mule-trip overnights (w/all meals and mule ride included) $369 for 1 person, $661 for 2 people. 2-night trips available Nov–Mar. **Amenities:** Restaurant (American); lounge. *In room:* No phone.

Yavapai Lodge   Located in several buildings at the east end of Grand Canyon Village (a 1-mile hike from the main section of the village, but convenient to the Canyon View Information Plaza), the Yavapai is the largest lodge in the park and thus is where you'll likely wind up if you wait too long to make a reservation. Unfortunately, it's also the least-appealing hotel in the park. There are no canyon views, which is why Yavapai is less expensive than the Thunderbird and Kachina lodges. If you must stay here, try for a room in the nicer Yavapai East wing, which is set under shady pines. Rooms in this wing have air-conditioning. However, we recommend that you plan ahead and try to stay at one of the lodges right on the rim.

358 units. $97–$126 double; $76–$89 double in winter. **Amenities:** Cafeteria; tour desk. *In room:* TV.

IN TUSAYAN (OUTSIDE THE SOUTH ENTRANCE)

If you can't get a reservation for a room in the park, this is the next closest place to stay. Unfortunately, this area can be very noisy because of the many helicopters and airplanes taking off from the airport. Also, hotels outside the park are very popular with tour groups, which during the busy summer months keep many hotels full. All of the hotels listed here are lined up along US 180/Arizona 64.

Best Western Grand Canyon Squire Inn ⭐⭐ *Kids*   If you prefer playing tennis to riding a mule, this may be the place for you. Of all the hotels in Tusayan, this one has the most resortlike feel due to its restaurants, lounges, and extensive recreational amenities. With so much to offer, it almost seems as if the hotel were trying to distract guests from the canyon itself. But even if you don't bowl or play tennis, you'll likely appreciate the large guest rooms with comfortable easy chairs and big windows. In the lobby, which is more Las Vegas glitz than mountain rustic, cases are filled with old cowboy paraphernalia. Down in the basement are an impressive Western sculpture, a waterfall wall, and even a bowling alley.

Ariz. 64 (P.O. Box 130), Grand Canyon, AZ 86023. ℃ **800/622-6966** or 928/638-2681. Fax 928/638-2782. www. grandcanyonsquire.com. 250 units. Mid-Mar to mid-Oct and late Nov to Dec $105–$195 double; mid-Oct to late Nov and Jan to mid-Mar $75–$155 double. Children 12 and under stay free in parent's room. AE, DC, DISC, MC, V. **Amenities:** 2 restaurants (Continental, American); 2 lounges; seasonal outdoor pool; 2 tennis courts; exercise room; Jacuzzi; sauna; game room; concierge; coin-op laundry. *In room:* A/C, TV, dataport, coffeemaker, hair dryer, iron, Wi-Fi, free local calls.

Grand Hotel ⭐⭐   With its mountain lodge–style lobby, this modern hotel lives up to its name and is your best bet outside the park. There's a flagstone fireplace, log-beam ceiling, and fake ponderosa-pine tree trunks holding up the roof. Just off the lobby are a dining room (with evening entertainment ranging from Native American dancers to country-music bands), a small bar that even has a few saddles for bar stools, and an espresso stand. Guest rooms are spacious, with a few Western touches, and some have small balconies.

Ariz. 64 (P.O. Box 3319), Grand Canyon, AZ 86023. © **888/634-7263** or 928/638-3333. Fax 928/638-3131. www. grandcanyongrandhotel.com. 121 units. $99–$223 double. Children 17 and under stay free in parent's room. AE, DISC, MC, V. **Amenities:** Restaurant (American/Southwestern); lounge; indoor pool; exercise room; Jacuzzi; concierge; coin-op laundry. *In room:* A/C, TV, dataport, coffeemaker, hair dryer.

Holiday Inn Express–Grand Canyon Hotel This hotel has modern, well-designed— if a bit sterile and characterless—guest rooms. The Holiday Inn Express also manages an adjacent 32-suite property whose rooms have a Western theme. Although these suites are fairly pricey, they're among the nicest accommodations inside or outside the park.

Ariz. 64 (P.O. Box 3245), Grand Canyon, AZ 86023. © **888/473-2269** or 928/638-3000. Fax 928/638-0123. www. grandcanyon.hiexpress.com. 194 units. $69–$162 double; $89–$250 suite. Rates include continental breakfast. Children under 18 stay free in parent's room. AE, DC, DISC, MC, V. **Amenities:** Indoor pool; Jacuzzi. *In room:* A/C, TV, dataport, hair dryer, iron, high-speed Internet access.

Quality Inn & Suites Canyon Plaza ✻ The setting behind the IMAX theater and surrounded by parking lots is none too pretty, but guest rooms are relatively luxurious and the hotel is built around two enclosed skylit courtyards, one of which houses a restaurant and the other a bar and whirlpool. Guest rooms are large and comfortable, with balconies or patios; most also have minibars. The suites contain separate small living rooms, microwaves, and fridges. The hotel is very popular with tour groups.

P.O. Box 520, Grand Canyon, AZ 86023. © **800/221-2222** or 928/638-2673. Fax 928/638-9537. www.grandcanyon qualityinn.com. 232 units. Mid-Mar to Oct $180 double, $240 suite; Nov to mid-Mar $100–$170 double, $160–$240 suite. Rates include continental breakfast. Children 18 and under stay free in parent's room. AE, DC, DISC, MC, V. **Amenities:** Restaurant (American); lounge; outdoor pool; 2 Jacuzzis. *In room:* A/C, TV, dataport, coffeemaker, hair dryer, high-speed Internet access.

Red Feather Lodge ✻*Kids* With more than 200 units, this motel is often slow to fill up, so it's a good choice for last-minute bookings. Try to get one of the newer rooms, which are a bit more comfortable than the older ones. The pool here makes this place a good bet for families.

Ariz. 64 (P.O. Box 1460), Grand Canyon, AZ 86023. © **800/538-2345** or 928/638-2414. Fax 928/638-2707. www. redfeatherlodge.com. 215 units. $80–$135 double. Rates include continental breakfast. Children under 18 stay free in parent's room. AE, DC, DISC, MC, V. Pets accepted ($50 deposit plus $10 per night). **Amenities:** Restaurant (American); seasonal outdoor pool; Jacuzzi. *In room:* A/C, TV, dataport, coffeemaker, hair dryer.

OTHER AREA ACCOMMODATIONS

Cameron Trading Post Motel ✻✻ *Finds* Located 54 miles north of Flagstaff on US 89 at the junction with the road to the east entrance of the national park, this motel offers some of the most attractive rooms in the vicinity of the Grand Canyon and is part of one of the best trading posts in the state. The motel, adjacent to the historic Cameron Trading Post, is built around the shady oasis of the old trading post's terraced gardens. The garden terraces are built of sandstone, and there's even a picnic table made from a huge slab of stone. Guest rooms feature Southwestern-style furniture and attractive decor. Most have balconies, and some have views of the Little Colorado River (which, however, rarely has much water in it at this point). Don't miss the Navajo tacos in the dining room; the small ones are plenty big enough for a meal.

P.O. Box 339, Cameron, AZ 86020. ℂ 800/338-7385 or 928/679-2231. Fax 928/679-2501. www.camerontrading post.com. 62 units. Jan–Feb $59–$69 double, $99–$129 suite; Mar–May $79–$89 double, $129–$159 suite; June to mid-Oct $99–$109 double, $149–$179 suite; mid-Oct to Dec $69–$79 double, $129–$159 suite. AE, DISC, MC, V. Pets accepted ($15 fee). **Amenities:** Restaurant. *In room:* A/C, TV, coffeemaker.

CAMPING
Inside the Park

On the South Rim, there are two campgrounds and an RV park. **Mather Campground,** in Grand Canyon Village, has more than 300 campsites. Reservations can be made up to 6 months in advance and are highly recommended for stays between March and mid-November (reservations not accepted for other months). Contact the National Park Service Reservation Center (ℂ **877/444-6777** or 518/885-3639; www.recreation.gov). Between late spring and early fall, don't even think of coming up here without a reservation; you'll just set yourself up for disappointment. If you don't have a reservation, your next best bet is to arrive in the morning, when sites are being vacated. Campsites are $18 per night ($15 per night mid-Nov to Feb; reservations not accepted).

Desert View Campground, with 50 sites, is 25 miles east of Grand Canyon Village and open from mid-May to mid-October only. No reservations are accepted. Campsites are $12 per night.

The **Trailer Village RV park,** with 84 RV sites, is in Grand Canyon Village and charges $27 per night (for two adults) for full hookup. Reservations can be made up to 13 months in advance by contacting **Grand Canyon National Park Lodges/ Xanterra Parks & Resorts,** 6312 S. Fiddlers Green Circle, Suite 600N, Greenwood Village, CO 80111 (ℂ **888/297-2757** or 303/297-2757; www.xanterra.com or www. grandcanyonlodges.com). For same-day reservations, call ℂ **928/638-2631.**

Outside the Park

Two miles south of Tusayan is the U.S. Forest Service's **Ten-X Campground.** This campground has 70 campsites, is open May through September, and charges $10. It's usually your best bet for finding a site late in the day. This campground is open May through October, depending on the weather.

You can also camp just about anywhere within the **Kaibab National Forest,** which borders Grand Canyon National Park, as long as you are more than a quarter-mile away from Arizona 64/US 180. Several dirt roads lead into the forest from the highway, and although you won't find designated campsites or toilets along these roads, you will find spots where others have obviously camped before. This so-called dispersed camping is usually used by campers who have been unable to find sites in campgrounds. One of the most popular roads for this sort of camping is on the west side of the highway between Tusayan and the park's south entrance. For more information, contact the **Tusayan Ranger District,** Kaibab National Forest, P.O. Box 3088, Grand Canyon, AZ 86023 (ℂ **928/638-2443;** www.fs.fed.us/r3/kai).

WHERE TO DINE
INSIDE THE PARK

If you're looking for a quick, inexpensive meal, there are plenty of options. In Grand Canyon Village, choices include **cafeterias** at the Yavapai and Maswik lodges and a **delicatessen** at Canyon Village Marketplace on Market Plaza. The **Bright Angel Fountain,** at the back of the Bright Angel Lodge, serves hot dogs, sandwiches, and ice cream and is always crowded on hot days. Our favorite place in the park to grab a quick bite is the **Hermit's Rest Snack Bar** at the west end of Hermit Road. The stone building that houses this snack bar was designed by Mary Elizabeth Jane Colter, who also designed several other buildings on the South Rim. At Desert View (near the east entrance to the park), there's the **Desert View Trading Post Cafeteria.** All of these places are open daily for all three meals, and all serve meals for $10 and under.

The Arizona Room SOUTHWESTERN   Because this restaurant has the best view of the three dining establishments right on the South Rim, it is immensely popular. Add to this the fact that The Arizona Room has a menu (pan-seared salmon with melon salsa, baby back ribs with prickly pear or chipotle glaze) almost as creative as that of El Tovar Dining Room, and you'll understand why there is often a long wait for a table here. To avoid the wait, arrive early, which should assure you of getting a table with a good view out the picture windows. Once the sun goes down, the view is absolutely black, which means you could be dining anywhere. Because this restaurant is open for lunch part of the year, you've got another option for dining with a billion-dollar view.

At the Bright Angel Lodge. (𝄫 **928/638-2631.** Reservations not accepted. Main courses $7.75–$12 lunch, $11–$26 dinner. AE, DC, DISC, MC, V. Daily 4:30–10pm (Mar–Oct also open for lunch daily 11:30am–3pm). Closed Jan–Feb.

Bright Angel Coffee Shop AMERICAN   As the least expensive of the three restaurants right on the rim of the canyon, this casual Southwestern-themed coffee-house in the historic Bright Angel Lodge stays packed throughout the day. Meals are simple and none too memorable, but if you can get one of the few tables near the windows, at least you get something of a view. The menu includes everything from burgers to Southwestern favorites such as tamales and fajitas to spaghetti (foods calculated to comfort tired and hungry hikers), but our favorite offerings are the bread bowls full of chili and stew. Wines are available, and service is generally efficient.

At the Bright Angel Lodge. (𝄫 **928/638-2631.** Reservations not accepted. Main courses $7–$16. AE, DC, DISC, MC, V. Daily 6:30–10pm.

El Tovar Dining Room ꩜꩜ CONTINENTAL/SOUTHWESTERN   If you're staying at El Tovar, you'll want to have dinner in the hotel's rustic yet elegant dining room. But before making reservations at the most expensive restaurant in the park, be aware that few tables have views of the canyon. However, despite the limited views, the meals served here are the best in the park. The menu leans heavily to the spicy flavors of the Southwest, though plenty of milder, more familiar dishes are offered as well. The New York steak with crispy onion rings is a good bet, as is the wild salmon. Start your meal with the interesting little roulades (flavorful bite-size tortilla roll-ups). Service is generally quite good. Have a drink in the bar before dinner.

At El Tovar Hotel. (𝄫 **928/638-2631,** ext. 6432. Reservations highly recommended for dinner. Main courses $10–$15 lunch, $19–$30 dinner. AE, DC, DISC, MC, V. Daily 6:30–11am, 11:30am–2pm, and 5–10pm.

IN TUSAYAN (OUTSIDE THE SOUTH ENTRANCE)

In addition to the restaurants listed below, you'll find a steakhouse and a pizza place, as well as familiar chains such as McDonald's, Pizza Hut, and Wendy's.

Canyon Star Restaurant and Saloon ꩜ AMERICAN/MEXICAN   This place aims to compete with El Tovar Dining Room and The Arizona Room, and serves the most creative Southwestern fare this side of the park boundary, plus you'll have live entertainment while you eat. Try the barbecued buffalo brisket (at lunch, go for the buffalo burger). Evening shows include performances of Native American songs and dances. This place is big, so there usually isn't too long a wait for a table, and even if there is, you can head for the saloon and saddle up a bar stool (some of the stools have saddles instead of seats) while you wait.

At the Grand Hotel, Ariz. 64. © **928/638-3333.** Reservations not accepted. Main courses $7–$13 lunch, $15–$28 dinner. AE, DISC, MC, V. Daily 7–10am and 11am–10pm.

Coronado Room ✦ CONTINENTAL/SOUTHWESTERN If you should suddenly be struck by an overpowering desire to have escargot for dinner, don't despair—head for the Best Western Grand Canyon Squire Inn. Now, we're well aware that Best Western and escargot go together about as well as the Eiffel Tower and rattlesnake fritters, but this place really does serve classic Continental fare way out here in the Arizona high country. You'll probably want to stick to the steaks, though (or the wild game such as elk tournedos). You might also want to try a few of the Southwestern appetizers on the menu.

At the Best Western Grand Canyon Squire Inn, Ariz. 64. © **928/638-2681.** Reservations recommended. Main courses $18–$29. AE, DC, DISC, MC, V. Daily 5–10pm.

2 Havasu Canyon ★/★ & Grand Canyon West

Havasu Canyon: 200 miles W of Grand Canyon Village; 70 miles N of Ariz. 66; 155 miles NW of Flagstaff; 115 miles NE of Kingman

With traffic congestion and parking problems becoming the most memorable aspects of many people's trips to the Grand Canyon, you might want to consider an alternative to the South Rim. For most travelers, this means driving around to the North Rim; however, the North Rim is open only from mid-May to late October and itself is not immune to parking problems and traffic congestion.

There are a couple of lesser-known alternatives. A visit to Havasu Canyon, on the Havasupai Indian Reservation, entails a 20-mile round-trip hike or horseback ride similar to that from Grand Canyon Village to Phantom Ranch, although with a decidedly different setting at the bottom of the canyon. Grand Canyon West, home to the much hyped SkyWalk, is on the Hualapai Indian Reservation and is primarily a tour bus destination for vacationers from Las Vegas. This is also the only place where you can fly down into the canyon, which accounts for all the air traffic.

ESSENTIALS

GETTING THERE Havasu Canyon It isn't possible to drive all the way to Havasu Canyon's Supai village. The nearest road ends 8 miles from Supai at Hualapai Hilltop. This is the head for the trail into the canyon and is at the end of Indian Route 18, which runs north from Arizona 66. The turnoff is 7 miles east of Peach Springs and 31 miles west of Seligman.

The easiest and fastest (and by far most expensive) way to reach Havasu Canyon is by helicopter from Grand Canyon Airport. Flights are operated by **Papillon Grand Canyon Helicopters** (© **800/528-2418** or 928/638-2419; www.papillon.com). The round-trip air-and-ground day excursion is $555; it's also possible to arrange to stay overnight. Lower rates are usually available on this company's website.

VISITOR INFORMATION For information on Havasu Canyon, contact the **Havasupai Tourist Enterprises,** P.O. Box 160, Supai, AZ 86435 (© **928/448-2121** or 928/448-2141; www.havasupaitribe.com), which handles all campground reservations. For information on Grand Canyon West, contact **Destination Grand Canyon,**

6206 W. Desert Inn, Suite B, Las Vegas, NV 89146 (© **877/716-9378** or 702/878-9378; www.destinationgrandcanyon.com).

HAVASU CANYON 🐾🐾

Havasu Canyon is the canyon of the Havasupai tribe, whose name means "people of the blue-green waters." For centuries, the Havasupai have called this idyllic desert oasis home.

The waterfalls are the main attraction here, and most people are content to go for a dip in the cool waters, sun themselves on the sand, and gaze for hours at the turquoise waters. A trail leads all the way down to the Colorado River, but this is an overnight hike.

The Havasupai entry fee is $35 per person to visit Havasu Canyon, and everyone entering the canyon is required to register at the tourist office in the village of Supai. Because it's a long walk to the campground, be sure you have a confirmed reservation before setting out from Hualapai Hilltop. It's good to make reservations as far in advance as possible, especially for holiday weekends.

If you plan to hike down into the canyon, start early to avoid the heat of the day. The hike is beautiful, but it's 10 miles to the campground. The steepest part of the trail is the first mile or so from Hualapai Hilltop. After this section, it's relatively flat.

Through **Havasupai Tourist Enterprises** (© **928/448-2121** or 928/448-2141; www.havasupaitribe.com), you can hire a horse to carry you or your gear down into the canyon from Hualapai Hilltop. Horse rental costs $75 each way. Many people who hike in decide that it's worth the money to ride out, or at least have their backpacks carried out. Be sure to confirm your horse reservation a day before driving to Hualapai Hilltop. Sometimes no horses are available, and it's a long drive back to the nearest town. There are also pack mules that will carry your gear into and out of the canyon.

If you'd like to hike into Havasu Canyon with a guide, **Arizona Outback Adventures,** 16447 N. 91st St., Suite 101, Scottsdale, AZ 85260 (© **866/455-1601** or 480/945-2881; www.azoutbackadventures.com), leads 3- to 5-day hikes into Havasu Canyon and charges $1,375 to $1,625 per person. **Discovery Treks,** 28248 N. Tatum Blvd., Suite B1, no. 414, Cave Creek, AZ 85331 (© **888/256-8731;** www.discovery treks.com), offers similar 3-day trips for $975 to $1,145 per person.

GRAND CANYON WEST

Located on the Hualapai Indian Reservation on the south side of the Colorado River, **Grand Canyon West** (© **877/716-9378** or 702/878-9378; www.destinationgrand canyon.com) overlooks the little-visited west end of Grand Canyon National Park. Although the view is not as spectacular as at either the South Rim or the North Rim, Grand Canyon West is noteworthy for one thing: It is one of the only places where you can legally take a helicopter ride down into the canyon. This is possible because the helicopters operate on land that is part of the Hualapai Indian Reservation. The tours are operated by **Papillon Helicopters** (© **888/635-7272** or 702/736-7243; www.papillon.com), which charges $149 to $204 per person for a quick trip to the bottom of the canyon and a boat ride on the Colorado River. *Note:* Lower rates may be available on their website.

Grand Canyon West is a self-styled major destination, with plans for a full-fledged resort and major airport in the future. In 2007, the first phase of this development, the much-publicized **Skywalk,** opened to the public. Contrary to what you may have read about this Vegas-style attraction, the SkyWalk is not over the Colorado River and is not in Grand Canyon National Park. The horseshoe-shaped glass observation platform juts over a side canyon of the Grand Canyon, and from the deck you can glimpse the Colorado River a short distance away and 4,000 feet below. However, you'll have to cough up $75 for the privilege of walking out on the SkyWalk for a view that is only marginally better than the view from solid ground. For your $75, you'll also get a guided **bus tour** along the rim of the canyon. Tours operate daily throughout the year and cost $50 per person (with lunch); $75 with lunch and the SkyWalk; $109 with a Hummer tour or horseback ride added on; and $199 with a helicopter ride down into the canyon and a brief boat trip on the Colorado River. Reservations are recommended. If you're coming from Kingman, allow at least 2 hours to get here.

While we can recommend a trip out to Grand Canyon West only as a side trip from Las Vegas or for travelers who absolutely must fly down into the canyon, the drive out here is almost as scenic as the destination itself. Along Diamond Bar Road, you'll be driving below the Grand Wash Cliffs, and for much of the way, the route traverses a dense forest of Joshua trees.

OTHER AREA ACTIVITIES

If you long to raft the Grand Canyon but have only a couple of free days in your schedule to realize your dream, then you have only a couple of options. Here at the west end of the canyon, it's possible to do a 1-day rafting trip that begins on the Hualapai Indian Reservation. These trips are operated by **Hualapai River Runners,** P.O. Box 246, Peach Springs, AZ 89434 (© **928/769-2219;** www.grandcanyonresort. com), a tribal rafting company, and run between March and October. Expect a mix of white water and flat water (all of it very cold). One-day trips cost $299 per person.

Also in this area, you can visit **Grand Canyon Caverns** (© **928/422-3223;** www. grandcanyoncaverns.com), just outside Peach Springs. The caverns, which are accessed via a 210-foot elevator ride, are open from Memorial Day to October 15 daily from 9am to 5pm (sometimes until 6pm), and other months daily from 10am to 4pm. Admission is $13 for adults, $9.95 for children 4 to 12. "Explorers' Tours" ($45) head off into parts of the caverns that aren't seen on the regular tour.

WHERE TO STAY & DINE
IN PEACH SPRINGS

Hualapai Lodge ⓕ *Finds*   Located in the Hualapai community of Peach Springs, this lodge offers by far the most luxurious accommodations anywhere in the region. Guest rooms are spacious and modern, with a few bits of regional decor for character. Most people staying here are in the area to visit Grand Canyon West, to go rafting with Hualapai River Runners, or to hike in to Havasu Canyon. The dining room is just about the only place in town to get a meal.

900 Rte. 66, Peach Springs, AZ 86434. © 888/255-9550 or 928/769-2230. Fax 928/769-2372. www.grandcanyon resort.com. 60 units. Mid-Mar to Oct $100–$110 double; Nov to mid-Mar $80–$84 double. Children under 15 stay free in parent's room. AE, DC, DISC, MC, V. **Amenities:** Restaurant (Mexican/Native American/American); outdoor saltwater pool; exercise room; tour desk; coin-op laundry. *In room:* A/C, TV, dataport, coffeemaker, hair dryer.

IN HAVASU CANYON

Havasupai Lodge   Located in Supai village, this lodge offers, aside from the campground, the only accommodations in the canyon. The two-story building features standard motel-style rooms that lack only TVs and telephones, neither of which is much in demand at this isolated retreat. The only drawback of this comfortable though basic lodge is that it's 2 miles from Havasu Falls and 3 miles from Mooney

Falls. The Havasupai Café, across from the general store, serves breakfast, lunch, and dinner. It's a very casual place, and prices are high for what you get because all ingredients must be packed in by horse.

P.O. Box 159, Supai, AZ 86435. (C) **928/448-2111** or 928/448-2201. www.havasupaitribe.com. 24 units. $145 double. MC, V. **Amenities:** Restaurant nearby. *In room:* A/C, no phone.

3 The Grand Canyon North Rim (★(★(★

42 miles S of Jacob Lake; 216 miles N of Grand Canyon Village (South Rim); 354 miles N of Phoenix; 125 miles W of Page/Lake Powell

Although the North Rim of the Grand Canyon is only 10 miles from the South Rim as the crow flies, it's more than 200 miles by road. Because it is such a long drive from population centers such as Phoenix and Las Vegas, the North Rim is much less crowded than the South Rim. Additionally, due to heavy snowfall, the North Rim is open only from mid-May to late October or early November. There are also far fewer activities or establishments on the North Rim than there are on the South Rim.

The North Rim is on the Kaibab Plateau, which is more than 8,000 feet high on average and takes its name from the Paiute word for "mountain lying down." The higher elevation of the North Rim means that instead of the mix of junipers interspersed with ponderosa pines of the South Rim, you'll see dense forests of ponderosa pines, Douglas firs, and aspens interspersed with large meadows. Consequently, the North Rim has a much more alpine feel than the South Rim. The 8,000-foot elevation—1,000 feet higher than the South Rim—also means that the North Rim gets considerably more snow in winter than the South Rim. The highway south from Jacob Lake is not plowed in winter, when the Grand Canyon Lodge closes down.

ESSENTIALS

GETTING THERE   The North Rim is at the end of Arizona 67 (the North Rim Pkwy.), reached from US 89A. **Trans Canyon** ((C) **928/638-2820**) operates a shuttle between the North Rim and the South Rim of the Grand Canyon during the months the North Rim is open. The trip takes 5 hours; the fare is $70 one-way and $130 round-trip (reservations required).

FEES   The park entry fee is $25 per car and is good for 1 week. Remember not to lose the little paper receipt that serves as your admission pass.

VISITOR INFORMATION   For information before leaving home, contact **Grand Canyon National Park**, P.O. Box 129, Grand Canyon, AZ 86023 ((C) **928/638-7888;** www.nps.gov/grca). At the entrance gate, you'll be given a copy of *The Guide*, a small newspaper with information on park activities. There's also an **information desk** in the lobby of the Grand Canyon Lodge.

(*Tips* An Important Note

Visitor facilities at the North Rim are open only from mid-May to mid-October. From mid-October to November (or until snow closes the road to the North Rim), the park is open for day use only. The campground may be open after mid-October, weather permitting.

EXPLORING THE PARK

While it's hard to beat the view from a rustic rocking chair on the terrace of the Grand Canyon Lodge, the best spots for seeing the canyon are Bright Angel Point, Point Imperial, and Cape Royal. **Bright Angel Point** is at the end of a half-mile trail near the Grand Canyon Lodge, and from here you can see and hear Roaring Springs, which are 3,600 feet below the rim and are the North Rim's only water source. You can also see Grand Canyon Village on the South Rim.

At 8,803 feet, **Point Imperial** is the highest point on the North Rim. A short section of the Colorado River can be seen far below, and off to the east the Painted Desert is visible. The Point Imperial/Nankoweap Trail leads north from here along the rim of the canyon. However, this area was burned in a forest fire in 2000.

Cape Royal is the most spectacular setting on the North Rim, and along the 23-mile road to this viewpoint you'll find several other scenic overlooks. Across the road from the **Walhalla Overlook** are the ruins of an Ancestral Puebloan structure, and just before reaching Cape Royal, you'll come to the **Angel's Window Overlook,** which gives you a breathtaking view of the natural bridge that forms Angel's Window. Once at Cape Royal, you can follow a trail across this natural bridge to a towering promontory overlooking the canyon.

Once you've had your fill of simply taking in the views, you may want to get out and stretch your legs on a trail or two. Quite a few day hikes of varying lengths and difficulty are possible. The shortest is the .5-mile paved trail to Bright Angel Point, along which you'll have plenty of company but also plenty of breathtaking views. If you have time for only one hike while you're here, make it down the **North Kaibab Trail.** This trail is 14 miles long and leads down to Phantom Ranch and the Colorado River. To hike the entire trail, you'll need to have a camping permit and be in very good physical condition (it's almost 6,000 ft. to the canyon floor). For a day hike, most people make Roaring Springs their goal. This hike is 9½ miles round-trip, involves a descent and ascent of 3,000 feet, and takes 7 to 8 hours. You can shorten this hike considerably by turning around at the Supai Tunnel, which is fewer than 1,500 feet below the rim at the 2-mile point. For a relatively easy hike away from the crowds, try the Widforss Point Trail.

If you want to see the canyon from a saddle, contact **Grand Canyon Trail Rides** (© 435/679-8665; www.canyonrides.com), which offers mule rides varying in length from 1 hour ($30) to a full day ($125).

EN ROUTE TO OR FROM THE NORTH RIM

Between Page and the North Rim of the Grand Canyon, US 89A crosses the Colorado River at **Lees Ferry** in Marble Canyon. The original **Navajo Bridge** over the river here was replaced in 1995, and the old bridge is now open to pedestrians. From the bridge, which is 470 feet above the Colorado River, there's a beautiful view of Marble Canyon. At the west end of the bridge, you'll find the Navajo Bridge Interpretive Center, which is operated by the National Park Service and is partly housed in a stone building built during the Depression by the Civilian Conservation Corps (CCC). At the east end of the bridge, which is on the Navajo Reservation, interpretive signs tell the story of Lees Ferry from the Native American perspective.

Lees Ferry is the starting point for raft trips through the Grand Canyon. This stretch of the river is legendary among anglers for its trophy trout fishing, and when the North Rim closes and the rafting season comes to an end, about the only folks you'll find up here are anglers and hunters. Lees Ferry has a 54-site campground (© **928/355-2320**); reservations are not accepted.

Lees Ferry Anglers (© **800/962-9755** or 928/355-2261; www.leesferry.com), 11 miles west of the bridge at Lees Ferry, is fishing headquarters for the region. Not only does it sell all manner of fly-fishing tackle and offer advice about good spots to try your luck, but it operates a guide service and rents waders and boats. A guide and boat costs $300 per day for one person, and $375 per day for two people. At Lees Ferry Lodge, there is also a fly shop, and you can hire a guide through **Ambassador Guides** (© **800/256-7596;** www.ambassadorguides.com), which charges $425 per day for one angler or two anglers if you go out in a boat. Lake Powell guide service is also available.

Along this same stretch of road, you'll find the gravel road that leads north to the **Coyote Buttes** ⚔⚔⚔, which are among the most unusual rock formations in Arizona. Basically, these striated conical sandstone hills are petrified sand dunes, which should give you a good idea of why one area of the Coyote Buttes is called The Wave. The buttes are a favorite of photographers. You must have a permit ($5 per person) to visit this area, and only 20 people are allowed to visit each day (with a maximum group size of six people). Reservations must be made 4 months in advance on the first of the month at exactly noon. With the exception of reservations for July and August, all available permits are usually reserved within a few minutes after noon. There's no actual trail to the buttes, so you have to navigate by way of the simple map that you'll be sent when you receive your permit. For more information, contact the **Arizona Strip Interpretive Association/Interagency Visitor Center,** 345 E. Riverside Dr., St. George, UT 84770 (© **435/688-3246;** www.az.blm.gov/asfo/asia.htm).

To learn more about the pioneer history of this remote region of the state (known as the Arizona Strip), continue west from Jacob Lake 45 miles on Arizona 389 to **Pipe Spring National Monument,** 406 N. Pipe Spring Rd., Fredonia (© **928/643-7105;** www.nps.gov/pisp), which preserves an early Mormon ranch house that was built in the style of a fort for protection from Indians. This "fort" was also known as Winsor Castle and occasionally housed the wives of polygamists hiding from the law. In summer, there are living-history demonstrations. The monument is open daily (except New Year's Day, Thanksgiving, and Christmas) from 7am to 5pm June through August, and from 8am to 5pm the rest of the year. Admission is $5 per adult.

WHERE TO STAY
INSIDE THE PARK
Grand Canyon Lodge ⚔⚔   Perched right on the canyon rim, this classic mountain lodge is listed on the National Register of Historic Places and is as impressive a lodge as any you'll find in a national park. The stone-and-log main building has a soaring ceiling and a viewing room set up with chairs facing a wall of glass, and on either side of this room are flagstone terraces furnished with rustic chairs. Accommodations vary from standard motel units to rustic mountain cabins to comfortable modern cabins. Our favorites are still the frontier cabins, which, although cramped and paneled with dark wood, capture the feeling of a mountain retreat better than any of the other options. A few units have views of the canyon, but most are tucked back away from the rim. The dining hall has two walls of glass to take in the awesome canyon views.

Xanterra Parks & Resorts, 6312 S. Fiddlers Green Circle, Suite 600N, Greenwood Village, CO 80111. © 888/297-2757 or 303/297-2757, or 928/638-2611 for same-day reservations. Fax 303/297-3175. www.grandcanyonnorthrim.com. 205 units. $102–$147 double. Children 16 and under stay free in parent's room. AE, DC, DISC, MC, V. Closed mid-Oct to mid-May. **Amenities:** 2 restaurants (American); lounge; tour desk; coin-op laundry.

OUTSIDE THE PARK

North of the national park, the next closest lodgings are the Kaibab Lodge and the Jacob Lake Inn. You'll also find lots of budget accommodations in Kanab, Utah, 37 miles west of Jacob Lake. If you don't have a reservation at the North Rim's Grand Canyon Lodge, you should call the places recommended below to see if you can get a reservation. If so, you can continue on to the North Rim the next morning. Lodges near the canyon fill up early in the day if they aren't already fully booked with reservations made months in advance.

Jacob Lake Inn   This is one of only two lodges outside the entrance to the North Rim of Grand Canyon National Park, and, because it is at the crossroads of Jacob Lake, it is always a busy spot in summer. While most of the units here are old cabins that tend to be cramped and old fashioned, there are also two dozen modern motel-style rooms in a contemporary mountain rustic lodge. It is these latter rooms, which are the inn's only rooms with TVs, telephones, and high-speed Internet access, that we recommend. Sure, they're more expensive than the cabins, but they are the nicest rooms in the area. Be sure to stock up on cookies at the inn's bakery.

Ariz. 67/US 89A, Jacob Lake, AZ 86022. ℭ **928/643-7232** or 928/643-7898. www.jacoblake.com. 69 units. $75–$122 cabin double; $94–$123 motel/lodge double. AE, DISC, MC, V. Pets accepted ($10 per night). **Amenities:** Restaurant (American); bakery; playground.

EN ROUTE TO THE PARK

Cliff Dwellers Lodge   There isn't much else out this way except this remote lodge, which is affiliated with Lees Ferry Anglers and tends to stay filled up with trout anglers and rafters. The newer, more expensive rooms are standard motel units with combination tub/showers, while the older rooms, in an interesting stone-walled building, have knotty-pine walls and showers only. Despite the rusticity of these latter rooms, they are among our favorites in the area. The lodge is close to some spectacular balanced rocks, and it's about 11 miles east to Lees Ferry. The views are unforgettable.

US 89A milepost 547 (H.C. 67, Box 30), Marble Canyon, AZ 86036. ℭ **800/962-9755** or 928/355-2261. Fax 928/355-2271. www.cliffdwellerslodge.com. 21 units. Mar–Nov $70–$80 double, $200 3-bedroom house; Dec–Feb $50 double, $150 3-bedroom house. AE, DISC, MC, V. **Amenities:** Restaurant (American). *In room:* A/C, TV, coffeemaker, no phone.

Lees Ferry Lodge at Vermilion Cliffs   Located at the foot of the Vermilion Cliffs, 3½ miles west of the Colorado River, Lees Ferry Lodge, built in 1929 of native stone and rough-hewn timber beams, is a small place with simple, rustic accommodations. However, the lodge's restaurant serves as a sort of de facto community center for area residents, and owner Maggie Sacher is usually on hand to answer questions and share stories. Also, the patio seating area in front of the lodge has fabulous views. Boat rentals and fly-fishing guides can be arranged through the lodge. The restaurant here has a great, old-fashioned atmosphere. With its rustic character and friendly feel, this is our favorite place to stay in the area. Don't miss it.

US 89A (H.C. 67, Box 1), Marble Canyon, AZ 86036. ℭ **800/451-2231** or 928/355-2231. www.leesferrylodge.com. 12 units. $53–$70 double. Children under 5 stay free in parent's room. AE, DISC, MC, V. Pets accepted. **Amenities:** Restaurant (American); game room. *In room:* A/C, coffeemaker, no phone.

Marble Canyon Lodge   The Marble Canyon Lodge, built in the 1920s just 4 miles from Lees Ferry, is popular with both rafters and anglers. Accommodations vary considerably in size and age, with some rustic units in old stone buildings and newer motel-style rooms available as well. These latter rooms are the best in the area. You're right at the base of the Vermilion Cliffs here, and the views are great. In addition to the restaurant, there's a general store and fly shop where you can rent a boat or hire a guide.

P.O. Box 6032, Marble Canyon, AZ 86036. © 800/726-1789 or 928/355-2225. Fax 928/355-2227. www.mcg-lees ferry.com. 56 units. $56–$72 double; $74–$88 cottage; $123–$136 apt. Children under 12 stay free in parent's room. AE, DISC, MC, V. Pets accepted. **Amenities:** Restaurant (American). *In room:* A/C, TV, no phone.

CAMPGROUNDS

Located just north of Grand Canyon Lodge, the **North Rim Campground,** with 75 sites and no hookups for RVs, is the only campground at the North Rim. It's open mid-May to mid-October. Reservations can be made up to 6 months in advance by calling the National Recreation Reservation Service (© 877/444-6777 or 518/885-3639; www.recreation.gov). Campsites cost $15 to $20 per night.

There are two nearby campgrounds outside the park in the Kaibab National Forest. They are **DeMotte Campground,** which is the closest to the park entrance and has 23 sites, and **Jacob Lake Campground,** which is 30 miles north of the park entrance and has 53 sites. Both charge between $14 and $16 per night and do not take reservations. They're open May 15 to November 1. You can also camp anywhere in the Kaibab National Forest as long as you're more than a quarter-mile from a paved road or water source. So if you can't find a site in a campground, simply pull off the highway in the national forest and park your RV or pitch your tent.

The **Kaibab Camper Village** (© 800/525-0924, 928/643-7804 May 15–Oct 15, or 928/526-0924 other months; www.kaibabcampervillage.com) is a privately owned campground in the crossroads of Jacob Lake, 30 miles north of the park entrance. It's open from mid-May to mid-October and has around 100 sites. Rates are $13 for tent sites, $27 for RV sites with full hookups. Make reservations well in advance.

WHERE TO DINE

INSIDE THE PARK

Grand Canyon Lodge has a dining room with a splendid view. Because this restaurant is so popular, reservations are required for dinner. More casual choices at the lodge include a cafeteria and a saloon that serves light meals.

OUTSIDE THE PARK

Your only choices for a meal outside the park are the **Kaibab Lodge,** just north of the entrance, and the **Jacob Lake Inn** (© 928/643-7232; www.jacoblake.com), 45 miles north at the junction with US 89A.

4 Flagstaff ✶✶

150 miles N of Phoenix; 32 miles E of Williams; 80 miles S of Grand Canyon Village

With its wide variety of accommodations and restaurants, the great outdoors at the edge of town, three national monuments nearby, one of the state's finest museums, and a university that supports a lively cultural community, Flagstaff makes an ideal base for exploring much of northern Arizona.

The San Francisco Peaks, just north of the city, are the site of the Arizona Snowbowl ski area, one of the state's main winter playgrounds. In summer, miles of trails through these same mountains attract hikers and mountain bikers, and it's even possible to ride the chairlift for a panoramic vista that stretches 70 miles north to the

Grand Canyon. Of the area's national monuments, two preserve ancient Indian ruins and one an otherworldly landscape of volcanic cinder cones.

It was as a railroad town that Flagstaff made its fortunes, and after several years of renovations, the historic downtown offers a glimpse of the days when the city's fortunes rode the rails. The railroad still runs right through the middle of Flagstaff, much to the dismay of many visitors, who find that most of the city's inexpensive motels (and even some of the more expensive places) are too close to the busy tracks to allow them to get a good night's sleep.

ESSENTIALS

GETTING THERE   Flagstaff is on I-40, one of the main east-west interstates in the United States. I-17 starts here and heads south to Phoenix. Arizona 89A connects Flagstaff to Sedona by way of Oak Creek Canyon. US 180 connects Flagstaff with the South Rim of the Grand Canyon, and US 89 connects the city with Page.

Pulliam Airport, 3 miles south of Flagstaff off I-17, is served by **US Airways** (© **800/ 428-4322**) from Phoenix. **Amtrak** (© **800/872-7245**) offers service to Flagstaff from Chicago and Los Angeles. The train station is at 1 E. Rte. 66.

VISITOR INFORMATION   Contact the **Flagstaff Visitor Center,** 1 E. Rte. 66 (© **800/842-7293** or 928/774-9541; www.flagstaffarizona.org). The visitor center is open Monday through Saturday from 8am to 5pm and Sunday from 9am to 4pm.

GETTING AROUND   Car rentals are available from **Avis** (© 800/331-1212), **Budget** (© 800/527-0700), **Enterprise** (© 800/261-7331), **Hertz** (© 800/654-3131), and **National** (© 800/227-7368).

Call **A Friendly Cab** (© 928/774-4444) if you need a taxi. **Mountain Line Transit** (© 928/779-6624) provides public bus transit around the city; the fare is $1.

GETTING OUTSIDE

Flagstaff is northern Arizona's center for outdoor activities. Chief among them is skiing at **Arizona Snowbowl** (© **928/779-1951;** www.arizonasnowbowl.com), on the slopes of Mount Agassiz, from which you can see all the way to the North Rim of the Grand Canyon. Conditions are, however, very unreliable, and the ski area can be shut down for weeks on end due to lack of snow. All-day lift tickets are $46 for adults, $25 for children 8 to 12, $25 for seniors, and free for children under 8 and seniors over 70. In summer, you can ride a chairlift almost to the summit of Mount Agassiz and enjoy the expansive views across seemingly all of northern Arizona. The round-trip lift-ticket price is $10 for adults, $8 for seniors, and $6 for children 8 to 12. To get here, take US 180 N from Flagstaff for 7 miles and turn right onto Snow Bowl Road.

When there's no snow on the ground, there are plenty of trails for hiking throughout the San Francisco Peaks, and many national forest trails are open to mountain bikes. Late September, when the aspens have turned a brilliant golden yellow, is one of the best times of year for a hike in Flagstaff's mountains. If you've got the stamina, do the **Humphreys Peak Trail,** which climbs 3,000 feet in 4.5 miles. Needless to say, the views from the 12,633-foot summit are stupendous. After all, this is the highest point in Arizona. To reach the trail head, take US 180 N out of Flagstaff for 7 miles, turn right on Snow Bowl Road, and continue to the parking area by the ski lodge. This is our favorite Flagstaff area hike and is nearly as awe inspiring in its own way as hiking down into the Grand Canyon.

If you'd like a short hike with a big payoff, hike to **Red Mountain.** This hike is only about 2.5 miles round-trip, but leads to a fascinating red-walled cinder cone that long ago collapsed to reveal its strange interior walls. To find the trail head, drive north from Flagstaff toward the Grand Canyon on US 180. At milepost 247, watch for a forest road leading west for about a quarter-mile to the trail-head parking area.

For information on other hikes in the Coconino National Forest, contact the **Peaks Ranger District,** 5075 N. Hwy. 89, Flagstaff (℃ **928/526-0866;** www.fs.fed.us/r3/ coconino).

SEEING THE SIGHTS

Downtown Flagstaff—along Route 66, San Francisco Street, Aspen Avenue, and Birch Avenue—is the city's **historic district.** These old brick buildings are now filled with shops selling Native American crafts, works by local artists and artisans, Route 66 souvenirs, and various other Arizona mementos such as rocks, minerals, and crystals. Don't miss **Jonathan Day's Indian Arts,** 21 N. San Francisco St. (℃ **928/779-6099;** www.traditionalhopikachinas.com), a small shop with what just might be the best selection of traditional Hopi kachinas in the state.

MUSEUMS, PARKS & CULTURAL ACTIVITIES

Lowell Observatory 𝕽   This historic observatory is located atop aptly named Mars Hill and is one of the oldest astronomical observatories in the Southwest. Founded in 1894 by Percival Lowell, the observatory has played important roles in contemporary astronomy. Among the work carried out here was Lowell's study of the planet Mars and the calculations that led him to predict the existence of Pluto. It wasn't until 13 years after Lowell's death that Pluto was discovered almost exactly where he had predicted it would be.

The facility consists of several observatories, a visitor center with numerous exhibits, and outdoor displays. While it can be interesting to visit during the day, the main attraction is the chance to observe the stars and planets through the observatory's 24-inch telescope. The telescope domes are not heated, so be sure to dress appropriately. Also, there are no programs on cloudy nights.

1400 W. Mars Hill Rd. (℃ **928/233-3211.** www.lowell.edu. Admission $6 adults, $5 seniors and students, $3 children 5–17. Mar–Oct daily 9am–5pm (tours on the hour 10am–4pm); Nov–Feb daily noon–5pm (tours on the hour 1–4pm). Telescope viewings: June–Aug Mon–Sat 5:30–9:30pm; Sept–May Wed and Fri–Sat 5:30–9:30pm. Closed Jan 1, Easter, Thanksgiving, and Dec 24–25.

Museum of Northern Arizona 𝕽𝕽   This small but surprisingly thorough museum is the ideal first stop on an exploration of northern Arizona. You'll learn, through state-of-the-art exhibits, about the archaeology, ethnology, geology, biology, and fine arts of the region. The cornerstone of the museum is an exhibit that explores life on the Colorado Plateau from 15,000 B.C. to the present. Among the other displays are a life-size kiva ceremonial room and a small but interesting collection of kachinas. The large gift shop is full of contemporary Native American arts and crafts, and in summer special exhibits and sales focus on Hopi, Navajo, and Zuni arts and crafts.

3101 N. Fort Valley Rd. (3 miles north of downtown Flagstaff on US 180). (℃ **928/774-5213.** www.musnaz.org. Admission $5 adults, $4 seniors, $3 students, $2 children 7–17. Daily 9am–5pm. Closed New Year's Day, Thanksgiving, and Christmas.

Riordan Mansion State Historic Park 𝕽   Built in 1904 for local timber barons Michael and Timothy Riordan, this 13,000-square-foot mansion—Arizona's finest example of an Arts and Crafts–era building—is actually two houses connected by a large central hall. Each brother and his family occupied half of the house (they had the rooflines constructed differently so that visitors could tell the two sides apart). Although the mansion looks like a log cabin, it's actually faced with log slabs. Inside, mission-style furnishings and touches of Art Nouveau styling make it clear that this family was keeping up with the times. The west wing of the mansion holds displays on, among other things, Stickley furniture. Guided tours provide a glimpse into the lives of two of Flagstaff's most influential pioneers.

409 W. Riordan Rd. (off Milton Rd./Ariz. 89A, just north of the junction of I-40 and I-17). ℂ 928/779-4395. www. azstateparks.com. Admission $6 adults, $2.50 children 7–13. May–Oct daily 8:30am–5pm; Nov–Apr daily 10:30am–5pm. Guided tours on the hour. Closed Christmas.

Sunset Crater Volcano National Monument ⚐   Dotting the landscape northeast of Flagstaff are more than 400 volcanic craters, of which Sunset Crater Volcano is the youngest. Taking its name from the colors of the cinders near its summit, Sunset Crater Volcano stands 1,000 feet tall and began forming in 1064. Over a period of 100 years, the volcano erupted repeatedly (creating the red-and-yellow cinder cone seen today) and eventually covered an area of 800 square miles with ash, lava, and cinders. A 1-mile interpretive trail passes through a desolate landscape of lava flows, cinders, and ash as it skirts the base of this volcano. If you want to climb to the top of a cinder cone, take the 1-mile Lenox Crater Trail. In the visitor center (at the west entrance to the national monument), you can learn more about the formation of Sunset Crater and about volcanoes in general. Near the visitor center is the small Bonito Campground, which is open from late May to mid-October.

14 miles north of Flagstaff off US 89. ℂ 928/526-0502. www.nps.gov/sucr. Admission $5 adults, free for children 16 and under (admission also valid for Wupatki National Monument). Daily sunrise–sunset; visitor center daily May–Oct 8am–5pm, Nov–Apr 9am–5pm. Visitor center closed Christmas.

Walnut Canyon National Monument ⚐   The remains of 300 small 13th-century Sinagua cliff dwellings can be seen in the undercut layers of limestone in this 400-foot-deep wooded canyon east of Flagstaff. These cliff dwellings, though not nearly as impressive as the ruins at Montezuma Castle National Monument (50 miles to the south) or Wupatki National Monument (20 miles to the north), are worth a visit for the chance to poke around inside the well-preserved rooms, which were well protected from the elements (and from enemies). The Sinagua were the same people who built and then abandoned the stone pueblos in Wupatki National Monument, and it is theorized that when the land to the north lost its fertility, the Sinagua began migrating southward, settling for 150 years in Walnut Canyon.

A self-guided trail leads from the visitor center on the canyon rim down 185 feet to a section of the canyon wall where 25 cliff dwellings can be viewed up close (some can even be entered). From Memorial Day to Labor Day three times each month, there are guided hikes into the monument's backcountry (reservations required). There's also a picnic area near the visitor center.

7½ miles east of Flagstaff on Walnut Canyon Rd. (take Exit 204 off I-40). ℂ 928/526-3367. www.nps.gov/waca. Admission $5 adults, free for children 16 and under. May–Oct daily 8am–5pm; Nov–Apr daily 9am–5pm; trail closes 1 hr. earlier. Visitor center closed Christmas.

Wupatki National Monument ⚐⚐   The landscape northeast of Flagstaff is desolate and windswept, a sparsely populated region carpeted with volcanic ash deposited in the 11th century. It comes as quite a surprise, then, to learn that this area contains

hundreds of Native American habitation sites. The most impressive ruins are those left by the Sinagua (the name means "without water" in Spanish), who inhabited this area from around 1100 until shortly after 1200. The Sinagua people built small villages of stone similar to the pueblos on the nearby Hopi Reservation, and today the ruins of these ancient villages can be seen in this national monument.

The largest of the pueblos is Wupatki Ruin, in the southeastern part of the monument. Here the Sinagua built a sprawling three-story pueblo containing nearly 100 rooms. They also constructed what is believed to be a ball court which, although quite different in design from the courts of the Aztec and Maya, suggests that a similar game may have been played in this region. Another circular stone structure just below the main ruins may have been an amphitheater or dance plaza.

The most unusual feature of Wupatki, however, is a natural phenomenon: a blow-hole, which may have been the reason this pueblo was constructed here. A network of small underground tunnels and chambers acts as a giant barometer, blowing air through the blowhole when the underground air is under greater pressure than the outside air. On hot days, cool air rushes out of the blowhole with amazing force.

33 miles north of Flagstaff off US 89. ☏ 928/679-2365. www.nps.gov/wupa. Admission $5 adults, free for children 16 and under (admission also valid for Sunset Crater Volcano National Monument). Daily sunrise–sunset. Visitor center daily 9am–5pm. Visitor center closed Christmas.

WHERE TO STAY
EXPENSIVE
The Inn at 410 ☆☆ This restored 1894 Craftsman home is one of the best B&Bs in Arizona, providing convenience, pleasant surroundings, comfortable rooms, and delicious breakfasts. Guests can lounge and enjoy afternoon tea on the front porch, in the comfortable dining room, or out on the pleasant garden patio. Each guest room features a distinctive theme; our favorites are Canyon Memories and the Southwest Suite, which conjure up the inn's Western heritage. All rooms have fireplaces, and three have two-person whirlpool tubs.

410 N. Leroux St., Flagstaff, AZ 86001. ☏ 800/774-2008 or 928/774-0088. Fax 928/774-6354. www.inn410.com. 9 units. $165–$230 double. 2-night minimum on weekends Apr Oct. Rates include full breakfast and afternoon refreshments. AE, MC, V. No children under 5. **Amenities:** Access to nearby health club; concierge; business center; massage; babysitting; guest laundry. *In room:* A/C, TV/DVD/VCR, fridge, coffeemaker, hair dryer, iron, Wi-Fi, no phone.

MODERATE
England House Bed & Breakfast ☆☆ This B&B, just 3 blocks from Flagstaff's historic downtown, is a beautiful two-story Victorian red-sandstone house built in 1902. This old house, which opened as an inn in 2004, was lovingly restored by owners Richard and Laurel Dunn, who are devoted to details. Consequently, this inn has a delightful period authenticity. The three large guest rooms are on the second floor and are furnished with 1870s French antiques. One room even has a Tempur-Pedic mattress, while another has a feather bed. Breakfasts are served in a bright sunroom just off the kitchen.

614 W. Santa Fe Ave., Flagstaff, AZ 86001. ☏ 877/214-7350 or 928/214-7350. www.englandhousebandb.com. 4 units. $125–$195 double. Rates include full breakfast. DISC, MC, V. No children under 12. **Amenities:** Jacuzzi; concierge. *In room:* A/C, hair dryer, iron, Wi-Fi, no phone.

Little America Hotel ☆ *Value* Set on 500 acres of pine forest and with a trail that winds for 2 miles through the property, this hotel on the east side of Flagstaff might seem at first to be little more than a giant truck stop. However, on closer inspection, you'll find a surprisingly luxurious and economical hotel set beneath shady pines. The decor is dated but fun, with a sort of French Provincial style predominating. Rooms vary in size, but all have small private balconies.

2515 E. Butler Ave., Flagstaff, AZ 86004. ⓒ 800/865-1410 or 928/779-7900. Fax 928/779-7983. www.littleamerica. com. 248 units. $89–$169 double; $99–$179 suite. Children 12 and under stay free in parent's room. AE, DC, DISC, MC, V. Take Exit 198 off I-40. **Amenities:** 3 restaurants (American, Continental, deli); lounge; outdoor pool; exercise room; Jacuzzi; children's playground; concierge; courtesy airport shuttle; business center; room service; coin-op laundry; laundry service; dry cleaning. *In room:* A/C, TV, dataport, fridge, coffeemaker, hair dryer, iron, safe, high-speed Internet access.

Radisson Woodlands Hotel Flagstaff 🐾🐾 With its elegant marble-floored lobby, the Woodlands Hotel is easily the most upscale lodging in Flagstaff. A white baby grand, a crystal chandelier, traditional European furnishings, and contemporary sculpture all add to the unexpected luxury in the public spaces, as do intricately carved pieces of furniture and architectural details from different Asian countries. Guest rooms are quite comfortable and have Sleep Number® beds.

1175 W. Rte. 66, Flagstaff, AZ 86001. ⓒ 800/333-3333 or 928/773-8888. Fax 928/773-0597. www.radisson.com/ flagstaffaz. 183 units. $99–$149 double; $129–$189 suite. AE, DC, DISC, MC, V. **Amenities:** 2 restaurants (Japanese, Continental); lounge; outdoor pool; exercise room; indoor and outdoor Jacuzzis; sauna; business center; room service; coin-op laundry; laundry service; dry cleaning. *In room:* A/C, TV, dataport, coffeemaker, hair dryer, iron, high-speed Internet access, Wi-Fi.

INEXPENSIVE
Historic Hotel Monte Vista This hotel is definitely not for everyone. Although it is historic, it is also a bit run-down and appeals primarily to young travelers who appreciate the low rates and the nightclub just off the lobby. So why stay here? In its day, the Monte Vista hosted the likes of Clark Gable, John Wayne, Carole Lombard, and Gary Cooper, and today, the hotel is haunted (ask at the front desk for the list of resident ghosts). Opened in 1927, the Monte Vista now has creatively decorated rooms that vary in size and decor. Although the hotel has plenty of old-fashioned flair, don't expect perfection. Check out a room first to see if this is your kind of place.

100 N. San Francisco St., Flagstaff, AZ 86001. ⓒ 800/545-3068 or 928/779-6971. Fax 928/779-2904. www.hotel montevista.com. 50 units, 5 w/shared bathrooms. May–Oct $70 double w/shared bathroom, $80–$130 double w/private bathroom, $120–$180 suite; Nov–Apr $65 double w/shared bathroom, $75–$125 double w/private bathroom, $115–$170 suite. AE, DISC, MC, V. Pets accepted ($25 deposit). **Amenities:** Restaurant (American); lounge; coin-op laundry. *In room:* TV, hair dryer.

WHERE TO DINE
EXPENSIVE
Brix 🐾🐾 NEW AMERICAN Although it's a bit hard to find (tucked into a corner of an old brick carriage house), Brix, Flagstaff's most contemporary restaurant, is well worth searching out. The menu relies on fresh, seasonal ingredients, so it changes regularly. However, any time of year, you'll find a great selection of artisanal cheeses, which make a good starter to a meal here. The chef's creativity shines through in such seasonal entrees as pork chops with rhubarb-ginger compote, pan-roasted duck breast with quinoa fritters, and house-made pappardelle pasta with fava beans, roasted mushrooms, and cippolini onions. There's an excellent wine list.

413 N. San Francisco St. ⓒ 928/213-1021. www.brixflagstaff.com. Reservations recommended. Main courses $8.50–$12 lunch, $22–$30 dinner. AE, DISC, MC, V. Mon–Thurs 11am–2pm and 5–9pm; Fri 11am–2pm and 5–10pm; Sat 5–10pm.

Cottage Place Restaurant 🕯🕯 CONTINENTAL/NEW AMERICAN   Cottage Place is just what its name implies—an unpretentious little cottage. But despite the casual appearance, dining here is a formal affair. The menu, which tends toward the rich side, is primarily Continental, with Southwestern and Middle Eastern influences as well. The house specialties are chateaubriand and rack of lamb (both served for two); there are always a couple of choices for vegetarians as well. The appetizer sampler, with herb-stuffed mushrooms, charbroiled shrimp, and *tiropitas* (cheese-stuffed phyllo pastries), is a winner. There's a long, award-winning wine list.

126 W. Cottage Ave. ℭ **928/774-8431.** www.cottageplace.com. Reservations recommended. 3-course meals $22–$34. AE, MC, V. Wed–Sun 5–9:30pm.

MODERATE

Jackson's Grill at the Springs 🕯🕯 NEW AMERICAN   Set on the outskirts of Flagstaff, this modern American bistro boasts the most attractive setting of any restaurant in town. The food here is also delicious, which makes this place well worth the 10-minute drive from downtown Flagstaff. Start with the spinach salad, which is made with prosciutto-wrapped shrimp, or the ahi tuna salad. The spit-roasted entrees are among the best bets here. If you are on your way between Flagstaff and Sedona late in the day, this makes a great place for dinner.

7055 N. US 89A. ℭ **928/213-9332.** www.jacksonsgrillrestaurant.com. Reservations recommended on weekends. Main courses $12–$34. AE, DC, DISC, MC, V. Mon–Thurs 5–9:30pm; Fri–Sun 11am–3pm and 5–9:30pm.

Josephine's 🕯🕯 REGIONAL AMERICAN   Housed in a restored Craftsman bungalow with wide front porch for summer dining, this restaurant combines a historical setting with excellent food that draws on a wide range of influences. For these reasons, this is our favorite downtown Flagstaff restaurant. The thinly sliced ancho-marinated steak is a real winner. At lunch, try the crab-cake po' boy sandwich. There's a good selection of reasonably priced wines also. Be sure to save room for the molten chocolate cake or the unusual half-baked peanut butter–chocolate chip cookie.

503 N. Humphrey's St. ℭ **928/779-3400.** www.josephinesrestaurant.com. Reservations recommended. Main courses $8.75–$13 lunch, $19–$28 dinner. AE, DISC, MC, V. Mon–Fri 11am–2:30pm and 5–9pm; Sat 5–9pm.

Pasto 🕯 ITALIAN   Located in downtown Flagstaff, Pasto has a lively urban feel and can get boisterous on the weekends. The food is some of the best in town and is always reliable. Casual yet sophisticated, Pasto is less formal than Cottage Place or Josephine's, so if you don't feel like getting dressed up after a day at the canyon, come here. As the restaurant's name implies, the menu includes a good assortment of pastas; however, we always go for the *osso buco.*

19 E. Aspen St. ℭ **928/779-1937.** www.pastorestaurant.com. Reservations recommended. Main courses $16–$28. AE, DC, DISC, MC, V. Tues–Sun 5–9pm.

INEXPENSIVE

Beaver Street Brewery *Value* BURGERS/PIZZA   This big microbrewery, cafe, and billiards parlor on the south side of the railroad tracks serves up several good brews, and it also does great pizzas and salads. The Beaver Street pizza, made with roasted-garlic pesto, sun-dried tomatoes, fresh basil, and goat cheese, is particularly tasty. Robust salads include a Mongolian beef version with sesame-ginger dressing. This place stays packed with college students, but a good pint of ale helps any wait pass quickly, especially if you can grab a seat by the woodstove.

Moments White Buffalo

As you drive north to the Grand Canyon on US 180, about 20 miles north of Flagstaff, be sure to watch for **Spirit Mountain Ranch,** mile marker 236.5 (*©* **928/ 606-2779;** www.sacredwhitebuffalo.com), which is home to a small herd of white buffalo. These animals are considered sacred by Native Americans. The buffalo can be visited daily between 9am and 4pm, and admission is $5.

---

11 S. Beaver St. *©* **928/779-0079.** www.beaverstreetbrewery.com. Reservations not accepted. Main courses $9.50–$15. AE, DISC, MC, V. Sun–Thurs 11:30am–11pm; Fri–Sat 11:30am–midnight.

Macy's European Coffee House & Bakery COFFEEHOUSE/BAKERY   Good espresso and baked goodies draw people in here the first time, but there are also decent vegetarian pasta dishes, soups, salads, and other college-town standbys. This is Flagstaff's counterculture hangout, attracting both students and professors. For the true Macy's experience, order one of the huge lattes and a scone or other pastry.

14 S. Beaver St. *©* **928/774-2243.** Meals $4–$7.75. MC, V. Daily 6am–10pm.

5 Williams

32 miles W of Flagstaff; 58 miles S of the Grand Canyon; 220 miles E of Las Vegas, NV

Although it's almost 60 miles south of the Grand Canyon, Williams is still the closest real town to the national park. Consequently, it has dozens of motels catering to those unable to get a room in or just outside the park. Founded in 1880 as a railroading and logging town, Williams also has a bit of Western history to boast about, which makes it an interesting place to explore for a morning or afternoon. Old brick commercial buildings dating from the late 19th century line the main street, while modest Victorian homes sit on the tree-shaded streets. In recent years, mid-20th–century history has taken center stage: Williams was the last town on historic Route 66 to be bypassed by I-40, and the town plays up its Route 66 heritage.

Most important for many visitors, however, is that Williams is where you'll find the Grand Canyon Railway depot. The excursion train that departs from here not only provides a fun ride on the rails, but serves as an alternative to dealing with traffic congestion in Grand Canyon National Park.

Named for famed mountain man Bill Williams, the town sits at the edge of a ponderosa pine forest atop the Mogollon Rim. Surrounding Williams is the Kaibab National Forest. Within the forest and not far out of town are good fishing lakes, hiking and mountain-biking trails, and a small downhill ski area.

ESSENTIALS

GETTING THERE   Williams is on I-40 just west of the junction with Arizona 64, which leads north to the South Rim of the Grand Canyon.

Amtrak (*©* **800/872-7245**) has service to Williams on its *Southwest Chief* line. There's no station, though—the train stops on the outskirts of town. However, a shuttle van from the Grand Canyon Railway Hotel will pick you up and drive you into town, and since most people coming to Williams by train are continuing on to the Grand Canyon on the Grand Canyon Railway, this arrangement works well.

For information on the **Grand Canyon Railway** excursion trains to Grand Canyon Village, see "Exploring the Area: Route 66 & Beyond," below.

VISITOR INFORMATION   For information on the Williams area, including details on hiking, mountain biking, and fishing, contact the **City of Williams/Forest Service Visitor Center,** 200 W. Railroad Ave. (© **800/863-0546** or 928/635-4707; www.williamschamber.com). The visitor center, which includes some interesting historical displays, is open daily from 8am to 5pm (until 6:30pm in the summer). The shop carries books on the Grand Canyon and trail maps for the adjacent national forest.

EXPLORING THE AREA: ROUTE 66 & BEYOND

These days, most people coming to Williams are here to board the **Grand Canyon Railway** ⟨⟨, Grand Canyon Railway Depot, 233 N. Grand Canyon Blvd. (© **800/ 843-8724** or 928/773-1976; www.thetrain.com), which operates vintage steam and diesel locomotives and 1920s and 1950s coaches between Williams and Grand Canyon Village. Round-trip fares (not including tax or the national park entrance fee) range from $60 to $170 for adults, $40 to $145 for children 11 to 16, and $30 to $95 for children 2 to 10. Although this is primarily a day-excursion train, it's possible to ride up one day and return on a different day—just let the reservations clerk know. If you stay overnight, be sure you have a reservation at one of the hotels right in Grand Canyon Village.

Route 66 fans will want to drive Williams's main street, which, not surprisingly, is named Route 66. Along this stretch of the old highway, you can check out the town's vintage buildings, many of which house shops selling Route 66 souvenirs. There are also a few antiques stores selling collectibles from the heyday of the famous highway.

WHERE TO STAY
MODERATE

Grand Canyon Railway Hotel ⟨⟨   This hotel is operated by the Grand Canyon Railway and combines modern comforts with the style of a classic Western railroad hotel. The high-ceilinged lobby features a large flagstone fireplace and original paintings of the Grand Canyon. The very comfortable guest rooms feature Southwestern styling; ask for a unit in the wing with the fitness room, pool, and hot tub. The hotel's elegant lounge, which features a 100-year-old English bar, serves simple meals, and there's a cafeteria-style restaurant adjacent.

233 N. Grand Canyon Blvd., Williams, AZ 86046. © 800/843-8724 or 928/635-4010. Fax 928/773-1610. www.the train.com. 298 units. Mid-Mar to mid-Oct and holidays $179 double; mid-Oct to Dec $119 double; Jan to mid-Mar $99 double. Railroad/hotel packages available (mid-Mar to mid-Oct and holidays $159 per person; mid-Oct to mid-Mar $119 per person). Children under 16 stay free in parent's room. AE, DISC, MC, V. **Amenities:** Restaurant (American); lounge; indoor pool; exercise room; Jacuzzi; children's playground; tour desk; room service; coin-op laundry. *In room:* A/C, TV, dataport, coffeemaker, hair dryer, iron, free local calls.

The Red Garter Bed & Bakery ⟨ *Finds*   The Wild West lives again at this restored 1897 bordello, but these days the only tarts that come with the rooms are in the bakery downstairs. Located across the street from the Grand Canyon Railway terminal at the top of a steep flight of stairs, this B&B sports high ceilings, attractive wood trim, and reproduction period furnishings. Walls in a couple of rooms have graffiti written by bordello visitors in the early 20th century. The great historical atmosphere makes this our favorite place to stay in Williams.

137 W. Railroad Ave., Williams, AZ 86046. © 800/328-1484 or 928/635-1484. www.redgarter.com. 4 units. $120– $145 double. Lower rates off season (and online). Rates include continental breakfast. DISC, MC, V. No children under 8. **Amenities:** Bakery. *In room:* TV, Wi-Fi, no phone.

Get Your Kicks on Route 66

About 65 miles west of Flagstaff begins the longest remaining stretch of old Route 66. Extending for 160 miles from Ash Fork to Topock, this lonely blacktop passes through some of the most remote country in Arizona (and goes right through the town of Kingman). In Seligman, at the east end of this stretch of the highway, you'll find the **Snow Cap Drive-In** (© **928/422-3291**), which serves up fast food amid outrageous decor. Next door at **Angel & Vilma Delgadillo's Route 66 Gift Shop & Visitor's Center**, 217 E. Rte. 66 (© **928/422-3352**; www.route66giftshop.com), owned by John's uncle Angel, you'll be entertained by one of Route 66's most famous residents and an avid fan of the old highway. The walls of Angel's old one-chair barbershop are covered with photos and business cards of happy customers. Today, Angel's place is a Route 66 information center and souvenir shop.

After leaving Seligman, the highway passes through such waysides as Peach Springs, Truxton, Valentine, and Hackberry. Before reaching Peach Springs, you'll come to Grand Canyon Caverns, once a near-mandatory stop for families traveling Route 66. In Hackberry, be sure to stop at the **Hackberry Store & Old Route 66 Visitor Center** (© **928/769-2605**), which is filled with Route 66 memorabilia as well as old stuff from the 1950s and 1960s. At Valle Vista, near Kingman, the highway goes into a 7-mile-long curve. Some claim it's the longest continuous curve on a U.S. highway.

After the drive through the wilderness west of Seligman, Kingman feels like a veritable metropolis; its bold neon signs once brought a sigh of relief to the tired and the hungry. Today, it boasts dozens of modern motels and is still primarily a resting spot for the road weary. Mr. D'z Route 66 Diner, a modern rendition of a 1950s diner (housed in an old gas station/cafe), serves burgers and blue-plate specials. Across the street at 120 W. Andy Devine Ave. is a restored powerhouse that dates from 1907 and is home to the **Historic Route 66 Association of Arizona** (© **928/753-5001**; www.azrt66.com), the **Historic Route 66 Museum** (© **928/753-9889**; www.kingmantourism.org/route66museum), and the **Kingman Area Chamber of Commerce Visitor Center**. Each year over the first weekend in May, Kingman is the site of the Route 66 Fun Run, which consists of a drive along 150 miles of old Route 66 between Topock and Seligman.

The last stretch of Route 66 in Arizona heads southwest out of Kingman through the rugged Sacramento Mountains and passes through Oatman.

INEXPENSIVE

In addition to the following choices, there are numerous budget chain motels in Williams.

The Canyon Motel & RV Park 🎃 (Kids) (Finds) You'll find this updated 1940s Route 66 motor lodge on the eastern outskirts of Williams. While the setting and rooms in 1940s flagstone cottages are nice enough, the real attractions are the railroad cars. You can stay in a 1929 caboose or a 1950s Pullman car, which makes this a fun place to overnight if you plan to take the excursion train to the Grand Canyon. We prefer the caboose rooms, which have a more authentic feel. An indoor pool, a horseshoe pit, a swing set, and a nature trail provide plenty of entertainment for the whole family.

1900 E. Rodeo Rd., Williams, AZ 86046. © 800/482-3955 or 928/635-9371. Fax 928/635-4138. www.thecanyon motel.com. 23 units. $40–$79 double; $115–$139 caboose; $69–$116 Pullman double. Children under 11 stay free in parent's room. DISC, MC, V. Pets accepted ($7 per night). **Amenities:** Restaurant (American); small indoor pool. *In room:* TV, fridge, coffeemaker, microwave, Wi-Fi, no phone.

CAMPING

There are several campgrounds near Williams in the Kaibab National Forest. They include **Cataract Lake,** 1 mile northwest of Williams on Cataract Lake Road, with 18 sites; **Dogtown Lake,** 6½ miles southeast of Williams off Fourth Street/County Road 73, with 52 sites; **Kaibab Lake,** 4 miles northeast of Williams off Arizona 64, with 63 sites; and **Whitehorse Lake,** 19 miles southeast of Williams off Fourth Street/ County Road 73, with 94 sites. All campgrounds are first-come, first-served, and charge $10 to $15 per night.

WHERE TO DINE

Rod's Steak House STEAKHOUSE/SEAFOOD   For a good dinner in Williams, just look for the red neon steer at the east end of town. The menu here may be short, but the food is reliable. Prime rib au jus, the house specialty, comes in three different weights to fit your hunger. If you're not in the mood for steak, opt for barbecued ribs, trout, or fried chicken.

301 E. Rte. 66. © 928/635-2671. www.rods-steakhouse.com. Reservations recommended. Main courses $6–$15 lunch, $12–$40 dinner. AE, DISC, MC, V. Mon–Sat 11am–9:30pm.

16

Southern Utah's National Parks

For many people, the best part of a Utah vacation is exploring the state's national parks, which offer spectacular red-rock scenery, deep green forests, rivers, historic sites, and numerous opportunities for outdoor recreation.

Although visitation at some national parks has dropped in the past few years, Utah's parks remain popular. Zion National Park broke visitation records in 2004, and in 2006 Arches National Park recorded the highest number of visitors since 1999.

For those trying to avoid the crowds, go in the off season. The parks are busiest in summer, when most children are out of school, so visit at almost any other time. Fall is usually best. Spring is okay, but often windy; and winter can be delightful but chilly.

1 Zion National Park ★★

Early Mormon settler Isaac Behunin is credited with naming his homestead "Little Zion" because it seemed to be a bit of heaven on earth. Today, 150 years later, **Zion National Park** casts a spell over you as you gaze upon its sheer multicolored walls of sandstone, explore its narrow canyons, hunt for hanging gardens of wildflowers, and listen to the roar of the churning, tumbling Virgin River.

Here you'll discover a smorgasbord of experiences, sights, sounds, and even smells, from massive stone sculptures and monuments to lush forests and rushing rivers.

Zion is home to an abundance of wildlife, with mammals ranging from pocket gophers to mountain lions, hundreds of birds (including golden eagles), lizards of all shapes and sizes, and a dozen species of snakes. Mule deer are common, and you may also see foxes, coyotes, ringtails, beaver, porcupines, and plenty of squirrels and bats. Practically every summer visitor sees lizards, often the colorful collared and whiptail varieties, and hears the song of the canyon wren and the call of the piñon jay.

ESSENTIALS

Located in southwest Utah, at elevations ranging from 3,666 feet to 8,726 feet, Zion National Park has several sections: **Zion Canyon,** the main part of the park, where everyone goes, and the less-visited **Kolob Terrace** and **Kolob Canyons** areas.

GETTING THERE St. George and Cedar City are the closest towns with airport service. From either airport, it's easy to rent a car and drive to Zion. Utah 9 crosses the park, giving the main section of the park two entry gates, south and east. The drive into Zion Canyon from I-15 on the park's western side—following Utah 9 or Utah 17 and Utah 9 to the south entrance at Springdale—is the more popular route.

From the east, a spectacularly scenic 24-mile drive leads from Mt. Carmel on Utah 9, reached from the north or south on US 89. However, be aware that this route into the park drops over 2,500 feet in elevation, passes through the mile-long Zion–Mt.

Carmel Tunnel, and winds down six steep switchbacks. The tunnel is too small for two-way traffic that includes larger-than-standard passenger cars and pickup trucks. Buses, trucks, and most recreational vehicles must drive down the center of the tunnel, stopping all oncoming traffic. This applies to all vehicles over 7 feet 10 inches wide (including mirrors) or 11 feet 4 inches tall. These vehicles pay a $15 fee, good for two trips through the tunnel in a 7-day period. Contact park offices for details.

Kolob Terrace Road, with viewpoints and trail heads, is north off Utah 9 from the village of Virgin, about 15 miles west of the park's southern entrance. This road is closed in the winter. To reach the Kolob Canyons section, in the park's northwest corner, take the short Kolob Canyons Road off I-15 exit 40.

VISITOR INFORMATION   Contact **Zion National Park,** Springdale, UT 84767 (© **435/772-3256;** www.nps.gov/zion). You can order books, maps, and videos from the nonprofit **Zion Natural History Association,** Zion National Park, Springdale, UT 84767 (© **800/635-3959** or 435/772-3265; www.zionpark.org).

The **Zion Canyon Visitor Center,** near the south entrance, has outdoor exhibits, sells books and maps, and provides information. The smaller **Kolob Canyons Visitor Center,** in the northwest corner of the park off I-15, provides information, permits, books, and maps. The **Zion Human History Museum,** about 1 mile inside the south entrance, has museum exhibits, park information, and an orientation program, plus a bookstore. Both visitor centers and the museum are open daily (hours vary by season) except December 25.

FEES   Entry to the park (for up to 7 days), including unlimited use of the shuttle bus (Apr through Oct), costs $25 per private vehicle, $12 per individual on foot, bicycle, or motorcycle.

Oversize vehicles pay an additional $15 for use of the Zion–Mt. Carmel Tunnel on the east side of the park (see "Getting There," above).

Backcountry permits, available at either visitor center, are required for all overnight hikes in the park as well as all slot canyon hikes. Permits cost $10 for 1 or 2 people, $15 for 3 to 7, and $20 for 8 to 12.

RANGER PROGRAMS   A variety of free programs and activities are presented, mostly during the summer. Evening programs, which sometimes include a slide show, take place at campground amphitheaters and Zion Lodge. Topics vary but may include the animals or plants of the park, geology of the park, or perhaps some unique feature such as Zion's slot canyons. Rangers give short talks on similar subjects several times daily at the Zion Canyon Visitor Center and at other locations, and lead guided hikes and walks. Schedules are posted throughout the park. Children 6 to 12 can join the Junior Rangers to earn badges and patches.

SEEING THE HIGHLIGHTS

To get the most from your visit, your first stop should be the **Zion Canyon Visitor Center** (see "Visitor Information," above) for the orientation video and exhibits.

Then hop on the free **shuttle bus,** which takes you to the major roadside viewpoints. You'll be able to get off, look at the rock formations, take a short walk, then catch the next shuttle for a ride to the next stop. During the off season (Nov–Mar), you'll use your own vehicle.

We especially recommend stopping at the **Temple of Sinawava** and taking the easy 2-mile round-trip **Riverside Walk,** which follows the Virgin River through a narrow canyon past hanging gardens. Then head back to the lodge (total time: 2–4 hr.). At the lodge, stop by the gift shop and perhaps have lunch in the excellent restaurant.

Near the lodge, you'll find the trailhead for the **Emerald Pools.** Especially pleasant on hot days, this hike is discussed below under "Outdoor Pursuits." If you still have time and energy, head back to the south park entrance and stop at **Watchman** (east of Watchman Campground), for the 2-mile, 2-hour round-trip, moderately strenuous hike to a plateau with beautiful views of several rock formations and the town of Springdale.

OUTDOOR PURSUITS

Zion offers a wide variety of hiking trails, ranging from easy half-hour walks on paved paths to grueling overnight hikes over rocky terrain. Hikers with a fear of heights should be especially careful when choosing trails; many include steep drop-offs.

The **Weeping Rock Trail,** among the park's shortest hikes, is a .5-mile round-trip walk from the Zion Canyon Scenic Drive to a rock alcove with a spring and hanging gardens of ferns and wildflowers. Although paved, it's steep and not suitable for wheelchairs.

Another short hike, the **Lower Emerald Pools Trail** *ᴋ*, is an easy 1-hour walk. If you want to extend your trip to a moderately strenuous 2-hour hike, you can continue along the loop. A .6-mile paved path from the Emerald Pools parking area, suitable for those in wheelchairs with assistance, winds through a forest of oak, maple, fir, and cottonwood to a waterfall, a hanging garden, and the Lower Emerald Pool. From here, a steeper, rocky trail (not appropriate for wheelchairs) continues past cactus, yucca, and juniper another .5 mile to Upper Emerald Pool, with another waterfall. A third pool, just above Lower Emerald Pool, offers impressive reflections of the cliffs. The pools are named for the green color of the water, which is caused by algae.

A particularly scenic hike is the **Hidden Canyon Trail,** a 2-mile moderately strenuous hike that takes about 3 hours. Starting at the Weeping Rock parking area, the trail climbs 800 feet through a narrow water-carved canyon, ending at the canyon's mouth. Those wanting to extend the hike can go another .6 mile to a small natural arch. Hidden Canyon Trail includes long, dizzying drop-offs.

For a strenuous 4-hour, 5-mile hike — one that's definitely not for anyone with even a mild fear of heights—take the **Angel's Landing Trail** *ᴋ* to a summit that offers spectacular views into Zion Canyon. But be prepared: The final .5 mile follows a narrow, knife-edge trail along a steep ridge, where footing can be slippery even under the best of circumstances. Support chains have been set along parts of the trail.

Hiking **The Narrows** *ᴋᴋᴋ* is not hiking a trail at all. It involves walking or wading along the bottom of the Virgin River, through a spectacular 1,000-foot-deep chasm that, at a mere 20 feet wide, definitely lives up to its name. Passing fancifully sculpted sandstone arches, hanging gardens, and waterfalls, this moderately strenuous 16-mile one-way hike can take less than a day or several days. The Narrows are subject to flash flooding and can be very treacherous, and park service officials remind hikers that they are responsible for their own safety and should check on current water conditions and weather forecasts. This hike is *not* recommended when rain is forecast. Permits are required for full-day and overnight hikes (check with rangers for details), but are not needed for short day hikes, which you can begin just beyond the end of the 2-mile **Riverside Walk.**

Zion is one of America's few relatively bike-friendly national parks. It permits bikes on the paved **Pa'rus Trail,** which runs several miles along the Virgin River. Bikes are also allowed on the park's established roads, except in the Zion–Mt. Carmel tunnel;

from April through October, **Zion Canyon Scenic Drive** north of the Zion–Mt. Carmel Highway is open only to shuttle buses, bicyclists, and hikers, plus tour buses and motorists going to Zion Lodge.

Guided horseback rides in the park are available from late spring through early fall from **Canyon Trail Rides,** P.O. Box 128, Tropic, UT 84776 (℃ **435/679-8665;** www.canyonrides.com), based near Zion Lodge. A 1-hour ride along the Virgin River costs $30, and a half-day ride on the Sand Beach Trail costs $65. Riders must weigh no more than 220 pounds. Children must be at least 7 years old for the 1-hour ride, and 10 years old for the half-day ride.

WHERE TO STAY

The only lodging in Zion National Park is Zion Lodge. The other properties listed here are in Springdale, at the park's south entrance.

For additional information on lodging, dining, and area attractions, contact the **Zion Canyon Visitors Bureau,** P.O. Box 331, Springdale, UT 84767 (℃ **888/518-7070;** www.zionpark.com).

Canyon Ranch Motel   This series of two- and four-unit cottages set back from the highway looks old-fashioned on the outside but provides modern motel rooms inside. Some units have showers only, while others have shower/tub combos. Some units have kitchenettes. Room no. 13, with two queen-size beds, offers great views of the national park's rock formations; views from most other rooms are almost as good. There's a lawn with trees and picnic tables. All rooms are nonsmoking.

668 Zion Park Blvd. (P.O. Box 175), Springdale, UT 84767. ℃ 866/946-6276 or 435/772-3357. www.canyonranch motel.com. 22 units. Apr–Oct $64–$94 double; Nov–Mar $49–$79 double; kitchenettes $10 more year-round. AE, DISC, MC, V. Pets accepted; $10 fee. **Amenities:** Outdoor pool; hot tub. *In room:* A/C, TV, Wi-Fi.

Cliffrose Lodge & Gardens 🗘   With river frontage and 5 acres of lawns, shade trees, and flower gardens, the Cliffrose offers a beautiful setting just outside the entrance to Zion National Park. The architecture is Southwestern adobe style, with redwood balconies, and the outdoor rock waterfall Jacuzzi is a delight. The modern, well-kept rooms and suites have all the standard motel appointments, plus unusually large bathrooms with combination shower/tubs. Units accommodate two to six; most sleep four.

281 Zion Park Blvd., Springdale, UT 84767. ℃ 800/243-8824 or 435/772-3234. Fax 435/772-3900. www.cliffrose lodge.com. 40 units. Apr–Oct and holidays $139–$199 per unit. Off-season discounts available. AE, DISC, MC, V. **Amenities:** Large heated outdoor pool; whirlpool tub; coin-op laundry. *In room:* A/C, TV/VCR, fridge, Wi-Fi.

Flanigan's Inn 🗘🗘   A mountain-lodge atmosphere pervades this attractive complex of natural wood and rock, set among trees, lawns, and flowers just outside the entrance to the park. Parts of the inn date from 1947, and all rooms have been renovated. They have Southwestern decor, wood furnishings, and local art. One room has a fireplace; other units have whirlpool tubs. Some units have kitchenettes. All units are nonsmoking. A nature trail leads to a hilltop vista, and the inn has an excellent restaurant.

428 Zion Park Blvd., Springdale, UT 84767. ℃ 800/765-7787 or 435/772-3244. Fax 435/772-3396. www.flanigans. com. 34 units. Mid-Mar to mid-Nov and holidays $109–$139 double; $149–$259 suite. Off-season discounts available. AE, DISC, MC, V. **Amenities:** Restaurant (regional cuisine); heated outdoor pool; outdoor hot tub; full-service spa. *In room:* A/C, TV, Wi-Fi.

Zion Lodge 🗘🗘   The motel units and cabins here occupy a splendid location with equally splendid views. Each charming cabin has a private porch, stone (gas-burning) fireplace, two double beds, pine-board walls, and log beams. The comfortable motel rooms have two queen-size beds, a private porch or balcony, and all the usual amenities except TVs. Suites have one king bed, a sitting room, and a wet bar with a small refrigerator.

Zion National Park, UT. © **435/772-7700**. Information and reservations: Xanterra Parks & Resorts, Central Reservations, 6312 S, Fiddlers Green Circle, Ste. 600N, Greenwood Village, CO 80111. © **888/297-2757** or 303/297-2757. Fax 303/297-3175. www.zionlodge.com. 121 units. Mid-Mar to Nov motel $151 double; cabin $161 double; suite $171 double. Winter discounts and packages available AF, DISC, MC, V **Amenities:** Restaurant (see below). In room: A/C.

CAMPING

Both of Zion's main **campgrounds** 🐾🐾🐾 have paved roads, well-spaced sites, and lots of trees. Facilities include restrooms with flush toilets but no showers, and a dump station. The fee is $16 per night for basic sites, $18 to $20 per night for sites with electric hookups.

South Campground has 127 sites and no hookups. It's usually open from March through October. Reservations are not accepted, and it often fills by early afternoon in summer. **Watchman Campground** (© **877/444-6777** or www.recreation.gov for reservations, for an additional $10 fee) has 145 sites, with electric hookups at 63 sites. It is open year-round (reservations available spring to early fall only).

Lava Point, which has only six sites, is on the Kolob Terrace. It has fire grates, tables, and toilets, but no water, and there's no fee. Vehicles are limited to 19 feet. It's usually open from June through mid-October.

If you can't get a site in the park, or if you prefer hot showers or complete RV hookups, several campgrounds are in the surrounding area. The closest, **Zion Canyon Campground & RV Park,** 429 Zion Park Blvd., Springdale, UT 84767 (© **435/772-3237**; www.zioncamp.com), is a half-mile south of the park entrance. It's open year-round and has 220 sites, many of which are shaded. Although it gets crowded in summer, the campground is clean and well maintained; in addition to the usual showers and RV hookups, you'll find a self-service laundry, dump station, convenience store, and restaurant. Tenters are welcome; rates range from $22 to $27 for two people.

WHERE TO DINE

Red Rock Grill 🐾🐾 AMERICAN   A mountain-lodge atmosphere prevails here, complete with large windows that face the park's magnificent rock formations. The menu changes periodically, but specialties often include excellent slow-roasted prime rib and the popular wild Alaskan salmon. There are also steaks, several chicken dishes, and vegetarian items such as roasted vegetable tortellini. At lunch, you'll usually find grilled salmon burgers, beef burgers, sandwiches, and salads; breakfasts offer all the usuals, including a good buffet. Full liquor service is available. For something quick and cheap, Zion Lodge's **Castle Dome Café** serves burgers, deli sandwiches, hot dogs, pizza, and ice cream on an outdoor patio.

In Zion Lodge, Zion National Park. © **435/772-7760**. www.zionlodge.com. Dinner reservations required in summer. Breakfast $3.50–$8.95, lunch $5.95–$8.95, dinner main courses $13–$21. AE, DC, DISC, MC, V. Daily 6:30–10am, 11:30am–3pm, and 5:30–9pm.

Zion Park Gift & Deli 🐾 *Value* SANDWICHES   This is our choice for a top-quality deli-style sandwich at an economical price. You can eat at one of the cafe-style tables inside or on the outdoor patio, or carry your sandwich off on a hike. All baked goods are made in-house. In typical deli style, you order at the counter and wait as your meal is prepared with your choice of bread, meats, cheeses, and condiments. Stop here at breakfast for fresh-baked cinnamon rolls, muffins, banana nut bread, and other goodies. Locally made candy, including excellent fudge, and 24 flavors of ice cream and frozen yogurt are also offered, along with espresso. No alcohol is served.

866 Zion Park Blvd., Springdale. ⓒ 435/772-3843. Main courses $5–$10. AE, DISC, MC, V. Summer Mon–Sat 8am–9pm; reduced hours in winter.

Zion Pizza & Noodle ⓡ ⓚⁱᵈˢ PIZZA/PASTA In a former Mormon church with a turquoise steeple, this casual place has small, closely spaced tables. Baked in a slate stone oven, the 12-inch pizzas are our favorites. You can get practically any type you want, including Southwestern burrito pizza and barbecued chicken pizza. You can also design your own with a variety of toppings, from pepperoni to green chiles to pineapple. Options on the noodle side of the menu include pastas such as penne with grilled chicken, broccoli, carrots, fresh cream, and cheese. Calzones and stromboli are available. Beer is served inside and in the delightful year-round beer garden.

868 Zion Park Blvd., Springdale. ⓒ 435/772-3815. www.zionpizzanoodle.com. Reservations not accepted. Main courses $7.95–$15. No credit cards. Summer daily from 4pm; shorter hours in winter.

2 Bryce Canyon National Park ⭐⭐⭐

If you could visit only one national park in your lifetime, we'd suggest it be **Bryce Canyon.** Here you'll find magic, inspiration, and spectacular beauty. The main draw of the park is the thousands of intricately shaped hoodoos: those silent rock sentinels and congregations gathered in colorful cathedrals, arranged in formations that invite your imagination to run wild.

Hoodoos, geologists tell us, are pinnacles of rock, often oddly shaped, left standing after millions of years of water and wind erosion. But perhaps the truth really lies in a Paiute legend. These American Indians told of a "Legend People" who lived here in the old days and because of their evil ways, were turned to stone by the powerful Coyote. Even today, they remain frozen in time.

Although the colorful hoodoos first grab your attention, it isn't long before you notice the deep amphitheaters that enfold them, with their cliffs, windows, and arches, all in shades of red, brown, orange, yellow, and white. Beyond the rocks are the other faces of the park: three separate life zones, each with its own unique vegetation; and a kingdom of animals, from the busy chipmunks and ground squirrels to the stately mule deer and their archenemy, the mountain lion.

The park is named for Mormon pioneer Ebenezer Bryce, who moved to the area in 1875 with his wife Mary and tried raising cattle. Although they stayed only a few years, Bryce left behind his name and his oft-quoted description of the canyon as "a helluva place to lose a cow."

ESSENTIALS

GETTING THERE The closest major towns with airports are **St. George** (130 miles southwest on I-15) and **Cedar City** (on I-15 about 80 miles west of the park).

From St. George, travel north on I-15 for 10 miles to exit 16, then head east on Utah 9 for 63 miles to US 89, north 44 miles to Utah 12, and east 13 miles to the park entrance road. The entrance station is 3 miles south of Utah 12. From Cedar City (I-15 exits 57, 59, and 62), follow Utah 14 west 41 miles to its intersection with US 89, and take US 89 north 21 miles to Utah 12, then east 17 miles to the park entrance road.

Utah 12 runs east-west across the park. The bulk of the park, including the visitor center, is accessible from Utah 63, which branches off from Utah 12 and goes south into the main portions of the park. Utah 89 runs north to south, west of the park, and Utah 12 heads east to Tropic.

INFORMATION/VISITOR CENTER   Contact **Bryce Canyon National Park,** P.O. Box 640201, Bryce, UT 84764-0201 (© **435/834-5322;** www.nps.gov/brca). You can order books, maps, and videos from the nonprofit **Bryce Canyon Natural History Association,** P.O. Box 640051, Bryce, UT 84764-0051 (© **888/362-2642** or 435/834-4601; www.brycecanyon.org).

The **visitor center,** at the north end of the park, has exhibits on the geology and history of the area and a short introductory program. Rangers provide information and backcountry permits. The visitor center is open daily year-round except Thanksgiving and December 25.

FEES   Entry to the park (for up to 7 days) costs $25 per private vehicle, $12 per individual on foot, bicycle, or motorcycle, which includes unlimited use of the park shuttle (when it's operating).

Backcountry camping permits ($5 per trip for one or two individuals), available at the visitor center, are required for all overnight trips into the backcountry.

RANGER PROGRAMS   Evening talks, which may include a slide show, take place most nights at campground amphitheaters. Topics vary but may include such subjects as the animals and plants of the park, geology, and the role of humans in the park's early days. Rangers also give half-hour talks on similar subjects several times daily at various locations in the park. They also lead hikes and walks, including a moonlight hike (reservations required) and a wheelchair-accessible 1-hour canyon rim walk. Schedules are posted on bulletin boards at the visitor center, general store, campgrounds, and Bryce Canyon Lodge. During the summer, children under 13 can join the Junior Rangers, participate in a variety of programs, and earn badges and certificates.

SEEING THE HIGHLIGHTS

Because this is our favorite national park, we would be happy to spend our entire vacation here. But if you insist on saving time for the many other fascinating areas in the Southwest, there are ways to see a good deal of Bryce in a short amount of time.

Start at the **visitor center** and watch the short program that explains the area's geology. Then drive the 18-mile (one-way) dead-end **park road,** stopping at viewpoints to gaze down into the canyon. An alternative is to take the free **shuttle,** which will take you to most of the main viewpoints.

Whichever way you choose to get around, make sure you spend at least a little time at **Inspiration Point,** which offers a splendid (and, yes, inspirational) view of **Bryce Amphitheater** and its hundreds of statuesque pink, red, orange, and brown hoodoo stone sculptures.

After seeing the canyon from the top down, it's time to get some exercise. Walk at least partway down the **Queen's Garden Trail.** If you can spare 3 hours, hike down the Navajo Loop and return to the rim on the Queen's Garden Trail, as discussed below. An alternative is to take an easy walk along the **Rim Trail,** which provides spectacular views into the canyon. It's especially gorgeous about an hour before sunset.

Bryce Canyon Area Tours & Adventures (© **866/834-0043** or 435/834-5357; www.brycetours.com) offers 1½-hour sunrise and sunset tours. Reservations are required and cost is $26 per person.

OUTDOOR PURSUITS

One of the things we like best about Bryce Canyon is that you don't have to be an advanced backpacker to really get to know the park. However, all trails below the rim have at least some steep grades, so wear hiking boots with a traction tread and good ankle support to avoid ankle injuries. During the hot summer months, you'll want to hike either early or late in the day, carry plenty of water, and keep in mind that the deeper you go into the canyon, the hotter it gets.

The **Rim Trail,** which does not drop into the canyon but offers splendid views from above, meanders along the rim for over 5 miles. Overlooking Bryce Amphitheater, the trail allows excellent views along most of its length. An easy to moderate walk, it includes a .5-mile section between two overlooks—Sunrise and Sunset—that is suitable for wheelchairs. This trail is a good choice for an after-dinner stroll, when you can watch the changing evening light on the rosy rocks below.

Your best bet for getting down into the canyon and seeing the most with the least amount of sweat is to combine two popular trails—**Navajo Loop** *꼬꼬꼬* and **Queen's Garden.** The total distance is just under 3 miles, with a 521-foot elevation change. Most hikers take 2 to 3 hours to complete the trek. It's best to start at the Navajo Loop trailhead at Sunset Point and leave the canyon on the less-steep Queen's Garden Trail, returning to the rim at Sunrise Point, .5 mile to the north. The Navajo Loop section is fairly strenuous; Queen's Garden is moderate. Along the Navajo Loop you'll pass Thor's Hammer and wonder why it hasn't fallen, then ponder the towering skyscrapers of Wall Street. Turning onto the Queen's Garden Trail, you'll see some of the park's most fanciful formations—including the trail's namesake, majestic Queen Victoria—and Gulliver's Castle.

Those looking for more of a challenge might consider the **Hat Shop Trail,** a strenuous 3.8-mile round-trip with a 900-foot elevation change. Leaving from the Bryce Point Overlook, you'll drop quickly to the Hat Shop, so named because it consists of hard gray "hats" perched on narrow reddish-brown pedestals. Allow 4 hours.

For die-hard hikers who don't mind rough terrain, Bryce has two backcountry trails, usually open in summer only. The **Under-the-Rim Trail** runs for some 23 miles, providing an excellent opportunity to see the park's spectacular scenery. **Riggs Spring Loop Trail,** 8.8 miles long, offers splendid views of the pink cliffs in the southern part of the park. The truly ambitious can combine the two trails for a weeklong excursion. Permits are required for all overnight trips.

To see Bryce Canyon the way the early pioneers did, you need to view the landscape from a horse. **Canyon Trail Rides,** P.O. Box 128, Tropic, UT 84776 (© **435/679-8665;** www.canyonrides.com), offers a close-up view of Bryce's spectacular rock formations from the relative comfort of a saddle. The company has a desk inside Bryce Lodge. A 2-hour ride to the canyon floor and back costs $40 per person, and a half-day trip farther into the canyon costs $65 per person. Rides are offered April through November. Riders must be at least 7 years old for the 2-hour trip, at least 10 for the half-day ride, and weigh no more than 220 pounds.

Bryce is beautiful in winter, when the snow creates a perfect white frosting on the red, pink, orange, and brown rock statues. **Cross-country skiers** will find several marked, ungroomed trails (all above the rim), including the Fairyland Trail, which leads 1 mile through a pine and juniper forest to the Fairyland Point Overlook. From here, you can take the 1-mile Forest Trail back to the road, or continue north along the rim for another 1.2 miles to the park boundary. **Snowshoes** may be used above the rim, but not on cross-country ski tracks.

WHERE TO STAY

Note that room taxes add about 10% to the total cost.

Best Western Ruby's Inn *Kids*   This large Best Western provides most of the beds used by tired park visitors. The lobby is among the busiest places in the area, with an ATM, liquor store, beauty salon, 1 hour film processor, and activities desks where you can book excursions of all sorts, from horseback rides to helicopter tours. Off the lobby are a restaurant, an art gallery, a post office, and a huge general store. Outside are car rentals and two gas stations.

Spread among nine buildings, the modern motel rooms feature wood furnishings, art showing scenes of the area, and shower/tub combos; some have whirlpool tubs. Rooms at the back of the complex are a bit quieter, but you'll have to walk farther to the lobby. All rooms are smoke free.

1000 S. Utah 63 (at the entrance to Bryce Canyon), Bryce, UT 84764. ℂ 866/866-6616 or 435/834-5341. Fax 435/834-5265. www.rubysinn.com. 368 units. June–Sept $135–$159 double, $185 suite; Oct–May $70–$130 double, $135 suite. AE, DC, DISC, MC, V. Pets accepted. **Amenities:** Restaurant (p. 573); 2 indoor pools; 1 indoor and 1 outdoor Jacuzzi; game room; concierge; multiple activities desks; car-rental desk; courtesy transportation from Bryce Airport; business center; general store; liquor store; salon; 2 coin-op laundries. *In room:* A/C, TV, coffeemaker, hair dryer, iron, Wi-Fi.

Bryce Canyon Country Cabins   There's something special about staying in a log cabin during a national park vacation, but there's also something very appealing about hot showers and warm beds. Bryce Canyon Country Cabins offers the best of both worlds, with six recently constructed log-style cabins and a historic two-room pioneer cottage, set on a 20-acre farm. The grounds surrounding the cabins and cottage are nicely landscaped, and you get views out over the national park, although we wish the units were farther back from the highway. The intriguing part of the facility, though, is the farm behind the buildings, where cattle graze in the fields and the chickens think they own the place.

The comfortable cabins have knotty pine walls and ceilings, exposed beams, and ceiling fans. Each has two queen-size beds, a table with two chairs, a private porch, and outdoor barbecues. Bathrooms have showers only. The cottage, built in 1905, has two spacious rooms with country-style decor, each with its own entrance. Both of the rooms have two queen-size beds and full bathrooms with shower/tub combos. The cottage's two rooms can be rented together or individually.

320 N. Utah 12 (P.O. Box 141), Tropic, UT 84776. ℂ 888/679-8643 or 435/679-8643. www.brycecountrycabins.com. 8 units. Summer $85 double, $175 for both rooms of the cottage; lower rates at other times. AE, DC, MC, V. *In room:* A/C, TV, fridge, coffeemaker, hair dryer, microwave.

Bryce Canyon Lodge   Location is what you're paying for here, and there's no denying that this is the perfect place to stay while visiting Bryce Canyon. The handsome sandstone and ponderosa pine lodge, opened in 1924, contains a busy lobby, with information desks for horseback riding and other activities, and a well-stocked gift shop.

The lodge suites are luxurious, with ceiling fans and separate sitting rooms. The motel rooms are simple; although the outside of the building looks like a hunting lodge, the guest units are pleasant, modern accommodations, quite spacious, with two queen-size beds and either a balcony or a patio. However, we'd choose the "rustic luxury" of one of the cabins. They're fairly small, with tall ceilings that give a feeling of spaciousness, stone (gas-burning) fireplaces, two double beds, and log beams. It's the right place to stay in a beautiful national park setting like Bryce Canyon. All units are smoke free.

Bryce Canyon National Park, UT. © 435/834-5361. Information and reservations: Xanterra Parks & Resorts, Central Reservations, 6312 S, Fiddlers Green Circle, Ste. 600N, Greenwood Village, CO 80111. © 888/297-2757 or 303/297-2757. Fax 303/297-3175. www.brycecanyonlodge.com. 114 units (110 in motel rooms and cabins; 3 suites and 1 studio in lodge). $120–$150 double. AE, DISC, MC, V. Closed Nov–Mar. **Amenities:** Restaurant (p. 573); activities desk.

Bryce View Lodge *(Value* This basic modern American motel gets our vote for the best combination of economy and location. It consists of four two-story buildings, set back from the road and grouped around a large parking lot and attractively landscaped area. The simply decorated rooms are comfortable and quiet. Guests have access to the amenities at Best Western Ruby's Inn, across the street.

991 S. Utah 63 (P.O. Box 64002), Bryce, UT 84764. © 888/279-2304 or 435/834-5180. Fax 435/834-5181. www.bryceviewlodge.com. 160 units. Summer $78–$93 double, rest of the year $54–$65 double. AE, DC, DISC, MC, V. Pets accepted. **Amenities:** See Best Western Ruby's Inn, p. 571. *In room:* A/C, TV.

Foster's *(Value* You'll find quiet, economical lodging at Foster's. A modular unit contains small rooms, each with either one queen or two double beds, decorated with posters showing scenery of the area; bathrooms have showers only. Refrigerators and microwaves are available for a fee. Also on the grounds is a grocery store with a rather nice bakery.

1150 Utah 12 (P.O. Box 640010), Bryce, UT 84764. © 435/834-5227. Fax 435/834-5304. www.fostersmotel.com. 52 units. Summer $50 double; winter $35 double. AE, DISC, MC, V. 1½ miles west of the national park access road turnoff. **Amenities:** Restaurant (p. 573). *In room:* A/C, TV.

CAMPING

Typical of the West's national park campgrounds, the two campgrounds at Bryce offer plenty of trees for a genuine "forest camping" experience, easy access to trails, and limited facilities. **North Campground** has 107 sites and is open year-round; **Sunset Campground** has 101 sites and is open May through September only. We prefer North Campground because it's closer to the Rim Trail—making it easier to rush over to catch those amazing sunrise and sunset colors—but we would gladly take any site in either campground. They have modern restrooms with running water, but no RV hookups or showers. Reservations are available for some sites in North Campground (© 877/444-6777; www.recreation.gov) for an additional $10 fee. Camping at Sunset Campground is first come, first served; get there early to claim a site. Cost is $10 per night.

Pay showers, a coin-operated laundry, a snack bar, food and camping supplies, and souvenirs are available in the summer at the **General Store** (for information, contact Bryce Canyon Lodge © 435/834-5361), which is a healthy walk from either campground. The park service operates an RV dump station (fee) in the summer.

Those seeking a commercial campground with hot showers, RV hookups, and all the usual amenities won't do any better than **Ruby's Inn RV Park & Campground**, 1280 S. Utah 63, Bryce, UT 84764 (© 866/866-6616 or 435/834-5301), right outside the park along the park's shuttle-bus route. Many of the 200 sites are shaded and there's an attractive tent area. Facilities include a pool, two coin-op laundries, a game room, horseshoes, barbecue grills, and a store with groceries and RV supplies. Also on the grounds are several camping cabins ($50 double) and tepees ($28 double), which share the campground's bathhouse. Campsite rates for two people are $28 to $31 for RV sites and $20 for tent sites. The campground is open from April through October.

WHERE TO DINE

Bryce Canyon Lodge ☆☆ AMERICAN   We would come here just for the mountain-lodge atmosphere, with two large stone fireplaces and large windows looking out on the park. But the food's good, too. The menu changes periodically, but may include dinner specialties such as the slow-roasted pork loin with cherry glaze and the grilled trout amandine, which is dusted with a seasoned mix and topped with toasted almonds. The menu also offers steaks—including a wonderful bourbon saloon steak (a grilled flat iron steak prepared with a bourbon-mustard marinade and topped with a spicy mushroom sauce and onion straws), chicken, and several vegetarian selections. At lunch, you'll find sandwiches, salads, and other lighter items. Breakfasts offer the usual American standards and an excellent buffet. The restaurant has full liquor service.

Bryce Canyon National Park. ⓒ **435/834-8760.** www.brycecanyonlodge.com. Reservations required for dinner. Main courses $4.95–$10 breakfast and lunch, $11–$22 dinner. AE, DC, DISC, MC, V. Daily 6:30–10:30am, 11am–3:30pm, and 5:30–9:30pm. Closed Nov–Mar.

Cowboy's Buffet & Steak Room STEAK/SEAFOOD   The busiest restaurant in the Bryce Canyon area, this place moves 'em through with buffets at every meal, plus a well-rounded menu and friendly service. The breakfast buffet offers more choices than you'd expect, and at the lunch buffet you'll find country-style ribs, fresh fruit, salads, soups, and vegetables. The dinner buffet features charbroiled rib-eye steak and other meats, pastas, potatoes, and salads. Regular menu dinner entrees include prime rib, steaks, ribs, grilled Utah trout, burgers, and salads. In addition to the large, Western-style dining room, a patio is open in summer. There is full liquor service.

At the Best Western Ruby's Inn, 1000 S. Utah 63, Bryce. ⓒ **435/834-5341.** www.rubysinn.com. Reservations not accepted. Breakfast and lunch $6.95–$16, dinner main courses and buffets $8.95–$26. AE, DC, DISC, MC, V. Summer daily 6:30am–10pm; winter daily 6:30am–9pm.

Foster's Family Steak House STEAK/SEAFOOD   The simple Western decor here provides the right atmosphere for a family steakhouse. Locally popular for its slow-roasted prime rib and steamed Utah trout, Foster's also offers several steaks (we like the 14-oz. T-bone), sandwiches, a soup of the day, and homemade chili with beans. All the pastries, pies, and breads are baked on the premises. Bottled beer is available with meals.

At Foster's motel, 1150 Utah 12, about 1½ miles west of the park entrance road. ⓒ **435/834-5227.** www.fostersmotel. com. Most breakfast and lunch items $3.75–$9.95, dinner main courses $9.95–$25. AE, DISC, MC, V. Mar–Nov daily 7am–10pm; call for winter hours.

3 Capitol Reef National Park ☆☆☆

A wonderful little-known gem, **Capitol Reef National Park** offers loads of that spectacular southern Utah scenery, but with a unique twist and a geologic personality all its own. You'll see the aptly named Hamburger Rocks, sitting atop a white sandstone table; the silent, eerie Temple of the Moon; and the commanding Castle. The colors of Capitol Reef's canyon walls are spectacular, which is why Navajos called this "The Land of the Sleeping Rainbow."

But Capitol Reef is much more than brilliant rocks and barren desert. The Fremont River creates a lush oasis in an otherwise unforgiving land, with cottonwoods and willows along its banks. The area is also rich in history, with thousand-year-old rock art, historic buildings, and other traces of the past.

ESSENTIALS

GETTING THERE   The park straddles Utah 24, which connects with I-70 to the northeast and northwest. Those coming from Bryce Canyon National Park can follow Utah 12 northeast to its intersection with Utah 24, and continue east into Capitol Reef. If you're approaching from the Four Corners area, follow Utah 276 or Utah 95 (or both) north to the intersection with Utah 24, where you'll then go west into the park.

INFORMATION/VISITOR CENTER   Contact **Capitol Reef National Park,** HC 70 Box 15, Torrey, UT 84775 (℗ **435/425-3791;** www.nps.gov.care).

The **visitor center** is on the park access road at its intersection with Utah 24. It's open daily except for several major holidays, and has exhibits on the area's geology and history. You can get information and backcountry permits, pick up free brochures, and purchase books, maps, and videos.

FEES   Entry to the park (for up to 7 days) costs $5 per vehicle. Free permits, available at the visitor center, are required for all overnight hiking trips into the backcountry.

RANGER PROGRAMS   Rangers present a variety of free programs and activities from spring through fall. Campfire programs take place most evenings at the outdoor amphitheater next to Fruita Campground. Topics vary but may include animals and plants, geology, and human history in and of the area. Rangers also lead hikes and walks and give short talks on history at the pioneer Fruita Schoolhouse and the Mormon homestead. Schedules are posted on bulletin boards at the visitor center and campground. Kids can become Junior Rangers or Junior Geologists; they'll learn to map ancient earthquakes, inspect water bugs, and so on.

SEEING THE HIGHLIGHTS

Start at the **visitor center,** where you will learn about the park's geology and early history. From there, the paved 25-mile round-trip **Scenic Drive** leads south into the park, offering good views of its dramatic canyons and rock formations. Pick up a free copy of the Scenic Drive brochure at the entrance station and set out, stopping at viewpoints to gaze out at the array of colorful cliffs and commanding rocks.

If the weather's dry, drive down the gravel **Capitol Gorge Road** (5 miles round-trip) at the end of the paved Scenic Drive for a look at what many consider the best backcountry scenery in the park. If you're up for a short walk, the relatively flat 2-mile (round-trip) **Capitol Gorge Trail,** which starts at the end of Capitol Gorge Road, takes you to the historic **Pioneer Register,** a rock wall where traveling pioneers "signed in."

HISTORIC SITES

In the park, you'll find evidence of man's presence through the centuries. The **Fremont** people lived along the river as early as A.D. 700, and their petroglyphs (images carved into rock) and pictographs (images painted on rock) are visible on the canyon walls. Prospectors and other travelers passed through **Capitol Gorge** in the late 1800s, leaving their names on a wall of rock that came to be known as the **Pioneer Register.** You can reach it on a 2-mile loop; see p. 575.

Mormon pioneers established the appropriately named community of **Fruita** when they discovered that this was a good spot to grow fruit. The tiny 1896 **Fruita Schoolhouse** served as a church, social hall, and meeting hall, in addition to being a one-room schoolhouse. The school closed in 1941, and it has been restored and furnished with old wood-and-wrought-iron desks, a wood stove, a chalkboard, textbooks, and even the hand bell that used to call students to class. Nearby, the **orchards** planted by the settlers continue to flourish, tended by park workers who invite you to sample the "fruits" of their labors.

The historic **Gifford Farmhouse,** built in 1908, is a typical early-20th-century Utah farmhouse. It offers displays of period objects and often schedules demonstrations of pioneer skills, such as quilting and rug making. Park across the road at the picnic area, a short path leads to the farmhouse.

OUTDOOR PURSUITS

This is the real Wild West; little has changed from the way cowboys, bank robbers, settlers, and gold miners found it in the late 1800s. Among the last areas in the continental United States to be explored, many parts of Capitol Reef National Park are still practically unknown, perfect for those who want to see this rugged country in its natural state. Several local companies offer guide and shuttle services. They include **Hondoo Rivers and Trails,** 90 E. Main St. (P.O. Box 98), Torrey, UT 84775 (© **800/ 332-2696** or 435/425-3519; www.hondoo.com); and **Wild Hare Expeditions,** 116 W. Main St. (P.O. Box 750194), Torrey, UT 84775 (© **888/304-4273** or 435/425-3999; www.color-country.net/~thehare).

For those who want to strike out on their own, the park's hiking trails offer panoramic views of colorful cliffs and soaring spires, eerie journeys through desolate steep-walled canyons, and cool oases along the tree-shaded Fremont River. Watch for petroglyphs and other reminders of this area's first inhabitants.

Among the best short hikes is the 2-mile round-trip **Capitol Gorge Trail.** It's easy, mostly level walking along the bottom of a narrow canyon, but looking up at the tall, smooth walls of rock conveys a strong sense of what the pioneers must have seen and felt 100 years ago, when they moved rocks and debris to haul their wagons up this canyon. Starting at the end of the dirt Capitol Gorge Road, the hiking trail leads past the **Pioneer Register,** where prospectors and other early travelers carved their names. The earliest legible signatures were made in 1871 by J. A. Call and "Wal" Bateman.

A more strenuous hike is the 3.5-mile round-trip **Cassidy Arch Trail.** This route offers spectacular views as it climbs steeply from the floor of Grand Wash to high cliffs overlooking the park. From the trail, you'll see Cassidy Arch, a natural stone arch named for outlaw Butch Cassidy, who is believed to have used the Grand Wash as a hideout. The trail is off the Grand Wash dirt road, which branches off the east side of the highway about halfway down the park's Scenic Drive.

As in most national parks, **bikes and four-wheel-drive vehicles** must stay on established roads, but Capitol Reef has several so-called roads—actually little more than dirt trails—that provide exciting opportunities for those using 4WD or pedal-power. ATVs are not permitted. Both the Grand Wash and Capitol Gorge roads, plus several much longer dirt roads, are open to mountain bikes as well as four-wheel-drive vehicles. Details are available at the visitor center.

WHERE TO STAY

There are no lodging or dining facilities in the park; the town of Torrey, just west of the park entrance, can take care of most needs. Room tax adds 9% to lodging bills.

Austin's Chuckwagon Motel This attractive family-owned and -operated motel offers a wide range of options. The well-maintained property includes modern motel rooms, which have Southwestern decor, phones, and two queen-size beds; and a family suite with a large living room, fully equipped kitchen, and three bedrooms that sleep six. Our choice here, however, is one of the plush but still Western-style cabins. Measuring 576 square feet, each cabin has two bedrooms (each with a queen-size bed), a living room with a queen-size sofa bed, a complete kitchen, a full bathroom with shower/tub combo, a covered porch, and a small yard with a barbecue grill and a picnic table. The grounds are attractively landscaped, with a lawn and large trees; also on the property is a grocery store/bakery with a well-stocked deli that prepares hot and cold sandwiches. All rooms are smoke-free.

12 W. Main St. (P.O. Box 750180), Torrey, UT 84775. ⓒ 800/863-3288 or 435/425-3335. Fax 435/425-3434. www. austinschuckwagonmotel.com. 24 units. Motel rooms $69 double (lower rates Mar and Nov); cabins $125 for up to 4; family suite $135 double. AE, DISC, MC, V. Closed Dec–Feb. **Amenities:** Deli; outdoor pool; whirlpool; salon; coin-op laundry. *In room:* A/C, TV.

Capitol Reef Inn & Cafe   This older, Western-style motel—small, beautifully landscaped, and well maintained—offers homey, comfortable guest rooms. The furnishings are handmade of solid wood. One unit has a shower/tub combo; the rest have showers only. Facilities include a playground and a lovely desert garden. The book and gift shop offers American Indian crafts, guidebooks, and maps.

360 W. Main St. (Utah 24), Torrey, UT 84775. ⓒ 435/425-3271. www.capitolreefinn.com. 10 units. $48 double. AE, DISC, MC, V. Closed Nov–Mar. **Amenities:** Restaurant (p. 577); large hot tub. *In room:* A/C, TV, fridge, coffeemaker.

SkyRidge Inn Bed & Breakfast 👫👫   This combination B&B and art gallery offers a delightful alternative to the standard motel. Rooms in the three-story Territorial-style inn are distinctively decorated with an eclectic mix of antiques and contemporary art. Two have private decks with hot tubs; another has a two-person whirlpool tub inside and a private deck. The inn sits on 75 acres, with hiking trails and spectacular views. Full breakfasts include homemade granola, fresh-baked coffeecake or muffins, and a hot entree such as pecan griddlecakes served with maple breakfast sausage. Smoking is not permitted.

950 E. Utah 24 (P.O. Box 750220), Torrey, UT 84775. ⓒ 800/448-6990 or 435/425-3222. www.skyridgeinn.com. 6 units. Apr–Oct $109–$159 double; Nov–Mar $95–$135 double. Rates include breakfast and evening hors d'oeuvres. AE, MC, V. **Amenities:** Whirlpool tub. *In room:* A/C, TV/VCR, hari dryer, CD player, Wi-Fi.

CAMPING

The 71-site **Fruita Campground,** open year-round, offers modern restrooms, drinking water, picnic tables, fire grills, and an RV dump station (open in summer only), but no showers or RV hookups. It's along the main park road, 1 mile south of the visitor center. Water may be turned off in winter, leaving only pit toilets. Camping costs $10; reservations are not accepted.

The park also has two **primitive campgrounds,** free and open year-round on a first-come, first-served basis. Both have tables, fire grills, and pit toilets, but no water. Check for directions and road conditions before going, because unpaved roads may be impassable in wet weather.

Backcountry camping is permitted in much of the park with a free permit, available at the visitor center. Fires are forbidden in the backcountry.

For a commercial campground with hot showers and RV hookups, we especially like the **Sandcreek RV Park,** 540 Utah 24 (P.O. Box 750276), Torrey, UT 84775 (ⓒ **435/425-3577,** 407/363-1622 in winter; www.sandcreekrv.com). Five miles west of the park entrance, this 24-site campground has an open, grassy area, numerous young trees, and great views. Facilities include a large, clean bathhouse; horseshoe pits; a gallery; a dump station; and coin-op laundry. Rates are $12 for tents and $16 to $18 for RVs. It's open April through mid-October.

WHERE TO DINE

Cafe Diablo 🐴🐴 SOUTHWESTERN Looks are deceiving. What appears to be a simple small-town cafe in a converted home is in fact a very fine restaurant, offering innovative beef, pork, chicken, seafood, and vegetarian selections, many created with a Southwestern flair. The menu varies but could include pumpkin seed–crusted local trout served with cilantro-lime sauce and wild-rice pancakes; Utah lamb marinated with sage and rosemary; and artichoke and sun-dried tomato tamales. Pastries and ice creams, all made on the premises, are spectacular. Beer, wine, and cocktails are served.

599 W. Main St., Torrey. 🕐 **435/425-3070.** www.cafediablo.net. Main courses $18–$32. MC, V. Daily 5–10pm. Closed mid-Oct to late Apr.

Capitol Reef Inn & Cafe 🐴🐴 *Finds* AMERICAN This local favorite offers fine, fresh, healthy cuisine that's among the best you'll find in Utah. Known for its locally raised trout, the cafe is equally famous for the 10-vegetable salad served with all dinner entrees. Vegetables are grown locally, and several dishes—such as spaghetti and excellent fettuccine primavera—can be ordered vegetarian or with meat or fish. Steaks and chicken are also served. The atmosphere is casual, with comfortable seating, American Indian crafts, and large windows. The restaurant offers wine and beer.

360 W. Main St. 🕐 **435/425-3271.** www.capitolreffinn.com. Main courses $4.95–$11 breakfast and lunch, $8.95–$19 dinner. AE, DISC, MC, V. Daily 7am–9pm. Closed Nov–Mar.

4 Arches & Canyonlands National Parks

Massive sandstone spires and arches that seem to defy gravity, all colored by iron and other minerals in shades of orange, red, and brown, define these two national parks. On opposite sides of the town of Moab, the parks offer numerous opportunities for hiking, mountain biking, and four-wheeling.

No lodging facilities, restaurants, or stores are inside either national park; most visitors stay and eat in Moab. For lodging, camping, and restaurant information for Moab, see "A Base Camp in Moab" (p. 582).

Moab is on US 191, 30 miles south of I-70 (take exit 180 at Crescent Junction) and 53 miles north of Monticello.

ARCHES NATIONAL PARK

Natural stone arches and fantastic rock formations, which look as if they were sculpted by an artist's hand, are the defining features of this park, and they exist in remarkable numbers and variety. Best of all, the formations here seem more accessible and less forbidding than the spires and pinnacles at nearby Canyonlands National Park. Arches is visitor-friendly, with relatively short, well-maintained trails leading to most of the park's major attractions.

Some people think of arches as bridges, but to geologists there's a big difference. Bridges are formed when a river slowly bores through solid rock. The often bizarre and beautiful contours of arches result from the erosive force of rain and snow, which freezes and thaws, dissolving the "glue" that holds sand grains together and chipping away at the stone, until gravity finally pulls a chunk off.

ESSENTIALS

GETTING THERE   From Moab, drive 5 miles north on US 191.

VISITOR INFORMATION   Contact **Arches National Park,** P.O. Box 907, Moab, UT 84532 (© **435/719-2299;** www.nps.gov/arch). **Canyonlands Natural History Association,** 3031 South US 191, Moab, UT 84532 (© **800/840-8978** or 435/259-6003; www.cnha.org), sells books, maps, and videos.

The visitor center, just inside the park entrance gate, provides maps, brochures, and information. It's open daily except December 25.

FEES   Entry to the park (for up to 7 days) costs $20 per vehicle, $10 per person on foot, bicycle, or motorcycle.

RANGER PROGRAMS   From March through October, rangers lead guided hikes on the Fiery Furnace Trail twice daily (see "Outdoor Pursuits," below), as well as daily nature walks at various park locations. Evening campfire programs (Apr–Oct) cover topics such as rock art, geological processes, and wildlife. A schedule of events is posted at the visitor center. Kids between 6 and 12 can pick up a Junior Ranger booklet at the visitor center. After completing the activities in the booklet and participating in several programs, they'll earn a badge.

SEEING THE HIGHLIGHTS

Arches is the easiest of Utah's national parks to see in a day, if that's all you can spare. An 18-mile (one-way) **scenic drive** offers splendid views of countless natural rock arches and other formations, and several easy hikes reveal additional scenery. Allow 1½ hours for the round-trip drive, adding time for optional hikes. Start by viewing the short program at the **visitor center** to get a feel for what lies ahead. Then drive north along the scenic drive, stopping at viewpoints and for occasional short walks. The scenic drive ends at the often-crowded parking area for the **Devils Garden Trailhead.** From here, you can hike to some of the park's unique arches, including **Landscape Arch,** which is among the longest natural rock spans in the world. From the trailhead parking lot, it's 18 miles back to the visitor center.

OUTDOOR PURSUITS

Most of the hiking trails here are short and relatively easy. Because of the hot summer sun and lack of shade, it's wise to carry water on even the shortest hike.

One easy walk is to **Sand Dune Arch,** a good place to take kids who want to play in the sand. It's only .3 mile (round-trip), but you can add 1.2 miles by continuing to Broken Arch. Sand Dune Arch is hidden among and shaded by rock walls, with a naturally created giant sandbox below the arch. Those continuing to Broken Arch should watch for mule deer and kit foxes along the way. Allow about 30 minutes to Sand Dune Arch and back; to Broken Arch, 1 hour.

From the **Devils Garden Trail,** you can see about 15 to 20 arches on a fairly long, strenuous, and difficult hike, or view some exciting scenery by following only part of the route. We suggest taking at least the easy to moderate 1.6-mile round-trip hike to **Landscape Arch**✿, a long, thin ribbon of stone that's one of the most beautiful arches in the park. Watch for mule deer along the way, and allow about an hour. Past Landscape Arch, the trail becomes more challenging, but it offers numerous additional views, including panoramas of the curious Double O Arch and a large, dark tower known as Dark Angel. From the section of the trail where Dark Angel is visible, you are 2.5 miles from the trailhead. If you turn back at this point, the round trip will take about 3 hours.

Considered by many to be the park's most scenic hike, the 3-mile round-trip **Delicate Arch Trail** *☞* is a moderate-to-difficult hike, with slippery slickrock, no shade, and some steep drop-offs along a narrow cliff. Hikers are rewarded with a dramatic and spectacular view of Delicate Arch. Allow 2 to 3 hours.

The **Fiery Furnace Guided Hike** is a difficult and strenuous 2-mile round-trip naturalist-led hike to some of the most colorful formations in the park. Guided hikes venture into this restricted area twice daily from spring through fall, by reservation, and last 2¼ to 3 hours. The cost is $10 for adults, $5 for children 6 to 12.

CAMPING IN THE PARK

At the north end of the park's scenic drive, **Devils Garden Campground** is Arches's only developed camping area. The 52 well-spaced sites nestle among rocks, with plenty of piñon and juniper trees. From March through October, the campground accepts reservations (© **877/444-6777;** www.recreation.gov), with a $9 additional booking fee. In summer, the campground fills early, often by 9am, with people trying to garner the 24 first-come, first-served sites; make reservations or get to the campground early, often by 7:30am. Sites cost $20 per night. There are no showers or RV hookups.

CANYONLANDS NATIONAL PARK

Utah's largest national park is not for the sightseer out for a Sunday afternoon drive. Instead, it rewards those willing to spend time and energy—*lots* of energy—exploring the rugged backcountry. Sliced into districts by the Colorado and Green rivers, this is a land of extremes: vast panoramas, dizzyingly deep canyons, dramatically steep cliffs, broad mesas, and towering spires.

The most accessible part of Canyonlands is the **Island in the Sky District,** in the northern section of the park. A paved road leads to sites such as Grand View Point, which overlooks some 10,000 square miles of rugged wilderness.

The **Needles District,** in the southeast corner, offers only a few viewpoints along the paved road, but it boasts numerous possibilities for hikers, backpackers, and high-clearance four-wheel-drives. Named for its tall red-and-white-striped rock pinnacles, this diverse district is home to impressive arches, including 150-foot-tall Angel Arch, as well as grassy meadows and the confluence of the Green and Colorado rivers.

Most park visitors don't get a close-up view of the **Maze District;** they see it off in the distance. That's because it's practically inaccessible. You'll need a lot of endurance and at least several days to see even a few of its sites, such as the appropriately named Lizard Rock and Beehive Arch.

ESSENTIALS

GETTING THERE   To reach the Island in the Sky Visitor Center, 34 miles west of Moab, take US 191 north to Utah 313, and follow it south into the park. To reach the Needles Visitor Center, 75 miles southwest of Moab, take US 191 south to Utah 211, and follow it west into the park. Getting to the Maze District is a bit more interesting. From I-70 west of Green River, take Utah 24 south. Watch for signs and follow two- and four-wheel-drive dirt roads east into the park.

VISITOR INFORMATION   Contact **Canyonlands National Park,** 2282 SW Resource Blvd., Moab, UT 84532 (© **435/719-2313;** www.nps.gov/cany). Books,

> ### Moments A Bird's-Eye View of Canyonlands
>
> Canyonlands is beautiful, but many of its most spectacular sections are difficult to get to—to say the least. One solution is to take to the air. **Slickrock Air Guides, Inc.** (© **866/259-1626** or 435/259-6216; www.slickrockairguides.com), offers 1-hour scenic flights over Canyonlands National Park and nearby areas for $125 per person; 2½-hour flights that take in Canyonlands and Monument Valley cost $230 per person.

very useful maps, and videos are available from the nonprofit **Canyonlands Natural History Association,** 3031 South US 191, Moab, UT 84532 (© **800/840-8978** or 435/259-6003; www.cnha.org).

Island in the Sky Visitor Center, in the northern part of the park, and **Needles Visitor Center,** in the southern section, provide maps, free brochures on hiking trails, and, most important, advice from rangers. We can't overemphasize how brutal the terrain at Canyonlands can be. It's important to know not only your own limitations, but also the limitations of your vehicle and other equipment.

FEES   Entry to the park (for up to 7 days) costs $20 per vehicle, $10 per person on foot, bike, or motorcycle.

Permits, available at visitor centers, are required for all overnight stays except at the established campgrounds. Call © **435/259-4351** or check the park website (see "Visitor Information," above) for rates and reservations.

RANGER PROGRAMS   On summer evenings at Squaw Flat and Willow Flat campgrounds, rangers offer campfire programs on various aspects of the park. Short morning talks take place in summer at the Island in the Sky Visitor Center and at Grand View Point.

SEEING THE HIGHLIGHTS

Canyonlands is not an easy place to see in a short time. In fact, if your schedule permits only a day or less, we suggest skipping the Needles and Maze districts entirely and going directly to the **Island in the Sky Visitor Center.** After looking at the exhibits, drive to several of the overlooks, stopping along the way for a short hike or two. Make sure you stop at the **Grand View Point Overlook,** at the south end of the paved road. Hiking the **Grand View Trail,** which is especially scenic in the late afternoon, literally gives you the "Grand View" of the park. Allow about 1½ hours for the easy 2-mile walk. We also recommend the **Upheaval Dome Overlook Trail,** which should take about half an hour and will bring you to a mile-wide crater of mysterious origins.

OUTDOOR PURSUITS

Canyonlands has little shade and no reliable water sources, and temperatures soar to 100°F (38°C) in summer. Rangers strongly advise that hikers carry at least a gallon of water per person per day, along with sunscreen, a hat, and all the usual hiking and emergency equipment. If you expect to do serious hiking, try to plan your trip for the spring or fall, when conditions are much more hospitable. Because some trails may be confusing, hikers attempting the longer ones should carry good topographic maps.

In the Island in the Sky District, the **Mesa Arch Trail** provides the casual visitor with an easy .5-mile (round-trip) self-guided nature walk among piñon and juniper trees, cactus, and a plant called Mormon tea, from which Mormon pioneers made a tealike beverage. The loop trail's main scenic attraction is an arch, made of Navajo sandstone, that hangs precariously on the edge of a cliff, framing a spectacular view of nearby mountains. Allow about a half-hour.

An easy 2-mile hike, especially pretty at sunset, is the **Grand View Trail** ✦, which follows the canyon rim from Grand View Point and shows off numerous canyons and rock formations, the Colorado River, and distant mountains. Allow about 1½ hours.

A bit more strenuous is the 5-mile **Neck Spring Trail,** which starts about .5 mile south of the Island in the Sky Visitor Center. Allow 3 to 4 hours for this hike, which follows old paths to two springs. You'll see water troughs, hitching posts, rusty cans, and the ruins of an old cabin. Climb to the top of the rim for a great view of the canyons and the Henry Mountains, some 60 miles away.

In the Needles District, one relatively easy hike is the **Roadside Ruin Trail,** a short (.3-mile), self-guided nature walk that takes about a half-hour round-trip. It leads to a prehistoric granary, probably used by the Anasazi (ancestral Puebloans) some 700 to 1,000 years ago to store corn, nuts, and other foods.

For a bit more of a challenge, try the **Slickrock Foot Trail,** a 2.4-mile loop that leads to several viewpoints and takes 2 or 3 hours. Slickrock—a general term for any bare rock surface—can be slippery, especially when wet. Viewpoints show off the stair-step topography of the area, from its colorful canyons and cliffs to its flat mesas and striped needles.

From **Elephant Hill Trailhead,** you can follow several interconnecting trails into the backcountry. The road to the trailhead is gravel, but it is graded and drivable in most two-wheel-drive passenger cars; those in large vehicles such as motor homes, however, will want to avoid it. The 11-mile round-trip **Elephant Hill–Druid Arch hike** ✦ can be done in 4 to 6 hours and is moderately difficult, with some steep drop-offs and quite a bit of slickrock. But the views are well worth it. You hike through narrow rock canyons, past colorful spires and pinnacles, and on to the huge Druid Arch, which somewhat resembles the stone structures at Stonehenge.

The **Confluence Overlook Trail,** an 11-mile round-trip day or overnight hike, leads to a spectacular bird's-eye view of the confluence of the Green and Colorado rivers and the 1,000-foot-deep gorges they've carved. The hike is moderately difficult, with steep drop-offs and little shade, but it splendidly reveals the many colors of the Needles District, as well as views into the Maze District of the park. Allow 4 to 6 hours.

Unlike most national parks, where all motor vehicles and mountain bikes are restricted to paved roads, Canyonlands has miles of rough roads for four-wheel-drive vehicles. Four-wheelers must stay on designated 4WD roads, but keep in mind that the term "road" can mean anything from a graded, well-marked, two-lane gravel byway to a pile of loose rocks.

Mountain bikes are also allowed on these roads, but they share space with motor vehicles and occasional hikers and horseback riders. Because some of the four-wheel-drive roads have spots of deep sand—which can turn into quicksand when wet—mountain biking may not be as much fun here as you'd expect.

The best four-wheel-drive adventure in the Island in the Sky District is the **White Rim Road** ✦✦. It winds some 100 miles through the district and affords spectacular views, from broad panoramas of rock and canyon to close-ups of red and orange towers and buttes. A high-clearance 4WD is necessary. Allow 2 to 3 days for the entire trip. There are primitive campgrounds along the way, but reservations and backcountry permits are needed. Mountain bikers also enjoy this trail, especially when accompanying a four-wheel-drive support vehicle with supplies.

Four-wheel-drive fans going into the Needles District will find one of their ultimate challenges on the **Elephant Hill Jeep Road,** which begins at a well-marked turnoff near Squaw Flat Campground. Although most of the 10-mile trail is only moderately difficult, the stretch over Elephant Hill itself (near the beginning of the drive) can be a nightmare. It has steep, rough slickrock, drifting sand, loose rock, and treacherous ledges. Coming down the hill, you'll reach one switchback that requires you to back to the edge of a steep cliff. This road is also a favorite of mountain bikers, although bikes will have to be walked on some stretches because of the abundance of sand and rocks. The route offers views of numerous rock formations, plus panoramas of steep cliffs and rock "stairs." Allow 8 hours to 3 days. Backcountry permits are needed for overnight trips.

For a spectacular view of the Colorado River, the **Colorado River Overlook Road** in the Needles District can't be beat. This 14-mile round-trip is popular with four-wheelers, backpackers, and mountain bikers. Considered among the park's easiest 4WD roads, the first part, which is accessible by high-clearance two-wheel-drives, is very easy indeed. But the second half has a few rough and rocky sections that require four-wheel-drive. The road features numerous panoramic vistas and a spectacular 360-degree view of the park and the Colorado River, some 1,000 feet below.

CAMPING IN THE PARK

The park has two developed campgrounds, both first come, first served. In the Island in the Sky District, **Willow Flat Campground** has 12 sites, picnic tables, fire grates, and vault toilets; camping is $10. In the Needles District, **Squaw Flat Campground** has 26 sites, fire grates, picnic tables, flush toilets, and drinking water; the fee is $15 per night.

A BASE CAMP IN MOAB

Most visitors to Arches and Canyonlands national parks stay in Moab, which offers easy access to both parks, plenty of other opportunities for outdoor recreation, and an abundance of places to sleep and eat. For information, contact the **Moab Area Travel Council,** P.O. Box 550, Moab, UT 84532 (© **800/635-6622** or 435/259-6281; www.discovermoab.com). When you arrive, stop by the **Moab Information Center,** at the corner of Main and Center streets.

WHERE TO STAY

Moab has most of the major medium-priced chains, located on Main Street. Our favorite of the franchises here is the very well maintained **La Quinta Inn,** 815 S. Main St., Moab, UT 84532 (© **435/259-8700;** www.laquintamoab.com), which is pet friendly and has summer rates of $99 to $114 double, with off season discounts. Moab's room tax of about 12.25% applies.

Aarchway Inn   Two miles from the entrance to Arches National Park, this well-maintained modern motel has large rooms with great views, decorated in Southwestern style. Photos on the walls depict the area's scenic attractions. Rooms contain two queen beds or one king, and eight family units also have queen sofa beds. The suites have whirlpool tubs. Facilities include a courtyard with barbecue grills, covered and locked bike storage, conference rooms, and a gift shop. The entire property is smoke free.

1551 N. US 191, Moab, UT 84532. (C) **800/341-9359** or 435/259-2599. Fax 435/259-2270. www.aarchwayinn.com. 97 units. Mar–Oct $110–$120 double, $139–$179 suite. Off-season discounts available. Rates include continental breakfast. AE, DC, DISC, MC, V. **Amenities:** Large heated outdoor pool; exercise room; indoor Jacuzzi. *In room:* A/C, TV, dataport, fridge, coffeemaker, microwave.

Bowen Motel   This family-owned and -operated motel offers fairly large, comfortable, basic rooms with attractive wallpaper, a king or one or two queen beds, and combination shower/tubs. Refrigerators and microwaves are available. Two family rooms sleep up to six persons each.

169 N. Main St., Moab, UT 84532. (C) **800/874-5439** or 435/259-7132. Fax 435/259-6641. www.bowenmotel.com. 40 units. $60–$85 double. Off-season discounts available. Rates include continental breakfast. AE, DC, DISC, MC, V. Pets accepted. **Amenities:** Heated outdoor pool. *In room:* A/C, TV.

Red Stone Inn *Value*   This centrally located motel is comfortable and quiet, and offers quite a bit for the price. The exterior gives the impression that these are cabins, and the theme continues inside, where colorful posters and maps of area attractions decorate attractive knotty pine walls. Rooms are a bit on the small side, although perfectly adequate and spotlessly maintained. All units have kitchenettes with microwaves, coffeemakers (with coffee supplied), and refrigerators. Three rooms accessible to travelers with disabilities have combination shower/tubs; the rest have showers only. There's a covered picnic area with tables and gas barbecue grills, and a mountain bike work stand and bike wash. Guests have free access to the pool at a motel across the street.

535 S. Main St., Moab, UT 84532. (C) **800/772-1972** or 435/259-3500. Fax 435/259-2717. www.moabredstone.com. 52 units. Summer $70–$75 double; winter $39–$45 double; prices higher in Sept and during special events. Check for Internet specials. AE, DISC, MC, V. Pets accepted; $5 fee. **Amenities:** Access to heated outdoor pool; indoor hot tub; coin-op laundry. *In room:* A/C, TV, dataport, kitchen.

Sunflower Hill Luxury Inn *★★*   This country-style retreat is our top choice in Moab for a relaxing escape. Located 3 blocks off Main Street on a quiet dead-end road, it offers elegant rooms and lovely outdoor areas. The rooms are individually decorated—for instance, the Summer House Suite boasts a colorful garden-themed mural—and have handmade quilts. Deluxe rooms have jetted tubs and private balconies. The grounds are grassy and shady, with fruit trees and flowers in abundance, plus a swing, picnic table, and barbecue. There's also locked, covered bike storage. The substantial breakfast buffet includes homemade breads and fresh-baked pastries, honey-almond granola, fresh fruits, and a hot entree such as a garden vegetable frittata, blueberry pancakes, or asparagus quiche. All units are smoke free.

185 N. 300 East, Moab, UT 84532. (C) **800/662-2786** or 435/259-2974. Fax 435/259-3065. www.sunflowerhill.com. 12 units. Mid-mar to Oct and holidays $145–$215 double; Nov to mid-Mar $90–$180 double. Rates include full breakfast and evening refreshments. AE, DISC, MC, V. Children under 10 are usually not accepted. **Amenities:** Heated outdoor pool; hot tub; coin-op laundry. *In room:* A/C, TV/VCR, hair dryer, CD player, no phone.

CAMPING

A number of commercial campgrounds in Moab offer hot showers, RV hookups, and other amenities. Among those we especially like are **Arch View Camp Park,** US 191, at the junction with US 313, 9 miles north of town (P.O. Box 938), Moab, UT 84532 (C) **800/813-6622** or 435/259-7854; www.archviewresort.com). It has 60 sites as well as great views into Arches National Park. For two people, tent sites cost $18 and full-hookup RV sites cost $27 to $30. Rates for cabins start at $40 for two people. Another good choice, especially for those who want to be downtown, is **Canyonlands Campground & RV Park,** 555 S. Main St., Moab, UT 84532 (© **800/522-6848** or 435/259-6848; www.canyonlandsrv.com). This quiet, shady campground has 138 sites. For two people, it charges $19 to $21 for tent sites, $30 to $32 for RV sites, and $42 for cabins.

WHERE TO DINE

Buck's Grill House ✦ AMERICAN WESTERN   This popular restaurant is our top choice in Moab for steak. The dining room's subdued Western decor is accented by exposed wood beams and local artwork. The attractive patio, away from the road, has trees and a delightful rock waterfall. Especially good is the grilled 12-ounce New York strip steak, either plain or rubbed with the restaurant's "cowboy" spices. We also recommend buffalo meatloaf, with black onion gravy and mashed potatoes. South-western dishes include duck tamale with grilled pineapple salsa. Buck's offers full liquor service and a good wine list, and serves a variety of Utah microbrews.

1393 N. US 191, about 1½ miles north of town. © **435/259-5201.** www.bucksgrillhouse.com. Main courses $7.95–$27. DISC, MC, V. Daily 5:30pm–closing.

Eddie McStiff's AMERICAN   This bustling, noisy brewpub is half family restaurant and half tavern, with a climate-controlled garden patio as well. You'll find Southwest decor in the dining room, and the tavern looks just as a tavern should—long bar, low light, and lots of wood. The menu includes a good variety of charbroiled meats, excellent pizzas, and a selection of pasta dishes. Specialties include grilled wild Alaskan salmon and slow-smoked barbecued ribs. About a dozen fresh-brewed beers are on tap. Mixed drinks, wine, and beer are sold in the dining room with food only; the tavern sells beer with or without food. (You must be at least 21 to enter the tavern.)

In McStiff's Plaza, 57 S. Main St. (just south of the information center). © **435/259-2337.** www.eddiemcstiffs.com. Main courses $6–$19. DISC, MC, V. Mon–Fri 5pm–midnight, Sat–Sun noon–midnight.

Moab Diner *(Kids* AMERICAN/SOUTHWESTERN   Breakfast—among the best in town—is served all day here. It features all the usual egg dishes, biscuits and gravy, and a spicy breakfast burrito. The decor is definitely diner, but the place does have lots of green plants (real, not plastic). Hamburgers, sandwiches, and salads are the offerings at lunch. For dinner, there are steak, shrimp, and chicken, plus liver and onions. In addition to ice cream, you can get malts and shakes. No alcoholic beverages are served.

189 S. Main St. (2 blocks south of Center St.). © **435/259-4006.** Main courses $4.75–$18. MC, V. Daily 6am–10pm. Closed Jan 1, Thanksgiving, and Dec 25.

Las Vegas

Las Vegas is a true original; there is nothing else like it in the world. In other cities, hotels are built near the major attractions. Here, the hotels *are* the major attractions. What other city has a skyline made up of buildings from other cities' skylines? You can also enjoy great works of art, world-renowned chefs, and rock clubs and arenas that attract major acts.

But Vegas is first and foremost a gambling destination. And though the hotels aren't undercharging for everything anymore in an effort to lure you into gambling round the clock, they still do their best to separate you from your cash. The cheap buffets and meal deals still exist, as do some cut-rate rooms, but both are likely to prove the old adage about getting what you pay for. Nevertheless, free drinks are handed to anyone lurking near a slot, and if show tickets aren't in the budget, you won't lack for entertainment. Free lounge shows abound, and the people-watching opportunities alone never disappoint.

Depending on which areas of the southwest you plan to visit, Las Vegas might make a convenient beginning or ending point to your vacation. Because it's such a popular destination, you can often find bargains on airfare and car rental rates. And in its own way, Vegas is as amazing as the nearby Grand Canyon and every bit as much a must-see. It's one of the Seven Wonders of the Artificial World. And everyone should experience it at least once—you might find yourself coming back for more.

1 Essentials

GETTING THERE

BY PLANE Almost every major domestic airline, and some international airlines, fly into **McCarran International Airport** (© **702/261-5211;** TDD 702/261-3111; www.mccarran.com), just a few minutes' drive from the southern end of the Strip.

Bell Trans (© **702/739-7990**) runs 20-passenger minibuses daily between the airport and all major Las Vegas hotels and motels all day (7:45am–midnight). The cost is $5 per person each way to Strip and Convention Center area hotels, $6.50 to Downtown or other Off-Strip properties.

Even less expensive are **Citizen's Area Transit (CAT)** buses (© **702/CAT-RIDE;** www.rtcsouthernnevada.com/cat). The no. 108 bus departs from the airport and takes you to the Stratosphere, where you can transfer to the no. 301, which stops close to most Strip- and Convention Center–area hotels. The no. 109 bus goes from the airport to the Downtown Transportation Center (at Casino Center Blvd. and Stewart Ave.). The fares for buses on Strip routes are $2 for adults, 60¢ for seniors and children 6 to 17, and free for children under 6.

Taxis are also plentiful, and a ride to the Strip costs $12 to $20.

BY CAR   The main highway connecting Las Vegas with the rest of the country is I-15 from the northeast (Salt Lake City) and southwest (Los Angeles and San Diego). Lots of folks drive up from Los Angeles, and thanks to the narrow two-lane highway, it can get very crowded on Friday and Sunday afternoons. Other major routes are US 93 from the southeast (Phoenix) and US 95 from the northwest (Reno).

VISITOR INFORMATION

For advance information, call or write the **Las Vegas Convention and Visitors Authority,** 3150 Paradise Rd., Las Vegas, NV 89109 (© **877/VISIT-LV** or 702/892-0711; www.visitlasvegas.com). Or stop by when you're in town. They're open daily from 8am to 5pm. Another excellent information source is the **Las Vegas Chamber of Commerce,** 3720 Howard Hughes Pkwy., no. 100, Las Vegas, NV 89109 (© **702/735-1616;** www.lvchamber.com). They're open Monday through Friday from 8am to 5pm.

GETTING AROUND

BY CAR   We highly recommend that visitors rent a car. The Strip is too spread out for walking, and public transportation is often ineffective in getting you from Point A to Point B. All the major hotels offer free parking.

BY BUS & TROLLEY   The no. 301 bus operated by **CAT** (© **702/CAT-RIDE;** www. rtcsouthernnevada.com/cat) plies a route between the Downtown Transportation Center (at Casino Center Blvd. and Stewart Ave.) and a few miles beyond the southern end of the Strip. The fare is $2 for adults, 60¢ for seniors 62 and older and children 6 to 17, and free for those under 6. A low $5 buys an all-day pass. CAT buses run 24 hours a day and are wheelchair-accessible. Exact change is required.

Las Vegas Strip Trolley (© **702/382-1404;** www.striptrolley.com) operates a classic streetcar replica that runs northward from Hacienda Avenue, stopping at all major hotels en route to the Sahara, and then looping back via the Las Vegas Hilton. They do not, however, go to the Stratosphere Casino Hotel & Tower or Downtown. Trolleys run about every 15 minutes daily between 9:30am and 1:30am. The fare is $2.50 for a single one-way ride or $6.50 (free for children under 5) for an all-day pass, and exact change is required.

There are also a number of free transportation services, courtesy of the casinos. A free monorail connects Mandalay Bay with Luxor and Excalibur, and a free tram shuttles between The Mirage and TI at the Mirage. Given how far apart even neighboring hotels can be, thanks to their size, and how they seem even farther apart on really hot (and cold and windy) days, these are blessed additions.

BY TAXI   Cabs line up in front of all major hotels. They charge $3.20 at the meter drop and 25¢ for each additional ⅛ mile. A taxi from the airport to the Strip will run you $12 to $20, from the airport to Downtown $15 to $20, and between the Strip and Downtown about $10 to $15. Up to five people can ride for the same fare.

If you want to call a taxi, any of the following companies can provide one: **Desert Cab Company** (© **702/386-9102**), **Whittlesea Blue Cab** (© **702/384-6111**), or **Yellow/Checker Cab/Star Company** (© **702/873-2000**).

FAST FACTS

For minor problems, try the **Harmon Medical Urgent Care Center,** the closest to the Strip, with doctors and X-ray machines; it's located at 105 E. Harmon at Koval, near the MGM Grand (© **702/796-1116;** www.harmonmedicalcenter.com). It's open 24 hours. Emergency services are available 24 hours a day at **University Medical Center,**

Las Vegas

1800 W. Charleston Blvd., at Shadow Lane (ⓒ **702/383-2000;** www.umc-cares.org). **Sunrise Hospital and Medical Center,** 3186 Maryland Pkwy., between Desert Inn Road and Sahara Avenue (ⓒ **702/731-8080**), also has a 24-hour emergency room. There's a 24-hour **Walgreens** (which has a 1-hr. photo service) at 3765 Las Vegas Blvd. S. (ⓒ **702/895-6878**), almost directly across from the Monte Carlo.

The sales tax on meals, goods, and some services is 7%. Clark County hotel room tax is 9%, and in Henderson it's 10%.

2 Where to Stay

If there's one thing Vegas has in spades, it's hotels. Big hotels. The hotels here are the city's biggest tourist attraction, and they pack in the crowds accordingly. A last-minute Vegas vacation can turn into a housing nightmare, so make reservations in advance.

First-time visitors will most likely stay on the Strip, although Downtown is a lot nicer than it used to be, and the rates there are cheaper. The **Las Vegas Convention and Visitors Authority** runs a room reservations hot line (ⓒ **877/VISITLV** or 702/892-0711; www.visitlasvegas.com) that can be helpful.

Vegas does have hotels that eschew the theme scheme. Unlike many of the casino hotels, they are far more likely to cater to kids, making them good choices for families. One of two great selections is the luxurious **Four Seasons** (ⓒ **877/632-5000** or 702/632-5000; www.fourseasons.com), inside the Mandalay Bay, although it has its own entrance and facilities. The **Residence Inn by Marriott,** 3225 Paradise Rd., Las Vegas, NV 89109, between Desert Inn Road and Convention Center Drive (ⓒ **800/331-3131** or 702/796-9300; www.marriott.com), offers clean apartment-like accommodations with full kitchens and sitting rooms.

All the usual budget chains, including Motel 6, Days Inn, Howard Johnson, Fairfield by Marriott, and Econo Lodge, are in Las Vegas.

VERY EXPENSIVE

Bellagio ⭐⭐   This $1.6 billion luxury resort is a big, grand, state-of-the-art Vegas hotel. Here you'll find fabulous fountains, classical gardens, an art gallery, and the best collection of restaurants in town. There is even an 8-acre Lake Como stand-in out front, complete with a dazzling choreographed water ballet extravaganza. Rooms are nicely decorated and the roomy bathrooms are even more luxurious. Service is surprisingly good given the size of the place. The pool area is exceptional and the spa is marvelous, if overpriced.

3600 Las Vegas Blvd. S. (at the corner of Flamingo Rd.), Las Vegas, NV 89109. ⓒ **888/987-6667** or 702/693-7111. Fax 702/693-8546. www.bellagio.com. 3,933 units. $149 and up double. Extra person $35. No discount for children. AE, DC, DISC, MC, V. Free self- and valet parking. **Amenities:** 14 restaurants; nightclub; 6 outdoor pools; large health club & spa; concierge; tour desk; car-rental desk; business center; elegant shopping arcade; salon; 24-hr. room service; in-room massage; laundry service; dry cleaning; casino; showrooms; wedding chapel; executive-level rooms. *In room:* A/C, TV w/pay movies, dataport, hair dryer, iron/ironing board, safe, high-speed Internet access (for a fee).

Caesars Palace ⭐⭐   Caesars is the spectacle that every Vegas hotel should be. A combination of Vegas luxury and a good dose of camp, the hotel is graced by Roman colonnades, marble fountains, and staff members attired in gladiator outfits and togas. But the hotel has a confusing layout, and it takes forever to get anywhere. Accommodations occupy five towers; art in the rooms keeps to the Greco-Roman theme. The newest rooms are handsome, if not as giggle-inducingly overwhelming as the classic ones, and have floor-to-ceiling windows that offer a hypnotizing panoramic view.

You'll likely enjoy a lavish bathroom with marble floor, European fixtures, and over-size marble tubs (about half are whirlpools). The **Garden of the Gods** pool area is a tasteful masterpiece.

3570 Las Vegas Blvd. S. (just north of Flamingo Rd.), Las Vegas, NV 89109. © 877/427-7243 or 702/731-7110. Fax 702/697-5706. www.caesarspalace.com. 3,348 units. $129 and up double; $549 and up suite. Extra person $30. Children under 18 stay free in parent's room. AE, DC, DISC, MC, V. Free self- and valet parking. **Amenities:** 25 restaurants; nightclub; 4 outdoor pools; health club & spa; concierge; tour desk; car-rental desk; business center; extensive shopping arcade; salon; 24-hr. room service; laundry service; dry cleaning; casino; 4 wedding chapels; executive-level rooms. *In room:* A/C, TV w/pay movies, dataport, hair dryer, iron/ironing board, safe, robe/slippers, high-speed Internet access (for a fee).

Hard Rock Hotel & Casino ✪✪ *Note:* At press time, the hotel's new owners had announced plans for $750 million worth of new hotel towers, including one that is all suites for VIPs. The hip flock to the Hard Rock, drawn by the cool 'n' rockin' ambience that pervades the place, from the piano-shaped roulette tables to the "backstage pass" room keys. The new and newly updated rooms are still a bit too '60s-futuristic hip to come off as posh, but they're certainly less immediately drab than the older versions, and they're more comfortable. Bathrooms are a big step forward—bigger, brighter, shinier. On warm days and nights the Hard Rock's beach-party pool is *the* hangout scene.

4455 Paradise Rd. (at Harmon Ave.), Las Vegas, NV 89109. © 800/473-ROCK (473-7625) or 702/693-5000. Fax 702/693-5588. www.hardrockhotel.com. 657 units. $119 and up double; $250 and up suite. Extra person $35. Children under 13 stay free in parent's room. AE, DC, MC, V. Free self- and valet parking. **Amenities:** 6 restaurants; 2 outdoor pools w/lazy river and sandy-beach bottom; small health club & spa; concierge; tour desk; salon; 24-hr. room service; laundry service; dry cleaning; casino; showroom; executive-level rooms. *In room:* A/C, TV w/pay movies, dataport, hair dryer, iron/ironing board, high-speed Internet access (for a fee).

Las Vegas Hilton ✪✪ This classy hotel is magnificent, from its lobby, glittering with massive chandeliers and gleaming marble, to its 8-acre recreation deck. The Hilton's location next to the convention center makes it the preferred choice of business travelers, and its Star Trek attraction—with its own space-themed casino—beams in the leisure crowd. The comfortable rooms have bathrooms with large marble tubs; some rooms offer views of an adjacent golf course. A new owner recently took over the Hilton and has done some major spiffing up. The lobby and older casino areas have been completely remodeled, giving the whole place a much more modern feel.

3000 Paradise Rd. (at Riviera Blvd.), Las Vegas, NV 89109. © 888/732-7117 or 702/732-5111. Fax 702/732-5805. www.lvhilton.com. 3,174 units. $49 and up double. Extra person $35. Children under 18 stay free in parent's room. AE, DC, DISC, MC, V. Free self- and valet parking. **Amenities:** 8 restaurants; outdoor pool; 6 night-lit tennis courts; health club & spa; video-game arcade; car-rental desk; business center; free Wi-Fi in coffee shop; shopping arcade; salon; 24-hr. room service; laundry service; dry cleaning; casino; showrooms; executive-level rooms. *In room:* A/C, TV w/pay movies, dataport, hair dryer, iron/ironing board, high-speed Internet access (for a fee).

Paris Las Vegas Casino Resort ✪ *Sacre bleu!* The City of Light comes to Sin City in this Strip fantasy hotel. It's theme-run-amok time again, and we are so happy about it. You can stroll down a mini Rue de la Paix, ride an elevator to the top of the Eiffel Tower, stop at an overpriced bakery for a baguette, take your photo by several very nice fountains, and snicker at dubious French signage ("le car rental"). Rooms are disappointingly uninteresting, with furniture that only hints at mock French Regency, and with small but pretty bathrooms that have deep tubs. Try to get a Strip-facing room so you can see the Bellagio's fountains across the street. Overall, not a bad place to stay but a great place to visit.

3655 Las Vegas Blvd. S., Las Vegas, NV 89109. © **888/BONJOUR** (266-5687) or 702/946-7000. www.parislv.com. 2,916 units. $119 and up double; $350 and up suites. Extra person $30. Children 17 and under stay free in parent's room. AE, DC, DISC, MC. V. Free self- and valet parking. **Amenities:** 12 restaurants; outdoor pool; health club & spa; concierge; tour desk; business center; shopping arcade; 24-hr. room service; laundry service; dry cleaning; casino; showrooms; 2 wedding chapels; executive-level rooms. *In room:* A/C, TV w/pay movies, dataport, coffeemaker, hair dryer, iron/ironing board, safe, high-speed Internet access (for a fee).

The Venetian 👧👧   The Venetian falls squarely between an outright adult Disney-land experience and the luxury resort sensibility of other Vegas hotels. The hotel impressively re-creates the city of Venice, including the outrageous prices. Rooms are the largest and probably the most handsome in town. They are all "suites," with a good-size bedroom giving way to steps down to a sunken living area, complete with pullout sofa bed. Bathrooms feature glassed-in showers, deep soaking tubs, double sinks, fluffy towels, and lots of space. A branch of the famous Canyon Ranch Spa is on the premises. If there's a weak point, it's the hotel's pool area, which is disappointing and bland.

3355 Las Vegas Blvd. S., Las Vegas, NV 89109. © **888/2-VENICE** (283-6423) or 702/414-1000. Fax 702/414-4805. www.venetian.com. 4,027 units. $169 and up double. Extra person $35. Children under 13 stay free in parent's room. AE, DC, DISC, MC, V. Free self- and valet parking. **Amenities:** 18 restaurants; 6 outdoor pools; health club & spa; video-game arcade; concierge; tour desk; car-rental desk; business center; extensive shopping arcade; 24-hr. room service; laundry service; dry cleaning; casino; showroom; wedding chapels; executive-level rooms. *In room:* A/C, TV w/pay movies, fax, dataport, fridge, hair dryer, iron/ironing board, safe, high-speed Internet access (for a fee).

EXPENSIVE

The Flamingo Las Vegas 👧   Gradually, all the Flamingo's dated rooms are getting upgraded. Rushing headlong into the Dean Martin/Rat Pack retro vibe, they are kicky candy modern, with hot pink accent walls, hot pink lights in the bathroom where you can also find TV screens embedded in the mirror, candy striped wallpaper, black and white photos of the Flamingo from its early days, squishy white beds with chocolate accents and vinyl padded headboards, huge flat screens with HDTV, iPod docking stations, and more. Two-bedroom suites scream classic playboy bachelor pad. The Flamingo's exceptional pool area encompasses fishponds, two water slides, five swimming pools, two whirlpools, waterfalls, and a flamingo enclave—plus its spa and tennis courts are a big draw.

3555 Las Vegas Blvd. S. (between Sands Ave. and Flamingo Rd.), Las Vegas, NV 89109. © **800/732-2111** or 702/733-3111. Fax 702/733-3353. www.flamingolv.com. 3,517 units. $75 and up double; $350 and up suite. Extra person $30. Children under 12 stay free in parent's room. Timeshare suites available. AE, DC, DISC, MC, V. Free self- and valet parking. **Amenities:** 8 restaurants; 5 outdoor pools; 3 night-lit tennis courts; health club & spa; small video-game arcade; car-rental desk; UPS Store; shopping arcade; 24-hr. room service; laundry service; dry cleaning; casino; showrooms; wedding chapels; executive-level rooms. *In room:* A/C, TV w/pay movies, dataport, hair dryer, iron/ironing board, safe, high-speed Internet access (for a fee).

Golden Nugget 👧👧   The Grande Dame of Downtown got some much-needed attention, with new restaurants, remodeled rooms and public spaces, a big new pool, and even an entire new hotel tower going in across the street (or more specifically, on the street—they got permission to take over a small, rarely used lane just to the north of the existing property). The completed phases look terrific; a new color scheme has given it a rich, deep look that is most posh and fresh. Everything feels brighter, lighter, and more spacious. Rooms are comparable to mid-range on the Strip, which makes them quite good for Downtown. You don't have to walk through the casino to get to your room, but you do have to walk a distance to get to the pool, which now has an aquarium where you can get up close and personal with various marine life (with only a glass wall separating you). The presence of the pool, and general overall quality, makes this the best hotel Downtown for families.

129 E. Fremont St. (at Casino Center Blvd.), Las Vegas, NV 89101. (C) 800/846-5336 or 702/385-7111. Fax 702/386-8362. www.goldennugget.com. 1,907 units. $69 and up double; $275 and up suite. Extra person $20. No discount for children. AE, DC, DISC, MC, V. Free self- and valet parking. **Amenities:** 5 restaurants; outdoor pool; health club & spa; tour desk; car-rental desk; salon; 24-hr. room service; laundry service; dry cleaning; casino; showroom; executive level rooms. *In room:* A/C, TV w/pay movies, dataport, hair dryer, iron/ironing board, safe, robe/slippers, high-speed Internet (for a fee).

Harrah's Las Vegas *⚅* There is much to like here, and occasional quite good rates might make the so-so bits worth overlooking. Guest rooms are slowly being refurbished at press time—make sure to ask for a newly renovated room. The rooms have undergone some cosmetic fluffing to the tune of good new mattresses and those white bed covers now more or less standard in most local hotels. Dark masculine decor is an odd choice for such a festive place. The rooms aren't flashy, but they are reliable for what is ultimately a gamblers' hotel. The hotel's health club is one of the best on the Strip, but its pool is underwhelming.

3475 Las Vegas Blvd. S. (between Flamingo and Spring Mountain roads), Las Vegas, NV 89109. (C) 800/HARRAHS (427-7247) or 702/369-5000. Fax 702/369-5283. www.harrahs.com. 2,526 units. $99 and up double; $199 and up suite. Extra person $20. No discount for children. AE, DC, DISC, MC, V. Free self- and valet parking. **Amenities:** 9 restaurants; outdoor pool; health club & spa; concierge; tour desk; car rental desk; business center; shopping arcade; salon; 24-hr. room service; laundry service; dry cleaning; casino; showrooms; executive-level rooms. *In room:* A/C, TV w/pay movies, dataport, hair dryer, iron/ironing board.

Mandalay Bay *⚅⚅* *(Kids* Mandalay Bay is one of our favorite hotels. It doesn't really evoke Southeast Asia, but the Mandalay Bay actually looks like a resort hotel rather than just a Vegas version of one. You don't have to walk through the casino to get to any of these public areas or the guest room elevators, the pool area is spiffy, and the whole complex is less overwhelming than some of the neighboring behemoths. Rooms are perhaps the finest on the Strip, spacious and subdued in decor. The large bathrooms, stocked with a host of fabulous amenities, are certainly the best on the Strip and maybe the best in Vegas. The hotel's highly touted wave pool isn't very surf-friendly, but it does offer a nice afternoon's relaxation. Note that a topless swimming area opened in 2003.

3950 Las Vegas Blvd. S. (at Hacienda Ave.), Las Vegas, NV 89119. (C) 877/632-7000 or 702/632-7000. Fax 702/632-7228. www.mandalaybay.com. 3,309 units. $99 and up double; $149 and up suite; $149 and up House of Blues Signature Rooms. Extra person $35. Children 14 and under free in parent's room. AE, DC, DISC, MC, V. Free self- and valet parking. **Amenities:** 22 restaurants; 4 outdoor pools w/lazy river & wave pool; health club & spa; Jacuzzi; sauna; watersports equipment/rentals; concierge; tour desk; business center; 24-hr. room service; in-room massage; laundry service; dry cleaning; casino; 12,000-seat events center; 1,700-seat performing-arts theater; aquarium; wedding chapels; executive-level rooms. *In room:* A/C, TV w/pay movies, dataport, hair dryer, iron/ironing board, safe, high-speed Internet (for a fee).

MGM Grand Hotel/Casino *⚅⚅* *(Kids* We've grown very fond of this hotel. Although the original standard rooms in the main tower with their 1930s-era Hollywood glam styling have been replaced by somewhat more blandly upscale decor, they are generously proportioned and equipped with pretty much everything you might need. A second section of the tower is now known as the West Wing, and it is here that you'll find the memorable accommodations. These rooms are smaller (a rather tiny 350 sq. ft.) but full of the trendy touches we are complete suckers for. There is no counter space in the open bathroom plan, but frosted green glass doors preserve privacy. DVD and CD players, TVs in the bathroom mirrors, and fluffy bedding, plus liberal use of electronic "gee whiz" moments like lamps that turn on and off if you touch them, while all lights in the rooms are controlled by the insertion of your room key. The Lion Habitat and fabulous pool area make this place popular with families.

3799 Las Vegas Blvd. S. (at Tropicana Ave.), Las Vegas, NV 89109. © **800/929-1111** or 702/891-7777. Fax 702/891-1030. www.mgmgrand.com. 5,034 units. $99 and up standard double; $159 and up suite. Extra person $30. Children under 13 stay free in parent's room. AE, DC, DISC, MC, V. Free self- and valet parking. **Amenities:** 15 restaurants; 5 outdoor pools w/lazy river; large health club & spa; Jacuzzi; video-game arcade; concierge; tour desk; car-rental desk; business center; shopping arcade; salon; 24-hr. room service; in-room massage; laundry service; dry cleaning; casino; events arena; showroom; Lion Habitat; cabaret theater; 2 wedding chapels; nightclub; executive-level rooms. *In room:* A/C, TV w/pay movies, dataport, high-speed Internet access (for a fee), hair dryer, iron/ironing board, safe, high-speed Internet (for a fee).

The Mirage *★★*   You walk into the Mirage and breathe the faintly tropically perfumed air, and it's just a different experience from most Vegas hotels. The hotel, fronted by waterfalls and tropical foliage, centers on a very "active" volcano that erupts every 15 minutes after dark. Inside, you'll find a verdant rainforest. The rooms have been redone and while the results are not distinctive, they are handsome. The overall effect is more beach than Caribbean. Super-deluxe rooms have whirlpool tubs. The staff is genuinely helpful; any problems that may arise are quickly smoothed out. The pool is one of the nicest in Vegas.

3400 Las Vegas Blvd. S. (between Flamingo and Spring Mountain roads.), Las Vegas, NV 89109. © **800/627-6667** or 702/791-7111. Fax 702/791-7446. www.mirage.com. 3,044 units. $119 and up double; $249 and up suite. Extra person $30. No discount for children. AE, DC, DISC, MC, V. Free self- and valet parking. **Amenities:** 11 restaurants; beautiful outdoor pool; health club & spa; concierge; tour desk; car-rental desk; business center; shopping arcade; salon; 24-hr. room service; laundry service; dry cleaning; casino; showrooms; executive-level rooms. *In room:* A/C, TV w/pay movies, dataport, hair dryer, iron/ironing board, safe, high-speed Internet (for a fee).

Monte Carlo Resort & Casino *★*   This European-styled hotel casino is not as theme-intensive as its Strip brethren—a nice change of pace from the usual Vegas kitsch. Its pool area, once the very last word in local pool fun, is now put to shame by better versions at Mandalay Bay and the MGM Grand. We love that the guest rooms are accessible without going through the casino, but we don't really love the rooms themselves, which are unimaginatively decorated and smaller than what we've grown accustomed to, especially in terms of bathroom square-footage.

3770 Las Vegas Blvd. S. (between Flamingo Rd. and Tropicana Ave.), Las Vegas, NV 89109. © **800/311-8999** or 702/730-7777. Fax 702/730-7250. www.montecarlo.com. 3,002 units. $99 and up double; $149 and up suite. Extra person $25. No discount for children. AE, DC, DISC, MC, V. Free self- and valet parking. **Amenities:** 7 restaurants plus a food court; outdoor pool w/wave pool & lazy river; health club & spa; Jacuzzi; watersports equipment/rentals; video-game arcade; concierge; tour desk; business center; shopping arcade; salon; 24-hr. room service; in-room massage; laundry service; dry cleaning; casino; showroom; wedding chapel; executive-level rooms. *In room:* A/C, TV w/pay movies, dataport, hair dryer, iron/ironing board, high-speed Internet (for a fee).

New York–New York Hotel & Casino *★★ (Kids)*   A visit to this spectacular hotel, which looks like the New York City skyline (complete with a roller coaster running through it) is a must. Subtle it isn't. You can gamble in a casino done up as Central Park or play games in the Coney Island arcade. Recently redecorated rooms come in 64 different styles, with the original Deco-inspired decor having been replaced by something they call '40s inspired. Light sleepers should request a room away from the roller coaster. If you're a pool person, go elsewhere—the one here is pretty mediocre.

3790 Las Vegas Blvd. S. (at Tropicana Ave.), Las Vegas, NV 89109. © **800/693-6763** or 702/740-6969. Fax 702/740-6920. www.nynyhotelcasino.com. 2,023 units. $79 and up double. Extra person $30. No discount for children.

AE, DC, DISC, MC, V. Free self- and valet parking. **Amenities:** 9 restaurants plus a food court; outdoor pool; small health club & spa; Jacuzzi; video-game arcade w/carnival midway games; concierge; tour desk; business center; salon; 24-hr. room service; laundry service; dry cleaning; casino; showrooms; executive-level rooms. *In room:* A/C, TV w/pay movies, dataport, hair dryer, iron/ironing board, safe, high-speed Internet (for a fee).

Planet Hollywood Resort & Casino ⁂

Those looking for the pop kitsch sensibility of the Planet Hollywood restaurants will be disappointed; it's actually kind of classy and design intensive. What it really offers that's different are the rooms. Each has a movie or entertainment theme. Beds have purple velour padded headboards and the beds themselves are the Sheraton Four Comforts pillow-top thing. Baths are larger than the standard bathroom but neither the largest on the Strip nor special enough to match the sleeping areas. The hotel also has its own arena, the **Center for the Performing Arts,** which is attracting big names back to Vegas. Finally, there is the **Mandera spa** ⁂⁂⁂, maybe aesthetically our hands-down local favorite. All in all, the place teeters on the brink of a higher rating but it's still a little early to say for sure.

3667 Las Vegas Blvd. S., Las Vegas, NV 89109. ℂ 877/333-9474 or 702/785-5555. Fax 702/785-5558. www.planet hollywood.com. 2,600 units. $99 and up double. Extra person $30. No discount for children. AE, DC, DISC, MC, V. Free self- and valet parking. **Amenities:** 19 restaurants; 7 bars/lounges; 2 outdoor pools; health club & spa; 2 Jacuzzis; concierge; tour desk; car-rental desk; business center; extensive shopping arcade; 24-hr. room service; in-room massage; babysitting; laundry service; dry cleaning; Casino; performing-arts center; showroom; chapel; executive-level rooms. *In room:* A/C, TV w/pay movies, dataport, hair dryer, iron/ironing board, safe, high-speed Internet access (for a fee).

Rio All Suite Hotel & Casino ⁂

Although it's not on the Strip, the Rio Suite has a carnival atmosphere that packs in the crowds—and the accompanying noise. In addition to its tropically themed resort, the Rio has an immensely popular 41-story tower and Masquerade Village that simulate a European village, complete with shops, restaurants, and a bizarre live-action show in the sky. The "suites" are actually one rather large room with a sofa and coffee table. Rooms feature amenities such as fridges, and floor-to-ceiling windows offer views of the Strip. Note that the hotel actively discourages guests from bringing children.

3700 W. Flamingo Rd. (just west of I-15), Las Vegas, NV 89103. ℂ 888/752-9746 or 702/777-7777. Fax 702/777-7611. www.riolasvegas.com. 2,582 units. $99 and up double-occupancy suite. Extra person $30. No discount for children. AE, DC, MC, V. Free self- and valet parking. **Amenities:** 12 restaurants plus additional sports-book dining; 4 outdoor pools; golf course; health club & spa; concierge; car-rental desk; business center; shopping arcade; salon; 24-hr. room service; in-room massage; laundry service; dry cleaning; casino; showrooms; executive-level rooms. *In room:* A/C, TV w/pay movies, fridge, coffeemaker, hair dryer, iron/ironing board, safe, high-speed Internet (for a fee).

TI at the Mirage ⁂⁂

Huh? What happened to Treasure Island? What happened to the pirates? Why, Vegas grew up, that's what. Originally the most modern family-friendly hotel, the former Treasure Island was a blown-up version of Disneyland's Pirates of the Caribbean. But that's all behind them now, and the name change is there to make sure you understand this is a grown-up, sophisticated resort. What remains, after they stripped the pirate gilt, are good-size rooms in modified French Regency style that are much nicer than most in their price range. The pool is not that memorable, however.

3300 Las Vegas Blvd. S. (at Spring Mountain Rd.), Las Vegas, NV 89177-0711. ℂ 800/944-7444 or 702/894-7111. Fax 702/894-7446. www.treasureisland.com. 2,891 units. From $69 double; from $109 suite. Extra person $25. No discount for children. Inquire about packages. AE, DC, DISC, MC, V. Free self- and valet parking. **Amenities:** 11 restaurants; outdoor pool; health club and spa; very well-equipped game and video arcade; concierge; tour desk; car-rental desk; business center; shopping arcade; 24-hr. room service; laundry service; dry cleaning; casino; showrooms; executive-level rooms. *In room:* A/C, TV w/pay movies, fax, dataport, hair dryer, iron and board, safe.

MODERATE

Luxor Las Vegas *(Kids)*   It would be hard to miss the Luxor's 30-story pyramid, even without the 315,000-watt light beam at the top. The hotel is, despite outward appearances, inviting, classy, and functional. The Egyptian Revival lobby has been redone in marble and cherrywood and is one of the nicest lobbies in town. The pyramid rooms cross Egyptian kitsch with Art Deco stylings, including gleaming inlaid wood furniture and a hilarious hieroglyphic bedspread. Marvelous views are offered through the slanted windows (the higher up, the better, of course), but the bathrooms are shower-only, no tubs. Tower rooms are even heavier on the Egyptian motif, pleasing in a campy way but not as aesthetically successful. High-speed "inclinator" elevators run on a 39-degree angle, making the ride up to the Pyramid rooms a bit of a thrill. Two notable attractions here are **King Tut Museum** and the **Luxor IMAX Theater and Ridefilm.** Another child-pleaser is the 18,000-square-foot Games of the Gods Arcade.

3900 Las Vegas Blvd. S. (between Reno and Hacienda aves.), Las Vegas, NV 81119. *(C)* **888/777-0188** or 702/262-4000. Fax 702/262-4478. www.luxor.com. 4,400 units. $59 and up double; $149 and up whirlpool suite; $249–$800 other suites. Extra person $25. Children under 12 stay free in parent's room. AE, DC, DISC, MC, V. Free self- and valet parking. **Amenities:** 7 restaurants plus a food court; 5 outdoor pools; health club & spa; 18,000-sq.-ft. video-game arcade; concierge; tour desk; car-rental desk; business center; shopping arcade; 24-hr. room service; dry cleaning; casino; showrooms; nightclub; executive-level rooms. *In room:* A/C, TV w/pay movies, dataport, hair dryer, iron/ironing board, high-speed Internet access (for a fee).

Stratosphere Casino Hotel & Tower *(Kids)*   At 1,149 feet, the Stratosphere is the tallest building west of the Mississippi; it's also in the middle of nowhere on the Strip, which explains the lack of crowds (and lower prices). The panoramic views available from the top of the tower and some amazing thrill rides (see "What to See & Do," later in this chapter) are the big attractions here. The smaller-size rooms here are basically motel rooms—really nice motel rooms, but with that level of comfort and style. Then again, you can often get such a room for around $39 a night. Perfect if you are coming to Vegas with no plans to spend time in your room except to sleep (if even that). Of course, the place just sold, so who knows what's in store for it? Other elements to like include an area with kiddie-oriented rides, a pool with a view, and some of the friendliest, most accommodating staff in town. You can still ride the following incredible thrill rides (provided the wind isn't blowing too hard that day) on top of the tower: the **Big Shot,** a fabulous free-fall ride that thrusts passengers up and down the tower at speeds of up to 45 mph; **X-Scream,** a giant teeter-totter-style device that gives you the sensation of falling off the side of the building; and **Insanity: the Ride,** a whirly-gig contraption that spins you around more than 900 feet above terra firma, and another to-be-announced ride to replace the now-closed roller coaster.

2000 Las Vegas Blvd. S. (between St. Louis and Baltimore aves.), Las Vegas, NV 89104. *(C)* **800/99-TOWER** (998-6937) or 702/380-7777. Fax 702/383-5334. www.stratospherehotel.com. 2,444 units. $39 and up double; $69 and up suite. Extra person $15. Children under 13 stay free in parent's room. AE, DC, DISC, MC, V. Free self- and valet parking. **Amenities:** 9 restaurants plus several fast-food outlets; large pool area w/great views of the Strip; children's rides and games; concierge; tour desk; car-rental desk; shopping arcade; 24-hr. room service; laundry service; dry cleaning; casino; showrooms; wedding chapel; executive-level rooms, free Wi-Fi in coffee shop in casino. *In room:* A/C, TV w/pay movies, dataport, hair dryer, iron/ironing board, safe, high-speed Internet access (for a fee).

INEXPENSIVE

Circus Circus Hotel/Casino *(Kids)*   Circus Circus, once the epitome of kitsch, is trying to be taken more seriously. The bright primary colors and garish trims have vanished in favor of subtle, muted tones and high-rent touches that appeal more to the Cirque du Soleil crowd. Nevertheless, the world's largest permanent circus and indoor theme park are still here, and kids will love it. Tower rooms have newish, just slightly better-than-average furnishings; the Manor section comprises five white three-story buildings out back. These rooms are usually among the least expensive in town, but you get what you pay for. A recent renovation of these rooms added a coat of paint and some new photos on the wall, but not much else. The hotel also has its own RV park.

2880 Las Vegas Blvd. S. (between Circus Circus and Convention Center drives), Las Vegas, NV 89109. ℂ 877/434-9175 or 702/734-0410. Fax 702/734-5897. www.circuscircus.com. 3,774 units. $59 and up double. Extra person $12. Children under 17 stay free in parent's room. AE, DC, DISC, MC, V. Free self- and valet parking. **Amenities:** 7 restaurants and several fast-food outlets; 2 outdoor pools; video-game arcade; tour desk; car-rental desk; shopping arcade; 24-hr. room service; laundry service; dry cleaning; casino; circus acts; midway-style carnival games; wedding chapel; executive-level rooms. *In room:* A/C, TV w/pay movies, hair dryer, safe, high-speed Internet access (for a fee).

Main Street Station ⭐⭐ *Finds*   The Main Street Station, one of the best bargains in the city, is just 2 short blocks away from Fremont Street in Downtown, barely a 3 minute walk. The overall look is turn-of-the-20th-century San Francisco, and the details, from the ornate chandeliers to the wood-paneled lobby, are outstanding. The long and narrow rooms are possibly the largest in Downtown, decorated with French provincial furniture. A 2005 overhaul gave them positively modern furnishings, new carpet and wall coverings, and updated fixtures in the bathrooms. The bathrooms are small but well appointed. If you're a light sleeper, request a room on the south side.

200 N. Main St. (between Fremont St. and I-95), Las Vegas, NV 89101. ℂ 800/465-0711 or 702/387-1896. Fax 702/386-4466. www.mainstreetcasino.com. 406 units. $59 and up double. AE, DC, DISC, MC, V. Free self- and valet parking. **Amenities:** 3 restaurants; access to outdoor pool at nearby California Hotel; car-rental desk; gift shop; dry cleaning; casino; free Wi-Fi available in lobby. *In room:* A/C, TV w/pay movies, coffeemaker.

3 Where to Dine

The dining scene in Las Vegas is a melting pot of midnight steak specials, cheap buffets, and gourmet rooms that rival those found in New York or Los Angeles. One word of warning: You can eat well in Vegas, and you can eat cheaply in Vegas, but it's hard to do both at the same time.

Theme restaurant buffs can chow down at **House of Blues,** in Mandalay Bay, 3950 Las Vegas Blvd. S. (ℂ 702/632-7607); the **Hard Rock Cafe,** 4475 Paradise Rd., at Harmon Avenue (ℂ 702/733-8400); **ESPN** in New York–New York, 3790 Las Vegas Blvd. S. (ℂ 702/933-3776); the **Harley-Davidson Cafe,** 3725 Las Vegas Blvd. S., at Harmon Avenue (ℂ 702/740-4555); the **Rainforest Café** in MGM Grand, 3799 Las Vegas Blvd. S. (ℂ 702/891-8580); or Jimmy Buffett's **Margaritaville** in The Flamingo, 3555 Las Vegas Blvd. S. (ℂ 702/733-3302).

For those wanting to sample one of the many hotel buffets, some of the better bets include **Luxor's Pharaoh's Pheast Buffet,** 3900 Las Vegas Blvd. S. (ℂ 702/262-4000); **Mirage Cravings Buffet,** 3400 Las Vegas Blvd. S. (ℂ 702/791-7111); **Rio's Carnival World Buffet,** 3700 W. Flamingo Rd. (ℂ 702/252-7777); **Le Village Buffet** in Paris Las Vegas, 3665 Las Vegas Blvd. S. (ℂ 888/266-5687); **Golden Nugget Buffet,** 129 E. Fremont St. (ℂ 702/385-7111); and **Main Street Station Garden Court,** 200 N. Main St. (ℂ 702/387-1896). The best Sunday brunch buffet in Vegas is **Bally's Sterling Sunday Brunch,** 3645 Las Vegas Blvd. S. (ℂ 702/967-7999), which costs $50 per person.

VERY EXPENSIVE

Aureole ★★★ NOUVELLE AMERICAN This branch of a New York City fave is noted for its glass wine tower. It's four stories of probably the finest wine collection in Vegas. The menu is a three-course prix fixe, though if you are winsome enough, they might send out luxurious extras like pâté on brioche topped with shaved truffles. Expect marvels like a tender roasted lamb loin and braised shoulder, or a rack of venison accompanied by sweet-potato purée and chestnut crisp. Everything demonstrates the hand of a true chef in the kitchen, someone paying close attention to his work and to his customers. Service is solicitous; desserts are playful, including a bittersweet chocolate soufflé with blood-orange sorbet and a Bartlett pear crisp with toasted cinnamon brioche and lemongrass foam. There is also an excellent cheese plate.

In Mandalay Bay, 3950 Las Vegas Blvd. S. ✆ 877/632-1766. www.aureolelv.com. Reservations required. Fixed-price dinner $75; tasting menu $95. AE, DISC, MC, V. Sun–Thurs 6–10:30pm, Fri–Sat 5:30–10:30pm.

Picasso ★★★ FRENCH Madrid-born chef Julian Serrano's cooking stands proudly next to the $30 million worth of Picassos that pepper the dining room's walls, making a meal here a truly memorable experience. This may well be the best restaurant in Vegas. The menu changes nightly and is always a choice between a four- or five-course fixed-price dinner or tasting menu. We were bowled over by roasted Maine lobster with a "trio" of corn—kernels, sauce, and flan. Hudson Valley foie gras was crusted in truffles and went down smoothly. And finally, the lamb rôti was an outstanding piece of lamb, crusted with truffles—just hope it's on the menu the night you're there. For dessert, a molten chocolate cake leaves any other you may have tried in the dust.

In Bellagio, 3600 Las Vegas Blvd. S. ✆ 877/234-6358. Reservations recommended. Fixed-price 4-course dinner $105; 5-course dégustation $115. AE, DC, DISC, MC, V. Wed–Mon 6–9:30pm.

EXPENSIVE

Border Grill ★★★ MEXICAN For our money, here's the best Mexican food in town. This big cheerful space houses a branch of the much lauded L.A. restaurant, conceived and run by the Food Network's "Two Hot Tamales," Mary Sue Milliken and Susan Feniger. This is truly authentic Mexican home cooking. Consequently, don't expect precisely the same food you would encounter in your favorite corner joint, but do expect fresh and fabulous food, arranged as brightly on the plates as the decor on the walls. Don't miss the dense but fluffy Mexican chocolate cream pie (with a meringue crust).

In Mandalay Bay, 3950 Las Vegas Blvd. S. ✆ 702/632-7403. www.bordergrill.com. Reservations recommended. Main courses $15–$28. AE, DC, DISC, MC, V. Sun–Thurs 11:30am–10pm; Fri–Sat 11:30am–11pm.

Canaletto ★★ ITALIAN Come here for solid, true Italian fare—and that means less sauce-intensive than the red-checked-tablecloth establishments of our American youths. Here, the emphasis is on the pasta, not the accompaniments. This place is all the more enjoyable for being perched on the faux St. Mark's Square; in theory, you can pretend you are sitting on the edge of the real thing, a fantasy we don't mind admitting we briefly indulged in. A risotto of porcini, sausage, and white-truffle oil was full of strong flavors, while the wood-fired roast chicken was perfectly moist. You know, a properly roasted chicken should be a much-celebrated thing, and that alone may be a reason to come here.

In The Venetian Grand Canal Shoppes, 3377 Las Vegas Blvd. S. ✆ 702/733-0070. Reservations recommended for dinner. Main courses $14–$36. AE, DC, MC, V. Sun–Thurs 11:30am–11pm; Fri–Sat 11:30am–midnight.

Rosemary's Restaurant ✦✦✦ NOUVELLE AMERICAN   A 15-minute (or so) drive down Sahara is all it takes to eat what the *Vegas-Review Journal* calls the best food in Las Vegas. Rosemary's cuisine covers most regions of the U.S., though Southern influences dominate. Seared foie gras with peach coulis, candied walnuts, and vanilla bean–scented arugula is like a quilt, with distinct flavors that all hang together nicely. Interesting sides include ultrarich bleu-cheese slaw, slightly spicy crispy fried tortilla strips, and perfect cornmeal jalapeño hush puppies. A recent visit found the crispy striped bass fighting it out with the pan-seared honey-glazed salmon for "best fish dish we've ever had." Desserts are most pleasant. We also recommend trying some of the restaurant's beer suggestions.

8125 W. Sahara. ✆ 702/869-2251. www.rosemarysrestaurant.com. Reservations strongly recommended. Lunch $14–$17; dinner $24–$39. AE, MC, V. Mon–Fri 11:30am–2:30pm and 5:30–10:30pm; Sat–Sun 5:30–10:30pm.

Second Street Grill ✦ *Finds*   INTERNATIONAL/PACIFIC RIM   One of the better-kept secrets of Las Vegas, this Downtown jewel is a lovely bit of romantic, cozy class with excellent food to boot. You are probably best off with grill dishes, though here might be your best ratio of quality to price for lobster tail. Play around with the Hunan pork and beef lettuce wrap appetizers, and the Peking duck and shrimp tacos. The waist-conscious will be very pleased with the bamboo-steamed snapper in a nice broth, while others may want to try the grilled salmon with goat cheese Parmesan crust. Desserts are disappointing, unfortunately. Overall, a nice place for a family event dinner Downtown, and certainly more affordable than fancy places on the Strip.

In Fremont Hotel & Casino, 200 E. Fremont St. ✆ 702/385-3232. Reservations recommended. Main courses $17–$30. AE, DC, DISC, MC, V. Sun–Mon and Thurs 6–10pm; Fri–Sat 6–11pm.

MODERATE

Grand Wok ✦✦ *Value* ASIAN   No longer thoroughly pan-Asian but still a solid choice for sushi and, more importantly, budget fare in the form of the combo soup full of noodles and different kinds of meat. It's particularly nice and more affordable than the usual hotel restaurant—and the primarily Asian clientele clearly agrees. Note that soup portions are most generous; four people could easily split one order and have a nice and very inexpensive lunch, an unexpected bargain option for the Strip.

In MGM Grand, 3799 Las Vegas Blvd. S. ✆ 702/891-7777. Reservations not accepted. Main courses $9–$19; sushi rolls and pieces $4.50–$15. AE, DC, DISC, MC, V. Restaurant Sun–Thurs 11am–10pm, Fri–Sat 11am–1am; sushi bar Mon–Thurs 5–10pm, Fri–Sat 11am–midnight, Sun 11am–10pm.

INEXPENSIVE

Capriotti's ✦✦✦ DELI   It looks like a dump but there's a reason that Capriotti's is one of the fastest growing businesses in town. They roast their own beef and turkeys on the premises and stuff them (or Italian cold cuts, or whatever) into huge sandwiches—the "large" is 20 inches, easily feeding two for under $10 total. And deliciously so; the "Slaw B Joe" (roast beef, coleslaw, and Russian dressing) is fabulous. They even have veggie varieties. We never leave town without a stop here, and you shouldn't, either.

322 W. Sahara Ave. (at Las Vegas Blvd. S.). ✆ 702/474-0229. www.capriottis.com. Most sandwiches under $10. No credit cards. Mon–Fri 10am–5pm; Sat 11am–5pm.

Rincon Criollo CUBAN   Located beyond the wedding chapels on Las Vegas Boulevard, Rincon Criollo has all the right details for a good, cheap ethnic joint: It's full of locals and empty of frills. It's not the best Cuban food ever, but it gets the job done.

The main courses (featuring Cuban pork and chicken specialties) are hit-or-miss; try the marinated pork leg or, better still, ask your server for a recommendation. Paella is offered, but only for parties at least five people (and starts at $25). The side-course *chorizo* (a spicy sausage) is excellent, and the Cuban sandwich (roast pork, ham, and cheese on bread, which is then pressed and flattened out) is huge and tasty. For only $3.50, the latter makes a fine change-of-pace meal.

1145 Las Vegas Blvd. S. (C) 702/388-1906. Reservations not accepted. Main courses $7.50–$13; paella (for 5) $25. AE, DISC, MC, V. Tues–Sun 11am–9:30pm.

Tiffany's 𝒌𝒌 *Value* DINER   This decidedly unflashy soda fountain/lunch counter was Las Vegas's first 24-hour restaurant, and it has been going strong for 60 years. Plunk down at the counter and watch the cooks go nuts trying to keep up with the orders. The menu is basic comfort food: standard items (meatloaf, ground round steak, chops, and so on), fluffy cream pies, and classic breakfasts served anytime—try the biscuits and cream gravy at 3am. But the best bet is a ⅓-pound burger and "thick, creamy shake," both about as good as they get. At around $6, this is half what you would pay for a comparable meal at the Hard Rock Cafe. Places like this are a vanishing species—it's worth the short walk from the Stratosphere. Note, however, that the neighborhood remains stubbornly rough in appearance, and that can be a turnoff. Stay alert if you come here at night.

1700 Las Vegas Blvd. S. (at East Oakey Blvd.). (C) 702/444-4459. Reservations not accepted. Most items under $8. No credit cards. Daily 24 hr.

4 What to See & Do

You can't sit at a slot machine forever. (Or maybe you can.) In any event, it shouldn't be too hard to find ways to fill your time between poker hands. Many of the hotels offer free entertainment in the form of light shows, animal-filled parks, and strolling musical performers. Can't-miss shows include the **Bellagio's dancing fountains,** a musical ballet of water and light that is the best free show in town; the **talking statues in Caesars' Forum Shops;** and the **Mirage's exploding "volcano."** Couch potatoes can watch the MGM Grand's 80-foot outdoor video screens, while adventurers head for a roller coaster celebrating that most daredevil of drivers—the New York cabbie. (This last one's not free, but that only heightens the reality of the experience.)

Nevertheless, when you finally tire of Strip-gazing (or your brain shuts down from the overload), there are plenty of other things to see and do in Las Vegas.

The Arts Factory 𝒌𝒌 *Finds*   Believe it or not, Las Vegas has a burgeoning art scene (what some would consider soul-crushing is what others consider inspirational), and this complex, located in the Gateway district, is the place to find proof. It features a few galleries and a number of work spaces for local artists. Several of the spaces are closed to the public. On the first Friday of each month, they have a party event (unimaginatively named "First Friday") showcasing local artists and arts-oriented businesses, with live music, street performances, and other entertainment and activities. Visit their website for further details.

101–107 E. Charleston Blvd. (C) 702/676-1111. www.theartsfactory.com. Free admission. Hours vary by gallery.

Fremont Street Experience 𝒌𝒌   The Fremont Street Experience in the heart of Downtown Vegas is a 5-block open-air pedestrian mall, a landscaped strip of outdoor cafes, vendor carts, and colorful kiosks purveying food and merchandise. Overhead is a 90-foot-high steel-mesh "celestial vault"; at night, it's the **Viva Vision,** a high-tech light-and-laser show enhanced by a concert-hall-quality sound system that takes place five times nightly. The canopy also cools the area through a misting system in summer and warms you with radiant heaters in winter. It's a place where you can stroll, eat, or even dance to the music under the lights. The crowd it attracts is more upscale than in years past, and of course, it's a lot less crowded than the hectic Strip.

Fremont St. (between Main St. and Las Vegas Blvd.), Downtown. www.vegasexperience.com. Free admission. Shows nightly.

King Tut's Museum ⊕

This full-scale reproduction of King Tutankhamen's tomb was all handcrafted in Egypt by artisans using historically correct gold leaf and linens, pigments, tools, and ancient methods. It's hardly like seeing the real thing, but if you aren't going to Egypt any time soon, it's a surprisingly enjoyable Vegas fake. A 4-minute introductory film precedes a 15-minute audio tour (available in English, French, Spanish, and Japanese).

In Luxor Las Vegas, 3900 Las Vegas Blvd. S. ✆ 702/262-4000. www.luxor.com. Admission $10. Daily 10am–11pm.

Las Vegas Mini Gran Prix ⊕⊕⊕ (Kids

Part arcade, part go-kart racetrack, this is exactly what you want to help your kids (and maybe yourselves) work their ya-ya's out. The arcade is well stocked, with a better quality of prizes than one often finds, but we suggest not spending too much time in there and instead hustling outside to the slide, the little roller coaster, and best of all, the four go-kart tracks. The staff is utterly friendly, and the pizzas at the food court are triple the size and half the price of those found in your hotel. The one drawback: It's far away from main Strip action—here's where you'll need that rental car, for sure. *Note:* Kids have to be at least 36 inches tall to ride any of the attractions.

1401 N. Rainbow Rd., just off US 95 N. ✆ 702/259-7000. www.lvmgp.com. Ride tickets $6.25 each, $29 for 5. Sun–Thurs 10am–10pm; Fri–Sat 10am–11pm.

Liberace Museum ⊕⊕⊕ (Moments

You can keep your Louvres and Vaticans and Smithsonians; *this* is a museum. Housed in a strip mall, this is a shrine to the glory and excess that was the art project known as Liberace. You've got your costumes (bejeweled), your many cars (bejeweled), your many pianos (bejeweled), and many jewels (also bejeweled). The museum is now better than ever, thanks to a costly renovation. Unless you have a severely underdeveloped appreciation for camp or take your museum going very seriously, you shouldn't miss it. The museum is 2½ miles east of the Strip on your right.

1775 E. Tropicana Ave. (at Spencer St.). ✆ 702/798-5595. www.liberace.org. Admission $13 adults, $8.50 seniors over 64 and students, free for children 10 and under. Mon–Sat 10am–5pm; Sun noon–4pm. Closed Thanksgiving, Dec 25, and Jan 1.

MGM Grand Lion Habitat ⊕⊕ (Kids

Hit this attraction at the right time—when the crowds aren't here—and it's one of the best freebies in town. It's a large, multi-level glass enclosure, in which lions frolic throughout the day. In addition to regular viewing spots, you can walk through a glass tunnel and get a worm's eye view of the underside of a lion (provided one is in position); note how very big Kitty's paws are. Multiple lions share show duties, so what you observe is definitely going to depend on who is in residence when you drop by.

In MGM Grand, 3799 Las Vegas Blvd. S. ✆ 702/891-7777. Free admission. Daily 11am–10pm.

Secret Garden & Dolphin Habitat 𝓇𝓇𝓇 *Kids* Get up close and personal with white tigers, lions, and plain old gray elephants here at this mini-zoo; or better still, watch dolphins frolic in the neighboring Dolphin Habitat. There is nothing quite like the kick you get from seeing a baby dolphin play. Ask the staff to play ball with the dolphins; they toss large beach balls into the pools, and the dolphins hit them out with their noses, leaping out of the water cackling with dolphin glee.

In The Mirage, 3400 Las Vegas Blvd. S. ℂ 702/791-7111. www.mirage.com. Admission $15 adults, $10 children 4–10, free for children under 4 if accompanied by an adult. Mon–Fri 11am–5:30pm; Sat–Sun and major holidays 10am–5:30pm. Hours subject to change and vary by season.

Speed: The Ride/Las Vegas Cyber Speedway 𝓇𝓇 This popular stop has two attractions. The first is a remarkable 8-minute virtual-reality ride, **Cyber Speedway,** featuring a three-quarter-size replica of a NASCAR race car. **Speed: The Ride** is a new roller coaster that blasts riders out through a hole in the wall by the new NASCAR Cafe, then through a loop, under the sidewalk, through the hotel's marquee, and finally straight up a 250-foot tower. At the peak, you feel a moment of weightlessness, and then you do the whole thing backwards! Not for the faint of heart.

In the Sahara, 2535 Las Vegas Blvd. S. ℂ 702/737-2111. www.nascarcafelasvegas.com. $20 for all-day pass on both rides. Cyber Speedway (simulator) $10 (you must be at least 54 in. tall to ride); SPEED: The Ride (roller coaster) $10 for single ride. Sun–Thurs 11am–midnight; Fri–Sat 11am–1am; hours may vary.

Stratosphere Thrill Rides 𝓇𝓇 *Kids* Atop the 1,149-foot Stratosphere Tower are three marvelous thrill rides. The **Big Shot** is a breathtaking free-fall ride that thrusts you 160 feet in the air along a 228-foot spire at the top of the tower, and then plummets back down again. Amping up the terror factor is **X-Scream,** a giant teeter-totter-style device that propels you in an open car off the side of the 100-story tower and lets you dangle there weightlessly before returning you to relative safety. And now they have the aptly named **Insanity,** a spinning whirly-gig of a contraption that straps you into a seat and twirls you around 1,000 feet or so above terra firma. Insanity is right. *Note:* The rides are shut down in inclement weather and high winds.

Atop Stratosphere Las Vegas, 2000 Las Vegas Blvd. S. ℂ 702/380-7777. Admission: Big Shot $9; X-Scream $9; Insanity $9; plus fee to ascend Tower: $10 for adults; $6 for locals, seniors, hotel guests, and children 4–12; free for children 3 and under and those dining in the buffet room or Top of the World. Multiride and all-day packages also available for varying costs. Sun–Thurs 10am–1am; Fri–Sat 10am–2am. Hours vary seasonally. Minimum height requirement for Big Shot is 48 inches, minimum height requirement for X-Scream and Insanity are 52 inches.

WHERE TO ROLL THE DICE

What? You didn't come to Las Vegas for the Liberace Museum? We are shocked. *Shocked.*

Yes, there are gambling opportunities in Vegas. Let's not kid ourselves; gambling is what Vegas is about. You should casino-hop at least once to marvel (or get dizzy) at the decor/spectacle and the sheer excess of it all. Beyond decoration, there isn't too much difference. All the casinos have slot and video poker machines and offer games such as blackjack, roulette, craps, poker, Pai Gow, keno, and baccarat. If you're a novice, many casinos offer free gambling lessons that include low stakes games, so you won't lose much while you learn.

Some notable places to gamble include the **MGM Grand,** the largest casino (you will get lost); **New York–New York,** where the change carts look like yellow cabs; the light and airy **Mandalay Bay;** the tasteful **Venetian;** the **Las Vegas Hilton,** where the space-themed casino has light beam–activated slots; **Harrah's,** where the "party pits" offer the most fun in town; **Paris Las Vegas,** where you'll find a kitschy Disneyesque atmosphere; and **Binion's,** where all serious gamblers head, thanks to low minimum bets and single-deck blackjack.

Downtown, stakes are lower, pretensions are nonexistent, and the clientele are often friendlier. You don't have to be a high roller. You would not believe how much fun you can have with a nickel slot machine. You won't get rich, but neither will most of those guys playing the $5 slots, either.

5 Las Vegas After Dark

THE SHOWS

You won't go wrong seeing one of **Cirque du Soleil's** productions—they're among the best in town. *O,* at the Bellagio (© **888/488-7111**), is a breathtaking mix of artistry and acrobatics over a 1.5-million-gallon pool; *Mystère,* at TI at the Mirage (© **800/288-7206**), is a sophisticated and surreal circus extravaganza. *Folies Bergère,* at the Tropicana, is the longest-running production show in town and has recently undergone a "sexier than ever" face-lift. The **Blue Men Group** at the Luxor is performance art for the masses, but don't let that prevent you from going and laughing your head off (© **702/262-4000**). And if you want to see a classic Vegas topless revue—oh, why not?—check out *Jubilee!* at Bally's (© **800/237-7469** or 702/739-4567).

Magic fans will love **Lance Burton: Master Magician,** at the Monte Carlo (© **877/386-8224**), whose sleight-of-hand tricks are extraordinary.

THE CLUB & BAR SCENE

Most Las Vegas bars and clubs don't even get going until close to midnight. **Body English,** in the Hard Rock Hotel, 4455 Paradise Rd. (© **702/693-5000;** www.body english.com), is one of the hottest clubs in town. **Jet,** in The Mirage, 3400 Las Vegas Blvd. S. (© **702/792-7900**), a three-dance-floor, four-bar club, opened in 2006. **Light,** at the Bellagio, 3600 Las Vegas Blvd. S. (© **702/693-8300**), is a grown-up nightclub that caters to the silver spoon crowd but has a party atmosphere that doesn't feel exclusive.

Country music fans might want to wander on over to **Toby Keith's I Love This Bar & Grill,** Harrah's, 3475 Las Vegas Blvd. S. (© **702/369-5084**), which offers live music Wednesday through Saturday.

The **Buffalo,** 4640 Paradise Rd. (at Naples Dr.; © **702/733-8355**), is a leather/ Levi's gay bar, while **Gipsy,** located nearby at 4605 Paradise Rd. (© **702/731-1919;** www.gipsylv.net), is the gay dance club that draws the biggest crowds.

Some good comedy clubs on the Strip are **Comedy Stop,** in the Tropicana, 3801 Las Vegas Blvd. S. (© **800/829-9034**); **The Improv,** at Harrah's, 3475 Las Vegas Blvd. S. (© **800/392-9002**); and **Comedy Club,** in The Riviera, 2901 Las Vegas Blvd. S. (© **800/634-6753**).

Nighttime Is the Right Time

For a great selection of nightlife on the Strip, head for Mandalay Bay; **Aureole, Red Square,** and the **House of Blues** are all popular. You might also check out the incredible nighttime view at the bar atop the **Stratosphere**—nothing beats it.

Appendix:
The Southwest in Depth

In the Hopi creation myth, the Spider Woman fashioned of clay all the birds and beasts, men and women. With Tawa, the sun god, she sang a song and brought forth life. In the American Southwest, the magic of that story is apparent wherever you turn. A colossal elephant, camel, or medicine man fashioned from stone might dominate the landscape; great canyons cut through the earth's crust, laying bare centuries of rock-layer stories. And human artifacts tell their own stories: spear points left some 9,000 years ago, centuries-old cliff dwellings where the scent of smoke still lingers, and grand missions and fortresses where Catholicism once ruled. It's a land with its own song, one the traveler can't help getting caught up in, stepping to the Spider Woman's ancient rhythm.

1 More Than Desert & Saguaro Cactus

Those who have never visited the American Southwest tend to have some misconceptions. The most common one is that the whole place is a hot desert studded with saguaro cactus. In fact, the Southwest has varied terrain, encompassing all seven of the earth's life zones, from the low Sonoran cactus country, through the higher plateaus studded with piñon and juniper, to the rich forested sections and even high alpine country. And rather than year-round heat, the Southwest has a range of temperatures, including blistering desert climes, midland regions with warm summers and cold winters, and high mountains where the air is always cool and winter brings world-class skiing.

Major landforms traverse the region. The southern Rocky Mountains cut down through central Colorado and northern New Mexico. The Grand Canyon slices across northern Arizona, as do other prominent canyons, which stretch into Utah. Dramatic stone formations carved by weather and erosion stud this region, including those you've likely seen in movies filmed in Monument Valley, as well as others such as Shiprock and Natural

Bridges National Monument. In the south, volcanic mountains, called "sky islands," dot the desert and are home to abundant wildlife, especially bird populations.

Water is the language of the region, enunciating the fate of what grows and what dies here. Rain is scarce. Rivers are scarcer. The Rio Grande cuts New Mexico nearly in half, barely feeding the towns and cities along its banks. The Colorado River snakes from its namesake state across Utah, Arizona, and Nevada before heading south to the Gulf of California. Over the years it's been heavily dammed, resulting in grand lakes, which supply the desert with electricity and irrigation.

What water there is feeds a remarkable array of plant and animal life. In the Sonoran Desert, the notable saguaro cactus, which can reach 40 feet tall and weigh several tons, stands as a symbol for the entire region. Many other kinds of cactuses thrive here as well, as does a range of vegetation, from delicate wildflowers such as the reddish-pink columbine and purple aster to hearty pines such as blue spruce and ponderosa. They help feed and house a broad variety of animal life, from tropical birds such as the elegant trogon to hearty mammals such as prong-horn antelopes, brown bears, and moun-tain lions. But the desert's most notorious creatures are those that crawl and creep: scorpions, tarantulas, and rattlesnakes. You should avoid these, but don't lose sleep over them—generally, if you leave them alone, they'll do the same to you.

2 How the Southwest Was Won—& Lost

IN THE BEGINNING   Archaeologists say that humans first migrated to the Southwest, moving southward from the Bering Land Bridge, around 12,000 B.C. Sites such as Sandia Cave and Folsom—where weapon points have been discov-ered that clearly established that our prehistoric ancestors hunted now-extinct mammals such as woolly mammoths—are internationally known. When large prey animals died off during the late Ice Age (about 8000 B.C.), people turned to hunting smaller game and gathering wild food.

Stable farming settlements, as evi-denced by the remains of domestically grown maize, date from around 3000 B.C. As the nomadic peoples became more sedentary, they built permanent resi-dences, known as pit houses, and made pottery. Cultural differences began to emerge in their choice of architecture and decoration: The Mogollon people, in the southwestern part of modern New Mex-ico, created brown and red pottery and built large community lodges; the Anasazi (also called ancestral Puebloans), in the Four Corners region, made gray pottery and smaller lodges for extended families. In Arizona, the Sinagua and Hohokam cultures farmed the land, crea-ting extensive irrigation systems.

By about A.D. 700, and perhaps a cou-ple of centuries earlier, the Anasazi had built villages throughout what is now known as the Four Corners region (where New Mexico, Arizona, Utah, and Colo-rado come together). Chaco Culture National Historic Park and Aztec Ruins National Monument in New Mexico; Mesa Verde National Park in Colorado; and Betatakin, Keet Seel, and Canyon de Chelly in Arizona, among other sites, all exhibit an architectural excellence and skill, and a scientific sensitivity to nature, that marks this as one of America's classic pre-Columbian civilizations.

The sites include condominium-style communities of stone and mud adobe bricks, three and four stories high. The villages incorporated circular spiritual chambers called kivas. The Anasazi also developed the means to irrigate their fields of corn, beans, and squash by con-trolling the flow of water from area rivers. From Chaco Canyon, they built a com-plex system of well-engineered roads lead-ing in four directions to other towns or ceremonial centers. Artifacts found dur-ing excavation, such as seashells and macaw feathers, indicate that they had a far-reaching trade network. The incorpo-ration of solar alignments into some of their architecture has led modern archaeo-astronomers to speculate on the importance of the equinoxes to the Anasazi religion.

The diminishing of the Anasazi cul-ture, and the emergence of the Pueblo culture in its place, is something of a mys-tery today. Scholars disagree about why the Anasazi left their villages around the 13th century. Some suggest drought or soil exhaustion; others, invasion, epi-demic, or social unrest. But by the time the first Spanish explorers arrived in the 1500s, the Anasazi were long gone and the Pueblo culture was well established throughout northern and western New Mexico, from Taos to Zuni, near Gallup. The Hopi had also established their home in northeastern Arizona.

Certain elements of the Anasazi civilization had clearly been kept alive by the Pueblos, including the apartment-like adobe architecture, the creation of rather elaborate pottery, and the use of irrigation or flood farming in their fields. Agriculture, and especially corn, was the economic mainstay.

Each village fiercely guarded its independence. When the Spanish arrived, there were no alliances between villages, even among those with a common language or dialect. No more than a few hundred people lived in any one pueblo, an indication that the natives had learned to keep their population down in order to preserve their soil and other natural resources. But not all was peaceful: They alternately fought and traded with each other, as well as with nomadic Apaches.

THE ARRIVAL OF THE SPANISH
The Spanish controlled the Southwest for 300 years, from the mid–16th to the mid–19th century—longer than the United States has. The Hispanic legacy in language and culture is still strong in the region.

The spark that sent the first European explorers into the region was a fabulous medieval myth that seven Spanish bishops had fled the Moorish invasion of the 8th century, sailed westward to the legendary isle of Antilia, and built themselves seven cities of gold. Hernán Cortés's 1519 discovery and conquest of the Aztecs' treasure-laden capital of Tenochtitlán, now Mexico City, fueled belief in the myth. When a Franciscan friar 20 years later claimed to have sighted, from a distance, "a very beautiful city" in a region known as Cíbola while on a reconnaissance mission for the viceroyalty, the gates were open.

Francisco Vásquez de Coronado, the ambitious young governor of New Spain's western province of Nueva Galicia, was commissioned to lead an expedition to the "seven cities." Several hundred soldiers,

accompanied by servants and missionaries, marched overland to Cíbola with him in 1540, along with a support fleet of three ships in the Gulf of California. What they discovered, after 6 hard months on the trail, was a bitter disappointment: Instead of a city of gold, they found a rock-and-mud pueblo at Hawikku, the westernmost of the Zuni towns. The expedition wintered at Tiguex, on the Rio Grande near modern Santa Fe, before proceeding to the Great Plains seeking more treasure at Quivira, in what is now Kansas. The grass houses of the Wichita Indians were all they found.

Coronado returned to New Spain in 1542, admitting failure. Historically, though, his expedition was a great success, contributing the first widespread knowledge of the Southwest and Great Plains, and encountering the Grand Canyon.

By the 1580s, after important silver discoveries in the mountains of Mexico, the Spanish began to wonder if the wealth of the Pueblo country might lie in its land and people rather than its cities. They were convinced that they had been divinely appointed to convert the natives of the New World to Christianity. And so a northward migration began, orchestrated and directed by the royal government. It was a mere trickle in the late 16th century. Juan de Oñate established a capital in 1598 at San Gabriel, near San Juan Pueblo in New Mexico, but a variety of factors led to its failure. Then in 1610, under Don Pedro de Peralta, the migration began in earnest.

It was not dissimilar to America's schoolbook stereotype. Bands of armored conquistadors did troop through the desert, humble robed friars striding by their sides. But most of the pioneers came up the valley of the Rio Grande with oxcarts and mule trains rather than armor, intent on transplanting their Hispanic traditions of government, religion, and material culture to this new world.

RELIGION & REVOLT The 17th century in the Southwest was essentially a missionary era, as Franciscan priests attempted to turn the Indians into model Hispanic peasants. Their churches became the focal point of every pueblo, with Catholic schools a mandatory adjunct. By 1625 there were an estimated 50 churches in the Rio Grande valley, and by 1670, the Franciscans had founded several missions among the Hopi pueblos.

But the Native Americans weren't enthused about doing "God's work"— building new adobe missions, tilling fields for the Spanish, and weaving garments for export to Mexico—so soldiers backed the padres in extracting labor, a system known as *repartimiento*. Simultaneously, the *encomienda* system mandated that a yearly tribute in corn and blankets be levied upon each Indian. The Pueblos were willing to take part in Catholic religious ceremonies and proclaim themselves converts. To them, spiritual forces were actively involved in the material world. If establishing harmony with the cosmos meant absorbing Jesus Christ and various saints into their hierarchy of *kachinas* and other spiritual beings, so much the better. But the Spanish friars demanded that they do away with their traditional singing and masked dancing, as well as with other "pagan practices." When the Pueblo religion was violently crushed and driven literally underground, resentment toward the Spanish grew. In 1680, the Pueblo Revolt erupted.

Popé, a San Juan shaman, catalyzed the revolt. Assisted by other Pueblo leaders, he unified the far-flung Native Americans, who had never confederated before. They pillaged and burned the province's outlying settlements, then turned their attention to Santa Fe, besieging the citizens who had fled to the Palace of the Governors. After 9 days, having reconquered Spain's northernmost American province, they let the refugees retreat south to Mexico.

Popé ordered that the Pueblos return to the lifestyle they had had before the arrival of the Spanish. All Hispanic items, from tools to livestock to fruit trees, were to be destroyed, and the blemish of baptism was to be washed away in the river. But the shaman misjudged the influence of the Spanish upon the Pueblos. They were not the people they had been a century earlier, and they *liked* much of the material culture they had absorbed from the Europeans. What's more, they had no intention of remaining confederated; their independent streak was too strong.

In 1692, led by newly appointed Gov. Don Diego de Vargas, the Spanish recaptured Santa Fe without bloodshed. Popé had died, and without a leader to reunify them, the Pueblos were no match for the Spanish. Vargas pledged not to punish them, but to pardon and convert. Still, when he returned the following year with 70 families to recolonize the city, he used force. And for the next several years, bloody battles persisted throughout the Pueblo country.

By the turn of the 18th century, the Southwest was firmly in Spanish hands. This time, however, the colonists seemed to have learned from some of their errors. They were more tolerant of other religions, and less ruthless in their demands and punishments.

ARRIVAL OF THE ANGLOS In 1739, the first French trade mission entered Santa Fe, welcomed by the citizenry but not by the government. For 24 years, until 1763, a black-market trade thrived between Louisiana and New Mexico. It ended only when France lost its toehold on its North American claims during the French and Indian War against Great Britain.

The Native Americans were more fearsome foes. Apache, Comanche, Ute, and Navajo launched repeated raids against each other and the Rio Grande settlements for most of the 18th century, which led the Spanish and Pueblos to pull closer together for mutual protection. Pueblo and Hispanic militias fought side by side in campaigns against the invaders. But by the 1770s, the attacks had become so savage and destructive that the viceroy in Mexico City created a military jurisdiction in the province, and Gov. Juan Bautista de Anza led a force north to Colorado to defeat the most feared of the Comanche chiefs, Cuerno Verde ("Green Horn"), in 1779. Seven years later, the Comanches and Utes signed a lasting treaty with the Spanish and thereafter helped keep the Apaches in check.

France sold the Louisiana Territory to the young United States in 1803, and the Spanish suddenly had a new intruder to fear. The Lewis and Clark expedition of 1803 went unchallenged, much as the Spanish would have liked to do otherwise. But in 1807, when Lt. Zebulon Pike built a stockade on a Rio Grande tributary in Colorado, he and his troops were taken prisoner by Spanish troops from Santa Fe. Pike was transported to the New Mexican capital, where he was interrogated extensively, and then to Chihuahua, Mexico. The report he wrote upon his return was the United States' first inside look at Spain's frontier province.

At first, pioneering American merchants—excited by Pike's observations of the region's economy—were summarily expelled from Santa Fe or jailed, and their goods confiscated. But after Mexico gained independence from Spain in 1821, traders were welcomed. The wagon ruts of the Santa Fe Trail soon extended from Missouri to New Mexico, and from there to Chihuahua. (Later, it became the primary southern highway to California.)

As the merchants hastened to Santa Fe, Anglo-American and French Canadian fur trappers headed into the wilderness. Their commercial hub became Taos, a tiny village near a large pueblo a few days'

ride north of Santa Fe. Many married into native or Hispanic families. Perhaps the best known was Kit Carson (1809–1868), a sometime federal agent and sometime scout whose legend is inextricably interwoven with that of the early Southwest.

In 1846, the Mexican War broke out and New Mexico (which included Arizona) became a territory of the United States. There were several causes of the war, including the U.S. annexation of Texas in 1845, disagreement over the international boundary, and unpaid claims owed to American citizens by the Mexican government. But foremost was the prevailing U.S. sentiment of "manifest destiny," the belief that the Union should extend "from sea to shining sea." Gen. Stephen Kearny marched south from Colorado; on the plaza in Las Vegas, New Mexico, he announced that he had come to take possession of the area for the United States. His arrival in Santa Fe on August 18, 1846, went unopposed.

An 1847 revolt in Taos resulted in the slaying of the new governor of New Mexico, Charles Bent, but U.S. troops defeated the rebels and executed their leaders. That was the last threat to American sovereignty in the territory. In 1848, the Treaty of Guadalupe Hidalgo officially transferred title of New Mexico, along with Texas, Arizona, and California, to the United States.

Kearny promised that the United States would respect religion and property rights and would safeguard homes and possessions from hostile Indians. His troops behaved with rigid decorum. The United States upheld Spanish policy toward the Pueblos, assuring the survival of their ancestral lands, their traditional culture, and their old religion—which even 3 centuries of Hispanic Catholicism could not do away with.

Meanwhile, on a broad valley of what is now southeastern Nevada, Spanish explorers found a new route to Los Angeles. Named Las Vegas (the meadows), the place had abundant wild grasses and plentiful water. It was also the home to the Paiute Indians. With hopes of teaching the Paiutes to farm, in 1855 Brigham Young assigned 30 Mormon missionaries to build a fort in the valley. It was raided and left in ruins just a few years later, but a precedent was established. By the 1880s, precious minerals had been found, bringing miners to the area. And the land itself proved fertile, attracting farmers. The phenomenon that would one day be Las Vegas had begun.

THE CIVIL WAR As conflict between the North and South flared east of the Mississippi, the Southwest found itself caught in the debate over slavery. Southerners wanted to expand slavery to the western territories, but abolitionists fought a bitter campaign to prevent that from happening. In 1861, the Confederacy, after seceding from the Union, laid plans to make the region its own as a first step toward capturing the West.

In fact, southern New Mexicans, including those in Tucson (Arizona was still part of the New Mexico Territory), were disenchanted with the attention paid them by Santa Fe and already were threatening to form their own state. So when Confederate Lt. Col. John Baylor captured Fort Fillmore, near Mesilla, and on August 1, 1861, proclaimed all of New Mexico south of the 34th parallel to be the new territory of Arizona, there were few complaints.

The following year, Confederate Gen. Henry Sibley assembled three regiments of 2,600 Texans and moved up the Rio Grande. They defeated Union loyalists in a bloody battle at Valverde, near Socorro; easily took Albuquerque and Santa Fe, which were protected only by small garrisons; and proceeded toward the federal arsenal at Fort Union, 90 miles east of Santa Fe. Sibley planned to replenish his supplies there before continuing north to Colorado, then west to California.

On March 27 and 28, 1862, the Confederates were met head-on in Glorieta Pass, about 16 miles outside Santa Fe, by regular troops from Fort Union supported by a regiment of Colorado Volunteers. By the second day, the rebels were in control, until a detachment of Coloradoans circled behind the Confederate troops and destroyed their poorly defended supply train. Sibley was forced into a rapid retreat back down the Rio Grande. A few months later, Mesilla was reclaimed for the Union, and the Confederate presence in the New Mexico Territory ended.

THE LAND WARS The various tribes had not missed the fact that whites were fighting among themselves, and they took advantage of this weakness to step up their raids on border settlements. In 1864, the Navajos, in what is known in tribal history as "The Long Walk," were relocated to the new Bosque Redondo Reservation on the Pecos River at Fort Sumner, in east-central New Mexico. Militia Col. Kit Carson led New Mexico troops in this venture, and was a moderating influence between the Navajos and those who called for their unconditional surrender or extermination. The experiment failed, and within 5 years the Navajos were returned to their homeland, though they were forced to live on a reservation.

Corralling the rogue Apaches in the south presented the territory with its biggest challenge. Led by chiefs Victorio, Nana, and Geronimo, these bands wreaked havoc upon the mining towns. Eventually they succumbed, and the capture of Geronimo in 1886 was the final chapter in the region's long history of Indian wars.

As the Native American threat decreased, more and more livestock and sheep ranchers established themselves on the vast plains east of the Rio Grande, in the San Juan basin of the northwest, and in the area around present-day Phoenix. Cattle drives up the Pecos Valley, on the Goodnight-Loving Trail, are the stuff of legend; so, too, is Roswell cattle baron John Chisum, whose 80,000 head of beef probably represented the largest herd in America in the late 1870s.

Mining grew as well. Albuquerque blossomed in the wake of a series of major gold strikes in the Madrid Valley, close to ancient turquoise mines. Other gold, silver, and copper discoveries through the 1870s gave birth to boomtowns—infamous for their gambling halls, bordellos, and shootouts in the streets. Tombstone and Bisbee in Arizona, Silver City in New Mexico, and Leadville and Cripple Creek in Colorado remain legendary.

In the late 1870s, the railroads arrived. Now linked by rail to the great markets of America, the region enjoyed an economic boom period. In 1905, the main railway connecting southern California with Salt Lake City was completed. Las Vegas, Nevada, became an important refueling point and rest stop on the route.

But ranching invites cattle rustling and range wars, mining beckons feuds and land fraud, and the construction of railroads has often been tied to political corruption and swindles. The Southwest had all of this, especially during the latter part of the 19th century. One of the central figures was William "Billy the Kid" Bonney, a headstrong youth (b. 1858) who became probably the best-known outlaw of the American West. He blazed a trail of bloodshed from Silver City to Lincoln to Fort Sumner, where he was finally killed by Sheriff Pat Garrett in July 1881.

By the turn of the 20th century, most of the violence had been checked. The mineral lodes were drying up, and ranching was taking on increased importance. Economic and social stability were coming.

AGRICULTURE & ATOMS In the late 19th and early 20th century, official statehood came to the Southwest: Nevada in 1864, Colorado in 1876, Utah in 1896, and New Mexico and Arizona in 1912. This was an exciting era for the West. Theodore Roosevelt set aside great tracts of land as national forests and established what is now called the Theodore Roosevelt Dam on the Salt River in Arizona, which enabled large-scale agriculture to take root.

In 1931, the state of Nevada legalized gambling, a decision that forever changed the face of the one-time agricultural and railroad town, Las Vegas.

But the most dramatic development in 20th century occurred during World War II. In 1943, the U.S. government sealed off a tract of land on the Pajarito Plateau, west of Santa Fe, that had been an exclusive boys' school. On this site, in utter secrecy, it built the Los Alamos National Laboratory, otherwise known as Project Y of the Manhattan Engineer District—the "Manhattan Project." Its goal: to split the atom and develop the world's first nuclear weapons.

Under the direction of J. Robert Oppenheimer, later succeeded by Norris E. Bradbury, a team of 30 to 100 scientists and hundreds of support staff lived and worked in almost complete seclusion for 2 years. Their effort resulted in the atomic bomb, tested for the first time at the Trinity Site, north of White Sands, on July 16, 1945. The bombings of Hiroshima and Nagasaki, Japan, 3 weeks later, signaled to the world that the nuclear age had arrived.

3 The Southwest Today—from Flamenco to Craps

GROWING PAINS The Southwest is experiencing a reconquest of sorts, as the Anglo population soars, and outside money and values make their way in. The process continues to transform the region's many distinct cultures and their unique ways of life, albeit in a less violent manner than during the Spanish conquest.

Certainly, the new arrivals—many of them from large cities—add a cosmopolitan flavor. The variety of restaurants has greatly improved, as have entertainment options. For their small size, towns such as Taos, Santa Fe, and Flagstaff offer a broad variety of restaurants and cultural events. Santa Fe, Tucson, and Phoenix have developed strong dance and drama scenes, with treats such as flamenco and opera that you'd expect to find in cosmopolitan centers such as New York and Los Angeles. Albuquerque and Tucson have exciting nightlife scenes with a wealth of jazz, rock, country, and alternative music.

Yet many newcomers, attracted by the exotic feel, often bring only a loose appreciation for the area. Some tend to romanticize the lifestyle of other cultures and trivialize their beliefs. Native American symbology, for example, is employed in ever-popular Southwestern decorative motifs; New Age groups appropriate valued rituals, such as sweats (in which believers sit in a very hot, enclosed space to cleanse their spirits). The effects of cultural and economic change are even apparent throughout the countryside, where land is being developed at an alarming rate, often as lots for new million-dollar homes.

Transformation of the local way of life and landscape is also apparent in the stores continually springing up in the area. For some of us, these are a welcome relief from Western clothing stores and provincial dress shops. The downside is that city plazas, which once contained pharmacies and grocery stores frequented by residents, now overflow with T-shirt shops and galleries appealing to tourists. Many locals in these cities now rarely visit their downtown areas except during special events such as fiestas.

The region's biggest addition is the $225-million Airport America spaceport near Truth or Consequences in southern New Mexico. In its embryonic stages now, it will include one or more runways, hangars, a control building, and launch pads. Test flights have already begun, with plans for Virgin Galactic to send tourists into space from here by 2009.

Environmental threats are another regional reality. Nuclear-waste issues form part of an ongoing conflict affecting the entire Southwest, and a section of southern New Mexico has been designated a nuclear-waste site. Colorado has its own nuclear-waste woes; cleanup of Rocky Flats nuclear weapons facility has been an ongoing problem.

Still, new ways of thinking have brought positive changes, and many locals have directly benefited from the influx of newcomers and the region's popularity as a tourist destination. Businesses and industries large and small have come to the area. Today, electronics manufacturing, aerospace engineering, and other high-tech industries employ thousands. Local artists and artisans also benefit from growth. Many craftspeople—furniture makers, silversmiths, and weavers—have expanded their businesses. The influx of people has broadened the sensibility of a fairly provincial region. You'll find a level of creativity and tolerance here that you would generally find in very large cities but not in smaller communities.

CULTURAL QUESTIONS Faced with new challenges to their ways of life, both Native Americans and Hispanics are marshaling forces to protect their cultural identities. A prime concern is language. Through the years, many Native Americans have begun to speak more and more English, with their children getting little exposure to their native tongue. To counter the effects, many villages have implemented language classes.

Some of the pueblos have introduced programs to conserve the environment, preserve ancient seed strains, and protect religious rites. Because their religion is tied closely to nature, a loss of natural resources would threaten the entire culture. Some area pueblos have limited outsider access to their villages and ceremonies. Jemez Pueblo, for instance, no longer allows visitors, while Zuni has limited the access to their notable Shalako ceremonies.

Hispanics, through art and observance of cultural traditions, are also embracing their roots. Throughout the region, murals depicting important historic events, such as the Treaty of Guadalupe Hidalgo of 1848, adorn walls. The Spanish Market in Santa Fe has expanded into a grand celebration of traditional arts, from tin working to santo carving. Public schools have bilingual education programs, allowing young people to embrace their Spanish-speaking roots.

Hispanics are also making their voices heard, insisting on more conscientious development of their neighborhoods and rising to positions of power in government. The region's best example of a prominent Hispanic citizen is Bill Richardson, who was appointed U.S. ambassador to the United Nations and left that post to become energy secretary in President Clinton's cabinet. Now he is New Mexico's governor and is running for U.S. President in the 2008 campaign.

GAMBLING WINS & LOSSES   Gambling, a fact of life and a source of much-needed revenue for Native American populations across the country, has been a center of controversy in the Southwest for a number of years, and now is well entrenched throughout the region.

Many are concerned about the tone gambling sets in the Southwest, fearing a fate similar to that of Las Vegas, Nevada. Since World War II, Las Vegas has expanded rapidly to become a world center for gambling, with attendant problems such as corruption and what some see as lax moral standards.

The Native American casinos aren't as flashy as those in Las Vegas, though they are, for the most part, large and unsightly. The neon-bedecked buildings stand out sorely on some of the region's most picturesque land. Though most residents appreciate the boost that gambling can ultimately bring to the Native American economies, many critics wonder where gambling profits actually go—and if the casinos can possibly be a good thing for the pueblos and tribes.

A number of pueblos and tribes, however, are showing signs of prosperity, and they are using newfound revenues to buy firefighting and medical equipment and to invest in local schools.

4 Art & Architecture

It's all in the light—or at least that's what many artists claim drew them to the Southwest. In truth, the light is only part of the attraction: Nature in this part of the country, with its awe-inspiring thunderheads, endless expanse of blue skies, and rugged desert, is itself a canvas. To record the wonders of earth and sky, early natives imprinted images (in the form of petroglyphs and pictographs) on the walls of caves and on stones, as well as on the sides of pots they shaped from clay dug in the hills.

Today's Native American tribes carry on that legacy, as do the other cultures that have settled here. Life is shaped by the arts. Everywhere you turn, you'll see pottery, paintings, jewelry, and weavings. You're liable to meet an artist whether you're having coffee in a Sedona cafe or walking along Canyon Road in Santa Fe.

The area is full of little villages that maintain their own artistic specialties. Each Indian pueblo has a trademark design, such as **Santa Clara's** and **San Ildefonso's** black pottery and the **Navajo's** geometric emblazoned weavings. Bear in mind that the images often have deep meaning. When purchasing art, you may want to talk with the maker about what the symbols signify.

Hispanic and Native American villagers take their goods to the cities, where for centuries people have bought and traded. Under the portals along plazas, you'll find a variety of works in silver, stone, and pottery for sale. In the cities, you'll find streets lined with galleries, both slick and modest. Trading posts, most notably Arizona's Hubbell Trading Post in Ganado and Cameron Trading Post in Cameron, offer excellent variety and quality. At major markets, such as the **Spanish Market** and **Indian Market** in Santa Fe, some of the top artists from the area sell their works. Smaller shows at the pueblos also attract artists and artisans. The **Northern Pueblo Artists and Craftsman Show,** revolving each July to a different New Mexico pueblo, continues to grow.

Drawn by the beauty of the local landscape and respect for indigenous art, artists from all over have flocked here, particularly during the 20th century. They have established locally important art societies; one of the most notable is the **Taos Society of Artists.** Santa Fe has its own art society, begun in the 1920s by a nucleus of five painters who became known as **Los Cinco Pintores.** Meanwhile, Scottsdale, Tucson, Sedona, Tubac, and Jerome have developed into rich founts for Southwestern and Western art.

The visitor interested in art should exercise some caution, however; there's a lot of schlock out there, targeting tourists. If you persist, you're likely to find much inspiring work as well. The museums and many of the galleries are excellent repositories of local art. Their offerings range from small-town folk art to works by major artists who show internationally.

A RICH ARCHITECTURAL MELTING POT   Nowhere else in the United States are you likely to see such extremes of architectural style as in the Southwest. The region's distinctive architecture reflects the diversity of cultures that have left their imprint on the region.

The first people to build in the area were the Anasazi (ancestral Puebloans), who made stone and mud homes at the bottoms of canyons and inside caves. **Pueblo-style adobe architecture** evolved and became the basis for traditional homes: sun-dried clay bricks mixed with grass for strength, mud-mortared, and covered with additional protective layers of mud. Roofs are supported by a network of vigas—long beams whose ends protrude through the outer facades—and *latillas,* smaller stripped branches layered between the vigas. Other adapted Pueblo architectural elements include plastered adobe-brick kiva fireplaces, *bancos* (adobe benches that protrude from walls), and *nichos* (small indentations within a wall that hold religious icons). These adobe homes are characterized by flat roofs and soft, rounded contours.

Spaniards wedded many elements to Pueblo style, such as portals (porches held up with posts, often running the length of a home) and enclosed patios, as well as the simple, dramatic sculptural shapes of Spanish mission arches and bell towers. They also brought elements from the Moorish architecture found in southern Spain: heavy wooden doors and elaborate corbels—carved wooden supports for the vertical posts.

The next wave of building came with the opening of the Santa Fe Trail in 1821 and the 1860s gold boom, both of which brought more Anglo settlers. New arrivals contributed architectural elements such as neo-Grecian and Victorian influences popular in the middle part of the United States at the time. Distinguishing features of what came to be known as **Territorial-style** architecture can be seen today; they include brick facades and cornices as well as porches, often placed on the second story. You'll also note millwork on doors and wood trim around windows and doorways, double-hung windows, and Victorian bric-a-brac.

Santa Fe Plaza is an excellent example of the convergence of these early architectural styles. On the west side is a Territorial-style balcony, while Pueblo-style vigas and oversize Spanish/Moorish doors mark the Palace of Governors. Outside Tucson, one of the most noted examples of Mission-style architecture still stands at Mission San Xavier del Bac.

In the mid–20th century, architect Frank Lloyd Wright designed several buildings in the Phoenix area, ushering in innovative building concepts. In the desert north of Phoenix, one of his students, Paolo Soleri, built an environmentally sensitive, ideal city called Arcosanti, which is open to the public.

5 Recommended Books & Films

FICTION Many well-known writers made their homes in the Southwest. In the 1920s, the most celebrated were **D. H. Lawrence** and **Willa Cather,** both short-term Taos residents. Lawrence's *Mornings in Mexico* and *Etruscan Places* capture the flavor of the region. Inspired by her stay in the region, Cather, a Pulitzer Prize winner famous for her depictions of the pioneer spirit, penned *Death Comes for the Archbishop.* It's a fictionalized account of the 19th-century Santa Fe bishop Jean Baptiste Lamy.

Many contemporary authors also live in and write about the region. John Nichols of Taos, whose *Milagro Beanfield War* (Henry Holt, 2000) was made into a Robert Redford movie in 1987, writes insightfully about the problems of poor Hispanic farming communities. For the past two decades, Albuquerque's Tony Hillerman has woven mysteries around Navajo tribal police in books such as *Listening Woman* (HarperCollins, 1990) and *A Thief of Time* (HarperCollins, 2004). Of the desert environment and politics, no one wrote better than the late Edward Abbey; *The Monkey Wrench Gang* (HarperPerennial, 2000) told of an unlikely gang of ecoterrorists, which helped inspire the founding of the radical Earth First! movement. Zane Grey fans should pick up a copy of *Riders of the Purple Sage* (Pocket Books, 1974). Set in southern Utah toward the end of the 19th century, it explores polygamy and the restraints it placed on women.

NON-FICTION Marshall Trimble and Joe Beeler's *Roadside History of Arizona* (Mountain Press Publishing, 1986) is an ideal book to take along on a driving tour of the Grand Canyon State. For general histories of New Mexico, try Myra Ellen Jenkins and Albert H. Schroeder's *A Brief History of New Mexico* (University of New Mexico Press, 1974) and Marc Simmons's *New Mexico: An Interpretive History* (University of New Mexico Press, 1988). Get some Colorado history from the short, easy-to-read *Colorado: Bicentennial and History Guide* (W.W. Norton, 1996), by Marshall Sprague. John Wesley Powell's 1869 diary, the first account of travels through the canyon, offers an exciting viewpoint of the Grand Canyon. You can read a recent republication of it titled *The Exploration of the Colorado River and Its Canyons* (Penguin, 1997), with an introduction by Wallace Stegner. For an interesting account of the recent human history of the canyon, read Stephen J. Pyne's *How the Canyon Became Grand* (Viking Penguin, 1999).

To catch the mood of southern Utah, read Abbey's *Desert Solitaire* (New York: Ballantine, 1968), a nonfiction work based on time Abbey spent in Arches National Monument, before it gained national-park status.

MOVIES Hundreds of movies have been filmed in the region. One of the most notable classics is director John Ford's *Stagecoach* (1939), filmed in Monument Valley. The valley has also shown up in such non-Western films as *2001: A Space Odyssey, Thelma and Louise,* and *Forrest Gump.* Many films have been made in Tucson at what's now called Old Tucson Studios, including *Arizona, Tombstone,* John Wayne's *Rio Lobo,* Clint Eastwood's *The Outlaw Josey Wales,* Kirk Douglas's *Gunfight at the O.K. Corral,* and Paul Newman's *The Life and Times of Judge Roy Bean.* New Mexico landscapes have set the scene for Westerns such as *The Cowboys, Silverado, Young Guns, City Slickers,* and *Wyatt Earp,* as well as two miniseries based on popular Larry McMurtry novels, *Lonesome Dove* and *Buffalo Girls.* The science fiction movies *Armageddon* and *Contact* were shot in New Mexico as well.

Index